C000161947

ISBN 978-0-331-08348-4
PIBN 11012264

FB &c Ltd, Dalton House, 60 Windsor Avenue, London, SW19 2RR.
Company number 08720141. Registered in England and Wales.

For support please visit www.forgottenbooks.com

CHEMAINUS

CHEMAINUS FIR

Clear Kiln Dried B. C. Douglas Fir

We can make prompt shipment on straight or mixed cars of clear kiln dried B. C. Douglas Fir in all sizes rough or dressed. Also flooring, ceiling, mouldings and siding.

If quality can talk to you — get in touch with us.

VICTORIA LUMBER & MFG. CO., LIMITED

Head Office and Mill
CHEMAINUS, B. C.

Eastern Representatives:
KNOX BROS.,
Bank of Hamilton Building, Toronto,
and
Drummond Building, Montreal.

High Grade Lumber and Timber

SPRUCE *Ready for Shipment*

2 x 4"	10/16'	3 x 5"	12/16'
2 x 5"	10/16'	3 x 6"	12/16'
2 x 6"	10/16'	3 x 7"	12/16'
2 x 7"	10/16'	3 x 8"	12/16'
2 x 8"	10/16'	3 x 8"	17/24'
2 x 9"	10/16'	3 x 9"	12/16'
2 x 10"	10/16'	3 x 9"	17/24'
2 x 10"	17/24'	3 x 10"	12/16'
		3 x 11"	12/16'

Douglas Fir & B.C. Spruce
Ready for Shipment

8 x 8 to 16 x 16" 16/32'

Pitch Pine

6 x 8"	14/20'
8 x 8"	12/20'
8 x 10"	14/16'
10 x 10"	18/20'

Derrick Stock
B.C. FIR

12 x 12"	1/60, 2/65
14 x 14	3/52, 6/60
16 x 18	5/60, 5/65
18 x 18	5/65
8 x 16	20/20, 16/36
10 x 16	1/20, 10/36

200,000' No. 1 Common and Better Basswood 1¼ x 4" and up, mostly 1sts and 2nds.

Spruce Flag poles, 25', 30', 35 and 40 long, 4½ to 5½" at bottom, 2" at top.

Pattern Pine a Specialty

Can Re-saw the above in any size required, rough or planed. Mail us your enquiries.

Cars of Fir Timber always in transit

The James Shearer Co., Limited

Wholesale and Retail Dealers in Lumber and Timber

OFFICE AND YARDS: 225 St Patrick St. **MONTREAL**

SPECIALS

1½ x 32" M.R. Hemlock Lath	300,000 Pcs.
1½ x 32" M.R. Hemlock and Spruce Lath	160,000 Pcs.

Ex. Bracebridge, Ont.

1¼ x 4 and up—6/16' White Pine Mill Culls	45,000'
2 x 4 " " " " " "	26,000'
1¼ x 4 " " " " No. 2 Culls	15,000'
2 x 4 " " " " " "	13,000'

Ex. Midland, Ont.

1 x 4 and up No. 3 Common and Better Birch	80,000'
1¼ x 4 " " " " " "	5,000'
2 x 4 " " " " " "	75,000'
22½ x 7 " " " " " "	4,000'

Ex. Caspadedia, P.Q.

INTERESTING PRICES FOR IMMEDIATE SHIPMENT

1918 SAWING

Complete Stock of White and Red Pine at Midland, Ont.

PLANING MILL FACILITIES

TERRY & GORDON

VANCOUVER BRANCH:
513 Metropolitan Bldg.
A. S. Nicholson,
Western Manager.

Head Office:
704 Confederation Life Bldg.
TORONTO, ONT.
Ontario Representatives of
The British Columbia Mills, Timber & Trading Co. of Vancouver, B.C.

U. S. Representatives:
Berry Lumber Company,
80 Church Street,
New York City.

We are Now in Toronto

AT

630 Confederation Life Building

PHONE MAIN 3153

with better facilities than ever to give you Quality and Service

Our Specialty

WHITE PINE STRIPS

Hocken Lumber Co., Limited

Formerly of Otter Lake Station, Ont.

"British Columbia Fir" TIMBERS

Rough Clears
Flooring, Ceiling and Finish

Alberta Lumber Co., Limited
VANCOUVER, B. C.

We are in the Market for

Railroad Ties, Piling and Posts

Canadian Tie & Lumber Co., Ltd.
510 and 511 Temple Building,
Phone Main 1151
TORONTO, ONTARIO

Fraser Bryson Lumber Co., Ltd.

Office, Castle Building 53 Queen St. Ottawa, Can.

Wholesale Lumber Dealers
and Selling Agents for

Fraser & Co.

Mills at
DESCHENES - - - QUEBEC

White Pine
Red Pine
Spruce
Lumber and Lath

HEMLOCK
AT MIDLAND

80,000 ft. 1.x.4 and up—6 to 16 ft. Merchantable.
35,000 " 2 x 6—10 and 12 ft. "
10,000 " 2 x 6—14 ft. "
30,000 " 2 x 8—10 and 12 ft. "
10,000 " 2 x 8—14 ft. "
10,000 " 2 x 8—16 ft.
20,000 " 2 x 10—10 and 12 ft. "
20,000 " 2 x 10—14 ft.
20,000 " 2 x 10—16 ft. "
20,000 " 2 x 12—10 and 12 ft. "
20,000 " 2 x 12—14 ft.
30,000 " 2 x 12—16 ft. "
15,000 " 2 x 6 and 8"—18 ft. "
60,000 " 2 x 10 and 12—18 ft. "

Write for prices. We can save you money.

The Long Lumber Co.
TORONTO BRANCH: 25 Toronto Street.
Head Office, HAMILTON, ONT.

California White Pine
California Sugar Pine
and Arizona Soft Pine

Best Stock for Factory and Pattern Lumber

Ask **LOUIS WUICHET**
Room 716 Railway Exchange, CHICAGO, ILLINOIS

Milling in Transit

A Well Equipped Mill
C.P., G.T., & C.R. Railway Connections

Large Dry Kilns *Special Millwork*

J. R. Eaton & Sons, Limited
ORILLIA, ONT.

Austin & Nicholson

CHAPLEAU, ONTARIO

Largest Producers of RAILROAD TIES in the Dominion

Pine and Spruce Lumber
Lath Piling
Railroad Ties
Pulpwood

First Class Planing-mill Equipment

Facilities for delivering Pulpwood to Michipicoten Harbour, Lake Superior

Splendid facilities for Dressing and Matching in straight car lots, one or more widths

Mills at NICHOLSON, ONTARIO, Main Line C.P.R.

Basswood

1 in., 1¼ in., 1½ in., 2 in., and 3 in., Dry Basswood

Dry Birch Stock

All thicknesses and grades in

Maple, Birch, Elm, Basswood and **Brown Ash**

Also **Cottonwood, Tupelo, Gum, Magnolia** and **Buckeye**

Spruce, Hemlock and Pine

Can saw to order at MacDonald's Siding

Let us quote on your requirements

HART & McDONAGH

Temple Building, Cor. Bay and Richmond Streets
TORONTO, ONT.

SOUTHERN HARDWOODS Dry Stock at Buffalo for Quick Shipment

BROWN ASH

	1 & 2	Clear Strips	No. 1 Com.	No. 2 Com.
1 in.	20,000	....	5,000	22,000
1¼ in.	29,500	5,300	6,200	6,300
1½ in.	11,500	....	....	....
2 in.	1,500	....	13,000	600

BASSWOOD

	1 & 2	Clear Strips	No. 1 Com.	No. 2 Com.
1 in.	35,700	2,200	172,000	24,000
1¼ in.	144,300	12,000	146,500	65,800
1½ in.	30,600	....	24,800	11,000
2 in.	20,900	....	15,000	4,500
2½ in.	75,000	....	20,900	13,000
3 in.	5,500	....	6,500	3,900

TENESSEE SCENTED RED CEDAR

	1 & 2	No. 1 Com.	No. 2 Com.	No. 3 Com.
1 in.	18,500	15,800	1,500	1,100
1¼ in.	4,400	800	....	....

RED GUM

	1 & 2	No. 1 Com.	No. 2 Com.
1 in.	60,300	13,200	......
1¼ in.	8,200	9,200	......
1½ in.	9,000	11,300	......
2 in.	7,100	4,800	......

PLAIN SYCAMORE

	1 & 2	No. 1 Com.
1 in.	5,600	....
2 in.	1,900	....
2½ in.	2,000	....

SAP GUM

	1 & 2	No. 1 Com.	No. 2 Com.
1 in.	47,400	6,000	......
1¼ in.	......	......	......
1½ in.	......	......	......
2 in.	......	......	......
2 in.	11,000 qtd.	7,500 qtd.	......

WHITE ASH

	1 & 2	Clear Strips	No. 1 Com.	No. 2 Com.
1 in.	57,300	800	130,000	89,000
1¼ in.	41,000	15,500	9,000	1,000
1½ in.	68,000	5,200	43,000	26,100
2 in.	48,300	500	79,000	44,000
2½ in.	....	....	11,500	1,500
3 in.	7,000	....	33,500	4,300
4 in.	4,500	....	....	....

HICKORY

	1 & 2	No. 1 Com.	No. 2 Com.
1 in.	2,200	2,300	800
1¼ in.	......	400	350
1½ in.	6,000	2,300	1,000
2 in.	12,350	13,600	10,700
2½ in.	7,000	5,000	......
3 in.	400	5,580	......
4 in.	200	200	......

QUARTERED RED OAK

	1 & 2	Clear Strips	No. 1 Com.	No. 2 Com.
¾ in.	....	....	......	....
1 in.	72,200	8,300	38,800	800
1¼ in.	500	....	400	....
1½ in.	....	....	550	150
2 in.	1,000	....	7,400	....

QUARTERED WHITE OAK

	1 & 2	Clear Strips	No. 1 Com.	No. 2 Com.
½ in.	5,500	....	....	....
¾ in.	84,500	25,400	128,000	....
⅝ in.	....	....	....	....
1 in.	29,400	12,800	4,000	15,000
1¼ in.	10,000	....	6,400	1,800
1½ in.	1,500	....	2,000	2,300
2 in.	6,500	350	5,100	2,700
2½ in.	800	....	....	....

POPLAR

	1 & 2 18 in. & up	1 & 2 13 in. & up	Box Boards	Bright Saps
¾ in.	....	3,000	....	2,300
1 in.	16,200	30,000	11,600	40,200
1¼ in.	2,800	3,000	....	11,600
1½ in.	5,300	7,000	....	21,000
2 in.	....	32,000	....	22,000
2½ in.	....	25,800	....	28,000
3 in.	....	3,900	....	32,000
4 in.	....	27,000	....	1,300

	Stained Saps	Clear Strips	No. 1 Com.	No. 2 Com.
¾ in.	9,800	....	34,300	2,000
1 in.	23,600	....	103,900	55,300
1¼ in.	8,600	....	11,000	6,000
1½ in.	0,700	....	45,000	2,700
2 in.	7,000	....	141,500	27,300
2½ in.	3,700	....	1,000	....
3 in.	1,300	....	48,000	32,000
4 in.	700	....	750	....

QUARTERED POPLAR

	1 & 2	Clear Strips	No. 1 Com.	No. 2 Com.
1 in.	....	....	....	....
1¼ in.	250	....	....	....

POPLAR SQUARES

	1 & 2	No. 1 Com.
4x4	3,300	700
5x5	8,700	2,900
6x6	9,450	4,200
7x7	2,100	500
8x8	9,000	....

BLACK WALNUT

	1 & 2	No. 1 Com.	No. 2 Com.
1 in.	150	14,000	3,100
1¼ in.	100	300	200
1½ in.	250	200	100
2 in.	300	800	500
3 in.	110	120	250
4 in.	....	500	1,200

PLAIN RED OAK

	1 & 2	Selects	No. 1 Com.	No. 2 Com.
4/4	10,000	......	40,000	48,000
5/4	1,000	......	3,000	......
6/4	......	......	6,000	2,000
8/4	......	......	41,000	2,000
10/4	......	......	3,000	......
12/4	1,000	......	......	......
16/4	5,500	......	8,500	......

20,000' 4/4" Wormy Oak.

PLAIN WHITE OAK

	1 & 2	No. 1 Com.	No. 2 Com.
4/4	1,500	......	......
8/4	......	......	......
6/4	6,000	18,000	32,000
12/4	2,000	8,000	7,000
10/4	2,000	4,000	......
5/8	4,000	1,000	......

QUARTERED WHITE OAK

	1 & 2	Clear Strips	No. 1 Com.
4/4	32,000	......	10,000
5/4	......	......	......
6/4	......	......	......

POPLAR

	1 & 2	Bright Saps	No. 1 Com.	No. 2 Com.
4/4	3,000	......	43,000	50,000
5/4	......	7,000	27,000	60,000
6/4	......	20,000	73,00	......
8/4	......	14,000	41,000	57,000
12/4	......	1,000	7,000	248,000
5/8	......	......	2,000	......

PLAIN WHITE OAK

	1 & 2	No. 1 Com.	No. 2 Com.	Wormy
4/4	......	29,000	20,000	38,000
6/4	......	......	4,000	......
8/4	......	......	......	......
10/4	......	......	......	......
12/4	......	......	......	......
16/4	......	......	......	......

Also Large Stock of BEECH, BIRCH and MAPLE

THE ATLANTIC LUMBER CO., Inc., 310 MANNING CHAMBERS, TORONTO

MANUFACTURERS SOUTHERN HARDWOOD LUMBER

Head Office: BOSTON, MASS. Yards: BUFFALO, N.Y. Mills: KNOXVILLE, TENN.; FONDE, KENTUCKY

SAW MILL MACHINERY

Firstbrook Bros.
Limited

Having decided to discontinue saw mill operations at Penetang have the following machinery for sale. This machinery is all in operating condition and is open for inspection at Penetang, Ont.

Mill Machinery

Extra heavy log haul-up works with inch round and flat chain, 128 ft. centres.
2—Waterous log unloaders or kickers, 3 arms, 10 in. cylinders.
1—Waterous log loader, 3 arms, 10-in. cylinders.
1—Waterous right-hand double cutting band mill, 11 in. saws, 8 ft. wheel, with 3-block carriage; 24 in. opening; Payette set works and dogs; 8 in. x 36 ft. steam feed.
1—Waterous double edger for 20-inch saws, lever shifter.
1—Payette double edger for 18-in. saws, lever shifter.
48—live rolls about 8 ft. long by 10 in. dia.; extra heavy, sprocket drive.
4—High cars with roller tops, 24 in. heavy wheels on 2 in. axles, standard gauge.
1—Mershon 4 saw gang resaw, takes squared cants or just one face, ideal machine to cut small logs and centres of large after good has been taken off.
1—Payette picket machine, made specially for shade roller stock, will feed pieces 16 in. long, also sorting table with chain top.
1—Rogers Iron Works circular resaw for making box lumber from slabs; fool-proof machine.
1—Payette edger for box and short stock.
1—Rogers twin circular or tie maker.
1—Payette lath bolter and lath machine.
1—Pair lath trimmers.
1—Picket trimmer (bunch trim).
Conveyor drives and chains.
Pulleys, gears, heavy line shafting and countershafting with bearings.
Send us your requirements.
We have a large stock of double and triple leather belting in widths from 10 in. to 18 in.

Power House Equipment

3—Return Tubular Boilers, Goldie McCulloch make, 66 x 16, Dutch oven settings, 85 lbs. steam allowance Ontario Government.
Breeching and smoke stack for above boilers, 60 in. dia., newly painted, 600 ft. new ½-in. guy and plate for brick pier.
1—Pair Polson "Brown" type engines, coupled on quarters, 22 in. x 30 in., with 16 ft. x 48 in. belt, balance wheel. Excellent engines.
1—Pair American feed water heaters for above engines; 10 in., copper coils.
1—8 x 10 Centre Crank Engine
1—10 x 14 Cowan Slide Valve Engine

Filing Equipment

1—Waterous band saw grinder for 6 in. saws.
1—Baldwin retoother for band saws.
2—Reversible saw levelling blocks.
2—Chilled band saw anvils.
Hanchet band saw swages; Crescent circular saw swages; shapers and dressers.

Yard Equipment

Booms and boom chains, ½, ⅝ & ¾.
Winches and other mill supplies.

Prompt shipments and bargains for quick sale. Will send all particulars and prices on application.

Firstbrook Bros.
Limited
Penetang, Ont.

"WELL BOUGHT IS HALF SOLD"

Can You Use Any of the Following Dry High Grade White Pine

1 x 4	—10/16'	No. 1 Stocks	
1 x 5	"	"	"
1 x 6	"	"	"
1 x 8	"	"	"
5/4 x 5	"	"	"
5/4 x 6	"	"	"
5/4 x 8	"	"	"
5/4 x 10	"	"	"

6/4 x 6 and up No. 1 and 2 Cuts

6/4 x 8 and up Canada Dressing and Better

Cut by GRAVES, BIGWOOD & CO.
at BYNG INLET

Canadian General Lumber Co.
Limited

FOREST PRODUCTS

TORONTO OFFICE :— 712-20 Bank of Hamilton Bldg.
Montreal Office :—203 McGill Bldg.
Mills : Byng Inlet, Ont.

PETRIE'S LIST
of
NEW and USED
WOOD TOOLS
for Immediate Delivery

Wood Lathes

20" Sidney, Famous
16" Cowan.
16" Sidney, Famous, patternmakers.
14" Sidney, Famous.

Band Saws

36" West Side, pedestal.
30" Cowan, bracket.
60" Fay & Egan, band re-saw.

Saw Tables

No. 6 Sidney, Famous, variety.
No. 2 Sidney, Famous, variety.
No. 2 Crescent, combination.
Fisher, iron frame rip.
MacGregor-Gourlay power feed cut-off.
Greenlee automatic cut-off.
7½' Fay & Egan, swing saw.
7' Williams, swing saw.
Bench type, jig or scroll saw.
No. 4 Canadian, steel frame, pole saw.

Wood Planers

30" Whitney pattern single surfacer.
26" double surfacer, with chip breaker.
24" Hermance, double surfacer.
24" Sidney, Famous, single surfacer.
24" Crescent, single surfacer.
24" MacGregor-Gourlay.
24" pony planer.
24" Champion planer and matcher, with moulding attachment.
24" Galt, planer and matcher.
18" Sidney Famous, single surfacer.
12" Buzz, with slotted head (2).
12" Petrie, buzz planers, safety heads (6)

Moulders

13" Clark-Demill four side.
12" Cowan four side.
12" Woods, four-side, inside.
10" Houston four side.
8" Dundas four side.
6" Dundas sash sticker.

Mortisers

Cowan, upright power.
Galt, upright, compound table.
No. 5 New Britain chain.
No. 2 Smart, foot power.
No. 2 Osborne, foot power.

Boring Machines

No. 8 Sidney, Famous, gear driven.
No. 7 Sidney, Famous, belt driven.
No. 920 Canada Machinery Corporation (2).
Fay, single spindle.

Clothespin Machinery

Humphrey automatic lathes (6).
Humphrey double slotters (3).

Miscellaneous

No. 30 Sidney, universal woodworker.
Vaughan, portable drag saw.
Champion, drag saw.
Cowan moulder and panel raiser.
MacGregor Gourlay 12 spindle dovetailer.
Fay & Egan 12 spindle dovetailer.
No. 1 Ballantine dowel machine.
12" Canada Mach. Corp. sander.
24" Fay, double drum.
No. 2 Defiance belt sander.
M135 Cowan, sash and door relisher.
2-spindle Cant-Gourlay shaper.
No. 1 Defiance, axle shoulder shaper.
Superior saw arbors, 6"-30" saws (7).
M63 Cowan spindle carver.
Hall, automatic shingle machine.
Ross automatic shingle machine.
No. 2 Dominion, lath machine & bolter.
No. 3 Defiance, rim and felloe rounding machine.
No. 1 Defiance, automatic, spoke driver.
8' Linderman, automatic, glue jointer.
8' McKeough & Trotter, hoop cutter.
No. 2 Reynolds, power screw driver.
No. 4 Lion, universal, wood trimmer.
Dundas, wood frame tenoner.
20" American wood scraper.

Ask to see our large stock of used supplies—belting, pulleys, machine shop equipment, mill supplies, pipe and fittings. Most of this material is as good as new and can be bought at greatly reduced prices.

H. W. PETRIE, LTD.
Front St. W., TORONTO, ONT.

Introducing You to the Lumber Users of Your Community

On this page are reproductions of three full page advertisements appearing in magazines that circulate in every community in the United States. They have been read by thousands of lumber users—lumber users all living within the trade territory of some retail lumberman. They all carry the line: **ASK YOUR DEALER FOR LONG-BELL LUMBER.** They carry a message to every reader that Long-Bell lumber has an outstanding quality.

Did you ever stop to think that, if you were a dealer in LONG-BELL lumber, these widely read advertisements would serve as a guide to **your** lumber yard? The name LONG-BELL and LUMBER are becoming synonymous. Dealers in that brand are coming to have a tremendous advantage—an asset that cannot be over-estimated.

The Long-Bell Lumber Company

R. A. Long Bldg. Kansas City, Mo.

OUR PRODUCTS

Southern Pine Lumber	**Creosoted Posts**
Oak	**Poles**
Oak Flooring	**Piling**
Gum	**Ties and Wood Blocks**
Creosoted Lumber	**California White Pine**

LONG-BELL

The Long-Bell Lumber Company

R. A. LONG BLDG. KANSAS CITY, MO.

Frank H. Harris Lumber Company, Limited

Manufacturers and Wholesalers of

Yellow Pine and Southern Hardwoods

Yellow Pine in Transit at all Times

Mills: { **High Point, Miss.** / **Lake, Miss.**

Office: 814 Excelsior Life Building, TORONTO, Canada.

Southern "Insurance" for Future Labor Supply.

Southern Products

Including long leaf Yellow Pine, short leaf Yellow Pine, Ash, Oak, Elm, Gum, Tupelo, Cottonwood, Louisiana Red Cypress, Kiln Dried End Matched Red and White Oak Flooring, etc., all of best quality. Manufactured by men of experience in splendidly equipped mills. Let us show you the value of our service---try us.

Annual Capacity

	Feet
Yellow Pine	350,000,000
Cypress Lumber	50,000,000
Cypress Shingles	15,000,000
Cypress Lath	15,000,000
Hardwoods	20,000,000
Oak Flooring	10,000,000

Let us quote you.

CHICAGO LUMBER & COAL COMPANY

Manufacturers

Yellow Pine, Cypress and Oak Flooring Sales Offices: East St. Louis, Ill.
Hardwood Sales Offices: Exchange Bldg., Memphis, Tenn.

J. B. WELLER & CO.,

LUMBER MERCHANTS

Trenton, - Ontario

Dealers in All Kinds of Long Timbers, Round or Square

OAK, ELM, PINE AND A SPECIALTY IN BRITISH COLUMBIA FIR.

QUICK ACTION

Can be assured if you will let the CANADA LUMBERMAN "Wanted and For Sale" department take care of your miscellaneous business needs.

We receive constant testimony from advertisers as to the value they have received from this far-reaching and inexpensive method of publicity in the lumber trade and allied industries.

Try these columns. The result will surprise you.

CANADA LUMBERMAN

and WOODWORKER

347 Adelaide St. West - - TORONTO

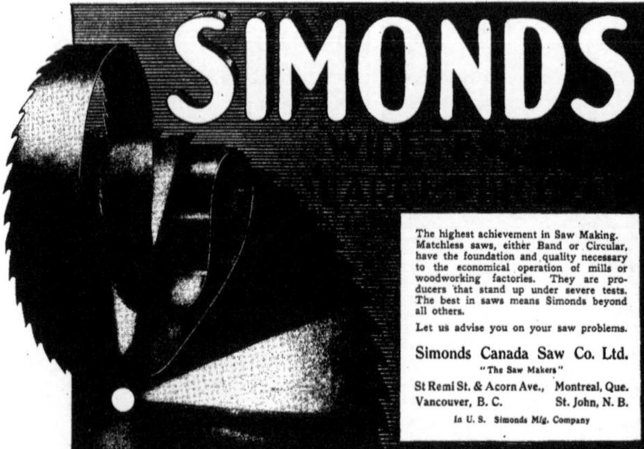
SIMONDS
The highest achievement in Saw Making. Matchless saws, either Band or Circular, have the foundation and quality necessary to the economical operation of mills or woodworking factories. They are producers that stand up under severe tests. The best in saws means Simonds beyond all others.
Let us advise you on your saw problems.
Simonds Canada Saw Co. Ltd.
"The Saw Makers"
St Remi St. & Acorn Ave., Montreal, Que.
Vancouver, B. C. St. John, N. B.
In U. S. Simonds Mfg. Company

Canada Lumberman and Woodworker

Issued on the 1st and 15th of every month by

HUGH C. MACLEAN, LIMITED, Publishers

HUGH C. MacLEAN, Winnipeg, President.

THOS. S. YOUNG, Toronto, General Manager.

OFFICES AND BRANCHES:

TORONTO - - Telephone A. 2700 - - 347 Adelaide Street West
VANCOUVER - - Telephone Seymour 2013 - - Winch Building
MONTREAL - - Telephone Main 2299 - - 119 Board of Trade
WINNIPEG - Telephone Garry 856 - Electric Railway Chambers
NEW YORK - - Telephone 3108 Beekman - - 1123 Tribune Building
CHICAGO - Telephone Harrison 5351 - 1413 Great Northern Building
LONDON, ENG. - - - - - - - - - - 16 Regent Street, S.W.

TERMS OF SUBSCRIPTION

Canada, United States and Great Britain, $2.00 per year, in advance; other foreign countries embraced in the General Postal Union, $3.00.

Single copies 15 cents.

"The Canada Lumberman and Woodworker" is published in the interest of, and reaches regularly, persons engaged in the lumber, woodworking and allied industries in every part of Canada. It aims at giving full and timely information on all subjects touching these interests, and invites free discussion by its readers.

Advertisers will receive careful attention and liberal treatment. For manufacturing and supply firms wishing to bring their goods to the attention of owners and operators of saw and planing mills, woodworking factories, pulp mills, etc., "The Canada Lumberman and Woodworker" is undoubtedly the most direct and profitable advertising medium. Special attention is directed to the "Wanted" and "For Sale" advertisements.

Authorized by the Postmaster-General for Canada, for transmission as second-class matter.

Entered as second-class matter July 18th, 1914, at the Postoffice at Buffalo, N.Y., under the Act of Congress of March 3, 1879.

Vol. 39 Toronto, July 1, 1919 No 12

Why Building Costs Keep Soaring

In the columns of the "Canada Lumberman" there have appeared from time to time many articles, of both an editorial and news character, urging retail lumbermen to enter upon an aggressive campaign, so far as their customers are concerned, to build now.

There is implanted in every human breast a desire to possess a roof over one's head. Paying rent comes to be regarded in the course of a few years as a monotonous, stereotyped and unprofitable proceeding. A city of home owners is generally a much more prosperous, contented, happy and progressive community than one where the residents are of that migratory and irresponsible class who are here today and away tomorrow. These remain in one centre as long as seasonable conditions are favorable, or fancy dictates, but depart at the first beckoning call of newer communities or larger centres, only to discover in the end that "distance lends enchantment to the view." After all there is not such a vast difference in localities where one resides if there is evidence of public spirit and local loyalty and a sincere desire to co-operate in any organized effort for the upbuild, advancement and prosperity of the hamlet, village, town or city.

The United States Department of Labor, through its Information and Educational Service, did particularly effective and timely work in stimulating "the build now," "buy now," and "own your own home" campaign. It pointed out that the man who owns his own home, is a valuable asset to the community in which he resides and has, all things considered, a better standing than the man who is content to keep his family in a rented house. It also urged that where an employer learns that a man owns his own dwelling or is paying for one, he has greater respect for him and is more willing to trust and advance him.

There is not only the patriotic side, but also the sentimental and the aesthetic as well. This is found in the memories and associations, happy reunions and joyous celebrations around the old homestead.

The aggressive and up-to-date lumber dealer should, in his publicity campaign, emphasize the fact that the ordinary family derives great pleasure, comfort and security in its home and is accorded the highest respect in the community. If the dealer states that he has in his office all sorts of plans and ideas that other people have found useful and that these will be of help to any prospective builder, the truth is being driven home that right now is the time to build, that prices are advancing all the while, that labor is going to cost more and all materials that enter into the equipment of an attractive residence are on the upward grade, such as lighting fixtures, plumbing, hardware, etc.

The cost of construction has been steadily increasing in the last twenty years, and it has been the record of builders that each delay in the hope of better prices has resulted in added cost to the projected improvement. From the lessons of the past surely one can learn a great deal and be guided by the experience and insight of the days that have passed.

One of the most effective slogans of the campaign already referred to sets forth that after the American civil war, building costs never came down to pre-war prices, and concludes: "Any man who takes opportunity by the horns will not be disappointed and will be far ahead of the man who waits. You will find when you investigate that owning your home is a very simple thing and not nearly so formidable as you once thought it. Every man has it in his power to own a cosy place which he calls "My home."

Making Your Business Earn Money

The weather is always a fruitful topic of conversation. It is the one common plane on which high and low, rich and poor, educated and illiterate, can meet and discuss with safety and ease. The only danger, perhaps, lies in the fact that a topic which is in the mouth of everyone is apt to grow threadbare and monotonous. By the same process of reasoning there has been so much said in the columns of the "Canada Lumberman" of late in regard to figuring costs and knowing overhead, that one may easily err on the side of presenting readers with too much of a good thing, or talking an otherwise interesting subject to a slow and painful death.

It is from the successful and prosperous business firms that the smaller operator can learn many lessons, and on this point one dealer, who for many years had been marking time and making a little money occasionally, but not in any way equal to the amount he should have earned on his investment and turnover, states that for several months now he has been reaping splendid results. He has raised the selling prices of his lumber so that he knows definitely that the "spread" between the wholesale figure and th retail figure is sufficient to take care of all proper charges and expenditures. In the first place, a proper system of checking has been adopted, and when an estimate is given and a contract secured, each item is checked up and, more particularly, the labor end, so that a close tab is kept on costs.

Not only is this method followed in the yard itself, but in the planing mill, and if labor costs on any contract are found too high there is an investigation and an effort made to locate the weakness so that the mistake will not be repeated. Every item of purchase and expenditure comes under close inspection. Now, as a result of system, foresight, sound business sense and sane judgment, the annual returns are most encouraging. Buying is carefully done, advantage taken of all discounts, collections promptly made, and the best service possible rendered. In this way the plant in question, which is located in a prosperous Ontario town, is building up a splendid and rapidly expanding connection. Nothing is taken for granted and every car of lumber is measured and a close watch kept to see that all stock is up to specifications and grade. This may seem a rather elaborate program, but it has paid the firm many thousands of dollars and is another exemplification of the oft reiterated declaration that success comes, not by accident or a turn in the wheel of fortune, so much as by thought, system, care, patience and perseverance and, last but by no means least,—service.

How Great Industry Has Expanded

Going back over ten years, the progress of the Canadian pulpwood, pulp and paper industries has been phenomenal. There are two principal reasons for this expansion—the practical removal of the tax upon paper going into the United States—(the duty on paper is above 5c. per pound)—and the policy of prohibiting the export of pulpwood cut on Crown lands. The possibilities of the pulp and paper industry have not been lost sight of by many of our large lumber companies, and in Eastern Canada particularly we have seen the construction of immense plants by lumber companies and the extension of others established in the earlier years. After all, it is a logical expansion by lumber concerns—they possess the raw material, and in many cases suitable sites adjacent to water powers, and the organization to handle efficiently such a rapidly growing industry.

The official figures of the exports of pulpwood, pulp and paper for the fiscal year ended March 31 last are now available. They tell the story of progress at a glance:—

Paper and manufactures of	$26,123,215	$37,865,330	$49,165,795
Wood pulp, mechanical	14,032,920	19,133,813	30,226,856
Wood pulp, mechanical.	6,371,133	6,487,079	4,479,915
	$46,527,268	$63,486,222	$83,872,566
Pulpwood, unmanufactured.	6,448,189	8,339,278	15,386,600
Total	$52,975,457	$71,825,50?	$99,259,16?

The United States were our largest customers for pulpwood, pulp and paper, so will be seen by the following tables. Canadian printing paper was exported as under:

	Cwt.	Value
United Kingdom	9,310	$ 38,484
United States	11,880,069	36,031,358
Australia	643,101	2,081,911
New Zealand	242,336	862,402
Other countries	473,726	1,703,866
	13,248,542	$40,718,021

The chief foreign markets for Canadian pulp during the year were:

Chemical Pulp	Cwt.	Value
United Kingdom	140,364	$ 611,399
United States	7,414,825	26,256,265
Japan	639,997	2,775,486
Other countries	137,744	583,706
Mechanical Pulp		
United Kingdom	2,528	3,033
United States	3,453,149	4,418,555
Other countries	53,049	58,327

The value of the United States as a buyer of these commodities is made doubly so at present by reason of the financial situation, and the adverse trade balance against us with the United States. It is urgent that we should sell more and more goods to our neighbors, and so redress the balance which unfortunately has been so largely against us for years. The falling off in ground wood pulp sold last year was due to the high water in the Eastern States and the increased supply of pulpwood.

The pulpwood figures are of interest in connection with the agitation in the States for the removal of the embargo on wood cut from Crown limits. The figures show how the United States mills are becoming more and more dependent upon Canadian supplies, and explain the anxiety of those connected with the U. S. paper industry to tap more freely our pulpwood resources, which are not so extensive as were at one time thought. Our own paper people, on the other hand, are not gratified at the increasing exports of raw material, it being contended that if exports of all pulpwood were prohibited it would compel more U. S. companies to build plants in Canada or give increased work to our present plants—thus materially benefiting our country. There is, however, the danger of retaliatory measures which must not be overlooked. Many things which are desirable are not always expedient, and the total prohibition of the export of pulpwood would certainly lead to an agitation for retaliation in some form or another.

In connection with this subject, the following information is significant as showing the increase in the exports to the United States of pulpwood. The total has grown from 982,671 cords, valued at $6,448,189 in 1917, and 1,002,127 cords, valued at $8,339,278, in 1918, to 1,597,042 cords, valued at $15,386,600, in 1919, an increase in one year of practically 100 per cent. It is estimated that the quantity of manufactured pulpwood exported last year was sufficient to have made 1,064,694 tons of paper, or about one-half the total quantity of newsprint used in the United States where the wood was sent. Sold at $75 a ton, the present market price in the States, this quantity of paper would have brought into Canada $79,852,050, instead of the $15,386,600 received for it in the form of wood.

The Badge of the Happy Home Owner

It is noted by the Musicians' Journal that the Trades Council Union News of St. Louis in an editorial in the current issue advocates a policy of each worker owning his own home. Better advice could not be given. Success in life depends upon thrift, and thrift is best cultivated through ambition and proper surroundings.

It is properly contended that the man who owns the house he lives in is going to take care of it, and at the same time take better care of those who live in it. Find the man who owns his home and you find the man who gives his children better educational opportunities, clothes and feeds them better.

Attention is also called in the St. Louis Trade Council News to the campaign of the United States Department of Labor to "Own Your Own Home." This campaign is conducted through local committees composed of town or city officials and representatives of leading associations interested in civic progress; through bankers, ministers, editors, teachers and members of women's clubs; through mercantile associations and labor unions. Thus is interest aroused in the building of dwellings and other structures. Community houses of various sorts are focusing attention. These include libraries, club houses and recreation centres.

Building gives employment to men of many trades, and it has the advantage of stimulating business enterprises of various sorts. The materials close at hand are likely to be used, and as every community has a certain proprietary interest in each new structure nothing more surely awakens civic pride than extensive building operations.

Consider for a moment the raw materials to be found in the average town and district for building purposes. Any move made in the erection of houses either for personal or company or renting purposes is a goo done and many allied trades are given employment. There is no better time to build than the present, whether one undertakes the enterprise on a big or small scale.

What the Yardman Should Observe

It is said that statistics make dry reading and it does seem that too few retail lumbermen and others give proper consideration to the study of costs on the ground, perhaps, that it is easier to guess or to estimate, or mayhap they have no definite idea of how costs should be figured or on what basis. Many firms do not know what their overhead amounts to, and if asked to tabulate what constitutes overhead charges, they would either be at a complete loss, or would eliminate—perhaps unintentionally—some of the most important items. How many men in their inventories ever deduct ten per cent. for depreciation on buildings, machinery, fixtures, etc., or take into consideration that their waggons, motor trucks, horses, harness, etc., are wearing out. Do they make proper allowance for all this?

Then again, certain lumber dealers own the buildings in which they do business, or the yards in which their stock is piled, and fail to charge up a specific amount annually for rent. By all means this should be done, as the money invested in land and buildings should bring in an adequate return, and if leased to a tenant, would certainly do so.

How many yard men fail to place a just estimate upon the value of their own services, or those of the members of their family? Perhaps there is a son or daughter, a nephew or niece, employed in the office, or some other department, and because it happens to be in the family no definite charge is made in the salary account to cover the work done by these persons. This is all a mistake. The retailer who fails to include a salary for himself equal to what he would be worth to anyone else—and, also, what the work done by members of his own family, or relatives would cost him if performed by outsiders—is certainly not figuring his overhead costs on the proper basis. By all means, salaries should be included for the proprietor and any working member of his household, and he should also make allowance for a reasonable percentage to cover his investment. The subject of figuring costs and knowing overhead expenses is, in these days, a very practical and pertinent problem with every retail lumber dealer, who wishes even to hold his own, let alone forge ahead in the game. As one authority has said, the man who does not know that he is selling his merchandise at a loss—or deliberately does so—is the type of competitor who brings bankruptcy to the trade.

Telephone Service Needs Gingering Up

The cost of Bell Telephone service in Canada has been increased, but so far as Toronto is concerned there is no evidence that this service has improved. The cold fact is that the service is bad. These are busy days and business men cannot afford to spend the time frequently required to get in touch with customers. There is delay in getting the operator's attention, a very big percentage of the calls are wrong numbers, many conversations are interrupted and the administration, generally, seems to be very loose.

These are times when people expect "service" and for the most part are ready to pay for it. However, there is no disguising the fact that there is a very general feeling that we are paying for a satisfactory service and getting a decidedly unsatisfactory one. Is the management inefficient? If so, it is due the Canadian public that the weak points be strengthened up without further delay.

Oh! What a Fall From Days of Old

The general public, having become accustomed in past years to respect the utterances of the Canadian Manufacturers' Association, as the result of the prominent connection with this association of such names as Senator Frederic Nicholls, Mr. W. K. McNaught, C.M.G., Mr. W. H. Rowley, Hon. Nathaniel Currie, Sir Chas. Gordon, Mr. Lloyd Harris, Mr. Robert Hobson, Hon. C. C. Ballantyne and others scarcely less prominent industrial figures, must have noted with considerable disappointment the recent explosion of one of the members at the annual convention, in which he made use of language not generally accepted, to say the least, as forming part of a gentleman's vocabulary. That the president of the association, Mr. W. J. Bulman, an insignificant Winnipeg manufacturer, sat quietly by and allowed the member to proceed, makes him equally responsible. The incident doubtless is without significance in itself beyond the fact that it indicates that the standard of C.M.A. officials is, temporarily we hope, at a very low ebb.

The Canadian Manufacturers' Association is an organization on whose shoulders grave responsibilities regarding the industrial development of our country rest. We do not believe the members of that association, even a small fraction of them, are favorable to the use of such unbridled and offensive utterances as those made by a Mr. Harris on the occasion referred to. If the Canadian Manufacturers' Association is to become an arena for such disgraceful brawls as the recent demonstration of this man's boorishness, the influence of the organization cannot fail to deteriorate very rapidly from the high standard of past years.

B. C. Lumber Commissioner Arrives

Major James Brechin, of Vancouver, who returned some time ago from overseas and was recently appointed by the British Columbia Government Lumber Market Commissioner for Ontario and the east, has arrived in Toronto and opened an office at 409 Kent Bldg., corner of Yonge and Richmond streets, which will be his headquarters.

Major Brechin is an experienced lumberman and was for some years manager of the King Lumber Company at Cranbrook, B.C. His mission to the east is to develop trade and increase the demand for forest products from both the Coast and Mountain regions. He has already called upon several leading builders, contractors, architects, retail lumbermen and others, and by his gentlemanly bearing and earnest, quiet manner has created a large number of friends. Major Brechin will undertake work of the same scope and character in the propaganda line as was carried out by L. B. Beale, former British Columbia Lumber Commissioner for Ontario, and later representative of the British Columbia administration in Great Britain. Mr. Bale is now one of His Majesty's Trade Commissioners, with headquarters at Winnipeg.

Major Brechin is associated with the trade extension department of the B. C. Forest Branch, and will conduct an aggressive campaign on behalf of that branch. The work will be undertaken on a broad basis. Major D. D. Young is the B. C. Lumber Market Commissioner for the prairie provinces, and was appointed at the same time as Major Brechin.

Canada's Remarkable Lumber King

Mr. J. R. Booth, the veteran "lumber king," of Ottawa, who is now in his 93rd year, had the misfortune to fall recently and break one of his arms, but this was only a mere trifle to a man of the sturdy physical frame and vigorous build of Mr. Booth. He made his appearance at his mammoth plants next day in spite of his fractured arm.

It will be remembered that about five years ago Mr. Booth, when supervising some construction work, was hit by falling timbers and had one of his legs broken, besides receiving internal injuries. He rallied from the effects and was out again in a few weeks. The many friends of Mr. Booth confidently believe that his iron constitution and open air life will carry him long past the century mark.

It will also be recalled that Sir James Ball, British Timber Controller, on his recent visit to Ottawa, took a walk over the extensive lumber yards at the Chaudiere Falls, in company with Mr. Booth. Just as he was departing, Sir James jocularly remarked, "Well, Mr. Booth, I am coming back ten years from now and hope to have the pleasure of having another stroll with you."

"All right," rejoined "J. R." with a smile, "you'll find me on deck and I'll be glad to give you a hearty welcome."

Some Editoral Short Lengths

Japanese lead pencil manufacturers will try out British Columbia cedar. The low land timber has been found too soft for this purpose, but it is hoped that the cedar on the benches and in the drier districts will prove satisfactory. Recently Japan has been taking considerable quantities of British Columbia cedar for finishing purposes.

It takes 15,000 feet of lumber to build the average dwelling. Suppose the price of lumber advances $1.00 a thousand. Suppose it advances $2.00. Suppose it advances $3.00. The first means an increased construution cost of only $15.00; the second, $30.00; the third, $45.00. Honestly, now, would that stop anyone from building who really wanted to build? remarks "The Retail Lumberman."

"The interest of Labor is not in the reward which can be obtained after accidents have happened, though that is important; the real interest of labor lies in preventing accidents," says the President of the Trade & Labor Congress of Canada. These are terse and timely words spoken at the annual meeting of the Ontario Safety League. While we may have been unfortunate enough to have left the barn door open, it is good sense to lock it before another horse is stolen.

A resolution on "trade relations" created a lively discussion recently among lumbermen and, for the present no definite agreement has been arrived at by the wholesalers and the retailers in regard to their respective status and definite sphere of action. On retail lumber dealer, when the subject of "trade relations" was mentioned, enthusiastically endorsed the proposition and intimated that he would gladly trade his mother-in-law and sister-in-law for a carload of 2 x 4 mill run white pine.

Making National Survey of Canada's Timber

What Stock Has The Dominion On Hand, What Future Crops Can Be Looked For, and By What Means Can Production Be Sustained and Measured

By James White, Ottawa, Commission of Conservation

James White, Ottawa, Ont.

Regarding the survey of the forest resources of Ontario, the Commission of Conservation has been assured of the fullest co-operation of the Ontario Government in this undertaking and proposes to start at once on the compilation of the data.

It took practically four years to complete the report on the "Forests of British Columbia" which has lately been issued and it is expected to take nearly as long to prepare a similar report for Ontario. Much will depend on the assistance received from the various departments of the government and from the timber owners. It is, of course, impossible for the Commission to attempt to cruise the whole province and since such a large proportion of the merchantable timber is in private holdings, for which the owners have detailed cruises, it would be extremely wasteful both of time and money, to duplicate this work. The Commission is therefore depending on the lumbermen, as it did in British Columbia, to supply the information they possess. It may be pointed out that, in British Columbia, detailed cruises were secured on 70 per cent. of the alienated lands and in only two or three unimportant instances was the information withheld when available.

Access to Cruises and Reports

Through the courtesy of the Minister of Lands, Forests and Mines of Ontario, the Commission will have access to all the cruises and reports in his department. Other sources of information will be cruisers, rangers, surveyors, explorers, etc., who have knowledge of local conditions, and, in addition, a considerable amount of field work will be conducted to check and connect up the data received from other sources.

The individual reports will be treated as confidential and used only as a basis for arriving at totals for large drainage areas embracing many holdings. It is hoped that sufficient data will be collected to permit of a general classification of the land as to whether it is wasteland or is suitable for agriculture or for forestry. Maps will be prepared, showing in a broad way the various forest types as regards composition and yield.

The report on the "Forests of British Columbia" has been received with the marked appreciation of the timber owners, lumbermen and others interested in the development of the forest resources of that province and it is felt that informatian of a similar nature should be available for the rest of the Dominion.

Similar Surveys in Other Provinces

The Commission of Conservation has completed a survey of the forest resources of Saskatchewan but, owing to the illness of the forester who conducted the investigation, the completion of the report has been much delayed. It is hoped, however, that it will be in the hands of the printer at an early date. In 1909-10, a similar survey of the forests of Nova Scotia was made by the Government of that province. When completed, the report was published by the Commission of Conservation.

Much data respecting the forests of Alberta and Manitoba have been obtained by the Forestry Branch, Dept. of the Interior, and when supplemented by some further investigations, will be available for publication. The forests of New Brunswick are being surveyed by the Government of that province. Ontario and Quebec, therefore, are the only provinces in which a very large amount of investigatory work is required and, if the survey of Quebec'c forests is undertaken by the Quebec Government, we may look forward with confidence to the completion, at a comparatively early date, of the survey of the forest resources of Canada. Then and then only, will we be able to formulate with confidence specific measures for the areas of Canada that contain forests and for the areas that are suitable only for the growth of forests. Unfortunately, when completed, thus survey will demonstrate that the optimistic statements respecting our "illimitable" and "inexhaustible" forest resources have no foundation in fact.

Canada Needs Increased Production

Forests are primarily valuable for the production of wood. At the present time, Canada needs increased production as never before, but the fact must not be overlooked that we shall require sustained production for several generations in order to meet the obligations which the war has imposed on us. That our forests may be used to the best advantage, it is necessary that we first know what stock we have on hand; second, what future crops can be looked for; and third, what means can best be adapted to sustain and increase production. This knowledge is perhaps more valuable to those engaged in the forest industries than to the governments since a knowledge of the available supplies will enable them to so plan their operations that their plants may be kept running. The increasing shortage of supplies is becoming a serious matter, especially for the pulp industry and the problem of reproduction either naturally or by planting, has become a live issue. The Commission of Conservation is conducting an extensive investigation of this subject and with a knowledge of the virgin supplies, basic information will be available as to the practical possibility or advisability of adopting means of maintaining the productivity of their timberlands.

The Commission appreciates the support which it has received in the past from the "Canada Lumberman" and from the other technical papers and the newspapers of Canada, and desires to thank them for their offer of co-operation in this project.

City Repeals Anti-Shingle Ordinance

The anti-shingle ordinance, prohibiting the use of shingles for wooden roofing and requiring roofs to be made of fire resistive materials was repealed recently by Dallas, Texas. The city commission was called into extra session by Mayor Wozencraft. The ordinance was repealed by an ordinance carrying with it the proviso that a secondary fire zone will be established in which fire resistive materials and not shingles must be used on roofs.

The anti-shingle ordinance was passed Aug. 2, 1918, "regulated the construction of roof covering for certain buildings in the city of Dallas, and requiring the use of fire resistive roofing to be used in the construction or repairing of such buildings." Existing houses with shingle roofs were allowed to stand under the ordinance, but houses constructed from the date of the passing of the ordinnance could not be constructed with wooden shingles.

Mayor Wozencraft made the following statement in regard to the repealing ordinance:

"The ordinance was passed by the commission in order that the relief which is urgently needed in order that building may not be unwarrantably delayed might be given.

"The commission, and more especially Police and Fire Commissioner McGee, will look into the proposition of extending the fire limits into a secondary fire zone where five-resistive roofs will be required, and all other regulations complied with.

"But it is not felt that this ordinance repealing the old ordinance should be held up until the details of the plan are completed.

"The commission satisfied itself that the use of fire-resistive materials adds materially to the construction of homes, and created considerable additional expense in the building of modest-priced homes. Upon further study we reached the conclusion that the cheaper grades of fire-resistive roofs were not satisfactory."

Section 3 of the ordinance passed yesterday says:

"Whereas, by reason of the unsatisfactory roofing required to be used by the citizens because their houses are to some extent rendered uninhabitable on account of rain and wind by reason of such unsatisfactory roofing; because it causes an interruption in building of homes by the citizens of the city of Dallas by reason of the operation of said ordinance, an emergency is created for the immediate preservation of the public peace, health and safety requiring that this ordinance shall take effect immediately and it is accordingly ordained that this ordinance shall take effect from and after its passage and approval."

Sawing Lumber for Export—Speed vs. Quality

The Question Arises Which Pays the Best—Some Observations on Swedish Methods in Comparison With Those Which Are Followed in Canada

By J. Ander, Montreal

J. Ander, Montreal, Que.

The "Canada Lumberman" of June 15th contained an interesting article by Mr. James H. Lane, entitled "Some Things Canadians Can Learn in Sawing". He points out, that Canadian exporters of lumber are up against a keen competition on the British market, particularly by Swedish shippers, and urges the Canadian shippers to study the methods of their Swedish competitors to enable them to secure a greater share of the trade with Great Britain than they have in the past.

Mr. Lane states that Swedish lumber is preferred by British buyers, and that £1 to £2 per standard more is willingly paid for Swedish lumber than for corresponding qualities of Canadian lumber. The reason for the preference accorded Swedish lumber is the regularity with which it is sawn, the neatness of the cross-cutting, the attractive way of marking the lumber and the strict adherence to qualities indicated by different marks. Mr. Lane's article is very instructive and deserves every attention. I wish to add a few remarks, based on more than twenty years' experience in the lumber business, twelve years thereof in Canada and several in Sweden.

They Never Go Hand in Hand

For the Canadian sawmill owners, there seems to be one consideration that outweighs every other—speed, with, as a consequence, low cost of manufacture. In a lumber mill, however, great speed and high quality of work never go hand in hand. Our modern Canadian sawmills cut lumber very fast and very cheap, but no one can deny that the lumber is very irregular. Anyone having had experience with resawing and planing Canadian lumber knows that it often varies in thickness all the way up to 1/4 in. Some pieces are 1 3/4 or 1 7/8 in. thick; others 2 1/8 in. or 2 1/4 in. Other pieces are 2 in. in one end, 1 7/8 in. in the middle, 2 1/8 in. in the other end. If such an irregularity were only an exception it would not be so important, but irregularity is the rule and precision is the exception. This is what British and French buyers object to. For a number of purposes, they demand lumber perfect in thickness and width, and for such lumber they are willing to pay a higher price, and in order to get it, they turn to Sweden.

Swedish lumber of standard makes is absolutely exact in thickness and width. It does not vary 1/16 in. It is cut plump, so that when the deal is dry, it is exact in size. Consequently, when the British buyer resaws this lumber into boards for shooks or for other purposes, he knows to a fraction of an inch what he is going to get out of it; there is no waste, no "last piece" that is useless. With Canadian lumber a considerable waste must always be figured on when working it. The British buyer figures it pays him better to give the Swedish shippers from $2.50 to $5.00 per M. S. ft. more; it not only means money in his pocket, but he preserves also his peace of mind, which he finds seriously threatened handling uneven lumber.

The Canadian producer sacrifices quality to speed—the Swedish, speed to quality. The question is, which pays the best?

The Precision of Swedish Cuts

All the larger Swedish mills are equipped with log frames built to turn out perfect lumber and to get as much lumber out of the log as possible. The foremost manufacturers of Swedish sawmill machinery, the Bolinder Company of Stockholm, Sweden, build a "precision log-frame," using very thin sawblades for all diameters. It produces a faultless cut and the saw blades used are from No. 18 to No. 20 B.W.G. and the sawkerf only about 1/16 in. A log frame of this kind, coupled with the Swedish procedure of sawing, about which more below, not only cuts perfect lumber, but the logs will yield from 6 to 10 per cent. more lumber than what can be got out of them even with the best Canadian band mills.

On a cut of say, twenty million feet of lumber per year, this saving would amount to at least 1,200,000 S. Ft., worth, with present prices, about $40,000: Considering further, that the Swedish producer will get on an average, $3.50 per M.S. Ft. more for his lumber, c.i.f. British port, his system of sawing will assure him of another gain of $70,000, or $110,000, in all, on a cut of twenty million feet.

The Swedish shipper has a lower freight to contend with, but we do not take that matter into consideration, as our object is only to make a comparison between Swedish and Canadian sawing methods. That the Swedish exporter is closer to the British market is something in his favor, which cannot be overcome.

Incidentally, we might mention that the lower freight rates for the Swedish exporters, are offset by the higher cost of their logs. The larger Swedish lumber corporations keep whole armies of men taking care of their forests. The Swedish forests get the same attention as an average mortal gives his children—with the result of course, that the logs, delivered at the mills, stand in a very high price, but also with the result that the forests are preserved and their wealth will never give out.

Yearly Gain vs. Increased Sawing Cost

Against the extra profit of $110,000, mentioned above, the Swedish manufacturer has to figure on a considerably higher cost of sawing the lumber. He employs a larger number of men in his mill than what a Canadian manufacturer does for cutting an equal quantity of lumber.

The whole question in a nutshell is, therefore, this: Which amounts to more, the $110,000 yearly gain on a twenty million feet cut, or the increased cost of sawing? That is a matter for Canadian manufacturers to study.

The Swede swears by his methods and claims that not only do they bring more money into his pocket, but they insure him also a world market. South Africa and Australia are large buyers of Swedish lumber and the reasons for this, as was clearly shown by an article in the "Canada Lumberman," a year or so ago, are exactly the same as those that make the Swedish lumber preponderant on the British market.

One or two attempts have been made to employ Swedish sawmill machinery in Canada, but the results of those attempts have not been very satisfactory. In the first place the machines employed were not modern, but very much out of date, and in the second place, the Swedish methods were not carried through in a consistent way. The success of the Swedish machines depends upon their being used for the working prcedure they are designed for.

The Swedish Methods in Detail

The Swedish method of sawing starts in the boom, where the logs are sorted as to sizes. A 10 in. log is not cut with the same saw-setting as a 9½ in. or 10½ in. log, from which slightly different sizes are taken out. The Swedish manufacturer has diagrams, showing to a fraction of an inch, what sizes are to be derived from all different log diameters.

The larger Swedish mills are equipped with quite a number of log frames, so that the different sizes of logs are easily handled. In smaller mills, the saw-setting is changed for different sizes, morning and noon, to prevent accumulation. This method requires very extensive booms with numerous pockets but the quantity of slabs and edgings going out from a Swedish sawmill is extremely small. Burners for taking care of sawmill waste, would be considered a monstrosity.

Wherever possible, the waste, after every foot of lumber that could be utilized for shooks or similar purposes, has been taken care of, is cut up by slab-chippers, and used by the pulp mills. At other sawmills, situated too far from a pulpmill, the edgings and slabs are converted into charcoal.

How the Appearance is Preserved

The lumber is not cross-cut in the mills. The cross-cutting or trimming is done by portable electric trimmers just before the lumber goes into the vessel. At the same time, the marking, which Mr. Lane speaks about, takes place. The trimming of the lumber, after it is dry, means that the ends are bright and neat, and not split, which all considerably improves the appearance of the lumber.

I trust that the above remarks may be of interest to progressive Canadian manufacturers. It would, no doubt, be of a tremendous interest to the Canadian lumber trade, if some large Canadian corporation would adopt the "Swedish system" in one of their mills, installing modern Swedish machinery in order to manufacture lumber, which would be able to compete with the Swedish on the British market. If carried through in the right way, there is no reason why such an attempt should not turn out a success. It would demonstrate how the Canadian forests could be made to yield from 6 to 10 per cent more lumber from the same amount of logs, and it would open up for Canada a larger market for its lumber.

It would undoubtedly take some little time to convince the British public that the Canadian lumber cut by Swedish methods would compare with the Swedish lumber in quality, and the old question would, no doubt, be asked: "Can anything good come from Nazareth?" By degrees, however, this incredulity would be overcome, as "seeing is believing."

Laurentide Dividends Grow Still Larger

When Laurentide Paper securities were bid down to 218 in the Montreal stock market recently it was hardly expected that an announcement would be made late in the afternoon that with the regular quarterly dividend of 3 per cent. the company would declare a bonus of 3 per cent. on its $9,600,000 capital stock.

The company increased its distribution to shareholders to 12 per cent. in December last, after paying 10 per cent. for the previous year. In some quarters it is considered a sort of preparation for the divison of the stock, making with what is now practically a 15 per cent dividend, new shares with dividends at 5 per cent., the stock, at present market value, to be quoted around 70.

There was a tendency when the news first became known to connect the 3 per cent. bonus with the dividends which the Laurentide Company is in receipt of from its prosperous subsidiary, Laurentide Power, but this was put aside as improbable in view of the fact that only one quarterly disbursement had been made by the latter, representing but 3/4 of 1 per cent. on the outstanding capital shares of the parent enterprise. The bonus, therefore, is, in all probability, the outcome of the earnings of the Pulp and Paper Company, the Grand Mere plant, as President Chahoon announced some time ago, being operated at capacity for several months past.

The action of the Laurentide executive, in the matter of the bonus distribution, would seem to render prospects particularly bright for shareholders, in view of the fact that officials of the enterprise are more or less committed to the policy of turning over to the holders of the pulp and paper stock annually the dividends received by the company from Laurentide Power. As these represent some 3 per cent. per year on the stock of the parent company, this would appear to be the equivalent to placing the shares on an 18 per cent. dividend basis, providing, of course, the bonus just declared becomes permanent.

Some Newsy Briefs from Ottawa

The principle of collective bargaining, as meaning the dealing by woodworking factory officials and heads with all the employees of such factories at Ottawa, has been flatly refused, according to information given the "Canada Lumberman."

The situation from the labor end with the woodworking factories at the date of writing, remained indefinite. The workers were asking for a further increase in wages and requested of the mills that they set a flat or general rate for all labor employed in woodworking plants. Negotiations which have been under way for some time, continued up to practically the end of the month when the workers staged a meeting at the Windsor Hotel and invited the employers to it. The employers did not appear.

The best information from the mills that the lumbermen could receive was that the mills, while willing to consider the demands of labor for an advance in salary, would not listen to the workers collectively, but were willing to discuss the situation, each mill for itself, with its own employees.

Secretary McLellan, of the New Brunswick Lumbermen's Association, recently returned fom England where he was in the interests of the association. He predicts great things for the New Brunswick product and says that there will be fine opportunities for a good market for many years to come. He says the housing problem in the Old Country is acute and large quantities of lumber will be needed for building purposes.

Wholesalers Discussed Trade Ethics

All Members Will Do Everything in Their Power to Protect Each Retail Customer

The Wholesale Lumber Dealers' Association, Incorporated, held its monthly meeting on June 13th, at the Albany Club, Toronto, and had one of the lragest turnouts of the season. Mr. A. E. Clark occupied the chair. Matters of a routine nature occupied the attention of the members chiefly during the evening.

The greater portion of the evening was devoted to an interesting discussion on the subect of trade ethics, being centered chiefly upon the proper field of operation for the wholesaler. Every member present expressed his views on the subject and it was the unanimous feeling of all the members that wholesale lumber dealers should do everything in their power to protect the interests of their retail customers.

The discussion showed, however, that it would be neither practical nor advisable to handle this matter by anything in the nature of definite regulations which might be considered as restraining trade, but rather that it should be left to each individual member.

It was brought out also by the discussion that practically every member of the Wholesale Lumber Dealers Association, Inc., is scrupulously careful to protect the interests of the retail lumber dealers, and that such complaints as may develop from time to time relate to firms or individuals who are not members of the Association.

The Wholesale Lumber Dealers' Association, Incorporated, has from the first, co-operated extensively with the Ontario Retail Lumber Dealers' Association, in order to assist the latter in its difficult work of organization, and the members felt that the goodwill they had shown to the retailers should be accepted by the latter as a definite indication of their desire to promote the welfare of the retail trade.

One of the interesting features was the passing of a resolution, moved by Mr. Alex. Gordon, and seconded by Mr. H. G. McDermid, that the Association should hold a picnic sometime during the summer. Details for the event were left in the hands of the Entertainment Committee, which consists of Messrs. F. Oliver, chairman; A. K. Johnson, D. C. Johnston, and D. Barclay.

At the conclusion of the meeting it was decided that no meetings should be held during the ensuing summer months.

St John Desires More Ships for Export

One of the biggest problems that lumbermen in New Brunswick have had to cope with in years is that of tonnage. For many months past the situation could be termed as acute for every available bit of space on wharves and in their yards was taken up with piles and there was very little, and in some instances, no room for this season's cut. The British controller of timber supplies purchased many hundreds of millions of feet of all kinds of lumber in New Brunswick and the vast majority of it is still piled up waiting shipment. Adequate tonnage was said to be available, but the price asked was too large. Representations were made to the controller and he promised to take immediate steps in the matter; for a time there was no change and much dissatisfaction resulted. To date there has been a slight change for the better and a promise is held out that more tonnage will be released later in the season to carry the many millions of feet overseas. Within the last fortnight there have been several sailings and this has helped to a great extent to lessen the strain.

Two cargoes of lumber went across within the past few days, the S. S. War Country and the S. S. War Ottawa taking away over four million feet at a value of over $100,000. This is for reconstruction work in the British Isles and in Belgium. The S. S. Everilda also took away a large quantity and the S. S. Trojan and the War Niagara are now in port loading, while a new schooner, Irma, is expected from New York in a few days to load for the United Kingdom. It is estimated that there are still many hundreds of million feet to be removed and a large number of steamers will be necessary.

Farnworth and Jardine's Wood Circular, of Liverpool, for June 1 had the following on New Brunswick and Nova Scotia spruce and pine deals and birch: "The total import to the Mersey, including the Manchester Canal, was 2790 standards, Liverpool receiving a small proportion. Satisfactory consumption, considering the depleted condition of stocks is noticeable. The demand is fairly steady for early arrivals, but business is difficult to arrange for more distant delivery, chiefly due to the very large quantities to come forward on government account. Tonnage, particularly for private business, is strictly limited. Pine deals-stocks practically exhausted. Birch-logs nominal import to Liverpool, deliveries accounted for the bulk of the stock on the quay at the end of last month, leaving the present holdings extremely light, viz: 6,000 cubic feet. Planks, arrived freely, good consumption; stocks not excessive."

Work of Lumbermen's Safety Association

Principle of Current Cost Plan Endorsed—Adoption of Merit Rating System and Placing Doctors Under Direction of Employers Advocated

The fourth annual meeting of the Lumbermen's Safety Association was held at 16 Castle Building, Ottawa. H. I. Thomas, the president, presided and there were also present: Messrs. Sir Henry K. Egan, W. E. Bigwood, John S. Gillies, T. E. Clendinnen representing the Hon. W. C. Edwards, and J. L. Martin of Kars. In addition, proxies had been received from 184 members.

President H. I. Thomas addressed the meeting as follows: "During the month of February, your president, in common with other representatives of the Canadian Manufacturers' Association, had an interview with Sir William Hearst and Mr. Lucas, the Attorney-General of Ontario, relative to the amendments which it was proposed to make to the Workmen's Compensation Act of Ontario during the session of the legislature this year. At this interview a number of more or less important considerations were laid before the Ontario Government and special attention was paid to the desirability of allowing the Safety Associations to represent before the Workmen's Compensation Board their respective groups of employers in any matter affecting such group as a whole. This suggestion was favorably considered and it was pointed out that no amendment to the

Mr. H. I. Thomas, Ottawa, Ont.

Act was required to permit such procedure and that steps would be taken to allow same in the future. It was also pointed out by the deputation that it was desirable that, on certain general points, an appeal should lie from the Board to some judicial tribunal. No desire was expressed for litigation with regard to awards made by the Board, but only for a final and decisive ruling on general principles. No indication was given by the Ontario Government as to the possibility of granting this request. Another matter which was brought forward by the deputation was the inclusion, in some cases, of the salaries of clerical employees in the assessments made by the Board. Unfortunately, this representation did not have the desired effect, as it became evident that, under the Act, as it then stood, such inclusion was not permitted, but it was evidently felt by the Ontario Government that clerical employees should be protected and their salaries assessed, so that an amendment to this effect has now been incorporated in the Workmen's Compensation Act.

Abandon Idea of Big Reserve Fund

"Perhaps the most important fact in the year's experience of the working of the Act has been the implicit abandonment by the Board of the principle of building up a large reserve fund to take care of deferred liabilities. It was felt that the representations made by your Association and other similar bodies to the effect that these reserve funds were already large enough and that it was unfair to burden the employers, at this time, with assessments larger than were necessary to take care of the current cost of the operation of the Act, had great weight and, as a consequence, we may look, in future, to an assessment only sufficient to pay the current cost.

"It should also be pointed out to the members of our Association that merit rating has now been established and employers, whose accident record is bad, will be penalized. This modification we have constantly asked for, and it is gratifying that our efforts in this direction have met with success."

The president also stated that the capitalized value of outstanding pensions in Class 1, as of December 31st, 1918, was $237,-273.04, and that a letter had been received from Mr. Samuel Price, chairman of the Board, dated April 10th, 1919, stating that it was the intention of the Board in the near future to have a re-valuation of outstanding pensions.

Some Data From Secretary's Report

The following extracts are taken from the secretary's report:

In the fall of 1918 it was decided to have your inspector visit the lumber camps, not alone for the purpose of safety inspection work, but also to inspect camps from a hygenic and sanitary point of view to avoid as far as possible industrial diseases. We incorporated with these ideas, the further one of First Aid—having secured diagrams, books, etc., from the St. John Ambulance Association—realizing that this would be a most important addition to the inspector's safety work.

Comparing the results of 1917 and 1918 cases finally disposed of by the Workmen's Compensation Board, the figures are as follows:

	1917		1918	
Temporary Disability				
Medical aid only	63		212	
Compensation	810	873	857	1069
Permanent Disability		76		69
Deaths		26		22
		975		1160

The report by the Workmen's Compensation Board of receipts and expenditures shows a net shortage on Class 1 operations for the year of $24,147.17, which explains why it will be necessary to increase the rate of assessment on saw mills from $1-.50 to $1.60 for both 1918 and provisionally for 1919. The logging or lumbering rate will remain the same $1.20 for each of the two years.

Average of $73 Paid per Accident

We understand that the total number of accidents in all classes for 1918 was 47,848 with paid claims amounting to $3,514,648, or an average per accident of $73.45.

In Class 1 the average per accident (not including the estimated amount required to complete all claims for the year 1918) is $123.88.

This emphasizes in graphic fashion the urgent necessity which exists, not only to reduce the number but the seriousness of accidents in Class 1, apart entirely from the humanitarian standpoint. It is to be noticed that lumbering and logging accidents were responsible for nearly 44 per cent of the awards and estimated requirements to settle all 1918 claims, while the percentage of saw mill accidents is nearly 55 per cent.

With reference to the subject of Merit Rating, it is felt by the Board that its adoption will go a long way towards attaining the objects sought by this industry. The following extracts from a circular issued by the Board in November, 1918, have special application at this time.

"It may be pointed out that employers who are so careless or reckless in regard to safety conditions as to be inadequately dealt with by the merit rating provisions are still subject to application of the penalties provided for by Section 74 (4) of the Act, namely, to be specially assessed for the cost of the accidents which they produce."

With regard to the subject of Medical Aid it says:

"The cost of medical aid, like the cost of compensation, has proved to be much less than wes feared or anticipated when the law was being framed. The year 1918 is the first full year of medical aid experience. The figures to date show that it has added less than 15 per cent. to what would otherwise have been the burden of the Act, the compensation awarded in Schedule 1 industries during the first ten months of 1918, amounting to $2,104,378.77, and the medical aid payments to $304,683.62. While, of course, some increase of rate will be inevitable by reason of medical aid, it is hoped that the figures of 1918 when finally ascertained will show the same satisfactory results as those of previous years."

Then with reference to the average rate per $100 of pay roll, we note the following:

"When the Act was going into effect in 1915, the average rate per $100 of pay roll which it was estimated would be required was $1.64, after the experience of 1915 had been ascertained, the rate were adjusted to an average of $1.27; the average rate for 1916 as finally adjusted was $1.09, and the average rate for 1917 was 98 cents; and the latter will,, as the figures now show, be slightly further reduced. These reductions have taken place while expenditures in almost every direction were very greatly increasing."

No Abuse of Provisions of Act

"The Board also, while giving the workmen entitled to it the full measure of compensation provided for it by the Act, has been careful to use every reasonable effort to avoid imposition and unwarranted payment of claims. For assistance in this, credit is due to the co-operation of employers in making careful reports, and notifying the Board of any attempted abuse of the provisions of the Act."

The net balance to the credit of Class 1 in the Pension Fund, December 31st, 1918, was $237,273.04.

The balance carried from 1917 was $153,980.13.
The amount transferred in 1918 was $94,065.75.
Interests received, $9,542.76.
Pensions payments, $20,315.60.

The books of the Association have been certified correct by Mr. Alex. F. Chamberlain, chartered accountant.

Inspections made in 1918:

In Class 4 to April 1st, 1918	190
In Class 1 to December 31st, 1918	506
In Camps, Nov. 18th to Dec. 31st, 1918	25
	721

Services Performed by the Association

Amongst the various services which have been rendered by this Association since its inception, may be mentioned the following:

The acknowledgement of the principle of the Current Cost Plan. That is, this Association objected to the building up of a huge reserve fund by the Board by means of capitalizing deferred payments.

We also have agitated that in connection with medical aid the doctors should be placed under the directions of the employers.

We have also urged the adoption of some sort of appeal by any group of industries from any decision of the Board, which might be regarded as unfair or unworkable.

We have urged the adoption of the Merit Rating System, which is now being done by the Board.

Another matter that we have consistently advocated is a provision whereby corporations able to give satisfactory evidence of financial stability should be allowed to stand outside the group in which they would naturally fall, and pay individually the actual amount of compensation awarded to their injured employees by the Board.

The summary of accidents forwarded by Mr. J. R. Booth of Ottawa was presented to the meeting, and it was decided to suggest in the report that all our members should send in a similar report. This report covers amount paid for accidents happening during the year ending December 31st, showing saw mill operations and bush operations separately, also accidents which happened in the previous year, compensation for which was received during the current year, then the amounts paid for doctors, hospitals, undertakers and ambulance accounts during the current year; pensions paid during the current year on accidents happening in previous years. This would give a total paid by the Workmen's Compensation Board in any one year, and then should be shown the amount of the assessment paid to the Workmen's Compensation Board during that year. Then the summary should contain the number of accidents during the calendar year, and which were reported to the Workmen's Compensation Board with detail to the number of accidents which happened in the various departments.

Officers and Directors for 1919

The following directors and officers were elected to serve for the year 1919:

Mr. H. I. Thomas, president.
Mr. W. E. Bigwood, vice-president.
Directors—Hon. W. C. Edwards, Mr. Dan McLachlin, Sir Henry K. Egan, Hon. George Gordon, Mr. John S. Gillies.
Frank Hawkins, secretary.

Fourteen Mills Wiped Out by Fire

Continued fine weather throughout New Brunswick for the greater part of the last month or two has made the outdoor world attractive, but it also has made the country dangerously dry, with the inevitable toll of forest fires as a result. Just as new fires were springing up in all directions a short time ago, a providentially heavy downpour of rain averted the danger but everything was so dry that the destruction of a big lumber mill and its supplies of lumber occurred during the rainstorm. Since then dry weather has given the fires another opportunity. The most serious was that at Kedgewick, where an entire village was wiped out, leaving many homeless people and doing damage to the extent of $250,000.

In recent weeks no less than fourteen lumber mills have been destroyed by fire, mostly in the northern part of the province. The annual recurrence of these fires, with the great loss not only in buildings and goods, but in the standing timber swept by forest fires, shows how necessary is the policy of the provincial Department of Mines and Lands which has been devoting more time and money to safeguarding the greatest provincial asset by the development of the forest protection service.

The recent decision that the government railways should be required to observe the same safeguards against the spreading of fire that have been required of privately owned roads, was a notable victory for the province and will play an immediate part in lessening the fire risk.

General News Notes From the West

The Tanner Lumber Co., at Camrose, Alta., has been succeeded by the H. J. Wells Lumber Co.

The launching of the 1,500-ton wooden schooner Gunn at the Cholberg shipyards at Victoria, V. C., marks the practical completion of the first vessel constructed on the Pacific coast of the Dominion for Norwegian registry. Two additional ships of the same type are being built at the Cholberg yard.

It is likely that an amendment will be made to the Forestry Act which proposes to withdraw certain portions of the Porcupine Forest Reserve in Saskatchewan, which are suitable for soldier settlement. It is estimated that the portions which may be withdrawn this year will aggregate about 200,000 acres. It is now the intention to take from the reserve land that ought to remain and be used for forestry purposes but it is intended to make available all that is especially suitable for crop production.

The Hammond Cedar Mill, of Hammond, B. C., is now entirely electrically driven. The daily output is about 70M feet of bevelled siding, and 200M shingles. Messrs. Hartnell, the heads of the enterprise, report business as being exceptionally good. The mill gives employment to about 100 men. New furnaces, a new filing room and machine shop 48 by 48 have been constructed. The erection of a new burner for taking care of the refuse and reducing the fire risk is almost completed, and the company is also installing a new underwriter's fire pump of 1,000-gallon capacity. Among other new machinery set up are a Yates power-feed rip saw, a Yates fast-feed motor, a six inch planing mill resaw and a Yates No. 10 timber sizer. There are also being installed a duplicate set of trimmers.

The H. W. Wilson Co., Ltd., has been incorporated at Edmonton, Alta.

The Robertson-Hackett Saw Mills, Ltd., of Vancouver, will shortly have added to them a modern fully electrically driven planing mill. The old mill on False Creek will be torn down as soon as the new structure is completed, and with its elimination will pass one of the old landmarks of Vancouver.

Another particularly successful launching was staged at the Foundation Yards, Victoria, B. C., recently when the good ship Ottawa was consigned to Neptune's domain in the presence of one of the largest crowds that has yet turned out for a twilight affair. The Ottawa marks the eighth ship to be launched by the Foundation Company to fly the tricolor of France, the shipbuilding corporation holding a contract for the construction of twenty wooden vessels.

Bad forest fires are raging forty to fifty miles northwest of Calgary in the Sheep Creek Valley. A forest fire is also reported in the valuable timber in the Porcupine Hills.

A recent despatch from Fernie says: 'After fighting for twenty-four hours forest fires which threatened to sweep the town, the inhabitants of Nataal, B. C., were removed from the town in a special train early Sunday morning, while a volunteer fire corps, under Chief MacDougall, extinguished blaze after blaze within the town itself, until the fire in the immediate vicinity had spent itself. No serious casualties were reported. Forest fires are reported from many districts near here, and some ranching property is threatened. A fire one mile east of Hosmer is confined to cut-over land, and the fire wardens have been successful so far is protecting valuable timber lands.

Something Wrong with Distribution System

It is Costing Too Much to Get Manufactured Products to Consumer, Declares Mr. Nicholson, Chairman of High Cost of Living Committee

Geo. B. Nicholson, M.P., East Algoma, Ont.

George B. Nicholson, M.P., of East Algoma, who is a member of the firm of Austin & Nicholson, Chapleau, Ont., lumbermen, pulpwood and tie dealers, delivered a stirring address at the annual banquet of the Canadian Manufacturers' Association, held recently in Toronto. Mr. Nicholson is chairman of the High Cost of Living Committee in the House of Commons. To meet the heavy financial burdens imposed upon her, Canada, the speaker said, must do as any individual would, take stock of her resources, and make up her mind how to develop them to meet the obligations. "We cannot take our place as a divided people," he said, "We must find some way to become united. At the present time we find that there is utter chaos. There seems to have grown up amongst our people a feeling of resistance against constituted authority or restraint. There is absolutely nothing in the form of unity.

"Unless we can find a basis upon which the workingman and his employer can get together we are going to end in utter and complete chaos. The unrest is due to three prime causes. There is the natural nervousness through which the whole world is passing because of the war. There is the economic pressure, which is bearing perhaps more heavily on the workingman than any other class, and there is the irresponsible agitator. The last of these I would consider first." He agreed that the time came long ago when Canadians should have said that people who were not willing to become Canadians should not have been allowed to enter; also that those who are here and are not willing to subscribe to our institutions should not be permitted to stay here.

Consumer Pays Too Much.

Dealing with the second cause, that of economic pressure, Mr. Nicholson gave it as his opinion that the less control the Government exercises over the normal things of earth the better it would be for the country. He believed there was something wrong in the distribution system, in that it may cost too much to get things from the producer to the ultimate consumer. "I believe there are instances where it is costing too much to get the things you men produce from the producer to the consumer. The Canadian Manufacturers' Association are bearing a very large part of the odium that is cast upon people who are producing things. It should be your business to see that the channel through which your goods pass to the utimate consumer is made as clear of obstruction as it is possible to make it, and I mean the distribution system within our own borders."

Referring to the nervousness existent at present, Mr. Nicholson said that great patience was necessary. It was manifest that conditions could not continue as at present, because it was impossible to produce anything in competition with the world and have the class war such as there is in Canada to-day.

"Canada cannot establish a different basis than other countries and compete with other countries," he declared. "Our workingmen have the right to the best standard workingmen can possibly get, but if they get on a pedestal above the other workingmen of the world then the things they are making cannot compete with the rest of the world. There must be an effort to bring about a reasonable world standard."

Rebellion Against Constittued Authority

Mr. Nicholson referred to the jaralysis in Winnipeg as an illustration of what the rest of the country should steer clear of. "The Winnipeg strike is not a strike at all in the accetped sense of the term," he said. "It is rebellion against constituted authority in organized labor itself. Those who are responsible for that movement know that the only way they could accomplish the purpose they had in mind—and that was the overthrow of constituted authority—was, first of all, by overthrowing organized labor. The thing that has saved the situation in Western Canada is that organized labor has been able to see through the whole thing. The men at the head of that Winnipeg movement were not workingmen at all, but they were grafters on the workingmen of this country and the workingmen in every other country."

However, the speaker declared, there is a place for organized labor, and many of the employers in Canada are, to a large degree, responsible for placing the club in the hands of those agitators that they have been able to use, because many employers in Canada have refused to recognize the good they are getting out of organized labor, properly constituted, and because they have refused to allow the workers to get together. Mr. Nicholson came out strongly in favor of labor having the right to organize; also in favor of collective bargaining. The Winnipeg strike struck at the foundation on which collective bargaining rests to be successful. It rests on two principles, the first being the recognition that employers may organize, and the second is the inviolability of a contract.

What Education Should Do For Masses

The Canadian Pulp & Paper Association some months ago appointed J. N. Stephenson, of Montreal, a committee of one for the purpose of considering certain aspects of educational matters in Canada. It was felt that one of the underlying causes of industrial unrest is the lack of proper appreciation on the part of the people of Canada for their rightful obligations and responsibilities in respect to social, political and industrial matters. It is believed that this is largely due to a lack of training on all ethical lines in our common schools, and that the present tendency for better facilities for technical education will fill a great want in the training of those who work in mills and factories, but this does not reach the great mass of future citizens.

It is stated by the Canadian Pulp & Paper Association that the dangers of Bolshevism, just as the dangers of Teutonism, really lie in the lack of ethical standards of the people and the failure of individuals to realize and accept their responsibilities to the community. It is only by proper training of the youth that an improvement of these conditions can be accomplished.

There has been drawn up by Mr. Stephenson, after a year of hard work and deep thought on the quetsion, a comprehensive memorial. This memorial will be presented to the various educational authorities in Canada for the local committees. The memorial has already been approved by the Canadian Mining Institute, Canadian Fisheries' Association and the Society of Chemical Industries. It is hoped that every member of the Pulp & Paper industry will express his approval of the sentiment contained in the resolution, which will be forwarded to the Ministers of Education for the different Provinces of Canada. The memorial states that it is of vital importance, in the development of the Canadian nationality with high ideals and efficient performance, that there should be an early and thorough training for citizenship in all schools throughout the Dominion.

To be effective this training should be based upon the ordinary activities and occupations of the children and young people; and it is pointed out that the success of this method is well shown in the Boy Scout movement, and that any attempt to teach abstract principles of citizenship and moral conduct solely through text-books, notes or lectures is sure to be futile. The committee is of the opinion that compulsory education should be universal throughout Canada up to the age of fourteen years, at least, and declares that illiteracy, even in a minor degree, is a great handicap. One reason why the masses in Russia cannot be reached and rescued from the present error of their ways is that they cannot read, and it is thus impossible to influence them as an educative populace can be influenced.

The question should also be considered whether some form of continuation education should not be compulsory for a further period of two years or more. To secure the desired results it would be necessary to pay the teachers larger salaries in order to make it worth while for the best men and women to devote themselves to the profession.

The committee also endorses improvements in text-books to make them more interesting and more closely related to the natural knowledge and the ordinary activities and occupations of children and parents. This would open up the opportunity of character building and training in citizenship.

Lumberman Legislator Talks on Labor Unrest

Stirring Address Delivered in Commons by Major Power, Lumberman, Who Charges Government with Negligence on Several Problems

Major Chas. G. Power, M.C., Federal representative for Quebec South

Major Chas. G. Power, M.C., who is the Federal representative in parliament of Quebec South, and a son of Wm. Power, the veteran lumberman of Quebec, recently made an able and logical address in the House of Commons on the question of industrial unrest in Canada. He discussed the situation in a clear manner and brought out many strong points in the matter of dealing with present conditions. Major Power, who is a brother of W. Gerard Power of St. Pacome, Que., president of the Canadian Lumbermen's Association, served with the Canadian forces overseas and was seriously wounded on two occasions. He was with the 14th Batt. and was later transferred to the Cyclists Corps. In his remarks in the House, he spoke in part as follows:

We have, as one of the approximate causes of the present unrest the difficulty which the Government has found in demobilization. I do not intend to go into this question at any great length. Many theories have been advanced as to whether demobilization should proceed more rapidly or more slowly, but we have found this: The Government, despite all its agencies—its employment agencies, its land settlement scheme, its war-service gratuity scheme, and even its pension scheme—has been unable to find work for the returned soldier, and unable to provide for the dislocation of industry conseqeunt on the armistice. The Government have been unable in any way to prevent or forestall the unrest which it was patent to any one of us would follow the conclusion of the war.

How Living Costs Have Aviated

The cost of living has been going up by leaps and bounds, and there has been no attempt to prevent or control it on the part of the Government. I do not wish to tire the House by quoting the figures of the percentage of rise for all the countries in the world, but I might mention the increase that has taken place since 1914 in the following countries: United Kingdom, 120 per cent; France, 137 per cent; Sweden, 220 per cent; Canada, 84 per cent; United States, 75 per cent; One hon. gentleman stated today that in New Zealand the cost of living had gone up higher than my figures show, but if my figures are correct, and I have reason for thinking so, the cost of living in New Zealand in October, 1918, had increased only 42 per cent. So it will be seen that the increase in the cost of living in Canada has been exceeded only in European countries subject to blockade conditions. Compared with all other countries except these the increase in the cost of living in Canada is by far the highest.

It has increased considerably more than in the United States. There is twice the increase suffered by New Zealand and nearly two and a half times that in Australia.

For four years our Government has permitted and even fostered one of the most nefarious following to become organized into a band of middlemen, which is as great a curse upon the country as the cold storage octopus. It has an army of agents running wild through the country buying up everything in and out of sight upon the farms, giving the farmers such fabulous prices that it not only unsettles and sometimes prevents them from taking advantage of the normal prices, but they themselves are admitting that the product is not worth the price that they are being sold for in the city of Quebec.

The excuse is that there is a shortage of food in Europe. If there is a shortage of food in Europe, where there is revolution and strife, is that any reason why we should export more of our surplus and create the same labor unrest at home? Would it not be better to take the bull by the horns and bring down the high cost of living by spending immediately in building cold storage houses and controlling the farmer's produce, so that there may be normal prices, only charging sufficient commission to pay the working expenses of the cold storage plants? Then, again, can we not make a law to imprison the dishonest promoter and speculator by making it an offenee punishable by imprisonment for middlemen to engage in speculation.

Wealthy People Flaunt Their Riches

There is another reason for this general unrest. I think the Government is, in some extent at least, responsible for it. The wealthy people of Canada have not been judicious in the manner in which they have enjoyed their wealth.

The wage-earner is measuring his income against the evidences of luxury, advertisements of ladies' dresses at prices that have to support a family for a year, and not too much of them at that. Gentlemen's neckties at from five to fifteen dollars, and all else in proportion—goods whose commendation evidently is their dearness. Daily appear such appeals to fashion luxury in the newspapers as might well be called immoral in their encouragement to ungainly waste. Meantime, the wage-earner reads with rage of millions made out of war necessities, and of one claim upon the government, that he has to support, for eighteen million dollars, which a contractor would have made had his product not been rejected. He stands aghast at such figures, and, in his corporate capacity of trades unionists, he rebels against it. Here is the way the Winnipeg worker sees it: "During all these fearful years the rich became richer and the poor poorer, and with the increase of wealth the arrogance of the wealthy increased. Their wealth did not make them more beneficient. It made them mad for still more wealth. They became more and more callous."

The condition of the worker is primarily of the utmost concern to the State. He should not be allowed to be exploited by capital as a mere instrument for the making of money; hence it is unjust that the fruits of man's sweat and labor should not belong to him. As a rule it is quite legitimate for the worker and the capitalist to bargain; but there comes t time when, driven by fear, necessity or otherwise, the laborer finds it impossible to make a bargain which will give him sufficient to gain a frugal, honest and honorable living. When that time comes it is the duty of the State to see that the laborer is not oppressed by the capitalist—to enable the employee to make a fair bargain with his employer.

What Standard of Living Should Be

Further, the standard of living should not be the minimum at which the worker can keep body and soul together, there should be given to him a wage sufficient to provide him with comfort and recreation, to enable him to educate his family and to provide against accident and old age. To establish this standard, it is essential that the workers unite, for experience teaches us that man is naturally greedy, and the rich and powerful will rarely concede anything to the poor unless coercion is applied. It is the duty of the State, therefore, to foster and encourage such unions when the poor have not the same facilities for protecting themselves as the rich. It is also the duty of the State as much as possible to remove all causes of complaint between employer and employee, to prevent by remedial measures, taken beforehand, any resources to the strike, which is invariably a great economic loss, in many cases most seriously affecting those not intimately concerned in the struggle, and always leaving rancour and bitterness in its train. It is neither justice nor humanity to grind men down and stunt their minds with labor of their bodies. Daily labor must be regulated so that it is not protracted beyond the strength of the workers. In all agreements between master and workman it is implied that proper leisure be left to the workman for rest, recuperation and recreation.

The laborer must come to realize that he owes his employer and society an honest day's work in return for a fair wage, and that conditions cannot be substantially improved until he roots out the desire to get a maximum of return for a minimum of service. The capitalist must likewise get a new viewpoint. He needs to learn the long-forgotten truth that wealth is stewardship, that profit-making is not the basic justification of business enterprise, and that there are such things as fair profits, fair interest and fair prices. Above and before all, he must cultivate and strengthen within his mind the truth which many of his class have begun to grasp for the first time during the present war; namely, that the laborer is a human being, not merely an instrument of production; and that the laborer's right to a decent livelihood is the first moral charge upon industry.

Do Not Delay Building Say Many Lumbermen

The Hope That Prices of Material and Labor Will Come Down in Near Future is Illusive One—Building Operations in the East

The opinion of many retail lumber dealers and representative builders' supply men is that now is the auspicious time to build, that nothing can be gained by delay, and those who are deferring structural undertakings or postponing the erection of homes, in the hope that lumber will soon come down in price, or labor become cheaper, are being deceived. Those who have given close study to the present situation and taken into consideration all the contributing factors are firmly of the belief that all signs point to increased quotations on many lines.

Some further reports of an interesting character have come to hand with respect to building prospects in the Eastern provinces and they will be read with timely interest:

George A. Christie of Truro, N.S., reports that operations in the building line are quiet at the present time owing to the high price of material. Many are hanging back, thinking there will be a drop in quotations. Mr. Christie does not believe this is likely to occur for a year or two yet. There is some repairing going on and a few homes will be built this summer, while others are talked of. There is a great demand for dwellings to rent. In Truro rents are not only very high, but help is scarce, and on account of so many strikes all over the country building has been tied up.

D. Porter & Son, Westville, N.S., state that there are not many houses being erected in their locality, as,, owing to the high cost of material, the people do not feel in a position to build and are waiting in the hope that price and labor conditions will ameliorate. The firm think that business is rather more quiet than usual on account of vessels not being available for shipping..

Many New Houses Going Up

In regard to building operations in Halifax, Wm. Watt states there are many houses going up in his section of the city, and that many more will follow. If it had not been for the outbreak of labor troubles, much greater progress would have been made. Everything was tied up for several weeks owing to the carpenters' strike. Now that a settlement has been effected, the outlook is much more promisng.

A. Duchemin & Co., of Charlottetown, report they find building prospects only fair for the coming season, owing to the high prices of material. Considerable extension and repair work and jobs are being carried out, but there is not a great deal of new work. The company say that building for investment is almost unknown just at present, so they expect in the near future, as soon as conditions are more settled, to become busy.

J. L. Black & Sons, of Sackville, N.B., state that the usual amount of building and repair work is being undertaken this season. They add that a considerable increase in new structures would undoubtedly be witnessed were it not for the prevailing feeling among prospective builders that the cost of materials and labor will be lower next season. From the lumbermen's point of view the situation is good. Prices are high; the demand is active, and while there is more stock on hand than usual, it is moving satisfactorily. The firm do not look for any radical alterations in prices for some months to come.

Considerable Repairs in Progress

Geo. A. Ryan, of Grand Falls, N.B., declares that the building prospects in his section are about normal. There appears to be considerable building and repairing going on, in spite of the high cost of labor and supplies, which, he asserts, does not seem inclined to drop. Lumber is high, and the general outlook not very encouraging for a reduction in prices, owing to the lumber cut last season. Mr. Ryan says that the Burgess & Sons' lumber mills are only cutting with a day crew, against a night and day crew last year.

Musgrave & Co., Halifax, after referring to the unsettled conditions generally in the building trade in that city occasioned by the strike, report that some of the contractors paid exceptionally high figures to workmen in order to have rush jobs completed on time, but outside of those isolated cases, there had been practically nothing doing in the building line for some weeks. The devastation caused by the explosion, in 1917, has not been fully replaced, and there are still hundreds of residences and tenements to be erected. In addition to this there are several additions to banks, hospitals, shipyards, etc., for immediate construction. The firm add that the general opinion is that materials will not be lower for some time to come, but on the other hand, with the increase in wages they may be higher. In any event, labor and building will be higher, and now that the strike is over a lot of work will be carried out. All local dealers are pretty well loaded up with ordinary stocks, but there are some enquiries coming in for large dimension material. The exporters in that community are not buying at the present time either for the West Indies or England, which makes the local market dull at this juncture.

Where Everybody is Rebuilding

J. E. Humphreys, Petitcodiac, N. B., states that a big fire in March last destroyed the greater part of the business houses in the village and that there is unusual activity there this summer. Practically everybody is rebuilding and on a better and bigger scale than before, and work has already commenced. The present cost of labor and materials has had no appreciable deterrent effect; although occasional comment is heard on the high prices of labor and supplies, but very little complaint. There is also more than the usual amount of repairs and extensions under way, while a great many new buildings are planned. Mr. Humphreys says that his sales this year have greatly exceeded those of last, (which was the largest in his history) and that everyone seems prosperous and optimistic. Mr. Humphreys concludes that one of the great difficulties is in getting dry lumber, or in fact green lumber, in right sizes and sufficient quantities. Stocks of last year have all been marketed and shipped, and although this season's cut is fully up to normal, much has already been shipped, and all the remainder has been practically contracted for by St. John exporters. The only difficulty has been in securing the business for transportation. The feeling seems to be that labor will continue high all the year, and that lumber quotations will prevail at an exalted level for some years to come.

Dodge That Storm

Lumber prices have NOT YET advanced in proportion to other commodities, but they are headed that way. The production is below normal on account of labor shortage. The demand is far in excess of the supply. Therefore, the best opinion available is that lumber prices WILL NOT COME down, but in ALL PROBABILITY will advance still farther. The sensible thing, then, for people to do who want to build, is to BUILD NOW. Come to our office and we'll talk it over.

From the "Retail Lumberman"

The lumber industry of the Province of New Brunswick is having troubles of its own. Shortage of shipping continues to be a serious problem and one which should be coped with as soon as possible. It is estimated that 600,000,000 feet of lumber have been sold in the Eastern section of this country through the British timber controller, but the vast majority of this is still piled up about the mills and on every available lot where it is possible to place a run, waiting for bottoms. The dealers are not under any expense holding the lumber, but the quantity of it lying about is causing considerable inconvenience and blocking up space, which should be used for this season's cut. Unless some relief is offered the mills may have a hard time to keep running for they have no place to carry the lumber to as it comes from the mills. There is a report heard that there will be a lot of shipping released in July, and if this is true it will undoubtedly ease the situation.

Mr. George R. Gray Elected Director

George R. Gray, Sault Ste. Marie, Ont.

George R. Gray, manager of wod operations of the Spanish River Pulp & Paper Mills, Limited, who have plants at Sault Ste. Marie, Espanola and Sturgeon Falls, has been elected a director of the company in succession of the late Ben. Tooke of Montreal. Mr. Gray has been associated with the Spanish River Company for many years and is well known in the pulp and paper industry, enjoying the confidence of a large circle of friends. He has been a resident of the "Soo" for the past two years and was a director of the original Lake Superior Paper Company several years ago. Mr. Gray is also a director of National Grocers, Limited, and Cochrane Hardware Limited. He is thoroughly familiar with lumbering and logging conditions in Northern and North-western Ontario, and reports that the drives of pulpwood during the past season have been brought down to the various plants of the company more expeditiously than in a long period, owing to the high water and splendid driving conditions. The company have ample pulpwood for the operation of their plants for the coming season. Mr. Gray is the nominee of the Ontario Pulp & Paper bondholders on the board of the Spanish River Company and will add strength to that representative body, of which Geo. H. Mead, of Dayton, Ohio, is president.

Gillies Bros. Lose Big Mill by Fire

The large and well equipped saw mill of Gillies Bros., Braeside, Ont., which is three miles west of Arnprior, was destroyed by fire on June 23rd. A harness-shop belonging to the firm and the C.P.R. station were also consumed by the flames. It is estimated that the loss is $300,000, mostly covered by insurance.

Gillies Bros., Limited, are one of the oldest established lumber firms in the Ottawa Valely, having started business in 1873. David Gillies is the president of the company; J. S. Gillies, vice-president and managing-director and D. A. Gillies, secretary-treasurer. It may also be stated that J. S. Gillies is the president of the Canadian Forestry Association.

The equipment of the mill, which was destroyed, was thoroughly overhauled two years ago by S. F. Caldwell, head millwright for the firm. The plant had two single bandsaws; one pair of twin circulars, 60 in. diameter, one 24 in. gang, which runs 260 R.P.M., and two, four saw edgers. There were many labor-saving devices about the mill. For putting logs on the twin carriage the firm had steam log loaders and similar equipment for the band carriages. They also had one steam nigger with steam set works for each carriage, which they found worked out well. The band saws, while of the older type, had many improvements on them, which made them as good as some of a later date.

Hudson's Consolidated Unissued Capital

The directors of the Hudson's Consolidated, Ltd., in a circular state that they have decided to provide additional working capital to complete the financial arrangements necessary to place the newly-acquired manganese properties in Great Britain on a largely-increased profit-earning basis, in order to secure the results anticipated in the various reports received from the company's managers and consulting engineers. The company now offers for subscription 70,000 7½ per cent. cumulative and participating preference shares of £1 each at par, and 141,693 ordinary shares at £1 5s. per £1 share.

After the payment of a fixed dividend of 7½ per cent. to the preference shares, the balance of the total profits distributed in dividends in each year is applied as to 10 per cent. to the preference, and as to 90 per cent. to the ordinary shareholders.

The directors have taken the opportunity of reviewing certain other of the company's enterprises, and publish valuations and reports by the manager, Mr. H. H. Riddle, and by Mr. F. A. Salaman, the well-known timber expert, on the St. Anne timber property in Canada, situated on the St. Lawrence River.

Mr. Riddle states that the property is equipped with a circular saw-mill having a capacity of 10,000 ft. per day. The mill has been running to full capacity since November last, supplying timber to specification at less than £8 per standard, and similar timber is now selling in England at £34 per standard upwards. He calculates that there exists over 300,000,000 ft. of good timber on the property, and that with an expenditure of from £20,000 to £30,000, the necessary dam and additional sawmill can be erected in five months. The completion of this work should easily allow of 100,000 board feet of first quality timber being cut per day, equal to 50 standards, on which there should be a profit of £15 to £25 per standard. The minimum of £15 per standard (based upon pre-war prices) would give a profit of over £112,500 per annum, working only 150 days in the year. This is considered an extremely conservative estimate.

Ontario Lumber Dealers Do Cash Business

It will be remembered that at the last annual meeting of the Ontario Retail Lumber Dealers' Association that a resolution was unanimously carried, as follows:

> "Whereas the retail lumber dealer must buy his lumber in car lots, carry for a considerable period and distribute in small lots to his customers, and
>
> Whereas the amount of capital required in the retail lumber business is now so large, and
>
> Whereas the public is continually demanding increased service from the retail yards,
>
> Be it resolved that the "terms of sale" in the retail lumber business in the Province of Ontario should be net cash, with ledger accounts carried only with people of absolute approved credit, and who agree to pay each month's account in net cash on or before the tenth of the following month, and Be it resolved further that a card containing this resolution in printed form be sent by the secretary to each member."

In accordance with the action then taken that a card should be issued containing the substance of the foregoing in printed form and that it should be sent out by the secretary to each member, Mr. Boultbee has carried out the instructions. The card, which is neatly printed, reads as follows:—

> "**Terms of Sale—Net Cash.** No discount. Ledger accounts only with customers of approved credit who will agree to pay each month's account in net cash on or before the tenth of the following month. Sales for amounts under $25,000—cash with order.—The Ontario Retail Lumber Dealers' Association.

Ten Million Dollars For New Homes

Under the Ontario Government's housing scheme 300 houses are now under construction in different parts of the province, and within another month it is anticipated that another 1,100 dwellings will be erected. No fewer than 19 cities, 29 towns, 13 villages and 9 townships have come under the scheme to date.

Government officials estimate that about $10,500,000 will be loaned to municipalities this year, of which sum the Dominion Government will furnish about $8,500,000. Five million dollars of this money will actually be expended this year, and it is likely that next year the figure will jump to $15,000,000.

In Toronto very little progress has been made in building homes owing to the difficulty in securing suitable sites, but had the Toronto City Council agreed to the Government supervision of its plans the local housing commission could now have been expropriating the land on which it could erect reasonably priced dwellings.

The Timber Requirements of Japan

A. E. Ryan, Canadian Government Trade Commissioner to Japan, in a recent report to the Trade and Commerce Department, Ottawa, says:

Considerable quantities of red cedar are imported into Japan. It usually comes in square cut logs ready for immediate use, without treatment except for slight planing. The squares must not be under 5-inch by 5-inch and not shorter than 10 feet. Before the armistice there was a strong demand for Douglas fir for shipbuilding. It was imported in heavy timbers of 20 feet to 40 feet long and 18 inches to 24 inches square. Most of the imports were from the Pacific Coast States of America. But there is no reason why British Columbia lumber should not fill the demand if our producers can give as attractive terms.

United States Forestry Situation

The United States has used up about half the forests originally possessed. Although there are forest associations in nearly every state supplementing the excellent work of the national forest service, trees are being used up faster than they are being grown. When a tree is cut less than half of it reaches the consumer. The sawmill wastes amount to 40 per cent. of the tree. Forest fires cause a loss of $25,000,000 to $50,000,000 yearly. There are 147 national forests in the United States, consisting of 155,166,619 acres.

Woodlands Section Summer Meeting

New Regulations Favored Governing the Cutting of Timber on Crown Lands of Quebec

Reafforestation was the keynote of the summer meeting of the Woodlands section of the Canadian Pulp and Paper Association, held at Berthierville and Grand 'Mere, on June 25 and 26. The attendance was very large, many members going from Montreal, Quebec and Ottawa, and others motoring in from Three Rivers and other points.

On arrival at Berthierville the members were entertained at luncheon, and afterwards inspected the Provincial Government nurseries, under the guidance of Mr. G. C. Piche, chief forester. This was followed by a discussion, under the chairmanship of R. Kernan, president of the Section.

The chairman referred to the question of artificial and natural reafforestation, and also discussed the subject of who should pay the cost of the former—the government or the limit holders. He advocated the burning of slash, even although it would involve a certain amount of expenditure.

The Hon. Jules Allard, Minister of Lands and Forests, reviewed the work of his department in fire protection, the suppression of the fake settler, and the general conservtion of forest resources. He was, he said, in favor of the co-operative method of limit holders in fire fighting. Mr. Allard also spoke of the establishment of the government nurseries, with a view to assisting the lumber and pulp companies and the private citizens.

Mr. Piche described in detail the history, operations, and extent of the nurseries, and also the reclamation of the shifting sands at Lachute. The present stock of trees in the nursery, he said, exceeds four million, and they were preparing to ship out annually two to three million plants. Mr. Piche then referred to the question of a progressive policy of reforestation in the province, in view of the rapid disappearance of trees from the shores of the St. Lawrence and also the increase in the cost of pulpwood and lumber. There was no use in hiding the truth that millions of acres of land had been impoverished either by improper cultivation or by wasteful lumbering, whilst others had been ruined by repeated fires. Mr. Piche, in enumerating the reasons for planting waste lands, declared that the increased development of the lumbering industries had produced such a big demand upon the forest that within a relatively short time some of the companies would either have to reduce their production or to purchase new holdings. The speaker was of opinion that reforestation would pay, basing his conclusion on American and European figures. As to lands leased from the Government, he had not come to a satisfactory conclusion as to who should do the work, the government or the limit holder, or both, co-operative. The forests should be protected from fire, and a systematic inventory made of the forests in order to organize a definite working plan of operation which would be based upon growth studies and also upon the analysis of the past lumbering operations. The time had come for the Government to exercise full control over the wood-working establishments of the province, as too often sawmills were located in localities where there was not enough wood to justify their appearance. All the woodworking establishments should be licensed and compelled each year to obtain a permit to operate. The Government would thus be in a position to determine if they had sufficient timber lands to justify the operation of the mills and to prevent enlargements where there was no supply in sight. The prevention of waste in the forest and in transit to the mill should be aimed at—in fact economy all the way round. Mr. Piche concluded by advocating that those who wasted the forests by bad lumbering should replant the limits at their expense.

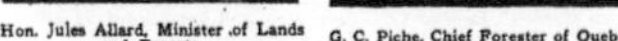

Hon. Jules Allard, Minister of Lands and Forests.

G. C. Piche, Chief Forester of Quebec Province.

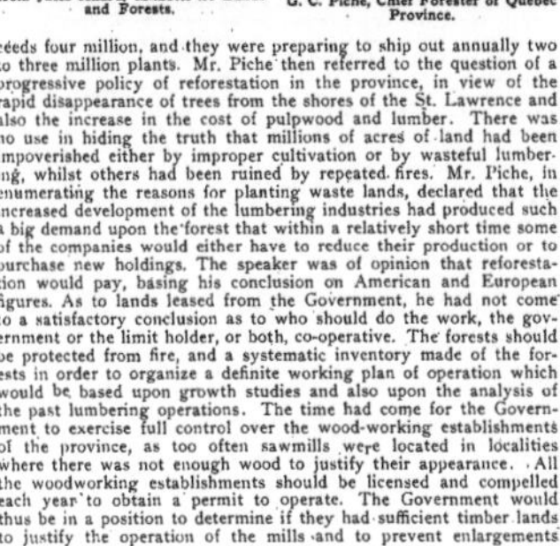

Mr. Ellwood Wilson urged that the Government should deal immediately with the slash question, the cost of which would, in the end, be borne by the consumer. It was impossible, he sad, to secure natural afforestation unless the system of lumbering was changed, and he favored the removal of the diameter limit and the cutting of certain areas absolutely clean.

Mr. W. Gerard Power, president of the Canadian Lumbermen's Association, said that if the Government would amend their regulations as to clean cutting the disposal of slash was a comparatively easy matter.

Mr. F. W. Reed of the U. S. Forest Service, gave details of the regulations of slash burning in the States.

The members left in the evening for Grand 'Mere, and slept on board the train. Next morning, with Mr. Ellwood Wilson as guide, they visited the Lauretnide Company's nurseries at Proulx. The delegates also visited Lac a Tortue, where Lieut. S. Graham gave a demonstration in one of the hydroplanes loaned to the St. Maurice Forest Protective Association for fire protection work. The delegates were entertained at luncheon by the Laurentide Co.

The delegates passed a resolution favoring certain changes in the regulations of the lands and forests, governing the cutting of timber on crown lands as essential to the preservation and perpetuation of the forests, and suggesting the appointment of a committee of the Association to wait upon the Government urging the necessity of an early revision of these regulations to meet present-day conditions.

Votes of thanks were passed to the Quebec Government, the Hon. Jules Allard, Mr. Piche, the Laurentide Co. and Mr. Ellwood Wilson for their hospitality and efforts to entertain the members.

Mr. Dollar Visits Eastern Ports

Robert Dollar, of the Dollar Shipping Company, owner and operator of a line of steamships which ply between Canadian and American ports, West India, and Oriental ports, was in Sydney, N.S., recently, on a business trip. Mr. Dollar said he was there to look over the situation from a shipping standpoint solely, and see what Sydney had to offer in the way of natural advantage and products of industries. The company plans to run a line of steamships, calling at Singapore and other ports in the Orient, and through the Panama Canal to some port on the Atlantic Coast. That port has not as yet been decided upon.

Lumber Company Will Not Use Aeroplanes

The Bathurst Lumber Co., Limited, of Bathurst, N.B., say that they have not made any arrangements for patrolling their forests by aeroplanes, as they do not consider this problem has been properly worked out as yet. They believe that during the experimental stage the matter will have to be handled in some way under Government patronage.

With respect to the demand for sulphite and sulphate pulp, the company declare that it is improving rapidly and prospects are that the trade will soon be back again good and strong, as at present nearly all the paper mills in Canada and United States are quite active and are in the market for raw material.

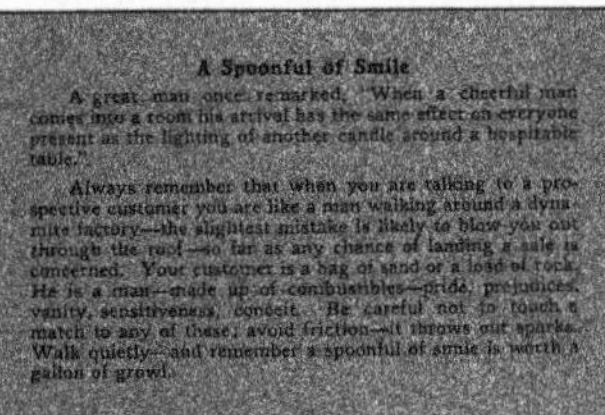

A Spoonful of Smile

A great man once remarked, "When a cheerful man comes into a room his arrival has the same effect on everyone present as the lighting of another candle around a hospitable table."

Always remember that when you are talking to a prospective customer you are like a man walking around a dynamite factory—the slightest mistake is likely to blow you out through the roof—so far as any chance of landing a sale is concerned. Your customer is a bag of sand or a load of rock. He is a man—made up of combustibles—pride, prejudices, vanity, sensitiveness, conceit. Be careful not to touch a match to any of these; avoid friction—it throws out sparks. Walk quietly—and remember a spoonful of smile is worth a gallon of growl.

Personal Paragraphs of Interest

Chas. H. Russell, of Montreal, was a recent visitor to New York on business.

Angus McLean, of the Bathurst Lumber Co., Bathurst, N.B., paid a short visit to Buffalo, recently.

Frank Hawkins, secretary of the Canadian Lumbermen's Association, Ottawa, visited Montreal last week on business.

W. R. Beatty, secretary-treasurer of the Colonial Lumber Company, Pembroke, spent a few days in Toronto recently on business.

L. C. Tatham of Churchill, Sims & Co., the London, Eng., wood brokers, has been on a business visit to Montreal and St. John, N.B.

Hugh A. Rose of Toronto, representing Mason, Gordon & Company, is on an extended business trip throughout the Maritime Provinces.

James W. Sewall and Joseph D. Latno, of the Sewall Co., Old Town, Maine, have returned from a short cruising trip in the Adirondacks.

W. A. Hadley of Chatham, Ont., president of the Southwestern Ontario Retail Lumber Dealers' Association, was in Toronto recently and called upon a number of members of the trade.

In the recent election in Maskinonge, Que., Rodolphe Tourville, lumberman, was successful in being returned in the Liberal interests, defeating his opponent, A. Lamy, Conservative, by over 700 majority.

Frank A. Kent, of Seaman Kent Co., Limited, Toronto, attended the twenty-second annual convention of the National Hardwood Lumber Association, which was held in Chicago on June 19 and 20.

Prof. B. E. Fernow, Dean of the Faculty of Forestry, University of Toronto, has asked to be relieved of his work, owing to poor health, and requests that his resignation take effect as soon as possible.

J. D. McCormack, General Manager of the Canadian Western Lumber Company, Fraser Mills, B.C., arrived in Toronto recently to spend a few days with L. D. Barclay, eastern representative of the firm. Mr. McCormack called upon a large number of friends while in Toronto.

In the recent Quebec Provincial election H. Biermans, general manager of the Belgo-Canadian Pulp & Paper Co., Shawinigan Falls, Que., contested the riding as an Independent candidate in St. Maurice, against Geo. Delisle, Liberal, and Dr. Dufresne, Conservative. Mr. Delisle was the successful candidate.

Claude Villiers and F. W. Wigg, of the Canadian General Lumber Co., Montreal, have been on visits to the New England States. Mr. Villiers reports that conditions have materially improved in these States, that building is proceeding very briskly, and that the outlook for Canadian lumber is decidedly better.

Miss Beatrice Maud Tobin, youngest daughter of Edmund W. Tobin, M.P., vice-president of the Brompton Pulp & Paper Company, and a well-known lumberman, was married recently to Joseph Omer Asselin, of Quebec, formerly of Sherbrooke. The ceremony was quietly celebrated at Bromptonville. Mr. Asselin and bride will reside in Quebec City.

George R. Gray, manager of wood operations of the Spanish River Pulp & Paper Mills, Limited, has been elected a director of the company in succession of the late Benjamin Tooke of Montreal. Mr. Gray has been associated with the Spanish River Company for many years and is receiving the congratulations of his many friends on his recent appointment.

George Edward Petry of Toronto, who is associated with R. G. Chesbro, representing the Allen-Stoltze Lumber Co., of Vancouver, has joined the ranks of the benedicts. Mr. Petry was married on June 24th to Miss Emeline Margaret, daughter of Rev. Dr. and Mrs. Abraham, Winchester St., Toronto. The many friends of the esteemed young couple will join in hearty felicitations.

With the recent incorporation of the Boston Plastic Fire Brick Co., Frank J. Jewell was elected President and Secretary, and Nelson Adams, vice-president and treasurer. The new corporation name is the Betson Plastic Fire Brick Co., Inc., Rome, N.Y. The company's products are Plastic Fire Brick for boiler furnace linings and baffle walls and Hi-Heat Cement for use in the boiler room.

H. R. MacMillan has been appointed representative of the British Timber Buyer in Western Canada, with offices in Vancouver, B.C. He has been on a trip to New York, Philadelphia, Montreal, and Ottawa, looking into shipping and other conditions. Prior to being appointed, Mr. MacMillan was in the aeronautical supplies (lumber) department of the Imperial Munitions Board.

Lieut.-Col. Frank J. Carew, who was the officer commanding No. 1 District, Canadian Forestry Corps, in France, and was sometime ago made an officer of the Order of the British Empire, recently returned from overseas and resumed his work with the John Carew Lumber Company, Lindsay, Ont., of which he is secretary-treasurer. Lieut.-Col. Carew is son of John Carew, M.L.A., of South Victoria and, previous to enlisting for service abroad, was engaged with his father in the lumber business.

Ed. Ouellette, vice-president and general manager of the Tourville Lumber Mills, Ltd., Montreal, and Louiseville, has been re-elected by acclamation for Yamaska, in the Province of Quebec elections. Rodolphe Tourville, the president of the company, had to fight for his seat in Maskinonge County. N. P. Tanguay, another lumberman, who represented Wolfe, retired after many years' service.

And. P. Shand passed away recently at Windsor, N.S. For many years Mr. Shand has been closely associated with the business life of Windsor. He was formerly connected with the Windsor Furniture Co., The Windsor Lumber Co., The Hants County Mfg. Co., Falmouth, N.S., barrel manufacturers; in addition he was a governor of the Acadia College, and President of the Commercial Bank of Windsor.

Albert E. Dyment, who was recently elected vice-president and chairman of the board of directors of the Canadian General Electric Company, to fill the vacancy caused by the death of W. D. Matthews, is a well-known figure in the financial and business world. He is senior partner of the firm of Dyment, Cassels & Company, stock-brokers, Toronto, and is identified with a number of progressive organizations. Mr. Dyment, who was born in Wentworth county, is a son of the late Nathaniel Dyment, and learned the lumber business with his father's concern, Mickle, Dyment & Son, who have several saw mills throughout Ontario, and also operate large industries in Toronto, Brantford and other cities. The headquarters of the firm are at Barrie, Ont. Albert E. Dyment holds a large interest in the organization. He is also well known to the Canadian turf, having, with his brother, established the Brookside Stable, which produced "King's Plate" winner at the Woodbine in Toronto some years ago.

Lumbermen Elected to C. M. A. Offices

At the annual meeting of the Maritime Branch of the Canadian Manufacturers' Association, which was held at Halifax recently, Angus MacLean of the Bathurst Lumber Co., Bathurst, N.B., was elected president. Mr. MacLean is a live wire in several organizations and under his direction the Maritime Branch of the Canadian Manufacturers' Association should enjoy a year of prosperity and increasing usefulness.

The British Columbia Branch of the Canadian Manufacturers' Association, at their recent annual meeting, elected J. H. McDonald, of the British Columbia Mfg. Company, New Westminster, E. W. Hamber, of the British Columbia Mills Timber and Trading Co., Vancouver, and J. O. Cameron of the Cameron Lumber Co., Limited, Victoria, members of the executive.

New Eastern Representative Appointed

A. W. Barnhill, who has been appointed Eastern representative of the "Service" Lumber Co., Vancouver, and has opened an office at 20 St. James Street, Montreal, is a well-known sawmill man and operator. He started in the lumber business with B. B. Barnhill of Two Rivers, Cumberland County, Nova Scotia, and spent fourteen years with the firm from the stump to the finished product and was also engaged in the marketing of the same. Mr. Barnhill was manager of the Ruby Lake Lumber Co., Hudson Bay Junction, Sask., for eight years, and was Forest Supervisor for the Dominion Government in that province for three years. He was president of Barnhill Bros., shipbuilders, at Goggins Mines, N.S., during the past year. The "Service" Lumber Co., which he now represents in the East, specializes in rough and dressed timber, fir, spruce and cedar, fir tank stock, B. C. red cedar shingles and all forest products from the Pacific Province.

A recent despatch from St. John, N.B., says: Capt. Dan Owen, late of the Royal Air Force, and now surveyor of the lumber lands for a United States firm, is on his way to the United States. He said he expected to command an expedition to Labrador in the interests of his firm, with the purpose of surveying the vast lumber lands owned by them in that country. Two aeroplanes will be used, one a seaplane and the other a landplane, and flying at a high altitude, photographs will be taken and maps made of the various forests.

Fire breaking out at the plant of James Davidson's Sons, Davidson, Quebec, recently, caused a loss of around $7,500. The sawmill was not injured Two cars of hay and some stables were burned. The loss is partly covered by insurance. On June 25th a fire swept through the Shepard and Morse yards at Ottawa and did $17,000 damage.

And Great is the Soul of Britain!

By A. C. Manbert, Toronto

Editor, "Canada Lumberman":

I should like to respect your request for comments upon conditions here, but I feel some restraint.

I am not unlike a motorist in a strange country, who from considerable study, has a theoretical knowledge of where the roads probably do go. There are reasonable doubts, however, until they are actually travelled.

To carry the analogy farther, the map shows some roads to be more important than others and that the more important ones control the access to lesser, but necessary, paths. Shipping seems the travel artery immediately vital to the export trade and opinion is varied as to probable developments in this road. Only "after whiles" can tell.

To abandon figurative speech, I am sure lumber trade confidence and expectation are much higher than when I reached England. The relatively small, but gradually increasing stocks arriving seem "appetizers," and future commitments are now being ventured, or considered, beyond anything thought possible a month ago.

When the Timber Controller ceased purchasing and released control on March 31st, it was generally believed that his stocks would have to be pretty well placed before new and private purchasing would resume. Not so! Already private trading is competing with the Controller's stocks, and, what is more, prices are both maintained and firmer.

Fundamentally, the situation is strong. The future is becoming somewhat clearer. It is a question of time and mechanism, and none now waste breath debating the ultimately vast demands. All woods are readily placed in consumer's hands as fast as they come forward. Customers literally stand in line for white pine. So keen is the demand, the Controller publicly gives notice that parties receiving his stocks must not sell above maximum prices named by him in March last.

Commercial and social life is here so complex one hesitates to speak with assurance, but the general business of the country is undoubtedly stabilizing itself—not so rapidly as some had hoped, to be sure.

Retail business is wonderfully good—too good for the satisfaction of the shopper, for war-time prices prevail. Few prices have lowered and many have advanced. This is unfortunate, for it adds fuel to the flame of labor's unrest, because of high living costs. How long this will continue is any man's guess.

He who knows the action of shipping and other productive agencies may answer. But it will not end immediately. It is a process and not an event, and in this clearing-house of world affairs, processes are not simple.

The marvel to me here is the wonderful patience of the people. Restrictions, interferences, discomforts. All are accepted with a good nature, a cheerfulness that quite amounts to a fine philosophy; perhaps better than any conscious philosophy, it is so spontaneous.

I have heard much of the "tension" of war times. Peace times have not removed it all. A very great deal remains. Scant housing, scant transportation, scant food, scant employment. When I hear of our disturbances at home, our grumbling, our attack of "nerves," it makes me fair ashamed at our lack of poise and perspective. Compared with this country, we have known nothing of war. "Nerves" would be justified here.

But undoubtedly it is this capacity to endure which has made Britain the outstanding bulwark in the great struggle. Also its inherent instinct toward fair play makes for it self-centered assurance, its imperturbable self-confidence. If there is unrest, there is little hysteria. If there be disagreement there is little ill-feeling. It is reflected everywhere—this respect for order and fair play; in the thronged Strand, the packed "busses," the crowded congregations—no ill-natured jostling, no recriminations.

It is not the good nature of indifference. It is the good nature of habit—a quality, not an attainment. Some prate of British stolidity. I like not the term. Stability suits me better. Temperamental? Perhaps not. But unimaginative? No. Rather an imagination that thinks in practicalities instead of abstractions, that visualizes integrity, honesty, justice.

Great is the soul of the man who is sure of himself. And great is the soul of Britain.

Small wonder, then if this great people with its heritage of centuries, goes serenely on in its national life undisturbed by doubts which paralyze.

Certain of purposes which sustain, it reaffirms, if deprecatingly, its unalterable conviction that it will "muddle through."

It is difficult for us of the Western Continent to understand all this. In our alertness, we are continually on the "qui vive." We react quickly to externals and, in the cumulative play of mass psychology, we rise to great enthusiasms or descend to marked despondencies with equal abandonment.

But without disparaging this awareness in which lies the root of our great energy, you will, I hope, understand me when I confess that in this time of stress and adjustment through which we are passing, there is a grateful sense of comfort and security in the ponderosity of this great people who accept things as they are and with undisturbed self-confidence meet their problems as they come.

(Signed) A. C. Manbert.

London, Eng., June 5, 1919.

LUMBERMEN LEGISLATORS IN QUEBEC PROVINCIAL ELECTIONS

Ed. Ouellette, M.L.A., Liberal candidate, who was returned by acclamation in Yamaska.

Rodolphe Tourville, M.L.A., who was successful in Liberal interest in Maskinonge.

N. P. Tanguay, M.L.A., late representative for Wolfe who has retired from public life.

Death of Mr. William J. Smith

Mr. William J. Smith, a well-known lumberman, passed away on June 26th at his residence, 15 Denison Ave., Weston, Ont., in his 57th year. He had been ailing since May, 1916, and heart trouble was the cause of his death.

Mr. Smith had been engaged in the wholesale lumber business in Weston for some fourteen years, and previous to that was associated with the late Robert Stewart in Guelph for some time. Prior to locating in Guelph the deceased conducted a successful contracting and carpenter business in Grand Valley for a number of years.

The late Mr. Smith was a member of the Wholesale Lumber Dealers' Association, Inc., of Toronto, and was widely known in the industry, enjoying the confidence and esteem of a large circle of friends. He was a member of the Masonic Order and also of the Canadian Order of Foresters. His wife died some two years and a half ago and a family of four sons and two daughters are left to mourn his passing. The sons are Lieut. Arthur L. (who enlisted with the 75th Batt. for overseas and was later transferred to the 4th Machine Gun Brigade, returning to Toronto recently); Alvin E., of the selling staff of Read Bros., Limited, Toronto; Arnold R., accountant in the office of his father at Weston, and Percy G. of the C. P. R. telegraph department, Vancouver; two daughters, Illa and Milda, reside at ohme.

The funeral took place on Saturday, June 28th, the remains being interred in Riverside Cemetery. The last sad rites were attended by a large number of lumbermen in both the wholesale and retail ranks, and many beautiful floral tributes bore silent evidence of the respect in which the late Mr. Smith was held.

Forestry Methods as Applied in Canada

At the invitation of the Pennsylvania Forestry Association, Mr. Robson Black, Secretary of the Canadian Forestry Association, addressed a large gathering of Amercans on Canadian forestry problems and the methods of operation of the Canadian association. Great interest was displayed in the rapid progress of forest fire preventive work throughout the Dominion, and particularly in the success of educational work for which the Canadian Forestry Association is responsible.

Mr. Black explained to his audience that unlike ordinary propaganda, the advancement of forestry could not promise a quick, tangible profit. People accustomed to political and commercial policies, based upon immediate likelihood of gain were slow to take up cudgels for a cause that spoke of a social and national profit fifty or a hundred years hence. Yet, in a country where 90 per cent. of the forest lands were owned and governed by the people and where timber operators were merely annual tenants, any advancement of state control of forest policies depended absolutely upon arousing the masses of citizens to their public privileges and responsibilities. The Canadian problem was, therefore, in sharp contrast to that of the average American state, where only a small fraction of the forest wealth had not been alienated and placed beyond public control.

The methods employed by the Canadian Forestry Association were explained in detail by the speaker, who claimed that one of the basic reasons for success in forestry propaganda is to keep the organization free from any governmental or commercial affiliation. This allowed perfect liberty to carry on constructive agitation, which, at times, must run counter to governmental tradition, and perhaps displease certain commercial interests. Mr. Black described reforms in province after province of Canada due largely to educational campaigns.

The Forestry Association, he said, devoted the greater part of its attention to improvement of public policies and administration. At the same time, it initiated and carried out scores of educational enterprises aimed at securing the good will and co-operation of the individuals responsible for setting forest fires. Scores of thousands of school children and teachers, settlers, railroad men, and other classes were reached year by year with attractive literature, and by motion pictures and special public speakers. This was a branch of work, said Mr. Black, which plays directly into the hands of practical rangers and their scheme of patrol, for it went far deeper than mere fear of the law and gained voluntarily what under no circumstances can be compelled by magistrates and fines.

The Lessening Supply of White Pine

William Little, of Westmount, Que., writes the press as follows: In corroboraton of the facts mentioned in your issue of June 2, relating to the building boom then existing in the United States, and the rapidly advancing prices of all kinds of lumber used in home building, the "Canada Lumberman," in its issue of June 1, shows that in the Ottawa lumber district of Canada a similar condition exists with regard to our old familiar friend, the white pine, known to be the most valuable in the North American forests, especially for building purposes, when its Ottawa price list shows that within the two weeks from May 15 to June 1 the mill prices for good pine sidings had been advanced from a mean of $65 per M. ft. b.m. for 1-inch lumber to $75, and for 1¼ and 1½ from $72.50 to $90, and for 2-inch from $74 to $95 or over $20 per M. increase within two weeks. In the lower grades dressing sidings are advanced from $50 to $55; dressing strips from $45 to $50, and dressing shorts from $40 to $47.

The price of mill run spruce 12 to 16 ft. has also been advanced from $34 to $40 per M. ft. You will also note on page 33 of the same issue of the "Canada Lumberman" some remarks contained in a letter from Mr. A. C. Manbert, of Toronto, who has been in England for some weeks conducting propaganda work in the interest of Ontario lumber products, who states: "There is literally a famine of white pine (or yellow pine, as it is called here). I went over the Surrey docks this past week and where in ordinary pre-war times vast stocks were stored there was not now five standards. In fact, I was told by a competent authority in the pine trade that he doubted if there was in all London 50 standards of pine that is for sale."

Of course, this state of the trade is largely due to the high rates of ocean freights, but it gives little comfort to those who are persistently trying to delude the public with their vagaries of unexhaustible forests, and pine timber enough to last for a hundred years, for here they get no help from the coast range of British Columbia, where there is no western pine and the mere trifle of only one half of one per cent. of white pine. Indeed, it may not be long before they will be competing with us for the limited stock now left us. The more this question of the supply of white pine is enquired into the clearer is it seen that we are close to the time when our at one time magnificent forests of white pine, the most valuable timber in existence, are destroyed through the rapacity of our too avaricious lumbermen.

Dr. Howe on N. B. Forest Survey

Dr. C. D. Howe, professor of forestry at the University of Toronto, has gone East to supervise the study of the annual growth on the Crown lands of New Brunswick. He joins the party on the forest survey which is working about thirty-five miles from Doaktown, and it is expected Dr. Howe will spend about a month in the province. He is employed by the Commission of Conservation to study annual growth in Canada, and his services have been loaned to New Brunswick in the interests of investigative work there.

The annual rate of growth will be studied so that the number of board feet of growth which takes place each year in the forests may be found out. When this is known it is proposed to regulate annual cut so as to keep it below the annual growth and thereby preserve the forests of the country. Dr. Howe was in New Brunswick last year and will continue the work which he started at that time.

Send in Your Boards for the Exhibit

The exhibition of timber grown within the British Empire, to be held in London next October, should have a special interest for Canada, which is by far the largest producer of lumber among British countries.

The collection and preparation of samples for display at this hibition and the preparation of information to be included in the catalogue are being made by the Forest Products Laboratories of Canada at Montreal.

Each kind of wood will be represented by four boards 1 inch thick by 8 feet long and of reasonable width, two boards in clear stuff and two boards in merchantable quality. One board of each quality will be planed smooth, and in some cases polished. Some boards have already been received at the Laboratories from members of the Canadian Lumbermen's Association, but others have yet to arrive.

The collection of information for the catalogue of this exhibition is a more urgent matter, as this information must be in London next month. Besides a general description of each kind of wood, the results of tests and a list of uses, it is desired that a list of commercial sizes and qualities suitable for export of each species should be given, together with the names of ports of shipment. Such commercial information can only come from the industry itself and it would be of considerable value if all exporters would send such information as to their own products without delay to Mr. W. B. Stokes, Forest Products Laboratories of Canada, 700 University Street, Montreal.

Bill of Lading—Joint Rail and Ocean Form

After receiving an expression of views from various members throughout the country in connection with the bill of lading—joint rail and ocean form—a letter was addressed to the various railway companies asking for a re-instatement of the through rail and ocean bill of lading. After due consideration the railway companies stated that they could not make such arrangements at that time owing to the difficulties in regard to space, but that they hoped to do so by midsummer. It has just been announced by the Canadian railway companies that, effective July 1st, they will re-instate this form of bill of lading. This should be of great assistance to many interested in export trade.

Mr. Laughlin Begins Important Work

H. S. Laughlin, Chatham, N. B.

Mr. H. S. Laughlin who has entered upon his duties as chief forester for the J. B. Snowball Co., Limited, lumber manufacturers, of Chatham, N.B., is a graduate of the University of New Brunswick, taking his Science degree in Forestry in 1914. After leaving this institution of learning he went into the British Columbia forest service, where he was forest assistant until he enlisted in November, 1915. He served overseas in the 104th Batt. under Lt.-Col. (Senator) G. W. Fowler, and was eventually transferred to the Canadian Forestry Corps, in May, 1917. Mr. Laughlin served as a forester and supervisor of logging under Lt.-Col. G. M. Strong, D.S.O., in No. 5 District, C.F.C., France, from May, 1917, to Aug. 1918, when he had a general break down and was taken to England for treatment. A few days before the signing of the armistice he was discharged from the hospital, but did not return to France. Lt.-Col. Grace of the 5th District, C.E.F., Commanding Officer, made the following mention of Mr. Laughlin in the Army Book No. 439. "This officer, Lieut. Laughlin, has been our forester and his services to No. 5 District, Canadian Forestry Corp., have been most valuable. It is regretted he leaves us owing to ill health."

In regard to his present work, Mr. Laughlin has been acquainting himself with the different regions of the J. B. Snowball Co.'s holdings. He is entering the field this month and will carry on a five per cent. cruise of about ninety square miles of the limits of the company on the Tabusintac River. Two cruising parties, each of three men, will be used for this work.

Arbitrator in Disputes is Parish Priest

The parish priest, is the sole arbitrator in case of disputes between a local manufacturing company and its men, representatives of a pulp and paper corporation and its employes told the Industrial Relations Commission at a meeting recently at Grand Mere, Que. The witnesses who gave evidence were George Chahoon, Jr., President of the Laurentide Company, who testified on behalf of the company owning the mill; Joseph DesLaurier, a carpenter; F. J. Gauthier, for the employes, and Father LaFleche, who decides the disputes.

Mr. Chahoon said that the company employed 1,700 men. By a raise that was to be given in a few days the minimum salary paid would be $3.50 a day. The men had received a fifty per cent. increase since 1914, and the increase in the cost of living in Grand-Mere had not gone up so rapidly. The company itself owned seventy houses, which it rented to employes at six per cent. on the cost. Clubs for athletics and amusement were also maintained.

Father LaFleche said that every time he had asked for something from the company for the men they got it. He considered their claims very carefully and he never asked for something that he felt the men were not entitled to.

Pulp Men Go After Tonnage Facilities

If there is one organization that is alive in the industrial life of Canada and is making strong, steady strides in the way of developing export business, it is the Canada Pulp & Paper Association, who have not only appointed a representative in the person of A. L. Dawe, Montreal, to go abroad and represent them in London, acting in conjunction with the Canadian Mission, but have also taken another decisive step in the way of securing adequate ocean tonnage.

A large number of companies have several thousand tons of ground wood pulp and paper awaiting transportation and representations have been made to the Federal authorities asking them to provide the necessary tonnage on conditions and under arrangements they will permit the industry to meet foreign competition, which under the present circumstances, is practically impossible. The industry finds that its products are welcomed in Great Britain and is anxious to take advantage of the opportunity which apparently exists at this time, and establish a permanent market overseas, both for its own advantage and that of the country.

Assurances have been received from the Minister of Marine and Fisheries that the Government is exerting every reasonable effort to the end that transportation facilities for Canadian pulp products should be provided and that vessels, now owned by the Government, are to be operated by the Canadian National Railways. It is probable that a generous amount of space in these Government owned ships will be placed at the disposal of the pulp and paper interests.

Fire Destroys Three Eastern Sawmills

The dread forest fires have again put it an appearance despite the vigilance of the rangers and within the past few days over a quarter of a million dollars damage resulted at Kedgewick, a settlement along the International Railway in Restigouche County, N. B. It is said that the fires resulted from carelessness on the part of farmers who were clearing lands and the flames got beyond their control. When the fire was noticed the villagers turned out and battled with the flames, which threatened to wipe out the entire village. Fifteen homes were demolished as well as three mills, one owned by the Richards Lumber Company, and two by the Poulay Lumber Company in addition to a large territory of lumber lands. When the flames were at their height and a call for help was being sent broadcast a providential rain checked the conflagration.

Edward Burtt, a New Brunswick lumberman, received word word recently that the Bridges Lumber Company's mill at Fort Steel, B. C., which he has been operating, was completely destroyed by fire. The loss is estimated at $50,000.

Newsy Happenings from the East

The five-masted schooner Jane Palmer, arrived in New York recently, en route to St. John, where she has been chartered to load deals for England at 300 shillings per standard. This is an exceptionally high rate and should prove lucrative to the owners of the vessel, which is 2,800 tons register.

There have been several serious lumber fires in the Maritime Provinces during the past few weeks and the loss will be great.

One June 9 a serious fire broke out in the yard of the Edward Sinclair Lumber Company in Newcastle, N.B., and did damage estimated at $50,000. The fire was so serious that a call was sent to Chatham, N.B., for assistance. Fortunately the fire was checked before it reached the large mill, which had been in operation since May 6th.

Ottawa Lumberman Takes Step Higher

D. K. Edwards, Ottawa, Ont.

D. Kemp Edwards, who has occupied the position of secretary-treasurer of Geo. M. Mason, Limited, Ottawa, for many years, has been made general manager of the company. It will be remembered that Geo. M. Mason, head of the organization, passed away recently, after a long and successful career in the lumber business. Mr. Edwards is well and favorably known to the trade in the Capital City and has always taken a warm interest in the welfare and progress of the industry. Geo. M. Mason, Limited, who are proprietors of the Bayswater planing mill, corner Wellington St. and Bayswater Ave., Ottawa, also have a branch yard at Woodroffe and deal in timber, scantling, rough and dressed lumber, lath, shingles, sash, doors and general factory work. A new board of directors was recently elected. W. T. Mason, of Montreal, is president of the company; Geo. I. Dewar, of the Montreal Lumber Company and the Export Lumber Co., Boston, vice-president and D. Kemp Edwards, secretary-treasurer and general manager. The company have developed a large and growing business and report prospects for the present season as being exceptionally good.

Receipts at the Crown Timber office, New Westminster, B. C., during May were $24,644, or nearly double those of May, 1916, when the total was $12,873. According to Assistant Agent Walmsley, this is due partly to the increased scale of rentals and royalties that went into effect on May 1st.

PUBLISHER'S NOTICE

Advertisements other than "Employment Wanted" or "Employees Wanted" will be inserted in this department at the rate of 20 cents per agate line (14 agate lines make one inch), $2.80 per inch, each insertion, payable in advance. Space measured from rule to rule. When four or more consecutive insertions of the same advertisement are ordered a discount of 25 per cent. will be allowed.

Advertisements of "Wanted Employment" will be inserted at the rate of one cent a word, net. Cash must accompany order. If Canada Lumberman box number is used, enclose ten cents extra for postage in forwarding replies. Minimum charge 25 cents.

Advertisements of "Wanted Employees" will be inserted at the rate of two cents a word, net. Cash must accompany the order. Minimum charge 50 cents.

Advertisements must be received not later than the 10th and 20th of each month to insure insertion in the subsequent issue.

Wanted–Lumber

Basswood Wanted

No. 2 Common and Mill Cull. Winter cut preferred. Apply Firstbrook Brothers, Ltd., Toronto, Ont. 8-t.f.

Posts and Slabs Wanted

Wanted to buy—Spruce and Pine, cedar Posts, also Pine Slabs. Hamilton Lumber & Coal Co., Ltd., Hamilton, Ont. 13

Bass Wood Blocks

Wanted 10" to 24" in. diameter, cut in multiples of 8 feet, for immediate or next winter's delivery. Address Auger & Son, Limited, Quebec. 13

Lath Wanted

Wanted—4' No. 3 White Pine Lath. State commission allowed. Mills interested please wire Charles H. Stewart, 45 Lothrop Ave., Detroit, Mich. 13

For Sale–Lumber

Oak Timbers For Sale

Oak timber from 6 x 8 to 20 x 20, lengths 10 to 30, for boat and dock work. D. A. Webster, 50 Vernon St., Brookline, Mass. 8-13

Beech For Sale

One hundred thousand feet of No. 1 Beech. Will cut to dimensions. For particulars write

E. S. THOMPSON,
13 Applin, Ont.

FOR SALE

100 Doors, 2-6 x 6-6 No. 3 White Pine, 5 panels 1¼.
100 Doors, 2-8 x 6-8-1¼, No. 3.
400 M. pcs. 48" Jack Pine, No. 3.
400 M. pcs. 48" Spruce, No. 3.
300 M. pcs. 32" Mill Run Spruce.
220 M. pcs. 32" Mill Run Jack Pine.
5 Cars Cedar Posts.

F. McGIBBON & SONS,
13 Sarnia, Ont.

SPRUCE FOR SALE
For immediate shipment

300 M. ft. 3" 5th quality and better.
200 M. ft. 3" 5th and 6th quality.
This lumber can be resawed and dressed in transit if desired. Write for attractive quotation.

J. GEO. CHALIFOUR,
13-14 Quebec, Can.

FOR SALE

About 300 M. ft. Birch, Red Oak and Maple, ready for immediate shipment.
Also ¾" Crating Spruce, and 1", 2" and 3".

Apply: J. P. ABEL, FORTIN & CO.,
379 Desjardins Avenue,
13 Maisonneuve, Montreal.

FOR SALE

A few carloads of small Hemlock and Cedar Ties.
Two carloads of XX Cedar Shingles.
Two carloads of 32" Lath.
One carload of 4' Lath.
Three carloads of Pine Dressing Strips.
Three carloads of Spruce Dressing Strips.
Three carloads of 6 x 6 to 10 x 10 timbers,—18 to 30 ft.

The John Carew Lumber Co., Ltd.,
13-14 Lindsay, Ont.

Wanted–Machinery

Wanted

Second-hand wood burner for mill with capacity of 30M to 35M. Communicate with Pierce Lumber Co., Timmins, Ont. 13

Bolting Machine

WANTED — 1 Bolting Machine, with carriage, for 4 to 5 foot wood, with 36 in. saw. Box 5, Papineauville, Que. 12-13

Wanted

Slab slasher in good repair, cash or exchange for light carriage or lath mill. Apply Box 939, Canada Lumberman, Toronto. 12-13

For Sale–Machinery

FOR SALE—SAWMILL

25 H. P. Engine, 50 H. P. return tubular boiler. Three log seat carriage, overhead set, friction feed works, single edger and slab saw. All in fair order. Price $1,000. Box 915, Canada Lumberman, Toronto. 12-15

For Sale

Berlin No. 177 Double Surfacer.
Berlin No. 90 High Speed Matcher.
Mershon 44 in. Band Rip Saw.
Berlin No. 88 Hardwood Matcher.

Box 948, Canada Lumberman, Toronto. 12-13

High Speed Matchers

1—Berlin No. 00 High Speed Matcher with Profilers and several extra heads.
1—American No. 77 High Speed Matcher without Profiler but having several extra heads.
Two real bargains.

Box 803, Canada Lumberman, Toronto, Ont. 6-t.f.

Band Saw Mill For Sale

One Waterous 9 ft. Band Saw Mill, gunshot feed, complete with extra saws and filing equipment. Used about one year, excellent condition. The Geo. F. Foss Machinery & Supply Co., Ltd., 305 St. James St., Montreal, Que. 7-t.f.

Logging Equipment

Phoenix Caterpillar Log Haulers.
Logging Sleighs.
Rutters.
Hoisting Engines.
12 lb. and 16 lb. Relaying Rails.

J. L. NEILSON & CO.,
13-t.f. Winnipeg, Man.

Here's Your Opportunity!
For Sale

"Canada Machinery Corporation", New No. 107 Planer and Matcher. New price $1,750. Our Price $800.

"Canada Machinery Corporation" New No. 110 Planer and Matcher and Moulder. New Price $1,400. Our Price $750.

"C.M.C." No. 610 Gang Edger. New price $900. Our Price $400.

"C.M.C." No. 303-10" Heavy Four-Sided Moulder, just like new. New price $1,750. Our Price $950.

Further particulars if so desired will be cheerfully furnished.

WILLIAMS & WILSON LIMITED,
84 Inspector Street,
13-16 Montreal, P.Q.

Machinery For Sale

20 to 25 h.p. portable horizontal boiler and engine on skids, good condition. Easy terms to responsible party. Box 973, Canada Lumberman, Toronto. 13-16

For Sale

1—17 x 24 Atlas Engine, with 36 in. x 10 ft. flywheel.
3—No. 94 Berlin Matchers, 15 in., fitted with hard steel knives on top and bottom cylinders—one pair shiplap, jointer and flooring heads with bits for each machine.
1—No. 182 Berlin Double Surfacer, 30 in. x 8 in.
1—No. 199 Berlin Buzz Planer.
1—No. 290 Berlin Picket Header.

The Otis Staples Lumber Company, Ltd.,
19-t.f. Wycliffe, B.C.

Building Sold, Machinery Must be Sol

Iron Pipe Valves, etc., guaranteed.
Boiler, 72 x 16 ft. 100 lbs.
Twin engine, bore 13¼", stroke 17".
3 Stickers.
17 Saws (various styles).
5 Sanders.
2 Automatic turning tables.
2 Tenoners.
2 Chain Mortisers.
4 Filing Machines (automatic).
2 Fans and Blower system.
Pulley and Shafting.
Many other Planing Mill machines.

Apply: Dominion Lumber & Coal Co. Ltd., Hamilton, Ont. 11-14

Wanted–Employment

Advertisements under this heading one cent a word per insertion. Box No. 10 cents extra. Minimum charge 25 cents.

First Class Band Sawyer wants position. 14 years experience in hard and soft woods, right or left hand rig. Box 964, Canada Lumberman, Toronto. 13-14

A Practical Lumberman, years of experience in Bush, just returned, wants position as foreman or licensed log or pulpwood scaler. Best of references. Box 978, Canada Lumberman, Toronto. 13-14

Man with long experience in export of deals, planed boards and box shooks for United Kingdom, Africa, Australia, and other countries, is open for engagement. Write Box 958, Canada Lumberman, Toronto. 12-14

POSITION WANTED by a well educated young man, 15 years' experience with wholesalers and manufacturers; competent inspector either hard or soft wood; will consider any other capacity. Apply Box 956, Canada Lumberman, Toronto. 12-16

WANTED—Position as Superintendent or Foreman of planing mill or woodworking factory by thoroughly capable experienced man who has handled big work and large gangs, knows the business and machines thoroughly, and gets results. Box 950, Canada Lumberman, Toronto. 12-15

First Class Man on Rip Saw.

JOHN B. SMITH & SONS,
13-16 Toronto, Ont.

SALESMAN with Eastern connection to sell B. C. Timbers, Yard Stock and Shingles, on Commission. Box 929, Canada Lumberman, Toronto. 10-11

Wanted—Man who has had some experience on band saw and jointer on ordinary work. Prefer man from village or small country town. Apply Box 967, Canada Lumberman, Toronto. 13

Wanted—One Foreman for Sash and Door Department; experienced on solid and veneered doors; four bench men, experienced on hard and soft wood; two cabinetmakers.

J. R. EATON & SONS, LIMITED,
13-16 Orillia, Ont.

FOR SALE

30 H.P. Bell Engine.
30 H.P. Waterous Return Tubular Boiler.
Three Log Seat Carriage.
Henry Disston inserted tooth saw, single edger and slab saw, Long shingle mill knife and saw edger; all in good order. Price $1,00 at railway switch. Box 144, Schomberg, Ont. 12-13

Saw Mill Plant For Sale

Practically new and modern Saw Mill Plant, capacity about 30 Million feet per annum, located in the Interior of British Columbia, on a beautiful Inland lake and on the main line of the Grand Trunk Pacific Railway. About 500 Million feet of timber on and adjacent to Lake (about 90% Spruce) and another Billion feet available at reasonable prices. Natural conditions ideal for economical logging, manufacturing, piling and shipping. An advantage of about $4 per thousand feet in freight rates to the Prairie Provinces over Coast shipments.

This property offers unlimited possibilities as a lumber, pulp and paper property. Would consider selling a half interest. Terms reasonable.

A. C. FROST COMPANY,
134 South LaSalle Street,
5-t.f. Chicago, Ill.

Two Timber Limits

34,000,000 ft. Virgin Timber, and 3,000,000 cords of Spruce Pulpwood. For all desirable information write to D. McDonald, La Salle, N.Y. 12-15.

For Sale

Building and machinery of good Double Cut Band Sawmill, well equipped with steam feed, canter, loaders, etc.

Also two storey Brick Factory on large lot, convenient to two railways; splendid location. Address Box 949, Owen Sound, Ont. 12-t.f.

Saw Mill Wanted

Wanted.—second-hand saw mill with capacity 25,000 to 30,000 ft. Up-to-date equipment. Box 971, Canada Lumberman, Toronto. 13

Saw Mill Property FOR SALE

Picnic Island sawmill plant at Little Current, Georgian Bay, 37 acres, for sale or lease for a term of years, or might put it in a good sized company, part cash, part stock; cutting capacity 140 M. a day, two thousand feet stone-filled lumber docks, 16 ft. water, Algoma railway station less than a mile distant, log booming capacity 10 million, telegraph and telephone, school taxes only, title from Crown, no debts or disputes; one of the best mills on the Bay, selling cheap to wind up an estate. For further particulars as to the mill and about twenty other buildings, etc., apply to Thomas Conlon, 44 Church Street, St. Catharines, Ont. 13-16

Miscellaneous

For Sale

One Detroit Hot Blast, Dry Kiln System, complete with Fan and Engine, also 36 feet of 9" double leather belt, used two weeks.

Port Hope Veneer & Lumber Co.,
13-t.f. Port Hope, Ont.

Sale of Timber Berths

Tenders will be received by the undersigned up to and including Wednesday, the 16th day of July next, for the right to cut the timber of various descriptions on the Townships of Groves and St. Louis in the District of Sudbury.

Terms and conditions of the sale containing full particulars, and maps showing the position of the Berths offered for sale, may be obtained upon application, to the undersigned, or from Mr. Charles Henderson, Crown Timber Agent, Sudbury.

G. H. FERGUSON,
Minister of Lands, Forests and Mines,
N.B.—No unauthorized publication of this notice will be paid for. 12-14
Toronto, June 11th, 1919.

Sale of Timber Berths

Tenders will be received by the undersigned up to and including Wednesday, the 16th day of July next, for the right to cut the Red and White Pine Timber on the following Townships, viz.:

DISTRICT OF ALGOMA

Mississaga Forest Reserve.
Township "C".

DISTRICT OF SUDBURY

Township of Teffer.
Township of McConnell.
Township of McNish.
Township of McNamara.

DISTRICT OF NIPISSING

Township of Kenny.
Township of Sisk,
Township of McCallum,
Township of McLaren,
Township of Charlton.

Also, tenders will be received by the undersigned up to and including Wednesday, the sixteenth day of July next, for the right to cut various classes of timber on Township "U", in the Mississaga Forest Reserve, in the District of Algoma.

The terms and conditions of the sale containing full particulars, and also maps showing the berths offered for sale, may be obtained upon application to the undersigned, or from Mr. Charles Henderson, Crown Timber Agent, Sudbury, or from Mr. J. T. McDougall, Crown Timber Agent, North Bay.

G. H. FERGUSON,
Minister of Lands, Forests & Mines.
Toronto, May 14th, 1919.

N.B.—No unauthorized publication of this notice will be paid for. 11-14

WANTED

LIGHT RAILS

State whether complete with splice or angle bars.

Give size, quantity, location, condition and best cash price f.o.b. cars loading point.

Box No. 966, Canada Lumberman, Toronto.
13-14

How Trees Make the City Beautiful

The Galtonian has for the past few days been looking on scenes of rare beauty about him. Spring coming with a rush has displayed Nature in her most glorious garb, says the Galt, Ont., "Reporter." Panaromic is the view from every hill in the city. Verdure is wonderfully fresh and inviting. Budding trees are everywhere. The late Hon. Jas. Young was wont to take his visitor to the west side of his house on the MacKenzie street elevation and ask him if in all his travels he had ever looked on a prettier landscape, crowned as our western hills are—terrace-like in their appearance—with hard and soft maples, oak, elm, ash, beech, cedar, spruce, pine and walnut, with a white birch here and there to add to Nature's color scheme. Other citizens champion the view from High Park as the one to feast one's eyes upon; and still others contend that from a point on Rose street near the C.P.R. station the eye receives a very vivid impression of Picturesque and Industrial Galt, an impression ineffaceable in its effect upon the sightseer. The fact is that from every hill overlooking the valley that is bisected by the Grand river this jewel spot of the valley glistens in spring and summer, with a riot of color in the fall that requires the artistic temperament and mental equipment of the painter to fashion a description. Today we are looking out on a picture that embraces many shades of green—from the dark hues of the pine and spruce to the lighter ones of the maple, elm, oak and ash. In her possession of pine groves and clumps of cedar and spruce this city is conspicuous in older Canada. Of them the hills and every piece of undulating land show natural groupings. When blended with Nature's handiwork in the valley and man's contribution to the picture in the form of stone, stucco, brick and frame structures they create a series of panoramic views of which Galtonians are justly proud.

Private Side Track Agreement

It is announced by the National Wholesale Lumber Dealer's Association, New York, that they have been doing a considerable amount of preliminary work with the United States Railroad Administration, and with various railroads, in an effort to secure a uniform and modified private side track agreement.

The following is a modified liability clause suggested by the National Wholesale Lumber Dealers' Association for incorporation in a uniform private track agreement:—

It is understood that the movement of the railroad's locomotives over said track involves some risk of fire, and as between the parties, the industry assumes all responsibility for loss or damage arising from fire caused by locomotives on said track ;except to the premises of the railroad and to rolling stock belonging to the railroad, or to others.

As to loss arising from any other cause each party shall indemnify the other for ,and save the other harmless from, all loss of life and injury to property and persons arising out of the use of, or occasioned by, the construction or maintenance of said track as follows:

The railroad assumes all responsibility for loss of or damage to rolling stock belonging to the railroad, or to others; and for injury to or death of agents or employees of the railroad, when acting as such; except such loss, damage, injury or death as may be caused by the sole negligence of the industry, or the agents, or employees of the industry, when acting as such.

The industry assumes all responsibility for loss or of damage to all other property; and for injury to or death of its agents or employees, when acting as such; except such loss, damage, injury or death as may be caused by the sole negligence of the roalroad, or the agents or employees of the railroad, when acting as such; the intent of this agreement being that in the case of joint negligence, each party shall bear its own loss; except in case of fire, and then only as set forth above; and in case of loss or damage to property of third parties (other than rolling stock) or injury or death of licensees caused by joint negligence of the industry and the railroad, the industry and the railroad shall share responsibility for such loss, damage, injury or death equally.

Review of Current Trade Conditions

Ontario and the East

There have been no material changes in the general market situation during the past few days. Business, on a whole, continues good in spite of industrial interruptions at various centres. While housing propositions have been called off in a number of places there is a great deal more building developing than was anticipated a few weks ago. The conviction is now firmly settled in the mind of many contractors and would-be house owners that nothing is to be gained by delay in undertaking the erection of new dwellings. Prices are growing firmer all the time and there is an inordinate demand for hemlock, dry stock being very scarce.

Retail lumber yards declare that business on the whole is good and reassuring reports reach wholesalers from various parts of the country. Manufacturing conditions of the mills are exceptionally favorable, and so far as can be learned, there have been no labor troubles. Driving and towing operations have been auspicious, and it looks as if last winter's cut of logs will be completed at a comparatively early period in the fall. There is a good demand for hardwood and the advanced prices are now being accepted as a matter of course. Automobile concerns are buying freely, while furniture factories are exceptionally busy, some of them being far behind in getting out their orders. For interior trim chestnut is being used to a large extent and is decidedly popular with house-builders at present.

There is a general movement of stock to the other side of the line and some improvement in the general export situation. There have been a number of sales of the season's cut at about the same figure as last year and, in certain instances, higher. Everything points to stiffer figures in order to keep pace with the increased cost of production.

The eastern representatives of coast mills have not been able to sell lately for several reasons, among them the labor tie-up in the West, the abnormal demand from the prairies, the recent rise in prices, (which will have to adjust themselves to new conditions in the east), and precariousness in the shipping situation in the prairie provinces, occasioned by the troubles in Winnipeg, Calgary, Vancouver and other cities. While orders for shiplap, boards, "V" jointing, flooring and ceiling are not being filled at present, due to the foregoing causes, there is a very good demand for timbers. It is hoped, however, that the mills will shortly be operating again in the west, and that eastern representatives will be permitted to resume business. Shingles are still high and scarce and many orders are unfilled. There is a shortage of No. 1 and No. 2 white pine lath, and building trades are using up supplies as fast as they can be secured. Dry lumber is getting scarcer every day, and until the season's present cut is released, there is likely to be witnessed the spectacle ot smaller stocks. For thick ash and elm there is a good demand and agricultural implement firms have been buying quite freely, while smaller stocks of drywood have induced them to go into the market to secure timber for seasoning.

It is announced in retail lumber circles that lumber will go from two to three dollars per thousand feet higher at the first of the month, and that one of the causes is the recent advance made by mills, and the fact that there is a lively requisition at the present time, particularly in Toronto, for all kinds of material. The steady advances in shingles and the scarcity of lath also add to the tenseness of the existing situation. The opinion of those who have given close study to conditions, causes and effects, is that the man who builds now is "wise in his day and generation." Everything betokens stiffer quotations, and that there will ever be a return to pre-war prices is largely a matter of conjecture. There is one safe prediction, however, and that is prices are certainly going higher before they take a drop.

Writing the "Canada Lumberman" an Ontario manufacturer states that business is very brisk just now and all stocks, especially shingles, are in great demand. General conditions on the drives, towing and saw-milling are good, and nearly all the lumbermen have completed their drives. The water has been high in most cases and the weather favorable. As a result, the timber has been landing at the mill considerably earlier than in any corresponding period for some years past.

It is announced that more space is now available for the shipment of pulp and paper to Great Britain and other European countries, and that two or three steamships have already been placed at the disposal of the manufacturers. This is encouraging for the trade in general, as the absence of tonnage up to the present time has seriously interfered with heavy export business. Indications are that from this out the situation will gradually improve. While ocean tonnage rates are no lower, the tendency is in the desired direction, so that a hopeful feeling now prevails regarding the overseas business.

Within the past two or three days eastern representatives of Coast mills have received advices of another advance of $2.00 per thousand on fir boards of all kinds, and $3.00 on cedar products. This makes several increases during the past few weeks, and it is not known whether or not the top has yet been reached. The latest messages from Vancouver would indicate that the strikes will soon be settled and the saw mills, along with other industries, resume operations.

United States

Activity characterizes the general situation in the lumber market and continued expansion is evidenced on all sides. The volume of current transactions is large. The building boom keeps up in a great many cities in spite of the labor unrest and strikes of certain trades. Building permits issued for May were more than double of those taken out during the corresponding month of a year ago. General reports from various agricultural centres indicate that the crop outlook is promising, and should no set back be received the harvest will be a very large one. Prices have advanced on a number of the better grades of hardwood and most of the yards in the border cities are doing a satisfactory business, with dry stocks especially in good demand. The requisition for hardwood lumber of all species is brisk and weather conditions have been favorable to increased output. There is a marked activity in birch, which is being largely used for interior trim. Gum, oak, poplar and birch of the better grades are moving most freely. There is really no fixed price governing at the present time, as quotations change from day to day. The figure which one has to pay depends upon how anxious he is to secure the stock. In southern pine there is still a shortage owing to the excessive demand. There is a call for the better grades of flooring, siding and finish and prices are governed by the promptness of the shipments. One outstanding feature is the increased demand for dimension and timbers for the east.

There is no material change in the shingle situation. The demand for white cedar shingles continues good and prices have not been lowered or advanced on the whole. In the southeast the demand for pine shingles is better and all along the southern coast, where cypress shingles are manufactured, it is impossible fully to supply the demand. Stocks of 4-foot plastering lath are scarce in manufacturers' hands in all sections and buyers are having trouble in securing all that they need. Lath prices have advanced considerably lately, and evidently lath are going to be mighty good property before long. It is significant to note that the wood lath or rather, a strip of wood similar to a lath, is preferred by many concerns putting up stucco houses. A house can be put up more cheaply with the use of wood than with metal lath and, furthermore, the wood lath is not subject to the attack of acids that are now put in some of the stuccos that give the best results. This means, of course, that strips of wood similar to lath, and also Byrkit lath are sure to be in great demand.

Speaking of the general situation, one authority says: "The new discount sheet on Douglas fir, showing advances of approximately $3 on the general list, is more effective in the eastern distributing centres than in the west or at manufacturing points, indicating that while much of the demand in the latter section has been accounted for, it is just beginning to manifest itself in the former. Another evidence that the demand which the territory west of the Mississippi has been experiencing since early spring is extending to the New England states is found in the action of eastern spruce and hemlock manufacturers in marking up prices generally, some mills withdrawing from the market until higher values are definitely established. Southern pine and hardwoods continue in an impregnable position, demand greatly exceeding supply and output and prices showing firmness. Stocks are short everywhere and buyers are not haggling over prices."

In regard to northern hemlock there is an exceptionally alert demand for all grades, which comes from the consuming industrials, and dealers in many sections of the country. Prices are strong and advancing. Northern pine, tamarac and all the white cedar products are having an exceptionally good call with no surplus of dry stocks at the mills. The eastern trade is drawing heavily on the present available supply of northern softwoods, water shipments at this time

View of Mills in Sarnia.

BUY THE BEST

Retailers and woodworking establishments who like to get A1 NORWAY and WHITE PINE LUMBER always buy their stocks from us because we can ship them on quick notice. It pays to have the goods, but it pays better to "deliver" them.

We also make a specialty of heavy timbers cut to order any length up to 60 feet from Pine or B. C. Fir.

"Rush Orders Rushed"

Cleveland-Sarnia Sawmills Co., Limited

SARNIA, ONTARIO

B. P. Bole, Pres. F. H. Goff, Vice-Pres. E. C. Barre, Gen. Mgr. W. A. Saurwein, Ass't. Mgr.

being heavy to many of the port distributing points. Northern manufacturers to-day can see no weakness in any of the markets for such available items now in pile at the mills.

Great Britain

The general phases of merchandising in lumber in the British Isles are admirably summed up in the article by A. C. Manbert of Toronto, lumber commissioner for Ontario. This timely contribution appears in another page of the "Canada Lumberman," and will be read with interest. On the whole, Mr. Manbert takes an encouraging view of the situation and gives a keen analysis of the contending forces that are now at play. Reports from Manchester and other centres indicate no material change in the timber trade, and a correspondent from that city writing "Timber" says:

At the present moment forward buying is very unsettled, and importers and merchants are not willing purchasers on the shippers' present f.o.b. prices from Sweden, which are about 20s. to 30s. per standard higher than the prices paid by the Government buyer.

Finnish shippers, through their agents, have been offering some decent specifications, including a big percentage of 3 x 9 in., at reasonable f.o.b. prices, but the great difficulty in securing suitable tonnage for some considerable time has caused the importers to decline business for the present.

The freight market continues very firm, with a marked tendency to go higher. Tonnage is very difficult to secure, and holders of stocks in Sweden and Norway are very anxious to arrange shipments, and are practictlly willing to pay the rates quoted for early delivery.

The Government purchases of spruce and pine from Canada are now getting shipped, and in the near future big shipments will be arriving. Pine stocks are very depleted, and what shipments that have arrived have been very meagre. There is bound to be a big demand for pine deals, boards and sidings for joinery work, and the Manchester merchants are hoping that some good-sized parcels will be arriving at an early date, so that they will be prepared to meet the requirements of the housing scheme, which will be started shortly.

Most of the large contractors have plenty of contract work on hand, and several large jobs are expected to be given out any day now. The amount of repair work which was left over on account of the war has found plenty of work for the jobbing joiners, and large quantities of timber are getting consumed. Several buildings in the city of Manchester, which were partly erected previous to the war, are now getting completed. Joiners, bricksetters and plumbers are still scarce, and work is consequently only going slowly.

We have had glorious weather this last month, which has considerably assisted all outside work.

In the hardwood section of the trade business still continues very good, and most of the parcels arriving belonging to the Government are selling freely at prices ruling for current importation. There is a big demand for No. 1 common oak. Whitewood and gum lumber are in good request, especially in sizes under 1 in. thick. Freight rates are very firm, and shipping space very difficult to secure. The rate of freight ruling to-day is 2 dols. per 100 lbs.

The advices from the Government buyer of many charters for Swedish goods has put new life into the market. Merchants are still only inclined to deal with goods which are either in stock, on passage, or being loaded, and unless an importer can offer on c.o.f. terms with a named steamer, he finds but a small inquiry. We have several times connected on what has hitherto proved to be an ultra-cautious policy on the part of inland firms. Prices, instead of weakening with the larger import of timber, are as firm as and, indeed, firmer than ever, and there is yet no sign whatever of a fall either in f.o.b. prices or in spot values in this country. The longer the merchants have waited the higher the prices they have paid, but most of them have preferred to do this rather than take the risk of the market, even for a few months ahead.

A recent edition of the London Times says: The Government stocks of timber now are about 140,000 standards. About 117,000 standards have been bought in the Baltic and White Sea regions, and will be delivered by June and July. Another 200,000 standards of European timber have been bought and will be delivered later in the year. A further 250,000 standards of Canadian timber have been bought, and a number of ships have been allocated for its shipment. The total stock lying in the Baltic ports is 1,400,000 standards,

Market Correspondence

SPECIAL REPORTS ON CONDITIONS AT HOME AND ABROAD

Montreal Reports Show Trade Improvement

Business in Montreal has picked up. This is especially true in connection with American orders. Building in the Eastern States is active, according to representatives of Canadian lumber firms visiting that territory, and the demand is improving right along the line Quite a change has come over this section of the market, the people in the Eastern States having apparently come to the conclusion that it is futile to wait for lower prices of building material.

Locally, there is a little more doing, but the position is still far from satisfactory. There is a large amount of industrial unrest, and at one time it looked as if the entire building trades would come out on a sympathetic strike with the electricians, who have quit on account of being unable to obtain an advance of 50 per cent. All this makes for hesitancy in construction.

Prices are very firm. Then general view is that quotations will still further rise. Manufacturers are stated to be holding out very persistently for their prices. Lath, which for such a long time was almost a drug on the market, is exceptionally strong, with a good demand.

B. C. stock is, speaking generally, difficult to obtain, owing to the closing of many mills and, in some instances, manufacturers have withdrawn from the market.

Woodworking plants are fairly busy, outside orders helping to keep the factories going. The millwork employees have secured an advance in wages.

Exports on Government account are being shipped at a good rate. In addition to the shipments on the ordinary liners, a tramp has left the port with a large cargo of pine. There is a very insistent demand for pine on the other side, comparatively little going from Montreal last season. A small amount of lumber for commercial account is also being sent this season, the high freight rates being a deterrent factor in limiting this class of exports.

The pulpwood, pulp and paper exports for March continue to show gains—the figures for the fiscal year are dealt with in another column. Pulpwood in March increased from $560,520 to $1,408,143, and chemical pulp from $1,190,082 to $2,041,884. Mechanical pulp, however, was again lower, being $226,554, as against $606,683 in the corresponding month last year.

All Lumber Prices are Stiffening at St. John

The last two weeks has seen a further stiffening in prices of all sawn lumber at St. John. The United States buyers have awakened to the fact that there is not nearly so much lumber for sale as they anticipated and that the English market had bought about everything in sight at good prices; also that if steamers could be chartered to carry lumber, very little would be left in Canada which could not be sold at good prices, much over the present offers of the United States buyers.

All the mills are running full time at St. John and labor troubles are insignificant, there being plenty of men at the high wages being paid. Some increase in movement of stock has taken place during the last few days but it only seems temporary. As no information is given out by the shipping board all the producers of deals are in the dark and all they can do is patiently await boats. Laths and spruce boards which have been slow sellers, are now b ing purchased at much higher prices than offered any time to date nd should the increase of building permits in United States keep pace with the last month, a further advance in price is not unlikely.

Cedar shingles are very firm and scarce. The box tade is also reported good, with prices keeping pace with advances in rough timber. Refuse lumber is still unsteady. Stocks of white pine are low and no abnormal quantity will be offered this year, in fact, it will no doubt be less than usual.

All the logs have about reached the Fredericton boom limit as the last drive of the season has left Grand Falls on the Main St. John and it should be only a short time reaching boom limits as the bulk of the logs are now into safe keeping; men are also plentiful for rafting.

Ottawa is Pleased With Bright Prospects

The greatest improvement for many months to occur in the Ottawa lumber market took place during the month of June. The whole tone of the market increased in firmness. Prices in the better grades advanced and there was a general optimistic feeling that, after months of patient waiting by the lumbermen, that war conditions were be-

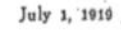

ginning to right themselves, and tend somewhat toward normal business as it was carried on in pre-war years.

The greatest improvement in the market began to be felt during the closing period of June, when it was reported that the wholesalers had or were beginning to be convinced that the price of this year's saw cut was not going to go down, and accordingly began to buy at higher prices.

Most importance was attached to the generally improved "tone" of the market. This was not confined to manufacturers' reports alone, but from some wholesalers as well, with a retailer here and there stating that business was "improving."

Little or no doubt existed that the demand for lumber was going to come back strong, and even with business being lower so far this year than had been expected, there was a strong undercurrent of feeling that business was on the up grade.

Not only were there sales of this year's saw cut at higher prices, but the demand showed more activity especially in the direction of the United States. Export business otherwise also brightened, though it did not open up to its pre-war extent. Considerable stocks of red and white pine deals and some spruce were shipped to Europe during the month of June, on what is known as "Government account."

Though the movement of stock for export went forward much faster when it was on "government account," the lumbermen, who have ideas as to the re-opening of the export trade, were a long way from being downhearted. They would have liked to have seen their own orders going over as fast.

They pointed out or seemed to take satisfaction in the belief that the faster the stock on "government account" was moved the sooner it would get over "there," and when such transporting was done that it would mean the freeing of more cargo space later on which some of them hope to be able to take advantage of at lower rates than those at present existing.

Some of the manufacturers and dealers were of the opinion that stocks in the Ottawa district at the present time are not as heavy or complete as they should be in view of the prabibility of a sudden opening up of export trade.

The "Canada Lumberman" can say that the saw cut of the Ottawa Valley mills this season will be less than last. The general cause given for this was that the sawmills generally did not open as early as usual. The real reason is that logs are not as plentiful as in former years.

"The effect of not being able to secure labor to send into the woods and get out the logs, last year and the year before, is beginning to make itself felt. There is plenty of water to float the logs, the thing is the logs are not in the river for us," was the general comment of a leading lumberman. Consequently without having logs at hand to saw, the sawmills have had to reduce or confine their operations. During the closing period of June, John R. Booth was only operating his mill on the usual day shift system which has been in vogue at his plant for the last two years. His sawmill is not operating to capacity.

Increased orders and inquiries from the United States indicated that the demand was for mill run, board, and better.

In connection with the increased demand from the United States exporters pointed out that in the U. S. building could be carried on the whole year round and that the wholesale dealers and yards realized this, whether there was snow on the ground in Canada or not, and consequently began to stock up.

Local transportation remained good. Lath and shingle held their previous prices and in this regard reports indicated continued firmness, or perhaps higher prices. There were no "over" stocks of either lath or shingle on the Ottawa market.

One of the most interesting inside reports was that the British Government order, purchased through Sir James Bell, the British Timber Controller, had in the Ottawa valley considerably exceeded early estimates. It was rumored unofficially that the pine output of Booth, Hawkesbury and some other Ottawa Valley mill had been entirely sold.

The furniture trade was exceptionally strong and factories were kept busy. General quotations were about twenty per cent. in advance of a year ago. Stocks for furniture manufacture remained satisfactory. The increase in manufacturing cost was attributed largely to higher wages of labor, which, it was stated, ran this item up from twenty-five to thirty per cent.

Building activity in Ottawa during the latter part of June showed little or no change.

Importation of Deals Still Light

An interesting circular was issued recently by Alfred Dobell & Company, of Liverpool, Eng., giving a report on the timber market. The firm declare that the market is still in a position of uncertainty. Notwithstanding the termination of the government control of the timber trade, the trade is still being dominated to a considerable extent by the operations of the Timber Supply Dept. In connection with the some of its foreign purchases the Department is absorbing most of the tonnage that would otherwise be available for shippers' operations. It is not yet definitely known what course will be adopted and what level of prices will be established in the disposal of the supplies to come forward on Government account.

Dealing specifically with the various kinds of wood, the firm furnish the following timely information:

Nova Scotia and New Brunswick Spruce Deals, etc.—The stocks are very light, and bare of several imported sizes. The importations have been light, and chiefly for account of the Timber Controller. Operations for Shippers' account have been very restricted in consequence of the difficulty in securing tonnage. Hardwood planks have been arriving freely for some time, and they have been needed, but buyers relying upon a steady supply being continued are likely to be disappointed.

Douglas Fir.—The stock of planks and decking is light, and that of logs practically exhausted. The importation has been almost entirely for Government account. There is a good enquiry for logs, decking, and planks of good dimensions in No. 2 common and better.

Scandinavian Deals, Boards, etc. are lightly stocked. Deals have arrived very sparingly and have gone direct into consumption. Flooring boards have arrived freely, and have met with a good demand. Shippers are quoting higher prices for forward-delivery in consequence of the increasing difficulty of the position of freights, etc.

Pitch Pine.—The stocks in the country are very limited, and the import is restricted in consequence of the lack of tonnage, a position which it is feared will continue for some time. There is a good demand, the descriptions more particularly required being, sawn timber, half timbers (6 by 12), deals and prime lumber.

States Hardwoods, etc., have arrived freely during the past month, and have consisted chiefly of oak, walnut, whitewood, red and sap gum, and cypress lumber. No Government hardwood auction sales have been held since the 13th March, but substantial quantities have been sold privately. The general enquiry is good, particularly for prime and No. 1 common grading West Virginia white oak, 1 in. and 2 in. thick, and planed and unplaned lumber of all descriptions in thickness of 7/8 in. and under. Freighting continues to be a difficult problem, but buyers are disposed to meet the advanced rates of freight which are demanded.

Bright Prospects For Lumber Abroad

R. W. McLellan, Fredericton, N. B.

"I have the greatest faith in what the next five or ten years has in store for New Brunswick's forest products," declared R. W. McLellan, of Fredericton, N, B., secretary of the New Brunswick Lumbermen's Association, who has just returned from a business trip to Great Britain and Ireland.

Mr. McLellan declared there was nothing more needed or wanted in the United Kingdom and throughout the devastated regions of Europe than lumber. "But," he declared, "the ships which will carry New Brunswick's lumber overseas are yet to be built." In spite of the lack of bottoms, Mr. McLellan sees a bright immediate future for the lumber trade with the British market and believes the British buyers will allow their stock to become seasoned here before shipment instead of holding it over for a year or more when it reaches an overseas port.

Regarding the overseas lumber market condition, Mr. McLellan said:

Lumber is a staple article greatly needed in Great Britain. During the war very little, if any, new building, except for military purposes, was carried on. The result is that housing conditions in all the large centres are in bad shape. It is impossible to secure the necessary accommodation to supply this demand. Relief will only come when the necessary ships are provided to carry Canadian lumber to the English market, and many of these have yet to be built. The large shipbuilding firm of Harland & Wolf, in Belfast, are desirous to add thousands of employees to their staff, but are prevented from doing so as no tenements are obtainable. The necessary demand for our forest products will be enormous when shipping facilities improve, and the outlook in the lumber situation is bound to be good for years to come.

Uniform Hardwood Inspection Rules

Report of Rules Committee to National Association says that Differences Between It and American Association are Trivial

In its report to the twenty-second annual convention of the National Hardwood Lumber Association in Chicago on June 19 and 20, the inspection rules committee expressed the hope and the belief that the day of single standard is almost here. Referring to the old controversy between the former Hardwood Manufacturers' Association and the National on the subject of uniform inspection, the absorption of the former by the American Hardwood Manufacturers' Association and the action of the latter in adopting its own set of inspection rules, the committee report declared that "in compiling their new rules, the American Association gave evidence of the very large duplication of membership between that organization and our own by paying us the compliment of adopting our rules practically in toto.

The main point which should be emphasized and which marks a long step forward toward a single standard of inspection is the fact that the new rules follow our principles of inspection and abandon the old idea of the Hardwood Manufacturers' Association, which was the bone of contention in the hardwood for so many years." Among other things, the report of the inspection rules committee said:

Rules Not Infallible

However fair and equitable a set of inspection rules may be, they have not, in themselves, the power to prevent errors in shipping or sharp practices among either buyers or shippers of hardwoods. There must be an inspection department composed of honest, experienced, efficient men who will apply the rules fairly and fearlessly when called open. Our inspection department is organized primarily to act as arbitrator between buyer and seller in case of dispute. The position of an arbitrator is never a pleasant one, but the continual growth of our organization and the prestige which we have acquired in the consuming trade evidence the confidence which our inspection department has established throughout the trade. That the great majority of official inspections are are satisfactory is shown by the small percentage of demands for reinspection. It is perfectly natural, however, that there should be some criticism of our inspection service, but of constructive criticism there is very little. The fact that the critics are about equally divided between the buyers and sellers would seem to indicate that our inspection department is following a straight line and keeping in the middle of the road.

Scientific Inspection Rules

Much has been said regarding scientific inspection rules, the intimation being that our present standards of inspection are in some degree unscientific. Your committee pleads guilty to the charge that we are lumbermen and not scientists. The practice of counting defects in the best grades while computing the cutting value of the lower grades is a custom as old as the trade itself and is embodied in our present system of inspection. If this is unscientific, then our rules are to the same extent unscientific. Whenever changed customs of the trade require that all grades be made on basis of the cutting value of lumber, then will the demand come for a similar change in the rules. Perhaps, some day, a real scientist may devise or discover a scientific method of rule making, but we feel that before accomplishing this result, the said scientist will devote himself to growing trees more scientifically than nature has evolved. A regularity in the growing of knots and other defects would be most desirable and would greatly facilitate the solution of inspection problems, or perhaps the simplest method would be the elimination from timber growth of all defects. But this is a problem for the future and in the meantime if the science of inspection rules can be measured by the successful and practical application of rules which are satisfactory and acceptable to the trade as a whole, then our entire membership, who in the last analysis, are the actual rule makers of our organization, may lay some claim to the scientific attainment.

Single Standard of Inspection

Since our last annual meeting, a new phase has developed in the organized opposition to our system of inspection. The Hardwood Manufacturers' Association which had for years promulgated a set of inspection rules opposed to our own, discontinued its organization for reasons best known to itself, and the individual members affiliated themselves with the American Hardwood Manufacturers' Association, an organization which had previously adopted the policy of neutrality as to inspection rules and which, from its inception, had expressed the desire for a single uniform standard of inspection. At the first meeting of the combined membership, in Louisville during December, 1918, the American Association revealed the change in the complexion of the organization with reference to inspection rules by voting to adopt and publish a new set of rules and to organize an inspection service along entirely different lines from the National. However, in compiling their new rules, the American Association gave evidence of the very large duplication of membership between that organization and our own, by paying us the compliment of adopting our rules practically in toto—with some slight changes which need not be discussed here in detail. The main point which marks a long step forward toward a single standard of inspection is the fact that the new rules follow our principles of inspection and abandon the old idea of the National Hardwood Manufacturers' Association which was the bone of contention in the hardwood trade for so many years. Although the rules adpted by the American Association are admittedly only temporary rules to be used until such time as a more scientific method of inspection may be developed by them, it is to be hoped that nothing will be done to revive the spirit of rivalry which formerly existed on the part of the H. M. A. toward the National, and there are grounds for hope that these two organizations, through the large duplication of membership, may reach a mutual understanding which will lead to uniform inspection. In fact, the rules, as they are now, are practically uniform, so that the differences are now largely in the methods of applying the rules. Perhaps these differences may be overcome in the course of time. It should be borne in mind also that the American Association has for its principal functions the advertising and market work and the compiling and dissemination of information regarding supplies of lumber and sales records. These two functions in themselves will doubtless require the greater part of the time and effort of that organization so that the question of inspection rules and service will not be emphasized in the sense of becoming an active competitor with our organization.

Laurentide Company is Extending

Extensive additions in the way of a new finishing-room, a storage and shipping building and a steel bridge are being carried out at Grand Mere, Que., by the Laurentide Co., Limited. Construction has begun on the new finishing-room and work on the other buildings will be under way in the near future. The improvements being carried out will afford the Company the most up-to-date facilities for handling their pulp and paper from the machines direct to the shipping point in their yards. The finishing-room has concrete foundations, brick facing and steel superstruction. Inside of the building there is room for the elevator shaft. This shaft is about 120 feet high. The capacity of the elevator will be about six 90-inch paper rolls or twelve 45-inch rolls. The paper will be delivered to a steel bridge connecting the elevator to the storage and shipping building. Its length is 170 feet by 31 feet wide. The last ninety feet of the bridge will contain scales for weighing the paper rolls and will provide space for wrapping them. This section is to be called the wrapping aisle. The bridge is of the lattice braced girder type and is supported on a central column of steel resting on a concrete pier.

The new storage and shipping building will be 92 feet wide by 280 feet long. Its foundation will be of concrete, the walls of solid brick and the super-structure of steel. The flooring will be of concrete on steel I-beams. The building is so designed that the maximum trucking space will be approximately sixty feet in length. An electric hoist will be installed to handle the paper rolls to the cars.

Charters Granted Housing Companies

The Listowel Housing Co., Limited, is a new organization which has been granted a provincial charter. The capital stock is forty thousand dollars, divided into eight hundred shares of fifty dollars, and the headquarters are at Listowel, Ont. The incorporators are Max K. Becker, Wm. Climie, J. H. Bender, Aaron Ringler, John M. Campbell and F. W. Hay, all of Listowel. The objects of the company are to acquire land and erect thereon dwelling houses of modern size and improvements, to be sold at moderate prices, or to be rented at moderate rates. The company will come under the purview and be subject to the provisions of the housing accommodation act.

The Canadian Co-operative Building Society, Limited have been granted a charter with headquarters in Toronto and the object of the organization is to buy, sell, transfer, hold, mortgage and possess real estate, to erect thereon buildings of every kind and to buy and sell building materials of all descriptions. The incorporators are L. H. Starrett, L. D. Corbett, Edward H. Wilson, Claude Warrington and others.

National Dealers Will Meet in Detroit

The next annual convention of the National Lumber Dealers association will be held at the Hotel Ponchartrain, Detroit, Mich., on September 11th and 12th.

EDGINGS

Ontario

The warehouse of the C. E. Gallagher Company, general storekeepers and lumber dealers, Bath, Ont., was recently burned to the ground.

Work will shortly start on the new sawmill of F. M. Wallingford, Timmins, Ont., and the mill will be rushed rapidly to completion.

R. E. Truax & Son, Walkerton, Ont., are remodelling their sawmill at a cost of several thousand dollars. Two new water wheels to develop 250 h.p. each will be installed.

On the suggestion of Controller Cameron, the Board of Control, Toronto, has decided to have a survey of the lumber yards in the city. He said that some were operating without permits.

The Ontario Department of Lands, Forests and Mines are advertising for tenders for the right to cut timber of various descriptions in the townships of Groves and St. Louis, the time for receiving such bids expiring on July 16th.

Supplementary letters patent have been granted by the Ontario Government to the Sturgeon River Improvement Company, Limited, extending the period of its existence for a further period of ten years, the extension to date from August 12th, 1919.

The Seamen, Kent Company, at Meaford, have received a large order from Liverpool, England, for hardwood flooring. They have found labor very scarce in Meaford and every effort has been made to induce help to come in from outside points.

The annual meeting of the Ottawa Lumbermen's Credit Bureau will likely be held some time next month. It will be remembered that Geo. M. Mason, president of the Bureau, passed away recently and in the meantime Grant P. Davidson, vice-president, is acting.

The Moose Lake Lumber Company, Limited, with headquarters at Cobalt, and a capital stock of forty thousand dollars, has been granted a charter to carry on the business of a lumber, saw and planing miller, etc. Among the incorporators of the company are John Ough, Alfred W. Herrington and Bruce Williams and others, of Cobalt.

The Frontier College has been incorporated with head offices in Toronto, to promote the education and welfare of Canadian frontiersmen, lumberjacks, miners and other working men. Among the incorporators are Alfred Fitzpatrick, educationalist; R. C. Dearle, lecturer; L. E. Westman, editor, and David A. Dunlop, barrister, all of Toronto, and James Playfair, of Midland, shipbuilder.

The Kingston Navigation Company, with headquarters at Kingston, and a capital stock of forty thousand dollars, has been granted a charter to operate boats and other ships or craft, and, generally, to continue a business of carrying passengers or freight by vessel or otherwise. The incorporators are John M. Campbell, John A. Carnegie, Robert E. Burns, John T. Bain and Chas. J. Bolton, all of Kingston.

It is authoritatively denied at the Toronto office of the Lake Superior Corporation that the Spanish River Pulp & Paper Company are negotiating for the large block of 682,000 acres of pulp lands owned by the Lake Superior Corporation. A report to this effect was recently published, but the statement is offered that negotiations with other interests have been in progress for some time, and are expected to come to a satisfactory conclusion before long.

Eastern Canada

The Tourville Lumber Company will erect a machine shop at Louiseville, Que.

Fire which broke out in lumber stored near the Edward Sinclair Company mill, near Newcastle, N.B., caused damage estimated to be between $150,000 and $200,000.

J. & W. Duncan, Limited, 1801 Ontario St. E., Montreal, are asking permission from the city council to erect a sawmill on Beaufort St., Montreal. They are also erecting a two-storey addition to their office.

The Tobique Lumber Company's mill at Eel River was totally destroyed by fire recently. The loss is about $15,000 and is partially covered by insurance. The lumber piles were not damaged. Work of rebuilding has commenced.

Serious forest fires are reported from the lower part of Matane County, Que. A sawmill belonging to Mr. J. A. Boulay, former member of the House of Commons for Rimouski, was burned to the ground. A number of box and flat cars and huge quantities of lumber were also destroyed.

A Federal charter has been granted the Minneapolis Steamship Co., Limited, with a capital stock of $50,000, and headquarters in Montreal. The company is empowered to build, acquire, charter, sail and operate steamships and other vessels and to carry on a business as freighters and forwarders between ports of Canada and Great Britain, or any foreign country.

A provincial charter has been granted H. C. Johnston Co., Limited, with a capital of $20,000 and headquarters in Montreal. The company is empowered to carry on the business of contractors, engineers and builders, and, also, to deal in timber, lumber, wood and pulp; to buy, acquire and operate sawmills, planing mills, etc., and to hold and sell forest and timber lands.

La Compagnie de Pulpe du Chicoutimi have been granted supplementary letters patent to increase the preference stock of the company from th sum of $2,500,000 to $3,000,000. The new stock will be divided into shares of $100 each and the common stock of the company will be decreased from the sum of $900,000 to $400,000.

Beauchemin & Rivet, Limitee, of Amos, Que., have been incorporated with a capital stock of $49,000, to own and operate sawmills, shingle mills, pulp and paper plants and carry on the business of lumber merchants and manufacturers. The incorporators are Joseph A. Beauchemin, Pierre E. Beauchemin, Alexis Rivet, Dr. Jos. A. Biague, and others.

A charter has been granted Three Rivers Lumber Co., Limited, with a capital stock of $300,000, and headquarters in Three Rivers. The incorporators are Germain Beaulieu; Reigner Brodeur; Chas. Holdstock and others. The company is authorized to carry on the business of manufacturers of and dealers in lumber and other wood, and to own, operate and control lumber operations, stores, mills, etc.

The Harvester Navigation Co., of Sussex, N.B., with a capital stock of $128,000, has been federally incorporated. The organization is empowered to build, lease, charter and operate ships, tugs, barges, etc. Among the incorporators of the company are M. Garfield White, lumber merchant, of Sussex, N.B.; Edgar Taylor, lumberman, of Apple River, N.S.; Whitfield Smith and Walter A. Keirstead, of Apple River, N.S., and Judson A. Cleveland, of Alma, N.B.

R. W. McLellan, of Fredericton, N. B., secretary of the New Brunswick Lumbermen's Association, who recently returned from an extended business trip to Great Britain and Ireland, states that conferences which were held in New York on his return, have convinced him that the pulp and paper business is now in that condition which means there is no prospect of advancing prices or even a return to last year's figures. The pulp and paper industry must await a return to something nearer normal conditions before its future can be accurately forecasted.

Supplementary letters patent have been granted by the Province of Quebec changing the name of the Saguenay Power Company to that of the Saguenay Pulp & Power Company, and granting additional powers of manufacturing pulp and paper and all articles in the making of which wood, pulp and paper may be utilized; to manufacture lime, bricks and to work quarries and to lease houses for and to employees, etc. The capital stock has been increased from $3,000,000 to $9,500,000. The principal place of business of the Corporation will be in Montreal instead of Chicoutimi, Que.

The revenue from the Department of Lands and Forests in the Province of Quebec for the last fifty years, ending June 30th, 1919, will, according to Hon. Jules Allard, show an increase of one million dollars. This is due to the recent order-in-council increasing the stumpage and other dues. In referring to the forest fire protection policy of the government, Hon. Mr. Allard said that if the plans which the administration now had in view succeeded in regard to forest fires, it would mean that no matter what exploitation of forests there was, Quebec would have forests in perpetuity.

The wooden cargo vessel "C-16" of 1500 tons, was launched recently by Fraser, Brace & Co., from their yard in Cote St. Paul, Que., this making the sixth vessel of a series of eight, which the firm are building for the French Government. Three of them were launched in March last. The dimensions of these ships are as follows: 1,500 tons; length, 202 ft.; 40 ft. 6 ins. beam; 17 ft. moulded depth. They are equipped with twin screw engines, Scotch marine boilers; crew quarters, 24 men; equipped with six cargo winches. The eight vessels are to be delivered this summer. They are all built of British Columbia fir.

Western Canada

A charter has been granted to United Aircraft Limited, of Vancouver, with a capital stock of $100,000.

The Arbuthnot & Helmer sash and door factory, 993 Sixth Avenue West, Vancouver, was recently destroyed by fire.

The Lanan Logging Co., Ltd., of Vancouver, capital $25,000, and United Logging Co., Ltd., of Vancouver, capital $10,000, have lately been incorporated.

The Abbotsford Lumber Company, of Abbotsford, have completed a record month's business, having shipped during May one hundred and twenty-eight cars of lumber containing some three million feet.

The Belgo Lumber Company, Limited, of Vancouver, with a capital stock of $40,000, and E. C. Walsh Lumber Co., Ltd., of Vancouver, with a capital stock of $50,000, have recently been granted provincial charters.

At a meeting of the Greater Vancouver and Lower Mainland Bureau of the Vancouver Board of Trade, the erection of a pulp mill in the Fraser Valley was proposed. It is believed that if such a mill is established, a large amount of the small standing timber could be used. The seeding down of logged-off lands in the valley was also another proposal.

The Mann & Wright lumber mill, which was recently erected on a triangular piece of land near Kennedy Station, B.C., formerly owned by the Timberland Lumber Company, is now in operation. The mill is run by electricity and ties, dimension timbers and rough and dressed lumber will be turned out. The company expect to have enough standing timber on their five hundred acre limits to keep the mill running for over three years.

A recent report from Winnipeg is to the effect that the lumber industry throughout the prairies has reached such proportions that car facilities are inadequate for getting the stock from British Columbia mills. On account of the scarcity of cars, yard labor and other trade conditions, Winnipeg wholesalers are being handicapped in securing sufficient stock. A large number of orders have been received from the country, particularly in the rural communities and small towns. There has been quite an advance in price during the last few days, owing to the augmented cost of production.

A. L. Mattes, manager of the Prince Albert Lumber Co., Ltd., Prince Albert, Saskatchewan, recently spent some time in the pine districts of Oregon and Washington studying manufacturing and logging methods. The Prince Albert Lumber Co. will cut out its timber this season and is planning on removing to some point on the Pacific Coast. Prince Albert is on the edge of the great Canadian prairie, on the line of the Canadian Northern. The timber is entirely small spruce, running about 20 logs to the thousand feet. The mill is a double cutting band with fast feed planers and other modern equipment.

The big plant of the Whalen Pulp & Paper Mills at Mill Creek has closed down because of conditions caused by the Vancouver strike. It has been found impossible to get the large product cut on account of lack of shipping facilities and thus 300 men have been thrown out of employment although it is not expected the shut down will last more than a few days. The Whalen Company found it would be impossible to keep going owing to the congested condition of their warehouses and made an arrangement with the Britannia Mining Company, whose mines are situated only a few miles from Mill Creek, to take as many of the men as desired to go. Quite a number took advantage of the offer and those who did were told that they were at liberty to remain in their houses rent free during the period of the shut down.

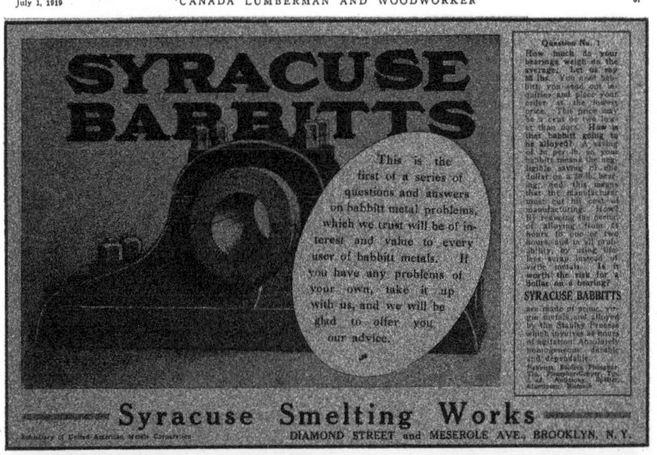

GREATER BUYING POWER

That is what the trade paper represents to the man who is a regular and careful reader of it.

In its editorial columns he finds useful ideas that help him in his business—helps and hints that smooth out many of the rough spots—plans the other fellow has tried and found successful.

The advertising pages are also a source of valuable information. Here he learns what the manufacturer has to offer—how those goods are made—the materials that enter into their manufacture—when salesmen are on the road—special opportunities, etc.

He keeps thoroughly posted on the market, because the trade paper is in close touch with the situation and gives him accurate knowledge of conditions—when and what to buy.

Read your trade paper thoroughly each issue and make a reference file of it. You will often have occasion to refer to it.

CURRENT LUMBER PRICES—WHOLESALE

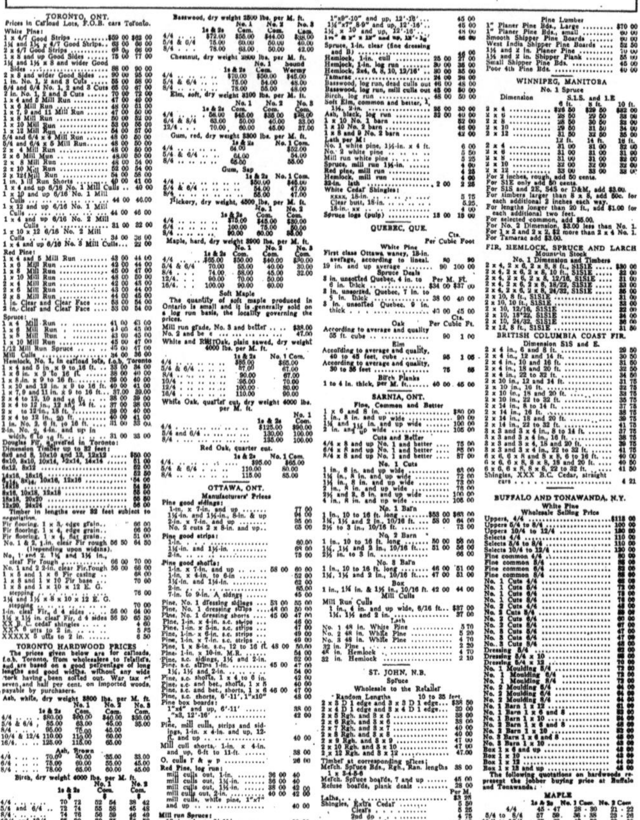

TORONTO, ONT.

Prices in Carload Lots, F.O.B. cars Toronto.

White Pine:

1 x 4/7 Good Strips	$59 00	$62 00
1¼ and 1½ x 4/7 Good Strips	63 00	66 00
2 x 4/7 Good Strips	68 00	66 00
1 x 8 and up Good Sides	75 00	77 00
1¼ and 1½ x 8 and wider Good Sides	88 00	90 00
2 x 8 and wider Good Sides	90 00	95 00
1 in. No. 1, 2 and 3 Cuts	55 00	58 00
5/4 and 6/4 No. 1, 2 and 3 Cuts	65 00	67 00
2 in. No. 1, 2 and 3 Cuts	70 00	72 00
1 x 4 and 5 Mill Run	47 00	49 00
1 x 6 Mill Run	48 00	51 00
1 x 7, 9 and 11 Mill Run	47 00	50 00
1 x 8 Mill Run	50 00	52 00
1 x 10 Mill Run	53 00	55 00
1 x 12 Mill Run	54 00	57 00
5/4 and 6/4 x 4 Mill Run	48 00	50 00
5/4 and 6/4 x 5 Mill Run	48 00	50 00
2 x 4 Mill Run	48 00	50 00
2 x 6 Mill Mun	48.00	50 00
2 x 8 Mill Run	48 00	54 00
2 x 10 Mill Run	52 00	54 00
2 x 12 Mill Run	54 00	58 00
1 in. Mill Run Shorts	40 00	41 00
1 x 4 and up 6/16 No. 1 Mill Culls		40 00
1 x 10 and up 6/16 No. 1 Mill Culls	44 00	46.00
1 x 12 and up 6/16 No. 1 Mill Culls	44 00	46 00
1 x 4 and up 6/16 No. 2 Mill Culls	31 00	32 00
1 x 10 x 12 6/16 No. 2 Mill Culls	34 00	36 00
1 x 4 and up 6/16 No. 3 Mill Culls		22 00

Red Pine:

1 x 4 and 5 Mill Run	43 00	44 00
1 x 6 Mill Run	42 00	44 00
1 x 8 Mill Run	45 00	47 00
1 x 10 Mill Run	48 00	50 00
2 x 4 Mill Run	42 00	43 00
2 x 6 Mill Run	43 00	44 00
2 x 8 Mill Run	44 00	45 00
1 in. Clear and Clear Face	53 00	54 00
2 in. Clear and Clear Face	53 00	54 00

Spruce:

1 x 4 Mill Run	41 00	43 00
1 x 6 Mill Run	43 00	45 00
1 x 8 Mill Run	43 00	45 00
1 x 10 Mill Run	45 00	47 00
1/12 Mill Run Spruce	45 00	47 00
Mill Culls	34 00	36 00

Hemlock, No. 1, in carload lots, f.o.b. Toronto

1 x 4 and 5 in. x 9 to 16 ft.	33 00	34 00
1 x 6 in. x 9 to 16 ft.	38 00	40 00
1 x 8 in. x 9 to 16 ft.	39 00	40 00
1 x 10 and 12 in. x 9 to 16 ft.	40 00	41 00
1 x 7, 9 and 11 in. x 9 to 16 ft.	37.00	39.00
2 x 4 to 12, 10 and 16 ft.	38 00	39 00
2 x 4 to 12 in., 12 and 14 ft.	37 00	38 00
2 x to 12 in., 18 ft.	39 00	40 00
2 x 4 to 12 in., 20 ft.	40 00	41 00
1 in. No. 2, 6 ft. to 16 ft.	31 00	33 00
2-in. No. 2, 4-in. and up in width, 6 to 16 ft.	31 00	33 00

Douglas Fir, delivered in Toronto:
Dimension Timber up to 32 feet:

6x6 and 8, 10x10 and 12, 12x12	$50 00
6x10, 8x10, 10x14, 12x14, 14x14	51 00
6x12, 8x12	52 00
14x16, 16x16	53 50
6x14, 8x14, 10x16, 12x16	54 00
14x16	54 50
8x18, 10x18, 12x18	55 00
18x18, 20x20	55 50
12x20, 24x24	56 00

Timber in lengths over 32 feet subject to negotiation.

Fir flooring, 1 x 3, edge grain		66 00
Fir flooring, 1 x 4, edge grain		66 00
Fir flooring, 1 x 4, flat grain		51 00
No. 1 & 2, 1-in. clear Fir rough (Depending upon widths).	56 50	64 50
No. 1 and 2, 1¼ and 1½ in., clear Fir rough	66 00	70 00
No. 1 and 2 2-in. clear Fir rough	56 00	66 00
1 x 5 and 1 x 6 Fir casing		68 00
1 x 8 and 1 x 10 Fir base		70 00
1 x 8 and 1 x 10 x 12 E. G. stepping		76 00
1¼ and 1½ x 8 x 10 x 12 E. G. stepping		70 00
1-in. clear Fir, d 4 sides	56 00	64 00
1¼ x 1½ in. clear Fir, d 4 sides	56 50	65 50
XX B. C. cedar shingles		4 60
XXX 6 butts to 2 in.		5 85
XXXXX 5 butts to 2 in.		6 50

TORONTO HARDWOOD PRICES

The prices given below are for carloads, f.o.b. Toronto, from wholesalers to retailers, and are based on a good percentage of long lengths and good widths, without any wide stock having been sorted out. War tax of seven and half per cent. on imported woods, payable by purchasers.

Ash, white, dry weight 3800 lbs. per M. ft.

	1s & 2s	No. 1 Com.	No. 2 Com.	No. 3 Com.
4/4	$80.00	$60.00	$40.00	$30.00
5/4 & 6/4	85.00	63.00	45.00	35.00
8/4	95.00	75.00	45.00	
10/4 & 12/4	110.00	110.00	60.00	
16/4	125.00	115.00	65.00	

Ash, Brown

4/4	70.00	50.00	35.00	33.00
6/4	75.00	60.00	55.00	45.00
8/4	78.00	65.00	60.00	45.00

Birch, dry weight 4000 lbs. per M. ft.

	1s & 2s $	No. 1 Com. $	No. 2 Com. $
4/4	70 72	52 54	38 42
5/4 and 6/4	72 74	55 58	45 48
8/4	74 76	56 59	46 49
10/4 and 12/4	85 90	70 75	55 58
16/4	95 100	80 85	55 60

Basswood, dry weight 2500 lbs. per M. ft.

	1s & 2s	No. 1 Com.	No. 2 Com.	No. 3 Com.
4/4	$72.00	$55.00	$44.00	$38.00
5/4 & 6/4	75.00	60.00	50.00	40.00
8/4	78.00	63.00	50.00	42.00

Chestnut, dry weight 2800 lbs. per M. ft.

	1s & 2s	No. 1 Com.	Sound Wormy
4/4	$70.00	$50.00	$45.00
5/4 & 6/4	75.00	54.00	48.00
8/4	78.00	55.00	48.00

Elm, soft, dry weight 3100 lbs. per M. ft.

	1s & 2s	No. 1 Com.	No. 2 Com.	No. 3 Com.
4/4	58.00	$45.00	$35.00	$28.00
6/4 & 8/4	63.00	50.00	40.00	33.00
12/4	70.00	60.00	45.00	37.00

Gum, red, dry weight 3300 lbs. per M. ft.

	1s & 2s	No. 1 Com.
4/4	64.00	$52.00
5/4 & 6/4	64.00	54.00
8/4	65.00	55.00

Gum, Sap

	1s & 2s	No. 1 Com.
4/4	$50.00	$45.00
5/4 & 6/4	54.00	47.00
8/4	55.00	47.00

Hickory, dry weight, 4500 lbs. per M. ft.

	1s & 2s	No. 1 Com.	No. 2 Com.
4/4	$75.00	$45.00	$30.00
6/4	100.00	75.00	50.00
8/4	90.00	60.00	35.00

Maple, hard, dry weight 3900 lbs. per M. ft.

	1s & 2s	No. 1 Com.	No. 2 Com.	No. 3 Com.
4/4	$65.00	$50.00	$40.00	$30.00
5/4 & 6/4	70.00	55.00	40.00	30.00
8/4	74.00	58.00	45.00	32.00
12/4	90.00	70.00	50.00	
16/4	100.00	90.00	60.00	

Soft Maple

The quantity of soft maple produced in Ontario is small and it is generally sold on a log run basis, the locality governing the prices.

Mill run grade, No. 3 and better	$38.00
No. 2 and better	47.00

White and Red Oak, plain sawed, dry weight 4000 lbs. per M. ft.

	1s & 2s	No. 1 Com.
4/4	$85.00	$65.00
5/4 & 6/4	87.00	67.00
8/4	90.00	67.00
10/4	95.00	70.00
12/4	100.00	80.00
16/4	110.00	90.00

White Oak, quarter cut, dry weight 4000 lbs. per M. ft.

	1s & 2s	No. 1 Com.
4/4	$125.00	$90.00
5/4 and 6/4	130.00	100.00
8/4	135.00	100.00

Red Oak, quarter cut.

	1s & 2s	No. 1 Com.
4/4	$95.00	$65.00
5/4 & 6/4	110.00	80.00
8/4	115.00	85.00

OTTAWA, ONT.

Manufacturers' Prices

Pine good sidings:

1-in. x 7-in. and up		77 00
1¼-in. and 1½-in., 8-in. & up		94 00
2-in. x 7-in. and up		95 00
No. 2 cuts 2 x 8-in. and up		65 00

Pine good strips:

1-in.		60.00
1¼-in. and 1½-in.		69 00
2-in.		75 00

Pine good shorts:

1-in. x 7-in. and up	58 00	60 00
1-in. x 4-in. to 6-in		52 00
1¼-in. and 1½-in.		62 00
2-in.		65.00
7-in. to 9-in. A sidings		45 00
Pine, No. 1 dressing sidings	53 00	55 00
Pine, No. 1 dressing strips	48 00	50 00
Pine, No. 1 dressing shorts	45 00	47 00
Pine, 1-in. x 4-in. s.c. strips		46 00
Pine, 1-in. x 5-in. s.c. strips		47 00
Pine, 1-in. x 6-in. s.c. strips		49 00
Pine, 1-in. x 7-in. s.c. strips		49 00
Pine, 1 x 8-in. s.c., 12 to 16 ft.	48 00	50.00
Pine, 1-in. x 10-in. M.R.		54 00
Pine, s.c. sidings, 1½ and 2-in.		52 00
Pine, s.c. strips 1-in.	45 00	47 00
1¼, 1½ and 2-in.		54 00
Pine, s.c. shorts, 1 x 4 to 6 in.		42 00
Pine, s.c. and bet., shorts, 1 x 5		40 00
Pine, s.c. and bet., shorts, 1 x 6	46 00	47 00
Pine, s.c. shorts, 6'-11', 1"x10"		48 00

Pine box boards:

1"x4" and up, 6'-11'		38 00
1"x3, 12'-16'		42 00
Pine, mill culls, strips and sidings, 1-in. x 4-in. and up, 12-ft. and up		40 00
Mill cull shorts, 1-in. x 4-in. and up, 6-ft to 11-ft.		38 00
O. culls r & w p		26 00

Red Pine, log run:

mill culls out, 1-in.	36 00	40
mill culls out, 1¼-in.	36 00	40
mill culls out, 1½-in.	38 00	42 00
mill culls out, 2-in.	40 00	42 00
mill culls, white pine, 1"x7" and up		40 00

Mill run Spruce:

1"x4 and up, 6'-11'		38 00
1"x4" and up, 12'-16'		40 00
1"x9"-10" and up, 12'-16'		45 00
1¼"x7" 8-9" and up, 12'-16'		45 00
1½ x 10 and up, 12'-16'		48 00
1½" & 2" x 12" and up, 12'-16'		46 00
Spruce, 1-in. clear (fine dressing and B)		46 00
Hemlock, 1-in. cull	25 00	27 00
Hemlock, 1-in. log run	30 00	35 00
Hemlock, 2x4, 6, 8, 10, 12/16'	30 00	35 00
Tamarac	24 00	28 00
Basswood, log run, dead culls out	46 00	48 00
Basswood, log run, mill culls out	45 00	50 00
Birch, log run	48 00	50 00
Soft Elm, common and better, 1, 1¼, 2-in.	25 00	30 00
Ash, black, log run	32 00	40 00
1 x 10 No. 1 barn		52 00
1 x 10 No. 2 barn		46 00
1 x 8 and 9 No. 2 barn		42 00

Lath per M:

No. 1 white pine, 1½-in. x 4 ft.		6 00
No. 2 white pine		5 50
Mill run white pine		5 25
Spruce, mill run 1½-in.		4 00
Red pine, mill run		4 25
Hemlock, mill run		4 00
32-in. lath	2 00	2 25

White Cedar Shingles:

xxxx, 18-in.		5 75
Clear butt, 18-in.		5.25
18-in. xx		4 00
Spruce logs (pulp)	18 00	15 00

QUEBEC, QUE.

White Pine

	Cts. Per Cubic Foot	
First class Ottawa waney, 18-in. average, according to lineal	80	90
19 in. and up average	90	100 00

Spruce Deals

	Per M. Ft.	
3 in. unsorted Quebec, 4 in. to 6 in. thick	$34 00	$37 00
3 in. unsorted, Quebec, 7 in. to 5 in. thick	38 00	40 00
3 in. unsorted Quebec, 9 in. thick	40 00	45 00

Oak

	Cts. Per Cubic Ft.	
According to average and quality 55 ft. cube	90	1 00

Elm

According to average and quality, 40 to 45 feet, cube	95	1 05
According to average and quality, 30 to 35 feet	75	85

Birch Planks

1 to 4 in. thick, per M. ft.	40 00	45 00

SARNIA, ONT.

Fine, Common and Better

1 x 6 and 8 in.	$80 00
1 in., 8 in. and up wide	90 00
1¼ and 1½ in. and up wide	100 00
2 in. and up wide	105 00

Cuts and Better

4/4 x 8 and up No. 1 and better	75 00
6/4 x 8 and up No. 1 and better	85 00
8/4 x 8 and up No. 1 and better	87 00

No. 1 Cuts

1 in., 6 in. and up wide	65 00
1¼ in., 8 in. and up wide	72 00
1½ in., 8 in. and up wide	73 00
2 in., 8 in. and up wide	78 00
2½ and 3, 8 in. and up wide	100 00
4 in., 8 in. and up wide	105 00

No. 1 Barn

1 in., 10 to 16 ft. long	$53 00	$63 00
1¼, 1½ and 2 in., 10/16 ft.	58 00	64 00
2½ to 3 in., 10/16 ft.		73 00

No. 2 Barn

1 in., 10 to 16 ft. long	50 00	56 00
1¼, 1½ and 2 in., 10/16 ft.	51 00	56 00
2½ in. to 3 in.		66 00

No. 3 Barn

1 in., 10 to 16 ft. long	46 00	51 00
1¼, 1½ and 2 in., 10/16 ft.	47 00	51 00

Box

1 in., 1¼ in. & 1½ in., 10/16 ft.	42 00	44 00

Mill Culls

Mill Run Culls

1 in., 4 in. and up wide, 6/16 ft.	$37 00
1¼, 1½ and 2 in.	37 00

Lath

No. 1 48 in. White Pine	5 70
No. 2 48 in. White Pine	5 20
No. 3 48 in. White Pine	4 70
32 in. Pine	2 20
48 in. Hemlock	4 70
32 in. Hemlock	2 10

ST. JOHN, N.B.

Spruce

Wholesale to the Retailer

Random Lengths 10 to 35 feet.

2 x 3 D 1 edge and 3 x 3 D 1 edge	$38 50
2 x 4 D 1 edge and 3 x 4 D 1 edge	39 00
2 x 5 Rgh. and 3 x 5	38 00
2 x 6 Rgh. and 3 x 6	38 00
2 x 7 Rgh. and 3 x 7	40 00
2 x 8 Rgh. and 3 x 8	40 00
2 x 9 Rgh. and 3 x 9	47 00
2 x 10 Rgh. and 3 x 10	47 00
2 x 12 Rgh. and 3 x 12	47.00

Timber at corresponding prices:

Merch. Spruce Bds., Rgh., Ran. lengths 1 x 3-4-5-6	38 00
Merch. Spruce boards, 7 and up	45 00
Refuse boards, plank deals	28 00
	Per M.
Laths	$3 75
Shingles, Extra Cedar	5 50
Clears	5 25
2nd do	4 75
Ex. No. 1	3 25
Spruce	4 00

Pine Lumber

1" Planer Pine Bds., Large	$70 00
1" Planer Pine Bds., small	60 00
Smooth Shipper Pine Boards	60 00
West India Shipper Pine Boards	52 50
1¼ and 2 in. Planer Pine	70 00
1¼ and 2 in. Shipper Plank	55 00
Small Shipper Pine Bds.	45 00
Poor 4th Pine Bds.	40 00

WINNIPEG, MANITOBA

No. 1 Spruce

Dimension	S.1.S. and 1.E 6 ft.	8 ft.	10 ft.
2 x 4	$26 50	$29 50	$32 00
2 x 6	28 50	29 50	33 00
2 x 8	28 50	30 50	33 00
2 x 10	29 50	31 50	34 00
2 x 12	31 50	32 50	35 00
	12 ft.	14 ft.	16 ft.
2 x 4	31 00	31 00	32 00
2 x 6	31 00	31 00	31 00
2 x 8	31 00	31 00	32 00
2 x 10	32 00	32 00	32 00
2 x 12	33 00	33 00	33 00

For 2 inches, rough, add 50 cents.
For S1E only add 50 cents.
For S1S and 2E, S4S or D&M, add $3.00.
For timbers larger than 8 x 8, add 50c. for each additional 2 inches each way.
For lengths longer than 20 ft., add $1.00 for each additional two feet.
For selected common, add $5.00.
For No. 2 Dimension, $3.00 less than No. 1.
For 1 x 2 and 2 x 2, $2 more than 2 x 4 No. 1.
For Tamarac add $3.00.

FIR, HEMLOCK, SPRUCE AND LARCH

Mountain Stock

No. 1 Dimension and Timbers

2 x 4, 2 x 6, 2 x 8, 8 ft., S1S1E	$30 00
2 x 4, 2 x 6, 2 x 8, 10 ft., S1S1E	32 00
2 x 4, 2 x 6, 2 x 8, 12/16, S1S1E	31 00
2 x 4, 2 x 6, 2 x 8, 18/22, S1S1E	33 00
2 x 4, 2 x 6, 2 x 8, 24/32, S1S1E	35 00
2 x 10, 8 ft., S1S1E	31 00
2 x 10, 10 ft., S1S1E	33 00
2 x 10, 12/16, S1S1E	32 00
2 x 10, 18/22, S1S1E	34 00
2 x 10, 24/32, S1S1E	36 00
2 x 12, 8 ft., S1S1E	31 50

BRITISH COLUMBIA COAST FIR.

Dimension S1S and E.

2 x 4 in., 6 and 8 ft.	29 50
2 x 4 in., 12 and 14 ft.	30 50
2 x 4 in., 10 and 16 ft.	31 50
2 x 4 in., 18 and 20 ft.	32 50
2 x 4 in., 22 to 32 ft.	34 50
2 x 10 in., 12 and 14 ft.	31 75
2 x 10 in., 10 ft.	32 75
2 x 10 in., 18 and 20 ft.	33 75
2 x 10 in., 22 to 32 ft.	35 75
2 x 14 in., 8 to 14 ft.	37 75
2 x 14 in., 16 ft.	38 75
2 x 14 in., 18 and 20 ft.	39 75
2 x 14 in., 22 to 32 ft.	41 75
3 x 3 and 3 x 4 in., 8 to 14 ft.	37 75
3 x 3 and 3 x 4 in., 16 ft.	38 75
3 x 3 and 3 x 4, 18 and 20 ft.	39 75
3 x 3 and 3 x 4 in., 22 to 32 ft.	41 75
6 x 6, 6 x 8 and 8 x 8, 6 to 16 ft.	40 00
6 x 6, 6 x 8, 8 x 8, 18 and 20 ft.	40 50
6 x 6, 6 x 8, 8 x 8, 22 to 32 ft.	41 50
Shingles, XXX B.C. Cedar, straight cars	4 21

BUFFALO AND TONAWANDA, N.Y.

White Pine

Wholesale Selling Price

Uppers, 4/4	$118 00
Uppers 5/4 to 8/4	100 00
Uppers 10/4 to 12/4	130 00
Selects 4/4	110 00
Selects 5/4 to 8/4	110 00
Selects 10/4 to 12/4	120 00
Fine common 4/4	80 00
Fine common 5/4	85 00
Fine common 6/4	83 00
Fine common 8/4	85 00
No. 1 Cuts 4/4	65 00
No. 1 Cuts 5/4	73 00
No. 1 Cuts 6/4	73 00
No. 1 Cuts 8/4	76 00
No. 2 Cuts 4/4	48 00
No. 2 Cuts 5/4	60 00
No. 2 Cuts 6/4	60 00
No. 2 Cuts 8/4	67 00
No. 3 Cuts 5/4	47 00
No. 3 Cuts 6/4	47 00
No. 3 Cuts 8/4	48 00
Dressing 5/4	63 00
Dressing 5/4 x 10	66 00
Dressing 5/4 x 12	70 00
No. 1 Moulding 5/4	73 00
No. 1 Moulding 6/4	73 00
No. 1 Moulding 8/4	73 00
No. 2 Moulding 5/4	64 00
No. 2 Moulding 6/4	64 00
No. 2 Moulding 8/4	64 00
No. 1 Barn 1 x 12	61 00
No. 1 Barn 1 x 6 and 8	53 00
No. 1 Barn 1 x 10	56 00
No. 2 Barn 1 x 6 and 8	48 00
No. 2 Barn 1 x 10	52 00
No. 3 Barn 1 x 6 and 8	48 00
No. 3 Barn 1 x 10	43 00
Box 1 x 6 and up	42 00
Box 1 x 10	42 00
Box 1 x 12	44 00
Box 1 x 13 and up	45 00

The following quotations on hardwoods represent the jobber buying price at Buffalo and Tonawanda:

MAPLE

	1s & 2s	No. 1 Com.	No. 2 Com.
4/4	45 - 47	28 - 30	21 - 22
5/4 to 8/4	57 59	36 - 38	23 - 26
10/4 to 16/4	67 - 69	48 - 50	29 - 30

(Continued on page 64

Why Dominion Friction Surface Belting Keeps Employees Satisfied

There are few manufacturers who haven't discovered that satisfied employees are an absolute necessity to low cost of production.

But poor equipment will not keep employees contented—it will not permit maximum production—it increases upkeep cost—it creates needless waste of time for operators and machines while making repairs.

Dominion Friction Surface Belting, in eliminating these conditions, does much to keep employees satisfied, for it enables operators to turn out maximum production at low cost—does away with most transmission troubles and saves power by taking a grip on pulleys that practically prevents all slipping.

Our Belting Experts are ready to show you how this "plus service" belting will keep your employees satisfied, just as they have for many other manufacturers. Phone, wire or write to our nearest service branch—there is no obligation.

Makers of

Dominion Hose, Packing and Industrial Rubber Goods and Dominion Tires, the GOOD Tires for every purpose.

Services Branches

Halifax,	Fort William,
St. John,	Winnipeg,
Quebec,	Brandon,
Montreal,	Regina,
Ottawa,	Saskatoon,
Toronto,	Edmonton,
Hamilton,	Calgary,
London,	Lethbridge,
Kitchener,	Vancouver,
North Bay,	Victoria

Maple Leaf SAWS

Are Good Saws.

Maple Leaf Circular Saws are made of Special High Grade Steel, accurately ground; have hard-tempered center which makes a stiff blade that will stand up under the most severe conditions, and is less liable to push over in case of accident.

Let us prove it to you if you have not discovered it already.

EVERY SAW GUARANTEED.

The Largest ALL Canadian Saw Manufacturers

Shurly Dietrich Company
Limited

Ottawa Vancouver Galt

CURRENT LUMBER PRICES—Continued

RED BIRCH

4/4	60 - 62	40 - 42	24 - 26
5/4 to 8/4	62 - 64	42 - 44	26 - 28

SAP BIRCH

4/4	54 - 56	32 - 34	20 - 22
5/4 and up	56 - 58	34 - 36	22 - 24

SOFT ELM

4/4	45 - 47	30 - 32	22 - 24
5, 6 & 8/4	47 - 49	32 - 34	22 - 24

BASSWOOD

4/4	50 - 52	40 - 42	27 - 29
Thicker	53 - 55	42 - 44	28 - 29

PLAIN OAK

4/4	62 - 64	38 - 40	24 - 26
5/4 to 8/4	64 - 66	42 - 44	26 - 28

ASH, WHITE AND BROWN

4/4	62 - 65	35 - 38	25 - 27
5/4 to 8/4	70 - 72	40 - 42	26 - 28
10/4 and up	85 - 95	47 - 55	29 - 31

BOSTON, MASS.

Quotations given below are for highest grades of Michigan and Canadian white pine and Eastern Canadian Spruce as required in the New England market in carloads.

White pine uppers, 1 to 2 in.		134 00
White pine uppers, 2½ and 3 in.		149 00
White pine uppers, 4 in.		160 00
Selects, 1 to 2 in.		125 00
Selects, 2½ and 3 in.		140 00
Selects, 4 in.		155 00
Fine common, 1 in., 30 per cent. 12 in. and up		92 00
Fine common, 1 x 8 to 11 in.		87 00
Fine Common, 1¼ to 2 in.		100 00
Fine Common, 2½ and 3 in.		130 00
Fine Common, 4 in.		145 00
1 in. shaky clear		72 00
1¼ to 2 in. shaky clear		75 00
1 in. No. 2 dressing		64 00
1¼ to 2 in. No. 2 dressing		68 00
No. 1 Cuts, 1 in.		80 00
No. 1 Cuts, 1¼ to 2 in.	85 00	87 00
No. 1 Cuts, 2½ and 3 in.		115 00
No. 2 Cuts, 1 in.		60 00
No. 2 Cuts, 1¼ to 2 in.	70 00	71 00

Barn Boards, No. 1, 1 x 12		69 00
No. 1, 1 x 10		64 00
No. 1, 1 x 8		61 00
No. 2, 1 x 12		64 00
No. 2, 1 x 10		61 00
No. 2, 1 x 8		58 00
No. 3, 1 x 12		58 00
No. 3, 1 x 10		57 00
No. 3, 1 x 8		55 00
Can. spruce, clear, 1 x 4 to 9 in.	46 50	48 50
1 x 10 in.		50 50
No. 1 1 x 4 to 7 in.		53 50
No. 1 1 x 8 & 9 in.		54 50
No. 1 1 x 10 in.		55 50
No. 2 1 x 4 & 5 in.		38 50
No. 2 1 x 6 & 7 in.		43 50
No. 2 1 x 8 & 9 in.	43 50	44 50
No. 2 1 x 10 in.		46 50
No. 2 1 x 12 in.		50 50
Spruce, 12 in. dimension		48 00
Spruce, 10 in. dimension		47.00
Spruce, 9 in. dimension		46 00
Spruce, 8 in. dimension		45 00
2 x 10 in. random lengths, 8 ft. and up	45 00	46 00
2 x 12 in., random lengths	47 00	49 00
2 x 3, 2 x 4, 2 x 5, 2 x 6, 2 x 7	38 00	40 00
3 x 4 and 4 x 4 in.		40 00
2 x 8 in.		43 00
All other random lengths, 7-in. and under, 8 ft. and up		38 00
8-inch and up merchantable boards, 8 ft. and up, p 1s		42 00
1 x 2		40 00
1 x 3		40 00
1-⅜ in. spruce lath		5 00
1-½ in. spruce lath		4 75

New Brunswick Cedar Shingles

Extras		5 50
Clears		4.00
Second Clears		4 00
Clear Whites		4 30
Extra 1s (Clear whites in)		[illegible]
Extra 1s (Clear whites out)		1 50
Red Cedar Extras, 16-in. 5 butts to 2-in.	5 05	5 18
Red Cedar Eurekas, 18-inch 5 butts to 2-in.		[illegible]
Red Cedar Perfections, 5 butts to 2¼		6 00
Washington 16-in. 5 butts to 2-in. extra red cedar		5 50

BOX MAKING MACHINERY
We Manufacture
Nailing Machines,
Shook Splicers for Driving Corrugated Fasteners,
Lock Corner Box Machines,
Box Board Matchers,
Box Board Printers.
Every manufacturer of boxes, every manufacturer who has nails to drive in any article, or packages of any kind to manufacture, should write the Morgan Machine Company for latest developments in machinery for the Box Industry.
Morgan Machine Company
ROCHESTER, N.Y.
Wood Tanks
All kinds and sizes
Estimates will be submitted promptly. Ask for our "Tank and Water Supply" catalogue
ADDRESS
Ontario Wind Engine and Pump Company, Ltd.
TORONTO, ONTARIO
Branches: Montreal, Winnipeg, Regina, Calgary

BOILERS
We make a specialty of Horizontal Return Tubular, Vertical Tubular and Locomotive Type Boilers for Saw Mills and Lumbering operations.
Send us your inquiries
Engineering & Machine Works of Canada, Limited
ST. CATHARINES, ONT.
STANDARD HORIZONTAL RETURN TUBULAR BOILER

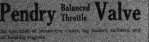

Do You Know That Lumbermen Have Been Saved

MILLIONS OF DOLLARS

By the

Manufacturing Lumbermen's Underwriters

Organized in 1898

The Pioneer Lumber Insurance Association

For 20 YEARS the best example of the RECIPROCAL or INTER-INSURANCE plan successfully applied to the lumber industry, and still the LARGEST AND STRONGEST CO-OPERATIVE EXCHANGE furnishing AT COST ideal fire insurance for Saw Mill plants and giving the best service, which includes

Liberal and Correct Policy Forms
Improvement Suggestions for Reducing Rates
Practical, Efficient, Frequent Inspections and Fire Prevention Service
The Certainty of Prompt and Equitable Adjustment

ARE YOU ONE OF THIS ASSOCIATION'S 735 MEMBERS?
ARE YOUR POLICIES PART OF THE SIXTY MILLIONS INSURANCE IN FORCE?
DO YOU OWN A PORTION OF THE SURPLUS FUND OF OVER ONE MILLION?
HAVE YOU RECEIVED ANY OF THE SAVINGS OF OVER 1¼ MILLIONS RETURNED?
HAVE YOU RECEIVED ANY OF THE 5¼ MILLION DOLLARS IN THE FIRE LOSSES PAID?

Do You Know of Any Other Insurance Medium That Never Had a Law Suit?

Help yourself and your fellow lumbermen by joining our membership, or if already a member, by giving us more of your business.

THIS ASSOCIATION HAS BENEFITED EVERY SAW MILL OWNER AND SO DESERVES YOUR FULL SUPPORT. Ask your neighbor or

Our representative will call on you at your convenience

Rankin-Benedict Underwriting Company
Attorney and Manager
Licensed in Canada **KANSAS CITY, MO.**

No. 134 Dimension Planer and Matcher

Here is a general purpose machine for general Planing Mill work. Will give steady sturdy service under all conditions. No. 134 has always made good and is the machine to consider when purchasing new equipment.

Write for Circular

Hall & Brown Wood Working Machine Co
Saint Louis, U.S.A.
Home Office and Factory, 1913 to 1933 North Broadway

BELL LOCOMOTIVES
are Built for Economy, Safety and Greater Tractive Power

Bell Locomotive weighing 12 tons hauls 285 ton logging train at plant of W. C Edwards Co., Rockland, Ontario, Canada

Made in sizes from 2 to 25 tons in working order. Tested material and thorough workmanship enter into every part of Bell Locomotives and their construction is accessible, simple and compact.

CHEAPEST FUEL—Will operate on Kerosene, fuel oil, distillate or crude oils.

NO HOT ASHES OR SPARKS can fly out so that fire hazard is eliminated.

50% GREATER TRACTIVE EFFORT than direct connected type locomotive of equal weight.

ONE MAN OPERATED—One valve fire control.

STANDARDIZED DESIGN—All parts interchangeable and kept in stock for immediate delivery.

WRITE FOR CATALOGUE AND PRICES TO-DAY.

Low First Cost
Low Fuel Cost
Long Life

Bell Locomotive Works Inc.

Founded 1908
11 Pine Street, NEW YORK, N.Y.

The General Supply Company of Canada
356-360 Sparks St., OTTAWA, Canada
Also at
MONTREAL, TORONTO, WINNIPEG and VANCOUVER

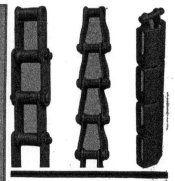

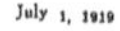

FIRE BRICK

We make five Brands of Elk Fire Brick in order to supply the many requirements of furnaces, boilers with stokers, Dutch ovens, refuse burners, kilns, etc. Our experience of many years enables us to specify the most reliable grade of Fire Brick for any purpose and this service is entirely free to our customers.

We manufacture the following well-known brands:

"Elkco Special," "Elk Steel," "St. Marys," "Keystone" and "Rotex"

Write for copy of our catalogue, "Refractory Efficiency Engineering."

Elk Fire Brick Co. of Canada, Ltd.

HIGH GRADE FIRE BRICK and CLAY

Sun Life Bldg., Hamilton, Canada

Representatives for Maritime Provinces:
RHODES, CURRY COMPANY, LTD., Head Office, AMHERST, N. S.
Branches at Halifax, Sydney and New Glasgow, N.S.

DIXIE DRAG SAW

A 4 H. P. Portable Single Cylinder 2 Cycle, Gasoline Rig, upon skids. Weight, 280 Lbs. Makes 125 strokes per minute. Cuts Logs 7" to 72" Diameter.

Easily started and moved. Runs as smoothly as the **Liberty Motor.**

The Solution of the present and future **Fuel, Labor and Car Shortage.**

Economical of fuel and never grows weary.

Saves Labor. May be taken to the Forest for cutting Logs, Fuel and Short Bolts for Stave, Heading, Shingle Bolts, Handle, Charcoal and Alcohol Wood.

When not required for sawing, Dixie Engine may be used for driving Pumps, Dynamos, Churn, Feed Cutters, Mixer, etc.

Price $225.00

Extra 5 ft. or 6 ft. Saws, each $12.00
Extra 6½ ft. or 7 ft. Saws, each $14.00

F. O. B. Cleveland.

Manufactured By

The Peter Gerlach Company

Cooperage Machinery and Saw Makers

Established 1854 CLEVELAND, OHIO, U. S. A.

A CONTENTED HORSE IS A BETTER WORKER

Your horse will do more work and better work if kept in condition with the proper equipment.

Tapatco Collar Pads

protect horses from the galls, bruises and chafes on their necks and shoulders which so often result from inferior and ill fitting harness.

Behind the manufacture of Tapatco Collar Pads is 37 years' experience and the practical knowledge of the conditions under which the horse gives best service. Tapatco Collar Pads are made with Patent Hook attachment.

See that your horses have this protection. Sold by dealers everywhere.

The American Pad & Textile Co.

Chatham, Ontario, Canada

"ASBESTOL" Gloves are on the Honor Roll of Service—

In the estimation of countless thousands of workers "ASBESTOL" gloves are on the Honor Roll for they have proven their loyalty in service wherever and whenever worn Lumbermen who appreciate the value of perfect hand protection always wear "ASBESTOL" gloves.

There are many styles particularly designed for work in the lumber camp.

EISENDRATH GLOVE CO.

2001 Elston Ave., CHICAGO, ILL.

ALPHABETICAL INDEX TO ADVERTISERS

Disston's four Invincibles

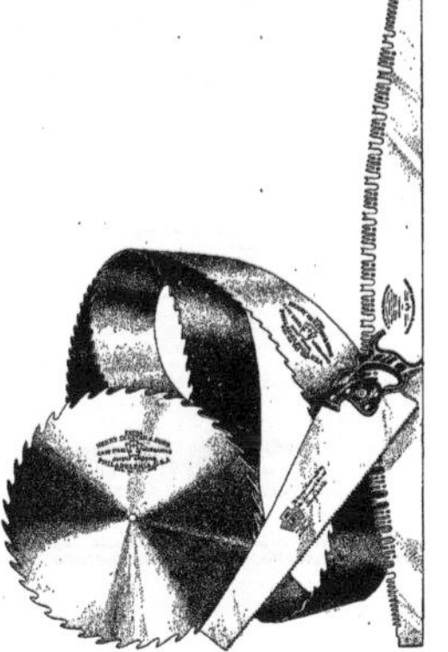

HENRY DISSTON & SONS
Incorporated
Keystone Saw, Tool, Steel and File Works
Philadelphia, U. S. A.

Pyrene Fire Extinguishers

Are the Ideal Fire Protectors for your mill, for the following reasons:—

1st—Pyrene is death to all inflammable fires.
2nd—Pyrene does not freeze at fifty degrees below zero.
3rd—Pyrene does not deteriorate.
4th—Pyrene is easily operated and ever ready.
5th—Pyrene reduces your Fire Insurance rate 15 per cent when installed on your Automobile or Motor Truck.
6th—Pyrene has seaved with the boys at the front.
7th—Pyrene in one of our Holsters is ideal for your watchman in case he locates a fire in your building.

We also carry the 2½ Gal. Soda Acid Extinguisher

Ask for our Catalogue which contains a full line of fire appliances, also for our book on how to protect your factory. This book contains valuable information.

Pyrene Mfg. Co. of Canada, Limited
3 St. Nicholas St. Montreal

GEO. W. REED & COMPANY, LTD.

Thomson Improved Spark Extinguisher

is an appliance for the tops of chimneys and stacks that is warranted to extinguish all dangerous sparks without choking the draft. Where wood is used as fuel, they are a positive necessity.

It is no untried experiment, as there are hundreds in use at the present time which are giving complete satisfaction.

Insurance companies make substantial reductions in their rates where this device is used.

Send for particulars.

Manufactured by

Geo. W. Reed & Co., Montreal
Established 1852

Aloxite Saw Gumming Wheels

Save Time and they cut Wheel Costs

KEEPING saws in shape costs money.

Real saw gumming wheels will cut these costs to a minimum without sacrificing efficiency.

When we say *real* saw-gumming wheels we mean wheels that cut fast and cool. That cut free without any dragging action. Wheels that hold their shape and require but little dressing. These are just the sort of wheels that will reduce your saw gumming costs and increase the efficiency of your filing room.

These are just the sort of wheels you will find in

Aloxite Saw Gumming Wheels

Made in all of the standard sizes, shapes, grits and grades

THE CARBORUNDUM COMPANY
NIAGARA FALLS, N. Y.

CANADA LUMBERMAN BUYERS' DIRECTORY

The following regulations apply to all advertisers:—Eighth page, every issue, three headings; quarter page, six headings; half page, twelve headings; full page, twenty-four headings.

ASBESTOS GOODS
Atlas Asbestos Company, Ltd.

AXES
Canadian Warren Axe & Tool Co.

BABBITT METAL
Canada Metal Company.
General Supply Co. of Canada, Ltd.
Syracuse Smelting Works

BALE TIES
Laidlaw Bale Tie Company.

BALL BEARINGS
Chapman Double Ball Bearing Co.

BAND MILLS
Hamilton Company, William.
Waterous Engine Works Company.
Yates Machine Company, P. B.

BAND RESAWS
Mershon & Company, W. B.

BELT CEMENT
Graton & Knight Mfg. Company.

BELT DRESSING
Atlas Asbestos Company, Ltd.
General Supply Co. of Canada, Ltd.
Graton & Knight Mfg. Company.

BELTING
Atlas Asbestos Company, Ltd.
Beardmore Belting Company
Canadian Consolidated Rubber Co.
General Supply Company
Goodhue & Co., J. L.
Goodyear Tire & Rubber Co.
Graton & Knight Mfg. Company.
Gutta Percha and Rubber Company.
Main Belting Company
Manhattan Rubber Mfg. Co.
D. K. McLaren Limited.
McLaren Belting Company, J. C.

BELTING (Transmission, Elevator, Conveyor, Rubber)
Dunlop Tire & Rubber Goods Co.

BLOWERS
Sheldons Limited.
Toronto Blower Company.

BOILERS
Hamilton Company, William.
Jenckes Machine Company.
Marsh Engineering Works, Limited
Waterous Engine Works Company.

BOILER PRESERVATIVE
Beveridge Paper Company
International Chemical Company

BOX MACHINERY
Garlock-Walker Machinery Co.
Morgan Machine Company.
Yates Machine Company, P. B.

BOX SHOOKS
Davison Lumber & Mfg. Company

CABLE CONVEYORS
Jeffrey Manufacturing Company.
Jenckes Machine Company, Ltd.
Waterous Engine Works Company.

CAMP SUPPLIES
Canadian Milk Products Limited.
Davies Company, William.
Dr. Bell Veterinary Wonder Co.
Harris Abattoir Company
Johnson, A. H.
Turner & Sons, J. J.
Woods Manufacturing Company, Ltd.

CANT HOOKS
Canadian Warren Axe & Tool Co.
General Supply Co. of Canada, Ltd.
Pink Company, Thomas.

CARS—STEEL BODY
Marsh Engineering Works, Limited

CEDAR
Fesserton Timber Co.
Foss Lumber Company
Genoa Bay Lumber Company
Muir & Kirkpatrick.
Long Lumber Company.
Terry & Gordon.
Thurston-Flavelle Lumber Company.
Vancouver Lumber Company.
Victoria Lumber and Mfg. Co.

CHAINS
Canadian Link-Belt Company, Ltd.
General Supply Co. of Canada, Ltd.
Hamilton Company, William.
Jeffrey Manufacturing Company.
Jenckes Machine Company, Ltd.
Pink & Co., Thomas.
Waterous Engine Works Company.
Williams Machinery Co., A. R., Vancouver.

CHINA CLAY
Bowater & Sons, W. V.

CHEMICAL PLANTS
Blair, Campbell & McLean, Ltd.

CLOTHING
Grant, Holden & Graham.
Kitchen Overall & Shirt Company
Woods Mfg. Company

COLLAR PADS
American Pad & Textile Co.

COLLARS (Shaft)
Bond Engineering Works

CONVEYOR MACHINERY
Canadian Link-Belt Company, Ltd.
Canadian Mathews Gravity Carrier. Company.
General Supply Co. of Canada, Ltd.
Jeffrey Mfg. Co.
Waterous Engine Works Company.

CORDAGE
Consumers Cordage Company.

COTTON GLOVES
American Pad & Textile Co.

COUNTERSHAFTS
Bond Engineering Works

COUPLINGS (Shaft)
Bond Engineering Works
Jenckes Machine Company, Ltd.

CRANES FOR SHIP YARDS
Canadian Link-Belt Company.

CROSS ARMS
Genoa Bay Lumber Company

CUTTER HEADS
Shimer Cutter Head Company.

CYPRESS
Blakeslee, Perrin & Darling
Chicago Lumber & Coal Company.
Long Lumber Company.
Wistar, Underhill & Nixon.

DERRICKS AND DERRICK FITTINGS
Marsh Engineering Works, Limited

DOORS
Genoa Bay Lumber Company
Harrington, E. I.
Long Lumber Company.
Mason, Gordon & Co.
Rutherford & Sons, Wm.
Terry & Gordon.

DOUGLAS FIR
Allan-Stoltze Lumber Co.
British American Mills & Timber Co.
Coal Creek Lumber Company.
Fesserton Timber Co.
Foss Lumber Company
Grier & Son, G. A.
Heeney, Percy E.
Knox Brothers.
Long Lumber Company.
Mason, Gordon & Co.
Shearer Company, Jas.
Terry & Gordon.
Timberland Lumber Company.
Timms, Phillips & Co.
Vancouver Lumber Company.
Victoria Lumber and Mfg. Co.

DRAG SAWS
Gerlach Company, Peter
Pennoyer & Company, J. C.

DRY KILNS
Sheldons Limited.

DRYERS
Philadelphia Textile Mach. Company.

DUST COLLECTORS
Sheldons Limited.
Toronto Blower Company.

EDGERS
William Hamilton Company, Ltd.
Garlock-Walker Machinery Co.
Green Company, G. Walter
Haight, W. L.
Long Mfg. Company, E.
Waterous Engine Works Company.

ELEVATING AND CONVEYING MACHINERY
Canadian Link-Belt Company, Ltd.
Jeffrey Manufacturing Company.
Jenckes Machine Company, Ltd.
Waterous Engine Works Company.

ENGINES
Hamilton Company, William.
Jenckes Machine Company.
Waterous Engine Works Company.

EXCELSIOR MACHINERY
Elmira Machinery and Transmission Company.

EXHAUST FANS
Garlock-Walker Machinery Co.
Reed & Company, Geo. W.
Sheldons Limited.
Toronto Blower Company.

EXHAUST SYSTEMS
Reed & Company, Geo. W.
Sheldons Limited.
Toronto Blower Company.

FILES
Disston & Sons, Henry.
Simonds Canada Saw Company.

FIRE BRICK
Beveridge Paper Company
Elk Fire Brick Company of Canada.

FIRE FIGHTING APPARATUS
Dunlop Tire & Rubber Goods Co.
Pyrene Mfg. Company.
Waterous Engine Works Company.

FIR FLOORING
Genoa Bay Lumber Company
Rutherford & Sons, Wm.

FLAG STAFFS
Ontario Wind Engine Company

FLOORING (Oak)
Long-Bell Lumber Company.

GALVANIZING
Ontario Wind Engine Company

GASOLINE ENGINES
Ontario Wind Engine Company

GEARS (Cut)
Smart-Turner Machine Co.

GRATE BARS—Revolving
Beveridge Paper Company

GRAVITY LUMBER CARRIER
Can. Mathews Gravity Carrier Co.

GRINDERS (Bench)
Bond Engineering Works
Garlock-Walker Machinery Co.

HARDWOODS
Anderson Lumber Company, C. G.
Atlantic Lumber Co.
Bartram & Ball.
Bennett Lumber Company.
Blakeslee, Perrin & Darling
Cameron & Co.
Cardinal & Page
Davison Lumber & Mfg. Company
Dunfield & Company
Edwards & Co., W. C.
Fassett Lumber Company.
Fesserton Timber Co.
Fraser Limited.
Gillespie, James.
Gloucester Lumber Company
Grier & Son, G. A.
Heeney, Percy E.
Knox Brothers.
Long Lumber Company.
McLennan Lumber Company.
Moores, Jr., E. J.
Nicholson & Co., E. M.
Pedwell Hardwood Lumber Co.
Powell-Myers Lumber Co.
Russell, Chas. H.
Spencer Limited, C. A.
Stearns & Culver Lumber Co.
Summers, James R.
Taylor Lumber Company, S. K.
Webster & Brother, James.

HARDWOOD FLOORING MACHINERY
American Woodworking Machinery Company
Garlock-Walker Machinery Co.

HANGERS (Shaft)
Bond Engineering Works

HARDWOOD FLOORING
Grier & Son, G. A.
Long Lumber Company.

HEMLOCK
Anderson Lumber Company, C. G.
Bartram & Ball.
Bourgouin, H.
Callander Sawmills
Canadian General Lumber Company
Cane & Co., Jas. G.
Davison Lumber & Mfg. Company
Dunfield & Company
Edwards & Company, W. C.
Fesserton Timber Co.
Foss Lumber Company
Grier & Son, G. A.
Hart & McDonagh.
Long Lumber Company.
Mason, Gordon & Co.
Spencer Limited, C. A.
Terry & Gordon.
The Long Lumber Company.

HOISTING AND HAULING ENGINES
Garlock-Walker Machinery Co.
General Supply Co. of Canada, Ltd.
Marsh Engineering Works, Limited

HORSES
Union Stock Yards.

HOSE
Dunlop Tire & Rubber Goods Co.
General Supply Co. of Canada, Ltd.
Goodyear Tire & Rubber Co.
Gutta Percha and Rubber Company.

INDUSTRIAL CARS
Marsh Engineering Works, Limited

INSURANCE
Hardy & Co., E. D.
Rankin Benedict Underwriting Co.

INTERIOR FINISH
Eagle Lumber Company.
Hay & Co.
Mason, Gordon & Co.
Renfrew Planing Mills.
Terry & Gordon.

KNIVES
Disston & Sons, Henry.
Peter Hay Knife Company.
Simonds Canada Saw Company.
Waterous Engine Works Company.

LATH
Austin & Nicholson.
Callander Sawmills
Canadian General Lumber Company
Cane & Co., Jas. G.
Cardinal & Page
Dupuis Limited, J. P.
Eagle Lumber Company.
Fraser Limited.
Fraser-Bryson Lumber Company.
Genoa Bay Lumber Company
Gloucester Lumber Company
Grier & Son, G. A.
Harris Tie & Timber Company, Ltd
Long Lumber Company.
McLennan Lumber Company.
New Ontario Colonization Company
River Ouelle Pulp and Paper Co.
Spencer Limited, C. A.
Terry & Gordon.
Union Lumber Company.
Victoria Harbor Lumber Company.

LATH BOLTERS
Garlock-Walker Machinery Co.
General Supply Co. of Canada, Ltd.
Green Company, C. Walter.

LOCOMOTIVES
Bell Locomotive Works
General Supply Co. of Canada, Ltd.
Jeffrey Manufacturiing Company.
Jenckes Machine Company, Ltd.
Climax Manufacturing Company.
Montreal Locomotive Workks.

LATH TWINE
Consumers' Cordage Company.

LINK-BELT
Canadian Link-Belt Company
Canadian Mathews Gravity Carrier Company.
Jeffrey Mfg. Co.
Williams Machinery Co., A. R., Vancouver.

LOCOMOTIVE CRANES
Canadian Link-Belt Company, Ltd.
LOGGING ENGINES
Dunbar Engine and Foundry Co.
Jenckes Machine Company.
Marsh Engineering Works, Limited
LOG HAULER
Green Company, G. Walter
Jenckes Machine Company, Ltd.
LOGGING MACHINERY AND EQUIPMENT
General Supply Co. of Canada, Ltd.
Hamilton Company, William.
Jenckes Machine Company, Ltd.
Marsh Engineering Works, Limited
Waterous Engine Works Company.
LUMBER TRUCKS
Waterous Engine Works Company.
LUMBERMEN'S CLOTHING
Woods Manufacturing Company, Ltd.
METAL REFINERS
Canada Metal Company.
Hoyt Metal Company.
Sessenwein Brothers.
MILLING IN TRANSIT
Renfrew Planing Mills.
Rutherford & Sons, Wm.
MOLDINGS
Genoa Bay Lumber Co.
Rutherford & Sons, Wm.
MOTOR TRUCKS
Duplex Truck Company
OAK
Chicago Lumber & Coal Company.
Long-Bell Lumber Company.
Weller, J. B.
OAKUM
Stratford Oakum Co., Geo.
OIL CLOTHING
Leckie, Limited, John.
OLD IRON AND BRASS
Sessenwein Brothers.
PAPER
Bowater & Sons, W. V.
PACKING
Atlas Asbestos Company, Ltd.
Consumers Cordage Co.
Dunlop Tire & Rubber Goods Co.
Gutta Percha and Rubber Company.

PAPER MILL MACHINERY
Bowater & Sons, W. V.
PILLOW BLOCKS
Bond Engineering Works
PINE
Anderson Lumber Company, C. G.
Atlantic Lumber Co.
Austin & Nicholson.
Bourgouin, H.
Callander Sawmills
Cameron & Co.
Canadian General Lumber Company
Cane & Co., Jas. G.
Cardinal & Page
Chicago Lumber & Coal Company.
Cleveland-Sarnia Sawmills Company.
Davison Lumber & Mfg. Co.
Donogh & Co., John.
Dudley, Arthur N.
Dunfield & Company
Eagle Lumber Company.
Edwards & Co., W. C.
Excelsior Lumber Company.
Fesserton Timber Company
Fraser-Bryson Lumber Company.
Fraser Limited.
Gillies Brothers Limited.
Gloucester Lumber Company
Gordon & Co., George.
Grier & Sons, Ltd., G. A.
Harris Tie & Timber Company, Ltd.
Hart & McDonagh.
Hettler Lumber Company, Herman H.
Long-Bell Lumber Company.
Long Lumber Company.
Mason, Gordon & Co.
McLennan Lumber Company.
Montreal Lumber Company.
Moores, Jr., E. J.
Muir & Kirkpatrick.
Parry Sound Lumber Company.
Russell, Chas. H.
Shearer Company, Jas.
Spencer Limited, C. A.
Summers, James R.
Terry & Gordon.
Union Lumber Company.
Watson & Todd, Limited.
Weller, J. B.
Williams Lumber Company
Wuichet, Louis.

PLANING MILL EXHAUSTERS
Garlock-Walker Machinery Co.
Reed & Company, Geo. W.
Sheldons Limited.
Toronto Blower Co.
PLANING MILL MACHINERY
American Woodworking Machinery Company
Garlock-Walker Machinery Co.
Mershon & Company, W. B.
Sheldons Limited.
Toronto Blower Co.
Yates Machine Company, P. B.
PORK PACKERS
Davies Company, William
Harris Abattoir Company
POSTS AND POLES
Auger & Company
Dupuis Limited, J. P.
Eagle Lumber Company
Harris Tie & Timber Company, Ltd.
Long-Bell Lumber Company.
Long Lumber Company.
Mason, Gordon & Co.
Terry & Gordon.
PULLEYS AND SHAFTING
Bond Engineering Works
Canadian Link-Belt Company
Garlock-Walker Machinery Co.
General Supply Co. of Canada, Ltd.
Green Company, G. Walter
Hamilton Company, William
Jeffrey Mfg. Co.
Jenckes Machine Company, Ltd.
PULP MILL MACHINERY
Canadian Link-Belt Company, Ltd.
Hamilton Company, William.
Jeffrey Manufacturing Company
Jenckes Machine Company, Ltd.
Waterous Engine Works Company
PUMPS
General Supply Co. of Canada, Ltd.
Hamilton Company, William
Jenckes Machine Company, Ltd.
Smart-Turner Machine Company
Waterous Engine Works Company
RAILS
Gartshore, John J.
Sessenwein Bros.

ROOFINGS
Reed & Company, Geo. W.
ROOFINGS
(Rubber, Plastic and Liquid)
Beveridge Paper Company
International Chemical Company
ROPE
Consumers Cordage Co.
Leckie, Limited, John
RUBBER GOODS
Atlas Asbestos Company
Dunlop Tire & Rubber Goods Co.
Goodyear Tire and Rubber Co.
Gutta Percha & Rubber Company
SASH
Genoa Bay Lumber Company
Renfrew Planing Mills.
SAWS
Atkins & Company, E. C.
Disston & Sons, Henry
General Supply Co. of Canada, Ltd.
Gerlach Company, Peter
Green Company, G. Walter
Hoe & Company, R.
Shurly-Dietrich Company
Simonds Canada Saw Company
SAW MILL LINK-BELT
Williams Machinery Co., A. R., Vancouver.
SAW MILL MACHINERY
Canadian Link-Belt Company, Ltd.
Dunbar Engine & Foundry Co.
Firstbrook Bros.
General Supply Co. of Canada, Ltd.
Haight, W. L.
Hamilton Company, William
Huther Bros. Saw Mfg. Company
Jeffrey Manufacturing Company
Long Manufacturing Company, E.
Mershon & Company, W. B.
Parry Sound Lumber Company
Payette Company, P.
Waterous Engine Works Company
Yates Machine Co., P. B.
SHEATHINGS
Beveridge Paper Company
Goodyear Tire & Rubber Co.
SHINGLE MACHINES
Marsh Engineering Works, Limited

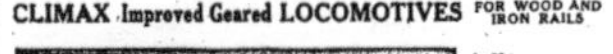

CLIMAX Improved Geared LOCOMOTIVES FOR WOOD AND IRON RAILS

A 82-ton Climax Locomotive Designed Especially for Heavy Logging Work.

Climax Locomotives are successfully operated on steep grades and sharp curves. Any weight or gauge. Locomotives in stock for immediate shipment. Get Catalog "H."

CLIMAX MANUFACTURING CO., 313 W. Main Street, CORRY, PA.
VANCOUVER MACHINERY DEPOT, LTD., VANCOUVER, B.C.

Peace Year 1919

Finds us optimistic for the future and well stocked with Horse Blankets, Feed Bags, Tarpaulins, Oil Clothing Tents, Flags, Straw Ticks and Grey Blankets

We Guarantee Prompt Shipment of Orders Entrusted to us

J. J. Turner & Sons
Limited
PETERBOROUGH, ONT.

PUT YOUR PROBLEM UP TO US

We are specialists in building locomotives. We build all types and sizes, also all kinds of repair parts for locomotives and tenders.

Our experience puts us in a position to give you expert advice as to what particular type and size of locomotive is best suited to your needs.

Put your locomotive problem up to us.

MONTREAL LOCOMOTIVE WORKS, LIMITED
DOMINION EXPRESS BUILDING, MONTREAL, CANADA.

PRATT & WHITNEY CO.
OF CANADA, LIMITED

SMALL TOOLS

Taps — Dies — Reamers — Cutters — Drills
MADE IN CANADA
As good as money can buy—Guaranteed absolutely!

Head Office and Works, DUNDAS, ONT.

SALES OFFICES:
MONTREAL, Drummond Bldg. VANCOUVER WINNIPEG, Bank of Hamilton Bldg.

DRYERS FOR PROFIT

A Proctor Dryer represents the most efficient and economical method of drying. It embodies air re-circulation, utilization of exhaust steam. Requires minimum time for drying. Saves floor space, labor, power, etc. The capacity and degree of drying are not affected by weather variations.

"Proctor" DRYERS for VENEERS
give a perfectly flat and pliable product without checks or splits

Made by the oldest and largest builders of dryers.
Ask for Proctor Dryer Catalog for your materials.

PHILADELPHIA TEXTILE MACHINERY CO.
Builders of Drying Machinery
SEVENTH STREET AND TABOR ROAD, PHILADELPHIA, PA., U.S.A.
Hamilton, Ont., Canada,—W. J. Westaway, 5 Sun Life Building.

SAW MANDRELS
Bond Engineering Works

SAW SHARPENERS
Garlock-Walker Machinery Co.
Waterous Engine Works Company.

SAW SLASHERS
Waterous Engine Works Company.

SAWMILL LINK-BELT
Canadian Link-Belt Company

SHEET METALS
Syracuse Smelting Works

SHINGLES
Allan-Stoltze Lumber Co.
Campbell-MacLaurin Lumber Co.
Cardinal & Page
Dominion Lumber & Timber Co.
Eagle Lumber Company
Foss Lumber Company
Fraser Limited.
Genoa Bay Lumber Company
Gillespie, James.
Gloucester Lumber Company
Grier & Sons, Ltd., G. A.
Harris Tie & Timber Company, Ltd.
Heeney, Percy E.
Long Lumber Company.
Mason, Gordon & Co.
McLennan Lumber Company.
Miller Company, Ltd., W. H.
Service Lumber Company
Shingle Agency of B. C.
Terry & Gordon.
Timms, Phillips & Co.
Vancouver Lumber Company.
Victoria Lumber and Mfg. Co.

SHINGLE & LATH MACHINERY
Dunbar Engine and Foundry Co.
Garlock-Walker Machinery Co.
Green Company, C. Walter
Hamilton Company, William.
Long Manufacturing Company, E.
Payette Company, P.

SILENT CHAIN DRIVES
Canadian Link-Belt Company, Ltd.

SILOS
Ontario Wind Engine Company

SLEEPING ROBES
Woods Mfg. Company, Limited

SMOKESTACKS
Marsh Engineering Works, Limited
Waterous Engine Works Company.

SNOW PLOWS
Pink Company, Thomas.

SPARK ARRESTORS
Jenckes Machine Company, Ltd.
Reed & Company, Geo. W.
Waterous Engine Works Company.

SPRUCE
Bartram & Ball.
Bourgouin, H.
Cane & Co., Jas. G.
Cardinal & Page
Davison Lumber & Mfg. Company
Donogh & Co., John.
Dudley, Arthur N.
Dunfield & Company
Exchange Lumber Company.
Foss Lumber Company
Fraser Limited.
Fraser-Bryson Lumber Company.
Gillies Brothers.
Gloucester Lumber Company
Grant & Campbell.
Grier & Sons, Ltd., G. A.
Hart & McDonagh.
Lauder, Spears & Howland.
Long Lumber Company.
Mason, Gordon & Co.
McLennan Lumber Company.
Muir & Kirkpatrick.
New Ontario Colonization Company.
Nicholson & Co., E. M.
River Ouelle Pulp and Lumber Co.
Russell, Chas. H.
Service Lumber Company
Shearer Company, Jas.
Snowball Co., J. B.
Spencer Limited, C. A.
Terry & Gordon.

STEEL CHAIN
Canadian Link-Belt Company, Ltd.
Jeffrey Manufacturing Company.
Waterous Engine Works Company.

STEEL PLATE CONSTRUCTION
Marsh Engineering Works, Limited

STEAM PLANT ACCESSORIES
Waterous Engine Works Company.

STEEL BARRELS
Smart-Turner Machine Co.

STEEL DRUMS
Smart-Turner Machine Co.

SWEAT PADS
American Pad & Textile Co.

SULPHITE PULP CHIPS
Davison Lumber & Mfg. Company

TANKS
Ontario Wind Engine Company

TARPAULINS
Turner & Sons, J. J.
Woods Manufacturing Company, Ltd.

TAPS AND DIES
Pratt & Whitney Company.

TENTS
Turner & Sons, J. J.
Woods Mfg. Company

TIES
Auger & Company
Austin & Nicholson.
Harris Tie & Timber Company, Ltd.
Long Lumber Company.
McLennan Lumber Company.
Terry & Gordon.

TIMBER BROKERS
Bradley, R. R.
Cant & Kemp.
Farnworth & Jardine.
Hillas & Co., W. N.
Hunter, Herbert F.
Smith & Tyrer, Limited

TIMBER CRUISERS AND ESTIMATORS
Sewall, James W.

TIMBER LANDS
Department of Lands and Forests.

TRACTORS
British War Mission

TRANSMISSION MACHINERY
Bond Engineering Works
Canadian Link-Belt Company, Ltd.
General Supply Co. of Canada, Ltd.
Jenckes Machine Company, Ltd.
Jeffrey Manufacturing Company.
Waterous Engine Works Company.

TRIMMERS
Garlock-Walker Machinery Co.
Green Company, C. Walter
Waterous Engine Works Company

TUGS
West & Peachey.

TURBINES
Hamilton Company, William.
Jenckes Machine Company, Ltd.

VALVES
Bay City Foundry & Machine Co.
Mason Regulator & Engineering Co.

VENEERS
Webster & Brother, James.

VENEER DRYERS
Philadelphia Textile Mach. Co.

VENEER MACHINERY
Garlock-Walker Machinery Co.
Philadelphia Textile Machinery Co.

VETERINARY REMEDIES
Dr. Bell Veterinary Wonder Co.

WATER HEATERS
Mason Regulator & Engineering Co.

WATERPROOFING
Beveridge Paper Company

WATER WHEELS
Hamilton Company, William.
Jenckes Machine Company, Ltd.

WIRE
Laidlaw Bale Tie Company.

WOOD DISTILLATION PLANTS
Blair, Campbell & McLean, Ltd.

WOODWORKING MACHINERY
American Woodworking Machy. Co.
Garlock-Walker Machinery Co.
General Supply Co. of Canada, Ltd.
Jeffrey Manufacturing Company.
Long Manufacturing Company, E.
Mershon & Company, W. B.
Waterous Engine Works Company.
Yates Machine Company, P. B.

WOOD PRESERVATIVES
International Chemical Company

WOOD PULP
Austin & Nicholson.
New Ontario Colonization Co.
River Ouelle Pulp and Lumber Co.

Vol. 39 Toronto, July 15, 1919 No. 14

Canada Lumberman & Wood Worker

JOHN LECKIE LIMITED
77a Wellington St. West, TORONTO, ONT.

CHAINS

Black, galvanized, all kinds, Blocks Steel and Wood, Oiled Clothing, Manila Rope, Wire Rope, Tents, Dunnage Bags, Canvas, Etc.

PRICES ON REQUEST

EDGAR D. HARDY JAS. E. REYNOLDS

E. D. HARDY & CO.
INSURANCE

Specialists in LUMBER and WOODWORKING Plants

HEAD OFFICE: OTTAWA, ONT.

Galvanizing Work OF ALL CLASSES

OUR galvanizing plant is the largest of its kind in Canada. All contracts, large and small, for Hot or Electro Galvanizing can be completed promptly. Satisfaction guaranteed.

Ask for quotations

Ontario Wind Engine and Pump Company, Limited
TORONTO - ONTARIO
Branches: Montreal, Winnipeg, Regina, Calgary

GENUINE "TURBROS"

Balata Belting

Waterproof and Stretchless.
The best belt for sawmills.

Atlas Asbestos Co., Limited
MONTREAL

PUMPS
for the most exacting requirements

Send us your next specification

THE SMART-TURNER MACHINE CO., LIMITED
HAMILTON CANADA

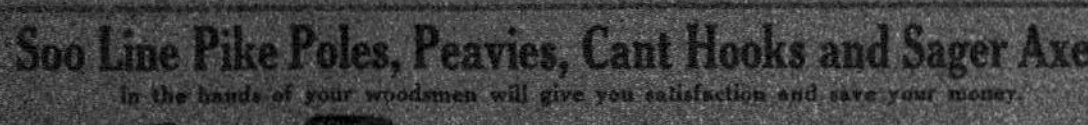

in the hands of your woodsmen will give you satisfaction and save your money.

Ask your dealer or order direct.

Made by
Canadian Warren Axe & Tool Co.
ST. CATHARINES, ONT.

Alphabetical Index to Advertisers, Page [illegible] Classified Directory to Advertisements, Page [illegible]

AMERICAN WOOD WORKING MACHINERY CO.

ROCHESTER, N. Y.

SALES OFFICE FOR BRITISH COLUMBIA, PORTLAND, OREGON
AGENTS FOR THE REST OF CANADA GARLOCK-WALKER MACHINERY CO., TORONTO
AGENTS FOR GREAT BRITAIN THE PROJECTILE CO., LONDON

FIRST IN QUALITY

The Inside of the Columbia No. 2

The sander with the real automatic take-up for sandpaper

Send for copy of Sander Booklet fully illustrating and describing this machine

CANADIAN SALES AGENTS

Garlock-Walker Machinery Company

32-34 FRONT STREET WEST, TORONTO LIMITED

TORONTO **MONTREAL** **WINNIPEG**

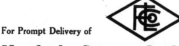

Geo. Gordon & Co.

Limited

Cache Bay - Ont.

White and Red Pine

Stock on Hand for quick shipment

6 x 6-	12/16	50,000	6 x 12-	12/16'	7,000
8 x 10-	12/16	30,000	8 x 12-	12/16'	14,000
10 x 10-	12/16	100,000	10 x 12-	12/16'	25,000'
4 x 12-	12/16	60,000	12 x 12-	12/16	150,000

Complete assortment 1"- 2"- and 3" White Pine

WRITE US FOR PRICES

Vancouver Lumber Co.

LIMITED

MANUFACTURERS OF

B. C. Fir, Cedar and

B. C. Hemlock Products

TWO LARGE MODERN MILLS AT YOUR SERVICE

View of our Fir Mill from log pond, Vancouver, B.C.

Fir Finish

Fir Flooring

Fir Timbers

"BIG CHIEF BRAND" SIDING

RITE GRADE SHINGLES

Eastern Sales Office:

701 EXCELSIOR LIFE BUILDING

TORONTO, ONT.

Representative—C. J. BROOKS

QUALITY

SERVICE

QUALITY

SERVICE

British Columbia

Dry

CLEAR HEMLOCK

Can guarantee quick shipment:

Size	Length	Quantity
1 x 6"	—8/18'	30,000'
8"	— "	13,000'
10"	— "	5,000'
8/12"	— "	5,000'
2 x 4"	— "	15,000'
6"	— "	25,000'
8"	— "	50,000'
10"	— "	17,000'
12"	— "	20,000'

Planing Mill Point of Shipment, and can mill, resaw and dress, to Ontario Standards.

INTERESTING PRICES FOR IMMEDIATE SHIPMENT

1918 SAWING

Complete Stock of White and Red Pine at Midland, Ont.

PLANING MILL FACILITIES

QUALITY

SERVICE

QUALITY

SERVICE

TERRY & GORDON

VANCOUVER BRANCH:
515 Metropolitan Bldg.
A. S. Nicholson,
Western Manager.

Head Office:
704 Confederation Life Bldg.
TORONTO, ONT.

U. S. Representatives:
Berry Lumber Company,
30 Church Street,
New York City.

Ontario Representatives of
The British Columbia Mills, Timber & Trading Co. of Vancouver, B.C.

HOCKEN HLC LUMBER

The Quality of Our Product is Our Best Advertisement

We Solicit Your Enquiries for Lumber in Any Quantities

WHITE & NORWAY PINE

2 x 6 Bone Dry

For Silo Construction

Hocken Lumber Co., Limited

630 Confederation Life Building - TORONTO

PHONE MAIN 3153

Austin & Nicholson

CHAPLEAU, ONTARIO

Largest Producers of

RAILROAD TIES

in the Dominion

Pine and Spruce Lumber

Lath Piling

Railroad Ties

Pulpwood

First Class Planing-mill Equipment

Facilities for delivering Pulpwood
to Michipicoten Harbour, Lake Superior

Splendid facilities for Dressing and Matching
in straight car lots, one or more widths

Mills at NICHOLSON, ONTARIO, Main Line C.P.R.

Basswood

1 in., 1¼ in., 1½ in., 2 in., and 3 in.,
Dry Basswood

Dry Birch Stock

All thicknesses and grades in

Maple, Birch, Elm, Basswood and **Brown Ash**

Also **Cottonwood, Tupelo, Gum, Magnolia**
and **Buckeye**

Spruce, Hemlock and Pine

Can saw to order at MacDonald's Siding

Let us quote on your requirements

HART & McDONAGH

Temple Building, Cor. Bay and Richmond Streets
TORONTO, ONT.

SOUTHERN HARDWOODS Dry Stock at Buffalo for Quick Shipment

BROWN ASH

	1 & 2	Clear Strips	No. 1 Com.	No. 2 Com.
1 in.	20,900	....	5,000	22,000
1¼ in.	29,500	5,300	6,200	6,300
1½ in.	11,500	....	....	....
2 in.	1,500	....	13,000	500

WHITE ASH

	1 & 2	Clear Strips	No. 1 Com.	No. 2 Com.
1 in.	57,300	800	130,000	89,000
1¼ in.	41,000	15,500	9,000	1,000
1½ in.	63,900	5,200	43,000	26,100
2 in.	48,300	500	79,000	44,700
2½ in.	....	....	11,500	1,500
3 in.	7,000	....	23,500	4,300
4 in.	4,500	....	....	....

BASSWOOD

	1 & 2	Clear Strips	No. 1 Com.	No. 2 Com.
1 in.	35,700	2,200	172,000	24,000
1¼ in.	144,300	12,000	146,500	65,800
1½ in.	36,000	....	24,800	11,000
2 in.	20,900	....	15,000	4,500
2½ in.	75,000	....	20,900	13,000
3 in.	5,550	....	6,500	3,000

BUTTERNUT

	1 & 2	No. 1 Com.	No. 2 Com.
1 in.	15,300	35,900	10,600
2½ in.	3,000	3,000	.....

TENESSEE SCENTED RED CEDAR

	1 & 2	No. 1 Com.	No.2 Com.	No. 3 Com.
1 in.	18,500	15,800	1,300	1,100
1¼ in.	4,400	800	....	....

CHERRY

	1 & 2	Clear Strips	No. 1 Com.	No. 2 Com.
1 in.	154,000	24,000	129,200	66,500
1¼ in.	3,500	.....	3,600	6,400
1½ in.	81,000	.....	17,700	73,300
2 in.	10,100	.....	17,200	30,000
2½ in.	4,500	.....	.....	800
3 in.	6,700	.....	.....	2,300
4 in.	3,000	.....	1,200	1,000

CHESTNUT

	1 & 2	Clear Strips	No. 1 Com.	No. 2 Com.
¾ in.	......	......	1,500	62,000
1 in.	147,000	10,700	21,300	94,500
1¼ in.	88,800	1,300	10,200	38,200
1½ in.	45,500	.....	4,000	.....
2 in.	28,200	.....	52,300	107,200
2½ in.	2,700	.....	850	.....
3 in.	1,800	.....	1,300	.....
4 in.	900	.....	.....	.....

RED GUM

	1 & 2	No. 1 Com.	No. 2 Com.
1 in.	60,300	13,200	....
1¼ in.	8,200	9,200	....
1½ in.	9,000	11,300	....
2 in.	7,100	4,800	....

SAP GUM

	1 & 2	No. 1 Com.	No. 2 Com.
1 in.	47,400	6,000	......
1¼ in.	......	......	......
1½ in.	......	......	......
2 in.	......	......	......
2 in.	11,000 qtd.	7,500 qtd.	......

HICKORY

	1 & 2	No. 1 Com.	No. 2 Com.
1 in.	2,200	2,300	600
1¼ in.	......	400	350
1½ in.	5,000	2,300	1,000
2 in.	12,350	13,600	10,700
2½ in.	7,000	5,000	......
2 in.	400	5,580	......
4 in.	200	200	......

PLAIN RED OAK

	1 & 2	Clear Strips	No. 1 Com.	No. 2 Com.
¼ in.	30,200	.....	.....	.....
¾ in.	97,000	.....	25,400	6,200
⅝ in.	8,500	.....	.....	.....
1 in.	220,200	2,700	10,500	10,400
1¼ in.	11,700	2,400	14,500	7,200
1½ in.	73,900	4,300	20,200	24,000
2 in.	38,100	.....	43,800	.....
2½ in.	23,100	.....	4,000	.....
3 in.	23,800	.....	8,500	.....
4 in.	3,600	.....	3,000	.....

PLAIN WHITE OAK

	1 & 2	Clear Strips	No. 1 Com.	No. 2 Com.
⅜ in.	23,400	.....	.....	.....
½ in.	11,500	.....	.....	.....
⅝ in.	28,150	.....	21,800	.....
¾ in.	39,000	.....	22,000	17,000
1 in.	22,300	.....	13,000	15,200
1¼ in.	76,300	.....	17,000	6,000
1½ in.	30,500	.....	30,400	10,000
2 in.	49,000	.....	101,000	2,000
2½ in.	118,500	.....	35,500	.....
3 in.	54,800	.....	39,800	4,400
4 in.	21,000	.....	1,500	.....

QUARTERED RED OAK

	1 & 2	Clear Strips	No. 1 Com.	No. 2 Com.
¾ in.	....	....	......	....
1 in.	72,200	8,300	38,800	800
1¼ in.	500	....	400	....
1½ in.	....	....	550	150
2 in.	1,000	....	7,400	....

QUARTERED WHITE OAK

	1 & 2	Clear Strips	No. 1 Com.	No. 2 Com.
½ in.	5,500	....	....	....
⅝ in.	84,500	25,400	128,600	....
¾ in.	....	....	....	....
1 in.	29,400	12,500	4,000	15,000
1¼ in.	10,080	....	6,400	1,300
1½ in.	1,500	....	2,000	2,300
2 in.	6,500	350	5,100	2,700
2½ in.	800	....	....	....

POPLAR

	1 & 2 18 in. & up	1 & 2 13 in. & up	Box Boards	Bright Saps
¾ in.	....	3,000	....	2,800
1 in.	16,200	36,000	11,600	40,200
1¼ in.	2,800	3,900	....	11,000
1½ in.	5,300	7,800	....	21,000
2 in.	....	32,000	....	22,000
2½ in.	....	25,800	....	28,000
3 in.	....	5,900	....	32,600
4 in.	....	27,000	....	1,300

	Stained Saps	Clear Strips	No. 1 Com.	No. 2 Com.
¾ in.	9,800	....	34,300	2,600
1 in.	23,600	....	105,900	55,300
1¼ in.	8,600	....	11,600	6,000
1½ in.	9,700	....	45,000	2,700
2 in.	7,000	....	141,500	27,500
2½ in.	3,700	....	1,000	....
3 in.	1,300	....	43,000	32,000
4 in.	700	....	750	....

QUARTERED POPLAR

	1 & 2	Clear Strips	No. 1 Com.	No. 2 Com.
1 in.	....	....	....	....
1¼ in.	250	....	....	....

BLACK WALNUT

	1 & 2	No. 1 Com.	No. 2 Com.
1 in.	150	14,000	3,100
1¼ in.	100	300	200
1½ in.	250	200	100
2 in.	300	800	500
3 in.	110	120	250
4 in.	....	500	1,200

Also Large Stock of **BEECH, BIRCH and MAPLE**

THE ATLANTIC LUMBER CO., Inc., 310 MANNING CHAMBERS, TORONTO

MANUFACTURERS SOUTHERN HARDWOOD LUMBER

Head Office: BOSTON, MASS. Yards: BUFFALO, N.Y. Mills: KNOXVILLE, TENN.; FONDE, KENTUCKY

JOHN MCKERGOW, President — W. K. GRAFFTEY, Managing-Director

The Montreal Lumber Co. Limited

Wholesale Lumber

Ottawa Office: 46 Elgin St. — Montreal Office: 759 Notre Dame St., W

H. CARDINAL — O. PAGE

Cardinal & Page

180 St. James St. Montreal

Large Quantity of Eastern Spruce and Ottawa White Pine on Hand.

Try a sample shipment and you will become a regular Customer.

Lake Lumber Co. Ltd.

Manufacturers of

Fir, Cedar, Hemlock, Spruce

QUALICUM QUALITY LUMBER

Rough Fir Timbers

Any size up to 60 feet long

Select Grades a Specialty

FIR PIPE and TANK STOCK

Market wanted for Rough Cedar Timbers
Inquire for prices

Office and Mills:
Qualicum Beach, V. I., B. C.

WE ARE BUYERS OF

Hardwood Lumber

Handles

Staves Hoops

Headings

James **WEBSTER** & Bro. Limited

Bootle, Liverpool, England

London Office
Dashwood House 9 New Broad St. E. C.

SPECIALTIES

Sawed Hemlock
Red Cedar Shingles
White Pine Lath
Bass and Poplar Siding

James Gillespie

Pine and Hardwood

Lumber

Lath and Shingles

North Tonawanda, N. Y.

LUMBER

Dry Ready to Ship

Midland Stock

White Pine

All Dimensions

WANTED

We are in the market for

ONTARIO HARDWOOD CUTS

ADVANCES MADE DURING OPERATIONS

C. G. Anderson Lumber Company, Limited

Manufacturers and Strictly Wholesale Dealers in Lumber

SALES OFFICE

705 Excelsior Life Building

Toronto

JACK PINE

HEMLOCK

SPRUCE

JAMES R. SUMMERS

Wholesale Lumber

95 King St. East TORONTO, Ont.
Main 7329

Lumber, Lath

Flooring, Cedar Poles and Posts

Railway Ties

Doors, Windows, Architraves and all kinds of Mill Work, done by experts.

Ask for our prices and services of our architect

J. P. DUPUIS, LTD.

592 Church Ave., Verdun, Montreal, P.Q.

Pulpwood of all kinds

Bought and Sold for Canadian or American delivery.
Quotations furnished on request.

The Jost Company, Limited

Successors to
F. M. Jost & Co.

285 Beaver Hall Hill, MONTREAL

Robt. Coltart & Co.

Royal Liver Building

Liverpool - England

Agents for the sale of Pine, Spruce and Hardwoods. Correspondence invited.

Cables—"COLTART" Liverpool

Cant & Kemp

82 St. Enoch Square
GLASGOW

Timber Brokers

Cable Address, "Tectona," Glasgow
A1 and A B C Codes used

FARNWORTH & JARDINE

Cable Address: Farnworth, Liverpool

WOOD BROKERS and MEASURERS

2 Dale Street, Liverpool, and Seaforth Road, Seaforth, Liverpool, England

SAW MILL MACHINERY

Firstbrook Bros.
Limited

Having decided to discontinue saw mill operations at Penetang have the following machinery for sale. This machinery is all in operating condition and is open for inspection at Penetang, Ont.

Mill Machinery

Extra heavy log haul-up works with inch round and flat chain, 128 ft. centres.
2—Waterous log unloaders or kickers, 3 arms, 10 in. cylinders.
1—Waterous log loader, 3 arms, 10-in. cylinders.
1—Waterous right-hand double cutting band mill, 11 in. saws, 8 ft. wheel, with 3-block carriage; 24 in. opening; Payette set works and dogs; 8 in. x 36 ft. steam feed.
1—Waterous double edger for 20-inch saws, lever shifter.
1—Payette double edger for 18-in. saws, lever shifter.
48—live rolls about 8 ft. long by 10 in. dia.; extra heavy, sprocket drive.
4—High cars with roller tops, 24 in. heavy wheels on 3 in. axles, standard gauge.
1—Mershon 4 saw gang resaw, takes squared cants or just one face, ideal machine to cut small logs and centres of large after good has been taken off.
1—Payette picket machine, made specially for shade roller stock, will feed pieces 16 in. long, also sorting table with chain top.
1—Rogers Iron Works circular resaw for making box lumber from slabs; fool-proof machine.
1—Payette edger for box and short stock.
1—Rogers twin circular or tie maker.
1—Payette lath bolter and lath machine.
1—Pair lath trimmers.
1—Picket trimmer (bunch trim).
Conveyor drives and chains.
Pulleys, gears, heavy line shafting and countershafting with bearings.
Send us your requirements.
We have a large stock of double and triple leather belting in widths from 10 in. to 18 in.

Power House Equipment

3—Return Tubular Boilers, Goldie McCulloch make, 66 x 16, Dutch oven settings, 85 lbs. steam allowance Ontario Government.
Breeching and smoke stack for above boilers, 60 in. dia., newly painted, 600 ft. new ½-in. guy and plate for brick pier.
1—Pair Polson "Brown" type engines, coupled on quarters, 22 in. x 30 in., with 10 ft. x 48 in. belt, balance wheel. Excellent engines.
1—Pair American feed water heaters for above engines; 10 in., copper coils.
1—8 x 10 Centre Crank Engine
1—10 x 14 Cowan Slide Valve Engine

Filing Equipment

1—Waterous band saw grinder for 6 in. saws.
1—Baldwin retoother for band saws.
3—Reversible saw levelling blocks.
2—Chilled band saw anvils.
Hanchet band saw swages; Crescent circular saw swages; shapers and dressers.

Yard Equipment

Booms and boom chains, ½, ¾ & ⅞.
Winches and other mill supplies.

Prompt shipments and bargains for quick sale. Will send all particulars and prices on application.

Firstbrook Bros.
Limited
Penetang, Ont.

"WELL BOUGHT IS HALF SOLD"

Dry Hardwood

133 M' 1" No. 3 Com. & Btr. Hard Maple
70 M' 6/4" No. 2 Com. & Btr. Hard Maple
25 M' 2" No. 2 Com. & Btr. Hard Maple
48 M' 3" No. 2 Com. & Btr. Hard Maple
(3" practically No. 1 Com. & Btr.)
36 M' 1" No. 3 Com. & Btr. Beech
3 M' 6/4" No. 2 Com. & Btr. Beech
14 M' 2" No. 2 Com. & Btr. Beech
8 M' 1" No. 3 Com. & Btr. Soft Elm
10 M' 3" No. 2 Com. & Btr. Soft Elm
14 M' 1" Wormy Chestnut
4 M' 8/4" Wormy Chestnut

We make special price on block for prompt shipment or sell in single carloads.

Canadian General Lumber Co.
Limited

FOREST PRODUCTS

TORONTO OFFICE:—712-20 Bank of Hamilton Bldg.
Montreal Office:—203 McGill Bldg.
Mills: Byng Inlet, Ont.

Quick Action

You Can Have It

Try the Canada Lumberman Wanted and For Sale Department. Have you anything you wish to buy or sell in the Lumber Industry? You will find this department inexpensive, and a very effective business getter.

Our Classified Advertisers do not repeat the ad, often. They don't have to. They report immediate results. Use these columns to your own advantage.

CANADA LUMBERMAN and WOODWORKER
347 Adelaide St. W.
TORONTO

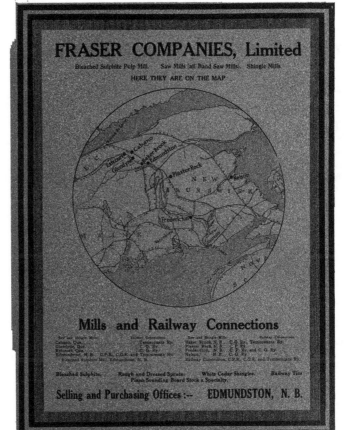

Feeding the Camp

IF that is your problem, remember that it is our business, too. We do a tremendous lumber camp trade and are fully acquainted with the food requirements of logging camps. We shall be glad to quote you on any lines you need this year, and will submit special quotations if you will drop us a card. We can supply you with all that's best in provisions and fresh meats, and give you a service you will appreciate.

WRITE OR WIRE US AT OUR EXPENSE—TODAY

LONG CLEAR BACON
BARRELED PORK
SAUSAGE
DAVIES PURE LARD
"PEERLESS" SHORTENING
MINCEMEAT, ETC.

THE WILLIAM DAVIES COMPANY LIMITED

MONTREAL TORONTO WINNIPEG

Canada Lumberman and Woodworker

Issued on the 1st and 15th of every month by
HUGH C. MACLEAN, LIMITED, Publishers
HUGH C. MacLEAN, Winnipeg, President.
THOS. S. YOUNG, Toronto, General Manager.

OFFICES AND BRANCHES:
TORONTO - - Telephone A. 2700 - - 347 Adelaide Street West
VANCOUVER - - Telephone Seymour 2013 - - Winch Building
MONTREAL - - Telephone Main 2299 - - 119 Board of Trade
WINNIPEG - Telephone Garry 856 - Electric Railway Chambers
NEW YORK - - Telephone 3108 Beekman - - 1123 Tribune Building
CHICAGO - Telephone Harrison 5351 - 1413 Great Northern Building
LONDON, ENG. - - - - - - - - - - 16 Regent Street, S.W.

TERMS OF SUBSCRIPTION
Canada, United States and Great Britain, $2.00 per year, in advance; other foreign countries embraced in the General Postal Union, $3.00.
Single copies 15 cents.

"The Canada Lumberman and Woodworker" is published in the interest of, and reaches regularly, persons engaged in the lumber, woodworking and allied industries in every part of Canada. It aims at giving full and timely information on all subjects touching these interests, and invites free discussion by its readers.

Advertisers will receive careful attention and liberal treatment. For manufacturing and supply firms wishing to bring their goods to the attention of owners and operators of saw and planing mills, woodworking factories, pulp mills, etc., "The Canada Lumberman and Woodworker" is undoubtedly the most direct and profitable advertising medium. Special attention is directed to the "Wanted" and "For Sale" advertisements.

Authorized by the Postmaster-General for Canada, for transmission as second-class matter.
Entered as second-class matter July 18th, 1914, at the Postoffice at Buffalo, N.Y., under the Act of Congress of March 3, 1879.

Vol. 39 Toronto, July 15, 1919 No. 13

A Great Economic Loss and Why

It is reported that within the past six weeks more than a score of sawmills, large and small, have been destroyed by fire. Some of these have been caught up in the flames that have spread from a neighboring bush, while others have been wiped out owing to the blaze originating from some unknown cause.

The loss of so many mills is a serious blow to the Canadian industry at this juncture, when there is such great need of increased production in order to meet the abnormal demand for lumber, caused by reconstruction activities since the close of the war.

It is not a pleasing fact to record that Canada has the distinction of having the highest known pro rata fire loss of any country in the world. In round figures the Canadian loss is $4 per capita per annum, while in the United States it is only $3 per capita, and in Europe the average has been as low as 33c for each person in the country. Last year it was estimated that the fire loss in Canada was about $33,000,000. The wiping out of so much valuable property and numerous flourishing industries means a direct economic setback in many more ways than the mere obliteration of the plants themselves.

As pointed out by a contemporary, it has been asked if the insurance company is willing to assume the risk and the owner is amply protected in a monetary sense whose business is it anyway? Why should the manufacturer go to the additional expense of installing the latest appliances in order to safeguard his premises against elimination by flame? It is only necessary to state that even if the damage is covered by insurance, it does not alter the fact that the loss is a decidedly serious one and that the wealth of the country has been decreased by more than the amount of the destruction. There is the wage loss to be considered; the period of idleness by reason of wiping out of the industry; the loss to the community as a whole through decreased production, not to speak of loss of customers, credit, trade connections, local and foreign markets and other factors. The material used for re-building and equipping a plant could have been employed to greater advantage in producing commercial commodities and thus contributing to the wealth of the nation. Outside of this there is the menace to surrounding buildings which an inadequately protected plant imparts.

That the authorities at Ottawa realize the serious menace of the annual loss is shown by amendments that were recently made to the criminal code of Canada. It provides for the penalizing of carelessness and negligence in respect to fire. Any person who by negligence causes a fire may be fined $1,000 or imprisoned for two years or both. Negligence is further defined as follows: any owner or occupant of property who has failed to maintain his property as provided for by the by-laws of the community where the property is situated or by any statutory requirement, shall be deemed guilty of negligence. This brings the responsibility home to the person who fails to take the necessary precautionary measures.

The New Aerial Patrol of Forests

What are the possibilities of aeroplanes and hydroplanes in relation to the protection of forests from fires? The question arises in connection with the loan by the Federal Government of two hydroplanes to the St. Maurice Forest Protective Association, which has undertaken to maintain the machines and to bear the cost of the work.

There is a marked divergence of opinion as to the value of the machines having regard to expenditure. The sceptics declare that at the best the machines can only be regarded as a costly auxiliary; they cannot take the place of rangers, lookout stations, telephones, etc., and no part of the present organization can be dispensed with. The working cost, it is claimed, is likely to be very heavy, and if hydroplanes are to be purchased, the outlay will be prohibitive. It is further contended that there will be great difficulty in landing, although Major H. E. Kennedy, a well-known aviator, is of opinion that this side of the subject is exaggerated.

Against these objections must be put the fact that machines can cover an immense area—Major Kennedy put it at 8,000 square miles per machine each day—and the location and reporting of fires thereby made more efficient. The objection as to cost is met by the argument that the prevention of fires, even at an enhanced cost, is an economical measure, and that one large fire will do more damage, measured in dollars and cents, than the entire cost of the aeroplanes to the Association.

The fact is, the employment of the machines is in the nature of an experiment; we have no reliable data as to their cost or as to their ability to do the work efficiently. Innovations of all kinds meet with criticisms from those who are of a conservative temperament, and who are convinced that a system giving good results should not be interfered with. It must not, however, be forgotten that the present protective system has been gradually built up—the addition of portable telephones and the introduction of portable fire pumps being instances where the system has been immensely improved. Looking at the question as a whole, there is no reason why the fire protective associations should not make the experiment of utilizing aeroplanes, particularly when the Federal Government is willing to co-operate by the loan of the machines. The cost falls upon the limit owners, who at the end of the season will be in a position to say whether the expenditure has been justified and whether the advocates of aeroplanes have had their faith confirmed by the results.

An Enemy That Will Not Stay Still

With the advent of warm, dry weather we always have the mosquito, the house fly, the drowning accident, the upset canoe, the inane individual who inquires "if it is hot enough for you," and the destructive forest fire.

Great as has been the progress of late years in scientific forestry and effective measures in safeguarding the wooded wealth of Canada, there appears to be no deterrent to the extent and frequency of fires in the bush, particularly when once they get well under way. From practically every province of the Dominion have come reports during the past few days of much damage done to industrial plants, mining camps, settlers' homes, growing timber and agricultural crops, through the ravages of an agency which has destroyed more valuable commercial timber in Canada than has been cut in the long history of lumbering, or been wasted by the none too economical methods of pioneer sawmill operators.

Every summer that is dry brings about forest fires, which in many cases are not checked until the fall of heavy rains. While steady advancement has been made in stamping out this enemy of our forests, recent events have only served to demonstrate that greater care, more effective and efficient co-operation and an extension of the facilities already at the command of the rangers, are needed in order to render the timber regions as immune as possible from any further visitations of the devouring enemy.

Progressive and far-seeing as Quebec is in her policy of conservation and preservation of her natural resources, yet at the recent meeting of the Woodlands Section of the Canadian Pulp and Paper Association, some constructive criticism was engaged in by the members. It was decided to urge upon the provincial authorities the advisability of taking, not only further steps in the husbandry of the arboreal assets of the province, but also the enforcement of better regulations covering the cutting of timber on Crown lands.

The keynote of the gathering was reafforestation and the recent fires which have swept certain portions of Northern Ontario, Quebec, New Brunswick, Alberta and British Columbia, cannot but tend to drive home the conviction for the necessity of greater vigilance. While a decade or two ago certain people who spoke of the not far-distant future when the apparently inexhaustible timber wealth of Canada would be but a memory, were regarded as day dreamers or forestal fanatics, they had a vision of what we are now being called upon to witness. They saw the menace which has been driven home in late years, by the ravaging element. While much has been effected in the line of protection, much more remains to be done. Any movement—any agitation—that tends to stamp out the fiery foe is worthy of every encouragement and support, from the private citizen, the business man, the manufacturer, the provinces and the Canadian commonwealth.

The Upbuild of the Lumber Industry

It is always interesting to review the past and contrast what was going on a generation or more ago, with the present. Only by linking up by-gone days with those that are now can one get a proper and comprehensive grasp and perspective of the development and progress of any industry, community or country. The historical is ever inviting to the student of the trend and tendencies of the times. By an adequate appreciation and thorough knowledge of what took place in past periods can one realize and appraise the privileges, opportunities and possibilities of the present.

It is a long way from the ox-cart to the high powered automobile, as a means of locomotion, and from travelling by foot to speeding through the air in an aeroplane at one hundred and twenty-five miles per hour. These instances afford a conception of how rapidly transportation facilities have developed in the last few decades. What applies to this sphere of action, can with equal point and effectiveness, be made to bear upon industrial growth and progress.

The "Canada Lumberman" believes that in presenting a short review every month of what was doing in the trade thirty years ago it will provide a pleasant and enlightening feature for, not only the newer exponents of the great lumber industry of Canada, but also the old-timers—the pioneers—who love to haunt the picture gallery of memory and gaze mentally upon the scenes indelibly mirrored upon the walls of that structure—the human tenement—which will not crumble until the call comes—whether it be sooner or later. A modern philosopher has said that you can rob a man of his wealth and his business; of his professional standing and of his friends; of his family and his associations. Calamity, disaster and disease can do many things, but it cannot take from his, who lingers on earth, the memories of delightful scenes and associations of the days that are gone and of the good times enjoyed in the fast receding and dimly distant past. The historical appeals keenly to all, and what is the record of expansion and uplift in any trade or industry but the regular narrative of the thoughts, movements and aspirations of its exponents, separately and collectively.

Editorial Short Lengths

Any man is better in every way for a holiday now and then. It gives him larger vision, greater perspective and a better sense of the proportion of things. The annual midsummer outing of the Ontario Retail Lumber Dealers will be held this season on August 1 and 2 to the busy lumbering towns of Penetanguishene, Midland and Victoria Harbor. All retailers, whether members of the Association or not, will be cordially welcomed on this educational tour, where there will be much to be heard, seen and learned.

Handling costs in many woodworking establishments are frequently too high by reason of poor planning in the expansion of the plant by the addition of incongruous wings and sheds to a nucleus which the business has outgrown, necessitating shafting mounted at various angles to accommodate machines set wherever floor room is found. The lumber travels a tortuous route to receive the various operations of planing, mortising, etc., sometimes doubling back on its course, until handling costs more than machine processes and much power is wasted turning unnecessary shafting, etc.

According to the Hon. Jules Allard, Minister of Lands and Forests for the Province of Quebec, the revenue from his department for the fiscal year ending June 30, 1919, will show an increase of a million dollars. This is due to the recent Order-in-Council increasing the stumpage and other dues. The Minister, in referring to the forest fire protection policy of the government, asserted that if the plans of the government succeeded in regard to forest fires it would mean that no matter what exploitation of forests there was Quebec would have forests in perpetuity.

There is nothing like optimism, but it can run to extremes. One newspaper in a small town with reckless abandon announces that the sawmill has started operations for the season and the local plant will cut one billion feet in 1919. Considering that the capacity of the average small mill is from 15,000 to 30,000 a day, and the number of working days at the most is possibly 175, the output would not be more than 500,000 feet—to say nothing of a billion. This is the day of big undertakings, big ideas, big companies, and big capitalization. The words millions and billions slip off the tongue without any adequate appreciation of what the terms involve or imply.

Chinese customs are quaint and their beliefs equally peculiar. It was stated by a speaker in Toronto recently that the railroad men of China expect a dead man for every tie placed in the construction of steel highways in that country. If such a superstition prevailed in Canada there would be at the end of one year practically no lords of creation in existence, as one Canadian concern alone has a contract for supplying millions of ties annually to the transportation companies, and this is only a portion of what is required for keeping the roadbeds in repair. The railroad tie business is exceptionally active at the present time, and there is a steady demand for all kinds, owing to extensive construction work.

A warning note has been sounded by a British weekly recently. It brushes aside the popular rumor that a coal famine is approaching, and draws attention instead to the waning forests of the world. Barring Russia and Scandinavia, it point out, no European country has had timber enough for her own needs for a long time past. The United Kingdom has been spending over $25,000,000 a year for many years on imported timber, most of it coming from Norway and the United States. The latter, it continues, are rapidly coming to the end of their own resources. During the past thirty years they have cut over seven hundred thousand million feet. This is equivalent in weight to 1,400,000,000 tons, or enough to load 250,000 large steamers. Canada, it warns, is now becoming badly off. Pine has doubled in cost since the outbreak of the war, and its price is four times what it was ten years ago. Honduras, once considered a treasure house of tropical timber, is cut almost clear, while Cuba and San Domingo are in a similar plight. The only great forest remaining, this paper points out, is that of the Amazon, and much of that timber is quite inaccessible. Such being the world's condition in timber resources, it is up to the foresters and lumbermen of today to conserve and replant, and to protect their virgin forests. The inevitable result, otherwise, will be to do without.

There are always many solutions offered for every perplexing problem. Ask a dozen different men the cause of the present industrial unrest and labor disturbances and one will obtain a dozen different replies, everyone firmly convinced that his own analytical review of the situation is accurate. Plenty of theory and surmise exist in this world, but too little of the practical. One journal intimates that the present cause of unrest can be largely laid at the door of the demand for too much efficiency in the operation of industrial, commercial and business enterprises. Another attributes it to the spirit of Bolshevism, another to selfishness, and still another to a reaction of the strained relations and high tension prevailing during the war. Other exponents declare that the high cost of living, the avarice of landlords, the greed of gain on the part of capitalists, the offensiveness and vulgar display of the rich, not to speak of war profiteering, predatory wealth and other manifestations of the times, are the chief factors. In the colloquial expression of the present day "You pay your money and take your choice."

With the progress and development of the lumber industry it seems as if this important Canadian activity is being linked more closely each succeeding year with pulp and paper enterprises. The number of outstanding Canadian concerns who are devoting their attention to pulp and paper production is increasingly large and each season witnesses many of the most important lumber corporations branching out into the paper field, which is placing Canada on the map as one of the leading exporters in this great present-day commodity.

The total exports of pulp and paper from the Dominion during the last year reached the huge sum of one hundred million dollars, which is more than double of what the returns were two years ago. The more Canada becomes an exporting country, the more stability and permanence will be given to our Canadian institutions and the development of our own resources.

Previous to the war Canada was largely an importing country and the balance of trade was always on the wrong side. Any nation which becomes aggressive in the foreign field and goes out into the wider avenues of the world's domains and captures business, is able at all times to hold its own in industrial and national life.

A kind of almost limitless possibilities is of little potential worth unless its natural resources are developed. As the wilderness may be made to blossom like the rose, so a country may become prosperous. The one factor which spells development and prosperity is its people, says "Conservation of Life."

As its people are healthy, vigorous and happy, so in proportion is the national vitality enhanced. Upon the men and women of Canada rests the responsibility of making or inhibiting its future greatness.

The period of reconstruction is here. Each man and woman must realize now their duty as citizens and, having realized, must strive to their utmost to co-operate each with his neighbor, in making Canada the best in this western hemisphere.

The need is for good, clean, healthy men and women; therefore, be healthy. Strive your utmost to maintain the best of health. Make your home, your workshop, your office and the children's school healthy, not forgetting that the unit of the town or city is the home; and, as we each make our home and its environment healthy, we are each doing our bit to improve the health of the community in which we live and the country generally.

The great advance cannot be made certain without the co-operation of individuals. Make Canada's success a sure thing by joining in the effort at once and building and owning your own home.

The French Government advises that fully 1,500,000 acres of woodland were wiped out by the war in the north an east of that country. Much of this wood was used in trench, road and barracks building, while great portions were blasted to pieces by shells. Nearly 1,000,000 French people were dependent upon these forests for their livelihood six months in the year and the French Government now faces a great economic problem in providing them with other resources until the forests are restored.

One of the most rapidly developing industries in Canada is that of the pulp and paper. The exports of pulp, paper and pulpwood during the past fiscal year will exceed $100,000,000, nearly all of which went to the United States. While the development of the industry in Canada has been steady, there is not a little conjecture regarding how much more wonderful would have been the expansion, had not the Federal authorities stepped in to regulate and control the price of the finished product. For a long period it was a matter of speculation which would end first—the war or the newsprint investigation at Ottawa, and the war has won out. It seems there is a disposition now on the part of certain publishers interested to have the control of the industry adapted as a war measure, and continued indefinitely. The Canada Pulp and Paper Association, in a recent announcement sent out to the shareholders of pulp and paper companies, states that it is now nearly two and a half years since the federal paper commissioner was appointed, and the Ottawa authorities authorized him to conduct an investigation as to what should be a fair price for paper. That inquiry is still going on, and has cost the government $75,000, and laid a heavy burden upon the manufacturers. The Association points out that the newsprint producers are still compelled to sell their product in Canada below the market price, and that whatever justification existed during the war for the control of the paper industry, now no longer exists. It is further emphasized that the government should relinquish its control in order to allow this great national undertaking on the part of the Dominion to develop, and particularly to increase the export trade. No other industry in Canada is or has been subject to federal control. The agitation that is now being waged on the part of certain interests across the line to have the embargo lifted on the exportation of unmanufactured pulpwood from Crown lands, in Ontario, Quebec and New Brunswick, is not likely to succeed. Canada has the raw material and will see that it is converted into the finished product within her own domains.

Suggested Policy of the Navy League of Canada

1. To disseminate among the people of Canada a knowledge of the necessity and use of sea power as the keystone of Empire and National defence and commercial prosperity.
2. The advocacy of a policy that Canada shall assume her proper share of the cost and maintenance of protecting her own trade routes and coast defences.
3. The advocacy of a marine policy that will tend to build up our mercantile tonnage.
4. The advocacy of the establishment of a naval reserve force composed of Canadian officers and men who have served in either the Imperial or Canadian Naval forces.
5. The support of all just claims of officers and men of the Royal Canadian Navy and its auxiliaries with regard to pay and pensions, and that merchant officers and men in times of war be put on an equal footing with regard to pay and pensions with officers and men of the Royal Canadian Navy.
6. The support of sailors' institutes in Canadian ports to better the conditions of merchant seamen when ashore.
7. The application of steady pressure upon Parliament and the Government for a better and more efficient administration of the Department of Naval Service, and the abandonment of the present system of the portfolio of Marine, Fisheries and Naval Defence being under the Minister.
8. The application of steady pressure upon all people enjoying the Canadian franchise to see to it that our public men and Members of Parliament insist upon it that all matters pertaining to our maritime policy shall be free from political bias.
9. The encouragement and extension of Naval Colleges and of the Boys' Naval Brigade movement, and the establishment of proper training institutions, with a view to the preparation of boys and men for a seafaring career to the ultimate end that all Canadian ships shall be manned by British-born and the elimination of aliens from the Mercantile Marine.

What Quebec is Doing to Conserve its Timber

Perpetuation of Forests Strongly Advocated by Woodlands Section—Practical Suggestions on Logging, Slash Burning and Tree Planting

A brief summary of the recent meeting of the Woodlands section of the Canadian Pulp and Paper Association at Berthierville and Grand Mere, P. Q., was given in the last edition of the "Canada Lumberman." The following is a fuller report of the proceedings, which are of timely and practical interest to lumbermen, limit holders, pulp and paper manufacturers and others.

The meeting was a success, thanks to the arrangements made by Mr. A. L. Dawe and Mr. E. Beck, of the Canadian Pulp & Paper Association, and the co-operation of the Provincial Government and the Laurentide Company.

The committee of the section decided that afforestation should be the subject to be discussed, and in order to demonstrate what is being done from the practical end, visits to the Government nurseries at Berthierville, and to the Laurentide Co.'s nurseries at Proulx, were arranged. The visitors were able to see hundreds of thousands of trees of many varieties being raised from seed—later to be transplanted in the woods. Mr. G. C. Piche, the chief of the P. Q. forest service, was the guide at Berthierville, and Mr. Ellwood Wilson, forester of the Laurentide Co., at Proulx, both explaining the methods of raising the trees. The Government and the Laurentide Co., both explaining the methods of raising the trees. The Government and the Laurentide Co. entertained the members in good style.

On arrival at Berthierville, the members were entertained at luncheon, and after an inspection of the nurseries, a meeting was held, presided over by Mr. R. P. Kernan, who in discussing the question of afforestation—artificial and natural—said that there was no doubt that opinions as to the supposed unlimited extent of our forests had changed. Some were of opinion that under certain conditions the forest would take care of itself; but when they came to consider artificial reafforestation, the question arose who should pay for the work—the Government or the limit holders? It was essential that the cost should be reasonable—not only for this work, but for clearing up the land by slash burning."

Hon. Mr. Allard Outlines Work

Hon. Jules Allard, in reviewing the work of his department, referred to the establishment of the Berthierville nurseries and the school of forestry. This was done with a view to perpetuate the forests—and he claimed that the department had secured good results. They had endeavored to get rid of the fake settler, and had also taken measures to protect the forests from fires. In that connection he pointed out the growth of the co-operative societies for protecting the forests, and while he did not desire to criticize the methods in other provinces, he believed that the system by which the associations controlled the rangers, etc., was the best. The nurseries had this year furnished over 700,000 trees to companies and private individuals, and had raised altogether over three million trees, which had been sold at cost price. Discussing the stumpage dues, the Minister remarked that a limit holder had said that they were not high enough (laughter), an observation that would not be lost sight of when the next revision was made. He claimed that Quebec Provinee was, in matters connected with the forest, as far advanced as any other, the great idea being to maintain an asset of immense value to the people.

Scope of the Forest Service

Mr. G. C. Piche, chief forester of Quebec, delivered a thoughtful and instructive address on the history, operation and extent of the nurseries at Berthierville. In the course of his remarks he said:

It affords us a great pleasure to welcome your coming to the Government Nursery at Berthierville, as it shows the great interest which the lumbermen, and more particularly the members of the Canadian Pulp and Paper Association, are taking in the welfare of our forests. It means also that the ideas of reafforestation are receiving a public recognition of their value and, therefore, it eases my task to give you some information about the work that has been carried on here during the past ten years.

The nursery of Berthierville was established in 1908, by Hon. Mr. Turgeon, then Minister of Lands and Forests, in view of furnishing planting material to the private owners of waste lands, and to enable the Government to make objective and practical demonstrations in reafforestation. At the origin, it was a farm of 70 arpents, which had been abandoned for many years, with the result that the buildings and the land were in a very bad order; even the woodlot exhibited evident signs of mismanagement. The first years were devoted towards re-establishing order throughout the property, and to raise, on a small scale, forest trees seedlings. Consequently, on the 22nd of May, 1908, the first sowings were done, and, in the autumn, we found that the nursery contained a little over 200,000 plants, of which the white pine, the Scotch pine, the Norway spruce and the European larch formed the bulk. I must say that, at first, the neighbouring farmers were very skeptical about the success of our enterprise, but many of them began, during the second year, to admit that there was something in the idea which the Government had endeavored to propogate in the Province, and very soon the nursery was, and is still, the favorite spot where they bring their visitors to see the great curiosity, each spring.

To give to our forestry students a practical knowledge in reafforestation, it was arranged that they would work two months each spring at the nursery. We must congratulate each class of the Laval Forest School for the good qualities that they displayed during their stay here; indeed, it was very hard for these college boys to be put on the spade, to harrow, or to weed, under the burning sun, but they accepted their instructions cheerfully and worked ten hours per day, just as the ordinary laborers, faithfully and with great interest, and I must, in justice, attribute to them a good deal of the success that we have obtained so far.

It would have been impossible to carry on our programme which meant to increase the production more and more every year, in order to cope with the increasing demand for trees, if we had not obtained the continuous support and the encouragement of the present Minister of Lands and Forests, the Honorable Jules Allard, who, as you know, has helped so much to the development of a sound forest policy in this Province. It was he who obtained for us, each year, the necessary credits from the Government and, with the sinews of war, we were able to increase every year the areas under cultivation.

On the Shifting Sands of Lachute

In 1910, some of the seedlings were big enough to be shipped, and we started the reclamation of the shifting sands in the parish of Lachute. These shifting sands, as you are no doubt aware, are the result of poor methods of cultivation that have exhausted some of the farm lands in that section; gradually the grass cover began to disappear and the sand to show up, and very soon the wind caused the displacement of its particles. Every year things went from bad to worse till finally there was a dune of about 3½ miles in length, broadening in its middle to about one-half mile. The sand not only prevented any cultivation upon the area affected, but also invaded with persistance the adjoining farms so that the area of waste land was increasing year by year. The Government of the Province passed an agreement with seven owners to buy their land at $1.00 per acre, in order to reforest same, giving them the option to buy it back after 15 years for $10.00 an acre. We began our work by planting on the western edge of the sand dune, some 20,000 pines and spruces, with a few elms and ashes; these broad leaf trees were used exclusively for experimental purposes. The next year 50,000 more pines were set in to replace part of the treess that had died (about 20 per cent.), and also to increase the surface planted, which is now equal to 45 acres. To-day, the trees have not only maintained their hold on the pure sand, but have grown up to five feet in average—many are ten feet in height; the sand has been stopped from shifting, and a grassy vegetation is exhibiting itself here and there. The result is so satisfactory that the former owner of the land has assured us that he would buy back the land at the expiration of the contract. Similar work has been done at Berthier Junction, in recent years, and it will pay to visit this plantation before leaving here.

The same year we began shipments of trees in various lots to private individuals, colleges, etc., and we have continued this ever since.

In 1911, the Seignior of Perthuis ordered fifty thousand pine and spruce trees to be set near Notre-Dame-des-Anges, and every year since he has repeated his order for about the same quantity. I have just received a report of these plantations and the white pine trees thereon show a fine growth. According to all those who have seen

Members of the Woodlands Section, Canadian Pulp and Paper Association, photographed on steps of Laurentide Inn at Grand Mere, Que.

these plantations they are a real success and a good example to follow.

Shipped Over 3,000,000 Plants

I believe it was in 1912 that we received our first order from the Laurentide Company, and it is a great pleasure for us to thank the authorities of this progressive society, with our other patrons, for their continuous and generous encouragement. And since, we have received orders from every section of the Province, even from the Province of Ontario, with the result that since the creation of the nursery we have shipped over three million plants.

At the present time the stock of trees in the nursery exceeds four million plants, and, we are preparing ourselves to be in a position to ship every year from two to three million plants, as we believe the demands will not only reach this amount, but will most likely exceed it before long. As a consequence of this undertaking of the government, similar nurseries have been established by the limit holders.

With a few exceptions, all the seeds used at the nursery have been purchased either in America or in Europe, but we would like very much to be able to use the indigenous seeds as they offer us, as you know, greater chances of success.

Therefore I will take advantage of the fact that so many of the limit holders are gathered here to ask for their co-operation in this matter. Gentlemen, we would like to obtain each year from the various parts of the Province a sufficient supply of the seeds of our white and red pine, of our spruce, hemlock, cedar, white and yellow birch. I will ask all those who wish to help us in this matter to give me their names and I will arrange with them for a plan to gather the tree seeds at the right moment, i.e., when they are matured. We will obtain, by this co-operation, not only better seed, but also cheaper seed. It is our ambition to produce, at this nursery, all the seed needed, not only for our work, but also for the other nurseries in the province, and to meet this purpose we intend to build, in the near future, a large seed house, where we would extract the seeds collected after the most modern methods.

The Intensive Production of Plants

Having attained this object, we could then realize our second aim, which is to produce not only two or three million plants per year, but ten to twenty million plants, if needed, in the Province, and I think that before long we may be planting more than that. This intensive production of plants would greatly diminish the cost price, and I calculate that if we could produce here ten million plants per year, we would be in position to sell them, after caring them for two years, for $1.50 per thousand, whereas we are now asking from three to five dollars per thousand for the same material. These young plants could be transplanted on the various flying nurseries that would be established in the neighborhood of the lands to be reforested, so that they would be acclimatized before the final setting.

During your visit to the nursery, you will see many trees of foreign origin; for example, you will come across the Scotch pine, which will appear to you as a sturdy tree. In fact it gives us great hopes for the reforestation of our waste lands. The Norway spruce, though not always as good as our native white spruce, will also give excellent results, as it grows fairly well. The European and the Japanese larchs will certainly interest you, as they appear to be more immune from the attacks of the large saw fly that annihilated our tamarac some thirty years ago. These foreign trees have been tried and we can recommend them to the planters. We have also extended this research to most of the forest trees growing under the same climatic conditions as we have studied also the bull pine of the Rockies, the black pine of Austria, which is excellent for the plantation on limy soil, the Englemann spruce and the blue spruce of Colorado have been found to be of more value for ornamental purposes than for reforestation; the Douglas fir does not appear yet to be acclimatized enough to our conditions to justify its plantation extensively, yet we have found it to be hardy in some cases, and should this experiment come to a good conclusion I think the nursery will have achieved very much, as it is a first-class tree.

We have also endeavored to produce trees for ornamental purposes. As you are aware the building of the national highways in the Province will necessitate a great amount of plantations, and we expect to have some some ten thousand trees to devote, per year, to this purpose. Everywhere, people desire more and more to beautify the surrounding of their property by the plantation of hedges and trees, and during your travelling from the station to here you will notice that many farmers have called upon us to secure a few trees which we have gladly given them.

The railway companies have also been on the market of late, and we have sold to the Canadian Pacific Railway, the Temiskaming and Northern Ontario Railway, the Canadian Northern railway, many thousand trees for the beautifying of the stations, the holding of the railway banks, etc.

The Arboretum and the Woodlot

Next to the nursery you will come to the arboretum, which has an area of some five acres. It is located between the nursery and the woodlot. It may be interesting to you to learn that ten years ago this land was pastured and covered only with a meagre grass. By preventing the grazing we have allowed the forest to re-establish itself solidly on the eastern half, and you will find there some grey birch of about twenty feet in height with a diameter of three inches. Here and there, we have made plantations of several foreign trees, in order to study their development under these conditions.

Coming to the woodlot, you will find a good example of what could be done similarly by each farmer in this province. Its area is close to twenty-five acres; it rests on a soil formed by a coarse sand of the poorest quality; yet you will find the trees to be in good health, tall, and of a fair size. The composition of the stand is also interesting, as almost each species growing in the Province is represented. In the first half, we have aimed to develop a mixture of maple and white pine, favoring, however, the production of white pine. The other half is devoted to the best trees as they appear.

This woodlot was divided into eight compartments of equal size, and contains 4139 hardwood, 1,228 softwood trees, with a total volume of over 500,000 feet board measure. Two excellent roads, made by the students, divide the property equally. Each tree measuring four inches and up was calipered and numbered, last year, and record is kept of its healthy condition. We expect to continue these measurements every two or three years, so as to judge of the progress and increases in the growth. Each tree that is removed during the year for sylvicultural purposes is calipered and scaled, so that we prepare a volume table.

Already one quarter of the forest has been culled under a rigid system of sylviculture, and you will see that the forest does not appear to be in a bad state, though the cutting on one compartment yielded seventy-two cords of firewood and two thousand five hundred feet of sawlogs: the whole being valued at eighty-four dollars. These operations will not only increase the value of the stand by the selection made of the best species and of the best trees, but the growth will also be increased and stimulated by the treatment.

We believe that this study will prove of great value to the farmers and we intend to publish the results of this experiment very soon.

Progressive Forestry Policy Advocated

Having briefly described the work done at the nursery, we must now consider the question of a progressive policy of reafforestation for this Province. It is rather surprising that in a country as rich in forests as our province, it is already necessary to discuss this question, but those who have travelled somewhat throughout the country have been surprised to see how quickly the forest has disappeared from the shores of the St. Lawrence and also how the cost of lumber and pulpwood has always been on the increase. First of all we must say that the plantations require so many decades to produce results that it will prevent many persons from investing part of their money in this operation. Yet in Europe many of the old families have retained their rank through the revenues that they derive in the management of forests planted by their ancestors.

There is no reason why farmers, large corporations, the towns and the Government should not consider this matter in a broad view. There is no use in hiding the truth: there are in this province millions of acres of land that have been impoverished either by improper cultivation or by wasteful lumbering, whilst others have been ruined by repeated fires. According to the census reports there would be about three million acres of such lands owned by private people here that would require immediate reforestation. It is certain that upon the timber limits there is also a certain quantity, but as we have no definite survey of same we can only say that its area is very large, perhaps equivalent to that of the private lands.

Why Should We Plant the Waste Lands?

The reason that would induce us to plant the lands not fit for cultivation would be the following:

1. To establish a forest cover on these lands so that they may be again put into value and rendered productive of revenue.
2. To prevent, as in the case of shifting sands, the devastation of the adjoining lands.
3. To increase the amount of timber per acre in the woodlots or timber limits. The studies made of cut over lands show that in numerous sections the stock left is very low, and if we consider the forest as a capital it will naturally take many years before the compound interest accruing each year by the annual growth of the tree will form a sufficient amount of timber to pay the expenses of lumbering the tract a second time.
4. It will be necessary, in many cases, to introduce new species in the forest, especially in the glades, which will increase its wealth.
5. To protect the headwater of streams. It is a well known fact that the forest has a great power to retain the moisture and regulate thereby the seepage.
6. To shelter the basin of the water works. It is not necessary for me to insist upon the good qualities of the water that is found in the gentle streams shadowed by trees in comparison to the poor water found in the ugly brooks running in the open.
7. To furnish the necessary supply of timber for the farmers, and also for lumbermen or paper makers. The increased development of the lumbering industries, especially that of pulp and paper mills, has produced such a big demand upon the forest that we can see, within a relatively short time, some of the companies having either to reduce their production or to purchase new timber holdings. Owing to the enormous amount of capital invested, the interested must necessarily seek for a continuous supply of their raw material.
8. The ownership of waste lands by a private owner is such a burden that, too often, they are abandoned and fall to the charge of the rural municipality, whereas if they were stocked with trees they would have a suffiicent future value to induce the owner to pay his taxes.

Does it Pay to Replant ?

There has not yet been a complete survey made of the plantations executed in Canada, as many of these plantations are either too young or of too small a size, or made exclusively for experimental purposes. Therefore we are compelled to seek our information. however, from the studies made here upon the growth of trees in height and diameter, we can see that the results recorded elsewhere will certainly be obtained in this country. The State of Massachusetts has published a booklet entitled "The Older Plantations in the Commonwealth of Massachusetts," in which you will find information that will please anyone interested in the matter. For example, a plantation made by John Tingwick of white and Scotch pines, has produced in thirty-eight years from 10,000 to 17,000 feet per acre. Those made fifty-five years ago, on the property ning from 6 to 17 inches in diameter, and the yield was estimated at 43,000 feet per acre. As you see these results are very good; the tabulation of all these various inventories has enabled the Forest Service of that State to publish an estimate of the future production of white pine, and we find that same, on an average quality of soil, will be as follows:

At the end of 25 years, 32,800 feet board measure.
At the end of 50 years, 46,500 feet board measure.
At the end of 60 years, 53,200 feet board measure.

The Financial Returns Outlined

It will be interesting to know what will be the financial return of this investment, and a good forester could not induce anyone to plant without saying what will be the ultimate results of the work. In the above cases the forester has first taken into account the value of the land, calculated at four dollars per acre, and which naturally must pay a rental; then come the expenses of planting, which were estimated at seven dollars per acre; the taxes must be paid as well as the annual charges of maintenance and protection against fires. Then, all the money spent at the start and afterwards must necessarily pay a rate of interest which was calculated at five per cent. We find that, after deducting all these expenses from the gross returns of the sale of the timber produced, the plantations would give the following net profit:

At the end of 30 years, $24.85 per acre.
At the end of 40 years, $102.57 per acre.
At the end of 50 years, $248.50 per acre.
At the end of 60 years, $90.17 per acre.

But if the rate of interest was 6 per cent., instead of five, the financial returns would be as follows:

After 30 years, a loss of $4,44 per acre.
After 40 years, a profit of $15.76 per acre.
After 50 years a profit of $151.97 per acre.
After 60 years, a loss of $114.30 per acre.

It will be seen by all these examples that the best time to cut a white pine plantation would be when it has reached the age of about fifty years, that is when the annual increment in volume will begin to diminish.

The Reproduction of Spruce Plantation

Of course, the pulp and paper makers are more interested in the question of spruce plantations. Here I must say that we have no positive American data on this subject, and must use the European figures, which are also very satisfactory. We find that, on an average quality of soil and locality, a spruce plantation may produce the following quantities of timber. Taking all the material over three inches in diameter at the small end:

At the end of 30 years, 6,700 feet b.m. or 11 cords per acre.
At the end of 40 years, 21,600 feet b.m. or 35 cords per acre.
At the end of 50 years, 36,700 feet b.m. or 61 cords per acre.
At the end of 60 years, 50,600 feet b.m. or 88 cords per acre.

In admitting that these figures could not yet be obtainable in this Province, we can, by reducing them to, say, one third, arrive at good conclusions, as:

After 20 years the stand would furnish 7 cords per acre.
After 40 years the stand would furnish 20 cords per acre.
After 50 years the stand would furnish 36 cords per acre.
After 60 years the stand would furnish 50 cords per acre.

Those who had the chance to see the national forests of France and Germany will admit that these figures are not exaggerated because every spot of these forests is devoted entirely to the production of trees, and of good trees, whereas in this country the good trees will only form, too often, an insignificant proportion of the stand, the remainder being occupied by swamps, inferior species or blanks.

It would be, therefore, of capital importance for the future operators to be assured that, instead of culling, as we do now, from four to ten cords per acre, they could find from twenty-five to fifty cords after an interval of thirty to fifty years. I need not insist upon the effect that such a yield per acre would have on the cost price of lumber; and also on the value of the forest property.

Who Must Do the Reforestation ?

A subject of vital interest is "who will do the reforestation?" Owing to the fact that no practical returns can be expected before at least, thirty years after the plantation, it requires, therefore, continuity, or almost permanency in the possession of the property to be reforested. The problem is easily solved as regards the private lands: it will be a sound and profitable investment for the farmer, the towns and the corporations owning some private lands not fit for cultivation, to go into this business as they will do a national work and also create an excellent and steady source of revenue for themselves.

But when we come to the question of reforesting the timberlands leased from the government, the problem is more complex. Though

I have studied it for a long while I have not yet come to a satisfactory conclusion. Will it be better for the Government to do this work exclusively, or should they rather allow or compel the limit holder to make it for and by himself, or should both co-operate in the planting? The later alternative may be the more logical since the Government owns the soil and keeps the tilte of the property; it might then furnish all the planting material required, and also the technical direction to do the work, whereas the limit holder would defray the expenses of replanting. Someone has raised the important question "Would the limit holder continue to pay the ground rent on the parts of his limits that have been reforested? I think he should continue to do so, if he wants to retain his lease, but I believe that his share of expense, that is the cost of planting, should be kept separated and returned to him as a deduction on stumpage charges either at the moment of the plantation or with the accrued interest of, say, three or four per cent., when the trees planted will have reached maturity. This plan is not altogether satisfactory to me, and I just present it as a basis for discussion rather than as a remedy for the difficulty.

Measures to Promote Reforestation

The first measure to adopt for the welfare of the plantations is unquestionably to give them a satisfactory protection against fires. It would be ridiculous to make a plantation on a tract that would not be easily reached and defended against forest fires. We must carry on further the policy of protection against forest fires. We have already done a good deal in that direction, but we find that much of our forests is still vanishing away in smoke, and this spring we have had several big fires in the Lake St. John and the St. Maurice districts, most of them being caused directly by the railways. Nobody can dispute that fact as we have secured complete evidence in each case establishing that the railway engines have been the cause of two large fires, one at Vandry and the other at Timbrell on the Transcontinental Railway. I firmly believe that we cannot allow our forest wealth to be depleted in such a manner, and the time has come to compel each engine travelling thorugh a forested district to burn something different from coal or wood.

We have water powers in abundance and we should study the electrifying of the railways in the forested regions. Someone will say that this may be too expensive, but it will be less expensive than the burning of fifty square miles of timber limits per year, and, besides, we will be thereby developing our natuarl resources and diminishing at the same time our dependency for coal upon our neighbors. If we cannot electrify the locomotives, we should have them burn oil, as is done in the Adirondacks and as was done, with success, by the contractors who built the Gouin dam. Anyhow, the railways wil have to burn something else than coal or wood, and I hope the Pulp and Paper Association will support any movement in this direction. Many fires may be attributed to the poachers, the fishermen and hunters. Nobody should be allowed to roam at will in the forest. We should make it a close property and oblige everyone to have a permit before entering. More preventive, effective organization should be made. It is much easier to prevent an ill than to cure it, and this is specially true of forest fires. We should have more patrols, telephone lines connecting all depots, etc.

To facilitate the work of the hydroplane service which is being inaugurated, we should establish, in connection with the Geodetic Survey more lookout stations.

Much has been done by the different protective associations, which are doing splendidly, but we must complete our protective service so that the fire danger will be eliminated totally; then we can plant but not before.

In regard to private lands, an important point is that of the taxes. The valuation of the properties reforested should not be modified after trees have been set, as it has been done. A law should be enacted, as early as posisble, to protect the citizens who have the courage to reforest against the unjust raising of the land valuation and, thereby, of their taxes. I contend that, for, at least, thirty years, the first valuation of the land planted should not be modified. The appraisal could take place to determine then the actual value of the forest crop separately from that of the soil and this valuation should stand for one decade at least. The ideal would be to repeat these appraisals at intervals of ten years, after the first period has elapsed. We must encourage the work and not prevent foolishly and unjustly the beneficial action of the reforesters.

Control Over Woodworking Plants

I think the time has come for the Government to exercise a full control over the wood working establishments in this Province, as we find, too often, sawmills being located in a locality where there is not enough wood to justify their appearance. Naturally the mill owner, to obtain his raw material, must get it at the expense of the adjoining limits, and this is the beginning of the timber speculation from which we have suffered so much. All the wood working establishments in the province should be licensed and compelled each year to obtain a permit to operate. The Government will then be in a position to determine if they have enough timber lands to justify their operating and to prevent enlargements when there is no supply in sight.

Up to the present we have found the lumbermen of this province ready to co-operate heartily with the Government in all the reforms made by the administration. Our province can boast, with justice, of having made great progress through this co-operation. Now that the lumber industry in this province is in a rather stable state of equilibrium we can look ahead and adopt a definite policy of reforestation and of management of our forests. We should cause those who waste their forest through bad lumbering to replant their holdings at their expense, while those who have done all they could to timber correctly should be helped to the fullest extent. We should endeavor to make every acre of waste land and of timber land produce the fullest quantity of timber possible. We can make this province the largest timber producer in the world, not only in lumber but also in pulp and paper products, and I am sure that with the spirit, the energy, and the co-operation of all we will realize our ambition.

Robt. P. Kernan,
Chairman of the Woodlands Section

Ellwood Wilson,
Director of the Woodlands Section

Necessity of Destroying the Slash

Mr. Ellwood Wilson declared that they knew very little about artificial or natural regenaration, but they were gradually gaining knowledge. He was firmly convinced that this work must be carried on if the productivity of the forests was to be maintained. He also felt very strongly on the question of destroying the slash. A recent fire which covered 20 square miles, was over an area piled wtih logging debris, and it was impossible to cope with a fire under such conditions. The cost of fighting these fires and the waste that occurred was a gerat deal more than the cost of burning the slash. Even should the cost be heavy, it would be borne by the ultimate consumer of the lumber. As to natural reafforestation, he was of opinion that it could not be secured unless there was a change in the system of lumbering. It was an exploded idea that the companies could go back to the woods and cut fresh lumber after a period of 25 years. He was in favor of the total removal of the diameter limit regulation, and would cut certain areas absolutely clean. Mr. Wilson suggested that the question of slash disposal be taken up at once. The cost was a matter of efficiency, for if the employees understood that the work was to be thoroughly done, the cost would be small.

Mr W. Gerard Power of St. Pacome, agreed with Mr. Wilson as to the urgency of dealing with the slash question. If the Government would amend their regulations as to clean cutting, slash disposal was comparatively easy.

Mr. T. W. Reed described some of the methods in the U. S. for disposing of slash. He also said that in New Hampshire their experience in cutting spruce was that there they cut to diameter, a large number of the smaller trees were subsequently blown down.

After the meeting the members proceeded by train to Three Rivers, and from there to Grand Mere, sleeping on the train.

The Visit to Laurentide Operations

The following morning, after breakfast in the Laurentide Inn of the Laurentide Co., the delegates inspected the Proulx Nurseries of the company. From there they went to Lac a Tortue, where they were entertained at luncheon by the company. Lieut. S. Graham then gave a demonstration in one of the hydroplanes loaned to the St. Maurice Forest Protective Association for the purpose of reporting fires.

At a subsequent meeting the following resolution was passed:

"That in the opinion of this meeting certain changes in the regulations of lands and forests, governing the cutting of timber on Crown lands, are essential to the preservation and perpetuation of the forests, and it respectfully requests that the executive committee of the Canadian Pulp & Paper Association appoint a committee to co-operate with the existing committee of the Province of Quebec Limit Holders' Association in waiting upon the Government with a view to urging upon it the necessity of an early revision of these regulations to meet present-day conditions."

Another resolution expressed thanks to the Province of Quebec Government and the Hon. Jules Allard for their invaluable work in organizing the preservation and perpetuation of the forests; further,

The hydroplane loaned to the St. Maurice Forest Protective Association for fire patrol work

that in view of the vital value of this organization in the interests of the future welfare of the Province, it was urged that the Government should preserve its present status, in order to ensure the various developments being brought to a satisfactory conclusion.

Votes of thanks were passed to the Provincial Government, Mr. Allard, Mr. Piche, the Laurentide Co., and Mr. Ellwood Wilson for their hospitality and work in connection with the meeting.

Mr. Allard and Mr. Wilson briefly replied.

A Most Representative Gathering

Among those who attended were Hon Jules Allard, Minister of Lands and Forests, Quebec; Messrs. W. G. Power, president of the Canadian Lumbermen's Association, St. Pacome; R. P. Kernan, Donnacona Paper Co., Quebec; P. G. Owen, Quebec, Timber Limit Holders' Association, Quebec; J. M. Dalton, St. Maurice Paper Co., Three Rivers; D. G. A. Galarneau, Three Rivers; H. T. Ham, St. Maurice Paper Co., Three Rivers; S. Beaudoin, St. Emelie; B. C. McLaren, St. Michel des Saints; Louis Marcil, St. Michel des Saints; T. E. Mack, La Tuque; J. A. Roussau, St. Anne de Perade; T. A. Tremblay, Quebec; G. E. Pelletier, Riviere Manie; Rockett Power, Rivere Manie; F. Demers, St. Pacome; J. H. Page, La Tuque; J. D. Brule, Val Brilliant; J. S. Rouleau, Matane; E. S. Coleman, St. Maurice Paper Co., Montreal; J. M. Swaine, Ottawa; H. S. Fleming, Ottawa; W. Little, Montreal; Ben Deacon, Laurentide Co., Grand Mere; R. W. Craig, Ottawa; J. P. MacLaurin, St. Maurice Paper Co., Montreal; H. Sorgius, St. Maurice Forest Protective Association, Three Rivers; R. Liagre, Van Bruyssel; G. G. Blyth, Dominion Parks Branch, Ottawa; S. W. Carter, Laurentide Co., Grand Mere; P. W. Buchanan, Brompton Pulp & Paper Co., East Angus; L. H. Prince, N.B. Forest Service; G. Roy, Mont Joli; H. E. Howe, Belgo-Canadian Pulp & Paper Co., Shawinigan; C. Burrill, Riverside Manufacturing Co., Three Rivers; R. H. Campbell, Director of Forestry, Ottawa; A. McLaurin, St. Maurice Paper Co., Montreal; J. D. Valiquette, St. Laurent; T. E. Draper, Riordon Pulp & Paper Co., St. Jovite; A. J. Ferguson, J. R. Booth, Ottawa; G. E. Loranger, Three Rivers; F. J. Ritchie, Wayagamack Pulp & Paper Co., Three Rivers; T. W. Reed, U. S. Forest Service; H. Kieffer, Montreal; B. F. Avery, Spanish River Pulp Co; Sanche, Abitibi Co.; Ellwood Wilson, Laurentide Co., Grand Mere; G. C. Piche, chief Forester, Province of Quebec; Anderson, Canada Paper Mills, Windsor Mills; R. O. Sweezy, Montreal; J. Stadler, Belgo-Canadian Pulp & Paper Co., Shawinigan, and others.

One of the largest evergreen orders in the history of the nursery trade was recently shipped to a northern lumber company for reforestation of the concern's cut-over lands. The shipment consisted of 1,500,000 Norway spruce trees, enough to line a 280-mile road, as from Chicago to St. Louis, if planted only one foot apart. The nursery company kept a gang of more than 50 men at work on this order for two weeks, digging, counting, and packing.

Maj. Brechin Outlines His New Work

British Columbia Lumber Commissioner Intends Opening Forest Products Show Room in Toronto

Major James Brechin, of Victoria, who has been appointed British Columbia Lumber Commissioner for Ontario, as announced recently in the "Canada Lumberman," is still occupying his temporary office at 409 Kent Bldg., Toronto. He is, however, looking for another location where he can have a permanent show-room displaying various forest products of the Pacific Coast province.

Major Brechin has already met a large number of architects, contractors, carpenters, retail and wholesale lumbermen. His mission to the east is solely in the interests of making the merits and qualities of British Columbia stock more widely known and to give definite information and advice regarding the character of coast and mountain woods and the different purposes for which they are best adapted. He will conduct no sales, directly or indirectly, and all the firms requiring Pacific Coast wood goods will place their business through regular wholesale or retail channels, as in the past. Considerable literature will, of course, be distributed and some extensive advertising done. This part of the work will be looked after by Mr. Wm. Turnbull, of Victoria, who is a former widely known newspaper man. Mr. Turnbull is expected in the east in a few days in the interest of a propaganda program.

Major Brechin is of direct Scotch decent, being born near Dundee, and after completing his education at St. Andrew's University, came to Canada nineteen years ago. After spending a short time in various towns in the west, he finally located in Kitchener, B. C., where he engaged in the contracting business, taking out telephone poles, fence posts, etc. He next entered the bridge and building department of the C. P. R. and was in this service for three years, after which he joined the staff of the King Lumber Co., at Cranbrook, B. C., being head accountant for five years and later occupied the responsible post of assistant manager for another five years.

Major Brechin has always taken a deep interest in military matters and enlisted in March, 1916, for overseas service, having raised in Cranbrook "B" Company, 225th B. C. Infantry. Although holding the rank of captain, the subject of this reference reverted to a lieutenancy in order to get to France and take part in the fray. He crossed the English channel in April, 1917, with the 102nd Canadians and participated in the scrapping round Vimy Ridge. Some three months later, while doing outpost work in the trenches he and a sergeant who was with him were blown up by a high explosive. On being invalided out, Major Brechin was posted to the Canadian Forestry Corps and put in charge of one of the companies, getting out timber for army huts. He was given the rank of captain and later had supervision of the aeroplane spruce operations in France near the border of Switzerland. He was then given his Majority and was in full command of this work until he left France on Feb, 10th to return to Canada in April last. Shortly after he was offered by the Department of Lands the position of British Columbia Lumber Commissioner for the East and is doing much the same work as was undertaken by L. B. Beale, (now one of his Majesty's Trade Commissioners in Winnipeg) a couple of years ago. Major Brechin's mission is to develop trade and increase the interest and demand for British Columbia products in the east.

Charter Granted McGibbon Lumber Co.

The McGibbon Lumber Co., Limited, of Penetanguishene, Ont., has been incorporated with a capital stock of $100,000 to conduct the business of timber merchants, sawmill proprietors and timber growers, as well as to carry on operations as ship owners, dealers in wood and builders' supplies, etc. The incorporators are Chas. Archibald McGibbon, Finlay T. McGibbon, Norman C. McGibbon and David D. McGibbon, lumbermen, of Penetanguishene. It will be remembered that Charles McGibbon, head of the company, passed away suddenly on March 22nd last at Glenwood Springs, Colorado, while en-route to visit his son, Lieut. Finlay T. McGibbon, of the McGibbon-Hodgson Lumber Co., Vancouver.

Douglas fir forests are to furnish the seeds for reforesting the denuded areas of France. In working out a plan for reforestation the French Government considered numerous species of trees but finally selected Douglas fir which is known in France as it is in this country as "America's most important wood." It is believed that the soil and climate of France are suitable to the rapid growth and development of Douglas fir forests.

Begins Work on Timber Survey in Ontario

Roland D. Craig of Commission of Conservation Outlines the Plan of Operation—What the Inventory Will Show and Its Great Worth to the Province

Roland D. Craig, Ottawa
Who is conducting the timber survey of Ontario

Roland D. Craig of the Commission of Conservation, Ottawa, who recently completed a valuable and comprehensive survey of forest resources of British Columbia is, as has already been announced in the columns of the "Canada Lumberman," now engaged in similar work in Ontario.

The wisdom and necessity of taking inventories of the wooded wealth of the various provinces of the Dominion has long been recognized, but up until the last few years many Canadians believing that the forest assets of the Dominion were practically inexhaustible and that the supply, like Tennyson's book, would "go on forever," suddenly began to waken up and become conscious that the former cherished hope was both illusive and dangerous. The average citizen in this connection is like the ordinary adult, who refused to admit, in spite of premonitory symptoms, that he is growing old but gets up some morning to find by a sudden visitation of disease, or other weakness, that he is nearing the final lap of his journey; then recuperative methods are resorted to and every effort put forth to prolong his length of days.

What is true of the individual in this regard is now finding expression in the attitude and policy of Canadians toward the timber possessions of the Dominion.

Belated as has been the start made in this direction, it is gratifying to learn that commendable progress is being made. Not only will Canada know when the task is completed where she is at, so far as sylvan appraisal is concerned, but she will know what stock she has on hand, what future crops can be looked for and by what means reproduction can best be secured and the productivity of the forests sustained.

Mr. Craig who is charge of the work of making a survey of the resources of Ontario—which will occupy about three years—brings to bear upon his task a wide knowledge of the subject in hand.

Has Good Grasp of the Work

He will be calling upon leading limit holders of Ontario and doubtless will be accorded a warm welcome. Since he is working under the direction of a federal body of a non-political and purely investigative character, and one that has wrought much for the advancement and conservation of the resources of Canada the purpose of his mission is worthy of hearty support. The Ontario Government has assured the Commission of Conservation of the fullest measure of sympathy and co-operation. It may be stated that all figures or other information of confidential nature which may be given to the Commission will be treated as such and will be used only for the purpose of enumeration and in arriving at the desired results.

Mr. Craig, who is an Ontario boy, was born in Ailsa Craig and after spending a few years in that town, his parents moved to Guelph where he attended the Collegiate Institute and took a course in the Ontario Agricultural College, graduating with the degree of B. S. A. This was in 1898. After being on the staff of that institution a couple of years he left for Cornell University where he was awarded the degree of Forest Engineer. In 1903-4 he was engaged with the U. S. Forest Service in California; returning to Canada he became identified with the Dominion Forestry Branch and spent three years as inspector of forest reserves; in 1907 he was offered an attractive connection in the West and left Ottawa to take up his residence in Vancouver, where he was managing-director of the Adams-Powell Timber Company for three years and for the succeeding five was with the Dominion Lumber & Timber Company. In 1915 he joined the Commission of Conservation, being engaged for two years in making a survey of the forests of the Pacific Coast province. While pursuing this work he was requested by the Imperial Minister of Munitions to undertake the inspection the areoplane spruce lumber and until the operation terminated he occupied the position of district inspector. Since then he has been laboring for the Commission of Conservation on the forest survey of Ontario.

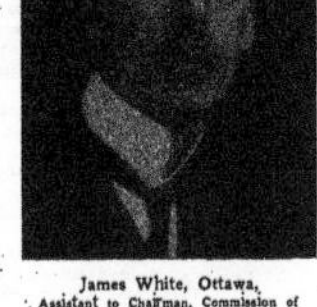

James White, Ottawa,
Assistant to Chairman, Commission of Conservation

In undertaking this task the province will be divided into five large drainage areas. These will consist of the southern portion of Ontario; the Ottawa Valley; the Georgian Bay district; the Lake Superior region and the north. The survey when completed, will not only furnish a reliable estimate of the present amount standing timber in the province, its location, distribution of species etc., but data and maps will be supplied showing the area covered by the forests, the area suitable for agriculture, the waste land and the areas which should be devoted to the production of forests.

This basic information, which has never before been available, will afford some concrete facts relating to the timber resources of Ontario. It may be stated that no attempt will be made to cruise the whole province—since a large proportion of the merchantable timber is in private holdings, for which the holders have detailed cruises—but reconnaisance work will be undertaken to supplement the detailed data which is available. There is no intention, however, to duplicate work that has already been carried out by private interests. The lumbermen of the west, Mr. Craig says, were extremely considerate and helpful, and there is no doubt but that the same degree of courtesy and assistance will be extended by the limit holders and saw mill operators in Ontario.

Mr. Craig is the gentleman whose portrait appears on the left in this article. It is true that this likeness was used in the last edition of the "Canada Lumberman" but through an error the name of Mr. James White, of Ottawa, Assistant to the Chairman of the Commission of Conservation, appeared below the picture. However, no unpleasant complications have followed, as both Mr. White and Mr. Craig are working for the highest and best interests of Canada in conducting the important enterprise in hand. This is not the first time, either on the street or in the press, that one good man has been mistaken for another. On the right is a photograph of Mr. White.

Mr. Craig will be visiting the leading wooded centres of Ontario and calling personally upon the lumbermen of the province during the coming months in the timely and important mission that he is undertaking under the direction of the Commission of Conservation.

New Eastern Sawmill Begins Operations

The new sawmill at Newcastle, N. B., built by James Robinson, of Millerton, began operations a short time ago, and for the first day's work produced forty thousand feet of lumber without mishap or any delays due to necessary alterations or readjustments and has been successfully operating since. The structure itself is 200 feet long by 60 feet wide, two stories high with a smaller plan third floor for filing room. It is a band mill with Yeats resaw, twin edgers, slash-ers, cut off saws, box board machine, and lath machine with a system of live rolls to distribute the manufactured lumber to all parts of the piling yard. The equipment is driven by two 150 horse power engines which make it a direct drive mill throughout. The capacity of the plant is seventy-five thousand superficial feet for each shift. The construction work was done by James Sullivan, of Newcastle, N. B., who remains in Mr. Robinson's employ as operating superintendent.

Standardization of Lumber and Mouldings

Representative Gathering Endorses Uniform Sizes and General Plan for Grading— Progressive Step Taken on Basis of Manufacture on New Lines.

The first American Lumber Congress, held some months ago, in Chicago, Ill., adopted a resolution that there should be uniformity of sizes in all lumber and mouldings manufactured in the United States, and that for the accomplishment of this purpose the Secretary-Manager of the National Lumber Manufacturers' Association, be requested to call a meeting of the proper representatives of all associations represented in the Congress at Chicago.

In compliance with this resolution representatives of lumber associations, manufacturers, wholesalers, retailers, architects, engineers, etc., met lately in Chicago, to discuss the points involved. Dr. Wilson Compton, Secretary-Manager of the National Lumber Manufacturers' Association, called the assembly to order and introduced Mr. William E. Tuttle, of Westfield, New Jersey, who acted as Chairman.

The discussion was divided into the following topics:

Need of standardization of sizes, grades and forms, by the manufacturer, as well as the consumer.

Confusion in the present nomenclature used in grading rules and by the industry.

Arrangement and order of presentation of articles in a standard form of specification.

A basis of standard lumber sizes among all manufacturers which will meet the need of the consumer, as well as the condition of manufacture and marketing as experienced by the producer.

A general plan of procedure for standardization of grades of lumber, which will place, if possible, material of equal or similar quality under a definite and common term, with clearly stated exceptions where needed.

Standard moulding forms which will elminiate multiplicity in designs having small differences in contour.

Standard grades for wood shingles.

Uniformity is the Watchword

As a result of the discussion on the points named above, the following resolutions were adopted by the conference:

Whereas: There is at present no uniform nomenclature for the different grades in the separate species of woods used in the building and other industries, and

Whereas: This condition is the cause of confusion and loss to the trade and to the public. Be it therefore

Resolved: That this meeting earnestly recommends, and pledges its best efforts to bring about uniformity in the various grades and names of grades in the separate species of woods, and be it further

Resolved: That the manufacturers and wholesale dealers in white pine, yellow pine, hemlock, fir, spruce and all other woods be urged to adopt for their separate woods, uniform grades and names of grades, and that these grades be made uniform for all woods, so far as practicable.

The Standardization of Grades

Resolved, that, approving the idea of uniform size, both in width and thickness, the question of uniform size of lumber be submitted to the Engineering Bureau of the National Lumber Manufacturers' Association, and that after a careful investigation they submit their conclusions to both retailers and manufacturers and to all those represented at this meeting and others interested.

Resolved, that the Engineering Bureau of the National Lumber Manufacturers' Association be requested in consultation with the wholesalers, manufacturers, retailers, architects, engineers, Forest Products Laboratory and other people and organizations interested, to prepare a plan for grading lumber which will include the names of grades, definitions of grades, definitions of defects, sizes, patterns of mouldings and submit it with complete arguments to the various manufacturing associations.

Resolved, that the question of the most logical form and arrangement of the general classification of data now common to all grading rules, be referred to the Engineering Bureau of the National Lumber Manufacturers' Association for study and recommendation to the various associations issuing such rules.

Standard Moulding Forms

Resolved, that the National Lumber Manufacturers' Association be instructed to prepare standards for mouldings and wood forms. The work to be supervised by a committee comprised of representatives of the lumber manufacturers associations, Wholesale Sash and Door Associations and American Institute of Architects. Templates of forms thus standardized to be prepared by the National Lumber Manufacturers' Association, for distribution to the manufacturers.

Standard Grade for Wood Shingles

Resolved, that it is the sence of this meeting, that inasmuch as shingles are manufactured by only five of the associations that the matter of standardizing shingle grades be referred to the Shingle Committee, which is a sub-committee of the Trade Extension Committee of the National Lumber Manufacturers' Association.

The desire for true co-operation among the representatives of the manufacturers, distributors, and consumers of lumber present in making needed changes in sizes and methods of grading, was apparent in all the discussions, and the National Lumber Manufacturers' Association was evidently recognized by all as the proper medium through which such changes should be suggested. The representatives of the manufacturers stated their willingness to furnish material according to definite standards to be determined by a thorough investigation of manufacturing and marketing conditions carried out by practical lumbermen and engineers.

The result of the meeting was to bring the producer and distributor to a closer understanding of the needs of the consumer, as well as to show the consumer the difficulties faced in meeting these requirements in some cases. Also, to impress upon the lumber industry the value of a central organization which may act as a forum for all interested in the product, and be in a position to advise the industry and the public through its various departments of specialized work.

Lumber Firm Appoints Traffic Manager

J. E. Green, who for sixteen years was in the employ of the Canadian Pacific Railway, has been appointed traffic manager for Terry & Gordon, wholesale lumbermen, Toronto, and has entered upon his new position. The rapidly expanding local and foreign busines of this firm has necessitated this progressive step in the service and Mr. Green brings to bear upon his new duties a wide acquaintance and thorough grasp of all transportation problems. For six years he was travelling freight agent for the C. P. R. in the Maritime provinces with headquarters at St. John, N. B., and during the past year has resided in Toronto, filling the position of travelling freight agent for the C. P. R. between Toronto and Smith's Falls and later acting as contracting agent for the eastern portion of the city. Mr. Green will devote special attention to the export and eastern trade of Terry & Gordon.

Moose Lake Lumber Company Organize

The Moose Lake Lumber Company, Limited, are the successors to C. J. Price, lumber dealer, Cobalt, Ont., and a charter has been granted the new firm with a share capital of $40,000. The officers of the company are C. J. Price, president; John Ough, vice-president; and A. W. Harrington, sec.-treas. and manager for the present. The Moose Lake Lumber Company will operate timber limits and cut logs, manufacturing the same into lumber which will be sold to the local trade and also wholesale. The company have a good sawmill which is located at Moose Lake. Mr. Price, head of the organization, has for many years been a widely known dealer in everything in rough and dressed lumber, sash, doors, stull and lagging timber and has carried out important contracts.

Kinds of Wood Used in Ontario

A total of thirty-four diffetent kinds of wood are reported as being used by the wood-using industries of Ontario, as stated in a bulletin issued by the Forestry Branch, Department of the Interior. Of the woods used, the greater part is grown in the province, particularly pine, spruce, maple, hemlock, and oak, which ars used in greater quantity than any others. Elm, basswood, birch, beech, the group which comes next in quantity used, are also mostly purchased in Ontario. Ash, balsam, fir, hickory, cypress and gum, which stand next in quantity used, are mostly imported, with the exception of the first two named, while the next group, chestnut, poplar ironwood, tulip, and Douglas fir, are nearly all home-grown except the last two. The other groups are walnut, Spanish cedar, butternut; apple and willow and sycamore, red cedar, ebony and sumac.

Just Thirty Years Ago

Interesting items from the fyles of the July edition of the "Canada Lumberman" away back in 1889

To trace the history, expansion and development of any trade is instructive and entertaining. In this issue of the "Canada Lumberman" is presented a comprehensive summary of the activities, enterprises and trade problems of the Canadian lumber industry, as recorded in our columns some thirty years ago. It is believed that this feature will be one of timely interest and, in view of the many questions arising today in the industrial, manufacturing and transportation arenas, will be perused each month with appreciation.

* * * * *

Messrs. Gillies Bros., of Braeside, intend cutting a lot of logs and dimensions at their Coulonge depot the coming season.

* * * * *

Large quantities of lumber, especially cut for the South American market, are now going forward from Ottawa to the United States for export for Buenos Ayres.

* * * * *

The lumber interests are extending in British Columbia but lack of shipping facilities somewhat curtails the export trade in this line, freights being high.

* * * * *

There is an active demand for ocean tonnage at Quebec, which is likely to be brisk for some time. The scarcity of stevedores and longshotemen is likely to cause considerable delay in loading vessels now in port.

* * * * *

The cedar industry is a prominent factor in the rapid advancement of that smart little town in the Manitoulin district, known as Gore Bay. This class of wood is not only plentiful but is of a superior quality.

* * * * *

The Canadian Gazette of July 20th, officially proclaims the reduction of the export duty on pine logs from $3 to $2 per thousand feet board measure, the same to be deemed to have gone into effect upon the first day of July.

* * * * *

Mr. J. D. Shire, of Bracebridge, has got out his full stock of logs, about four million feet; which will take a good season to cut. He has the work well forward, however, and if it be possible the whole will be run through before the snow flies.

* * * * *

There has been considerable activity in the freight market during the past month. Rates are now running at: Quebec to Liverpool, deals 68s 9d; timber 28s; Quebec to Bristol channel, deals 75s; Quebec to Cork, deals 71s 3d; Montreal to Buenos Ayres, lumber $18.

* * * * *

The wages paid workers in the woods and sawmills in British Columbia are: Mill hands, $35 to $65 per month; axemen and swampers, $35 to $45 per month; teamsters at mills, $2 to $2.50 per day; teamsters in the woods, $60 to $65 per month. Board is from $8 to $10 per week.

* * * * *

The bulk of the square timber which came from the Upper Ottawa lumbering districts this spring, was sold before it left the bush to speculators on the American side. Mr. William Wade left with his raft on the 10th. It consisted of 150 cribs and was sold to Quebec parties.

* * * * *

The lack of rain for several weeks has dried up the small streams in the Moncton section of New Brunswick, and seldom has the water been so low as it now is. As a consequence nearly all the water mills are shut down or about to do so, and some of the steam mills are short of logs. Messrs. Wright & Cushing, however, managed to get half a million feet of logs down the Little River to their mills near Salisbury. They had taken the precaution to build a dam across the river behind their logs, and on the dam being opened, the logs were carried down in fine style.

* * * * *

Another new method of utilizing sawdust has recently come to light in the Ottawa district. At Deseronto bricks are now being made of sawdust and are known as the terra cotta brick. The bricks composing the flooring of the printing bureau at Ottawa are of this kind. The flooring is all arched, and the planking on the top. The sawdust bricks are very light and are porous.

* * * * *

Some rafts of square timber belonging to Messrs. Klock passed through Long Sault rapids last month. The first portion of the raft came through all right, but the second detachment struck a rock and went to pieces, the men managing to get ashore. The pilot immediately after banded together eight cribs and took them down safely, a performance that has never been done before.

* * * * *

Some of the Canadian papers are taking up the question of a national currency for Canada. We see no just reason why Canada cannot have a currency that will circulate at its face value all over the Dominion, and be just as good in the States as the United States money is in Canada, but we would prefer to have it based on a more honest footing than the national banking system of the United States

* * * * *

A very sensible suggestion has been made by the Canadian Institute. A deputation from that body waited upon the Hon. A. S. Hardy, the Ontario Commissioner of Crown Lands, last week to explain a scheme for a great provincial park for Ontario. They propose a tract of land 36 miles long by 28 miles wide, comprising about 1,000 square miles, back of Haliburton in the Nipissing district, should be set apart and called the Algonquin Park.

* * * * *

The lumber trade at Ottawa has assumed large proportions and is constantly increasing. At this time of the year the Ottawa district is a veritable hive of industry. The driving and sorting of logs, the hum of a score or more of mills, the loading of cars and steamers all tend to give it a busy appearance. Ottawa lumbermen carried over 150,000,000 feet last winter, very little of which is now in first hands. wintered for many years, very little of which is now in first hands.

* * * * *

The Picnic Island Mills, at Little Current, owned by Messrs. J. & T. Conlon, have been in operation since the 10th of May and have already cut 1,500,000 feet of lumber and are at present cutting about 100,000 feet per day. They employ about 100 men. The mill is 154 x 50 feet with engine and boiler attached, and consists of two circular saws and gang saws. The firm export large quantities of pine lumber, using a steam barge and consort and steam tug for the purpose.

* * * * *

The statement which has been going the rounds that there is more or less fraud perpetrated upon the St. John and St. Croix rivers under the special provision made whereby Maine logs are floated to St. John and the lumber re-admitted duty free, is denied by the St. John Globe. It says stories of this kind are not true. The United States revenue authorities made many efforts to discover whether any reported frauds have any evidence and that they have been unable to discover them.

* * * * *

The Victoria Lumber Manufacturing Company, Chemainus, last week placed the order with the Wm. Hamilton Mfg. Co., of Peterborough, for five steel boilers 60 x 20 and a lot of other machinery for the new mill. The largest shareholder was out West lately and said that he had no idea that Canadian manufacturers could turn out such machinery as he has seen in British Columbia; but could not understand why prices should be so much higher than the Americans, the wages in the States being only slightly higher.

* * * * *

Taking the trade and navigation returns for 1888 it appears that no distinction as to quality is made under the heading of dutiable lumber imported from the United Statees into Canada, which, however, in value only reached $90,, 723, upon which $18,164 was collected as duty. On the free list, lumber and timber, plank and boards, sawed, not shaped, planed and otherwise manufactured, of boxwood, cherry, chestnut, gum, hickory, whitewood, there was imported 1,986,-000 feet; mahogany, 1,750 feet; oak, 3,744,000 feet; pitch pine, 3,-490,000 feet; walnut, 5,714,000 feet, and other woods, 470,000 feet.

* * * * *

The following comparative statement shows the quantity of timber measured and culled at Quebec during the first six months of the present year and the two preceding years:

	1887	1888	1889
Waney white pine	407,706	235,112	690,490
White pine	119,756	142,139	1,312,959
Red pine	328,709	88,993	156,076
Oak	293,263	368,707	412,340
Elm	140,635	103,758	356,499
Ash	25,528	46,963	178,048
Birch and maple	114,228	123,969	231,291

* * * * *

The changes in the lumber duty, which are receiving so much attention in the East, are not affecting British Columbia for exporting to us here amounts to nil and vice versa; but in foreign markets, according to the American Commissioner's report, British Columbia woods command a better price than Puget Sound lumber or Oregon pine, necessitating the "Sound" shippers culling all their loads to enter into competition with Douglas fir. The owner of the largest mills on the "Sound," is through the press, forcing this fact on the people of the United States for what object cannot be ascertained—commercial union probably or annexation.

* * * * *

The following statement shows the quantity of lumber imported into the United States from Canada, and duty paid during the past nine years, the quantity of pine logs exported to the United States, and export duty paid, and the total duty on all lumber imported into Canada from the United States, during the period indicated:

	Lumber exported to United States		Pine Logs exported to to United States		Duty paid on lumber imported from U. S.
	Quantity Feet	Duty paid in U. S.	Quantity Feet	Export Duty	
1880	563,963,000	$1,127,026	2,075,000	$2,075	$13,636
1881	562,827,000	1,125,654	2,640,000	2,640	42,913
1882	602,821,000	1,205,642	1,313,000	1,313	74,584
1883	537,517,000	1,075,034	2,863,000	2,863	128,692
1884	557,266,000	1,114,532	974,000	974	40,563
1885	562,542,000	1,125,084	380,000	380	17,522
1886	541,777,000	1,083,554	2,869,000	2,869	16,549
1887	508,304,000	1,016,608	6,350,000	13,107	19,123
1888	553,939,000	1,107,878	468,000	926	18,164
Total	14,990,956,000	9,981,912	19,932,000	27,357	371,736

* * * * *

An Ottawa despatch to the New York Tribune says: The Dominion Government has been informed that R. C. Gibbs, a lumberman of Manistee, Mich., intends this season to test the legality of Canada's action in imposing duty on Canadian sawlogs. The duty was levied by the Dominion Government for the prevention of the destruction of Canadian Forests. The Gibbs firm intend bringing 38,000,000 feet of Georgian Bay logs to Bay City for sawing. They contend that through a treaty between the United States and Canada, signed in 1855, they will not have to pay the duty of $2 per 1000 feet. Restitution of duties already paid is also talked of. A careful investigation of the case discloses the fact that a treaty placing all kinds of timber on the free list was adopted in 1854 but was terminated in 1866 by the United States. Upon inquiry at the Customs department it was learned that Canada could not be held responsible, as the United States had themselves terminated the treaty in question.

* * * * *

The Chicago Lumber Trade Journal referring to the recent action of the Canadian Government in taking off the duty from lumber under eleven inches in diameter, and reducing the export duty on saw logs from $3 to $2 per thousand as it had previously been, says it is a step in the right direction, but does not go far enough to satisfy the Amercan government. "Ask for what you want and take what you can get," was the advice of a great reformer, and it would probably be wise to act upon that advice in the present case. We have not the least doubt but it would answer the purpose of the American government to get all the Canadian logs they require free of duty, to be manufactured in American mills, and at the same retain their import duty on Canadian lumber. The journal referred to says: "Nothing short of a repeal of all export duties on logs and timber by the Dominion can satisfy the lumbermen of this country. The Constitution of the United States prohibits retaliation by the imposition of export duties, but it is within the province of Congress to add to the import duty a sum, equal if need be, to double the export duty charged by a government which is disposed to discriminate against this country, and a strong pressure will be brought to bear next winter to this end, if the wisdom of the Canadian officials, in the meantime, does render it unnecessary." The proposition of the Dominion gov ment to remove all import duties on logs and lumber, providing the American government will reciprocate, is a wise one; but it can hardly be expected that the present tariff Congress will consent to the abolishing of the import duty on Canadian timber.

British Government Timber Representatives

Mr. L. C. Fisher is the representative along with Mr. S. G. Denman, of the British Government Timber Buyer's office in Eastern Canada. Mr. Fisher was born at Horsley, Surrey, England. He lately arrived in this country to take up the above position. For 12 years he has been connected with Mr. Montague L. Meyer's lumber business in London. After being in the office, he went on to the road, and since 1914, when Mr. Meyer was appointed to buy lumber for the British government, has been engaged in government work. He was chief inspector, inspecting lumber cargoes arriving in England to see that the lumber compiled with the specifications.

L. C. Fisher, Montreal

S. G. Denman, Montreal

Mr. S. G. Denman began his commercial career in 1905 as office boy in the General Purchasing Department of the C. P. R. In 1912 he went to B. C. as lumber clerk in the same department, and was later promoted to chief clerk B. C. Division, and afterwards relieving purchasing agent, then assistant purchasing agent for the Alberta division with headquarters at Calgary. In 1917 he joined the Imperial Munitions Board, wooden shipbuilding department, at Victoria, under Mr. R. P. Butchart, Director, and in the same year he was asked by Mr. FitzGerald to take charge, in Ottawa, of the lumber section of the Imperial Munitions Board. In May last Mr. M. L. Meyer appointed him joint Eastern Canada representative, (with Mr. L. C. Fisher) of the British Timber Buyer, with offices in Montreal.

Bandits Rob Northern Logging Camp

Armed bandits recently entered the office of the Schroeder Mills and Timber Co., at Pakesley, Ont., on the line of the C. P. R., and held up the manager, James Ludgate, and his staff. The robbers got away with about $3,000 in cash. Pakesley is located 206 miles north of Toronto and has been the headquarters of the Schroeder Mills and Timber Co's. camps for the past two years. Masked men entered the premises at dusk and pointing loaded revolvers at the head of Mr. Ludgate and two of his assistants, demanded "hands up..' George Knight, the bookkeeper, fired at the men and wounded one of them, but the man was able to accompany his chum and they chased Mr. Ludgate and others at the point of their guns some distance up the C. P. R. tracks and forced Mr. Knight to accompany them, saying they were going to dispose of him, but he escaped and was able to return to the camp.

The first consignment of Douglas fir seeds was taken to France a few weeks ago by P. S. Ridsdale, Secretary of the American Forestry Association, and will be sufficient to grow 50,000 trees, valued, it is estimated, at $1,000,000.

Big Opportunity for All Joinery Work

Mr. Manbert Declares There is Great Demand in Britain for Canadian Woodenware Lines

Editor, "Canada Lumberman."

Among my other activities I am making some enquiries into the market for wood manufacturers, such as joinery work, turned goods and all wares made largely or primarily of wood. There has been more or less discussion of this business at home, and in my knowledge a certain amount of export trade has run between Canada and this country; but, so far as I can learn, it has always been of minor volume and conducted in too casual a fashion.

At the present moment an undoubted opportunity exists. It would be most unfortunate if we were not to take full advantage of the present situation and I, therefore, bring this subject to your notice as one warranting some publicity in your paper; thereby I am sure you can do the situation much good. Furthermore, I would suggest that if you know of any other means of giving the matter publicity, you pass the good word along.

Heretofore this trade has been very largely controlled by Sweden, Germany and the United States. At the present moment all goods of this kind are either prohibited from importation outside of the Empire, or are subject to licenses which are difficult of securing. Quite apart then from any sympathetic attitude this gives a substantial preference to Canadian sources of supply, a preference which I repeat, it would be unfortunate if Canadians in general, and Ontario in particular, did not take advantage of. Furthermore, it seems particularly opportune at this hour, when so many of our industries in the wood-working line are establishing themselves after unsettlement of the war period. I have received several tangible indications of interest by parties here in developing this trade with Canada. Among these I have before me a letter from F. A. Perrin, of Winther, Perrin & Company, 52 Great Eastern Street, London, following an interview which Mr. Perrin had with me.

In this letter Mr. Perrin confirms his purpose of going to Canada within the next week or ten days to pursue the renewal of some old relationships existing before the war, and the establishing of new ones. He is interested in purchasing the following items:

Dowels.
Broom handles, made from soft wood, such as basswood, spruce.
Ash hay fork handles.
Ash rake handles.
Hickory and maple pick handles.
Hickory and ash hammer handles.
Hickory sledge hammer handles.
Clothes pins.
Wash-boards.
Maple skewers.
Chairs.
Household utensils made in wood.
Practically anything in the turnery and woodware lines.

Other Lines That are Desired

In addition there is an active demand for many other items such as:

Rakes.
Step-ladders.
Pails.
Garden barrows.
Washing machines.
Ironing boards.
Wooden trays.
Paint brush handles.
Ets., etc.

My conviction is that we cannot be too aggressive in getting a full measure of the possibilities of this trade, because if we fail to do our part to meet the demand, it must sooner or later turn to other sources for satisfaction, and a decided opportunity be lost to us.

Yours very truly,
A. C. Manbert,
Timber Commissioner for Ontario.

163 Strand, London, W. C.
June 23, 1919.

Association Will be Represented in Eastern Canada

One of the main objects of the recently-formed Associated Mills, Ltd., of Vancouver, B.C., is to take care of the Eastern Canadian lumber trade. Attention is being devoted, at the outset by the management of this new organization, to the prairie and American trade but it is expected that, within a short time, the association will appoint capable representatives in Ontario and Quebec, as well as other provinces in the east. It had been felt for some time by the concerns which are affiliated with this association, that combined action was advisable in order to more thoroughly serve the eastern market. The formation by the half dozen mills of one general sales organization was the result and the following are now identified with this new in corporation:—Eburne Sawmills Ltd., Robertson and Hackett Ltd., Dominion Creosoting and Lumber Company Ltd., False Creek Lumber Co., Craig Taylor Lumber Co. and the Alberta Lumber Co. The incorporators are: Messrs. P. D. Roe, George R. Hackett, Dan McLeod, C. McRae, J. A. McMillan and F. C. Taylor, all of whom are connected with the concerns mentioned. The aggregate of these six mills is in the neighborhood of 450,000 feet daily, the output consisting ol all lines of Coast common and upper grade lumber, lath, mouldings, etc.

As already stated, the prairie points and some districts in the United States will be organized by the association and representatives have already been appointed. The association, however, believes that it can be of equal service to the retailers in Eastern Canada as well as on the prairies and tentative plans are now under consideration for the placing of capable representatives in some of the larger centres in the east of which due announcement will be made.

Mr. A. T. Robson, formerly manager for the Canford Mills in the Nicola Valley, B. C., has been appointed manager of the association. It should be mentioned that each of the mills referred to has rail connection on either one or more lines, north, south and east.

The Work and Worth of Dr. Fernow

Dr. B. E. Fernow, Toronto, Ont.

Dr. B. E. Fernow, Dean of the Faculty of Forestry, University of Toronto, has retired from that position after having filled it faithfully and efficiently for the last twelve years. He is one of the foremost forestry experts on the continent and his work and worth are well summed up in the epigrammatic utterance of a representative Canadian journal "There is no abler man in his own department than Dr. Fernow."

The honored head of the forestry department of the Provincial University is now nearing the alloted span of three score years and ten and feels that he needs a well deserved rest as his health has not been of the best for some time, and with the hope of enjoying more freedom from care and a larger measure of leisure asked that he be relieved of his charge. He will return to the United States and hopes if health permits to resume his labors in authorship.

To enter in detail upon the success of the important work that has been carried out in the department of which Dr. Fernow presides, what it has accomplished during the past few years, the splendid records of its graduates, the status to which forestry has been raised and the deepening interest aroused in this important branch of the public service, would be reciting a tale that is familiar to all in any way connected or interested in the conservation and protection of the wooded wealth of the Dominion. He has undertaken most important timber surveys and now, practically, every province in the Dominion is conducting work along this line.

Dr. Fernow resided for a number of years in United States where he occupied leading positions in the service. He was first engaged in the metallurgical business and became chief of the Division of Forestry in the United States Department of Agriculture, which post he held from 1886 until 1898. He was secretary and later chairman of the Executive Committee and subsequently first vice-president of the American Forestry Association, and, also edited for a considerable time their publications. He was Director and Dean of New York State College of Forestry for Cornell University for five years and also consulting engineer and lecturer for the Yale Forest School. Subsequently he was professor of Forestry in the State College of Pennsylvania and since leaving that institution in 1907 has been actively identified with Forestry work in Canada. Among the important positions the duties of which he has discharged with credit to himself and distinction to the organization, are president of the Canadian Society of Forest Engineers and president of the Canadian Forestry Association. A few years ago he donated to the Forestry department of Toronto University, his entire collection of more than 2,500 books, pamphlets and magazines, dealing with Forestry and kindred subjects.

Forest Fires Visit Many Provinces

Dangers at One Time Were Great but Rains Came Suddenly—Timber Losses in the West

The forest fires which threatened to do a great deal of damage in Alberta, British Columbia, Northern Ontario, Quebec and Nova Scotia have all ben practically wiped out by providential rain falls. Even from far off Newfoundland comes word that the forests along the Reid line, in the ancient colony, have been ablaze. One of the visitors to that island recently concluded that Newfoundland had lost from forest flames during the last few years, $500,000,000 worth of timber.

In Northern Ontario the fires assumed menacing proportions around Cochrane, Haileybury, Iroquois Falls, Timmins, Porcupine, Boston Creek and other districts. So thick was the smoke at times that trainmen declare that their trains ran blindly, the engineers being unable to see a hundred feet ahead of them. A dense pall of smoke hung over Sault Ste Marie.

In the Cobalt district the outlook for a time was alarming, and while calamity howlers are not welcomed in the north, the most optimistic entertained grave fears for a week that the dread holocaust of 1916 would again visit the country. Fortunately, few, if any, lives, were lost in the recent outbreak of flame. The sweep was due, principally, to the long dry, hot spell, which prevailed for several weeks, interspersed with but few showers of rain and these only local in their extent.

Following the disastrous fires of 1916 better fighting organization was brought into use and much progress has been made in equipping this defensive force so far as rapid transit is concerned, and with observation towers at the various points of vantage. The summers of 1917 and 1918 was comparatively wet and but little damage was done by forest fires.

According to forest superintendent E. H. Finlayson the forest fire in Alberta was the worst in many years. He declared that 30,000,000 feet of valuable timber had already been destroyed. The worst part of the blaze was in the north-west corner of the Stoney Indian Reserve, and it menaced Banff National Park northern outskirts.

The most serious damage was done in the district around Porquois Junction in Northern Ontario. Some 17 miles out of Cochrane the railway section house and other buildings were burned and 10,000 cords of pulpwood destroyed.

For a while the situation around Timmins was very serious, and was watched with a great deal of anxiety. The pulpwood contractors, J. O'Loughlin and T. Lawlor, were the greatest sufferers in that vicinity. Several saw mills had a narrow escape and heavy clouds of smoke filled the atmosphere. Word from New Liskeard says that the saw mill of James McBrayne in Firstbrook Township, with 7,000 feet of lumber and the barn and machinery shed on the farm of Prof. John Sharp, two miles south of the town were destroyed by bush fires.

Ferguson's mill there was partly affected from the same cause. In the case of the Sharp farm, the fire jumped the railway tracks, the main road and a broad field, missing a barn, from which the contents had been removed, and attacking the other building on the lake shore.

Forest fires entered into the Ottawa Valley in the Kippewa district during early July, two of them attacking the limits of the Shepard and Morse Lumber Co.

In the northern district of the Province the Forest Protective Association successfully brought suit against a settler for starting a fire to burn slash without first having secured a permit. The settler was fined $25. The Association pressed for a conviction as a matter of example.

A recent despatch from Calgary says that the Porcupine Hill forest fire is now under control, but that the flames had destroyed 15,000,000 and 18,000,000 feet of lumber. At Natal, B. C., several people left the town by special train, so threatening did the bush fire become. Forest fires were reported from many districts near Fernie, but the damage was confined mainly to cut-over land and the fire wardens were successful in protecting valuable timber lands.

Forest fires also raged along the line of the Quebec and Lake St. John Railway, doing considerable damage.

When the forest fires broke out in Northern Ontario, the Department of Lands, Forests and Mines, Toronto, sent specific instructions to many of the settlers there how to cope with the danger. The Department has reason to believe that these instructions were not followed out in a number of cases and that there was wanton carelessness on the part of a number of settlers which caused fires to spread over a wider area than they otherwise would have. Hon. G. Howard Ferguson has issued instructions that drastic action be taken against all such settlers and two officers are already at work rounding up those who are believed to have been careless with regard to these destructive fires.

Reports reaching the Department of Lands, Forests and Mines indicate that further rain fell between Kapuskasing and O'Brien. While the heavy winds caused the flames to spread in a number of districts, there is evidence that in all districts fire-swept the flames were brought under complete control. Porquois Junction was reported absolutely safe and the Cochrane district is freed from smoke.

A Budget of Briefs From the East

The cry sent out from New Brunswick for shipping relief and for the release of bottoms for the transportation of lumber to the United Kingdom has been heard, for [illegible]lions of feet are weekly being sent overseas. Steamers and sailing vessels of all kinds are now loading or are on the ocean wave carrying cargos of lumber consigned to the British controller. During the past two weeks several steamers left St. John, N. B., with many millions of feet, while a number of sailing vessels also set sail carrying full cargos to destinations in the United Kingdom. As a result conditions are beginning to become normal, and while there is still a large quantity to be shipped the amount already sent away has greatly relieved the situation. At the present time there are several schooners loading for overseas, among their number being the Jane Palmer, a large five master of 2,823 tons regitser, which is taking over four million feet.

A four-masted schooner, Herbert Black, 594 tons register, was driven ashore in Preston, England, and from latest advices is a total wreck. She sailed from St. John with a full cargo of lumber and was reported as having arrived safely, but a few days later word came that she had met with a mishap. The lumber was shipped by Dun field & Co., St. John, N. B. There was nearly a half million feet on the vessel and this was valued at over $30,000. It is felt that the vast majority of the lumber will be salved.

H. Mobbs, of Kettering, England, was in St. John recently interviewing officials of the Provincial Department of Lands and Mines regarding the securing of leases of hardwood lands on which a supply would be available for manufacturing purposes.

Another serious forest fire broke out recently on crown lands in the vicinity of Wapske, a lumbering centre in Victoria County on the Transcontinental Railway. The lands were under lease to the Wapske Lumber Company. Heavy rains quenched the flames or the damage would have been much greater. The damage is estimated at $25,000, but this figure may be low when a detailed report is available.

Every effort to cope with forest fires in New Brunswick is being made. As a result of a system inaugurated a fire is soon detected and men rushed to the scene to fight the blaze. This system has already proven invaluable and the extra precautions have undoubtedly saved large tracks of valuable timber lands.

A sale of unmarked logs for the province was held recently in St. John, N. B., and resulted in Stetson, Cutler & Company bidding in for all spruce, cedar and pine picked up during the season, and Randolph & Baker for all hemlock.

A report from Grand Falls, N. B., says that the water in the St. John River at that point is very low and few logs are running, a large number being held up in coves and eddies. A crew of men are being put to work to dislodge some of the large joints which have jammed. About a mililon feet at present lie in the "churn" and alcove below the large falls. This place is considered dangerous for the men who are dislodging the logs with the aid of wire hawsers and donkey engines. The logs are packed in like sardines and some are believed to be resting on the bottom.

There has been an exceptionally heavy movement of logs along the St. John River and the firm of James Holly & Sons, who have charge of all movements on the lower river, report that business has been brisk. They have charge of South Bay where millions of feet are stored and after being surveyed are towed to the mills for manufacture. This firm is one of the oldest in Eastern Canada.

Must Have Provincial Charter

It has been debated in various provinces in Canada whether a company operating under a Dominion charter could be required by law to take out a provincial charter. The Supreme Court of Canada has handed down a judgment deciding in favor of the provinces, which means that a Dominion company can be compelled to bring itself under a provincial companies' act as a condition of carrying on business in the province. The effect of the decision appears to be to make a Dominion charter valueless for practical purposes in those provinces which require such companies to take out a provincial license. The decision would appear to apply to all classes of Dominion companies, including insurance companies. The provinces requiring provincial licensing are Ontario, Manitoba, Saskatchewan, British Columbia and New Brunswick.

Securing Co-operation Against Fires

New Brunswick Enlists the Interest of Boys and Girls to Keep Forests Green and Growing

The "Canada Lumberman" has received from Hon. E. A. Smith, Minister of Lands and Mines for the Province of New Brunswick, two attractive and well-printed booklets, with colored illustrations on the covers, one scene depicting the growth of several fine spruce trees, and the other revealing the destructive work of the fire fiend in the bush. The title of these brochures are "About Camp Fires" and "A Camp Fire Book for Boys and Girls".

The Department of Lands and Mines, New Brunswick, believes in a campaign of education, and instruction in the interest of forest protection, and is of the opinion that upon the plastic minds of the youth of the province many useful and timely lessons may be impressed. Hon. Mr. Smith, in association with the Chief Superintendent of Education of New Brunswick, has recently issued an appeal to the school teachers and school children of the Province for their active co-operation in forest fire protection. All teachers have been requested to read to their pupils an effective and forceful letter and other literature dealing with forest fires. This has already been done in most cases.

The letter is so direct and pointed in its appeal and application that the "Canada Lumberman" believes it is worthy of consideration in other provinces of the Dominion and reproduces the communication, which is signed by Hon. E. A. Smith, Minister of Lands and Mines.

The Government appeals to the assistance of every boy and girl in the fight against the great enemy of our forests—FIRE. Forest Rangers and Fire Wardens are constantly travelling through the forests watching for signs of fire, but these men have vast areas to cover and cannot be in more than one place at a time. At any moment some careless camper or smoker, by neglecting a burning match, may cause a serious fire that will rage for days and destroy thousands of dollars' worth of timber and sometimes houses and even the lives of the people. Ask your parents to tell you about the Great Miramichi Fire of 1825.

A careless farmer, while clearing his land, may neglect to take precautions against the spread of his bush fire into the surrounding woods. Or a spark from a railway locomotive may fall in the dry leaves and needles on a dry, windy summer's day, and soon be fanned into a raging flame, destroying everything in its path. These things are happening every year. If people only knew how wonderfully valuable the forests are to New Brunswick and how easily they are destroyed by acts of thoughtlessness and neglect, we would soon get rid of this terrible enemy of our forests.

The fire rangers of New Brunswick ask for the help of every boy and girl in this school in preventing forest fires from starting and in instantly notifying a fire ranger, road supervisor, or any official if a forest fire is discovered.

When you go into the woods this summer on a holiday, picnic or camping party, and require a fire, build it on rocks or gravel, and away from the trees or old logs. Make a small fire in the same manner as the first inhabitants of our woods, the Indian, who says, "White man, he build big fire, keep long way back—too hot. Injun make him small fire, get close." A small camp fire is always best for cooking purposes. When leaving the woods, put your fire completely out with pails of water or earth. If by chance you should see anyone toss a lighted match or burning tobacco in the woods or where it is liable to cause serious results, do not hesitate to warn him of his dangerous act.

New Brunswick must keep her forests green and growing, her logging, pulp and saw mill industries in operation, if she can hope to employ the thousands of returning heroes from overseas, and if she is to supply her share of the lumber required for the reconstruction of Europe.

In addition to the direct loss to the people of New Brunswick through forest fires, there is still another inheritance, viz., the dwellers of the forest, moose, caribou, deer, and also the fur-bearing animals and birds. These require protection from forest fires. They have attracted many sportsmen to our land, and brought prosperity to many of our people.

New Look-out Station Now in Use

Mount Hope look-out, near Penniac, is the first look-out to be utilized by the New Brunswick Forest Service. The tower is about 75 feet high, and a territory is visible at least thirty miles in all directions. A returned soldier will act as look-out man. Arrangements have been made to hook the line up by telephone with the New Brunswick Telephone Co's. office at Fredericton.

In all, about thirty fires have been reported in New Brunswick this season, the greater majority of which were caused by the operation of trains on the railroads, and by farmers neglecting slash fires. Exert gangs of men were employed on about ten of these fires and they were extinguished before reaching any great size, and only in two cases was any serious damage done.

The Minister of Public Works is co-operating with the Minister of Lands and Mines in the important matter of Fire Protection, 474 road supervisors being instructed in case of forest fires to leave their work and employ their men fighting fire at any time. This will undoubtedly result in a considerable assistance in all parts of the province of New Brunswick.

Live Association Does Good Work

One of the most progressive and enthusiastic organizations in the retail lumber line is that of the Quebec City Retail Dealers' Association, the second annual meeting of which was held recently. The officers of this body are well pleased with the results of the past year, and there have been bonds of unity and evidences of friendship and co-operation such as has not been witnessed in the retail ranks for many years.

One of the most important moves made by the Association was in deciding to levy a uniform charge for the delivery of all lumber. This charge is made independent of the price of the stock, and the plan has been found to work out admirably. Another advanced step was taken when it was unanimously agreed that all parties except well-known and highly responsible citizens should pay spot cash for their purchases. The new terms of settlement have been satisfactory all around.

OFFICERS OF QUEBEC CITY RETAIL LUMBER DEALERS ASSOCIATION

L. C. Marquis, President — O. A. Gignac, Director — Nap. Gignac, Director — J. O. Chalifour, Secy.-Treas.

Personal Paragraphs of Interest

L. Rolland, of Blair & Rolland, Montreal, was a reecnt visitor to Boston.

Walter Mason, of Mason, Gordon & Co., Montreal, is on a business visit to the Pacific Coast.

Lieut. Frank J. MacGibbon, of Fredericton, N.B., who recently returned from overseas, has taken a position with the Snowball Lumber Company of Chatham.

A. D. Huff, formerly traffic manager of the Canadian Export Paper Co., Monteral, has been appointed traffic manager of the Riordon Sales Co., Montreal.

A. E. Gordon, of Terry & Gordon, Toronto, has returned from spending a few weeks in the Muskoka district, where he is erecting a summer home near Whiteside.

Among Toronto lumbermen enjoying a holiday at present with their families are W. J. Lovering, at Port Severn; Alex. Greig, at Bala, and A. E. Cates, at Lake Muskoka.

Maurice Welsh of Campbell, Welsh & Paynes, wholesale lumber dealers, Toronto, is spending the holidays with his family, including "The Twins," at his summer home in Bobcaygeon, Ont.

C. Riordon, of the Riordon Pulp & Paper Co. Ltd., Montreal, signed the majority report of the Royal Commission, on Industrial Relations, and F. Pauze, of U. Pauze & Fils, Montreal, the minority report.

John Stewart, one of the pioneers of West Toronto, who was for some years engaged in the lumber business, died recently in his 69th year. He had resided in Toronto or vicinity all his life and was a well-known citizen. He is survived by one daughter.

Tadashi Hamaski, acting director of the Tokio Trading Co. Ltd., Toyko, is on a visit to Canada, with a view of securing large amounts of pulp for use in Japan. He states that his firm can dispose of 50,000 tons per annum; hitherto a large amount has been purchased in the United States.

A. E. Mackney, manager of the Atlantic-Pacific Lumber Co., Vancouver, and associated with Muir & Kirkpatrick, of Toronto, spent a few days in Toronto, recently, on his way east, on a business trip to Montreal, New York and other centres. He called upon a number of friends in the trade.

Among those who attended the big annual meeting of the National Hardwood Lumber Association, which was held recently in Chicago, were J. W. Jacobson; Frank A. Kent, W. R. Youmans, and J. M. Donovan, Toronto; J. H. Hall, Kitchener, and Geo. Goodfellow, Montreal, and others.

John McComb died recently at St. Stephen, N.B., after an illness of seven months. He was 85 years of age and the last of a family of nine. Mr. McComb was one of the pioneer lumbermen on the St. Croix River and had resided in St. Stephen for about 63 years. He leaves a son and a daughter.

John McDonald, late of Grand View, Man., who for the past three years was engaged in the contracting and lumber line, there, has returned to Ontario, and is at present residing at 63 Duke St., Toronto. It is his intention to re-enter the lumber business in the Haliburton district at an early date.

D. C. A. Galarneau has resigned his position with the Algoma Central and Hudson Bay railway, and has been appointed forester to the St. Maurice Pulp and Paper Company with headquarters at Three Rivers, P.Q. He is now conducting an extensive forest survey upon the limits of this company.

Herman G. Schanche has arrived at Iroquois Falls, where he is establishing his headquarters as chief forester of the Abitibi Power & Paper Co.. He will leave shortly for an extended trip through the limits, planning ways and means to be adopted to carry out the reforestation program of the company.

The death of Steele Lewis, only son of E. A. Lewis, St. Thomas, Ont., occurred recently from the after effects of a severe attack of influenza. For some years the late Mr. Lewis carried on a successful law practice in Buffalo, but returned over a year ago to engage in the lumber and coal business with his father. Besides his parents, he leaves one sister to mourn his loss.

Dr. Murdock M. Graham, of Boston, left that city recently with a party of aviators, mechanics, foresters and photographers, and will conduct an exploration by aeroplane of the timber resources of Labrador. Boston lumbermen are reported to have assisted in financing the expedition with a view to the possible development of new sources of supply of pulpwood and lumber.

A. C. Volkmar has severed his connection with the Riordon Pulp and Paper Company, to become forester to the Canada Paper Company, with headquarters at St. Raymond, P.Q. Walter ab Yberg, who has been connected with the Riordon company for some years, and has lately been in charge of their cruising operations in the Kipawa district, has been placed in charge of the forestry operations of the company, including the nursery and planting work.

Hon. Jules Allard, Minister of Lands and Forests for the Province of Quebec, will, it is stated, retire to become prothonotary of the district of Montreal. At the meeting of the Woodlands section of the Canadian Pulp & Paper Association, Mr. Allard strongly hinted that he might leave the Government, adding that it would be for purely personal reasons.

F. A. Perrin, managing director of Winther, Perrin & Co., Limited, London, Eng., is spending a few days in Montreal, Toronto and other cities. The firm are large importers of all kinds of woodenware, and the object of Mr. Perrin's visit is to arrange contracts with concerns with whom his company have previously dealt, and also to interest other manufacturers in many articles which it is desirable to import from Canada.

Gillies Bros. Will Rebuild Sawmill

How Historic Plant at Braeside was Completely Wiped Out — Firm Had Excellent Protective System

The large and well-equipped sawmill of Gillies Bros., Limited, located at Braeside, Ont., was recently wiped out by fire, as announced in the last edition of the "Canada Lumberman." The company have decided to rebuild and expect to have their new mill, which will be of the latest type, ready for next season's operations.

Further particulars regarding the destruction of the historic plant of Gillies Bros. have been received and will prove of much interest in showing how, in spite of the most efficient fire protection system, it is impossible, at times, to overcome the onrush of flames.

The fire started late in the afternoon within a few feet of the south end of the mill, immediately below the sawing floor, when the plant was in full operation. Water was available immediately from two stand pipes, but this had no effect, the flames flashing up to the filing room floor almost immediately and the mill had fallen in less than an hour afterwards. About three hundred and twenty men were on the pay roll the day of the fire. The mill is a total wreck, even the refuse burner having telescoped and slipped down some fifteen feet from its original height.

As stated, the men were all in their places in the mill at the time the blaze occurred, and there was no delay in discovering it or getting water on it. In addition to the fire which was visible, and on which the water was turned, it must have been burning along the bottom of the sawing floor, where it was not reached by water, and not noticed by the men with the hose.

There were twelve standpipes in the mill and adjoining it, within reach, with from 50 to 100 feet of hose and a nozzle attached to each and ready for immediate use. Full pressure was on at the time the flames were discovered.

There were three pumps in the boiler house, all fitted so as to connect up the main water pipe with a 6 in. supply and a 6 in. discharge, but the water supply failed as soon as the steam pipe between the boilers and engines collapsed, about thirty minutes after the fire started, leaving the mill water supply useless. The fire was so hot, however, that the men could not stand near enough to throw water on it.

Gillies Bros. had their own steam fire engine, which was immediately put in use between the mill and the lumber yards to protect the latter, and later on, after the danger to the yards was over, it was used to extinguish the embers of the fire. The engine is equipped with some 1,200 feet of standard rubber-lined hose, and it ran steadily for about twelve hours. They also had the fire engine from the town of Arnprior, about three miles distant, and the fire boat from McLachlin Bros., Arnprior, which gave assistance in keeping the devouring element from spreading, and in quenching the embers. The hose connections of Gillies Bros. are interchangeable with McLachlin Bros., and those of Arnprior, so that in case of necessity all can be used together.

The mill was built in 1870, and was purchased by Gillies Bros. in 1873, and rebuilt and enlarged in 1893, and had a record of 300,000 feet per day of ten hours. The company had only been sawing from May 15th, and have a full season's supply of logs in the water.

Lumberman Retires from Public Life

N. P. Tanguay, who has represented Wolfe in the Quebec legislature since 1904, retired in the recent provincial contest after long and faithful public service. Mr. Tanguay is a well-known lumberman and general storekeeper of Weedon, Que. He is a Liberal in politics. His successor in Wolfe is J. E. Rheault, Liberal, who was elected by acclamation.

Midsummer Trip Retail Lumbermen

Ontario Party will Visit the Large Mills at Penetang, Midland and Victoria Harbor First Two Days in August

The annual midsummer outing of the members of the Ontario Retail Lumber Dealers' Association will be held on Friday and Saturday, August 1 and 2, to Penetanguishene, Midland and Victoria Harbor. The busy saw mills and wood products industries in these towns will be visited and it is expected there will be a large and representative attendance from all parts of the province. The trip will prove a delightful and instructive week-end jaunt.

The party will leave Toronto by the G. T. R. at 5 o'clock in the afternoon of July 31 and will reach Penetanguishene at 9.55 the same evening. They will spend the night in the hotels in that town.

On the morning of Friday, August 1, the members will visit the manufacturing plants in Penetanguishene and in the afternoon will inspect the various woodworking industries of Midland.

On Saturday, August 2, the retail lumbermen will journey to Victoria Harbor to view the mill and yards of the Victoria Harbor Lumber Co. and will be tendered a luncheon as guests of the Victoria Harbor Lumber Co.

Mr. Manley Chew, of Midlands, has kindly placed his tugs at the disposal of the party in making the trips from Penetanguishene to Midland and from Midland to Victoria Harbor. Persons desiring to return to Toronto may do so on the 2.54 train on the afternoon of Saturday, August 2, but it is expected that a large number will spend Sunday and Monday at some of the delightful resorts on the Georgian Bay as Monday, August 4, is civic holiday not only in Toronto but in several other cities and towns in Ontario.

Every retail lumberman whether a member of the association or not is invited to take in this educative and pleasant excursion and will be afforded an excellent opportunity of learning how the lumber that he sells is produced. All those who do not find it convenient to join the company leaving Toronto on the afternoon of Thursday, July 31, should make arrangements to reach Penetanguishene by some other route so as to be there on the morning of August 1. "Come one, come all" is the slogan.

Four Hundred Houses Being Erected

The number of municipalities in the Province of Ontario now operating under the Ontario Housing Act has grown to 74, and includes 17 cities, 35 towns, 14 villages and 10 townships. About 40 municipalities are actually building houses. Over 1,200 plans have been approved by the director, Mr. J. A. Ellis, and over 400 houses are in the course of construction.

The village of New Toronto has let contracts for over 50 houses. They are building a six-roomed solid brick house for $3,000. It is probable that Windsor will erect the largest number of houses of any municipality in the Province.

Travelling inspectors were appointed recently, and they are visiting the various municipalities which are erecting houses. Seven of the nine inspectors are returned soldiers.

Price Bros are Making Extensions

Judgment has been delivered in the case of Price Bros. & Co., of Quebec, against whom information was laid sometime ago for operating one of their paper plants at Kenogami on Sunday. The Court of Appeal rendered judgment against the company on the question of Sunday labor on June 27th and Price Bros. are now considering the advisibility of carrying the matter to a higher tribunal.

The installation of a further unit at the company's paper mill at Kenogami is proceeding satisfactorily and it is expected it will be in operation about December. The high scale of wages prevailing and the excessive cost of all camp material is bound, in the opinion of Price Bros., to raise the price of wood. The company are building a new and thoroughly up-to-date sawmill at Matane, Que., which will be ready for next season's cut.

Quebec Lumbermen Retain Their Seats

Ed. Ouellette, who was recently returned by acclamation for Yamaska in the Quebec province elections, is vice-president and general manager of th Tourville Lumber Mills, Limited, Montreal and Louiseville. He was first elected a member of the Quebec legislature in 1905 and has been returned at each subsequent election. Mr. Ouellette, who is past president of the Quebec Limit Holders' Association, is a director of several large concerns and a wire awake and progressive citizen. He resides at Pierreville Mills, Que., and is a Liberal in politics.

Rodolphe Tourville, president of the Tourville Lumber Mills Company, won his political fight and retains his seat in Maskinonge Co. He was first honored with the confidence of his constituents in 1912 and since then has always been able to write M.L.A. after his name. Mr. Tourville was born in Montreal in 1878 and is an aggressive and broad minded business man, interested in a large number of companies. In politics he is a Liberal.

It will also be of interest to his many friends in the lumber trade that Hon. Jules Allard, Minister of Lands and Forests, will be a member of the next legislature. He has a seat in the Legislative Council. Other widely known lumbermen who hold seats in the Legislative Council are Hon. Geo. Bryson, Fort Coulogne, Pontiac Co., and Hon. John C. Kaine, of Stadacona Division, Quebec City.

Mr. Stewart Pays Visit to the West

E. Stewart, Toronto

Elihu Stewart, of Toronto, managing director of the Canada Timber and Lands Company, left recently on a business trip to British Columbia and will spend some time in the West in the interests of the organization which he represents. At the annual meeting of the company, which was held lately, L. A. Hamilton of Toronto was elected president; F. F. Telfer, of Toronto, vice-president; Elihu Stewart, managing director and secretary-treasurer; and R. R. Grant, of Toronto, assistant secretary.

It has been decided to start logging operations on the limits of the company which are located on the main coast line, 140 miles, north of Vancouver, along the Toba River. The company own 23 sq. miles of heavily wooded lands of fir, cedar, spruce and some hemlock. The latest logging equipment has been purchased consisting of three donkey engines and all other accessories and it is expected that 100,000 feet will be taken out every day. Logging will be begun at once and will be pushed vigorously.

It is some years since Mr. Stewart paid a visit to the West. He is vice-president of the Spruce Falls Pulp and Paper Co., who intend erecting a hundred and fifty ton pulp and paper mill at Kapuskasing, Ont., and was superintendent of Forestry for Canada from 1899 to 1907. Mr. Stewart is also a former president of the Ontario Land Surveyors Association and of the Canadian Forestry Association, being a delegate from the federal government to the American Forestry Congress in 1905 and during that year making a tour of inspection of the forests of France and Germany. For many years he was engaged on Crown land surveys in Ontario and the prairie provinces and was a Commissioner appointed by the Dominion government in delimiting the boundary between Ontario and Manitoba. Mr. Stewart resides at Collingwood, of which town he is a former Mayor and his office is at 88 King Street East, Toronto.

Would Eliminate All Orientals in Mills

Some phases of the present industrial condition in Victoria, B. C., from the standpoint of labor, were represented to the royal commission on industrial relations, which sat in that city recently.

Robert Donachie, representing the carpenters and mill employees, referred to the efforts made recently to eliminate Orientals from working in the mills and the fixing of a wage scale there and claimed labor found it difficult to enter into any negotiations on the subject with the employers. If the unions could not secure satisfaction they were prepared, he said, to take the same stand as was taken by the Australian unions seven years aga, when large orders were given by Britain to Australian firms.

There were nine mills, employing 2,000 Orientals in the Victoria district. It was proposed to substitute whites for Orientals.

"Does your request embrace a clean sweep of the Orientals?" asked Chairman Mathers.

"Absolutely," was the reply. "There are some 2,500 whites idle in Victoria."

Witness stated that with some rare exceptions employers of labor in this district have confidence in organized labor. So far as the sawmills were concerned, sanitary conditions were very bad, and he believed the law prohibiting any but whites to operate certain machines was being violated and Chinese utilized thereon.

The Forest Reserve of Alberta

The Province of Alberta has 16,711,000 acres of timber lands under Forest Reserve. This comprises about 14 per cent. of the total area of the province. With reasonable protection from fires, the supply of timber products is assured for all time. Most of the land under Forest Reserve is not well adapted for agriculture. It is, therefore, the policy of the Government to preserve the existing species and propagate new types in order to supply adequately the needs of the people for home consumption, and export for the future. Moreover, the Reserves are generally situated near the sources of the rivers and streams of the Province, and thereby ensure the natural regulation and conservation of the water supply and water power.

The estimated stand of the timber as far as surveyed in the existing Reserves, reaches the enormous estimate of 21,000,000,000 board feet. For the last year in which figures are available (namely the fiscal year ending March 31st, 1918), the annual production was as follows:

	Ft. B. M.
Lumber	67,024,000
Lath	3,488,400
Railway ties	50,955
Shingles	1,276,250
Piling props	2,197,000

Besides these products, great numbers of fence posts, telephone and telegraph poles, and fence rails are cut each year. The cutting of timber of Forest Reserves is strictly regulated by the Government under license. At the present time, there are 2,030 square miles of timber lands under license, for which the licenses pay a revenue to the Government for the pirivilege of taking timber.

A system of permits to settlers and homesteaders is in vogue, whereby they may secure timber supplies for fencing and building, and during the last fiscal year, over 11,613,000 feet B.M. of logs and lumber have been cut by the homesteaders for improvements on their homesteads. This is a very important consideration to the new settler in Alberta. Timber for building and fencing is generally close at hand in the northern half of the province, at very little cost for these necessary improvements.

Systematic Burning of Logging Slash

A recent discussion of logging costs in national forests in the United States refers to the question of brush disposal. In California, for example, it is the general practice to require operators to pile and burn all brush resulting from the felled timber and snags. The work of piling is often subcontracted at rates ranging from 17 cents to 25 cents per thousand feet of timber cut. Records of brush-piling work done directly under the supervision of the company show that the cost ranges from 11 cents to 26 cents per thousand feet of timber cut. Brush burning is usually done by the operator at a cost of from 2 cents to 5 cents per thousand feet of the timber cut, with an average of possibly 4 cents per thousand. There has recently been a sharp advance in labor costs. A fair present average, therefore, for piling and burning is 30 cents per thousand feet.

Corresponding costs in eastern Canada would, of course, be higher, due to the smaller size of the timber, with consequent larger amount of brush per unit of timber cut. However, the importance of brush disposal from the standpoint of decreasing damage to the forest, due to fire, insect and fungi, is so great that the problem calls imperatively for solution at an early date. Under the auspices of the Woodlands Section of the Canadian Pulp and Paper Association, experiments are to be made on a number of operations this year to determine the feasibility and cost of reducing the menace by systematic burning of the logging slash, under safe conditions. Logging slash is the garbage of the forest, and its disposal is as essential to the health of the forest as is the disposal of city garbage to the health of the community of human beings.

Coopers Look for Good Year's Business

James Innes of the Sutherland-Innes Co., Chatham, Ont., in a recent report, says; We are pleased to say that trade is opening up very nicely this year, and it looks as if we would have at least a normal year's business. Perhaps not just as much rush as some of the war years, but a good, steady business. There, of course, will not be the very high prices that were maintained during the war, but in spite of the high wages and high freight rates, it looks as if the manufacturers and the coopers would have a good year.

While there is no great export trade yet, on account of shortage of room, it is opening up very promisingly, and as soon as ocean room is available, we expect a large demand for all kinds of slack and tight barrel stock for export.

Prices are now fairly steady, although stock is not moving as rapidly as we would like to see it, and there are some accumulations at the mills. The hoop situation is the weakest, as there are more hoops being manufactured than are required for present consumption, and a great many of these hoops are being made by mills that cannot hold their goods until they are actually wanted.

The outlook for cereal crops is excellent, and reports, so far, on the fruit trees, are better than they have been for years. I think, on the whole, the manufacturers have reason to feel a little optimistic at the present time.

Tight barrel stock especially is in good demand, and as the production has been very light lately, there have been no stocks accumulating. In fact, in some lines, there has been an entire clearance, at the mills and yards, and little prospect of replacing for some time to come. Prices are being maintained. In fact, the tendency is for higher prices, on account of the difficulty of obtaining raw material, at the present time. What tight barrel stock men want now is some way to enable them to replenish their stocks at the mills.

Fraser Valley Wants Pulp Industry

An important meeting was held in the Board of Trade rooms, New Westminster, recently when representatives of several boards of trade throughout the Fraser Valley met to consider the ultimate clearing and seeding of 400,000 acres of arable, uncleared, uncultivated land in the Fraser Valley, and the establishment of a pulp mill.

The one great drawback to the agricultural development of this, one of the most fertile valleys in the world, has always been the cost of clearing the land, and the second great drawback has been to keep the logged-off lands clear after the timber has been taken therefrom.

Up to this time practically no effort has been made to have these logged-off areas seeded down and in this way make them available for pasturing thousands of cattle and hundreds of thousands of sheep.

Brush that springs up after the land has been logged is hard enough to deal with, but this can be slashed and burned. The real enemy that renders this land valueless for pasturage purposes are the ferns. These cannot be got rid of till the land is ploughed, and it is a much more expensive proceedure to take the green stumps out of the land than stumps that have been allowed to rot for a few years while the land has been used for pasture.

The first object of the meeting was to bring pressure on the governments to enact legislation making it compulsory for any party removing timber from land to clear the land of everything but the stumps and to seed it down with suitable grass seed.

The second object of the meeting looked to the establishment of a pulp plant at the most convenient point in the valley which will enable a man to take every stick of wood not suitable for mill purposes, off his land at a profit on his work.

Cordwood selling at $4 to $4.50 a cord f.o.b. Vancouver, will not do this, and if it did, the demand for cordwood is limited. A number of public spirited citizens have been making enquiries about pulp manufacture, and the information they have secured has been most promising.

Pulp wood sells in the east for from $8 to $14 a cord, and after making all necessary allowances, the corresponding price in B. C. would be a profitable one.

Unique Table Made of All Native Woods

The Directors' and General Conference table in the offices of the Eastern Forest Products Association at Bangor, Maine, is an article most unique and at the same time a beautiful piece of furniture. Every piece that shows is different, all of native Maine woods.

H. G. Wood, Executive Secretary of the Association, conceived the idea that such a table would be most appropriate for the committee room, besides serving as an advertisement for Maine lumber products and what could be done with them.

The table is eight feet long and three feet wide, and has five legs. The top is made up of six boards, six inches wide, and of the following woods: White ash, Bird's-eye rock maple, black cherry, curly yellow birch, beech, and quartered white oak.

The legs are of elm, hickory, chestnut, butternut and mahoganized yellow birch. The ledge boards are of Sycamore, white birch, brown ash and cherry birch. Under the margin of the top is a plate to give a thick top effect, which is made of white pine, hemlock, white cedar and red spruce. With the exception of the mahoganized leg, each piece is in natural finish, and the effect is beautiful. The mahoganized leg illustrates the possibility of securing a most deceiving imitation of mahogany wood by using birch.

Morse and Company, of Bangor, who are members of the Association, made the table, and carefully selected each piece from their extensive stock of lumber. The boards of bird's-eye maple and curly birch are exceptionally choice and pretty specimens of those woods, and said by many to be the best ever seen.

Caspar's Air Patrol and How He Felt!

Editor Lumberman Canayenne:

It are some tam since Im wrote you few linę so mebee praps it be better sen you few word now.

Im spose you have hear bout dat airplane patrolle for watch de fire on de bush so dat gone make good subjec for one letter an mebee it gone ope your eye leetle bit too.

Im be read good deal bout dat air beezness an have tink so much on dat affair it bodder me an Im not slip very well for couple wik.

Ma wife Glorianna she have lot de fun wit me on de subjec de airplane an she laff wen Im mention it but it are no matter for de laff, special after ma experience las Sunday.

Las Sunday Im get up early for go on de church an have put may bes close, for Glorianna are gone wit me. De course Glorianna are not ready so soon like me for she not be long enuff marry for not take interes on her person, so Im seat mesef on nice beeg chair wat are stop on de gallerie on de front our house.

Mebbe you not know dat but Im got one de bes house on dis part de contree. It are build wit de stone an Im get her from ma ole Fadder wen he sell de res de lan on de Boss for her mill.

We have few apple tree on front de house an one place have piece nice flat ground for play de "croquet" wit de visite wen dey come on our place.

Well; Im seat mesef on dat chair an Im fine it very comfortable too for it have beeg shipskin over it an Im begin tink on dat airplane proposition.

Good Place For Kip Ma Plane

You mebee wonder for why Im bodder mesef wit such ting but dats easy answer. Im be "fire ranger" for die part de contree an Im spen mos ma time on de bush each summer.

Dis sort de work not spoil me for make de log on de winter for it give me good chançe to see de good tree, an place for make good road each winter. De Govermin she hire me but de Boss he pay ma wage.

Dis make explanations de ma reason for tink on de airplane for Im expec mos any tam get one dose machine from Monsieur Gouin, wit leetle book for tel how shes go.

Im look on dat piece groun wat are for play de "croquet" an Im tink it make good place for kip ma plane wen Im not use it, an den Im make de plan for "hangar" for place her wen it rain.

Jus bout de tam Im get plan for hangar wit door on each end Im hear fonny soun not far away.

Im tink one dose labor wat are make de beeg pay on de mill, have inves some hees monee on motor boat an have place it on de lac but de soun not come from dat direction. It are more like it are high on de air an Im look up an dere she are—one dose beeg airplane.

She come along jus like one does dev needle bog wat are catch de fly on de summer.

Ba Gosh; shes look pretty, but shes not look strong enough on ma eye for make me tink it carry Caspar Lamarche wat are weight more as two hunder poun.

Dere are feller on board wat are wave hees han on me an den he begin make de circle on de air an soon shes lan on ma croquet place.

Im go down for shake de han dat mans wat Im never see before an Im aks her on de house, but he say he not have time for visit an dat he have message for me from de Govermin.

Say; Dats make me feel fonny on ma stomack wat are empty too for we not eat before go on de Church, but Im ope dat lettre and read wat are say on her.

Im Asks Her Wat Shes Do Fir

He say dis feller are deliver me ma airplane an he are gone give me few lesson before go away an give lesson on nodder mans, an it asks me take ma lesson without make de delay.

Im asks dat feller give me chance for go on de Church, for Im begin tink Im have neglec ma duty lettle bit too much, special wen Im not sure Im gone arrive safe on ma home after make one trip wit her but he say he not take long dat he bring me back on time for 10 o'clock.

Well; Im fine wen de Govermin say you do one ting, dats bes for do it without make de fuss, so Im asks her what shes do firs.

Dat feller he show me roun dat machine an he show me lot de instrument an den he shaw me hows she start. He say Im put on nodder coat and cap wat he are han me an den he show me ma place on de cabin near her side. Den he say Im twis her screw for make de start an Im on dat but shes nearly catch me with one her claw. She make me tink de Mercedes an Im begin call her Mercedes on ma mine.

After Im place mesef on de cabin an have tie leetle strap roun ma wais which are plentee small now becaus ma inside have all rise on ma shoulder, dat feller let her go.

De firs motion are not so bad for we run on de groun for piece but wen she make couple jomp an not return on de groun after de las jomp, Im close ma eye. De las ting Im notis for lettle wile are wen we pass over de stable an ma Jersey cow are try race wit her calf on de back pasture, de bot hole dere tail on de air an wave it on us.

Dat feller are so busy move de instrument he not say nottin for minute but after wile he say "hole tight, Im gone do few trick" so Im do ma possible for kip de tight hole but it are hard job.

Wen he are busy do de trick Im look over de side an den Im close ma eye queek for we are more as one mile high.

Im begin tink how Glorianna are look wen she are dress in black, an de neighbor come on her house for cry wit her an tel her wat a good mans were Caspar, an asks her have he leave much insure.

Jus bout de time Im cry for mesef dat feller make queek turn an we are fly on our back. I look up an Im see de lac an de village, on de sky.

Dats plenty for me an Im asks her return on ma house but he say he not finish wit de lesson an he head her straight on de groun an ma inside fly on nodder end agen.

He try so many trick Im lose track of mesef an ma inside do jus wat dey like de bes, so wen he say he are gone make de "pancake" dats wat happen for me.

Ma Inside Fly on Nodder end Agen

We are have gone one awful tam an he show me how fine de fire an how Im gone put her out an lots de nodder ting but Im not pay much tenshun on wat he say for Im have plentee troub mesef.

Bime bye he tel me take de steerwheel an we go home an wen he have head for ma house Im take de wheel.

Wen we arrive near ma house he say we gone make nodder "pancake" for lan but Im tink one pancake are nuff for one trip an Im try an go down straight. We go down alright but Im not able to make de queek stop an jus wen Im prepare mesef for break beeg hole on ma house wit ma face, Im hear de voice ma wife Glorianna, an she say, "Caspar, you Ole Fool. For why you make de bad temper like dat, just becaus Im kip you wait few minute?"

You never see somebody more glad as me wen Im here Glorianna say dose word, for Im expec Im be kill an have jomp on de gallerie "plein vente" like we say on French.

Im ope ma eye an wen Im see her stan dere like one angel, Im jomp ma feet an give her one beeg kiss on his mout. Den Im excuse mesef an go on de house for change de collar wat are bus, an few nodder ting.

Dere are ole pine tree on de back ma house an one dose "pic de bois" woodpecker you call her are look for his breakfas on it and are make noise like wat Im tink are airplane, but it have bad effec for me spose it are only dream.

Im have one satisfy anyway. Im gone quit de read bout dose air patrolle beezness for Im fine it are bad for nodderstan leetle bit and not nuff bout her. Nooder ting wat are give me pleasure are dere gone be only two dose machine try dis summer an de feller wat run her are gone be custom make dose "pancake" drop, an dis are mos important.

Bien a vous,
Caspar Lamarche

Lac au Loup, Que., June 4, 1919.

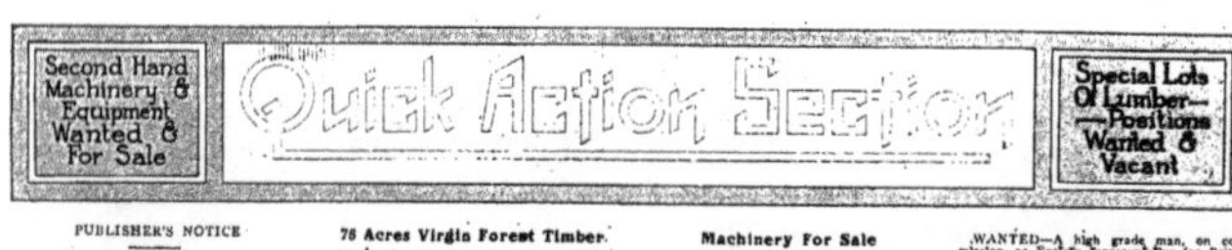

PUBLISHER'S NOTICE

Advertisements other than "Employment Wanted" or "Employees Wanted" will be inserted in this department at the rate of 20 cents per agate line (14 agate lines make one inch), $2.80 per inch, each insertion, payable in advance. Space measured from rule to rule. When four or more consecutive insertions of the same advertisement are ordered a discount of 25 per cent. will be allowed.

Advertisements of "Wanted Employment" will be inserted at the rate of one cent a word, net. Cash must accompany order. If Canada Lumberman box number is used, enclose ten cents extra for postage in forwarding replies. Minimum charge 25 cents.

Advertisements of "Wanted Employees" will be inserted at the rate of two cents a word, net. Cash must accompany the order. Minimum charge 50 cents.

Advertisements must be received not later than the 10th and 20th of each month to insure insertion in the subsequent issue.

Wanted–Lumber

Basswood Wanted

No. 2 Common and Mill Cull. Winter cut preferred. Apply Firstbrook Brothers, Ltd., Toronto, Ont. 8-t.f.

Wanted To Buy

1 x 4 and up Cull Spruce, also a merchantable grade; Cedar Posts and Hemlock. Hamilton Lumber & Coal Co., Limited, Hamilton, Ont. 14

Hemlock Wanted

Will buy (for cash) mill stock of Hemlock up to one and a half million feet; advise what you have. Box 986, Canada Lumberman, Toronto. 14

Wanted

We are in the market for Spruce Lumber, 50% 3 x 7 and 8", also 2", 2½" and 3" birch, 6" and wider, and quantity of white pine and Douglas fir. Will purchase entire mill cut. Also want aspen wood in forest or lots. Tell us what you have. Box 981, Canada Lumberman, Toronto. 14-15

For Sale–Lumber

FOR SALE

80,000 ft.	2 x 4 x 10/16'	Jack Pine	& Spruce
100,000 "	2 x 5 x 10/16'	"	"
100,000 "	2 x 6 x 10/16'	"	"
100,000 "	2 x 7 x 10/16'	"	"
100,000 "	2 x 8 x 10/16'	"	"
2 cars	6 x 6 x 10/16'	"	"
2 "	6 x 8 x 10/16'	"	"
2 "	8 x 8 x 10/16'	"	"
1 "	10 x 10 x 10/16'	"	"

The above stock cut and piled ready for shipment. Write or Wire

NORTHERN LUMBER MILLS,
14-17 North Cobalt, Ont.

FOR SALE

A few carloads of small Hemlock and Cedar Ties.
Two carloads of XX Cedar Shingles.
Two carloads of 32" Lath.
One carload of 4' Lath.
Three carloads of Pine Dressing Strips.
Three carloads of Spruce Dressing Strips.
Three carloads of 6 x 6 to 10 x 10 timbers,—18 to 30 ft.

The John Carew Lumber Co., Ltd.,
13-14 Lindsay, Ont.

75 Acres Virgin Forest Timber.

Maple, Basswood, Rock Elm, Soft Elm. Within 2½ miles of railroad. Apply,

H. G. COCKBURN & SON,
14 Guelph, Ont.

SPRUCE FOR SALE
For immediate shipment

200 M. ft. 3" 5th quality and better.
200 M. ft. 3" 5th and 6th quality.
This lumber can be resawed and dressed in transit if desired. Write for attractive quotation.

J. GEO. CHALIFOUR,
13-14 Quebec, Can.

For Sale–Machinery

FOR SALE—SAWMILL

24 H. P. Engine, 50 H. P. return tubular boiler. Three log seat carriage, overhead set, friction feed works, single edger and slab saw. All in fair order. Price $1,000. Box 915, Canada Lumberman, Toronto. 12-15

High Speed Matchers

1—Berlin No. 90 High Speed Matcher with Profilers and several extra heads.
1—American No. 77 High Speed Matcher without Profiler but having several extra heads.
Two real bargains.
Box 893, Canada Lumberman, Toronto, Ont. 6-t.f.

Band Saw Mill For Sale

One Waterous 9 ft. Band Saw Mill, gunshot feed, complete with extra saws and filing equipment. Used about one year, excellent condition. The Geo. F. Foss Machinery & Supply Co., Ltd., 305 St. James St., Montreal, Que. 7-t.f.

Logging Equipment

Phoenix Caterpillar Log Haulers.
Logging Sleighs.
Rutters.
Hoisting Engines.
12 lb. and 16 lb. Relaying Rails.

J. L. NEILSON & CO.,
13-t.f. Winnipeg, Man.

Here's Your Opportunity!
For Sale

"Canada Machinery Corporation", New No. 107 Planer and Matcher. New price $1,750. Our Price $800.

"Canada Machinery Corporation", New No. 110 Planer and Matcher and Moulder. New Price $1,400. Our Price $750.

"C.M.C." No. 610 Gang Edger. New price $900. Our Price $400.

"C.M.C." No. 308-10" Heavy Four-Sided Moulder, just like new. New price $1,750. Our Price $950.

Further particulars if so desired will be cheerfully furnished.

WILLIAMS & WILSON LIMITED,
84 Inspector Street,
13-15 Montreal, P.Q.

Building Sold, Machinery Must be Sold

Iron Pipe Valves, etc., guaranteed.
Boiler, 72 x 16 ft. 100 lbs.
Twin engine, bore 13¼", stroke 17".
8 Stickers.
17 Saws (various styles).
5 Sanders.
2 Automatic turning tables.
2 Tenoners.
2 Chain Mortisers.
4 Filing Machines (automatic).
2 Fans and Blower system.
Pulley and Shafting.
Many other Planing Mill machines.

Apply: Dominion Lumber & Coal Co. Ltd., Hamilton, Ont. 11-14

Machinery For Sale

20 to 25 h.p. portable horizontal boiler and engine on skids, good condition. Easy terms to responsible party. Box 973, Canada Lumberman, Toronto. 13-16

For Sale

1—17 x 24 Atlas Engine, with 36 in. x 10 ft. flywheel.
3—No. 94 Berlin Matchers, 15 in., fitted with hard steel knives on top and bottom cylinders—one pair shiplap, jointer and flooring heads with bits for each machine.
1—No. 182 Berlin Double Surfacer, 30 in. x 8 in.
1—No. 190 Berlin Buzz Planer.
1—No. 290 Berlin Picket Header.

The Otis Staples Lumber Company, Ltd.,
19-t.f. Wycliffe, B.C.

Wanted–Employment

Advertisements under this heading one cent a word per insertion. Box No. 10 cents extra. Minimum charge 25 cents.

First Class Band Sawyer wants position. 14 years experience in hard and soft woods, right or left hand rig. Box 964, Canada Lumberman, Toronto. 13-14

A Practical Lumberman, years of experience in Bush, just returned, wants position as foreman or licensed log or pulpwood scaler. Best of references. Box 978, Canada Lumberman, Toronto. 13-14

Man with long experience in export of deals, planed boards and box shooks for United Kingdom, Africa, Australia, and other countries, is open for engagement. Write Box 958, Canada Lumberman, Toronto. 12-14

POSITION WANTED by a well educated young man, 15 years' experience with wholesalers and manufacturers; competent inspector either hard or soft wood; will consider any other capacity. Apply Box 956, Canada Lumberman, Toronto. 12-16

WANTED—Position as Superintendent or Foreman of planing mill or woodworking factory by thoroughly capable experienced man who has handled big work and large gangs, knows the business and machines thoroughly, and gets results. Box 950, Canada Lumberman, Toronto. 12-15

Wanted–Employees

WANTED—Salesman for lumber yard. Apply Box 985, Canada Lumberman, Toronto. 14

First Class Man on Rip Saw.

JOHN B. SMITH & SONS,
13-16 Toronto, Ont.

SALESMAN with Eastern connection, to sell B. C. Timbers, Yard Stock and Shingles, on Commission. Box 929, Canada Lumberman, Toronto. 10-11

Wanted—One Foreman for Sash and Door Department; experienced on solid and veneered doors; four bench men, experienced on hard and soft wood; two cabinetmakers.

J. R. EATON & SONS, LIMITED,
13-16 Orillia, Ont.

LUMBER EXPORT HOUSE has opening for intelligent young man, 19-23 years of age. Applicant must be ambitious, willing, and have a good education. Competent stenographer and typist, and be accurate at figures. Moderate salary to start, but good opportunity for advancement and to learn the business. Apply giving references, experience, etc., to Mr. S. Bick, P. O. Box 284, Montreal. 14-17

WANTED—A high grade man, on commission, as Eastern representative for British Columbia organization handling a daily output of 500,000 feet. Must have first class connections and wide experience. Box 238, Canada Lumberman, 212 Winch Bldg., Vancouver, B.C.

WANTED—SALESMAN—Man competent to visit Lumber Mills and Woodworking Plants generally, with some knowledge of Saw Mill operation. Must have fairly good education, native Canadian, returned soldier preferred. In writing give full particulars, experience and references. Apply Box 990, Canada Lumberman, Toronto. 14

Good reliable saw mill man with portable mill to cut two million feet or more Birch and Hemlock in Patterson Township. Warren Ross Lumber Co., Jamestown, N.Y. 14-15

Birch Dowels

Firm of Liverpool Timber Merchants would be pleased to get into touch with a Canadian firm manufacturing Birch Dowels, with a view to handling their output in England. Box 979, Canada Lumberman, Toronto. 14

Saw Mill Plant For Sale

Practically new and modern Saw Mill Plant, capacity about 30 Million feet per annum, located in the Interior of British Columbia on a beautiful inland lake and on the main line of the Grand Trunk Pacific Railway. About 500 Million feet of timber on and adjacent to Lake (about 90% Spruce) and another Billion feet available at reasonable prices. Natural conditions ideal for economical logging, manufacturing, piling and shipping. An advantage of about $4 per thousand feet in freight rates to the Prairie Provinces over Coast shipments.

This property offers unlimited possibilities as a lumber, pulp and paper property. Would consider selling a half interest. Terms reasonable.

A. C. FROST COMPANY,
134 South LaSalle Street,
5-t.f. Chicago, Ill.

Two Timber Limits

34,000,000 ft. Virgin Timber, and 3,000,000 cords of Spruce Pulpwood. For all desirable information write to D. McDonald, La Salle, N.Y. 12-15

For Sale

Building and machinery of good Double Cut Band Sawmill, well equipped with steam feed, canter, loaders, etc.

Also two storey Brick Factory on large lot convenient to two railways; splendid location. Address Box 949, Owen Sound, Ont. 12-t.f.

For Sale—100 Acres Land

within 2½ miles of railroad.
75 acres Virgin Forest, Maple, Basswood, Rock Elm, Soft Elm. Apply

H. G. COCKBURN & SON,
14 Guelph, Ont.

Pine Doors Wanted

I want to buy 5,000 No. 2 pine doors, for delivery this summer; design to be 5 or 6 flat cross panels, sound knotted, no plugs permitted; may be dowelled or tenoned, cove and bead sticking solid; sizes standard in both 6' 6" and 6' 8" heights. Quote F.O.B. Cars, Toronto, Ont. Terms must be 60 days net. Apply Box 982, Canada Lumberman, Toronto. 14

Opportunity in Lumber Business

Will contract self-red cedar timber as cut—150,000,000-foot tract. Quality and accessibility good. Grand Trunk Railroad.

J. RANDALL BLACK,
14-17 Edmonton, Alberta.

Saw Mill Property FOR SALE

Picnic Island sawmill plant at Little Current, Georgian Bay, 37 acres, for sale or lease for a term of years, or might put it in a good sized company, part cash, part stock; cutting capacity 140 M. a day, two thousand feet stone-filled lumber docks; 16 ft. water, Algoma railway station less than a mile distant, log booming capacity 10 million, telegraph and telephone, school taxes only, title from Crown, no debts or disputes; one of the best mills on the Bay, selling cheap to wind up an estate. For further particulars as to the mill and about twenty other buildings, etc., apply to Thomas Conlon, 44 Church Street, St. Catharines, Ont. 13-16

Miscellaneous

For Sale

One Detroit Hot Blast, Dry Kiln System, complete with Fan and Engine, also 35 feet of 9" double leather belt, used two weeks.

Port Hope Veneer & Lumber Co.,
13-14. Port Hope, Ont.

Sale of Timber Berths

Tenders will be received by the undersigned up to and including Wednesday, the 16th day of July next, for the right to cut the timber of various descriptions on the Townships of Groves and St. Louis in the District of Sudbury.

Terms and conditions of the sale containing full particulars, and maps showing the position of the Berths offered for sale, may be obtained upon application to the undersigned, or from Mr. Charles Henderson, Crown Timber Agent, Sudbury.

G. H. FERGUSON,
Minister of Lands, Forests and Mines,

N.B.—No unauthorized publication of this notice will be paid for. 12-14

Toronto, June 11th, 1919.

Sale of Timber Berths

Tenders will be received by the undersigned up to and including Wednesday, the 16th day of July next, for the right to cut the Red and White Pine Timber on the following Townships, viz.:

DISTRICT OF ALGOMA

Mississaga Forest Reserve,
Township "C".

DISTRICT OF SUDBURY

Township of Teffer.
Township of McConnell.
Township of McNish.
Township of McNamara.

DISTRICT OF NIPISSING

Township of Kenny,
Township of Sisk,
Township of McCallum,
Township of McLaren,
Township of Charlton.

Also, tenders will be received by the undersigned up to and including Wednesday, the sixteenth day of July next, for the right to cut various classes of timber on Township "U", in the Mississaga Forest Reserve, in the District of Algoma.

The terms and conditions of the sale containing full particulars, and also maps showing the berths offered for sale, may be obtained upon application to the undersigned, or from Mr. Charles Henderson, Crown Timber Agent, Sudbury, or from Mr. J. T. McDougall, Crown Timber Agent, North Bay.

G. H. FERGUSON,
Minister of Lands, Forests & Mines.

Toronto, May 14th, 1919.

N.B.—No unauthorized publication of this notice will be paid for. 11-14

WANTED

LIGHT RAILS

State whether complete with splice or angle bars.

Give size, quantity, location, condition and best cash price f.o.b. cars loading point.

Box No. 900, Canada Lumberman,
13-14 Toronto.

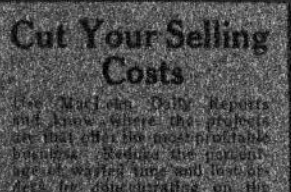

Coolidge & Carlisle

Forest Engineers

Timber Estimates and Maps
Plans for Logging Operations

Bangor, Maine

$2.00 a Year

24 Issues

Big value to any Lumber Manufacturer or Dealer.

ARE YOU A SUBSCRIBER?

CANADA LUMBERMAN
347 Adelaide St. W., TORONTO

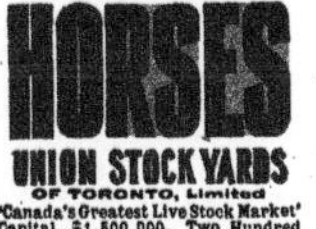

Correspondence Solicited.

WALTER HARLAND SMITH
Manager Horse Dept.

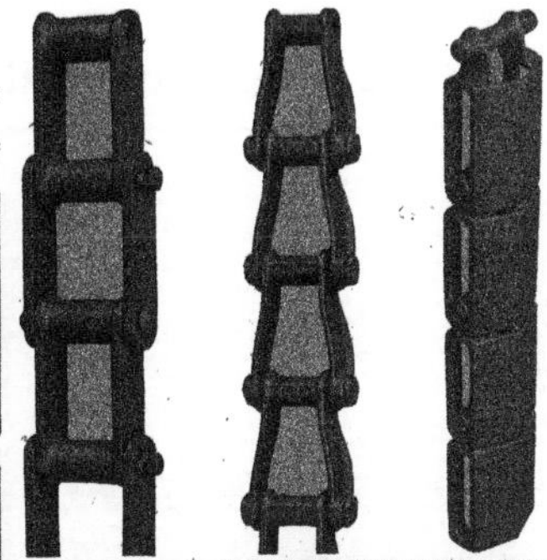

LINK-BELT
FOR EVERY PURPOSE

Whether your problem is one of power transmission, elevating or conveying, we have a type of Link-Belt especially designed for the purpose.

And when we say "especially designed" we mean it. For our engineers have spent years in the study of the peculiar conditions and requirements which various industries place upon Link-Belt. Each type has been designed not with the thought of how cheaply it can be made, but how perfectly it can serve its purpose. We show a few types. Our Catalog shows many others. Send for a copy.

Look for this Mark on Every Link ⟩——⟨ It is your guarantee of service and satisfaction.

CANADIAN LINK-BELT CO., LTD.

WELLINGTON & PETER STREETS, TORONTO

Stock also carried at 1195 St. James Street, Montreal

Review of Current Trade Conditions

Ontario and the East

The general tone of the lumber business has been improving steadily, and shipments across the border have been growing larger all the while. Building is imparting activity to the local demand, and there have been brisk requisitions for hemlock and spruce. The new stocks of this season's cut are beginninng to come on the market, and none too soon, for dry lumber has been growing scarce.

There is every indieation that prices will go higher and quotations on all lines are very firm. Much progress is being made in the house building plans under the government housing act and a fuller reference to the development along this line is made in another column. Costs of manufacturing are advancing all the while and preparations will soon be made for sending men to the bush for the coming season. There is every likelihood that the cut during the fall months will be considerably larger than any year since the outbreak of the war. Every week new concerns are being organized in the lumber business to undertake operations and manufacturing conditions are good. There have been very few labor troubles at any of the saw mills, and stocks are being gotten out in good shape. One large Ontario concern states that during the past month they shipped more lumber than any year since they have been in business. Predictions are being freely made that there will be a decided scarcity in certain lines before many weeks advance. There have been several large sales closed for this season's cuts at augmented figures over 1918, and prices in the East have taken another jump.

The cost of boarding men in the camps will this winter be heavier than ever and wages still show no signs of dropping, all of which means added expense in getting out the logs. The situation in the west has greatly improved and a brisk demand is springing up from the prairies. The B. C. mills, which were closed down owing to labor disturbances and strikes, have resumed operations. Some of the plants are now operating night and day to catch up. Loggers have made another advance in prices, and quotations for Coast forest products have been aviating all the while. The increases in the past two months have averaged about twenty-five per cent., and since the outbreak of the war the figures on most lines have shown raises well on to one hundred per cent. Certain lines on which the mills have an abundance of stock are being sold in the east, and there is a fair demand for timbers. Shingles from British Columbia are still a scarce article, but a few carloads are coming through. Prices keep soaring. Lath are more plentiful than they were some time ago, and the market is strong.

The hardwood situation is staunch and birch and oak are in active requisition with prices stiffening all the while. What has added to the gravity of the situation in the east during the past few days have been the menacing forest fires. Fortunately for limit holders the rain came in time to avert a repetition of the scourge of two or three years ago. In the east a number of sawmills have been destroyed and this is not good news at a time when all the lumber in the country will be needed. The export situation improves, but slowly, owing to high rates of carriage.

Referring to the export problem, a recent despatch from London, Eng., says:

A prediction made that the Ministry of Shipping would shortly commandeer more shipping space, which is so urgently required for Canadian trade, has been soon realized. The reality is a little worse than was anticipated, however. During July the Ministry will require seventy per cent. of all cargo space, and in August and September this will be increased, leaving practically no room for ordinary commercial shipments.

This space will be required largely for the shipment of timber and bacon bought in Canada. It includes 75,000,000 tons per month of bacon. A strong protest has been addressed to the Ministry of Shipping by the Candian Trade Mission, and the request has been made that a proportion of the tonnage now arranged to go to the United States ports be transferred to Canadian routes. It was recently discovered that some of this commandeered space was being used for the shipment of scrap iron ordered in Canada by the Ministry of Munitions and unsaleable there at a sufficiently high price to Britain. Compaint was made and this has accordingly been discontinued.

It has been reported that some very extensive sales have been made by leading lumber companies during the past few days. One mill in Northern Ontario is reported to have sold its output of white pine merchantable at a top notch figure to a leading Michigan firm. It was an exceptionally high price and would indicate that values are increasing all the time. It is understood that the R. Laidlaw Lumber Co. of Toronto has purc[illegible]sed ten million feet from Manley Chew, Midland, Ont., consisting of white and Norway pine, hemlock and spruce. It is understood that about three-quarters of the output consists of white pine.

Gum has now gone so high in price that Canadian birch is a strong competitor with it and several heavy sales are taking place in the latter wood.

The Toronto Housing Commission announces that 200 applications have been received to date from those desirous of getting homes under the ruling of the commission. Land has been purchased and erections planned for a number which will exceed the applications. According to Manager Swaine a large number of inquiries are being received in this connection at the Temple Building offices.

Mr. W. M. Neal, of the Canadian Railway War Board, in respect to the loading of cars, states as follows:

"I might add from now on the car situation will become more acute, and the shortage will probably reach the extreme point about the middle of next fall. Any situation along these lines which may come about will be ameliorated if all concerned will continue the policy of placing the maximum load in each car."

United States

So far as supply and demand are concerned there is not much change in the general situation. Many mills are unable to meet requisitions and stocks are low. Word comes from hardwood dealers across the line that there has been a further advance of from two to eight dollars, and some think that the top has almost been reached. The new stocks are beginning to come forward and will dry out rapidly during the summer months. Northern pine operators lately advanced their prices and the increase on selects ranges from two to five dollars per thousand. In some instances, orders have had to be declined as the mills have all the business they can turn out. Southern pine prices continue strong with an advancing tendency.

The upward trend continues in hardwoods and the best grades are commanding the highest quotations ever known.

The largest supplies are held by the manufacturers of birch, but the stocks of birch in the hands of jobbers have been pretty well cleaned out. The furniture manufacturers are the best customers of the birch owners. Ash has been picking up of late, due to a large demand from the refrigerator manufacturers for the softer quality and an increased demand from the makers of automobiles for the tougher kinds of this wood. Prices have been going up with the demand. Short supplies of all hardwoods at southern mills, and particularly of oak, have sent quotations on this wood to unheard of heights. Buyers are bidding for the stock that is to be had, and there seems no limit, but the sky. Manufacturing conditions in the south have been so bad for the past six months that the cut has been way below normal, and there is no telling when the mills will be able to approach normal activity.

The call for hemlock is particularly brisk in view of so much home construction. The revival of building in the East is progressing rapidly and thus the hemlock producers are patricularly favored in being near an eager market and one that it is impossible to satisfy at present. Eatsern buyers continue to take a great deal of interest in hemlock from the North and are also paying attention to the Pacific coast stocks of this wood. Prices are very firm and stocks in the hands of manufacturers are small, especially of lumber that is in shipping condition.

Lath show a steady increase from week to week and supplies in the hands of manufacturers are really getting badly reduced. Lath prices advanced this week in many sections, the advances ranging from 25 cents to 50 cents a thousand. The red cedar shingle market has been a little steadier this week and with the close of the mills resulting from the Fourth of July celebration the market is sure to remain firm, as the demand for shingles has not decerased. The supply of cedar logs at the mills is not large and most of the producers have more orders than they can fill, and with the restricted output of the next two or three weeks the demand is very apt to cause an increase in the market. The demand for cypress shingles continues in excess of the supply and thus very good prices are obtained. With the growing scarcity of cypress and red cedar shingles

the interest of retailers in redwood, white cedar and pine shingles increases and sales naturally show a corresponding increase.

The sash and door business, from the standpoint of the producer and wholesale distributor, is very satisfactory even when compared with pre-war conditions. This applies to the amount of orders on hand, trade that is being proffered and future prospects. In every commercial and industrial centre there is a pronounced scarcity of quarters in which to house the people. Rents have advanced radically, which has encouraged capital to make investments. Flats and apartment buildings are being constructed in very much larger proportions than ever before. In the country most every farmer has ready money, and with the assurance of abundant yields and higher prices for his product, the granger is disposed to be a liberal buyer. The up-to-date dealer is taking advantage of this situation to sell the farmer a new home, barn or other structure before the automobile salesman and distributor of luxuries gets all the farmers' cash. The demand in the cities is calling for a large amount of special woodwork. In some cases the contractors have to suspend operations to wait until they get this special material.

Great Britain

With the signing of Peace Treaty there is a general feeling of relief and business will now go on actively in all lines. There is a good opening in the Old Country just now for Canadian woodenware. A leading firm, in writing the "Canada Lumberman" says: "We were large importers in this line before the war, but unfortunately we found it necessary to get our supplies from Scandinavian and American firms, although we have done considerable business with Canadian manufacturers. We realize the fact that Canadian produce articles to compete with foreign countries, and we see no reason whatever why we should not get all our supplies from Canada alone. We hope soon to arrange contracts with firms with whom we have previously dealt, and also interest other manufacturers in the lines we wish to import. There is undoubtdly at the present time a fine opportunity for Canadian manufacturers to supply the British market if they will only specialize in the export trade."

Speaking of transportation an English exchange says:

Some may naturally ask why it is we do not anticipate a big trade this year, considering that the construction must increase as Europe becomes more settled, and as our men in this country get back into their old employment. There are, it is argued, plenty of goods in Canada, Finland and Sweden, and if the demand in the importing countries increases, as all anticipate it will, why should we not also anticipate a large consumption of timber during the current shipping season. To those importers who have carefully studied the position the answer is only too obvious. There will not be sufficient tonnage available to bring over the wood. It is not even a question of rates. In all quarters, and in all trades, the same cry for more shipping is heard, and important as wood is for national developments, food and other raw materials are sometimes more so; and, what is more to the point, nearly all other commodities can afford to pay higher freights. Timber importers and merchants should, therefore, make up their minds that, however favorably the labor and national situation develops, timber will be short in supply. There could have been no more powerful influence over the shipping of wood than that of the Timber Controller and of the Government Buyer, and yet these two officials, even with the help of the Ministry of Shipping, have not been altogether successful. We hear of firms among those who left the chartering of their goods in the hands of the Government Timber Buyer, who have not yet been allocated tonnage for more than a proportion of their f.o.w. contracts..

Regarding Canadian goods, there is no change of note. Freights continue very high, and the Government buyer is allocated the bulk of the space. The situation depends almost entirely on what arrangements will be made for disposal of the very large purchases of Canadian timber made by the Government. The market could do with shipments of birch lumber and logs, as there is no large supplies of these woods in store. Pine deals and sidings are also urgently needed, as the modest shipments that have already arrived came in on a practically bare market and went into consumption direct. There has been a fair demand for Oregon pine in fair widths, in the absence of other woods that might have been preferred if available.

Although there is an urgent need for at least 300,000 new houses in Great Britain, no big start has been made in building them. The high cost of building materials is considered to be the chief deterrent to the revival of the building trade. At an interview recently granted to a representative of the London Times the Minister of Supply indicated that ample supplies of building materials, except slates, are available for all local housing schemes as they develop, and that when allowance has been made for the probable requirements of the Government housing authorities there will still be adequate supplies for private builders.

The government stocks of timber are now about 140,000 standards (28,000,000 board feet.) Some 117,000 standards have been bought in the Baltic and White Sea regions and will be delivered very soon. Another 200,000 standards of European timber have been purchased for delivery later in the year. A further 250.000 standards of Canadian timber have been bought and a number of ships have been allocated for their shipment.

Transport difficulties are considered to be second only to high prices as an obstacle to the resumption of building operations. About 40,000 freight cars, which were taken from the British railways ,are in northern France and Belgium, and it is believed doubtful if they will ever be brought back. Because of the high cost, the private builder can not, without aid, build houses of a class that formerly rented for about $200 a year that could now profitably be let at less than about $450 The greater part of the work will, therefore, probably be done with the assistance of government housing authorities

Market Correspondence

SPECIAL REPORTS ON CONDITIONS AT HOME AND ABROAD

St. John Shipments Are Moving More Freely

A much better tone has come over the lumber market at St. John during the past two weeks; large shipments are moving forward both by steamer, but largely by sailing vessels. One large five masted schooner now loading here will carry away 2½ million feet, other small vessels are also loading, practically all water shipments being for United Kingdom parts and chiefly British government orders. Largely all of the stock being shipped is coming from rotary mills from the interior of the province. The mills at St. John are not being used to supply cargoes to amount to anything, but nevertheless it has its effect and will be felt later on as it clears up stocks in the interior of the country.

One great factor in the better tone here is the buying for the American market at good prices and every day sees an improvement in these American prices; if it were possbile to purchase larger quantities the American market would certainly take much more stock but as the British government had bought up practically all the mills' cuts here very little remains to be offered to United States and it looks very much as if the buyers must go short of their requirements.

Prices are well maintained 2 x 3-4-5-6 being quoted at $40.00 on cars; 2 x 8 at $42.50; 2 x 9-10 $45 and $47 on cars here—net cash. Refuse stocks are being bought at around $27 on cars and stocks of these grades will also be much depleted before long. Pine lumber also remains very firm, anything in pine bringing around $40 on cars, or in some cases, as the British government and foreign buyers are purchasing all they can find. It appears as if there would be a large shortage of pine. Laths have taken a jump and are scarce at $3.50 on wharf at St. John. Shingles are also very scarce and are selling extras $5.50; clears $5.75; 2nd clears $4.75; Ex. No. 1 $3.25 city delivery.

Logs are coming forward out of the booms as rapidly as possible and all mills at St. John are running full time.

Ottawa Business is Looming Up Encouragingly

"Getting better all the time," describes the situation as regarding the Ottawa market during the opening period of July. Trading, sales, and orders continued to increase over even the exceptionally good period during the last two weeks of June.

The entire general outlook during the last fortnight underwent a considerable alteration for the better. The market, while largely pine, when judged as to sales, orders, and inquiries from the United States also showed an increased demand for spruce stocks.

United States business was the principal factor to govern the increase in the volume of trade done. Ottawa wholesalers and manufacturers all reported an increased volume. The wholesalers, if anything, increased their purchases in cetrain grades from the manufacturers, buying this year's saw cut.

One of the best informed lumbermen in the Ottawa Valley stated that the possibilities of the present outlook was little short of

Advertising is Business Insurance

A large manufacturer who, during the war, devoted his entire plant to war-work, kept his advertising running continuously, although he could not fill a single order. When asked why he did it, he said that he was insuring a market for his product when he returned to his regular lines. He has since reverted to his pre-war products and his plant is running to full capacity with more business in sight than he can handle.

Advertising was business insurance for him.

"wonderful." The basis back of this assertion was that the saw-cut of the Ottawa Valley mills, this year, was going to be considerably below that of last season. The cost of production from the camp end had risen, and for next year's operations would likely be higher.

A suggestion was made by those outside of the trade that the increased buying in the United States might, in a measure, be attributed to the securing of a large contract by Americans for the rebuilding of Nancy and other devastated cities in France. It is, at the time of writing, impossible to definitely state whether the lumber now being purchased in the Ottawa Valley for export to the U. S. is eventually going to land in France or not.

Factory labor conditions as between mill hands and employers continue to hang fire. No move by either side was definitely made up to July 9th. Thus the acceptance or rejection of the principle of collective bargaining remained in abeyance.

Sash and door remained about the same. Lath and shingle showed more activity. Building trades showed some strengthening.

Domestic business showed improvement. Prices indicated a general advance. Western lumber, it was reported from Eastern sources, had showed a recent jump of from $3 to $4 per M. This season's wood operations are expected to be thirty-three and one-third per cent. over the season of 1918-1.

Montreal Finds Conditions Getting Better

A still further improvement in business in Montreal is to be reported. As noted in the last notes, the chief increase is in trade with the United States. The building trade in the Eastern States is brisk; and Canadian firms are feeling the benefit of this revival.

Prices rule high, and the outlook is for a continuance of this condition. The general idea is that we may expect still stiffer quotations, having regard to the upward tendency of most commodities and of labor. "In my opinion," said a local wholesaler, "we may look for a lumber famine in October or September. Spruce is getting scarcer every day, and with the large amount taken off the market by the British governmen tand the good buying of the Americans, there is certain to be a shortage. Under these circumstances prices are bound to advance." Lath is an exceptionally strong market, with a good demand. B. C. stock is also firm.

Local trade is better. A fair amount of building work is coming out, and there are also reports that other jobs of a good size will soon be let. The building permits continue to improve. Last month the total was $731,417, an increase of $433,857, as compared with 1918; for the half year the total was $2,887,424 a gain of $847,859. This was in spite of the labor unrest, which is holding up a certain amount of work.

Reports from the province indicate that building is satisfactory, and that lumber dealers are doing a fair business. The housing problem, however, is still serious, and in Montreal practically no progress has been made with the municipal scheme.

The Canadian War Board has issued a notice to the effect that there is likely to be a car shortage next month, and asking that cars be filled to capacity, so as to relieve the situation.

A very large amount of lumber is being shipped to the United Kingdom for the government from this port, Quebec, and Three Rivers, the commercial consignments being restricted. The goods are being shipped by liners and by tramp boats. It is expected that the bulk of the Eastern purchases for the government will be sent by October. There is an increasing demand for space for all kinds of commodities, and certain criticisms have been made as to the intention of the Ministry of Shipping to commandeer additional space, principally, it is stated, for the shipment of lumber and bacon.

Enterprising Lumber Company Issues Paper

The Long-Bell Lumber Co., Kansas City, Mo., have begun the publication of the "Long-Bell Bulletin," a miniature newspaper for retail lumbermen. The reading matter is bright, timely and interesting. This is another advanced step in the service department of this progressive organization, which has for a long time been conducting a national advertising campaign on behalf of retail dealers who sell Long-Bell products. The company believe in co-operating with the dealer in making sales to the consumer. The "Bulletin" appears under the editorial direction of Paul E. Kendall, the aggressive, advertising manager of the company, who announces that the publication is more than a newspaper, for it will help create and maintain friendly relations with the company's customers. The "Bulletin" will be issued once a month and will be a medium for the exchange of ideas on trade-marked lumber and northern merchandising methods.

Forest fires in various sections of Newfoundland destroyed valuable timber tracts and threatened isolated settlements. Later reports received indicate that rain storms have extinguished most of the fires.

Sir James Ball Scores Profiteers

Says If Yellow Pine Dealers Continue to Charge Excessive Prices the Government Will Get Busy

Sir James Ball, London, Eng.

Sir James Ball, British Timber Controller, who recently visited Canada, has returned to England, and has just retired from the position which he so ably and impartially filled during the war. He resumed his railway duties on July 1st. In his intercourse and interviews with the lumbermen in all parts of the Dominion, Sir made many friends in the industry who will read with interest the subjoined statements from the press of Great Britain.

The "Timber News" says Sir James made the acquaintance of many trade organizations and the principal exporters in the districts covered. We understand that Sir James has made arrangements for supplies of British Columbia fir and spruce, the former (largely sleepers), coming from the West and the latter from the East Coast. Transport has already been arranged for at favorable rates.

In an interview which Sir James Ball accorded the press on June 27, he announced that his position as Controller of Timber Supplies will terminate at the end of the month, and he will resume his railway duties on July 1. He said that during his visit to British Columbia he had been struck with the potentialities of Douglas fir, of which he believed we should see far larger stocks in this country during the year than ever before. His associations with the trade, despite little differences which soon yielded to treatment, had been most cordial, and, as a whole, he had been loyally assisted in his work. He expressed the hope that the trade would now be loyal to itself, and set its face against the profiteering instincts of a few who, if left to themselves, would put up prices unduly. Should this continue the Government will not hesitate to step into the breach, and sell to the consumer direct.

It may be recalled at this moment that Sir James Ball, then Mr. Ball, was apointed Controller of Timber Supplies on Whit Saturday, 1917, in succession to Sir Bampfylde Fuller, K.C.I.E. Though none will pretend to regret the passing of control, all who know Sir James and his work will recognize that he has acquitted himself well, and will take with him into his retirement the best wishes for his future of those with whom he has come in contact.

Is Canada Barred in The Timber Trade?

Despite the urgent need of timber for the huge house building program of the Government and municipalities here, Canadians see little chance of supplying the market in competition with the Scandinavians, says a recent press despatch from London, Eng. The chief difficulty is shipping. Before the war Canadian rates were nearly double those from lower Scandinavia. To-day they are almost trebled, thus helping the Scandinavian intention to control the British market, especially now the large Russian competition is quiescent.

A. C. Manbert, Ontario Timber Commissioner, says that until the British Government's economic policy is announced and Government stocks of timber are distributed, individual purchases from Canada or elsewhere are bound to be deferred, moreover the present freights make all private timber importation very hazardous unless for a definitely arranged outlet. Canada must devise some means of controlling transportation as well as producing wares. It is incongruous to expect Canada to compete successfully with Sweden and Norway in timber products and at the same time to look to these countries for a large proportion of the bottoms to carry Canadian goods.

The huge building program now being formulated in all parts of Britain needs large supplies of white pine. The quality of Ontario's product is well recognized, but the price bears a prominent part in the introductory stages of any extension of its use here. Everything says Mr. Manbert, depends on the shipping facilities and the prices announced. French and British timber merchants together agreed to put the demands of practically all importers of Baltic timber in England and France into the hands of a central chartering bureau at great St. Helens, London City. This alliance is designed to reduce freights and encourage Baltic trade.

EDGINGS

Ontario

James Davidson's Sons, Ottawa, recently shipped to France one of their cut houses consisting of two rooms and a shed.

The sawmill of James McBrayne in Firstbrook Township and 7,000 feet of lumber were destroyed in the recent forest fires near Haileybury.

A fire occurred in the planing mill of Jacob Kauffman, Limited, Kitchener, Ont. The blaze was extinguished promptly, the loss being very slight.

The Union Navigation Co., Limited, Montreal, has been incorporated to build, equip and furnish vessels and boats of all descriptions. Capital $50,000.

Duncan Graham, of Renfrew, and P. Shannon, of Booth & Shannon, Biscotasing, Ont., have bought the old Milne mill at Brennan Harbor and are operating the same this season.

The Canadian Barking Drum Company has just received a contract for another American barking drum for the Lake Superior Paper Co., making the sixteenth drum for this concern.

The Dickson Co., Limited, of Peterboro, have been receiving tenders for their old sawmill, which is located on the east bank of the river at Lakefield. The structure will be dismantled.

The Lang Mfg. Co., Limited, Guelph, Ont., has been incorporated to manufacture and deal in wood, iron and steel and all products which these materials enter into. Capital $40,000.

The National Standard Co. of Canada, Ltd., Guelph, Ont., have been incorporated to manufacture and deal in any article made in whole, or in part, from wood, glass or fabric. Capital $30,000.

It is learned that the order for "knock down" houses which the Canadian Timber Products Association was to receive some months ago from the French government, did not materialize, the high ocean freight rates killing the business.

A fatal accident was narrowly averted in the plant of Austin & Roberts, Haliburton, Ont. The night watchman while attempting to put a belt on the saw-dust carrier became entangled in the shaft, his clothes were all torn off and one arm was twisted out of joint, but, fortunately, by this time the machinery had stopped. Other employees hearing him call came and quickly released him from his predicament.

The Allied Aeroplanes, Limited, Brantford, Ont., have been incorporated to manufacture and deal in aeroplanes on a commercial scale; also to manufacture and deal in automobiles, trucks and other vehicles. Capital $40,000. It is the intention of the company to run an aerial jitney and two machines willl be put into service at an early date. Lieut. G. Russell, late of the Royal Air Force, has been appointed official pilot.

Information from the Abitibi Power and Paper Co., of Iroquois Falls, leads to the belief that this year's business will stand well ahead of last year's, a condition that will have an important bearing on the payment of the arrears on the preferred, dating back to April 1, 1915. As the preferred stock amounts to only $1,000,000, this would not be a heavy tax on the company. The whole output of the paper mills is sold for the present year.

The Canadian Soo Lumber Co., Limited, has been incorporated with a capital stock of $500,000 and head offices in Sault Ste. Marie, Ont. The company is empowered to buy, sell and operate timber lands and to manufacture and deal in lumber, timber and all and sundry wood articles. Among the incorporators are William Herman Rath and Peter P. DuKet, lumberman, of Chicago, and Geo. A. A. Allen and James McEwan, of Sault Ste. Marie, Ont.

The total number of municipalities which have come under the Ontario Housing Act now amounts to 74. This number included 17 cities, 35 towns, 14 villages and 10 townships. Actual construction operations are at present being carried on by 40 of these municipalities. Mr. J. A. Ellis, the Provincial Director has approved over 1200 plans and the houses in the course of construction exceed 400. Nine travelling inspectors were recently appointed to visit the various municipalities that are conducting building operations; out of the nine men appointed, seven were returned soldiers.

A provincial charter has been granted the Kingston Road Lumber Company, Limited, with a capital stock of $150,000 and headquarters at Toronto. The provisional directors are W. M. Miskelly; F. J. Cummings and Jas. G. Shaw. The new organization has taken over the stock, plant and business formerly conducted by the W. C. Charters Lumber Company, at 828 Kingston Road. Mr. Miskelly is the manager of the Kingston Road Lumber Company, while the manufacturing end is being looked after by Mr. Cummings, who has been in the building and lumber line of the Queen City for a score or more of years.

In recent fires which did considerable damage in Northern Ontario the residents of Cochrane hal a bad scare for a few days. The muskeg south of the town ignited and was fanned along by a high wind until it assumed a dangerous aspect. The whole town turned out and, assisted by the fire brigade, soon had the flames under control. Several settlers' shacks at Lamarche went up in smoke. Many logs belonging to K. Belick on the Frederickhouse River were consumed. The flames also crossed the boundary line into Quebec and around LaReine and Lasarre considerable destruction of property ensued. A conservative estimate places the loss of pulpwood at these places at 7000 acres.

Eastern Canada

Poissen & Frere, Chartierville, Que., registered recently as lumber dealers.

The F. R. Seale Lumber Co., Limited, were recently registered at Quebec.

The partnership known as the National Timber Co., Quebec, has been dissolved.

About 300 acres of N. B. crown lands have been burned over by the forest fire which has been raging on crown lands in the vicinity of Wapske, a lumbering centre in Victoria county on the National Transcontinental Railway. The damage is said to be approximately $25,000.

Wm. Coppling Lumber Co., Limited, Joliette, Qu., were recently granted a charter.

F. W. Duncan, 1801 Ontario St., Montreal, is contemplating the erection of a saw and planing mill.

The Allen Lumber Co., of Waterloo, Que., was registered recently. George E. Allen is the proprietor.

J. and W. Duncan, lumber manufacturers and wholesalers, are erecting a sawmill at Beaufort St., Montreal.

The plant and planing mill of the Tobique Lumber Co., Limited, Eel River Crossing, N. B., were destroyed by fire.

The plant and planing mill of the Richards Mfg. Co., Limited, Whites Brook, N. B., were completely destroyed by fire.

T. A. Morrison & Co., Montreal, has been incorporated to manufacture and deal in building material of all kinds. Capital $10,000.

The plant of L. B. Amos, Doaktown, N. B., woodworker and contractor, was recently destroyed by fire. The loss was partially covered by insurance.

Geo. C. Goodfellow, 511 St. Catharine St. W., Montreal, has let a contract for a two storey frame construction building 60 x 61 ft., to be used as a sawmill.

Riverside Realty Co., Limited, Sherbrooke, Que., have been incorporated to do business as builders and contractors and to deal in lumber and other building material. Capital $49,000.

A large number of fires have occurred in the province of Quebec, particularly in the Saguenay district, and the fire protective associations have been very busy in preventing their spreading.

Legara Automobiles, of Sorel, Limited, have been incorporated to manufacture and deal in automobiles, motor trucks, carriages, furniture, woodenware and musical instruments. Capital $100,000.

LaReine Lumber Co., Limited, Quebec City, have been incorporated to manufacture and deal in lumber, timber, pulp and wood products of all kinds and to take over as a going concern the manufacturing business known as Welford, Laliberte & Frere, St. Remi, P. Q.; capital $49.000.

La Compagnie de Pulpe du Chicoutimi have been granted supplementary letters patent to increase the preference stock of the company from the sum of $2,500,000 to $3,000,000. The new stock to be divided into shares of $100 each and decreasing the common stock of said company from the sum of $900,000 to $400,000.

At a meeting of the Saguenay Pulp & Paper Company, held last week, Hon. F. L. Beique, Hon, J. Marcelin Wilson and Hon. Nemese Garneau, and Edward C. Pratt, Louis Chable, J. E. A. Dubuc, Joseph Quintal, R. A. Hammond and John T. Steel, were elected members of the board of directors. Senator Beique was named president and Hon. N. Garneau, vice-president.

Doheny, Quinlan & Robertson, Limited, Montreal, have recently been incorporated. Among the powers conferred on this company are to manufacture and deal in timber, lumber ,and all manufactures of wood and to acquire or build ships, barges, tugs, and other vessels. The incorporators are H. Doheny, H. Quinlan and A. W. Robertson, contractors; G. A. Campbell and J. Kerry, all of Montreal; capital $2,000,000.

Gates Refractories, Limited, Montreal, has been formed to take over the business of John W. Gates. The company have acquired a factory at Montreal East, where they manufacture Gates' patent boiler furnace lining blocks and special shapes in refractories. The company are also engineering contractors,' specializing in furnace building. The capital is $250,000. Mr. John W. Gates is the president, Mr. E. T. Jeffrey, vice-president, and Mr. L. G. Black, secretary.

Western Canada

A fire recently occurred in the plant of the Victoria Lumber & Mfg. Co., Chemainus, B. C. Fortunately the blaze was extinguished before any serious damage had been done.

The Fillmore Building Co., Limited, Fillmore, Sask., has been incorporated with a capital of $10,000, to carry on a building and contracting business and to manufacture and deal in building supplies.

The Alberta Pioneer Canning Co., Limited, Edson, Alta., was recently incorporated. Among the powers conferred by the charter is to manufacture barrels, boxes, kegs and other forms of packages, whether of wood or other materials. The capital stock is $40,000.

Sidney Mills, Limited, Sidney, B. C., have found it necessary to install additional equipment in their box factory. The new machines consist of a 6-in. Mershon band resaw; an automatic tumbler saw for cut-off saw and a circular rip saw for the sizing of box lumber.

A provincial charter has been granted to the Lount Engineering Co., Limited, with a capital stock of $60,000 and headquarters in Winnipeg. The new organization will take over the business of Chas. T. Lount and among other powers is authorized to carry on the business of acquiring and holding timber limits, timber licenses and timber lands and to engage in the cutting and manufacture of lumber and, generally, carry on a saw mill, planing mill and other lines.

The Great West Lumber Mills, Limited, have been granted a provincial charter with headquarters in Winnipeg and a capital stock of $100,000. Among the incorporators are Wm. P. Dutton and Geo. U. Bacon, lumbermen; John W. Brown, traveller and others. The company are empowered to carry on the general business of lumber and timber merchants, sawmill proprietors and timber drawers, and buy, sell and deal in all articles in the manufacture of which timber or wood is used.

In order to keep pace with the growing demand for their products the Robertson Hackett Saw Mills, Limited, Vancouver, B.C., are constructing a new planing mill, 100 x 100 ft. The building will be one story in height with what is known as a truss roof. The construction of this roof will be such that its weight will be supported by 4 posts leaving a 56 ft. span in the centre of the mill where the machinery will be located. The equipment will consist of 5 planers and matchers; 2 rip saws and a band resaw for bevel siding. Individual electric drive will be used throughout. Last year this firm constructed a 40 x 120 ft. north coast dry kiln.

Eighteen Replies

were received recently to a small advertisement in the Quick Action Section of the "Canada Lumberman and Wood-Worker." At a trifling outlay this advertiser got in touch with eighteen interested parties.

Are you making use of the

QUICK ACTION SECTION ?

Whether a mill, a piece of machinery, an odd lot of lumber, a timber limit, an employer or employee, this department usually gets the right parties, and will get them for you at a minimum cost.

We will gladly give you full particulars if you will write us your requirements.

CANADA LUMBERMAN
347 Adelaide St. West - TORONTO

SAVOIE & CO. MANSEAU, QUE.

Lumber Dealers

Spruce, Hemlock, Hardwood, Lath, Cedar Posts, Pulp Wood

MILLING IN TRANSIT

We have facilities for milling lumber in transit, Manseau is on the Intercolonial Ry., 110 miles East of Montreal

BELTING FOR SALE

We have a large quantity of Second-Hand Rubber and Leather Belting in all sizes and plys up to 24 inches in width, which we can sell at interesting prices. Send us your requirements.

N. SMITH
138 York St. - Toronto, Ont.

TIMBER LANDS

Bought and Sold

Timber and Pulp Wood Estimates

R. R. BRADLEY
Consulting Forester
58 Telegraph Building
Hospital St., MONTREAL

Timber Estimates

James W. Sewall
OLD TOWN, - MAINE

BELL LOCOMOTIVES

Bell Locomotive weighing 12 tons hauls 285 ton logging train at plant of W. C Edwards Co., Rockland, Ontario, Canada

Made in sizes from 2 to 25 tons in working order. Tested material and thorough workmanship enter into ever part of Bell Locomotives and their construction is accessible, simple and compact.

CHEAPEST FUEL—Will operate on Kerosene, fuel oil, distillate or crude oils.

NO HOT ASHES OR SPARKS can fly out so that fire hazard is eliminated.

50% GREATER TRACTIVE EFFORT than direct connected type locomotive of equal weight.

ONE MAN OPERATED—One valve fire control.

STANDARDIZED DESIGN—All parts interchangeable and kept in stock for immediate delivery.

Compare First Cost, Fuel Cost, Tractive Power and Length of Service with Any Other Type of Locomotive

A Sure Investment

Bell Locomotive Works Inc.
Founded 1908
11 Pine Street, NEW YORK, N.Y.

The General Supply Company of Canada
356-360 Sparks St., OTTAWA, Canada
Also at
MONTREAL, TORONTO, WINNIPEG and VANCOUVER

CURRENT LUMBER PRICES—WHOLESALE

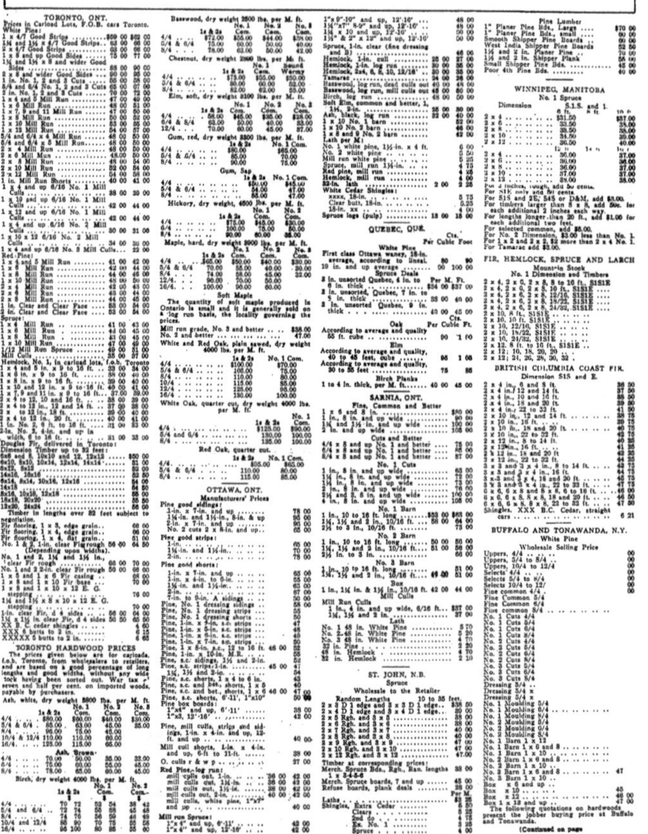

TORONTO, ONT.

Prices in Carload Lots, F.O.B. cars Toronto.

White Pine:

1 x 4/7 Good Strips	$59 00	$62 00
1¼ and 1½ x 4/7 Good Strips	63 00	66 00
2 x 4/7 Good Strips	63 00	66 00
1 x 8 and up Good Sides	75 00	77 00
1¼ and 1½ x 8 and wider Good Sides	88 00	90 00
2 x 8 and wider Good Sides	90 00	95 00
1 in. No. 1, 2 and 3 Cuts	56 00	58 00
5/4 and 6/4 No. 1, 2 and 3 Cuts	65 00	67 00
2 in. No. 1, 2 and 3 Cuts	70 00	72 00
1 x 4 and 5 Mill Run	47 00	49 00
1 x 6 Mill Run	48 00	51 00
1 x 7, 9 and 11 Mill Run	47 00	50 00
1 x 8 Mill Run	50 00	52 00
1 x 10 Mill Run	53 00	55 00
1 x 12 Mill Run	54 00	57 00
5/4 and 6/4 x 4 Mill Run	48 00	50 00
5/4 and 6/4 x 5 Mill Run	48 00	50 00
2 x 4 Mill Run	48 00	50 00
2 x 6 Mill Mun	48.00	50 00
2 x 8 Mill Run	48 00	54 00
2 x 10 Mill Run	52 00	54 00
2 x 12 Mill Run	54 00	58 00
1 in. Mill Run Shorts	40 00	41 00
1 x 4 and up 6/16 No. 1 Mill Culls	38 00	39 00
1 x 10 and up 6/16 No. 1 Mill Culls	42 00	44 00
1 x 12 and up 6/16 No. 1 Mill Culls	42 00	44 00
1 x 4 and up 6/16 No. 2 Mill Culls	30 00	31 00
1 x 10 x 12 6/16 No. 2 Mill Culls	34 00	36 00
1 x 4 and up 6/16 No. 3 Mill Culls		22 00

Red Pine:

1 x 4 and 5 Mill Run	41 00	42 00
1 x 6 Mill Run	42 00	44 00
1 x 8 Mill Run	44 00	46 00
1 x 10 Mill Run	48 00	50 00
2 x 4 Mill Run	42 00	43 00
2 x 6 Mill Run	43 00	44 00
2 x 8 Mill Run	44 00	45 00
1 in. Clear and Clear Face	53 00	54 00
2 in. Clear and Clear Face	53 00	54 00

Spruce:

1 x 4 Mill Run	41 00	43 00
1 x 6 Mill Run	43 00	45 00
1 x 8 Mill Run	43 00	45 00
1 x 10 Mill Run	47 00	49 00
1/12 Mill Run Spruce	49 00	51 00
Mill Culls	35 00	37 00

Hemlock, No. 1, in carload lots, f.o.b. Toronto

1 x 4 and 5 in. x 9 to 16 ft.	33 00	34 00
1 x 6 in. x 9 to 16 ft.	38 00	40 00
1 x 8 in. x 9 to 16 ft.	39 00	40 00
1 x 10 and 12 in. x 9 to 16 ft.	40 00	41 00
1 x 7, 9 and 11 in. x 9 to 16 ft.	37.00	39.00
2 x 4 to 12, 10 and 16 ft.	38 00	39 00
2 x 4 to 12 in., 12 and 14 ft.	37 00	38 00
2 x to 12 in., 18 ft.	39 00	40 00
2 x 4 to 12 in., 20 ft.	40 00	41 00
1 in. No. 2, 6 ft. to 16 ft.	31 00	33 00
2-in. No. 2, 4-in. and up in width, 6 to 16 ft.	31 00	33 00

Douglas Fir, delivered in Toronto:

Dimension Timber up to 32 feet:

6x6 and 8, 10x10 and 12, 12x12	$50 00
6x10, 8x10, 10x14, 12x14, 14x14	51 00
8x12, 8x12	52 00
14x16, 16x16	52 50
6x14, 8x14, 10x16, 12x16	54 00
14x18	54 50
8x16, 10x18, 12x18	55 00
18x18, 20x20	55 50
12x20, 24x24	56 00

Timber in lengths over 32 feet subject to negotiation.

Fir flooring, 1 x 3, edge grain		68 00
Fir flooring, 1 x 4, edge grain		66 00
Fir flooring, 1 x 4, flat grain		51 00
No. 1 & 2, 1-in. clear Fir rough (Depending upon widths).	56 60	64 50
No. 1 and 2, 1¼ and 1½ in., clear Fir rough	68 00	70 00
No. 1 and 2 2-in. clear Fir rough	56 00	66 00
1 x 5 and 1 x 6 Fir casing		68 00
1 x 8 and 1 x 10 Fir base		70 00
1 x 8 and 1 x 10 x 12 E. G. stepping		76 00
1¼ and 1½ x 8 x 10 x 12 E. G. stepping		70 00
1-in. clear Fir, d 4 sides	56 00	64 00
1¼ x 1½ in. clear Fir, d 4 sides	56 50	65 50
XX B. C. cedar shingles		4 60
XXX 6 butts to 2 in.		6 15
XXXXX 5 butts to 2 in.		6 65

TORONTO HARDWOOD PRICES

The prices given below are for carloads, f.o.b. Toronto, from wholesalers to retailers, and are based on a good percentage of long lengths and good widths, without any wide tock having been sorted out. War tax of seven and half per cent. on imported woods, payable by purchasers.

Ash, white, dry weight 3800 lbs. per M. ft.

	1s & 2s	No. 1 Com.	No. 2 Com.	No. 3 Com.
4/4	$80.00	$60.00	$40.00	$30.00
5/4 & 6/4	85.00	63.00	45.00	35.00
8/4	95.00	75.00	45.00	
10/4 & 12/4	110.00	110.00	60.00	
16/4	125.00	115.00	65.00	

Ash, Brown

4/4	70.00	50.00	35.00	33.00
6/4	75.00	60.00	55.00	45.00
8/4	78.00	65.00	60.00	45.00

Birch, dry weight 4000 lbs. per M. ft.

	1s & 2s $		No. 1 Com. $		No. 2 Com. $	
4/4	70	72	52	54	38	42
5/4 and 6/4	72	74	55	58	45	48
8/4	74	76	56	59	46	49
10/4 and 12/4	85	90	70	75	55	58
16/4	95	100	80	85	55	60

Basswood, dry weight 2600 lbs. per M. ft.

	1s & 2s	No. 1 Com.	No. 2 Com.	No. 3 Com.
4/4	$72.00	$55.00	$44.00	$38.00
5/4 & 6/4	75.00	60.00	50.00	40.00
8/4	78.00	63.00	50.00	42.00

Chestnut, dry weight 2800 lbs. per M. ft.

	1s & 2s	No. 1 Com.	Sound Wormy
4/4	$75.00	$55.00	$50.00
5/4 & 6/4	80.00	60.00	52.00
8/4	82.00	62.00	55.00

Elm, soft, dry weight 3100 lbs. per M. ft.

	1s & 2s	No. 1 Com.	No. 2 Com.	No. 3 Com.
4/4	58.00	$45.00	$35.00	$28.00
6/4 & 8/4	63.00	50.00	40.00	33.00
12/4	70.00	60.00	45.00	37.00

Gum, red, dry weight 3300 lbs. per M. ft.

	1s & 2s	No. 1 Com.
4/4	$80.00	$65.00
5/4 & 6/4	85.00	70.00
8/4	90.00	75.00

Gum, Sap

	1s & 2s	No. 1 Com.
4/4	$50.00	$45.00
5/4 & 6/4	54.00	47.00
8/4	55.00	47.00

Hickory, dry weight, 4500 lbs. per M. ft.

	1s & 2s	No. 1 Com.	No. 2 Com.
4/4	$75.00	$45.00	$30.00
6/4	100.00	75.00	50.00
8/4	90.00	60.00	35.00

Maple, hard, dry weight 3900 lbs. per M. ft.

	1s & 2s	No. 1 Com.	No. 2 Com.	No. 3 Com.
4/4	$65.00	$50.00	$40.00	$30.00
5/4 & 6/4	70.00	55.00	40.00	30.00
8/4	74.00	58.00	45.00	32.00
12/4	90.00	70.00	50.00	
16/4	100.00	90.00	60.00	

Soft Maple

The quantity of soft maple produced in Ontario is small and it is generally sold on a log run basis, the locality governing the prices.

Mill run grade, No. 3 and better	$38.00
No. 2 and better	47.00

White and Red Oak, plain sawed, dry weight 4000 lbs. per M. ft.

	1s & 2s	No. 1 Com.
4/4	$100.00	$70.00
5/4 & 6/4	105.00	75.00
8/4	110.00	80.00
10/4	115.00	85.00
12/4	125.00	95.00
16/4	130.00	100.00

White Oak, quarter cut, dry weight 4000 lbs. per M. ft.

	1s & 2s	No. 1 Com.
4/4	$125.00	$90.00
5/4 and 6/4	130.00	100.00
8/4	135.00	100.00

Red Oak, quarter cut.

	1s & 2s	No. 1 Com.
4/4	$05.00	$65.00
5/4 & 6/4	110.00	80.00
8/4	115.00	85.00

OTTAWA, ONT.

Manufacturers' Prices

Pine good sidings:		
1-in. x 7-in. and up		78 00
1¼-in. and 1½-in., 8-in. & up		95 00
2-in. x 7-in. and up		95 00
No. 2 cuts 2 x 8-in. and up		65 00
Pine good strips:		
1-in.		65 00
1¼-in. and 1½-in.		70 00
2-in.		78 00
Pine good shorts:		
1-in. x 7-in. and up		65 00
1-in. x 4-in. to 6-in.		55 00
1¼-in. and 1½-in.		65 00
2-in.		67 00
7-in. to 9-in. A sidings		50 00
Pine, No. 1 dressing sidings		58 00
Pine, No. 1 dressing strips		55
Pine, No. 1 dressing shorts		50
Pine, 1-in. x 4-in. s.c. strips		47
Pine, 1-in. x 5-in. s.c. strips		48
Pine, 1-in. x 6-in. s.c. strips		49
Pine, 1-in. x 7-in. s.c. strips		50
Pine, 1 x 8-in. s.c., 12 to 16 ft.	48 00	52
Pine, 1-in. x 10-in. M.R.		55
Pine, s.c. sidings, 1½ and 2-in.		52
Pine, s.c. strips, 1-in.	45 00	47
1¼, 1½ and 2-in.		54
Pine, s.c. shorts, 1 x 4 to 6 in.		43
Pine, s.c. and bet., shorts, 1 x 5		40
Pine, s.c. and bet., shorts, 1 x 6	46 00	47 00
Pine, s.c. shorts, 6'-11', 1"x10"		50 00
Pine box boards:		
1"x4" and up, 6'-11'		38 00
1"x3, 12'-16'		42 00
Pine, mill culls, strips and sidings, 1-in. x 4-in. and up, 12-ft. and up		40 00
Mill cull shorts, 1-in. x 4-in. and up, 6-ft to 11-ft.		38 00
O. culls r & w p		27 00
Red Pine, log run:		
mill culls out, 1-in.	36 00	42 00
mill culls out, 1¼-in.	36 00	42 00
mill culls out, 1½-in.	38 00	42 00
mill culls out, 2-in.	40 00	42 00
mill culls, white pine, 1"x7" and up		40 00
Mill run Spruce:		
1"x4" and up, 6'-11'		42 00
1"x4" and up, 12'-16'		42 00
1"x9"-10" and up, 12'-16'		48 00
1¼"x7" 8-9" and up, 12'-16'		48 00
1¼ x 10 and up, 12'-16'		50 00
1½" & 2" x 12" and up, 12'-16'		50 00
Spruce, 1-in. clear (fine dressing and B)		46 00
Hemlock, 1-in. cull	25 00	27 00
Hemlock, 1-in. log run	30 00	35 00
Hemlock, 2x4, 6, 8, 10, 12/16'	30 00	35 00
Tamarac	24 00	26 00
Basswood, log run, dead culls out	40 00	48 00
Basswood, log run, mill culls out	45 00	50 00
Birch, log run	48 00	50 00
Soft Elm, common and better, 1, 1¼, 2-in.	25 00	30 00
Ash, black, log run	32 00	40 00
1 x 10 No. 1 barn		52 00
1 x 10 No. 2 barn		46 00
1 x 8 and 9 No. 2 barn		42 00
Lath per M:		
No. 1 white pine, 1½-in. x 4 ft.		6 00
No. 2 white pine		5 50
Mill run white pine		5 25
Spruce, mill run 1½-in.		4 75
Red pine, mill run		4 25
Hemlock, mill run		4 00
32-in. lath	2 00	2 25
White Cedar Shingles:		
xxxx, 18-in.		5 75
Clear butt, 18-in.		5.25
18-in. xx		4 00
Spruce logs (pulp)	15 00	18 00

QUEBEC, QUE.

Cts. Per Cubic Foot

White Pine

First class Ottawa waney, 18-in. average, according to lineal.	80	90
19 in. and up average	90	100 00

Spruce Deals

Per M. Ft.

3 in. unsorted Quebec, 4 in. to 6 in. thick	$34 00	$37 00
3 in. unsorted, Quebec, 7 in. to 5 in. thick	38 00	40 00
3 in. unsorted Quebec, 9 in. thick	40 00	45 00

Oak — Cts. Per Cubic Ft.

According to average and quality 55 ft. cube	90	1 00

Elm

According to average and quality, 40 to 45 feet, cube	95	1 05
According to average and quality, 30 to 35 feet	75	85

Birch Planks

1 to 4 in. thick, per M. ft.	40 00	45 00

SARNIA, ONT.

Fine, Common and Better

1 x 6 and 8 in.		$80 00
1 in., 8 in. and up wide		90 00
1¼ and 1½ in. and up wide		100 00
2 in. and up wide		105 00
Cuts and Better		
4/4 x 8 and up No. 1 and better		75 00
6/4 x 8 and up No. 1 and better		85 00
8/4 x 8 and up No. 1 and better		87 00
No. 1 Cuts		
1 in., 8 in. and up wide		63 00
1¼ in., 8 in. and up wide		72 00
1½ in., 8 in. and up wide		73 00
2 in., 8 in. and up wide		78 00
2½ and 3, 8 in. and up wide		100 00
4 in., 8 in. and up wide		105 00
No. 1 Barn		
1 in., 10 to 16 ft. long	$53 00	$63 00
1¼, 1½ and 2 in., 10/16 ft.	58 00	64 00
2½ to 3 in., 10/16 ft.		73 00
No. 2 Barn		
1 in., 10 to 16 ft. long	50 00	56 00
1¼, 1½ and 2 in., 10/16 ft.	51 00	56 00
2½ in. to 3 in.		66 00
No. 3 Barn		
1 in., 10 to 16 ft. long		51 00
1¼, 1½ and 2 in., 10/16 ft.	49 00	51 00
Box		
1 in., 1¼ in. & 1½ in., 10/16 ft.	42 00	44 00
Mill Culls		
Mill Run Culls		
1 in., 4 in. and up wide, 6/16 ft.		$37 00
1¼, 1½ and 2 in.		37 00
Lath		
No. 1 48 in. White Pine		5 70
No. 2 48 in. White Pine		5 20
No. 3 48 in. White Pine		4 70
32 in. Pine		2 20
48 in. Hemlock		4 70
32 in. Hemlock		2 10

ST. JOHN, N.B.

Spruce

Wholesale to the Retailer

Random Lengths 10 to 35 feet.

2 x 3 D 1 edge and 3 x 3 D 1 edge	$38 50
2 x 4 D 1 edge and 3 x 4 D 1 edge	39 00
2 x 5 Rgh. and 3 x 5	38 00
2 x 6 Rgh. and 3 x 6	38 00
2 x 7 Rgh. and 3 x 7	40 00
2 x 8 Rgh. and 3 x 8	40 00
2 x 9 Rgh. and 3 x 9	47 00
2 x 10 Rgh. and 3 x 10	47 00
2 x 12 Rgh. and 3 x 12	47.00
Timber at corresponding prices:	
Merch. Spruce Bds., Rgh., Ran. lengths 1 x 3-4-5-6	38 00
Merch. Spruce boards, 7 and up	45 00
Refuse boards, plank deals	28 00
	Per M.
Laths	$3 25
Shingles, Extra Cedar	5 50
Clears	5 25
2nd do	4 75
Ex. No. 1	3 25
Spruce	4 00

Pine Lumber

1" Planer Pine Bds., Large	$70 00
1" Planer Pine Bds., small	60 00
Smooth Shipper Pine Boards	60 00
West India Shipper Pine Boards	52 50
1½ and 2 in. Planer Pine	70 00
1½ and 2 in. Shipper Plank	58 00
Small Shipper Pine Bds.	45 00
Poor 4th Pine Bds.	40 00

WINNIPEG, MANITOBA

No. 1 Spruce

Dimension S.1.S. and 1.

Dimension	6 ft.	8 ft.	10 ft.
2 x 4	$31.50		$37.00
2 x 6	33.50		35.00
2 x 8	33.50		35.00
2 x 10	34.50		39.00
2 x 12	36.50		40.00
	12 ft.	**14 ft.**	**16 ft.**
2 x 4	36.00		37.00
2 x 6	36.00		36.00
2 x 8	36.00		37.00
2 x 10	37.00		37.00
2 x 12	38.00		38.00

For 2 inches, rough, add 50 cents.
For S1E only add 50 cents.
For S1S and 2E, S4S or D&M, add $3.00.
For timbers larger than 8 x 8, add 50c. for each additional 2 inches each way.
For lengths longer than 20 ft., add $1.00 for each additional two feet.
For selected common, add $5.00.
For No. 2 Dimension, $3.00 less than No. 1.
For 1 x 2 and 2 x 2, $2 more than 2 x 4 No. 1.
For Tamarac add $3.00.

FIR, HEMLOCK, SPRUCE AND LARCH

Mountain Stock

No. 1 Dimension and Timbers

2 x 4, 2 x 6, 2 x 8, 8 to 16 ft., S1S1E
2 x 4, 2 x 6, 2 x 8, 10 ft., S1S1E ....
2 x 4, 2 x 6, 2 x 8, 12/16, S1S1E ....
2 x 4, 2 x 6, 2 x 8, 18/22, S1S1E ....
2 x 4, 2 x 6, 2 x 8, 24/32, S1S1E ....
2 x 10, 8 ft., S1S1E ....
2 x 10, 10 ft. S1S1E ....
2 x 10, 12/16, S1S1E ....
2 x 10, 18/22, S1S1E ....
2 x 10, 24/32, S1S1E ....
2 x 12, 8 ft. to 16 ft., S1S1E ..
2 x 12; 10, 18, 20, 20 ..
2 x 12; 24, 26, 28, 30, 32 .

BRITISH COLUMBIA COAST FIR.

Dimension S1S and E.

2 x 4 in., 6 and 8 ft.	36 50
2 x 4 in., 12 and 14 ft.	37 50
2 x 4 in., 10 and 16 ft.	38 50
2 x 4 in., 18 and 20 ft.	39 50
2 x 4 in., 22 to 32 ft.	41 50
2 x 10 in., 12 and 14 ft.	38 75
2 x 10 in., 16 ft.	39 75
2 x 10 in., 18 and 20 ft.	40 75
2 x 10 in., 22 to 32 ft.	42 75
2 x 12 in., 8 to 14 ft.	40 25
2 x 12 in., 16 ft.	41 25
2 x 12 in., 18 and 20 ft.	42 25
2 x 12 in., 22 to 32 ft.	44 25
3 x 3 and 3 x 4 in., 8 to 14 ft.	43 75
3 x 3 and 3 x 4 in., 16 ft.	44 75
3 x 3 and 3 x 4, 18 and 20 ft.	45 75
3 x 3 and 3 x 4 in., 22 to 32 ft.	47 75
6 x 6, 6 x 8 and 8 x 8, 6 to 16 ft.	46 00
6 x 6, 6 x 8, 8 x 8, 18 and 20 ft.	46 50
6 x 6, 6 x 8, 8 x 8, 22 to 32 ft.	47 50
Shingles, XXX B.C. Cedar, straight cars	6 21

BUFFALO AND TONAWANDA, N.Y.

White Pine

Wholesale Selling Price

Uppers, 4/4	00
Uppers, 5/4 to 8/4	00
Uppers, 10/4 to 12/4	00
Selects 4/4	00
Selects 5/4 to 8/4	00
Selects 10/4 to 12/	00
Fine common 4/4	00
Fine Common 5/4	
Fine Common 6/4	
Fine common 8/4	
No. 1 Cuts 4/4	
No. 1 Cuts 5/4	
No. 1 Cuts 6/4	
No. 1 Cuts 8/4	
No. 2 Cuts 4/4	
No. 2 Cuts 5/4	
No. 2 Cuts 6/4	
No. 2 Cuts 8/4	
No. 3 Cuts 5/4	
No. 3 Cuts 6/4	
No. 3 Cuts 8/4	
Dressing 5/4	
Dressing 5/4 x	
Dressing 5/4 x	
No. 1 Moulding 5/4	
No. 1 Moulding 6/4	
No. 1 Moulding 8/4	
No. 2 Moulding 5/4	
No. 2 Moulding 6/4	
No. 2 Moulding 8/4	
No. 1 Barn 1 x 12	
No. 1 Barn 1 x 6 and 8	
No. 1 Barn 1 x 10	
No. 2 Barn 1 x 6 and 8	
No. 2 Barn 1 x 10	
No. 3 Barn 1 x 6 and 8	47
No. 3 Barn 1 x 10	
Box x 6 and up	
Box x 10	45
Box x 12	46 00
Box 1 x 13 and up	47 00

The following quotations on hardwoods present the jobber buying price at Buffalo and Tonawanda.

(Continued on page

CURRENT LUMBER PRICES—Continued

MAPLE	1s & 2s	No. 1 Com.	No. 2 Com.
4/4	47 - 50	30 - 32	22 - 24
5/4 to 8/4	60 - 62	38 - 40	26 - 28
10/4 to 16/4	70 - 72	50 - 52	30 - 32
RED BIRCH			
4/4	62 - 64	42 - 44	26 - 28
5/4 to 8/4	64 - 66	44 - 46	28 - 30
SAP BIRCH			
4/4	56 - 60	34 - 36	22 - 24
5/4 and up	59 - 62	36 - 38	24 - 26
SOFT ELM			
4/4	47 - 49	32 - 34	24 - 26
5, 6 & 8/4	49 - 51	34 - 36	24 - 26
BASSWOOD			
4/4	52 - 54	42 - 44	29 - 31
Thicker	55 - 58	44 - 46	29 - 32
PLAIN OAK			
4/4	67 - 72	44 - 48	28 - 30
5/4 to 8/4	72 - 76	48 - 52	32 - 34
ASH, WHITE AND BROWN			
4/4	68 - 70	37 - 40	27 - 30
5/4 to 8/4	73 - 77	43 - 47	30 - 32
10/4 and up	100 - 90	58 - 62	31 - 33

BOSTON, MASS.

Quotations given below are for highest grades of Michigan and Canadian white pine and Eastern Canadian Spruce as required in the New England market in carloads.

White pine uppers, 1 to 2 in.		134 00
White pine uppers, 2½ and 3 in.		149 00
White pine uppers, 4 in.		160 00
Selects, 1 to 2 in.		125 00
Selects, 2½ and 3 in.		140 00
Selects, 4 in.		155 00
Fine common, 1 in., 30 per cent. 12 in. and up		92 00
Fine common, 1 x 8 to 11 in.		87 00
Fine Common, 1¼ to 2 in.		100 00
Fine Common, 2½ and 3 in.		136 00
Fine Common, 4 in.		145 00
1 in. shaky clear		72 00
1¼ to 2 in. shaky clear		75 00
1 in. No. 2 dressing		64 00
1¼ to 2 in. No. 2 dressing		68 00
No. 1 Cuts, 1 in.		80 00
No. 1 Cuts, 1¼ to 2 in.	85 00	87 00
No. 1 Cuts, 2½ and 3 in.		115 00
No. 2 Cuts, 1 in.		60 00
No. 2 Cuts, 1¼ to 2 in.	70 00	71 00

Barn Boards, No. 1, 1 x 12		69 00
No. 1, 1 x 10		64 00
No. 1, 1 x 8		61 00
No. 2, 1 x 12		64 00
No. 2, 1 x 10		61 00
No. 2, 1 x 8		58 00
No. 3, 1 x 12		59 00
No. 3, 1 x 10		57 00
No. 3, 1 x 8		55 00
Can. spruce, clear, 1 x 4 to 9 in.	45 00	48 00
1 x 10 in.		[illegible]
No. 1 1 x 4 to 7 in.		[illegible]
No. 1 1 x 8 & 9 in.		[illegible]
No. 1 1 x 10 in.		[illegible]
No. 2 1 x 4 & 5 in.		[illegible]
No. 2 1 x 6 & 7 in.		[illegible]
No. 2 1 x 8 & 9 in.	45 00	[illegible]
No. 2 1 x 10 in.		[illegible]
No. 3 1 x 12 in.		[illegible]
Spruce, 12 in. dimension		54 00
Spruce, 10 in. dimension		52 00
Spruce, 9 in. dimension		51 00
Spruce, 8 in. dimension		50 00
2 x 10 in. random lengths, 8 ft. and up		50 00
2 x 12 in., random lengths		51 00

2 x 3, 2 x 4, 2 x 5, 2 x 6, 2 x	45 00
3 x 4 and 4 x 4 in.	45 00
2 x 8 in.	48 00
All other random lengths, 7-in. and under, 8 ft. and up	38 00
5-inch and up merchantable boards, 8 ft. and up, D 1s	42 00
1 x 2	42 00
1 x 3	42 00
1-⅝ in. spruce lath	5 00
1-½ in. spruce lath	5 50
New Brunswick Cedar Shingles	
Extras	6 [illegible]
Clears	5 [illegible]
Second Clears	4 75
Clear Whites	4 [illegible]
Extra 1s (Clear whites in)	3 [illegible]
Extra 1s (Clear whites out)	1 [illegible]
Red Cedar Extras, 16-in. 5 butts to 2-in.	
Red Cedar Eurekas, 18-inch 5 butts to 2-in.	
Red Cedar Perfections, 5 butts to 2¼	
Washington 18-in. 5 butts to 2-in. extra red cedar	

The Secret
of
Successful
Sawing

ATKINS

EFFICIENCY

WHENEVER you see an Atkins you will see its STERLING QUALITY reflecting efficiency in the highest degree.

Supreme in all kinds of woodworking, these saws are the first essentials in keeping pace with the progressive spirit of reconstruction.

Send for Free Catalogue

E. C. ATKINS & CO.

Factory: HAMILTON, ONT. Branch: 109 Powell St., VANCOUVER, B.C.

ALPHABETICAL INDEX TO ADVERTISERS

GOODHUE BELTING

For

Saw and Planing Mills

In a Goodhue Belt you get only the best leather with the stretch taken out of it. A Goodhue Belt will always run evenly and "clings" to the pulley transmitting 100% of your power

For the wet places in the mill we have a special waterproof leather belt—"Acme." Other Goodhue Belts are "Extra" and "Standard" recommended according to the conditions under which the belt has to run.

Goodhue Belts stretch less than any other belt by 15 to 25 per cent.

Send for prices and particulars

J. L. Goodhue & Company, Limited

DANVILLE, QUEBEC

WINNIPEG AGENTS—Bissett & Webb, Ltd., 151 Notre Dame Avenue East, Winnipeg, Man.
VANCOUVER AGENTS—Fleck Bros., Ltd., 1142 Homer Street, Vancouver, B.C.
Standard Machinery & Supplies, Ltd., Bank of Toronto Bldg., St. James St., Montreal, Que., Agents for the Island of Montreal.

Quality Sells

HENRY DISSTON & SONS
Incorporated
Keystone Saw, Tool, Steel and File Works
PHILADELPHIA, U. S. A.

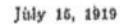

The Ideal Edger for Light Mills

Specifications

Our new Double Edger is built on entirely new lines and possesses many features that commend it to mill men. The saving in material alone will soon pay for the machine. The output of a mill with this machine can be increased by one-third. It is best adapted for medium-sized or portable mills that cut from 5,000 to 25,000 feet of lumber per day.

SAWS—This Edger is fitted with either two or three saws as required. The saws are 16 in. in diameter, and 10 in. gauge. The greatest distance between saws is:—Two saw machines, 24 in.; three saw machine, 20 in.; the least distance between saws, 2 in.

DRIVE PULLEY—The Drive Pulley is 8 in. x 8 in., affording a good belt grip, and is supported by an outside bearing.

SAW ARBOR—The Saw Arbor is made of 2½ in. steel, and has very wide bearings.

For Shingle, Lath and Portable Saw Mill Machinery

write the well known manufacturers

The G. Walter Green Co.
Limited
PETERBOROUGH, ONT.

Send for Catalogue

Algoma LIGHT STEEL RAILS

For Mining and Lumbering Purposes

All Complete with Splice Bars

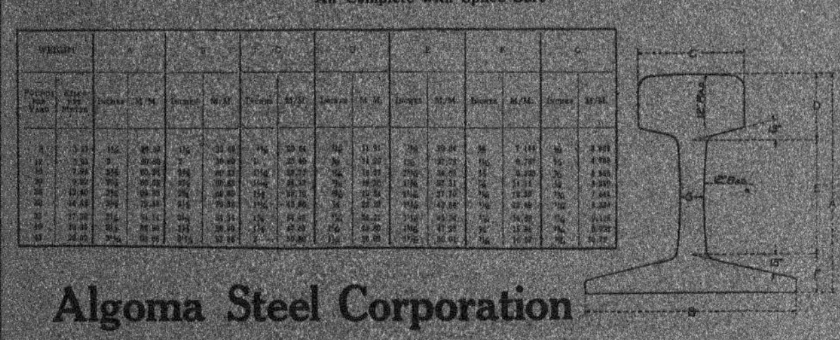

Weight		A		B		C		D		E		F		G	
Pounds per Yard	Kilos per Metre	Inches	M/M	Inches	M/M	Inches	M/M	Inches	M/M	Inches	M/M	Inches	M/M	Inches	M/M
[illegible]	[illegible]	[illegible]	[illegible]	[illegible]	[illegible]	[illegible]	[illegible]	[illegible]	[illegible]	[illegible]	[illegible]	[illegible]	[illegible]	[illegible]	[illegible]

Algoma Steel Corporation
Limited

Sault Ste. Marie, Ontario

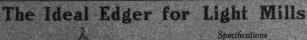

GATES REFRACTORIES, LIMITED

382 St. James Street - - - MONTREAL

CANADA LUMBERMAN BUYERS' DIRECTORY

The following regulations apply to all advertisers:—Eighth page, every issue, three headings; quarter page, six headings; half page, twelve headings; full page, twenty-four headings.

ASBESTOS GOODS
Atlas Asbestos Company, Ltd.

AXES
Canadian Warren Axe & Tool Co.

BABBITT METAL
Canada Metal Company.
General Supply Co. of Canada, Ltd.
Syracuse Smelting Works

BALE TIES
Laidlaw Bale Tie Company.

BALL BEARINGS
Chapman Double Ball Bearing Co.

BAND MILLS
Hamilton Company, William.
Waterous Engine Works Company.
Yates Machine Company, P. B.

BAND RESAWS
Mershon & Company, W. B.

BELT CEMENT
Graton & Knight Mfg. Company.

BELT DRESSING
Atlas Asbestos Company, Ltd.
General Supply Co. of Canada, Ltd.
Graton & Knight Mfg. Company.

BELTING
Atlas Asbestos Company, Ltd.
Beardmore Belting Company
Canadian Consolidated Rubber Co.
General Supply Company
Goodhue & Co., J. L.
Goodyear Tire & Rubber Co.
Graton & Knight Mfg. Company.
Gutta Percha and Rubber Company.
Main Belting Company
Manhattan Rubber Mfg. Co.
D. K. McLaren Limited.
McLaren Belting Company, J. C.

BELTING (Transmission, Elevator, Conveyor, Rubber)
Dunlop Tire & Rubber Goods Co.

BLOWERS
Sheldons Limited.
Toronto Blower Company.

BOILERS
Hamilton Company, William.
Jenckes Machine Company.
Marsh Engineering Works, Limited
Waterous Engine Works Company.

BOILER PRESERVATIVE
Beveridge Paper Company
International Chemical Company

BOX MACHINERY
Garlock-Walker Machinery Co.
Morgan Machine Company.
Yates Machine Company, P. B.

BOX SHOOKS
Davison Lumber & Mfg. Company

CABLE CONVEYORS
Jeffrey Manufacturing Company.
Jenckes Machine Company, Ltd.
Waterous Engine Works Company.

CAMP SUPPLIES
Canadian Milk Products Limited.
Davies Company, William.
Dr. Bell Veterinary Wonder Co.
Harris Abattoir Company
Johnson, A. H.
Turner & Sons, J. J.
Woods Manufacturing Company, Ltd.

CANT HOOKS
Canadian Warren Axe & Tool Co
General Supply Co. of Canada, Ltd.
Pink Company, Thomas.

CARS—STEEL BODY
Marsh Engineering Works, Limited

CEDAR
Fesserton Timber Co.
Foss Lumber Company
Genoa Bay Lumber Company
Muir & Kirkpatrick.
Long Lumber Company.
Service Lumber Company
Terry & Gordon.
Thurston-Flavelle Lumber Company
Vancouver Lumber Company.
Victoria Lumber and Mfg. Co.

CHAINS
Canadian Link-Belt Company, Ltd.
General Supply Co. of Canada, Ltd.
Hamilton Company, William.
Jeffrey Manufacturing Company.
Jenckes Machine Company, Ltd.
Pink & Co., Thomas.
Waterous Engine Works Company.
Williams Machinery Co., A. R., Vancouver.

CHINA CLAY
Bowater & Sons, W. V.

CHEMICAL PLANTS
Blair, Campbell & McLean, Ltd.

CLOTHING
Grant, Holden & Graham.
Kitchen Overall & Shirt Company
Woods Mfg. Company

COLLAR PADS
American Pad & Textile Co.

COLLARS (Shaft)
Bond Engineering Works

CONVEYOR MACHINERY
Canadian Link-Belt Company, Ltd.
Canadian Mathews Gravity Carrier Company.
General Supply Co. of Canada, Ltd.
Jeffrey Mfg. Co.
Waterous Engine Works Company.

CORDAGE
Consumers Cordage Company.

COTTON GLOVES
American Pad & Textile Co.

COUNTERSHAFTS
Bond Engineering Works

COUPLINGS (Shaft)
Bond Engineering Works
Jenckes Machine Company, Ltd.

CRANES FOR SHIP YARDS
Canadian Link-Belt Company.

CROSS ARMS
Genoa Bay Lumber Company

CUTTER HEADS
Shimer Cutter Head Company.

CYPRESS
Blakeslee, Perrin & Darling
Chicago Lumber & Coal Company.
Long Lumber Company.
Wistar, Underhill & Nixon.

DERRICKS AND DERRICK FITTINGS
Marsh Engineering Works, Limited.

DOORS
Genoa Bay Lumber Company
Harrington, E. I.
Long Lumber Company.
Mason, Gordon & Co.
Rutherford & Sons, Wm.
Terry & Gordon.

DRAG SAWS
Gerlach Company, Peter
Pennoyer & Company, J. C.

DRY KILNS
Sheldons Limited.

DRYERS
Philadelphia Textile Mach. Company.

DUST COLLECTORS
Sheldons Limited.
Toronto Blower Company.

EDGERS
William Hamilton Company, Ltd.
Garlock-Walker Machinery Co.
Green Company, G. Walter
Haight, W. L.
Long Mfg. Company, E.
Waterous Engine Works Company.

ELEVATING AND CONVEYING MACHINERY
Canadian Link-Belt Company, Ltd.
Jeffrey Manufacturing Company.
Jenckes Machine Company, Ltd.
Waterous Engine Works Company.

ENGINES
Hamilton Company, William.
Jenckes Machine Company.
Waterous Engine Works Company.

EXCELSIOR MACHINERY
Elmira Machinery and Transmission Company.

EXHAUST FANS
Garlock-Walker Machinery Co.
Reed & Company, Geo. W.
Sheldons Limited.
Toronto Blower Company.

EXHAUST SYSTEMS
Reed & Company, Geo. W.
Sheldons Limited.
Toronto Blower Company.

FILES
Disston & Sons, Henry.
Simonds Canada Saw Company.

FIR
Associated Mills, Limited
Allan-Stoltze Lumber Co.
British American Mills & Timber Co.
Coal Creek Lumber Company.
Fesserton Timber Co.
Foss Lumber Company
Grier & Sons, Ltd., G. A.
Heeney, Percy E.
Knox Brothers.
Long Lumber Company.
Mason, Gordon & Co.
Reynolds Company, Limited
Service Lumber Company
Shearer Company, Jas.
Terry & Gordon.
Timberland Lumber Company.
Timms, Phillips & Co.
Vancouver Lumber Company.
Victoria Lumber and Mfg. Co.
Weller, J. B.

FIRE BRICK
Beveridge Paper Company
Elk Fire Brick Company of Canada.

FIRE FIGHTING APPARATUS
Dunlop Tire & Rubber Goods Co.
Pyrene Mfg. Company.
Waterous Engine Works Company.

FIR FLOORING
Genoa Bay Lumber Company
Rutherford & Sons, Wm.

FLAG STAFFS
Ontario Wind Engine Company

FLOORING (Oak)
Long-Bell Lumber Company.

GALVANIZING
Ontario Wind Engine Company

GASOLINE ENGINES
Ontario Wind Engine Company

GEARS (Cut)
Smart-Turner Machine Co.

GRATE BARS—Revolving
Beveridge Paper Company

GRAVITY LUMBER CARRIER
Can. Mathews Gravity Carrier Co.

GRINDERS (Bench)
Bond Engineering Works
Garlock-Walker Machinery Co.

HARDWOODS
Anderson Lumber Company, C. G.
Atlantic Lumber Co.
Bartram & Ball.
Bennett Lumber Company.
Blakeslee, Perrin & Darling
Cameron & Co.
Cardinal & Page
Davison Lumber & Mfg. Company
Dunfield & Company
Edwards & Co., W. C.
Fassett Lumber Company.
Fesserton Timber Co.
Fraser Limited.
Gillespie, James.
Gloucester Lumber Company
Grier & Son, G. A.
Heeney, Percy E.
Knox Brothers.
Long Lumber Company.
McLennan Lumber Company.
Moores, Jr., E. J.
Nicholson & Co., E. M.
Pedwell Hardwood Lumber Co.
Powell-Myers Lumber Co.
Russell, Chas. H.
Spencer Limited, C. A.
Stearns & Culver Lumber Co.
Summers, James R.
Taylor Lumber Company, S. K.
Webster & Brother, James.

HARDWOOD FLOORING MACHINERY
American Woodworking Machinery Company
Garlock-Walker Machinery Co.

HANGERS (Shaft)
Bond Engineering Works

HARDWOOD FLOORING
Grier & Son, G. A.
Long Lumber Company.

HEMLOCK
Anderson Lumber Company, C. G.
Bartram & Ball.
Bourgouin, H.
Callander Sawmills
Canadian General Lumber Company
Cane & Co., Jas. G.
Davison Lumber & Mfg. Company
Dunfield & Company
Edwards & Company, W. C.
Fesserton Timber Co.
Foss Lumber Company
Grier & Sons, Ltd., G. A.
Hart & McDonagh.
Long Lumber Company.
Mason, Gordon & Co.
Spencer Limited, C. A.
Terry & Gordon.
The Long Lumber Company.

HOISTING AND HAULING ENGINES
Garlock-Walker Machinery Co.
General Supply Co. of Canada, Ltd.
Marsh Engineering Works, Limited

HORSES
Union Stock Yards.

HOSE
Dunlop Tire & Rubber Goods Co.
General Supply Co. of Canada, Ltd.
Goodyear Tire & Rubber Co.
Gutta Percha and Rubber Company.

INDUSTRIAL CARS
Marsh Engineering Works, Limited

INSURANCE
Hardy & Co., E. D.
Rankin Benedict Underwriting Co.

INTERIOR FINISH
Eagle Lumber Company.
Hay & Co.
Mason, Gordon & Co.
Renfrew Planing Mills.
Terry & Gordon.

KNIVES
Disston & Sons, Henry.
Peter Hay Knife Company.
Simonds Canada Saw Company.
Waterous Engine Works Company.

LATH
Austin & Nicholson.
Callander Sawmills
Canadian General Lumber Company
Cane & Co., Jas. G.
Cardinal & Page
Dupuis Limited, J. P.
Eagle Lumber Company.
Fraser Limited.
Fraser-Bryson Lumber Company.
Genoa Bay Lumber Company
Gloucester Lumber Company
Grier & Sons, Ltd., G. A.
Harris Tie & Timber Company, Ltd
Long Lumber Company.
McLennan Lumber Company.
New Ontario Colonization Company
River Ouelle Pulp and Paper Co.
Spencer Limited, C. A.
Terry & Gordon.
Union Lumber Company.
Victoria Harbor Lumber Company

LATH BOLTERS
Garlock-Walker Machinery Co
General Supply Co. of Canada, Ltd
Green Company, C. Walter.

LOCOMOTIVES
Bell Locomotive Works
General Supply Co. of Canada, Ltd
Jeffrey Manufacturing Company
Jenckes Machine Company, Ltd.
Climax Manufacturing Company
Montreal Locomotive Workks.

LATH TWINE
Consumers' Cordage Company.

LINK-BELT
Canadian Link-Belt Company
Canadian Mathews Gravity Carrier Company.
Jeffrey Mfg. Co.
Williams Machinery Co., A. R., Vancouver.

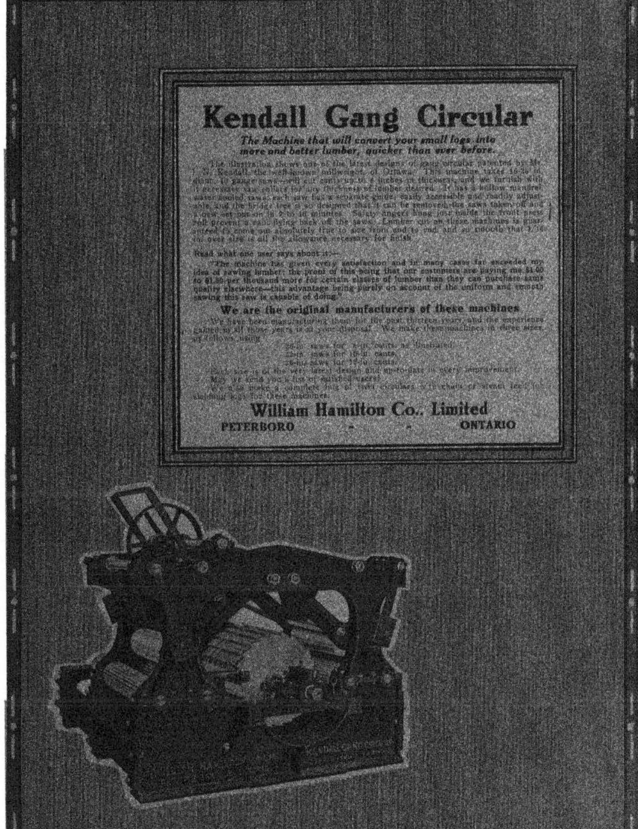
Kendall Gang Circular
The Machine that will convert your small logs into more and better lumber, quicker than ever before.
Read what one user says about it:—
"The machine has given every satisfaction and in many cases far exceeded my idea of sawing lumber; the profit of this being that our customers are paying me $1.00 to $1.50 per thousand more for certain classes of lumber than they can purchase same quality elsewhere—this advantage being purely on account of the uniform and smooth sawing this saw is capable of doing."
We are the original manufacturers of these machines
William Hamilton Co., Limited
PETERBORO - - ONTARIO

LOCOMOTIVE CRANES
Canadian Link-Belt Company, Ltd.

LOGGING ENGINES
Dunbar Engine and Foundry Co.
Jenckes Machine Company.
Marsh Engineering Works, Limited

LOG HAULER
Green Company, G. Walter
Jenckes Machine Company, Ltd.

LOGGING MACHINERY AND EQUIPMENT
General Supply Co. of Canada, Ltd.
Hamilton Company, William.
Jenckes Machine Company, Ltd.
Marsh Engineering Works, Limited
Waterous Engine Works Company.

LUMBER TRUCKS
Waterous Engine Works Company.

LUMBERMEN'S CLOTHING
Woods Manufacturing Company, Ltd.

METAL REFINERS
Canada Metal Company.
Hoyt Metal Company.
Sessenwein Brothers.

MILLING IN TRANSIT
Renfrew Planing Mills.
Rutherford & Sons, Wm.

MOLDINGS
Genoa Bay Lumber Co.
Rutherford & Sons, Wm.

MOTOR TRUCKS
Duplex Truck Company

OAK
Chicago Lumber & Coal Company.
Long-Bell Lumber Company.
Weller, J. B.

OAKUM
Stratford Oakum Co., Geo.

OIL CLOTHING
Leckie, Limited, John.

OLD IRON AND BRASS
Sessenwein Brothers.

PAPER
Bowater & Sons, W. V.

PACKING
Atlas Asbestos Company, Ltd.
Consumers Cordage Co.
Dunlop Tire & Rubber Goods Co.
Gutta Percha and Rubber Company.

PAPER MILL MACHINERY
Bowater & Sons, W. V.

PILLOW BLOCKS
Bond Engineering Works

PINE
Anderson Lumber Company, C. G.
Atlantic Lumber Co.
Austin & Nicholson.
Bourgouin, H.
Callander Sawmills
Cameron & Co.
Canadian General Lumber Company
Cane & Co., Jas. G.
Cardinal & Page
Chicago Lumber & Coal Company.
Cleveland-Sarnia Sawmills Company.
Davison Lumber & Mfg. Co.
Donogh & Co., John.
Dudley, Arthur N.
Dunfield & Company
Eagle Lumber Company.
Edwards & Co., W. C.
Excelsior Lumber Company.
Fesserton Timber Company
Fraser-Bryson Lumber Company.
Fraser Limited.
Gillies Brothers Limited.
Gloucester Lumber Company
Gordon & Co., George.
Grier & Sons, Ltd., G. A.
Harris Tie & Timber Company, Ltd.
Hart & McDonagh.
Hettler Lumber Company, Herman H.
Long-Bell Lumber Company.
Long Lumber Company.
Mason, Gordon & Co.
McLennan Lumber Company.
Montreal Lumber Company.
Moores, Jr., E. J.
Muir & Kirkpatrick.
Parry Sound Lumber Company.
Russell, Chas. H.
Shearer Company, Jas.
Spencer Limited, C. A.
Summers, James R.
Terry & Gordon.
Union Lumber Company.
Watson & Todd, Limited.
Weller, J. B.
Williams Lumber Company
Wuichet, Louis.

PLANING MILL EXHAUSTERS
Garlock-Walker Machinery Co.
Reed & Company, Geo. W.
Sheldons Limited.
Toronto Blower Co.

PLANING MILL MACHINERY
American Woodworking Machinery, Company
Garlock-Walker Machinery Co.
Mershon & Company, W. B.
Sheldons Limited.
Toronto Blower Co.
Yates Machine Company, P. B.

PORK PACKERS
Davies Company, William
Harris Abattoir Company

POSTS AND POLES
Auger & Company
Dupuis Limited, J. P.
Eagle Lumber Company
Harris Tie & Timber Company, Ltd.
Long-Bell Lumber Company.
Long Lumber Company.
Mason, Gordon & Co.
Terry & Gordon.

PULLEYS AND SHAFTING
Bond Engineering Works
Canadian Link-Belt Company
Garlock-Walker Machinery Co.
General Supply Co. of Canada, Ltd.
Green Company, G. Walter
Hamilton Company, William
Jeffrey Mfg. Co.
Jenckes Machine Company, Ltd.

PULP MILL MACHINERY
Canadian Link-Belt Company, Ltd.
Hamilton Company, William.
Jeffrey Manufacturing Company
Jenckes Machine Company, Ltd.
Waterous Engine Works Company

PUMPS
General Supply Co. of Canada, Ltd.
Hamilton Company, William
Jenckes Machine Company, Ltd.
Smart-Turner Machine Company
Waterous Engine Works Company.

RAILS
Gartshore, John J.
Sessenwein Bros.

ROOFINGS
Reed & Company, Geo. W.

ROOFINGS
(Rubber, Plastic and Liquid)
Beveridge Paper Company
International Chemical Company

ROPE
Consumers Cordage Co.
Leckie, Limited, John

RUBBER GOODS
Atlas Asbestos Company
Dunlop Tire & Rubber Goods Co.
Goodyear Tire and Rubber Co.
Gutta Percha & Rubber Company

SASH
Genoa Bay Lumber Company
Renfrew Planing Mills.

SAWS
Atkins & Company, E. C.
Disston & Sons, Henry
General Supply Co. of Canada, Ltd.
Gerlach Company, Peter
Green Company, G. Walter
Hoe & Company, R.
Shurly-Dietrich Company
Simonds Canada Saw Company

SAW MILL LINK-BELT
Williams Machinery Co., A. R., Vancouver.

SAW MILL MACHINERY
Canadian Link-Belt Company, Ltd.
Dunbar Engine & Foundry Co.
Firstbrook Bros.
General Supply Co. of Canada, Ltd.
Haight, W. L.
Hamilton Company, William
Huther Bros. Saw Mfg. Company
Jeffrey Manufacturing Company
Long Manufacturing Company, E.
Mershon & Company, W. B.
Parry Sound Lumber Company
Payette Company, P.
Waterous Engine Works Company
Yates Machine Co., P. B.

SHEATHINGS
Beveridge Paper Company
Goodyear Tire & Rubber Co.

SHINGLE MACHINES
Marsh Engineering Works, Limited

SAW MANDRELS
Bond Engineering Works

SAW SHARPENERS
Garlock-Walker Machinery Co.
Waterous Engine Works Company.

SAW SLASHERS
Waterous Engine Works Company

SAWMILL LINK-BELT
Canadian Link-Belt Company

SHEET METALS
Syracuse Smelting Works

SHINGLES
Allan-Stoltze Lumber Co.
Associated Mills, Limited
Campbell-MacLaurin Lumber Co.
Cardinal & Page
Dominion Lumber & Timber Co.
Eagle Lumber Company
Foss Lumber Company
Fraser Limited.
Genoa Bay Lumber Company
Gillespie, James.
Gloucester Lumber Company
Grier & Sons, Ltd., G. A.
Harris Tie & Timber Company, Ltd.
Heeney, Percy E.
Long Lumber Company.
Mason, Gordon & Co.
McLennan Lumber Company.
Miller Company, Ltd., W. H.
Reynolds Company, Limited
Service Lumber Company
Shingle Agency of B. C.
Terry & Gordon.
Timms, Phillips & Co.
Vancouver Lumber Company.
Victoria Lumber and Mfg. Co.

SHINGLE & LATH MACHINERY
Dunbar Engine and Foundry Co.
Garlock-Walker Machinery Co.
Green Company, C. Walter
Hamilton Company, William.
Long Manufacturing Company, E
Payette Company, P.

SILENT CHAIN DRIVES
Canadian Link-Belt Company, Ltd.

SILOS
Ontario Wind Engine Company

SLEEPING ROBES
Woods Mfg. Company, Limited

SMOKESTACKS
Marsh Engineering Works, Limited
Waterous Engine Works Company.

SNOW PLOWS
Pink Company, Thomas.

SPARK ARRESTORS
Jenckes Machine Company, Ltd.
Reed & Company, Geo. W.
Waterous Engine Works Company.

SPRUCE
Bartram & Ball.
Bourgouin, H.
Cane & Co., Jas. G.
Cardinal & Page
Davison Lumber & Mfg. Company
Donogh & Co., John.
Dudley, Arthur N.
Dunfield & Company
Exchange Lumber Company.
Foss Lumber Company
Fraser Limited.
Fraser-Bryson Lumber Company.
Gillies Brothers.
Gloucester Lumber Company
Grant & Campbell.
Grier & Sons, Ltd., G. A.
Hart & McDonagh.
Lauder, Spears & Howland.
Long Lumber Company.
Mason, Gordon & Co.
McLennan Lumber Company.
Muir & Kirkpatrick.
New Ontario Colonization Company.
Nicholson & Co., E. M.
River Ouelle Pulp and Lumber Co.
Russell, Chas. H.
Service Lumber Company
Shearer Company, Jas.
Snowball Co., J. B.
Spencer Limited, C. A.
Terry & Gordon.

STEEL CHAIN
Canadian Link-Belt Company, Ltd.
Jeffrey Manufacturing Company.
Waterous Engine Works Company.

STEEL PLATE CONSTRUCTION
Marsh Engineering Works, Limited

STEAM PLANT ACCESSORIES
Waterous Engine Works Company.

STEEL BARRELS
Smart-Turner Machine Co.

STEEL DRUMS
Smart-Turner Machine Co

SWEAT PADS
American Pad & Textile Co.

SULPHITE PULP CHIPS
Davison Lumber & Mfg. Company

TANKS
Ontario Wind Engine Company

TARPAULINS
Turner & Sons, J. J.
Woods Manufacturing Company, Ltd.

TAPS AND DIES
Pratt & Whitney Company.

TENTS
Turner & Sons, J. J.
Woods Mfg. Company

TIES
Auger & Company
Austin & Nicholson.
Harris Tie & Timber Company, Ltd.
Long Lumber Company.
McLennan Lumber Company.
Terry & Gordon.

TIMBER BROKERS
Bradley, R. R.
Cant & Kemp.
Farnworth & Jardine.
Hillas & Co., W. N.
Hunter, Herbert F.
Smith & Tyrer, Limited

TIMBER CRUISERS AND ESTIMATORS
Sewall, James W.

TIMBER LANDS
Department of Lands and Forests.

TRACTORS
British War Mission

TRANSMISSION MACHINERY
Bond Engineering Works
Canadian Link-Belt Company, Ltd.
General Supply Co. of Canada, Ltd.
Jenckes Machine Company, Ltd.
Jeffrey Manufacturing Company.
Waterous Engine Works Company.

TRIMMERS
Garlock-Walker Machinery Co.
Green Company, C. Walter
Waterous Engine Works Company

TUGS
West & Peachey.

TURBINES
Hamilton Company, William.
Jenckes Machine Company, Ltd.

VALVES
Bay City Foundry & Machine Co.
Mason Regulator & Engineering Co.

VENEERS
Webster & Brother, James.

VENEER DRYERS
Philadelphia Textile Mach. Co.

VENEER MACHINERY
Garlock-Walker Machinery Co.
Philadelphia Textile Machinery Co.

VETERINARY REMEDIES
Dr. Bell Veterinary Wonder Co.

WATER HEATERS
Mason Regulator & Engineering Co.

WATERPROOFING
Beveridge Paper Company

WATER WHEELS
Hamilton Company, William.
Jenckes Machine Company, Ltd.

WIRE
Laidlaw Bale Tie Company.

WOOD DISTILLATION PLANTS
Blair, Campbell & McLean, Ltd.

WOODWORKING MACHINERY
American Woodworking Machy. Co.
Garlock-Walker Machinery Co.
General Supply Co. of Canada, Ltd.
Jeffrey Manufacturing Company.
Long Manufacturing Company, E.
Mershon & Company, W. B.
Waterous Engine Works Company.
Yates Machine Company, P. B.

WOOD PRESERVATIVES
International Chemical Company

WOOD PULP
Austin & Nicholson.
New Ontario Colonization Co.
River Ouelle Pulp and Lumber Co.

Pink's Lumbering Tools

The Standard Tools in every province of the Dominion, New Zealand, Australia, etc.
We manufacture all kinds of lumber tools. Light and Durable.

Long Distance Phone, No. 87

Send for Catalogue and Price List.

Sold throughout the Dominion by all Wholesale and Retail Hardware Merchants.

The Thomas Pink Company, Limited

Manufacturers of Lumber Tools

PEMBROKE . . . . . **ONTARIO**

MADE IN CANADA

It's a Pink anyway, you take it, and it's the best Peavey made.

Not altogether what we say, but what users say

"We have used the Alligator or Warping Tug manufactured by you for the last 7 or 8 years, and consider them indispensable to lumbermen on waters of French River or similar streams."

Will move a bag containing 60,000 logs, in calm weather, 30,000 in a head wind.

West & Peachey - Simcoe, Ont.

FOR THE TOPS OF CHIMNEYS

The Thompson Improved Spark Extinguisher will extinguish all dangerous sparks without choking the draft.

There are hundreds now in use giving complete satisfaction—conclusive proof of their practicality.

Substantial reductions in rates are the insurance companies endorsements of this spark extinguisher.

Send for particulars and specifications.

Manufactured by

Geo. W. Reed & Co., Montreal

Established 1852

Vol. 39 Toronto, August 1, 1919 No. 15

Canada Lumberman & Wood Worker

Alphabetical Index to Advertisers, Page 66 Classified Directory to Advertisements, Page 80

QUALITY

SERVICE

Dry White Pine and Norway

QUALITY

SERVICE

We have many lines in stock of 1918 sawing. Choice small log stock ready for prompt shipment. Special prices to make piling room for new cut.

Now sawing White, Red and Jack Pine, Spruce and Hemlock, Send us your inquiries.

Four cars British Columbia Shingles in transit.

QUALITY

SERVICE

TERRY & GORDON

QUALITY

SERVICE

Head Office:

704 Confederation Life Bldg., TORONTO, ONT.

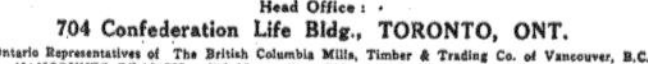

Ontario Representatives of The British Columbia Mills, Timber & Trading Co. of Vancouver, B.C.

VANCOUVER BRANCH: 513 Metropolitan Bldg.—A. S. Nicholson, Western Manager.

HOCKEN LUMBER

The Quality of Our Product is Our Best Advertisement

We Solicit Your Enquiries for Lumber in Any Quantities

We have on Hand Bone Dry

65,000' 2 x 4 — 10/16 Mill Run White Pine
100,000' 2 x 6 — 10/16 Mill Run White Pine
150,000' 2 x 8 — 10/16 Mill Run White Pine
50,000' 2 x 10 — 10/16 Mill Run White Pine

3 Cars 1 x 4 One Face Flooring Strips
Dressing Grade
Very Moderate Price

All Above Small Red Knotted Stock—No Shake

Hocken Lumber Co., Limited

630 Confederation Life Building - TORONTO

PHONE MAIN 3153

SOUTHERN HARDWOODS Dry Stock at Buffalo for Quick Shipment

BROWN ASH

	1 & 2	Clear Strips	No. 1 Com.	No. 2 Com.
1 in.	20,000	....	5,000	22,000
1¼ in.	20,500	5,300	6,200	6,300
1½ in.	11,500	....	....	....
2 in.	1,500	....	13,000	500

WHITE ASH

	1 & 2	Clear Strips	No. 1 Com.	No. 2 Com.
1 in.	57,300	800	130,000	89,000
1¼ in.	41,000	15,500	9,000	1,000
1½ in.	63,900	5,200	43,000	26,100
2 in.	48,300	500	79,000	44,000
2½ in.	....	....	11,500	1,500
3 in.	7,000	....	23,500	4,300
4 in.	4,500	....	....	....

BASSWOOD

	1 & 2	Clear Strips	No. 1 Com.	No. 2 Com.
1 in.	35,700	2,200	172,000	24,000
1¼ in.	144,300	12,000	146,500	65,800
1½ in.	36,000	....	24,800	11,000
2 in.	20,900	....	15,000	4,800
2½ in.	75,000	....	20,900	13,000
3 in.	5,350	....	6,500	3,900

BUTTERNUT

	1 & 2	No. 1 Com.	No. 2 Com.
1 in.	15,300	35,800	19,600
2½ in.	3,000	3,000	.....

TENESSEE SCENTED RED CEDAR

	1 & 2	No. 1 Com.	No. 2 Com.
1 in.	18,500	15,800	1,500
1¼ in.	4,400	800	.....

CHERRY

	1 & 2	Clear Strips	No. 1 Com.	No. 2 Com.
1 in.	154,000	24,000	129,200	66,500
1¼ in.	3,500	.....	3,600	6,400
1½ in.	31,000	.....	17,700	73,300
2 in.	10,100	.....	17,200	30,000
2½ in.	4,500	.....	.....	800
3 in.	6,700	.....	.....	2,300
4 in.	3,000	.....	1,200	1,000

CHESTNUT

	1 & 2	Clear Strips	No. 1 Com.	No. 2 Com.
¾ in.	.....	.....	1,500	62,000
1 in.	147,900	10,700	21,300	94,500
1¼ in.	88,800	1,300	10,300	38,200
1½ in.	45,500	.....	4,000	.....
2 in.	23,200	.....	52,300	107,200
2½ in.	2,700	.....	850	.....
3 in.	1,800	.....	1,300	.....
4 in.	900	.....	.....	.....

RED GUM

	1 & 2	No. 1 Com.	No. 2 Com.
1 in.	60,300	13,200	......
1¼ in.	8,200	9,200	......
1½ in.	9,000	11,300	......
2 in.	7,100	4,800	......

SAP GUM

	1 & 2	No. 1 Com.	No. 2 Com.
1 in.	47,400	6,000	......
1¼ in.	......	......	......
1½ in.	......	......	......
2 in.	......	......	......
2 in.	11,000 qtd.	7,500 qtd.	......

HICKORY

	1 & 2	No. 1 Com.	No. 2 Com.
1 in.	2,200	2,300	600
1¼ in.	......	400	350
1½ in.	5,000	2,300	1,000
2 in.	12,350	13,600	10,700
2½ in.	7,000	5,000	......
3 in.	400	5,580	......
4 in.	200	200	......

PLAIN RED OAK

	1 & 2	Clear Strips	No. 1 Com.	No. 2 Com.
⅜ in.	30,200	.....	.....	.....
½ in.	97,000	.....	25,400	6,200
⅝ in.	8,500	.....	.....	.....
1 in.	220,200	2,700	10,500	10,400
1¼ in.	11,700	2,400	14,500	7,200
1½ in.	73,900	4,300	20,200	24,000
2 in.	38,100	.....	45,800	.....
2½ in.	23,100	.....	4,000	.....
3 in.	23,800	.....	8,800	.....
4 in.	3,600	.....	3,900	.....

PLAIN WHITE OAK

	1 & 2	Clear Strips	No. 1 Com.	No. 2 Com.
⅜ in.	23,400	.....	.....	.....
½ in.	11,800	.....	.....	.....
⅝ in.	28,150	.....	21,300	.....
¾ in.	39,900	.....	22,000	17,000
1 in.	22,300	.....	13,000	15,200
1¼ in.	76,300	.....	17,000	6,000
1½ in.	30,500	.....	50,400	10,000
2 in.	40,000	.....	101,000	2,000
2½ in.	113,800	.....	35,500	.....
3 in.	54,800	.....	39,800	4,400
4 in.	21,000	.....	1,500	.....

QUARTERED RED OAK

	1 & 2	Clear Strips	No. 1 Com.	No. 2 Com.
¾ in.	....	....	......	....
1 in.	72,200	8,300	38,800	800
1¼ in.	500	....	400	....
1½ in.	....	....	550	150
2 in.	1,000	....	7,400	....

QUARTERED WHITE OAK

	1 & 2	Clear Strips	No. 1 Com.	No. 2 Com.
⅜ in.	5,500	....	....	....
½ in.	84,500	25,400	128,600	....
⅝ in.	....	....	....	....
1 in.	29,400	12,800	4,000	15,000
1¼ in.	10,000	....	6,400	1,300
1½ in.	1,500	....	2,000	2,300
2 in.	6,500	350	5,100	2,700
2½ in.	800	....	....	....

POPLAR

	1 & 2 18 in. & up	1 & 2 13 in. & up	Box Boards	Bright Saps
⅝ in.	....	3,000	....	2,300
1 in.	16,200	30,000	11,000	40,200
1¼ in.	2,800	3,000	....	11,000
1½ in.	5,300	7,000	....	21,000
2 in.	....	32,600	....	22,000
2½ in.	....	25,800	....	28,000
3 in.	....	5,000	....	32,600
4 in.	....	27,000	....	1,300

	Stained Saps	Clear Strips	No. 1 Com.	No. 2 Com.
⅝ in.	9,800	....	34,300	2,600
1 in.	23,600	....	105,900	55,300
1¼ in.	8,800	....	11,000	6,000
1½ in.	9,700	....	45,000	2,700
2 in.	7,000	....	141,500	27,500
2½ in.	3,700	....	1,000	....
3 in.	1,500	....	43,000	32,000
4 in.	700	....	750	....

QUARTERED POPLAR

	1 & 2	Clear Strips	No. 1 Com.	No. 2 Com.
1 in.	....	....	....	....
1¼ in.	250	....	....	....

BLACK WALNUT

	1 & 2	No. 1 Com.	No. 2 Com.
1 in.	150	14,000	8,100
1¼ in.	100	300	200
1½ in.	250	200	100
2 in.	300	800	500
3 in.	110	120	250
4 in.	....	500	1,200

Also Large Stock of BEECH, BIRCH and MAPLE

SAW MILL MACHINERY

Firstbrook Bros.
Limited

Having decided to discontinue saw mill operations at Penetang have the following machinery for sale. This machinery is all in operating condition and is open for inspection at Penetang, Ont.

Mill Machinery

Extra heavy log haul-up works with inch round and flat chain, 128 ft. centres.
2—Waterous log unloaders or kickers, 8 arms, 10 in. cylinders.
1—Waterous log loader, 8 arms, 10-in. cylinders.
1—Waterous right-hand double cutting band mill, 11 in. saws, 8 ft. wheel, with 8-block carriage; 24 in. opening; Payette set works and dogs; 8 in. x 36 ft. steam feed.
1—Waterous double edger for 20-inch saws, lever shifter.
1—Payette double edger for 18-in. saws, lever shifter.
48—live rolls about 8 ft. long by 10 in. dia.; extra heavy, sprocket drive.
4—High cars with roller tops, 24 in. heavy wheels on 8 in. axles, standard gauge.
1—Mershon 4 saw gang resaw, takes squared cants or just one face, ideal machine to cut small logs and centres of large after good has been taken off.
1—Payette picket machine, made specially for shade roller stock, will feed pieces 16 in. long, also sorting table with chain top.
1—Rogers Iron Works circular resaw for making box lumber from slabs; fool-proof machine.
1—Payette edger for box and short stock.
1—Rogers twin circular or tie maker.
1—Payette lath bolter and lath machine.
1—Pair lath trimmers.
1—Picket trimmer (bunch trim).
Conveyor drives and chains.
Pulleys, gears, heavy line shafting and countershafting with bearings.
Send us your requirements.
We have a large stock of double and triple leather belting in widths from 10 in. to 18 in.

Power House Equipment

3—Return Tubular Boilers, Goldie McCulloch make, 66 x 16, Dutch oven settings, 85 lbs. steam allowance Ontario Government.
Breeching and smoke stack for above boilers, 60 in. dia., newly painted, 600 ft. new ½-in. guy and plate for brick pier.
1—Pair Polson "Brown" type engines, coupled on quarters, 22 in. x 30 in., with 16 ft. x 48 in. belt, balance wheel. Excellent engines.
1—Pair American feed water heaters for above engines; 10 in., copper coils.
1—8 x 10 Centre Crank Engine
1—10 x 14 Cowan Slide Valve Engine

Filing Equipment

1—Waterous band saw grinder for 6 in. saws.
1—Baldwin retoother for band saws.
2—Reversible saw levelling blocks.
2—Chilled band saw anvils.
Hanchet band saw swages; Crescent circular saw swages; shapers and dressers.

Yard Equipment

Booms and boom chains, ½, ¾ & ⅞.
Winches and other mill supplies.

Prompt shipments and bargains for quick sale. Will send all particulars and prices on application.

Firstbrook Bros.
Limited
Penetang, Ont.

"WELL BOUGHT IS HALF SOLD"

UNIQUE !

This word applies to

OUR

WHITE PINE

Why?

BECAUSE:

Logs—Come from best White Pine section in Ontario.

Manufacture—Unsurpassed. Modern, up-to-the-minute mill equipment insures this.

Grading—Careful, uniform and of sufficiently wide range to give the customer just what he requires.

Have you used our White Pine?
A trial order will convince you that it really does stand in a class by itself.

Canadian General Lumber Co.
Limited

FOREST PRODUCTS

TORONTO OFFICE :— 712-20 Bank of Hamilton Bldg.
Montreal Office :—203 McGill Bldg.
Mills : Byng Inlet, Ont.

PETRIE'S LIST
of
NEW and USED
WOOD TOOLS
for Immediate Delivery

Wood Lathes

20" Sidney, Famous
16" Cowan.
16" Sidney, Famous, patternmakers.
14" Sidney, Famous.

Band Saws

36" West Side, pedestal.
30" Cowan, bracket.
60" Fay & Egan, band re-saw.

Saw Tables

No. 6 Sidney, Famous, variety.
No. 2 Sidney, Famous, variety.
Fisher, iron frame rip.
MacGregor-Gourlay power feed cut-off.
Greenlee automatic cut-off.
7½' Fay & Egan, swing saw.
7' Williams, swing saw.
Bench type, jig or scroll saw.
No. 4 Canadian, steel frame, pole saw.

Wood Planers

30" Whitney pattern single surfacer.
26" double surfacer, with chip breaker.
24" Hermance, double surfacer.
24" Sidney, Famous, single surfacer.
24" Crescent, single surfacer.
24" MacGregor-Gourlay.
24" pony planer.
24" Champion planer and matcher, with moulding attachment.
24" Galt, planer and matcher.
18" Sidney Famous, single surfacer.
12" Buzz, with slotted head (2).
12" Petrie, buzz planers, safety heads (6)

Moulders

13" Clark-Demill four side.
12" Cowan four side.
12" Woods, four-side, inside.
10" Houston four side.
8" Dundas four side.
6" Dundas sash sticker.

Mortisers

Cowan, upright power.
Galt, upright, compound table.
No. 5 New Britain chain.
No. 2 Smart, foot power.
No. 2 Osborne, foot power.

Boring Machines

No. 8 Sidney, Famous, gear driven.
No. 7 Sidney, Famous, belt driven.
No. 920 Canada Machinery Corporation (2).
Fay, single spindle, horizontal.
Jardine hub boring machine.

Clothespin Machinery

Humphrey automatic lathes (6).
Humphrey double slotters (3).

Miscellaneous

No. 30 Sidney, universal woodworker.
Vaughan, portable drag saw.
Champion, drag saw.
Cowan moulder and panel raiser.
MacGregor Gourlay 12 spindle dovetailer.
Fay & Egan 12 spindle dovetailer.
No. 1 Ballantine dowel machine.
12" Canada Mach. Corp. sander.
24" Fay, double drum.
No. 2 Defiance belt sander.
M135 Cowan, sash and door relisher.
2-spindle Cant-Gourlay shaper.
No. 1 Defiance, axle shoulder shaper.
Superior saw arbors, 6"-30" saws (7).
M63 Cowan spindle carver.
Hall, automatic shingle machine.
Boss automatic shingle machine.
No. 2 Dominion, lath machine & bolter.
No. 3 Defiance, rim and felloe rounding machine.
24" Defiance shaft and pole tapering machine.
No. 1 Defiance, automatic, spoke driver.
8' Linderman, automatic, glue jointer.
8' McKeough & Trotter, hoop cutter.
No. 2 Reynolds, power screw driver.
No. 4 Lion, universal, wood trimmer.
Dundas, wood frame tenoner.
20" American wood scraper.
Horizontal bracket carving machine.

Ask to see our large stock of used supplies—belting, pulleys, machine shop equipment, mill supplies, pipe and fittings. Most of this material is as good as new and can be bought at greatly reduced prices.

H. W. PETRIE, LTD.
Front St. W., TORONTO, ONT.

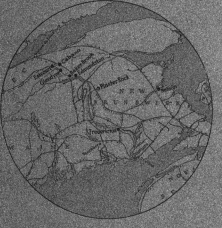

Canada Lumberman

and Woodworker

Issued on the 1st and 15th of every month by

HUGH C. MACLEAN, LIMITED, Publishers

HUGH C. MacLEAN, Winnipeg, President.

THOS. S. YOUNG, Toronto, General Manager.

OFFICES AND BRANCHES:

TORONTO - - Telephone A. 2700 - - 347 Adelaide Street West
VANCOUVER - - Telephone Seymour 2013 - - Winch Building
MONTREAL - - Telephone Main 2299 - - 119 Board of Trade
WINNIPEG - Telephone Garry 856 - Electric Railway Chambers
NEW YORK - - Telephone 3108 Beekman - - 1123 Tribune Building
CHICAGO - Telephone Harrison 5351 - 1413 Great Northern Building
LONDON, ENG. - - - - - - - - - - 16 Regent Street, S.W.

TERMS OF SUBSCRIPTION

Canada, United States and Great Britain, $2.00 per year, in advance; other foreign countries embraced in the General Postal Union, $3.00.

Single copies 15 cents.

"The Canada Lumberman and Woodworker" is published in the interest of, and reaches regularly, persons engaged in the lumber, woodworking and allied industries in every part of Canada. It aims at giving full and timely information on all subjects touching these interests, and invites free discussion by its readers.

Advertisers will receive careful attention and liberal treatment. For manufacturing and supply firms wishing to bring their goods to the attention of owners and operators of saw and planing mills, woodworking factories, pulp mills, etc., "The Canada Lumberman and Woodworker" is undoubtedly the most direct and profitable advertising medium. Special attention is directed to the "Wanted" and "For Sale" advertisements.

Authorized by the Postmaster-General for Canada, for transmission as second-class matter.

Entered as second-class matter July 18th, 1914, at the Postoffice at Buffalo, N.Y., under the Act of Congress of March 3, 1879.

Vol. 39 Toronto, August 1, 1919 No 15

Gauging Conditions in Lumber Industry

One of the most important resolutions adopted at the last annual meeting of the Canadian Lumbermen's Association was that monthly reports should be presented on manufacturers' shipments and sale, in order that market conditions might be gauged more accurately and matters affecting the industry as a whole be stabilized and strengthened. The producers, if these returns were regularly and promptly made, would know where they were at in regard to stock, production, demand, transportation, etc.

It was pointed out by several of the leading representatives that there was not sufficient definite information regarding the annual available supply of manufactured lumber in Canada—on hand or to be cut, and that more facts should be known with respect to cuts, costs and sales.

In accordance with these facts it was decided that all manufacturers who are members of the Association, be requested to furnish on specific dates the total board feet of lumber, showing what spruce, pine, etc., also lath and shingles, are on hand and unsold at a particular period, and that a similar monthly statement should be issued throughout the sawing season, together with the aggregate amount in feet and sales each month.

It was asserted that all mills making such returns would be acting in a spirit of helpfulness and co-operation; that nothing was to be gained by withholding the figures which would, in any event, be private, and only the recapitulations would be sent out to the members from month to month. The totals would afford the trade a clear conception of where matters stood, of what had taken place during the past thirty days, and how the market, as based upon supply and demand, shaped up.

Although this important and aggressive step was taken over five months ago, it is learned that not much headway has been made. The proper forms were prepared by the officers of the Canadian Lumbermen's Association and sent to the different members, to be returned to the secretary, properly filled in. It is reported that the statistical returns have not been coming in very satisfactorily and an officer of the Association recently stated that there was little progress to report in this direction. He did not know whether or not it is because the mills are so busily occupied in trying to work out satisfactorily the unusual problems which each day present themselves, yet the fact remains that the Canadian Lumbermen's Association has not been receiving replies from some of the largest producers and, without these returns, the result will not be of much value.

It is true there have been many things cropping up to distract the attention of lumber manufacturers, among them being the labor unrest, the shortage of ships for export, the uncertainty regarding the building situation and the added cost of production and distribution. While these are of themselves most important, still a constructive, creative department, such as the monthly statistical returns of manufacture, shipments and sales should not be neglected. It is hoped that all the manufacturers will fall in line and in the true spirit of co-operation and mutual helpfulness, which is characterizing many present day movements, they will manifest sufficient interest to see that the proposition is crowned with success.

The Adoption of the Cash Basis

Almost anyone can sell goods at a cut price; it requires real salesmanship to dispose of them at regular values. Like the poor man, the price cutter has always been with each trade and in every community, and will, possibly, continue until the end of time. When one bargain shouter or cut-rate "artist" goes down and under in the business game there is always someone else to rise up and take his place. Lessons of the past, the failures of others, the mercantile ruins that are witnessed on all sides, count for nothing in the judgment and experience of some. They imagine they are immune from such reverses and, while certain persons have been baffled, they know a better way, and wish to demonstrate the faith which they have in themselves to push ahead, (and, parenthetically, it might be remarked, they should have equal faith in their goods and sell them at a proper valuation). However, this is outside the issue under discussion.

The retailer who places his business to-day upon a cash basis, is the one who is forging ahead, expanding and making money. Never were artisans, skilled mechanics, farm help and all classes of labor in receipt of such generous remuneration for their services as at the present time, and the products of the farmer are also commanding a higher figure than at any period in the history of the world. What more auspicious occasion than the present to usher in a cash business. Many men are fearful about taking the first step, but after the initial plunge has been made they realize that the move was not a very difficult one after all, and soon learn that the people will come up to the higher standards of merchandising if tradesmen will only lead with calmness, courage and decision.

The retail lumberman has to pay cash for his lumber, has to carry a representative stock, has to purchase in increasingly large quantities and distribute in small lots. Values were never as high, rents were never so stiff, taxes so excessive and labor so insistent in its demands as at this juncture and, in the face of all these exactions, the public is clamoring for specialized and more efficient service. Yet there are many retail lumbermen who are allowing farmers, carpenters, contractors and private builders all sorts of time in which to settle their bills. The day has practically arrived when, instead of large accounts carried from mnoth to month with various people making (or not making,) payments at such times as suits their convenience, that all patrons will have to pay cash.

If the Ontario Retail Lumber Dealers' Association had not done anything in the year and a half of its successful history other than inaugurate better terms and place business on a cash basis, it would have justified its existence. There is now displayed in practically every retail lumber yard office a conspicuous sign to the effect that "no discount is allowed," that terms are "net cash" and that the only accommodation extended is with customers of approved credit who will agree to pay each month's account in "net cash" on or before the 10th of the following month. Now that cards have been printed to that effect and posted prominently in every office, it is the duty of each member of the Association to live up to the high standard which it is sought to establish.

There is no doubt that industrially and financially the world is undergoing radical changes—not to employ the term revolution, to describe adequately the shifting state of affairs. Early closing is here, the eight-hour day has been ushered in and may soon become universal; the Saturday half holiday is generally observed; labor men are demanding more leisure and better pay in order to live decently and comfortably. If, in in the face of all the opposition that has been raised, industrial workers can accomplish so much during the period of readjustment and re-construction following the war, surely the employer, as typified in the retail lumber dealer, can also raise the status and dignity of his business, not only by rendering better service and keeping more attractive yards, a better selected stock and a wider range of supplies, but also by inaugurating the cash system with practically every patron. There is no doubt that as the eight hour day has practically arrived and will extend from one end of the Dominion to the other, so the retail yardman must fall in line and keep step to the music of cash accounts, or, otherwise, he will fall behind in the financial race and be numbered among the "also rans." It takes initiative, energy, persistence, aggressiveness and co-operation, and last, but by no means least, cash to win any present day business struggle.

Mr. Retail Lumbermen, you will never have a more auspicious opportunity to place your affairs on a cash basis than at this very moment, and it behooves you, in the progress of economic events to do so without further delay or ado.

Naturalness in Publicity Appeals

Natural expression in print, as in conversation, carries with it, says D. A. Reidy, in "Printers' Ink," a certain weight and confidence that adds 100 per cent. to its selling effect. Why not? The natural language of business is the language of the street as ordinarily heard. Men do not sit at a business deal and conjure up symphonic sentences to impress the other fellow with their meticulosity of words, or write business letters that sound as if every sentence was written with the aid of Webster's Unabridged. The salesman who would talk to his customers in the stilted language of the ordinary kiln-dried ad. would be looked upon as a martinet. Nobody but a literary gent would undertake to sell goods to any ordinary prospect by indulging in set sentences set forth. In salesmanship, as in other human relations, if the touch of human nature is lacking, the effort is very liable to lose weight. Why not apply this same rule to salesmanship in print ? In truth, whenever this very thing has been done, the effect has not only been refreshing to the mind of the reader and carried complete confidence, but in some notable instances that occur offhand, you will agree it has produced remarkable response.

We remember, with what relish some years ago, we swallowed the blithe business messages of a big St. Louis hardware house written by "Mike the Teamster" in a style and language we all could understand and some of us happen to know how said hardware concern in a short time trebled its business as a result of the house organ being written and edited entirely by "Mike." Also we recall with gusto the first time a daring young Lochinvar broke into print with the longshore vernacular and abjured us gentlemen of the upper crust to pack our old Jimmy pipes with that sure enough baccy stuff called for convenience P. A., which, being only human, several million of us immediately proceeded to do and have kept on doing ever since.

That there is something more than mere novelty or cleverness in getting off the pedestal and chucking the rules for a change, was still more recently proved by "Jim Henry" who, so to speak, took off his coat and collar and dared to talk everyday salesman's language with the result that the Post Office was fairly gummed up for a while sending out millions of sample shaves ordered by people who didn't feel at all resentful at the every-day naturalistic conversation of Jim. People do like to feel that they can touch elbows with a business concern in print, just as they would in a Pullman smoker or the lobby of a hotel. Every time it has been tried out, within reasonable bounds of course, the natural note in copy has made a hit and the wonder is that it is not being done a great deal more, considering the undeniable fact that the Colonel's Lady and Judy O'-Grady are now, always have been, and always will be sisters under the skin.

As an example of this sort of free-hand treatment applied to a serious appeal, every one who saw it will recall a Victory Loan ad. that appeared in New York newspapers the other day. It told of a boy who struck his foot through the Victory Arch on Fifth Avenue and found it was only papier-mache. As you read it, you could almost see the boy pulling his foot out of the mock marble pillar with a look of sorrow on his face. This ad. was not written according to rule or sat on by a Board of Experts, or changed twenty different times, or passed from one judge to another to see where it could be improved. As a matter of fact, it was dictated red hot to a typist, never read a second time by the author, and went into print with all its original barbs and burrs, and maybe that very fact explains why it left such a fetching impress on the reader's mind. One cannot help admiring the audacity that dared to use the expression, "stuck his foot," instead of "penetrated with his boot" or "punctured with his shoe" or some other Sunday school phrase that might be suggested by the rules. This piece of copy broke all the ten commandments as to length of sentences and selection of words, but it drove straight home even among advertising men and on account of its unusualness carried the reader right along.

Thus are we being gradually shown in various ways that the book. "How to Write Good Copy," may soon be on its way to the waste basket and that the first, last and middle rule for writing good copy is to be, first of all, a good business thinker, and then express your business thoughts easily, naturally, spontaneously and sincerely—thus making your own rules.

Better Support to Worthy Institution

The Federal Government of Australia has established a Bureau of Science and Industry for the purposes of industrial research. Included in the scope of the Bureau's functions will be a Forest Utilization Laboratory, which will be located at Perth, Western Australia, and with a view to securing the latest data, preliminary to the establishment of the laboratory, the Government has commissioned Mr. I. H. Boas to visit the research laboratories in the U. S., Canada, England, France and India. Mr. Boas will be the head of the institution.

The Australian Government is planning to develop the country's forest resources on an extensive scale. At present the country has large stands of hardwoods, but it is felt there is an opportunity to produce softwoods in considerable quantities. Experiments are now being carried out with Maritime pine, on sand waste areas.

Mr. Boas visited institutions in the United States, paying particular attention to the work and equipment of the Forest Products Laboratory at Madison, and was very favorably impressed by the work carried on there. Mr. Boas also visited the Forest Products Laboratories of Canada at Montreal, and left on July 11th for England.

In connection with his visit we desire to emphasize a point to which we have made previous reference. It is this—the necessity of Canada adequately supporting the Forest Products Laboratories. While the Australian Government is evidently alive to the possibilities of developing the country's forest products, and is spending a large sum in securing the latest information as to what is being done in other parts of the world, Canada is very parsimonious in her support of an institution which has done, and is doing, excellent work in investigating scientifically her forest products. The Laboratories train men, and promptly lose them to lumber and pulp and paper compaines, owing to the inadequate salaries paid by the Government. The subject has been ventilated in the House of Commons, and the Department recognizes that the country is being deprived of the services of good men, but so far nothing has been done in the way of increasing their remuneration. Until that is done the country cannot hope to retain men who possess technical knowledge relating to industries which are rapidly expanding, and who can find a ready market for their knowledge in service outside the Government.

Editorial Short Lengths

If the report of the impending resignation of the Hon. Jules Allard, Minister of Lands & Forests for the Province of Quebec, be confirmed, the lumbermen of the province will lose a good friend. Mr. Allard has the reputation of considering questions with an open mind, and with a desire to conserve the natural resources of the province. His work in connection with the protection of forests from fire may be cited as an instance of progressive policy. Mr. Allard rightly regards the forests as one of the most valuable assets of the province, and his aim has been to preserve them from wanton destruction. Quebec has been a pioneer in the campaign for the perpetuation of forests, and no man has done more than Mr. Allard towards achieving that object.

* * *

In view of the large sales of lumber to the U. K. the decline in sterling exchange is of more than ordinary interest to the Canadian lumber trade. Unless sterling shows more strength, trade between Canada and the U. S. and the United Kingdom is likely to be considerably restricted, as British importers will only buy the barest requirements under the circumstances. A committee of foreign bankers in New York has been considering the question. In the lumber trade, exports for private account have been curtailed owing to the uncertainty of the exchange market, combined with the high freights. The demand for space for all kinds of commodities is abnormal, and the steamship lines are able to command rates which are out of the question so far as lumber is concerned. As one exporter put it: "There is no use shipping for the sole benefit of the steamship companies. All our profit is swallowed up by the freight charges."

* * *

The visit of the Woodlands section of the Canadian Pulp and Paper Association to Laurentide, P. Q., recalls what is being done by lumber and pulp and paper companies in the matter of erecting houses for the workpeople, and in other ways providing better conditions for the men. This is a question of vital importance, in view of the universal industrial unrest, which fortunately has not affected these industries to any extent. The Laurentide Co. has been a notable leader in this work, and Mr. F. A. Sabbaton, of that company, in a paper read before the first meeting of the Woodlands section, strongly advocated companies giving increased attention to the subject. The Laurentide Co. has a model town at Grand 'Mere, and has spent large sums in efforts to make life more tolerable, providing a hotel, club-houses, free school, skating rink, tennis courts, playgrounds, golf links, and a large farm and truck garden.

Other companies are also working on the same lines, particularly in the direction of good housing. We may allude to the St. Maurice Paper Co. at Three Rivers, P.Q.; the Donnacona Paper Co. at Donnacona, P.Q., the Abitibi Co., in Northern Ontario; the Kipawa Co. at Temiskaming, and the Riordon Company at Hawkesbury.

Looked at merely from the point of the companies, such schemes are of value, in that they engender a feeling of attachment to the various firms, and thus ensure a continuity of employment which makes for efficiency. Men who have pleasant surroundings and comfortable houses are more likely to remain in a town than when such conditions are unsatisfactory. The companies are putting up well-designed and laid out houses. and do not look upon such schemes as revenue producers. The central idea is to afford excellent accommodation, and to keep the labour, giving, in some instances, opportunities for the men to fill responsible positions. The outlay has been large, but according to Mr. Sabbaton, the results have more than justified the expenditure.

* * *

The Laurentide Co., Grand Mere, has instituted a safety first departmental honor roll which might be copied, with advantage, by other large firms. A bulletin-board, placed in a conspicuous position, records during each month, departmentally, accidents as they occur, the department sustaining a lost time accident having its name transferred from the left or honor side to the right of the board and remaining there until the end of the current month.

The following table shows the standing of the "honor roll" from May 1st to June 30th, 1919, inclusive:

Department	No. of Accidents	Average No. of employees	P.C. of accidents per 100 men.
Miscellaneous	....	170.0	..
Wood mill	....	160.2	..
Sulphite	....	112.4	..
Village	....	107.9	..
Ground Wood	....	106.3	..
Mill Supply	....	32.7	..
Real Estate	....	30.0	..
Electrical	....	22.4	..
General Mills	2	426.4	.47
Paper	2	341.5	.59
Steam Plant	1	53.0	1.89
Total	5	1563.	

The institution of such an honor roll is calculated to impress on the employees the value of carefulness in their work, and to inspire each department with a desire to figure on the safety side of the roll.

* * *

As in the other industries, scientific research work is of prime importance in connection with those industries using wood as a raw material. Such work furnishes accurate knowledge of the characteristics of the different kinds of wood, reveals new uses for them, shows how to reduce waste and decay, and brings to light by-products that can be secured from otherwise wasted materials.

This work in Canada is carried on in connection with the Forest Products Laboratories, conducted by the Forestry Branch of the Department of the Interior, in co-operation with McGill University, Montreal. The laboratories are laboratories of practical research. As the benefits of the work done will only be realized when the results are made use of in the industries, every effort is made to maintain a close co-operation with the industries. The laboratories are furnished with very complete and up-to-date equipment, particularly for testing the strength of timbers, for the manufacture of paper from wood, and for the preservative treatment of ties and posts. The semi-commercial experimental paper machine is the most complete in America.

The work carried on includes the study of the physical and chemical structure of the different kinds of Canadian woods, the testing of their strength, the study of the agencies destructive to wood and the best means to preserve the wood from decay and to properly and quickly season it, the study of the methods of wood distillation and of the manufacture of paper from wood. The last line of work is particularly important at the present time on account of the fact that during the war the cutting off of European manufacture greatly increased the demand from the United States for Canadian wood pulp and paper. The existence in Canada of very large forests of spruce and balsam, which are the kinds of trees most used for paper manufacture, assures her an important place in this industry if she can develop methods to produce pulp and paper of sufficiently high quality and cheap enough to meet all competition.

The importance of the timber resources of the province of British Columbia and the necessity of investigation at close range problems in connection with the timbers peculiar to that province led last year to the establishment of a branch forest products laboratory in Vancouver. The establishment of this laboratory was especially urged by the Imperial Ministry of Munitions, who wished to secure information in regard to the properties of woods used in the construction of airplanes. Since the conclusion of hostilities this work has been proceeded with on account of the importance of complete knowledge of the woods suitable for airplanes in view of the probable development in the use of these in the near future for other than military uses.

Some Present Day Problems of Lumbermen

How Enterprising Yardmen May Extend Business and Improve Their Facilities —Getting After Rural and Town Customers—Practical Pointers

For several days lately I have been passing a place where an old fourteen-room residence was being taken down to give place to a brick business building. I have been greatly interested in watching the con dition of the lumber that came from it. The house was built over fifty years ago, and at the time was one of the finest in the town. The lumber that went into its construction was, of course, white pine, which was all that could be had at that period. Both the sheathing and dimension were rough and of full size in width and thickness, and some of the boards were equal in quality of grade to the present "C" Select. It looked a waste of good lumber to use such for sheathing purposes, says C. H. Ketridge in the "Mississippi Valley Lumberman."

It was remarkable to note the perfect condition of the entire lot of lumber as it was taken down. I made a special investigation in this matter of preservation and found only a few instances where there was decay, and these were at the ends of some of the sills and under the porch and bay window. And all of this, I don't think, would amount to a hundred feet. The nails were of the old-fashioned cut type and as good in condition as the day they were driven. The house had been reshingled but once since it was built and white pine shingles used each time.

I made some inquiries about the cost of lumber here at that time, and as near as I could ascertain, common lumber was selling in bills at $10 and $12 a thousand. A good deal of this stuff was being sold as it was taken down from the building. It was sold by the piece at 2 cents a lineal foot for 2 x 4's; 3 cents for 2 x 6's; 4 cents for 2 x 8's, and 5 cents for 2 x 10's. So, you see, the wreckers were getting a little over $30 a thousand for lumber that originally cost about one-third of this. A man who was buying some of this stuff said they asked him 95 cents for a yellow pine 2 x 8-14 at the local yard. Compare this with the selling price of fifty years ago. It may be said, however, that the low price here at that time was owing to its being bought at a yard that was near the lake dock that was here at the time, but which was removed many years ago. You can estimate what lumber was selling at in the country towns of this section of the state.

Remodelling is Paying Proposition

I was talking with one of our local real estate dealers the other day who makes a business of erecting buildings and selling them. He said he was not building any new ones now, but he was buying old houses and remodelling them to suit the more modern requirements. He was doing this because it involved a less investment and with the strong demand for houses he found little trouble in selling them. I took occasion to write something about this matter of remodelling old houses some weeks ago, but I believe it of such importance to mention it again, because, as I view it, it is going to be a paying proposition for the retailers to take hold of the matter and develop it, especially in the country towns. As I have said before, most of these places have done growing in population and the houses now there are sufficient. Very few new houses are being built in these towns, and this will continue for some time to come if people wait for prices of material to be much lower than they are. There are few of the older towns in which there are not people of means living in these old houses who are able to have them remodelled so as to give them the more modern conveniences. Then again, there are more or less of these houses that are occupied by tenants, and are generally in a run-down condition. The owners can't sell them, and so they rent for what they can get and doing as little repairing as possible on them.

In a Kansas town the business men's club took this matter up and after investigating the possibilities, thought it worth while to salvage these old houses. And so they went at it and raised a fund to purchase these neglected places and make them over into new and attractive homes and put them on the market for sale. This action served to arouse interest among those living in their old houses and started some of them on the work of remodelling them. My information does not extend to giving the particulars, but I'm pretty sure it was the lumber dealers of the town that first started the proposition and worked up the interest of the community in the project.

As a rule people in most of these old towns have grown disheartened about attracting new enterprises to come there. Many have tried it and made a failure, but there is no good reason why they cannot go at it and improve what they have in the town, and as this is mostly buildings, a concerted action to make improvements on these would result in making the whole town more attractive and arouse a greater civic pride in the inhabitants. The more attractive a town is in its business and home buildings and the general upkeep of the place, the more likely it is to induce other people to come and build new homes there, because such a town is more desirable to live in. The hardest part of this proposition is to arouse a sufficient degree of interest to induce people to give it the attention to examine into it, and this work naturally falls on the lumber dealers of the town. Combining together for this purpose undoubtedly they will be able to induce a few more of the progressive spirits to join them in the initial work of starting it, but the lumbermen will have to furnish the steam to carry it on.

Would Rather Erect New Houses

I am well aware of the chronic state of mind of lumber dealers and carpenter-contractors regarding old houses. It is generally the case that when the owner of an old house consults them about the feasibility of remodelling it, they usually seek to advise him to pull it down or remove it to another lot and build a new one. Lumbermen do this for the reason that they will sell more material and the carpenter-coutractor because he don't like the job of tearing out the inside of an old building and working over old lumber. They prefer to use new lumber as long as others are paying for it. But both of these parties must change their attitude in this regard, because lumber is getting too valuable to let old buildings go to waste, as a great many are now doing. And paradoxical though it may seem, it is to the interest of the lumbermen to prevent this as much as possible, for a lot of old dilapidated buildings invariably operates to discourage the growth of a town, not only from the outside but also from the inside for the continued appearance of these old "shacks" exerts a depressing effect on the community. It makes one feel "blue" to look at them, and gives him the feeling that the town is "going to the dogs."

We are effected and educated more through the sense of sight than by anything else, though we do not realize it. No individual can do his best when in a depressed condition of mind Neither can a town make progress where there is a chronic depression caused by the sight of general neglect and dilapidation of its buildings Go into some of your old stores with their dingy fronts and unkempt condition of the interiors, and you'll never find the storekeeper occupying one of these in anything but a pessimistic frame of mind He can't be cheerful in the face of such surroundings.

The Effects of Our Envirous

It is a well known fact that during a continued period of cloudy weather business is not so good as it is on sunshiny days. There is a lack of ozone in the atmosphere to stimulate activity. So it is with the effect a dingy looking town has upon its inhabitants. The surroundings of such a place deaden the spiritual ozone that produces activity in a community. A town that is backward in making itself attractive in appearance does not get the share of the trade it ought to have. Farmers and their families like to go to an attractive looking town and a good many will obey this impulse and take their trade from their unattractive home town and drive farther to where the surroundings are more pleasing to the eye and there is a sense of enjoyment of the change from the dull environments of their own farms. And they are justified in their action in so doing, although they may be barely conscious of their reasons for it.

Business men in these old ramshackle towns of course complain of this loss of trade, and they attribute it to the lower prices obtainable in these more attractive towns. This is more imaginary than anything else, as they would find out if they took the trouble to investigate. Every town wants more farmers to come there and do their trading, but only a few of them ever seem to think that farmers enjoy going to a town where the business men act as though they wanted them and the community does things that will attract and insure their making it their regular trading place. And now the farmers have got their riding machines, they are going to more and more leave the unattractive towns in the lurch and go where it is manifested they are wanted.

Keeping Farm Buildings in Repair

When I lived in the country, I have been out on some of the rented farms and seen the conditions under which some of the renters were compelled to live. Some places were better than others, but the large majority of the houses were hardly fit for a family to live in, and the other buildings, limited in number to the veriest needs, were of the same character. I always felt sorry for these people. Some of them had been accustomed to better things, but misfortune had compelled them to take what they could get. The owners of these farms had no interest in the living of their tenants and cared less. Getting their rent was about all that interested them.

I presume there has been some improvement in these conditions since then, but even now, I guess, the houses and buildings on tenant farms are not what they should be, considering the better times for farming. Farm owners complain of the general poor character of tenants. Farm leases are generally for one year, and the tenant never expects to stay on the place. Consequently he has little interest in spending his own time and money in making improvements, and so the next tenant takes the place as he has left it. The better class will not live in these places, and therefore these farms with their rundown living places, are left to be occupied by the poorer class of tenants. And the influence of such home surroundings on the families is not conducive to developing a progressive spirit.

With the increase of tenant farming, it is becoming more and more to the interest of the lumbermen in country towns to promote a movement for improving the living conditions on these tenant farms for the continuance in growth of their business depends on it.

Just figure up the number of tenant farms there are in your territory, and then estimate the difference in volume of your trade if these farms were kept up in improvements on the same scale as those that are occupied by their owners, and also the additional trade in other lines it would bring to the town. Consider, too, the improved morale it would produce in the farming community and this better spirit would want to come to an attractive town, for like seeks like in everything in human relations.

Securing Future Forest Crops of Quality

The Necessity of Aggressive Conservation Methods in Keeping British Columbia in the Forefront as Great Timber Producing Province

There are many differing opinions as to the necessity for conservation in order to secure future forest crops of the same high quality for which B. C. is becoming justly famed. Some say that climate conditions at the Coast will continue to bring up similar forests to take the place of those logged-off and burned, as for thousands of years in the past. Others, on the contrary, claim that with the logger have come changed conditions against which the naturally reproductive elements are waging a losing fight. The advocates of both sides are worthy of attention, more especially at this time when we are planning to make British Columbia not only the main source of the Empire's lumber supply, but also the foremost lumber producing country in the world.

It may be interesting, then, to recall some of the results of an investigation conducted by C. D. Howe, Ph.D., some years ago, to discover the present state of reproduction of commercial timber (more especially Douglas fir) in the Coast region of B. C. The investigation

Old growth timber in Squamish district, Howe Sound, B.C.

was made on the eastern side of Vancouver Island as far north as Union Bay, and on the mainland as far north as Powell River. It was carried out five miles inland, and a total area of 1,000 sq. miles was thus explored.

Of the mature forests, Mr. Howe found that up to an elevation of 2,000 feet Douglas fir was the predominating tree species, comprising between 70 and 80 per cent. of the stand, and topping its forest companions in growth. Taking all the trees into consideration, Western hemlock outranked the fir in numbers. It was in good development along streams, on north facing slopes, in gullies and depressions, and on the flats at the head of lakes. Western cedar was a less common associate of the Douglas fir. Balsam, spruce and western white pine occurred only scatteringly in the Douglas fir forests.

A large number of stands of mature fir were observed in which the trees were nearly all of the same age, viz., 315, 173 and 124 years, and it was evident, from examination, that these stands had been established as the result of fires. It was also noticed that practically all the reproduction of commercially important Douglas fir was taking place on areas cleared once by fire alone, or by logging and fire combined. On areas swept more than once by fire, or not burned at all, the growth was insufficient to insure the re-establishment of the commercial forest.

Judging by the age of the fire scars on the older trees, it was determined that during the past 20 years a fire had occurred once in five years. From 20 to 100 years ago the average interval between fires was 27 years, while from 100 to 360 years ago severe fires took place at intervals of 86 years. The rate of fire occurrence had therefore increased enormously in recent years, and practically all of these fires were upon logged-over areas.

Now, one burning stimulates the reproduction of Douglas fir. It is, in fact, regarded as necessary for the establishment of dense stands; but a second burning is disastrous, as it kills more of the seed trees and the young growth following the first fire. There are not sufficient seed trees left to start another plentiful crop of trees on the area.

Crowded young growth, of course, produces the best quality of lumber, as the shade is so dense that the side branches are killed off early in the life of the tree, and the wood laid down on the stem afterwards is free from knots. Crowding also forces the young trees to grow more rapidly in height and more uniformly in thickness, which means more logs to a tree and less taper to a log. There is good evidence for the belief that the dense stands of Douglas fir which follow the first fire do not come only from one crop of seeds, but from several crops that have accumulated on the ground waiting for a favorable opportunity to germinate when the over-shading trees and undergrowth have been removed. Dr. Hofmann demonstrated this in the Columbia national forest, Washington. An extensive area was burned in 1902, and all the seed trees were killed. In 1913, dense stands of young fir of from 5 to 11 years old were found. Since the seed from which the younger trees sprang could not have been blown in by the wind, they must have lain on the ground and retained their germinating capacity for from one to six years after the fire. This capacity of Douglas fir seeds to retain their vitality for at least six years gives an opportunity for the accumulation of several seed crops from which the dense stands arise.

Mr. Howe found that the reproduction of forest after logging without burning was "scrappy." The removal of the over-shading trees stimulated the growth of the under vegetation, such as bracken fern, salal, etc. These together with the slash, formed such a shade that most of the fir seedlings which sprang up had soon died. The young seedlings to grow must have overhead light, and to grow vigorously they must have considerable light.

Mr. Howe, therefore, recommends the light burning of slash and undergrowth after logging operations.

An exhaustive investigation into the forest resources of British Columbia has recently been completed by the commission of conservation. The preliminary report made public shows that of the total land area of the province (355,855 square miles), approximately 200,000 square miles is incapable of producing forest of commercial value. About 145,000 square miles lie above the merchantable timber line, and on 55,000 square miles the soil is either too rocky or too wet, or the forests have been so completely destroyed by fire that there is no hope for the natural re-establishment of forest conditions for centuries to come. Of the remaining 155,855 square miles which is capable of producing forests, only about 28,000 square miles carries sufficient timber to be classed as statutory timber land. The timber on about 100,000 square miles has been totally destroyed by fire, and that on over half of the remaining 55,855 square miles has been seriously damaged.

New Chief Forester of Abitibi Co.

H. G. Schanche, Iroquois Falls, Ont.

Mr. H. G. Schanche has recently been appointed Chief Forester of the Abitibi Power & Paper Co., Ltd., of Iroquois Falls, Ont. He is a graduate of the Pennsylvania State College at which institution he pursued the course in forestry. Prior to the entrance of the United States in the war he was connected for over three years with the Forestry Division of the Laurentide Co., Ltd., of Grand Mere, P. Q. He was also for a time engaged in logging and lumbering in Central Pennsylvania. Enlisting in the U. S. Engineers, he later transferred to the Air Service and was subsequently promoted to a lieutenancy in that branch.

Since taking up his new duties, Mr. Schanche has selected a site for a Forestry Nursery and the clearing and preparation of the same, is now in progress. The output of the nursery will be made to satisfy the demands of the reforestration program of the Forestry Department. Mr. Schanche will leave shortly on an extended trip over the limits of the company in order to gain a first hand knowledge of the same, following which a working plan will be drawn up for the surveying and mapping of the holdings, work on which will be begun this fall. A regeneration survey on virgin and cut-over areas is at present being carried on within the company limits. The work is under the direction of Dr. C. D. Howe of the Commission of Conservation and is similar to the investigations of a like nature recently conducted by him on the Laurentide and Riordon limits.

Invents New Method of Lumber Shipping

John Arbuthnot, who was mayor of Winnipeg from 1903 to 1905 and has since been living in Vancouver, has invented a new method of transporting lumber across the ocean. His clever device is described in the Industrial Progress and Commercial Record, the official organ of the Manufacturers' Association of British Columbia.

The idea is to make a ship of the lumber itself, first laying down a keel, then piling on a superstructure of timber and bolting the whole securely together. Sails and auxiliary engines are to be supplied and there will be quarters to accommodate the crew. When the "ship" is taken apart and marketed, the engine, sails and crew will take a regulation steamship back to Canada. It is calculated that whereas an ordinary freighter carries about 1,500,000 feet of lumber, this will carry 5,000,000 feet at one trip.

The experiment is to be tried immediately in transporting to England the first consignment of a large order which has been secured by Mr. Arbuthnot's firm through the British Purchasing Commission, to supply lumber for rebuilding devastated areas of Europe.

Brompton Company Shows Good Earnings

The half yearly statement of the Brompton Pulp and Paper Co., Limited, of East Angus, Que., has been issued for the period ending April 30. J. A. Bothwell, who is president of the Canadian Pulp and Paper Association, is the general manager of the Brompton Co. The statement reveals gross profits of $517,355 against a total for the full previous fiscal year of $1,051,275, or at practically the same rate. After deductions of expenses, bond and bank interest, as well as preferred dividends, net available on the common stock is $343,118, as compared with $1,114,000 in the full previous year, or at a somewhat lower annual rate. The carry forwards for the half year amounts to $168,118.

President F. N. McCrea, commenting on the figures, says: "Under the circumstances the earnings statement, showing, as is does, the common dividend earned nearly twice over, may be considered a satisfactory indication of the company's earning power under adverse conditions. The results were due largely to the diversified nature of the company's activities.

Suggests Gas Bombs for Forest Fires

If the suggestion of a settler in Northern Ontario as to the best method of putting out forest fires had been acted upon by the Department of Lands, Forests and Mines, the Provincial Treasurer would have had to impose a tax on the use of tooth picks to meet the financial expenditures of the current year. The Department is in receipt of a letter from a settler suggesting that the best method of putting out the fires would be to drop bombs of carbonic acid gas on the burning areas. It was figured out that it would cost the province $375,000 an acre to extinguish fires by this method and, with several thousand acres of forest involved, it would have cost the province millions of dollars.

During the recent forest fires, the Department has taken every precaution and every step to stamp them out as soon as possible. The system adopted is, with the possible exception of France, the best in the world. Hundreds of men were sworn in by the Department to help fight the flames. In the Cochrane district alone one hundred men were engaged, and at Porquois Junction there were fifty additional men. There have been cases where settlers actually refused to help the fire rangers. These settlers have been arrested and are now awaiting trial. Under the statutes the Department is given full authority to swear in extra men in case of such an emergency, and they have done so to the fullest extent of the capacity during recent fires.

The Market for Pit Props in Britain

J. E. Ray, Canadian Government Trade Commissioner of Manchester, Eng., in a recent report to the Department of Trade and Commerce, Ottawa, in speaking of the outlook of the pit prop, railway sleeper and telegraph pole says:

Previous to the outbreak of war British timber merchants drew practically all their supplies of pit timber from European countries. Approximately three million loads were imported annually, half of which quantity was furnished by Russia and one-third by France. Sweden, Norway and Portugal contributed on a smaller scale to the total. The proximity of these countries to the consuming centres of the United Kingdom gave them an advantage over transatlantic competitors, so that no serious attempt to compete was made by either Canada or Newfoundland. With supplies from the usual sources curtailed, purchasers naturally turned their attention to Canada and Newfoundland, with the result that in 1915 timber limits were taken up even by colliery proprietors, if not in the former country certainly in the latter, and small supplies came from that source for two years. In 1917, however, supplies ceased, and only limited quantities have since been brought in. In 1916 there were signs that Canada might take advantage of the shortage in Great Britain, but it is understood that lack of tonnage prevented the development of a promising trade. The imports from Canada in 1916 exceeded 21,000 loads, but they fell to 1,280 loads in the following year.

At the present time, importers are turning their attention to the old sources of supply again, but with Russia still in a chaotic condition the collieries are managing on scanty supplies. Strenuous efforts have been made to draw timber from the home forests, but transportation difficulties continue to impede progress.

The trade is still under partial Government control, and is likely to remain so until October next at any rate. To what extent Canada will be able to export to the United Kingdom in the future depends upon her ability to compete with countries nearer to the British collieries. Naturally prices can never be so low as they were in pre-war days, and the curtailment of supplies from Russia, the main contributor prior to 1914, prevents any hope of an immediate decline in prices. France appears to be taking full advantage of the situation, for it is stated that her exporters reap a profit of 13s. per ton, while the pitwood importers in South Wales obtain but 2s. per ton.

Compared with pit props, the imports of railway sleepers are comparatively small. In 1914 the total imports were 216,231 loads, of which Russia furnished 106,096 loads. Canada attempted to capture a portion of this trade in 1916, but her supplies only reached 8,816 loads, and in the following year they fell to nil. The United States took advantage of the decline in imports from Russia by increasing her sale from 1,229 loads in 1914 to 105,890 loads in 1915, and to 155,226 loads in the following year. In 1917, however, her sales fell to 1,025 loads, due to lack of transportation facilities. The effect of the dearth of tonnage is reflected in the total British imports of that year, which were 21,298 loads against 216,321 loads in 1914.

It is felt by timber importers that the forests of Canada should make possible a larger export of sleepers, although the question of competition again with European countries will have to be confronted.

The British Government is usually in the market for about 50,000 telegraph poles a year. Tenders are solicited in the month of July, and specifications are invariably sent out to recognized contractors to the Government. Before the war it was specified that all poles should be of Russian or Scandinavian red pine. During the last three or four years this stipulation has been somewhat modified owing to circumstances associated with the curtailment of supplies from pre-war sources. It should be stated that Scandinavian exporters found it necessary to utilize the services of British pole merchants, due to the stringent clauses in the specifications, and a similar course should be adopted by Canadian firms anxious to obtain a share of the trade. The leading pole merchants will furnish copies of the specifications.

Difficulties Lumber Salesmen Have to Face

The Fellow Who is Waiting For Something to Happen, the Doubter of Increased Cost, the Kicker on Service and the Business Bolshevik

It is needless for me to review what has taken place within the lumber industry during the past four years to convince you that an evolution of more than ordinary importance has taken place, that the lumber industry, as an industry, is a far better merchant, in a much better position to render service and more efficient than it was in 1914, said H. T. Kendall recently before the American Lumber Congress. The great lesson the war has taught the world at large and the lumber industry in particular, is the value of unified strength and co-operative effort. It cannot be more than five years ago when a shivering few met in this room to witness the death throes of the National Lumber Manufacturers' Association. Since that time the National Lumber Manufacturers' Association and all of its component regional associations have so developed and have become so needful to the industry that their positions are secure and their future assured.

This development of co-operative effort has moved along two lines. First, co-operative effort within the divisions of the industry, and second, within the last few months co-operative effort among the great primary divisions of the industry.

From the manufacturers' standpoint, the salesman comes in closest touch with the other two branches of the industry, and therefore he can readily see the need for such a council and the value of the work that has already been done.

In this reconstruction period there are certain definite situations that every salesman of lumber has to face, and from these many perplexing problems. I have selected for brief review the following:

First, the problem of the man who is waiting for something to happen.

Second, the problem of the man who does not believe that costs have increased.

Third, the problem of the man who kicks on wartime service.

Fourth, the problem of the man who is a business bolshevik.

I will take these up in the order I have named them, and first consider the problem of the man who is waiting for something to happen.

The war was over, the armistice was signed. Now surely things were going to happen. Days passed and lengthened into weeks, and the business world began to rub its eyes, and wipe its spectacles. Nothing happened.

Everybody agreed that something was going to happen, but nothing did happen. Now the reason that nothing has happened is because no colletcive progress can be made without the full appreciation by each individual that he has certain definite responsibilities. Having accepted these responsibilities it is up to each one of us to do something so that the whole structure may move forward.

The manufacturer must stop worrying about and figuring over his costs. He must get out and do something in a creative way that will assist in reducing costs. The retailer has got to get out of his chair atilt against the sunny side of his shed, and stir up something. The wholesaler has got to quit telling his hard luck story to both the manufacturer and the retailer and use his genius in creating some demand.

Having concluded that we, as individuals, have a definite responsibility, and that we must accept and act under that responsibility, before we can look for general progress, the question naturally occurs: What can I do? The very first thing that any of us in the lumber industry can do is to become convinced that there is prosperity ahead, and that now is a good time to do business.

Let us assume that we are convinced that now is the time to move forward, the first thing to do, as I have already mentioned, is to sell this idea to the other fellow. This means not only other salesmen, but the buyer and the ultimate consumer. In other words, the first thing to do is to advertise our belief and our convictions to the world.

The problem of the man who does not believe that costs have increased:

The salesman of any commodity is at the present time spending a large portion of his time explaining the price of his goods. So far as the lumberman is concerned the buyer will admit that he needs lumber or that he would build if he did not believe that prices would be lower later on. I have argued this point of costs out to a finish with retailers and wholesalers, with my friends who are figuring on building, and with the retailer's cutsomer, when opportunity afforded, and after failing to get a decision in many bouts of this kind, I stumbled upon a method that is at least productive of some results. It does not always bring a knockout, but sets the other fellow to thinking. It is the simple old-fashioned method of muddying the water by doubting the other fellow. Most men with whom we do business are producing something, and I care not what line it is, costs and sales prices have increased, consequently after a few moment's discussion of lumber costs and value, I permit the subject to be changed and gradually work the other fellow around to his line of business, and casually ask him about the price of his commodity.

Turn the Talk in Different Direction

After you have permitted your erstwhile victim to expiate for a few moments upon the cost of his product and selling price of it, it is perfectly proper for you to quietly ask him why, if his costs have increased from 150 to 300 per cent., is it not reasonable to suppose that the cost of lumber has advanced 87 per cent. I will leave it to you whether or not the lumberman has any apology to make.

The problem of the man who kicks on war-time service:

At a glance this problem would seem to be a dead issue, but it is only the salesman on the firing line that can appreciate just how much of a factor this is at present. It is peculiar how willing we all are to excuse our own deficiencies, but how slow we are to excuse the same deficiencies in others.

No business man should be asked to explain or apologize for the service rendered during the war, because we are all living in the same glass house. The buyer of lumber should be fair enough to at least credit the manufacturer or retailer with the intent to do the best he could under most trying circumstances. Everyone's energies were concentrated in one direction. Nothing else counted. Aside from the handling of the emergency orders created by the war, every business man should have the right to ignore any criticism of wartime service, but at the same time he must accept and forget the record of the other fellow.

The problem of the Business Bolshevik:

In every line of effort we run across the man who will not cooperate in anything. He does not believe in modern methods—in short he is an obstructionist. The doctrine of the Bolshevik has been defined as a doctrine of selfishness. In the lumber business the line of demarcation is becoming more and more clearly marked. There is a distinct divison between those who do and those who don't. This type of business man is not peculiar to the manufacturer, the wholesaler or the retailer. He is not peculiar to the lumber business. You will find him in every line of human endeavor.

Men of this character most generally respond to an appeal based on possible profits. The "build a home" campaign offers a particularly good starting point, because it brings in a direct and visible return. After you have demonstrated the possibilities of co-operative effort by direct returns, it will be easier for you to interest him in the general association work. If possible harness him and put him to work. The associations in this country that have made the greatest success to-day have made it through their ability to keep busy along some line, every one of their members. Never overlook the fact that the measure of success of co-operative effort depends upon the value and strength of the individual effort.

Making Competitor See His Defects

If you continue to outgeneral and outsell your competitor you are sooner or later going to make him see the defects of his own salesmanship, and when he comes knocking at your door asking for assistance, do not remember the days that you spent trying to get him to work with you on your "build a home" campaign, or urging him to join your association, but remember the day when you sat in your own little office, confronted with seemingly unsurmountable difficulties and then when you went abroad and got a wider viewpoint you saw your own troubles dwindle to nothing; your own problems solved in the solving of the major problems of the industry. "If you will remember that, you will know how to handle the repentant blshevik."

In conclusion I wish to again suggest that this meeting seriously considers such an organization as a national lumber council, composed of retailers, wholesalers and manufacturers. As the scope of association work broadens and as we gradually come to recognize our inter-dependence, such a council as this seems to me to be a clear necessity. On the other hand and while considering a further development of organized effort, I also wish to again call your attention to the necessity for a continued individual effort. Do not for a moment think that your association, or your community is going to get along without something from you. There are two kinds of labor: productive and nonproductive. In a sense this definition may be applied here. If the majority of an industry or community are alive, hustling, wideawake, aggressive business men, willing to get away from their own business for awhile and do something for the common good, you will find a prosperous group of people, but if in that prosperous body the drones, or non-producers, gradually increase until they are in the majority, you will see a decaying industry and a shrivelling community. One of the great dangers besetting the success of association work is the overlooking of this simple truth. We get to recognize the association as a great force and being a great force, we expect it to continue without effort from us. So finally, I leave before you this broad principle, that no great co-operative success can be permanent without continued individual effort.

The man who is waiting for something to happen; the man who does not believe costs have increased; the man who kicks on wartime service, and the business bolshevik, are problems respecting which co-operative effort only can point out possible solutions. It is up to you and me as individuals using the knowledge in our possession to meet these situations and move forward.

Yardmen to Sell Lumber at Cost to Soldiers

Through the agency of the Ontario Retail Lumber Dealers' Association an arrangement has been made which will result in important assistance being given to the Soldiers' Settlement Board of Canada, in connection with the settlement of returned soldiers upon farms in Ontario. Representatives of the Board have had a number of conferences with the secretary of the Association. They have explained the workings of the Board and asked the Association to assist by furnishing lumber to soldier settlers at the cost price, plus the actual cost of handling.

The proposal was laid before the directors of the Association and it was decided to ask each dealer in Ontario to express his own opinion regarding it and to co-operate if he so desired. Many replies to the association's circular have been received and others are coming in daily, all showing that the retail lumber dealers of Ontario are ready to do their best in the direction of assisting in getting those soldiers who desire to take up farming settled upon their land at the least possible expense. In a number of cases the dealers are stating the amount of discount from their list prices which they will give. The average is in the neighborhood of 10 per cent. In other cases no specified reduction is stated, but the lumber will be furnished at cost price plus the actual cost of handling.

The Soldiers' Settlement Board is taking every precaution to ensure that the soldiers are placed upon farms to the best possible advantage. Careful enquiry is being made into the fitness of soldiers who apply for farms, as to their farming ability. Those who have not had experience at farming are being given a course of actual farm training before being placed. Careful selection of farms is provided. Free farm land in Ontario is no longer available for the Dominion Government and it is purchasing farms in the settled districts.

Adequate loans to meet all the essential requirements of the soldier settlers are being made by the government upon terms which make it as easy as possible for the soldiers to repay out of the proceeds of the farm. Careful enquiry is being made also into the requirements of each settler, in the line of machinery, equipment and buildings. When the requirements of this nature have been passed upon by the Board, a requisition is given by the Board upon the nearest local dealer. The soldier, upon presentation of the requisition to the dealer, secures his material and receipts the requisition. The receipted requisition together with the bill is sent by the dealer to the Board and the latter pays the bill within 30 days. By this plan the soldier gets exactly what he requires. He runs no risk of making unnecessary purchases on account of lack of experience, and the dealer is certain of receiving payment for what he sells.

From a business point of view the dealers, although they make no profit upon the lumber supplied to the soldiers in connection with this plan, are assisting in a most important part of the work in establishing returned soldiers, and are bringing to their neighborhood a most desirable class of settlers who will enlarge their market for future business. The reduction in price, of course, applies only to the first requirements of the settlers, or whatever is required in order to set them up in an adequate manner for successful farming. Future requirements will be paid for at current market prices.

Arrangements are being made by the Board for the purchase of all the other requirements of the soldiers at cost, including such machinery and equipment as they may need. Arrangements are also being made in all the other provinces of Canada for assistance on similar lines. The Board has already received applications for farms from a large number of soldiers and is now engaged in settling about 500 in Ontario

Spruce stand in New Brunswick containing trees up to 15 inches in diame Land burned in 1825 by great Miramichi fire upon which no returns were possible for at least eighty years

"Goodyear Get-together Meeting"

On Monday and Tuesday of last week the Goodyear Lumber Company of Buffalo, N.Y., had a meeting of their representatives at their Buffalo office, which was attended by G. A. Townsend, Sales Manager of the Great Southern Lumber Co., H. L. DeMuth, Manager, Goodyear Lumber Company's New Orleans office, and W. E. Farnan, Manager of their New York office; also, A. Booth of Albany, B. E. Fitzgerald, Reading; W. E. Sloan, Williamsville, N.Y., J. D. Stewart, Toronto, Canada, and A. J. Hartmann, Newark, N. J.

The Goodyear Company, in addition to having the exclusive sale of the Great Southern Lumber Co.'s stock in the East, has also acquired the output of the Moore Timber Company at Bay Harbor, Florida, and represent exclusively in this section the Dunlevie Lumber Company of Allenhurst, Ga.

The purpose of the meeting was to discuss conditions generally with a view to giving the trade the best possible service. The reports of the gentlemen referred to above were unanimous in that they all expect a continuance of the very heavy demand for lumber throughout the summer and fall. Inasmuch as the Goodyear Company is now specializing in yellow pine, having a splendidly diversified source of supply as indicated above, they believe that meetings of this kind are necessary in order to serve the trade's interests and they will be held quarterly hereafter. While business was the watchword, the social and recreative features were not by any means overlooked by President Ganson Depew and Vice-Presidents C. W. Goodyear and J. W. Trounce.

Will Steel Supplant Wood Ties?

Practical railroad builders and experts from the Bureau of Forestry, Washington, were called on to enlighten the House interstate commerce committee which is trying to find out whether steel could be substituted for wooden cross ties, in use since the first roads were operated. They were called to testify at a hearing on a resolution by Representative Dyer, Republican, Missouri, providing for an investigation by the committee as to the advisability of the plan.

Most Prolific Producing Species of Wood

White Spruce is Most Important for Pulp While Douglas Fir Leads in Lumbering —Ontario Has Most Hardwoods—What Different Provinces Possess

The woods most commonly used in pulp manufacture in Canada vary but slightly from year to year. The increased manufacture of sulphate, or kraft, pulp has enabled the manufacturers to use increasing proportions of jack pine. The use of balsam fir has increased steadily in past years. Hemlock is used to a greater extent than any other wood in British Columbia. In every other province but British Columbia, spruce heads the list of woods converted into pulp, says a recent bulletin issued by the Forestry Branch, Department of the Interior.

Spruce pulpwood in the Maritime Provinces is composed mostly of red spruce (Picea rubra), a tree the distribution of which is confined to this region in Canada.. With this are mixed smaller quantites of white spruce (Picea canadensis) and black spruce (Picea mariana).

In Ontario and western Quebec the red spruce is almost unknown, and forms only a small part of the wood used in pulp manufacture. White spruce grows in Canada from the Atlantic to the Yukon, and is undoubtedly the most important pulp species in the forests of this country. It probably forms 90 per cent. of the spruce pulpwood cut in Ontario and Quebec. Smaller quantities of black spruce and red spruce are also cut. In British Columbia, the place of these three eastern spruces is taken by typical British Columbia species. The spruce pulpwood produced in this province at the present time is cut in the coast region, and is the wood of the Sitka spruce (Picea sitchensis). The Engelmann spruce of the Selkirk and the Rocky Mountains (Picea Engelmanni) is not utilized for this pur-spruce (Picea sitchensis). The Englemann spruce of the Selkirk and the Rocky Mountains (Picea Engelmanni) is not utilized for this purpose at the present time, not because of its lack of satisfactory pulp-producing qualities, but simply because the pulp industry has not been developed in interior of British Columbia.

The Balsam Fir in East

In Eastern Canada only one species of balsam fir occurs, and this tree (Abies balsamea) forms the entire production of balsam fir pulpwood in Ontario, Quebec, New Brunswick, and Nova Scotia. In British Columbia the most commonly used balsam fir species are amabalis fir (Abies amabilis) and lowland fir (Abies grandis).. In the interior of the province and on the Rocky Mountain slopes the common species is mountain fir (Abies lasiocarpa), which has a similar distribution to Engelmann spruce and, like it, is not used for pulp at the present time.

Eastern-hemlock (Tsuga canadensis) is not used extensively in the east for pulp manufacture, although it is reported from Ontario, Quebec, and Nova Scotia. The western species (Tsuga heterophylla) is the most important pulpwood in British Columbia at the present time, and forms almost half of the wood used in that province. It is said to be superior to the eastern species for pulpwood as well as for lumber and other products.

Jack pine (Pinus Banksiana) is used only in Quebec and Ontario, and only in the manufacture of sulphate or kraft pulp. Poplar is also used only in Quebec and Ontario, but is made into groundwood pulp, sulphite, and kraft fibre. Two species are utilized, aspen poplar (Populus tremuloides) forming the greater part of the pulpwood consumed, and balsam poplar(Populus balsamea) being used in smaller quantities. Common cottonwood (Populus deltoides) and large-toothed aspen (Populus grandidentata) are probably also used occasionally. Pulp manufactured from the wood of the poplar species lacks the high tensile strength of that made from spruce, balsam fir, and other coniferous woods, and is used chiefly to give body to book and magazine paper. Mixed with a stronger, coarser pulp it fills in the interstices between the coarser fibres and makes the paper smooth and opaque.

In the same Forestry Branch bulletin is given an outline of tree species generally utilized for the manufacture of lumber. In part it is as follows:

"Canada's lumber-producing trees are largely softwoods. British Columbia cuts more softwood than Ontario, although its total production of lumber is less. In Quebec, the Maritime Provinces, and the Prairie Provinces the most important softwood is spruce. In Ontario white pine has always headed the list, and in British Columbia, Douglas fir.

Ontario Leads in Hardwoods

Ontario is the most important hardwood-producing province, cutting over twice as much as Quebec, which comes second on the list. The other provinces in order of their importance as producers of hardwood are as follows: Nova Scotia, New Brunswick, British Columbia, Prince Edward Island, Manitoba, Alberta, and Saskatchewan. In Quebec and the three Maritime Provinces birch is the most important hardwood. In Ontario maple heads the list and in the three Prairie Provinces aspen poplar. Cottonwood poplar is the most important deciduous-leaved tree in British Columbia.

"Hard" maple is cut from one tree only (Acer saccharum), "soft" maple lumber may be cut either from silver maple (Acer saccharinum or red maple (Acer rubrum).

The ash is divided into two classes, the harder wood being that of the American ash (Fraxinus americana) and the softer material black ash (Fraxinus nigra). There are three elms in Quebec of commercial importance, white elm (Ulmus americana), rock elm (Ulmus racemosa), and red or slippery elm (Ulmus fulva).

Poplar in Quebec apart from aspen poplar may be either balm poplar (Populus balsamifera), large-toothed aspen (Populus grandidentata), or common cottonwood (Populus deltoides). In the reports received the aspen is usually the only one separated from the other poplars.

Red oak (Quercus rubra) is the most important oak species in Quebec in point of quantity of lumber produced, although the wood of the white oak (Quercus alba) is more valuable. There are other oak species of only minor importance.

There are four hickories that contribute to the supply of hickory lumber, but the wood of these is so closely related that they are seldom separated in the market.

The Greatest Lumber Producing Tree

Douglas fir, the most important single species of lumber-producing tree in Canada, is known botanically as Pseudotsuga mucronata.

The cedar in British Columbia is a different species from that of the eastern provinces. This is called western red cedar, or sometimes giant cedar (Thuja plicata).

The greater part of the spruce lumber sawn in British Columbia is cut from Engelmann spruce (Picea Engelmenni) and Sitka spruce (Picea sitchensis).

The black spruce of the East is fairly common in northern British Columbia and the eastern white spruce is also found in the province.

The tamarack of the province is usually called western larch (Larix occidentalis) and is a distinct Pacific coast species. Mountain larch (Larix lyallii), the Rocky Mountian species, is of little or no commercial importance. The British Columbia yellow pine is the wood of one species often called bull pine (Pinus ponderosa). The hemlock (Tsuga heterohylla), western white pine (Pinus monticola) black cottonwood (Populus trichocarpa), jack or lodgepole pine (Pinus murrayana), maple (Acer macrophyllum), birch (Betula occidentalis), yellow cypress (Chamaecyparis nootkatensis), and red alder (Alnus oregona) are all cut from single species, each a distinct western tree, differing from its eastern relatives. The balsam fir lumber is made up of wood from Alpine fir (Abies lasiocarpa) and Amabilis fir (Abies Amabelis) with perhaps a smaller quantity of lowland fir (Abies grandis).

Two Million Feet of Lumber in Arena

The largest arena ever constructed in modern times was erected by Tex Rickerd, in Toledo, Ohio, on the occasion of the heavy weight championship bout between Jess Willard and Jack Dempsey.

The structure was built entirely of lumber and required nearly 2,000,000 ft. The actual cost of material and labor on the huge building was $150,000, and yet when tenders were asked for the demolition of the arena the highest bid was from the American Housewrecking Co., of Chicago, their figure being $25,000. The immense edifice, which was intended to seat 97,000 persons and yet on the only occasion on which it was used it was less than one-quarter filled. This means that had the promoters of the great fistic contest known in advance of the comparatively limited number who would be present at "the attraction" they could have erected a building sufficiently large to accommodate all with half a million feet of lumber instead of using four times this quantity.

Why Forest Fires Endanger the No

Frame Houses of Settlers Invite the Flames—Fire Wardens Cannot Wipe Out the Peril—Precautions That Would Prove Effective

Wm. Henderson, of Toronto, superintendent of the Shantymen's Christian Association, for many years in the interest of the work of that organization, has travelled all through Northern Ontario. He has witnessed many forest fires and given close study to their cause and prevention, and on several occasions has presented the facts to the provincial authorities. Mr. Henderson states that most of the houses in the Northland invite the fiend and that until all slash is burned and wide clearings made around the various homes that settlers will be in constant peril whenever there is a dry summer, the same as they have had this season.

Writing on the recent outbreak of flames in the bush, when several settlers in Northern Ontario lost their homes and a holocaust similar to that of the summer of 1916 was prevented only by the timely descent of heavy rains which extinguished the menacing embers, Mr. Henderson presents some pertinent and logical truths in the subjoined sketch:

"This is a nice little home you have," I exclaimed as I walked into a small cottage west of Cochrane, where a young couple with baby were living.

"Well, it's good enough to burn," was the young man's reply.

Wm. Henderson, Toronton, Ont.

"You see," he continued, "all this country will be burnt over twice before it is cleared, so there is no use spending too much on a house."

"What about the wife and baby when the fire comes?" I enquired.

"Oh, the river is only about 100 yards away and they would be quite safe under the bridge," was the answer.

"Indeed," chimed in the wife, "you won't find me here when the dry season comes, as I'll go to town."

For miles into the forest away from the river settlers were putting up their little shacks to secure the 80 acres of land on easy terms being offered by a land company, by arrangement with the Ontario Government.

This company guaranteed work for the men in their mills and camps, and employed them to cut down and utilize all the marketable timber, and these homes were being built surrounded by the slash made in these operations.

As Safe as in Powder Factory

Most of the settlers were French or foreign with large families of small children, and in a dry, hot summer like the present they would be as safe living in a powder factory as amongst this dry spruce, slash and timber.

In conversation with the doctor of the settlement he remarked: "It seems almost criminal to put families into these conditions." "It is not 'almost,' but quite criminal," was my response.

In other Northern districts that are open for homesteading the chief inducement to take up the land is the revenue to be derived by cutting and selling the pulpwood on it, and this brings in the French-Canadians by the hundred. They are good bush men, and do well as long as the wood lasts, but have not much idea of real farming, so the hot summer weather finds them away from home working in some saw mill or construction camp, while wife and children live by themselves among the stumps.

Possibly there is an acre of ground with a few potatoes and garden stuff round the house, but this is no protection at all when the bush fire comes along with a sixty mile an hour wind, carrying flame and blazing embers before it. The fire of 1916 jumped the Abittibi river, which is a wide stream, as if it were only a ditch in its path. In the Porcupine fire the flames licked the surface of the lake for many yards, killing many who were seeking safety in its waters.

For the benefit of those unacquainted with conditions it may be well to explain just what happens, and this will best be done by telling what did occur in 1911 and 1916.

When the fire occurred in 1911, all the country surrounding Porcupine, Cochrane, Matheson and adjacent settlements was covered by green brush with slashes here and there to start the fires.

Through all this great territory the fire ran and towns were burnt and scores of lives lost.

For five years this whole country was a wilderness of dry, dead trees with a heavy undergrowth of fire weed and similar ideal fodder for the flames.

In the winter of 1913-1914 I travelled all through that country. At this time all round Porquis Junction and Iroquois Falls and most of the country between there and Cochrane was still green bush, and the new print mills with the local market thus open for pulp wood had led settlers to take up every available homestead near the railroad. Their little shacks in the clearings were everywhere, and all in close proximity to the standing timber.

One Wilderness of Burnt Trees

I walked one day from Matheson to a camp on the Abittibi river some 26 miles east. Until I came within eight miles of the river there was nothing but a wildernes of burnt trees. Among these trees up to about ten miles from Matheson were the little homes of the settlers, in some cases quite close together, but none far from the burnt timber, getting drier year by year, and with each years added undergrowth to make it the more dangerous.

When the great fire of 1916 occurred it was in this district that had been previously burnt over that it raged fiercest, and where most lives were lost, in all about 300.

A great many of the settlers in all this district were young Englishmen, and when war broke out in 1914 nearly all left their homesteads and enlisted. When they went overseas the wives of such as were married followed them. Consequently the names of few English were found among the victims of the fire.

All through the green bush already referred to round Porquois, etc., this fire went, and it has been standing since then awaiting such a summer as we are now having to jeopardize the lives of such as have rebuilt the homes burnt down in 1916 or taken up new homesteads since. I might explain that lots of this timber, being only blackened outside, was still valuable as pulpwood, and many thousands of cords in these past three years have been cut and sold at good prices, thus making a good living for the settlers.

Why Fire Wardens are Helpless

It is simply folly to think that these fires can be prevented by any number of fire wardens in the summer time. Unless the slash is burnt every winter and wide clearings made round the various homes, settlers in the forest will be in constant peril whenever a dry summer occurs.

Very many miles have been cleared by the fires, but most of it is growing up again for want of settlement in it.

After the 1916 fire the land for miles round Mathieson was so well cleared that one man single-handed could clear an acre a day have it ready for the plough.

The early frosts prove the enemy of most field crops and in view of the history of the past three years it is not to be wondered at that there is no great rush of farmers into some new district. The one sure crop, (until the fire comes) is the pulpwood and consequently the settlers will naturally take up the lots in the bush with all the risks entailed by living there instead of the fine cleared lands that the fire has already travelled over.

What Forest Conservation Really Implies

Unless Different Handling of the Timber of Canada is Resorted to its Exhaustion Will Make Direct Taxation Necessary, Declares Dr. Fernow

There has been a mischievous story afloat about the "unlimited and "inexhaustible" timber supply of the Dominion of Canada, and public men who ought to have known better have repeated it. It is mischievous because it insures wasteful use and delays the rational, conservative management of the forest resources with regard to future needs. Our knowledge of probable supplies, to be sure, is for much of the forest area, still mere guess work, but it is sufficiently well based to enable us to see that an end is in sight, says Dr. B. E. Fernow, Dean of the Faculty of Forestry, University of Toronto.

The easiest way to make one realize the exhaustibility of the timber ready for the axe in Canada is to state that the present sawmill capacity of the United States would suffice to dispose of it in less than a decade, and that, according to the best information, the timber supply of the States is about four times that of the Dominion.

Since the forest resource is looked to, to play a not insignificant role in the reconstruction of the Dominion's world trade, it is indicated to analyze the situation.

The commercial timber of Canada is found in two widely separated regions: the eastern forest and that of British Columbia. In the case of the latter the merchantable stand has been estimated recently by the Commission of Conservation on the basis of an exhaustive survey at 360,000 million feet, and enough is known to place the eastern stand at considerably less.

It is not usually recognized that the forests stand second as a basis for our manufacturing industries, that the annual value of our forest products equals that of our wheat crop, and that our forest industries supply around 15 per cent. of our foreign trade and an equal percentage of railway traffic. It is evident that the handling of such a resource is a matter of high economic importance.

Spruce White Pine and Fir Lead

The sawmill lumber cut alone for the Dominion has reached as high as 5,000 million feet annually, and for the last decade has averaged over 4,000 million feet, worth around 60 million dollars at the mill. An analysis of the figures brings out the fact that spruce, white pine and Douglas fir make up three-fourths of the annual lumber cut of the Dominion; this comes in the sequence of their output from the forests of Ontario, British Columbia, Quebec and New Brunswick, which provinces, indeed, furnish some 90 per cent. of all our lumber. Our interest accordingly in general narrows down to a consideration of the white pine forests of Ontario and Quebec, the spruce forests of Quebec and New Brunswick, and the Douglas fir forests of British Columbia.

Turning our attention to eastern Canada alone, we may give a few figures to indicate the place of its forests in the economic life of this section. To begin with, there are some 30,000 men of the eastern provinces who gain a livelihood in the operations between the tree and mill. There are over 3,000 mills engaged in converting the logs into lath, lumber, shingles, staves, etc. These mills, according to 1911 census, represented a capital of over $96,000,000, and employed over 58,000 men, whose earnings amounted to around $18,000,000. The wood-using industries in eastern Canada number over 3,000 firms, which require roughly, 2,000 million feet of raw material annually, and since this is largely of domestic origin, the industries are doubly important. While these industries could exist on imported wood material, the logging and milling industries mentioned above must pass with the exhaustion of the forest.

The pulpwood industry in the east has become of growing importance of late years, due in some measure to the waning supply in the northeastern states. The home consumption of pulpwood has risen from 480,000 cords in 1908, valued at around $3,000,000, to 1,765,000, cords in 1916, valued at over $13,000,000. In addition, in that year 1,000,000 cords were exported, valued at nearly $7,000,000. The pulpwood manufactured into pulp in home mills has been above 1,000,000 cords annually the past six years, and has exceeded the cordage exported in the raw state since 1913. Some fifty mills are concerned, and over 85 per cent. of the consumption is in Ontario and Quebec.

What Forests Typify and Signify

Enough has been said to indicate that the eastern forests are of very great economic importance, especially so when we bear in mind that these forests are very largely found on non-agricultural lands, and that these lands comprise from two-thirds to three-quarters of the provincial areas. They mean the livelihood of many thousands of men, the raison d'etre of several thousand mills and wood factories together with various subsidiary industries, to say nothing of the direct provincial revenues, which aggregate some four million dollars annually. Every business man in eastern Canada is directly interested in the maintenance of such a prosperous state of affairs, and in the question of whether this great resource is handled in the most intelligent way. Every citizen is interested with his own pocket as to whether this forest resource is going to continue in furnishing revenue or whether its exhaustion will make direct taxation a necessity. To all appearances, unless different handling of the timber is resorted to soon, such necessity will arise in not a distant time.

The economic importance to Canada of her great forest areas is no less apparent. The value of our primary forest products exported from the country during the past year totalled some $200,000,000. The pulp and paper industry export products valued at some $85,000,000 annually. The importance of perpetuating a resource that assists so largely in redressing our unfavorable trade balance can scarcely be over-emphasized.

The first and most vitally necessary step toward handling our forests as crops, rather than mines, is, of course, the prevention of fires. Great progress has been made in this direction during recent years, though much still remains to be accomplished.

The next step should be the adoption and strict enforcement of improved cutting regulations in connection with all logging operations on crown lands. The situation in this respect is least satisfactory in the Province of Ontario and on Dominion licensed timber lands in the west.

Good Salesmanship in Lumber Yard

A customer dropped into a certain retail lumber office one day and told the dealers that he wanted some 12-foot and 16-foot drop siding, along with a little dimension, and some 1 x 4 flooring 12 feet long.

The dealer had the material in the lengths specified, but he also had a good assortment of short length stock which he wanted to sell where it could be worked to advantage. He knew that his short cut stock graded a little better than the standard lengths and that the customer would be getting better stock if he would take the short stuff.

So he asked what the lumber was to be used for. The customer said he wanted to build a small out-house. He gave the dimensions of the building. The dealer took him out in the yard and showed him the short stock.

"Why, I didn't know you had that short stuff. Sure, I'll take it. It looks good to me."

This incident is one of real lumber yard salesmanship. Some dealers never let a bit of lumber go out of their yards without learning what it is to be used for. Others hesitate to ask. Occasionally a customer may show a little resentment if the dealer begins questioning him, in which case the dealer can say: "My only purpose in asking these questions is to help you get the kind of lumber that will give you the best results." Usually that statement removes the customer's objection to telling what he is going to build.

By following these lines lumber dealers will soon educate their customers to accept advice and suggestions, with the result that the dealers will be in a position to give better service, and at the same time strengthen their own position as authorities on all matters relating to building.

That lumber dealers, or building material merchants should be generally recognized as reliable building authorities, is the idea put forth by the Retail Lumberman years ago, at a time when dealers seemed perfectly satisfied to let the public get its help from carpenters. We have kept up our work in this connection and today the lumber dealers pretty generally recognize the logic of our position, and are rapidly educating the public to the same view. The time will come when prospective builders will instinctively go to the building material merchants first for building advice and helps of all kinds, and the dealers will then be better able to develop new business and promote building, thus providing work for the carpenters that otherwise might never develop, or at the best would be long deferred.

Lumber yard salesmanship is a very important matter, and one that dealers are giving more attention to now than formerly.

Lumbermen Would Welcome Inquiry

The Calgary Contractors' Association at its annual meeting, sent a wire to Sir Robert Borden, urging that a prompt and thorough investigation be held into the prices of lumber charged by the British Columbia Manufacturers' Association. The Calgary contractors charge that there is profiteering, and that Canadian consumers are discriminated against, while American buyers are favored. As a result, they claim, industrial discontent is being increased, work in Western Canada is being held up and business is badly handicapped.

"We shall welcome the fullest and most reaching investigation into the affairs of the mills comprised in the Mountain Lumber Manufacturers' Association," said H. H. Ross, president of the association.

"The Mountain Lumber Manufacturers' Association wants the whole truth known," Mr. Ross added, "and with the facts before the public and before the Government we shall have no apprehension as to the verdict respecting our profits."

Mr. Ross said that the British Columbia mills had lost money for the last ten years, and some had gone into liquidation, for example the Fernie Lumber Company, with liabilities of $200,000.

Respecting the charge that the British Columbia Lumber Manufacturers were discriminating against the prairie consumers, Mr. Ross declared that it was untrue.

When an explanation of the Calgary despatch was asked from R. H. H. Alexander, secretary of the British Columbia Lumbermen's Association, Mr. Alexander said: "Hot air; nothing but hot air. Why the prairie market fell down on us and the vast orders which were promising early in the season failed to mature. Practically all the Albertan market is filled from the mountain lumber division, but there have been no orders worth while recently from Alberta. When they talk of lumber being expensive they are ignorant of the market because the American market is as high as $10 per thousand over us now. As for profiteering," said Mr. Alexander, "why these people must realize that when labor and all other commodities go up it naturally raises the cost of producing lumber."

Several lumbermen expressed the opinion that they did not consider it good business to sell lumber in Canada at $10 per thousand cheaper than they can market it for on the U. S. side of the boundary. One man said: "We are out for business and all things being equal Canada will get the lumber, but when Washington lumber buyers offer $10 per thousand more than Canada then we sell to Washington"

Stumpage Rates are Increased

Notification is given in the Royal Gazette, of New Brunswick, of an increase in the rates on practically all softwood saw logs cut on the crown lands of New Brunswick.

The increase is approximately one-third and will be effective from Aug 15th next, thus being operative before next season's cutting operations.

The new rates are published in connection with a long statement of regulations under which licensees of Crown Timber Lands shall operate. Spruce, pine, hacmatac and cedar logs will pay $3.50 instead of $2.50, while hemlock, fir and poplar lags will pay $3 instead of $2 stumpage. Other classes of lumber are not affected.

Whalen Company Elects New Directors

Announcement was made recently of the addition of three new directors to the board of the Whalen Pulp and Paper Mills, Limited, Vancouver, of which company Sir George Bury recently assumed the presidency. The three new members of the board are W. N. Harlbut, of Dayton, Ohio; Alexander Smith, of Chicago; and I. W. Killam, of this city.

Mr. Harlbut is connected with the George H. Mead Company, of Dayton, Ohio, and was for many years associated with the Backus paper interests. He has in recent years been prominent in the affairs of the Spanish River Pulp and Paper Company, working with George H Mead, president of that company.

Mr. Smith is president of the well-known financial house of Peabody, Houghteling and Company, of Chicago, who is well and favorably known in Canada.

Mr. Killam, who is president of the Royal Securities Corporation, has taken an active part in the organization and financing of other important pulp and paper enterprises.

General Survey of Lumber Activity

The "Labor Gazette" of Ottawa in its last edition in referring to general lumbering conditions in Canada, says: Westville reported great activity in the lumber mills. Charlottetown reported that the industry had a very quiet month. Fredericton reported that the mills were in full operation and gave employment to a large number of men. Quebec reported that river driving was in full swing under favorable conditions, but that the mills had not yet started the season's cut. Sherbrooke reported that river drivers were well employed and that saw and shingle mills were busy. Three Rivers reported that the St. Maurice Lumber Co. were preparing their mill for the season. Ottawa reported that the sawmills ran about ten days in May only, the high water closing them down, but that as soon as the water permitted they would again run at full capacity. Fernie reported that in every section of the district there was remarkable stimulation of the lumber market and that operators were finding it exceedingly difficult to fill the orders placed, the unfavorable winter and late spring and high water conditions having retarded progress. Vancouver reported that the saw and shingle mills were busy. New Westminster reported that all the sawmills in the district were running and that many of the shingle mills were working double shifts. Victoria reported that the lumbering and logging industry was fairly active with indications of improvement in the near future. Nanaimo reported that the logging camps of the district were working steadily and that the sawmills were also operating normally.

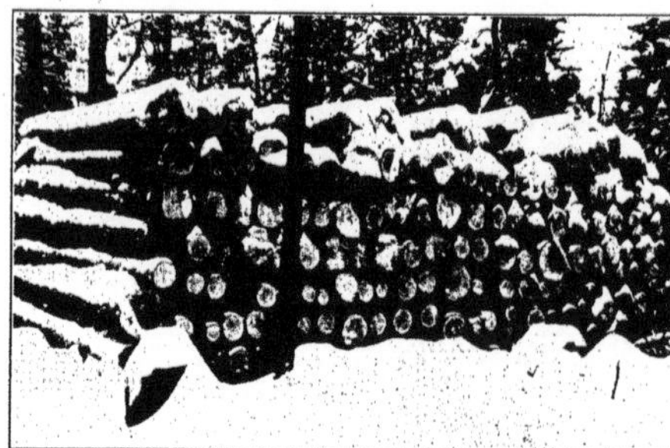

A yard of spruce logs on Sevogle River, in New Brunswick, containing 148 pieces. It takes about twenty of these logs to scale 1000 ft. board measure, N. B. rule.

Why Some Men Never Make Business "Go"

Contributing Factors Which Undermine the Foundation of Lumber and Other Undertakings—Analysis of the Various Causes

Why do men fail in business—not only in the retail lumber business, but in all other lines? Various reasons are presented and attempts have been made to analyze and group the causes. The six principal factors given are:

1. Lack of skill, which includes unpreparedness for the business; inefficiency, inaptitude, and the general subject of buying and selling.
2. Lack of capital.
3. Over-extension.
4. Unwise credits.
5. Speculation.
6. Dishonesty.

One recognized writer does not agree at all with this summary and declares that fundamentally the failures of most merchants are due to overstocking, inefficient and indifferent service, inability or indisposition to figure profits properly, senseless price slashing and lack of backbone and foresight.

Another authority asserts that many reverses have been contributed to by not advertising. Bradstreets is a great commercial agency, and recently compiled, after thorough investigation—not hearsay or guess work—a table showing that eighty-four per cent. of the business failures during the past year occurred among firms which did no advertising. The information was gathered by this well-known commercial agency at a considerable outlay of time and money, and the statement is worthy of careful deduction. One does not mean to infer that had these eighty-four per cent. of merchants, who went down in the business race spent money in publicity plans, they would have succeeded and been in a flourishing state today, but, nevertheless, the lesson to be drawn from the statistics presented is obvious.

A Recapitulation of Defects

Here again is the sextette of causes given in their order of precedence in contributing to business skill, lack of capital, over-extension, unwise credits, speculation and dishonesty. A writer in "System" says there are a few other causes, such as bad habits, and personal extravagance, but more often than not these grow out of a lack of skill; few failures are, in the last analysis found to be due to either of these frequently assigned reasons.

Every failure due to the causes which I have enumerated is preventable. Even "dry rot," which catches more creditors than any other kind of failure, may be discovered by the wary. I know one large wholesale house which had been a leader in business for three-quarters of a century; successive generations had come and gone with ample fortunes. It was a Rock-of-Gibraltar sort of concern; bank officers accompanied the partners out to the steps when they called for accommodations. They had started business in the days when the request for a financial statement by a bank or mercantile agency was considered impertinent and meddlesome. No one had the hardihood to ask them for a statement. Their affairs went on quietly and smoothly; customers received exactly the same consideration as the postal clerk gives to the man buying stamps; you might take or leave their goods without disturbing the even progress of their ways.

One morning the business world awoke to the conservative firm's failure for more than a million dollars. The accountants found affairs in a tangled mass; the members of the firm had not the slightest notion how much they owed; they had goods to the inventory value of several million dollars, but the goods were old-fashioned and unsalable—they brought less than a hundred thousand dollars.

The public was informed that the shifting of business from the firm's location, together with a failing demand for the character of goods carried by the house, had brought about the bankruptcy. As a matter of fact, the firm had stood with its back to the progress of the world; the old members, who had bought and sold with shrewdness, had been succeeded by men who bought and sold by convention. The condition of the firm would have been apparent to any man who cannily watched operations without being blinded by the glories of the past. On a complete reorganization, with new buying and selling heads and a careful system of accounts, the firm paid all its debts within three years.

Look Well After Buying End

Lack of skill in buying is one of the most prolific causes of failure; too many concerns put all their stress on the selling end of the game. Of course, a concern cannot make money unless it sells, but it does not take much of a salesman to dispose of goods which have been bought right and which therefore can be offered at the right price to the right market. No amount of selling skill will permanently cover up deficiencies in the buying department. And this principle applies just as truly to the individual who is buyer, salesman and bookkeeper all in one as it does to the million-dollar business.

Failures from lack of capital are really failures from lack of skill because the money and the business have not been kept in their proper relations, but the heading is such a large one that it deserves separate consideration.

Over-extension is closely related to lack of capital, but true over-extension is not so much an outdistancing of capital by business as it is an outdistancing of business by organization. A concern doing a good business starts new branches in districts where there is not enough business to support the branch. Often the house will not have sufficiently mastered system, and the skill which made the home office succeed is not transferred to the sub-office. Perhaps localities or transportation methods have not been sufficiently considered.

Very few men start in business with the idea of being dishonest. Dishonesty comes usually when the man is at bay and is usually suggested by someone outside. Then comes a succession of false statements, sharp dealing, and all the other unlovely practices of the crook.

Some concerns honestly enough add the increase in plant and realty values to their statements, on the supposition that the plant is worth what it will bring. Of course, that is the worth on liquidation—although plants rarely bring more than a fraction of their value as a going business and not in liquidation. A plant is generally worth what it can be mortgaged for, because that is the only sum of money which can be quickly raised for the purpose of business.

Ontario Retail Dealers' Summer Outing

The annual, midsummer, educational trip of the Ontario Retail Lumber Dealers' Association is being held from July 31st to August 4th to Penetanguishene, Midland, Victoria Harbor and Parry Sound. Some seventy-five members from all parts of the province are taking in the outing. This is the largest party of retail men, who have ever gone on a tour of the association and the busy lumber plants on the Georgian Bay will be visited. Preparations on an extensive scale have been made for the reception of the guests by all the forest products manufacturers of the Midland district and an enjoyable time is assured every one. There will be a sail to Honey Harbor on the afternoon of August 2nd. The majority of the company of yardmen intend going on the jaunt to Parry Sound where they will visit the mills in that town and incidentally do some fishing on Civic Holiday, August 4th. The excursionists left Toronto on the G. T. R. by private car on Friday afternoon, July 31st, and arrangements for the outing were most complete. A full report of the proceedings will appear in the next edition of the "Canada Lumberman."

All Furniture Prices Still Going Up

At a recent meeting of the furniture section of the Canadian Manufacturers' Association it was decided to increase furniture prices from 10 to 20 per cent. The larger increase will apply to pieces in which the mirror forms an important part. Increased cost of labor and materials is the reason given for this advance. As an instance, shellac which was selling three months ago at $4.40 per gallon is now quoted at $6.60, an advance of $2.20. A pane of glass costing seven cents in 1914 increased to 37c during the war and is now quoted at 50c.

The Largest Spruce Log in the West

The largest spruce log ever brought out of the forest of Washington was carried from near Hoquiam on a 3½-ton Federal truck operated by the Spruce Division of the United States army. It measured 99 inches at butt, 86 inches at top and was 24 feet long. The log contained more than 13,000 feet of lumber and weighed over 39 tons.

If the truth were known, it is frequently the under dog that begins the fight; he started something he was not able to finish successfully.

Personal Paragraphs of Interest

L. Henderson, of James Davidson's Sons, Ottawa, was on a recent business visit to Montreal.

J. A. Culligan, the New Brunswick lumber manufacturer, was in Montreal on a business visit.

H. C. Campbell, of C. H. Russell, Montreal, has been on a business trip to Eastern Quebec.

Claude Villiers, of the Canadian General Lumber Co., Montreal, has been on a business trip to the Eastern States.

James Shearer, president of the James Shearer Co., Ltd., Montreal, has gone to the Laurentian Mountains, owing to illness.

J. B. Knox, of Knox Bros., Ltd., Montreal, has just returned from a trip to England. This is Mr. Knox's second visit this year.

Paul Day, treasurer of the Federal Lumber Co., Vancouver, was in Montreal, Quebec, Toronto and other cities recently on a business trip.

Guy Tombs, assistant freight manager of the Canadian Government Railways, Montreal, has been appointed transportation manager of the Canadian Export Paper Co., Ltd., Montreal.

John B. Reid, of Toronto, vice-president of the Ontario Retail Lumber Dealers' Association, has returned from a successful and enjoyable fishing trip in the vicinity of Bobcaygeon.

Ellwood Wilson, chief forester of the Laurentide Co., Grand Mere, P. Q., and Dr. Howe, of the Conservation Commission, Ottawa, attended a meeting of the Association of Eastern Foresters, at Mont Kineo.

Jas. D. McCormack, general manager of the Canadian Western Lumber Co., Fraser Mills, B. C., spent a short time in Toronto recently on his return from a visit to his boyhood home in Prince Edward Island.

F. C. Nunnick, an expert of the Conservation Commission, Ottawa, has been loaned to the New Brunswick Government to make an examination of the soil on the crown lands in that province. This will be Mr. Nunnick's third trip to New Brunswick.

The Wilson Lumber Co., Ltd., previously at the foot of Spadina Ave., Toronto, are situated in offices at 333a Confederation Life Bldg., Richmond St. E., with Mr. J. B. Meech as manager. Mr. Meech was formerly western representative of James G. Cain & Co., of Toronto.

Clarence Hyde and C. O. Maus, of the Hyde Lumber Co., South Bend., Ind., and Chas. Hyde, of Lake Providence, La., have been on an angling expedition in the Bruce Peninsula. The party met with splendid luck and are loud in their praises of the black bass fishing qualities of the Georgian Bay waters.

Edmund Hind, formerly with the Beaver Lumber Co., of Hamilton, has opened a retail yard on Gerrard St. E., Toronto, under the name of the Edmund Hind Lumber Co. Several lumbermen in Ontario are interested in the new enterprise which has been placed on a firm basis and has good prospects for developing a large trade.

Dr. C. D. Howe, Professor of Forestry at Toronto University, recently returned from New Brunswick. Dr. Howe has been collecting statistics on the annual growth of the forests of New Brunswick, spending part of his time on the Renous Survey about forty miles north of Boiestown. In company with Mr. G. H. Prince, chief forester of New Brunswick, he visited the limits of the Pejebscot Lumber Co. in St. John County and also the limits of the Bathurst Lumber Co. on the Nipisiquit River. When Dr. Howe resumes his duties at the University next fall he will become Dean of the Forestry School succeeding Dr. Fernow who retired recently to take up forestry journalistic work in the United States.

John P. Mosher, buyer and travelling representative for L. N. Godfrey Co., wholesalers of lumber with offices in Boston, Mass., and New York City, is back again in the Maritime Provinces calling upon the lumber manufacturers with the purpose of making several good sized purchases for both immediate and future deliveries. This reputable lumber firm are looking for merchantable spruce in sizes 2 x 3 and up and also shingles, as well as hemlock boards in random or stock lengths. L. N. Godfrey Co. buy large amounts of Canadian lumber during the year and have various sources from which they regularly buy but the constantly increasing demand for spruce in the New England markets has compelled this firm to seek a more plentiful supply in the better lines of stock.

Lieut.-Col. John A. Cooper, of Toronto, who went overseas in command of the 198th Canadian Buffs, saw service in France, and later attained the position of transportation officer of the 5th Infantry Brigade, has gone to New York where he will have charge of the Publicity Bureau which is being opened by the Dominion Government. For some time past it has been felt that Canada's interest in the United States had reached the stage where it required careful and well organized attention. The new Bureau will furnish all the information relating to the progress and development of the Dominion along commercial, industrial, financial and agricultural lines, and will be a permanent source of information for United States news agencies, publishers, etc. Col. Cooper is a past President of the Canadian Press Association and is widely known in newspaper ranks.

C. E. Huddert, of San Francisco, has been appointed manager of the Associated Timber Exporters of British Columbia. This association was formed to cover practically all export sales of British Columbia lumber. The majority of the large concerns have affiliated with the association and most of those who have not are working in close conjunction with it. Since its inception a few months ago the affairs of the association have been administered by R. H. H. Alexander, Secretary of the Lumber & Shingle Manufacturers' Association. In the interview Mr. Huddert stated that the shortage of tonnage which has stood in the way of big developments in the lumber industry will be overcome shortly through the release of ships from the Government service and expects that the next four or five years will see the largest volume of business transacted the world has ever known

I. H. Boas, chief of the Forest Products Laboratories of the Forestry Department of Australia, was in Montreal recently and made a study of the pulp and paper trade, with special reference to the efforts being made to capture the European market. Mr. Boas was delegated by the Australian Government to look into forest products business all over the world. He has spent considerable time in the United States examining the methods of the industry there and while in Montreal evinced a great interest in the forest products laboratory of the McGill University. He stated that the Australian Government is making extensive plans to assist forest production and proposed to establish a modernly equipped forest laboratory. At present Australia is importing all her pulp and paper but the Australian Government has already undertaken the work of planting the vast sand areas with pulpwood trees,

J. E. Ray, Canadian Trade Commissioner in Manchester, England, was a visitor to Toronto recently. Mr. Ray is very optimistic as to the prospects before the Canadian woodworking industry. There is a marked shortage of woodenware of all kinds in Britain today and British manufacturers are very anxious to secure large quantities of Canadian wood products. As an instance, a Manchester firm asked him to inquire into the prospects of securing 2,000,000 blocks 2 in. square to be used for teaching children the alphabet. There is a marked demand for tool handles, washboards, tubs and wooden toys, including blocks, toy houses, wooden trains, cart wheels, checkers and chess sets. Mr. Ray states that the shortage of furniture is very marked and that stocks of doors, windows and building material are very low. In his opinion the markets of the Old Country are open to Canadian manufacturers for the next three or four years and after that competition will be keener and it will be a case of quality, service and price.

Death of Mr. Robert M. Cox

Many friends in the lumber industry will regret to learn of the death of Robert M. Cox, of Ottawa, Ont., who was at the head of the large exporting firm which bears his name. Mr. Cox was a pioneer lumber merchant of Liverpool, Eng., and Ottawa. He had attained the advanced age of 83 years and passed away at his residence, 381 Stewart St., in the Capital City. He was a prominent and highly respected figure in forest products circles in Ottawa and the Ottawa Valley for over half a century and enjoyed the confidence of his associates and numerous personal friends. The late Mr. Cox was a frequent visitor to England where his trade connections were extensive, Liverpool being the headquarters of his firm in the Old Land.

In the passing of Mr. Cox, who was born in England, an outstanding figure in the Canadian lumber arena has departed. He leaves a record of achievement and success, which should be an inspiration to many younger concerns and his firm developed a trade of large proportions and enviable prestige in foreign and local markets

Mr. Alfred Mitchell Passes Away

Mr. Alfred Mitchell, one of the well known lumbermen of Powassan, Ont., passed away recently. Mr. Mitchell was born in Markham township sixty-six years ago, and came to Powassan when he was thirty years of age. During his stay there, he owned several saw mills in the neighborhood. Recently he had given all his attention to his sawmill in town, with which a sash and door factory and a planing mill are connected. He served efficiently at different times on the Township Council and the Town Council, and was at the time of his death a member of the School Board, and an elder in the Union Church. He has been ailing for several months, parts of which time he spent in Toronto, where he received special treatment. He returned home for a while, but went back to the General Hospital, where an operation was performed. He leaves a wife, one son and two daughters.

Why Western Lumber Prices are High

There is an Absolute Shortage and Yard Stocks Cannot be Sold Below Costs This Year

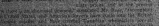

Hugh A. Rose, Toronto, Ont.

"In calling on retailers we find there is some criticism of Western manufacturers and wholesalers for not protecting and supplying the Eastern market with stocks, which owing to low prices existing in the past, Eastern retailers were induced to buy. Numerous articles have appeared in your publication and others regarding increased costs for logging and the manufacture of lumber, but these reasons do not appear sufficient to satisfy buyers that Western manufacturers are entitled to the present level of prices in order to make a profit on their operations," said Mr. Hugh A. Rose, of Toronto, representing Mason, Gordon & Co., in a recent interview with the "Canada Lumberman."

"Supply and demand really regulate prices, and at the present time there is an abnormal demand," continued Mr. Rose, "throughout the United States, and American buyers have come into the British Columbia market and have overbid Canadian wholesalers for all lines of stock, with the result that in spite of the fact that the Prairie markets are not taking their normal supply of lumber, there is an absolute shortage of all lines of stock at the mills in British Columbia and many of the mills are oversold for some weeks to come. This in itself is a justification of high prices, but one of our friends has put the matter up to us in another light.

"The sales manager of this mill says that unless he can sell at prices equal to those paid by American buyers he is not doing justice to his principals, and points out that prices this year are not averaging as high at the mill as last year. He gives the following figures as an illustration:

E. G. Decking, 100M per month at	$70.00	$ 7000.00
Ship Timbers, 400M per month at	40.00	16000.00
Jap. Flitches and large sq., 100M per month at	55.00	5500.00
Balance cut to yard stock, including uppers, 1000M per month at	18.00	18000.00
Total 1600M per month		$46300.00
Average price	$29.00 per month	

"This year up to the end of June their average selling price was $[illegible] or $3.00 per M below last year, whereas the cost of manufacture has increased. This is accounted for by the fact that all the high average lumber sold last year is not in demand this year at all. Last year it was common knowledge yard stocks all sold away below cost, but the mill could still make money with the other stocks to offset the loss, but this year the tables have turned and yard stocks must at least carry themselves, which apparently the mills are not finding it difficult to do on account of the American demand," concluded Mr. Rose.

Newsy Happenings from the West

The Prince Albert Lumber Company, Prince Albert, Sask., of which A. E. Mattes is manager, have practically cut all their timber and disposed of their saw and planing mill. They expect that it will be moved west, but as to the location the company are unable at present to state. The Prince Albert Lumber Company have operated their plant at Prince Albert for some thirteen years, and the output has been all marketed in western Canada.

A syndicate of Eastern capitalists has acquired the Canadian Puget Sound Lumber Company's saw mill at Rock Bay, B.C. W. D. Connor, of Marshfield, Wis., is head of the newly formed corporation and the big plant will soon be in operation. The cut will be about 150,000 feet daily. The company has been completely reorganized with the capital placed at $1,500,000. The officers are: President, Mr. W. D. Connor; secretary, Mr. George H. Reynolds; treasurer, Mr. H. A. Bly. The other directors are Mr. John W. Harter and Mr. W. G. Langley.

The Pacific Coast Shippers Organization recently held a meeting at Portland, Oregon. Practically all the wholesale lumber dealers of Portland were in attendance as well as a large number from Seattle. It was decided to extend the organization of this association, more particularly in its relation to the wholesale lumber business. Under the new plans the association will promote the interests of the wholesale lumbermen as well as those of the industry as a whole. L. D. Carpenter of Seattle is the president.

The Redonda Island Timber Company, Limited, a company incorporated under the laws of the State of Delaware, recently registered to do business in British Columbia.

H. H. Stevens, one of the B. C. members of the Federal House stated, in an interview, recently that the Government would continue the construction of ships, but not on such a scale as during the last few years. He said that $10,000,000 had recently been voted for additional vessels.

It is expected that the City Council of New Westminster, B.C., will shortly commence work on its housing programme. A workable scheme has been evolved and submitted to the Provincial Government and it is not anticipated there will be any further delay in carrying out this work. At present there are thirty applicants for loans and it is anticipated that this number will be increased as soon as construction commences.

The following companies were recently incorporated in B. C.: The Newton Logging Co., Limited, Vancouver, capital, $15,000; the Miller Grant Construction Co., Limited, Vancouver, capital, $50,000; the Melrose Shingle Co., Limited, Crescent, B.C., capital $50,000.

The Fullerton, Fawcett Lumber Co., Limited, Battle Lake, Alta., was recently granted a charter.

The partnership known as the Rowley, Bennett Lumber Co., Millet, Alta., has been dissolved and Mary A. Rowley and Victor C. Rowley, two of the partners, have registered as Rowley & Son.

Among the companies recently incorporated in Saskatchewan were the Aerial Service Co., Limited, Regina, Sask., capital $20,000; The Paskwegin Lumber Co., Limited, Paskwegin, Sask., capital $20,000, and the Battleford Aviation Co., Limited, North Battleford, Sask., capital $10,000.

Canadian Western Cordage Co., Vancouver, B. C., are planning to erect a factory at New Westminster to manufacture wooden pulleys, binder twine, etc.

The City Council of Winnipeg is working on an extensive housing scheme. It was proposed to spend at least $2,000,000 this year and the plan embraces the erection of between 3,000 and 4,000 houses. At a recent meeting it was urged that this work be undertaken at once so that no time may be lost and fullest advantage taken of the balance of the present building season. It is proposed to finance this scheme by collecting 10 per cent. of the total cost from the prospective purchasers and placing a mortgage for 60 per cent. with the regular mortgage on insurance companies and to finance a second mortgage of 30 per cent. with funds obtained from the Dominion, Provincial and Civic Governments and other sources.

The two vessels C-34 and C-39, which were built by the Northern Construction Co. for the French Government have successfully passed their tests and been accepted. These steamers are now at the Johnston Wharf, Vancouver, B.C., and will shortly commence loading lumber and spelter for the United Kingdom.

The manner in which British Columbia was able to respond to the call for airplane spruce has given an advertisement in the Old Country for the northern Sitka spruce that will have a marked effect on providing a future market in Great Britain for that wood, according to Mr. F. L. Buckley of the Masset Timber Company, who returned recently to Vancouver from a trip through England and Scotland. Mr. Buckley's company supplied the bulk of the spruce that was cut in this province to meet the demand for that wood for the construction of airplanes. "The quantity and quality of the light, strong and white northern grown spruce which was sent over to the Old Country from British Columbia has given that product a great reputation in Great Britain," said Mr. Buckley, "and I feel safe in predicting that the demand which has been created will be enlarged as new uses are found for a wood that is peculiarly adapted for a number of uses. Northern spruce from British Columbia will be called for carriage work, box manufacturing and other uses for which it is suitable, while it will of course remain sought after for airplane construction."

The International Coal & Coke Co., Limited, Coleman, Alta., were recently granted a Dominion charter. Wide powers have been conferred on this company. Among others to construct and operate steamers and vessels of all kinds and to build sawmills, wood working factories, etc.; capital stock, $3,000,000.

The Department of Labor, Ottawa, has been advised that the Commission named by the Minister of Labor to deal with the dispute between the Coghlan ship yards, Vancouver, and its employees, has brought about a satisfactory adjustment of the difficulty. Mr. Justice Murphy was Chairman of the Commission.

Record Sale of Ontario Timber Limits

High Prices Were Secured and There Were Numerous Tenders for all the Holdings Offered

The Ontario Department of Lands, Forests and Mines recently held a very successful sale of timber limits in several townships bordering principally on the Great Lakes. The returns are highly satisfactory and there was keen competition for a number of the concessions.

The successful tenderers for the respective limits, together with the prices for the timber, as bid, are:

Township	Per M. ft. B.M.
McCallum—J. B. Smith & Sons, Toronto	18.20 plus 2.00 dues.
Telfer—Manley Chew, Midland,	15.50 plus 2.00 dues.
Kenny—J. R. Booth, Ottawa,	17.50 plus 2.00 dues.
Charlton—J. B. Smith & Sons, Toronto,	13.20 dues. 2.00 dues.
"C"—W. J. Bell, Sudbury	8.45 plus 2.00 dues.
MacLaren—Gillies Bros., Ltd., Braeside	9.57 plus 2.00 dues.
McConnell—Gillies Bros., Ltd., Braeside	11.29 plus 2.00 dues.
McNamara—Marshay Lumber Coy., Sudbury,	14.65 plus 2.00 dues.
McNish—J. B. Smith & Sons, Toronto,	18.20 plus 2.00 dues.
Sisk—Pierce Lumber Co., Timmins,	20.57 plus 2.00 dues.

"U"—J. J. McFadden, Renfrew.

$2.50 per M. Ft. B.M. plus $2.00 dues for pine including Jackpine and spruce.

15c per tie plus 5c dues.

40c per cord for spruce pulpwood plus 40c dues.

25c per cord for other pulpwood plus 20c dues.

5c per cedar post plus 1c dues, and the following rates on cedar poles, namely.

30 ft. and less in length, 30c plus 15c dues each.
31 ft. to 40 ft. in length, 50c plus 25c dues each.
41 ft. to 50 ft. in length, 80c plus 50c dues each.
51 ft. and over, $1.25 plus $1.00 dues each.

Townships of Groves and St. Louis

Spanish River Pulp & Paper Mills, Ltd., Sault Ste. Marie.

On Red and White Pine $5 per M. ft B.M. plus $2 dues, or $7 per M. Ft. B.M.
On Jackpine, $4 plus $2 per M. ft. B.M., or $6 per M. ft. B.M.
On Ties, 10c per tie, plus 5c dues, or 12c per tie.
On Spruce Pulpwood, 40c per cord, plus 40c dues, or 80c per cord.
On other pulpwood, 40c. per cord, plus 20c dues, or 60c per cord.
On Cedar posts, 3c per post, plus 1c dues, or 4c per post.
On Poles:
30 ft. & less in length, 27c plus 15c dues, or 42c per pole.
31 ft. to 40 ft. in length, 47c plus 25c dues, or 72c per pole.
41 ft. to 50 ft. in length, 85c plus 50c dues, or $1.35 per pole.
51 ft. & over in length, $1.50 plus $1 dues or $2.50 per pole.

Budget of Briefs from the East

A forest fire broke out a few days ago in timber lands in York County, N. B. It was discovered by men in the vicinity and later an alarm was sent out from one of the towers of the Department of Lands and Mines and crews were rushed to the scene to combat the flames. Latest reports were to the affect that the fire was under control.

An expedition which marks a new era in commercial flying, left Annapolis Royal, N. S., recently for Labrador, under command of Captain Dan Owen, late of the Royal Air Force. The expedition is being sent out by the Belle Isle Straits Lumber & Pulp Company, Ltd., of Canada. The purpose of the expedition is to explore and survey 2,400 square miles of forest lands by airplanes. The whole future of lumber surveys by airplanes rests on the result of this expedition, which is being watched with interest all over the country.

Export figures of lumber shipments to the United States showed a falling off in comparison with the same period in 1918. The figures compiled show shipments from St. John, N. B., for three months ending June 30, as follows:

Laths: 10,500 m., $35,473.81.
Lumber: 3,527 m. feet, $122,742.48.
Pulpwood: 5,614 cords, $54,248.72.
Wood pulp: 3,980 m. lbs. $241,305.18.
Shingles: 111 m. $699.35.
Staves: 4,160 bundles, $3,131.66.
Spruce piling: 2,805 pieces, $6,944.
Total, $464,545.20.

Exports of lumber for three months ending June 30, 1918, were: $966,281.47.

Lumber shipments from the province are heavy. Daily schooners and steamers are carrying large quantities to the United Kingdom and the situation, so trying in the spring, is greatly relieved. Sailing vessels of all kinds are being chartered to carry lumber overseas.

Three Hollanders, Messrs. Pauw, Trip and Ponnis, were in St. John recently en route to British Columbia. They are repreesnting a large lumber firm in Holland, which has been in business more than 300 years, and which is known as the William Pont Timber Trading Co., Ltd., of Saandam, Holland. In conservation with a representative of the "Canada Lumberman" they said they had come to Canada in order to get an insight into the lumber industry of this country and to ascertain how conditions were in the lumber trade here. They said they planned on purchasing large quantities for shipment to their firm. They also declar[illegible] that there is a great demand for lumber, not only in their own country, but also in France and Belgium and if they could get the kind they wanted they would supply these countries through their firm in Holland

Taking Advantage of Cash Discounts

A large wholesale firm in a progressive city in New York State who deal in building materials furnish some illuminating facts in the matter of always "taking the discounts" on purchases. Here is their important announcement which is worth reading carefully and pondering well.

The merchant who fails to take advantage of cash discount on bills is missing an opportunity to increase his yearly profits materially. Is it not better to borrow the necessary funds at your bank at 6 per cent. interest annually and save the cash discount that amounts to sometimes over 36 per cent annually? As an example: Jones purchases $100.00 worth of goods and receives a bill thereof allowing 2 per cent discount if paid within 10 days. Jones is careless and waits 30 days and pays $100.00. If Jones was wise he would go to his bank and borrow $100.00 on his note for 30 days. He would deduct 2 per cent discount remitting $98.000. At the end of 30 days he would pay the bank $100.50. He has saved $1.50, or enough to pay the interest on $100.00 for three months.

2 per cent. cash discount, net 60 days, means over 14 per cent. per annum.

5 per cent cash discount, net 60 days, means over 36 per cent. per annum.

Do you make the above profits on the sale of your goods,
Think it over.

Stand of Timber in B. C. Province

The stand of timber in British Columbia is estimated to be as follows:

Species.	Total. Million b.f.	Per cent.
Western red cedar	77,968	22.2
Douglas fir	75,973	21.2
Spruce (all species)	73.064	20.8
Western hemlock	64,112	18.3
White fir (balsam)	32,953	9.4
Lodgepole pine	11.861	3.4
Western yellow pine	4,208	1.2
Yellow cypress		
Western larch	3,152	.9
Western white pine	2,700	.8
Cottonwood		.2
Total saw material	350,835	
Piling, poles, pulpwood, etc	15,465	
Total forest resources	366.300	

Forest Fires in Western Canada

The municipality of West Point Grey, a suburb of Vancouver, B. C., was threatened by a bush fire which broke out in the surrounding timber. At one point, twelve or fifteen houses were the nearest being a mere half block from the fire. The fire brigade assisted by a detachment from the Vancouver force and a large number of citizens, succeeding in extinguishing the blaze. About 500 acres were burned over.

A number of fires are reported in the Nelson district. In the Salmon River Valley a large fire trapped three men in a tunnel at the second relief mine near Erie. It is known that the men have enough provisions to last for three or four days and it is thought that they are safe, although there is the danger that they may be suffocated.

Slocan City, about 25 miles from Nelson, is completely surrounded by fires. Fire hose have been stretched to all outlying sections of the town in an attempt to save the city. Fire rangers in this district say that the fires are due to the spontaneous combustion of the gases generated, by the heat, from the resin in the trees.

Yardman Should Give Good Service

Should Never Resort to Price Cutting Which is Confession of Inefficient Salesmanship

Mr. Retail Lumberman, do things in the community that will get you talked about. I do not mean eccentric things. You do not have to wear your coat wrong side out, or go bare foot in the winter time. Remember always that you are working for yourself, even though you may be managing the business of another. If you keep this in mind your course of action will be the same as though you owned the business yourself and were ambitious to go to the top of the ladder, says one who has given the subject of publicity for the retail lumberman much thought and attention.

So, it is a good idea to at least be in the front rank of those who are boosting for the community—if not at the top.

Some dealers make a practice of giving away souvenirs. If this is done indiscriminately, it is of doubtful value as an advertisement. In giving souvenirs it is well to have them of a useful sort, and it is also well to do it in a manner which will make them appreciated. Souvenirs of any kind cost money, and giving them away is a charge against the cost of operation. It is also true that people attach less value to something that does not cost them anything. Some such plan as giving a souvenir to every cash customer, or to every customer who meets his obligations promptly, will have the effect of making collections easier, particularly if the souvenir is of some value, and useful.

An exception to this rule may be made in relation to the young people—the children of the community. Most children are "pleased with a whistle and tickled with a straw." So, it is not necessary to give them expensive presents; but it is necessary to give them something they want. It has often been said that "the children of today are the customers of tomorrow," and it pays to cultivate them and gain their good will. They will have an influence with their parents, too, and if they hear the old people talking about buying building material, or building something, they will probably get in a good word for the dealer who has done them a favor.

I will not attempt to go into all the details of the publicity part of the selling plan. Not everything is suitable in every community, and the dealer must be his own guide. He must depend on his own ingenuity and perception.

In many lines of business "bargain sales" are common, but I do not think that they are a legitimate part of the selling plan for staple building material. Neither is price cutting. A general merchandise store can offer goods at a bargain for a week and then go back to the old prices, and nothing is thought of it. The goods they offer at such sales are usually slow moving stock or an accumulation from over-stocking. To that extent, a lumber dealer can offer bargains, provided he makes it definitely plain that he is offering an accumulation of "dead" stock.

But if he offers bargains for a week on a regular staple merchandise, he is laying up trouble for the future. He creates the impression that his regular prices are too high, and he will find that the customer who has bought at a low price will be mighty hard to sell to at a higher price. Other customers who did not take advantage of the "sale" will hear about it, for such news travels fast in a small community, and will expect to buy as cheaply.

Price-cutting to get competitive business is foolish—and unnecessary. In the first place it is a confession of poor salesmanship. Good salesmanship does not necessarily mean ability to get prices that represent more than the worth of the goods sold. Good salesmanship is the selling of things that give the buyer so much satisfaction that he does not remember what he paid for them.

A man may buy a two-dollar watch that either loses or gains a half an hour a week, but he never brags of it. He may say, "Well, I only paid two dollars for it." But if he pays a hundred dollars for a watch that does not vary a minute a month from being accurate, he will be proud of it, and will never regret the hundred dollars.

Cheap goods will not give service, and the man who is a constant price-cutter will avoid loss by delivering poor quality. He has got to do this, or go broke. The ability to guarantee what you sell, with the knowledge that it will give the service desired, makes the seller respect himself, and creates respect in the mind of the buyer.

This does not mean that you should try to sell every customer building material that is better than he requires for his purpose; but it does mean that you must not sell him material that will not give the service desired.

The farther you can get away from talking prices, and the more you can impress the customer with the service he is to get from what he buys, the larger will be your volume of trade—and your profits.

The Lobstick Lumber Co., Limited, Edmonton, Alta., was recently incorporated.

Camp Fires are Forest Destroyers

In almost every part of Canada, the camp fire of picnic and fishing parties continues to destroy more of public-owned timber than could be grown by the planting of scores of millions of trees, says a recent leaflet issued by the Canadian Forestry Association.

From every direction comes urgent suggestions that governments start to re-plant the waste forest areas. This procedure may profitably apply to certain sections of Canada. The main consideration, however, is to stop the destruction of timber requiring a century to grow. Planting is a highly expensive alternative to fire prevention. If camp fires were invariably extinguished, there would be less need for asking the public treasury to assume the cost of rebuilding the forests by the use of millions of seedlings. Camp fires in Canada have stolen more public wealth than would have transported the guilty campers around the world on a luxurious free trip. Veteran woodsmen always build their fires small and build them in a safe spot, such as along a rocky shore or on a gravel or sand base, never among leaves or against a log.

Why are Wooden Labels Imported?

We have recently published reports, says the "Weekly Bulletin" of Ottawa, from the Canadian Trade Commissioners in the United Kingdom to the effect that there is a great demand for woodenware in the United Kingdom and great opportunities for Canadian manufacturers of wooden articles to secure trade in that market. In connection with this we have reeived a letter from a well-known Canadian scientific man in which he points out that wooden labels for plants used by florists and sticks for the support of rose bushes are imported into Canada from the United Kingdom. He wonders that these articles are not made in Canada.

The "Movie" as Sawmill Benefactor

There probably is not a grown man today who cannot recall the day of the tramp actor—the artist of the canvas wagon and the town hall, attempting in grotesque manner to portray the greatness and the grandeur of life. His acting was a travesty, his talent was a vacuum, his getting money for his work was a crime. Yet from coast to coast, and from the sawmills of the cold North to the logging camps of the balmy South, the advent of these burlesques on human existence was a call for man, woman and child to dig out their quarters and their half dollars and pack a smelly tent or an unsanitary hall to greet him. He neither entertained nor educated. He was not a faithfull portrayer of good or evil; he left behind nothing to be remembered by but a vacancy in the purse. Yet he drew full houses, small as they were, wherever he went. says "Lumber."

To the man who has lived his life in the sawmill town of the United States the old Hamletian ham is a whimsical memory; he has been replaced by the greatest educator of the common people (and most of us are common people), that the world has ever seen—The Movie.

The water boy in the woods nowadays can, for a dime, see the great actors whose every move is a benediction; the loose-lipped ignoramus can have brought before him the greatest builder of human life; the seasoned and intelligent southern man worker can see the great trees cut down and crash through woods to Pacific Coast mills, every detail a perfection; can see the flitches they themselves, perhaps, sent the band saw through rear themselves into place in Gulf shipyards: can see his brothers of the snowy North guiding their loads of logs down frozen pathways to their resting place until the spring winds sweep along, on the banks and breasts of the solid rivers, the women of the household can see perfection in form and dress, and sweetness of life talk to them out of the screen. The world is no longer bounded to them by the railroad where it dies away in the distance, or by narrow walls that shut out the bigness of life. All life and greatness and goodness and brains are brought to them and poured, like treasurers of the Incas, at their feet.

What the movie has done to help make sawmill workers better contented is but a promise of what it can do. Its worth is recognized by the modern mill builder and a movie show is part of the building plans of every mill that arises in a tract of timber. The operators of sawmills can give their working force an education that will result in nothing but betterment of community life, of precision and efficiency in their labors; an interest in life that will make the littlest strip of "shorts" that ever was sent out on a car an inspiration.

The National Wholesale Lumber Dealers' Association, whose headquarters are at New York City, have secured a substantial reduction in the present high demurrage rates. The new schedule went into effect a few days ago and the charges are now $2 per car per day for the first four days after the expiration of the free time and $5 per car per day thereafter.

Second Hand Machinery & Equipment Wanted & For Sale

Special Lots Of Lumber— —Positions Wanted & Vacant

PUBLISHER'S NOTICE

Advertisements other than "Employment Wanted" or "Employees Wanted" will be inserted in this department at the rate of 20 cents per agate line (14 agate lines make one inch). $2.50 per inch, each insertion, payable in advance. Space measured from rule to rule. When four or more consecutive insertions of the same advertisement are ordered a discount of 25 per cent. will be allowed.

Advertisements of "Wanted Employment" will be inserted at the rate of one cent a word, net. Cash must accompany order. If Canada Lumberman box number is used, enclose ten cents extra for postage in forwarding replies. Minimum charge 25 cents.

Advertisements of "Wanted Employees" will be inserted at the rate of two cents a word, net. Cash must accompany the order. Minimum charge 50 cents.

Advertisements must be received not later than the 10th and 20th of each month to insure insertion in the subsequent issue.

Wanted–Lumber

Basswood Wanted

No. 2 Common and Mill Cull. Winter cut preferred. Apply Firstbrook Brothers, Ltd., Toronto, Ont. 8-t.f.

Wanted

We are in the market for Spruce Lumber, 50% 3 x 7 and 8", also 2", 2½" and 3" birch, 6" and wider, and quantity of white pine and Douglas fir. Will purchase entire mill cut. Also want aspen wood in forest or lots. Tell us what you have. Box 981, Canada Lumberman, Toronto. 14-15

Wanted

Spruce Plastering Lath

J. E. Harroun & Son
Watertown, N.Y.

For Sale–Lumber

FOR SALE

80 M Basswood, 4/4.
14 M Basswood, 6/4.
35 M Maple and Birch, 4/4.
20 M Red Oak, 4/4.
4 M Red Oak, 2/4.
75 M Elm and Ash, 4/4.

We have some 2 x 6, 28 and 30 B. C. Cedar Silo Stock.

F. McGibbon & Sons,
15 Sarnia, Ont.

FOR SALE

2 cars 2½" Log Run Pecan.
2 cars 2" Log Run Pecan.
2 cars 3" Log Run Sycamore.
1 car ⅝" Log Run Elm.
2 cars 1" Soft Maple Crating.
1 car 1" Beech and Maple Crating.
1 car ¾" Beech and Maple Crating.
1 car ¾" Elm Crating.

John I. Shafer Hardwood Co.,
Farmers' Trust Building,
15-16 South Bend, Indiana.

Ties For Sale

Ties for sale at a bargain. 5,000 small cedar ties for immediate delivery.

ST. LAWRENCE LUMBER CO.,
81 St. Peter Street,
15 Quebec, Que.

Lumber For Sale
This Season's Cut

300 M Basswood, 1" and 1½".
75 M Black Ash, 1".
100 M Soft Elm, 1", 2", 3" and 4".
150 M Hard Maple, 1", 2" and 3".
15 M Birch, 4" and 2".
Ontario White Cedar Shingles, 16".
Box 982, Canada Lumberman, Toronto. 15

FOR SALE

50,000 ft.	2 x 4 x 10/16'	Jack Pine	&	Spruce
100,000 "	2 x 5 x 10/16'	"		"
100,000 "	2 x 6 x 10/16'	"		"
100,000 "	2 x 7 x 10/16'	"		"
100,000 "	2 x 8 x 10/16'	"		"
2 cars	6 x 6 x 10/16'	"		"
2 "	6 x 8 x 10/10'	"		"
2 "	8 x 8 x 10/16'	"		"
1 "	10 x 10 x 10/16'	"		"

The above stock cut and piled ready for shipment. Write or Wire

NORTHERN LUMBER MILLS,
14-17 North Cobalt, Ont.

For Sale–Machinery

FOR SALE–SAWMILL

25 H. P. Engine, 50 H. P. return tubular boiler. Three log seat carriage, overhead set, friction feed works, single edger and slab saw. All in fair order. Price $1,000. Box 915, Canada Lumberman, Toronto. 12-15

High Speed Matchers

1—Berlin No. 90 High Speed Matcher with Profilers and several extra heads.
1—American No. 77 High Speed Matcher without Profiler but having several extra heads.

Two real bargains.

Box 893, Canada Lumberman, Toronto, Ont. 6-t.f.

Band Saw Mill For Sale

One Waterous 9 ft. Band Saw Mill, gunshot feed, complete with extra saws and filing equipment. Used about one year, excellent condition. The Geo. F. Foss Machinery & Supply Co., Ltd., 305 St. James St., Montreal, Que. 7-t.f.

Logging Equipment

Phoenix Caterpillar Log Haulers.
Logging Sleighs.
Rutters.
Hoisting Engines.
12 lb. and 16 lb. Relaying Rails.

J.-L. NEILSON & CO.,
13-t.f. Winnipeg, Man.

Here's Your Opportunity!
For Sale

"Canada Machinery Corporation" New No. 107 Planer and Matcher. New price $1,750. Our Price $890.

"Canada Machinery Corporation" New No. 110 Planer and Matcher and Moulder. New Price $1,400. Our Price $750.

"C.M.C." No. 610 Gang Edger. New price $900. Our Price $400.

"C.M.C." No. 303-10" Heavy Four-Sided Moulder, just like new. New price $1,750. Our Price $950.

Further particulars if so desired will be cheerfully furnished.

WILLIAMS & WILSON LIMITED,
84 Inspector Street,
13-15 Montreal, P.Q.

FOR SALE

One twenty-four inch Combined Planer and Matcher, Clark-Demill make.

Three Gas Engines, from 1 to 6 H.P.

Two twenty-six inch Barnes Sliding Head Drills. Good as new. Bargain prices.

W. H. Sumbling Machinery Co.,
7 St. Mary Street,
15-16 Toronto, Ont.

For Sale

1—17 x 24 Atlas Engine, with 36 in. x 10 ft. flywheel.
3—No. 94 Berlin Matchers, 15 in., fitted with hard steel knives on top and bottom cylinders—one pair shiplap, jointer and flooring heads with bits for each machine.
1—No. 182 Berlin Double Surfacer, 30 in. x 6 in.
1—No. 199 Berlin Buzz Planer.
1—No. 290 Berlin Picket Header.

The Otis Staples Lumber Company, Ltd.,
10-t.f. Wycliffe, B.C.

Equipment For Sale

1—Yates No. 177 30 x 12 double surfacer, with round cylinders, Jointer and power cylinder grinder. In A1 condition.
1—Fay & Egan No. 217 Continuous Feed Glue Jointer, with 2 set Shimer Heads; 1 set Square Jointing Heads; 1 set Tongue and Groove Heads. Machine new; was installed but never operated.
1—6' Linderman Glue Jointer and Matcher in A1 condition.

The above machines are real bargains, subject to inspection.

Box 400, Canada Lumberman, 119 Board of Trade Bldg., Montreal. 15

Wanted–Machinery

Wanted

Log Haul-Up Complete
120 Centres
in good condition

Clarke Brothers, Ltd.
Bear River, Nova Scotia

Wanted–Employment

Advertisements under this heading one cent a word per insertion. Box No. 10 cents extra. Minimum charge 25 cents.

WANTED—POSITION AS BAND-SAW FILER—The kind you can depend on to get results. At present in Upper Michigan; prefer Canada. Box 980, Canada Lumberman, Toronto, Ont. 15-16

POSITION WANTED by a well educated young man, 15 years' experience with wholesalers and manufacturers; competent inspector either hard or soft wood; will consider any other capacity. Apply Box 956, Canada Lumberman, Toronto. 12-16

Thoroughly experienced sawmill and lumberman as assistant manager or general superintendent of operations on coast or interior; age 30, married, an English Canadian and speaks French; satisfactory references. Write Box 988, Canada Lumberman, Toronto. 15-17

WANTED POSITION by representative and superintendent, still employed with large wholesale firm, with twenty-five years' experience in the lumber business. Can give reference as to capabilities and take charge on a month's notice. Box 991, Canada Lumberman, Toronto.

WANTED—Position as Superintendent or Foreman of planing mill or woodworking factory by thoroughly capable experienced man who has handled big work and large gangs, knows the business and machines thoroughly, and gets results. Box 950, Canada Lumberman, Toronto. 12-15

WHOLESALERS—MANUFACTURERS—ATTENTION! Fifteen years in the business; territory Windsor to Halifax, New York and New England, buying and selling. Know trade thoroughly, Eastern and Western stocks. Highly educated, both languages. Would make first class office manager or secretary or traveller. Real correspondent. Employed. Desire change. Start at once. Hard worker. Age 37. Your chance to secure a producer. Apply Box 50, Canada Lumberman, Montreal. 15-16

First Class Man on Rip Saw.

JOHN B. SMITH & SONS,
13-16 Toronto, Ont.

Salesman with Eastern connection to sell Hardwood and Softwood lumber on salary or commission. Box 987, Canada Lumberman, Toronto.

Wanted—One Foreman for Sash and Door Department; experienced on solid and veneered doors; four bench men, experienced on hard and soft wood; two cabinetmakers.

J. R. EATON & SONS, LIMITED,
13-16 Orillia, Ont.

WANTED—A high grade man, on commission, as Eastern representative for British Columbia organization handling a daily output of 500,000feet. Must have first class connections and wide experience. Box 238, Canada Lumberman, 212 Winch Bldg., Vancouver, B.C. 14-15

LUMBER EXPORT HOUSE has opening for intelligent young man, 19-23 years of age. Applicant must be ambitious, willing, and have a good education. Competent stenographer and typist, and be accurate at figures. Moderate salary to start, but good opportunity for advancement and to learn the business. Apply giving references, experience, etc., to Mr. S. Bick, P. O. Box 284, Montreal. 14-17

Salesman and Purchasing Abent—A bright and energetic young man with knowledge of lumber wanted to represent us in Ontario with headquarters in Toronto. Must know lumber; previous selling experience not absolutely necessary. Good salary and future for right man. Reply stating experience and salary wanted.

Campbell, MacLaurin Lumber Company,
Board of Trade Building,
13-16 Montreal, Que.

Business Chances

Wanted

Good reliable saw mill man with portable mill to cut two million feet or more Birch and Hemlock in Patterson Township. Warren Ross Lumber Co., Jamestown, N.Y. 14-19

Two Timber Limits

34,000,000 ft. Virgin Timber, and 3,000,000 cords of Spruce Pulpwood. For all desirable information write to D. McDonald, La Salle, N.Y. 12-15.

For Sale

Building and machinery of good Double Cut Band Sawmill, well equipped with steam feed, canter, loaders, etc.

Also two storey Brick Factory on large lot convenient to two railways; splendid location. Address Box 949, Owen Sound, Ont. 12-t.f.

Timberlands For Sale

2½ million ft. Birch and Maple.
½ million ft. Hemlock and Pine.
Situated 100 miles north of Toronto, 1 mile from railroad. For particulars write

E. J. WHITE,
15-18 15-16th St., Buffalo, N.Y.

For Sale

Hardwood Timber Limits of about seven million feet, with up-to-date sawmill.

BEDFORD MANUFACTURING CO.,
15-18 Waterloo, Que.

Opportunity in Lumber Business

Will contract sell red cedar timber as cut—150,000,000-foot tract. Quality and accessibility good. Grand Trunk Railroad.

J. RANDALL BLACK,
14-17. Edmonton, Alberta.

Timber Limit For Sale

Situated in Northern Ontario, 27¼ square miles. Estimated quantity of pine thereon upwards of 10,000,000 feet, as well as spruce and other timber. For full information apply to W. E. Bigwood, Bank of Hamilton Building, Toronto, or Byng Inlet, Ontario. 15-18

Sawmill For Sale

Portable outfit in first class condition, 3 block carriage, track, saw frame, double edger, slab saw, lath machine and trimmer, boiler and engine, complete with shafting, pulleys, belting, saws and all equipment. Purchased new, ran 12 months.

Capacity 10 to 12 M. ft. per day. Now set in town of Arnprior. Must be moved this fall.

A. F. CAMPBELL & SON,
15-16 Box 455, Arnprior, Ont.

Saw Mill Plant For Sale

Practically new and modern Saw Mill Plant, capacity about 30 Million feet per annum, located in the Interior of British Columbia on a beautiful inland lake and on the main line of the Grand Trunk Pacific Railway. About 500 Million feet of timber on and adjacent to Lake (about 90% Spruce) and another Billion feet available at reasonable prices. Natural conditions ideal for economical logging, manufacturing, piling and shipping. An advantage of about $4 per thousand feet in freight rates to the Prairie Provinces over Coast shipments.

This property offers unlimited possibilities as a lumber, pulp and paper property. Would consider selling a half interest. Terms reasonable.

A. C. FROST COMPANY,
134 South LaSalle Street,
5-t.f. Chicago, Ill.

Saw Mill Property FOR SALE

Picnic Island sawmill plant at Little Current, Georgian Bay, 37 acres, for sale or lease for a term of years, or might put it in a good sized company, part cash, part stock; cutting capacity 140 M. a day, two thousand feet stone-filled lumber docks, 16 ft. water, Algoma railway station less than a mile distant, log booming capacity 10 million, telegraph and telephone, school taxes only, title from Crown, no debts or disputes; one of the best mills on the Bay, selling cheap to wind up an estate. For further particulars as to the mill and about twenty other buildings, etc., apply to Thomas Conlon, 44 Church Street, St. Catharines, Ont. 13-16

FOR SALE
Saw and Shingle Mill

20 H.P. Bell Engine.
30 H.P. Waterous Return Tubular Boiler.
Three Log Seat Carriage.
Henry Disston inserted tooth saw, single edger and slab saw, Long shingle mill knife and saw edger; all in good order. Price $1,000 at railway switch. Box 144, Schomberg, Ont. 15

A Business Opportunity

A company located in a mixed population, nearly all speaking English, wishes to dispose of its business, consisting of Saw, Planing and Shingle Mills, with timber standing and in sight for several years. A good Custom Sawing and Dressing in Transit trade is established. Reason for selling, illness of principals. Address Box 990, Canada Lumberman, Toronto, Ont. 15-16

Virgin Timber For Sale

I have for sale, on very easy terms, in Virginia, 3,000 acres of Virgin Timber, mostly Shortleaf Pine, with some Oak. It is estimated to cut about 17 million feet of pine and oak, with a percentage of white wood, cherry and ash. Railway runs through the centre of it. The land will be worth $50.00 an acre after it is cleared. Apply

DON. M. CAMPBELL,
15-18 Preston, Ont.

1300 Acres of Standing Timber FOR SALE

It consists of Birch, Basswood, Ash, Maple, Pine, Spruce, Cedar, Hemlock. Camps, logging equipment and sawmill on the ground; owner not a lumberman, engaged in other business. The said lands are located right on C. P. R. and C. N. R. sidings, six miles west of North Bay, better known as the Indian Reserve. Apply to

P. ADAMS,
15-18 North Bay, Ont.

Miscellaneous

Canadian National Railways

CENTRAL LINES

Sealed tenders, addressed to the undersigned and endorsed "Tender for Ties," will be received at this office until twelve o'clock noon, Monday, 25th day of August, for 1,375,000 Railway Ties to be made and delivered between October 1st, 1919, and October 1st, 1920, in accordance with tie specification No. 3956, dated March 18th, 1819.

1,000,000 to be delivered on Canadian National lines between Port Arthur and Pembroke.

50,000 to be delivered on Canadian National lines in Central Ontario.

25,000 to be delivered on Canadian National lines between Ottawa and Quebec.

200,000 to be delivered on Canadian National lines between O'Brien and Quebec.

100,000 to be delivered on Canadian National lines Lake St. John District.

Tender forms and specifications can be obtained at the office of the General Tie Agent, No. 9 Toronto Street, Toronto.

Tenders will not be considered unless made on forms supplied by the Railway.

No tender for quantities less than 10,000 ties will be considered.

The lowest or any tender not necessarily accepted.

E. LANGHAM,
General Purchasing Agent,
Canadian National Railways,
13-16 Toronto.

For Sale

One Detroit Hot Blast, Dry Kiln System, complete with Fan and Engine, also 35 feet of 9" double leather belt, used two weeks.

Port Hope Veneer & Lumber Co.,
13-t.f. Port Hope, Ont.

WANTED
LIGHT RAILS

State whether complete with splice or angle bars.

Give size, quantity, location, condition and best cash price f.o.b. cars loading point.

Box No. 966, Canada Lumberman,
13-14 Toronto.

WATER STORAGE ON ST. MAURICE RIVER

The great benefit derived from water storage is soon to be further demonstrated on the St. Maurice river where a large water-power undertaking will soon be started.

The increased power made possible at the various sites on this river by the La Loutre reservoir, the largest but one in the world, is a strong incentive to prospective power users. It is estimated that the conserved water thus made available represents a total increase of over 500,000 h.p.

The proposed development above referred to is reported to be in connection with the operations of the St. Maurice Paper Company, the latter having leased two sites in the lower portion of the river, known as Les Forges and La Gabelle. It is intended to combine these two, giving a total effective head of 33 feet, while the regulated flow from the La Loutre reservoir increases the power now available at this site, namely 20,000 h.p., to 42,000 h.p.

Another proposition reported in this connection is the construction of a hydro-electric plant utilizing the combined sites of La Gabelle and Les Gres, the latter site being controlled by the Shawinigan Water & Power Company. The latter power company would carry out the development and supply hydro-electric power to the St. Maurice Paper Company under a special contract.

BELTING FOR SALE

We have a large quantity of Second-Hand Rubber and Leather Belting in all sizes and plys up to 24 inches in width, which we can sell at interesting prices. Send us your requirements.

N. SMITH
138 York St. - Toronto, Ont.

TIMBER LANDS

Bought and Sold

Timber and Pulp Wood Estimates

R. R. BRADLEY

Consulting Forester
58 Telegraph Building
Hospital St., MONTREAL

Timber Estimates

James W. Sewall
OLD TOWN, - MAINE

Manufacturers of
WIRE
For TYING, BUNDLING and many other purposes.
NAILS, Etc.

LAIDLAW BALE-TIE CO., Ltd.
HAMILTON, ONT.

Cut Your Selling Costs

Use MacLean Daily Reports and know where the projects are that offer the most profitable business. Reduce the percentage of wasted time and lost orders by concentrating on the most likely opportunities.

Rates and Samples on Request.

MacLEAN DAILY REPORTS, Ltd.
345 Adelaide Street West, TORONTO

Coolidge & Carlisle

Forest Engineers

Timber Estimates and Maps
Plans for Logging Operations

Bangor, Maine

DR. BELL'S
Veterinary Wonder Remedies

10,000 one dollar ($1.00) bottles Free to horsemen who give the Wonder a fair trial. Guaranteed for Colic, Inflammation of the Lungs, Bowels, Kidneys, Fevers, Distemper, etc. Send 25c for Mailing Package, etc. Agents wanted. Write your address plainly. DR. BELL, V.S., Kingston, Ont.

HORSES

UNION STOCK YARDS
OF TORONTO, Limited

"Canada's Greatest Live Stock Market"
Capital, $1,500,000. Two Hundred Acres. Dundas St. cars to Keele St., West Toronto. Auction Sales every Wednesday. Private Sales Daily.

Correspondence Solicited.

WALTER HARLAND SMITH
Manager Horse Dept.

Review of Current Trade Conditions

Ontario and the East

Business in the lumber line continues brisk and there is an active demand from various centres in the United States where building activities are particularly brisk. Prices in all ranges of material, particularly that used in house construction, remain very firm. As the season advances there is considerably more structural work being carried out in Ontario than appeared possible this spring. Then throughout the country and in various small towns a great deal of repair work, extensions and renovations is going on. Dry stock is getting scarcer all the while and it begins to look as if there might be a decided shortage in certain lines of lumber before the season closes.

Mill stocks are now pretty well bought up and this year's cut is coming on to the market. Manufacturing and labor conditions are on the whole quite satisfactory and distribution is not presenting much difficulty to shippers at the present time. Those persons who have been hesitating about building or laying in additional stock in the hope that prices would come down, have reckoned without their host; production expenses are aviating all the while and there is no immediate indication of any decline in the value of wood goods.

That the future is viewed with assurance is evidenced by the recent successful sale of several township rights in northwest Ontario when the timber holdings brought as high as $22.50 per thousand feet on the stump, while $20.00 was a general figure. Most of the wood in the township sold, consists of white and Norway pine.

The export situation is improving somewhat but not as rapidly as certain big firms would like. More available space is now at the disposal of shippers and the Federal Government is doing all in its power to increase tonnage facilities but it will be well on in the fall or the beginning of next year before ordinary commercial business can be arranged without a great deal of difficulty, delay and uncertainty.

In regard to the demand for Pacific Coast products, there is a fair market with some improvement in the requisitions for timbers. Ontario representatives of B. C. Coast and Mountain mills complain of trouble in getting shipments through in a prompt manner owing to the car shortage which is an aftermath of the strike in Winnipeg. Shingles are constantly advancing and while a few carloads are coming though the demand is much above the supply. There have been three advances during the last fortnight and XXX are now quoted at $6.40 and XXXXX at $7.00. Since the middle of June there has been an advance of $5.00 on all clear fir items such as flooring, ceiling, trim, etc., while recently there was another jump of $2.00 on boards and shiplap. Just now it is a case of prices adjusting themselves to conditions or conditions to prices so far as the eastern demand is concerned. How high quotations will ascend is a matter of conjecture.

Owing to the marked shortage of all kinds of lumber and the increased demand due to improved building conditions and large orders from other users, American buyers are coming to Canada and buying all the stock they can possiby secure. High prices do not seem to deter them at all, providing they can get the lumber. To this one feature, perhaps, more than any other, can be attributed the steady increase in lumber values in Canada. The building situation is much more active in the States than in Canada and this has materially increased the demand for Canadian spruce, hemlock and other soft woods. The American buyers are trying to keep up diminishing hardwood stocks with shipments from this country and are buying birch, beech and maple in large quantities. The local demand is all that is to be desired. Wood users, such as furniture, sash, door and box men, builders, etc., are all seeking material. It is hard to forecast the future but if the present movement continues it looks as if available stocks will be exhausted before the next winter cut is on the market.

United States

Generally speaking there is not much change in the situation except that prices are soaring all the while and trade on market stock is good. Business is firming up all along and building activities are remarkably active in many centres. One eastern firm states that it is useless to try and keep up with the constant change in prices and any correction that is made in the list today may look like a back number to-morrow. Much depends upon how badly a customer wants his stock so far as the figure at which it changes hands is concerned. In the hardwood field it is gratifying to note that there will be only one set of rules for inspection and this will eliminate much of the trouble of the past. Oak in the better grades is probably in the best demand today of the native American hardwoods. There is a great scarcity of mahogany, and the demand for this wood is very keen. Supplies of walnut are comparatively large and the demands for this wood is not equal to the supply of some grades offered. From an inspection trip to the mills, both North and South, an uninformed observer might conclude that the stocks are fairly large, and while this is true it does not signify that there is a great deal of lumber for sale. A very large part of the lumber still stacked at the mills is sold and is only awaiting shipment. The result is that the volume of lumber appears to be greater than it is, so far as that available for making sales is concerned.

The demand for white pine continues to increase. Some very heavy sales have recently been made in the North and the activity, especially among retail buyers, shows no sign of the usual midsummer slackness. On the whole, orders are not accepted for future delivery though there have been some large orders placed for delivery from time to time during the fall months. Buying of this character is customary at these mills and such orders are accepted only from old time customers of the manufacturers. There has been a considerable speeding up in production and it begins to appear as though production this year will be heavier than expected.

The demand for red cedar shingles continues good and manufacturers could well sell more shingles than they are producing. The supply of red cedar logs which at no time this season has been heavy has been further decreased by the Fourth of July shutdown and there is no apparent reason to believe that production will be materially increased for some time. The result is that prices are very firm and in a number of markets advances were made this week. Supplies of lath in manufacturers' hands in all sections of the country are small and as the home building boom increases in volume, the call for lath increases and prices go up.

A broad survey of the southern pine situation reveals a stabilizing tendency. The policy is becoming more and more general for manufacturers to accept orders which can be delivered within a short time and there is a growing tendency to set prices for a definite time and hold to them for that time. There is no tendency toward price recession and there have been price advances upon numerous items, but abrupt and constant revision in prices, notably in the better grades, especially of flooring, are less evident. In the Southeast buying continues brisk and the abnormal spread in price between certain grades is being smoothed out somewhat by the revision upward of price lists on the lower grades.

Great Britain

In a general report on the timber market an admirable summary is given in a recent letter sent out by Alfred Dobell & Co., which succintly presents all the leading features.

In Nova Scotia and New Brunswick spruce deals, etc., the stocks are still very light, and depleted of several important dimensions. Operations continue restricted owing mainly to the difficulty in obtaining tonnage. Hardwood planks are wanted, and have not arrived as freely as during the previous month.

In Douglas fir, the arrivals have been practically all for account of the Timber Controller. The consumption has been well maintained, and the light stocks consist chiefly of Planks. Timber of good length and size, also decking, would meet with a ready sale. Prices are firmer.

In Scandinavian deals, boards, etc., flooring boards have arrived freely. The consumption has been satisfactory. Stocks remain light and values very firm.

There is very little alteration in the position of pitch pine. The demand continues satisfactory at advanced prices. Imports have again been light, and the offerings for forward shipment have been parcel lots in limited quantities.

During the past month there has been an increase in imports of all classes of lumber, the arrivals having been chiefly under contracts. Operations have been a good deal interfered with by the congested state of the quays and the difficulty experienced by merchants in obtaining railway facilities. Consignments of red and sap gum and whitewood lumber in thicknesses of one inch and up have been sold at slightly lower prices than previously. The demand for thin lumber of all descriptions is well maintained.

The auction sales of mahogany held during the past month were well attended, and keen competition ruled for all classes of mahogany with the exception of round Honduras.

African—Lagos, Benin and Grand Balsam were in strong demand, and the moderate quantities on offer cleared at prices showing an upward tendency. Sapeli.—The small quantity offered met with spirited competition, and extreme prices were realized for sound, roey logs. Axim.—High values were obtained for the shipments from this district.

Honduras. Square logs sold readily at good prices. Round logs failed to interest buyers at the auction sales, but substantial quantities have been sold by private treaty.

Market Correspondence

SPECIAL REPORTS ON CONDITIONS AT HOME AND ABROAD

St. John Reports Serious Shipping Conditions

A much better feeling prevails in the eastern spruce market than for some time past, and if it were not for both rail and water transportation difficulties, business would be extra good, as the American market is advancing from week to week, and to-day any random spruce of short lengths can be sold at $40.00 on cars St. John, paying in American funds, which is equal to another $1.00 per M., but the whole trouble is to get foreign cars in which to make shipments.

This on top of no water transportation makes a double hardship which the lumber manufacturer is compelled to bear; certainly it is not fair to both the public who want the material and the shipper who wishes to forward his goods. The C. P. R. refuse to allow any of their cars to go into the United States from the Eastern Provinces further than the western and southern boundary of the State of Maine, claiming that 5,000 cars are needed for grain shipments from the West during the coming fall; then the United States Government, who are handling the railways in the United States, have not forwarded the usual number of empty cars from their country into Canada. Just when this car situation will clear itself cannot be told and until it does shipments of lumber to United States points must be very limited.

The base for spruce at Boston is now $55.00, and many claim it will reach $60.00 per M. Stocks are very scare both in Maine, Vermont, New Hampshire and the Eastern Provinces and many mills in eastern Maine are now about sawed out, having only cut a limited quantity of logs during the past winter. To be very frank there is a scarcity of lumber which is being felt all over the continent and prices and conditions on the west coast of Canada are very similar to those on the East, B. C. fir being almost impossible to buy for shipment to the east; in some cases an advance of $5.00 per car has taken place during the past four weeks. In fact to-day all prices on B. C. fir are withdrawn as no stocks can be found.

All mills at St. John are running and are well sold up, in some cases oversold, and buyers are coming every day looking for stocks and finding none; laths are oversold and to-day the ordinary 1-3/8 in. lath are selling at $4.00 f.o.b. St. John. Shingles are very scrace and cannot be found at any price as manufacturers are oversold. Short stocks, such as stavesheading and shooks are very firm and orders plentiful.

Ottawa Reports Continuous Improvement

Continued improvement, as to tone, price and conditions, was shown in the Ottawa lumber market during the closing period of July Summarized for the whole month, the business so lumbermen reported was the best that had been witnessed since the boom years before the war.

Prices remained absolutely firm. In some instances they advanced though not in all the grades. Rail transportation tightened up a little, though there were plenty of cars available to carry shipments consigned to U. S. Points.

The cut of the Ottawa valley with the sawmills this year will fall away below normal, but from the woods end, it is an understood fact, that the operators are going to rush unto the woods during the coming season every man they can get, in an attempt to turn out the biggest log output since 1914.

Stocks on the Ottawa market during the last two weeks of July which period is recognized as being a dull one, were not exactly low as things go, but the market on the other hand was a long way from being overstocked—especially in dry lumber.

The export demand to the United States continued good and showed improvement over the preceeding two weeks. The middle grades and mill run were chiefly in demand. Indications pointed at Ottawa from the demand for this quality of lumber that building operations were about to commence on a big scale across the border.

Inquiries showed improvement and increased in range and in the quality of stock desired. The European export situation showed little or no change. The general impression was that the freeing of cargo space was an indefinite matter which rested entirely with the British Ministry of Shipping. Lumber on Government account continued satisfactory, for transportation to Europe.

Hopes were held out on one hand that with the British Ministery holding up approximately seventy per cent. of the available shipping space for the transhipment of merchandise on Government account that there might be a break in the rules before long. Others were sceptical pointing out that even if the Government did relax on the shipping space as at present requisitioned, that the movement of the western grain crop together with bacon and other food stuffs would use up what margin of space might be released.

Some lumbermen and exporters in the Ottawa Valley, so the "Canada Lumberman" understands, are even now looking ahead as far as the spring months of next year for the real opening up of the European export trade. Shipments of lumber or even deck cargoes they point out are not feasible during the winter period.

Lath remained strong and shingles firm. In some instances there was a scarcity reported in the latter.

The labor situation with both the sawmills and the woodworking plants showed no change. Some of the operating companies began making preparations for the sending of the men to their woods-camps. The outlook for the securing of labor this year while better on the main than last seemed early in the season to indicate that there was still a considerable shortage.

Building activity during the month of July did not show any great change with the exception of the letting of the half million dollar contract to Bate-McMahon Company for the new Loew theatre. For the first half of the year building permits at the city hall in comparison with the July-December period last fall more than doubled increasing by $655,366. During the last six months of 1918 the amount was $404,771, and from January to July this year $1,660,137.

With the woodworking factories conditions remained about same most of the plants having enough to keep them going. exceptional increase in business was reported. The furniture plants reported good business with prices keeping up.

Situation Getting Much Better in Montreal

The improvement in the Montreal market referred to in our last report has continued, and conditions are now better than at any time this seaon. Buying for American account is the great factor in the revival, and in this respect the market has undergone a wonderful change. Wholesalers report that the buying orders from the Eastern States are on a very large scale, due to the extensive building there. Heavy inquiries and orders come in by every mail. Naturally prices have taken a jump, with the outlook for still higher quotations. Lath is being bought freely, prices touching record. Some firms who were loaded up with lath and who at one time would have gladly sold at a loss have cleared out all their stock at very good prices, and are unable to supply the demand.

B. C. stock continues to advance. The mills are now working to capacity, and have turned down orders from the East. Against this, the prices of certain lines have increased to such an extent that Eastern customers decline to purchase.

The local demand for lumber is better Montreal buyers have done very little for months, but they will now have to pay the enhanced values which are ruling, due to the more general activity in the lumber market. Building is undoubtedly picking up, and contractors express the opinion that work will steadily increase and that the fall will see a rush. The number of contracts let is on the upward plane, while supply dealers state that the number of inquiries is large. These do not always lead to business. There is, however, a tendency to recognize the fact that costs are likely to go higher—lumber certainly will not be cheaper. The Montreal Housing Commission has run into two or three snags, and very little progress has been made with the scheme for industrial dwellings. The Provincial Government has suggested that a tax of 2¼ per cent. be levied on the loan of $5,000,000, for the purpose of paying the expenses of a provincial technical committee. The commission has declined to agree to this proposal.

Lumber is being sent by the British Timber Buyer's office to

Woods Manufacturing Co., Limited - Ottawa

Will give you prompt shipment and best prices on van supplies, of everything your men require from head to foot, consisting of **Mackinaw Clothing**, Underwear, Wool Socks and Mitts, Caps and Moccasins.

Toronto
Welland

Montreal
Winnipeg

A Double Sure Grip

Bond Patent "Spiro" Compression Coupling

The Bond Patent Spiro Compression Coupling has 50% more gripping power than any other Compression Coupling on the market. Use it in installing new shafting or extending your present line. The price is reasonable. It will save you money. No keys or keyseating are necessary. Why not order now?

ASK FOR CATALOGUE W-C.W.
WHEN WRITING

B
D-S
BOND Double-Sure Quality

Bond Engineering Works, Limited

Sole Makers,
BOND DOUBLE-SURE POWER TRANSMISSION MACHINERY

Harbour Industrial District
TORONTO, CANADA

JOHNSON'S
Veterinary Remedies

are the surest, the most economical and the best medicines with which to equip your stables. They have been on the market for twenty-five years and still retain their superiority over all others.

The quality never varies, it is our first consideration.
Prices in effect at the present time are as follows:

Johnson's Horse Liniment No. 1	Per Gal.	$7.00
Johnson's Horse Liniment No. 1	Quarts, Per Doz.	19.00
Johnson's Horse Liniment No. 1	Pints, Per Doz.	10.00
Johnson's Horse Colic Remedy	Per Gal.	10.00
Johnson's Horse Colic Remedy	Quarts (8 Doses each) Doz.	30.00
Johnson's Horse Colic Remedy	Pints (4 Doses each) Doz.	15.00
Johnson's Veterinary Healing Ointment (Gall Cure)		
2 lb. Tins	each 2.25 Doz.	24.00
¼ lb. Tins	Per Doz.	4.00
Johnson's Concentrated Condition Powders, 1 lb. Pkgs.	Doz.	6.00
Johnson's Condition Powder, No. 2	doz.	3.75
Johnson's Horse Worm Powders	Pkgs., Per Doz.	4.00
Johnson's Purging Balls	Per Doz.	2.80
Johnson's Antiseptic Dusting Powder (For Drying and Healing Sores, Proud Flesh, etc.)	Per Doz.	5.00
"Kreoline," antiseptic, deodorizing	Gal. Tin	1.50

Our Family and Van Remedies are as follows:—

Pine and Tar Cough Syrup	Big 4 Liniment—Mosquito Oil
Purgative Pills	X Ray Liniment
Little Liver Pills	Cholerine Mixture (Diarrhoea)
Porous Plasters	Headache Powders
Stomach Bitters	Sarsaparilla
Laxative Cold Tablets	All Healing White Ointment

All Drugs and Patent Medicines at Market Prices.
Mail orders solicited — Prompt shipments made.

A. H. JOHNSON WHOLESALE DRUGGIST
Collingwood, Ontario

the United Kingdom at a great rate, the goods being shipped from all the principal ports of the St. Lawrence, by liners and tramps. If the present rate continues, the greater part of the lumber by liner space will have vanished by the end of August. The exporters are very busy —a contrast to the experience of last year. The decline in sterling exchange is a serious matter for those who have received Government orders, and for those who are sending goods on private account. The basis of the Government business was sterling, and the unexpected drop involves a considerable decrease in the amounts receivable. This, with the high freights, has restricted shipments by private exporters.

Lumber Conditions in the West

C. S. Battle of the C. S. Battle Timber Co., Vancouver, sends the following highly interesting letter to the "Canada Lumberman" on Pacific Coast conditions, production, prices and outlook:

Heretofore I have written in rather a constrained and conservative manner, but at present I feel more optimistic regarding the general lumber situation.

Export lumber.—The demand for export number is increasing, bottoms are getting more plentiful and rates are gradually declining, but are still too high to bring the best results.

Northwest trade.—Owing to the short crop in the Northwest millmen do not look for a large business until another crop is made.

United States trade.—The demand for lumber from the other side is more than sufficient to take care of the lumber produced in this section and all mills have plenty of orders.

Local trade.—The local demand for lumber is about double what it was one year ago. Houses are being built and added to. In fact, the country is underbuilt and it looks as if there would be a good demand for lumber for the next three to five years.

Price of Lumber.—The wholesale price f.o.b. the mills on lumber ranges from $22 to $54 per M.

Price on Shingles.—The wholesale price f.o.b. the mills on shingles ranges as follows:

Three X	$4.70 to $4.80
Five X	$5.30 to $5.40
Eureka	6.10 to 6.20
Perfection	6.75 to 6.80

Standing Timber.—The price of standing timber has remained almost stationery for the last five years except for small tracts handy to log, but we are on the eve of a bull market. There is a large deal on to the South of us which, if consummated, will be the biggest deal ever pulled off in timber on the Pacific Coast, and will start the ball to roll.

Price of Logs.—Fir logs are worth $12, $16 and $21 per M delivered at the mill. Cedar logs are worth from $18 to $31 per M. delivered at the mill, depending on the quality. The above prices are checked up on to-day's market and are dependable.

The yellow pine situation in the south, judging from Government reports, is almost alarming. During the next five years 86 per cent. of the standing yellow pine will have been cut. The market for Pacific Coast lumber is broadening all the time. Watch the price of standing timber for 1920.

As stated above while this report may look optimistic it does not hardly represent the true facts, and if this information is of any value use it as you see fit.

No Excuse for Inflating Prices

"Timber," in a recent issue, says: Sir James Ball, who lately returned to England from a trip to Canada, said in an interview that he felt constrained in the interests of fair play, to speak his mind plainly on the subject of excessive price charging for yellow pine by a section of the trade. To the credit of the great bulk of the timber industry, said he, there has been a loyal adherence to the maximum values laid down by the Control, and which, up to the end of March, were not exceeded, but, he added smilingly, human nature is the same everywhere, and the temptation to make a bit is no doubt strong. "I leave the Controllership at the end of the present month, and return to my pre-war avocation, but before I go I should like to impress upon all concerned the necessity, in their interests, of observing the prices laid down for their guidance. Before these prices were fixed there was quite enough made in the shape of abnormal profits, and the Control came not a day too soon. I may say," added Sir James, with emphasis, "that if heed be not taken of my warning—the last which I shall probably give—the government will take steps to restore the balance in a way that will be an unpleasant surprise to the profiteers. There is really no excuse for sellers inflating their prices for yellow pine, and its shortage at the present time ought to deter any tendency to do so. We have provided for a liberal profit to the vendor and, compared with the pre-war conditions of trading, the margin is a handsome one. I want to impress upon one and all," he continued, "that it is a most misguided policy to seek for big profits under present conditions." Sir James said the Control would continue after his departure. Its continuity was absolutely necessary until such time as the purchases made recently were disposed of. The object of making these purchases was a measure of protection against the anticipated high values which would doubtless be quoted by Continental exporters. It was the case that the Government had initiated the policy of handing over all goods to the trade, and the Government was quite willing to adhere to its policy, but it must provide a safeguard for the least as well as the greatest, and he felt that this had been done. Our purchases, said he, will be brought to England, and buyers from us will be in a position to undersell outsiders.

As to his successor, Sir James was not in a position to discuss this phase of the Control. Take it from me, he added, the Government is not going to let its helpful sympathy with the trade diminish, and if I were to continue as Controller I would make very short work of the profiteer. As regarded the more recent phases of restricted trading, he mentioned the purchase of some sleepers, which did not affect the general question.

Touching upon industrial conditions, Sir James gave it as his opinion that the undue stiffening of prices in the timber trade tended to create labor unrest and reacted upon the community as a whole. People felt uncertain of their position in matters of supply and demand, with the result that business languished and all suffered. The timber trade was a great industry, and was capable of yielding abundant profits based upon fair and equitable lines. It remained for its followers to rise to the occasion and be satisfied with legitimate results.

Sir James said he visited Montreal, Quebec, Toronto, Ottawa, and other centres, and bought largely. He met many members of the trade, and discussed with them the present and future of the woodgoods industry, and in that way was enabled to clear up many points which were previously obscure. He had made arrangements to ship his purchases rapidly, and when these arrived they would be sold to consumers at the lowest possible profits, and it would be seen that the prices were reduced to the extreme limits. He had bought some 23,000 standards of good quality, well-seasoned yellow pine and the great point was to get the stuff into circulation. It was not the intention to raft the goods; shipping facilities would be availed of. These purchases were all made since the signing of the Armistice, and the sleepers which he had referred to would be disposed of to the railways.

Indulging in a brief retrospect on Timber Control, Sir James said he was now leaving, after two years' association with the trade, and he believed he was right in believing that throughout his relations with the greatest and the least had been cordial. Since he took up office at Whitsuntide, 1917, in succession to Sir Bampfylde Fuller, K.C.S.I., K.C.I.E., he had tried to do his best for one and all, and he wished it to go forth that he had experienced from big and little in the indutsry the maximum of loyalty and whole-hearted co-operation. He desired to associate with that expression of approval his sense of the unfailing and untiring exertions of the Trade Press, which was always ready to help and never slow to point out where the Control could be improved, and the conditions of commerce bettered. They owed much to the timber newspaper Press, which although now and then severe in its criticism, was a healthy tonic to the trade.

An interesting conversation ensued on the merits of Douglas fir as a substitute for yellow pine, in the course of which reference was made by Sir James to the use and utility of Douglas fir. There was no reason why the latter should not be extensively used at home as well as abroad. In point of fact, there was more Douglas fir brought home now than ever, and one had only to view the fine spar in Kew Gardens to realize the magnificent proportions of the wood. There were enormous possibilities in the future for Douglas fir.

Small Percentage of Sawdust

A recent edition of a weekly publication of Price Bros. & Co., Quebec, says: The percentage of sawdust in cutting logs is one-half of one per cent. The usual percentage in other mills is one per cent. The sawdust percentage of our chips is 1.98, whereas in most mills it runs from 2.5 to 3 per cent. Considerable satisfaction is felt in this showing.

Will Add to Provincial Revenue

With lumber at its present prices, and no sign of a downward tendency, the provincial government, according to a recent despatch from St. John, N. B., has decided that it might as well have a share in the extra profits. Stumpage rates on Crown lands always have been lower than the rates charged by private owners and recently the discrepancy has become more marked. An order-in-council has put into effect a new rate of $3.50 per thousand for spruce instead of $2.30, with other rates in proportion. It is estimated that this will add $150,000 to the provincial revenue, while leaving the rates lower than those charged on private timber lands.

Shipbuilding Active in Nova Scotia

The Supply of Tonnage is Inadequate to Meet the Demand for Carriers—Rates Still High on Lumber

By E. Woodworth, Parrsboro, N. S.

The revival of wooden ship-building in Nova Scotia was largely caused and promoted by the great war, but the boom did not cease when the armistice was signed and it is not likely to terminate now the peace terms are accepted. Of course, many vessels were in course of construction when the fighting ceased and they obviously had to be completed, but many new keels have been laid since that time and probably many more vessels will be built before the shipyards become idle.

It is true that, with the prospect of immediate peace, many builders hesitated about making further investments. Wages and the cost of materials remained as high as ever, while on the other hand they anticipated a speedy reduction in freight rates and a corresponding falling off in the demand for vessels. At first freights showed a slight tendency downward and some ship owners were afraid the bottom was falling out, but at no time did prices show any inclination to revert to pre-war levels. Early this year a new schooner was chartered at Parrsboro, N. S., to load three cargoes of deals for Great Britain at three hundred shillings per standard. This was considered a big drop, for freights had soared to four hundred shillings last year, but it did nothing in the way of fixing rates, for freights soon climbed to three hundred and fifty shillings, or at least ten times what the rate was five years ago.

The fact is that the supply of tonnage is totally inadequate to meet the demand for carriers. The stock of lumber on hand is exceptionally large and prices are extremely high, but very few bottoms are to be had. The Imperial Govrenment has purchased many million feet of deals in Nova Scotia and New Brunswick, but practically all their immense holdings await transportation. Freights to South America and to the West Indies are as high as they are to cross the Atlantic, and more vessels seem to be needed everywhere. Shipbuilding costs far too much at present, and there is always the possibility of a big slump in values, but, while present demand for tonnage continues, men will continue to build ships.

The number and tonnage of the vessels registered within a definite period at any port of registry furnish the best possible means of determining the extent of the shipbuilding boom in that vicinity. Judged by this rule Parrsboro, N. S., is one of the ports that can boast a new record. The number of vessels entered on the registry books of the port of Parrsboro during the first half of the current year was thirteen. These were all tern schooners and averaged more than four hundred net tons each. Several of them have changed owners since being registered, and one has been sold to foreigners and has been taken off the registry books. At least seven more vessels will be added to the Parrsboro books before the year ends. One or two of these will be four-masters, and one will be a steamer of about 500 tons. In most of the yards where these vessels were built others will be commenced immediately, and it is said that the steamer will be replaced by another of more than double her tonnage.

In the southern part of Nova Scotia it is probable that there are several ports of registry that will exceed Parrsboro's record with regard to the number of entries, but the vessels built there are chiefly of a different class and will average little more than one hundred tons each. They are built for fishing, and are first-class of their kind, but, of course, do not require to be large. New vessels have to be built every year to replace losses and to meet the growth of the business, but more were required this season than ever to make up for the depredations of the U-boats. Some fine tern schooners are also built along the southern and south-western coasts, but their number is small in comparison with the fishing craft. In other ports of the province the ships built are chiefly tern schooners with an occasional four-master, and the tendency seems to be to increase their size without greatly diminishing their numbers.

How Eastern Lumber Firm Gives Service

Two pictures rise up. In one there is a big pile of lumber scatterer about an open field. There seems no special order or regularity in the way the lumber is piled. Snow and ice is in evidence everywhere and it would seem difficult to get a load of that lumber without having to cut away the ice which clings to each stick of lumber, each board and each portion of that big lumber pile. Some of the boards are warped and twisted from exposure to the sun and rain. Some of the timber looks soaked with water, while evidences of approaching decay are apparent says, "The Busy East."

But look again and see an entirely different picture. This time we see great piles of lumber, but under conditions altogether different. A huge warehouse contains the lumber which is piled in orderly bays or sections. There is no snow or ice on the neatly piled boards, which are clean and dry. All kinds of lumber, both rough and finished, wide and narrow, hard and soft, planed and unplaned, are there. Every kind of lumber is in a special place and can be easily located. Boards of the same width and quality are piled together. Driveways run through the big shed and teams can be loaded under cover no matter what kind of weather is prevailing outside.

The first picture gives the old-fashioned way of conducting a lumber yard. The second picture shows the modern method as inaugurated and carried out by the Dartmouth Lumber Company, of Dartmouth, N. S. There can be no possible doubt in any one's mind which is the better way. Ask the man who is building and see what he says.

In former years Dartmouth was a sort of appendage to Halifax. Some people looked upon the town as a good place in which to sleep. But times change and Dartmouth is fast waking up from the lethargy of the past. One of the real needs of the town for many years has been a "Building Supply House" where one could obtain all the essential materials for the construction of a residence, store or factory. To fill this need, in the early part of the year 1918, The Dartmouth Lumber Company, Limited, was organized, the directorate being composed of Messrs. H. R. Silver, president; Hamilton Lindsay, vice-president and A. A. McDonald. The secretary-treasurer and general manager is Mr. Harold Brownhill, a man of energy and ideas, who is undoubtedly "making good." He has proved it possible to sell as cheaply as the Halifax firms and when the advantage of quicker delivery is considered, "going to Halifax" results in loss instead of gain. The business of the past year has been eminently satisfactory. More and more room has been found necessary to house the varieties of stock which this enterprising firm are constantly adding, and customers have expressed their entire satisfaction with the service given.

This season promises to be especially busy with the Dartmouth Lumber Company, which is making preparation for the eager demand for all sorts of building material. Many houses will be built; much repair work will be done and it looks as though the Dartmouth of next year would be an altogether different Dartmouth from that of recent years.

The company's office is located in a large two storey building, part of which is used to store doors and sashes. A separate shed at the rear contains large quantities of shingles of different grades, designed to meet the requirements of the people.

The big idea in connection with the Dartmouth Lumber Company is the fact that its supplies are kept under cover, fully protected from the elements; always in first class condition; always ready for use. The big sheds covering acres of ground, stand out prominently. The idea seems so fine that one wonders why every lumber dealer does not do likewise. The introduction of up-to-date methods is always appreciated by a discerning public.

Fight Fires With Gasoline

The value of the new engine with which to fight forest fires has been amply demonstrated. It was first tried at the Gibson mine on the south fork of Kaslo creek, B. C., recently when it not only put out a bad forest fire but saved $20,000 worth of mine property. It is stated this would have kept ten men busy for a week had the pump not been available.

The engine and pump can be packed anywhere up a mountain by a couple of men and has a great force. The pump and gasoline engine only weigh 120 lbs, but develop 45 h.p. The stream from the inch and a quarter hose has a nozzle velocity of 120 lbs, per square inch—sufficient to knock a man down at 100 feet distance.

Through the efficacy of this pump another forest fire, on Pass creek, which has spread over 2,000 acres was greatly got under control and saved several ranches.

Protecting the Trade by Stable Prices

yellow pine lumber will be after that date, but it shall be our policy to endeavor to protect our trade by stable prices on yellow pine lumber for successive periods of thirty days, if humanly possible. It being the policy of our company to render prompt service, it shall not be our thought to take orders that we cannot reasonably expect to ship within thirty days after acceptance.

Handle it Mechanically

with

JEFFREY CONVEYERS

The Standard Equipment for Handling Mill Refuse, Logs, Lumber, Etc.

"V" SHAPED TROUGH for large capacities of Refuse, Blocks, Etc. An all-steel trough with re-enforcing angles on the top edges may be used in place of the wood trough with steel lining illustrated above.

JEFFREY GAPPED SHEAVE WHEELS with Solid Rim and Single Flexible Teeth. Also furnished in Adjustable Rim—Double Flexible Teeth.

Jeffrey Wire Cable Conveyers

are especially adapted to economical handling of large capacities and to long distance handling of Sawdust and Mill Refuse.

Long Link Coil Chain with U-Bolts and Cross Bars carrying Slabs from Mill to Fire Pot.

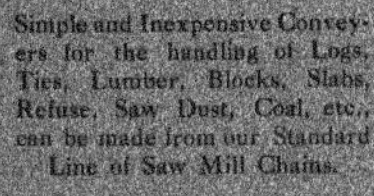

Simple and Inexpensive Conveyers for the handling of Logs, Ties, Lumber, Blocks, Slabs, Refuse, Saw Dust, Coal, etc., can be made from our Standard Line of Saw Mill Chains.

LET US FIGURE ON YOUR CONVEYING REQUIREMENTS

The Jeffrey Mfg. Co.

Canadian Branch and Warerooms

MONTREAL

Long Link Coil Chain with S-1½ Log Spur—handling Logs to Mill.

K-1 Attachment

Lumber Carrier between Mill and Yard Storage consisting of two strands of Jeffrey Plain Chain.

S-1½ Log Spur

Ontario

struction of a pulp mill.

capital stock of $15,000 has been granted a charter.

a serious one.

ated
$100,000.

Midland Woodworkers, Limited, Midland, Ont., have been granted a provincial charter to carry on business in Ontario, the capital used not to exceed the sum of $366,000.

Chase Tractors Corporation, Limited, Toronto, Ont., have been incorporated to manufacture and deal in lumber and to carry on the business of woodworkers; capital $2,000,000.

The Goderich Mercantile Co., Limited, Goderich, Ont., were recently incorporated to manufacture and deal in baby-carriages, go-carts, toys and furniture of all kinds. Capital $40,000.

York Steamship Co., Limited, Toronto, have been incorporated to build, construct or otherwise deal in steamships and vessels of any classes. Minimum capital to be used not less than $5,000.

The Fergus Housing Company, Limited, Fergus, Ont., have been incorporated for the purpose of carrying on the business of builders, contractors, merchants, manufacturers and general agents. Capital $40,000.

The Riordon Annex Housing Company, Limited, Hawkesbury, Ont., have been incorporated for the purpose of carrying on the business of builders, contractors, merchants, manufacturers and general agents; capital $50,000.

Beattie Bros., Fergus, Ont., are adding two new wings to their factory; one to be 144 x 96 and the other 192 x 96, saw tooth construction. They are also erecting a dry kiln 120 x 96. Considerable new equipment will be installed.

Canada Petroleum & Refining Corp., Limited, Toronto, have recently been incorporated. One of the powers conferred on this company is to acquire and purchase, lease, or otherwise, timber limits or timber licenses. Capital $2,500,000.

Mr. Rittenhouse, of the Financial Advertising Co., Toronto Stock Exchange Building, Toronto, is representative for a company who are calling for tenders for the erection of a 150 ton pulp and paper mill and power plant equipped to develop 5000 horsepower.

D. G. Steinman, who was a partner in the B. & N. Planing Mill Co., Milverton, Ont., died recently. He had retired, apparently in the best of health, and during the night passed away suddenly. Mr. Steinman was one of the most highly esteemed citizens of Milverton.

Canadian Aero Co., Limited, Brantford, Ont., have been incorporated to manufacture and deal in aeroplanes and other forms of aircraft on a commercial scale and to carry passenger mails, express, for hire between points and places within or without the Dominion. Capital $50,000.

The will of the late William J. Smith, lumber merchant, of Weston, was filed for probate recently. The estate amounts to $36,115.89, the bu'k of which is held in promissory notes and book debts. The will apportions the estate between the four sons and two daughters of the testator.

Harry J. Strong, Limited, Toronto, has been incorporated to engage in the lumber business in all its branches, acquire timber limits and licenses and to erect lumber mills, saw mills or other woodworking plants for the manufacturing of lumber and wood in any form. Capital $30,000.

John B. Smith & Sons, Toronto, have bought 144 sq. miles of timber limits from the Ontario government. The holdings are in McNish, Charlton, McCallum and Sturgeon townships. The timber is principally white and Norway pine and the company intend to start logging operations this fall.

Eastern Shipping Co., Limited, Toronto, have been incorporated to build or otherwise deal deal in steamships and other vessels of any class. The capital stock to be divided into 1000 shares of no nominal or par value, provided the company must carry on business with a capital of not less than $5,000.

Premier Paper Products, Limited, Sarnia, have been incorporated to manufacture and deal in paper made from any material including manufacturers of pulp, straw board and other similar products. Also to manufacture and deal in lumber, boxes, barrels, and all other articles manufactured from wood. Capital $50,000.

The McGibbon Lumber Co., Penetanguishene, Ont., which was recently incorporated with a capital stock of $100,000 full paid up, has elected the following officers: President, Archie McGibbon; vice-president, Norman McGibbon; and secretary-treasurer, Finlay McGibbon; directors, Archie, Norman, Finlay, John and D. D.

Work has been resumed in the plant of the Beaver Board Co. at Thorold after a strike of four weeks. The working period has been divided into three shifts of eight hours each, with a working agreement for six months. The men have been invited to form a shop committee which will meet the officers of the company to discuss conditions and grievances.

Forest fires southwest of Fort William have done great damage to timber limits and property. Archie Bishop lost his whole saw mill plant and the fires badly encroached on his timber limits. Mr. Bishop, his wife and family were driven from their home by the flames and had to spend the night in a rowboat in the middle of North Lake. Mr. Bishop's many friends will sympathize with him in his loss.

In the serious fires which recently prevailed in Northern Ontario the store of Pellow & McMeekin, lumbermen, of Hearst, Ont., was completely destroyed. Luckily all the other buildings of the firm escaped. Pellow & McMeekin report that there is not a very active demand for lumber in their district at the present time and that the outside market is also quiet. Conditions, however, may pick up considerably in the near future.

The plant of the Ontario Paper Co., Thorold, Ont., was recently threatened with destruction. A fire broke out in the large paper machine room and gained considerable headway. Assistance was brought from Merritton, St. Catharines and Niagara Falls, N. Y., and after a stubborn fight the firemen succeeded in bringing the flames under control. Considerable damage was done to the roof and to a large stock of felts and paper stored in that building.

Provincial Police Inspector Storey reports he has captured one of the two men who entered the office of Schroeder Mills & Timber Company at Pakesley, Ont., several weeks ago, and after holding up the clerk with a revolver, decamped with over $3,000 in cash. The police report that in all they have recovered over $5,000, including $3,000 in cash, Victory Bonds and a considerable quantity of stamps. The clerk at the lumber office shot one of the robbers in the arm, but the other made the clerk surrender everything.

Eastern Canada

The partnership known as the Northern Lumber Co., Montreal, has recently been dissolved.

The sawmill of the Leclaire Shipbuilding Company at St. Joseph de Sorel, P. Q., has been destroyed by fire.

John & C. R. Ross, who have been operating a saw mill at Baxter's Harbor, N. S., have dissolved partnership.

Three River Ship Yards Co., are constructing a new machine shop. This building is of frame and brick construction.

A contract has been awarded for the erection of a saw mill for Geo. C. Goodfellow, 511 St. Catharine St. W., Montreal.

Omer Lamothe, St. Louis De Champlain, Que., whose sawmill was completely destroyed by fire intends to erect a new building.

D. Sweeney, Yarmouth, N. S., is building a 150 ton schooner and McLean & McKay, Central Economy, N. S., have commenced work on a wooden ship.

Fire destroyed the plant and planing mill of the Tobique Lumber Co., Limited, Eel River Crossing, N. B. The loss was fully covered by insurance.

Fire visited the Richards Mfg. Co., Limited, Whites Brook, N. B., completely wiping out the plant and planing mill. The loss is fully covered by insurance.

Clovis Naud, La Chevrotiere, Terrebonne Co., Que., contemplates the erection of a sawmill and is in the market for sawmill machinery, including planer, matcher and steam power plant.

Hugh Doheny & Co., Limited, Montreal, P. Q., have been incorporated to acquire timber limits and to carry on the business of lumbermen, paper makers and woodworkers. Capital $2,000,000.

Wonham, Bates & Goode, Inc., 145 St. James Street, Montreal, P. Q., have sold at 15 ton eight-wheel Orton & Steinbrenner locomotive crane, with electric magnet 40 in., to the Canadian Rolling Mills, Montreal, for quick delivery.

Chas. H. Russell Co., Limited, Montreal, was recently incorporated to manufacture and deal in lumber, timber, and wood products of all kinds and to purchase or otherwise acquire timber lands and licenses; capital stock $50,000.

Albert Vickers died recently at Eastbourne, England. Mr. Vickers was chairman of Vickers, Limited, who are one of Britain's largest manufacturers of steel products and aeroplanes. The Vickers, Limited, have also a large plant in Montreal.

Pure Cane Molasses Co. of Canada, Limited, Montreal, P. Q., were recently incorporated with power to manufacture and deal in barrels, boxes and packages and to acquire saw mills, planing mills, cooperages and box factories. Capital $250.000.

The St. Omer Lumber, Limited, Quebec, was recently incorporated to manufacture and deal in lumber, pulpwood and wood products and to acquire and hold timber limits and timber leases; capital $70,000. Alfred P. Boisseau, lumber merchant, is one of the incorporators.

The American Import, Limited, was recently incorporated with head office at Montreal. Among the powers granted under this charter are to purchase or lease timber limits or licenses and to manufacture and deal in lumber, pulpwood or any article made of wood; capital $20,000.

Carrying out its policy of providing good housing accommodation for its employees, the Laurentide Co., Ltd., is building three houses, of eight rooms each, at the logging headquarters at La Tuque. One is for Mr. B. Baxter, the assistant superintendent of La Tuque, and the other two for members of his staff.

W. H. Miller & Sons, Tomifobia, Que., who recently formed a partnership to engage in the lumber and pulpwood busines, report that not as much wood is being peeled in their district as last year and that the price, f.o.b. cars, is $14 for spruce. The firm expect to handle 5,000 cords of spruce this season and 1,000 cords of poplar, all peeled.

A charter has been awarded to Beauchemin & Rivet with a capital stock of $49,000 and headquarters at Amos, Que., to own and operate saw mills, shingle mills and lath mills, etc., and generally to conduct the business of lumber merchants and manufacturers. The incorporators are Joseph A. Beauchemin, Pierre E. Beauchemin, Alex Rivet and Dr. Joseph A. Bigue, all of Amos.

A charter has been granted to the La Reine Lumber Co., Limited, with headquarters in Quebec and a capital stock of $49,000. The incorporators are Roch Julien and Alex Faguy, of Quebec City, and W. Laliberte, P. Laliberte and A. Laliberte, of Saint-Remi, Portneuf county. The company is empowered to take over the business now operated by Wilfrid Laliberte and Frere and carry on the same and to manufacture, buy, sell and deal in timber and lumber and to equip and operate mills for the manufacture of pulp, etc.

Makers of

BABBITT

SOLDER

PHOSPHOR-TIN

PHOSPHOR-COPPER

Dealers in

TIN

LEAD

COPPER

SPELTER

ANTIMONY

ALUMINUM

Syracuse Smelting Works

Diamond St. and Meserole Ave.
BROOKLYN, N.Y.

Does This Name of McClary's Mean Anything to You When Purchasing Your Requirements ?

The character of McClary's" from 1847 to 1919 demonstrates a powerful determined attitude of rigid faithfulness to a dominating standard of quality. Never failing to maintain that high standard of quality McClary's name stands to-day where it stood in 1847; in the forefront of Range manufacturers. This vigorous, robust organization concentrates into every article manufactured the value of its seventy-two years' experience, thus

McClary's Algoma Range

has absorbed into its manufacture not only high grade materials but also the valuable experiences gained from the manufacture of thousands of similar articles.

For the Camp, Boarding House, Hotel, or other large establishments where a big sure service is constantly required, the extensive cooking and baking abilities of the Algoma will be warmly appreciated. When stripped for action this Range astonishes the discriminating Cook by the amount of work it will accomplish without strain. The Algoma is made with a heavy Steel body and a strong, rigid cast-iron top. There are three different sizes of Oven with adjustable top to suit. A complete detail of its massive construction will be furnished on request to our nearest Branch.

McClary's

LONDON, TORONTO, MONTREAL, WINNIPEG, VANCOUVER, ST. JOHN, N.B., HAMILTON, CALGARY, SASKATOON, EDMONTON

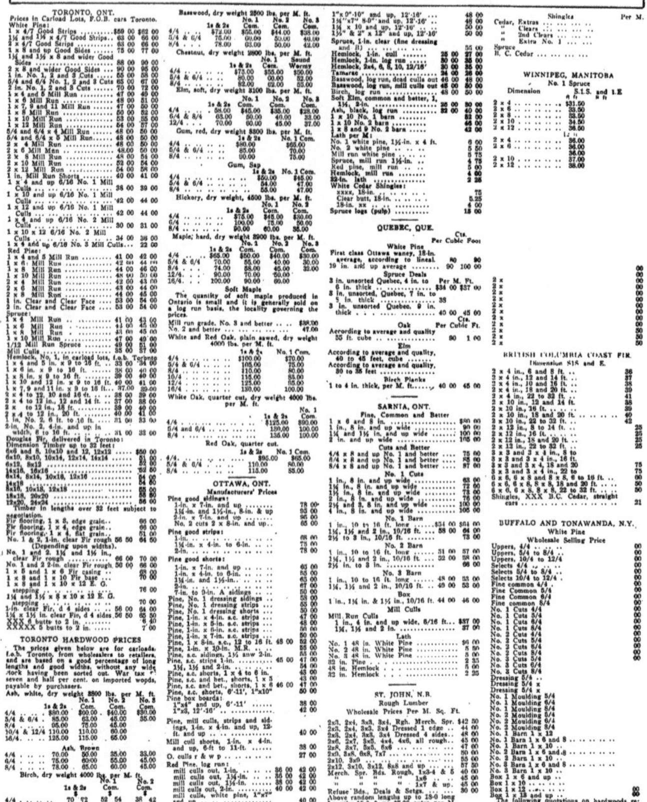

CURRENT LUMBER PRICES—WHOLESALE

TORONTO, ONT.

Prices in Carload Lots, F.O.B. cars Toronto.

White Pine:

1 x 4/7 Good Strips	$59 00	$62 00
1¼ and 1½ x 4/7 Good Strips	63 00	66 00
2 x 4/7 Good Strips	63 00	66 00
1 x 8 and up Good Sides	75 00	77 00
1¼ and 1½ x 8 and wider Good Sides	88 00	90 00
2 x 8 and wider Good Sides	90 00	95 00
1 in. No. 1, 2 and 3 Cuts	55 00	58 00
5/4 and 6/4 No. 1, 2 and 3 Cuts	65 00	67 00
2 in. No. 1, 2 and 3 Cuts	70 00	72 00
1 x 4 and 5 Mill Run	47 00	49 00
1 x 6 Mill Run	48 00	51 00
1 x 7, 9 and 11 Mill Run	47 00	50 00
1 x 8 Mill Run	50 00	52 00
1 x 10 Mill Run	53 00	55 00
1 x 12 Mill Run	54 00	57 00
5/4 and 6/4 x 4 Mill Run	48 00	50 00
5/4 and 6/4 x 5 Mill Run	48 00	50 00
2 x 4 Mill Run	48 00	50 00
2 x 6 Mill Man	48.00	50 00
2 x 8 Mill Run	48 00	54 00
2 x 10 Mill Run	52 00	54 00
2 x 12 Mill Run	54 00	58 00
1 in. Mill Run Shorts	40 00	41 00
1 x 4 and up 6/16 No. 1 Mill Culls	38 00	39 00
1 x 10 and up 6/16 No. 1 Mill Culls	42 00	44 00
1 x 12 and up 6/16 No. 1 Mill Culls	42 00	44 00
1 x 4 and up 6/16 No. 2 Mill Culls	30 00	31 00
1 x 10 x 12 6/16 No. 2 Mill Culls	34 00	36 00
1 x 4 and up 6/16 No. 3 Mill Culls		22 00

Red Pine:

1 x 4 and 5 Mill Run	41 00	42 00
1 x 6 Mill Run	42 00	44 00
1 x 8 Mill Run	44 00	46 00
1 x 10 Mill Run	48 00	50 00
2 x 4 Mill Run	42 00	43 00
2 x 6 Mill Run	43 00	44 00
2 x 8 Mill Run	44 00	45 00
1 in. Clear and Clear Face	53 00	54 00
2 in. Clear and Clear Face	53 00	54 00

Spruce:

1 x 4 Mill Run	41 00	43 00
1 x 6 Mill Run	43 00	45 00
1 x 8 Mill Run	43 00	45 00
1 x 10 Mill Run	47 00	49 00
1/12 Mill Run Spruce	49 00	51 00
Mill Culls	35 00	37 00

Hemlock, No. 1, in carload lots, f.o.b. Toronto

1 x 4 and 5 in. x 9 to 16 ft.	33 00	34 00
1 x 6 in. x 9 to 16 ft.	38 00	40 00
1 x 8 in. x 9 to 16 ft.	39 00	40 00
1 x 10 and 12 in. x 9 to 16 ft.	40 00	41 00
1 x 7, 9 and 11 in. x 9 to 16 ft.	37.00	39.00
2 x 4 to 12, 10 and 16 ft.	38 00	39 00
2 x 4 to 12 in., 12 and 14 ft.	37 00	38 00
2 x to 12 in., 18 ft.	39 00	40 00
2 x 4 to 12 in., 20 ft.	40 00	41 00
1 in. No. 2, 6 ft. to 16 ft.	31 00	33 00
2-in. No. 2, 4-in. and up in width, 6 to 16 ft.	31 00	33 00

Douglas Fir, delivered in Toronto:

Dimension Timber up to 32 feet:

6x6 and 8, 10x10 and 12, 12x12	$50 00
6x10, 8x10, 10x14, 12x14, 14x14	51 00
6x12, 8x12	52 00
14x16, 16x16	52 50
6x14, 8x14, 10x16, 12x16	54 00
14x18	54 50
8x16, 10x18, 12x18	55 00
18x18, 20x20	55 50
12x20, 24x24	56 00

Timber in lengths over 32 feet subject to negotiation.

Fir flooring, 1 x 3, edge grain		66 00
Fir flooring, 1 x 4, edge grain		66 00
Fir flooring, 1 x 4, flat grain		51 00
No. 1 & 2, 1-in. clear Fir rough (Depending upon widths).	56 50	64 50
No. 1 and 2. 1¼ and 1½ in., clear Fir rough	66 00	70 00
No. 1 and 2 2-in. clear Fir rough	56 00	66 00
1 x 5 and 1 x 6 Fir casing		68 00
1 x 8 and 1 x 10 Fir base		70 00
1 x 8 and 1 x 10 x 12 E. G. stepping		76 00
1¼ and 1½ x 8 x 10 x 12 E. G. stepping		70 00
1-in. clear Fir, d 4 sides	56 00	64 00
1¼ x 1½ in. clear Fir, d 4 sides	56 50	65 50
XXX 6 butts to 2 in.		6 40
XXXXX 5 butts to 2 in.		7 00

TORONTO HARDWOOD PRICES

The prices given below are for carloads, f.o.b. Toronto, from wholesalers to retailers, and are based on a good percentage of long lengths and good widths, without any wide stock having been sorted out. War tax of seven and half per cent. on imported woods, payable by purchasers.

Ash, white, dry weight 3800 lbs. per M. ft.

	1s & 2s	No. 1 Com.	No. 2 Com.	No. 3 Com.
4/4	$80.00	$60.00	$40.00	$30.00
5/4 & 6/4	85.00	63.00	45.00	35.00
8/4	95.00	75.00	45.00	
10/4 & 12/4	110.00	110.00	60.00	
16/4	125.00	115.00	65.00	

Ash, Brown

4/4	70.00	50.00	35.00	33.00
6/4	75.00	60.00	55.00	45.00
8/4	78.00	65.00	60.00	45.00

Birch, dry weight 4000 lbs. per M. ft.

	1s & 2s $		No. 1 Com. $		No. 2 Com. $	
4/4	70	72	52	54	38	42
5/4 and 6/4	72	74	55	58	45	48
8/4	74	76	56	59	46	49
10/4 and 12/4	85	90	70	75	55	58
16/4	95	100	80	85	55	60

Basswood, dry weight 2500 lbs. per M. ft.

	1s & 2s	No. 1 Com.	No. 2 Com.	No. 3 Com.
4/4	$72.00	$55.00	$44.00	$38.00
5/4 & 6/4	75.00	60.00	50.00	40.00
8/4	78.00	63.00	50.00	42.00

Chestnut, dry weight 2800 lbs. per M. ft.

	1s & 2s	No. 1 Com.	Sound Wormy
4/4	$75.00	$55.00	$50.00
5/4 & 6/4	80.00	60.00	52.00
8/4	82.00	62.00	55.00

Elm, soft, dry weight 3100 lbs. per M. ft.

	1s & 2s	No. 1 Com.	No. 2 Com.	No. 3 Com.
4/4	58.00	$45.00	$35.00	$28.00
6/4 & 8/4	63.00	50.00	40.00	33.00
12/4	70.00	60.00	45.00	37.00

Gum, red, dry weight 3300 lbs. per M. ft.

	1s & 2s	No. 1 Com.
4/4	$80.00	$65.00
5/4 & 6/4	85.00	70.00
8/4	90.00	75.00

Gum, Sap

	1s & 2s	No. 1 Com.
4/4	$50.00	$45.00
5/4 & 6/4	54.00	47.00
8/4	55.00	47.00

Hickory, dry weight, 4500 lbs. per M. ft.

	1s & 2s	No. 1 Com.	No. 2 Com.
4/4	$75.00	$45.00	$30.00
6/4	100.00	75.00	50.00
8/4	90.00	60.00	35.00

Maple, hard, dry weight 3900 lbs. per M. ft.

	1s & 2s	No. 1 Com.	No. 2 Com.	No. 3 Com.
4/4	$65.00	$50.00	$40.00	$30.00
5/4 & 6/4	70.00	55.00	40.00	30.00
8/4	74.00	58.00	45.00	32.00
12/4	90.00	70.00	50.00	
16/4	100.00	90.00	60.00	

Soft Maple

The quanity of soft maple produced in Ontario is small and it is generally sold on a log run basis, the locality governing the prices.

Mill run grade, No. 3 and better	$38.00
No. 2 and better	47.00

White and Red Oak, plain sawed, dry weight 4000 lbs. per M. ft.

	1s & 2s	No. 1 Com.
4/4	$100.00	$70.00
5/4 & 6/4	105.00	75.00
8/4	110.00	80.00
10/4	115.00	85.00
12/4	125.00	95.00
16/4	130.00	100.00

White Oak, quarter cut, dry weight 4000 lbs. per M. ft.

	1s & 2s	No. 1 Com.
4/4	$125.00	$90.00
5/4 and 6/4	130.00	100.00
8/4	135.00	100.00

Red Oak, quarter cut.

	1s & 2s	No. 1 Com.
4/4	$95.00	$65.00
5/4 & 6/4	110.00	80.00
8/4	115.00	85.00

OTTAWA, ONT.

Manufacturers' Prices

Pine good sidings:

1-in. x 7-in. and up		78 00
1¼-in. and 1½-in., 8-in. & up		93 00
2-in. x 7-in. and up		95 00
No. 2 cuts 2 x 8-in. and up		65 00

Pine good strips:

1-in.		68 00
1¼-in. x 4-in. to 6-in.		73 00
2-in.		78 00

Pine good shorts:

1-in. x 7-in. and up		65 00
1-in. x 4-in. to 6-in.		55 00
1¼-in. and 1½-in.		65 00
2-in.		67 00
7-in. to 9-in. A sidings		50 00
Pine, No. 1 dressing sidings		58 00
Pine, No. 1 dressing strips		55 00
Pine, No. 1 dressing shorts		50 00
Pine, 1-in. x 4-in. s.c. strips		47 00
Pine, 1-in. x 5-in. s.c. strips		48 00
Pine, 1-in. x 6-in. s.c. strips		50 00
Pine, 1-in. x 7-in. s.c. strips		50 00
Pine, 1 x 8-in. s.c., 12 to 16 ft.	48 00	52 00
Pine, 1-in. x 10-in. M.R.		55 00
Pine, s.c. sidings, 1½ and 2-in.		55 00
Pine, s.c. strips 1-in.	45 00	47 00
1¼, 1½ and 2-in.		54 00
Pine, s.c. shorts, 1 x 4 to 6 in.		43 00
Pine, s.c. and bet., shorts, 1 x 5		43 00
Pine, s.c. and bet., shorts, 1 x 6	46 00	47 00
Pine, s.c. shorts, 6'-11', 1"x10"		50 00

Pine box boards:

1"x4" and up, 6'-11'		38 00
1"x3, 12'-16'		42 00
Pine, mill culls, strips and sidings, 1-in. x 4-in. and up, 12-ft. and up		40 00
Mill cull shorts, 1-in. x 4-in. and up, 6-ft to 11-ft.		38 00
O. culls r & w p		27 00

Red Pine, log run:

mill culls out, 1-in.	36 00	42 00
mill culls out, 1¼-in.	36 00	42 00
mill culls out, 1½-in.	38 00	42 00
mill culls out, 2-in.	40 00	42 00
mill culls, white pine, 1"x7" and up		40 00

Mill run Spruce:

1"x4" and up, 6'-11'		42 00
1"x4" and up, 12'-16'		42 00
1"x9"-10" and up, 12'-16'		48 00
1¼"x7" 8-9" and up, 12'-16'		48 00
1¼ x 10 and up, 12'-16'		50 00
1½" & 2" x 12" and up, 12'-16'		50 00
Spruce, 1-in. clear (fine dressing and B)		55 00
Hemlock, 1-in. cull	25 00	27 00
Hemlock, 1-in. log run	30 00	35 00
Hemlock, 2x4, 6, 8, 10, 12/16'	30 00	35 00
Tamarac	24 00	26 00
Basswood, log run, dead culls out	46 00	48 00
Basswood, log run, mill culls out	48 00	50 00
Birch, log run	48 00	50 00
Soft Elm, common and better, 1, 1¼, 2-in.	25 00	30 00
Ash, black, log run	32 00	40 00
1 x 10 No. 1 barn		52 00
1 x 10 No. 2 barn		46 00
1 x 8 and 9 No. 2 barn		42 00

Lath per M:

No. 1 white pine, 1½-in. x 4 ft.	6 00
No. 2 white pine	5 50
Mill run white pine	5 75
Spruce, mill run 1½-in.	4 75
Red pine, mill run	5 00
Hemlock, mill run	4 00
32-in. lath	2 25

White Cedar Shingles:

xxxx, 18-in.	75
Clear butt, 18-in.	5.25
18-in. xx	4 00
Spruce logs (pulp)	15 00

QUEBEC, QUE.

White Pine

	Cts. Per Cubic Foot	
First class Ottawa waney, 18-in. average, according to lineal.	80	90
19 in. and up average	90	100 00

Spruce Deals

	Per M. Ft.	
3 in. unsorted Quebec, 4 in. to 6 in. thick	$34 00	$37 00
3 in. unsorted, Quebec, 7 in. to 8 in. thick	38	
3 in. unsorted Quebec. 9 in. thick	40 00	45 00

Oak

	Cts. Per Cubic Ft.	
According to average and quality 55 ft. cube	90	1 00

Elm

According to average and quality, 40 to 45 feet, cube

According to average and quality, 30 to 35 feet

Birch Planks

1 to 4 in. thick, per M. ft.	40 00	45 00

SARNIA, ONT.

Fine, Common and Better

1 x 6 and 8 in.		$80 00
1 in., 8 in. and up wide		90 00
1¼ and 1½ in. and up wide		100 00
2 in. and up wide		105 00

Cuts and Better

4/4 x 8 and up No. 1 and better		75 00
6/4 x 8 and up No. 1 and better		85 00
8/4 x 8 and up No. 1 and better		87 00

No. 1 Cuts

1 in., 8 in. and up wide		63 00
1¼ in., 8 in. and up wide		72 00
1½ in., 8 in. and up wide		73 00
2 in., 8 in. and up wide		76 00
2½ and 3, 8 in. and up wide		100 00
4 in., 8 in. and up wide		105 00

No. 1 Barn

1 in., 10 to 16 ft. long	$54 00	$64 00
1¼, 1½ and 2 in., 10/16 ft.	58 00	64 00
2½ to 3 in., 10/16 ft.		73 00

No. 2 Barn

1 in., 10 to 16 ft. long	51 00	57 00
1¼, 1½ and 2 in., 10/16 ft.	52 00	58 00
2½ in. to 3 in.		66 00

No. 3 Barn

1 in., 10 to 16 ft. long	48 00	53 00
1¼, 1½ and 2 in., 10/16 ft.	49 00	53 00

Box

1 in., 1¼ in. & 1½ in., 10/16 ft.	44 00	46 00

Mill Culls

Mill Run Culls

1 in., 4 in. and up wide, 6/16 ft.	$37 00
1¼, 1½ and 2 in.	37 00

Lath

No. 1 48 in. White Pine	$6 00
No. 2 48 in. White Pine	5 50
No. 3 48 in. White Pine	5 00
32 in. Pine	2 35
48 in. Hemlock	5 00
32 in. Hemlock	2 25

ST. JOHN, N.B.

Rough Lumber

Wholesale Prices Per M. Sq. Ft.

2x3, 2x4, 3x3, 3x4, Rgh. Merch. Spr.	$42 50
2x3, 2x4, 3x3, 3x4 Dressed 1 edge	44 00
2x3, 2x4, 3x3, 3x4 Dressed 4 sides	48 00
2x6, 2x7, 3x5, 4x4, 4x6, all rough	45 00
2x8, 3x7, 5x5, 6x6	47 00
2x9, 3x8, 6x8, 7x7	50 00
2x10, 3x9	55 00
2x12, 3x10, 3x12, 8x8 and up	57 50
Merch. Spr. Bds. Rough, 1x3-4 & 5	40 00
" " " " 1x6	45 00
" " " " 1x7 & up.	45 00
Refuse Bds., Deals & Setgs.	30 00

Above random lengths up to 18-0 long Lengths 19-0 & up $5.00 extra per M.

For planing Merch. and Refuse Bds. add $2.00 per M to above prices.

Laths $4.25 per M pieces.

Shingles	Per M.
Cedar, Extras	
" Clears	
" 2nd Clears	
" Extra No. 1	
Spruce	
B. C. Cedar	

WINNIPEG, MANITOBA

No. 1 Spruce

Dimension	S.1.S. and 1.E 8 ft	8 ft
2 x 4	$31.50	
2 x 6	33.50	
2 x 8	33.50	
2 x 10	34.50	
2 x 12	36.50	
	12 ft	
2 x 4	36.00	
2 x 6	36.00	
	36.00	
2 x 10	37.00	
2 x 12	38.00	

	00
2 x	00
2 x	00
2 x	00
2 x	00
2 x	00
2 x	00
2 x	00
2 x	00
2 x	00
2 x	50
2 x	50
2 x	50

BRITISH COLUMBIA COAST FIR.

Dimension S1S and E.

2 x 4 in., 6 and 8 ft.	36	
2 x 4 in., 12 and 14 ft.	37	
2 x 4 in., 10 and 16 ft.	38	
2 x 4 in., 18 and 20 ft.	39	
2 x 4 in., 22 to 32 ft.	41	
2 x 10 in., 12 and 14 ft.	38	
2 x 10 in., 16 ft.	39	
2 x 10 in., 18 and 20 ft.	40	
2 x 10 in., 22 to 32 ft.	42	
2 x 12 in., 8 to 14 ft.		25
2 x 12 in., 16 ft.		25
2 x 12 in., 18 and 20 ft.		25
2 x 12 in., 22 to 32 ft.		25
3 x 3 and 3 x 4 in., 8 to		
3 x 3 and 3 x 4 in., 16 ft.		
3 x 3 and 3 x 4, 18 and 20		75
3 x 3 and 3 x 4 in., 22 to		75
6 x 6, 6 x 8 and 8 x 8, 6 to 16 ft.		00
6 x 6, 6 x 8, 8 x 8, 18 and 20 ft.		50
6 x 6, 6 x 8, 8 x 8, 22 to 32 ft.		50
Shingles, XXX B.C. Cedar, straight cars		21

BUFFALO AND TONAWANDA, N.Y.

White Pine

Wholesale Selling Price

Uppers, 4/4	00
Uppers, 5/4 to 8/4	00
Uppers, 10/4 to 12/4	00
Selects 4/4	00
Selects 5/4 to 8/4	00
Selects 10/4 to 12/4	00
Fine common 4/4	00
Fine Common 5/4	00
Fine Common 6/4	00
Fine common 8/4	00
No. 1 Cuts 4/4	00
No. 1 Cuts 5/4	00
No. 1 Cuts 6/4	00
No. 1 Cuts 8/4	00
No. 2 Cuts 4/4	00
No. 2 Cuts 5/4	00
No. 2 Cuts 6/4	00
No. 2 Cuts 8/4	00
No. 3 Cuts 5/4	00
No. 3 Cuts 6/4	
No. 3 Cuts 8/4	
Dressing 5/4	
Dressing 5/4 x	
Dressing 5/4 x	
No. 1 Moulding 5/4	
No. 1 Moulding 6/4	
No. 1 Moulding 8/4	
No. 2 Moulding 5/4	
No. 2 Moulding 6/4	
No. 2 Moulding 8/4	
No. 1 Barn 1 x 12	
No. 1 Barn 1 x 6 and 8	
No. 1 Barn 1 x 10	
No. 2 Barn 1 x 6 and 8	
No. 2 Barn 1 x 10	
No. 3 Barn 1 x 6 and 8	
No. 3 Barn 1 x 10	
Box 1 x 6 and up	
Box 1 x 10	
Box 1 x 12	00
Box 1 x 13 and up	00

The following quotations on hardwoods represent the jobber buying price at Buffalo and Tonawanda.

(Continued on page 64

CURRENT LUMBER PRICES—Continued

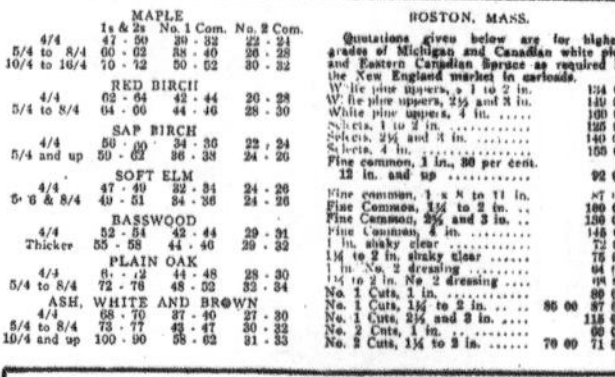

MAPLE	1s & 2s	No. 1 Com.	No. 2 Com.
4/4	47 - 50	30 - 32	22 - 24
5/4 to 8/4	60 - 62	38 - 40	26 - 28
10/4 to 16/4	70 - 72	50 - 52	30 - 32
RED BIRCH			
4/4	62 - 64	42 - 44	26 - 28
5/4 to 8/4	64 - 66	44 - 46	28 - 30
SAP BIRCH			
4/4	56 - 60	34 - 36	22 - 24
5/4 and up	59 - 62	36 - 38	24 - 26
SOFT ELM			
4/4	47 - 49	32 - 34	24 - 26
5/6 & 8/4	49 - 51	34 - 36	24 - 26
BASSWOOD			
4/4	52 - 54	42 - 44	29 - 31
Thicker	55 - 58	44 - 46	29 - 32
PLAIN OAK			
4/4	6[illegible] - [illegible]2	44 - 48	28 - 30
5/4 to 8/4	72 - 76	48 - 52	32 - 34
ASH, WHITE AND BROWN			
4/4	68 - 70	37 - 40	27 - 30
5/4 to 8/4	73 - 77	43 - 47	30 - 32
10/4 and up	100 - 90	58 - 62	31 - 33

BOSTON, MASS.

Quotations given below are for highest grades of Michigan and Canadian white pine and Eastern Canadian Spruce as required in the New England market in carloads.

White pine uppers, 1 to 2 in.		134 00
White pine uppers, 2½ and 3 in.		149 00
White pine uppers, 4 in.		160 00
Selects, 1 to 2 in.		125 00
Selects, 2½ and 3 in.		140 00
Selects, 4 in.		155 00
Fine common, 1 in., 30 per cent. 12 in. and up		92 00
Fine common, 1 x 8 to 11 in.		87 00
Fine Common, 1¼ to 2 in.		100 00
Fine Common, 2½ and 3 in.		130 00
Fine Common, 4 in.		145 00
1 in. shaky clear		72 00
1¼ to 2 in. shaky clear		75 00
1 in. No. 2 dressing		64 00
1¼ to 2 in. No. 2 dressing		68 00
No. 1 Cuts, 1 in.		80 00
No. 1 Cuts, 1¼ to 2 in.	85 00	87 00
No. 1 Cuts, 2½ and 3 in.		115 00
No. 2 Cuts, 1 in.		60 00
No. 2 Cuts, 1¼ to 2 in.	70 00	71 00

Barn [illegible]		69 00
[illegible]		64 00
[illegible]		61 00
[illegible]		64 00
[illegible]		61 00
[illegible]		58 00
[illegible]		00
[illegible]		00
[illegible]		00
Com. spruce, clear, 1 x 4 to 9 in.	46 50	48 50
1 x 10 in.		50 50
No. 1 1 x 4 to 7		53 50
No. 1 1 x 8 & 9		54 50
No. 1 1 x 10 in		55 50
No. 2 1 x 4 & 5		36 50
No. 2 1 x 6 & 7		43 50
No. 2 1 x 8 & 9 in.	43 50	44 50
No. 2 1 x 10 in.		46 50
No. 2 1 x 12 in.		50 50
Spruce, 12 in. dimension		54 00
Spruce, 10 in. dimension		52 00
Spruce, 9 in. dimension		51 00
Spruce, 8 in. dimension		50 00
2 x 10 in. random lengths, 8 ft. and up		50 00
2 x 12 in., random lengths		51 00

2 x 3, 2 x 4, 2 x 5, 2 x 6, 2 x 7	48 00
3 x 4 and 4 x 4 in.	45 00
2 x 8 in.	45 00
All other random lengths, 7-in. and under, 8 ft. and up	38 00
5-inch and up merchantable boards, 8 ft. and up, p 1s	42 [illegible]
1 x 2	[illegible]
1 x 3	[illegible]
1-¼ in. spruce lath	[illegible]
1-½ in. spruce lath	[illegible]
New Brunswick Cedar Shingles	
Extras	[illegible]
Clears	[illegible]
Second Clears	[illegible]
Clear Whites	[illegible]
Extra 1s (Clear whites in)	[illegible]
Extra 1s (Clear whites out)	[illegible]
Red Cedar Extras, 16-in. 5 butts to 2-in.	[illegible]
Red Cedar Eurekas, 18-inch 5 butts to 2-in.	[illegible]
Red Cedar Perfections, 5 butts	
Washington 16-in. 5 butts to 2 in. extra red cedar	4 80

ALPHABETICAL INDEX TO ADVERTISERS

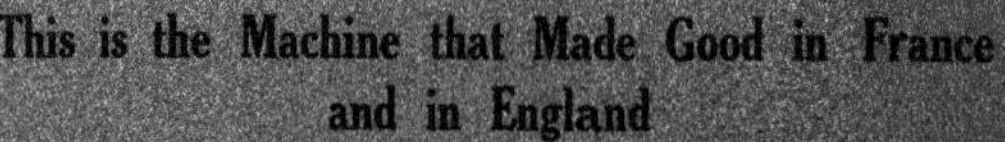

DIXIE DRAG SAW

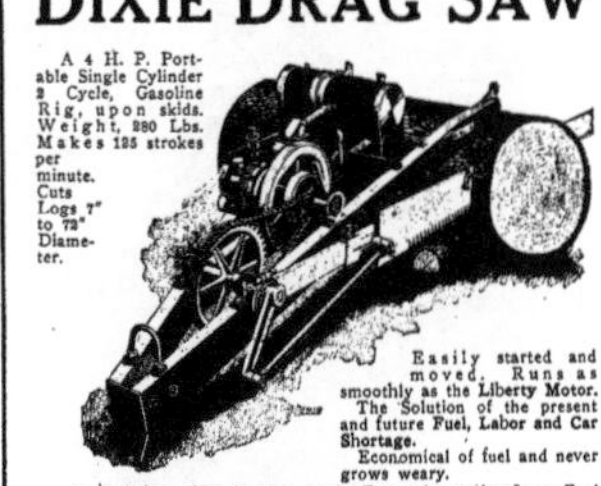

HORSE COLLAR PADS
TAPATCO
BRAND

TAPATCO
REGISTERED BRAND TRADE MARK

The Secret of Successful Sawing

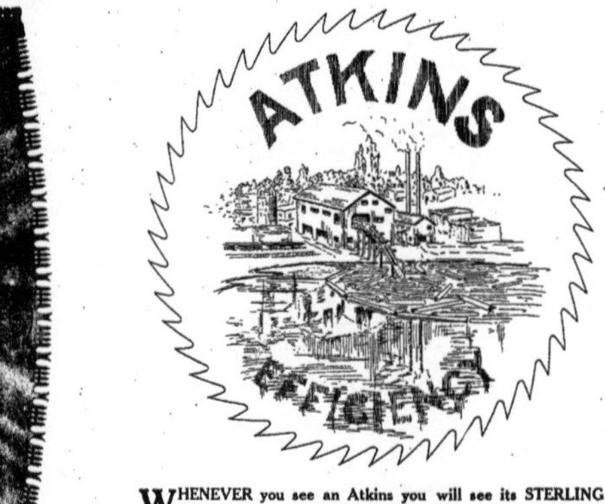

WHENEVER you see an Atkins you will see its STERLING QUALITY reflecting efficiency in the highest degree.

Supreme in all kinds of woodworking, these saws are the first essentials in keeping pace with the progressive spirit of reconstruction.

Send for Free Catalogue.

E. C. ATKINS & CO.

Factory: HAMILTON, ONT. Branch: 109 Powell St., VANCOUVER, B.C.

The Carriage You

Our No. 1 Size

CARRIAGE—Has three head blocks, as shown in cut, usually set 9 and 6 feet apart, will be placed any distance apart to suit purchaser. Knees open 38 in. from saw, and is fitted with Knight or Peel dogs, as desired. Taper movement on each knee. 1 15-16 in. steel set bar with steel pinions and coil spring receder, and friction lever brake for stopping knees where required. Timbers are 5 x 6 in., or heavier if desired, well bolted and braced. Diameter of truck wheel, 12 in. Axles 1¾ in. diameter, and extend clear across carriage, are furnished with self-oiling bearings. Front block is fitted with timber rule, placed as desired; 54 feet of V and flat track furnished with each carriage.

SET WORKS—As shown in cut, is made up of ratchet wheel 12 in. diameter, 4 in. face, with set lever carrying 7 steel pawls of varying lengths; also, same number of check pawls set in quadrant. Both sets of pawls are disengaged from either side of carriage when required to recede knees. This is a positive set, without lost motion.

FEED WORKS—As shown in cut, consists of 16 x 12 in. drum, with spur gear keyed to shaft. Pinion or friction shaft in saw frame engages with this gear. Cable takes two or three turns around drum, and is passed around end sheaves and attached to carriage. We also furnish 26 in. drum with internal gear in place of 16 in. drum when desired.

For Shingle, Lath and Portable Saw Mill Machinery write the well known manufacturers

The G. Walter Green Co.,

Send for Catalogue

PETERBOROUGH, ONT.

Algoma LIGHT STEEL

For Mining and Lumbering Purposes

All Complete with Splice Bars

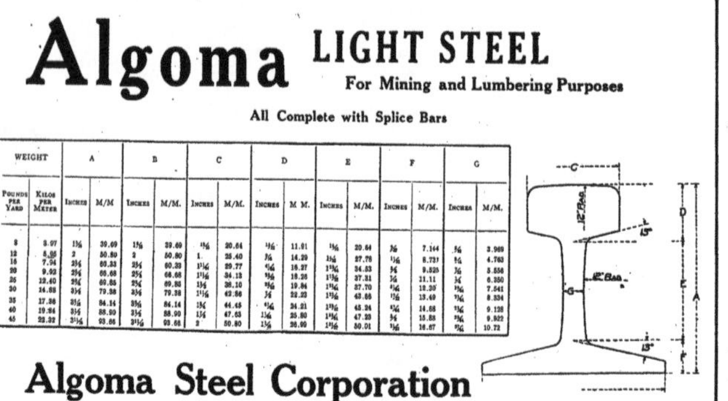

WEIGHT		A		B		C		D		E		F		G	
Pounds per Yard	Kilos per Meter	Inches	M/M	Inches	M/M.	Inches	M/M.	Inches	M M.	Inches	M/M.	Inches	M/M.	Inches	M/M.
8	3.97	1 9/16	39.69	1 9/16	39.69	13/16	20.64	7/16	11.01	13/16	20.64	9/32	7.144	5/32	3.969
12	5.95	2	50.80	2	50.80	1	25.40	9/16	14.29	1 3/32	27.78	11/32	8.731	3/16	4.763
16	7.94	2 3/8	60.33	2 3/8	60.33	1 11/64	29.77	41/64	16.27	1 23/64	34.53	3/8	9.525	7/32	5.556
20	9.92	2 5/8	66.68	2 5/8	66.68	1 11/32	34.13	23/32	18.26	1 15/32	37.31	7/16	11.11	1/4	6.350
25	12.40	2 3/4	69.85	2 3/4	69.85	1 1/2	38.10	25/32	19.84	1 31/64	37.70	31/64	12.30	19/64	7.541
30	14.88	3 1/8	79.38	3 1/8	79.38	1 11/16	42.86	7/8	22.23	1 23/32	43.66	17/32	13.49	21/64	8.334
35	17.36	3 5/16	84.14	3 5/16	84.14	1 3/4	44.45	61/64	24.21	1 25/32	45.24	37/64	14.68	23/64	9.128
40	19.84	3 1/2	88.90	3 1/2	88.90	1 7/8	47.63	1 1/64	25.80	1 55/64	47.23	5/8	15.88	25/64	9.922
45	22.32	3 11/16	93.66	3 11/16	93.66	2	50.80	1 1/16	26.99	1 31/32	50.01	21/32	16.67	27/64	10.72

Algoma Steel Corporation

Limited

Sault Ste. Marie, Ontario

Put Your

Veneer Cutting and Drying Problems

up to us

Lathe

Have you investigated the many advantages and economies in cutting logs into rotary cut veneer? Rotary cut veneer is being extensively used in the manufacture of boxes, baskets, fruit packages, crates, furniture, door panels, airplane construction, etc., etc. We are specialists in building complete veneer equipment. Our [illegible] years' experience puts us in position to give you expert advice as to what equipment is the most economical and best suited for your needs.

Write today for Catalogue

The Coe Manufacturing Co.

Painesville, Ohio, U. S.

The Oldest and largest manufacturers of complete veneer equipment in the world since 1852

Pyrene Fire Extinguishers

Are the Ideal Fire Protectors for your mill, for the following reasons:—

1st—Pyrene is death to all inflammable fires.

2nd—Pyrene does not freeze at fifty degrees below zero.

3rd—Pyrene does not deteriorate.

4th—Pyrene is easily operated and ever ready.

5th—Pyrene reduces your Fire Insurance rate 15 per cent when installed on your Automobile or Motor Truck.

6th—Pyrene has served with the boys at the front.

7th—Pyrene in one of our Holsters is ideal for your watchman in case he locates a fire in your building.

We also carry the 2½ Gal. Soda Acid Extinguisher

Ask for our Catalogue which contains a full line of fire appliances, also for our book on how to protect your factory. This book contains valuable information.

Pyrene Mfg. Co. of Canada, Limited

3 St. Nicholas St. Montreal

Aloxite Saw Gumming Wheels Sing the Song of Clean Cutting

THEY sound good to the filer's ear, because they cut clean and free. No drag—no undue heat. The keen, sharp, tough Aloxite grains stand right up to their job—and how they cut!

The bond breaks at just the right time to keep the wheel free—yet the wheel stands up to insure against waste—against the wheel losing shape.

And, remember—that Aloxite Wheels are uniform in grit and grade.

Made in all of the standard sizes, shapes and grits

THE CARBORUNDUM COMPANY

NIAGARA FALLS, N. Y.

NEW YORK CHICAGO BOSTON PHILADELPHIA CLEVELAND CINCINNATI PITTSBURGH GRAND RAPIDS MILWAUKEE

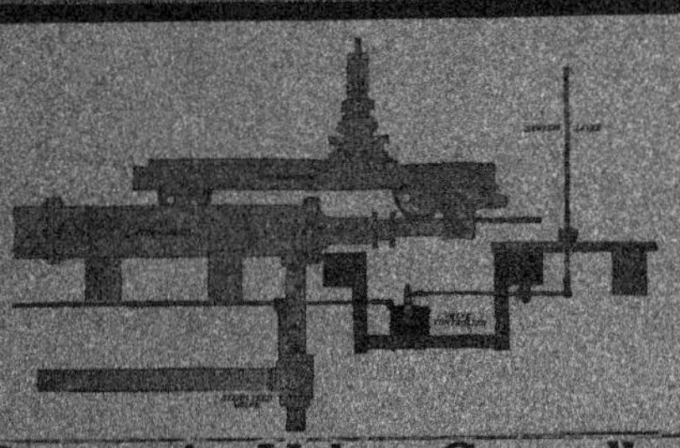

Prescott's Valve Controller

Patented June 6, 1916

The Machine You Have Been Waiting for.

WHAT IS IT?

PRESCOTT'S VALVE CONTROLLER

To eliminate every trouble with your Steam Feed Valves install one of these machines.

Six Real Reasons for Doing So:

1—Gives the sawyer the easiest kind of control of valve.
2—Hand lever stays put, making them safe against any jerk or kick of valve.
3—Gives the sawyer every confidence in handling valve.
4—Will prevent accidents—is easier on the nerves and carriage runs steadier.
5—Water flowing into valves from foaming boilers does not fret the sawyer.
6—This relief from all troubles of which sawyers have complained enables them to give closer attention to the logs they are cutting and a better inspection of the lumber they produce.

Read what one of the largest lumber companies on the north shore has to say about it.

We are sole Canadian manufacturers of these machines.

Pamphlets with full description and prices on application.

Let us quote you also on our new "Hamilton" Vertical Steam Feed Valves.

William Hamilton Co., Limited

Peterboro, Ontario

Agents: J. L. Neilson & Co., Winnipeg, Man.

CANADA LUMBERMAN BUYERS' DIRECTORY

The following regulations apply to all advertisers:—Eighth page, every issue, three headings; quarter page, six headings; half page, twelve headings; full page, twenty-four headings.

ASBESTOS GOODS
Atlas Asbestos Company, Ltd.

AXES
Canadian Warren Axe & Tool Co.

BABBITT METAL
Canada Metal Company.
General Supply Co. of Canada, Ltd.
Syracuse Smelting Works

BALE TIES
Laidlaw Bale Tie Company.

BALL BEARINGS
Chapman Double Ball Bearing Co.

BAND MILLS
Hamilton Company, William.
Waterous Engine Works Company.
Yates Machine Company, P. B.

BAND RESAWS
Mershon & Company, W. B.

BELT CEMENT
Graton & Knight Mfg. Company.

BELT DRESSING
Atlas Asbestos Company, Ltd.
General Supply Co. of Canada, Ltd.
Graton & Knight Mfg. Company.

BELTING
Atlas Asbestos Company, Ltd.
Beardmore Belting Company
Canadian Consolidated Rubber Co.
General Supply Company
Goodhue & Co., J. L.
Goodyear Tire & Rubber Co.
Graton & Knight Mfg. Company.
Gutta Percha and Rubber Company.
Main Belting Company
Manhattan Rubber Mfg. Co.
D. K. McLaren Limited.
McLaren Belting Company, J. C.

BELTING (Transmission, Elevator, Conveyor, Rubber)
Dunlop Tire & Rubber Goods Co.

BLOWERS
Sheldons Limited.
Toronto Blower Company.

BOILERS
Hamilton Company, William.
Jenckes Machine Company.
Marsh Engineering Works, Limited
Waterous Engine Works Company.

BOILER PRESERVATIVE
Beveridge Paper Company
International Chemical Company

BOX MACHINERY
Garlock-Walker Machinery Co.
Morgan Machine Company.
Yates Machine Company, P. B.

BOX SHOOKS
Davison Lumber & Mfg. Company

CABLE CONVEYORS
Jeffrey Manufacturing Company.
Jenckes Machine Company, Ltd.
Waterous Engine Works Company.

CAMP SUPPLIES
Canadian Milk Products Limited.
Davies Company, William.
Dr. Bell Veterinary Wonder Co.
Harris Abattoir Company
Johnson, A. H.
Turner & Sons, J. J.
Woods Manufacturing Company, Ltd.

CANT HOOKS
Canadian Warren Axe & Tool Co.
General Supply Co. of Canada, Ltd.
Pink Company, Thomas.

CARS—STEEL BODY
Marsh Engineering Works, Limited

CEDAR
Fesserton Timber Co.
Foss Lumber Company
Genoa Bay Lumber Company
Muir & Kirkpatrick.
Long Lumber Company.
Service Lumber Company
Terry & Gordon.
Thurston-Flavelle Lumber Company.
Vancouver Lumber Company.
Victoria Lumber and Mfg. Co.

CHAINS
Canadian Link-Belt Company, Ltd.
General Supply Co. of Canada, Ltd.
Hamilton Company, William.
Jeffrey Manufacturing Company.
Jenckes Machine Company, Ltd.
Pink & Co., Thomas.
Waterous Engine Works Company.
Williams Machinery Co., A. R., Vancouver.

CHINA CLAY
Bowater & Sons, W. V.

CHEMICAL PLANTS
Blair, Campbell & McLean Ltd.

CLOTHING
Grant, Holden & Graham.
Kitchen Overall & Shirt Company
Woods Mfg. Company

COLLAR PADS
American Pad & Textile Co.

COLLARS (Shaft)
Bond Engineering Works

CONVEYOR MACHINERY
Canadian Link-Belt Company, Ltd.
Canadian Mathews Gravity Carrier Company.
General Supply Co. of Canada, Ltd.
Jeffrey Mfg. Co.
Waterous Engine Works Company.

CORDAGE
Consumers Cordage Company.

CORN SYRUP
Canada Starch Company

COTTON GLOVES
American Pad & Textile Co.

COUNTERSHAFTS
Bond Engineering Works

COUPLINGS (Shaft)
Bond Engineering Works
Jenckes Machine Company, Ltd.

CRANES FOR SHIP YARDS
Canadian Link-Belt Company.

CROSS ARMS
Genoa Bay Lumber Company

CUTTER HEADS
Shimer Cutter Head Company.

CYPRESS
Blakeslee, Perrin & Darling
Chicago Lumber & Coal Company.
Long Lumber Company.
Wistar, Underhill & Nixon.

DERRICKS AND DERRIC FITTINGS
Marsh Engineering Works, Limited

DOORS
Genoa Bay Lumber Compa
Harrington, E. I.
Long Lumber Company.
Mason, Gordon & Co.
Rutherford & Sons, Wm.
Terry & Gordon.

DRAG SAWS
Gerlach Company, Peter
Pennoyer & Company, J. C

DRY KILNS
Sheldons Limited.

DRYERS
Philadelphia Textile Mach. Company.

DUST COLLECTORS
Sheldons Limited.
Toronto Blower Company.

EDGERS
William Hamilton Company, Ltd
Garlock-Walker Machinery Co.
Green Company, G. Walter
Haight, W. L.
Long Mfg. Company, E.
Waterous Engine Works Compan

ELEVATING AND CONVEYIN MACHINERY
Canadian Link-Belt Company, Ltd.
Jeffrey Manufacturing Company.
Jenckes Machine Company, Ltd.
Waterous Engine Works Compan

ENGINES
Hamilton Company, William.
Jenckes Machine Company.
Waterous Engine Works Compan

EXCELSIOR MACHINERY
Elmira Machinery and Transmission Company.

EXHAUST FANS
Garlock-Walker Machinery Co.
Reed & Company, Geo. W.
Sheldons Limited.
Toronto Blower Company.

EXHAUST SYSTEMS
Reed & Company, Geo. W.
Sheldons Limited.
Toronto Blower Company.

FILES
Disston & Sons, Henry.
Simonds Canada Saw Compan

FIR
Associated Mills, Limited
Allan-Stoltze Lumber Co.
British American Mills & Timber Co.
Coal Creek Lumber Compan
Fesserton Timber Co.
Foss Lumber Company
Grier & Sons, Ltd., G. A.
Heeney, Percy E.
Knox Brothers.
Long Lumber Company.
Mason, Gordon & Co.
Reynolds Company, Limite
Service Lumber Company
Shearer Company, Jas.
Terry & Gordon.
Timberland Lumber Company.

Weller, J. B.

FIR FLOORING
Genoa Bay Lumber Company
Rutherford & Sons, Wm.

FLAG STAFFS
Ontario Wind Engine Company

FLOORING (Oak)
Long-Bell Lumber Company.

GALVANIZING
Ontario Wind Engine Company

GASOLINE ENGINES
Ontario Wind Engine Company

GEARS (Cut)
Smart-Turner Machine Co.

GRATE BARS—Revolving
Beveridge Paper Company

GRAVITy LUMBER CARRIER
Can. Mathews Gravity Carrier Co.

GRINDERS (Bench)
Bond Engineering Works
Garlock-Walker Machinery Co.

HARDWOODS
Anderson Lumber Company, C. G.
Atlantic Lumber Co.
Bartram & Ball.
Bennett Lumber Company.
Blakeslee, Perrin & Darling
Cameron & Co.
Cardinal & Page
Davison Lumber & Mfg. Company
Dunfield & Company
Edwards & Co., W. C.
Fassett Lumber Company.
Fesserton Timber Co.
Fraser Limited.
Gillespie, James.
Gloucester Lumber Company
Grier & Son, G. A.
Heeney, Percy E.
Knox Brothers.
Long Lumber Company.
McLennan Lumber Company.
Moores, Jr., E. J.
Nicholson & Co., E. M.
Pedwell Hardwood Lumber Co.
Powell-Myers Lumber Co.
Russell, Chas. H.
Spencer Limited, C. A.
Stearns & Culver Lumber Co.
Summers, James R.
Taylor Lumber Company, S. K.
Webster & Brother, James.

HARDWOOD FLOORING MACHINERY
American Woodworking Machinery Company
Garlock-Walker Machinery Co.

HANGERS (Shaft)
Bond Engineering Works

HARDWOOD FLOORING
Grier & Son, G. A.
Long Lumber Company.

HEMLOCK

Anderson Lumber Company, C. G.
Bartram & Ball.
Bourgouin, H.
Callander Sawmills
Canadian General Lumber Company
Cane & Co., Jas. G.
Davison Lumber & Mfg. Company
Dunfield & Company
Edwards & Company, W. C.
Fesserton Timber Co.
Foss Lumber Company
Grier & Sons, Ltd., G. A.
Hart & McDonagh.
Long Lumber Company.
Mason, Gordon & Co.
Spencer Limited, C. A.
Terry & Gordon.
The Long Lumber Company.

HOISTING AND HAULING ENGINES

Garlock-Walker Machinery Co.
General Supply Co. of Canada, Ltd.
Marsh Engineering Works, Limited

HORSES

Union Stock Yards.

HOSE

Dunlop Tire & Rubber Goods Co.
General Supply Co. of Canada, Ltd.
Goodyear Tire & Rubber Co.
Gutta Percha and Rubber Company.

INDUSTRIAL CARS

Marsh Engineering Works, Limited

INSURANCE

Hardy & Co., E. D.
Rankin Benedict Underwriting Co.

INTERIOR FINISH

Eagle Lumber Company.
Hay & Co.
Mason, Gordon & Co.
Renfrew Planing Mills.
Terry & Gordon.

KNIVES

Disston & Sons, Henry.
Peter Hay Knife Company.
Simonds Canada Saw Company.
Waterous Engine Works Company.

LATH

Austin & Nicholson.
Callander Sawmills
Canadian General Lumber Company
Cane & Co., Jas. G.
Cardinal & Page
Dupuis Limited, J. P.
Eagle Lumber Company.
Fraser Limited.
Fraser-Bryson Lumber Company.
Genoa Bay Lumber Company
Gloucester Lumber Company
Grier & Sons, Ltd., G. A.
Harris Tie & Timber Company, Ltd.
Long Lumber Company.
McLennan Lumber Company.
New Ontario Colonization Company.
River Ouelle Pulp and Paper Co.
Spencer Limited, C. A.
Terry & Gordon.
Union Lumber Company.
Victoria Harbor Lumber Company.

LATH BOLTERS

Garlock-Walker Machinery Co.
General Supply Co. of Canada, Ltd.
Green Company, C. Walter.

LOCOMOTIVES

Bell Locomotive Works
General Supply Co. of Canada, Ltd.
Jeffrey Manufacturing Company.
Jenckes Machine Company, Ltd.
Climax Manufacturing Company.
Montreal Locomotive Workks.

LATH TWINE

Consumers' Cordage Company.

LINK-BELT

Canadian Link-Belt Company
Canadian Mathews Gravity Carrier
Company.
Jeffrey Mfg. Co.
Williams Machinery Co., A. R., Vancouver.

LOCOMOTIVE CRANES

Canadian Link-Belt Company, Ltd.

LOGGING ENGINES

Dunbar Engine and Foundry Co.
Jenckes Machine Company.
Marsh Engineering Works, Limited

LOG HAULER

Green Company, C. Walter
Jenckes Machine Company, Ltd.

LOGGING MACHINERY AND EQUIPMENT

General Supply Co. of Canada, Ltd.
Hamilton Company, William.
Jenckes Machine Company, Ltd.
Marsh Engineering Works, Limited
Waterous Engine Works Company.

LUMBER TRUCKS

Waterous Engine Works Company.

LUMBERMEN'S CLOTHING

Woods Manufacturing Company, Ltd.

METAL REFINERS

Canada Metal Company.
Hoyt Metal Company.
Sessenwein Brothers.

MILLING IN TRANSIT

Renfrew Planing Mills.
Rutherford & Sons, Wm.

MOLDINGS

Genoa Bay Lumber Co.
Rutherford & Sons, Wm.

MOTOR TRUCKS

Duplex Truck Company
Chicago Lumber & Coal Company
Long-Bell Lumber Company.
Weller, J. B.

OAKUM

Stratford Oakum Co., Geo.

OIL CLOTHING

Leckie, Limited, John.

OLD IRON AND BRASS

Sessenwein Brothers.

PAPER

Bowater & Sons, W. V.

PACKING

Atlas Asbestos Company, Ltd.
Consumers Cordage Co.
Dunlop Tire & Rubber Goods Co.
Gutta Percha and Rubber Company.

PAPER MILL MACHINERY

Bowater & Sons, W. V.

PILLOW BLOCKS

Bond Engineering Works

Anderson Lumber Company, C. G.
Atlantic Lumber Co.
Austin & Nicholson.
Bourgouin, H.
Callander Sawmills
Cameron & Co.
Canadian General Lumber Company
Cane & Co., Jas. G.
Cardinal & Page
Chicago Lumber & Coal Company.
Cleveland-Sarnia Sawmills Company.
Davison Lumber & Mfg. Co.
Donogh & Co., John.
Dudley, Arthur N.
Dunfield & Company
Eagle Lumber Company.
Edwards & Co., W. C.

CLIMAX Improved Geared LOCOMOTIVES FOR WOOD AND IRON RAILS

A [illegible]-ton Climax Locomotive Designed Especially for Heavy Logging Work.

Climax Locomotives are successfully operated on steep grades and sharp curves. Any weight or gauge. Locomotives in stock for immediate shipment. Get Catalog "B."

CLIMAX MANUFACTURING CO., 313 W. Main Street, CORRY, PA.
VANCOUVER MACHINERY DEPOT, LTD., VANCOUVER, B.C.

Peace Year 1919

Finds us optimistic for the future and well stocked with Horse Blankets, Feed Bags, Tarpaulins, Oil Clothing Tents, Flags, Straw Ticks and Grey Blankets

We Guarantee Prompt Shipment of Orders Entrusted to us

J. J. Turner & Sons Limited
PETERBOROUGH, ONT.

PUT YOUR PROBLEM UP TO US

We are specialists in building locomotives. We build all types and sizes, also all kinds of repair parts for locomotives and tenders.

Our experience puts us in a position to give you expert advice as to what particular type and size of locomotive is best suited to your needs.

Put your locomotive problem up to us.

MONTREAL LOCOMOTIVE WORKS, LIMITED

DOMINION EXPRESS BUILDING, MONTREAL, CANADA.

PRATT & WHITNEY CO.
OF CANADA, LIMITED

SMALL TOOLS

Taps — Dies — Reamers — Cutters — Drills
MADE IN CANADA

As good as money can buy—Guaranteed absolutely!

Head Office and Works, DUNDAS, ONT.

SALES OFFICES:
MONTREAL Drummond Bldg. VANCOUVER WINNIPEG Bank of Hamilton Bldg.

IMPROVING YOUR PRODUCT

The engineering experience of 50 years has made it possible for the Proctor Organization to build dryers for every individual drying need. The usual results are an improved product and improved working conditions. That's why users of Proctor dryers are always ready to recommend and demonstrate their dryers.

Proctor DRYERS for VENEERS

give a perfectly flat and pliable product without checks or splits

Made by the oldest and largest builders of dryers.
Ask for Proctor Dryer Catalog on your materials.

PHILADELPHIA TEXTILE MACHINERY CO.
Builders of Drying Machinery
SEVENTH STREET AND TABOR ROAD, PHILADELPHIA, PA., U.S.A.
Hamilton, Ont., Canada,—W. J. Westaway, 1 Sun Life Building.

Excelsior Lumber Company.
Fesserton Timber Company
Fraser-Bryson Lumber Company.
Fraser Limited.
Gillies Brothers Limited.
Gloucester Lumber Company
Gordon & Co., George.
Grier & Sons, Ltd., G. A.
Harris Tie & Timber Company, Ltd.
Hart & McDonagh.
Hettler Lumber Company, Herman H.
Long-Bell Lumber Company.
Long Lumber Company.
Mason, Gordon & Co.
McLennan Lumber Company.
Montreal Lumber Company.
Moores, Jr., E. J.
Muir & Kirkpatrick.
Parry Sound Lumber Company.
Russell, Chas. H.
Shearer Company, Jas.
Spencer Limited, C. A.
Summers, James R.
Terry & Gordon.
Union Lumber Company.
Watson & Todd, Limited.
Weller, J. B.
Williams Lumber Company
Wuichet, Louis.

PLANING MILL EXHAUSTERS
Garlock-Walker Machinery Co.
Reed & Company, Geo. W.
Sheldons Limited.
Toronto Blower Co.

PLANING MILL MACHINERY
American Woodworking Machinery Company
Garlock-Walker Machinery Co.
Mershon & Company, W. B.
Sheldons Limited.
Toronto Blower Co.
Yates Machine Company, P. B.

PORK PACKERS
Davies Company, William
Harris Abattoir Company

POSTS AND POLES
Auger & Company
Dupuis Limited, J. P.
Eagle Lumber Company
Harris Tie & Timber Company, Ltd.
Long-Bell Lumber Company.
Long Lumber Company.
Mason, Gordon & Co.
Terry & Gordon.

PULLEYS AND SHAFTING
Bond Engineering Works
Canadian Link-Belt Company
Garlock-Walker Machinery Co.
General Supply Co. of Canada, Ltd.
Green Company, G. Walter
Hamilton Company, William
Jeffrey Mfg. Co.
Jenckes Machine Company, Ltd.

PULP MILL MACHINERY
Canadian Link-Belt Company, Ltd.
Hamilton Company, William.
Jeffrey Manufacturing Company
Jenckes Machine Company, Ltd.
Waterous Engine Works Company

PUMPS
General Supply Co. of Canada, Ltd.
Hamilton Company, William
Jenckes Machine Company, Ltd.
Smart-Turner Machine Company
Waterous Engine Works Company

RAILS
Gartshore, John J.
Sessenwein Bros.

ROOFINGS
Reed & Company, Geo. W.

ROOFINGS
(Rubber, Plastic and Liquid)
Beveridge Paper Company
International Chemical Company

ROPE
Consumers Cordage Co.
Leckie, Limited, John

RUBBER GOODS
Atlas Asbestos Company
Dunlop Tire & Rubber Goods Co.
Goodyear Tire and Rubber Co.
Gutta Percha & Rubber Company

SASH
Genoa Bay Lumber Company
Renfrew Planing Mills.

SAWS
Atkins & Company, E. C.
Disston & Sons, Henry
General Supply Co. of Canada, Ltd.
Gerlach Company, Peter
Green Company, G. Walter
Hoe & Company, R.
Shurly-Dietrich Company
Simonds Canada Saw Company

SAW MILL LINK-BELT
Williams Machinery Co., A. R., Vancouver.

SAW MILL MACHINERY
Canadian Link-Belt Company, Ltd.
Dunbar Engine & Foundry Co.
Firstbrook Bros.
General Supply Co. of Canada, Ltd.
Haight, W. L.
Hamilton Company, William
Huther Bros. Saw Mfg. Company
Jeffrey Manufacturing Company
Long Manufacturing Company, E.
Mershon & Company, W. B.
Parry Sound Lumber Company
Payette Company, P.
Waterous Engine Works Company
Yates Machine Co., P. B.

SHEATHINGS
Beveridge Paper Company
Goodyear Tire & Rubber Co.

SHINGLE MACHINES
Marsh Engineering Works, Limited

SAW MANDRELS
Bond Engineering Works

SAW SHARPENERS
Garlock-Walker Machinery Co.
Waterous Engine Works Company.

SAW SLASHERS
Waterous Engine Works Company

SAWMILL LINK-BELT
Canadian Link-Belt Company

SHEET METALS
Syracuse Smelting Works

SHINGLES
Allan-Stoltze Lumber Co.
Associated Mills, Limited
Campbell-MacLaurin Lumber Co.
Cardinal & Page
Dominion Lumber & Timber Co.
Eagle Lumber Company
Foss Lumber Company
Fraser Limited.
Genoa Bay Lumber Company
Gillespie, James.
Gloucester Lumber Company
Grier & Sons, Ltd., G. A.
Harris Tie & Timber Company, Ltd.
Heeney, Percy E.
Long Lumber Company.
Mason, Gordon & Co.
McLennan Lumber Company.
Miller Company, Ltd., W. H.
Reynolds Company, Limited
Service Lumber Company
Shingle Agency of B. C.
Terry & Gordon.
Timms, Phillips & Co.
Vancouver Lumber Company.
Victoria Lumber and Mfg. Co.

SHINGLE & LATH MACHINERY
Dunbar Engine and Foundry Co.
Garlock-Walker Machinery Co.
Green Company, C. Walter
Hamilton Company, William.
Long Manufacturing Company, E.
Payette Company, P.

SILENT CHAIN DRIVES
Canadian Link-Belt Company, Ltd.

SILOS
Ontario Wind Engine Company

SLEEPING ROBES
Woods Mfg. Company, Limited

SMOKESTACKS
Marsh Engineering Works, Limited
Waterous Engine Works Company.

SNOW PLOWS
Pink Company, Thomas.

SPARK ARRESTORS
Jenckes Machine Company, Ltd.
Reed & Company, Geo. W.
Waterous Engine Works Company.

SPRUCE
Bartram & Ball.
Bourgouin, H.
Cane & Co., Jas. G.
Cardinal & Page
Davison Lumber & Mfg. Company
Donogh & Co., John.
Dudley, Arthur N.
Dunfield & Company
Exchange Lumber Company.
Foss Lumber Company
Fraser Limited.
Fraser-Bryson Lumber Company.
Gillies Brothers.
Gloucester Lumber Company
Grant & Campbell.
Grier & Sons, Ltd., G. A.
Hart & McDonagh.
Lauder, Spears & Howland.
Long Lumber Company.
Mason, Gordon & Co.
McLennan Lumber Company.
Muir & Kirkpatrick.
New Ontario Colonization Company.
Nicholson & Co., E. M.
River Ouelle Pulp and Lumber Co.
Russell, Chas. H.
Service Lumber Company
Shearer Company, Jas.
Snowball Co., J. B.
Spencer Limited, C. A.
Terry & Gordon.

STEEL CHAIN
Canadian Link-Belt Company, Ltd.
Jeffrey Manufacturing Company.
Waterous Engine Works Company.

STEEL PLATE CONSTRUCTION
Marsh Engineering Works, Limited

STEAM PLANT ACCESSORIES
Waterous Engine Works Company.

STEEL BARRELS
Smart-Turner Machine Co.

STEEL DRUMS
Smart-Turner Machine Co.

SWEAT PADS
American Pad & Textile Co.

SULPHITE PULP CHIPS
Davison Lumber & Mfg. Company

TANKS
Ontario Wind Engine Company

TARPAULINS
Turner & Sons, J. J.
Woods Manufacturing Company, Ltd.

TAPS AND DIES
Pratt & Whitney Company.

TENTS
Turner & Sons, J. J.
Woods Mfg. Company

TIES
Auger & Company
Austin & Nicholson.
Harris Tie & Timber Company, Ltd.
Long Lumber Company.
McLennan Lumber Company.
Terry & Gordon.

TIMBER BROKERS
Bradley, R. R.
Cant & Kemp.
Farnworth & Jardine.
Hillas & Co., W. N.
Hunter, Herbert F.
Smith & Tyrer, Limited

TIMBER CRUISERS AND ESTIMATORS
Sewall, James W.

TIMBER LANDS
Department of Lands and Forests.

TRACTORS
British War Mission

TRANSMISSION MACHINERY
Bond Engineering Works
Canadian Link-Belt Company, Ltd.
General Supply Co. of Canada, Ltd.
Jenckes Machine Company, Ltd.
Jeffrey Manufacturing Company.
Waterous Engine Works Company

TRIMMERS
Garlock-Walker Machinery Co.
Green Company, C. Walter
Waterous Engine Works Company

West & Peachey.

TURBINES
Hamilton Company, William.
Jenckes Machine Company, Ltd.

Bay City Foundry & Machine Co.
Mason Regulator & Engineering Co.

VENEERS
Webster & Brother, James.

VENEER DRYERS
Coe Manufacturing Company
Philadelphia Textile Mach. Co.

VENEER MACHINERY
Coe Manufacturing Company
Garlock-Walker Machinery Co.
Philadelphia Textile Machinery Co.

VETERINARY REMEDIES
Dr. Bell Veterinary Wonder Co.

WATER HEATERS
Mason Regulator & Engineering Co.

Beveridge Paper Company

WATER WHEELS
Hamilton Company, William.
Jenckes Machine Company, Ltd.

Laidlaw Bale Tie Company.

WOOD DISTILLATION PLANTS
Blair, Campbell & McLean, Ltd.

WOODWORKING MACHINERY

WOOD PRESERVATIVES
International Chemical Company

WOOD PULP
Austin & Nicholson.
New Ontario Colonization Co.
River Ouelle Pulp and Lumber Co.

Toronto, August 15, 1919 No. 16

Canada Lumberman & Wood Worker

Alphabetical Index to Advertisers, Page 68 Classified Directory to Advertisements, Page 76

AMERICAN WOOD KING MACHINERY CO.

ROCH , N. Y.

SALES OFFICE FOR B IA. PORTLAND. OREGON
AGENTS FOR THE REST OF CANA WALKER MACHINERY CO., TORONTO
AGENTS FOR GREAT B ROJECTILE CO., LONDON

FIRST IN QUALITY

The Inside of the Columbia

The sander with the real automatic take-up for s

Send for copy of Sander Booklet fully illustrating describing this machine

CANADIAN SALES AGENTS

Garlock-Walker Machinery Company

LIMITED

32-34 FRONT STREET WEST, TORONTO

TORONTO MONTREAL WINNIPEG

Davison Lumber & Manufacturing Co., Ltd.

Bridgewater, N. S.

THE LARGEST LUMBERING INDUSTRY IN NOVA SCOTIA **PRODUCTION 40 MILLION FEET PER ANNUM**

Send us your enquiries for

Spruce, Pine, Hemlock or Hardwood Lumber
Box Shooks and
Dry Pressed Baled Sulphite and Sulphate Pulp Chips

OUR SPECIALTIES:

Nova Scotia White Spruce and Hardwood Flooring

We are equipped with everything appertaining to Modern Saw Milling and operate from the Woods to the finished product.
If you want something special quickly, try us. We will cut, dry, work and ship within a few days from receipt of order.
We are located on the main line of the Halifax and South Western Railway and on Tidewater.

We Operate:

A Double Band Mill at Springfield, N.S., Capacity 120,000 ft. per day
A Rotary and Gang at Mill Village, N.S. " 40,000 ft. per day
A Rotary and Gang at Bridgewater, N.S., " 80,000 ft. per day
A Planing Mill at Bridgewater, N.S., " 100,000 ft. per day

A Box Shook Factory at Bridgewater, N.S., Capacity 50,000 ft. per day
A Dry Kiln at Bridgewater, N.S., " 100,000 ft. per day
A Chipping Mill at Bridgewater, N.S., " 100 cords per day
A Ground Wood Pulp Mill at Charleston, N.S., Capacity 40 tons Spruce Pulp per day.

PHONE: BRIDGEWATER 74

DUNFIELD & CO., Limited

Exporters of Nova Scotia and New Brunswick

Spruce, Pine, Hemlock and Hardwood

in 1 in., 2 in., 3 in., 4 in.

Spruce Laths and Railway Ties

***Head Office:* 8 Prince St., Halifax, N.S.** ***Branch Office:* 8 Market Square, St. John, N.B.**

U. K. Brokers: Duncan, Ewing & Co., K21 Exchange Bldg., Liverpool. Telegraphic Address: Dunfield, Halifax. Codes: ABC 5th Ed. Western Union

Austin & Nicholson

CHAPLEAU, ONTARIO

Largest Producers of
RAILROAD TIES
in the Dominion

Pine and Spruce Lumber
Lath Piling
Railroad Ties
Pulpwood

First Class Planing-mill Equipment

Facilities for delivering Pulpwood
to Michipicoten Harbour, Lake Superior

Splendid facilities for Dressing and Matching
in straight car lots, one or more widths

Mills at NICHOLSON, ONTARIO, Main Line C.P.R.

Basswood

1 in., 1¼ in., 1½ in., 2 in., and 3 in.,
Dry Basswood

Dry Birch Stock

All thicknesses and grades in
Maple, Birch, Elm, Basswood and **Brown Ash**
Also **Cottonwood, Tupelo, Gum, Magnolia**
and **Buckeye**

Spruce, Hemlock and Pine

Can saw to order at MacDonald's Siding

Let us quote on your requirements

HART & McDONAGH

Temple Building, Cor. Bay and Richmond Streets
TORONTO, ONT.

SOUTHERN HARDWOODS Dry Stock at Buffalo for Quick Shipment

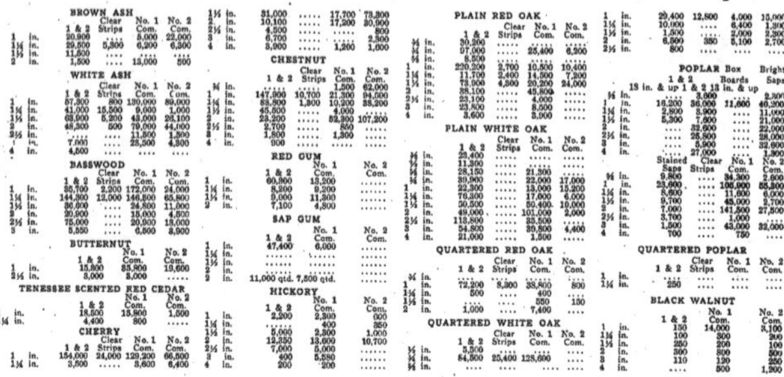

BROWN ASH

	1 & 2	Clear Strips	No. 1 Com.	No. 2 Com.
1 in.	20,900	....	5,000	22,000
1¼ in.	29,500	5,300	6,200	6,300
1½ in.	11,500	....	....	....
2 in.	1,500	....	13,000	500

WHITE ASH

	1 & 2	Clear Strips	No. 1 Com.	No. 2 Com.
1 in.	57,300	800	130,000	89,000
1¼ in.	41,000	15,500	9,000	1,000
1½ in.	63,900	5,200	43,000	26,100
2 in.	48,300	500	79,000	44,000
2½ in.	....	....	11,500	1,500
3 in.	7,000	....	28,500	4,300
4 in.	4,500	....	....	....

BASSWOOD

	1 & 2	Clear Strips	No. 1 Com.	No. 2 Com.
1 in.	35,700	2,200	172,000	24,000
1¼ in.	144,300	12,000	146,500	65,800
1½ in.	36,600	....	24,800	11,000
2 in.	20,900	....	15,000	4,500
2½ in.	75,000	....	20,900	13,000
3 in.	5,550	....	6,500	3,900

BUTTERNUT

	1 & 2	No. 1 Com.	No. 2 Com.
1 in.	15,800	85,800	19,600
2½ in.	3,000	3,000	.....

TENESSEE SCENTED RED CEDAR

	1 & 2	No. 1 Com.	No. 2 Com.
1 in.	18,500	15,800	1,500
1¼ in.	4,400	800	.....

CHERRY

	1 & 2	Clear Strips	No. 1 Com.	No. 2 Com.
1 in.	154,000	24,000	129,200	66,500
1¼ in.	3,500	.....	3,600	6,400
1½ in.	31,000	.....	17,700	73,300
2 in.	10,100	.....	17,200	30,900
2½ in.	4,500	.....	.....	800
3 in.	6,700	.....	.....	2,300
4 in.	3,900	.....	1,200	1,000

CHESTNUT

	1 & 2	Clear Strips	No. 1 Com.	No. 2 Com.
¾ in.	.....	.....	1,500	62,000
1 in.	147,900	10,700	21,300	94,500
1¼ in.	83,800	1,300	10,200	38,200
1½ in.	45,500	.....	4,000	.....
2 in.	23,200	.....	52,300	107,200
2½ in.	2,700	.....	850	.....
3 in.	1,800	.....	1,300	.....
4 in.	900	.....	.....	.....

RED GUM

	1 & 2	No. 1 Com.	No. 2 Com.
1 in.	60,300	13,200	......
1¼ in.	8,200	9,200	......
1½ in.	9,000	11,300	......
2 in.	7,100	4,800	......

SAP GUM

	1 & 2	No. 1 Com.	No. 2 Com.
1 in.	47,400	6,000	......
1¼ in.	......	......	......
1½ in.	......	......	......
2 in.	......	......	......
2 in.	11,000 qtd.	7,500 qtd.	......

HICKORY

	1 & 2	No. 1 Com.	No. 2 Com.
1 in.	2,200	2,300	600
1¼ in.	......	400	350
1½ in.	5,000	2,300	1,000
2 in.	12,350	13,600	10,700
2½ in.	7,000	5,000	......
3 in.	400	5,580	......
4 in.	200	200	......

PLAIN RED OAK

	1 & 2	Clear Strips	No. 1 Com.	No. 2 Com.
⅜ in.	30,200	.....	.....	.....
½ in.	97,000	.....	25,400	6,200
⅝ in.	8,500	.....	.....	.....
1 in.	220,200	2,700	10,500	10,400
1¼ in.	11,700	2,400	14,500	7,200
1½ in.	73,900	4,300	20,200	24,000
2 in.	38,100	.....	45,800	.....
2½ in.	23,100	.....	4,000	.....
3 in.	23,800	.....	8,500	.....
4 in.	3,600	.....	3,900	.....

PLAIN WHITE OAK

	1 & 2	Clear Strips	No. 1 Com.	No. 2 Com.
⅜ in.	23,400	.....	.....	.....
½ in.	11,300	.....	.....	.....
⅝ in.	28,150	.....	21,300	.....
¾ in.	39,900	.....	22,000	17,000
1 in.	22,300	.....	13,000	15,200
1¼ in.	76,300	.....	17,000	6,000
1½ in.	30,500	.....	50,400	10,000
2 in.	49,000	.....	101,000	2,000
2½ in.	113,800	.....	35,500	.....
3 in.	54,800	.....	30,800	4,400
4 in.	21,000	.....	1,500	.....

QUARTERED RED OAK

	1 & 2	Clear Strips	No. 1 Com.	No. 2 Com.
¾ in.	....	....	......	....
1 in.	72,200	8,300	38,800	800
1¼ in.	500	....	400	....
1½ in.	....	....	550	150
2 in.	1,000	....	7,400	....

QUARTERED WHITE OAK

	1 & 2	Clear Strips	No. 1 Com.	No. 2 Com.
½ in.	5,500	....	....	....
¾ in.	84,500	25,400	128,600	....
⅝ in.	....	....	....	....
1 in.	29,400	12,800	4,000	15,000
1¼ in.	10,000	....	6,400	1,300
1½ in.	1,500	....	2,000	2,300
2 in.	6,500	350	5,100	2,700
2½ in.	800	....	....	....

POPLAR

	1 & 2 18 in. & up	1 & 2	Box Boards 13 in. & up	Bright Saps
⅝ in.	....	3,000	....	2,300
1 in.	16,200	36,000	11,600	40,200
1¼ in.	2,800	3,900	....	11,000
1½ in.	5,300	7,600	....	21,000
2 in.	....	32,600	....	22,000
2½ in.	....	25,800	....	28,000
3 in.	....	5,900	....	32,600
4 in.	....	27,000	....	1,300

	Stained Saps	Clear Strips	No. 1 Com.	No. 2 Com.
⅝ in.	9,800	....	34,300	2,600
1 in.	23,600	....	105,900	55,300
1¼ in.	8,600	....	11,600	6,000
1½ in.	9,700	....	45,000	2,700
2 in.	7,000	....	141,500	27,500
2½ in.	3,700	....	1,000	....
3 in.	1,500	....	43,000	32,000
4 in.	700	....	750	....

QUARTERED POPLAR

	1 & 2	Clear Strips	No. 1 Com.	No. 2 Com.
1 in.	....	....	....	....
1¼ in.	250	....	....	....

BLACK WALNUT

	1 & 2	No. 1 Com.	No. 2 Com.
1 in.	150	14,000	3,100
1¼ in.	100	300	200
1½ in.	250	200	100
2 in.	300	800	500
3 in.	110	120	250
4 in.	....	500	1,200

Also Large Stock of BEECH, BIRCH and MAPLE

THE ATLANTIC LUMBER CO., Inc., 310 MANNING CHAMBERS, TORONTO

MANUFACTURERS SOUTHERN HARDWOOD LUMBER

Head Office: BOSTON, MASS. Yards: BUFFALO, N.Y. Mills: KNOXVILLE, TENN.; FONDE, KENTUCKY

John McKergow, President — W. K. Grafftey, Managing-Director

The Montreal Lumber Co. Limited

Wholesale Lumber

Ottawa Office: 46 Elgin St. — Montreal Office: 759 Notre Dame St., W

H. Cardinal — O. Page

Cardinal & Page

180 St. James St. Montreal

Large Quantity of Eastern Spruce and Ottawa White Pine on Hand.

Try a sample shipment and you will become a regular Customer.

Lake Lumber Co. Ltd.

Manufacturers of

Fir, Cedar, Hemlock, Spruce

QUALICUM QUALITY LUMBER

Rough Fir Timbers

Any size up to 60 feet long

Select Grades a Specialty

FIR PIPE and TANK STOCK

Market wanted for Rough Cedar Timbers
Inquire for prices

Office and Mills:
Qualicum Beach, V. I., B. C.

WE ARE BUYERS OF

Hardwood Lumber

Handles

Staves Hoops

Headings

James **WEBSTER** & Bro.
Limited

Bootle, Liverpool, England

London Office
Dashwood House 9 New Broad St. E. C.

SPECIALTIES

Sawed Hemlock
Red Cedar Shingles
White Pine Lath
Bass and Poplar Siding

James Gillespie

Pine and Hardwood

Lumber

Lath and Shingles

North Tonawanda, N.Y.

LUMBER

WANTED

ONTARIO HARDWOOD CUTS

ADVANCES MADE DURING OPERATIONS

C. G. Anderson Lumber Company, Limited

Manufacturers and Strictly Wholesale Dealers in Lumber

SALES OFFICE

705 Excelsior Life Building

Toronto

JACK PINE

JAMES R. SUMMERS
Wholesale Lumber
95 King St. East TORONTO, Ont.

Manufacturers of

WIRE For TYING, BUNDLING and m ay other purposes. NAILS, Etc.

LAIDLAW BALE-TIE CO., Ltd.
HAMILTON, ONT.

Timber Estimates

James W. Sewall
OLD TOWN. - MAINE

TIMBER LANDS
Bought and Sold

Timber and Pulp Wood Estimates

R. R. BRADLEY
Consulting Forester
58 Telegraph Building
Hospital St., MONTREAL

USED SAW MILL

MACHINERY

FOR SALE

Extra heavy log haul-up works with inch round and flat chain, 128 ft. centres.
2—Waterous log unloaders or kickers, 3 arms, 10 in. cylinders.
1—Waterous log loader, 3 arms, 10-in. cylinders.
1—Waterous right-hand double cutting band mill, 11 in. saws, 8 ft. wheel, with 3-block carriage; 24 in. opening; Payette set works and dogs; 8 in. x 36 ft. steam feed.
1—Waterous double edger for 20-inch saws, lever shifter.
1—Payette double edger for 18-in. saws, lever shifter.
48—live rolls about 8 ft. long by 10 in. dia.; extra heavy, sprocket drive.
1—Payette picket machine, made specially for shade roller stock, will feed pieces 16 in. long, also sorting table with chain top.
1—Payette edger for box and short stock.
1—Rogers twin circular or tie maker.
1—Payette lath bolter and lath machine.
1—Pair lath trimmers.
1—Picket trimmer (bunch trim).
—Pair Polson "Brown" type engines, coupled on quarters, 22 in. x 50 in., with 16 ft. x 48 in. belt, balance wheel. Excellent engines.
1—8 x 10 Centre Crank Engine.
1—10 x 14 Cowan Slide Valve Engine.
Pulleys, gears, heavy line shafting and countershafting with bearings.
Booms and boom chains, ½, ⅝ & ¾.
Winches and other mill supplies.
Prompt shipments and bargains for quick sale. Will send all particulars and prices on application.

Firstbrook Bros.
Limited
PENETANG

"WELL BOUGHT IS HALF SOLD"

UNIQUE !

This word applies to

OUR

WHITE PINE

Why?

BECAUSE:

Logs—Come from best White Pine section in Ontario.

Manufacture—Unsurpassed. Modern, up-to-the-minute mill equipment insures this.

Grading—Careful, uniform and of sufficiently wide range to give the customer just what he requires.

Have you used our White Pine?
A trial order will convince you that it really does stand in a class by itself.

Canadian General Lumber Co.

Limited

FOREST PRODUCTS

TORONTO OFFICE :— 712-20 Bank of Hamilton Bldg.
Montreal Office :—203 McGill Bldg.
Mills : Byng Inlet, Ont.

Quick Action

You Can Have It

Try the Canada Lumberman Wanted and For Sale Department. Have you anything you wish to buy or sell in the Lumber Industry? You will find this department inexpensive, and a very effective business getter.

Our Classified Advertisers do not repeat the ad, often. They don't have to. They report immediate results. Use these columns to your own advantage.

CANADA LUMBERMAN and WOODWORKER
347 Adelaide St. W.
TORONTO

FRASER COMPANIES, Limited

Bleached Sulphite Pulp Mill. Saw Mills (all Band Saw Mills). Shingle Mills.

HERE THEY ARE ON THE MAP

Mills and Railway Connections

Saw and Shingle Mills	Railway Connections	Saw and Shingle Mills	Railway Connections
Cabano, Que.	Temiscouata Ry.	Baker Brook, N. B.	C. G. Ry., Temiscouata Ry.
Glendyne, Que.	C. G. Ry.	Plaster Rock, N. B.	C. P. Ry.
Estcourt, Que.	C. G. Ry.	Fredericton, N. B.	C. P. Ry. and C. G. Ry.
Edmundston, N. B.	C.P.R., C.G.R. and Temiscouata Ry.	Nelson, N. B.	C. G. Ry.
Bleached Sulphite Mill, Edmundston, N. B.		Railway Connection	C.P.R., C.G.R. and Temiscouata Ry.

Bleached Sulphite. Rough and Dressed Spruce. White Cedar Shingles. Railway Ties

Piano Sounding Board Stock a Specialty.

Selling and Purchasing Offices :-- EDMUNDSTON, N. B.

SERVICE

Fir, Cedar and Spruce

LUMBER

"Service" Lumber Co.

Pacific Building, VANCOUVER, B.C.

Eastern Representative, A. W. BARNHILL, 20 St. James Street, Montreal.

Ontario Representative, A. R. MASURET, 60 King St. W., Toronto. Telephone Adelaide 3071

International Land & Lumber Company, Limited

Lumber, Railway Ties Shims, Shingles, etc.

Head Offices, Ottawa, Ont.

Limits and Mills: ST. FELICIEN, LAKE ST. JOHN DISTRICT, QUEBEC

Our NEW TIMBER MILL

(Capacity 100,000 Feet Ten Hours.) NOW IN OPERATION

We solicit your enquiries for

Heavy Construction Material and Yard Stock

ANY SIZE TIMBERS UP TO 100 FT.

Give us an opportunity to prove to you that we have earned a reputation for Quality and Service.

Timberland Lumber Co., Limited

Head Office: Westminster Trust Bldg., NEW WESTMINSTER, B.C.

Mills at South Westminster, on B.C.E.R.

Shipments by C.P.R., C.N.R., G.N.R., N.P.R. and C.M. & St. P. Ry.

Arrow Brand Shingles Hit the Mark

Shingle Bolts in Reserve—RUSKIN, B.C.

ALLEN-STOLTZE LUMBER CO., LTD.

C. C. BOCKUS, 17 Knox Street, MONTREAL, P.Q.

VANCOUVER, B.C.

R. G. CHESBRO, 1304 Bank of Hamilton Bldg., TORONTO, ONT.

Atlantic Lumber Company
HARDWOODS

WEST VIRGINIA SOFT RED AND WHITE OAK
Our Specialty: West Virginia and Pennsylvania Cherry

1055 Seneca Street

Standard Hardwood Lumber Co.
Hardwoods

Prompt Shipment { From Buffalo Yards or from Mill direct to you

8 Million Feet Dry Stock on Hand 1333 Clinton St.

Hugh McLean Lumber Co.
Hardwoods of All Kinds

Our Specialties—QUARTERED WHITE OAK
SAP AND RED GUM

Established 25 Years 940 Elk Street

Miller, Sturm & Miller
1142 SENECA STREET

Hardwoods of All Kinds

G. Elias & Bro., Inc.
Established 1881

All Kinds of Hardwood Lumber

And in addition we carry a full line of
White Pine, Yellow Pine, Spruce, Hemlock and Fir Timber, Lumber, Millwork and Boxes—Maple and Oak Flooring

CAREFUL ATTENTION TO MIXED CAR ORDERS

Taylor & Crate
Hardwoods of All Kinds

A stock of 18,000,000 to 20,000,000 feet of hardwoods carried at all times at our two big Buffalo Yards

Established 50 Years Rail or Cargo Shipments

T. Sullivan & Co.
HARDWOODS

We Specialize in Brown Ash and Elm

Car or Cargo Shipments Cor. Niagara and Arthur Sts.

Yeager Lumber Company, Inc.
SPECIALTIES

Oak, Poplar, Ash, Maple

932 Elk Street

BUFFALO

Buffalo Hardwood Lumber Dealers

Buffalo Hardwood Lumber Co.
940 Seneca St.

We specialize in White Ash, Plain Oak, Qtd. Oak, Maple and Poplar. We also carry a complete stock of Native Hardwoods.

Blakeslee, Perrin & Darling
A Complete Stock of Seasoned Hardwoods

including Ash, Basswood, Birch, Cherry, Chestnut, Cypress, Elm, Gum, Hickory, Maple, Plain and Quartered Oak, Poplar and Walnut.

1100 Seneca Street

Canada Lumberman and Woodworker

Issued on the 1st and 15th of every month by

HUGH C. MACLEAN, LIMITED, Publishers

HUGH C. MacLEAN, Winnipeg, President.

THOS. S. YOUNG, Toronto, General Manager.

OFFICES AND BRANCHES:

TORONTO - - Telephone A. 2700 - - 347 Adelaide Street West
VANCOUVER - - Telephone Seymour 2013 - - Winch Building
MONTREAL - - Telephone Main 2299 - - 119 Board of Trade
WINNIPEG - Telephone Garry 856 - Electric Railway Chambers
NEW YORK - - Telephone 3108 Beekman - - 1123 Tribune Building
CHICAGO - Telephone Harrison 5351 - 1413 Great Northern Building
LONDON, ENG. - - - - - - - - - - 16 Regent Street, S.W.

TERMS OF SUBSCRIPTION

Canada, United States and Great Britain, $2.00 per year, in advance; other foreign countries embraced in the General Postal Union, $3.00.

Single copies 15 cents.

"The Canada Lumberman and Woodworker" is published in the interest of, and reaches regularly, persons engaged in the lumber, woodworking and allied industries in every part of Canada. It aims at giving full and timely information on all subjects touching these interests, and invites free discussion by its readers.

Advertisers will receive careful attention and liberal treatment. For manufacturing and supply firms wishing to bring their goods to the attention of owners and operators of saw and planing mills, woodworking factories, pulp mills, etc., "The Canada Lumberman and Woodworker" is undoubtedly the most direct and profitable advertising medium. Special attention is directed to the "Wanted" and "For Sale" advertisements.

Authorized by the Postmaster-General for Canada, for transmission as second-class matter.

Entered as second-class matter July 18th, 1914, at the Postoffice at Buffalo, N.Y., under the Act of Congress of March 3, 1879.

Vol. 39 Toronto, August 15, 1919 No 16

The Revival of Building Operations

All classes of lumbermen are vitally interested in construction. This is a truism that requires no elaboration. Hence the lumber trade will note with satisfaction the revival that is taking place in building. Reports from all over the Dominion indicate that the long depression, dating from the outbreak of war, is passing away, and that there are signs of a new era.

There is plenty of scope for this return to better conditions. There is no doubt that the public lost confidence in building. During the war the Federal, provincial, and municipal authorities, as well as companies, firms and private people restricted their investments in brick and mortar and in other work to the barest necessities. Of course, a considerable amount of construction, in the form of factories, was compelled by the rise of the ammunition industry, but in other directions the expenditure was very small.

An adverse factor was the steady rise in the cost of building material. Lumber, it is true, did not advance in proportion to some other materials, but the general tendency was upwards. Many people postponed work in the vain hope that prices would come down—the contrary was the case, and for the best of all reasons—labor, which is the main factor in the cost of building, demanded more pay, and got it. Some classes of material, too, were scarce, and advanced.

Apparently many of the projects which were postponed are now being proceeded with. Many of the public which have money to spend on building have, it would seem, come to the conclusion that prices will not be scaled down, and that construction will not be cheaper for some time. Some commodities have fallen, but others and labor have, per contra, advanced; it is likely, moreover, that lumber, to take one item, will be dearer. Some architects and engineers state that if materials were on a lower basis more work would come out, particularly in the way of houses, as at the present cost it is almost impossible to build and obtain an adequate return on the expenditure. While this may be true in many instances, the fact remains that all conditions are against reduced costs. The increase in the volume of contracts let is evidence that this is being recognized. In Montreal and Toronto the building permits for July were the largest since the war.

Canada is following the example of the States, which are now freely buying our lumber. The outlook here is decidedly good, with indications of a substantial recovery this fall and next year.

Eliminating the Narrow Viewpoint

The vision of some men, as well as of some communities, is lamentably restricted. They judge the importance and significance of all problems largely from a selfish and narrow standpoint. Certain organizations, like certain individuals, are seemingly incapable of taking a broad and comprehensive grasp of any phase of activity or development that partakes of a national character or upbuild. They have not developed the facility of seeing the other fellow's viewpoint. It is wise to look upon both sides of every question and, after weighing the pros and cons come to a calm, dispassionate decision.

For a number of years now the Ontario Department of Lands, Forests and Mines, like similar departments in New Brunswick and Quebec, has been exercising rigid regulations so far as the burning of slash by the settlers is concerned. Slash has been described as "the garbage of the forest." Its ignition at ill advised times and under unfavorable conditions has resulted in untold damage. Like many stupendous events in life, which have a small beginning and expand through the course of time and action, so a forest fire may start from a tiny brush blaze—the perpetrator little thinking of the immense havoc that may be wrought by a strong wind, dry undergrowth or other contributing agencies.

Considering the ravages of flame in 1911 and also the great holocaust in 1916 in Northern Ontario it is difficult to believe that after these terrible experiences anyone would come forward with the suggestion of continuing menacing practices. The agitation for free running fires, in order to clear off the land for settlement, is still in the air and letters appear in the columns of the press in Northern Ontario, from alleged "friends of the settlers," setting forth the right of the struggling farmer to fire his slashes whenever he feels so disposed, irrespective of time, conditions, preparations or surroundings. The latest of these newspaper pleas appears in the Cobalt Nugget of recent date, signed "Settler." In two columns of complaint regarding the hardship of having to take out a permit before lighting his land-clearing fires, "Settler" never once mentions the fact that unbridled freedom in setting fire to forests in Northern Ontario has on more than one occasion established a chain of graveyards from New Liskeard to Cochrane, says the Canadian Forestry Journal. In countries with the peculiar conditions of Northern Ontario no method has yet been discovered for "burning off the country" without burning up the people. The 1916 disaster which supplied columns of anguishing details was the product of unrestricted settlers' fires. Any modification of the present provisions would deliberately withdraw the chief safeguard thrown about the thousands of men, women and children now resident in the Claybelt.

Should Pulpwood Embargo be Extended?

The press of Northern Ontario is clamouring for the Legislature to pass a measure shutting off the exportation of pulpwood, even from freehold lands, to the United States. This problem has long received consideration and sporadic efforts have been made from time to time to induce the Federal government to take a determined stand in this direction. French Canadian representatives and other M.P.'s have always contended strenuously against the passing of such a bill. It was feared the United States, which in 1918 obtained from Canada 1,325,565 cords of the value of $8,339,278, might retaliate by placing an embargo on anthracite coal or pursuing some other course in reprisal that would be inimical to the expansion and operation of Canadian industries. Drastic measures have to be considered from more than a selfish standpoint and moderate means are always preferable to extreme ones, except in isolated cases. The sectional viewpoint largely prevails in the agitation now and then heard for restrictions to be placed on all wood coming off private lands.

For some years legislation has been in effect in Ontario, Quebec and New Brunswick, distinctly setting forth that no pulpwood can be shipped from Crown lands except that it first be converted into pulp or paper. To extend the embargo to private holdings aroused the opposition of certain members of parliament, who were apprehensive of retaliatory measures from "Uncle Sam." They also feared that the settlers in certain portions of Northern Ontario, as well as in the province of Quebec—if absolutely no export of pulpwood was permitted—would be at the mercy of local pulp and paper companies who could possibly dictate terms and make their own prices for wood. As it now is, the settler has the United States market open to him and is not confined in his negotiations for the sale of his annual cut to one source only. Monopoly is frequently the fruit of restriction and, as the settler depends a great deal on the revenue obtained from his wood in order to carry him through the first few years of his struggle he desires to sell in the dearest market, and if this were shut off existence would be all the more trying and difficult.

One paper in Northern Ontario in upholding the contention for the total prohibition for the export of pulpwood, takes the following view of the situation:—

"The war came and revealed the really desperate condition in which many of the mills in the United States find themselves. The wood from Canada is keeping them alive. If the supply were shut off the mills would either go out of business or remove to this country. We hold the situation in the hollow of our hand. The question for the government to decide is whether it is better to take all there is in the trade, or be the simple hewer of wood. This question must be settled and settled in the true interests of the north country, which is the interests of the province as a whole.

"The answer must not be left until the forests are depleted as was the case with the pine, but must be answered now when there is yet time to establish the paper business on the basis which our resources warrant."

Speaking along this line, J. A. Bothwell, of East Angus, Que., who is president of the Canadian Pulp and Paper Association, says: "The moral for Canada is that not only must this country continue the restrictions now imposed upon the exportation of pulp wood, but we must, if we would enjoy the full benefits of our heritage, apply them more intensively. This becomes all the more important when we realize that our supply of wood, far from being inexhaustible, is diminishing at a rate which threatens its complete exhaustion within a comparatively few years. The inroads made by the paper manufacturing industry are not the only source of diminution of our pulpwood forests. Fires, insects, and fungus growths all contribute to the destruction. A blight known as the budworm has recently worked an enormous amount of damage to the pulpwood limits of Quebec, destroying practically the entire stock of balsam and injuring other forest species. Neither the natural re-growths nor artificial propagation, as at present carried on, can possibly overtake the rate at which our pulpwood resources are being depleted by these several means. The most serious problem in the industry to-day is how to bring to bear ways and means that will result in perpetuating our pulpwood supplies and thus continue the industry as one of the premier wealth-producing agencies of the Dominion. The larger the returns we receive for our pulp and paper exports the better able will we be to provide these ways and means.

"Most of the wood now exported in its manufactured state is cut from freehold lands and settlers' lots, and while it is in great demand and furnishes a source of temporary income appreciated by the owners and settlers, the policy which permits it to be done is short-sighted in the extreme and the practice one that ought to be discouraged."

It would appear that the question of placing an embargo on all pulpwood is about as vexatious in character and complex in effecting a satisfactory solution as the tariff issue, total prohibition, collective bargaining, national ownership of public utilities or the reconstruction and re-establishment processes following the war. All require much thought, labor and study to adjust wisely and well and with the idea in view of effecting the "greatest good to the greatest number."

The Value of Educational Outings

The business man who can unshackle himself from the cares and worries of his own immediate interests and betake himself to another scene for a holiday, generally comes back refreshed and invigorated to resume his work where he left it off. On his return he discovers that things have gone on just about as well or even better than if he were "Johnny-on-the-spot." It is almost impossible for some of us to get away from delusions. The more we are inclined to think along certain lines and raise mental barriers, the more convinced we become that our business could not really go along without us and that it is quite impossible to take a vacation like other fellows and, amid new associations and other scenes, while away a few days or weeks. To shatter this hallucination sometimes requires the visitation of a prevalent malady or accident; then the average mortal suddenly realizes in his isolation and detachment of how little consequence he is after all in the scheme of mundane affairs.

It is often difficult to displace personal prejudice, uproot distorted ideas or undermine cherished traditions, yet it is being done on every side by the progressive sweep of world-wide events. Capital and labor are learning to appreciate that more time is needed for recreation and play. The trouble with most of us is that we take ourselves too seriously and in order to get out of this frame of mind or self centred groove there is nothing like a genuine, care-free holiday.

What good-will, unity and co-operation is doing in commercial and industrial ranks is evidenced on all sides. The midsummer annual outing of the Ontario Retail Lumber Dealers' Association is more largely patronized each year and the recent educational trip saw some seventy representatives gathered from various points in the province. They visited a dozen sawmills and woodworking plants and witnessed, under the most favorable auspices, the methods of manufacture of all kinds of forest products; gained a wider and more thorough acquaintance of the goods they handle and were enabled to gauge the other fellow's problems as well as give some heed to their own.

Too frequently in our own restricted interests, we are inclined to believe that the barriers and snags are along our own journey and the retailer is disposed to think the other fellow, such as the manufacturer and wholesaler, follow a primrose path. It is only by the interchange of views, visits and visions that one's conceptions grow larger, one's sympathies broader and the grasp of the great game of business more kind.

Then there is the social side of such jaunts, where fellow dealer meets fellow dealer and swaps experiences. Each comes away feeling that the other is a pretty good sort after all and that the struggle is really worth while. The man from the east who converses with the man from the west and the chap from the south who chats with one from the north, discovers, in mutual interchanges, that all retail lumbermen have about the same triumphs and trials, successes and failures, hopes and disappointments, no matter where they are located.

In other words, the lumber business is like a great human family. In aims and achievements, purposes and pursuits, all its exponents find the same incentives and emotions, pleasures and perplexities. The one who is inclined to grow weary or downhearted, or halt by the wayside, is stimulated to greater activity and fresh endeavor on hearing a narrative of some other fellow's struggle, and comes to the conclusion, "Well, if he conquered so can I." At he goes again with stout heart, clear conscience and determined ort—and, best of all, he wins out.

The railways are making ready for another advance in freight rates but not a word is heard from them regarding more efficient service.

Ontario Lumber Retailers Visit Many Mills

Midsummer Educational Outing Attracts Representative Dealers from all Parts of Province—Enjoyable Trip to Busy Georgian Bay Towns

Well managed, enjoyable and successful in every respect was the annual midsummer educational outing of the Ontario Retail Lumber Dealers' Association, which was held from Thursday evening, July 31st, to Monday evening, August 4th.

The objective points were Penetanguishene, Midland, Victoria Harbor and Parry Sound. The welcome accorded the visitors at all of these centres, both by the lumbermen and the citizens, was cordial and sincere and the memory of the trip will live long in the minds of the seventy representatives of the retail ranks who had the pleasure of participating in the proceedings. Everything was admirably arranged and each event was carried out promptly and agreeably. There were no delays and no disappointments—in fact, the itinerary from the time that the party left Toronto by G. T. R. in a special pullman car at 5.50 on Thursday afternoon, July 31, until the return home at the same hour on Monday evening, August 4, was closely followed. The retailers were loud in their expressions of satisfaction at the enjoyable associations of the journey. Many of them learned and saw a great deal more in the few days' jaunt than they would hanging around their own yards in a year. They gathered much information anent the various processes of manufacturing lumber from the stump to the pile and became acquainted with the different kinds of mill equipment—cutting, edging, trimming, grading, sorting, piling, shipping, etc. They grew familiar with all these problems, first-hand, and came home with a wider knowledge of the importance and greatness of the industry they represent and a more adequate appreciation of the difficulties and handicaps which manufacturers have to overcome—particularly during the present trying period when labor is restless, the market particularly active and men in some centres difficult to procure.

The First Leg of the Journey

Arriving at Penetang at 10 o'clock the party were met by W. F. Beck, chairman of the local reception committee, and Mayor C. E. Wright and members of the city council and board of trade. The delegates were soon comfortably quartered at the different hotels in that progressive town. After all had been assigned to their respective rooms, word was passed round that a reception was to be tendered the visitors in the spacious Sunday-school Hall of All Saints Church. There the lumbermen repaired and found a tasty and varied menu awaiting them, both for the intellectual and the inner man. The tables were laden with all the good things that could be provided and amid the exhalation of smoke from the fragrant havanas, the yardmen and their friends sat down to enjoy an hour or more of song, music and speech. Local talent contributed materially to the enjoyment of the occasion and Penetang certainly has some clever artists.

The retail lumbermen aboard Manley Chew's tug at Midland

C. E. Wright, Mayor, welcomed the retail lumbermen on the occasion of their first visit to Penetanguishene, and said that the municipal council and the board of trade had joined together in tendering them the reception at which they were present and in providing the repast of which they had just partaken. He assured the lumbermen that the freedom of Penetang was theirs and that the town constable had been locked up for the night. It was, indeed, a pleasure to greet so many representative business men and he trusted that their stay—brief though it was—would be both profitable and instructive.

In the absence of Thos. Patterson, of Hamilton, president of the Ontario Retail Lumber Dealers' Association, who was on a trip to the south, John B. Reid, of Toronto, vice-president of the Association, delivered one of his optimistic and breezy addresses. On behalf of the organization he thanked the Mayor and the people of Penteang for their cordial welcome. The reception was certainly something that the lumbermen had not been looking for, and it was, therefore, all the more pleasant, coming as it did in the nature of a surprise. Mr. Reid stated that the retail lumbermen were there this evening as a result and as the fruit of an organization which has been formed less than two years ago. It was the custom of the members to take trips now and then for educational purposes and also to cultivate the spirit of co-operation and sociability.

Viewing yards and stock of lumber at Victoria Harbor

The Broadening Effect of Organization

Mr. Reid enlarged upon the benefits of friendship and mutual confidence in business, and how associations broadened a man's ideals and sympathies. He came to realize that there was some good in the other fellow, as well as in himself. Three years ago the members of the retail lumbermen in Toronto were composed largely of grouches and cranks, and today you could not find one in the ranks; that was what association had done for the dealers of the Queen City and the movement had extended throughout the province and even to the ranks of the wholesalers. They had learned a lot and been taught to appreciate one another and, in the spirit of harmony and co-operation were marching on to better and brighter things. Life was larger than the dollar, and sordid self should not take possession of men's souls. The fellow who shed gladness and sunshine about him and gave a cheery smile and a welcome word to his fellowman was worth much more to himself and the community than the miserable wretch who chased life only for all the gold he could get out of it and in the end passed away mourned by none of his fellows.

In a more humorous vein Mr. Reid pointed out that some of the retail lumbermen present had been handling lumber all their lives, yet had never seen the inside of a sawmill. They had come up to Penetang to find out things, and, more particularly, discover the firms who made the culls. He was certain that no one would dare ship out culls to members of the Association after their trip to Penetang, as the offenders would be spotted.

It appears that Penetang is organizing a Board of Trade, and

Mr. Reid was asked by Mayor Wright to give the citizens some ideas of how to undertake the work successfully and to outline in what way the institution might be of the greatest benefit and service to the community. Mr. Reid then took up in detail the work of the Toronto Board of Trade, informing those present how it is divided into sections, each having its own particular interests and dealing with its own peculiar problems, yet on the larger and more vital questions having the backing and support of the whole body or institution. He referred to the formation of the Lumbermen's Section, which had in three years become the most influential section of the Toronto Board of Trade.

The Benefits of the Credit Bureau

Everything relating to the lumber industry is now harmonious and the members have ceased cut-throat practices and eliminated petty jealousies and distrust. Out of the Lumbermen's Section has grown the Credit Bureau, which is a distinctly useful institution, and any member can speedily tell when an application is made for credit whether to extend it or not. So valuable has become its work and worth that, at the last annual meeting, the membership fee was raised to $100, and the regular dues had to be paid by the members, as well, added Mr. Reid, who went on to say that owing to the well balanced service and operation of the bureau losses had been practically wiped out. Out of the credit bureau of the retailers had grown the credit bureau of the wholesalers, who had also formed the Wholesale Lumber Dealers' Association. The big men had seen how well smaller ones had got along through association and had decided to copy their example. The retailers had built up their present prosperous body upon the principles of sociability, honesty and integrity, all of which formed a solid foundation. They had confidence in themselves and in one another and believed that the other chap should have a chance to go ahead and prosper as long as he conducted his business on a fair and honorable basis.

Taking in the beautiful vistas of the Georgian Bay

Horace Boultbee, secretary of the Retail Lumber Dealers' Association, followed in a short address recounting his early visits to Penetanguishine many years ago. He dwelt appreciatively on the hospitality of the town and referred to the encouraging progress of the Ontario Retail Lumber Dealers' Association, which now had 166 members in good standing and is growing all the while. Mr. Boultbee said they had a large program to carry out during their stay and it was important that everybody should be on time for each event. He also spoke hopefully regarding the Wholesale Lumber Dealers' Association, which had become incorporated and now had 35 members. Both the wholesalers and retailers, through the mediums of organization, were learning to appreciate and know one another better. The attitude of the wholesalers toward the retail men had changed considerably so that any small man was now assured of courteous treatment and consideration of just claims when presented.

G. B. Van Blaricom, editor of the "Canada Lumberman," made a few closing remarks, speaking briefly on the advantages of organization and the importance and educational value of the trips taken by the retail lumbermen. The attendance every year showed a gratifying increase, which was indicative of the benefit of such outings.

The proceedings closed with the singing of the National Anthem and three hearty cheers for the chief magistrate and lumbermen of Penetanguishene.

The next morning automobiles were at the hotels shortly after eight o'clock. The cars were kindly placed at the disposal of the visitors by the local lumbermen and merchants, and for three hours the various industrial plants of Penetang were visited. The first mill that was inspected was that of W. J. Martin, which is driven by [illegible] h.p. motor and is the only electrically-driven sawmill in the province. Then followed in succession visits to the industries of Gropp Bros., Fibre Products, Limited, which is greatly increasing its output; Firstbrook Bros.' box plant; McGibbon Lumber Co.'s mill, and the two sawmills, the planing mill, pail and tub factory, box plant and other departments of the C. Beck Mfg. Co. Then a stop was made at the Gidley Boat Works and the next industry inspected was the Dominion Stove & Foundry Co. Afterwards a drive was enjoyed round town and a visit paid to the asylum for the insane (which years ago was a provincial reformatory for incorrigible boys). W. F. [illegible], G. A. Beck, Finlay McGibbon, W. J. Martin and others did all in their power to make the industrial tour pleasant and instructive.

The travelling lumbermen were next conveyed by automobile to the neighboring town of Midland, where they had dinner at the Queen's Hotel. Afterwards, in motor cars provided by the town and the citizens, visits were paid to the busy plant of Manley Chew, ex-M.P., who extended hearty greetings to the guests. This is, undoubtedly, the fastest producing sawmill in the whole Georgian Bay district, turning out one-quarter of a million feet of lumber every twenty-four hours, the plant running day and night. The enterprise of the Georgian Bay Shook Mills (now Midland Woodworkers, Limited), of which R. H. Scribener is in charge, next came under the review of the sightseers. Various processes of manufacture were closely followed, and the output of the company afforded much scope for inquiry and favorable comment. The motor cars were again filled and a trip taken through the extensive yards of Chew Bros. One outstanding feature of this plant is the splendid fire protection system. Ed. Letherby, managing-director of the firm, was on hand and made everything enjoyable for the visitors as they were conducted through the various departments, including the lath and picket sections. A visit was paid to the plant of the Midland Woodworkers, Limited, which turn out doors, columns, sash and mouldings of all kinds. M. J. Bray acted as guide, counsellor and friend, and the neatness, order and arrangement of all departments aroused more than passing interest.

The Boat Trip to Honey Harbor

Returning to the Queen's Hotel the members of the party soon made their way to the wharf, where the steamer "Tenno" was boarded for a trip down the inside channel of the 30,000 islands of the Georgian Bay, and after a sail of a little over an hour, a short call was made at the Royal Hotel, of which Grise Bros. are proprietors. It had been arranged that the retail lumbermen should partake of dinner there at a later hour, and, pending its preparation, the journey among the many islands was resumed, the boat travelling amid scenes and narrow waterways not usually witnessed by the average tourist. Everywhere salutes and greetings were exchanged with the cottagers, and at 7.30 o'clock a return was made to the hotel, where the guests sat down to an admirably prepared and splendidly served dinner. It was one of the best arranged and excellently conducted social affairs.

At the close a vote of thanks, moved by J. B. Reid, and seconded by W. B. Tennant, was moved to Ed. Letherby, of Midland, for his kindness and courtesy in doing so much to make the lumbermen's visit entertaining and edifying. Mr. Reid spoke in the highest terms of Mr. Letherby's integrity, kindliness and useful public career, he having for several years been Mayor of Midland, of which town he is one of its most influential and upright citizens.

Mr. Letherby in replying disclaimed any special praise for what little part he has played in the entertainment of the party. He trusted that they would have, as a result of their visit, better ideas of the serious problems which manufacturers had to face. Getting out the timber, conveying it to the mill and sawing it into lumber was not all sunshine, as costs were increasing very rapidly and labor was becoming most insistent in its demands. The lumbermen's road had not been an alluring one during the years of the war, and many a dollar had been invested without the sight of another one in return. The disbursements for timber limits, logging, driving, towing and other overhead expenses, were increasing all the time and the total extra cost from the stump to the finished product would, he estimated, be all the way from 25 to 40 per cent. over that of a year ago. He was very glad to see so many lumbermen present on an occasion of this kind and was sure they would take away with them many happy and delightful memories of their visit to Midland.

C. A. McDowell, Mayor of Midland, added a few words of greeting, and told of the pleasure which it gave the town to entertain the visitors. After three cheers for mine host Grise, of the Royal Hotel, the party set sail on the "Tenno" on the return trip to Midland, which was reached shortly before midnight.

Early on Saturday morning, before the average citizen in Midland had withdrawn himself from the coverlets in his sleeping quarters,

Ed. Letherby,
of Chew Bros., Midland, Ont.

F. N. Waldie,
of Victoria Harbor Lumber Co.

Finlay McGibbon,
of McGibbon Lumber Co., Penetanguishene

Manley Chew, ex-M.P.,
Midland, Ont.

the sojourning lumbermen were wide awake and partaking of a hearty breakfast. Manley Chew had kindly placed one of his tugs at the disposal of the visitors and equipped the steamer with chairs so that all rode in comfort to Victoria Harbor, first paying a short visit to Port McNicoll, the eastern terminus of the Great Lakes Navigation Co. Arriving at Victoria Harbor about 9 o'clock the members of the delegation were cordially greeted by G. E. Spragge, sales manager of the Victoria Harbor Lumber Co., and Jerome Duckworth, manager of the manufacturing end. They were conducted through the saw and planing mills and afterwards made a tour of the extensive yards and stock. Everything around the premises, both interiorally and exteriorally, betokened neatness, method and dispatch. The great lumber industry of Victoria Harbor was founded many years ago by the late John Waldie, and around it has been built up a solid and contented village.

At noon in the Royal Victoria Hotel the sight-seeing yard-men sat down to a splendidly served and temptingly prepared repast as the guests of the Victoria Harbor Lumber Co., of which F. N. Waldie is president. The preparation of the viands and the execution of the service had been left in the hands of the good ladies of the Presbyterian church, who left nothing undone to see that all appetites were appeased. G. E. Spragge presided.

Mr. Wm. Laking, of Hamilton, head of the Wm. Laking Lumber Co., arose amid applause and stated that before taking departure, he, being the oldest member of the party, would like to say a few words in respect of the splendid treatment the manufacturers had accorded the retailers throughout this trip. "They have used us royally, not only here, but in Midland and Penetanguishene," continued Mr. Laking, "and we will all have the desire to come back again. The present outing has been a most successful one in every way. It has been a time of education and pleasure. I, myself, feel that I am a link between the past and the present, and as I have wandered around the yards here to-day, I have been reminded of the scores of years gone by and many old lumbermen friends in this

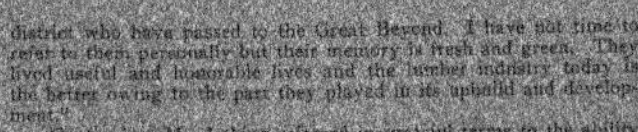

district who have passed to the Great Beyond. I have not time to refer to them personally but their memory is fresh and green. They lived useful and honorable lives and the lumber industry today is the better owing to the part they played in its upbuild and development."

Continuing, Mr. Laking referred in grateful terms to the ability and faithfulness of Mr. Boultbee, secretary of the Ontario Retail Dealers' Association, and the great benefits accruing from association. He felt that no small amount of praise, not only of the present enjoyable trip, but also of the credit bureau, was due largely to the energy and foresight of Mr. Boultbee. Reverting to the social side of such outings as the present, Mr. Laking said that sociability had been too much neglected in the past, and the present age is moving along in the direction of more sociability and co-operation. The speaker added that he had seen more of life than anyone else in the room and he believed that Canada was the best country on the face of the globe and that Canadians were as good a people as were to be found in any land.

Tendering Thanks to the Manufacturers

Mr. John B. Reid, in seconding Mr. Laking's vote of thanks to the manufacturers in general, and the Victoria Harbor Lumber Co. in particular, for their hospitality, naively said that the lumber manufacturers had, at least, learned to appreciate the hard work of the poor retail man. An association has been organized in the retail ranks to do good to the members as a whole and there was no necessity of dwelling at any length on the success which has characterized the association. They had evidence of it on all sides in the present gathering. The speaker praised the menu provided by the ladies and the warmth of welcome which had been extended by the Victoria Harbor Lumber Co. All members could, as individuals, do much to make the association an even greater success than it had developed into and to cultivate more brotherly love and friendship in the retail ranks. Mr. Reid said he was glad to hear Mr. Laking refer to the

A. E. Beck,
of the A. E. Beck Mfg. Co., Penetanguishene

G. A. Maclean,
of the Conger Lumber Co., Parry Sound

John B. Reid, of Toronto,
Vice-president of the Association

Horace Boultbee, of Toronto,
Secretary of the Association

social benefits derived from such gatherings and felt that all would re-echo the sentiment that, through co-operation and mutual helpfulness, cut-throat methods were among the relics of the past and today there had been ushered in friendship and brotherly love, which augured well for the future weal of the industry in all its varied activities.

Mr. Spragge, replying on behalf of the Victoria Harbor Lumber Co., said he felt extremely flattered by the remarks that had been made and added that the ladies of the Presbyterian Church were responsible for the high character of the luncheon. "It has been a great pleasure for us to have you with us," concluded the speaker, "and we hope you will all come back again when we will endeavor to give you an even better time than we have on the present occasion." A hearty vote of thanks was moved to the Ladies Aid by W. C. Irvin, who paid them not a few compliments in the course of a happy speech. This was seconded by T. E. Paterson and carried unanimously. Rev. A. E. Neilly, pastor of the Victoria Harbor Presbyterian Church, replied in a humorous vein.

Another resolution carried was that of appreciation of the work and worth of Secretary Boultbee, which was moved by Mr. Laking and seconded by Mr. Fred Taylor, of Hamilton.

On the Way Up to Parry Sound

The diners then made their way to the steamer, and once more aboard Manley Chew's tug set sail for Penetanguishene, where the twin-screw steamer "Waubic" of the Northern Navigation Co., was taken for a trip to Parry Sound. At Victoria Harbor about 15 or 20 members of the party, who could not remain over Sunday and Monday, departed for their respective homes, amid the hearty cheers of the remainder of the company.

Nearly fifty happy excursionists enjoyed the delightful voyage amid the 30,000 island route to Parry Sound, a distance of some 65 miles from Penetang. The steamer called at the summer resorts of Honey Harbour, Minnecog, Whalen's, Go-Home Bay, Wahwahtaysee, Manitou, Copper Head, Sans Souci and Rose Point, arriving at Parry Sound shortly after 9 o'clock in the evening. The various cottages all appeared to their best advantage and at every port of call there were gasoline launches and put-puts galore, while many witty sallies were exchanged between the tourists on the docks and the sightseers on the deck of the "Waubic." Arrived at Parry Sound the travellers were warmly greeted by Mr. Fitzgerald, representing the Conger Lumber Co., of which W. B. Maclean is president, and escorted to the Hotel Belvidere, which occupies a commanding position overlooking Georgian Bay. The two days at Parry Sound were spent pleasantly in visiting the mill and yards of the Conger Lumber Co. and in taking in the various points of interest of this progressive town. Through the kindness and generosity of the Conger Lumber Co., the steamer "Voyageur" was placed at the disposal of the visitors, a pleasing act which the members will not soon forget. The Conger Lumber Co. also provided refreshments. Under the guidance of Secretary Boultbee, some twenty-five members set out on a bass fishing jaunt. "The boys" were accompanied by Capt. E. E. Tedford, of Cork, Ireland, who is a British government inspector of the various steamers which are being turned out for overseas at the Midland Shipbuilding Co.'s plant. The captain has sailed all around the world, but it is doubtful if he ever fell in with more jolly fellows than he did on this angling expedition.

The arrival of the party at Honey Harbor for evening dinner

Some twelve or fifteen miles from Parry Sound anchor was weighed and small boats taken by a number of enthusiastic disciples of Izaac Walton, who were earnest enough in their pursuit of the finny tribe to depopulate the waters of Georgian Bay so far as the bass colony is concerned. A real, old-fashioned open air lunch was enjoyed on the island, and after a stay of a few hours, the whistle of the "Voyageur" sounded shrilly, which was the signal that the piscatorial party should return to the deck. The net result of the day's catch was not as satisfactory as it might have been, as only about a half dozen bass were captured, but the anglers had all done their best, and what more can be expected of any man, or body of men!

Just before departing it was suggested that the name of the island, which had been "discovered," should be perpetuated, and upon a huge rock, in black letters, two feet deep, were printed the words "Lumbermen's Island—No Fish." When the Ontario Department of Education issues a new geography in order to set forth accurately the new boundary lines of European countries which were altered during the war, there is no doubt but that the Minister of Education will see that there is shown prominently among the islands of the Georgian Bay the one which was charted and christened by the retail lumbermen.

While they may not have been able to "discover" fish, they were at least able to explore land, and names of the members will go down with those of Columbus, Champlain, Cabot, Cartier and other venturesome spirits of historic renown.

On the return to Parry Sound the half dozen fish secured were cooked at the Empire restaurant. There were about forty fish-loving lumbermen who thought that there should be ample quantity to go round, and like the miracle of old, the catch could be blessed and made to multiply until all appetites were satisfied. No miracle man was in the company—no super-lord of creation—and less than one-half of the assembly did not have the pleasure of feasting at the bass banquet.

After a restful night's sleep the happy but tired party set sail for home. When the steamer called at Copperhead Island, Secretary Boultbee left his associates to continue the rest of the journey alone. He decided to stay at this widely-known fishing resort for a few days in order to deplete the surrounding waters of the finest specimens and to show, on his return home, what a real angler can do when he sets out alone and unaided to capture the finny tribe.

The party reached home on Monday evening all loud in their praise of the success of the four days' educational and pleasure outing and unanimously declaring that next year they will be ready once more to join in a pilgrimage as bright and enjoyable as the one of 1919.

In connection with the narrative of the jaunt of the Ontario Retail Lumber Dealers' Association, no attempt has been made in this issue to describe in detail the operation of the various plants visited. Only the social and recreative side of the events has been touched upon, and in a later edition of the "Canada Lumberman" there will be presented illustrations and descriptive write-ups of the different lumber and woodworking industries.

The Members of the Party

The following is the register of those who lined up for the trip:

Piggott, P. G., Piggott Lumber Co., Chatham.
Anderson, Roy, Consumers' Lumber Co., Hamilton.
Anglin, F. R., S. Anglin & Co., Kingston.
Barnes, John T., Walter Davidson & Co., Ltd., Toronto.
Barrett, Wm., Canada Lumber Co., Ltd., Weston.
Bond, T. G., Batts, Limited, Toronto.
Boultbee, H., Toronto.
Bowden, H. V., Frank H. Bowden & Sons, Ltd., Toronto.
Bryan, F. W., The Bryan Mfg. Co., Ltd., Collingwood.
Bryan, G. E., The Bryan Mfg. Co., Ltd., Collingwood.
Burton, F. R., Consumers Lumber Co., Hamilton.
Cadenhead, J. K., R. Laidlaw Lumber Co., Toronto.
Campbell, John D., Cornwall.
Coates, Chas C., A. Coates & Sons, Burlington.
Crosthwaite, Harvey, Patterson & Crosthwaite, Hamilton.
DeLaplante, A. W., The Beaver Lumber Co., Hamilton.
Doty, C. F., Oakville.
Gillies, J. M., James Gillies & Son, Preston.
Harper, B. L., Consumers Lumber Co., Hamilton.
Harris, W. A., R. Laidlaw Lumber Co., Toronto.
Henderson, A., Cheltenham.
Henderson, Mrs. A., Cheltenham.
Howes, G. M., Harriston.
Ingleby, Chas. E., The Ingleby-Taylor Co., Brantford.
Irvin, W. C., The Irvin Lumber Co., Toront
Kalbfleisch. Emil., Kalbfleisch Planing Mill, Stratford.
Kent, F., Seaman, Kent Co., Toronto.
Laking, Wm., Riverdale Lumber Co., Toronto.
Merkle, W. J., Boake Mfg. Co., Toronto.

Morgan, J. M., F. A. Bowden & Sons, Toronto.
Mackenzie, J. B., Georgetown.
Mackenzie, Mrs. J. B., Georgetown.
McPherson, G. D., Merlin.
Nafziger, E. R., B. & N. Planing Mill, Milverton.
Paterson, T. A., Mickle, Dyment & Son, Toronto.
Press, R. J., The Alliance Lumber Co., Hamilton.
Reid, J. B., Reid & Co., Toronto.
Rhind, A., Simpson Planing Mill, Toronto.
Roper, C. H., John Poag & Co., Hamilton.
Smith, Clarence M., Aylmer.
Smith, Osborne, O. & W. R. Smith,Toronto.
Taylor, Edwin E., Ingleby-Taylor Co., Brantford.
Taylor, Fred D., Aitchison & Co., Hamilton.
Tupling, W. M., J. R. Eaton & Sons, Orillia.
Van Blaricom, G. B., "Canada Lumberman," Toronto.
Warren, W., R. Laidlaw Lumber Co., Toronto.
Waters, John P., Burks Falls, Riverdale Lumber Co., Toronto.
Watt, Allan, Watt Milling & Feed Co., Toronto.
Wells, C. M., Paris Station.
Wells, Mrs. C. M., Paris Station.
Williamson, Wm., Toronto.
Schmidt, C., R. Laidlaw Lumber Co., Toronto.
George, H., R. Laidlaw Lumber Co., Toronto.
Boake, Roy, Boake Mfg. Co., Toronto.
McCormack, J., Campbell, Welsh & Paynes, Toronto.
Tennant, W. B., J. B. Smith & Sons, Toronto.
Richards, C. F., R. Laidlaw Lumber Co., Sarnia.
Purse, A. J., R. Laidlaw Lumber Co., Toronto.
McDowell, J. S., Mayor of Midland, Midland.
Thuerck, W. C., Terry & Gordon, Toronto.
Letherby, Ed., Chew Bros., Midland.

Among the wholesalers, or the representatives who joined the party at Midland and took in the festivities, were: C. G. Anderson, Toronto; W. G. Paynes, Toronto; J. M. Donovan, Toronto; S. Dyment, C. Dyment and C. O. Cameron, of Mickle, Dyment & Son, Barrie.

Shall Sizes Continue to Shrink?

Retail lumber dealers in several of the Eastern States have been wondering why there should be a further shrinkage in the actual sizes of surfaced lumber. In some localities of New York consumers have protested against the scant sizes of lumber now being furnished by certain manufacturers. We refer to the surfacing of inch lumber below thirteen-sixteenths in thickness and to the reduction of lumber dressed four sides below one-fourth inch scant in width, says the "Lumber Co-operator."

Correspondence with associations of manufacturers indicates that the consensus of opinion is against a reduction of one-inch lumber, including flooring to less than thirteen-sixteenths in thickness. Some of the associations have rules to this effect.

The Southern Cypress Association says that for years at least 90 per cent. of the surfaced lumber has been 13/16, although it is still possible to secure 7/8 inch stock in Cypress, if it is so ordered and paid for.

The ruling of the Southern Pine Association is one inch dressed to 13/16, except for special stock, such as casings, bases, drop siding, and similar items.

The North Carolina Pine Association allows 1/8 inch for one side and 3/16 inch for dressing both sides.

The West Coast Lumbermen's Association says that it has been their practice to ship common lumber green, and their ruling now in one inch S1S or S2S, finished size 3/4 inch. Common boards S2S or shiplap to 3/4 inch. The moist climate plays an important part, and until recently no dry kilns have been successfully developed which will permit the drying of common lumber produced in that territory. This is a problem to which attention is being given at this time in the hope of finding a solution. We are informed that this organization does not contemplate any changes in its sizes in the direction of scant measures, but that on the other hand there is a growing sentiment on the part of West Coast manufacturers toward full size and a change to 13/16 inch boards.

The Western Pine Manufacturers' Association informs us that their mills are adhering to their standard sizes, viz.: inch lumber surfaced two sides is 25/32 inch in thickness; all lumber surfaced four sides is 1/2 inch scant, that is ten inch boards will actually measure 9 1/2 inches. This applies to lumber which is seasoned before surfacing. The California White and Sugar Pine Association does the same with reference to their shop and factory lumber.

The Retail Lumber Dealers' Association of the State of New York at the last meeting of its Board of Directors held on June 11, went on record as opposed to the reduction in thickness of inch lumber, including flooring below 13/16. It is also opposed to the loss of one-half inch in width in surfacing lumber four sides and believes that one-fourth inch scant should be the limit in that direction. Our position on this subject was emphasized by Vice-President Gould at the recent meeting held at Chicago to discuss the standardization of working of lumber and mouldings. He pointed out the fact that in many cases the cutting down on widths made it necessary for the contractors to use additional stock and caused additional labor. For this reason dealers would far rather pay more money if necessary for stock dressed 1/4 inch scant than to have the widths skinned down. Secretary James R. Moorehead of the South-western Lumbermen's Association, brought out the fundamental fact that the average yard does not object to the present standard of dimension, provided that it is lived up to. He further said that it is time for the manufacturers of lumber to get together and adopt the standard of 13/16 inch thick for all dressed lumber and flooring and to live up to the practice of dressing four sides 1/4 inch scant in width.

The viewpoint of the architects was voiced at this same meeting. Their representative said that it was highly important that sizes of timbers be lived up to so that architects could know how to figure their floor loads. This they are required to do by municipal ordinances for all buildings erected in many of the larger cities of the country.

We are not alone in our contention that lumber should not be further skinned down in working. Both of the leading retail associations of Pennsylvania have already taken action and it is quite likely that other neighboring organizations will be heard from shortly. President H. J. Meyers of the Pennsylvania Lumbermen's Association which has headquarters at Philadelphia, says:

"The fact that thinner lumber may cost less than that of a proper thickness is no excuse for retailers being satisfied with such material. We must protect the consumer, for he looks to his local dealer to give him something which meets his requirements. We are the only people he can appeal to and when he finds that we are indifferent to such things, he may become one of the many who are always ready to have the state or national government regulate business.

"I hope that every time we purchase a car of lumber we will insist on nothing less than thirteen-sixteenths thickness and not more than one-fourth inch waste in the width. Tell the salesmen who visit your offices that we are in earnest in this matter and that our campaign is not merely to have a question to talk about in our annual meetings. I have found many salesmen anxious to co-operate with us and not one who thought otherwise. When they come in contact with their sales managers, they will report our attitude and some good results will follow."

Destruction of Shade Trees

For years past there has been a gradual dying out of shade trees in the city, says the "Montreal Star." Spasmodic efforts have been made to save them, but little of a practical nature has been accomplished. One cause for this is the meagre amount set aside for tree culture and planting. This city spends less on such work than any other of its size on the continent. In many of the big United States cities the importance of making streets attractive by the planting of shade trees, is demonstrated by their appointing special commissions who have sole charge of this branch of the civic service. The results thus obtained have been most satisfactory.

So far as Montreal is concerned, there is room for great improvement in the system of caring for trees. A special tree commission is sorely needed here as elsewhere. Ir such a commission had ben appointed years ago the trees would not have been in their present forlorn condition.

In many of the streets running north from St. Catherine Street trees have been ruthlessly slaughtered. Electric companies and householders are both to blame for this. The spectacle of slowly dying trees can be seen all over the city. Unless a halt is called it will not be many years before Montreal will be peculiar for its lack of trees in the streets. The subject is important enough specially to occupy the attention of the Administrative Commission.

Will Construct Slides and Piers

A provincial charter has been granted the Sucker Creek Timber Slides Co., with a capital stock of $15,000, and headquarters in Port Arthur. The object of the company is to construct slides, piers, boom and other works necessary to facilitate the transmission of timber now in Sucker Creek in the unsurveyed area lying immediately west of the township of Hele in the district of Thunder Bay, from a point where the Creek enters the Black Sturgeon River to Sucker Lake, a distance of 17½ miles, and also the construction of a dam at Sucker Creek and a dam opposite the property of the Port Arthur Pulp & Paper Co. at a point 11 miles up the Creek from the entrance through into the Black Sturgeon River, with all the powers authorized by the Timber Slide Companies' Act.

New Position for Mr. Alex. Dick

Alex. Dick, Peterboro, Ont.

Alexander Dick, who for the past four years has been with the R. Laidlaw Lumber Co., Toronto, has been appointed manager of the estate of Alfred McDonald, lumber dealers and sawmill owners, Peterboro, Ont., and has entered upon his new duties. Mr. Dick is well known to the lumber industry, with which he has been identified all his life. Born in Scotland he came to Canada in 1905 and soon engaged in his regular vocation. He was associated with several leading firms and for four years was superintendent for John Lumsden, of Lumsden's Mills, Kippewa, Pontiac Co., Que. In 1915 he entered the service of the Laidlaw Lumber Co. and has covered the ground in western Ontario north of the main line.

A genial, earnest and likable representative he made many friends who will wish him every success in his new and responsible post. He has always taken a deep interest in the welfare and progress of retail dealers and in the contest, which was inaugurated among the lumber salesmen of the province a year and a half ago as to who could secure the greatest number of members within a given time for the Ontario Retail Lumber Dealers' Association, Mr. Dick was one of the winners, having corralled thirteen new members. Owing to his splendid efforts subsidiary branches of the parent organization have also been organized. In Peterboro Mr. Dick will, no doubt, continue the good work he has carried out in the west on behalf of unity and co-operation.

Alex. J. Purse, who for several years has been with the R. Laidlaw Lumber Co., and returned some time ago from overseas, since when he has been attached to the west end yard, 2268 Dundas St., has succeeded Mr. Dick on the selling force and is looking after the same territory.

Decreasing Timber Wealth Creates Alarm

Dr C. D. Howe of Toronto, and Ellwood Wilson of Grand Mere, P. Q., were the guests of the Eastern Forestry Association and the Great Northern Paper Co., at Mt. Kineo, on Moosehead Lake in Maine, and afterwards on an inspection trip over the timberlands of the latter.

The Foresters of the New England and Middle States, of the University Forest Schools, of large Companies, Railroads and a representative of the U. S. Forest Service were present. Means for improving the condition of the forests were thoroughly discussed, and also the scheme put forward by Col. Graves of the U. S. Forest Service, to encourage, and if necessary, to compel the practice of proper forestry methods on private lands, as is done in Sweden, Norway, France and Germany. The situation in the United States is becoming so serious that some action looking to the proper utilization of the forests so as to insure a permanent supply, is imperative. White pine has almost disappeared, chestnut has been attacked by a blight which threatens to destroy it, spruce and balsam in the paper making States of the East, it is said, will be exhausted in another fifteen years; the great Southern pine region will be cut over in another six to ten years, and then most of the timber must come from the West.

In view of this situation, steps must be taken to reduce the cut and begin reforestation. Lumbermen in the States have bought up, in the past, large tracts of virgin timber, often for speculative purposes. In order to carry their investments, they have put in sawmills and cut off the timber as fast as posible, striving to make money, not by quality but by quantity production.

Many Men Required for Logging in Ontario

Dr. W. A. Riddell, superintendent of the labor branch of the Public Works Department for the Province of Ontario, states that there will be ample work this fall for thousands of men in the lumber camps of Ontario as all the lumber and pulpwood companies intend carrying on logging operations more extensively than ever. There is a big demand for lumber of all kinds and a decided shortage in stocks at many centres. The result is that manufacturers intend to get out larger timber cuts during the coming season than at any period since the beginning of the war. Mr. Riddell says that the greatest difficulty facing the department at the present time is to secure sufficient men to go to the lumber camps. A few days ago he stated that 10,000 men could find employment in the bush if they could be rounded up. The wages run from $50 to $70 a month and board. Last year the department over which Dr. Riddell presides, placed some 1500 in the camps and the additional call this year is owing to the large amount of lumber purchased by the British government in Canada, as well as the overseas demand and the revival of building operations and carrying out of extensive repairs and alterations. Men who were in the forestry battalions in Great Bri and France are most desirable and available for the work, but any healthy, able bodied man, who can swing an axe or operate a saw is assured of steady employment in the bush during the coming fall and winter at a remunerative wage and under better housing and sanitary conditions than in any previous logging season.

Fraser Companies Will Build Another Mill

The Fraser Companies Limited are to erect another mill in New Brunswick and operations for same have already been commenced. The site of the old mill of the Scott Lumber Company at Upper Magaguadavic siding on the C. P. R., in western York County will be the location of the new mill. James M. Scott, of Fredericton, N. B., superintendent of logging operations for the company in that district, is in charge of the latest development project. The Fraser interests control about ten thousand acres of timber lands in the Magaguadavic district, including what were formerly the Scott Lumber Company's lands, as well as other limits which they have acquired from time to time. The new mill will be of a permanent character and will have a capacity of between five and six million superficial feet per season. Already crews are in the woods in the district which will supply the mill with logs and are getting out lumber as well as peeling bark. There will be a capacity cut of logs available for the mill by next spring and this fall will see the construction of the plant completed.

Eastern Happenings in Lumber Arena

Clarke Bros., of Bear River, N. S., who purchased material in the Mispec Pulp & Paper buildings at Mispec, N. B., are removing same to Nova Scotia where they intend erecting a new pulp mill.

Joseph Edward Lingley, an old and respected resident of St. John, N. B., who for more than forty years was associated with the firm of Holly & McLellan, lumber surveyors and tug boat owners, died at his home recently aged ninety years.

Upwards of $220,000 has been received by the Department of Lands and Mines according to a statement made recently by Lieut.-Col. T. G. Loggie, the Deputy Minister of Lands and Mines, Fredericton, N. B. Three quarters of the amount mentioned is in payment of stumpage rates and the balance is for charges for renewals of leases at $8 per mile, as well as the forest fire protection tax of half a cent an acre. The payments are said to be less than during a corresponding period of 1918.

A recent report from Perth, N. B., states that the water in river there has risen about three feet and the St. John River Driving Company's drive, which was abandoned there a few weeks ago will be resumed.

Hon. N. M. Jones, general manager of the Nashwaak Pulp & Paper Company, St. John, N. B., recently stated that the Amberson Hydraulic Construction Company, Ltd., of Montreal, will erect a new concrete dam, which the company propose building on the Nashwaak river at Marysville and which will be follwed by the construction of a pulp mill.

The late James S. Fairley, lumberman, of Bloomfield Ridge, N. B., who died recently, left an estate said to be worth from $15,000 to $20,000. The will is being contested.

Building Activity in New Toronto

Many foundations are completed and bricklayiing started recently on several houses being built in New Toronto by the New Toronto Housing Commission. More than half the material for the fifty houses contracted for is now on the grounds and the Commission confidently expects to have all the outside work finished by the fall at the very latest. The original grant of $200,000 has been exhausted, and the Commission will likely make application for $250,000 more.

With nearly 200 applications to date the New Toronto Housing Commission will likely make application for 250,000 more.

in any town in Ontario. The Commission follows the same plan as the Toronto Housing Commission, and advances money for the site as well as the buiilding. Thirty-six houses are being erected on one block while others are being built on single lots.

The houses are all being built of brick and tile, and the present plans are for five and six-roomed detached and semi-detached houses costing $3,000 to $3,600.

Getting After More Business in Retail Yard

Practical Plans That Have Been Followed by Representative Dealers With Gratifying Results—Things That Suggest Big Possibilities and Develop Trade

The average retail lumberman likes to retain not only the business that he has built up since starting out for himself, but to add materially to its volume from year to year. The live wire, aggressive yardman is neither content to mark time nor to eke out a bare existence. He desires to keep up with the procession and to feel that he is a real force and a vital factor in the community.

Unless his business shows a gratifying gain each year, he naturally comes to the conclusion that if he is not going forward he is practically falling behind. In this age of rapid transit and growing national development and expansion there is no such a thing as standing still. If the turnover of the average retail lumber merchant is correspondingly larger each year, he knows that things are moving in the right direction. If he did not cherish the ambition to become bigger and stronger in his activities and demonstrate that he is an increasingly useful, influential factor in the upbuild of the business community, he would scarcely be human. We all like to be well thought of and well spoken of; to have a clean record, an honorable name, firm friends and staunch customers.

Keeping Pace with the Times

In a rapidly growing centre the volume of the lumberman's trade will naturally increase with the branching out of the community, but what about doing business in a town which shows practically no growth from year to year, so far as increase in population or the number of industries is concerned? The yardman does not want to stand still and have his business show just about the same turnover as in the years before the war, for such a state of affairs virtually means that with values doubled he is only doing half what he did previous to 1914. All lumber prices have jumped practically 100 per cent. during the past five years and unless the turnover has been commensurate with the augmented investment, the balance of trade is on the wrong side of the books. New customers must be secured, older ones must see the need of expending money in repairs, alterations and additions, and the young men (and older ones, too), should have impressed upon them the desirability, economy and advantage of owning their own homes and not paying tribute to the landlord from month to month during the greater portion of their natural lives.

One leading authority states that concerning the development of new business by the retail dealer much has been written and presented periodically, but that when all is said and done, next to capital the right kind of personality, properly applied, is the greatest of all business assets and it is asked how shall it be applied? There are other considerations to be taken into account besides personality, and one of the most outstanding of these is service, prompt, efficient and satisfactory. The yardman may have a winning personality, a representative and complete stock and may dispose of his product at reasonable prices, but unless back of it all there is service and honest value and a sincere desire to maintain and strengthen the mutual relations between seller and buyer, retailer and customer, he will never get very far ahead in the race.

In regard to the plans to develop new business, many have been tried and found successful. One eastern dealer is a strong believer in the strength of the personal appeal. Periodically he sends a representative to call upon old and prospective customers in his trade territory. This representative calls upon some town people but spends most of his time among the farmers. He carries with him advertising literature and full information concerning the service offered by the firm but he DOES NOT COME WITH THE IDEA OF SELLING ANYTHING. His business is to get acquainted with the farmer, talk over his problems with him and be of any assistance possible.

Make Pencil Sketch Right There

If the farmer is thinking of making an improvement, he may make a pencil sketch of it right then and there. This service carries with it no feeling of obligation on the part of the prospect to purchase material from the firm. This fact is made clear at the start. There is no dotted line for signature at the close of the visit. Any suggestions given the farmers' wife in making changes in the home, such as adding a sleeping porch, laying down a hardwood floor over old pine boards, removing partitions between the time honored parlor and the sitting room and throwing them into one big light, airy living room, is most cheerfully given. The whole object is to be of service.

In the course of his conversation the caller picks up some valuable information relative to the needs of his prospect. If he has been putting up any buildings this is noted, as well as the name of the dealer furnishing the material. His future needs and the probable date of future improvements are also jotted down. This data is all entered on prospect cards on returning to the office, together with credit information and any additional facts secured from the books of the County Assessor and the County Auditor.

Special Mail Order or Inquiry

When taking his leave of the farmer, the caller gives him some advertising literature and an envelope which opens out flat on the reverse side into an order sheet similar to the illustration following:

Special Mail Order or Inquiry

IF YOU HAVEN'T IT IN STOCK,
YOU CAN GET IT FROM

Your Lumber Co. **Your Town, Busyville.**

... ...

PLEASE SHIP OR QUOTE ME AT ONCE

... ...

... ...

BE SURE TO SIGN

Above may be used for inquiry by crossing out the word ship

SIGNED ... ...

On the two ends which fold under is a list of several lines of builders' supplies and masons' supplies carried by the firm. The address of the firm is printed on the envelope so that all the sender has to do is to fill in his order or inquiry, sign it, fold, and seal with the gummed flap.

This form of advertising has paid big returns to this dealer who has used it for the past five or six years. The personal contact and service gets the attention of the prospect. It also gives the dealer definite information concerning the prospect. The envelope order blank left with the prospect provides a handy method for sending in orders and inquiries. What this means was illustrated by an order which this particular dealer received a few weeks ago for 32 M shingles. The order came in on an envelope order blank left with the farmer on August 31, 1914, almost five years ago. This is evidence which speaks for itself.

Another means of getting the inquiries is that used by a live Western concern. This firm has arranged a booklet of six post cards, each a blank request for quotations, the items to be filled in by the inquirer. With each card is a carbon and a duplicate slip which enables the inquirer to keep a definite record of the items upon which he has asked quotations. A list of items on which they can give immediate service is printed on the outside cover of the booklet. The last card is printed with red ink so that it acts as a signal that the inquirer is ready for another booklet. The principle is the same as that of the envelope order blank and can be adopted by any dealer with such modifications as he desires.

General Activity in Lumber Line

The last issue of the Labour Gazette of Ottawa reviews general conditions in the lumbering industry in Canada as follows:—

Westville reported that the lumber mills continued to be active. Charlottetown reported that lumbermen were very well employed. St. John reported that river driving and rafting had been completed, but that the saw and shingle mills were running steadiily. Fredericton reported that the lumber mills and booming operations were giving employment to large numbers of men. Quebec reported that the sawmills and the rossing mills were well on with their season's cut, which would give considerable employment during the whole season. River driving was practically completed. Sherbrooke reported that the saw and shingle mills were busy. Ottawa and Hull reported that the sawmills were busy. The sawmills at Peterborough were very active. Owen Sound reported that the tie mill was not running and that the shingle mill was quiet, but that the sawmill was busy. Fernie reported that part time only was worked in some of the mills.

Just Thirty Years Ago

Interesting items from the fyles of the July edition of the "Canada Lumberman" away back in 1889

Rathbun's big mill at Deseronto is cutting on an average 2,500 logs a day.

* * *

Mr. J. R Booth is having his depots and shanties on the Nipissing limits connected by telephone.

* * *

It is said the lumber cut on Lake Winnipeg this season will be 3,000,000 feet less than last year.

* * *

Wm. Milne's sawmill at Ethel, Ont., was burned August 18th. Loss about $5,000; insurance $1,500.

* * *

Messrs. Strickland & Co., Lakefield, have been fined $20 and costs for allowing sawdust to fall into the river.

* * *

McLachlin Bros., Arnprior, will build another large steam mill this winter. The ground is now being cleared for the purpose.

* * *

A Victoria, B.C., man, is said to have discovered a process by which lumber can be rendered fireproof at a cost of $1 per thousand.

* * *

Christie's mill at Brandon has been closed down, the logs brought down the Assiniboine last fall having been all used up. There is no prospect of getting more logs down at present.

* * *

The present scale of wages in the logging camps at Puget Sound are as follows: teamster, $75 a month; chopper, $65 to $70; hook tender, $45 to $50; barker, $40; swamper, $40; sawyer, $55.

* * *

The mill of the Parry Sound Lumber Co., Parry Sound, is run by water power furnished by the Sequin river. The company have some 400 square miles of timber limits around Parry Sound.

* * *

The Victoria Lumber Manufacturing Company, Victoria, will shortly proceed with the extension of their mill at Chemainus, Vancouver Island, enlarging it to a capacity of 250,000 feet per day.

* * *

The shingle mill lately built on Gambier Island, by W. L. Johnston & Co., of Westminster, is completed. The mill is turning out 30,000 shingles per day and this number will be largely increased.

* * *

The sawdust question has broken out again, and this time in the goodly town of Peterborough. Four of the sawmill men were fined $20 and costs for permitting sawdust to flow into the Otonabee River.

* * *

Gravenhurst, the centre of the lumber district of Northern Ontario, can boast of having 14 sawmills, all of which are busily engaged in manufacturing lumber. The principal mills are Mickle's, Cockburn's and McNeil's.

* * *

Mr. Alex. McCormack recently sold to Robt. Booth, of Pembroke, for $70,000, a valuable timber limit, 27 square miles on the Nipissing branch of the Petewawa river. The limit is partly in Devine and partly in Butt township.

* * *

During the shanty season, which is now about closed, upwards of 800 bushmen registered in Lower Town hotels, Ottawa. Many of these complain bitterly of the way they were treated both by the lumber firms and hotel men.

* * *

Ludlam & Ainslie's heading factory at Comber, Ont., was burned on August 3rd, together with two M.C.R. cars loaded with elm bolts for Detroit, which were standing on the siding near the mill. Loss on the mill $3,000. Cause of the fire unknown.

* * *

The last drive of the season is about out of
It belonged to McLachlan Bros., of Arnprior,
Ottawa, and Mr. Fraser. There is only one raft
Petewawa, and it will be impossible to get it out

* * *

Eighteen cribs of square timber and hemlock saw logs are on their way to Kingston for the dry dock. This is the first consignment of some forty-two cribs from Ottawa for the same purpose. The cribs will contain 700,000 feet of surface measure. The contractor receives 1½ cents per square foot for its delivery in Kingston.

* * *

The C. Beck Manufacturing Co., Ltd., Penetanguishene, with a paid up capital of $250,000, have three extensive mills, known as the "Penetanguishene Mills," the new Keene mill and the shingle and planing mill. They cut a daily average of 150,000 feet of lumber. They claim to have the fastest running circular saw in the world. They own a steam barge with a carrying capacity of 280,000 feet of lumber and a large steam tug.

* * *

The Roberval Lumber Company, of Roberval, consisting principally of Mr. Ross, of Quebec, Mr. Beemer and Mr. B. A. Scott, have just erected a magnificent steam sawmill, fitted with the most modern improvements, including a circular saw, revolving 10,000 ft. a minute, and gang saws making 22 strokes in the same brief period of time. Three logs are thus squared and cut every two minutes, and it is the intention of the company to saw 150,000 logs per season, 20 per cent. of which are said to be pine, and the balance spruce.

* * *

The wonderful resources of British Columbia are attracting the attention of capitalists, not only of Canada but also of America, and it is surprising to see how rapidly the country is advancing even in this rapidly advancing age. That it has a great future before it we have not the least doubt. Its splendid climate, its beautiful waters and harbors, together with its vast fisheries, immense forests and rich mineral lands, with the vim and push manifested by its people, all combined bid fair to make it the Fairy Land—the Eldorado of the West.

* * *

The French River Boom Company has given notice of its intention to apply for letters of incorporation from the Ontario government to enable it to carry out work and improvements to facilitate the transmission of timber on the French river. The company is also asking for power to erect mills for the purpose of carrying on a general lumber business. Toronto is to be the chief place of business. The capital stock of the company is to be $100,000, in shares of $100 each. The names of the applicants are as follows: H. H. Cook, H. J. Bohme, F. E. Macdonald, all of Toronto; C. Henderson, of Bracebridge, and N. Irvine, at French River.

* * *

A very influential and significant gathering of the lumber kings of the North Shore was held at Newcastle on the 25th of July, to consider and resolve on the question of stumpage on crown lands. It was resolved to insist upon the local government complying with the following demands: (1) Renewal of the present ten-year leases; (2) Reduction of the stumpage from $1.25 to $1 per thousand; (3) Reduction of mileage from $8 and $4 to $2; (4) Adoption of Quebec scale; (5) Making expenditure on streams to facilitate driving and constructing portage roads.

* * *

A number of mill owners of Cape Breton have entered an action against the Dominion Government to recover damages sustained. It is alleged that in the erection of the bridges for the Cape Breton railroad, the government has caused the water to be dammed and diverted, so that it is impossible to float logs with the same facility as before. The railway act, under which the claims are made, promises that in operations upon rivers, the latter shall be left in their former state, or equally as good. This has not been done in the case cited, and heavy damages are now demanded.

* * *

The sale of Mr. E. B. Eddy's timber limits took place at the Russel House, Ottawa, on August 14th. . The sale was the result of a determination of the Eddy Manufacturing Company to retire from the wholesale manufacture and sale of lumber and timber in order to devote more attention to the other branches of the manufacturing business at Hull. The property offered for sale comprised about 1,377 square miles of timber limits, with depots, farms, buildings, supplies, plant, etc. Some of the properties offered were exceedingly valuable, notably the large water power sawmill, splitting mill and filing room at Hull, the cutting capacity of which is estimated at from 35,000,000 to 40,000,000 feet per season. The other properties included lumber yards and piling grounds, and are supplied with tramways, engines and cars, slides and docks, also the steam mill at Nepean, surrounded by 32 acres.

* * *

The labor commission which was appointed by the Domiinion Government to inquire into the relations of capital and labor, might have been more explicit in its classification of wages paid to the employees of the lumber industry, inasmuch as the investigations of the commission have cost the country, with their publication of their report upwards of $50,000. The lumber trade is the second leading industry of the country, and we had hoped that the commission would have been able to furnish the country with valuable information in such a manner as it would at least be intelligible. On the question of lumbermen's wages it is too ambiguous, many of the statements are very indefinite, leaving the reader to do considerable guessing. At Ottawa, gangmen with eight months' work in the year are put down at from $8 to $10.50 a week; mill men, at from $1.25 to $1.50 a day a day; pilers, $1.25 to $2 a day; shanty men at $16 a month and board; slabbers, $1.50 a day and teamsters $7 a week.

* * *

The St. Catharines Milling and Lumber Company have sued the Dominion Government for $215,000 damages for the loss of logs, plant, etc. It appears that some six years ago, a number of gentlemen secured a license from the Dominion Government to cut timber and transact business of lumbering generally on Lake Wabigoon. After obtaining the license they formed a company, secured incorporation by letters patent, and started business. Some two million feet had been cut, when in 1884 the Ontario Government secured a decision of the Privy Council of England, the highest tribunal in the Empire, on the question of the ownership of the portion of the country in which the St. Catharines Milling Company were operating. On the strength of this decision, the Ontario Government served writs of injunction on each of the members of the St. Catharines Company restraining them from further operations, at the same time seizing their season's cut of logs and plant, which were subsequently sold. The Federal Government, using the name of the company, resisted the provincial authorities in the courts, claiming that although Ontario had a right to the land, to the Federal Government belonged the minerals and the timber. Judgment being given adversely in the Dominion, an appeal was again made to the Privy Council, which upheld the decision of the Supreme Court and gave judgment in favor of Ontario. The company subsequently waited on Sir John Thompson, Minister of Justice, and asked to have the matter referred to arbitiration; but the government decided to refer the matter to the Exchequer Court for settlement. Sir John Thompson denies that the company are entitled to anything. The outcome will be awaited with much interest.

Adequate Ocean Tonnage is Vital Problem

The Situation as Reviewed by Leading Manufacturer—Canada's Exporting Industries Should Receive Every Encouragement to Expand

Canadian pulp and paper manufacturers, like lumber exporters shipping on private account, are finding it difficult to secure space for the U. K. Mr. A. L. Dawe, of Montreal, secretary of the Canadian Pulp and Paper Association, is now in England with a view of securing additional space, and on this side the manufacturers have approached the Hon. C. C. Ballantyne, Minister of Marine, to see what can be done in the way of obtaining space. Mr. Ballantyne, while promising to do everything to improve the situation, declared that the Government could not afford any immediate relief. This Government could not influence the British Government to relax the restrictions which it has placed upon all tonnage under British charter, although he intimated that strong representations to this effect had already been made. He saw no bettering of the position regarding outgoing vessel room until Canada had her own merchant marine.

The situation is fully explained by the following statement by Mr. J. A. Bothwell, president of the Canadian Pulp and Paper Association.

"Criticism of the Canadian Government because there is insufficient shipping to get Canadian pulp and paper products to the European market is hardly justified by the facts of the situation," said Mr. J. A. Bothwell, when asked what grounds there were for holding the Government responsible for the difficulties which the industry is having in getting its goods into the overseas market. "The pulp and paper industry is certainly greatly hampered by the lack of ships and by the abnormal freight charges for such space as is available, but in that respect it is no better and no worse off than other Canadian industries.

"The Government," continued Mr. Bothwell, "has, through the Hon. Mr. Ballantyne, given a very sympathetic hearing to our case, and has promised to do everything possible to relieve our situation, and I believe it will carry out its promise. The difficulty arises from the fact that Great Britain controls practically all Canadian shipping, except such as is owned by the Canadian Government, which is almost a negligible amount at present. Canadian vessel owners placed their ships under the British Registry during the war in order to enjoy the protection of the British Government, and to meet other war conditions. So far all efforts to have some or all of the ships restored to the Canadian registry have failed.

"The British Government wants the ships for its own uses, and the Canadian Government, as Mr. Ballantyne frankly told our delegation, is powerless in the matter. The salvation of Canada's commerce, as the Minister also said, lies in building up a Canadian merchant marine, and that will take a considerable time to accomplish. The Government expects to have 20 ships in commission this year, and fifty within two or three years' time, but shippers fear that by that time their present market opportunity will have vanished. Other countries than Canada will have seized upon the trade that this country might have secured had we the facilities at present for securing it.

"The trouble with we Canadians is that we didn't look far enough ahead, and begin building ships early enough and in large enough numbers. That was probably due to the fact that we had our hands full in carrying on the war, and besides have neither the men nor the means, even if we had had the vision, to enter upon an extensive shipbuilding programme at a time when all concerned were concentrated upon the war effort. But if we didn't have these things other countries, much more sorely pressed than ours did, and to-day they are the ones that stand to benefit chiefly by construction.

"But if the pulp and paper men understand the difficulties of the Government, and are not inclined to visit upon them the responsibility for their present troubles, we, nevertheless, realize that the situation is one of very great hardship for our industry, as well as a drawback to Canadian trade expansion. In our own industry we are flooded with inquiries from Europe for quotations on pulp and paper products of almost every grade. The Minister of Marine and Fisheries, when inquiring into the situation, asked us for specific information as to what amounts of pulp and paper we had ready for export, where the shipments were located, their destination, and the amount the shippers would be willing to pay for ocean freights, having in mind all the circumstances at present surrounding ocean freight traffic. We were able to give him some information of this character, such as the fact that one Quebec producer of ground wood pulp has over 12,000 tons of pulp lying upon the docks waiting for ships to carry it to England, where it has a market, and has tried in vain for months to secure the necessary accommodation, but the real situation is that the producers are afraid to make contracts with the British buyers, because of the uncertainty as to being able to make delivery. Some, however, are taking orders and are running the chance of being able to get the necessary cargo space.

"The high freight rates are also an adverse factor in the situation," said Mr. Bothwell. "There is a differential of between $8.00 and $10.00 a ton against Canadian pulp and paper laid down in the

U. K., as compared with the same class of products exported thence from the Scandinavian countries, our chief competitors for the trade. We understand, too, that American pulp and paper are going overseas with a similar advantage in rates as compared with our own. But this again is a situation difficult to remedy, since we are told that for every ton of cargo space available at any Canadian port, from 2 to 6 times the amount of merchandise is offered. The Government tells us that when its ships are ready for business, profits on their operation will be made secondary to the question of Canadian trade expansion. This sounds like good policy, but its benefits are too far distant in the future to have any appreciable effect upon our present situation.

"Another thing that militates against Canadian foreign trade expansion is the fact that there are so few things that Canada wants to import from abroad, comparatively speaking. We are practically producing all of our our food stuffs and the greater part of our requirements in manufactured goods. But ships that leave our ports laden with Canadian goods cannot be expected to come here empty. There has got to be reciprocity in trade. A striking instance of this relates to the supply of print paper and pulp now going to Australia. There is no reason why Canada should not supply these commodities, except again the lack of ships; but as a matter of fact, since the war stopped, Scandinavia has been supplying Australia's needs of these things, taking Australian wheat in exchange. Australia has three years' crop of wheat stored up ready for the market, which she must get rid of. Canada, of course, isn't a wheat buying country, and we cannot trade our pulp and paper for wheat."

Asked as to the general outlook for this year's pulp and paper export business, Mr. Bothwell said:

"Our American market continues firm with a very strong demand. The market for kraft and other grades of wrapping paper, which slowed up considerably when the war stopped, probably in the mistaken expectation of a slump in prices, has firmed up to such an extent of late that the kraft mills some time since withdrew all quotations, and find some difficulty in filling orders. The market for newsprint is also strong, and some producers fear a runaway market may develop this fall, which they would very much deplore, as a stabilized market is the best for all concerned. The American demand for pulp is better than normal. A statement, however, printed a day or two ago that this year's exports of Canadian pulp would amount to $100,000,000 in value is somewhat exaggerated. Last year Canada exported pulps of all grades to the value of $34,706,771. We may show an increase over that this year, but we have to count upon competition with the European producers, which was non-existent last year. At any rate, prices show no indication of falling, nor will they so long as the present high price of labor, freight and raw materials keep up.

"Another misstatement going around that needs correction is that the British paper mills are practically out of business, and that it will take them two or three years to get back to normal production.

Our special representative in London cables that the British mills have gone to the three-tour system, which means that they are operating 24 hours a day with three shifts of workmen. At that rate it will take them but a very short time to overtake any undersupply that may exist, and any foreign made paper that gets into England will have to show good cause for doing so. The Imperial preference, you may be sure, will not be allowed to operate to the detriment of British manufacturers and British workmen, and there is no reason why it should. Great Britain is under even more of a necessity than we are to keep her industries alive, and to keep as much of her money as possible from leaving the country.

"These, however, are all reasons why Canadian exporting industries, such as pulp and paper manufacturing, should receive every possible encouragement at home, and why special efforts should be put forth to enable them to maintain and increase their foothold in the overseas market," concluded Mr. Bothwell.

New Project of Bathurst Lumber Co.

Dr. C. D. Howe, Dean of the Toronto Forest School, recently visited New Brunswick where he visited some of the parties engaged on the New Brunswick Forest Survey. The Conservation Commission, through Dr. Howe, is co-operating with the New Brunswick Forestry Department, and a special party, employed by the New Brunswick Government, is devoting the entire season to the study of annual growth and regeneration, under Dr. Howe's immediate supervision. Also, the limits of the Bathurst Lumber Company and the Pejebscot Lumber Company were visited, and it is possible that through the cooperation of the Bathurst Lumber Company, the Conservation Commission and the New Brunswick Government, a 600 acre experimental plot may be established. The Bathurst Lumber Company are especially interested in experimental work of this kind with a view to perpetuating their timber lands.

Will Reforest the British Isles

A recent despatch from London, Eng., says: When the last of three-decker men-of-war ran off the slips British forestry died. The oak forests planted after Trafalgar for the express purpose of building Britain's wooden ways, stood untouched at the beginning of the war. When the overseas' supplies of timber were cut off, the country had cause to bless the men who unconsciously planted for an emergency greater than any which they could have contemplated.

Serious effort now being made toward afforesting Great Britain
is the result of the hard lesson learned during the war
of many hopeful signs of the intelligent reconstructi
Britain can never be self-supporting in the matter
whatever success may attend the present endeavor,
she will import a single log the less for a generation.

But, thanks largely to the splendid work of the Ca
Corps, her woods are a picture of desolation, and, e
most successful attack, the area under timber was only four per cent. of the whole.

The proposal is to spend three and a half millions sterling in planting a quarter of a million acres during the next ten years, under centralized authority, possessing wide powers and capable of laying down a well-defined, far-reaching policy.

Britain has never had a real forestry department, and one of its advantages will be that education in forestry will be greatly stimulated, and a worthy career opened to experts.

The House of Lords, which has approved the scheme, knows
more about such subjects than the Commons, and it is hoped n
ous opposition will be encountered in the lower House.

The Prince of Wales as Soldier

Many charming little stories, demonstrating the great human and soldierly qualities, are being told about the Prince of Wales, who will open the Canadian National Exhibition in Toronto on Monday, Aug. 25th.

The Canadian boys overseas had plenty of opportunity to observe his actions and declare that he seemed to love danger, and at times his conduct bordered on the reckless.

This side of his character is well illustrated by the following extract from Ian Hay's book, The First Hundred Thousand.

"Bloikie lit his pipe—it was almost broad daylight now—and considered.

"Yes," he agreed. "Perhaps. Still, my son, I can't say I have ever noticed staff officers crowding into the trenches (as they have a perfect right to do) at four o'clock in the morning. And I can't say I altogether blame them. In fact, if ever I do meet one performing such a feat, I shall say: 'There goes a sahib—and a soldier,' and I shall take off my hat to him."

"Well, get ready now," said Bobby. "Look."

They were still standing at the trench junction. Two figures in the uniform of the staff were visible in Orchard Trench, working their way down from the apex, picking their steps amid the tumbled sandbags, and stooping low to avoid gaps in the ruined parapet. The sun was just rising behind the German trenches. One of the officers was burly and middle-aged; he did not appear to enjoy bending double. His companion was slight, fair-haired, and looked incredibly young. Once or twice he glanced over his shoulder, and smiled encouragingly at his senior

The pair emerged through the archway into the main trench, and straightened their backs with obvious relief. The younger officer—he was a lieutenant—noticed Captain Blaikie, saluted him gravely, and turned to follow his companion.

Captain Blaikie did not take his hat off, as he had promised. Instead he stood suddenly to attention, and saluted in return, keeping his hand uplifted until the slim, childish figure had disappeared round the corner of a traverse.

It was the Prince of Wales.

In the Abitibi, P.Q., region there are now fifty
pleted and another four are in course of constructio
six mills are completed; Dupuy, 3; La Sarre, 6; Mec
2; Privat, 4; Launay, 1; Trecesson, 2; Dalquier, 1;
Motte, 1; Amos, 5; Landr
terre, 2; Doucet, 2. It is
000 feet of lumber will be p
ment has spent large sums in developing

The Southern Pine Association, New Orleans, La., is issuing a bright and breezy monthly publication known as the "Southern Pines Salesman." It is filled with interesting and timely topics and is neatly printed.

"More Aggressive Policy in Business Life"

Waiting and Expecting That Trade Will Come Without Effort is Relic of Bygone Days—Cashing in on Big Demand for Building Material

By George C. Robson

Business, generally, is going through a period of reconstruction and it has now reached the point where business competition in all lines will be keener and an entirely different type of merchandizing must be adopted, which will include a more aggressive policy in your business life.

The idea of the retail dealers standing with our face before a mirror, smiling and kidding ourselves in the belief that we are the finest merchants in any business, and at the same time allowing the auto salesman and lightning rod agent and the likes to go out and "cop" Mr. Farmer's money, will not bring us any success in these times of readjustment and changes in business methods.

The retail lumber business is surely good for your health, but most of you, of course, are not in for this purpose alone. Your desire is not only to make a good living, but more, and you are entitled to more; however, waiting and expecting the business will come to you without effort is a relic of the by-gone days, and unless you stir yourselves, keen competition and progress are going to sell Farmer Jones his building material right under your nose; the auto agent will sell him an automobile, and someone else will entice him to buy something he does not need as much as buildings properly to house his family, grain machinery or stock. And quite possibly, while you are sitting idly in your warm office, he will use the money he owes you for some other material in purchasing these things, that, to a more or less extent, are side attractions to farming, and you, still sitting in your comfortable chair, are wondering how it happened and continue to cuss him because he does not pay his bills. The other fellow went and convinced him the article he had to sell was something Mr. Farmer needed, and sold it probably for the hard cash that really belonged to you.

Are you willing to admit that these fellows that travel around the country selling "Tin Lizzies" and lightning rods are better salesmen than you? If so, I suggest you take a few days off, let it be known that you are interested in buying an automobile, and it will not take you long to find out just how the other fellow did it.

Lumber manufacturers and retail lumbermen have, in the past, been entirely too well satisfied to sit in their warm office and figure they were handling a God-created material from which Mr. Farmer or anyone else who desired to build must create his housing for man and beast. To a greater or less extent, it has been compulsory for those who intended to build to come to you, but had this idle time been spent in working out plans to create a desire among the people to build more and better, and to promote the "own your own home" idea, it is certain many of us would have learned the lesson we are taugh by the auto salesman, and the lightning rod agent.

Promote the "Own-Your-Home" Idea

Many of you are depending, to a greater or less extent, on the farmer's trade for a considerable bulk of your business, and you will agree with me Mr. Farmer is a suspicious fellow when it comes to buying, and a most peculiar fellow when he comes to sell the product from his farm. He always feels he is over-charged for everything he buys and the only real honest fellow who has anything to sell is himself. You, as a retail lumber merchant, have a large duty to perform in connection with the handling of the farmer's trade, especially at this particular time when many of the building materials appear somewhat high in price and at a time when we must all urge more building to help during the reconstruction period.

Not only must you keep on most friendly terms with him, but at the same time you must be able to convince him you are giving him a square deal. If conditions have forced you to increase the prices on your lumber, it is therefore necessary that you sell at higher values, and it is your duty to convince him that, proportionately, the product you are selling is one of the best bargains a farmer can invest in; that he, to-day, even when paying more for lumber, is getting a much larger percentage of lumber for any article he has to market; that the building material you are selling him properly to house his crops, stock or family is a dividend producer for him; and we know he watches his profits much closer than do many lumbermen.

Make yourself believe you are doing this customer as great a favor by selling him as he is doing you in buying. And isn't this a fact, only more so, for you are persuading him to buy something that he really needs from which he expects to realize or increase his profits? When it is all said and done, the most successful sale is the one where both the buyer and the seller have made a profitable transaction.

Personality, good fellowship and enthusiasm, to-day, play a more important part in successful merchandising than ever before, and the successful retailer can well afford to arrange his affairs so he can give a considerable portion of his time to visiting the community which logically belongs to him, cultivate an interest not only in the entire community, but the individual friendship and acquaintance of those with whom he should deal. And, if I may add, he might well take some lessons in salesmanship from the old-time politician, who, to make a good fellow of himself, always jollied the farmer's wife by telling her what an excellent housekeeper she was, complimented the daughter on her good looks, cultivated the confidence and friendship of the old man himself, and lastly, but not least, did not forget to kiss the baby; however, I caution you against over-doing in attempting to practice the foregoing method by being sure you do not attempt to kiss other than baby, or allow Mr. Farmer to exchange all his victory bonds for your building material. He can much better afford to carry them than you, as you have already taken your full share, and his bank will gladly loan him money on them for building purposes.

Local Lumbermen Can Work Together Profitably

Help to keep him a 100 per cent. patriot by making him hold some of his country's bonds, the country that does more for him than any other merchant; for does it not guarantee him a fixed and extremely profitable price for his wheat, pork and other products?

Progress has been defeated many times and oftener arrested temporarily through the eternal belief in the survival of the fittest. All forward movements are the result of a keener foresight and the past may be well forgotten as a guide for the future, for it holds much that is valueless and harmful. A new power, long dormant in business, is awakening men to new undertakings and greater achievements, and the inspiration and enthusiasm of the new undertaking will accomplish the end we seek.

There are some matters of co-operation within the membership of your association on which I wish to touch, particularly as they apply to towns that have more than one yard, some of these being at points where there is plenty of room for legitimate competition, and others at points where the community is not well enough settled to make a successful business for more than one yard. I shall first mention the towns that have a sufficient population within and without their limits to support two or more retail yards, and shall first discuss those places where you will find the retailers in friendly competition. In such places you usually find success attending their efforts, and what a golden opportunity there is for them to plan together on all matters that are not only good for themselves, but for the community they serve.

How well they can work together in the exchange of stock, and just citing an example: Suppose the town did not require more than one car of siding, or possibly a car of another grade annually, and instead of each yard putting in a carload of these various items, why not arrange between themselves for each to take a portion and in this way not only be able to exchange if one is out of such items, but likewise exchange on other stock, which occasionally one or the other may be short? They are not only reducing the amount of their investment, but each such transaction brings them closer together. How much they can accomplish with contractors or architects by having these parties know there is not throat-cutting competition going on, which, as a rule, is very detrimental to the builders from the standpoint of quality.

A Concrete Example

I recall, many years ago, going to a western town and by prearrangement meeting four dealers in the office of the largest yard in town, and while we were sitting around one common board I succeeded in selling them 3,000,000 feet of lumber for their season's requirements all at the same price and on the same terms. Everyone of these dealers knew exactly what the other ptrty was paying for his material, and after the transaction was closed I could not refrain from remarking this was an unsual transaction and one of the gentlemen spoke up and said they conducted their lumber business in that community along these lines at all times, and I can tell you I positively knew every yard in that city was a success, each making money and having a confidence in the others that allowed a close cooperation on all matters that were of common interest to them. They know what it cost them to do business and realized that no one person can do all the business. Many times have I looked and thought of the many places where such conditions did not exist.

I recall another town where there were two dealers who were not even on speaking terms. One dealer in this place passed no comments about the other, while the other party not only talked freely in a detrimental way of his competitor, but did not buy from any salesman who sold the other party. I considered one of these men a perfect gentleman, and it was my pleasure to sell him considerable stock. I know he tried several times to get together with the other party, but his competitor happened to have a little more financial backing and declined at all times to have anything to do with him.

I hope there are not many places in Western Canada where these conditions exist, and if there are, I will vouch that neither party is making headway; and unless the business is going ahead, it certainly is going back. It is impossible for any business to stand stationary.

How much better it would be if the two unfriendly dealers mentioned could get together, talk over matters concerning their business and work in harmony for the good of their community and their pocketbooks! They surely would find life much sweeter and have a much better belief in humanity at large.

If any of you occupy either of the positions of the two lumbermen mentioned, I suggest and urge that you try to forget your difficulties and the fact that you are competitors in the same line and see if you cannot find a common ground on which you can co-operate. Nothing would give me more pleasure than, some day, to have two such competitors come to me and say that through this small word of advice I have mentioned they were able to get together. I can assure you each one of them would feel like handing me a good sized victory bond. Get to know each other; probably you are both good fellows; confide in him and he will trust you; tell him your troubles and you will find there are others.

Too Many Yards to Make Success

Let me touch shortly on the deplorable condition that exists where there are too many yards to enable any of them to make a business success. It would be much better for them to get together, possibly forming a partnership, thereby eliminating one of the yards, and in this way not only cut down the large overhead, but enable the interested parties at least to make more than their bread and butter out of the financial investment. Or possibly in some places it might be practicable for one of the yards to discontinue by selling out to the other, and in this way enable one not only to make a living but reap some advantages from his investment.

Let me suggest that, if such a transaction is attempted, extreme care should be used to make the proposition attractive to the competitor who discontinues. He is entitled to this consideration, and the purchaser, by enlarging on his sales, is enlarging on his profits, and any matter of false pride on such matters should be cast aside the same as it should be in a place where there is unfriendly competition.

Is not such a transaction, put through in good faith, much better for all parties concerned than to find, after doing business for a considerable length of time without profit, one or the other is forced through financial difficulties to discontinue? In such cases it is usually the survivor who has the longest pocket-book. After it is all over they can look back over a few wasted years without compensation to either and nothing to show for their efforts except "they gave the other fellow a good run for his money."

Retailers' Advertising

Judicious advertising is something many retailers, I believe, are neglecting, and while they do occasionally send out a calendar, or put up a few sign boards around the community in which they live, I do not believe this form of advertising brings them direct results.

I am impressed with the form of advertising used by a few of your members, and mention this in connection with the house organ. They believe this type of advertising brings them excellent results, and while not so much advertising what they have to sell, it dwells on matters that are of special interest to the farming community where most of their yards are located. It is information the farmers appreciate, for it gives them something of particular value which does not cost them anything—something every farmer appreciates. He journeys to the offices of Mr. Lumberman for further information, which gives the yard manager an excellent chance, not only to get acquainted, but to talk with the farmer concerning his building requirements and to interest him in some new buildings that possibly had not been considered until a new idea was brought to his attention.

You may say it is easy for me to make suggestions but impracticable in many places to carry them out, but, I charge you, many good live retailers are doing it successfully. It can be done anywhere if gone at in the proper spirit.

New Brunswick is Aggressive

The fire season in New Brunswick may be said to be more severe than 1918 owing to the extended period of dry hot weather. The organization of the Forest Service is proceeding favorably, but is not complete, owing to a considerable number of rangers' appointments not being firmed after the six months' probationary period.

A summary of the fires compiled to date is submitted, but does not include, of course, all the fires that have occurred to date.

Total number of fires repor ..	220
General causes	76
Railway causes	144

37 of railway fires occurred on right of way and 107 were reported as tie fires

The total estimated damage, is in the vicinity of $1

	Railway	Others	
April fires	2	2	
May fires	39	39	
June fires	125	33	158
			220 fires

Causes:

(a) Settlers neglecting slash fires or carelessness which resulted in $50,000 damage	30 fires
(b) Fishermen, campers, picnic parties	23 fires
(c) Railways	144 fires
(d) Accidental	3 fires
(e) Careless use of fire, industrial	12 fires
(f) Incendiary	5 fires
(g) Unknown	3 fires
	220 fires

The area of ground covered by all the fires in the province to date is approximately 10,000 acr

The Fire Protection Staff at present consists of·

Rangers and Inspectors .	
Temporary Fire Wardens	
Co-operative Fire Wardens	60
Voluntary Fire Wardens	154
Road Commissioners ...	
Total	

Splendid results have been secured by the co-operation of the Public Works Department of the Provincial Government, wherby the Minister of Public Works has authorized 490 Road Commissioners to act as Fire Wardens in case of fire in their vicinity. Also great assistance has been rendered by the lumbermen of New Brunswick, who have given the services of 60 of their woods superintendents and foremen as co-operative fire wardens.

1,000 school teachers have been circularized regarding fire protection; 14,000 camp fire books have been distributed.

15,000 fire posters have been placed in the field.

One look-out has been connected with telephone and watchman employed.

Preparations are being made for three others, and considerable amount of woods telephone lines.

Donnacona Will Make Big Extensions

Though no official announcement is as yet forthcoming, it is understood on good authority that during the past few days definite plans have been consummated for financing of several millions for expansion of the activities of the Donnacona Paper Company, Limited, Donnacona, Que. Though perhaps not so familiar to the Canadian investment markets as some other large Eastern paper manufacturers, the Donnaconna Company is known to the pulp and paper trade as one of the largest and most successful of Canadian manufacturers of newsprint paper, practically the whole of its thirty thousand ton output being absorbed by prominent newspaper publishers of the Eastern United States. In years past its output was sold to The New York Times.

Nothing definite is yet known regarding the exact nature of the securities to be issued, but it is believed that the new financing will take the form of a first mortgage bond issue of several millions.

Pacific Coast Forest Products at Big Fair

Major James Brechin, Toronto, B. C. Lumber Commissioner for the East

The Province of British Columbia will make an imposing and attractive display of forest products in the Canadian government building at the annual exhibition of the Canadian National Exhibition, Toronto, which will be held from August 25th to Sept. 6th. The space occupied will be 12 x 55 ft. and the booth will be representative in every respect of the forest wealth of British Columbia. There will be not only many photographic illustrations of the timber assets of that province, but also samples of B. C. flooring, ceiling, interior and exterior trim, panelings, cooperage, pulp products, etc. Not since 1916 has there been a display made by British Columbia at the big exposition, and the space which will be occupied this time will be much larger and the character of the showing more extensive than ever.

Major James Brechin, now of Toronto, late of Victoria, who was recently appointed British Columbia Lumber Commissioner for the East, will have charge of the booth, and will be glad to welcome all those interested.

It has been estimated by the Canadian Commission of Conservation that there are over 300,000,000,000 feet of saw-timber in British Columbia, which represents over one-half the total stand in Canada. The annual growth increment has been estimated at 6,000,000,000 feet.

The production of lumber in British Columbia has increased so rapidly in the last few years that some are predicting that the province will be marketing 250 million feet annually before long. The value of last year's production was $54,162,000, as against $48,300,000 for 1917, and $29,150,000 for 1916. The waterborne export of lumber from the province last year was 88,069,000 feet, or more than 100 per cent. over 1917. Of this 17,024,000 feet went to China and 10,803,000 feet to Japan. The year 1918 saw the province most prominent in connection with the war, the total shipment and production of aeroplane spruce and fir from January to November, 1918, totalling 25,124,000 and 9,224,000 feet respectively.

Forest Fire Smoke Impedes Navigation

On Lake Superior, and to a lesser extent on Lake Huron, the movements of vessels have been interfered with by the smoke from forest fires. During the day the captains are able to make way with a fairly clear view, but almost every night they are forced to anchor their vessels. Between the fog and the smoke it is impossible at times for the crews to see twenty-five yards, and to continue sailing would mean accidents. A few days ago, when morning broke on Whitefish Bay, at the head of the St. Mary's River, between 50 and 60 freighters were revealed anchored within a short distance of one another. For twenty hours one day last week not a vessel locked through the Canadian Soo because of the smoke.

Several small forest fires are burning within the city limits of Sault Ste. Marie. The city has men patrolling some of these areas, and the firemen have spent several nights in an endeavor to keep the flames from getting into the centre of the city. While no lives have been lost to date, there have been many settlers in these districts who have been ready to leave their homes on short notice should the fires get closer.

Logging Companies Will Increase Cut

There is every indication that operations will be carried on in the bush this year in Ontario, Quebec, and New Brunswick more extensively than ever. Some firms have already doubled the number of their camps and are engaging all the lumberjacks available in their representative districts, so as to get as much cutting done as possible by the end of 1919. There is no doubt that if labor conditions are propitious the timber taken out this winter will be greater than any year since the outbreak of the war. Wages show no disposition to come down and while there was a slight drop during the summer, the figure for the average lumberjack is running from $55 to $65 per month, with a strong upward tendency. Cooks are receiving $80 to $100 per month, and foremen $110 to $125.

On a number of items which enter into the running of the lumber camps there is an advance. Taken on the whole the expense of getting out the timber will be greater this season than last.

An indication of the extensive character of logging operations was furnished the other day when a harness manufacturer stated that his establishment was so crowded with orders for harness for lumbermen and loggers that he could not begin to make the number of sets required. Of late years business has been rather quiet, but it has now set in with a rush.

Oats are selling at $1.06 per bushel, whereas last year lumbermen were paying only from 65c to 80c. Hay is now $33 per ton and up, and was from $10 to $15 lower at this particular period in 1918; thus do logging costs keep avanting all the while, and dearer lumber is in sight again next season.

Portable Houses Will Be Costlier

It is understood that the Canadian Timber Products Association recently gave the Export Association of Montreal a price on a certain type of portable house, which might be used to advantage in Europe. This figure was to hold good until the middle of the present month, by the end of which time the price was to be void. It is understood that the Export Association is sincerely hoping that the offer will not be accepted, as the estimate, when given several weeks ago, was thought to be sufficient, but just now considering labor and lumber the quotation is away below the mark. "If we were figuring again on this house," remarked one leading member of the association, "we would want to increase the price by, at least, one-third, which will have to be done in order to protect the manufacturers so that they are assured of profit on their production."

Would Place Lumber on Free List

At the recent Liberal convention held in Ottawa, a tariff resolution was passed calling for substantial reductions of the burdens of Custom taxation with a view to accomplishing two purposes, viz., diminishing the high cost of living and reducing the cost of the instruments of production in the industries based on the natural resources of the Dominion. In this connection it was declared that sawmill machinery, rough and dressed lumber, etc., should be free from Custom duties, as well as the raw material entering into the same.

Housing Scheme Encounters Some Snags

The Province of Quebec Industrial Housing Scheme, in which lumbermen are interested, is meeting with difficulties. To begin with three of the original members of the Montreal Commission resigned on the ground that the plan is unworkable. Then the Commission objected to be taxed 2½ per cent. on the amount of the loan to meet the expense of a technical committee which has been appointed by the province to draw up plans and supervise the work. The general criticism of the scheme is that it cannot be carried out within the limits of expenditure—$4,500 per house—set by the Act. While houses may be built for this sum in rural districts, it is impossible to do so in a city like Montreal, where a large part of the money must be spent. The town planner of the Commission, however, is optimistic so far as this is concerned, provided that the houses are constructed on plans which will permit many dwellings to be built in terraces and in large numbers. But there are sceptics, who declare that houses worthy of the name cannot be built for the amounts specified.

Will Cruising Be Done by Aeroplane?

A sign of the times. A Nova Scotia Aerial Survey Company is offering to make photographs and to survey timber and pulpwood areas by aeroplane in any part of the world; also to undertake forest protective work. There are optimists who believe that the time is not far distant when we shall be surveying and cruising our forest lands by aeroplanes—that the work can be done more accurately and cheaper than by present methods. Those of the old school, however, are very sceptical. The company referred to is prepared to make contracts for the distribution of political and advertising literature. This opens up a new field of publicity, and in the future we may expect to find our cities, towns and villages bombarded with immense quantities of propagandist and trade literature by the rival political parties and enterprising commercial firms.

Three petitions for leave to appeal, involving important questions whether the Companies' Acts of Manitoba, Saskatchewan and Ontario are ultra vires of the provinces, were before the Privy Council recently in London, Eng. Before counsel opened their addresses, Lord Haldane intimated, on behalf of the Privy Council, that their Lordships were ready to grant leave, and expressed the desire that all three appeals be consolidated, and only one set of arguments be heard. Counsel promised to arrange this.

Personal Paragraphs of Interest

L. Rolland, of Blair & Rolland, Montreal, is on a business trip to the Eastern States.

H. J. Terry and family, of Toronto, have returned from a trip to Port Arthur, Duluth and other points.

W. T. Mason, of Mason, Gordon & Co., Montreal, spent a few days in Toronto recently with Hugh A. Rose, Ontario representative of the company.

H. J. Hall, of H. J. Hall & Sons, who conduct a general planing mill business at Kitchener, Ont., is spending a well earned vacation in the Muskoka district.

F. Dieulefet has left Montreal for France as representative of Mr. U. E. Germain, Montreal, the representative of Timms, Phillips & Co., Ltd., Vancouver.

R. G. Chesbro, Toronto, representing the Allen-Stoltze Lumber Co., of Vancouver, has been on an extended motor tour through Michigan and other States.

Frank W. Gordon, who has charge of the B. C. forest products department of Terry & Gordon, Toronto, has returned from an extended business trip to B. C.

L. D. Barclay, manager of the Toronto office of Canadian Western Lumber Co., Fraser Mills, B. C., left recently on an extended visit to Edmonton and the Coast.

Arthur Frerrault, of the Brown Corporation, La Tuque, was drowned while attempting to rescue his two sons in the Bastonnais River, near La Tuque. All three were drowned.

Chester H. Belton, of the R. Laidlaw Lumber Company, Sarnia, Ont., accompanied by his wife and family, has returned from spending a few enjoyable holidays at St. Andrew's, N. B.

C. H. Goodhand, of Lindsay, Ont., who is foreman for the John Carew Lumber Company, has been laid up for sometime with a cut arm but is now making good progress toward recovery.

Among the lumbermen from Ontario who attended the recent big Liberal convention in Ottawa, were A. J. Young, of North Bay and Toronto, and Norman C. Hocken, of Otter Lake, Ont.

Horace Hartley, representing J. & D. A. Harquail Co., Limited, lumber manufacturers, Campbellton, N.B., spent a few weeks in Toronto and other Ontario cities recently, calling upon members of the trade.

Arthur Marshall Rowles died recently in Toronto after a long illness in his 68th year.. He came to Canada from England in 1880. Prior to his illness he had completed fifteen years' service with the Canadian Shipbuilding Company, latterly as manager of the Boiler Department. Seven children survive him.

Thos. Patterson, of Hamilton, president of the Ontario Retail Lumber Dealers' Association, who is spending an enjoyable vacation in Oregon and California, is expected home from the south in the near future. Mr. Patterson has visited many points of interest and will have much to tell his friends on his return.

Albert V. S. Pulling, who is a graduate in Forestry of New York State College, has been appointed Dean of the Forestry School of the University of New Brunswick at Fredericton. He has been employed on practical work in New Hampshire for some time and was assistant professor during his course in New York.

J. L. MacFarlane, secretary of the Canadian General Lumber Company, Toronto, is spending his holidays at his summer home near Peterboro. Mr. McFarlane's many friends will regret to learn that his health has not been of the best during the past few weeks and hope that he will speedily regain his former vigor.

Joseph Oliver, of the Oliver Lumber Co., Toronto, and former president of the Canadian National Exhibition, Toronto, was a member of a deputation which recently waited upon the federal cabinet at Ottawa with the request that the government contribute one half of the million dollars required for a live stock arena in Toronto. The delegation reports that the request met with a sympathetic hearing.

G. N. Howes, son of John Howes, retail lumberman, Harriston, Ont., has taken a position with Campbell, Welsh & Paynes, Toronto, and will cover part of eastern and western Ontario in the interests of the firm. Mr. Howes has spent all his life in the lumber business of which he has a thorough experience and returned some time ago from overseas.

Mr. and Mrs. John K. Bell, of Toronto, were recently killed by a shunting C. P. R. engine while crossing the tracks of Riverdale Park on their way across the Don River to hear the band concert in the eastern section of the park. Mr. Bell, who was a retired lumberman, formerly lived in Peterboro and was in his 79th year and Mrs. Bell was 78. Although the flagman tried to warn the aged couple and shouted to them, he could not avert the terrible accident and both Mr. and Mrs. Bell lost their lives. The crossing is a very dangerous one and it is almost miraculous that more tragedies have not occurred at this point.

Wm. Turnbull, Victoria, B. C., lumber commissioner of British Columbia, who also has charge of the publicity work in connection with the Forestry branch of the Department of Lands for that province, spent a few days recently in Toronto, Ottawa, Montreal and other eastern centres in the interest of wood products of the Pacific Coast. While in Toronto, Mr. Turnbull, who is a former widely known newspaper man, being for several years engaged in journalism in Prince Rupert, spent some time in company with Major James Brechin, British Columbia Lumber Commissioner for the East. They called upon a large number of members of the trade.

J. L. Campbell, of Campbell, Welsh & Paynes, Toronto, has returned from a trip to Winnipeg. He reports that owing to the crop failure in many sections of the Province, the demand for lumber from the Coast will be light during the coming year, but that the B. C. manufacturers are not worrying as their stock is commanding an exceptionally high figure across the border with the demand greater than supply. So far as prices are concerned at the present time, the market is largely an auction one and the material goes to the highest bidder.

The Powell Lumber & Door Co., 133 Front St. W., Toronto, who have been in business for a number of years, having taken over the interests of the Rathbun Company in Toronto before the war, have disposed of their stock and gone out of business. The property on which their premises were located has been sold. The Oliver Lumber Co. have acquired the sidings of the Powell Company at the foot of Spadina Ave., where the latter maintained a hemlock yard. Richard Locke, manager of the company, has retired for the present and will take a well needed rest, but may re-enter the lumber business at a later date.

W. G. Clarke, of Clarke Bros., Limited, Bear River, N. S., accompanied by A. G. McIntyre, president and managing-director of the pulp division of the company, spent a few days in Toronto rerecently on their way west to Port Arthur, where they inspected the plant of the Port Arthur Pulp and Paper Co. Mr. Clarke and Mr. McIntyre have been spending sometime visiting pulp plants in the New England States with a desire to secure all the latest ideas and suggestions in construction and equipment. Clarke Bros., Limited, are erecting a sulphate pulp plant at Bear River, which will have a capacity of 30 tons per day and they are also enlarging their sawmill and woodworking operations. Good progress has been made on the construction of the new pulp mill. Mr. McIntyre was until recently news print expert of the American Publishers Association.

Big Increase of Timber Revenue

Upwards of $20,000 had been received at the Department of Lands and Mines of New Brunswick, according to a statement made recently by Lieut, Col. T. G. Loggie, the Deputy Minister of Lands and Mines.

Three-quarters of the amount mentioned is in payment of stumpage rates and the balance consists of charges for renewals of leases at $8 per mile, as well as the forest fire protection tax of half a cent an acre. These payments are due on August 1st annually, but many of the lumbermen pay their amounts in advance.

The Evolution of the Country Lumber Yard

Dealer Has Legitimate Right to Keep for Sale Anything He Can Make Profit on, but is it Good Policy for Him to do so—Law of Limitation

The country lumber yard has always been a place where the carrying of mixed stocks was the rule. The addition of the coal business was rendered necessary because of the limitation of the use of building materials during a large part of the year. But everything else that went into building construction was considered proper for the business of the yard, says C. H. Ketridge in the "Mississippi Valley Lumberman." Among these things, however, there were certain articles, such as paint and builders' hardware that many dealers did not handle, because they thought it didn't pay them to do it. In the earlier days though pretty near every country dealer was handling the mixed paints. But the hardware and drug stores thought it was a part of their business also to handle them and competition was such that gradually the lumbermen ceased to bother with the business.

There were other articles, too, such as implements and furniture that a few dealers thought they saw some money in handling. In fact, there were those who took up with most anything they saw a dollar in and didn't care whether they were infringing on the rights of other business men or not. As a rule, however, the stock of a lumber yard comprised building materials and coal, and where they took up anything else was chiefly in the little towns where there were more yards than were needed. Doubtless this same condition prevails in such towns at the present time and dealers have to sell anything they can to make any money at all.

There is no question but a dealer has a legitimate right to keep for sale anything he can make a profit on, but it is questionable whether in all cases it is good policy for him to do so. Take it in the average town, I believe it the best policy for a lumber dealer to include in his stock only those things which are used for building purposes. This, of course, includes paints, builders' hardware, and fencing. Drain tiling, also, would probably come under the head of construction. These, with others of like character, together with coal, constitute what may be termed the legitimate stock of a lumber yard.

Leaving out paints, hardware and fencing, it may be said that competition is confined to the two or more yards in the place. But when the yards go to dabbling into something which other business concerns think belong solely to them, the lumber yard, or yards, as the case may be, have a competitor in every one of those people, and naturally they are not going out of their way to throw business to a competitor. The druggist or the hardware dealer is not likely to influence a man to buy his lumber at a yard that competes with them for the sale of paints and hardware, and moreover, they are not overly friendly with the lumberman either. The result of this feeling is that prices are cut to get the business, and consequently no money is made out of it. Some yards even handle salt and flour, which can't help but antagonize the grocer. If he handles wagons or automobiles, the implement dealer and the garage man have got it in for the lumberman and would just as soon see a bill shipped in on him as not.

Creates an Unpleasant Atmosphere

So instead of having the business men friendly to the lumber yard and using their influence to persuade people to patronize the home lumber yard, their attitude is right the other way, and they and their friends are hostile to the dealer and his business. They may be in a personal way friendly and all that, but nevertheless, there is a feeling of business hostility existing which is always working to the detriment of the dealer's business interests. In a large place this does not matter so much but in a small town where everybody is more closely related, it matters a good deal to the lumberman, for much of his success depends on his having the good will of every unit of the community. This is something, of course, which does not concern the farmers, for the more competition there is in the town the better it suits them. But all the same they have their friends among the business men who can help or injure the lumber dealer as he chooses to.

You can form some idea of this feeling by how you feel yourself when one of the elevators puts in a stock of coal or perhaps lumber. You haven't the same feeling as you had before toward that concern. You think it is an unnecessary infringement on your business, and places you at a disadvantage as you are practically debarred from retaliating by handling grain. But you are not prevented from hinting to your farmer friends that grain prices are not what they ought to be. Anything like this plays the devil with an elevator. But it is human nature to retaliate. There's lots of it in these small country towns, and it is a game two can play at. So if the elevator man hears of the dealer's attitude, he is likely to come back by intimating that lumber yard prices are too high, and forthwith makes a cut on his coal and lumber, which he can easily make up for on his grain prices.

When lumber yards and elevators keep within the limits of their regular business they can be a great help to each other in forming public opinion. But if otherwise, they can make it mighty unpleasant for each other.

It is not to be reasonably expected that a state of harmony can always exist between the lumber and some of the other business men. For many years the hardware men have been handling things that more properly belong to the lumber business, such as building paper, roofing, screen doors, and in many instances, windows and storm sash and doors. The lumbermen have lost the sale of pine fencing and most of the wire substitute is sold at the hardware stores together with the steel posts also. In one way or another, substitutes for what the dealer handles are being carried for sale in other stores in the town, so that it has come about that every country dealer has several local competitors besides those of the lumber yards, and I think it is more of a general thing than it used to be. Every town of considerable size now has its department store where practically everything is handled that is carried by the smaller single stores. As a rule they have proven to be an economy in merchandising.

Becoming a Department Store

There is no question but that there is a tendency also toward making a department store of the lumber yard and including everything that goes into the composition of buildings, and in some places

Cutting the stalwart white pine in Northern Ontario

doubtless it will include some of the other heavier commodities of merchandise as the conditions will justify. If dealers generally accept the idea of selling the building instead of selling the items for it, contracting to furnish the job complete, it will become a department of the business. We don't generally think of a lumber yard as a department store, but in a way it really is, and should be considered so. The average yard is a conglomeration of building merchandise and all the sales are thrown together in one lump sum of each day's transactions and at the end of the year the whole is figured up and the profits of the yard supposed to be arrived at. Such yards have no way of telling whether they are making any money on coal, cement, plaster and lime, or any other item of stock, other than lumber which they may handle. They may be losing money on any one of these articles and don't know it. As a consequence this loss has to be made up by the rest of the stock. It is a well known fact that cement, as it has been handled in the past few years, is an expense instead of a profit with the average dealer, and doubtless other items are being sold in the same way.

I think I am warranted in saying that the majority of lumber dealers don't know for sure what it costs them to sell a ton of coal. They fix a certain price and guess that it is making them a profit, but

How two progressive firms at Sault Ste. Marie, Ont., get after business by attractive advts. in the local papers

they don't know whether they guess right or not. Some men seem to have the notion that if they come out at the end of the year with a profit it makes no difference whether it has been made out of the "side line" or lumber. So what is the use of bothering to keep separate accounts? When one gets into the habit of thinking and doing this way it is not an easy thing to change.

This, of course, is more apt to be the case with individual dealers who, having but the one yard, do not consider it necessary. But with a string of yards a systemized policy is essential to the success of the business, and most line yards have a divisional system also and by this they know whether they gain or lose on any item of stock they are carrying.

I am aware of the fact that it takes considerable extra bookkeeping to keep an account with so many stock items as are in the average yard, and so I have thought that this could be avoided by dividing the yard into departments, perhaps four of these would be sufficient, putting lumber and millwork into one; coal in another; cement, and all other plasterers' and masons' materials into another, and all the rest of the stock into a department of miscellany. This would cover the different stocks carried in the ordinary yard and by making these divisions it would economize labor in keeping the books, and at the same time afford the dealer the required knowledge of his business. He would then know whether lumber was bearing more than its share of the cost of carrying on the business and let him know which department is not bearing its proportionate share. I think this method would in some cases simplify a system which is now overloaded with system. This is not a new idea, although its application may be new to those country dealers who still follow the old system of "bunching" things as they do in the common general merchandise store in your town. Go into that store and ask the proprietor how much profit his groceries net him, or his shoes, clothing, or dry goods. Ten to one he can't tell you because he has no system for keeping a separate account of each line of goods.

Trouble From Lack of Proper Accounting

This lack of an accounting system has been the main trouble with the farmers. I well remember asking twelve representative farmers to let me know in writing their estimate of what it cost them to raise a bushel of wheat and corn respectively. After a time I got in all their answers and it was amusing to see the wide divergence in some of them. The majority had not counted in the interest on their investment and not one mentioned the labor of his wife and family. Not until recent years has there been an effort to bring system into the business of farming and it will be many years yet before the majority of farmers will know what their respective crops cost them to produce, and which is profitable or unprofitable. As a matter of fact, and generally speaking, farming of itself has not been a profitable business and the farmer has made what money he has chiefly from the rise in the value of his land. As a business investment farming has been a poor business. Very few landlords in the older states where land values are high have realized more than four per cent. on the investment.

The average lumber dealer is not getting all out of his business that he might because he is handling some lines that are unprofitable, and in this he is very much like the farmer. And like him, too, he has no system to show him where the trouble lies and his method of business in this respect puts him in a class with the farmer.

In the matter of buying and selling, a good many business men can learn something from the farmers, as most of you know.

The ready-cut house concerns in their advertising put great stress on their alleged saving in cutting up the material for a house, and like everything else in their claims, this is a false assumption. But I know it carries great weight with those who are ignorant of the details of construction, and this will include practically everybody but the building mechanics. Speaking myself from experimental knowledge of the details of construction. I can say that the only way these concerns can save in the material is by skimping the job, which is the identical way that some contractors follow when they take a job to furnish at a figure which would be a loss to them if they put up the building as it should be and as intended by those in competition for the job. Such a saving, however, is not in the interest of the owner who is paying for what he thinks he is getting but don't get.

Aircraft in Forest Protective Work

The following comment on the use of airplanes in forestry service is contained in the annual report of the Committee on Forests, Commission of Conservation:

A great deal of attention is being devoted throughout the world to the development of peace-time uses of aircraft. That there will be many such uses requires no argument.

Among the possibilities are forest fire patrol and aerial photography. It is now expected that fire patrols by flying boats will be established during the current year by the British Columbia Forest Branch and by one or more of the forest protective associations of Quebec, assisted by the Quebec Government. The St. Maurice Forest Protective Association is the leader in this respect in the East, as the British Columbia Forest Branch has already proved in the West. It is believed that there are large possibilities also in connection with aerial fire patrol on Dominion lands in the West, through the Dominion Forestry and Parks Branches. Many men whose experience in aviation overseas should qualify them to express thoroughly practical opinions state that, beyond question, these things are eminently feasible.

Similarly, there is undoubtedly a large field for developments along the line of aerial photography, both in connection with forest protection and independently. The recent address of Colonel Cull before the Geodetic Society of Ottawa showed some of the possibilities of aircraft in furthering the line of work with which the geodetic survey is particularly concerned.

The possibilities in connection with forestry work are also very great. There are vast areas in all our provinces, where only fragmentary data are available as to drainage and topography, or as to the extent, composition, and volume of the forests. As a result of war developments, the importance of our forests in the national economy is now recognized as never before. An adequate knowledge of the character, location, and extent of the forests of Canada is essential to the proper administration and exploitation of this vital resource.

The Commission of Conservation made a survey of the forest resources of British Columbia and Saskatchewan, although the data available as to extive areas were of the most fragmentary character. Similar work in other provinces is planned, as rapidly as the necessary funds can be secured. The prosecution of such projects would be enormously simplified and the results would be much more accurate and valuable, if necessary work on the ground could be supplemented by systematic surveys made by means of aerial photography. Such surveys might, of course, serve other public purposes as well. This suggests the extreme desirability of co-operation between all agencies interested, Dominion and provincial, as well as private.

The public interest involved in all these questions is undoubtedly very great. If adequate developments along these lines are to be anticipated on a par with those planned in other countries, it would seem logical that the Dominion Government should take the lead in making the necessary plans and in providing the equipment.

Use of Motor Truck in Logging Grows Rapidly

Proper Roads are Essential to Successful and Economic Operation—Good Make of Truck and Trailer is Desirable—Expense and Upkeep

It is only three years since logging trucks were first adopted at all generally by operators on the Pacific Coast, yet in that short time the number in use has jumped from about half-a-dozen to some five hundred. This rapid development of motor truck logging is mainly due to the adoption of a practicable trailer, which is necessary to the successful economic operation of the truck, because of the size of logs taken out in the Pacific Northwest. The advantages of the truck and trailer combination are many. Three times as great a load can be hauled as by the truck alone; fuel is saved, as an engine will pull a load to capacity where it can't so carry a load; time is saved, obviously, as increased loads lessen the number of trips; labor is saved, as the number of loading operations are, of course, less when each operation disposes of a greater quantity; and, finally, longer and bulkier logs can be taken out.

As to what can be done by means of truck and trailer haulage. One logger reports that on an eight-mile haul he averaged six trips daily, hauling from 3,000 to 5,000 feet a trip; another states that he makes four or five round trips daily for distances of from two to seven miles, and hauls anything from 15,000 to 40,000 feet of logs, depending on the length of haul and the condition of the road; on a seven mile haul another logger makes four round trips daily, averaging 4,000 feet a trip. A single truck and trailer was used in each instance.

The Question of Cost

As to the expense of operation, some interesting figures, giving the cost to a logging concern across the line, recently came to our notice. We give them hereunder:

Cost of truck (as basis), 5 ton	$5,000.00
Cost of trailer (as basis), 8½ ton	1,700.00
	$6,700.00
Depreciation at 25%	$1,675.00
Interest at 7%	469.00
License	50.00
Taxes	
Insurance	75.00
Total	$2,269.00
Per day, based on 300 working days	7.60
Variable Charges—per day.	
Tires, guaranteed 7,000 miles	$ 4.40
Gasoline (4 miles to gallon at 25c)	2.50
Oil and Grease (estimated)	.50
Wages	6.00
Repairs (costs averaged)	.80
	$ 14.20
	7.60
Total per day	$ 21.80

From the above it is easy to estimate what the cost would be on this side. Duty would have to be added to the original investment and to subsequent expenditures for tires, part renewals, etc. There would be little other difference, as some of our operations on the lower Mainland are conducted in similar timber and over much the same kind of ground.

Specially Constructed Roads Necessary

The road problem is important. In the States, pole roads and concrete roads are the two types favored by loggers. Where concrete is used, grades may be steeper, as concrete affords better traction than wood. Six per cent is as steep a grade as is advisable on a pole road; as high as twelve per cent is practicable on concrete. As the average width of a logging truck is 7 feet 6 inches, measuring from the outer edge of the wheels, at least 8 feet of road is necessary, or about 12 feet in all, with the sub-grade. Ditches should be made, and there should be outlets for the water flow every fifty feet.

A good pole road is made with heavy single poles for the main track and lighter poles on the outside for guard rails, and on the inside to support the steering wheels. The main poles should be about twenty inches in diameter, and the longer they are the more serviceable they will prove. The top sides of the main poles are hewn to a flat surface, 16 inches wide, and the poles are laid half buried. Every ten feet or so the poles rest on cross ties, to which they are securely spiked. The guard rails are firmly braced and spiked to the main poles. The inside poles are hewn flat and laid level with the main track.

In the concrete road two tracks of concrete, one for each wheel, are used. The concrete lies in ditches 26 inches wide and 6 inches deep, and it has a guard lip of about 4 inches in height and 4 inches in width along its outer edge. Where material is available, a concrete road probably costs twenty-five per cent more to build than a pole road.

Good roads are very necessary to the successful operation of trucks in logging, and in the experience of operators the initial expense in providing them is more than made up in subsequent saving of wear and tear and time. Trucks "live" much longer when run over good roads, they haul bigger loads, and logs are less often shaken off—a fruitful source of waste labor under unfavorable conditions.

"Lumber Export Bulletin" is the name of a new fortnightly periodical published by The Lumbermen's Bureau of Washington, D.C. The first issue contains current exporters' selling prices f.a.s. of pitch pine, hardwoods, Douglas fir, California sugar pine, and redwood; a Tonnage Review and Table of Current Ocean Rates; Foreign Exchange; Review of Foreign Markets, and Inquiries for Lumber from Foreign Importers.

Illustration shows rapid development in the use of motor trucks in logging operations.

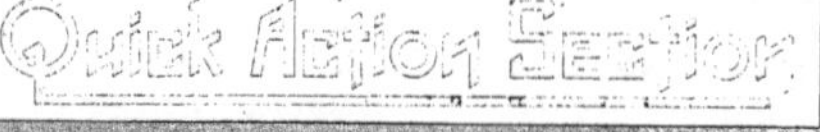

PUBLISHER'S NOTICE

Advertisements other than "Employment Wanted" or "Employees Wanted" will be inserted in this department at the rate of 20 cents per agate line (14 agate lines make one inch). $2.80 per inch, each insertion, payable in advance. Space measured from rule to rule. When four or more consecutive insertions of the same advertisement are ordered a discount of 25 per cent. will be allowed.

Advertisements of "Wanted Employment" will be inserted at the rate of one cent a word, net. Cash must accompany order. If Canada Lumberman box number is used, enclose ten cents extra for postage in forwarding replies. Minimum charge 25 cents.

Advertisements of "Wanted Employees" will be inserted at the rate of two cents a word, net. Cash must accompany the order. Minimum charge 50 cents.

Advertisements must be received not later than the 10th and 20th of each month to insure insertion in the subsequent issue.

Wanted–Lumber

Basswood Wanted

No. 2 Common and Mill Cull. Winter cut preferred. Apply Firstbrook Brothers, Ltd., Toronto, Ont. 8-t.f.

CEDAR LATH WANTED

We are in the market for clear Eastern Cedar Lath in the following sizes:

½" thick, 1½" wide, and lengths 4'-4'4"-4'8" and 5'.

⅜" thick, 2" wide, and lengths 4'-4'4"-4'8" and 5'.

½" x 2½" x lengths 5', 5' 4", 5' 8" and 6'.

Any lath manufacturers who are cutting cedar lath will find it to their advantage to communicate with us as we are offering a big price for clear lath.

The Peterboro Canoe Co., Limited,
16 Peterboro, Ont.

Wanted

10/4 and 12/4 No. 1 Common and Better Birch,

also

10/4 and 12/4 No. 1 Common and Better Soft Elm.

In quoting, state how the stock will run to 1st and 2nds and how long it has been cut. Box 996, Canada Lumberman, Toronto. 16-19

LUMBER WANTED

We are in the market for the following lumber and will make contracts for the quantities we require for delivery during the coming season.

1" Basswood, winter cut, 17 and 18' long, log run.
1" Basswood, winter cut, 8-16' long, log run.
1" Clear Eastern Cedar, 8-16' long, 4" wide and up.
1" Butternut, No. 1 Common and Better.
2" Rock Elm, No. 1 Common and Better, 10-16'
1¼" Hard Maple, winter cut, 1sts and 2nds.
1" Oak, No. 1 Common and Better, 10-16'.
1½" Oak 17 and 18' long, clear strip, 3" wide and up.
1½" Oak, 10-22', clear strip, 3" wide and up.
1½" Oak, 10-22', No. 1 Common and Better.

If you have any of the above stock to cut get in touch with us.

The Peterboro Canoe Co., Limited,
16 Peterboro, Ont.

For Sale–Lumber

For Sale

30,000 setts Cheese Box Veneer. Apply C. A. Moses, Osgoode Station, Ont. 16-19

FOR SALE

100 pieces White Oak Piling, 20 to 60 ft. For particulars write

E. S. THOMPSON,
16 Appin, Ont.

FOR SALE

About 300 Spruce Ties, 6" up face, 6" thick, 8' long, good sound spruce, balance of car cedar ties. Also 1", 2" and 3" merchantable spruce. Write for prices. Address Box 81, Mont Joli, P.Q.

FOR SALE

2 cars 2½" Log Run Pecan.
2 cars 2" Log Run Pecan.
2 cars 3" Log Run Sycamore.
1 car ¼" Log Run Elm.
2 cars 1" Soft Maple Crating.
1 car 1" Beech and Maple Crating.
1 car ¾" Beech and Maple Crating.
1 car ¾" Elm Crating.

John I. Shafer Hardwood Co.,
Farmers' Trust Building,
15-16 South Bend, Indiana.

FOR SALE

50,000 ft.	2 x 4 x 10/16'	Jack P[illegible]	& Spruce
100,000 "	2 x 5 x 10/16'	"	"
100,000 "	2 x 6 x 10/16'	"	"
100,000 "	2 x 7 x 10/16'	"	"
100,000 "	2 x 8 x 10/16'	"	"
2 cars	6 x 6 x 10/16'	"	"
2 "	6 x 8 x 10/16'	"	"
2 "	8 x 8 x 10/16'	"	"
1 "	10 x 10 x 10/16'	"	"

The above stock cut and piled ready for shipment. Write or Wire

NORTHERN LUMBER MILLS,
14-17 North Cobalt, Ont.

For Sale–Machinery

FOR SALE

One second-hand 8" band saw, complete with saws; also circular resaw, with two inserted tooth saws, 42" dia. Keenan Bros., Ltd., Owen Sound, Ont.

Machinery For Sale

20 to 25 h.p. portable horizontal boiler and engine on skids, good condition. Easy terms to responsible party. Box 973, Canada Lumberman, Toronto. 16

MACHINERY FOR SALE

surfacer. This machine is in good condition, but has been replaced by a large machine. Apply at once to

P. W. GARDINER & SON,

FOR SALE

One twenty-four inch Combined Planer and Matcher, Clark-Demill make.
Three Gas Engines, from 1 to 6 H.P.
Two twenty-six inch Barnes Sliding Head Drills. Good as new. Bargain prices.

W. H. Sumbling Machinery Co.,
7 St. Mary Street,
15-16 Toronto, Ont.

FOR SALE—SAWMILL

25 H. P. Engine, 50 H. P. return tubular boiler. Three log seat carriage, overhead set, friction feed works, single edger and slab saw. All in fair order. Price $1,000. Box 915, Canada Lumberman, Toronto. 16-19

Band Saw Mill For Sale

One Waterous 9 ft. Band Saw Mill, gunshot feed, complete with extra saws and filing equipment. Used about one year, excellent condition. The Geo. F. Foss Machinery & Supply Co., Ltd., 305 St. James St., Montreal, Que. 7-t.f.

For Sale

1—17 x 24 Atlas Engine, with 36 in. x 10 ft. flywheel.
3—No. 94 Berlin Matchers, 15 in., fitted with hard steel knives on top and bottom cylinders—one pair shiplap, jointer and flooring heads with bits for each machine.
1—No. 182 Berlin Double Surfacer, 30 in. x 6 in.
1—No. 109 Berlin Buzz Planer.
1—No. 200 Berlin Picket Header.

The Otis Staples Lumber Company, Ltd.,
19-t.f. Wycliffe, B.C.

FOR SALE
Saw Mill Machinery

Complete saw mill machinery; equipped with rotary, steam feed carriage, Gang Saw, Resaw, Edger, Butter, Lath Machine. Three Boilers and twin engine 300 H.P.; also saw gummers, filers and one shingle machine, with bolter and barker. For particulars apply:

CHICOUTIMI PULP CO.,
16-19 Chandler, Que.

Used Saw Mill Machinery FOR SALE

One McGregor & Gourlay endless bed Planer, knives 28" long, bed raises and lowers by power. Will plane 10" thick. In good condition. One B. F. Sturtevant Exhaust Fan, Intake 23" diameter, discharge 19" x 19" square, pulley 10" dia. x 8" face. In good working order, with an extra set of blades or fans. Also bonnet and piping for planer and discharge piping for fan.

Also two Moreau Rossers for peeling pulp wood. These are as good as new; used only one season. Will peel on an average 25 cords per day. Reason for selling, no more pulp wood to peel.

Complete Saw Mill for sale. Full particulars given on enquiry. All this machinery is at Kazubazua, Que., and belongs to Kazubazua Lumber Co. Any further information will be given by addressing

L. D. PHILIPS,
34 Thornton Ave.,
16-10 Ottawa, Ont.

Wanted–Employment

Advertisements under this heading one cent a word per insertion. Box No. 10 cents extra. Minimum charge 25 cents.

WANTED: Position as log culler or foreman in log camp, by experienced man. For further particulars apply Box 44, Orangeville, Ont. 16-19

WANTED—POSITION AS BAND-SAW FILER—The kind you can depend on to get results. At present in Upper Michigan; prefer Canada. Box 989, Canada Lumberman, Toronto, Ont. 15-16

POSITION WANTED by a well educated young man, 15 years' experience with wholesalers and manufacturers; competent inspector either hard or soft wood; will consider any other capacity. Apply Box 956, Canada Lumberman, Toronto. 12-16

Thoroughly experienced sawmill and lumberman as assistant manager or general superintendent of operations on coast or interior; age 36, married, an English Canadian and speaks French; satisfactory references. Write Box 988, Canada Lumberman, Toronto. 15-17

WANTED POSITION by representative and superintendent, still employed with large wholesale firm, with twenty-five years' experience in the lumber business. Can give reference as to capabilities and take charge on a month's notice. Box 991, Canada Lumberman, Toronto. 15-18

WHOLESALERS—MANUFACTURERS—ATTENTION! Fifteen years in the business; territory Windsor to Halifax, New York and New England, buying and selling. Know trade thoroughly, Eastern and Western stocks. Highly educated, both languages. Would make first class office manager or secretary or traveller. Real correspondent. Employed. Desire change. Start at once. Hard worker. Age 37. Your chance to secure a producer. Apply Box 50, Canada Lumberman, Montreal. 15-16

Wanted–Employees

First Class Man on Rip Saw.

JOHN B. SMITH & SONS,
13-16 Toronto, Ont.

Wanted—One Foreman for Sash and Door Department; experienced on solid and veneered doors; four bench men, experienced on hard and soft wood; two cabinetmakers.

J. R. EATON & SONS, LIMITED,
13-16 Orillia, Ont.

POSITION OPEN for a high-class man capable of organizing and assuming full management of all lumbering operations of a 500 mile timber limit for a Company operating a Saw-mill and a Pulp-mill. All replies will be treated confidentially. A permanent position with a good salary open for the right man. Box 983, Canada Lumberman, Toronto. 16-21

LUMBER EXPORT HOUSE has opening for intelligent young man, 19-23 years of age. Applicant must be ambitious, willing, and have a good education. Competent stenographer and typist, and be accurate at figures. Moderate salary to start, but good opportunity for advancement and to learn the business. Apply giving references, experience, etc., to Mr. S. Bick, P. O. Box 284, Montreal. 14-17

Business Chances

Lumber Yard

Excellent place in Montreal, for sale or to let. Room 8, LaPresse Building, Main 16-19

Wanted

Good reliable saw mill man with portable mill to cut two million feet or more Birch and Hemlock in Patterson Township. Warren Ross Lumber Co., Jamestown, N.Y. 14-19

Cruising and Reforestation

Operators desirous of preserving timber lands for future cutting can secure the services of two men experienced in cruising and reforestation. Send particulars first letter. Box 997, Canada Lumberman, Toronto. 16

FOR SALE

Saw, Heading and planing mill with electric light plant for lighting town. Will sell with or without electric light plant. Good supply of timber. For further information apply to Geo. Coultis & Son, Thedford, Ont. 16-19

Mill Wanted

Have 80 million feet good mixed timber near rail and good labor supply. Require good mill and man to log and cut on profit sharing basis. Capital and selling organization provided. Excellent opportunity. Full particulars available from Box 985, Canada Lumberman, Toronto. 16

STANDING TIMBER FOR SALE

A well located block of splendid standing timber, consisting of Pine, Cedar, Hemlock, Maple, Elm, Black and White Ash. About 20 to 25 million feet altogether. All or part will be sold by thousand on the stump. Could also arrange to cut one to two million feet to order. Box 994, Canada Lumberman, Toronto. 16

Sawmill For Sale

Portable outfit in first class condition, 3 block carriage, track, saw frame, double edger, slab saw, lath machine and trimmer, boiler and engine, complete with shafting, pulleys, belting, saws and all equipment. Purchased new, ran 12 months.

Capacity 10 to 12 M. ft. per day. Now set in town of Arnprior. Must be moved this fall.

A. F. CAMPBELL & SON,
15-16 Box 455, Arnprior, Ont.

For Sale

Building and machinery of good Double Cut Band Sawmill, well equipped with steam feed, canter, loaders, etc.

Also two storey Brick Factory on large lot convenient to two railways; splendid location. Address Box 949, Owen Sound, Ont. 12-t.f.

Timberlands For Sale

2½ million ft. Birch and Maple.
½ million ft. Hemlock and Pine.
Situated 100 miles north of Toronto, 1 mile from railroad. For particulars write

E. J. WHITE,
15-18 15-16th St., Buffalo, N.Y.

For Sale

Hardwood Timber Limits of about seven million feet, with up-to-date sawmill.

BEDFORD MANUFACTURING CO.,
15-18 Waterloo, Que.

Opportunity in Lumbe Business

Will contract sell red cedar timber as cut—150,000,000-foot tract. Quality and accessibility good. Grand Trunk Railroad.

J. RANDALL BLACK,
14-17 Edmonton, Alberta.

USED MACHINERY *FOR SALE*

Subject to previous sale we offer a lot of used engines, paper mill machinery, etc., as per list below.

Item No.	Machinery	Manufacturers
1.	1 Engine (Steam) Diam. Cyl. 18" Stroke 10" Center Crank R. P. M. 225	B. F. Sturtevant, Boston, Mass.
2.	2 Engines (Steam) McEwen Diam. Cyl. 15" Stroke 10" H. Power 204 Center Crank High Speed Fly Wheel 64 x 18 Gov. Wheel 64 x 12	Ridgway Dynamo & Eng. Co., Ridgway, Pa.
3.	1 Engine 24 x 42 Brown Corliss Fly Wheel 180" x 38" Run six months	
4.	1 Engine, McEwan, 22 x 20 Fly wheel 24 x 90 Gov. Wheel 17 x 84	
5.	2 Allen Mixers	Sandy Hill Brass & Iron Works, Sandy Hill, N. Y.
	Riverside Grinders	
6.	1 Complete Grinder, stone 27 x 54	Friction Pulley & Machine Co., Sandy Hill, N.Y.
7.	4 Complete Grinder, stone 26 x 54	Cedar Point Grinder, Ticonderoga, N. Y.
8.	5 Complete Grinder, stone 27 x 50	Cedar Point Grinder, Ticonderoga, N. Y.
	Cascade Grinders	
9.	10 Complete Grinders, stone 27 x 54	Holyoke Machine Co., Holyoke, Mass.
	Barkers	
10.	2 Right and 2 Left Hand Holyoke Barkers, 54"	Holyoke Machine Co., Holyoke, Mass.
11.	1 " " 1 " " Carthage Barkers, 48"	Carthage Machine Company
12.	8 " " 8 " " Portland Barkers, 66"	Portland Company, Portland, Maine.
13.	1 " " 1 " " Witham Attachment for Portland Barkers	
14.	1 Smidths Pulp Refiner	G. Hardman, Christiania, Norway.
15.	1 Pulp Shredder	Ryther & Pringle, Carthage, N. Y.
16.	4 Paul & Trombly 8 ft. Sulphur Burners	Ticonderoga Machine Co., Ticonderoga, N. Y.
17.	2 Reeves Variable Speed Transmission Drives, Size 8—No. 114 Class C.	Reeves Pulley Co., Columbus, Ind.
18.	3 Worm Washers with bronze frame and Copper Worm	Geo. F. Shevlin Mfg. Co. Saratoga Springs, N.Y.
19.	2 Wandall Screens	Otto Wandall, Walpole, Mass.
20.	4 Warren Winders 156"	Bagley & Sewall Co., Watertown, N. Y.
21.	2 Pusey & Jones Winders 96"	Pusey & Jones, Wilmington, Dela.
	Split Shives	
22.	1—36" face 6' 4" Diam. 20 Strand. 5-15/16 Bore.	
23.	1—10" " 5' 2" " 14 " 4-7/16 "	
24.	1—28" " 4' " 13 " 5-16/16 "	
25.	1—13" " 4' " 7 " 4-7/15 "	
26.	1—28" " 7' " 13 " 7-15/16 "	

Further Particulars on Request

BROWN COMPANY, Portland, Maine

Timber Limit For Sale

Situated in Northern Ontario, 27¼ square miles. Estimated quantity of pine thereon upwards of 10,000,000 feet, as well as spruce and other timber. For full information apply to W. E. Bigwood, Bank of Hamilton Building, Toronto, or Byng Inlet, Ontario. 15-18

ATTRACTIVE TIMBER PROPOSITION

has been placed in my hands for immediate sale; an exceptional opportunity to secure excellent timber lands at a moderate price. Call at office for particulars. W. Cooke, 203 Stair Building, Toronto. 16

Saw Mill Plant For Sale

Practically new and modern Saw Mill Plant, capacity about 30 Million feet per annum, located in the Interior of British Columbia on a beautiful inland lake and on the main line of the Grand Trunk Pacific Railway. About 500 Million feet of timber on and adjacent to Lake (about 90% Spruce) and another Billion feet available at reasonable prices. Natural conditions ideal for economical logging, manufacturing, piling and shipping. An advantage of about $4 per thousand feet in freight rates to the Prairie Provinces over Coast shipments.

This property offers unlimited possibilities as a lumber, pulp and paper property. Would consider selling a half interest. Terms reasonable.

A. C. FROST COMPANY,
134 South LaSalle Street,
5-t.f. Chicago, Ill.

Saw Mill Property FOR SALE

Picnic Island sawmill plant at Little Current, Georgian Bay, 87 acres, for sale or lease for a term of years, or might put it in a good sized company, part cash, part stock; cutting capacity 140 M. a day, two thousand feet stone-filled lumber docks, 16 ft. water, Algoma railway station less than a mile distant, log booming capacity 10 million, telegraph and telephone, school taxes only, title from Crown, no debts or disputes; one of the best mills on the Bay, selling cheap to wind up an estate. For further particulars as to the mill and about twenty other buildings, etc., apply to Thomas Conlon, 44 Church Street, St. Catharines, Ont. 13-16

A Business Opportunity

A company located in a mixed population, nearly all speaking English, wishes to dispose of its business, consisting of Saw, Planing and Shingle Mills, with timber standing and in sight for several years. A good Custom Sawing and Dressing in Transit trade is established. Reason for selling, illness of principals. Address Box 990, Canada Lumberman, Toronto, Ont. 15-16

Virgin Timber For Sale

I have for sale, on very easy terms, in Virginia, 3,000 acres of Virgin Timber, mostly Shortleaf Pine, with some Oak. It is estimated to cut about 17 million feet of pine and oak, with a percentage of white wood, cherry and ash. Railway runs through the centre of it. The land will be worth $50.00 an acre after it is cleared. Apply

DON. M. CAMPBELL,
15-18 Preston, Ont.

1300 Acres of Standing Timber FOR SALE

It consists of Birch, Basswood, Ash, Maple, Pine, Spruce, Cedar, Hemlock. Camps, logging equipment and sawmill on the ground; owner not a lumberman, engaged in other business. The said lands are located right on C. P. R. and C. N. R. sidings, six miles west of North Bay, better known as the Indian Reserve. Apply to

P. ADAMS,
15-18 North Bay, Ont.

Miscellaneous

For Sale

One Detroit Hot Blast, Dry Kiln System, complete with Fan and Engine, also 35 feet of 9" double leather belt, used two weeks.

Port Hope Veneer & Lumber Co.,
13-t.f. Port Hope, Ont.

FOR SALE—FIRE BRICK

4,150 Fire Brick Arch Blocks, 9 x 9 x 4¼" to 3¼", in first class condition, at Toronto, Ont., suitable for arch of Dutch Ovens. Elk Fire Brick Co. of Canada, Ltd., Hamilton, Ont. 16

Canadian National Railways

CENTRAL LINES

Sealed tenders, addressed to the undersigned and endorsed "Tender for Ties," will be received at this office until twelve o'clock noon, Monday, 25th day of August, for 1,375,000 Railway Ties to be made and delivered between October 1st, 1919, and October 1st, 1920, in accordance with tie specification No. 3856, dated March 18th, 1919.

1,000,000 to be delivered on Canadian National lines between Port Arthur and Pembroke.

50,000 to be delivered on Canadian National lines in Central Ontario.

25,000 to be delivered on Canadian National lines between Ottawa and Quebec.

200,000 to be delivered on Canadian National lines between O'Brien and Quebec.

100,000 to be delivered on Canadian National lines Lake St. John District.

Tender forms and specifications can be obtained at the office of the General Tie Agent, No. 9 Toronto Street, Toronto.

Tenders will not be considered unless made on forms supplied by the Railway.

No tender for quantities less than 10,000 ties will be considered.

The lowest or any tender not necessarily accepted.

E. LANGHAM,
General Purchasing Agent,
Canadian National Railways,
15-16 Toronto.

Code: A.B.C. 5th Edition
Member National Hay Association

Chs. E. DUCLOS

54 Notre Dame East
MONTREAL, QUE.

Receiver Shipper Exporter
Hay, Straw and Grain

Special Facilities for Shipping Camps
Write for Quotations

HORSES

UNION STOCK YARDS OF TORONTO, Limited

"Canada's Greatest Live Stock Market"
Capital, $1,500,000. Two Hundred Acres. Dundas St. cars to Keele St., West Toronto. Auction Sales every Wednesday. Private Sales Daily.

Correspondence Solicited.

WALTER HARLAND SMITH
Manager Horse Dept.

Review of Current Trade Conditions

Ontario and the East

There is no particular change in the general situation so far as the lumber market is concerned, except that manufacturing conditions are moving along smoothly, the demand is steady, stocks getting lower and prices growing firmer all the while. There is developing in some centres a pronounced scarcity of dry lumber, and hemlock is pretty well in the hands of a few who have been shrewd enough to buy up cuts of the mill. Building continues very active in Toronto, Montreal and other larger cities, and in some of the smaller towns there is quite a movement in favor of the Ontario house-building campaign. The demand from across the border is steady and heavy shipments of white pine are being made.

It is feared that car shortage may develop in a few weeks when the western grain crops begin to move. It will not be surprising to several of the larger lumber concerns of the East if an application is made to the Dominion Railway Board at an early date for an increase in freight rates, in order to meet the demands of the men for higher wages and to cope with the constantly increasing cost of operations. Everything portends an ascent in the value of lumber of all kinds for many months to come. Those builders and others who have been hanging back, thinking there would be recession in prices after the war, have to admit they have been sadly astray in their calculations. It does not do to go into the prophecy business, particularly in times like these, when old traditions are being shattered over night and ordinary methods revolutionized. The "Canada Lumberman" remembers hearing one of the shrewdest buyers remark on the day that the armistice was signed." Well, wait until you see lumber take a drop now, for the war demand was the strongest prop that the industry had to boost values. That prop is now removed and quotations will tumble rapidly; just you tarry and see." That was eight months ago and, instead of the decline, there has been a steady increase, and the end is not yet.

The export situation is looking up a little more favorably and there has been a slight reduction in ocean freight rates, which, small though it is in the right direction, and is being heralded as a good omen.

The woodworking and furniture factories are all operating, a number of them with orders ahead for several months, but there is a considerable handicap owing to the shortage of skilled labor. There has been a splendid demand for oak, elm, birch, maple and other hardwoods. Automobile concerns are rushed with business and piano manufacturers, phonograph producers and others, are having a busy season. The hardwood situation is on the whole very strong, and prices in some lines have jumped materially.

Western stock still continues to soar in price and flooring, casing, ceiling, jointing, and interior trim having recently undergone radical changes so far as values are concerned. Eastern representatives of Coast and Mountain mills wonder when the aviation will cease. Shingles are jumping by leaps and bounds and there does not seem to be any figure to which they may not reach. The result of the high prices is that ready-roofing manufacturers were never so busy in their careers and this demand will likely continue until shingles come down to somewhere near normal.

The only B. C. stock that remains stationary is dimension timber. All the operating companies are preparing to increase their output in Ontario and the east during the coming season—in fact, some concerns will more than double the number of their camps if sufficient men are available.

Wages are rating about the same as last year, and the cost of provisions is higher on a number of items of food, so that there will be no decrease whatever in the expense of getting out timber. It is predicted the quantity that will be felled during the coming fall and winter will be greater than any season since the outbreak of the war Even with the augmented production there will likely be a scarcity of forest products in 1920, as it is expected more space will be available on ocean steamers for commercial shipments and the present freight rates will be somewhat equalized. It will not be until next year that the great reconstruction campaign in France and Belgium and other countries gets underway, while the British house-building movement will have gained considerable impetus by the beginning of 1920.

The general situation is very strong and the demand keeps ahead of the supply. There is a scarcity in practically every line. There is a strong requisition for hardwood and, in many instances, the yield is not equal to the number of calls received for birch, bass, elm, ash and oak. Manufacturers are all busy and prices on many lines have soared sky-high.

The figure which certain sizes and grades command depends largely on how badly the purchaser wants the stock and for what purpose it is to be used, or if the seller can obtain a big consignment, or pretty well controls the stiuation in his own town or city.

A number of Ontario manufacturers of white pine are declining to sell American buyers a Tonawanda garding, such as No. 1, 2 and 3 barn, etc. They insist that all transactions shall be mill run with culls and clears out, or on a box and better basis. Those firms across the border who are taking deliveries on a mill run basis are well satisfied with the results. Recent outputs of mills show that white pine disposed of under this system runs in No. 3 barn and better, to a very large percentage of No. 2 barn.

During the month of May the exports of pulpwood decreased $828,587, the total being $608,199. For the two months of the fiscal year the total was $1,237,388, a decline of $834,542. During the same period exports of mechanical and chemical pulp declined, but newsprint showed a very large increase.

Owing to the abnormal state of the market and rapidly rising values on a number of lines, it is not possible to give stable market quotations in many instances. Prices and stocks fluctuate in many centres according to supply and demand. The market is largely an open one.

Great Britain

There is a measure of optimism observable in importing circles among those firms who are pulling together to bring about the downfall of freights, but, up to the present, it is not believed that there is anything of a tangible nature to base a conclusion upon a successful issue from the struggle. One outcome of the fight is noticeable in a sudden cessation of c.i.f. quotations for Swedish stocks, which makes it probable that the shippers themselves have feared to operate for fear of finding a slow market in the event of goods arriving upon this side unsold says "The Timber News."

From enquiries we have made in several directions, it can be clearly stated that all sections of the timber trade are anxious to see lower rates of freight, for it need hardly be pointed out how unsatisfactory it is to note the effect upon the market of rates which are eight to nine times as much as those existing in prewar days. Opinions, however, are decidedly mixed when the methods of fighting the shipowners are discussed.

Spruce deals, etc., have arrived for the Controller by the War Ottawa, from St. John; pine deals and boards by the Canada, from Montreal; and pitchpine lumber and logs by sundry steamers.

Freights by available tonnage from Canadian ports rule very high. The Government continues to practically monopolise the space in the regular liners, and there will be very little opportunity granted the usual importers to bring over supplies this season. The Government purchases in Canada are very considerable, and as yet only a small quantity have been shipped. Some shipments of pine have arrived this week. The demand for this wood is very strong, and it will need heavy additional arrivals to satisfy urgent needs. The Controller has practically fixed the price for pine, as the privately-imported wood will of necessity bring similar figures to the Government stock.

Stocks of birch at Liverpool are not heavy. A fair demand exists for planks. Occasional parcels are coming through at figures in the neighborhood of £43 c.i.f. for Quebec, and £32 c.i.f. for Halifax. Quebec logs are badly needed as there are none available to stock. Round logs are offered, but waney logs are scarce. There have been a few deliveries of sawn pitchpine timber. The demand is steady and values are firm.

There has been little moving with respect to Scandinavian and Finnish business. Freights fr the Baltic are still high, and the action of the importers in refusing to pay the exorbitant rates has not yet succeeded in its object.

Building operations have n exceedingly slow, and with no incentive to launch out housebuilders are not in the market for material. The Government scheme is apparently for the future, and certainly little benefit is likely to be felt until next year. Then, no doubt, the call for deals and the special building sizes will be greater than the supply. The signing of peace has not been marked by any

special development in timber circles. It means, however, that continental countries will soon become competitors as purchasers of wood goods. In the countries that were at war the quantity of lumber manufactured during the past three or four years was very low, even where timber was fairly plentiful. How the financial difficulty is to be overcome is a bit of a puzzle.

This country, rich as it is, does not look at the figures demanded at present for sawn wood with equanimity. The value of the wood imported on these prices imposes a strain on the country's resources, that is not lightened because the wood costs more to produce. It has to be paid for, and at a time when other demands are very heavy. How the countries that have suffered financially through the war are to carry out their transactions is a question difficult to answer today.

United States

The general market situation shows a steady improvement with strong tendencies to higher prices and the demand varying according to the building activity and local conditions at various points. In some localities there is not much change but in others the market is largely an auction one. It is interesting to note that taking 1913—the year before the war, as a normal one—and placing the output of lumber at 100 per cent., that there has been a decreasing annual cut during the past five years with the exception of 1916. The percentage as compared with 1913 is as follows: 93.4 in 1914; 86.3 in 1915; 90.9 in 1916; 81.8 in 1918; and 72.7 in 1918.

In the North there is very little hemlock available for sale. Perhaps nothing conveys a clearer idea of the true situation than the fact that for members cutting 91 per cent. of the hemlock produced by members of the Northern Hemlock & Hardwood Manufacturers' Association, shipments have excelled production by 61,000,000 feet so far this year. Furthermore, these same mills have on hand less than 33,000,000 feet of No. 3 hemlock, the smallest amount which the mills have had on hand since 1914.

In the North, the heaviest hardwood sawing season is past. Yet today in the field of the Northern Hemlock & Hardwood Manufacturers' Association, there are at least 25,000,000 feet less of No. 3 common and better hardwoods on hand than on March 1 of this year. Furthermore, production for the last six months of 1918 has been 45,000,000 feet less than in the corresponding six months of 1918. This condition prevails throughout the North, while in the South stocks in the hands of manufacturers have been depleted even more than they have in the North.

Taking the southern pine situation as a whole more men are available but this has had little or no influence upon production which is proceeding at a pace which does not keep up with the demand. Perhaps taking the country as a whole, the price situation has been a bit more settled, though any definite clean cut statement regarding prices is very different to make because there is no such thing as a price list and a seller knows what he is going to ask twelve hours in advance. Considerable advances have been made upon a few items which are very much in demand such as B&Better flat grain flooring, which has sold for as much as $70 f.o.b. mill.

The retail trade in the immediate vicinity of white pine producers is somewhat quieter and there is less of a tendency on the part of retailers to jump at lumber offered. On the other hand, the demand for industrial stock and for shipments east and south is good and the mills find no difficulty in disposing of all the lumber on hand even at the heavy advances in price recently put in effect. Reports from nine mills to the Northern Pine Manufacturers' Association show shipment of 6,459,053 feet of lumber and 1,874,200 lath for the week ended July 26, compared with 6,417,591 feet of lumber and 1,266,850 lath for the previous week. Orders received are reported at 2,665,568 feet compared with 3,916,309 feet for the week before. Production was 8,213,061 feet of lumber and 1,405,050 lath, compared with 6,200, 952 feet of lumber and 1,243,650 lath for the previous week.

Buyers of red cedar shingles are now reaping the benefit—if they so care to term it—of the Fourth of July close down on the Pacific coast. Red cedar shingles are scarcer than ever and have made rapid advances during the last two weeks. Efforts are being made to increase production on the Coast and there will be a larger supply of shingles available for sale, in two or three weeks. When more shingles are available for sale, the situation will steady down, but so long as the demand exceeds the supply advances are certain.

Market Correspondence

SPECIAL REPORTS ON CONDITIONS AT HOME AND ABROAD

Ottawa Reports Several Favorable Features

Increased firmness as to the tone coupled with a sharp advance in prices, featured the Ottawa lumber market during the opening period of August. From all sides come indications of trade picking up and business getting better. The building grades started to move, indicating that building activities are on the upward trend, though no great boom is on as yet.

As compared with a corresponding period a year ago the market all around was better even making allowances for the big consumption of shell box stock which was then in good demand. Another bright spot in the market was that of the free transportation of large cargoes of lumber to Europe on Government account.

Such shipments are going ahead fast on the Canadian order placed by Sir James Ball, the British Timber Controller, during his recent visit to Canada. Lumbermen generally look on the quick movement of this lumber as a good sign and predict that it is stimulating the home market, as stocks of dry lumber are already low and this year's saw mill cut will be below the average.

A hundred dollar figure per M. feet in the price list was reached in the second week of the month, the grade being 2 in. by 7 in. good pine sidings. A jump of six dollars per thousand feet in spruce occurred in the New York market and the advance had its effect locally. Pine prices throughout the valley advanced generally from $2 to $7 per M. The market was largely pine. The offerings of spruce stocks were small.

Stocks of dry lumber (while there is not yet exactly a scarcity if one cares to pay the price) are far from being plentiful. The cut of the manufacturers has been pretty well sold, and the wholesalers are standing pat or asking higher figures for whatever stock they have.

The labor situation did not show much change. Transportation remained good, and export conditions to Europe on consignments on other than government account did not show improvement. Many of the trade are quite satisfied with the way transportation to the Old Country is going. They point out that the sooner the orders on government account get across the quicker the ocean tonnage will be freed for private shipments.

With the sawmill season well advanced, and no great amount of stock yet unsold, lumbermen are generally agreed that every grade of stock is going to be scarce, and the indications are that prices will go still higher. The activity in the building lines, several of the dealers believed, was not for immediate use, but will likely be carried over until next spring, when the greatest revival of building since 1914 is expected.

Orders and inquiries continued good, the chief demand being from the United States. The domestic trade also showed improvement. The increase in the price of shingles is largely attributed to the limited production brought about by the decreased demand during the war years, and owing to the big shipments of this staple which are not being exported to England and other European countries..

Even western shingles are scarce. "The western shingle manufacturers have their hands full and are not able to produce any more." was the opinion expressed by one of the leading lumbermen. Shingle production in the Ottawa valley fell off last year, and indications are that this will be another lean year.

Activities with the woodworking plants and factories showed little or no change. The labor situation with such plants remained practically the same as in July.

Preparations for bush operations and the establishment of camps went ahead fast. The "Canada Lumberman" has been definitely informed that the larger operators in the Ottawa Valley this year are going to attempt to double last year's woods production if possible. There is, consequently, a great demand for woods labor with high wages being paid.

Buying Stimulates Higher Prices in Montreal

The American demand is still the outstanding feature of the on- treal market. Firms doing business across the border state th the threatened industrial upheaval there has not affected business; that

orders continue to be excellent; and that prices are very stiff, with an upward tendency. For a long time buyers refused to come into the market, holding that prices were too high. Now they are eager to purchase, and under this stimulus quotations have gone ahead. There are renewed inquiries for both, which is difficult to get.

Business in B. C. products is dull, the increased prices being against the taking of orders. The price of logs has again gone up.

Hardwoods and veneers have been slow, but are picking up.

Local trade is fair and promises to improve.

Building is broadening. The Montreal building permits for July were the highest in any one month since war broke out, totalling $1,484,999, an increase of $874,954; for the seven months the aggregate was $4,372,423, an increase of $1,703,013. Progress is being made with the Province of Quebec housing scheme. A technical commission has been appointed to supervise the planning of the houses and to see to the sanitary arrangements. The houses are to be mainly of the terrace type, built in squares, with gardens and community playgrounds. The cost of the commission is to be met by a tax of 2½ per cent. on the amount of the loan, which will total $7,000,000. Reports from the province show considerable building activity.

Owing to the strike in Liverpool, which has delayed unloading, there has been a scarcity of vessels arriving in the port. This has caused the shipment of lumber on Government account to ease off. All the U. K. ports are congested, the general labor conditions in the Old Country being adverse factors in the prompt dealing with cargoes. Little commercial lumber is going, the prices ruling not being sufficient to warrant sending at the present freight rates. Cables received from England report that the market for spruce and for American hardwoods has declined. A change has been made in the method of paying for freight. The steamship companies formerly were paid on the other side; they then stipulated that the freight should be prepaid, and have now gone back to the original method. The pulp and paper companies have for some time complained of the inability to secure tonnage, resulting in a loss of trade to the Dominion. Cables from London and also inquiries here show that there is likely to be relief in this respect, and that the mission of Mr. A. L. Dawe to London, has done something towards getting more space for this important Canadian industry.

How Lumber Prices are Ascending

Mr. Wm. Little, of Westmount, Que., who is a veteran lumberman but still active and keen in spite of his eighty odd years, sends the "Canada Lumberman" the following, which will be read with interest. Mr. Little says:—The prices of the Ottawa manufacturers on white pine as recorded in your paper for the years July 12th, 1899, and July 1st, 1919, are as follows:

Ottawa Manufacturers' Prices

	1899		1919		Mean Difference
Pine, good sidings, per M. ft. b.m.	$31.00	to $36.00	$77.00	to $95.00	$52.50
Pine, good strips	25.00	27.00	60.00	75.00	41.50
Pine, good shorts	17.00	28.00	58.00	65.00	39.00
Pine, No. 1 dressing sidings	15.00	21.00	53.00	55.00	36.00
Pine, No. 1 dressing strips	14.00	16.00	48.00	50.00	34.00
Pine, No. 1 dressing shorts	10.00	12.00	....	58.00	47.00
Pine, 10 s.c. and better stocks ..	13.50	15.00	mill run	55.00	40.75
Pine, 8 s.c. and better	11.00	12.50		52.00	40.25
Pine, 8 and up s.c. sidings	11.00	13.00		52.00	40.00
Pine, s.c. strips	8.00	10.00		47.00	38.00
Pine, s.c. shorts	7.00	8.50		45.00	37.25
Pine, box culls	9.00	10.50	38.00	42.00	30.25
Pine, mill culls	7.50	9.00	....	40.00	31.75
Lath, per M., No. 1	1.00	1.25	....	6.00	4.88
Lath, per M., No. 2	.85	1.00	....	5.50	4.00
1 x 10 No. 1 barn	....	18.00	....	52.00	34.00
1 x 10 No. 2 barn	....	16.00	....	46.00	30.00
1 x 8 No. 1 barn	....	17.00	....	42.00	25.00
1 x 8 No. 2 barn	....	15.00	....	40.00	25.00
Spruce, mill run	....	10.00	....	42.00	32.00

The foregoing shows the increased prices of white pine lumber, the product of Ottawa mills, and yet there are some wise people who wonder why spruce and hemlock must take the place of white pine. The latter is rapidly advancing in price while ordinary mill run spruce that was valued at about $10 per M. feet in 1899 is now, just 20 years after, valued at $42 per M. feet at the mills.

Imperial Forestry Conference Will be Held

A recent despatch from London, Eng., says: As the outcome of a suggestion emanating from Canada, which was cordially adopted here, an Imperial Forestry Conference will be held in London during the coming winter

It is proposed that the conference should coincide with the projected exhibition of Empire-grown timber, and as soon as the date of the latter is definitely fixed, and the necessary Treasury grant obtained, the Dominions will be invited to appoint delegates.

In order that the proceedings may be conducted on a business-like basis, a request will be made that the papers prepared by the delegates for submission to the conference should follow definite lines, viz.:

(1) Production of timber

(2) Conversion of timber (felling, conveyance to milling, grading, etc.)

(3) Organization of personnel.

The proposal is that the first two or three days should be spent in reading and discussing papers, followed by a couple of days' excursion to selected areas of the country, during which the delegates will have an opportunity of getting to know one another.

After their return another couple of days might be spent in formulating practical measures for the advancement of forestry in the Empire, such as training and exchange of personnel, and the establishment of a permanent bureau for disseminating information and encouraging research.

Importance of Careful Slash Burning

A large audience assembled at the office of Justice Lemieux of Kedgwick, N.B., July 16, to attend the trial of twenty-one offenders under the Forest Fire Law. The cases covered neglecting slash fires, neglecting to report forest fires to the fire warden, and neglecting to secure fire permits.

Justice Matherson, of Campbellton, presided, Justice Lemieux, of Kedgwick, acting as Clerk of Court. Forest Rangers Roy, Hocquard, Blanchard, Inspector Brophy, Caretaker Somers and Provincial Forester Prince were present. Asst. Chief Fire Inspector L. A. Gagnon acted as prosecutor on behalf of the Department of Crown Lands.

The evidence was taken in both French and English and the Department took the opportunity of explaining to the people that they did not wish to deal harshly with the residents but that the fire law must be observed in the interests of themselves as well as their neighbors and surrounding timber owners. Justice Matheson gave the offenders severe reprimands, pointing out not only the danger of neglecting slash fires, but the terrible destruction rendered by the recent fires in which nearly $122,000 damage resulted, and in which many of the settlers lost their homes and property.

It was stated that thirty buildings were burned and three sawmills. Insurance covered about one-half the damage. Justice Matheson ascertained carefully the amount of damage each of the offenders suffered by reason of the fire and the fines against those who lost heavily were allowed to stand. It is interesting to note that none of the defendants pleaded ignorance of the slash burning law, but claimed that they did not expect their fire would do any damage.

At the time of the fire, June 12th, the slash and ground was extremely dry and the fire swept over even hay and oat fields in which there was nothing to feed the flames excepting scattered stumps. In much of the area covered by the fire all vegetable matter is burned out of the soil and it is rendered almost useless.

It is hoped that in the future the residents of Kedgwick will carefully take every precaution in burning, as it is considered miraculous that some of them did not lose their lives in the recent fire as well as their property. Several spent the day in railway cuts to escape the smoke.

Newsy Briefs of General Interest

The Whalen Pulp & Paper Mills, of Vancouver, are making an issue of $1,500,000 6 per cent. first mortgage and refunding mortgage serial gold bonds, dated May 1, 1917, and May 1, 1919, and maturing in annual series from May 1, 1921, to May 1, 1934.

This is one of the largest Canadian producers of bleached, easy bleaching sulphite pulp, high-grade spruce lumber and cedar shingles. Apart from its mill at Mill Creek, it operates at Swanson, Swanson Bay and Port Alice, B. C. The British Columbia mill is designed for an ultimate capacity of 96,000 tons. The issue will be handled through the Royal Securities Corporation.

The request of the Canadian pulp and paper manufacturers recently made to the Minister of Marine in Canada for more transportation facilities for their products is being taken up in London, Eng. Inquiries have been made at the Ministry of Shipping as to the possibility of obtaining more cargo space. It has incidentally been found that the Harmsworth people now have four steamers with a tonnage of 22,000 engaged in shipping pulp and paper from Canada to Britain; the Becker interests have five vessels of 30,000 tons, and the Erikson interests one ship of 5,500 tons.

EDGINGS

Ontario

The Toronto Ferry Co., of Toronto, will build a new boat next season to replace the two lost by fire and not rebuilt during the war.

Ald. Burrows announced recently that the price of civic wood had been reduced $2 per cord in Brantford. No. 2 wood was now selling at $14 and No. 1 at $16.

The saw and shingle mill belonging to E. Leuck, Dornoch, Ont., was completely destroyed by fire. The loss is estimated at $4,000. The owner intends rebuilding.

The woodworking plant of Cargill, Limited, Cargill, Ont., is shut down due to the shortage of skilled operators. They expect to resume production about the first of the year.

The Crossen Car Co., Limited, Cobourg, Ont., who formerly manufactured a line of sleeping, parlor and passenger cars, etc., have discontinued business. The plant has been completely dismantled.

The sawmill belonging to Geo. Pinkerton, Eagle Lake, Ont., was completely destroyed by fire. The machinery is a total loss. The owner contemplates rushing a new mill to completion. Loss $10,000.

A. & C. Boehmer, box manufacturers, Kitchener, Otn., have awarded a contract for an addition to their factory. The new building will be two storey brick construction, 95 x 50 and will cost in the neighborhood of $10,000.

The Irvin Lumber Company, 26 Vine St., Toronto, have sold their property at 1114 Bathurst St., on which a branch yard is located to T. Kinnear & Co., wholesale grocers, who ,it is understood, will erect a large warehouse on the site.

The Beaver Lumber Company, of Hamilton, have erected an attractive and commodious new office on their premises on Ottawa Street in that city. The new quarters of the company represent the last word in comfort and convenience.

Pulpwood shipments from Northern Ontario in May were considerably less than half the volume in previous month, amounting to only 5,573 cords, decrease of 55.3 per cent. Woodpulp is also down some 187 tons or 24.4 per cent. to 579 tons. Paper shipments show an increase of 14.4 per cent. to 6,856 tons.

The Kalbfleisch Planing Mill, Stratford, who have been for many years in the woodworking and retail lumber line, have recently branched out and added a new department in the manufacture of bodies for motor hearses, ambulances, coupes, limousines and other equipages.

It is expected that work will shortly be started on the new pulp and paper mill of the Spruce Falls Pulp & Paper Co., which will be erected at Kapisskasing, Ont. The capacity of the plant will be 200 tons a day and the general contractors for the work and large dam which will be built on the river at this point are Morrow & Beatty, Limited, of Peterboro.

Building permits issued by the City Architect's Department, Toronto, during July were practically double, both in number and value, those for July, 1918. They included permits for 14 factories, eight warehouses, 181 stores, 511 dwellings and over ,1500 garages. The cost of these last structures alone totals over half a million dollars. Buildings erected last month total $2,155,250 in cost, as against a corresponding figure of $1,095,763 for July, 1918.

A charter has been granted to the Edmund Hind Lumber Co., Limited, with headquarters in Toronto and a capital stock of $40,000 to carry on the business of lumber merchants and dealers; to operate a saw mill and a planing mill and to do a general contracting business in the erection of all classes of buildings. The incorporators of the company are Edmund Hind, Joseph May and others. Mr. Hind was formerly connected with the Beaver Lumber Co., of Hamilton, and the yards of the new organization are on Gerrard St. E., Toronto.

The cabinet makers', millmen and inside woodworkers' union of Toronto have drafted a new schedule which they will attempt to put into effect. This schedule calls for an eight hour day, 44 hour week; time and a half for overtime; double time for Saturday afternoons, Sundays and legal holidays. Minimum wage of $26.00 per week; no piece work or contract work; the recognition of the union, a closed shop and a shop committee to be appointed by the men in each shop to meet the management and to adjust any grievances that may arise.

Eastern Canada

The Legare & Tremblay, carriage manufacturers ere recently registered in Quebec.

The partnership carried on under the name of e Milton Shipbuilding Co., Yarmouth, N.S., has been dissolved.

Lumber freight continues high at provincial ports, $41 per thousand feet being paid from Halifax to the United Kingdom.

The Lewis Lumber Co., Upper Newport, N. S., was recently formed. The partners are Edmund Lewis, Chas. Staples and Ralph Richards.

The Quebec Provincial Housing Commission are having plans prepared for a large number of residences. They propose to spend $7,000,000 in building houses.

The Scotia Shipbuilding Co., Yarmouth, N. S., was recently formed. The partners are E. B. Ehrgott; E. G. Baker, S. E. O'Brien, G. M. Goudey, G. C. Brown and H. K. Lewis.

Construction, Limited, Montreal, has been incorporated to carry on business as general contractors, builders, and engineers and to manufacture any lines used in connection with this business. Capital $20,000.

Quinlan, Robertson & Hanin, Limited, Montreal, have been incorporated to deal in timber, lumber and building material and to erect mills and factories suitable for the carrying on the company's business. Capital $500,000.

Phoenix Construction Co., Limited, Montreal, P. Q., were recently incorporated. Wide powers are conferred on the company under the charter, such as to manufacture and deal in woodworking tools and machinery, railway cars, automobiles and all articles made in whole or in part of wood and to build and repair vessels, tugs and barges of all descriptions. Capital $100,000.

Thirty-five members of the Technical Section of the Pulp and Paper Association attended the summer meeting held from July 28 to August 1. The members went by steamer and rail from Montreal to Quebec, Chicoutimi, Kenogani, St. Alphonse, returning to Montreal. The plants at Chicoutimi and Kenogami were inspected, the visitors being the guests of Price & Co., Ltd., at the latter place. On the boat a business session was held, at which papers were read by Messrs. O. F. Bryant and G. Meerbergen

The last of the wooden war time vessels built in Canada for the French government was launched recently at the Cote St. Paul ship yards of Fraser Brace & Co., Montreal. Canada undertook to build fifty wooden vessels for France and the work in this connection is practically completed. Of the fifty, twenty-five have been built on the Pacific Coast. The other twenty-five have been in the hands of the Eastern Construction Co. The wooden ships have no attractive names but are being called by numbers.

Plans of the big dam which is to be constructed on the Nashwaak river, near Marysville, N. B., by the Nashwaak Pulp and Paper Co., of which Hon. N. M. Jones is general manager, have been filed with the Lieut.-Gov. of the province in accordance with the provisions of the Act passed at the last session of the New Brunswick legislature. It is understood that the Nashwaak Co. will proceed with the erection of their big sulphite pulp plant at Marysville in the near future and will eventually remove the present plant from St. John to Marysville.

The plant of the Cape Breton Pulp and Paper Co. at St. Ann's, Victoria County, is very busy at the present time and about three hundred men are employed. The company is looking for additional help. A large new barking drum is being installed. Gangs of men are at work taking out large quantities of pulp wood and making roads in order to facilitate the movements of the motor trucks, which will deliver the product to the pulp mill. Shipments of pulp have been made by steamer to several points in the United States and it is the intention of the directors to erect eventually a paper mill, which will convert the raw material into the finished product.

Western Canada

The Empire Timber Products Co., Limited, of Vancouver, has been incorporated with a capital stock of $100,000.

The Redonda Island Lumber Company has just been incorporated in B. C. The headquarters are in the state of Delaware. The authorized capital is $200,000 and the head office in the province will be in Victoria.

One million shingles daily is the output of the Dominion Shingle and Cedar Mills at New Westminster. There are sixteen machines operating and still the demand is incessant.

Large shipments of shingles are being made daily by Cedars, Ltd., of Lynn Valley, to eastern Canadian points. Three motor-trucks are being used to haul the product of the mill to the south shore.

Recent rains have extinguished the forest fires on the Bow River, and according to information given out at the local office of the forestry Branch of the Dominion Government, all the fire fighters are being recalled.

The Beaver Cove Lumber & Pulp Co. will be operating their new plant at Beaver Cove, B. C., by Sept. 1st. W. O. King, treasurer of the company, and Mr. White, president and general-manager, recently paid a visit to the new industry.

Papers of incorporation have been granted to the Edgecumbe-Newham Company, Ltd., which acquired the old Stoltze shingle mill at Cedar Cove, Vancouver; the Great West Logging and Lumber Company and the Mc and Mc Logging Company.

James Whalen, of the Whalen Pulp & Paper Co., recently paid a visit to British Columbia on an inspection of the company's plants. Mr. Whalen is the pioneer pulp man of the coast and the founder of the Whalen Company. When the company was recently organized and Sir Geo. Bury became the president and active head, Mr. Whalen became chairman.

The North American Lumber Yards, Regina, Sask., were burned recently. The fire broke out in a nearby livery barn and spread rapidly owing to the fire engine refusing to work. By an extraordinary effort the flames were, however, confined to the lumber yard, the loss of which is partly covered by insuranec.

Due to the strong demand for tonnage on the Pacific coast, charter rates are remaining firm. They are approximately as follows: to Sydney, N.S.W., $32.50; Melbourne, Australia, $37.50; Chili, $32.50; South Africa, 225s.; United Kingdom, $52.50 to $55. The rates to Valparaiso and Callao have been increased by from 5 to 7½ per cent.

Reports from Vancouver Island indicate that they are having a busy time there. Five mills are operating in the Alberni district, four in the locality in and around Courtenay, the V. L. & M. Company at Chemainus is running to capacity, the New Ladysmith Lumber Company is operating two mills. At Qualicum there are two mills going full blast and at Duncan there are three. There is also one working at Cobble Hill.

The Sterling Lumber and Shingle Co., B. C., owned and operated by Munchi Ram, and J. Tack, the foreman, were fined $200 and $150 and costs, respectively, recently. The mill was charged with having operated a locomotive and donkey engine without the proper fire-fighting equipment, and the charge against the foreman was one of hindering and impeding the forest rangers in the performance of their duties.

Plans were completed and the work commenced recently to establish the Nicola Pine Mills, Ltd., in Merritt. It will be remembered that some months ago the splendid plant and yards of the company at Canford were completely destroyed by fire, since which time strenuous efforts have been made by the citizens to have this industry established at Merritt. With this object in view, a joint stock company was formed to purchase the Blair property, situated south of the Coldwater river, between Merritt and Middlesboro, immediately adjoining the city limits.

Two Hundred Years is Average Tree Age

Many Monsters are Much Older but Dimension of Trunk is no Guide Regarding its History

A tree's size is no guide to its age. A good many people fail to get a grip on that fact. From time to time articles make the rounds of magazines and papers, purporting to give instances of very old trees in various parts of the world; and the farther away these trees are, the greater interest some people take in them. In almost every such instance, the estimate of the tree's age is based on its size. However, a tradition is sometimes cited to give authenticity to the claims of great age.

There are two reliable methods of fixing a tree's age, and only two. One is, to count the growth rings from the centre to the bark. It will not do to count part of the rings an destimate the balance, because a tree does not generally grow at a uniform rate during its whole life, and some of the rings are wider than others. The number of rings gives the tree's age in years, because each year produces one ring. The other method of arriving at a tree's age is to consult a record of the time when it began its existence and of the time when it fell. The included period represents the tree's age. In some instances such records are obtainable for old trees, but usually they are not. It is not ordinarily practicable to count the rings of a standing tree, though it may occasionally be done. For that reason, the ages of standing trees are seldom determined by counting their rings.

The conclusion that because a tree is very large it must be very old, is the result of faulty reasoning; but there are many instances where such conclusions have been announced as facts. A certain cypress tree in Mexico, that Humboldt measured, is a familiar example. Because this tree is nearly forty feet in diameter, its age has been variously estimated from 5,000 to 7,000 years. The estimate is absolutely worthless. That massive trunk is made up of a dozen or so smaller trees which stood so closely together when young that they grew fast to one another, thus forming one bale of many smaller ones. The age, of course, is no greater than the age of the oldest of the individuals forming the trunk.

Certain South American trees are credited with being nearly 10,000 years old because they are very large; and in India and Australia there are others of the same sort. Yet those trees may be smaller than others in other parts of the world that are known to be less than a thousand years old.

What, then, is the greatest age that trees can attain? Nobody knows. Some kinds of trees live longer than others. Every tree lives until it meets a fatal accident. If it succumbs to "old age," even that is an accident that never fails to prove fatal, for it weakens the tree so that insects, fungus, or malnutrition kills it. So long as a tree bears leaves, it grows. The average ages of mature trees of certain kinds are pretty well known. The jack pine of our northern states and Canada lives from eighty to one hundred years, if it escapes fire and the axe. Some oaks may attain 500 years, but probably not one in ten thousand is that old. That is believed to be about the extreme limit of the age of white pine; but in the lumbered tracts one would likely count the rings on many thousand pine stumps before finding one as much as 400 years old. Bald cypress may attain an age of 800 years. Some stumps have nearly that many rings. Western red cedar has been known to exceed an age of 1,200 years, and that is about the limit of Douglas fir.

The sequoias or redwoods of California are generally conceded to be the longest-lived of American trees, but a great deal of fiction and guesswork concerning their ages has been published. They are said to be "the oldest living things," and that may be true; but no dependence should be placed in the claim of 4,000 or 5,000 years as the ages of these trees. It is true that John Muir counted 4,000 rings on one of these trees, and he was worthy of belief. He was so worthy of belief that he was careful not to state that the tree was 4,000 years old. He said the rings were so wavy and folded that he was uncertain. Ages exceeding 2,000 years for some of these trees appear to be well authenticated. An exact count and measurement of a tree less than 28 feet in diameter is a record in the United States Forest Service, showing an age of 1,245 years when that tree was cut in 1864. It was one of the largest sequoias on record, though not the oldest.

It is not possible to determine an average age of trees, without being particular to specify the kind of trees, their number, and several other factors. The average age of merchantable trees encountered by one walking through the forests in those parts of the United States east of the Rocky Mountains is probably less than 200 years, though many are much older. Persons who wish to have first-hand knowledge of forest trees will do well to cultivate the habit of counting rings in sawlogs and stumps in various localities and of different species. Such experience will lead to a good deal of practical knowledge of tree ages. It will assist in checking up on some of the wild guesses one often hears concerning ages of trees.

An oak tree that grew in the court yard at Monroe, La., was 49 inches in diameter and 55 years old. In northwestern Oklahoma and southern Kansas there are thousands of oaks older than that and not one inch in diameter. A pine near Monterey, California, was 35 inches and 42 years old. On the high mountains of the same state there are pines much older, yet not large enough for canes. These instances serve to emphasize the fact that size is not a reliable guide to the ages of trees.

Sand Will Do It

I observed a locomotive in the railroad yards one day,
It was waiting in the roundhouse where the locomotives stay;
It was panting for the journey, it was coaled and fully manned,
And it had a box the fireman was filling full of sand.

It appears that the locomotive cannot always get a grip
On their slender iron pavement, 'cause the wheels are apt to
And when they reach a slippery spot their tactics they comman
And to get a grip upon the rail, they sprinkle it with sand.

It's about the way with travel a long life's slippery track:
If your load is rather heavy, you're always slipping back
So, if a common locomotive you completely understand,
You'll provide yourself in starting with a good supply of

If your track is steep and hilly and you have a heavy grade,
If those who've gone before you have the rails quite slippery made,
If you ever reach the summit of the upper table land,
You'll find you'll have to do it with a liberal use of sand

If you strike some frigid weather and discover to your cost,
That you're liable to slip up on a heavy coat of frost,
Then some prompt decided action will be called into demand,
And you'll slip' way to the bottom if you have'nt any sand.

You can get to any station that is on life's schedule seen
If there's fire beneath the boiler of ambition's strong machine,
And you'll reach a place called Flushtown at a rate of speed that's grand,
If for all the slippery places you've a good supply of sand.

Philippines to Export Newsprint

The Philippines are in a position not only to supply newsprint for domestic needs, but to export large quantities of this product. According to a report just made by the Director of the Bureau of Forestry, the raw materials available, such as the bamboo and two kinds of grasses, the cogon and the talahib, are of such good quality and can be so cheaply secured that if this industry is given careful study the islands will not need to import annually $2,000,000 worth of paper as heretofore.

How Timber Raises All Farm Values

The man who is fortunate enough nowadays to have attached to his farm a wood lot containing a million feet or so of standing timber is envied by the man who allowed his farm to be stripped of logs fifteen or twenty years ago when the price was much lower than it is today, says the Fredericton, N.B., "Mail." While quitie a number of farmers living along the river have disposed of their standing timber within the past year or two at a price greater than that which they would have at one time readily accepted for the entire farm, there are others who seem to be in no hurry to sell. They reason that the land costs them nothing apart from the taxes which they pay on it and that every year adds to its value.

One man living in Kingsclear is said to estimate that he has two million feet of standing timber on his farm in addition to a large quantity of pulp wood and thousands of cords of hardwood suitable for fuel. He has received several temptiing offers for the lumber, but is in no hurry to dispose of it. A resident of Douglas estimates that he has a million feet of merchantable logs on his land and he plans to cut it next winter and haul it to the river. A number of other farmers have carefully conserved their lumber lands and stand to make a good thing out of it. A million feet of standing time on a St. John River farm these days is estimated to be worth anywhere from $12,000 to $15,000.

CURRENT LUMBER PRICES—WHOLESALE

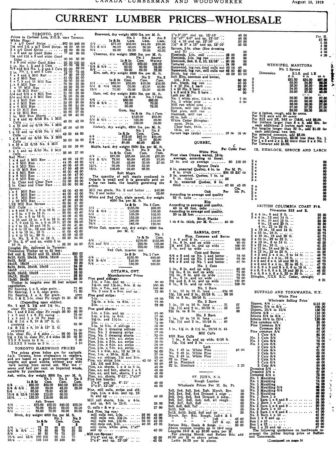

TORONTO, ONT.

Prices in Carload Lots, F.O.B. cars Toronto.

White Pine:

1 x 4/7 Good Strips $62 00 $65 00
1¼ and 1½ x 4/7 Good Strips. 66 00 68 00
2 x 4/7 Good Strips 66 00 69 00
1 x 8 and up Good Sides 77 00 80 00
1¼ and 1½ x 8 and wider Good Sides 90 00 95 00
2 x 8 and wider Good Sides .. 95 00 100 00
1 in. No. 1, 2 and 3 Cuts 65 00 68 00
5/4 and 6/4 No. 1, 2 and 3 Cuts 65 00 68 00
2 in. No. 1, 2 and 3 Cuts 72 00 75 00
1 x 4 and 5 Mill Run 47 00 49 00
1 x 6 Mill Run 51 00 52 00
1 x 7, 9 and 11 Mill Run 50 00 52 00
1 x 8 Mill Run 51 00 53 00
1 x 10 Mill Run 53 00 55 00
1 x 12 Mill Run 55 00 57 00
5/4 and 6/4 x 4 Mill Run 51 00 53 00
5/4 and 6/4 x 5 Mill Run 51 00 53 00
2 x 4 Mill Run 50 00 52 00
2 x 6 Mill Run 52 00 53 00
2 x 8 Mill Run 52 00 54 00
2 x 10 Mill Run 53 00 55 00
2 x 12 Mill Run 55 00 57 00
1 in. Mill Run Shorts 41 00 42 00
1 x 4 and up 6/16 No. 1 Mill Culls 40 00 42 00
1 x 10 and up 6/16 No. 1 Mill Culls 45 00 46 00
1 x 12 and up 6/16 No. 1 Mill Culls 42 00 44 00
1 x 4 and up 6/16 No. 2 Mill Culls 33 00 34 00
1 x 10 x 12 6/16 No. 2 Mill Culls 35 00 36 00
1 x 4 and up 6/10 No. 3 Mill Culls 25 00 27 00

Red Pine:

1 x 4 and 5 Mill Run 43 00 44 00
1 x 6 Mill Run 44 00 46 00
1 x 8 Mill Run 48 00 49 00
1 x 10 Mill Run 47 00 48 00
2 x 4 Mill Run 45 00 46 00
2 x 6 Mill Run 46 00 47 00
2 x 8 Mill Run 48 00 49 00
1 in. Clear and Clear Face 53 00 56 00
2 in. Clear and Clear Face 55 00 56 00

Spruce:

1 x 4 Mill Run 42 00 43 00
1 x 6 Mill Run 44 00 45 00
1 x 8 Mill Run 45 00 46 00
1 x 10 Mill Run 47 00 48 00
1/12 Mill Run Spruce 50 00 51 00
Mill Culls 36 00 37 00
1 x 4 and 5 in. x 9 to 16 ft. .. 34 00 35 00
1 x 6 in. x 9 to 16 ft. 39 00 40 00
1 x 8 in. x 9 to 16 ft. 40 00 41 00
1 x 10 and 12 in. x 9 to 16 ft. 40 00 41 00
1 x 7, 9 and 11 in. x 9 to 16 ft. 37 00 38 00
2 x 4 to 12, 10 and 16 ft. 40 00 41 00
2 x 4 to 12 in., 12 and 14 ft. .. 39 00 40 00
2 x 4 to 12 in., 18 ft. 41 00 42 00
2 x 4 to 12 in., 20 ft. 42 00 43 00
1 in. No. 2, 6 ft. to 16 ft. .. 33 00 34 00
2" No. 2, 4" and up, width 6 to 16 ft. 33 00 34 00

Douglas Fir, delivered in Toronto:
Dimension Timber up to 32 feet:

6x6 and 8, 10x10 and 12, 12x12 .. .. .. $50 00
6x10, 8x10, 10x14, 12x14, 14x14 .. .. .. 51 00
6x12, 8x12 .. .. 52 00
14x16, 16x16 .. .. 52 50
6x14, 8x14, 10x16, 12x16 .. .. 54 00
14x18 .. .. 54 50
8x16, 10x18, 12x18 .. .. 55 00
18x18, 20x20 .. .. 55 50
12x20, 24x24 .. .. 56 00

Timber in lengths over 32 feet subject to negotiation.

Fir flooring, 1 x 3, edge grain.. 71 00
Fir flooring, 1 x 4, edge grain. 71 00
Fir flooring, 1 x 4, flat grain. open
No. 1 & 2, 1-in. clear Fir rough 61 50 00 50

(Depending upon widths).

No. 1 and 2, 1¼ and 1½ in., clear Fir rough 71 00 75 00
No. 1 and 2 2-in. clear Fir rough 56 00 66 00
1 x 5 and 1 x 6 Fir casing .. 73 00
1 x 8 and 1 x 10 Fir base .. 75 00
1¼ & 1½ x 8, 10 & 12" E. G. stepping 85 00
1¼ & 1½ x 8, 10 & 12" E. G. stepping 75 00
1-in. clear Fir, d 4 sides 56 00 64 00
1¼ x 1¼ in. clear Fir, d 4 sides 56 50 65 50
XXX 6 butts to 2 in. 7 30
XXXXX 5 butts to 2 in. 8 10

TORONTO HARDWOOD PRICES

The prices given below are for carloads, f.o.b. Toronto, from wholesalers to retailers, and are based on a good percentage of long lengths and good widths, without any wide stock having been sorted out. War tax of seven and half per cent. on imported woods, payable by purchasers.

Ash, white, dry weight 3800 lbs. per M. ft.

	1s & 2s	No. 1 Com.	No. 2 Com.	No. 3 Com.
4/4	$80.00	$60.00	$40.00	$30.00
5/4 & 6/4	85.00	63.00	45.00	35.00
8/4	95.00	75.00	45.00	
10/4 & 12/4	110.00	110.00	60.00	
16/4	125.00	115.00	65.00	

Ash, Brown

4/4	$75.00	$55.00	$40.00	$33.00
6/4	80.00	65.00	50.00	50.00
8/4	83.00	70.00	53.00	50.00

Birch, dry weight 4000 lbs. per M. ft.

	1s & 2s $		No. 1 Com. $		No. 2 Com. $	
4/4	75	78	60	63	45	50
5/4 & 6/4	78	80	68	70	50	55
8/4	80	83	70	75	55	
10/4 and 12/4	100	105	90	95	70	
16/4	105	110	85	100	80	

Basswood, dry weight 2600 lbs. per M. ft.

	1s & 2s	No. 1 Com.	No. 2 Com.	No. 3 Com.
4/4	$77.00	$55.00	$44.00	$38.00
5/4 & 6/4	80.00	60.00	50.00	40.00
8/4	83.00	63.00	50.00	42.00

Chestnut, dry weight 2800 lbs. per M. ft.

	1s & 2s	No. 1 Com.	Sound Wormy
4/4	$75.00	$55.00	$50.00
5/4 & 6/4	80.00	60.00	52.00
8/4	82.00	62.00	55.00

Elm, soft, dry weight 3100 lbs. per M. ft.

	1s & 2s	No. 1 Com.	No. 2 Com.	No. 3 Com.
4/4	$63.00	$50.00	$40.00	$38.00
6/4 & 8/4	68.00	55.00	43.00	48.00
12/4	73.00	65.00	50.00	42.00

Gum, red, dry weight 3300 lbs. per M. ft.

	1s & 2s	No. 1 Com.
4/4	$80.00	$65.00
5/4 & 6/4	85.00	70.00
8/4	90.00	75.00

Gum, Sap

	1s & 2s	No. 1 Com.
4/4	$120.00	$85.00
5/4 & 6/4	125.00	90.00
8/4	130.00	95.00

Hickory, dry weight, 4500 lbs. per M. ft.

	1s & 2s	No. 1 Com.	No. 2 Com.
4/4	$75.00	$45.00	$30.00
6/4	100.00	75.00	50.00
8/4	90.00	60.00	35.00

Maple, hard, dry weight 3900 lbs. per M. ft.

	1s & 2s	No. 1 Com.	No. 2 Com.	No. 3 Com.
4/4	$70.00	$55.00	$45.00	$35.00
5/4 & 6/4	75.00	60.00	45.00	35.00
8/4	79.00	63.00	50.00	37.00
12/4	95.00	75.00	55.00	
16/4	105.00	95.00	65.00	

Soft Maple

The quantity of soft maple produced in Ontario is small and it is generally sold on a log run basis, the locality governing the prices.

Mill run grade, No. 3 and better ... $43.00
No. 2 and better 52.00

White and Red Oak, plain sawed, dry weight 4000 lbs. per M. ft.

	1s & 2s	No. 1 Com.
4/4	$135.00	$90.00
5/4 & 6/4	145.00	100.00
8/4	150.00	105.00
10/4	155.00	110.00
12/4	160.00	115.00
16/4	165.00	120.00

White Oak, quarter cut, dry weight 4000 lbs. per M. ft.

	1s & 2s	No. 1 Com.
4/4	$210.00	$155.00
5/4 and 6/4	220.00	165.00
8/4	225.00	170.00

Red Oak, quarter cut.

	1s & 2s	No. 1 Com.
4/4	$135.00	$90.00
5/4 & 6/4	145.00	95.00
8/4	150.00	100.00

OTTAWA, ONT.

Manufacturers' Prices

Pine good sidings:

1-in. x 7-in. and up 80 00
1¼-in. and 1½-in., 8-in. & up 100 00
2-in. x 7-in. and up 100 00
No. 2 cuts 2 x 8-in. and up.. 72 00

Pine good strips:

1-in. 68 00
1¼-in. x 4-in. to 6-in. 75 00
2-in. 78 00

Pine good shorts:

1-in. x 7-in. and up 63 00
1-in. x 4-in. to 6-in. 57 00
1¼-in. and 1½-in. 72 00
2-in. 72 00
7-in. to 9-in. A sidings 55 00

Pine, No. 1 dressing sidings .. 69 00
Pine, No. 1 dressing strips .. 57 00
Pine, No. 1 dressing shorts .. 52 00
Pine, 1-in. x 4-in. s.c. strips .. 45 00
Pine, 1-in. x 5-in. s.c. strips .. 50 00
Pine, 1-in. x 6-in. s.c. strips .. 52 00
Pine, 1-in. x 7-in. s.c. strips .. 52 00
Pine, 1 x 8-in. s.c., 12 to 16 ft. 54 00
Pine, 1-in. x 10-in. M.R. 57 00
Pine, s.c. sidings, 1½ and 2-in. 55 00
Pine, s.c. strips 1-in. 45 00 47 00
1¼, 1½ and 2-in. 54 00
Pine, s.c. shorts, 1 x 4 to 6 in. 45 00
Pine, s.c. and bet., shorts, 1 x 5 45 00
Pine, s.c. and bet., shorts, 1 x 6 49 00
Pine, s.c. shorts, 6'-11', 1"x10" 52 00

Pine box boards:

1"x4" and up, 6'-11' 40 00
1"x3", 12'-16' 44 00

Pine, mill culls, strips and sidings, 1-in. x 4-in. and up, 12-ft. and up 40 00
Mill cull shorts, 1-in. x 4-in. and up, 6-ft to 11-ft. 35 00
O. culls r & w p 27 00

Red Pine, log run:

mill culls out, 1-in. 36 00 42 00
mill culls out, 1¼-in. 36 00 42 00
mill culls out, 1½-in. 38 00 42 00
mill culls out, 2-in. 40 00 42 00
mill culls, white pine, 1"x7" and up 40 00

Mill run Spruce:

1"x4" and up, 6'-11' 42 00
1"x4" and up, 12'-16' 42 00
1"x9"-10" and up, 12'-16' 48 00
1¼"x7" 8-0" and up, 12'-16' .. 48 00
1¼ x 10 and up, 12'-16' 50 00
1½" & 2" x 12" and up, 12'-16' 50 00

Spruce, 1-in. clear (fine dressing and B) 00
Hemlock, 1-in. cull 25 00 00
Hemlock, 1-in. log run 30 00 00
Hemlock, 2x4, 6, 8, 10, 12/16' .. 30 00 00
Tamarac 24 00 00
Basswood, log run, dead culls out 46 00 48
Basswood, log run, mill culls out 46 00 50 00
Birch, log run 48 00 50 00
Soft Elm, common and better, 1¼, 2-in. 30 00
Ash, black, log run 40 00
1 x 10 No. 1 barn 52 00
1 x 10 No. 2 barn 46 00
1 x 8 and 9 No. 2 barn .. 00

Lath per M:

No. 1 white pine, 1½-in. x 4 ft. 7 00
No. 2 white pine 6 50
Mill run white pine .. ..
Spruce, mill run 1½-in.
Red pine, mill run ..
Hemlock, mill run .. ..
32-in. lath .. ..

White Cedar Shingles:

xxxx, 18-in. .. ..
Clear butt, 18-in. .. ..
18-in. xx .. ..

Spruce logs (pulp) 13 00 15 00

QUEBEC,

Per Cubic Foot

White Pine

First class Ottawa waney, 18-in. average, according to lineal.
19 in. and up average 90 100 00

Spruce Deals

3 in. unsorted Quebec, 4 in. to 6 in. thick .. .. Per M. Ft. $34 00 $37 00
3 in. unsorted, Quebec, 7 in. to 9 in. thick 38
3 in. unsorted Quebec, 9 in. thick 40 00 45 00

Oak — Per Cubic Ft. Cts.

According to average and quality 55 ft. cube .. ..

Elm

According to average and quality, 40 to 45 feet, cube .. .. ..
According to average and quality, 30 to 35 feet .. ..

Birch Planks

1 to 4 in. thick, per M. ft. 40 00

SARNIA, ONT.

Pine, Common and Better

1 x 6 and 8 in. $80 00
1 in., 8 in. and up wide 90 00
1¼ and 1½ in. and up wide .. 100 00
2 in. and up wide 105 00

Cuts and Better

4/4 x 8 and up No. 1 and better . 75 00
6/4 x 8 and up No. 1 and better . 85 00
8/4 x 8 and up No. 1 and better . 87 00

No. 1 Cuts

1 in., 8 in. and up wide 63 00
1¼ in., 8 in. and up wide 72 00
1½ in., 8 in. and up wide 73 00
2 in., 8 in. and up wide 76 00
2½ and 3, 8 in. and up wide .. 100 00
4 in., 8 in. and up wide 105 00

No. 1 Barn

1 in., 10 to 16 ft. long $54 00
1¼, 1½ and 2 in., 10/16 ft. .. 58 00
2½ to 3 in., 10/16 ft. .. .. ..

No. 2 Barn

1 in., 10 to 16 ft. long 51 57
1¼, 1½ and 2 in., 10/16 ft. .. 52 58
2½ in. to 3 in. 66

No. 3 Barn

1 in., 10 to 16 ft. long 48
1¼, 1½ and 2 in., 10/16 ft. .. 40

Box

1 in., 1¼ in. & 1½ in., 10/16 ft. 44

Mill Culls

Mill Run Culls
1 in., 4 in. and up wide, 6/16 ft.
1¼, 1½ and 2 in. .. ..

Lath

No. 1 48 in. White Pine $6 00
No. 2 48 in. White Pine .. ..
No. 3 48 in. White Pine .. ..
32 in. Pine .. ..
48 in. Hemlock .. ..
32 in. Hemlock 2 25

ST. JOHN, N.B.

Rough Lumber

Wholesale Prices Per M. Sq. Ft.

2x3, 2x4, 3x3, 3x4, Rgh. Merch. Spr. 50
2x3, 2x4, 3x3, 3x4 Dressed 1 edge .. 00
2x3, 2x4, 3x3, 3x4 Dressed 4 sides.. 00
2x6, 2x7, 3x5, 4x4, 4x6, all rough.. 00
2x8, 3x7, 5x5, 6x6 00
2x9, 3x8, 6x8, 7x7 00
2x10, 3x9 00
2x12, 3x10, 3x12, 8x8 and up .. 50
Merch. Spr. Bds. Rough, 1x3-4 & 5
" " " " 1x6 .. .. 45 00
" " " " 1x7 & up. 45 00
Refuse Bds., Deals & Setgs. 30 00

Above random lengths up to 18-0 long. Lengths 19-0 & up $5.00 extra per M.

For planing Merch. and Refuse Bds. add $2.00 per M to above prices.

Laths $4.25 per M pieces.

Per M.
$5 60
5 35
4 85
3 35
4 60
4 30

WINNIPEG, MANITOBA

No. 1 Spruce

Dimension	S.1.S. and 1.E 6 ft.	8 ft.	10 ft.
2	$31.50	$34.50	$37.00
2	33.50	34.50	38.00
2	33.50	35.50	38.00
2	34.50	36.50	39.50
2	36.50	37.50	40.00
	36.00	36.00	37.00
	36.00	36.00	38.00
	36.00	36.00	37.00
	37.00	37.00	37.00
	38.00	38.00	38.00

For 2 inches, rough, add 50 cents.
For S1E only add 50 cents.
For S1S and 2E, S4S or D&M, add $8.00.
For timbers larger than 8 x 8, add 50c. for each additional 2 inches each way.
For lengths longer than 20 ft., add $1.00 for each additional two feet.
For selected common, add $5.00.
For No. 2 Dimension, $2.00 less than No. 1.
For 1 x 2 and 2 x 2, $2 more than 2 x 4 No. 1.
For Tamarac add $3.00.

IR, HEMLOCK, SPRUCE AND LARCH

2 x 00
2 x 00
2 x 00
2 x 00
2 x 00
2 x 00
2 x 00
2 x 00
2 x 00
2 x 00
2 x 50
2 x 50

BRITISH COLUMBIA COAST FIR.

Dimension S1S and E.

2 x 4 in., 6 and 8 ft. 36 50
2 x 4 in., 12 and 14 ft. 37 50
4 in., 10 and 16 ft. 38 50
4 in., 18 and 20 ft. 39 50
4 in., 22 to 32 ft. 41 50
2 x 10 in., 12 and 14 ft. .. 38 75
2 x 10 in., 16 ft. 39 75
2 x 10 in., 18 and 20 ft. .. 40 75
2 x 10 in., 22 to 32 ft. 42 75
2 x 12 in., 8 to 14 ft. 40 25
2 x 12 in., 16 ft. 41 25
2 x 12 in., 18 and 20 ft. .. 42 25
2 x 12 in., 22 to 32 ft. 44 25
3 x 3 and 3 x 4 in., 8 to 14 ft. .. 43 75
3 x 3 and 3 x 4 in., 16 ft. 44 75
3 x 3 and 3 x 4, 18 and 20 ft. .. 45 75
3 x 3 and 3 x 4 in., 22 to 32 ft. .. 47 75
6 x 6, 6 x 8 and 8 x 8, 6 to 16 ft. .. 46 00
6 x 6, 6 x 8, 8 x 8, 18 and 20 ft. .. 46 50
6 x 6, 6 x 8, 8 x 8, 22 to 32 ft. .. 47 50
Shingles, XXX B.C. Cedar, straight 6 21

BUFFALO AND TONAWANDA, N.Y.

White Pine

Wholesale Selling Price

Uppers, 4/4 .. .. .. $115 00
Uppers, 5/4 to 8/4 .. 100 00
Uppers, 10/4 to 12/4 130 00
Selects 4/4 .. .. .. 110 00
Selects 5/4 to 8/4 .. 110 00
Selects 10/4 to 12/4 . 120 00
Fine common 4/4 . 82 00
Fine Common 5/4 87 00
Common 6/4 84 00
Fine common 8/4 87 00
1 Cuts 4/4 65 00
No. 1 Cuts 5/4 74 00
No. 1 Cuts 6/4 75 00
No. 1 Cuts 8/4 78 00
2 Cuts 4/4 47 00
2 Cuts 5/4 61 00
2 Cuts 6/4 62 00
2 Cuts 8/4 69 00
3 Cuts 5/4 49 00
3 Cuts 6/4 49 00
3 Cuts 8/4 50 00
Dressing 5/4 .. 64 00
Dressing 5/4 x 67 00
Dressing 5/4 x 72 00
No. 1 Moulding 74 00
No. 1 Moulding 74 00
No. 1 Moulding 74 00
No. 2 Moulding 5/4 66 00
No. 2 Moulding 6/4 66 00
No. 2 Moulding 66 00
No. 1 Barn 1 x 68 00
No. 1 Barn 1 x 6 and 8 .. .. .. 54 00
No. 1 Barn 1 x 10 .. .. 56 00
No. 2 Barn 1 x 6 and 8 .. .. .. 50 00
No. 2 Barn 1 x 10 .. 54 00
No. 3 Barn 1 x 6 and 8 .. .. .. 47 00
No. 3 Barn 1 x 10 .. 45 00
Box 1 x 6 and up .. 45 00
Box 1 x 10 .. .. .. 45 00
Box 1 x 12 .. .. .. 45 00
Box 1 x 13 and up 47 00

The following quotations on hardwoods represent the jobber buying price at Buffalo and Tonawanda.

(Continued on page 64

CURRENT LUMBER PRICES—Continued

MAPLE	1s & 2s	No. 1 Com.	No. 2 Com.
4/4	47 - 50	32 - 34	22 - 24
5/4 to 8/4	60 - 62	38 - 40	26 - 28
10/4 to 16/4	70 - 72	50 - 52	30 - 32
RED BIRCH			
4/4	62 - 64	42 - 44	26 - 28
5/4 to 8/4	64 - 66	44 - 46	28 - 30
SAP BIRCH			
4/4	58 - 60	36 - 38	22 - 24
5/4 and up	62 - 65	38 - 40	24 - 26
SOFT ELM			
4/4	47 - 49	32 - 34	24 - 26
5, 6 & 8/4	49 - 51	34 - 36	24 - 26
BASSWOOD			
4/4	52 - 54	42 - 44	29 - 31
Thicker	55 - 58	44 - 46	29 - 32
PLAIN OAK			
4/4	67 - 72	44 - 48	28 - 30
5/4 to 8/4	72 - 76	48 - 52	32 - 34
ASH, WHITE AND BROWN			
4/4	68 - 70	38 - 42	27 - 30
5/4 to 8/4	73 - 77	45 - 47	30 - 32
10/4 and up	100 - 90	90 - 95	31 - 33

BOSTON, MASS.

Quotations given below are for highest grades of Michigan and Canadian white pine and Eastern Canadian Spruce as required in the New England market in carloads.

White pine uppers, 1 to 2 in.		134
White pine uppers, 2½ and 3 in.		149
White pine uppers, 4 in.		160 00
Selects, 1 to 2 in.		125 00
Selects, 2½ and 3 in.		140 00
Selects, 4 in.		155 00
Fine common, 1 in., 30 per cent. 12 in. and up		[illegible]
Fine common, 1 x 8 to 11 in.		87 00
Fine Common, 1¼ to 2 in.		100 00
Fine Common, 2½ and 3 in.		130 00
Fine Common, 4 in.		145 00
1 in. shaky clear		72 00
1¼ to 2 in. shaky clear		78 00
1 in. No. 2 dressing		64 00
1¼ to 2 in. No. 2 dressing		68 00
No. 1 Cuts, 1 in.		90 00
No. 1 Cuts, 1¼ to 2 in.	85 00	87 00
No. 1 Cuts, 2½ and 3 in.		115 00
No. 2 Cuts, 1 in.		69 00
No. 2 Cuts, 1¼ to 2 in.	70 00	71 00

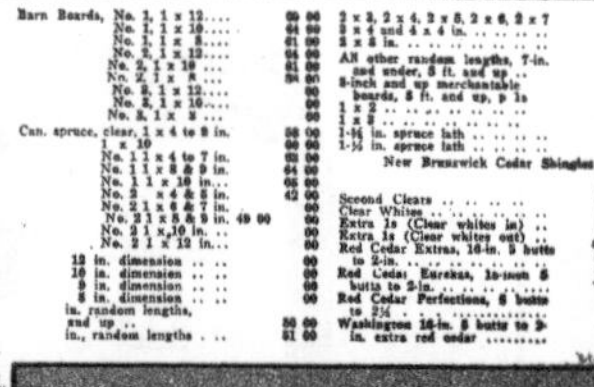

Barn Boards, No. 1, 1 x 12		[illegible] 00
No. 1, 1 x 10		64 00
No. 1, 1 x 8		61 00
No. 2, 1 x 12		[illegible] 00
No. 2, 1 x 10		61 00
No. 2, 1 x 8		[illegible] 00
No. 3, 1 x 12		[illegible] 00
No. 3, 1 x 10		[illegible] 00
No. 3, 1 x 8		[illegible] 00
Can. spruce, clear, 1 x 4 to 9 in.		58 00
1 x 10		[illegible] 00
No. 1 1 x 4 to 7 in.		[illegible] 00
No. 1 1 x 8 & 9 in.		64 00
No. 1 1 x 10 in.		65 00
No. 2 x 4 & 5 in.		42 00
No. 2 1 x 6 & 7 in.		[illegible] 00
No. 2 1 x 8 & 9 in.	49 00	[illegible] 00
No. 2 1 x 10 in.		[illegible] 00
No. 2 1 x 12 in.		[illegible] 00
12 in. dimension		[illegible] 00
10 in. dimension		[illegible] 00
9 in. dimension		[illegible] 00
8 in. dimension		[illegible] 00
in. random lengths, and up		50 00
in., random lengths		51 00

2 x 3, 2 x 4, 2 x 5, 2 x 6, 2 x 7	[illegible]
3 x 4 and 4 x 4 in.	[illegible]
3 x 5 in.	[illegible]
All other random lengths, 7-in. and under, 5 ft. and up	[illegible]
8-inch and up merchantable boards, 8 ft. and up, p 1s	[illegible]
1 x 2	[illegible]
1 x 3	[illegible]
1-⅝ in. spruce lath	[illegible]
1-½ in. spruce lath	[illegible]
New Brunswick Cedar Shingles	
Second Clears	[illegible]
Clear Whites	[illegible]
Extra 1s (Clear whites in)	[illegible]
Extra 1s (Clear whites out)	[illegible]
Red Cedar Extras, 16-in. 5 butts to 2-in.	[illegible]
Red Cedar Eurekas, 18-inch 5 butts to 2-in.	[illegible]
Red Cedar Perfections, 6 butts to 2¼	[illegible]
Washington 16-in. 5 butts to 2-in. extra red cedar	[illegible]

ALPHABETICAL INDEX TO ADVERTISERS

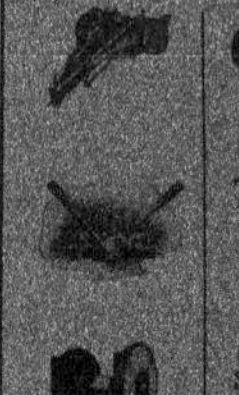

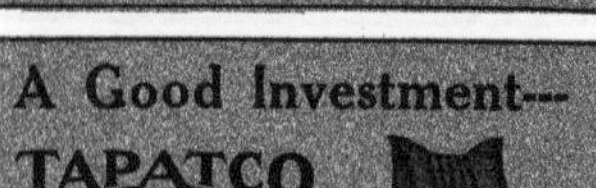

ASBESTOL
ASBESTOL

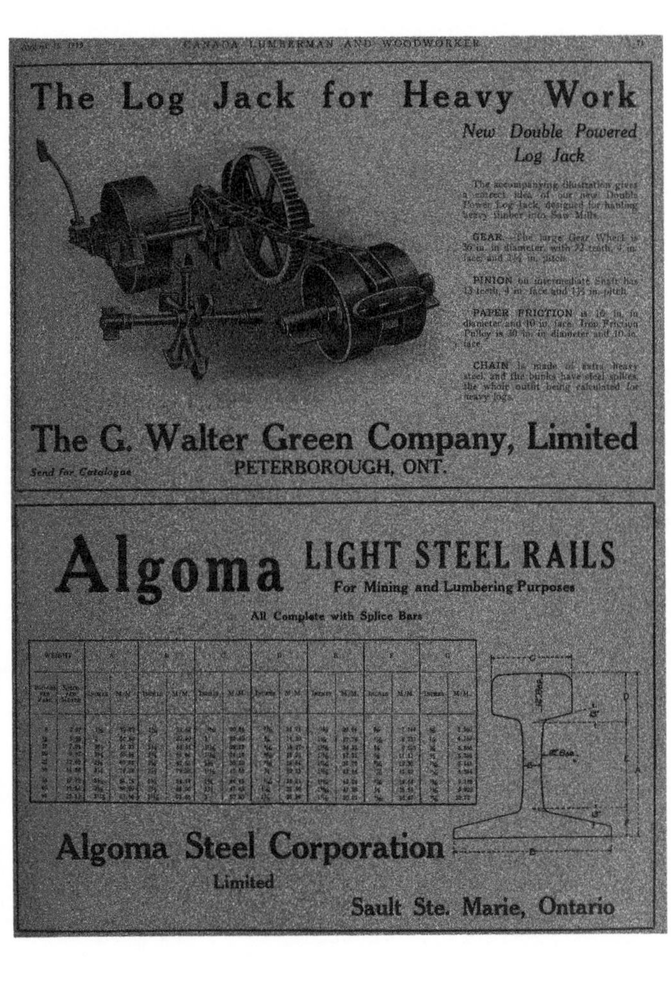
CANADA LUMBERMAN AND WOODWORKER
The Log Jack for Heavy Work
New Double Powered Log Jack
GEAR
PINION
PAPER FRICTION
CHAIN
The G. Walter Green Company, Limited
Send for Catalogue
PETERBOROUGH, ONT.
Algoma LIGHT STEEL RAILS
For Mining and Lumbering Purposes
All Complete with Splice Bars
Algoma Steel Corporation
Limited
Sault Ste. Marie, Ontario

The Old Timers' Favorite
Yates No. 108 Moulder
THE popularity of this machine is shown by the fact that one or more "108s" are to be found in over 1,500 mills and factories in North America.
It is the favorite of practical men whose experience enable them to compare the accessibility and sturdiness of the No. 108 with other machines designed for the same purpose.
This machine combines the sturdiness of an inside moulder with the accessibility of an outside moulder. All adjustments are placed in the most convenient positions. The jointing devices, one of which is shown above, make a fine finish possible by keeping the knives sharp and each doing its share.
Our new eight-page illustrated circular on the No. 108 will be sent free on request. Write for it today.
Yates
"The Invariable Choice of the Man Who Knows"
Yates
P. B. Yates Machine Company Ltd.
HAMILTON, ONT. CANADA
U. S. PLANT, BELOIT, WIS.

GATES REFRACTORIES, LIMITED

382 St. James Street - - - MONTREAL

CANADA LUMBERMAN BUYERS' DIRECTORY

The following regulations apply to all advertisers:—Eighth page, every issue, three headings; quarter page, six headings; half page, twelve headings; full page, twenty-four headings.

ASBESTOS GOODS
Atlas Asbestos Company, Ltd.

AXES
Canadian Warren Axe & Tool Co.

BABBITT METAL
Canada Metal Company.
General Supply Co. of Canada, Ltd.
Syracuse Smelting Works

BALE TIES
Laidlaw Bale Tie Company.

BALL BEARINGS
Chapman Double Ball Bearing Co.

BAND MILLS
Hamilton Company, William.
Waterous Engine Works Company.
Yates Machine Company, P. B.

BAND RESAWS
Mershon & Company, W. B.

BELT CEMENT
Graton & Knight Mfg. Company.

BELT DRESSING
Atlas Asbestos Company, Ltd.
General Supply Co. of Canada, Ltd.
Graton & Knight Mfg. Company.

BELTING
Atlas Asbestos Company, Ltd.
Beardmore Belting Company
Canadian Consolidated Rubber Co.
General Supply Company
Goodhue & Co., J. L.
Goodyear Tire & Rubber Co.
Graton & Knight Mfg. Company.
Gutta Percha and Rubber Company.
Main Belting Company
Manhattan Rubber Mfg. Co.
D. K. McLaren Limited.
McLaren Belting Company, J. C.

BELTING (Transmission, Elevator, Conveyor, Rubber)
Dunlop Tire & Rubber Goods Co.

BLOWERS
Sheldons Limited.
Toronto Blower Company.

BOILERS
Hamilton Company, William.
Jenckes Machine Company.
Marsh Engineering Works, Limited
Waterous Engine Works Company.

BOILER PRESERVATIVE
Beveridge Paper Company
International Chemical Company

BOX MACHINERY
Garlock-Walker Machinery Co.
Morgan Machine Company.
Yates Machine Company, P. B.

BOX SHOOKS
Davison Lumber & Mfg. Company

BUNKS (Steel)
Alaska Bedding Co. of Montreal.

CABLE CONVEYORS
Jeffrey Manufacturing Company.
Jenckes Machine Company, Ltd.
Waterous Engine Works Company.

CAMP SUPPLIES
Canadian Milk Products Limited.
Davies Company, William.
Dr. Bell Veterinary Wonder Co.
Harris Abattoir Company
Johnson, A. H.
Turner & Sons, J. J.
Woods Manufacturing Company, Ltd.

CANT HOOKS
Canadian Warren Axe & Tool Co.
General Supply Co. of Canada, Ltd.
Pink Company, Thomas.

CARS—STEEL BODY
Marsh Engineering Works, Limited

CEDAR
Fesserton Timber Co.
Foss Lumber Company
Genoa Bay Lumber Company
Muir & Kirkpatrick.
Long Lumber Company.
Service Lumber Company
Terry & Gordon.
Thurston-Flavelle Lumber Company.
Vancouver Lumber Company.
Victoria Lumber and Mfg. Co.

CHAINS
Canadian Link-Belt Company, Ltd.
General Supply Co. of Canada, Ltd.
Hamilton Company, William.
Jeffrey Manufacturing Company.
Jenckes Machine Company, Ltd.
Pink & Co., Thomas.
Waterous Engine Works Company.
Williams Machinery Co., A. R., Vancouver.

CHINA CLAY
Bowater & Sons, W. V.

CHEMICAL PLANTS
Blair, Campbell & McLean, Ltd.

CLOTHING
Grant, Holden & Graham.
Kitchen Overall & Shirt Company
Woods Mfg. Company

COLLAR PADS
American Pad & Textile Co.

COLLARS (Shaft)
Bond Engineering Works

CONVEYOR MACHINERY
Canadian Link-Belt Company, Ltd.
Canadian Mathews Gravity Carrier Company.
General Supply Co. of Canada, Ltd.
Jeffrey Mfg. Co.
Waterous Engine Works Company.

CORDAGE
Consumers Cordage Company.

CORN SYRUP
Canada Starch Company

COTTON GLOVES
American Pad & Textile Co.

COUNTERSHAFTS
Bond Engineering Works

COUPLINGS (Shaft)
Bond Engineering Works
Jenckes Machine Company, Ltd.

CRANES FOR SHIP YARDS
Canadian Link-Belt Company.

CROSS ARMS
Genoa Bay Lumber Company

CUTTER HEADS
Shimer Cutter Head Company.

CYPRESS
Blakeslee, Perrin & Darling
Chicago Lumber & Coal Company.
Long Lumber Company.
Wistar, Underhill & Nixon.

DERRICKS AND DERRICK FITTINGS
Marsh Engineering Works, Limited

DOORS
Genoa Bay Lumber Company
Harrington, E. I.
Long Lumber Company.
Mason, Gordon & Co.
Rutherford & Sons, Wm.
Terry & Gordon.

DRAG SAWS
Gerlach Company, Peter
Pennoyer & Company, J. C.

DRY KILNS
Sheldons Limited.

DRYERS
Philadelphia Textile Mach. Company.

DUST COLLECTO
Sheldons Limited.
Toronto Blower Company.

EDGERS
William Hamilton Company, Lt
Garlock-Walker Machinery Co.
Green Company, G. Walter
Haight, W. L.
Long Mfg. Company, E.
Waterous Engine Works Compan

ELEVATING AND CONVEYIN MACHINERY
Canadian Link-Belt Company, Ltd.
Jeffrey Manufacturing Company.
Jenckes Machine Company, Ltd.
Waterous Engine Works Company

ENGINES
Hamilton Company, William.
Jenckes Machine Company.
Waterous Engine Works Company.

EXCELSIOR MACHINERY
Elmira Machinery and Transmission Company.

EXHAUST FANS
Garlock-Walker Machinery Co
Reed & Company, Geo. W.
Sheldons Limited.
Toronto Blower Company.

EXHAUST SYSTEMS
Reed & Company, Geo. W.
Sheldons Limited.
Toronto Blower Company.

FILES
Disston & Sons, Henry.
Simonds Canada Saw Company.

FIR
Associated Mills, Limited
Allan-Stoltze Lumber Co.
British American Mills & Timber Co.
Coal Creek Lumber Compan
Fesserton Timber Co.
Foss Lumber Company
Grier & Sons, Ltd., G. A.
Heeney, Percy E.
Knox Brothers.
Long Lumber Company.
Mason, Gordon & Co.
Reynolds Company, Limited
Service Lumber Company
Shearer Company, Jas.
Terry & Gordon.
Timberland Lumber Company.
Timms, Phillips & Co.
Vancouver Lumber Company.
Victoria Lumber and Mfg. Co.
Weller, J. B.

FIRE BRICK
Beveridge Paper Company
Elk Fire Brick Company of Canada.

FIRE FIGHTING APPARATUS
Dunlop Tire & Rubber Goods Co.
Pyrene Mfg. Company.
Waterous Engine Works Company.

FIR FLOORING
Genoa Bay Lumber Company
Rutherford & Sons, Wm.

FLAG STAFFS
Ontario Wind Engine Company

FLOORING (Oak)
Long-Bell Lumber Company.

Ontario Wind Engine Company

GASOLINE ENGINES
Ontario Wind Engine Company

GEARS (Cut)
Smart-Turner Machine Co.

GRATE BARS—Revolving
Beveridge Paper Company

GRAVITY LUMBER CARRIER
Can. Mathews Gravity Carrier Co.

GRINDERS (Bench)
Bond Engineering Works
Garlock-Walker Machinery Co.

HARDWOODS
Anderson Lumber Company, C. G.
Atlantic Lumber Co.
Bartram & Ball.
Bennett Lumber Company.
Blakeslee, Perrin & Darling
Cameron & Co.
Cardinal & Page
Davison Lumber & Mfg. Company
Dunfield & Company
Edwards & Co., W. C.
Fassett Lumber Company.
Fesserton Timber Co.
Fraser Limited.
Gillespie, James.
Gloucester Lumber Company
Grier & Son, G. A.
Heeney, Percy E.
Knox Brothers.
Long Lumber Company.
McLennan Lumber Company.
Moores, Jr., E. J.
Nicholson & Co., E. M.
Pedwell Hardwood Lumber Co.
Powell-Myers Lumber Co.
Russell, Chas. H.
Spencer Limited, C. A.
Stearns & Culver Lumber Co.
Summers, James R.
Taylor Lumber Company, S. K.
Webster & Brother, James.

HARDWOOD FLOORING MACHINERY
American Woodworking Machinery Company
Garlock-Walker Machinery Co.

HANGERS (Shaft)
Bond Engineering Works

HARDWOOD FLOORING
Grier & Son, G. A.
Long Lumber Company.

HEMLOCK
Anderson Lumber Company, C. G.
Bartram & Ball.
Bourgouin, H.
Callander Sawmills
Canadian General Lumber Company
Cane & Co., Jas. G.
Davison Lumber & Mfg. Company
Dunfield & Company
Edwards & Company, W. C.
Fesserton Timber Co.
Foss Lumber Company
Grier & Sons, Ltd., G. A.
Hart & McDonagh.
Long Lumber Company.
Mason, Gordon & Co.
Spencer Limited, C. A.
Terry & Gordon.
The Long Lumber Company.

HOISTING AND HAULING ENGINES
Garlock-Walker Machinery Co.
General Supply Co. of Canada, Ltd.
Marsh Engineering Works, Limited

HORSES
Union Stock Yards.

HOSE
Dunlop Tire & Rubber Goods Co.
General Supply Co. of Canada, Ltd.
Goodyear Tire & Rubber Co.
Gutta Percha and Rubber Company.

INDUSTRIAL CARS
Marsh Engineering Works, Limited

INSURANCE
Hardy & Co., E. D.
Rankin Benedict Underwriting Co.

INTERIOR FINISH
Eagle Lumber Company.
Hay & Co.
Mason, Gordon & Co.
Renfrew Planing Mills.
Terry & Gordon.

KNIVES
Disston & Sons, Henry.
Peter Hay Knife Company.
Simonds Canada Saw Company.
Waterous Engine Works Company.

LARCH
Otis Staples Lumber Co.

LATH
Austin & Nicholson.
Callander Sawmills
Canadian General Lumber Company
Cane & Co., Jas. G.
Cardinal & Page
Dupuis Limited, J. P.
Eagle Lumber Company.
Fraser Limited.
Fraser-Bryson Lumber Company.
Genoa Bay Lumber Company
Gloucester Lumber Company
Grier & Sons, Ltd., G. A.
Harris Tie & Timber Company, Ltd.
Long Lumber Company.
McLennan Lumber Company.
New Ontario Colonization Company.
Otis Staples Lumber Co.
River Ouelle Pulp and Paper Co.
Spencer Limited, C. A.
Terry & Gordon.
Union Lumber Company.
Victoria Harbor Lumber Company.

LATH BOLTERS
Garlock-Walker Machinery Co.
General Supply Co. of Canada, Ltd.
Green Company, C. Walter.

LOCOMOTIVES
Bell Locomotive Works
General Supply Co. of Canada, Ltd.
Jeffrey Manufacturiing Company.
Jenckes Machine Company, Ltd.
Climax Manufacturing Company.
Montreal Locomotive Workks.

LATH TWINE
Consumers' Cordage Company.

LINK-BELT
Canadian Link-Belt Company
Canadian Mathews Gravity Carrier Company.
Jeffrey Mfg. Co.
Williams Machinery Co., A. R., Vancouver.

LOCOMOTIVE CRANES
Canadian Link-Belt Company, Ltd.

LOGGING ENGINES
Dunbar Engine and Foundry Co.
Jenckes Machine Company.
Marsh Engineering Works, Limited

LOG HAULER
Green Company, G. Walter
Jenckes Machine Company, Ltd.

LOGGING MACHINERY AND EQUIPMENT
General Supply Co. of Canada, Ltd.
Hamilton Company, William.
Jenckes Machine Company, Ltd.
Marsh Engineering Works, Limited
Waterous Engine Works Company.

LUMBER TRUCKS
Waterous Engine Works Company.

LUMBERMEN'S CLOTHING
Woods Manufacturing Company, Ltd.

METAL REFINERS
Canada Metal Company.
Hoyt Metal Company.
Sessenwein Brothers.

MILLING IN TRANSIT
Renfrew Planing Mills.
Rutherford & Sons, Wm.

MOLDINGS
Genoa Bay Lumber Co.
Rutherford & Sons, Wm.

MOTOR TRUCKS
Duplex Truck Company

OAK
Chicago Lumber & Coal Com y.
Long-Bell Lumber Compa
Weller, J. B.

OAKUM
Stratford Oakum Co., Geo.

OIL CLOTHING
Leckie, Limited, John.

OLD IRON AND BRASS
Sessenwein Brothers.

PAPER
Bowater & Sons, W. V.

PACKING
Atlas Asbestos Company, Ltd.
Consumers Cordage Co.
Dunlop Tire & Rubber Goods Co.
Gutta Percha and Rubber Company.

PAPER MILL MACHINERY
Bowater & Sons, W. V.

PILLOW BLOCKS
Bond Engineering Works

PINE
Anderson Lumber Company, C. G.
Atlantic Lumber Co.
Austin & Nicholson.
Bourgouin, H.
Callander Sawmills
Cameron & Co.
Canadian General Lumber Company
Cane & Co., Jas. G.
Cardinal & Page
Chicago Lumber & Coal Company.
Cleveland-Sarnia Sawmills Company
Davison Lumber & Mfg. Co.
Donogh & Co., John.
Dudley, Arthur N.
Dunfield & Company
Eagle Lumber Company.
Edwards & Co., W. C.

CLIMAX Improved Geared **LOCOMOTIVES** FOR WOOD AND IRON RAILS

A [illegible] Climax Locomotive Designed Especially for Heavy Logging Work

Climax Locomotives are successfully operated on steep grades and sharp curves. Any weight or gauge. Locomotives in stock for immediate shipment. Get Catalog "H."

CLIMAX MANUFACTURING CO., 312 W. Main Street, CORRY, PA.
VANCOUVER MACHINERY DEPOT, LTD., VANCOUVER, B.C.

Peace Year 1919

Finds us optimistic for the future and well stocked with Horse Blankets, Feed Bags, Tarpaulins, Oil Clothing Tents, Flags, Straw Ticks and Grey Blankets

We Guarantee Prompt Shipment of Orders Entrusted to us

J. J. Turner & Sons Limited
PETERBOROUGH, ONT.

PUT YOUR PROBLEM UP TO US

We are specialists in building locomotives. We build all types and sizes, also all kinds of repair parts for locomotives and tenders.

Our experience puts us in a position to give you expert advice as to what particular type and size of locomotive is best suited to your needs.

Put your locomotive problem up to us.

MONTREAL LOCOMOTIVE WORKS, LIMITED
DOMINION EXPRESS BUILDING. MONTREAL, CANADA.

PRATT & WHITNEY CO.
OF CANADA, LIMITED

SMALL TOOLS

Taps — Dies — Reamers — Cutters — Drills
MADE IN CANADA
As good as money can buy—Guaranteed absolutely!

Head Office and Works, DUNDAS, ONT.

SALES OFFICES:
MONTREAL Drummond Bldg. VANCOUVER WINNIPEG Bank of Hamilton Bldg.

"ABOVE ALL THE OTHERS"

[illegible]

Proctor DRYERS for VENEERS

give a perfectly flat and pliable product without checks or splits

Made by the oldest and largest builders of dryers. Ask for Proctor Dryer Catalog for your materials.

PHILADELPHIA TEXTILE MACHINERY CO.
Builders of Drying Machinery
SEVENTH STREET AND TABOR ROAD, PHILADELPHIA, PA., U.S.A.
Hamilton, Ont., Canada,—W. J. Westaway, 4 Sun Life Building.

Excelsior Lumber Company.
Fesserton Timber Company
Fraser-Bryson Lumber Company.
Fraser Limited.
Gillies Brothers Limited.
Gloucester Lumber Company
Gordon & Co., George.
Grier & Sons, Ltd., G. A.
Harris Tie & Timber Company, Ltd.
Hart & McDonagh.
Hettler Lumber Company, Herman H.
Long-Bell Lumber Company.
Long Lumber Company.
Mason, Gordon & Co.
McLennan Lumber Company.
Montreal Lumber Company.
Moores, Jr., E. J.
Muir & Kirkpatrick.
Otis Staples Lumber Co.
Parry Sound Lumber Company.
Russell, Chas. H.
Shearer Company, Jas.
Spencer Limited, C. A.
Summers, James R.
Terry & Gordon.
Union Lumber Company.
Watson & Todd, Limited.
Weller, J. B.
Williams Lumber Company
Wuichet, Louis.

PLANING MILL EXHAUSTERS
Garlock-Walker Machinery Co.
Reed & Company, Geo. W.
Sheldons Limited.
Toronto Blower Co.

PLANING MILL MACHINERY
American Woodworking Machinery Company
Garlock-Walker Machinery Co.
Mershon & Company, W. B.
Sheldons Limited.
Toronto Blower Co.
Yates Machine Company, P. B.

PORK PACKERS
Davies Company, William
Harris Abattoir Company

POSTS AND POLES
Auger & Company
Canadian Tie & Lumber Co.
Dupuis Limited, J. P.
Eagle Lumber Company
Harris Tie & Timber Company, Ltd.
Long-Bell Lumber Company.
Long Lumber Company.
Mason, Gordon & Co.
Terry & Gordon.

PULLEYS AND SHAFTING
Bond Engineering Works
Canadian Link-Belt Company
Garlock-Walker Machinery Co.
General Supply Co. of Canada, Ltd.
Green Company, G. Walter
Hamilton Company, William
Jeffrey Mfg. Co.
Jenckes Machine Company, Ltd.

PULP MILL MACHINERY
Canadian Link-Belt Company, Ltd.
Hamilton Company, William.
Jeffrey Manufacturing Company
Jenckes Machine Company, Ltd.
Waterous Engine Works Company

PUMPS
General Supply Co. of Canada, Ltd.
Hamilton Company, William
Jenckes Machine Company, Ltd.
Smart-Turner Machine Company
Waterous Engine Works Company

RAILS
Gartshore, John J.
Sessenwein Bros.

ROOFINGS
Reed & Company, Geo. W.

ROOFINGS
(Rubber, Plastic and Liquid)
Beveridge Paper Company
International Chemical Company

ROPE
Consumers Cordage Co.
Leckie, Limited, John

RUBBER GOODS
Atlas Asbestos Company
Dunlop Tire & Rubber Goods Co.
Goodyear Tire and Rubber Co.
Gutta Percha & Rubber Company

SASH
Genoa Bay Lumber Company
Renfrew Planing Mills.

SAWS
Atkins & Company, E. C.
Disston & Sons, Henry
General Supply Co. of Canada, Ltd.
Gerlach Company, Peter
Green Company, G. Walter
Hoe & Company, R.
Shurly-Dietrich Company
Simonds Canada Saw Company

SAW MILL LINK-BELT
Williams Machinery Co., A. R., Vancouver.

SAW MILL MACHINERY
Canadian Link-Belt Company, Ltd.
Dunbar Engine & Foundry Co.
Firstbrook Bros.
General Supply Co. of Canada, Ltd.
Haight, W. L.
Hamilton Company, William
Huther Bros. Saw Mfg. Company
Jeffrey Manufacturing Company
Long Manufacturing Company, E.
Mershon & Company, W. B.
Parry Sound Lumber Company
Payette Company, P.
Waterous Engine Works Company
Yates Machine Co., P. B.

SHEATHINGS
Beveridge Paper Company
Goodyear Tire & Rubber Co.

SHINGLE MACHINES
Marsh Engineering Works, Limited

SAW MANDRELS
Bond Engineering Works

SAW SHARPENERS
Garlock-Walker Machinery Co.
Waterous Engine Works Company.

SAW SLASHERS
Waterous Engine Works Company

SAWMILL LINK-BELT
Canadian Link-Belt Company

SHEET METALS
Syracuse Smelting Works

SHINGLES
Allan-Stoltze Lumber Co.
Associated Mills, Limited
Campbell-MacLaurin Lumber Co.
Cardinal & Page
Dominion Lumber & Timber Co.
Eagle Lumber Company
Foss Lumber Company
Fraser Limited.
Genoa Bay Lumber Company
Gillespie, James.
Gloucester Lumber Company
Grier & Sons, Ltd., G. A.
Harris Tie & Timber Company, Ltd.
Heeney, Percy E.
Long Lumber Company.
Mason, Gordon & Co.
McLennan Lumber Company.
Miller Company, Ltd., W. H.
Reynolds Company, Limited
Service Lumber Company
Shingle Agency of B. C.
Terry & Gordon.
Timms, Phillips & Co.
Vancouver Lumber Company.
Victoria Lumber and Mfg. Co.

SHINGLE & LATH MACHINER
Dunbar Engine and Foundry Co.
Garlock-Walker Machinery Co.
Green Company, C. Walter
Hamilton Company, William.
Long Manufacturing Company, E.
Payette Company, P.

SILENT CHAIN DRIVES
Canadian Link-Belt Company, Ltd.

SILOS
Ontario Wind Engine Company

SLEEPING ROBES
Woods Mfg. Company, Limited

SMOKESTACKS
Marsh Engineering Works, Limited
Waterous Engine Works Company.

SNOW PLOWS
Pink Company, Thomas.

SPARK ARRESTORS
Jenckes Machine Company, Ltd.
Reed & Company, Geo. W.
Waterous Engine Works Company.

SPRUCE
Bartram & Ball.
Bourgouin, H.
Cane & Co., Jas. G.
Cardinal & Page
Davison Lumber & Mfg. Company
Donogh & Co., John.
Dudley, Arthur N.
Dunfield & Company
Exchange Lumber Company.
Foss Lumber Company
Fraser Limited.
Fraser-Bryson Lumber Company.
Gillies Brothers.
Gloucester Lumber Company
Grant & Campbell.
Grier & Sons, Ltd., G. A.
Hart & McDonagh.
Lauder, Spears & Howland.
Long Lumber Company.
Mason, Gordon & Co.
McLennan Lumber Company.
Muir & Kirkpatrick.
New Ontario Colonization Company.
Nicholson & Co., E. M.
River Ouelle Pulp and Lumber Co.
Russell, Chas. H.
Service Lumber Company
Shearer Company, Jas.
Snowball Co., J. B.
Spencer Limited, C. A.
Terry & Gordon.

STEEL CHAIN
Canadian Link-Belt Company, Ltd.
Jeffrey Manufacturing Company.
Waterous Engine Works Company.

STEEL PLATE CONSTRUCTI
Marsh Engineering Works, Limi

STEAM PLANT ACCESSOR
Waterous Engine Works Company.

STEEL BARRELS
Smart-Turner Machine Co.

STEEL DRUMS
Smart-Turner Machine Co.

SWEAT PADS
American Pad & Textile Co.

SULPHITE PULP CHIPS
Davison Lumber & Mfg. Company

TANKS
Ontario Wind Engine Company

TARPAULINS
Turner & Sons, J. J.
Woods Manufacturing Company, Ltd.

TAPS AND DIES
Pratt & Whitney Company.

TENTS
Turner & Sons, J. J.
Woods Mfg. Company

TIES
Auger & Company
Austin & Nicholson.
Canadian Tie & Lumber Co.
Harris Tie & Timber Company, Ltd.
Long Lumber Company.
McLennan Lumber Company.
Terry & Gordon.

TIMBER BROKERS
Bradley, R. R.
Cant & Kemp.
Farnworth & Jardine.
Hillas & Co., W. N.
Hunter, Herbert F.
Smith & Tyrer, Limited

TIMBER CRUISERS AND ESTIMATORS
Sewall, James W.

TIMBER LANDS

TRIMMERS
Garlock-Walker Machinery Co.
Green Company, C. Walter
Waterous Engine Works Company

TUGS
West & Peachey.

TURBINES
Hamilton Company, William.
Jenckes Machine Company, Ltd.

VALVES
Bay City Foundry & Machine
Mason Regulator & Engineering C

VENEERS
Webster & Brother, James.

VENEER DRYERS
Coe Manufacturing Company
Philadelphia Textile Mach. Co.

VENEER MACHINERY
Coe Manufacturing Company
Garlock-Walker Machinery Co.
Philadelphia Textile Machinery

VETERINARY REMEDIES
Dr. Bell Veterinary Wonder Co.

WATER HEATERS
Mason Regulator & Engineering Co

WATER WHEELS
Hamilton Company, William.
Jenckes Machine Company, Ltd

Laidlaw Bale Tie Company.

WOOD

WOOD PRESERVATIVES
International Chemical Company

WOOD PULP
Austin & Nicholson.
New Ontario Colonization Co.
River Ouelle Pulp and Lumber Co.

PERFORMANCE

PERFORMANCE is what really shows the true worth of any machine. In February 1916 England appealed to Canada for help in producing timber for war needs.

That Canada's response took a practical form is evidenced by the fact that in April the first draft of the Canadian Forestry Corps landed in England, and in May two more drafts fully equipped with WATEROUS Machinery followed.

This Machinery, designed and built to cut from 15,000 to 20,000 ft. per day, has turned out as much as 58,000 ft. in 10 hours.

A Waterous Outfit in the Jura Mountains, France

That this is not an isolated case, or the record of one mill, is shown by the many letters we have received from different parts of England and France, of which the following is an extract

"....I have many WATEROUS mills running under me, each mill designed to fit into a different location, but all doing equally good work.

"I have no complaint to make of the WATEROUS Mills, in fact, I prefer them to anything I have been able to secure up to the present time, and I have many different kinds of machinery with which to do our work.

"To illustrate: I believe all records of the Forestry Corps, either in England or France, rest with ourselves in the Jara; one of our Company's output a few days ago was 51,300 ft. for one shift of 10 hours, cutting 3 x 9 plank. A mill of this kind that can put over a cut like the above I believe you canlook upon as a fairly successful outfit. To sum up, with the Waterous machinery that I have running in the Jara I feel confident that I can out cut any combination that is now running in the Forestry Corps. . . ."

What we have done for the Forestry Corps we can do for you.

Waterous

BRANTFORD, ONTARIO, CANADA

and Wood-Worker
Camp Supplies

Geo. Gordon & Co.

Limited

Cache Bay - Ont.

White Pine Red Pine

We can ship promptly Dimension Timber in sizes from 8 x 8 to 12 x 12, any length up to 24 feet.

Send us your inquiries

Hemlock, Spruce, Lath, Pulpwood and Hardwoods

The Year Round---In Any Quantity Dressed and Ripped to Your Orders

We specialize in Hemlock and Spruce Timbers. Let us know your requirements. We can assure you of immediate shipment through our splendid transportation facilities. Rail and water delivery.

Fassett Lumber Company, Limited FASSETT QUEBEC

SERVICE

Fir, Cedar and Spruce

LUMBER

"Service" Lumber Co.

Pacific Building, VANCOUVER, B.C.

Eastern Representative: A. W. BARNHILL, 20 St. James Street, Montreal.

Ontario Representative: A. E. MASURET, 30 King St. W., Toronto. Telephone Adelaide 3071.

International Land & Lumber Company, Limited

Lumber, Railway Ties Shims, Shingles, etc.

Head Offices, Ottawa, Ont.

Limits and Mills: ST. FELICIEN, LAKE ST. JOHN DISTRICT, QUEBEC

Our NEW TIMBER MILL

(Capacity 100,000 Feet Ten Hours.) NOW IN OPERATION

We solicit your enquiries for

Heavy Construction Material and Yard Stock

ANY SIZE TIMBERS UP TO 100 FT.

Give us an opportunity to prove to you that we have earned a reputation for Quality and Service.

Timberland Lumber Co., Limited

Head Office: Westminster Trust Bldg., NEW WESTMINSTER, B.C.

Mills at South Westminster, on B.C.E.R.

Shipments by C.P.R., C.N.R., G.N.R., N.P.R., and C.M. & St. P. Ry.

Arrow Brand Shingles Hit the Mark

Shingle Bolts in Reserve—RUSKIN, B.C.

ALLEN-STOLTZE LUMBER CO., LTD.

C. G. BOCKUS, 17 Knox Street, MONTREAL, P.Q.

VANCOUVER, B.C.

R. G. CHESBRO, 1404 Bank of Hamilton Bldg, TORONTO, ONT.

Manufacturers of

WIRE For TYING, BUNDLING and many other purposes. NAILS, Etc.

LAIDLAW BALE-TIE CO., Ltd.
HAMILTON, ONT.

Timber Estimates

James W. Sewall
OLD TOWN, - MAINE

TIMBER LANDS
Bought and Sold

Timber and Pulp Wood Estimates

R. R. BRADLEY
Consulting Forester
58 Telegraph Building
Hospital St., MONTREAL

USED SAW MILL
MACHINERY
FOR SALE

Extra heavy log haul-up works with inch round and flat chain, 128 ft. centres.
2—Waterous log unloaders or kickers, 3 arms, 10 in. cylinders.
1—Waterous log loader, 3 arms, 10-in. cylinders.
1—Waterous right-hand double cutting band mill, 11 in. saws, 8 ft. wheel, with 3-block carriage; 24 in. opening; Payette set works and dogs; 8 in. x 36 ft. steam feed.
1—Waterous double edger for 20-inch saws, lever shifter.
1—Payette double edger for 18-in. saws, lever shifter.
48—live rolls about 8 ft. long by 10 in. dia.; extra heavy, sprocket drive.
1—Payette picket machine, made specially for shade roller stock, will feed pieces 16 in. long, also sorting table with chain top.
1—Payette edger for box and short stock.
1—Rogers twin circular or tie maker.
1—Payette lath bolter and lath machine.
1—Pair lath trimmers.
1—Picket trimmer (bunch trim).
—Pair Polson "Brown" type engines, coupled on quarters, 22 in. x 30 in., with 16 ft. x 48 in. belt, balance wheel. Excellent engines.
1—8 x 10 Centre Crank Engine.
1—10 x 14 Cowan Slide Valve Engine.
Pulleys, gears, heavy line shafting and countershafting with bearings.
Booms and boom chains, ⅝, ⅝ & ¾.
Winches and other mill supplies.
Prompt shipments and bargains for quick sale. Will send all particulars and prices on application.

Firstbrook Bros.
Limited
PENETANG

Trade  Mark

Reg. U. S. A.

ALABAMA HEWN OAK TIMBER—

HARDWOOD LOGS:—
Ash, Hickory, Poplar, Oak, Satin Walnut, Mobile Bay Poplar, Dogwood

HARDWOOD LUMBER:—
Hewn Pitch Pine Timber, Pitch Pine Lumber

THE S. K. TAYLOR LUMBER COMPANY
Exporters Mobile, Alabama, U.S.A. Cables "Taylor, Mobile"

Austin & Nicholson
CHAPLEAU, ONTARIO

Largest Producers of
RAILROAD TIES
in the Dominion

Pine and Spruce Lumber
Lath Piling
Railroad Ties
Pulpwood

First Class Planing-mill Equipment

Facilities for delivering Pulpwood to Michipicoten Harbour, Lake Superior

Splendid facilities for Dressing and Matching in straight car lots, one or more widths

Mills at NICHOLSON, ONTARIO, Main Line C.P.R.

Emery and Corundum Wheels

Vitrified Silicate

You will find our product the best for quality and service in the lumber camp.

Send us your orders and we will ship promptly.

Brantford Emery Wheel Co.
Brantford . Ontario Limited

PETRIE'S LIST
of
NEW and USED
WOOD TOOLS
for Immediate Delivery

Wood Lathes
20" Sidney, Famous
16" Cowan.
16" Sidney, Famous, patternmakers.

Band Saws
30" Sidney, Famous, pedestal.
36" West Side, pedestal.
30" Cowan, bracket.
60" Fay & Egan, band re-saw.

Saw Tables
No. 6 Sidney, Famous, variety.
No. 5 Sidney, Famous, combination.
No. 4 Sidney, Famous, combination.
No. 2 Sidney, Famous, variety.
Fisher, iron frame rip.
MacGregor-Gourlay power feed cut-off.
Greenlee automatic cut-off.
7' Williams, swing saw.
Bench type, jig or scroll saw.
No. 4 Canadian, steel frame, pole saw.

Wood Planers
26" double surfacer, with chip breaker.
24" Hermance, double surfacer.
24" Sidney, Famous, single surfacer.
24" Crescent, single surfacer.
24" MacGregor-Gourlay.
24" pony planer.
24" Champion planer and matcher, with moulding attachment.
24" Galt, planer and matcher.
18" Sidney Famous, single surfacer.
12" Buzz, with slotted head (2).
12" Petrie, buzz planers, safety heads (6)

Moulders
13" Clark-Demill four side.
12" Cowan four side.
12" Woods, four-side, inside.
8" Dundas four side.
6" Dundas sash sticker.

Mortisers
Cowan, upright power.
Galt, upright, compound table.
No. 5 New Britain chain.
No. 1 Smart, foot power.
No. 2 Osborne, foot power.

Boring Machines
No. 7 Sidney, Famous, belt driven.
No. 920 Canada Machinery Corporation (2).
Fay, single spindle, horizontal.
Jardine hub boring machine.

Clothespin Machinery
Humphrey automatic lathes (6).
Humphrey double slotters (3).

Miscellaneous
No. 30 Sidney, universal woodworker.
Vaughan, portable drag saw, power driven.
Champion, drag saw, friction feed.
Cowan moulder and panel raiser.
MacGregor Gourlay 12 spindle dovetailer.
Fay & Egan 12 spindle dovetailer.
No. 1 Ballantine dowel machine.
12" Canada Mach. Corp. sander.
24" Fay, double drum.
No. 2 Defiance belt sander.
M135 Cowan, sash and door relisher.
2-spindle Cant-Gourlay shaper.
No. 1 Defiance, axle shoulder shaper.
Superior saw arbors, 6"-30" saws (7).
M63 Cowan spindle carver.
Hall, automatic shingle machine.
Boss automatic shingle machine.
No. 2 Dominion, lath machine & bolter.
No. 3 Defiance, rim and felloe rounding machine.
21" Defiance shaft and pole tapering machine.
No. 1 Defiance, automatic, spoke driver.
8' Linderman, automatic, glue jointer.
8' McKeough & Trotter, hoop cutter.
No. 2 Reynolds, power screw driver.
No. 4 Lion, universal, wood trimmer.
Dundas, wood frame tenoner.
20" American wood scraper.
Horizontal bracket carving machine.

Ask to see our large stock of used supplies—belting, pulleys, machine shop equipment, mill supplies, pipe and fittings. Most of this material is as good as new and can be bought at greatly reduced prices.

H. W. PETRIE, LTD.
Front St. W., TORONTO, ONT.

Bleached Sulphite Pulp Mill. Saw Mills (all Band Saw Mills). Shingle Mills.

HERE THEY ARE ON THE MAP

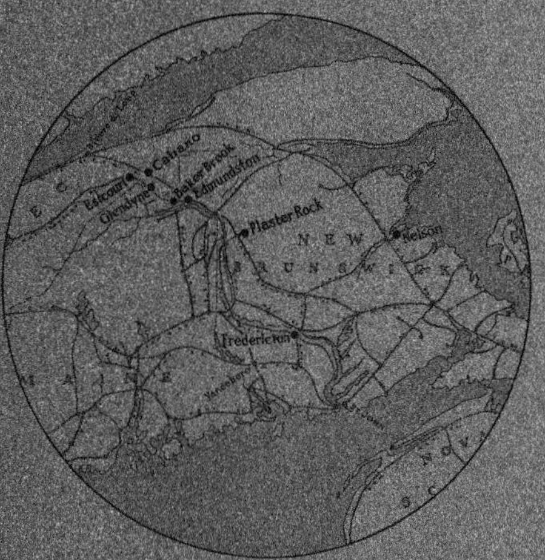

Mills and Railway Connections

Saw and Shingle Mills	Railway Connections	Saw and Shingle Mills	Railway Connections
Cabano, Que.	Temiscouata Ry.	Baker Brook, N. B.	C. G. Ry., Temiscouata Ry.
Glendyne, Que.	C. G. Ry.	Plaster Rock, N. B.	C. P. Ry.
Estcourt, Que.	C. G. Ry.	Fredericton, N. B.	C. P. Ry. and C. G. Ry.
Edmundston, N. B.	C.P.R., C.G.R. and Temiscouata Ry.	Nelson, N. B.	C. G. Ry.
Bleached Sulphite Mill, Edmundston, N. B.		Railway Connection, C.P.R., C.G.R. and Temiscouata Ry.	

Bleached Sulphite. Rough and Dressed Spruce. White Cedar Shingles. Railway Ties

Piano Sounding Board Stock a Specialty.

Selling and Purchasing Offices :-- EDMUNDSTON, N. B.

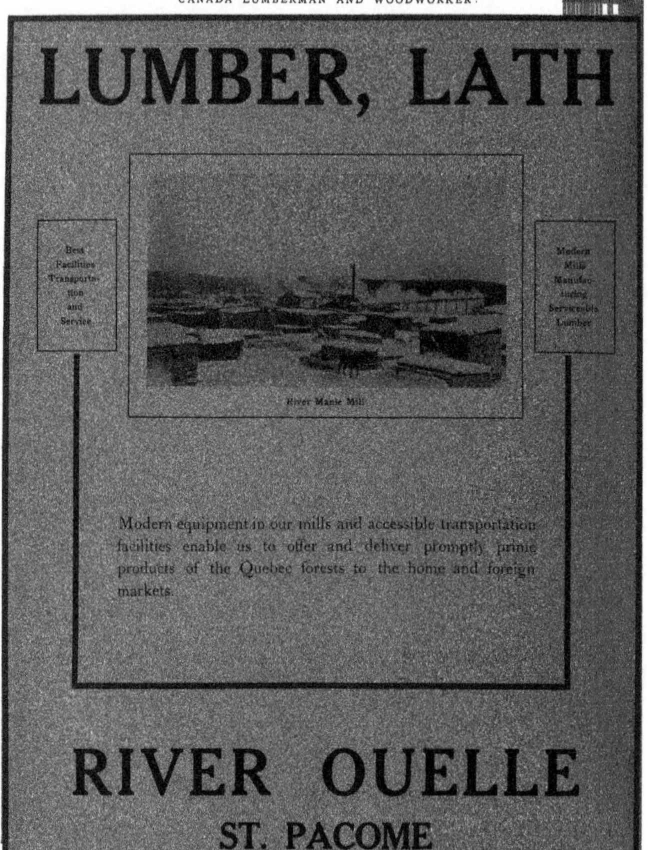
LUMBER, LATH
Best Facilities Transportation and Service
Modern Mills Manufacturing Serviceable Lumber
River Manie Mill
Modern equipment in our mills and accessible transportation facilities enable us to offer and deliver promptly prime products of the Quebec forests to the home and foreign markets.
RIVER OUELLE
ST. PACOME

Food Supplies for the Camp—

TEAS, COFFEES, PEAS, BEANS, LARD ETC.

Evaporated Apples, Dried Prunes, Raisins

We can quote you attractive prices on large or small shipments of fresh, wholesome stock. You will receive careful, intelligent attention from men who have been supplying Canadian Lumber Camps for many years.

Let us give you our quotations on the above items before placing your winter orders. Our reputation ought to be a guarantee for your satisfaction.

WHITEHEAD & TURNER, LIMITED
WHOLESALE GROCERS
QUEBEC

Special List of

Dr. Bell's Veterinary Wonder Medicines

	Price
Dr. Bell's Veterinary Medical Wonder	$1.00
Dr. Bell's Wonder Fire Blister, per box	1.00
Dr. Bell's Wonder Worm and Indigestion Powder (24 pds.)	.50
Dr. Bell's Wonder Kidney, Water and Blood Powder (24 pds.)	.50
Dr. Bell's Wonder Distemper Cough and Heave Powder (24 pds.)	.50
Dr. Bell's Wonder Condition Powders	.25 and .50
Dr. Bell's Wonder Worm and Physic Ball	.75
Dr. Bell's Wonder Liniment for Horses and Cattle	.75 and 1.00
Dr. Bell's Wonder Lotion for Horses and Cattle	.75 and 1.00
Dr. Bell's Wonder Eye Lotion	.50 and .75
Dr. Bell's Wonder Hoof Ointment and Gall Cure Combined	.50 and .75
Dr. Bell's Wonder Cow Physic (special)	.50
Dr. Bell's Wonder Pain Stop	(Unquoted)
Dr. Bell's Wonder Gall Cure	.25 and .50
Dr. Bell's Wonder Extract Liniment ... per qt., $1.75; per gallon,	$6.00
Dr. Bell's Wonder Extract Lotion ...... per qt., $2.00; per gallon,	$6.00
Dr. Bell's Wonder Stock Conditioner and Stock Food. Send for circular.	

Special Household Remedies for Camp use:

Dr. Bell's Wonder Liniment for Man (cures rheumatism and all sprains)	.50 and .75
Dr. Bell's Wonder Ointment	.25
Dr. Bell's Wonder Balsam of Pine Cough Syrup	.35 and .50
Dr. Bell's Wonder Kidney Pills	.25
Dr. Bell's Wonder Stomach and Liver Pills	.25
Dr. Bell's Wonder Rheumatism Tablets (something new).	

These medicines are all wonders. Agents wanted in every town and county in Canada. Can make good. Write for terms. Write name and address plainly; also nearest express office.

Dr. Bell's Veterinary Medical Wonder is composed of twenty of the most powerful and costly medicines in the world; and, according to reports from agents and those using it from coast to coast, including all the provinces (old and new) throughout the entire Dominion, also Newfoundland, Medical Wonder has saved in horses, cattle, sheep, and swine over $10,000,000 to the stock-owners of Canada during the past fifteen years, of which $2,500,000 worth were saved by Medical Wonder in 1918.

BANK REFERENCES.—Dr. Bell refers to Northern Crown and Toronto Banks of this city or any bank in Kingston.

A $1.00 bottle free to any Horseman sending 25c for mailing, packing, etc.

Special Wholesale Rates to Lumbermen

Dr. Bell Veterinary Wonder Co.
KINGSTON. ONT.

Keep Your Horses in Condition With

Johnson's Veterinary Remedies

They are invaluable equipment to your stables, and a stock of them would save you a lot of worry and expense when your horses get out of sorts and need medicine. With 25 years' reputation to back them, you can be sure they are reliable in obtaining the best possible results.

Prices in effect at the present time:

Johnson's Horse Liniment No. 1	Per Gal.	$7.00
Johnson's Horse Liniment No. 1	Quarts, Per Doz.	19.00
Johnson's Horse Liniment No. 1	Pints, Per Doz.	10.00
Johnson's Horse Colic Remedy	Per Gal.	10.00
Johnson's Horse Colic Remedy, Qu. (8 Doses ea.)	Doz.	30.00
Johnson's Horse Colic Remedy Pts. (4 Doses ea.)	Doz.	15.00
Johnson's Veterinary Healing Ointment (Gall Cure) 2 lb. Tins	each 2.25; Doz.	24.00
¼ lb. Tins	Per Doz.	4.00
Johnson's Concentrated Condition Powders, 1 lb. Pkgs.	Per Doz.	6.00
Johnson's Horse Worm Powders, Pkgs.	Per Doz.	4.00
Johnson's Purging Balls	Per Doz.	2.50
Johnson's Antisepting Dusting Powder (For Drying and Healing Sores, Proud Flesh, etc.)	Per Doz.	8.00
Kreoline—Deodorizer, Antiseptic, etc.	Gal. Tin	1.50

Our Family and Van Remedies are as follows:

Pine and Tar Cough Syrup
Purgative Pills
Little Liver Pills
Porous Plasters
Stomach Bitters
Laxative Cold Tablets
Chlorine Mixture (Diarrhoea)
Big 4 Liniment—Mosquito Oil
X Ray Liniment
Headache Powders
Mosquito Oil

All Drugs and Patent Medicines at Market Prices—Mail orders solicited—Prompt shipments made

A. H. JOHNSON, Wholesale Druggist

COLLINGWOOD, ONT.

THE BEST VALUE
IN
Pine, Hemlock, Cedar, Ash, Basswood, Elm, Spruce, Birch, Maple and Tamarac
We Specialize in
Doors, Sash, Frames, Moldings, Box Shooks, Crating
Wholesale and Retail
Ripping, Resawing, Dressing, and Making in Transit
Let us quote you
Dealers in
Lumber, Shingles, Lath Railway Ties, Posts, Hard and Soft Wood, Cement & Coal
THE JOHN CAREW LUMBER CO.
LIMITED
LINDSAY - CANADA
JOHN CAREW
President and General Manager
G. J. CAREW
Secretary and Treasurer

Ryther & Pringle Co.

Carthage, N. Y.

To the Lumbermen of Canada

AT a time like the present, when lumber activities are intensified to meet huge demands in the urgent reconstruction of Europe as well as for domestic needs, consideration has to be given to every means of improving conditions in the lumber camp. Serviceable equipment for the men is an important factor in satisfactory working conditions.

In addition to those engaged in the lumber work during the war are thousands of men returning from the army to the lumber field, and these men will require encouragement by the best provision for their future work.

Like many other big organizations, the firm of A. R. Clarke & Company were handicapped through the last four years by a large proportion of their staff serving their country. But it was realized that men and money were needed for the Empire's defence, and therefore, their employees were encouraged in the support of every means that contributed to the one end—VICTORY.

We are now back to full capacity, prepared in every way to meet the demands of present conditions. As to the quality and utility of our products, we believe they are so well known that special emphasis here is hardly needed. With our extensive facilities for the production of every article of clothing needed in the lumber camp and our determination to maintain the high standard by which our goods have always been recognized, we ask your enquiries for the equipment of your men.

We assure you your enquiries will receive every consideration and our best attention.

A. R. CLARKE & CO. LIMITED
TORONTO

Griffith B. Clarke.
President and General Manager

CLARKE'S
Established 1852
"A.R.C." Brand
clothing is favorably known in lumber camps all over Canada. It has a reputation for good materials, correct design and thorough workmanship.
Illustrated are a few A.R.C. brand garments—the line includes everything necessary for the lumberman's complete outfit. *Catalogue on request.*
A. R. Clarke & Co.
Toronto

PURITY FLOUR
98 lbs
WHEN PACKED
MILLS AT
WINNIPEG - GODERICH - BRANDON - CALGARY

THE WEST'S BEST
PURITY
ROLLED OATS
80 lbs
WHEN PACKED
MILLS AT
WINNIPEG - GODERICH - BRANDON - CALGARY

Striking For
68 Years

Sure, Safe
& Silent

The Only Safe Match for the Lumber Camp

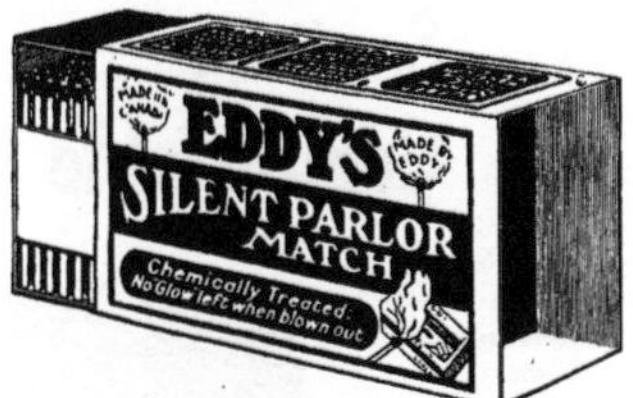

THE high tax upon matches makes it more than ever a matter of importance to the buyer that he realizes good match value. The self-extinguishing quality of the "silent 5's" has the heart-whole endorsation of all fire inspectors.

The Best
is the Cheapest

The Famous Eddy Fibreware
round-bottomed pail
Invaluable in Bush, Camp & Mill

The E. B. Eddy Company Ltd.

Hull - Canada

Woodsmen Of The World Look To "Pink"

FOR
ALL
LOGGING

TOOLS and HANDLES

Wherever the British flag flies and the lumbering industry flourishes, there you will find Pink's Tools.

The same uniformly excellent quality supplied year in and year out has earned for Pink's Tools the esteem of all lumbermen.

Exporters to Europe, and contractors to the Allied Armies.

The Thomas Pink Company have shipped vast quantities of tools to Britain and her Allies.

Lists free. All good hardware dealers sell our Tools and Handles.

Write for information. *Canada Long Distance Phone No. 87.*

THOMAS PINK CO. LIMITED

PEMBROKE, ONTARIO, CANADA.

We are also Makers of Car Movers.

Lumbermen, Railroad, Contractors and Miners Outfitters

We are Head to Foot Specialists for all kinds of Clothing, Mackinaws, Ettoffs and Untearable Wool Tweeds.

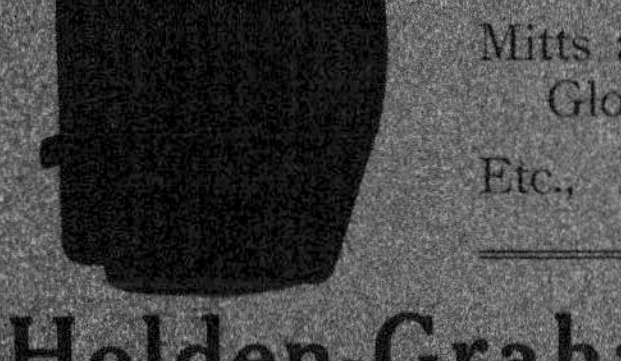

- Underwear
- Long Stockings
- Wool Socks
- Braces
- Caps
- Moccasins

- Rubber Footwear
- Snow Shoes
- Blankets
- Bedding
- Towels
- Table Oil Cloth
- Top Shirts
- Overalls
- Sweaters
- Mitts and Gloves
- Etc., Etc.

Grant-Holden-Graham Limited

Manufacturing Wholesalers and Importers

Ottawa 147-151 Albert Street **Canada**

KLIM
IN POWDER FORM
FOR ALL USES
Keep your men on the job
CANADIAN MILK PRODUCTS LIMITED
TORONTO
MONTREAL
WINNIPEG
ST. JOHN

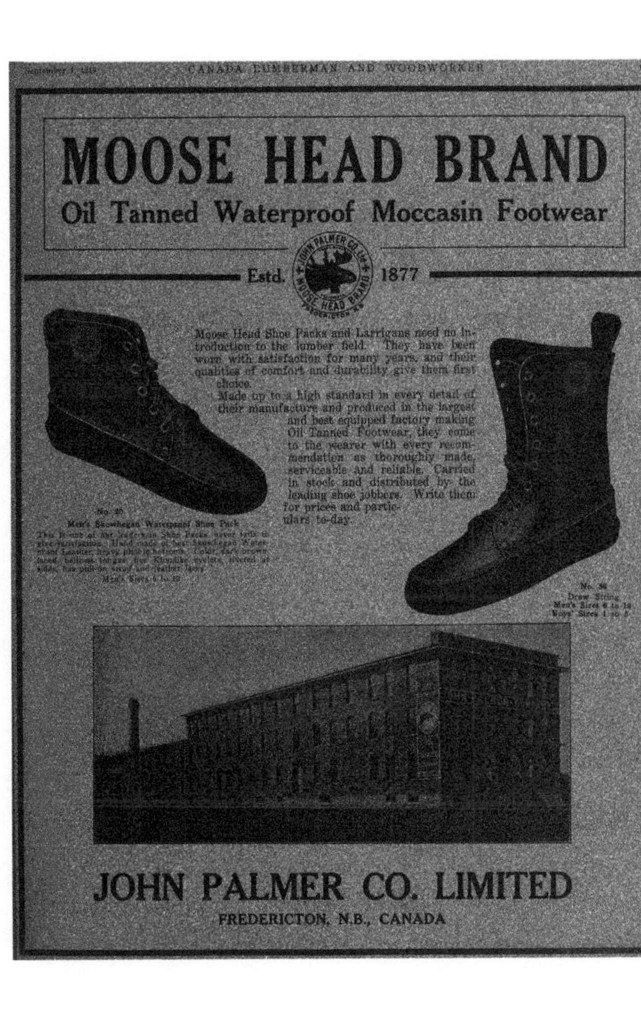
MOOSE HEAD BRAND
Oil Tanned Waterproof Moccasin Footwear
Estd. 1877
JOHN PALMER CO. LTD.
MOOSE HEAD BRAND
FREDERICTON N.B.
Moose Head Shoe Packs and Larrigans need no introduction to the lumber field. They have been worn with satisfaction for many years, and their qualities of comfort and durability give them first choice.
Made up to a high standard in every detail of their manufacture and produced in the largest and best equipped factory making Oil Tanned Footwear, they come to the wearer with every recommendation as thoroughly made, serviceable and reliable. Carried in stock and distributed by the leading shoe jobbers. Write them for prices and particulars to-day.
No. 20
Men's Skowhegan Waterproof Shoe Pack
Draw String
Boys' Sizes 1 to 5
JOHN PALMER CO. LIMITED
FREDERICTON, N.B., CANADA

ACME---Noun, the highest point
(Webster's Dictionary)

ACME
TRADE MARK

GLOVES

live up to their name

They have reached the highest point of perfection. Made from first grade leather tanned in our own plants; well stitched; full sized; liberal allowance of material. An article in which the quality is maintained to the highest standards.

That is why we call them "Acme Gloves."

To the purchasing agent:—

We will send a sample pair to any lumber company on request. For the teamster, the sawyer, the chopper, the foreman, or the boss of the camp "Acme" is the best glove investment, because they wear longer, and cost no more than inferior makes.

We also Manufacture a complete line of

Shoe Packs, Drawstrings, Driving Boots,
Horse-hide & Buckskin Moccasins
Sheep Socks, Lumbermen's Socks, Wool Mitts, Sweaters
Mackinaw Clothing, Overalls & Pants

INQUIRIES SOLICITED

BRANCHES:
CRAIG STREET
CLOTHING
MARIEVILLE
KNITTING MILL

HEAD OFFICE AND
MAIN FACTORY
MONTREAL

BRANCHES:
JOLIETTE
Tannery and Woolen Mill
ST. TITE
Tannery Larrigans
GLOVES

LUMBER and TIMBER

Carefully Selected and Graded

BASSWOOD
We offer subject to prior sale three cars of No. 1 Common & Better Basswood, 1½" x 9" and up x 6 to 16'

GOOD PINE SIDINGS
One care 3" x 14" and up, three year old stock.

STOCKED AT OUR MILL
105,000' Spruce, 2 x 9 and 10", mostly 10", 10 to 18' long, mostly 12'.
90,000' Spruce, 2 x 8" x 10/13', mostly 12'
70,000' Spruce, 2 x 7" x 10/13', mostly 12'
50,000' Spruce, 2 x 6" x 10/13', mostly 12'

FIR TIMBER
We have a fine stock of Fir timber up to 85' long, and have excellent connections in the West and are capable of handling business direct from the Coast.

The James Shearer Co., Limited

Wholesale and Retail Dealers in Lumber and Timber

OFFICE AND YARDS: 225 St Patrick St. MONTREAL

DAVIDSON'S

The "Premier" of Camp Ranges

It embraces every modern improvement and convenience that can be of practical use or advantage in a range.

The Body is made of extra heavy specially prepared steel, 14 and 16 gauge. It is hand riveted throughout with cone headed rivets.

The Oven is very large. Baking for fifty men can easily be done with this range. The oven bottom is made of extra heavy flat steel, and is stayed with angle iron, so that buckling or warping is impossible. The fire box is large and roomy, and the fire box door, being extra large, tough coarse wood can be used with ease.

The Reservoir is made of planished copper, and being set next to fire box, a good supply of hot water is ready soon after firing up.

No.	Size of Oven	Fire Box Door	Size of Top	Shipping Weight
10-27	25x27x16in	8 x 8½ in.	53 x 28 in	500 lbs.

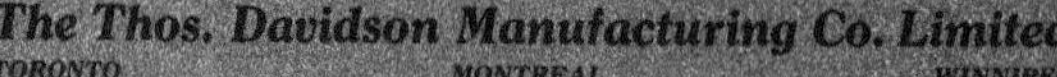

CAMP HOTEL RANGE
6 10-inch Pot Holes   Burns 33-inch Wood

The Thos. Davidson Manufacturing Co. Limited

TORONTO   *MONTREAL*   *WINNIPEG*

British Timber Importers and Merchants

Canada Lumberman and Woodworker

Issued on the 1st and 15th of every month by
HUGH C. MACLEAN, LIMITED, Publishers
HUGH C. MacLEAN, Winnipeg, President.
THOS. S. YOUNG, Toronto, General Manager.

OFFICES AND BRANCHES:

TORONTO - - Telephone A. 2700 - - 347 Adelaide Street West
VANCOUVER - - Telephone Seymour 2013 - - Winch Building
MONTREAL - - Telephone Main 2299 - - 119 Board of Trade
WINNIPEG - Telephone Garry 856 - Electric Railway Chambers
NEW YORK - - Telephone 3108 Beekman - - 1123 Tribune Building
CHICAGO - Telephone Harrison 5351 - 1413 Great Northern Building
LONDON, ENG. - - - - - - - - - - 16 Regent Street, S.W.

TERMS OF SUBSCRIPTION
Canada, United States and Great Britain, $2.00 per year, in advance; other foreign countries embraced in the General Postal Union, $3.00.

Single copies 15 cents.

"The Canada Lumberman and Woodworker" is published in the interest of, and reaches regularly, persons engaged in the lumber, woodworking and allied industries in every part of Canada. It aims at giving full and timely information on all subjects touching these interests, and invites free discussion by its readers.

Advertisers will receive careful attention and liberal treatment. For manufacturing and supply firms wishing to bring their goods to the attention of owners and operators of saw and planing mills, woodworking factories, pulp mills, etc., "The Canada Lumberman and Woodworker" is undoubtedly the most direct and profitable advertising medium. Special attention is directed to the "Wanted" and "For Sale" advertisements.

Authorized by the Postmaster-General for Canada, for transmission as second-class matter.

Entered as second-class matter July 18th, 1914, at the Postoffice at Buffalo, N.Y., under the Act of Congress of March 3, 1879.

Vol. 39 Toronto, September 1, 1919 No. 17

The Coming Days in the Lumber Field

This issue constitutes the Annual Camp and Supply Number of the "Canada Lumberman," and contains many features that should prove both interesting and helpful in all the numerous activities of the industry. Various phases of the logging situation, the amount of timber that will be taken off, operating expenses, management of men and camp administration generally are dealt with and discussed by representative lumbermen.

An effort has been made to present in instructive form, for the enlightenment of those firms who do not carry on bush operations, the progress that has been made in the way of efficient camp life and conveniences, and to show, in a convincing manner, that logging today is conducted under more sanitary, pleasant and comfortable surroundings than at any previous period.

There has been advancement all along in the lumber trade, and today quality, economy and production are the watchwords. In the opinion of those who have given close study to production problems it will take some years before enough lumber can be sawn to answer adequately all the at home and abroad requirements. An effort will be made this year to speed up production, and, in some instances, to double the cut of last season. Even should this desideratum be realized, there will still be a shortage in many avenues. The active building campaigns, the extensive character of repairs, the many new industrial undertakings and activity in the purchase of furniture, automobiles, phonographs, player-pianos and kindred lines will consume various kinds of woods at a more rapid rate than the manufacturers in this country can supply.

Then, export has only been begun. It will not attain its full status and development until next year, when the reconstruction of Europe will be under full sway. So long as Canada becomes more and more an exporting people instead of an importing one, will industry in all fields continue to grow. The balance of trade is at present very materially against the Dominion, and, if through its ship-building campaign, its tariff boards, [illegible]way commission, or other bodies, the federal government can render any stimulus and facilitate the means of export, a real national service will have been accomplished. The necessary tonnage to handle export trade should be speedily supplied.

There is now a great opportunity for the Dominion to reach out and come to its own in preeminence of commercial nationhood. The stream of prosperity has its source in the bush, and, through all the ramifications of the industry until the delivery of the finished cargo, there should be aggressiveness, co-operation and harmony. It is felt that Canada can now do much to place herself in the forefront of world-wide mercantile affairs by undertaking in a distinctly businesslike manner and with whole-hearted energy the work of developing foreign connections and retaining these through well established service, superiority of products and the abundance of materials at our command. In the lumber and woodworking branches there should be a "long pull, a strong pull and a pull altogether."

A Criticism and the Answer

In a recent issue of the "Quebec Telegraph" there appeared an interview with a "prominent local timber merchant," alleging discrimination against the port of Quebec in favor of Montreal by the Eastern representatives of the British Government Timber Buyer, in connection with the shipment of the lumber purchased on that Government's account. Quebec is, very properly, jealous in retaining every pound of traffic to which she believes the port is entitled, and naturally does not like to see business diverted to Montreal or elsewhere. Lumber is an important item in the port's trade, and the fact that several of the largest exporters to the United Kingdom have their headquarters in Quebec is significant of the standing of the port in the matter of this section of Canada's overseas business.

The allegation of the "prominent local timber merchant" is that the Montreal shipping companies are exercising an influence not only to the detriment of the port of Quebec, but to the detriment of Imperial interests. Further, it is asserted that lumber can be shipped as cheaply, if not cheaper, than via Montreal. It is argued that if the British Government Timber Buyer's representatives insist on loading deals at Montreal, they ought to take on deck loads of square timber at Quebec. The first need for construction in France and Belgium, it is said, is square timber for the building of foundations, and later the shipment of deals. But the advice given by the Quebec lumberman was, he asserts, ignored, as the British officials "would simply place themselves, as they have been doing all along since the outbreak of the war, in the power of their Montreal advisers without taking the trouble to learn the cost."

"The result is, in a majority of cases, the lumber and deals are being first shipped to European ports for construction and the square timber most needed for the beginning of foundation work left to follow, just like the shipment of the cart before the horse. But this is not the only disadvantage. Millions of feet of lumber and deals manufactured in the district of Quebec and purchased by the Imperial Ministry, is being transported by rail from here to Montreal and thence loaded on board the ships, an extra cost in handling and railway transportation that must be enormous, and still the agents sent over from England to supervise these shipments and protect the interests of those who employ them in cost, are influenced by the Montreal shipping agents to the detriment of honest competition and the port of Quebec.

"Every day it occurs that square timber that should be shipped out of Quebec is being transported from this port to Montreal for shipment on the European steamers, which is not only an extra expense in handling, but in railway freight. It is like going to London for merchandise and placing it on sale in Canada for the British public to come over and purchase, and this thing has been going on for some time and still the British officials sent over here to supervise the shipments of square timber and sawn lumber are either blind or too dense in intellect to realize conditions."

The assertion that the British Government Timber Buyer's representatives are under the influence of the Montreal steamship companies is, we are informed, absolutely incorrect, and in that connection it must not be overlooked that the allotment of space for government cargo on "Liner Steamships," including lumber, is under control of the British Ministry of Shipping, with offices in the Shaughnessy Building, McGill Street, Montreal.

All the regular liner cargo vessels that can be accommodated at Quebec are stopped at that port outward bound to load their lumber allotments, and, therefore, the allegation that millions of feet of lumber manufactured in the Quebec district is being transported by rail to Montreal at heavy additional expense for loading on steamships at that port is without foundation, and as a matter of fact the maximum quantity of lumber which can be shipped is being loaded on steamers at the port of Quebec.

In addition to the large number of liner cargo vessels which are loading lumber at Quebec regularly each week, about a dozen vessels specially chartered by the British Government Timber Buyer have loaded complete cargoes of lumber at Quebec during the months of July and August, and the shipment of lumber direct from that port will continue without intermission until all the contracts have been completed.

The statement that spruce lumber is being shipped overseas in preference to waney pine timber required in the construction of buildings is not, we understand, in accordance with facts, as all such timber now being shipped from Quebec is used almost exclusively for shipbuilding purposes.

Beautiful But Costly Ideals

Government operation and control of railways in the United States has been anything but a signal success. The mania for public ownership which swept the land, so far as the transportation facilities were concerned, found early accomplishment when "Uncle Sam" entered the war. Enthusiastic advocates came out with long articles praising the foresight, wisdom and initiative of the powers that prevail on the banks of the Patomac.

Now national control of the railways is like the leprosy—no cure. The authorities at Washington would shake off the incubus if they could and hand the roads back to the original owners. The deficits have amounted to millions and millions of dollars. Railway employees have been clamoring for more money until an office boy, a flagman or a stenographer now receives practically as much as did an engineer, station-master or conductor before the war. It has been stated that there are watchmen at crossings where only five or six trains a day pass, drawing $150 per month. Who is footing the bill for all this inflated and abnormal economic creation whereby a messenger now commands the salary of a former bank manager? Why, it is the people, and they are paying for it doubly, not only in increased freight and passenger rates, but also by direct taxation. Labor has become more and more insistent. It wants to reap all the sweets and partake of naught of the bitter.

Recently the plumb plan for ownership and operation of railways was proposed. It did not by any means score a bull's eye. The railway employees who advocated it were not willing to take any chances. They wanted their share of the dividends if there was a profit resulting from the operation of the roads, but if there was a deficit they desired the shortage to be made up by taxation. In other words, they were not willing to take a "sporting chance." They were eager to gamble on a "sure thing," which is not creditable to their spirit of justice and fair play. If government operation continues it looks as if there will be a permanent deficit, and hence taxation must be resorted to to make up the difference.

Rates on the United States carrying lines were increased twice during 1918 and it was thought at that time that sky-line had been reached, but there is an altitude higher yet, for it is learned that Walter D. Hines, director general of the United States railway administration, has in contemplation another advance in freight rates. As soon as such a move is made on the other side a similar shift will be pulled off in Canada, as there seems to be a remarkably sympathetic and reciprocal bond of union between the transportation companies when it comes to augmenting either freight or passenger fees.

The National Wholesale Lumber Dealers' Association has sent out through its traffic manager, notices to the members. Messrs. W. G. Power, of St. Pacome, Que., and Gordon C. Edwards, of Ottawa, are trustees of the National Wholesale Lumber Dealers' Association, and the announcement by that body has a direct appeal to Canada, the same as it has across the border. In this notice the situation is summed up succinctly by the association as follows:—Notwithstanding the increased tonnage expected from heavy crop movements and other sources, it is evident that the revenues to be derived therefrom will not be sufficient to offset the heavy increases in operating expenses. Apparently the only way in which another advance could be avoided would be by having Congress make further appropriations to the Railroad Revolving Fund. Are you in favor of a further advance in freight rates at this time? If so, how much, in your opinion, should the rates be advanced and what form should this advance take, i.e., should it be on a percentage basis or a flat increase? You will recollect that General Order No. 28, effective June 25, 1918, provided for a 25 per cent. advance, with a maximum advance of 5c in the commodity rates on lumber and forest products. In your opinion, should a further advance apply to all commodities, including lumber and forest products, or do you consider that lumber and forest products at present contribute more than their share to the transportation revenues of the railroads? From the broad view of quickly rehabilitating our country from the war basis will an increase in freight rates on lumber be another deterrent in our house building program?

It certainly does not look as if the price of lumber is going to recede when one considers the increased cost of li
wages, the shortened hours, the exactions of labor
ing charges, the outlet to Europe and the general active house-building campaign. Apparently the pendulum is swinging far in the direction of higher quotations on forest products.

Editorial Short Lengths

The housing problem, which is one of the most difficult with which Britain has to deal, is now being tackled by the government in earnest. Tenders have been called for the erection of 3,200 houses in London, costing in the aggregate £2,300,000 sterling.

The total annual freight bill of the United States lumber industry is estimated at about $215,000,000. Lumber and forest products furnish about 11 per cent. of the total tonnage of the American railroads, or about 215,000,000 tons yearly, according to Interstate Commerce Commission statistics. This total is greater than the movement of all agricultural products and is exceeded only by the tonnage of general manufactures and mine products.

There is an agitation on in one of the great political parties of Canada to have lumber placed on the free list. The platform adopted declares emphatically for free trade or near free trade in sawmilling machinery as requisite to the fullest development of the forest resources. At the same time it demands that if the party is returned to power at the next election there must be abolition of tariffs against United States lumber in all degrees of manufacture.

At the convention Hon. John Oliver, premier of British Columbia, challenged the free trade planks on the ground that to specify free sawmilling machinery was patchy and foolish. Sawmilling, he pointed out, was only one operation in converting logs to finished products. Logging machinery, cables, donkey engines, locomotives, axes, saws, etc., had quite as much right to be considered essential as the materials entering into a sawmill.

It has often been declared that free trade is the panacea of all economic ills. The query naturally arises at this particular juncture, would wood goods be any cheaper were all tariff bars let down and the circulation of lumber made as free as the air we breathe?

There will always be theorists, dreamers, faddists, visionaries and fanatics who want to try out everything and anything in the hope of realizing the economic dream of many a man. The dream is that it is his inalienable right to buy in the cheapest and sell in the dearest market. Respecting the best means how this belief or ideal can be accomplished, opinions and procedure will continue to differ until the dawn of the millenium.

Some Busy Sawmills on the Georgian Bay

Midland, Penetang, Victoria Harbor and Parry Sound all Have Progressive Plants —Features of Various Units Recently Visited by Ontario Yardmen

Midland has for many years been one of the most important lumber manufacturing towns in the Georgian Bay District. Its natural location, splendid shipping facilities and convenience to timber limits have marked it out as one of the busiest operating centres, so far as wood products are concerned, in the province of Ontario.

The largest producing mill in Midland, as well as one of the most efficient, compact and well equipped, is that of Manley Chew. Many important additions and improvements were made a few years ago to the plant which is a most active one, operating night and day. The mill generally starts up as soon as the ice leaves the bay and runs right through to the first of December. Two gangs of men are employed, each working ten hours a day.

The present mill building is 65 x 125 ft. with cement boiler house 44 x 16 ft. which is designed in the most modern manner with boilers fitted with Dutch ovens and fed with self-feeders. The sawing equipment consists of two double-cutting band saws, two gang edgers, lath and picket machines and all the other accessories of an up-to-date sawmill. The present capacity of the plant is one-quarter million feet every 24 hours, or, more properly speaking, every day of two shifts of 10 hours each. The lumber cut is pine and hardwood, fully 80 to 90 per cent. of the product being white pine. The mill has a splendid yard capacity, containing piling room for about 20,000,000 ft. with 5,000 ft. of track and lumber is shipped out both by rail and water. The motive power of the mill is steam and there is a sprinkler system of fire protection throughout the buildings and yards.

The mill was erected in 1899 by Geo. Chew & Son, the company being composed of the late Geo. Chew and his sons, A. G. Chew and Manley Chew. The latter has been the sole owner and manager for the past 18 years and is widely known throughout the industry for his business ability and aggressiveness. For some time Mr. Chew represented the riding of Simcoe in the Federal Parliament.

The dock for water shipment will hold about 5,000,000 ft. of lumber and 3,000,000 lath and has a depth of water from 14 to 30 ft.

Mr. Chew operates his own camps in the woods and this year will take out about the same quantity of timber as last. He makes a specialty of contract sawing and his mill is generally referred to as the "fastest operating one on the Georgian Bay."

In regard to the fire protection system, already referred to, it may be stated that there are four hydrants across the yard between the mill and where the lumber starts. Pipes are strung under the full length of each of the trams with four or five connections. At every connection throughout the yard and under the trams fire hose has been placed. By this efficient plan water can be directed against any outbreak of fire on any part of the yards within one minute.

The Plant of Chew Bros.

The mill of Chew Bros. is a well laid out and admirably managed one and is widely known throughout the whole of Ontario. The firm originally consisted of Geo. Chew (father of Manley Chew) and his brother, Thos. Chew. They dissolved partnership some years ago and the partnership now consists of Edwin Letherby and Manley Chew, the former acting in the capacity of manager as the latter has extensive interests of his own which requires the greater part of his attention. Mr. Letherby has been with the firm since 1885 when he took a position as office boy and has steadily risen by industry, perseverance and devotion to duty. Not only is he well liked in the lumber arena but by the citizens of Midland, Mr. Chew has been honored on more than one occasion in being elected to the position of Mayor.

F. C. Battrick is the mill superintendent of Chew Bros. and Wm. Nicholas the yard superintendent, while Elgin Gilmour has charge of the office and Thomas Pickering is wood superintendent. The company operates its own camps and owns its own limits. The mill has a sawing capacity of 15,000,000 to 18,000,000 ft. of lumber annually; 6,000,000 pieces of lath and 2,000,000 pieces of pickets. The sawing season is generally from May to November.

The equipment of the mill consists of two double-cutting bands, a Wickes gang, Fayette edger, lath and picket machines complete, together with all the smaller saws and essential equipment in connection with a modern mill. The principal timber sawn is white and red pine and the location of the mill gives it excellent facilities for shipment either by rail or water. The company has five private switches extending the full length of its lumber yards and also a dock for water shipments. Eight tramways extend throughout the yard for distribution and piling ground. The mill plant is equipped with an up-to-date automatic sprinkler system, the source of water supply is the town and there is a private 1,000 gallon capacity fire pump located near the mill, while fire mains and hydrants are installed for yard protection. Some years ago the entire lumber yards of Chew Bros. were twice consumed by the flames but of late years although a blaze has broken out now and then the fire has, through the splendid protection afforded, been speedily extinguished without any heavy loss.

Enterprising Woodworking Industries

One of the cleanest, most progressive and ably administered woodworking plants is that of the Midland Wood Products Company, Limited, which was organized in 1917. The officers at present are —president, Jas. Playfair; vice-president, D. S. Pratt; secretary-treasurer, N. L. Playfair; manager, M. J. Bray.

The company manufacture doors, columns, sash and mouldings in pine and hardwood, etc., and carry a large stock of rough lumber suitable for building purposes. The company also turn out window and door screens and wood rolling partitions suitable for dividing class rooms and assembly halls, Sunday-school halls, etc. The factory of Midland Wood Products, Limited, is well laid out, well lighted and the equipment is installed with a view to utilizing the minimum of space and giving the maximum of output. The company

Panoramic view of the mill property of Chew Bros., Midland, Ont., taken from the elevator and showing the extensive yards of the firm

Well equipped sawmill of Chew Bros., Midland, Ont., showing log pond in the foreground

manufacture mouldings of all kinds to details and their designs show a most representative line for general building purposes, while among other products are stairs, newels, dowels, porch rails, etc.

Another busy industry in Midland is that of Midland Woodworkers, Limited, formerly the Georgian Bay Shook Mills. The company manufacture planing mill products and box shooks of all kinds and have a particularly large and well established plant. The "Canada Lumberman" hopes at a later date to be able to present some pictures and full details of the equipment of this well known organization.

Busy Plants in Penetanguishene

The neighboring town of Penetanguishene has several busy industries, not only in the lumber and woodworking line but in other branches as well. The town has first class shipping facilities and is a thriving centre with a happy and contented people and a go-ahead spirit, an aggressive Board of Trade being recently organized.

The C. Beck Mfg. Co., Limited, have very extensive mills in Penetanguishene and turn out lumber, lath and timber, as well as boxes, box shooks, wooden pails and tubs. The company also do milling, resawing and their products in the woodworking line are known as the "horseshoe brand." The plant originated under the late Chas. Beck in 1877 when he acquired the Penetang Saw Mill and added to it from time to time until it embraces two splendid cawmills, planing mill, box factory and wooden pail factory. The saw mill capacity is 130,000 ft. in 10 hours with an equipment of one circular and one Wickes gang; one double-cut band saw and a gang edger.

The company cut principally pine and have this year a small stock of spruce and hemlock. The C. Beck Mfg. Co., of which W. F. Beck is president, A. E. Beck, vice-president and treasurer and G. A. Beck, secretary, manufacture lath in connection with their saw mills and from one mill a record cut of 128,000 pieces in 10 hours was produced. The Toronto box trade of the firm is supplied from the company's factory at the foot of Parliament St. The sales of the Beck Lumber Co. are under the supervision of Frank H. Horning, who makes his headquarters in Toronto.

The attractive and well laid out plant of Midland Wood Products, Limited, Midland, Ont.

The McGibbon Lumber Co. specialize in hemlock, as well as in white pine and hardwood and the industry has been established a great many years. In fact, it was in 1865 that the business was founded by the late Chas. McGibbon, who passed away a few months ago. The mill is equipped with a circular saw and the cutting capacity is 40,000 ft. per day, the product being white pine, hemlock, hardwood, lath and shingles.

The company was recently incorporated with a capital stock of $100,000 and the following officers elected: President, Archie McGibbon; vice-president, Norman McGibbon; secretary, Finlay McGibbon; directors, the foregoing and John and D. D. McGibbon.

Gropp Bros. have been established in the lumber business in Penetanguishene since 1900 and their establishment is known as the Penetanguishene Lumber & Shingle Mills. The firm manufacture rough and dressed lumber, pine and cedar shingles and are equipped to cut lath with an up-to-date lath mill. The shipping of Gropp Bros. is done principa rail. firm also manufacture crating and

The sawmill of Gropp Bros., Penetanguishene, showing a huge pile of logs in the foreground

have installed a plant for this purpose and operate machine to cut up slabs and mill refuse, which they lots for stove wood.

An Electrically Operated Sawmill

W. J. Martin who is one of the firm of Martin Bros., H Ont., has a small but well equipped mill at one end Penetanguishene. His plant is operated by 100 h.p. electric motor and is one of the few electrically driven mills in the province. Mr. Martin has been in the lumber business a life time and also in the slack cooperage and planing mill business at Hillsdale. The firm also operated a lumber plant at Martin's Siding, Muskoka, under the name of Martin Lumber Company and established a post office and station at that place, which is a few miles south of Huntsville. The Martin Lumber Company disposed of their interests some years ago to Mr. Alex Prowdfoot. The plants at Hillsdale and Craighurst have not been running for the last three years and Mr. W. J. Martin, not wishing to get out of touch with the lumber business, came to Penetanguishene and bought 300 acres of virgin timber from Geo. E. Copeland.

This timber was acquired by Mr. Copeland's father from the British government some 60 years ago and had never changed hands until it fell into the possession of Mr. Martin at the beginning of 1918 when he started operations and took out a stock of logs to build a mill and camps on the property and put in railway sidings. The first stock was put through the mill during the summer of 1918. The bush consists mostly of hardwood and the mill is a circular one complete, and run, as already stated, by electric power with one 100 h.p. motor. Mr. Martin states that this drive is very satisfactory and is a great saving on fuel. The sawdust is shipped by carload and also all other mill refuse for which there is a ready market. The capacity of the mill is from 15,000 to 20,000 ft. per day. Mr. Martin

The P. Payette foundry and machine shop, Penetanguishene, Ont.

expects to have all the timber cut on his 300 acres in about two more years and will turn out between 3,000,000 and 4,000,000 ft. besides 6,000 or 8,000 cords of hardwood.

Widely Known Saw Mill Machinery Firm

The P. Payette Company, of Penetanguishene, are manufacturers of general sawmill machinery, lath mills and boilers, carriages and set works, log decking machinery, etc. The business was established by Peter Payette 54 years ago and J. T. Payette, the present proprietor, has served 21 years apprenticeship, learning his trade in each shop, such as the moulding, machine and pattern shops. Then entering the office he worked his way up until he became office manager and latterly took a position on the road. On the death of his uncle, Peter Payette, he became manager of the whole factory, which was left to himself and eight other heirs. Geo. E. Copeland and J. T. Payette purchased the interests of the other heirs and four years ago last spring Mr. Payette acquired Mr. Copeland's interests making the former sole proprietor of the plant. The capacity of the industry is now five times what it was five years ago. J. T. Payette purchased some three years ago the gas engine plant of the Adams Launch & Engine Co. and has more than doubled its output. The Payette Company have been doing a great deal of shipyard work and at present have about a year's work ahead of them. They made all the rudder posts for six Toronto ships and also for three Midland ships and turned out all the cast iron slabs for the Dominion Shipbuilding Co. of Toronto and the Midland Shipbuilding Co. of Midland.

Mr. J. T. Payette is only 33 years of age and has always taken a deep interest in good horses. He keeps a number of fast stepping animals and a couple of years ago purchased the town park from Penetanguishene and transformed it into one of the finest racing establishments in northern Ontario. The half-mile track is one of the best that could be desired.

Historic Plant at Victoria Harbor

The Victoria Harbor Lumber Co., Ltd., whose mills are located at Victoria Harbor and whose head office is at 12 Wellington St. E., Toronto, is one of the historic industries on the Georgian Bay. The late John Waldie was the founder of the progressive enterprises of which his son T. N. Waldie is president, R. S. Waldie, vice-president and W. R. Harper, secretary. J. Duckworth is the manager of manufacture and G. F. Spragge, sales-manager.

The yards of the company are exceptionally well laid out, the

W. J. Martin, of Penetang, Ont., standing beside a few pine logs, 45 of which made over 30,000 ft. of lumber. One tree alone contained 6,000 ft.

stock being neat and regularly piled. The means of distribution are two yard locomotives and several miles of track. One locomotive is used for hauling lumber, lath, slabs and edgings from the mill to the piling yard and the other is employed in the shipping yard for shunting cars and hauling lumber from the yard to the planing mill. The shipping facilities of the Victoria Harbor Lumber Co. are by either rail or boat and the sheltered position which the mill occupies affords excellent booming ground for logs.

No. 1 mill which was destroyed by fire in May, 1918, was erected in 1877 and remodelled in 1902. It was equipped with one single cutting band saw and was used entirely for sawing timbers and all kinds of bill stuff.

No. 2 mill, which is idle this season owing to the scarcity of logs, was built in 1870 by Kean & Fowlie and remodelled in 1902 by the present owners. It contains one double cut band saw, as well as a circular and a gang saw.

No. 3 mill is the newest one and was put up in 1909. It is equipped with two double cutting band saws, a gang and gang edger and

The electrically-driven sawmill and part of the lumber yard of W. J. Martin, Penetanguishene. Five months before this picture was taken the site was a solid bush

is busy operating this season. The average daily cut is 125,000 ft. and 50,000 pieces of lath. The planing mill which was erected in 1897, contains two matchers, one double surfacer, one moulder, one re-saw, two rip saws and one siding machine. When the two sawmills of the Victoria Harbor Lumber Co. are in full operation the daily output is one-quarter million feet of lumber and 100,000 pieces of lath.

The Conger Lumber Co's. Activities

The Conger Lumber Co., Ltd., are manufacturers of pine and hemlock lumber, timber and lath, and their mill is located at Parry Sound, being one of the busy institutions of the north. W. B. Maclean is the president of the company, J. G. Maclean, secretary-treasurer and G. A. Maclean, manager of manufacture. The company was incorporated in 1884 and the original mill was equipped with a circular saw and a Wickes gang. This mill was destroyed by fire in April, 1901, but was rebuilt during the summer and is now equipped with two Waterous double-cutting band saws, together with edgers and a lath mill. The capacity of the plant is from 12,000,000 to 14,000,000 ft. annually. Owing to the scarcity of help and the impossibility of securing bush men to get out the usual quantity of logs, the cut will be rather small this year.

The Conger Lumber Co. was originally formed by W. H. Pratt, father-in-law of W. B. Maclean now president of the company. Mr. Pratt died in July 1905 and the industry has been carried on ever since under the able and progressive management of Mr. Maclean.

Rain Checks Menacing Fires in Ontario

The fierce forest fires which have been raging around Sault Ste. Marie, Ont., and other parts of northern and north-western Ontario have, at last, been extinguished by recent heavy downpours of rain. The protracted dry spell in many sections added to the flame hazard and kept many communities on tenderhooks owing to the proximity of the flames. Word received from the Soo says, now that the smoke cloud is lifted, the damage that the fires have caused is clearly apparent. Miles upon miles of bush land have been reduced to a barren debris. Here and there a farm has been destroyed, but the damage in this respect was astonishingly small. No towns were hurt. There is scarcely a trace of wild-animal life within a fifty mile radius, all the animals being driven to places of safety.

Settlers were working night and day in certain areas to save their house, as well as their fences and growing crops. In the vicinity of Deer Lake, 25 miles from Parry Sound, much damage was done

General view of the mills of the Victoria Harbor Lumber Company at Victoria Harbor, Ont.

Millions of feet of standing timber have been killed by the fires in Parry Sound region. This timber will have to be cut this winter in order to save the trees from the worms and rot which follow. Miles of fences were also consumed, as well as some firewood which had been cut and piled last winter. Forest fires in the north have been more numerous this year than at any period since 1916, when the great holocaust occurred. The damage, however, has not been nearly as great.

Careless Settlers Add to Danger

The Ontario Department has 1100 fire rangers scattered throughout the north country. These men can do much, but not everything, in safeguarding the wooded wealth of the various districts in which they labor. The Provincial Department of Lands, Forests and Mines declare that every precaution was taken this year, the same as in former ones, but the fires gained in numbers and strength owing to the long dry summer, rain not having fallen for weeks and weeks.

It is stated that some of the fires were started by settlers burning slash without first obtaining the necessary permit. E. J. Zavitz, the chief provincial forester of Ontario, in a recent interview, stated that the Department could control the fires in the towns and save lives, but was not able to control the fires on the big areas of bush when settlers and others go out and burn slash, despite the rigid regulations. It is understood that a number of settlers have been convicted of this offense, but the fine is a comparatively light one. At the next session of the Ontario Legislature the Act will probably be amended, through the initiative of Hon. G. H. Ferguson, Minister of Lands, Forests and Mines. The penalty will be increased and the offence made punishable by a term of imprisonment.

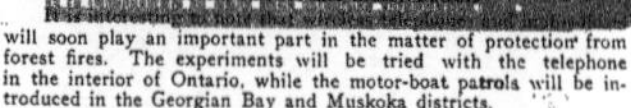

Wireless Phones and Motor Patrols

It is interesting to note that wireless telephones and [illegible] will soon play an important part in the matter of protection from forest fires. The experiments will be tried with the telephone in the interior of Ontario, while the motor-boat patrols will be introduced in the Georgian Bay and Muskoka districts.

In discussing the frequency, extent and damage done by forest fires, a leading paper ably summed up the situation recently by stating:—

Canada is experiencing one of the most destructive forest fire seasons in many years. From British Columbia to Nova Scotia comes the same story of vast timber limits wiped out, and it is an unfortunate feature of the conflagrations that the timber destroyed was on land that is of no use for agricultural purposes. Thus the loss to the various provincial treasuries, as well as to private owners, is heavy and total. Forest fire protection has been greatly expanded of recent years, even to the extent of utilizing aeroplanes in some districts; but despite these precautions the fire fiend annually transforms rich timber resources into barrens, that for scores of years will be of no use to man. Few problems are so vital to the prosperity and progress of the nation as forest conservation. Much has been done to protect our timber from this devastating agency, but it is clear that efforts on a still greater scale will have to be developed if we are to secure the upper hand.

The mill and part of the yards of the Conger Lumber Company at Parry Sound, Ont.

"Some Things That Our Association Has Done"

Benefits of Organization Are Shown in Almost Every Walk of Life But Nowhere More Thoroughly Than Among Retail Lumber Dealers of Ontario

By Thos. Patterson, Hamilton, Ont.

Thomas Patterson, Hamilton, President of O. R. L. D. A.

The year that has passed since the publication of the 1918 Camp Number of the "Canada Lumberman" has been one of those great periods which will come to be known in history as an epoch. The termination of hostilities was one of its first events and from the day of the armistice in Europe dates everything that is constructive for the new era into which we have entered.

For the Ontario Retail Lumber Dealers' Association these months have been alive with interest and pregnant with import. Until the early autumn of 1918 the work of the Association had of necessity been devoted almost entirely to organization. The Association had to make itself known, to secure members and to map out its work during the first few months of its existence. That this work was done to good effect is evidenced by the present healthy state of, the membership, which amounts to 167, and by the interest which the members are taking in the progress of the Association.

There are two things which account for most of the success which the Association has experienced. First, is the necessity for the work it is doing, and second, is the progressiveness and breadth of vision of the men who have so readily devoted their time and thought to its welfare. The benefits of organization are being impressively shown in almost every walk of life to-day, but nowhere more thoroughly than among the retail lumber dealers of Ontario. The dealers realize fully the truth of the statement recently made by the President of the National Federation of Construction Industries of the United States who said:—"Conjecture as to the world's future throws ORGANIZATION into high relief. With vast accumulated stores of knowledge and experience, we are upon the threshold of a new era in which OUR INHERITANCE WILL BE BROUGHT TO FULL FRUITION THROUGH CO-OPERATION."

Some of the chief public events of the past few months, so far as the Ontario Retail Lumber Dealers' Association is concerned, have already been fully reported by the "Canada Lumberman." Our two meetings, the first special general convention in September, 1918, and our first annual meeting in February of this year, are now matters of history, well known to all the trade. Their great success was a matter for pride on the part of those who were instrumental in their carrying out.

The Individual Units Count

The work of the Ontario Retail Lumber Dealers' Association, however, is not a matter solely of big conventions. These are only the periodical, though very necessary, illustrations of the force that lies within such an organization. It is in the effective and daily activity of the Association that its claim to existence lies. No amount of cheering and entertainment at an annual meeting will hold together an Association of this nature. The individual members must feel that the Association is a benefit to them, and in order that this may be the case there must exist among the members a determination to work for the promotion of the general interest of the trade. Happily, this is one of the strong features of the membership of the Association.

There are two broad divisions of work which the Association is carrying on; educative and protective. An educative factor in the work of the Association is that which is afforded by the meetings held by local branches. In Ottawa the members hold meetings nearly every week throughout the year. Toronto members hold meetings frequently. Hamilton has been the centre for meetings of the Western District. London, Sarnia, Windsor, St. Thomas and Chatham dealers have held several meetings. Local branches have been formed at Orangeville and Stratford. A good meeting was held at Georgetown early this year. At all these meetings the programme is a wide one, covering an informal discussion of many matters that are of vital importance to the trade. It is becoming increasingly evident from these meetings that only by such means can the members of the trade lift themselves out of the old rut of selfish individualism and get into the broad road of progressive co-operation, friendly respect and scientific business management, which are essential to success.

Some Big Propositions Weighed

Many matters were discussed at the annual meeting of the Association in February, and made the subjects of motions which outline a large field of work for the members. One of the most important was that which had to do with trade relations between wholesalers and retailers. The appointment of a special committee to deal with this matter was an important step. Conferences have been held between this committee and a similar committee of the wholesalers. While it has not been found practical or possible to draw up anything concrete in the nature of a definition of trade relations, important progress has been made in the direction of establishing greater mutual confidence and respect between the two branches of the trade. It has been amply demonstrated by these conferences that the Wholesale Lumber Dealers' Association, Inc., has the interests of the retail trade closely at heart and that the members of the Wholesale Association are doing all they can to promote the welfare of the retailers, both by campaigning for new members for the retail association and by adopting modern principles of trade ethics.

Trade ethics is a matter which has two sides to it. The retailers, realizing this and that they have a responsibility similar to that of the wholesalers have placed themselves on record in a strong resolution passed at the annual meeting in February which requires the directors to make a thorough investigation into any case in which a member is alleged to have cancelled orders on a falling market.

Among the most gratifying results which the Association has been able to obtain has been in connection with a large number of disputes between retailers and wholesalers or manufacturers about delay in shipment of stock, and sometimes about other matters which were making trouble. In this one direction alone we feel that the Ontario Retail Lumber Dealers' Association has justified its existence. These are invariably matters of a personal nature about which it would not do to make public statements, yet it can be said that in all cases, with only one exception, these difficulties have been overcome, and this one exception is still the subject of negotiations. Outstanding sources of trouble have been eliminated. Friendly relations have been restored. In short, while promoting the interests of our members in this direction it has been found possible to remove many causes of friction which formerly were permitted to remain.

Legislative Matters Requiring Attention

In the field of legislation there is much for the Ontario Retail Lumber Dealers' Association to watch. Several matters of importance have already received attention. The chief of these has had to do with the Mechanics' Lien Act of Ontario. Under the present Act, the retail lumber dealer and other material men, as well as the wage-earners, do not receive the protection to which they are entitled and which it was the intention of the framers of the Act that they should receive. Our Association brought this matter to the attention of the Ontario Government and has induced the Government to appoint a special committee of the Legislature for the purpose of hearing all parties who are interested in the passage of a new Act. It is expected that, upon the report of this committee, the Government will frame a new Act and have it passed at the next session. The Legislative Committee of our Association has devoted a great deal of time to this subject and has prepared its suggestions in definite shape for presentation before the Special Committee of the Legislature. The best possible legal talent has been retained by the Association for this purpose and the proposals which we desire to have laid before the committee will thus be presented in the most effective manner possible.

The Ontario Retail Lumber Dealers' Association may now be said to have amply demonstrated the wisdom of those who established it. It has secured a splendid start. Its membership is thoroughly representative of the best elements of the trade. There is room for considerable increase still in the membership list, and there is an ever-expanding field of usefulness for the Association. In the near future we should see it become the leading trade organization of its

"No Man Can Play Go-it-Alone Policy"

How Need for Closer Co-operation Among Members in Lumber Industry is Being Recognized and Growth of Unity and Mutual Helpfulness Encouraged

By Chas. A. Bowen, Detroit, Mich., Secretary National Retail Lumber Dealers' Association

Charles A. Bowen, Detroit, Mich.

I do not know exactly what I can say to you at this particular time which will be of any value to your readers. It does seem to me, however, that the conditions which have been surrounding the business men of the United States and the Dominion of Canada for the past two or three years have been of such a character that it is particularly emphasized to them in possibly a little clearer way than ever before, the great need for a closer co-operation among the members of the trades. I believe that to-day there is a larger spirit and a greater desire for co-operation on the part of business men with the fellows in their same line of business than there has ever been before, and that this has increased very much even during the past twelve months.

In the United States we notice particularly that the different associations of lumber dealers in the cities, in the states, the various regions and in the National, have grown very materially in membership, thus indicating that the retail lumbermen at least are awakening to the values of co-operation through organization and a co-ordination of interest.

The times are such that business men absolutely cannot play the "go it alone" policy, and the need of advice and association from and with their fellows is being brought home to them very clearly, because otherwise they would be "all at sea" as to what course to pursue in any direction.

The value of the National Association has been emphasized to them by the work which this Association has done of a national character, such as looking after their needs from a government standpoint; working out and securing national legislation to their particular interest; securing for them what business there was to be had from the government during the war period, and seeing that the surplus of material in lumber, etc., was turned back by the government into the proper channels, and not dumped upon the market to be sold at ruinous prices to the industry.

The matter of proper trade relations between manufacturers, wholesalers and dealers and between the dealers in the different localities, has also been of infinite value to them, and all of these things would not have had any bearing from any one district or group, but were brought about by the broad national co-operation represented through this Association.

Better Merchants and Community Leaders

Business generally, in the larger cities of the country, is getting back very nearly to a pre-war basis, although in some sections the high prices of material is still retarding building activities, but this is being gradually overcome.

Detroit probably stands out more clearly in this direction than any other city of the country. The activity of the building interests in this city are even greater than during the pre-war period, and the building permits of this city for the six months of the year 1919 show an increase of over $2,000,000 over the first six months of our banner year, which was 1916, when we had over $52,000,000 worth of buildings.

The public were taken into the confidence of the supply dealers, contractors, architects, bankers and others, through a general meeting early in the year, when it was clearly pointed out to all interests concerned, that what was considered high prices was not out of proportion; that there would be no lower prices for reasons which were definitely pointed out, and that if anything, prices would go up rather than down, and convincing arguments were presented from all sources to show that these statements were absolutely reliable. The result was, building has gone forward very rapidly, and had this course been pursued by those in the other cities, as recommended by our National Association, we believe it would have had the same effect, and [illegible]ing of all character would have been enhanced.

This in itself, we believe, shows that the tendency of the lumber industry is to be better merchants; to take a larger interest in the conditions which surround their localities, and to be leaders in the enterprises wherein they are interested, rather than followers.

Unfortunately the lumber dealers are not yet up to the standard which this Association hopes for them, but it is a condition which cannot be brought about overnight, and we believe that the continued agitation, educational features and other propaganda which is being put out by this Association, will ultimately bring about much better conditions, if not all that is hoped. We predict for the retail lumber business a bright future and good business for many months to come. There must, however, be no spirit of complacency, but one of close concentration and keen observation, together with a spirit of endeavoring to improve conditions individually and generally, if this prosperity comes, which we predict, and if it is to be of any particular advantage to the industry.

The Convention of the National Retail Lumber Dealers' Association of the United States, which will be held in the city of Detroit on September 11 and 12, will be, it is anticipated, one of the [illegible] gatherings of retail dealers, particularly of the larger centers, ever held in the United States, and is to be of a character which is to be a bigger and better helper to the dealers than they have had before. It is to be largely a Congress given up largely to discussions of pertinent matters of paramount interest to the dealers themselves, and discussed by them themselves, and in which some definite action can be taken looking to a future policy in these things before the conference closes.

We will welcome all of the dealers of the United States and Canada who can possibly find time to attend this conference, whether they are members of the Association or not, and take pleasure, through your publication, in extending this invitation to our Canadian friends.

Using Mill Waste for Making Paper

The manufacture of pulp and paper from wood is an industry which has proved itself stable and of increasing magnitude for a number of years. Almost every kind of wood has been proved suitable for the manufacture of some form of paper, but there are considerations affecting the use of each kind which must always be observed. Most of the pulp is made from the wood cut especially for the purpose, but almost any wood can be used, provided that it is reasonably free from dirt, knots, and bark, or that these can be easily removed from it.

Sawdust is an exception to this rule on account that the fibres are cut so short that the pulp produced will not felt properly and the cooking is made considerably more difficult. There are several mills in the United States at present using milllslabs, shavings, and other forms of waste more or less entirely. The advantages of waste wood are, of course, its cheapness and its quantity. There are several disadvantages; it is usually green and full of water, has a large percentage of bark, and comes in irregular shape. Shavings are rather better for the purpose, and, if in sufficient quantity, make very good raw material.

Another point to be taken care of in using waste material such as this is to use the raw material of only one species, or at least species sufficiently alike that they may respond to the same treatment. For instance, on account of the relatively large content of resin in long-leaf pine, it would not do to treat this in the same way as [illegible]. Neither will it be satisfactory to work hard and soft woods together in any one treatment, though any of these can be worked satisfactorily if kept separate. The process to be used will depend chiefly on the raw material at hand, and on the market for any particular variety of pulp, as stated in a circular entitled, "Chemical Methods of Utilizing Wood Wastes," by W. B. Campbell, B.Sc., issued by the Forestry Branch, Department of the Interior.

The manufacture of pulp has been started in various parts of Japan, and it is expected that within a few years home production will be sufficient to meet the demands. About 800,000 tons of pulp were consumed in 1918.

Eliminating Fire Hazards in Woodworking

Some Practical Suggestions Along the Line of Safeguarding the Industry and Installing Appliances That Will Reduce Rates and Insure Safety

By E. D. Hardy, Ottawa, Can.

E. D. Hardy, Ottawa, Ont.

Woodworkers may roughly be divded into two classes: First, those which deal with the raw material, such as saw mills, pulp mills, tie mills and shingle mills; second, those which deal with the products of the log, such as planing mills, carriage factories, organ factories, cabinet factories, and other plants of a more or less similar nature, which are known by different names, according to the kind of article manufactured.

The latter class may be subdivided under the head of planing mills city and country, and factories which specialize in some particular form of woodworking and turn out the finished product.

The construction of woodworkers differs materially, according to the nature of the operation and the particular processes employed.

The saw mill, taken as an example under the first general dealing with the raw material is usually constructed of frame with heavy rigid timbers and a metal or gravel roof. The power house of brick, stone or cement.

Planing mills are frequently constructed of brick, frame, or metal clad, with power house of same construction.

Factories are more often built of brick or cement with a power house of similar material.

All the more modern plants are using cement for foundations, walls, or the completed structure, inasmuch as this material offers greater economy in building and is more easily handled.

For the larger plants steam still furnishes the usual power, although electricity is now being used, particularly for the smaller woodworkers, on account of the economy involved, since by operating each machine under a separate motor, the usual wear and tear on the shafting, as a whole, is eliminated.

Lumber Yards

Among the faults common to lumber yards in connection with mill plants, there is probably no condition of the insurance policy which is more often violated than the clear-space clause. This violation of the clear space is usually due, first, to the ignorance on the part of employees as to the purpose and meaning of the clear space clause; second, to carelessness on the part of the management in allowing temporary piling within the clear space as a matter of convenience, and, third, to the absence of any suitable erection to define the limits of the clear space.

The clear space should properly be measured by an insurance inspector, or one who understands the purpose and conditions of this clause. Permanent "fire limit" signs to designate the confines of the clear space offer a simple, but effective, remedy for many of the existing evils.

The Hazards and Their Character

Primarily, there are two hazards which determine the character of woodworkers, as in fact any property which an insurance policy may cover. First, the normal hazard; second, the physical hazard.

In the case of the larger operations which handle the raw material, aside from the question of financial resources, the hazard is largely determined by the number of years' timber supply on which the life of the operation depends, the accessibility of the plant to the timber limits, the size and quality of the timber and the state of the lumber market.

Financial embarrassment and the necessity for ready cash often create the most serious kind of moral hazard. Therefore, insurance companies do well to avoid risks where, for any reason, there is doubt as to value or productivity.

According to one writer, not only the desire to destroy, but also the lack of a strong desire to preserve, creates moral hazard, so-called, and it is hard to say which condition is the more dangerous. The prospect of a profit from fire or the absence of a financial incentive to preserve a risk, make it impossible for an insurance company to rely upon the exercise of that due care and diligence for its protection which is essential if business is to be transacted at a profit.

Another situation which frequently incurs moral hazard is when the property insured becomes involved in litigation, or when there is a dispute as to ownership.

Any woodworker which may be considered objectionable or a menace to surrounding property may be subject to a moral hazard on account of the ill will of those to whom the property is objectionable, and not infrequently, a discharged employee becomes a dangerous menace.

Physical hazards may be divided into external and internal.

In addition to exposure, the external hazards include lightning, conflagrations, sparks, bon-fires, forest and prairie fires.

Of the external hazards affecting woodworkers which handle the raw material, such as saw mills, forest fires probably offer the greatest menace and are the least controllable.

Arousing of Public Sentiment

The causes of forest fires are numerous, but are usually the result of carelessness. Undoubtedly, the railroads are responsible for by far the largest number, while others may be attributed to careless campers and hunters who leave their fires without properly extinguishing them. The lumbermen themselves have also contributed to the destruction of the forests by leaving their slashings scattered over the ground where they easily become the prey to sparks from logging trains and donkey engines which are now used extensively in logging operations.

Fortunately, public sentiment has at last become aroused to the necessity for action if our forests are to be preserved and steps are now being taken to reduce the annual drain on our natural resources and the attendant waste to property subject to forest exposure.

Fire patrols, lookout towers equipped with telescope and telephone connecting with the merest settlement; laws requiring the right of way on either side of the railroad to be kept free from underbrush and inflammable material; the use of wire screens on locomotives; the greater care which lumbermen are using in burning their slashings, and the severe penalties imposed on the settler who endangers other property by his bush fire are all important means which should be encouraged to reduce the serious effect of these national bonfires.

Notwithstanding these precautions there seems to be no distance from which property is entirely free from such exposure.

In the larger towns and cities we have the exposure from old and dilapidated buildings and the conflagration hazard, the only remedy for which lies in the more rigid enforcement of the present building laws and greater co-operation between the insurer and the assured.

If more attention were paid to the subject of construction, the loss ratio on woodworkers, as well as on other classes of risks, would be appreciably reduced. Instead of consulting insurance experts before deciding on plans and building specifications, the assured usually decides how the plant should be constructed for the convenience of the operation, without considering the question of fire prevention until the matter is forcibly brought to his attention by the insurance companies' rate.

Pay More Attention to Construction

If there could be a better understanding between the insurance companies and property owners so that before erecting a new building the insurance companies could furnish the prospective builder with specifications calculated to reduce the fire hazard to a minimum and insure the lowest rate, a great advance would be made in reducing the present annual waste from preventable fires. While in theory the insurance companies are doing this, there does not seem to be the proper co-operation between the insurer and the assured calculated to produce the best results for both.

Of the most important external hazards, sparks play a very important part in increasing the number of fires affecting woodworkers. Locomotive sparks alone are responsible for a large number of the fires originating about a lumber plant, particularly where they are employed in a lumber yard.

Such steam motors should be equipped with closed ash-pan and outside bonnet spark arrester. Every saw mill plant should be equipped with standard refuse burner and standard spark arrester, unless smoke stack is constructed of brick.

The interior hazards are more numerous and differ according to the operation and the processes employed.

Of the internal hazards peculiar to woodworkers might be mentioned, faulty construction, which allows the shafting to be thrown out of alignment and permits friction of machinery, resulting in heated bearings, which often ignite any adjacent inflammable substances.

Open gas jets, unprotected electric lights, defective wiring, steam pipes passing through or adjoining unprotected wooden surfaces, stoves and forges without metal covering on floor beneath, sparks from emery wheels in contact with oily waste and smoking are a few of the many causes of preventable fires affecting woodworkers.

It is obvious that the best way to combat fires originating from such sources is to eliminate the cause.

Other Hazards which Should be Avoided

There are other hazards peculiar to certain classes of woodworkers on account of the various processes employed. The use of inflammable mixtures for painting or japanning, the improper use of fire heat under kettles and glue pots are all conducive to a fire unless proper care is exercised.

Spontaneous combustion is not uncommon wherever vegetable or animal fiber is handled or stored, especially when these substances become saturated with animal oil or grease.

The more hazardous the process, the greater should be the precaution against fire. In all factories where paints and oils are used, sand is the most effective means of preventing the spread of the fluid, and a hand extinguisher is usually sufficient to exterminate an incipient blaze.

The fine dust which accumulates on the interior walls and rafters of any building in which the process of woodworking is carried on, constitutes another serious hazard, inasmuch as it is susceptible to the smallest spark and, on account of its prevalence and ignitability, rapidly carries the fire to all parts of the structure, unless confined to a limited area by cut-off walls and automatic fire doors.

The most effective prevention for fire originating from this source is found in the steam cleaner, which is composed of a rubber hose connecting at one end with a valve attached to steam pipe. The other end of the hose is attached to an iron pipe with wooden handle, on the end of which is a flexible nozzle operated by a cord to direct or bend the nozzle in any direction.

This equipment can easily be installed in any woodworker at a small cost and will clean walls, ceilings, bearings, pulleys and machines.

The oil hazard was formerly a source of great danger, especially to saw mills and planing mills; but now, thanks to the more modern appliances, such as ball bearings, self-feeding drip cups and pans for catching the oil and grease which exudes from bearings, this hazard can largely be removed, provided there is the desire on the part of mill owners.

Fires Originating from Dry Kilns

One of the necessary evils in connection with woodworking plants is the dry kiln. The large number of fires resulting from the process of drying lumber and the severe loss to insurance companies has led to a careful investigation of the cause of fires originating in dry kilns and the proper remedy.

"Experience has demonstrated," says a recent writer on this subject, "that half the fires in woodworking shops start in the boiler room, the shavings vault or the dry room; also that steam is the best means of extinguishing fires in such small and confined places. However, as fire employees often forget the steam jet until the next day, automatic sprinklers have been demonstrated to be the most effective means of putting out fires. These facts have led to experiments with automatic steam sprinklers, and their very successful use in a large number of cases shows that they are not only entirely feasible, but the best possible aid in extinguishing fire. Steam has proven its value in boiler houses, shavings vaults and dry kilns, and is the only means of conquering fire in the dry room with small loss."

When all ascertainable hazards have been classified and the causes for fire set forth, so far as we can ascertain them, it is estimated that there yet remains about 16 per cent. of all fires for which the causes cannot be discovered.

Included among these are many incendiary fires, the only safeguards for which are efficient watchman services, fire alarm signals and private fire protection.

Lumber yards and woodworkers enclosed with a high board fence with gates, which are shut and locked at night, will help to keep out tramps and undesirable characters, which are always a menace to any property.

All of the foregoing facts are merely a general index to the subject of physical hazards. With the ever-changing conditions, the different materials used in construction, the hazards arising out of new processes of manufacture, and the modern inventions, it is only natural that, if the insurance companies are to keep pace with the times, the work of investigation and safeguarding of these hazards must be left more and more in the hands of experts.

In addition to technical men, we need a better adaptation by the assured of the knowledge and experience which we, as underwriters, have already acquired. We need not so much new building laws as a better enforcement of the present laws, a greater spirit of co-operation between the insurer and the assured, which can only be brought about by a thorough system of education, by which we will be able to impart to others the knowledge which we have acquired from our study and wide experience, and take from them whatever information will lead to a better understanding of their requirements.

We should encourage a wider use of the means for extinguishing fires, such as automatic sprinkler systems and other devices for fire protection, ever striving to inculcate in the minds of mill owners the old principle, that the best fire protection is prevention, which consists in eliminating, so far as possible, the causes of fire.

Will Paper Shingles Replace Wooden?

Paper shingles are rapidly taking the place of the wooden kind in Worcester, Mass. Architects and contractors as well as agents for the paper variety claim that paper shingles of first quality last as long as first quality cedar shingles. However, paper shingles have not been in use long enough to make this claim absolutely certain and tried out by experience, but the manufacturers solemnly add the weight of their word to the claim.

The best quality of paper shingles cost about 75 cents to $1 per 1,000 more than the best quality wooden shingles. Twenty years of actual endurance is guaranteed for some grades of the paper make. Old houses and barns in and around Worcester have had first quality pine shingles on the roofs now that lasted for fifty and sixty years without a leak.

Paper shingles, felt shingles, and metallic shingles made out of cast off tomato cans are the latest roofing features in Worcester. They are all fireproof and are intended to take the place of wood shingles. Owing to war time conditions the supply of wood shingles became short and manufacturers of the paper and tin can kinds have been doing their utmost to introduce the fireproofing sort. Wooden shingles are in three grades; one is known as the clear; another is called the clear butt, and the best quality is known as the extra clear. The butts have knot holes in the sections that are nailed out of sight.

There are scores of Worcester houses with paper shingled roofs, and they have been shedding rain and snow, some of them for several years, so that paper shingles are not strictly new, but the tomato can kind is new. Tin can shingles are not known under that name; what architect would specify a roof shingled with tomato cans for a client. The tin can shingles are known as metallic shingles; stamped metal roofing and composite metal shingles. It makes no difference whata they call them, they are often tomato cans in a new form.

The Growth of Forest Trees

Investigations carried out by the forestry officers of the Commission of Conservation show how extremely slow is the growth of our forests. It has been ascertained that a balsam with a diameter of 4 inches has taken on an average 55 years to grow. It would be 70 years old when 8 inches in diameter and 80 years when 10 inches. These measurements were taken breast-high.

And the balsam shows rapid growth by comparison with the more valuable spruce, which has but a diameter of 6 inches on attaining its century mark. The 12-inch log of the lumberman is rarely taken from a tree aged less than a couple of centuries. The foregoing measurements apply, however, strictly but to Quebec; in other provinces the growth may be either slower or quicker according to conditions.

Such statistics should cause us to think furiously ere cutting down a tree. The Canadian, like his emblem the beaver, is a tree-felling creature. Instead of invoking a blessing on the man who made two trees grow where there had been but one, he reserves his admiration for the axe that brings the greatest number of tops to the ground during a short winter's day. This was all very well, when men were scarce and trees prodigiously abundant, but men having increased wondrously as mature trees become less numerous, it is high time that we learned to acquire something of the respect in which the European, especially the Frenchman and the German, regards a tree —otherwise our descendants may have to import their timber from those who, while having an inferior stand to start with, yet manage it so well that generation after generation there is a sufficiency for local use, and even a little for export.

How the Timber Limits of Ontario are Held

Evolution in the Methods of Disposing of Licenses—The Various Species of Wood Found in the Province and Their Wide Distribution

Early in the nineteenth century much timber wealth was given away in the form of grants to lumbermen and speculators, although as far back as 1789 the government had reserved the timber and was issuing a form of timber cutting licenses. But no actual cutting fees were collected till 1826. To evade these dues lumbermen bought the land, stripped it of its timber and then let it revert to the government.

In 1841, each province in the Dominion was given control of its own timber. Then the "sales of land" were changed to "licenses to cut." To further increase the revenue, a little later the limits were sold by auction, the purchaser paying this auction price or "bonus" plus the "stumpage dues," as the timber was cut. In 1849, the term license was limited to one year, but these licenses were renewable. Two years later the ground rent system was inaugurated. That is an additional charge per square mile was collected annually.

Thus we have "bonus," "stumpage" and "ground rent" the basis, with modifications, for the method of securing the most of Ontario's timber limits, which are held at the present time.

The regulations of 1869 apply to most of these Ontario berths. The principal clauses of these regulations state:

The berth shall be surveyed at expense of licensee.

The berths shall be offered for sale at auction at an upset price.

License-holders complying with regulations shall be entitled to have licenses renewed.

Transfers shall be subject to approval of Commissioner of Crown Lands.

All licenses shall expire on April 20 and shall be renewed before July 1, when all dues must have been paid.

All licensees must make sworn statements of amount of cut.

A splendid stand of hemlock timber in Simcoe County, Ont.

After 1892, any new licenses issued were for pine only, and did not include hemlock, spruce and hardwoods, as did previous grants.

In 1871, the districts of Muskoka and Parry Sound were put on the market, when 487 square miles were sold at a bonus of $117,672, or an average of $241.60 per mile.

Ground rent was $2 per mile.

Stumpage dues for square timber 2½ cents per cubic foot.

Stumpage dues for saw logs $1.50 per M feet.

One report shows a bonus of $835 per square mile having been paid about 1885. In 1913, ground rent was $5 per mile and stumpage $2 per M feet.

The method of selling by square mile in Ontario has been replaced in late years by the better one of a price per thousand feet. But, as this change does not apply to already issued licenses, its effects are not yet far reaching. A complete history of the Crown timber regulations is given in the report of the Minister of Lands, Forests and Mines in1907 for Ontario. Each province in the Dominion has its own specific governing regulations, governing the sale of crown timber lands.

The Different Types of Forests

Three types of forest may be recognized in the Georgian Bay and North Shore region. The first is the mixed coniferous or ridge type. This is a two-storied forest with the upper story white and red pine, varying all the way from 30 per cent to 85 per cent. white pine and 10 to 35 per cent. red pine. The lower storey is composed of the following species, in varying percentages: white, spruce, balsam, black spruce, birch and poplar.

Toward the north of this type Jack pine, while not numerically prominent, comes in very thickly after fire, whether this occurs before or after logging. Toward the south, around the Parry Sound district, cedar and hemlock, as the two most tolerant species, form a great percentage of the lower story. The upper story is from 90 to 110 feet in height, while the lower is only 30 to 60 feet, with the white spruce somewhat higher wherever it occurs.

This type invariably occupies the poorer sites, the sides and tops of rocky ridges and on the poorer sand soils. Much of the white pine shows butt rot, which extends a long way up and often requires the culling of the butt log. Many experienced sawyers are able to locate the extent of this defect very well and saw a portion off a portion of the butt. This defect, as well as punk knots, seems to be confined to certain localities or exposures.

Estimates give 20 to 25 M board feet per acre as the maximum stand of pine, while the average is variously estimated at from 6 to 10 M board feet per acre, with 12 to 20 logs per M board feet.

The reproduction in this type when fire is kept out is chiefly balsam and spruce, with hemlock in the lower regions. However, when fire occurs Jack pine, poplar and birch come in very thickly.

A modification in this type occurs in places and might be made another type altogether. The upper story is a pure stand of red pine, even-aged and very old. As in the other, the reproduction is chiefly spruce and balsam, with a slight amount of red and white pine.

The Hardwood and Swamp Types

The hardwood types occur on the better soils, such as low ridges and flats. The principal species are maple, yellow and paper birch, poplar, and occasionally red oak and ash in the order named. Only in localities where there is a local demand for such class of material, is this type logged at all. However, as soon as closer utilization indicates an adequate return these species will make up a larger and larger proportion of the cut. Any coniferous young growth in this type is confined to white spruce and balsam, but in much of it the cover is too dence for any reproduction as yet.

The predominating species of swamp types are cedar, black spruce and tamarack. Black ash and yellow birch occur on the drier parts. Around the edges white spruce replaces the tamarack. The total stumpage is very small and forms a very minor part of the cut. In fact, it is only where closer utilization is possible that any material is logged in this type.

Cedar is usually large but very defective and where logged at all is used for poles, posts and ties. But cedar, as well as other swamp species, is more frequently used for road and other construction purposes. The first two types comprise 75 per cent. of the timbered area.

Hordes of Caterpillars Killing Pine Trees

Much Havoc Wrought by the Voracious Pest—Difficult to Fight as the Worms are Aggressive and Scattered on Some Tall Timber in Ontario

Editor, "Canada Lumberman":

There is a pest destroying our pine forests in Ontario—threatening their very exsterice at a number of points in the East and I think it is high time the attention of the provincial and federal government is forcibly called to this menace. The pest must be exterminated before it spreads all through Ontario and beyond and utterly ruins what is left of our Canadian pines.

The evil to which I refer, is a small worm or caterpillar which devours the foliage of the pines, thus killing the trees. By this mail I am sending you a few specimens of this worm in a small bottle and also some pictures showing in a small way some samples of the havoc wrought by these worms.

Last summer a friend wrote the Ontario Provincial authorities about these worms and sent a sample. He received a polite reply acknowledging receipt and endeavoring to name and classify the worm, but so far as we can ascertain no steps whatever have been taken to try and check the development and spread of the pest. Hence this letter to you.

These worms or caterpillars resemble in many respects the well-known "Tent Caterpillar" that is all too familiar a sight on our apple and pear trees, and has created such a terrible destruction in our orchards. These pine tree caterpillars are hatched out in families of a hundred or more. They cling closely together in a compact bunch or mass until the available food supply is exhausted when they separate and seek fresh pastures.

They Are Ravenous Eaters

Their appetite is insatiable. They eat constantly as long as there are any pine needles within reach. They grow very rapidly, and in two or three weeks attain a length of about an inch or a little more, by which time the portion of the tree in which they have been feeding is killed, and they are compelled to start on their travels in search of more pine needles. They do not waste time spinning a web or bulding a dwelling place as the tent caterpillars do. No, their time is wholly devoted to eating. If they would build a web or a "tent" it would be much easier to discover them. We have tried hard for three years now to rid this small island of the pests, but in spite of our almost daily search we find it impossible to get rid of them entirely as some of them are too high up for us to get at; so they can placidly continue their work of destroying the large pines without molestation from us.

We find there are three ways of locating a cluster or family of the worms. First, by actually seeing them; second, by noting their destructive work in the tree, and seeking in the close vicinity for the destroyers; third, by the yellowish green droppings on the ground under where they are working. These green droppings on the ground have betrayed the presence of many a nest of worms when a careful search of the tree had revealed none. For they are difficult at times to locate, as their bodies are of about the same color as the pine needles on which they feed.

They Multiply Very Rapidly

As an instance of the alarming rapidity of their increase, we first noticed them on this (Bear) island in 1917 and destroyed all we could find, probably a dozen or more nests. In 1918, in our last summer's vacation, we destroyed by actual count over one hundred clusters, and hoped that we would find the island reasonably free of them this year, but instead they are worse than ever, and to date we have destroyed 310 clusters or families this summer on this island, which is not more than a quarter of an acre in extent.

Harvey Gunter, provincial fire ranger for this district, says he has seen hundreds of acres of pines absolutely destroyed by these worms. "Harve" may at times be guilty of verbal camouflage, or even of exaggeration, especially when talking of hunting or fishing, having been much in the company of city bred hunters and fishermen and having thus absorbed somewhat of their ways. But in this case, I have no reason whatever to doubt his accuracy, as he has had especially good facilities for observing in his varied roles of fire ranger, game warden, guide, hunter, fisherman and lumberman. Besides, my own observation amply suppports his statement.

The pictures sent you were taken on Bear Island, situated approximately on lots 28 and 29 First Concession of the Township of of Ashby, Frontenac County. While picking huckleberries on this island the worms seemed to be everywhere. They were dropping off the trees they had destroyed on to the ground, on myself and in the berry pail (from which I extracted dozens).

In their search for more pine needles to devour they were crawling over the ground, up the berry bushes and shrubbery, up the poplars, birch or any other tree that came handy. In fact one would have to actually see them and have them crawl over his own person to appreciate their numbers. Bear Island is only one of many such places I have seen this season. Moreover I have noted them m quantities this year on shores where they were entirely absent last year showing that the plague is rapidly spreading.

Ever on the Search for Prey

As we are here for a few weeks only in the summer we have not had opportunity to learn or observe the whole cycle of the life of these caterpillars, but presume they came from a butterfly, moth, or other winged creature, owing to their presence on the islands, and also due to the fact that we are more apt to find them close to the shore, rather than inland in pastures that are new to them. In subsequent seasons they spread inland and destroy all as they go. It would thus appear that they fly across the waters often to find places to lay their eggs where the trees are not already destroyed, but will furnish plenty of food for the young when hatched.

I have no remedy to suggest for this plague of worms. We have highly paid experts for this purpose. It is a difficult proposition. They will be hard to fight, as they are scattered over quite an area, and on some pretty tall trees, but some attempt should be made to check them before they get so bad that the task will be absolutely impossible, and our pines destroyed.

In spite of the tremendous governmental war expenditures, Ottawa has been prevailed upon to make a grant to fight the white pine tree plister in southern Ontario. This summer several returned soldiers, university men, are heading expeditions to fight the blister; also to study its cause and to discover the best means to prevent it. If nothing better can be suggested, some such course could be adopted to fight this pine caterpillar plague, that is, a university man could be sent out with helpers to fight and study and observe and find remedies, same as they are doing for the blister.

The Norway Pine Suffers Most

The pine tree blister, so I have been informed, attacks only one variety of pine, but the worms eat any kind of pine needles, and seem to be more plentiful on the Norway or red pine.

The season for the caterpillars, in which they do their destructive work seems to be from about the last week in June to the middle or end of August. After that they disappear.

This letter has stretched out to a greater length than I had anticipated, but I sincerely hope you will be able to make use of, at least, some of the information given to start a publicity campaign against these pine tree caterpillars before it is too late. Too much time has been lost already through the apparent apathy and inaction of the provincial governmental authorities to whom the mattetr was referred. Somebody should do something to combat this plague.

This district was logged over some years ago, and there is here and there a splendid beginning of second growth pines, some only a foot high, and others several years old. It is these young pines that are suffering the most from these worms, although the older ones are also affected. But when we were too careless or indifferent to plant pines for future generations, to replace those we used, will we not, at least, make an effort to care for and preserve those which the Almighty has planted in His own way?

The specimen worms sent are bottled in coal oil. We have found that either coal oil or gasoline is fatal to the worms, and to make sure of destroying the whole cluster or nest of worms we simply cut off the end of the branch on which they are feeding and dip it in a can of coal oil. This is easier, quicker and safer than attempting to burn them. We sometimes throw the branch with the worms on it into the lake, but they live longer in the water and are apt to drift ashore alive, so have concluded that the coal oil is the most effectual.

Yours, etc.,
"EXTERMINATOR."

McCrae, Frontenac County, Ont.
August 19, 1919.

"Rambling Through the Region of Mystery"

Every Man Who Has Desire to Find Useful and Remunerative Occupation Can Have That Desire Satisfied in Greater Measure To-day Than Ever

By E. H. Newton, Vancouver, B.C.

E. H. Newton, Vancouver, B.C.

With the editor's permission, I would like to persuade you, dear reader, to lay down your work and cast aside your worries and go with me for a ramble.

I know that many of you will feel that you are too busily engaged with pressing obligations to spare the time, but never mind your obligations; come along and let us ramble along the enchanting arrow with blissful ignorance to the trail of mysteries, which is gladden our hearts and teach us the lesson that work is an abhorrent and needless punishment inflicted upon us by some profit-seeking boss, and that there is abundance for us without work, and that the more work we do the less we get. So what's the use of working? Come along.

We will have to travel fast and make few stops, as we have a long way to go, since the trail over which I wish to take you reaches out over the length and breadth of this great country and into other regions, even beyond the seas.

We will not go into those other regions though, because we want to get away from work and forget that there are such words as "trade" and "commerce," and we must also banish all thoughts of such sordid things as capital and profit. We must remember that we have been travelling along the narrow trail of useful citizenship until it has become a rut, and as we are now entering a new era in the world's history, we must broaden out and take notice as we ramble along this other trail and see the vast wealth, and we must realize and understand that we have an inherent right to all this wealth, not by any special effort or merit of our own, but by the natural laws of this paradise into which we have now entered.

How beautiful is the picture before us! Wealth everywhere! In the forests, in the hills, on the vastness of the prairies; down the slopes, in the streams; the ocean and the air. Yes, wealth everywhere, and it all belongs to us. Now, aren't you glad you came? Never knew before that you were so wealthy, did you?

Now, having seen and established our inherent right to all this, if we can only oust capital and keep it away from it, and keep people from making profit out of it, we have an inexhaustible inheritance. And hasn't it been restful to get away from railroads and steamships and industries of all kinds, which represent capital, our great arch-enemy? Capital! Relentless capital! It goes into our forests, and into our hills, and wherever else wealth is to be found, and delves deep and develops it and builds railways and steamships to carry our timber, our mineral, our coal, our oil, our grain and every other kind of wealth away for profit. We must rebel. We must! We must!

The Lost Key

We have now wandered a long way, dear reader, and we have seen wonderful things. But where is the key to the situation? Now I have said something. That is the question that the whole world is puzzled over to-day—where is the key? Millions of people have been hunting for that key for a long time, and many are becoming weary. It has been thought to have been discovered many times, but when it was tried it would not unlock the situation.

I am reminded of a game young folks used to play, called "Find-ing the Key." In that game the searcher was blindfolded. Is it not just possible that we also have some obstruction to our vision, or are following a delusion? Nobody seems able to describe a key that will turn smoothly and swing back the big door, that greater prosperity and contentment may enter.

There never was a time when greater opportunities presented themselves than the present. I believe that every man who has a desire to find a useful and remunerative occupation could have that desire satisfied in greater measure to-day than ever before, if he would endeavor to find his proper place and then "fall in."

Have you found the key yet, reader? If you have, you did not find it where most people are looking for it. It is not there, nor never was.

To develop the resources of the country without capital; to lower the cost of living by raising the cost of production; to do less work and get more for it; to abolish competition to the degradation of efficiency; to crowd into the cities and let the land lie waste; to stir up strife and discontent, and to block the wheels of progress whenever possible are some of the keys that are talked of or tried, but they will not fit.

I am asked the question as to whether present prices of lumber products are likely to be maintained. I answer yes, and they are going still higher, and why not? The trend in everything is upward. Labor is not yet satisfied. It wants shorter hours and more money, and still more. The employer grants it and advances his product to meet the added cost. What else can he do? The same applies in all other lines, and the men who got the advance that caused the other advance turn around and find their extra receipts absorbed by extra expenditures, and who has been benefited? In the lumber business labor is the big item in the cost sheet, and when labor soars, lumber must follow.

New Capital is Timid

Of one thing I am quite sure, all newspaper talk to the contrary—until things become more settled we are not likely to be overburdened with new capital seeking investment. Those firms now having their money invested are doing the only thing they can do. They are making a display of courage and are trying to make the most of conditions.

We talk about profiteering, and sometimes say uncomplimentary things about it, but I want to tell you that the man with capital to invest, if he will put it into any business where he has to employ labor and figure on a close margin of profit, that man is not wise, and should have a guardian.

I am not a capitalist, dear reader, nor do I hold any brief for that or any other class. I believe in playing the game manfully. I know that there are some employers, though they are not in the majority, nor are they representative of their class, whose grasping proclivities lead them to, and keep them at, the border of "just within the law."

I know also, that the employee is not always free from blame, but that he also is too often found just within the law. I have studied both sides of this question for years, and I have found that the man who is ever ready to cry "thief" or "robber" will stand watching. I find people claiming that they cannot exist on the wages they get, and yet these same people can afford to lose thousands of dollars, or perhaps hundreds of thousands, for the sake of demonstration.

Our industry will become normal some day, but when it does, it will not be alone. Just when we will reach the turn I cannot say, but the load is becoming top-heavy, and may topple over, perhaps when least expected. In the meantime there is nothing better to be recommended than peace and harmony between employer and employed. This is a good old world yet, and there are lots of good, honest employers in it. There is also a very large representation of honest labor, and instead of chaos as some might wish you to see, we are going to see a closer relationship and still greater sympathy and tolerance between the better class of labor and the better class of employer, and may God bless every effort in this direction.

Making Progress on Ontario Survey

Roland D. Craig, forest engineer, who has charge of the work of investigating and making a report of the timber wealth of Ontario, under the direction of the Commission of Conservation, is making satisfactory progress with the undertaking. Mr. Craig has secured a list of the timber limits and the owners of them from the Ontario Government and has started to interview leading lumbermen in various centres of the province. He states that he has found them, without exception, most willing to give any information desired. Mr. Craig has two men, Major G. H. Edgecombe and A. V. Gilbert, in the field making reconnaissance surveys of the Madawaska and Petawawa drainage areas. Though this survey is made in a somewhat [illegible] manner, remarkably good material is being secured for the mapping of the various types of forests of Ontario.

Picturesque Camp Life on the St. Maurice

Broad Steam Bears on its Bosom Some 14,000,000 Pieces Annually for the Different Mills—The Care-Free Jobber and How He Operates

By Romeo Morrissette, A.M.E.I.C.

The St. Maurice river is widely known for the log operations carried on in its territory. The area of its drainage basin is approximately fifteen thousand square miles, nearly all subdivided in timber limits, the boundaries of which were fixed in 1851. In 1870 some 250,000 logs were cut yearly and floated to the most important sawmills on the river. These mills were located at Les Grès Falls and at Trois Rivieres. Since then logging operations have increased. The actual quantity of logs cut yearly amounts to some 14,000,000 pieces which are driven to different saw and paper mills along the main stream from La Tuque to Trois-Rivieres, a distance of one hundred miles. The various companies turn out 500,000 tons of wood products annually. The principal going concerns interested in the logging operations over the St. Maurice territory are: Brown Corporation Ltd., La Tuque; Laurentide Company Ltd., Grand'Mere; Belgo-Canadian Pulp and Paper Company Limited, Shawinigan Falls; St. Maurice Paper Company, St. Maurice Lumber Company, Wayagamack Pulp and Paper Company Limited and J. H. Dansereau, Trois-Rivieres.

"Post" owned by the St. Maurice Paper Co., Three Rivers, Que., and situated at La Riviere aux Rats

These firms give employment to many thousand men who live for the great portion of the years in the woods and are employed hewing and log driving. Generally, they are engaged at the headquarters of the company, viz., Trois-Rivieres, Shawinigan Falls, Grand'Mere or La Tuque. They are directed towards a post or a section of logging operations in a certain part of the company's limits. This is done by rail or by boat, in the former case by using the National Transcontinental and in the latter by means of some small boats plying between Grand'Mere and La Tuque on the river which is navigable for a four-foot draught a distance of eighty miles.

At convenient points, in the heart of their respective territory, companies maintain posts, towards which radiate all their traffic. There each company maintains a staff of clerks, who receive reports on the progress of log operations in the sector to which they are attached. These posts are connected with the head office by telephone and telegraph. Generally such posts are located along the river St. Maurice or a railroad and there is also a general store or a kind of warehouse.

From Snowshoes to Patent Medicines

Groceries, snowshoes, boots, blankets, patent medicine, etc., are kept in store. A lumberjack or a jobber is supplied with a small account book in which is charged all the merchandise he may need in the course of his stay in the woods. At the end of the season, his book is checked and the total amount is credited in the company's book and deducted from his pay cheque.

The duty of clerks at the post is to receive orders from the head office and transmit the same to any jobber or camp foreman; to direct log cutters toward their proper field of operation; to forward any information for the proper execution of work and the welfare of the lumberjack.

When men have to wait at a post, there is also a cook and helper attached to the service. Men receive fresh meat, beef and lard. One of the accompanying illustrations shows a post along the St. Maurice river. This one is owned by the St. Maurice Paper Company, is situated at La Riviere aux Rats near Grand Anse and is a small village by itself. Every house has a stone foundation. The post is a frame building well wainscotted with clapboard and painted, and heated by stoves. In these posts clerks have private rooms as well furnished as any apartment in any ordinary country inn.

Log camps are operated in two ways—by the company or by jobbers. When operated by a company, the camp has many buildings, four, five or six and sometimes more than that. Another of the pictures presented gives an idea of an up-to-date log camp. In the back ground, there is the lunch house which is on the right; apart on the left is the stable and on the side are the sleeping houses. Some of these buildings have been built sixty to one hundred feet long by over twenty-five feet wide. They are one and a half-storey high and are provided with good windows. They are round-timber cabins in which the walls and partitions are made of well selected logs carefully laid down.

The Equipment of the Quarters

Granite and tin plates are used for crockery. Cooks wear their white linen aprons and caps when attending to their duty and the clerks in charge of the camp receive instructions from headquarters regarding the supervision of the cook's kitchen and the preparation of meals.

The companies feed men with pea and bean soup, salted lard and beef, corn beef, meat in can, pressed prunes, apples, pies, molasses, sugar, butter, condensed milk, preserves, pickles, home-made bread, etc. The menu for a meal includes: one sort of soup, roast or stewed meat with potatoes, bread, pickles, a dessert, apple or prune pies, preserves, cheese, tea or coffee with condensed milk.

A camp in the dead of winter. The large room on the right is the loggers' bedroom

In the sleeping house, beds are made with fir planks in a box shape with shallow sides. They are fastened to the walls and placed in two rows. The mattress is replaced by a couch of fir branches, and each man is supplied with a pair of grey camp blankets. It is estimated that it costs the companies $1.00 to $1.25 per day to feed each lumberjack. The St. Maurice Lumber Company employs on its own account some 525 men during logging operations and the entire St. Maurice operations require about 4,500 woodsmen.

On the St. Maurice territory, nearly every French-Canadian who owns a farm along the river is a jobber. During the summer he cultivates his farm, but when the harvesting seasoning season is over, and the tree leaves turn a golden shade, then the time is ripe for him to go to the "company" and get his log contract. He takes the work at a unit price. He will hew the tree, cut it in logs and haul to the nearest creek from his shanty.

The jobber hires his own men, three, four, five, sometimes to sixteen. Generally, they are brothers, cousins, or young men who contemplate saving enough to make a first payment in order to secure a patch of land on which to live in old days.

With the falling of the leaves the farmers quit their lands, take with them their wives, their children, their men, their horses—everything which renders their stay in the woods profitable and agreeable. This is advantageous to the company and to the men who are directly interested in their work and no strike can be feared.

Cleaning up after dinner at one of the busy logging camps in the St. Maurice district

The camp is built in the centre of the section granted by the company to the jobber. It is usually erected on the bank of a lake or creek, at a point reached by every trail or footpath. The buildings are the same as are the company's camp, but all live in the same house. There are two rooms, one used by the jobber and his family as a bedroom; the other converted into a kitchen, dining room and living room combined. In the back are located beds for the hired men. The stable is built apart and sometimes is adjacent to the camp.

The jobber enjoys in the camp family life as much as if he was staying on his farm with the difference that he converts the spare time when he could do no work on the farm into money.

The rationing of a family is by means of the section store at the post and is done without any loss of time. There the goods stocked are such that any lumberman's demand can readily be satisfied. For the season 1918-19, in one of its stores the Belgo-Canadian Pulp and Paper Company, Limited, had 450 articles permanently in stock. They are distributed under the headings: Provisions, clothing, mercery, iron mongery, tools, kitchen-utensils, tobacco, pharmacy, stationery, etc. The charges made by the companies are approximately the same as at any ordinary store in the vicinity. At any post there are fresh supplies of meat each week as well as fresh fish, etc.

Here is a table showing the amount of food required to are fresh supplies of meat each week as well as fresh fish, etc. develop the necessary calories to keep a forest inhabitant in good physical shape for one day when he is in the forest.

Potatoes	0.600 lbs.
Fresh and salt pork	0.600 "
Flour	0.400 "
Fresh beef	0.300 "
Beans	0.250 "
Peas	0.150 "
Sugar	0.100 "
Salt	0.060 "
Lard	0.050 "
Onions	0.040 "
Baking powder	0.013 "
Molasses	0.050 gal.

Next in smaller quantity: Rice, tea, raisins, apples, plums, milk, etc.

For the horses, they are fed on the following base:

Oats	22 lbs. per day
Hay	18 lbs. per day.

Hired men work at the job or per piece and some good workers get from $100 to $125 a month.

These jobbers who are generally French-Canadian, are healthy and good humored men and always in a mood to see things on the right side. They are fond of news, talking and stories. The writer, at the opening of the war, had to furnish many explanations on the development and the complications of the trouble in Europe. At that time he was in charge of surveying party. It is not a rare sight to see these men up late at night listening to some educated visitor discussing different themes. There is no theatre, no movie and no church but there are trees, white snow, icy lakes and far away neighbors.

The Joys of the Winter Evenings

These people enjoy their life. They organize dances, music and concerts. They visit among themselves and preserve a kind of social life which might be called woods society. They laugh, play and amuse one another, but when all have departed the whole family kneels on the floor. Then the winds carry on their wings a soft murmur. Far into the back country and in the deepness of the forest, the jobber's family thanks God for His care and protection over them in their daily struggle for bread.

The author of this aticle is indebted to J. M. Dalton, Robert F. Grant, Chas. Lebrun and R. Liagre for much of the data concerning the picturesque camp life on the St. Maurice river.

Publicity That is Worth While

"Money just thrown away," "No good whatever, I tried it once and got no results," "My goods are so well known that no publicity is needed," "Am doing all the trade I can attend to now," "Can't get the stock and have really nothing that I could advertise."

How often does the newspaperman advertising representative or director of publicity hear arguments like these advanced by manufacturers, wholesalers and merchants. One would think that there was no future for expansion, no service to maintain, no good-will to establish and that, by some hocus-pocus means, as soon as an announcement was inserted in the print it should bring magical returns and rich rewards.

One swallow does not make a summer and the effect of well directed, continuous and ably supervised advertising may apparently be slow in securing results, but the outcome is certain and satisfactory—backed up by the goods and the service. It takes time, effort, energy and perseverance nowadays to accomplish anything worth while. Instantaneous effects may be startling and speculative but rarely, if ever, are they permanent and substantial. Someone has said if he were asked to write the recipe for success he would do so in three words, "Repetition, Repetition, Repetition." And that applies very well to the kind of advertising that is successful.. Not repetition of one Ad, but of the arguments and good points you want to establish in the consumer's mind. In advertising it takes time and quantity to produce the full measure of results. It isn't fair to judge advertising as the Indian did the white man's feather bed. He saw the white man using a feather bed so he took a few feathers, put them on a rock and laid down on them. After a few minutes he arose and declared the white man was a "heap big fool."

Player Piano and an Orchestra Next?

"Forks, knives and spoons to be nickel silver" is one of the demands that the Loggers' Union has made on the operators in British Columbia. There is no mention of a player piano, a victrola, an orchestra or finger bowls and cut glass but these will likely be made in due course. The union sent a circular letter to every operator in the province setting forth a few of the things the loggers would like. Among them were the following—minimum wage of $5 per day and an eight-hour day, time and a half for overtime, semi-monthly pay for all camps, contract work piece system and bonus work stop, transportation paid for the worker and in case where the man is not kept long enough to earn $25 the employer pay his wages for the time occupied in travelling back.

And here are a few of the creature comforts the loggers asked—all bunkhouses with six beds not to be less than 18 by 24 feet, beds to be fitted with springs, mattresses, two double blankets, sheets, pillows and pillow slips, sheets to be washed once a week; wash-houses and drying houses and bath houses for each camp with antiseptic soap and towels. And listen to this—earthenware must take the place of enamelware, forks, knives and spoons to be nickel silver, six men only at a table, kitchen utensils to be copper, aluminum or pressed steel, zinc and dish-up table to be lined with zinc.. A reading room to be supplied to every camp and first-aid to be there also.. That's all.

Evolution in Logging Camp Construction

Some Features Which Have Been Carried Out in Sleeping and Eating Quarters— Buildings That May Be Moved From One Location to Another

There was published in the last annual Camp and Supply Number of the "Canada Lumberman" illustrations of the camp car idea, so far as the accommodation and shelter of men are concerned. These camp cars have been used at various points throughout the western States. They consist of dining-room, smoking-room, lavatories, bath-rooms, sleeping-quarters, etc. One of the first concerns to make use of these movable habitations on wheels was the Snoqualmie Falls Lumber Co., Snoqualmie Falls, Wash. The general manager at that time reported that the camp car for long operation in any one spot was very economical and that its equipment was decidedly convenient. It was also stated by him that the quarters are appreciated by the better class of men, "but there is a type in the logging camps of the country who even though they get the chance, are not going to appreciate Paradise. However, we still feel there is enough good left in the personnel of the entire crew to justify giving them econsideration and perhaps some day this element will awaken to the fact that one of the best things they can do is to assist in kicking off the job the class of men who preach discontent and trouble.

"We have two of these camps, known as Camp "A" and Camp "B," each of which consists of twelve ears; most of these cars are 14 feet by 60 feet. There are five bunk cars, thirty men per car, or ten men per room. Two dining cars, a kitchen, a commissary with a reading room in one end, an office and store car, a shop and power car and a car containing shower baths and a drying room."

Lately the "Canada Lumberman" made inquiry from Mr. W. W. Warren, general manager of the company, regarding his experience with this kind of camps, and he reports that there is no change in their logging conditions during the last twelve months. Since the first of the year the Snoqualmie Falls Lumber Company have had no complaint to make about the efficiency of their crews. They closed their camps on June 28th, shutting down six sides and settling up with all the men. They notified them that they would resume operations nine days later, or on July 7th. Mr. Warren asserts that sufficient help was on hand on that date to start four sides and that other men came in, in time to start the two remaining sides on the following morning. He adds, "whether the absence of liquor or the high cost of living away from the camp had anything to do with the men returning so promptly we do not know, but at any rate, they were on the job looking fit and our work is progressing satisfactorily."

Model Camps in the West

Among the most up-to-date and complete camps in Canada are those located at Port Neville, B.C., which are operated by the Vancouver Lumber Co., of Vancouver. The "Canada Lumberman" regrets that it has not been able to secure any photographs of these camps for the present issue, but hopes at a later date to be able to present some illustrations.

With the exception of the cookhouse, all of the buildings are constructed so that they can be picked up and put on the company's logging cars and moved from one location to another. The camp consists of a large cook shanty that will accommodate one hundred men at table without crowding; windows along each side. Tables run crosswise of the room so that it makes this building exceptionally light. For ventilation the roof of this building, as well as of all the other camp buildings, has a lantern or cupola the whole length of it on the same principle as a passenger coach. The kitchen is in the same building partitioned off from the main dining room, the ventilation of which keeps the room entirely free from the smoke and odor of the kitchen. The exceptional lighting given to this room by many windows makes a very cheerful and satisfactory dining-room. Right opposite and across the track from the cookhouse is the store and office building.

On the same side of the track as the cookhouse there are five sleeping shanties for the men. Each shanty contains eight double-deck iron beds with springs and mattresses. Each shanty will accommodate sixteen men without crowding and the beds are placed so that each man has a window at the head of his bed. In addition to these windows, as before stated, the shanty is furnished with the cupola the whole length of it the same as a passenger coach.

Across the track from these sleeping shanties there is a reading room for the men, also a wash room, laundry, modern toilets and shower baths. These buildings, with the usual warehouses, complete this camp outfit. Running water is piped to these buildings, and, furthermore, the company expect to heat the camps with steam in the winter.

The camps are simply built out of rough lumber and are not painted, but they have many features of comfort that are not found in any other logging centre.

Do Model Quarters Allay Unrest?

Another Western concern, which has done a good deal in the way of improving its camps from a sanitary and living standpoint, when asked if the work undertaken was appreciated by the men and if the spirit of unrest and dissatisfaction which prevails in many camps manifested itself amid better and more congenial surroundings, states, "We think the men appreciate the comfortable quarters, but as to whether it makes any difference in the length of their stay in our employ we cannot say definitely; it may have this effect eventually but just at present our loggers do not seem to remain in our camps any longer than do those with the other firms which have not such commodious and comfortable quarters."

Several western operators report that, in spite of what has been done for the ease and comfort of the loggers during the past few months, there is just as much "Red" in their camps as ever. Bolshevism flourishes to a certain extent, notwithstanding what may be carried out to satisfy the material needs of "the boys." However, it is thought that most of this talk is a good deal louder than it is sincere, and that the allegiance of some of the loggers to any new propaganda is like the loyalty of certain individuals in a national crisis—rather of an uncertain character and quantity. If the men who are "filled up" with all the doctrines of anarchy, socialism, individualism, etc., do not become too obnoxious or irksome, they are tolerated by the managers of the camps, as frequently such individuals are the very best woodsmen—in fact, far above the average. Their tongue is the worst part of them, and if the men are allowed enough rope in proclaiming this and that view, they generally manage to choke the thing which they would keep alive.

"The general feeling is that there is much more shouting than there is absolute faith in the adherence of some of these men to the cause that they professedly espouse," declares a leading Mountain firm.

Progressive Concern Opens Another Office

The Jeffrey Mfg. Co., of Columbus, Ohio, have opened a branch office in Detroit in the Book Building on Washington between State and Grand Ave. This step has been taken in order that the firm may look after, in a more efficient manner, the requirem of their customers in the Detroit district where the demand for Jeffrey products has been constantly increasing. The office is in charge of O. B. Westcott, who has had a long and successful engineering experience in the sales and engineering construction department of the company and is thoroughly qualified to render every assistance to clients in working out the most economical and practical material-handling equipments for their requirements. Mr. Westcott will give personal attention to inquiries for Jeffrey Portable Loading, Elevating, Conveying, Crushing, Pulverizing, Screening or Tipple Machinery.

An Insect Getting in Deadly Work

In certain sections of New Brunswick the young fir and spruce trees are being killed by an insect which first appeared in the province about four years ago. Lumbermen and guides from several of the interior districts report that there is hardly a green young fir tree standing in the big woods of New Brunswick and that many spruce trees have been almost completely destroyed. Trees, both large and small, are being rotted so as to be rendered almost unfit for profitable manufacture after they have been felled by the lumbermen.

The insect responsible for this damage is said to be still prevalent in some sections of the woods. It is a small white millar which lays an egg in the soft buds in the spring and from which a web is formed over the tender parts of the bowl and kill its growth. As yet it has not been found possible to successfully combat this trouble.

Will Promote Use of Home Grown Lumber

Representative Gathering in Great Britain Believes Supplies From Abroad are Limited and Some Steps Must Be Taken to Supplement Them

Great Britain is now giving serious consideration to the cultivation of home grown timber. Conferences on how to promote its use are being held. These gatherings are indicative of the spirit now actuating the home-grown timber merchant.

L. M. Ellis, formerly assistant superintendent of the Forestry Branch of the Canadian Pacific Railway at Calgary, but now Forestry Officer with the Board of Agriculture for Scotland, and headquarters in Edinburgh, states, in a letter to the "Canada Lumberman," that the trade is gradually getting together and working in co-operation with the consumers.

Mr. Ellis adds that he recently attended a conference promoted by the Timber Supply Department of the Board of Trade, Glasgow. A representative committee was appointed to further the objects desired, and among the subjects discussed were grading, seasoning, and how to secure the more general use of home grown timber.

Mr. Ellis observes that he was delighted with the earnestness and enthusiasm displayed in promoting the home-grown industry.

The Assistant Controller of Timber Supplies for Scotland, Sir John Stirling Maxwell, Bart., who presided at the gathering, made a comprehensive and instructive address which will be read with particular interest at the present juncture. Sir John remarked that he thought it was perhaps as representative a gathering as ever had assembled in Scotland to consider the question of home-grown timber. Besides a large representation of timber merchants, they had also representatives of architects, surveyors, the railway companies, the Office of Works, the Ministry of Health, the Department of Building Materials, the Interim Forest Authority, and other bodies interested in the subject.

Although it appeared that the government in future was going to take a very large part in the planting of woods, he hoped in this country the example of France would be followed, and that these woods would be exploited by the timber trade. Nothing in his experience in the Timber Supply Department led him to think that the government would be the best agent for the manufacture of timber.

Dwindling Foreign Supplies

The whole question they were considering ultimately depended upon how far home-grown timber really was required. Various views had been expressed on the question of our national supplies, but the government appeared to have taken the view at last that our supplies from abroad were precarious, and that some steps must be taken to supplement them at home.

The whole question of home-grown timber was apt to be prejudiced by very loose statements made from time to time as to the supplies of timber which the world possessed. The United States, with a very large area of woods, had been for many years in great anxiety about its timber supplies. The woods of the United States, vast as they seemed, were not large enough now for their own requirements, and the actual cutting of the wood was reckoned to be three times the annual growth, and the destruction by fire had also to be considered. They could therefore write off the United States as a source of supply. In Canada things had not got to the same point, but they must come to that point. The supplies of Russia, from which this country up to the time of the war was drawing half its whole supply of imported timber, were after all not much more than the United States and Canada added together. The point was that it took 75 years to prepare against a timber famine, and therefore anything that had to be done had to be done in good time. The whole subject was so often prejudiced by a belief, utterly unfounded, as he thought, that if we could get imports we could get all the timber we required. That, he believed, was not the case, and he believed the Russian Bolshevik had in his hands, if he liked to use it, an extraordinary weapon against the rest of the world by withholding the supplies of timber. Coming to the position of home-grown timber, he contended that the best timber we grew had never had a fair chance in our market. It had been treated as the refuse of the market. There had been the prejudice of the buyer and the want of organization among the producers, and they had to put these things right. The war had not put them right, although it had led to the use of an immense amount of home-grown timber. In some way it had emphasized the difficulties of the situation.

But he thought they had got a great opportunity during the next few years. Supplies of timber from the Baltic and elsewhere had been coming in, but not in very large quantities, and freights were certain to be very expensive for some time. There would also be great competition for coniferous timber from other countries. Therefore, he felt that those who were going to be users of timber, and especially the government departments who had to use large quantities, would not only be justified but really were bound to ensure themselves against shortage of supplies from abroad. They were in a position when they could and ought to make contracts on a large scale covering a period of years until things returned to the normal. Home-grown timber would never have its proper place in the market until it was properly graded and until it was sold seasoned. Of course that entailed considerable expense, and arrangements ought to be made between the trade and the users which would bridge over these difficulties and put the home timber trade in its proper place. This could not be done without a fairly close alliance between the home-grown timber trade and the importing merchants, who had the mills and machinery which were required for putting the timber in order for building and other purposes. An alliance of that kind might be very much to the advantage of both parties.

Hon. Jules Allard Has Retired

Hon. Jules Allard, Quebec, P. Q.

Honorable Jules Allard, Minister of Lands and Forests in the Province of Quebec since 1909, has resigned and has been succeeded by Hon, Honore Mercier, Minister of Colonization, Mines and Fisheries. The retirement of Mr. Allard will be generally regretted as he has many friends among the lumbermen and pulpwood operators of the province. His administration has always been aggressive and energetic and his desire to conserve the natural resources of the province has ever been to the forefront. Quebec has possibly the most advanced and enlightened policy of any of the provinces so far as the preservation of its wooded wealth is concerned and no man has done more toward achieving this object than Mr. Allard. He has been a good friend to all those who have wanted to see Quebec enjoy its rightful and natural heritage and save its resources from the hand of the profiteer, the spoiler and the devastator.

Mr. Allard was first elected for Yamaska in 1897 and also at the two subsequent provincial elections. He was called to the Legislative Council in 1905 and appointed Minister of Colonization and Public Works. In 1907 he was made Minister of Agriculture and in 1909 Minister of Lands and Forests. He resigned his seat in the Legislative Coucil in 1910 and was elected to the Legislative Assembly for the county of Drummond but was called back to the Legislative Council a few years ago.

The Industrial Value of Maple

Maple is the most important hardwood used by Ontario's wood-using industries, over three-quarters of a billion feet board measure being used every year. Accidental forms with the grain curled and contorted, known as curly maple and bird's-eye maple, are common and are highly prized for decorative work. Maple does not grow in any quantity north of the 49th parallel of latitude in Ontario. The material is used in twenty-eight industries. The greatest quantities are used for hardwood flooring, furniture, and wood distillation, as stated in a bulletin issued by the Forestry Branch, Department of the Interior.

Shantymen's Christian Association Expands

Work is Now Carried On Among the Logging Camps in B.C.—What the Organization Has Done in Allaying Unrest and Discontent Among the Men

By William Henderson, Toronto

Wm. Henderson, Toronto, Supt. Shantymen's Christian Association

As we were travelling home from the West a few weeks ago our train stopped at a station in Northern Ontario and a number of river drivers came aboard. Thinking that we might have some friends among them we walked through the smoker to find out.

As we looked them over and noticed the good clothes they were wearing, with light shirts and white collars, we recalled how different things were thirteen years ago.

Then, in place of these quiet, self-respecting, well-dressed men, the river drivers boarding the train were a reckless, noisy, roughly-dressed lot whom the quieter passengers wanted to avoid. At the first opportunity flasks of whiskey would have been secured and drunkenness and disorder would have been the rule on the whole journey.

As we thought of this contrast we felt that the interest we had taken in these men thirteen years ago had not been a vainly directed effort.

It is not merely in the drinking habits that the Ontario lumberjack has improved, but the religious work done among them by both Roman Catholic priests and Protestant missionaries, has kept them from being swept off their feet into the Bolshevist teachings prevailing elsewhere.

One Sunday morning in January we were sitting in a lumber camp in the far north when a Russian came into the office. After a few minutes' talk with him we asked "What do you think about the Bolsheviks?"

His answer was short but emphatic. "Damn fools."

"But," we continued, "there seems to be lots of them in Russia, how do you account for that?"

"All damn fools," again was the reply; then he added, "Lots of Bolshevik in this country. Government should take every man who talks this way and send him back to Russia."

These Bolsheviks in Ontario are to be found in the mines and on the railways, where seven days' work a week, or other conditions, make it hard for the missionary to reach them. It is high time those responsible for such industries awakened to the fact that it is poor business to treat a man as an animal who has no soul, as he soon gets to think that way himself, and casting aside all moral restraints will utilize the force of numbers to try and destroy all employers of labor.

The type of employer like one who said to the writer years ago "These men are like a lot of cattle, and the more like cattle you treat them the better results you get," is sadly lacking in discerning the signs of the times, and is largely responsible for the growing class hatred being shown by these men.

More up-to-date and businesslike was the recent action of the Northern Wisconsin Loggers' Association, who asked the Shantymen's Christian Association to send missionaries to their camps, and assessed their members a certain rate to help defray expenses.

All Changes for the Better

While the regular camp buildings and conditions in Ontario have changed but little, yet every change has been for the better in these thirteen years.

For example, breakfast during the sleigh haul at four, or sometimes three in the morning is a thing of the past, and five or five-thirty is considered now early enough.

The large log sleep camps are still the favorites in Ontario, and best adapted for the cold winters, but iron bedsteads, with spring mattresses are becoming quite common in place of the hard wooden bunks. In other parts of the continent the men have had all kinds of improvements, and by way of contrast, we may mention sleeping on a miserable bed in a poor little office of a camp in Michigan, where in the men's sleeping camp there were spring beds with white sheets and pillow slips.

However, it is on the west coast, in the British Columbia camps that the men's comfort has been mostly considered. Here is one camp that we spent a night in which is a good specimen of many others. On one side of the logging railway running through the camp were the cookery and bunk houses. Each bunk house had accommodation for ten or twelve men. The beds were double decker single iron beds, and so arranged that every man had a window at the head so that he could lie and read if he chose. A ventilator ran the whole length of each roof.

On the other side of the track was the office and a wash room with running water for the basins, and lavatories and shower baths. There was also a large reading room. In addition to the usual good food provided in every camp we noticed [illegible] with [illegible], also oranges that the men took as they left the table.

In common with other loggers the men only worked eight hours a day and all the heavy lifting was done by the donkey engines, and wages $90.00 a month and up. Surely here there ought to be found contented men. In the first place we noticed that the reading room was crowded with gamblers who absolutely refused to listen while we tried to speak. Then in the second place, after we had spoken in the open air and made every one hear whether they would or no, and went round the bunk houses offering our little books, we were abused by the usual Bolsheviks, for not assisting the laboring man to get his "rights."

Admitted Things Were Not So Bad

When we turned on one of these men and told him it beat us to know how much better they could have things than they were right there, he grudgingly admitted that they were not too bad.

It was quite expected that the loggers' union, which is under Bolshevik leadership, would strike for a six-hour day, and the employers had decided simply to shut down their works till they were ready to return to work for ten hours. The nonsuccess of the Winnipeg strike, and arrest of the leaders, discouraged this move, so the members have gone on working.

We now have eight splendid missionaries at work among the logging camps in British Columbia. Two of them are well-known in Toronto, viz., Rev. Oswald J. Smith and Dr. E. Ralph Hooper.

Our experience is that the preaching of the old fashioned fundamentals of Christianity does more to restore men to right mind than any amount of arguments, as nearly all received some such teaching in their boyhood. In the present condition of unrest all over the country we are firmly convinced that one good missionary makes more for the safety of the country than a regiment of soldiers.

Should any of the lumbermen in Canada desire to follow the good example of those in Wisconsin, our Treasurer's address is R. D. Richardson, 103 St. Clair Avenue, Toronto.

Great Growth of Pulpwood Disclosed

Cruising in airplanes over Labrador disclosed great timber lands from which millions of cords of pulp wood could be cut and rolled to streams for direct shipment, so members of a Boston expedition, which spent the past month there report. The expedition was forced to halt on its return when the steamer Granville struck an iceberg and experienced boiler trouble in the Gulf of St. Lawrence.

The expedition, which included in its equipment three airplanes and comprised a personnel of twenty persons, among them five aviators, operated seventy miles north of Battle Harbor. Two million acres of timber lands was explored by air and by the ordinary methods of timber cruising. Pictures taken from the air, numbering 13,000 were said to show dense growths of pulp material in such manner that the most available places could be located readily. The use of the airplane was looked upon as opening a new field for commercial aviation.

The plans cruised inland for more than 100 miles, flying at heights of 2,000 to 9,000 feet.

Eastern Lumbermen Call For More Vessels

The Future of the Dominion Depends Upon the Facilities With Which Forest Products Can be Marketed Abroad—Merchant Marine Must Expand

By Elihu Woodworth, Parrsboro, N.S.

The effects of the peace negotiations upon Canadian business conditions have been disappointing. When the armistice was signed it was believed by many that important changes in the business situation would take place immediately, but the results thus far have been very different from what was anticipated. Unfortunately, the anticipated effects of the peace negotiations led to a number of changes in business plans which succeeding events have failed to justify. This is particularly true of the wooden shipbuilding industry in Nova Scotia, which reached its greatest development during the last year of the war and which appeared to be capable of still greater expansion. The industry began in a small way with but few engaged in it, but as the war went on more shipyards were opened and larger vessels were built every year.

During the latter part of last year plans were made for building many vessels of increased tonnage as compared with those that had been turned off in preceding years, and the numbers seemed likely to be at least quite as large as ever before. Then the armistice was signed, and many builders reconsidered the plans they had formed. They believed that, with the war ended, the prevailing freight rates would be reduced immediately, and that consequently the abnormally high price of shipping would speedily decline. They held that with these reductions in prospect and likely to occur at any moment, it would be impossible, considering the almost prohibitory cost of materials and the exorbitant rate of wages, to build vessels that could be profitably sold or successfully operated.

As a consequence, some of the builders who had planned to put on larger vessels than before, changed their plans in favor of vessels of smaller dimensions, while a few others decided to stop building altogether for a time. Those who had vessels in course of construction rushed them to completion with as little delay as possible, and some of them were probably somewhat surprised to find they had no difficulty in making profitable sales, even before the vessels were ready for sea. Those who had built for their own use and refused to sell found it easy to secure profitable charters. Up to the present the demand has been much greater than the supply, and the indications are that the scarcity of bottoms will continue indefinitely.

Ships Called Upon to Carry Food

The close of the war released a large fleet of merchant ships which had been commandeered by the British Government, and it was natural to suppose the return of so many ships to peaceful avocations would speedily result in a large reduction in freight rates. But sufficient allowance was not made for the obvious fact that the armies from overseas would have to be sent home—a task that of itself would give employment to the big steamers for many months. It was generally known that vast quantities of lumber and other materials would be required in Europe for reconstruction purposes, and it was thought that the return of peace would furnish all the carriers needed at largely reduced rates, but it was not generally realized that food was more urgently needed than anything else in the war-ravaged lands and that practically all suitable ships were required to carry food to the starving millions.

Lumber was much needed in England and prices ruled high, while in Nova Scotia and New Brunswick there were large stocks on hand, but the matter of transportation was a difficult problem. Tramp steamers, which before the war were glad to accept deal charters : prices which seem ridiculous when compared with current rates, were not to be had at the present exorbitant figures. Wooden square-rigged vessels had practically disappeared from the seas, and there was nothing left to carry lumber but the staunch three-masted schooners, with an occasional four-master, which had been turned off during the shipbuilding revival. When it was proposed to utilize the schooners as deal carriers it was objected by some authorities that their rig rendered them unsuitable for ocean traffic, and that only square-riggers were fitted to go "off shore." However, the experiment was made, with such schooners as were then in commission, and the result proved highly satisfactory.

The largest schooners available at the time registered less than four hundred tons and the majority fell below the three-hundred-ton mark, but they made speedy voyages and easy money for their owners and, for a considerable period, escaped the ravages of the U-boats. When the shipment of deals to the United Kingdom was resumed this year very few steamers were to be had on any terms, but a fleet of schooners was available, and others that were yet unlaunched would soon be ready. The new schooners made a fine fleet of well-built, well-modelled, thoroughly up-to-date vessels, and most of them would average about twice the tonnage of the vessels they succeeded or replaced. The new schooners are not only supplying the urgent demand for lumber carriers, but they are establishing many new records, some of which would have been deemed impossible in the days when only square-riggers sailed the seas. The schooner has been proved beyond peradventure to be the best all-round rig, and it has practically no limitations with regard to size.

Excessive Freight Rates Continue

This province is undoubtedly handicapped at present by the lack of sufficient shipping. One proof of this fact is the continuation of the excessive rates of freight, which some predicted would shrink to pre-war dimensions as soon as the war came to an end. Early this year the freight on deals to the United Kingdom dropped to 300 shillings per standard, and several charters were fixed at that rate, but the price soon began to climb, and in a few weeks it had soared to 350 shillings. Of course, this is somewhat lower than the highest notch reached in war time, but it is, at least, ten times as high as the rate paid a few years before the war. It is evident that the scarcity of bottoms, rather than the high cost of living, is responsible for a considerable part of the advance in freights, and it would also appear that vessel property is a good investment at present. The excellence of the investment is really one cause of the scarcity of vessels in Nova Scotia.

During the last two or three years a number of large schooners were commenced in local shipyards with the intention of supplying the home demand, which was already becoming urgent. But the plans regarding these vessels were seldom carried out, for men from outside were ready, almost at the beginning, to make offers which in most cases proved irresistible. In this way many places—notably Newfoundland—acquired fine fleets of large, well-built schooners which they greatly needed, while the original shareholders received big returns for their investment—in many cases without effort on their part. Under such circumstances it is not surprising that the home fleet failed to grow, and, counting all the losses by shipwreck and German depredations, it is probable that this province had fewer bottoms a year ago than it had before the war.

Unsatisfactory Effect on Lumber Trade

During the present year, however, a great change has been made. Last winter was especially favorable for shipbuilding, and advantage was taken of it to turn off early in the year a number of vessels that were not expected to be launched until later in the season. These schooners and a large number that succeeded them have, almost without exception, been kept at home and have afforded almost the only means available for shipping lumber across the ocean. The scarcity of shipping has a particularly unsatisfying effect upon the lumber trade this season. The prices in the British market are so high that our shippers could afford to pay the excessive freights if they could be sure of getting such vessels as they want at the time when they want them. But this, unfortunately, they are seldom able to do, and more frequently they are compelled to wait for time and tide while the season for marketing their lumber is rapidly passing. In the meantime the Norwegians, who are able to ship much more cheaply, are rushing their lumber to market as quickly as possible, and if it were not for the fact that they too are suffering from a lack of bottoms, they would be able to secure what would practically be a monopoly of the trade.

The resources of Canada may be truthfully said to be unlimited, and it is equally true that the future of the Dominion depends upon the facility with which our products can be marketed. It is obvious that we have not enough vessels for our present needs, and that our merchant marine must be greatly enlarged in order to handle the increased production that must come. The matter has been taken in hand by the Canadian Government, and the Canadian Merchant Marine, Limited, is being rapidly constructed. This fleet consists of forty-five vessels of three types and seven sizes, ranging from 2800 tons to 10,500 tons. Two are of the size first mentioned and two of the largest size, while no less than sixteen will measure 8100 tons each. These ships are being built at Halifax, New Glasgow, Levis, Three Rivers, Montreal, Kingston, Welland, Collingwood, Port Arthur, Prince Rupert, Vancouver and Victoria, and are giving employment to many Canadian workmen. When the ships are named each will have the word "Canadian" prefixed, and will thus advertise the Dominion in every port they visit.

Seven of these steamers are already in commission and have made voyages to the West Indies, South America and across the Atlantic. By the end of this year it is expected that the Canadian Merchant Marine will have twenty ships afloat, aggregating 100,000 tons. It is hoped and believed that before the end of another year the present objective of 300,000 tons will be reached. This fleet will help to take care of the greatly increased production that is expected and of the increased imports that are sure to come, and at the same time will serve as a very necessary complement to our great lines of railways. Meanwhile, our provincial shipyards are as busy as possible turning out an entirely different class of vessel, but one that is very useful in its way, and whenever one is launched it may be taken for granted that no time will be lost in providing it with a cargo for the British market.

Historic Lumber Co. Re-organizes

J. R. McDonald, Peterboro, Ont.

The oldest son of the late Alfred McDonald, lumberman, of Peterboro, Ont., is J. R. McDonald, who for a number of years has taken an active interest in the business and will continue to do so. The estate of Alfred McDonald has now been wound up and the business handed over to his family consisting of Mrs. McDonald and three sons, J. R., A. D. and C. McDonald. The firm will be known in the future as the Alfred McDonald Lumber Co. and its business policy will be along the same modern lines as in the past. The plant consists of a sawmill, shingle mill, planing mill, box factory and sash and door factory. The sawmill is not operating this summer as it was considered advisable last fall, in view of labor conditions, etc., not to go into the bush. The company are, however, putting in several camps this year and will bring out a considerable cut of red pine, white pine, hemlock and cedar. Mr. McDonald reports that Peterboro anticipates a very active building season next year and the winter activities of the firm will be along the line of preparing for the rush in 1920.

Fear Congestion of Canadian Timber

A trade correspondent of a London, Eng., journal, who has been investigating the congestion of the docks in London, cites a high official of the port as saying: "The one danger point is in regard to large timber consignments coming on Government account for housing scheme. A million tons are to come from Canada. If it is shipped in steamers that do not require deep water docks it will not matter so much, but otherwise it will need lighters to move it to places where it will have to be stored, and that will accentuate the shortage of general cargo vessels."

Another authority said: "Much space has been used of late for foodstuffs that was formerly used for timber. If all this timber is brought in ahead of the housing scheme for which it is intended and is not stored elsewhere, there will be a direct effect on the food storage accommodation, and that may easily affect food prices."

May Open Branch in Montreal

Frank F. Fish, secretary and treasurer of the National Hardwood Lumber Association, Chicago, has been on a visit to Montreal and Quebec, with a view of making arrangements for opening a branch of the Association in Montreal. It is proposed to open an office and to appoint an official bonded inspector on the same basis as in Toronto during the past six years. Mr. Fish, who also visited Toronto on his way to Montreal, was successful in securing additional members in Ontario and Quebec. The present membership in Canada numbers 35.

Vision of Great Future of the Coast

By C. S. Battle, Vancouver, B.C.

The Dominion of Canada is supposed to contain about one thousand billion feet of saw timber, of which amount British Columbia is credited with one-half, but I am of the opinion that the estimates made are incorrect. I believe that we have about three hundred and fifty billion feet of saw timber in this province. It sounds a big amount of timber, and at the present rate of cutting would last a long time, but we have hardly got started in the manufacture of lumber in British Columbia.

The eyes of the East and South are turning toward the Pacific Coast, and British Columbia will get more than her share for the reason that most of the timber is close to the salt water, and mills will be built and the lumber shipped to the uttermost parts of the earth. One big factor in the consumption of timber in British Columbia will be pulp mills. We have five pulp mills already in operation, and there is talk of several others being built within the near future.

Varieties of Timber

In the coast district we have fir, cedar, hemlock, balsam, spruce and a limited amount of white pine, cottonwood and maple. Fir, of course, is put to more general use. We have hemlock as a good second, and speaking of hemlock will state that our Coast hemlock is almost as good as fir and cannot be compared with the eastern hemlock, which generally speaking has a bad name. British Columbia has almost the monopoly of cedar timber. You will find very little cedar in California, and while the state of Washington had a very heavy stand of cedar it is disappearing fast and British Columbia will be called upon to furnish shingles and cedar lumber for the greater part of the North American Continent.

While yellow cedar is limited in quantity, at the same time we have more of it than one would imagine. It is the highest priced timber grown in the United States and Canada, and there are several fortunes waiting for some progressive firm or individual, who will study this wood and manufacture and specialize on same.

Market for Standing Timber

There has been very little demand for standing timber for the last five or six years, except for small tracts, handy to log, but with the marked increase in the lumber business and with the prospect of it keeping up for the next five years, the lumbermen are beginning to sit up and take notice.

You will find men of means either in person or by representatives in British Columbia looking over timber conditions. These parties come from Eastern Canada, from the Eastern States, Northern States, Southern States, and even from the Pacific coast states. As stated before, we are on the eve of a rapid advance in standing timber. One or two big deals will start th ball to roll and as we have a down hill grade I predict the timber business will continue to advance for a number of years.

We want Canadians to realize that this great western province is the richest in Canada insofar as its natural resources are concerned, and these resources are waiting for the man of vision with well directed energy and capital. Our neighbors across the line discovered this "promised land" a number of years ago and have invested a great deal of capital. "Now is the accepted time" to purchase timber.

New Plant Will Make Hardwood Lasts

York County, N. B., is to have a new industry, which is one of the first after the war developments by British capital in Eastern Canada. Official announcement has been made that H. Mobbs, of Kettering, England, has finally decided to locate a plant for the manufacture of hardwood lasts on Mullins Brook on the Transcontinental route of the Canadian National Railways.

Extensive lumber privileges have been arranged for by the new company, under an agreement with the Nashwaak Pulp & Paper Company, and it is expected that from three to four million feet of maple lumber will be manufactured annually into last blocks. The company will eventually manufacture furniture in their new plant.

Mr. Mobbs, who is one of the largest manufacturers of last blocks in the world, selected the site for the location of his new mill after investigating the various hardwood sections in New Brunswick. Not only is he satisfied that the hardwood supply on the Upper Nashwaak waters is unsurpassed anywhere, but he has been able to make what he considers a reasonable arrangement with the Nashwaak Pulp & Paper Company. Work of erecting the mill is now under way and it is expected to be in operation before long. It is expected that 200 people will be employed in the plant.

Millmen along the Miramichi River, N. B., have formed a union following a recent walk-out. A meeting of lumber manufacturers was held in the Fraser Company's office in Chatham. As a result the men were given a nine hour day instead of ten and are to receive the same wages as formerly.

The Camp School and What it is Carrying Out

Educational Work Among Lumberjacks Has Been Tried Thoroughly and Found to Measure Up to the Best That was Expected—Policy of the Future

By Raymond C. Dearle, M.A., Ph.D., Eastern Inspector, Frontier College

Alfred Fitzpatrick, Toronto, Supt. Reading Camp Association

Once upon a time men laughed at the idea of night schools. It was visionary, it was impracticable, it was anything under the sun that has been said about every other idea that has been new to the time.

As a matter of fact one does not need to be a deep student of history to know that it required long years of effort to establish the principle that every child is not only entitled to an education but that it is to the interest of the state to insist that every child shall have an education. Having accepted this principle, our various provinces have built up educational systems, more or less imperfect perhaps, but still constantly tending toward improvement, despite their burden of officialdom and red tape. The night school was the logical outcome of the day school. There were bound to be thousands of boys and girls, of young men and young women who must leave school prematurely by reason of circumstances and many of these demanded an opportunity to make use of their spare hours in the improvement of their minds and the furthering of their studies. The private business colleges were among the first to realize the fertility of this field.

Such institutions are necessarily operated from a dollars and cents view, no matter how high their academic standards may be; nevertheless, the fact that the number of these institutions has increased rapidly and is still increasing, offers positive proof, if proof be needed, that supplementary education as represented by the night school is every bit as necessary and justifiable as the primary education of our public schools. The official mind works slowly, to be sure, but in the course of time the need and the opportunity stood revealed to the educational authorities and free night classes became an established principle, at least in the larger centres of population.

The Cause of the Frontier Laborer

Now, what has all this to do with logging camps? Why should I occupy the time of you who read this article with a resume of facts with which you are all pretty well acquainted? Simply because I want to plead with you from an educational point of view the cause of the frontier laborer. Presumably the majority of you who read this can be put in the class labelled "Hard Headed Business Men." You are accustomed to dealing with the frontier laborer as the representative of a class and that class pretty generally assumes to you the aspect of a bugbear. The frontiersman to you is an individual who is always demanding more money, always discontented, always "jumping" just when you need him most, in short, his chief purpose in life seems to be to bring grey hairs to the head of the man who employs him. Still, he is very useful to you when it comes to figuring that very tangible thing called production.

I do not need to quote figures to you—you know, or ought to know, how many million feet of lumber were cut in Canada last year, how much of it was exported and what was its value in dollars and cents. You may know, too, the productive value of the mines of Canada and earning power of the railroads. And yet all this would be impossible without the aid of that class represented by the frontier laborer—the man who swings an axe and pulls a saw in the bush, who delves into the bowels of the earth for our precious ores, and who labors in the rock-cut and tunnels to build our railways.

The Human Side of the Problem

Now I am not a socialist and have no socialistic iron to heat at your fire. I want merely to present to you something of the human aspect of that frontier laborer, to enlist your sympathies for a movement which may tend to bring about a better understanding on both sides. And this is where I come back to the beginning of my story and start afresh on the subject of night schools. It is the question of supplementary education for the men in the camps that I want to discuss with you. If we take for granted that night schools are an excellent thing to have for one portion of our country, is there any logical reason for saying that the other parts should not have them as well? Why should we offer educational facilities to one section of our population and refuse them to another? Why assume that individuals in cities and towns have the desire and ambition to improve themselves intellectually while individuals of identically the same race and nationality in the rural communities and in the backwoods have no such desire or ambition? I will defy any person to produce an argument in favor of such a distinction that will stand the test of logic. Is there anyone who doubts but that the man who spends his days in the forest or mine actually produces more wealth for the state than the young girl operating a typewriter in an office? Has not the former the right then to ask that the state shall spend at least as much money in providing him with educational facilities as it spends in providing such facilities for the latter?

In principle then, we must accept the idea of frontier education; in practice, I will admit, different circumstances must demand different methods. The difference however, is more apparent than real, as anyone may easily ascertain by going into a camp community and living with the men as one of themselves. In all of my various experiences in camp life gathered from a great many different kinds of camps I have always found the men essentially the same as a group of men in the city. If there is any difference as regards moral standards and intellectual capacity I will take my chances with the men in the camp.

Basic Policy Regarding the Foreigner

I know, of course, that someone will object that these arguments are of no use because of the great number of foreigners in the camps. But we have equally large numbers of foreigners in the cities. More than that, we have in such communities special night classes which cater to the foreign element. Why not do the same in the camps? As a matter of fact, the presence of the foreigners in our frontier camps in such large numbers is an argument in favor of camp education, not against it. For it is high time that we should take advantage of the present slackness in foreign immigration to formulate some more definite policy with regard to these people. Sooner or later we must realize, I hope we are realizing it, that we cannot go on filling up our country with men of alien birth unless we attach some definite conditions to the privilege of landing on our shores. A basic principle of these conditions should be compulsory attendance at some sort of night school for the purpose of learning to read and write English and for a fundamental training in Canadian citizenship, its privileges and its obligations. The folly of allowing foreign born men and women to enter our country and build up their own communities which are not nor never will be Canadian in either principle or practice, has been pretty well demonstrated by reason of late events. If we were to lay some sort of obligatory education upon the incoming alien with the penalty of deportation for non-compliance, one of our national problems would be simplified, if not completely solved. Hence another argument in favor of camp education.

Mr. Fitzpatrick Saw the Great Need

For upwards of nineteen years the Reading Camp Association has been carrying on a series of experiments along these lines, working in all the varied forms of frontier camps and over the whole extent of country from Atlantic to Pacific. The idea originated with Mr. Alfred Fitzpatrick, a graduate of Queen's University, who originally fancied himself for the Presbyterian ministry but later saw a crying need among his fellow-men in the camps and proceeded to answer that need to the best of his ability. Through Mr. Fitzpatrick's efforts the Reading Camp Association came into existence supported solely by a sublime faith in his ability to make people see the need and the opportunity as he saw it. In the face of circumstances that were at times almost heartbreaking the work has been financed through public subscriptions.

One by one the various governments, with the exception of Prince Edward Island, have been compelled to take notice of the work that was being done and an annual grant now comes through their educational departments. Even with this semi-official encouragement the bulk of the financial burden is carried only through the generc osity of private individuals. During this last spring it was thought advisable to emphasize the educational aims of the association and to this end a charter was secured under the name of the Frontier College. This name expresses admirably the underlying idea of its founder and present principal. It exists for the sole purpose of carrying education to the frontiersman, be he native-born or foreign. Unless you totally lack for imagination you must be thrilled by the audacity and boldness of such a scheme. What other college has such opportunities before it, such an extensive field from which to draw its students? The only regret is that with the present limited revenue only about sixty or seventy camps can be reached in one year.

Qualifications of the Teaching Staff

Now every well regulated college is provided with a staff of teachers, and the staff of the Frontier College is as unique as is the organization itself. Except under very unusual circumstances only university graduates or undergraduates are chosen and these are hand picked from the different universities of the Dominion. In choosing the instructors, as they are called, emphasis is, of course, laid upon a man's scholastic attainments, but more important still is his moral and physical stamina. The would-be instructor must above all else be filled with an abundance of real grit for his is to be no soft job. It was Mr. Fitzpatrick's idea from the first that if an instructor is to be of any use to his men he must understand their point of view. Consequently he takes his place with them in their daily labors—works with them, eats with them and sleeps with them. Only during the evenings does he become an instructor of the Frontier College, and even then his attitude is not so much that of a master to a pupil but rather of a chap who has struck it lucky, sharing up with his less fortunate fellows. No favors are asked and usually few are granted; occasionally an instructor does office work but not ordinarily. Sometimes the hard going proves too much for the young chap and he quits but on the whole it can be said that no finer body of young men could be gathered together anywhere than those who have made up the active teaching staff of the Frontier College.

Now that the organization has received formal incorporation greater stress than ever will be laid upon the educational side of the work. It will still be the policy of the Frontier College to provide daily newspapers and attractive reading material in the way of books and magazines. Also, during this summer an attempt has been made in some camps to provide athletic features, and this might be extended in some measures to the winter camps. However, that is not the main purpose for which the instructors are sent into the bush. These attractions may be used to draw the men but the evening classes are more than ever the strongest feature of reading camp work. Every instructor now signs an agreement to teach a minimum of ten hours a week which averages two hours a night for five nights. Saturday night is usually reserved for something special in the way of concert or entertainment, if possible Sunday is set apart for reading and writing letters, accommodation for the latter being provided in the reading room.

Co-operation and Support of Lumbermen

Naturally, the success or failure of any camp school must depend upon several factors, as for instance, the character of the men employed in the camp and the calibre of the instructor. But very important also is the need for co-operation on the part of the foreman or superintendent, and his attitude is generally a mere reflection of the views of his employer. Consequently my appeal is to the employers to lend their assistance and moral support wherever they come in contact with this work. And surely, of all men, the lumbermen of Canada have the very best opportunity to show their good-will, for in no other class of camps is the opportunity as great. Through the depths of the winter there is no possibility of long hours of overtime such as we meet with in the railroad camps; here the evenings are free, even if the men do retire very early. Then too the woodman as a rule comes of a sturdy stock with intelligence something above that of the average laborer, so that if camp education is to be a success anywhere it has its best chance in the lumber camps. Most employers are now quite willing to open their doors to this work but some opposition is still encountered. It is worth noting however, that some who were most sceptical at first are now among the most enthusiastic backers of camp education. But as I stated above, the field is too big to be covered with a limited income and direct government action is longed for. Camp education is not an experiment; it has been tried thoroughly and found to measure up fully to the best that was said of it. There is only one thing lacking and that is that there is not enough of it.

The Clark Picnic Was a Hummer

The annual picnic of A. R. Clarke & Co., of Toronto, who are extensive manufacturers of lumbermen's clothing and have built up a business from Coast to Coast in this line producing everything from moccasins to mackinaws, was held recently to Wabasso Park, Hamilton. The day was proclaimed a general holiday for everyone in the large establishment and all employees were given full pay and provided with free transportation and an excellent lunch on the grounds. In the case of married folks tickets for the ladies and children up to 12 years of age were presented. There was not a dull moment during the whole of the proceedings and the 29 sporting events were keenly contested. The trip from Toronto to the park and return was made on the "Corona." Mr. Griffith B. Clarke, president of the company, who is an enthusiastic motor boat devotee, treated the passengers to some thrills. He circled around the large steamer with the result that the people rushed from one side to the other in order to get a passing glance at the "Leopard." The 20th Bat. band furnished delightful music during the afternoon and the associations of the day will long be remembered for the brightness, pleasure and friendly spirit that prevailed. Mr. Griffith B. Clarke is exceptionally popular with all the employees and the result is that every man and woman in the establishment works with the company rather than for it.

The judges of the different events during the day were: J. Ross, sales manager, glove and clothing departments; J. Andrews, foreman of japan department (who had a great day seeing his boys clean up most of the prizes); R. Watson, glove leather dept., and H. Symonds, glove dept. The Main Committee, who worked hard to make this picnic a big success, was as follows: Chairman, Griffith B. Clarke, president of the company; J. G. Hoult, supt. of factory; C. A. Upper, accountant; H. A. Sailer, sales manager, patent leather dept.; Alf Collins, secretary.

The many friends of Mr. Clarke will extend congratulations on his recent marriage which took place at St. Mark's Rectory, Niagara-on-the-lake, his bride being Miss Kathleen Smith, only daughter of Mr. and Mrs. J. Norman Smith, of Montreal. Mr. and Mrs. Clarke left for a motor boat trip and since their return have taken up their residence in Toronto.

The magnificent harbor of St. John, N.B., recently visited by the Prince of Wales

Some fine Nova Scotia timber being hauled to the mill

"Necessity and Importance of The Retailer"

E. M. Trowern, Secretary of Dominion Board, R.M.A., Ottawa, Outlines Work and Worth of Merchants in Great Economic Plan of Sales and Distribution

Although the question of the increased cost of merchandise and the cost of distribution at retail may not be considered by your committee to properly come under the public enquiry that has been allotted to you to report upon, yet we feel that it is so closely related to the subject you have under consideration that we are taking the liberty of presenting to you a few facts on the subject of retail distribution as we see them, standing, as we do, between the producer, the manufacturer and the workman on the one hand, and the consumer on the other. So much has been said about the conditions of the producer and the manufacturer, and what is termed, for the sake of a better classification, the "working classes," and so little has been said about what is known as the distributing classes, that the whole subject has become confused and misunderstood.

It is not generally known that there are many more millions of dollars invested in distribution than there are in either manufacture or production. It could not be but otherwise; merchandise must always be manufactured ahead of the immediate demand. Goods produced or manufactured in Vancouver are of no value to people residing in Halifax unless they are transported to the latter point. To do this, it requires negotiation, purchase, transportation, warehouse facilities, retail facilities, etc., and final delivery to the ultimate purchaser in single items. A host of transactions take place before the goods are finally delivered. All these separate transactions cost money, and take time and intelligence, in addition to "capital," which cannot be regarded in any other light than "accumulated industry."

We are quite aware that arguments have been put forth for centuries, striving to discover some plan whereby goods produced or manufactured can be handed direct to the consumer, and to have the middleman—which means either the wholesaler or the retailer—removed. All efforts in this direction have been failures, and they always will be failures, because the present system has been a natural development that has grown out of actual necessity.

Value of Retails to the Community

The value of the land and buildings upon which retail stores are situated, together with the value of the wholesale properties, exceeds in value, and is more highly assessed than any other property in any municipality. Add the value of all the retail property in Canada together, couple with it the value of the stocks which are held waiting, ready and near at hand for the convenience of those who want the goods, and then add the value of all the wholesale property and merchandise to the retail property, and you have a volume of wealth that far exceeds the value of all our farming and manufacturing industries. This costly and expensive system exists because it is required and because there is no other legitimate system that can take the place of it. It has been found to be the most economic, convenient and elastic system that can be provided, and it has developed through necessity and experience. There is no practical proposal or scheme in sight that can take the place of our present system of distribution. It requires adjusting here and trimming there, but the underlying principles cannot be abolished. We are anxious to go on and develop it and make it more complete and convenient. This can only be attempted by those who practically understand the principles which guide and direct it. No improvement can come from any other source.

All attempts that have been made by those who operate "Co-operative Soieties" in any part of the world have proved to be nothing more than the old scheme of one merchant endeavoring to outwit his competitor by trying to tell the public that his goods and his system are far superior to those of his neighbor, whereas the so-called Co-operative Society system is clumsy in its operations, inferior in its service, and its method of handing back so-called dividends or bribes to its customers has all the deceptive elements of the trading stamp scheme.

The Disadvantages of Certain Methods

To those who are not acquainted with the problem of retail merchandisinz, and from the manner in which some of these Co-operative societies advertise themselves, and their supposed superior methods, it is not surprising that those who are unfamiliar with the "tricks of trade" see some virtue in their proposals, but those who are anxious to have all trade transactions based upon a sound, healthy, moral basis, know full well that any system of merchandising that is based upon the placing of a higher price on any article to a customer, and then handing the increased price back as a bonus or a dividend or a bribe to secure and hold the trade, by or through any pretext whatsoever, is wrong in principle and commercially unsound. It is for this reason that reputable and honorable retail merchants will have nothing to do with business methods of that character.

If the claims put forth by these so-called Co-operative Societies were true, and the principles upon which they are founded were correct, every one conducting a retail store would adopt the same system, but the co-operative system is not adopted because the principles upon which they are founded are commercially unsound, and their methods can never appeal to those retail merchants who want to see the retail trade of Canada placed upon a higher plane.

Believing, therefore, that we, as retail distributors, are an absolute necessity, and that our services cannot be dispensed with, we feel that we have an important duty to perform in every community throughout Canada, and we further believe that owing to our financial position, our absolute necessity, and our numerical strength in every city and town and village throughout Canada, that no question affecting what is termed the "working classes" or the "manufacturers" or "producers" can be intelligently considered without taking the great problem of distribution into consideration as well.

Their Place and Service Outlined

Retail merchants stand in a very unique position in every community. They reach out and take the goods from the producer and manufacturer and hand them to the consumer. Every increase that is made to an article, whether it is through increased wages, the increased cost of raw materials, increased transportation, increased rent or the increased overhead expenses of every class through whose hands any product passes, is collected again by the retail merchant from the consumer. The higher wages go, the higher will go the prices of the articles created by the wage earners. The circle is complete and no system of reasoning can alter this truth. The law of supply and demand is the basic law upon which everything is founded. The dearer goods are the less profit the retail merchant makes, as the demand is lessened, and his business turnover is, therefore, less.

In order that workmen may be able to purchase all those things that are necessary for their actual comfort, they must receive a salary more than equal to the value of the actual things required so as to enable them to lay aside sufficient for old age, etc. If wages keep climbing up, merchandise will go on climbing up, and there is no scheme that can be proposed that will prevent it. If wages climb higher on one class of goods than they do on others, the workmen will be limited to fewer classes of goods and their comfort will be affected thereby. If, for instance, a working man received twenty-five dollars a week, and with that sum he could pay his rent, buy groceries, meat, fuel, light, clothing, boots and other actual necessities, and his rent was doubled, he would be compelled to forego purchasing some of the other articles of necessity, and, having to do without these necessities, he would immediately become discontented. On the other hand, whatever necessities he economized on, it would injure the retail merchant who handled those lines, and he, in turn, would have to undergo the same weeding-out process as that undertaken by the wage earner.

Interest of One, Interest of All

These simple illustrations are made for the purpose of showing how closely the affairs of every community are inter-related, and whenever one class is affected all classes are affected.

Our purpose in submitting these brief views on the problem of retail distribution, which is one of the most difficult problems for those who have had no practical exeperience in it to understand, is to point out that there is more capital invested, and more people employed in distribution, than there is in production and manufacture combined, and that, in our opinion, no plan, no scheme and no device that can be suggested can ever alter it unless we turn our plan of civilization backward and all begin again to be tillers of the soil and makers of the things we use and require. No one would be satisfied to go back again to the simple life of making our own candles, and using flint instead of matches, and using a spinning wheel to make clothing out of sheeps' wool. We have experienced life's comforts and we want them, and if we want them and must have them, we must pay for them. A meal provided in a million dollar hotel will always cost more than a meal provided in a tent. There is a price ticket on everything. The best things cost the most, and if we desire them we must be prepared to pay for them or go without them.

To properly consider the subject we have before us, we must take conditions as we find them to-day, and not as they were a century or two ago. To-day we have public school systems all over the world. Boys and girls, and men and women, have been educated to try and think. In every sphere of activity we see development We find improved machinery in all lines of manufacture and production. We have labor-saving devices and we have transportation facilities that are unequalled in any age of the world. We have new devices for transportation, such as automobiles, automobile trucks, aeroplanes, bicycles, etc. In electric power and electrical devices we are in advance of anything in the history of the world. In telephones, telegraphs and cables, our advances are phenomenal, and all this with the many other new inventions such as gramophones, etc., which can produce the human voice, all these things have been brought about by those who have been educated to think, to diagnose, to investigate and to study.

Wrong Thinking and False Principles

It is said that a little learning is a dangerous thing. In many cases this has proved to be true. Not having had practical experience and an opportunity of giving any study to the great problem of distribution, the rock upon which thousands and thousands of persons engaged in other walks of life become shipwrecked is where they venture out upon its dangerous surface. These persons who have not had a proper commercial training advocate, among other things, the following:—

1. The abolition of the middleman.
2. Direct purchase and sale between producers and consumers.
3. Municipal trading in coal, wood, milk and other articles of common use.
4. Public retail markets to enter into competition with tax-paying retail merchants, who carry vegetables all the year round, whereas consumers cannot buy vegetables in the market when the temperature is below freezing point.
5. Without knowing the unsound, commercial basis upon which so-called "Co-operative Societies" are established, they advocate their adoption.

In our opinion, it is wrong thinking of this character that lies at the root of our present troubles and unrest to-day. The remedy for this false thinking lies at the door of the retail merchants themselves. Believing, as we do, that no intelligent system on earth can be devised to abolish the retail merchant, or whereby all means of retail distribution can be operated entirely by the State, and that all men must have the right to develop their own lives as they deem best for themselves, without injury or interference with the rights of others, it is our duty to make our claims known.

We wish, therefore, to repeat again that the most difficult problem of all problems for the average student of political economy to understand is that of the distribution of merchandise at retail. It has puzzled wise men before corn was sold in Egypt, and it will puzzle wise men and social economists until the crack of doom. Retail merchants have been on earth for centuries, and they will be here for all time. You can devise no plan that will abolish them because they are an important and essential part of every community. They comprise the active, independent and free men of every municipailty. Their chief desire is to be allowed to do their business on a sound, business basis, and their chief enemy is municipal and legislative restrictions that are proposed to be placed upon them by those who do not understand the simplest principles of buying and selling.

The Great Problem of Distribution

As to the labor troubles of retail merchants, they have very few. Most of their clerks are their friends. A young man who enters behind the counter of the average retail merchant's store must take an interest in the business. He must be pleasant and agreeable with the customers of the store. The proprietor knows his habits, knows his Christian name, he calls him Bill or Bob, and he interests himself in his work, and encourages him to develop his character. It has often been said, and we have never heard it disputed, that the best business college in the world for a young man to enter is behind the counter of an honest retail merchant.

A retail merchant who places his name over his door, and who is always before the public, has a stake in the community, and his influence is for good and not for evil. Strikes, lock-outs and hold-ups are never heard of in ninety-seven per cent. of the retail stores in Canada, nor will they ever be heard of because each store has its own plan of paying wages or giving commissions on profits, or giving bonuses or increasing salaries according to the ability of the clerk to earn. No system of paying all clerks the same salary, even in the same class of trade, could ever be adopted, because the clerks themselves would object to it. The principle that exists, and which always will exist, is to pay clerks according to their worth to the firm. This is the only fair system and the only one that will give them an incentive and an ambition to some day become their own masters. In Canada to-day, every young man who is ambitious and who is willing to devote his time and thought to the business of his employer in the retail trade can find an opportunity of advancing to the highest position in the store, or becoming a partner, or eventually entering into business for himself. The first thing, however, that must be done, and for this reason, chiefly, we are submitting this article, is to impress upon the public mind that the man behind the counter is performing equally as useful and important work in the community as the man behind the lathe or the man behind the plow.

As retail merchants, in the past we have been too docile and too unconscious of our own importance in the community, and we have allowed all sorts of reports to be circulated by those who know nothing about the problem of distribution, being of the opinion that the public would not believe the statements made. In the future we hope to remedy this condition by taking our proper place in the community and insisting upon equal recognition with all other kinds of useful employment. As stated before, we occupy the most important position in the life of every well ordered community. We are here because we are required, and we will be here for all time, and there is no other system of distribution that can supplant us.

For this reason, if for none other, the Dominion Government must recognize that it is essential that no unfair or discriminatory legislation should be passed that will hamper our progress or interfere with our rights as free citizens. At the present time we welcome the opportunity to be able to lay before the special committee of the House of Commons, which has been appointed to investigate the cost of living, all the facts concerning the retail trade that we have in our possession, as we feel that the more we make our condition public the more the public will respect and appreciate us.

Currency and Measurements Used in Export Markets

British and Foreign currencies and measures of length with their Canadian equivalent are as ofllows:—

Country	Monetary Unit	Canadian Equivalent		Measure of Length	Canadian Equivalent
United Kingdom	Pound or sovereign.	$4.86 2/3		Same as Canadian	
British Possessions, viz:—					
Antigua	Pound	4.86 2/3		Same as Canadian	
Australian Commonwealth	"	4.86 2/3		Same as Canadian	
Bahamas	"	4.86 2/3		Same as Canadian	
Barbados	"	4.86 2/3		Same as Canadian	
Bermuda	"	4.86 2/3		Same as Canadian	
British Guiana	"	4.86 2/3		Same as Canadian	
British S. Africa	"	4.86 2/3		Same as Canadian	
Dominica	"	4.86 2/3			
Grenada	"	4.86 2/3			
		W.	F.		
Hong Kong	Dollar	.8701	.900		
Jamaica	Pound	$4.86 2/3			
Montserrat	"	4.86 2/3			
Newfoundland	Dollar	1.01388			
New Zealand	Pound	4.86 2/3			
St. Kitts	"	4.86 2/3			
Nevis	"	4.86 2/3			
St. Lucia	"	4.86 2/3			
St. Vincent	"	4.86 2/3			
Trinidad & Tobago	"	4.86 2/3			
Argentine Republic	Peso	96.5 cents		Metric.	
Belgium	Franc	19.3 "		"	
Brazil	Milreis	54.61 "		"	
		W.	F.		
China	Shanghai tael. ‡Haikwan tael	1.20775 1.20975	.885 1.000 (See note)	10 fun = 1 tsun = 10 tsun = 1 chek = 10 chek=1 ch'euug=	1.41 E. in. 14.1 " 141 E. in. or nearly 4 yds.
Columbia	Dollar	$1.00		Metric.	
Cuba	"	100 cents		Vara Metric.	38.874 in.
Denmark	Krone	26.8 "		" Ell	2.06 ft.
France	Franc	19.3		Foot	1.03 ft.
German Empire	Mark	23.8 "		Metric.	
Japan	Yen	49.8 "		" 10 bu = 1 sun = 10 sun = 1 shaku = 10 shaku = 1 jo. =	 1.193 in. 11.93 in. 119.3 in.
Mexico	Peso	49.8 "		Metric.	
Netherlands	Floria	40.2 "		Vara Metric.	32.9 in.
Norway	Krone	26.8 "		"	
Russia	Rouble	51.5 "		Fot Sajene = 3 arshins Arshin=16 vershoks Russian inch	.974 ft. 7 ft. 28 inches. English Inch.

Note.—The average value of the Haikwan Tael for 1908 was 63 cents; 1909, 66 cents; 1910, 69 cents; 1911, 65 cents, and for 1912, 74 cents.

‡The values in Chinese Imperial Customs Returns are always given in Haikwan taels, which are relatively in value equal to about 1.113 Shanghai taels. The tael is in reality not a standard of value (there is no such coin), but of weight, and when used in the sense of a value it only represents its weight in gold or silver, as the case may be. The real difficulty is to establish its exact equivalent in grains.

From "Camboose" to Phonographs and Music

Camp Life and Associations in Ottawa Valley of Twenty Years Ago and Today—With Improvements There Has Been Steady Decline in Efficiency

By Everett Andrew, Ottawa, Ont

Improved sanitation, shorter working hours, more congenial laboring conditions, and, last but by no means least, a greater variety of food, coupled with considerable alterations to buildings and the camp layout, can be safely cited as instances, if anyone asks the question "How much have the woods camps changed in the Ottawa Valley in the last twenty years?"

Opinion, in some instances, differs as to whether today's camp is as good, as profitable and as satisfactory to the men, and the system of ventilation in the sleeping quarters is a healthful as in the olden days? Then again there are tendencies that point toward the gradual elimination of the famous picturesqueness of the old camp life.

This latter phase must not be reckoned in the terms of "today or tomorrow," for like the growth of the oak from the acorn it takes place steadily though gradually. More modern standards of civilization are being advanced and looked up to as time passes: Today in some camps there are phonographs, electric lights, telephones, with here and there gasoline apparatus. All of these inventions would have been looked upon with a certain amount of awe or suspicion by the grandfathers or pioneer lumberjacks of the valley, whose primary object in camp life then was to get out "big sticks" and "go down" on the drive.

Now comes the advent of the aëroplane as a means of forest patrol. Truly a newly developed protector to the forests brought about by the war, and as many decades ago described by Lord Alfred Tennyson as:

"The nations airy navies hurling down their ghastly dew."

Educational fire prevention propaganda is also helping greatly in and out of the camps to destroy "fire", the greatest enemy of lumbermen and their woodland tracts and berths.

Watch towers though many of them are still in existence and capably fulfilling the limited functions for which they were erected, are it seems gradually "passing out."

The efficiency of woods labor as rated on the output of so much per man, per day, has considerably fallen away. Some estimates are that the woodman of today only does from sixty to seventy per cent. so far as production goes as his predecessor of twenty or forty years ago. Consequently more hands have to be employed.

Regarding ventilation and sanitation as at present practised in the camps several of the old time lumbermen point to the serious influenza epidemic which swept over the camps last fall and winter. Some of them maintain that if the old "square" had been in the roof instead of the "stuffed up barrel" that the germs of the epidemic would not have spread through the camp so rapidly and there would have been fewer serious cases. Smallpox, on the other hand, which with vermin was the scourge of the lumbering camps for many years, has of late almost passed into oblivion.

Taken all around there is room for debate as to the old and new time camp; a brief history of and description of the lumbering camp of twenty years ago and today is as follows:

Two decades or so ago the woodsman before he arrived in camp had a pretty good mental bird's eye view of what the place was going to look like, and what he could expect to find there. Camps in those days were pretty much the same—and had been generally so, so far as appearance went for two score years before or more.

The woods domicles of the lumbermen were then known as "camboose" camps, with walls constructed of round logs with the chinks between filled in with moss. The roof which today is almost an interesting relic of the past, was made with small sapling with the heart hollowed out, and inverted every second space to shed the rain. A most capable and efficient roof it proved.

Not the least of the peculiarities about the roof of the "camboose" camp, which any old lumbermen today well remembers and don't forget to talk about, was the "smoke-hole" or "the flue." This was usually a square opening in the roof from which day and night eminated, if the wind were in the right direction,, all and sundry of the variegated odors from the cook's diligent operations, and such other scents, smells or perfumes as may have been created by one cause or another.

Then there was the other aspect of the "smoke hole." While it let the heat and whatever else was in the "camboose" out it also let the rain, snow and the atmospheric elements in. Of this latter the "old timers" do not now complain. The ventilation from the "flue" was better they believe than the "holes bored in the barrel."

The interior of the "camboose" showed the cook's stove and his utensils, and the wooden bunks ranged two tier deep much as they are today. The bunks, of course, were wooden, and upon them a mattress of balsam bows was placed. There were two men in a bunk. The resting places surrounded the cook's fire in the centre of the dwelling.

Keeping Up Production and Morale

Napoleon once said an army travelled on its stomach, and as applicable to the woods camp and its workers, there are many grains of truth in the remark, for nowhere perhaps is wholesome nourishing well-cooked food more needed than in the woods camp if the production aimed at is to be attained and the morale of the men kept up. Thus the cook of the "camboose" though he may not have been as well liked then on account of the smoke from his cooking fire and the odors of his viands being prevalent within the sleeping quarters, was an indispensable unit to the workers, just as he is today. He baked his bread then in the hot sand around his open fire in the centre of the dwelling and excellent and evenly "done" bread it was too. Of course, he didn't pour the dough into the sand but placed it in large metal pans which were covered over.

When the "eats" were ready the men assembled around a large pot for soup and each man helped himself, choosing such morsals from the general bowl as he could fortunately secure. Sometimes the bigger fellows got the tit- bits and the wee lad or the newcomer more than once went wanting.

After the tin vessels were loaded (some only partially loaded) the men hied themselves to three legged stools, held their tin plates on their lap or knees and figuratively "went to it." The standard ethics of etiquette prevailing as tradition has handed it down, were: get there first, grab the best bits, and get away with them as fast as you can. Nobody worried whether bouillon cups or soup plates were used, or whether some greedy soul drank his soup or sipped it from his spoon. Five o'clock tea was never poured except on the shortest and dullest of winter-evenings (if the men reached camp by that time)—and then man and not the cook or bis assistant attended to that function himself.

The food supplied in the days of the old time camp consisted almost wholly of the following bill of fare: pork, potatoes, beans, and flour. Sugar and soap were in the camp but were sold to the men instead of being supplied gratis.

How Food Costs Have Aviated

The cost of food supplies then as compared with present day prices provides an interesting table for all lumbermen.

Commodity	Prior to 1900	Present day	Increase %
Pork per bbl.	$10.00	$60.00	500
Beans per bush.	1.25	5.00	300
Potatoes per bag	.75	2.00	166 2/3
Flour per bbl.	4.00	12.00	200%
Tea per lb.	.14	.40	185%
Sugar per lb.	. 3½	.11	214%

In addition in most camps of the Ottawa Valley sugar and soap are now supplied gratis. Work for the men began at daybreak and ended at dark. "Starting" didn't mean getting out of your bunk, but having the axes to work on a tree with first streaks of dawn, after perhaps the men had already travelled two or three miles from the camp to be at "work."

Away back in the golden age when square timber manufacture was a profitable enterprise, there were usually two kinds of camps. One for the square timber and the other for the "waney." Most of

Pen and ink sketch, showing the layout and location of buildings in a Quebec logging centre

the square timber from upper part of the Valley was cribbed and rafted over the Chaudiere slides at Ottawa, and down the Ottawa River to Quebec.

Here much of the picturesqueness of lumbering life came in with the logs down the "rollway" on the shore of river or lake. The "drivers" from the headwaters or the "starting point" as the case may have been, adopted more or less a "sang froid" attitude and "set" themselves for the long trip to the waters below the "Plains of Abraham."

The "rollway" then was pretty much as it is today, built on the side of a hill or slope which before hand has been carefully cleared of obstruction. At the head of it the logs were piled so they might easily roll down in the spring. Before the logs got to the rollway the head "swamper" or the "roadmaker" had penetrated into the forest as the "lumberjacks advanced."

The Various Duties of the Gang

The "gang" of workers ranged anywhere from twenty to eighty hands, and the bush superintendent (a man usually of many affairs and of wondrous capacity and energy) drove in all kinds of weather from one camp to another to make sure that everything was keeping up and learn of the fluctuating conditions. The result of a day's operations was usually recorded by the gang foreman on a rough slate or a shingle.

Besides the cook and his assistant the "carpenters," "head teamster" and "sleight tender" were important functionaries. The "hewer" and the scorer" also figured largely in the operations before the "stick" was taken out.

Such a gang with half a score or a dozen horses and sleds would usually bring out from four to five thousand sawlogs within the period of a season. To haul some of the heavy pieces of timber through the bush from ten to twelve horses were required. Rollers or skids were often placed under them to lessen the friction.

"Snubbing" and other practices so well known to lumbermen as not to need mention were practiced then pretty much as they are today.

Perhaps one of the best descriptions of early logging life is presented by a few paragraphs in "Picturesque Canada," edited by Principal Grant of Queen's University, in its edition on lumbering entered under the copyright act of 1875. Pages 222-23 of Serial No. 9 describes old camp life as follows:

"The road to the landing is often far from level; when the descent is dangerously steep, what is called a gallery road, is constructed by driving piles into the hillside and excavating earth, which is thrown on the artificial terrace thus carried around the face of the hill. Down this the merry sleigh driver descends safely with incredible speed; above him the steep—beneath the precipice from which the wall of piles, logs, and earth secures him.

"When the descent is still steeper and that of the 'gallery road,' snubbing is practised. This consists in securing a rope at one end to the sleigh and at the other to a tree at the top of a hill, whence it is paid out slowly as the tree descends. The logs at the landing are marked on the end with the trademark of the owner; also with another mark indicating their value.

"The gang works from dawn till dark with an interval for dinner. This is often brought to them ready cooked in the woods. men sit round a fire, over which boils the fragrant tea. They despise milk and sugar, but the tea must be strong. After dinner and a few minutes smoking, work is resumed; the axe swings, the saw is plied, teams drive their loads to the landing until after sunset, when they are driven back and the weary horses are stabled and fed. Then after a hasty wash the men enter the shanty, where, close to the central fire, is a boiler full of strong tea, fresh made, flanked by a huge pan full of fat pork, fried and floating in gravy. There is also a dish equally large, of cold pork. On a corner shelf is a mammoth loaf of bread, than which all Canada can provide no better, with a large knife and a pile of basins stacked together. With admirable unanimity of purpose the men, one after another, select a pint basin and a huge slice of the hot, fresh bread." Passing to the camboose they fill their basins with hot tea, and secure as much of hot or cold pork as they desire. Then seated on benches beside the fire, each with the help of his caseknife discuss the pork and bread, washing the solids down with copious draughts of tea. The only light is that of the camboose fire, gleaming on swart figures and stalwart forms and reflected from the tin vessels in their hands."

Many Conflicts Between Nationalities

In the olden days as is the majority of cases today, the most of the lumberjacks were of French extraction. Many of them had Indian blood in their veins and some were the converts of Jesuit missionaries. The priest of the church came about once per season and carried with him a portable altar. After being received in camp with reverance by his co-religionists and with respect by all he heard confessions which, in many instances, lasted far into the night. Next morning the celebration of mass took place.

In the Ottawa Valley the remainder of the bushmen who were not of French extraction were Scottish Highlanders, descendants of Glengarry Scots. Then there was a good sprinkling of the sons of the land of Erin. Many a conflict in the woods for one reason or another took place between the creeds and nationalities, finally resulting in the separation of camps in which each was housed or what might be termed today a mode of "segregation."

Saturday night, if someone in charge did not lose track of the calendar, was the big night of the week. "Big" didn't mean what it means in a city, a summer resort, or the now decadent Ontario "waterin" places.

Axes were whetted, repairs to equipment made. mayhap a dance was on or a fiddler appeared. Such was the camp life of the old time lumberman, and by way of diversion or sport he looked forward to the spring when impromptu log rolling- contests requiring both strength and skill were staged, before and on the drive.

The Twentieth Century Camp

Now in the trend of present day events and in the establishment of a new order of things, a great deal has been changed. The buildings of the camp are different, very much so. Instead of the old camboose one now sees an almost scientifically arranged structure worked out and erected on the basis of so much space per man.

A modern woods camp today has its hospital, its recreation rooms, school houses in a few instances are fostered by the pulp and paper mills. The era of modernism, civilization, and last but by no means least education, and diversion from physical effort, coupled with sanitary and religious principles are steadily creeping into camp life.

In accordance with provincial legislation stables have to be situated a certain distance from the sleeping quarters of the men's or the cook's camp. The drinking water supply is practically under the supervision of the Provincial Board of Health who secured its authority for health regulation within the last ten years.

In short the woods camp be it situated in the Ottawa Valley today as regards sanitation, has virtually to meet with the approval of the Provincial Board of Health. There are also pretty much restrictions as to the size of the buildings, the number of men they may house, and generally supervision of the layout of the whole camp from a sanitation standpoint.

Another new point which is insisted upon by the department is that a doctor has to attend the camp at least once a month and has to be within reasonable call in the event of sickness, epidemic breaking out or serious accident occurring.

In the construction of the new camp buildings, the walls are largely built of logs as formerly, but the roof instead of being the inverted sapling is of sawn lumber usually covered over with tar papers or other manufactured roofing material. A regular box stove and not the cook's fire heats the abode and there is a regular chimney which usually consists of a stove or galvanized iron pipe protruding through the roof.

Sticking a Shirt in the Barrel

Ventilation in most cases is obtained by cutting openings in the roof and placing barrels up-side-down over them. In the "head" or uppermost part of the barrel auger holes are bored. Not infrequently on a draughty or chilly night some enterprising soul sticks a shirt in the barrel which cuts off draught from his particular person and at the same time impedes the ventilation for the rest of the men.

The arrangement of the bunks remains pretty much the same as in the old time "shanty;" only now instead of being of wood they are of metal. And instead of the fragrant and healthful odor from the old time balsam bows, the "jack" sleeps on a "tick" which is filled with straw or dried grass or a wire spring mattress. Even with these precautions aimed at the extermination of vermin, it is necessary to "disinfect" the camp.

The cook has a separate camp and cooks on a standard or regular cooking range and no longer, unless in some dire emergency, does he bake his bread in the sand. Considerable improvements for feeding the men have been made. Instead of each one picking out what he wanted from the big pot of the old days, the men sit down at a long table with seats on either side on which the food is placed, and at which dishes have been set. Such courses as soup are brought to them from the kitchen, the camp chore boys serving as waiters at meal time. Thus everyone gets a share of what is going and the distribution of "tit-bits" is a great deal more equitable. The list of camp supplies has undergone a considerable change and the bill of fare is now quite an extended one. The quality and variety of food has been much diversified. The following is a standard list of what the men now get in most of the camps of the Ottawa Valley:

Free sugar, free soap, beef in large quantities, bacon, cereals, beans, preserves, fruits, apples, prunes, raisins, jam, cakes, pies, syrup, molasses. In some camps condensed milk is provided from time to time.

The modern practise in most of the camps is to diversify the diet to the greatest possible extent. Such a practise it has been found has worked out in better satisfying the men, and last but by no means least, at present prices it is also cheaper. Pork, for instance, is now cited by lumbermen as being one of the dearest commodities on the food market. Thus to feed men pork as in the old days, would figuratively cost the operator a mint of money, and send his production costs away up.

Today, as in the past, the majority of the woodsmen in the Valley are native French-Canadians. The Glengarry Scotch is disappearing and the Irish log makers are becoming few. Though the war had considerable to do with the departure of the Scotch and Irish from the lumbering camps, it was not the main cause for diversion, as even before the war the sons of these two races had shown an inclination to quit the woods and follow other occupations or lines of industry.

Their Heart Not in Their Work

The places they have vacated before the war and during the war, and are being filled with that which is commonly termed in the woods as "foreign" labor, and with little consideration generally classified as "Polacks." Broadly speaking as compared with the old days they are "fair" workers. In a general way on this phase it is a question if the heart of all of them is in their work. As one of wide experience put it, some of them are working to get a stake to go home with, others are content to plod along and live, but rarely is there one of them who displays ambition or initiative to go ahead and overcome the varied obstacles of lumbering life and master it.

Another improvement that has come to camp conditions is in the lighting. In a very few camps electric light is the means of illumination, but at several others the acetylene process is being extensively used as against the system in days gone by, that of lanterns, the pine torch, or in individual instances, the candle.

The mode and method of transporting men from the city to the camps has undergone a considerable change in most instances. With the building of railways before the war it was the custom to put the steel in as far as possible and make the hike or tramp or portage into the woods for the men as short as could be. Sometimes the journey from the end of the steel to the camp had to be largely made by water. In some locations the railway now goes right "in."

Will 10 Hour Day Come in Camps?

The hours the men work have changed. Though there is not at present any general set hours in the camps, the operators state that woodsmen of today work less time. The belief has been expressed that the day is coming when a ten hour day will be the accepted as a recognized working day for the woodsman.

As a means of recreation or diversion from work now, gramaphones are in many camps and there is also usually a ball field or an athletic ground where contests may be held if desired. Such fields are in the main primative, but they fill the purpose well. Then there are dominoes, checkers, and other indoor games and amusements provided.

Twenty or more years ago the lumberjack worked for from thirteen to fifteen dollars per month and board and did a day's work, as a day's work meant in that time. Today the same class of labor is drawing around sixty-five dollars and board, and some operators estimate that even, at this figure, the class of help offering gets through only two-thirds of that performed a generation ago.

Canadian Deals Should be Marked

By York Long (Cox, Long & Co., Ltd.,) London, Eng.

With considerable interest I have perused the article by Mr. James H. Lane of this city, in your issue of June 15th last, and also that of Mr. J. Ander, of Montreal, in your issue of July 1st.

With a good deal that is said by both these gentlemen any thoughtful person conversant with the Canadian wood trade must necessarily agree, but both of these correspondents omit to make any particular allusion to Quebec stocks of spruce, etc. This is the more remarkable, knowing as they must do, that the manufacture from that locality is nearly all that could be desired, hence in this country there is an increasing demand for these supplies.

It would be helpful to get expressions of opinion from the large operators in the Lower Provinces as to why they do not manufacture their lumber as consistently as the Quebec men. I think, too, it must be admitted that the manufacturers in the Quebec district produce their deals just as well made as the Swedes, and their grading is usually quite satisfactory—possibly, however, the Archangel stocks are more attractively made than either.

As regards marking or stencilling deals, etc., on the ends, I very much wish the Eastern Canadian lumber manufacturers would give serious attention to this question, as suggested by Mr. J. H. Lane.

If they were to carry out this matter in the same way as the Swedes, they would remove some very serious difficulties that at present arise in the handling of their goods at the port of discharge.

I predict the time is not far distant when this must be demanded by the buyers, in order to expedite delivery at this end.

Gathering Moss Sometimes Pays Well

Persons owning swamp lands in the vicinity of Brockville, Ont., are likely to benefit through a lucrative trade just developed in moss gathered from the marsh or low swamp lands. George E. Johnston, of Newmanville, Grenville county, and a relative, Claude Armstrong, are at present engaged in shipping three carloads of moss to Rochester, N. Y., where it will be used by nurserymen and florists. The moss, which is found in abundance in low lands, conserves moisture, and is used by nurserymen to wrap around the roots of fruit trees intended for shipment. Some varieties of the moss are used by florists in preserving cut flowers. The moss is sold by the cord, and brings a good price.

Ready Cut Houses Higher in Price

Owing to Advances in Labor and Material During Past Fiw Weeks Cost Jumps Considerably

Jas. Davidson's Sons, Ottawa, recently shipped to France a ready-cut house, illustrations of which are presented on this page. One picture shows the ready-cut house in construction and the other reveals it after completion.

The domicile is called "Type 2," and the outside measurement is 13 ft. wide by 26 ft. long, divided into two rooms of equal size, ⅞ in. flooring, beaver board on the inside walls, shed adjoining 13 ft.

Type "2" house in course of construction, showing framing, sheathing, flooring and one wall and ceiling of one room covered with beaverboard

by 13 ft. outside measurement, but no flooring or beaver board on the shed.

The size of the material which went into the structure was as follows: Sills were 1⅝" x 5¼", finished size; joists, 1⅝" x3¼", finished size; studs, plates, braces, girths and trusses, 1⅝" x 2¼", finished size; rafters, 1⅝" x 4¼", finished size; facia, ¾" x 6¼", finished size; roofing, ¾" x 6" to 12", tongued and grooved; flooring, ¾" x 4" to 6", tongued and grooved; outside sheathing, ¾" x 6" to 12", tongued and grooved. Beaver board for inside with ⅜ x 1⅜ battens over joints, doors and shutters out of ¾" V joint with battens. French sash, 6 lights each.

The house contained altogether 5,000 feet of lumber and 1,070 feet of beaver board. The weight was 7,000 pounds, and the cubic measurement 370 cubic feet. The house cost $528, including crat-

The same house fully completed for shipment abroad. This house contains 5,000 ft. of lumber and cost $528.

ing, f.o.b. Montreal. As this was a sample house, the firm had the same erected in their own lumber yard. Should a large order come their way the manufacturers would get the material for the other houses out and cut to length and have it packed ready for shipment.

It is interesting to note the developments that have come about in the export situation so far as ready-made houses are concerned. The Canadian Timber Products Association some weeks ago gave the Export Association, of Montreal, a price of $375, f.o.b. Montreal, on type "A" house, which was to hold good until August 15th. At the end of that time, if the Canadian Timber Products Association did not receive the order, the price was void. The members were not very enthusiastic about executing any contracts at the figure originally presented, owing to the rapid advance in labor and lumber.

One member of the Canadian Timber Products Association stated recently if they were figuring again on this house they would put in a bid of nearer $500 than $375. Since the original estimate lumbe advanced over 10 per cent., while labor had gone up 30 per cent. The order was not accepted by the exporters and the Timber Products Association members are not disappointed. They are convinced that they would lose money if called upon to implement the original contract at the price put in at that time.

World Lumber Demand Not Yet Started

"One of our aims in making a guaranteed price is against the development of a speculative market, as we believe stability of prices is the need of the lumber market, as well as every other American industry," says W. M. Beebs, manager of the lumber sales for the Long-Bell Lumber Co., of Kansas City, Mo., which firm inaugurated a few weeks ago guaranteed price lists covering periods of one month. Some pertinent observations on general market conditions and the outlook present and prospective, are presented by the company in a recent announcement. The views expressed will be read with interest:

"As we have said many times, the world's supply of available lumber is almost nothing, taking into consideration Australia, China, South America. When these countries, to say nothing of Europe, can get boats to supply them with lumber, you will see that the real world wide demand for lumber has not as yet even started.

"The home demand for lumber is very much greater than the supply, and when the other countries, which depend upon us for their lumber supply, are in position to get boats, it is hard to figure just where the market will rest.

"The car builders and railroads must of necessity buy immense quantities of lumber in the near future. The U. S. Railroad Administration officials are out scouring the country now trying to buy lumber to finish up the cars which were bought a year ago last June, and are having a hard time in filling their requirements.

"It is safe to say that it will be several years before the price of lumber is, relatively, any cheaper than at the present time. In fact we have no doubt but what there will be great advances over present values.

"We are often asked the questions why we do not run nights. Will say that there is not much chance for ourselves, or the industry at large, to operate nights when it is almost impossible to secure labor to operate during the day.

"On account of the car shortage, every order must provide for a filler so that every car can be loaded to its full physical capacity.

"What the retailer wants above everything is a stable market. While we know full well that we are not able to supply all of our customers with their entire requirements, yet we are willing to go just as far as we can toward that end.

"The great benefit which seems to come to customers in having a guaranteed price is the definite knowledge of what the stock will cost them in estimating a bill of material for their customer. Changes have been so numerous as to make it rather hazardous for a dealer to make a price to a contractor on a bill of material. When prices were going up as rapidly as they have been, he had no definite basis on which to figure.

"We have noted from some lists that a few other manufacturers have put this same plan into effect, both in yellow pine and white pine.

"While it may be considered good business principles and the natural tendency is to always sell to the best advantage and the highest price obtainable, a broad view of the matter, under present conditions, leads us to believe that the highest price upon the immediate transaction is not always the best policy in the long run."

River Works Turned Over to Lumbermen

The policy of turning over the river works, booms and slides to the lumbering interests which use them, instead of having the government continue to pay for their upkeep, instituted by Hon. F. B. Carvell at Ottawa while he was Minister of Public Works, is being carried out and only one more lease, that for the Saguenay River Works, remains to be signed.

By this course officials of the Public Works Department estimate that the Government has been saved, ata least, $100,000 which it would have been necessary to expend in repairs to booms and slides this year, and which would have benefited only the lumber interests using them.

The lease for the improvements on the Ottawa River was signed a few days ago with the Ottawa River Improvement Company, and for those on the Gatineau with the Gilmour and Hughson and Edwards interests.

The St. Maurice River Driving & Boon Company took over the works on that river some years ago, and the Chicoutimi and other interests are at present operating the booms and slides on the Saguenay, although the leases have not yet been signed.

The Goal of Uniformity Attained

One Code of Grading Rules in Hardwood Lumber Now Prevails Throughout the Continent

On several occasions when the matter of grading rules for hardwood lumber and the desirability of uniformity has been discussed it has been suggested that the best way to arrive at that result was for the other organizations to adopt the rules of the National Hardwood Lumber Association. They have now done so and uniformity is an accomplished result, says the "Mississippi Valley Lumberman."

The National Hardwood Lumber Association has been perfecting its code of grading rules for a number of years. Other changes will probably be made in the future. The first rules were not perfect. Those who formulated them did not claim perfection for them. Errors and inconsistencies have been ironed out, and some changes have been made because of changing conditions or to meet the desires of considerable numbers of the members of the organization; but always there has been an advance.

Some years ago, a considerable percentage of the membership, composed chiefly of southern hardwood lumber manufacturers, believing that they were too much in the minority to obtain what they desired, or for some other cause, withdrew from the National organization and organized the Hardwood Manufacturers' Association of the United States, which later became the American Hardwood Manufacturers' Association of the United States, which later became the American Hardwood Manufacturers' Association. Under the latter title they made approaches to the directors of the National Association, suggesting that they might adopt the National rules, provided the National would agree to certain changes in its inspection system. The National Association could not agree to this, so the American organization decided to formulate a code of rules of its own.

Its rules committee could not find anything better as a guide than the National rules, so they formulated a code, which differed only in defects from the rules of the National Association. They could not copy them outright, because they were protected by copyright. Finding that they could only eliminate the defects in their rules by making them absolutely the same as those of the National Association, they finally agreed to adopt the National rules in toto, and the National Association directors agreed to waive the copyright privileges. The only difference between the two associations now, in the matter of grading rules and inspection is that the American Association will confine the work of its inspection department to the settlement of disputes, while the National organization uses its department in making original inspections.

The American Hardwood Manufacturers' Association appears particularly fortunate in respect to grading rules. Not only has it been able to find an entirely satisfactory code for the inspection of hardwood lumber, but it has adopted the rules of the Southern Cypress Manufacturers' Association for the grading of cypress; the rules of the Southern Pine Association for the grading of southern pine; the rules of the Maple Flooring Association for the grading of maple flooring; the rules of the Oak Flooring Manufacturers' Association for the grading of oak flooring; the rules of the Commercial Rotary Gum Association for commercial rotary cut veneer, and the rules of the Rotary Cut Box Lumber Manufacturers' Association for rotary cut box lumber.

When the National Hardwood Lumber Association was organized, it was composed of manufacturers and wholesalers representing all parts of the country, and it was hoped that a uniform set of rules could be formulated for the grading of all American hardwood lumber. Several times this seemed about to be accomplished, but fell just short of the mark. It now seems as though the goal of uniformity has been attained, and it is to be hoped that there will be no more kicking over the traces.

Big Problems for the Retail Lumberman

There is a great deal of work for any large or small association in the lumber arena to undertake. No matter what is accomplished new problems are always coming to the front, clamoring for adjustment and solution. It has been said that the poor will always be with us, and as long as trade and commerce continue there are bound to arise difficulties that will perpelx and annoy.

The same is quite true of our own isolated selves. We are never —for any lengthened period at any rate—wholly free from mental or bodily disturbance, pain or uneasiness. No life, no calling, no pursuit flows on calmly and quietly from its source to its destination without a few "ripples" or "rapids."

It has been asked what a retail lumber dealers' association, nation wide, could accomplish, and what future has it? Here are a number of things pointed out by the "American Lumberman," which are worthy of serious study by the yardmen of every province in the broad Dominion of Canada:

The subject of housing is one of great and increasing importance. The people of the U. S. are going to insist upon having more sunshine and fresh air in their houses, and larger lots upon which to place them. All this will help the lumber business, and the lumberman should be foremost in furthering every movement looking toward more and better homes. As a specialist in woods he should see that the residents of his city or community are thoroughly educated regarding the good points of lumber, its wide range of usefulness, and at the same time be on hand to combat any misrepresentations by distributers of substitute materials. The National association is constantly putting out literature along these lines for the use and benefit of the lumber dealers in serving their customers.

The increasing cost of distribution is another subject that has received and is receiving considerable attention by the association. In this connection it should be mentioned that the association has adopted a uniform system of cost accounting that is proving very helpful. A subject of importance to every retail lumber dealer, and to business men in other lines as well, is that of the amount that may be legitimately charged to expense. Accurate accounts are absolutely essential to success in business. Without a clear idea based on knowledge of this important matter a man is likely, in making his returns to the Government, to enter for expenses a smaller amount than he is entitled to deduct, not being fully informed with regard to all the many factors that enter into the expense of conducting a business or the proper methods of distributing that expense.

On the other hand, he is likely to enter too large an amount, through ignorance, and be unjustly accused as a profiteer. It is very easy, in these days of rising costs, to overlook the fact that expenses advance a little faster than income, and the only true basis for profit is a proper return on the investment, which is every one's due.

There also are the big questions of the best and most efficient methods of conducting a retail business; of deliveries, whether teams or motor trucks are the more economical; the question of labor, and many others. All of these subjects are very closely interrelated. Methods that have been found helpful in one city might, if applied in another, prove the very means needed to relieve an acute situation, and all these and many more are matters on which the National association is gathering data and distributing them to its members, as well as taking active steps toward eliminating many abuses in the business.

Only through co-operation can advancement be made by any group of men in their business matters. National associations in every line of business are accomplishing much for the industries. The retail lumber business is one of the largest and most extensive of the many lines and a very large amount of capital is invested in it. It needs associations, in city and State, but, above all, a strong national association, if it is to be recognized in national matters, and there is much need for work in this direction.

Making Paper From Cotton Linters

The Department of Agriculture of the United States has been distributing samples of a good quality of paper made from cotton linters by its forest products laboratory at Madison, Wis., and claims it can be commercially produced in large quantities. Speaking of the possibilities, it says:

"Second-cut cotton linters, the short fibers which are obtained from cotton seed after ginning and removal of the lint suitable for cotton mattress stuffing, can be made into high-grade book, writing, blotting and tissue paper. This possibility will probably reduce the price of all kinds of paper. Second-cut linters can be removed fairly easily from the seed, but this is not the present mill practice. The shorter fibres are left on, although they interfere with economical oil extractions and have no food value when mixed with the ground cotton seed meal.

"The possible supply of this new paper material is about 600 tons a day. Once it comes into the market its influence on paper prices should be decidedly beneficial.

Forest Fire Patrol Working Well

The recently established aerial forest fire patrol discovered 35 fires in one week in California and Oregon and made 79 flights for a total of 8,536 miles. The patrol service was extended recently to Oregon and 28 of the fires discovered were in that state.

Ninety-one fires have been discovered by the service since it was inaugurated seven weeks ago. The forestry service, the announcement said, was able to extinguish the greater number of these fires before they gained headway.

What Line Lumber Yards Have Done for West

How They Have Contributed in no Small Measure to Growth of Prairie Provinces— Their Management, Service and Operation Outlined

Theo. A. Sparks, Grandview, Man.

Theo. A. Sparks, General Manager of the Northern Lumber Co., Limited, who operate thirty-eight retail yards in the West, and have their headquarters in Winnipeg, is "to the manor born," as our old friend, Wm. Shakespeare, has so well put it. His father, Geo. Sparks, was for many years a logging contractor in the Ottawa district, and it was in 1882, in the village of Vars, that Theo. A. Sparks was born. The boy grew up, as most lads did in that section, now and then getting into trouble and getting out again as best he could, —running away from school occasionally and earning a few dollars during the holiday period by doing odd jobs in the neighborhood and working at them with the spirit to "get there."

When in his 24th year Mr. Sparks went West and took a position in the office of Theo. A. Burrows, who is now president of the Northern Lumber Co. Mr. Burrows was a spruce manufacturer in the province of Manitoba, where he has operated in that kind of timber for the past forty years. Mr. Sparks soon took a situation on the road, and for several years covered the prairies as a lumber salesman. Mr. Burrows had operated a lumber yard at Selkirk and Winnipeg in the early eighties, and in 1896 opened a yard in Dauphin, which is still in operation. Some eleven years ago Mr. Burrows decided to conduct an extensive line of retail yards in connection with his milling interests. Mr. Sparks was given the organization of them and expansion was the watchword until to-day the Northern Lumber Company have thirty-eight yards on the Prairies, principally in Nortthern Manitoba and Northeastern Saskatchewan. Mr. Sparks also retains the position of General Sales Manager for the wholesale end—the Theo. A. Burrows Lumber Co., who, of course, manufacture more than is absorbed by the subsidiary retail company. During the past year, five more retail yards were launched, and the sales office of the Theo A. Burrows Lumber Co. and the general office of the Northern Lumber Co. removed from Grandview to 411 Electric Railway Chambers, Winnipeg.

Back of every successful enterprise there is a story of a purpose and plan, as well as of policy. The Northern Lumber Co. attach much credit for the rapid development of their interests to the fact that their local managers have always been instructed to give the very best service and to be absolutely fair in their dealings with the foreign population as well as with those who readily know how many pieces make a thousand feet of lumber.

The Northern Lumber Co. state they were the first concern of their kind in the West, and, possibly in Canada, to employ a certified architect in connection with their Service Department, and to supply free plans of houses and barns to prospective customers. The company have tried also to create harmony and team-work in the staffs of all their retail yards and have instituted a bonus system to local managers over and above their regular salary. This bonus consists of 10 per cent of the net profits of the respective yards.

All stock when shipped to the yards is invariably dressed as the mills in the various districts operate their own planing plants. While the main source of supply for spruce in connection with the Northern Lumber Co.'s activities is naturally the Theo. A. Burrows Lumber Co., situated at Grandview, still the Northern Co. buy spruce in the open market, taking the cuts of several smaller mills and purchasing large quantities of B. C. fir.

Speaking of the methods and management of line lumber yards in the West, Mr. Sparks, in a recent interview, said—"The methods are possibly as advanced as those followed anywhere on the continent, with regard to perpetual stock sheet, collection department, the sales department, service department, etc. The operation of these is so well known and so uniform in character that I scarcely think I can tell you much that is new or useful. I might add that our service department, where necessary, is prepared to supply the farmer with a fully completed house, painted, with farm lighting plant installed, etc. We advertise "From Stump to Completed Home," and "Real Homes," rather than 2 x 4's and shiplap which enter into it.

"In regard to terms of settlement, we give substantial discount for cash, but necessarily have to make concessions extending to the Western settling date—that of the wheat harvest. These longer terms of the Western lumbermen have proved to be important factors in the building up of this great country. When the history of the West is written we feel that the Western Retail Lumber Dealers will be accorded their just meed in having contributed in no small way during the period of the making of the great prairie provinces. This has been done through these credits extending over times when the crops were bad, etc., and thus has helped to develop a great, progressive people."

Mr. Sparks has been for five years a director of the Western Retail Lumbermen's Association, which has a membership of some 1,400 live aggressive yardmen and, at the annual meeting held last winter in Calgary, was honored by being elected vice-president.

Endless Belts Smooth in Operation

One very important and valuable quality of the leather belt, to which sufficient attention is not given, is the facility with which it may be made endless, and the great advantages which characterize an endless belt in its smooth operation over the pulleys and its freedom from fastening troubles, says a recent publication of Sadler & Haworth. It is quite possible to make endless Rubber, Balata and Stitched Canvas belts, but this can be done satisfactorily only at the factory in the process of its manufacture, involving a delay of a week or ten days, which is in most cases prohibitory. Endless joints in these belts, too, are without the special convenience of the endless joint in the leather belt because of the fact that when they stretch, and shortening becomes necessary, it is impossible to do anything with the factory point. It cannot be opened and remade after a piece has been cut out, but the only recourse is to cut the belt, and make a new joint with laces or hooks, after which it is no longer an endless belt, and all the advantage of it once having been endless is lost. It also is not possible with these belts to make a satisfactory joint over the pulleys, but otherwise must be restricted to those places where it may be possible to open the shafting, or where the two pulleys are outside the hangers. There restrictions make it possible to use the fabric endless belts in comparatively few cases where an endless belt would be desirable.

The leather belt, on the other hand, can be successfully made endless by any good mechanic who is trained to work to line. After the possession of the proper belt clamps and other tools, and a good cement, all of which are readily obtainable, the only problem, and one easily mastered, is to have the belt drawn up straight and the ends square. With very little practice any intelligent mechanic can make a first-class joint on a belt in its proper position around pulleys, and to the proper tension. Furthermore, when this belt has stretched a little so that its tension has been decreased, the same intelligent mechanic can open the joint he has made, cut out such a number of inches as may be thought desirable, make a new joint in the same manner as before, all in very little time, and the belt is soon ready for continuous duty, without the objection of a lace or hook joint.

So much of all the belt trouble is due to deficient connection of the ends, that we think we should give some special consideration to the subject and inform the buyer how simple an operation it is to make a leather belt endless, and the advantage of so doing. These methods of fastening the ends, which require holes to be cut or punched through the material of the belt, necessarily weaken the belt at that point, and when one of them pulls out, as they are likely to do, there results a crooked belt which makes trouble. The various forms of wire lacing, both those inserted by machine and by hand, distribute the strain more evenly over the width of the belt, but are open to the objection that the perforation which they require becomes a point of weakness. No other form of joining the ends of a belt can compare in efficiency and permanency with the endless joint.

POINT FIFTEEN

Marie Corelli in Sunday Chronicle (Eng.)

"Reconstruction! Reconstruction!" This has become almost a parrot cry. What we have called "civilization" has had its little house of cards blown down by a hurricane, and we stand, more or less bewildered, looking at the bits of pasteboard lying about, and wondering how we shall begin to put them up into some sort of shape again.

"We must reconstruct!" we say, both in Press and Parliament. But how? Each man asks the question of his neighbor, and each offers a different opinion.

The continuous uncertainty, suspense, and general muddle make up the finest possible hunting-ground for loose-minded agitators and blustering demagogues, who are, of course, paid for their agitations and demagogue-isms either by British malcontents or German agents, and pocket their ill-gotten gains as cheerfully as lawyers who, if they lose their clients' cases, lose nothing themselves.

* * * * *

Amid all the turmoil one man from America assumes, or rather presumes a dictatorship for the rest of the world—though why he should be permitted this privilege will ever be a riddle and a mystery, save to the sneaking devil of finance.

With a quill from the American eagle's swooping pinion he sets down fourteen points of "reconstruction" which, like fourteen rays of light, are to emanate from himself as the central sun of social and political wisdom.

There would be something humorous in this if it were not, as a whole, so desperately tragic.

Think of it! One man, one poor, little, swiftly perishable microbe of humanity, setting down, as in a copybook for children, certain rules and laws for the brotherhood of nations and for the better behaviour of all the Cains and Abels of the race!

In this moral attitude, self-assumed, quill in hand, the complacent Pronouncer of Platitudes has none of the greatness or wisdom so foolishly attributed to him; he merely makes one of the most pathetic figures in all history. He would seem to imagine it possible to succeed where the Divine Christ failed!

Pitiful self-delusion!—immense effrontery!—the blind confidence of a gnat confronting flame!

* * * * *

For this simple platitudinarian of Fourteen Points, in his copy-book schemes for "reconstruction" and general fraternity, has forgotten the greatest point of all—the point which makes all such schemes impossible of workable fulfilment—Human Nature.

Human Nature is the untamed, and possibly for ever untamable, monster of life—the half-God, half-devil, that rejoices in its dual character and is at most times more satisfied to be devil than God—now revelling in the brute claims of its brutish desires, and anon springing to the pure height of a spiritual ideal so lofty as almost to touch the throne of God.

No copy-book precepts will control this strange product of the unfathomable mind of the Creator. It has to fight its way alone. As it emerged from Simian and cave-type men to its present doubtful state of semi-civilized savagery, so it must emerge of itself, if at all, with such mental and moral consciousness as will persuade it that its human brothers are not survivals and would-be destroyers.

* * * * *

The American Eagle will succeed in hustling this slow evolvement and most gradual phase of education—no, not if a hundred "Points" were pulled from its wings instead of Fourteen.

The unwritten, undeclared, and well-nigh forgotten number rules all the rest—Point Fifteen—otherwise Human Nature.

Human Nature, with a devil-impulse, has sunk the German Fleet in the Scapa Flow. Human Nature has likewise burnt the French flags captured in 1870. "Vulgar spite," says the Press. Certainly. But spite is a part of the devil side of human nature.

German human nature, which is, racially, fierce and cowardly at once, like Shakespeare's "bully Pistol," will eat its heart and all other hearts in its way for the purposes of vengeance.

British human nature, easy-going and phlegmatic, is, after much ox-like patience, beginning to resent the irritating insolence of Government control, which measures out its beef and denies it its beer, and means to "have it out with every man jack of the lot," according to street parlance, some day..

Every nation is ill at ease—every man and woman strung up to an unhealthy nerve-tension. Yet we mildly prattle of peace—"when there is no peace;" no, not under any German signature.

* * * * *

And our "reconstruction"? What is it worth?

Who will "reconstruct" the human nature of the beaten and baffled Hun? Who will temper the thirsty palate of the beer-loving Briton? Who will "reconstruct" the lost faith of Italy, and bind up the gaping wounds of France and brave little Belgium?—Belgium in particular, who sacrificed all to save her neighbors!

There is no sign as yet of any such "reconstruction."

Among ourselves there are evidences of violent hysteria, which displays itself in the delirium of our women who, casting off as much clothing as the police will allow, dance in a semi-nude condition night after night in public places, and offer themselves to immorality without shame; while the men, adrift from the clamour and horror of war, look about at home for something to kill—either their unfaithful women or their broken and disheartened selves.

In this sort of plight human nature is reverting to brute instincts merely; and as a sapient evening newspaper remarked in its columns the other day:—

There has been recently a considerable outcrop of crimes of violence which is not a little alarming, and it is to the interest of the community that the causes and possible cure of this social disease should be sought.

O wise judge! O learned judge! It is, indeed, "to the interest of the social community" that the "causes" of the utter downfall of women's modesty and the evidences of men's callousness should be probed to their root.

Look for them, then!—and find them in the weakness, timidity and inefficiency of the Church; in the criminal sufferance accorded to atheists and sexualists; in the indecencies of the "gutter" Press, pictorial and otherwise! It is difficult to find a newspaper nowadays without a "snapshot" of a nearly nude woman; and this is the sort of daily pictorial provender sent into the houses of Britain for the entertainment of growing girls and boys!

To quote again from the sagacious journal before mentioned:—

The high spirits of youth, if directed into healthy channels, are an asset to the nation; allowed to drift they become at once a grave danger and a sorry disgrace to the community.

Just so. And it is not any "League of Nations" or Wilsonian maxims that will amend social or political matters as they stand to-day both in Great Britain and America.

* * * * *

Intrigue and corruption are rife in both countries, and while intrigue and corruption are tolerated by any statesmen such a thing as our "reconstruction" is impossible.

It is a matter for each individual to consider deeply whether he or she is able and willing to aid in the task by "reconstructing" himself or herself.

At the moment society is merely "running amok," and there is no self-discipline. Personally, I do not wonder at it, for the tolerance shown by the public Press to atheism and blasphemy has deprived religion of its hold on the mind and robbed the afflicted of comfort, so that one constantly hears people say: "Oh, what does it matter? Nobody cares whether you're good or bad, dead or alive—it's all one.

The great unchanging Law of God, which never fails to recompense evil for evil and good for good, is seldom recognized or admitted; humanity all over the world seems bent on the swift "rush" to its end!

"Reconstruction" is a fair-sounding word—but the deed is in abeyance.

Some few things might be done for the help of the young—the bookstalls might be cleared of filthy fiction such as even Rabelais might have blushed to own; the Press might once more be clean, and refuse to deal with subjects only fit for medical discussion; and the stage might encourage legitimate drama decently clothed.

A skidway of pine logs in a Northern Ontario camp

First Band Mill Built in Canada Still in Use

A number of band mills, carrying narrow saw blades and designed to take the place of the hand saw and circular saw in woodworking establishments were shown at the first Paris Exhibition. At the second Paris Exhibition band mills carrying a good deal wider saw up to 6 inches were shown, which made it possible to cut small logs; consequently a French band mill was introduced in Quebec about 1860 by Mr. Peters, but did not prove satisfactory. At that time, no one knew how to handle band saws properly and the continual breaking of the saws made the use of the mill unprofitable.

About 1890 the Waterous Engine Works Co., of Brantford, Ont., made up a design of a band mill. This mill was especially designed for the eastern trade; in fact, the first mill went to the Gaspe Peninsula. In the course of the following three or four years the Waterous Company built seventeen of these band mills, some of which were placed in Ontario mills. Most of these have disappeared, but one is still at work at the Knechtel Furniture Company, Hanover, Ont. From a letter received lately comes the word that it is in as good condition and doing as good work today as it did in 1892.

The demand for band mills became general, and a number of band mill designs were developed in the United States.

Band saw built by Waterous Co. of Brantford, in 1890, and still in working order in Hanover, Ont.

One of the best, and one which attracted a good deal of attention on account of being exhibited at the Chicago Fair in 1893, was built by the A. P. Allis Company, of Milwaukee. As the Waterous Company saw the advantage of this machine and knew the prestige of the Allis Company, they made a contract to build the Allis mill in Canada for a royalty, though the band mill was never patented in the Dominion, and commenced to build these mills in 1894.

It must not be forgotten that, since the construction of the first French band mill in Canada, the steel plate manufacturers have made enormous improvements in the evenness of their band plates, so that by the time the Allis band mills were placed in the mills in Canada, there were few troubles experienced with breaking saws. Of course, a good deal of cracking of saws was still in vogue, but the cause of this was not entirely the saw-makers' fault, but inherited in the band mill construction.

The improvements in band mills were very slow and no decided changes took place till Mr. Fitzgerald, of the Allis Company, developed the telescopic band mill, which was brought on the market in 1898. The Waterous Company consequently started to build some in 1899. The telescopic features of the band mill promised a band mill of great efficiency, as it made possible the use of double cutting saws.

The adoption of the telescopic band mill in the United States was very quick, but unfortunately the machine did not produce the results expected. The underlying principle of the telescopic band mill was to use double cutting saws and to eliminate the use of saw guides by bringing the part of the saw leaving the top wheel as close as possible to the log.

As the logs are of varying diameter, it was necessary to lift and lower the whole band mill to suit the log, which had to be done often and quickly. To do it quickly it took considerable power, and the mill had to be fairly loose in the guides. This last condition proved the stumbling block for success, as it created vibration in the mill frame and consequently the mill cut poor lumber. To overcome this the sawyer clapped the frame tightly into the guides which prevented the mill from raising and lowering and made the mill a standard band mill. Not having saw guides the lumber made on this mill was not uniform in thickness, because no saw can be hammered to cut straight. Every saw has a tendency to c[illegible] either in or out. For this reason the double cutting band mill came in bad reputation in the United States.

The Waterous firm had built between 1899 and 1902 four telescopic band mills which were placed by them in different mills in Canada.

During the time they introduced band mills in Canada, they had established in their factory an instru[illegible] course for saw filers to come to Brantford during the wi[illegible] months and be instructed in the way of handling band [illegible].

The instructor in saw filing whom the company had in their shop for several years was Mr. Jack Grant, who happened to be filing in Parry Sound in 1901 with the Conger Lumber Company. He had ample opportunities of watching the telescopic band mill in use at the Parry Sound Lumber Company.

In the fall of 1891, Mr. Grant came to Brantford with the suggestion that he would undertake to run double cutting saws on the standard band mill if the firm could devise for him an upper and lower saw guide which would enable him to change saws quickly. They made a design for both, and in the spring of 1902 the first double cutting band mill was run in Canada on a standard band mill. The Waterous Company feel quite sure that no double cutting saw was run before this on a standard mill.

The success obtained in Parry Sound was so encouraging that from that date very few single cutting mills were placed in Canada, although the bad behaviour of the double cutting saws in the United States had not been forgotten.

The Waterous Company found that in double cutting band mills it was more essential than in any other band mill to have the saw guides adjustable around the centre of the saw plate and the firm consequently designed the first lower saw guide and the upper saw guide.

The Allis band saw had a number of weak points. The base was overhanging. The top arbor was only supported below; the saw guide lifting mechanism was placed on the top of the frame, consequently creating a big vibration after running several seasons, and the saw staining device was rather crude. There was designed in the fall of 1908 the new Waterous band mill, which gave the band mill an extended base. It carried the arbor boxes beyond the arbor, gave the mill column a more rigid construction and eliminated the saw guide raising mechanism by moving the same by steam or hydraulic pressure. Last, but not least, a very sensitive saw staining device was introduced. Some other minor improvements were made which are outside the scope of this paper.

It might interest the reader to know that since building the first band mill the Waterous Company have built up to date over 240 machines, made up as follows: 17 mills; 141 Allis mills; 78 new Waterous, which are built in four sizes.

How Leading Firms View Logging Outlook and Operations for 1919-20

Expansion is the watchword in logging operations, and from reports received by the "Canada Lumberman," extending over many parts of the Dominion, the majority of firms are preparing to take out more timber than at any period during the war.

The sawmill cut during the past season has been the smallest in many years, while the demand for forest products, owing to the heavy purchases in Canada by the British government, the active requisitions across the border, the big building campaign, and the calls from the various countries of Europe, has caused a decided shortage in numerous lines. Next spring it is expected that shipping conditions will be normal and ocean freight rates brought down to a reasonable basis, while the reconstruction campaign will have taken on added impetus, not only in Breat Britain, but in France, Belgium and other countries.

The past year has been an encouraging one so far as new buildings are concerned in the bigger cities, but the smaller centres have only begun to take advantage of the provincial housing schemes. In not a few cases excellent sites have been secured and the necessary organization got in shape to go ahead with projects in hand. By 1920 all this will be arranged and matters generally will be on a more stable and solidified basis. It is hoped that the unrest—not to say revolutionary spirit—which has been in the air, will have disappeared and that a calm, saner and more dispassionate state of affairs may prevail.

Many large industries, contractors and even private owners have held back during the past season, owing to an apprehensive attitude. They did not know exactly where they were at or what was forthcoming. They believed that things could not be any worse than they were so far as strikes, tie-ups and excessive demands were concerned. The talk of one big union, cumulative bargaining, Bolshevism, Soviet rule and other manifestations of the times naturally caused investors to hesitate. Capital is aggressive on certain occasions, but diffident in others, and the building campaign did not, owing to the reasons already outlined, enjoy as wide a sweep and large results as anticipated. Next season everything should be at its highest. There appears no possibility of the price of lumber, particularly hemlock, white pine and spruce, receding. The cost of production will be greater this winter than ever, judging by present indications, and thus any hope that may have existed with respect to cheaper building material has, by the logic of post-bellum events and the force of reconstruction circumstances, been sadly shattered.

What Others Are Doing

It is always interesting to ascertain the views of the other fellow and learn how he sizes up the situation. With this hope in view the "Canada Lumberman" got in touch with several extensive logging and lumbering companies regarding their programs during the coming season. It will be noticed that the majority of them intend taking out more timber, in fact, the operations of some will be limited only to the number of men available. There is no expectation, however, that costs will come down, either in the matter of wages or provisions or the up-keep of camps. The most agreeable features to be presented at this juncture are that a larger amount of help is available and the demand for lumber of all kinds during 1920 will be greater than at any period since the outbreak of the war. There is no danger of production satisfying the calls that will be made for all grades and classes of wood goods, either at home or abroad, while prices will steadily ascend, so far as one can prejudge the general situation. How high they will go no one is in a position to state. The feeling in the best informed circles is that values will not recede for at least another twelve months, and perhaps not then.

The Denis Canadian Co, of Whitney, Ont, say:—We expect to double our output of logs over last season if possible. The labor situation looks rather uncertain at present, although we do not anticipate any marked shortage of help when the movement for the woods gets under way later in the season. Wages are apparently going to be about the same as last season, but if any change it will be downward, as the wages of bushmen is now too high in comparison with other occupations where common labor is used. Costs of logging have much more than doubled during the past four years. Supplies and labor have about doubled, while the production per man has fallen off to an alarming extent. So many boys and poor men are employed that it lowers the standard for the whole crew. We think from now on a better class of men can be obtained and some of the culls weeded out."

* * *

Operating Expense Up Fifteen Per Cent.

Clarke Bros., of Bear River, N.S., observe:—We expect to be sending our full complement of men to the bush when the season opens. At the present time we are getting ready to put down the foundation of a pulp mill at the mouth of Bear River, where we expect to manufacture pulp. As soon as we can get this mill completed and ready to run, we intend devoting our attention at our Lake Jolly plant largely to the manufacture of hardwoods. Operating costs are from fifteen to twenty per cent, greater than they were in the winter of 1918-19, and while we can see no reason why there should be an increase in these items, we are not anticipating very much in the way of a decline for the present year. Of course, should the high cost of living continue, we must necessarily have an increase in the matter of wages. Then, there is no surplus of labor at the present time. We are, however, getting sufficient for our requirement, but unfortunately we do not regard labor today as being more than from sixty to seventy per cent. efficient. We are at the present time, and have always operated our camps in such a way as to put them at the head of all industries of this kind in Nova Scotia.' We believe this is generally acknowledged. In regard to figures relative to the cost of feeding men, this item has doubled in the last five years, and today we would not consider one dollar per day as being more than sufficient to pay the cost of rationing men in the bush. While ordinarily we used to put timber on the brows for $5, we discovered in the winter of 1918 it cost us $10.50.

* * *

Recent Fires Increase the Cost

A. E. Beck, of Thessalon, Ont., who is vice-president of the C. Beck Mfg. Co., of Penetanguishene, writes:—The cost of logging last year was very excessive and all the northern lumbermen had hoped that it would be greatly lessened this season. But from all present indications the logs will cost more than ever. The same wages are now being paid as held during last year. A feeble attempt was made by a few companies at the start to hold the wages down to a more reasonable rate for woods work, where the men are boarded free, and consequently do not worry about the high cost of food. Immediately the camps were opening in any number and there was an increase in the demand for men, some companies started hiring at the old rates and others had to follow or secure no help. The cost of camp supplies of all kinds is much higher than last year. Practically all lines of groceries have advanced in price, and I expect it will cost a great deal more to board the men this season. Horse feed is also very high. The only hope of getting cheaper logs this year will depend on the efficiency of the labor in the camps. So far we seem to be getting a more experienced class of labor and there appears to be no lack of men available for the camps. If we can get rid of the desire of men in the camps to get all pay and board and no work, or as little work as possible, it may result in logs at a more reasonable price than has been the cases during the past few years. The disastrous fires which have swept a large number of the limits will greatly increase the cost of this year's logs, as a great many camps have been burned, and will have to be rebuilt. Quantities of supplies and outfits have been lost and these will have to be replaced at greatly increased cost, while valuable time has been lost in getting at making logs.

* * *

Dry Weather Delays Starting

The Schroeder Mills & Timber Co., of Pakesley, Ont., report that the weather has been so dry that they have not started their camps yet, but will do so now as the country has had some rain during the past few days and bush fires appear to be pretty well over. "Men seem to be much more plentiful this year than last—that is when you think of the season. This time last year nobody had any men in the woods; today camps which have only been running a short time are over half filled, and some of the others are full up. Wages seem to be just the same as last year, with a slight tendency to be easier, as men are more plentiful, but the cost of board is enormous, and horse feed is almost out of sight. We will put in six or seven camps and will not take out any more than last year," say the company.

* * *

The Scale of Wages Being Paid

James Davidson's Sons, of Ottawa, declare:—The operating cost as regards wages are about the same as they were this time last year, and run from $55 to $65, general hands getting $65. This $55 and $65 per month is with board also. The prices on provisions and camp supplies compared with 1918 and 1919 have advanced, we find, about 10 per cent., and it does not look at the present time as if these commodities would come down. It seems that every time we send out a requisition for camp supplies, that invariably the prices are higher, so we do not know just where it is going to end. With regard to labor, we might say that as far as the bush is concerned it is plentiful, but as to its efficiency the men are not the same bushmen as we could have got ten years ago. The average bushman of today is inclined to take things easy as compared with his forefathers years ago. We are sorry that we are unable to give you figures relating to the cost of feeding men, getting out timber, etc., based on our operations of last season, for the reason that we do not keep these items separate."

* * *

Operations on the Georgian Bay

Manley Chew, of Midland, Ont., says that he intends to take out about the same quantity of timber as last year and advises that the cost of operation will be fully as high as during the past winter. Mr. Chew adds: Provisions are higher. Wages today are not quite so high, but it would not surprise me to see them almost as high as they were last year, later on. We have a little more labor than during the last three years, and get a little better satisfaction. We have made no changes in our camps, but always try to keep them up to the standard. With reference to feeding men, we may add it will cost more this year than ever before. About the cost of taking out timber, this altogether depends upon the location. Generally speaking, it will be equally as high as last year.

* * *

Dollar Per Day to Feed Each Man

The Colonial Lumber Co., Limited, of Pembroke, Ont., report:—We expect to put in six or seven camps this season, which is about the number we had last year. We will possibly have a few more men in our camp, in which case we will take out two or three more million feet; at any rate, we should take out about the same quantity as last year. As regards operating costs, would say that wages are now as high as they were last year, but we find that all supplies are much higher in price, so that as far as we can see, the outlook at the present is that logs will cost more this coming season than last. We cannot give you any figures relative to the cost of feeding men, but would say that according to our records, last season, it cost us about $1 per day per man in some camps and about $25 per month in others.

* * *

Will Double Number of Camps

Shepard & Morse Lumber Co. (Canada) Limited, Ottawa, say:—It is our intention to put in double the number of camps we had last season. While men were very plentiful a month ago, most all the operators are going in heavier this season, and as a consequence woods labor has become very scarce in the last two weeks. Wages are practically the same as last season with a likelihood of an advance, owing to the shortage of labor, although when the crops are harvested men will be more plentiful. No doubt it is going to cost the lumbermen more to take out logs this season than last, owing to the higher cost of provisions and materials used in the operations. Our camps are always built on the most sanitary lines and inspected by a qualified medical man early in the season and monthly thereafter. We cannot give you any figures as to the cost of feeding men this season, as it is too early, but in any event it will be higher than our last operations.

* * *

Logging Jumps Six Dollars Per M

The McGibbon Lumber Co., of Penetanguishene, state: We will take out a million feet more this year than last, and will put about fifty more men in the bush. The wages are running about the same as last year, and we have had no trouble getting men as yet. The good class of lumbermen that were around before the war have all disappeared and it takes at least three men to do two men's work. Provisions are up at least 20 per cent., and we do not look for a drop. It cost us last year 21½ cents per meal to feed our men and $6 per M. more to take out our logs, than it did the year before. What this year will bring forth we do not know, but we do not think it will be less than last year.

* * *

The Flu Helped Pile Up Costs

The Muskoka Wood Mfg. Co., Limited, Huntsville, will take out about the same amount of timber for 1920 as they did in 1919, and regarding the fact the company assert:—From the present outlook, the cost will even be higher than 1919, which was the worst year we ever had to take out stuff, as far as cost goes. Our cost for taking out logs for this year was $5 per thousand higher than the preceding year. Of course, a considerable part of the cost during the winter of 1918-19 was caused by so much sickness in the camps and the mildness of the early part of the winter. With a very favorable winter, we might take out logs for the same cost this winter as we did last.

* * *

Bath Tubs Which Few Men Us

The Crows Nest Pass Lumber Co., Limited, Wardner, B.C., furnish the following interesting review of the present situation:— For the past three years we have tried to in-

A log drive in one of the thickest timbered parts of New Brunswick crease our output of merchantable saw-logs, but instead of accomplishing an increase, each year has shown a decrease in the output. We are counting on getting all the logs we can, although we do not anticipate making any great investment in further equipment. Our experience is that costs are continually advancing. This includes wages, provisions, hay, oats, coal, tools and equipment. We doubt if we are competent to say whether or not there will be any reduction in the cost of these items. During the past two months there appears to have been an appreciable increase in the number of men willing to try a few days' work in the camp. Very few of these seem to have had any experience in logging or using logging tools. Some men whom the employment agencies sent out as teamsters have had to first learn to harness the team. It would be a conservative statement to say that labor is fifty per cent. efficient under the pre-war period. For a number of years our camps have been equipped with steel bunks, springs, and mattrsses. Last year we installed bath-tubs and bathing facilities as required under B. C. law. However, the men do not use them very much.

* * *

Labor Supply is None Too Plentiful

The Hocken Lumber Co., Limited, of Toronto, who have mills at West River and Deer Lake, say they expect to increase their operations this season by about twenty-five per cent. They are putting in more camps and expect to take more logs than any year since the war started. —"As to present operation costs, wages and camp supplies are steadily increasing and we do not anticipate that wages will decline, as to our mind there is nothing now in sight that indicates any noticeable drop in prices of camp supplies," add the company. "In regard to labor in our district, at present we find it very difficult to keep operations moving as we would like and do not notice any improvement in efficiency. Conditions seem at present somewhat peculiar in the country. Instead of the old immigration problem we now have a pretty extensive emmigration, which is causing some inconvenience and a drain on labor, but matters will adjust themselves in time. We are offering our men good wages and steady employment with as comfortable surroundings as we can conveniently supply, so as to induce them to stay with the job."

* * *

Lumberjack Goes on Individual Strike

The Spanish River Mills Co., of Cutler, Ont., furnish the following interesting review regarding the prospects for the coming season so far as production, wages and operating costs are concerned:—We are endeavoring to increase our cut of sawlogs this year if we can get a sufficient number of men. It is pretty hard to say at the present time just how much we will be able to do. The foreigner, upon whom we largely depend, is going back to Central Europe as soon as he can get passage, to look up his family or friends, whom he has not heard of for several years. Many of those who have not planned to go back are somewhat indifferent about going to the woods and are looking for a job where there is an eight-hour day at 45c to 50c an hour. We have already made a start at nine camps, which are as yet hardly half manned, but have done nothing much up to date, except fight bush fires, which are very serious just now in many parts of Northern Ontario.

With regard to the efficiency of the men this year, I think it will be much like last year. As an example, in one of our operations, where we have now one hundred and twenty-five men, we have paid railway fares since the middle of June for three hundred men, thus turning over the crew more than one and a quarter times in two months. While the lumberjack is unorganized, and cannot very well do so, owing to his drifting proclivities; and therefore cannot go on strike in the way the various unions have been doing, yet he goes on an individual strike quite often.

As to improvements in camps and that sort of thing, we have always kept them up to government requirements, but have not as yet tried the "Alfred Fitzpatrick Plan," which we saw published in your paper some time ago. As our facilities are not yet prefected for moving a whole town, with all the accompanying paraphernalia, such as steam boilers and tons of pipe, every one or two years over lakes, mountains and swamps, we are obliged to go ahead in much the same old way.. The cost of feeding men this season looks like an addition of 20 per cent. over last year, or from $1 to $1.10 per day per man, depending upon the location, and also the cook. Wages are now at the highest point they reached last year, namely, $65 per month and board. They may go higher, and even if they do not, additional cost of all plant and provision for both men and horses will add to the cost at least 10 per cent. over last year.

* * *

Look for Strong Hemlock Situation

The Conger Lumber Co., Parry Sound, report that their next season's cut, which they are now taking out, will be approximately the same as last year, with the exception of the amount of pine. The company hope to have 4,000,000 feet of hemlock and about 1,000,000 feet of pine. Of the latter they took out practically none last year.

Continuing, the company say:—Regarding operating costs, it now looks as though wages will reach $65 to $70 in the bush, which we consider a high figure, although last season was equally expensive. Earlier in the year the wages were down to $50 to $60, but as it now appears that some firms of this district are going to operate rather extensively, men are in great demand and the wages going up accordingly. Supplies are very high. Instance the prices on bacon, oats, sugar, etc., all of which have advanced from ten to fifteen per cent. Equipment, too, has reached abnormally high figures, while the prospects of any decrease do not seem to be at all bright. We have this year constructed a new camp in Gibson and are considering the putting in of another small one, our only other camp being in Freeman, which was built last year. Regarding the class of labor we are procuring, we cannot say it is of the best. The large foreign element seem an unstable lot, while the real bushman is such a scarce article as to be almost a man of the past. So far this season we have managed to get the requisite amount of hemlock peeled and the bark swamped, and do not anticipate having trouble in watering either this or the 45,000 pieces of small pine we are taking out. We are expecting a strong hemlock market for 1920 and judging from the rapidity of movement of this year's stock, do not think we will be disappointed.

* * *

What Contractors Got for Logs

A large operating concern of Fredericton states:—During spring and early summer we found labor quite plentiful in this district, but, of course, during the haying and harvesting seasons men are somewhat scarce, though the shortage is not serious. During the past winter we found the laborer very inefficient, but we look for this condition to improve this fall. As we do not operate our own camps we cannot tell you figures of the cost of feeding men or getting out logs, but could give you the prices paid to contractors in this district. We had one man whose logs cost $13.50, another, on practically the same chance, $12.75, and another $14.90. So you see the figures vary somewhat. In all of these cases we considered the difference to be in management, almost altogether, as provisions, wages, etc., were the same in all cases.

* * *

Will Contract for Most Pulp Wood

The Abitibi Power & Paper Co., of Montreal, say they have not decided how many camps they will open this year but in any event they will be less than last year as they hope to be able to contract for a very considerable portion of the wood they will cut this coming winter. The amount they propose getting out, however, will be less than for the last two years, as they have accumulated somewhat of a surplus during that period. According to the company it does not look as if there will be any appreciable reduction in operating costs or wages. The costs, however, will be larger dependent upon the prices for provisions and camp supplies. If the present high cost of living campaign results in any reduction in the prices of the former, the company state that they will feel the effects, but, in view of all the talk of reduced living conditions and lower wages, they have not experienced the same as yet.

In regard to the efficiency of men the company opine that as a general proposition this was much below what it was a year ago and, with the present world-wide labor unrest no marked improvement can be looked for at least for some time.

* * *

All Men Do Not Want Work

One of the largest lumbering organizations in northwest Ontario furnish the following:—We expect to use about 20 per cent. more men this year than we did last, and will probably take out about the same quantity of timber. We do not anticipate any drop in operating costs as supplies will be considerably higher than last year. The labor situation is fair only; there appears to be plenty of men but not all of them are at work. Efficiency is fair. We have made considerable improvements in camps during the last few years.

* * *

Experiencing Decided Scarcity in Help

The Bathurst Lumber Co. of Bathurst, N.B., declare:—Our logging season for 1919-1920 has scarcely commenced yet, as most of the men who usually go to the woods are still engaged on their farms and will not be ready until about September 1st. We are, however, having a serious labor shortage right now in our sawmills, and our shipping gangs are so short that we are not able to get our lumber and other products loaded, and are fully 50 per cent. short on this class of labor. What few are now coming for the woods are looking for high wages and easy jobs, and we must face a higher wage scale than last year, which we considered at the time a ruinous one. As near as we can judge, there will not be enough men available to get out a normal cut of logs even if all other conditions, such as weather and the health of the men, are good. Supplies of all kinds are fully as high as last year, so we can see no relief in sight so far as high costs are concerned, for at least another year. We are providing hospital accommodation and full equipment at convenient centres to care for our men in case of any epidemic such as we had last year.

* * *

Quality of Labor Should Improve

The J. D. Shier Lumber Co., Limited, Bracebridge, report that they expect to have about the same amount of timber cut as last season, or approximately 4,000,000 feet. "We cannot see where there can be much reduction made in the cost of getting out logs as all lines of camp supplies, with the exception of beef, are higher than last year. Wages will be about the same as last year, but as most of the men who served in Forestry work overseas are now home, the quality of labor procurable should be of a higher standard than that of last year," conclude the company.

* * *

What Other Concerns Are Doing

The Pembroke Lumber Co., Pembroke, Ont., state they expect to operate six camps this year which will be the same number as last year and the product of logs will undoubtedly be about the same. "It is impossible to make an intelligent prediction regarding the probable cost of logs this season. Suffice it to say that wages are as high as they were last year, and foodstuffs and material equally as high. There is no apparent probability of any reduction in cost," add the company.

* * *

Hay and Oats Are Away Up

The C. Beck Mfg. Co., Limited, of Penetanguishene, Ont., observe:—Re the situation in the camps this coming season, we are just commencing to start in and anticipate from present indications that prices will be as high, if not higher. All foodstuffs are higher and hay and oats are very much higher, so that the cost of feeding teams will be increased considerably. Men's wages will not be reduced to any extent. The biggest loss last year was in not having enough men, and consequently the output was very small, making the overhead enormously high. This year there should be better production, as we should get a better supply of men. A good many of our old hands were drafted in the Forestry Battalion. These will be back and should be as efficient, if not more efficient, than ever. We anticipate taking out about our usual cut if we can get as many camps under way as we contemplate.

Some splendid spruce logs felled in New Brunswick

* * *

Cost Will Be 10 Per Cent Higher

Austin & Nicholson, of Chapleau, Ont., observe:—We expect that our operations will be about the same this year as last, providing always that men are available. We can see no prospect of wages for lumberjacks being any lower than last year. Some men have been hired at rates a little lower than that prevailing in 1918, but it is our opinion that before the season's work gets well under way, we will be back to 1918 rates. The cost of food and general camp supplies has increased over 15 per cent. over 1918. The chief advances are in pork and dairy products, sugar, dried fruits, vegetables, hay, oats, and all lines of hardware. Men seem to be fairly plentiful, but if anything more unsettled, which means less efficient. To sum up, we would say that as things look at present, the cost of getting out logs will be 10 per cent. above the level of 1918.

* * *

St. John Lumbermen Will Be Active

The St. John, N.B., correspondent of the "Canada Lumberman" writes:—All the mills anticipate going into the woods for a full cut of logs, but no more. Should a depression come about, certainly a curtailment will be made, but should present prices remain in force a larger cut of logs will be made in New Brunswick than a year ago. Wages will be as high as they were last winter, but there will be a greater number of men to draw from. Supplies, such as pork, hay and oats, are higher at the present time, and if they keep at present quotations certainly it will cost more to cut logs than a year ago. Hay is now being held by farmers at $25 per ton in the barn loose. Pork, green, about 25c per lb. Beef is higher than a year ago, and oats are also up about 5c per bushel. The cut on the St. John River and in Maine will no doubt exceed last winter's by at least twenty to thirty million feet, but manufacturers are certainly not going to overload themselves with logs for anything over the coming year. Just at the present moment plans for logging are not completed, but by the middle of September it will be well known what the St. John river manufacturers will plan to cut. No abnormal cut of rotary sawn stock will be gotten out during the coming winter, although a greater quantity than a year ago will be made should prices remain firm.

* * *

Much Burned Timber to Take Care Of

The Holt Timber Co., Bolger Bridge, Ont., state that owing to the forest fires a great effort will be made to put in logs from the burned districts. Much of such timber will not reach the market next year. It will be [illegible] to save it. The rush to get men all at once and early has resulted in a mad scramble and needlessly high prices. It has also defeated its own purpose by unsettling the minds of jobbers and they wonder what is coming next and are waiting to see. The

Holt company will not take out as large an amount of timber as last year and about one-third as much as in 1915-16. Operating costs are likely to go higher as everything in the way of wages, provisions and camp supplies is now starting in at about the same figure as the highest that prevailed last year, and, naturally, things are bound to climb. So far the firm report a shortage of men and many of them are inefficient. The cost of feeding the lumberjack and getting out the timber during the past season was higher than the previous one and will likely exceed during the next few months.

* * *

Cost $1.20 Each to Board the Men

The logging department of the Genoa Bay Lumber Co., Victoria, B.C., provides the following comprehensive review: We are just starting another camp at Cowichan Lake, which will employ from forty to fifty men. The output during 1918 amounted to 21,000,000 feet, and we have already, to August 1st, taken out 15,000,000 feet this year. As it is our intention to continue operating the two camps for the balance of the year, it is likely that the output for 1919 will exceed 1918 by five or six million feet. The operating costs are getting higher all the time, and so far as we can find out, there is no likelihood of a drop in the prices during the balance of the year. The efficiency of the men is very low compared with 1915 and 1916, which condition we do not think will change until some time in the future when work is harder to get.

We have made quite a lot of improvements in our camps, viz., the building of the bath house and wash room, and reading room for the men. So far as the food is concerned, we have made no changes, considering it our duty to feed the men good food. During 1918 the board in camp was $1.20 per day, and all the previous years we lost 7c per meal for every meal furnished," continue the company.

"We expect that there will be another raise in wages before very long, as the 10c increase which went into effect in this coast on July 15th only brought the wages back to the basis they were receiving on January 1st, 1918.

"We are giving you an itemized statement of our cost for last year, which we are giving you for your private information in order that you may understand the cost. We may explain that our camp is located twenty miles up Cowichan Lake. We log in the lake, tow to the foot of the lake, and load on cars of the E. & N. Railway. We haul them thirty miles to our booming ground on the salt water at Crofton. From there they are towed to Genoa Bay mill, a distance of twelve miles, or if sold, can be towed to Victoria, Vancouver, or any other point in the Straits of Georgia."

* * *

Have Five Camps Now Operating

Graves, Bigwood & Co., Byng Inlet, Ont., report that they intend to extend greatly their operations in the woods during the coming season and already have five camps at work. Wages of men are about the same as last year, running from $60 to $82 per month, but the cost of supplies is very much higher. Oats at their depots cost around $1.06 per bushel, whereas last year the prevailing figure was 80c.; for hay the company is now paying $35 to $38 per ton, and last year the rate was $20 to $25. There have also been sharp advances in beans, barrelled pork, smoked hams, and many other lines, with a reduction in only a few items. The firm believe that the cost of getting out timber will this year average from 10 to 15 per cent. higher than during the past season.

* * *

Believes Good Board Pays Well

J. D. Irving, Limited, of Buctouche, N.B., assert:—We expect to be putting in as many men this year as usual and getting out equally as large a cut for next season. We also purpose installing some small portable mills this winter.

As to present operating and costs, these are about 20 per cent. above what they were last year—that is, with regards to wages in our lumber mills. The cost of equipment has gone up from 25 to 50 per cent., provisions in proportion, during the last few years. The cost of camp supplies has increased about 10 per cent. and we do not anticipate any drop. With regards to labor, we think we are about the same as everywhere else. There is an abundance of labor, but it is a very difficult question to get it harnessed. We had a strike in our lumber mill a little over a week ago, but made no concessions, and all the crew we are willing to accept are back again. We endeavor to keep our camps as clean and wholesome as possible, as we always find it enables us to get the best class of men, and the better men we get the cheaper the labor. We always try to have running water in our camps, have them well heated and lighted, and divided up into one or more buildings, as the more homelike the camp is the more satisfied the labor. As to the feeding of the men, it costs us about 80c per day per man. We find it a paying proposition to give them lots of sweets, such as pies and cakes, more particularly the first week they are in the woods. As yet we are using horses for handling our lumber, but are considering tractors, and would like to have your views regarding the matter, or anything you can give us. We have here on an average of from two to three feet of snow and our logs haul from three to six miles.

* * *

Are Well Equipped with Labor

The Brompton Pulp & Paper Co., of East Angus, Que., remark:—We anticipate getting our usual cut of wood this coming winter. The present outlook, however, is that it will cost considerably more this year than it did last. We are fully supplied with labor in this district at the present time.

* * *

Will Take Out the Same Quantity

The timber director of a large pulp and paper concern in Montreal says:—We are sending the same number of men to the bush this season that we sent last year and intend taking out about the same quantity of timber. Wages are about as last year. Provisions and camp supplies are slightly higher and we do not anticipate any drop in these items. The labor situation in this district so far as men and their efficiency are concerned is unchanged from last season. Men at the moment are not plentiful, but we anticipate no difficulty in getting the number we require.

* * *

Too Much Talking on Labor Matters

The New Ontario Colonization Co., Limited, of Jacksonboro, Ont., are of the opinion that quietude would reign for a while in the ranks of labor if less publicity and agitation was carried on through the press and less talking done by employers of labor. Just at present they think that the less said the better regarding wages, efficiency and the future. Regarding how long the period of adjustment will require the company report that it can only surmise and in the meantime they propose to put in their best efforts to aid in the adjustment and restore conditions to normal.

A busy logging scene in Nova Scotia woods

Importance of Interior Finish in the Home

The Potent Desire of People to Have Their Places of Abode as Attractive as Possible—Evolution in Style and Ideas—Demands of the Future

By Charles J. Brooks, Toronto

Charles J. Brooks, Toronto

A good many of those who read this article will remember a time, not so many years ago, when the interior woodwork of the average house was "grained" usually in imitation of quarter sawn oak. The effect was a good deal as though a bunch of polliwogs had wiggled at random through the paint before it had dried, finally to get stuck and expire, leaving sundry blotches to indicate the fatal spots. "Grained" finish belongs to the past and may be pointed to as an illustration of the fact that the beauty of nature cannot be successfully imitated by man.

The wood on which these fantastic creations of the old-time painter were perpetuated was usually white pine or spruce. Sound knots were not an insuperable defect, as a daub of shellac over the knot would make a surface to which the paint would stick. And so the potent desire in the bosoms of women and men to have their place of abode as attractive as possible, was in some measure satisfied.

The passing of the "grained finish period" in interior decoration was largely determined in Ontario, at least, by the introduction of Southern Yellow Pine. Here was a wood which, at a moderate price, provided a much more attractive finish with considerably less trouble. The natural grain and the natural color could be made a permanent addition to the beauty of the home. And while man was not successful in imitating nature in the production of natural effects, working on a beauty already provided he was able, by means of stain and varnish, to intensify and perpetuate that beauty. Thus "grained" finish departed and Yellow Pine reigned in its stead.

The Passing of Yellow Pine

It appears at this time that the day is not far distant when the passing of yellow pine finish will also be duly chronicled. Forestry reports indicate that the lumbermen of the South have gathered the harvest of the forest perhaps not wisely, but too well. That within a very few years yellow pine will cease to be a prominent factor in the streams of lumber which flow, impelled by the gravity of economic forces, hither and thither across and up and down this continent. The fact that it is estimated that well within the next ten years over 3,000 southern pine manufacturers will be obliged to close up shop on account of exhaustion of timber supply is significant, foreshadowing a continually diminishing volume and, as a natural consequence, a progressive reduction in the radius of distribution.

The "heir apparent" already beginning to be in evidence is British Columbia fir, whose contribution to the home's attractiveness is greater even than that of its beautiful southern contemporary. While a good deal similar to yellow pine in many respects B. C. fir presents a more pleasing appearance in grain effects, which are brought out more prominently by its greater adaptability in the way of taking stain.

The Popularity of Fir Finish

Fir finish has already come very largely into use in Eastern Quebec, New Brunswick and Nova Scotia, in other words, in those sections where distances from the producing centres and, consequently, a more even break in freight rates, have given a fair field, and no favors in the matter of southern pine competition. The geographical situation of Ontario, with respect to the yellow pine producing areas, has been greatly in favor of that wood holding its own in this market. Just now, however, when the southern manufacturers have more business than they can handle, nearer home, and aided to some extent by the adverse exchange situation, fir finish begins to move more freely into Ontario, indicating very clearly, when one keeps the general lumber situation on this continent in mind, what is to be the standard trim for the average dwelling here in the days that are to come.

Undoubtedly there will be further movements of yellow pine finish to this market. But, with an enormous home demand assured for the next few years, with prices that may well be depended on to stimulate further exhaustion of the yellow pine forests; and with a large enforced curtailment of production already in sight, it does not require the spirit of prophecy to predict that, within a very few years, B. C. fir finish must occupy the place of yellow pine in the homes of Ontario.

Looking to Future Requirements

In closing, I think it might be advisable to call attention to an instructive and attractively illustrated publication, which was issued a considerable time ago by the Forest Branch of the Department of Lands, entitled "How to Finish British Columbia Wood." This booklet has enjoyed wide distribution, and now that building operations are being carried on so extensively, it will no doubt be in greater demand than ever. The comprehensive work is designed to bring to the attention of wood-finishers, builders, architects, and prospective home-makers the desirability of selecting British Columbia woods for interior finishing of their homes, offices, and other buildings. It also gives instructions as to how the wood should be surfaced, stained, varnished, or painted.

Western woods are remarkable for their excellent wearing and time-resisting qualities. They have a beautiful figure and are especially suitable for inside and outside finish. Two entirely different styles of figure are possible. From lumber sawn flat-grained is obtained a beautiful watered-silk effect, and from that sawn vertically a restful, pleasing edge-grained effect. A cedar panelled room finished in wax polish with an edge-grained Douglas fir floor, natural shade, is a delight to behold, combining as it does, comfort, beauty, and durability.

Wood improves in appearance with age. Plaster for walls in many cases, is but a cheap and inefficient substitute for panelling or other form of wood covering; it is easily damaged, difficult to repair, is almost impossible to clean, and requires periodic decoration to give a presentable appearance. Wood has none of these disadvantages. Keep your floors and panelling clean and their beauty and usefulness will be more apparent every day. The various finishes, oil, stain, varnish, or polish, on woods serve to bring out the grain, protect the surface again wear, and enable it to be easily cleaned.

Handy New Oil Pump on Market

The Hamilton Motor Works Co., Limited, of Hamilton, Ont., have recently placed on the market a Hand Oil Pump. With this pump any desired quantity of oil may be drawn from a barrel and its use does away with oil soaked floor and waste of oil. The pump has two adjustable stops so that it can be set to pump any desired quantity up to one quart. There is a lock with two keys provided so that the apparatus can be locked up. The pump is supplied complete with suction pipe reaching to the bottom of the barrel and with bushing screwed for 1½ in. pipe tap, which is standard in steel barrels. The Hamilton Motor Works say that the same bushing can be used to screw into a wooden barrel if desired.

Labor Troubles in Eastern Mills

Practically every sawmill on the Miramichi River was closed down recently owing to a strike among the workmen. The firms involved were John Maloney; Jas. Robinson, O'Brien, Limited; Wm. Sullivan; Sinclair Lumber Co.; D. J. Buckley; John Burchill & Sons and D. & J. Ritchie, employing in all about 1500 men. The men secured a nine hour day.

The men engaged in loading ships at Nelson, Newcastle and French Port Cove on the Miramichi River struck recently for a 9 hour day and an increase in wages. They have been working for 55c an hour in the hold and 45c on the outside. The demand is for 65c inside and 55c on the outside and a 9 hour day. A deadlock resulted for several days as the employers were quite willing to grant the increase but not the shorter day.

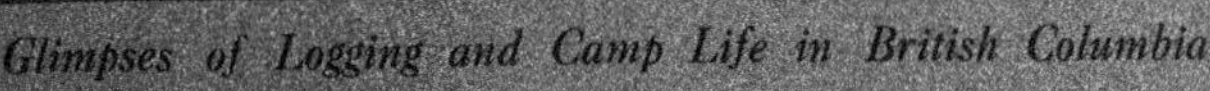

Glimpses of Logging and Camp Life in British Columbia

In the accompanying illustrations are presented several representative scenes of the timber wealth and logging operations in British Columbia. The views are exceptionally clear and afford some idea of the extensive character of the lumber industry in the Pacific Coast Province.

In the first row, from left to right, are seen a logging railway and up-to-date logging camp, an extensive rock cut and a trip on a logging train.

In the middle row, from left to right, there is witnessed the operation of loading the logs, and then comes a floating bridge connecting the camp with the foreman's house. In the next "snap" William Henderson of Toronto, superintendent of the Shantymen's Christian Association is observed seated on a log. All these logs were part of the slash formed during the night that the picture was taken. The next view shows a typical camp on the lake, all the hillside being on fire caused the smoke in the rear.

In the bottom row are five gentlemen all actively participating in, or sympathetic with, the work of the Shantymen's Christian Association. From left to right is Rev. Oswald J. Smith, late associate pastor of the Dale Presbyterian Church, Toronto, (who is now engaged in work on behalf of the Shantymen's Christian Association in British Columbia); Wm. Henderson, of Toronto, superintendent of the Shantymen's Christian Association; J. Matheson and Alexander Weir, missionaries of British Columbia, Wm. Sharpe, president of the Pacific Box Co., Vancouver, who is a director of the S.C.A. in that Province. Next to this party is a train load of logs and in the lower right hand corner (seated) are Messrs. Matheson, Smith and Weir.

Personal Paragraphs of Interest

J. B. Gregory, manager of the York & Sunbury Milling Co., Fredericton, N. B., has been ill for some time and not able to attend to business.

C. A. Morin, of L. P. Morin & Fils, St. Hyacinthe, Que., spent a few days in Toronto recently calling upon the members of the lumber trade.

W. W. Carter, president of the Fesserton Timber Co., Toronto, and family, who have been spending several weeks at their summer home, Honey Harbor, Georgian Bay, have returned to Toronto.

A. E. Eckardt, of the R. Laidlaw Lumber Company, Toronto, has returned to his desk after spending several weeks at Rosseau, Lake Muskoka, where he became an enthusiastic golf player.

G. H. Askwith, of the Riordon Sales Co., Montreal, is calling on the New York lumber trade in the interests of his company, who are large sellers of spruce by barge shipments.

R. N. Bates, of Ottawa, vice-president and managing director of the International Land and Lumber Co., is on a business trip to England. He is expected home about the middle of September.

Charles H. Russell has been appointed president and H. C. Campbell, vice-president, of the Charles H. Russell Co., Ltd., wholesale lumber merchants, Montreal. The company was recently incorporated to take over the business of Mr. Russell.

George C. Hurdman, M.P.P. for West Ottawa, who is a widely known lumberman, has again been nominated by the Liberals of the Capital to contest the riding at the next provincial election in Ontario.

Brigadier-Gen. J. B. White, of the Riordon Pulp & Paper Co., Ltd., Montreal, took part in the great welcome given in Montreal on August 21 to General Sir Arthur Currie on his return from overseas. A detachment of the Canadian Forestry Corps formed part of the parade.

Maurice Welsh, of Campbell, Welsh & Paynes, Toronto, has returned with his family from his summer residence at Bobcaygeon, Ont., to his new home, 56 Glenholme Ave., Toronto. Mr. Welsh reports that "the twins" reached the city by motor in fine form and had a most pleasant holiday.

Robson Black, of Ottawa, secretary of the Canadian Forestry Association and Wm. B. Stokes, of the Forest Products Laboratories, Montreal, spent a few days in Toronto recently supervising the splendid exhibit jointly made by these organizations in the Railway building at the Canadian National Exhibition.

L. C. Fisher, one of the Eastern representatives of the British Government Timber Buyer, is on a visit to Vancouver and Victoria in connection with the shipping of the government lumber. He will also visit Seattle and other U. S. ports. Mr. Fisher expects to leave for England early in October.

John Millin, 517 Crawford St., Toronto, was killed by lightning in his home during a recent severe electric storm. He was at his evening meal when a bolt struck the house. Mr. Millin was a carpenter, and his shop was where he lived. He had recently bought some timber limits and a sawmill near Parry Sound, and intended going north to reside.

H. A. Stewart, formerly of Buffalo, who for the past year has been manager of the hardwood department of C. G. Anderson Lumber Co., Toronto, left recently for Manilla, Philippine Islands, where he will supervise the manufacture and shipping of mahogany for the firm of Black and Yates of New York City, who specialize in this kind of wood. Mr. Stewart's many friends wish him every success in his new position.

Ralph E. Alling, representing the Wapskehegan Lumber Company, of Wapske, N. B., was in Toronto recently on a business trip and called upon a number of wholesalers in the interest of eastern spruce. Owing to a shortage of cars the shipping arrangements to the Eastern States have been somewhat interrupted and Mr. Alling's firm hopes to build up a strong connection for its products in Ontario.

Ex-Mayor Frank A. Kent, of Meaford, now of Toronto, who is general manager of the Seamen-Kent Co., Limited, recently took his initial trip in an aeroplane. The first aerial mail service out of Meaford occurred on August 20th when Mr. Kent left on a flight in company with an aviator who gave an exhibition of his skill in that town. He thoroughly enjoyed the rapid passage through the air.

Martin Valiquette, of Quebec, a forest engineer, lost his life recently in the northern wilds. He was drowned while surveying the forests on the shores of the Gulf for the Provincial Department of Lands and Forests. Had it not been for the prompt action of a guide who was following the canoe in which were Valiquette and others, two more deaths would have been added to the tragedy. The guide, Alf. Perrion, of St. Felicien, Lake St. John, struck out in the rushing waters of the river and rescued two of the men.

A basswood tree at Penetanguishene, Ont., which cut over 2,500 ft. of lumber. W. J. Martin is seen standing beside the tree.

Frank F. Fish, Chicago, secretary-treasurer of the National Hardwood Lumber Association spent a few days in Toronto recently calling upon a number of members of the trade. Mr. Fish states that the Amercian Hardwood Lumber Association has officially adopted the Inspection Rules of the National Hardwood Lumber Association, so that for the first time in nearly twenty years there is only one standard for the official inspection and measurement of hardwood lumber. This action on the part of the American Association will not in any way change the present policies of N. H. L. A.

Daniel J. Driscoll, a widely known wholesale lumberman, died recently at his home, 143 Gloucester St., Ottawa, in his 70th year. He had resided in the Capital since 1898 and in his commercial dealings was well known throughout all parts of the country. Mr. Driscoll was highly respected in business circles and was 70 years of age. Born in St. John, N. B., where he first entered the lumber business he followed it all his life. In St. John he carried on an extensive export trade for a number of years. Many old friends in that city will learn of his death with keen regret. Mr. Driscoll is survived by his widow and one son, Geo. F. Driscoll, of Montreal, who is prominent in theatrical circles.

Wm. Robertson, of Victoria, B. C., who is in charge of trade extension work in connection with the Forestry Branch, Department of Lands, is spending a few days in Toronto. Major James [illegible], B. C. Lumber Commissioner for the east, and Mr. Robertson are supervising the splendid exhibit of Coast and Mountain products which is being made in the Canadian government building at the Canadian National Exhibition. The display is a representative one in every respect and was brought east by Mr. Robertson. It is possible that, after the Exhibition, arrangements may be completed to have the various lines shown remain as a permanent exhibit in Toronto. Sergt. Robertson was a member of the Canadian Forestry Corps and was overseas for a considerable period. Previous to that he was located in Vancouver and had been identified with the Rat Portage Lumber Co., Kenora, Ont., for some 20 years, filling the position of assistant general manager.

Upward Scale of Camp Supplies

How Costs are Climbing Constantly on Many Commodities that are Daily Served Up to Lumberjacks

The cost of nearly all camp supplies is constantly on the increase. This is a broad statement to make, but a comparison of the prices paid for commodities previous to the war and four years later shows advances ranging from 75 to 150 per cent. In the 1918 Camp and Supply Number of the "Canada Lumberman" a comparative table was published of the average figures. In this edition the prices have been brought down to date and it will be observed that the trend of disbursements is still upward and on many articles of diet there has been a decided advance.

The figures have been obtained from reliable sources and are an index of how the camp commissariat is annually becoming a more serious problem and contributes in no small measure to the increased expense of logging.

The question is often asked "when will lumber take a drop." It certainly will not come about until the pendulum of values swings in the other direction and the cost of rations begins to descend. Just when this will occur one man's guess is as good as another. In the meantime, there does not appear on the horizon any visible omens of relief from the present stringent situation.

	June, 1914	June, 1918	August, 1919
Barrelled Pork Reg. Mess	26.00	54.50	55.00
Short Cut Back	28.50	58.50	64.00
Clear Fat Back 85/100	24.00	57.00	65.00
70/85	25.00	57.50	67.00
50/70	26.00	58.50	69.00
40/50	26.50	59.00	69.00
30/40	26.50	60.50	70.00
Bean Pork	24.00	51.50	49.00
S. P. Rolls	26.00	61.00	70.00
Barrelled Beef	23.00	42.00	45.00
	22.00	40.00	36.00
	28.00	32.00	32.00
	18.00	30.00	30.00
Smoked Hams 12/18	.18½	.36½	.48½
18/25	.17½	.34½	.46
25/35	.16½	.32½	.43½
35/up	.16	.30	.40½
Bacon 8/10	.18½	.44½	.56
10/12	.18½	.44½	.56
12/14	.18	.44½	.55½
14/20	.16½	.43	.55½
Pure Lard	.12½	.30	.36½
Eggs	.26	.44	.55
Cheese	.14½	.24	.29
Shortening	.10¼	.26	.31
Butter, Creamery Prints	.26	.45	.56
Creamery Solids	.25	.44½	.55
Dairy Prints	.22	.40	.48½
Dairy Solids	.21	.39	.47½
Mince Meat	.9	.12½	.15
Sausage	.9	.16	.17
Beef, Medium Steer Heifers, 450/550	.13½	.24	.21
Medium Cows, 450/550	.12½	.21	.17
Medium Bulls, 600/900	.12	.19½	.16½
Sugar (No. 1 standard granulated)	$4.51	$9.97	$10.50
Coffee (Rio)	17-18	24-29	37-39
Tea (Indian Pekoe Souchong)	19-20	46-48	45-47
Oatmeal (Standard 98 lb. bags)	$2.50-2.65	$5.75-7.00	$6.00-6.30
Beans (Canadian Whites)	$2.10-2.25	$6.75	$5.40-5.70
Flour (Manitoba White, sec. pats.)	5.10	10.95	11.00
New Potatoes (N. B., per bag)	$1.75	$2.00	$2.60
Prunes (60 to 70 to the lb., 50 lb. boxes)	10½-11	13¾-15	.25
Apples, (Evaporated)	9-10	20-21	.22
Rice (Rangoon)	3-4	9½-10	.13
Corn Syrup (barrels)	.3½	.7	.8¼

Ottawa Valley Will Double Log Output

A considerably increased woods cut for the season of 1919-20 with possibly a decreased sawmill cut for 1919, as compared with the previous years, is the best outlook one can predict for the production of the Ottawa Valley.

Attempts to double last year's log output in the woods is being generally made by the lumbermen and operators. In doing this it is pointed out that twice the number of hands will not be required, as last year many of the workers lost considerable time through being ill with the "flu."

The attempt to double the production of last year has been made necessity of getting down more logs and replenishing their reserves. the heavy drawing on reserves of logs and sawn lumber which are usually always kept ahead by most lumber manufacturers.

Stocks at the present time are low on the Ottawa lumber market particularly dry stock, and there is no great amount being held back of this year's cut by the manufacturers. To meet the demand which the manufacturers believe will arise next year, the lumbermen see the necessty of getting down more logs and replenishing their reserves.

The labor situation as gauged by the number of men offering is very satisfactory at the present time, but the rub comes when the question of efficiency is raised. Many men now offering themselves for bush or camp work were formerly employed in munition plants or in other jobs during the war. Numbers have little or no experience in log manufacture. Others want to go to certain camps, many of which are already filled and if they cannot they prefer to stay in the city or at home.

This consequently makes the situation all the more complicated, but advices to the "Canada Lumberman" indicate that there is not at the present time any anticipated shortage of woods labor. Wages run all the way from forty-five dollars per month for the inexperienced hand to sixty-five dollars for the old woodsman, with board.

The outlook all around seems favorable for a good season's operations and with an even break with the health of the camps keeping up and a fair standard of labor being available, there is not much doubt being expressed that the lumbermen will not be able to "double up."

The number and size of the camps are being increased. Operations toward getting the men into the camps in August indicated that they would be well filled and stocked promising a good season's operations.

The Pioneer Saw Mill in Northern Manitoba

The Finger Lumber Company, Limited, is the pioneer in the lumber industry in Northern Manitoba, that vast stretch of land hitherto considered as the Frozen Hinterland. With the advent of the Hudson's Bay Railway people are learning differently and the so-called frozen waste is now considered the richest part of Manitoba, as it is rich in mineral wealth, fish, fur, water power and lumber.

The Finger Lumber Company, Limited, commenced operations in the Spring of 1912. Its plant is located on the Saskatchewan river at the town of The Pas, Manitoba, which is the western terminus of the Hudson's Bay Railway. The Company owns extensive timber limits along the Saskatchewan and the Carrot rivers. Its logging thus far has been conducted on the limits along the Carrot river, where a number of camps last winter were operated. The logs are driven down the Carrot river into a storage boom located where this river empties into the Saskatchewan. They are then towed from this storage boom to the saw mill by the company's own tugs.

The mill is now equipped with a circular and gang, but as soon as conditions warrant it, it is the intention to increase the capacity considerably. The capacity now is 25,000,000 feet annually. This output is mostly spruce, there being only a sprinkling of cottonwood and tamarac. Carrot River spruce is considered high quality; has fine texture and compares favorably with white ine. The lumber is hauled from the sorting works to the yard by rail, and the planing mill is equipped with modern fast-feed machines and resaws.

The company operates its own electric light plant, and the motive power for both the sawmill and the planing mill is steam.

Most of the company's product is marketed in the Prairie Provinces, but during the last few years it has developed a market in the United States, where it is shipping as far east as New York City.

The officers of the company are: President and manager, H. Finger; vice-president, H. S. Smith; secretary-treasurer, W. H. Miner.

Thirty million feet of logs in the Miramichi river, N.B.

When Duty on Saw Logs Was Live Issue

Editor "Canada Lumberman",

Sir:—Feeling, as I do, the serious importance of the timber question to the interests of Canada, and desiring to assist, as far as in my power to do so, those who are advocating the preservation of our forests for the benefit of our own people, I have to say that on looking over some of our family papers, I found that on June 5th, 1851, the Toronto "Globe" had a long article headed "Duty on Saw-logs," based on a letter written by my father, James Little, who was then carrying on extensive lumbering operations from Caledonia on the Grand River, where he operated fulling mills and sawmills, being one of the first to export lumber in quantity from Canada to Buffalo, Albany, Cleveland, and Chicago.

You will see by an article published in the "Lumberman," thirty-one years later, December, 1882, that Sir Henri Joly de Lotbimere ably supported the views advocated by my father,

Gratefully yours,

William Little.

101 The Boulevard, Westmount, Que.

Under the heading of Duty on Saw Logs the "Globe" of Toronto, in its issue of June 5th, 1851, publishes the following article:

"Mr. James Little, the extensive pine lumber manufacturer of Caledonia has sent us a communication in reference to our remarks of last week on the proposal of the Middlesex County Council to lay an export duty on sawlogs. Mr. Little complains loudly of our statement that a good pine log will yield 1,500 feet of lumber, but he might have seen that this was a pure error—that we should have said a good pine tree will contain that quantity of lumber. But Mr. Little refers to other points and gives us some valuable information on the lumber merchant's side of the argument. Referring to our statement that "the best pine which a few years ago brought but $8, $9 and $10 per thousand feet, now sells readily for $16 for the Albany market. The cost of sawing is not more now than it was when the price was so much lower, therefore the prices of saw-logs should have greatly risen, but have not done so—, Mr. Little says: "The three upper qualities of lumber have for many years back ranged at less than from $10 to $12 per thousand feet, and all under these descriptions were higher when I first came to the river, seventeen years ago, than at present. At that time logs which now fetch a dollar and a dollar and a quarter did not bring more than from 1s. 3d. to 1s. 10½d. (=25c to 37½c) each. The description of logs now bringing from a dollar and a dollar and a quarter each, will only saw out 300 feet, and if we get a third or a fourth of clear out of the number of feet the log makes we are more than satisfied; indeed one-sixth is fully an average of these descriptions—so that you will see the quantity of clear dwindles down to less than a hundred feet. With reference to the cost of sawing, wages are higher, as are also coarse grain, hay and other feed for teams than the time you speak of.

Mr. Little next refers to our statement that "the Canadian manufacturer has a great natural advantage over the American, which should be quite sufficient,—he saws the logs on the spot, selects the best for the distant market, ships it in beautiful order, and pays no freight on refuse. The American manufacturer, on the other hand, pays freight on the tree with all its refuse, is exposed to much loss and trouble in the transport, and brings his timber to market in inferior condition."

And on this Mr. Little says: "If, sir, you would just reverse the whole of the above you would exactly have the truth. The Canadian manufactures on the spot, and carries his lumber in wagons, scows and vessels to market, with a deterioration in its quality which cannot be estimated at less than a dollar per thousand feet on every handling on the upper qualities, ships in "inferior order," and is met in the American market with an ad-valorem duty of 20 per cent. on sawn, and 30 per cent. on planed lumber, has commissions to pay for receiving, measuring, shipping, inspecting and selling. The American manufactre, on the other hand, floats his logs down the stream, rafts them at its mouth, and tows them across the lake (You surely don't suppose he freights his logs in vessels) for one-half the cost of transporting the lumber—pays an ad-valorem duty on logs, which is a mere trifle—saws them and disposes of his lumber at home, without any deterioration in quality from frequent handling, in "beautiful order," without the several commissions the Canadian manufacturer has necessarily to pay."

(From the "Canada Lumberman," December 1882.)

Hon. H. G. Joly de Lotbiniere, of Quebec; I cannot understand why there should be any doubt as to the wisdom of imposing an export duty on our logs. Many of those who with the hope of promoting their personal interests, advocated at one time its removal, are now in favor of its re-imposition. But let us look at the question as it affects the country at large. In giving us our forests Providence has given us a source of wealth which it is our duty to husband carefully and to turn to the best account. It is possible that we Canadians should have so little manliness left as to tell our neighbors: Come, cut down our trees, take them away, manufacture them at home and reap the golden harvest. We don't want it. We have got work enough to occupy us here. What would have become of England if she had invited the world to come and take away her coals and iron and manufacture abroad? We ought to treasure our forests. But how much more ought we to treasure the youth of our country, leaving us every year by thousands to seek work in the United States? Shall we force those who still remain with us to leave us, too, by sending the raw materials, the logs, in the manufacturing of which we can procure work for so many Send away our logs to the States and our mill-hands will follow them. In other words, while we cannot find employment at home for our own workmen, shall we provide work for those of the United States? Our neighbors want our lumber, they must have it, they threaten us with the imposition of higher duties if we insist upon manufacturing our own timber at home. We cannot complain, it is their right. Perhaps they may carry out their threat. As one interested in the exportation of sawn lumber to the United States, and naturally anxious to enter it there under favorable conditions, I appeal to those who are answerable for the welfare and prosperity of our country. I implore them to keep our logs here, and with our logs to keep here those who will earn their living by working them, and should I be called upon to pay a higher duty for my sawn lumber exported to the United States, I will then pay it cheerfully.

W. F. Beck, Penetanguishene, Ont. [illegible]

L. Hamel, Quebec City, Que. [illegible]

Dr. C. D. Howe, Toronto, Ont. [illegible]

See De Style Put On By De Chantierman

Editor Lumberman Canayenne.

It are mak me much soree Im not to on ma house we'n you come on Lac au Loup las w'ik. You see, I can' be on de house w'en Im be on de bush, an dats sure t'ing.

We are ope de camp now an have place a couple jobber. Im expec ope couple more jus so soon Im get de mans an cook, an mebbe two, t'ree wat you call "valet" for de mans.

Ba Gosh, dats mak me laff, wen Im not angree, for see de style wat are put on by de "chantierman" dese day, an it soon be we have get recommend before d'ey come work for us.

Im tel you Mon Ami, dere are beeg change tak place on our beezness on las few year an it cost much monee too.

Ma ole fadder he tel me he work, wen he be yong mans, for $9.00 mont an he bring hees own tea on de chantier too.

D'ey are not have any "gadondar," wat you call him, cross saw, on dose tam an he fall de beeg pine wit de axe an cut her on de log same way. Dats some job too, wen you tink de size dose ole pine tree. He are hire for de "run" which means he go up one summer an return on tam for go up nex' summer. A good steady job an las all de tam.

Den I 'member meser, run one small camp, an de bes pay are $18.00 mont'. We have one cook an he cut his wood for his sef an Im hav it haul on de camp for heem.

Get More Appetite for Eat Agen

Dose tam were better for mak de log as now, for good many reason. One reason were de strong grub we eat, pork and bean, pea soup an molasses an de good bread wat are mak from real flour. W'en a mans have fill hersef wit dat sort de grub, he wan do something pretty queek an he jomp on de log an work her off. Den he get more appetite for eat agen.

On dat tam Im mention, we have de good mans wat are work all de tam on de bush an not bodder with nodder kin' work. He not have much ceremonee wen he eat, an are satisfy for he'p hersef wit de dish an knife an spoon, an den go on de pot for fill her up. He tak a place on a bench an eat with de good conscience. He sl'ip well an work well an are good fren for have aroun wen troub come for bodder you, an he have excuse for tak leetle drink between job jus for get rid some dat grease wat are not diges'.

Wn we begin talk about de "chantierman" wat are work for us today dats annuder storee an mebbe praps you know better as me how she are. An you begin tink, Caspar are talk through her hat an are gone try give you lecture on "Troub' on de Camp," an "W'y de logs cos' so much dis year."

No Sir, Im not give you lecture for good reason. De Boss have visit me few wi'k ago an have give me lecture on how Im gone get out more as quarter million piece de log wit'out it cost me more as las year.

De Boss are good feller, an we are de good fren but he mus be cowboy on one tam, for he handle de bull lak he were 'custom.

Wen Im hope de firs camp dis year, it were easy for get de good mans for Im place mos ma neighbor on it, but wen Im try for get de mans, bout forty, for season camp, it are nudder ting an Im have sen notis everyw'ere an say we wan' de "chantiermans" an dat we pay de good wage for experience mans.

Say He Are Wan Job on de Bush

One feller come on me an say he are wan job on de bush an aks me how much Im pay. Im tel her we pay jus so much lak nudder company, but he mus mak de wage now so Im tel her $50.00 mont an board. He say he tak job for few day an if Im have good camp he stay for wile anyway. Im hire her an sen her on de camp wit nudder mans an wen Im go on de camp for see how it are go, Joe Larocque wat are foremans, tel me bout dat feller.

He say he arrive on de camp an go on office an see de "commis" wat are kip de book. Den he go on de chantier an look aroun' an come out agen. He go on commis agen an say he no lak stay on chantier an aks for bed on office. De commis tel her de office are for hissef an de foremans, also for de culler an de visite, an aks her wat are wrong wit de chantier. De mans say we not have de spring bed, an pillow mak wit de fedder. An nudder ting, he not use slip wi nudder feller an wan bed for his sef.

De commis are pretee smart yong feller an he lak have joke once a w'ile. He aks dat mans have he bring "valet" wit her an how offen he get her nail manicure but it no mak de laff. Dat feller were serious. He say he are use have de spring bed, d pillow an de sheet, an dat he are custom tak bat' once a wik. He also say he not custom wash hees clothes but are have it done for heem jus lak we live on city.

Now, how you lak dat, ma fren? An it are a fac dat feller wat are use have a bat' on de chantier once a wi'k, are good mans too an can mak de log with nudder mans an are better as mos mans on Joe Larocque's camp. He are not kicker but are custom have good accommodation w'ere he work.

On our camp we have de good bed. We not have de spring bed but have de straw mattress an pillow, an de chore boy he mak de bed each morning an swip de camp. He kip de place clean an wen it are cold he kip good fire an lots de wood. We not have a place for bat' but who wan tak bat' wen it are cold wedder? An for wash de clothes, it are not veree hard work was a few socks an mebbe some nudder clothes once a mont'.

De Tam Have Change in de Chanty

Anyhow, de tam have change an Im spose we have change too if we wan' kip our mans.

Im not mention de cookery w'ere de cook are boss but dats mos importan place too an we have de good table an bench an lots de dish an knife; an de fork also, den we have two cook an chore boy an some cook dey wan a boy for wash de dish an peel potatoe.

Yeh, De Boss have visit me before we ope de camp an we go on de bush on ma las' year cutting. We stop on de camp an have a bite an after we smoke a wile de Boss he say "Caspar, you smoke veree strong tubac dis year. Were you get him?"

Im say Im raise her mesef, las year but it are not too strong. "Well," he say, "it smell strong anyway," an jus den we see a skunk come on de door an de Boss he say "w'ere we go from here" but not give me chance for tel her for he go through de window an Im fin' her bout quarter mile below de camp wen Im get chance for come out. Im tink dat skunk have loss her mate an imagine he have foun her wen he smell dose cigaret de Boss are smoke.

Anyway, it are gone cost someting for mak de log dis year an you feller wat are live on de city an are buil' de house, gone pay for de bat', an spring bed, an wash de cloes ann few nudder ting wat are need on de bush now.

Tam have change an mebbe it are bes we not eat de strong food now for it are hard get a drink an we have notting for help us diges our food excep' work, an no one wan' do dat needer.

Bien a vous,

CASPAR LAMARCHE.

Lac au Loup, Que., August 21st, 1919.

Moving Picture Film of Timber Test

"Timber Testing at the Forest Products Laboratories of Canada, McGill University" is the title of a film that will be shown throughout Canada and is of considerable educational interest. The cinematographer of the British Canadian Pathe news recently photographed the first movie taken of showing work in progress as conducted at the Forest Products Laboratories of Canada, 700 University Street, Montreal. The film shows a test to determine how much weight was required to break a structural timber measuring 8 inches by 16 inches, by 16 feet long. The test piece was purchased from a local timber firm and was of Douglas fir. The British Columbia Forest Service desired to have exhibited at their section of forest exhibits of the National Exhibition, Toronto, a full-sized beam of Douglas fir as used for structural purposes, showing how it breaks and what weight it will carry. The Forest Products Laboratories of Canada, which has frequently made strength tests of various kinds of Canadian woods, reports the break occurred at 58,450 pounds in this case.

No Prospect of Lower Prices in West

By George B. Cross, New Westmins er, B. C.

Prices of all house building lumber are high and still advancing. This is accoutned for by the great building boom now on throughout the length and breadth of the United States and reaching into Canada.

The amount of house and farm building throughout Canada and the United States really controls the prices of that class of lumber. There is no prospect of lower prices for the balance of this year, or, at least, until the snow flies, and every indication points to high prices for 1920. There will be two or three months during the winter, perhaps beginning with December, when it may be possible to lay in a stock at somewhat lower prices than are in effect to-day.

It is probably well known to many of your readers that the British Columbia Coast Mills produce another class of lumber, viz.: timber, 8 x 8 in. and up. Without orders for such timber the mills are at a disadvantage in operating; first, because the heart of the log is much better fitted for timber, railway ties, etc., than for cutting up into lumber; and secondly, the capacity of the mill machinery, the trimmers, planers, sorting tables, etc., is usually arranged to take care of only about 50 per cent. of the cut of the mill, the balance going out in timber.

Owing to want of lumber carriers for the foreign market, and to the small domestic demand for timber and the stoppage of ship-building, timber has not advanced in price since last year, nor is it likely to avance until more ships are available. Railway companies are, therefore, securing their supplies of ties and timber at very favorable prices.

There is increased demand for Pacific Coast lumber for industrial purposes, such as doors, veneer, agricultural machinery, pianos, cooperage, crating, etc., and we hope to retain this business when the lumber business gets back to normal in other lumber centres.

No Reduction in Cost of Logging

By Wm. G. McKay, Madawaska, Ont.

The war is now over and the food regulations are somewhat modified. However, the rationing in force during the European conflict did not work any hardship on the men boarding in the lumber camps, as ample food of the various kinds was allowed and no complaints were heard either as to quantity or quality.

Now that the war is ended and conditions are on the way down to normal, the cost of provisions and board varies but little from last season. The only article of food used in the camps to any extent, in which there is much difference in price, is beans, they having dropped from $7 per bushel to $4.50. All other provisions remain much the same as last year, some slightly higher and some slightly lower. Flour is about the same, meat, in some cases, a little higher, and cheese is up about 3c per pound; so, when all is figured in, board will cost as much as last year.

Labor conditions are unsettled, the men being restless and moving around from one place to another. Wages are somewhat lower but not very much, the men being hired from $50 to $65 per month, the most of them getting the latter. Cooks, handy men and foremen are receiving more than at the same time last year. The quantity of work done is about the same, but more supervision is required to get it carried out as well as other seasons, which makes it harder for the men in charge of the operations.

Conditions may be somewhat better as far as the men settling down to work are concerned when the regular logging season comes in, about the 1st of September. During the summer months the hot weather, along with flies, makes it harder to keep men. I have not had much difficulty in keeping my camps full, as I have from 85 to 100 men in each camp.

It is pretty safe to say that the cost of logging will not be any lower than last season, unless conditions change very materially from what they are now. In regard to hiring men by the day in the lumber camps I have not given this very much consideration. I do not believe there would be very much gained in changing from the present plan of engaging them by the month.

Thinks West Should Move More Rapidly

That there are great calls for British Columbia lumber in overseas markets, and that B. C. lumbermen have failed to take anything like full advantage of their opportunities to secure big business there, is the opinion expressed by Sir Douglas C. Cameron, former lieutenant-governor of Manitoba, and president of the Rat Portage Lumber Company, who was recently in Vancouver.

"There are markets for British Columbia lumber, but the Vancouver dealers have not gone after them. It does not create a favorable impression to find that the order for 70,000,000 feet of lumber for Britain has not yet been moved," said Mr. Douglas.

That there is a great demand for British Columbia lumber in various parts of the States, was also stated by Sir Douglas, who added that the possibilities for the development of the lumber trade from Vancouver were very great indeed, and the outlook satisfactory in every way.

Correct Moisture Content of Lumber

Shrinking and swelling of wood, as well as warping and twisting, are caused by changes in moisture content. Such changes always take place when the wood is not in equilibrium with the surrounding atmosphere. This state of equilibrium depends mainly upon the humidity of the air and to some extent upon its temperature.

Knowing the average temperature and humidity of any given region, as given by the Weather Bureau records, it is possible to determine the moisture content of wood corresponding to these conditions. Wood dried to this moisture content will undergo the least possible amount of working in that particular region.

The following table, compiled from data secured by the Forest Products Laboratory of the U. S. Forest Service at Madison, Wis., shows the moisture content in wood corresponding to various temperatures and humidities:

When relative humidity of air is Per cent.	The moisture content of At temperature of 70 deg. F. Per cent.	At temperature of 140 deg. F. Per cent.
20	4.5	
30	6.0	4.5
40		
50		
60	11.2	
70	13.5	10.7
80	17.0	
90		
100	32.0	26.2

Airplane Forest Protection is Success

Protection of forests by airplanes, said Mr. G. C. Piche, in charge of the Forestry service of the province, has proved very effective, and he added, as soon as this new system proves to be possible in all regions of the province it is understood that it will be exclusively adopted.

"There has been a marked improvement this year in the protection of forests in the province of Quebec," stated Mr. Piche, "and this is due to the efforts made by the department to attain better results, because the conditions have been far from ameliorated with the dryness in certain regions."

Cafeteria Plan Gives Good Results

There appeared in the "Canada Lumberman" of May 1st, 1918, an illustrated description of the cafeteria plan, which had been adopted by the Kerr Lake Mining Co., Limited, of Cobalt, Ont., in regard to feeding men by this method. At that time the Food Control Board at Ottawa was thinking of instituting a system of rationing in the logging camps. Many lumbermen, who were eager to economize and conserve as much as possible both in the matter of food and labor, were thinking seriously of instituting the cafeteria system. However, before the new food regulations were promulgated the armistice was signed and the thought of the self-serve plan has, no doubt, faded from the minds of loggers.

H. A. Kee, manager of the Kerr Lake Mining Co., was asked recently how the cafeteria idea was working out and, in a reply, he states, "we have found this system perfectly satisfactory after a year and a half of experience with it and we would not care to alter it in any way. Even with the food regulations removed and more latitude in consequence allowed in consumption, the quantities per man have increased very slightly. The workers appear to be just as well pleased with our plan as they were eighteen months ago. If there is any particular point that any lumberman would like to be enlightened upon regarding the cafeteria service, we will endeavor to send as full particulars as possible."

MAKING THE PRINTED WORD EFFECTIVE

"If you have anything worth selling, it is worth advertising. If your business is not worth advertising, give it away and get into some other line of business." said the late Elbert Hubbard.

The message—the thing you have to say—is the main thing about a good advertisement. If it is strong, the rest is not so important. The mistake of trying to be original has ruined many an advertisement. The public is not interested in freak advertising.

People want the realities. They want to know why this merchandise was produced, in some cases how it was produced, and what are its good qualities and uses. And you can write a good advertisement if you are mightily interested in what you have to sell and then put a lot of that interest into your advertising copy. Feature the points that do or should appeal to the average customer.

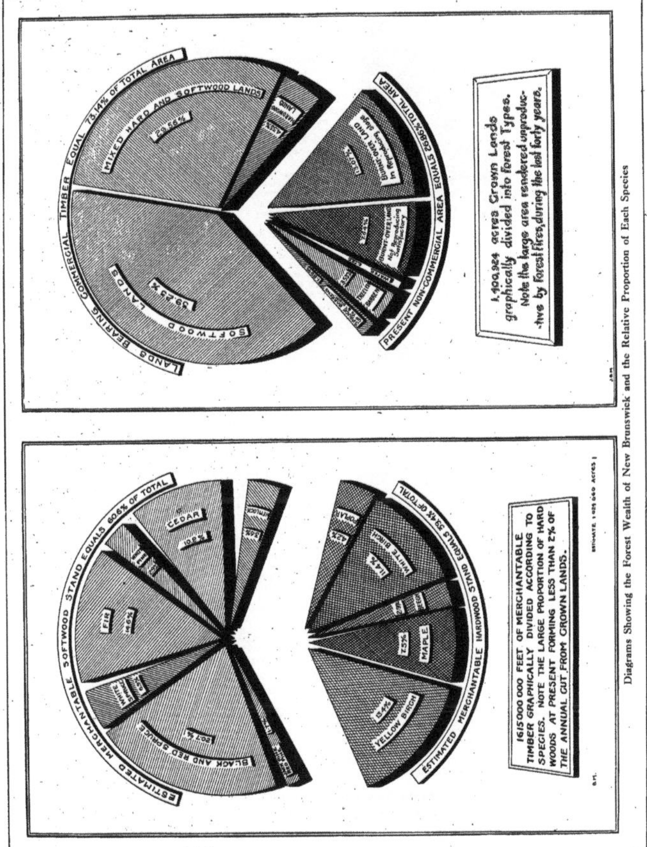

Diagrams Showing the Forest Wealth of New Brunswick and the Relative Proportion of Each Species

Mr. Mackin Goes to Australia

James N. Mackin, Sydney, Australia

James N. Mackin "started succeeding" when he entered the saw business as a young man scarcely out of his "teens." His happy, genial disposition was a valuable asset, and he eventually became an expert salesman. For twenty years he represented a Philadelphia house, during which time he travelled extensively throughout the world.

He acquired experience of great value, and became familiar with business conditions everywhere. But one of the greatest facts that he learned, because it was so repeatedly impressed upon him wherever he journeyed, was the unusual high quality and great popularity of Atkins Silver Steel Saws.

During the war he represented E. C. Atkins & Co., in Washington, D.C., and made hosts of friends both for himself and for the great firm for which he sold. His success here, due to his wonderful business ability coupled with a wealth of energy, vigor, and optimism, made him the logical man to care for the rapidly increasing business of the firm in the Far East.

Atkins Silver Steel Saws and tools have enjoyed a steady growth in Australia amounting to over fifty per cent. in the last three years. The Company very wisely selected Mr. Mackin to represent them there, and he is now superintendent of the entire Australian division. His headquarters are located at the E. C. Atkins & Co., Branch House, No. 5 Australasia Chambers, Martin Place, Sydney, N.S.W., Australia.

Mr. Cox Was Tower in Timber Trade

"The Timber Trades Journal" says: The Canadian, as well as the Liverpool trade, have sustained a great loss by the death of Mr. Robert M. Cox, who was the pioneer in the Canadian pine trade as it is today. Mr. Cox, who was a native of Bewdley, Worcestershire, and the son of Mr. John Cox, a timber merchant of that town, went to Canada for the benefit of his health, when he soon saw the opportunities the export trade offered, and from that time developed the special line of business in which he afterwards became so prominent, being at one time the largest shipper of Canadian pine goods. In the interest of his business, Mr. Cox had crossed the Atlantic as many as 300 times, having in some years travelled to and fro twice or thrice, but latterly he spent the greater part of his time in Ottawa, and had not been on this side for three years. Besides having commercial interests in Ottawa, Mr. Cox was a Freemason, at one time a member of the Bottle Town Council, and a staunch supporter of the Timber Trade Benevolent Society, acting as one of its vice-presidents, and to which he sent a substantial donation each year.

The "Timber News" remarks: Mr. Robert Montgomery Cox had stood like a tower in the midst of the timber trade for a quarter of a century or more. He was the creator if we may use the word of the Canadian pine deal industry as we know it today. In former times the pine deal was like the rest of Canadian sawn stuff, ill manufactured and ill sorted, and Canadian pine came to this country largely in the log, and was then converted into planks and boards to suit English requirements. Mr. Cox was a man with a vision and he saw what was wanted and seized the opportunity, and in a few years rose to fame and fortune. Since then others have entered the field, and they, too, have been firms with ideas, and have expanded in ways unthought of the Canadian pine trade. The log has largely vanished, but in its place we have infinite varieties of planks, deals, battens, and sidings. The surviving partner of Robert Cox & Co., Liverpool, Mr. Fred Burns, has been associated with Mr. Cox for more than 40 years. He is at present in Canada, where he will remain until the end of the shipping season. Meanwhile the interests of the firm on this side are being looked after by the Liverpool manager, Mr. W. E. Bell, who is well known to the trade.

What Quebec Can do for Europe

The possibilities of Canadian natural resources in reconstructing devastated Europe are outlined by Lieut.-Col. P. Pelletier, agent for the Province of Quebec in London, in an article in a London daily paper. While referring to the Dominion as a whole, Lieut.-Col. Pe-

An Attractive Logging Camp is Appreciated

The Last Word in Construction is the Equipment of Progressive Western Firm at Myrtle Point—Men Paid on Piece Basis and Output Increased

WHAT is undoubtedly one of the most up-to-date logging camps in British Columbia, or in Canada for that matter, has just been given its finishing touches and is now in full operation at Myrtle Point. In reality there are four camps, but they are so connected that they are called one. The bulk of the timber for these camps, which are owned by Messrs. Bloedel, Stewart and Welch, whose headquarters are at Vancouver with Mr. Frank Riley as manager, was bought in 1911, and the hauling of logs on one side was started on New Year, 1912. During that year the firm increased their operations two sides and ran along with that capacity until last January, when they purchased the holdings of the Straits Lumber Company at Lang Bay, adding to their timber holdings about eleven miles of railway with equipment.

Since that time a new terminal has been constructed, that at Lang Bay being eliminated, so that the pivotal point is at Myrtle Point. The firm now have over twenty miles of steel. About nine miles of this is a main line and five or six miles of branch lines, and at the present time they are operating on four sides. At Myrtle Point they enlarged their building ground and, in addition to that, constructed a breakwater to protect the booming ground from the southeast winds. New buildings have sprung up as if by magic, one of these being a combination warehouse and store, machine shop and so forth.

Steel Bunks for the Men

The camp itself where the men live and eat is the last work in camp construction. Each car is divided into two and each compartment contains eight double-decker steel bunks, which were supplied by the Alaska Bedding Company of Vancouver. The latest sanitary conveniences have been installed, embracing bath-rooms, while there is a billiard room run on the most approved lines.

While all the camps are called one, there are in reality four, and they are numbered 1, 2, 3 and 4, with headquarters at Myrtle Point. In what is designated Camp 1, there are 35 men. Camp 2 consists of modern cars, each 15 x 60 feet, on wheels. Camp 3, at Haslam Lake, the present terminal of the main line, is stationary. Camp 4 is at the head of the lake. Each of these camps is an example of what a logging camp ought to be for the accommodation of men who spend their lives in the open and who have not the daily amusements to which the people of a city are accustomed. So far as it is possible to do so, the arrangements are such that ample provision is made for the comfort and amusement of the employees.

View of the High-Lead unit that is in operation at the camp at Myrtle Point. This spar tree is about 190 feet high

This loader was specially constructed for the camp

Labor Troubles are Unknown

In regard to the equipment, Bloedel, Stewart and Welch use the most modern high-lead units with duplex loaders mounted on steel cars. The railway stock consists of one 180-ton Baldwin locomotive, one 42-ton Shay engine and a 45-ton Climax, with 50 air-equipped skeleton flats. The accompanying illustrations show the high-lead system at work and the type of loader that is in use, this loader being the product of the camp. It is named after the popular manager, Mr. Riley.

The firm have enough timber to carry on operations for the next ten years. There is aproximately 500,000,000 feet of it, consisting principally of fir and cedar. Of course this period depends on the state of the lumber market. All told there are 250 men at work, and it is interesting to hear the statement from Mr. Riley that the labor troubles in Vancouver did not effect Myrtle Point one iota. The camp is operated on what is known, so far as wages are concerned, as a piece basis. Under this system the men are paid in proportion to their earnings, based on a reasonable maximum output at the present wages. By this means, the men have largely increased their earnings and the output has been increased accordingly.

Lighting of the Camp

The camp is electrically lighted throughout. Current for this purpose is furnished by an installation of the Delco Light system, consisting of two automatic generating units, three-quarter kilowatt each, connected with a set of 160 ampere-hour storage batteies. The advantage of the two-unit system is, that most of the time a full load is not necessary, in which event one unit only need be operated, thus cutting the fuel cost very considerably. Another advantage is that, in the event of any mishap to one of the units, a plentiful supply of light is assured until repairs can be made, although this latter contingency is not so important as general experience with this particular system demonstrates that there is practically no danger of breakdown where ordinary care is given to the plant.

In passing, it may be noted that a serious objection to these isolated lighting plants might lie in the necessity for expert attention due to the liability of a breakdown. The experience of users, so far as can be ascertained, does away with the former of these objections, as usually the timekeeper, blacksmith or someone else, whose duties keep him around the camp, is capable of looking after the plant with perfect success. As to the latter objection, the local representatives of the Delco system state that, during last winter, with over thirty plants in operation in logging camps and similar places, only eight calls on them were made for service, three of these being from the same place, where gross carelessness was the cause.

Quick Action Section

PUBLISHER'S NOTICE

Advertisements other than "Employment Wanted" or "Employees Wanted" will be inserted in this department at the rate of 20 cents per agate line (14 agate lines make one inch). $2.80 per inch, each insertion, payable in advance. Space measured from rule to rule. When four or more consecutive insertions of the same advertisement are ordered a discount of 25 per cent. will be allowed.

Advertisements of "Wanted Employment" will be inserted at the rate of one cent a word, net. Cash must accompany order. If Canada Lumberman box number is used, enclose ten cents extra for postage in forwarding replies. Minimum charge 25 cents.

Advertisements of "Wanted Employees" will be inserted at the rate of two cents a word, net. Cash must accompany the order. Minimum charge 50 cents.

Advertisements must be received not later than the 10th and 20th of each month to insure insertion in the subsequent issue.

Wanted—Lumber

Basswood Wanted

No. 2 Common and Mill Cull. Winter cut preferred. Apply Firstbrook Brothers, Ltd., Toronto, Ont. 8-t.f.

Lumber Wanted

Spruce, Pine and Hardwoods, also sawdust in car lots, spot cash soon as on the cars. Apply Box 11, Canada Lumberman, Toronto. 17

DOWELS

Wanted to purchase several carloads. Quote F.O.B. or C.I.F. and state quantity offered. Frank Rosser, 226 Upper Brook Street, Manchester. 17

Birch Wanted

We require 400,000 ft. 4/4" Birch, No. 2 and No. 3 Common. Quote prices, name of shipping point, and delivery. Box 15, Canada Lumberman, Toronto. 17

Wanted Lumber

Hardwood Lumber wanted. Birch, Maple, Basswood and other Hardwoods. Dry or sawn to order. We send inspector. Box 14, Canada Lumberman, Toronto. 17-20

Rock Maple Blocks Wanted

Can use one million feet 13" to 16" in length, according to diameter, cut in bolts. Quote price per M. feet scale, loaded on cars. Box 18, Canada Lumberman, Toronto. 17-18

Wanted

10/4 and 12/4 No. 1 Common and Better Birch,

also

10/4 and 12/4 No. 1 Common and Better Soft Elm.

In quoting, state how the stock will run to 1st and 2nds and how long it has been cut. Box 996, Canada Lumberman, Toronto. 16-19

For Sale—Lumber

For Sale

30,000 setts Cheese Box Veneer. Apply C. A. Moses, Osgoode Station, Ont. 16-19

FOR SALE

100 pieces White Oak Piling, 20 to 60 ft. For particulars write

E. S. THOMPSON,
Appin, Ont.
10-t.f.

Lumber For Sale
This Season's Cut

300 M Basswood, 1" and 1½".
15 M Black Ash, 1".
75 M Soft Elm, 1", 2", 3" and 4".
130 M Hard Maple, 1", 2" and 3".
250 M 1" and 2" Hemlock.
15 M Birch, 1" and 2".
Ontario White Cedar Shingles, 16".

THE PEARCE CO., LIMITED,
Marmora, Ont.
17

FOR SALE

50,000 ft.	2 x 4 x 10/16'	Jack Pine & Spruce	
100,000 "	2 x 5 x 10/16'	"	"
100,000 "	2 x 6 x 10/16'	"	"
100,000 "	2 x 7 x 10/16'	"	"
100,000 "	2 x 8 x 10/16'	"	"
2 cars	6 x 6 x 10/16'	"	"
2 "	6 x 8 x 10/16'	"	"
2 "	8 x 8 x 10/16'	"	"
1 "	10 x 10 x 10/16'	"	"

The above stock cut and piled ready for shipment. Write or Wire

NORTHERN LUMBER MILLS,
North Cobalt, Ont.
14-17

Wanted—Machinery

Wanted

Steel Refuse Burner—Second hand—20 to 25 feet diameter. Write stating size, condition and lowest price and where situated, to Refuse Burner, Box 22, Canada Lumberman, Toronto, Ont. 17-18

Wanted

Large Horizontal Resaw for Sawmill, must be good condition. Also Swage for 18 gauge blades. Have for sale No. 177 Berlin Double Surfacer and a 44" Mershon Band Rip Saw. Box 999, Canada Lumberman, Toronto. 17

For Sale—Machinery

FOR SALE

One second-hand 8" band saw, complete with saws; also circular resaw, with two inserted tooth saws, 42" dia. Keenan Bros., Ltd., Owen Sound, Ont. 16-19

FOR SALE

1 Steam Feed Carriage with Steam Set Works, "Waterous Model."
1 Nigger, complete, "Waterous Model."
1 Wicks Gang Saw, complete with saws and steam engine, "Midland," 60 H.P.
2 Shingle Machines, complete with saws.
11 Pulpwood Barkers.

For particulars apply to

CHICOUTIMI PULP CO.,
Chandler, Que.
17-20

For Sale

1—17 x 24 Atlas Engine, with 36 in. x 10 ft. flywheel.
3—No. 94 Berlin Matchers, 15 in., fitted with hard steel knives on top and bottom cylinders—one pair shiplap, jointer and flooring heads with bits for each machine.
1—No. 132 Berlin Double Surfacer, 30 in. x 6 in.
1—No. 190 Berlin Buzz Planer.
1—No. 290 Berlin Picket Header.

The Otis Staples Lumber Company, Ltd.,
Wycliffe, B.C.
19-t.f.

FOR SALE—SAWMILL

25 H. P. Engine, 50 H. P. return tubular boiler. Three log seat carriage, overhead set, friction feed works, single edger and slab saw. All in fair order. Price $1,000. Box 913, Canada Lumberman, Toronto. 16-19

FOR SALE
Saw Mill Machinery

Complete saw mill machinery; equipped with rotary, steam feed carriage, Gang Saw, Resaw, Edger, Butter, Lath Machine. Three Boilers and twin engine 300 H.P.; also saw gummers, filers and one shingle machine, with bolter and barker. For particulars apply:

CHICOUTIMI PULP CO.,
Chandler, Que.
16-19

Band Saw Mill Complete

Waterous 9 ft. Band Mill, Gunshot Feed Carriage, with extra Saws complete.

Filing Equipment

Three Saw Edger, lot of live rolls, Engine, Shafting, Hangers, Pulleys, etc.

All of the above is Waterous equipment in good condition at a bargain.

The Geo. F. Foss Machinery & Supply Co., Limited,
305 St. James Street,
Montreal, Que.
17-t.f.

Used
Saw Mill Machinery
FOR SALE

One McGregor & Gourlay endless bed Planer, knives 28" long, bed raises and lowers by power. Will plane 10" thick. In good condition. One B. F. Sturtevant Exhaust Fan, Intake 23" diameter, discharge 19" x 10" square, pulley 10" dia. x 8" face. In good working order, with an extra set of blades or fans. Also bonnet and piping for planer and discharge piping for fan.

Also two Moreau Rossers for peeling pulp wood. These are as good as new; used only one season. Will peel on an average 25 cords per day. Reason for selling, no more pulp wood to peel.

Complete Saw Mill for sale. Full particulars given on enquiry. All this machinery is at Kazubazua, Que., and belongs to Kazubazua Lumber Co. Any further information will be given by addressing

L. D. PHILIPS,
34 Thornton Ave.,
Ottawa, Ont.
16-19

Wanted—Employment

Advertisements under this heading one cent a word per insertion. Box No. 10 cents extra. Minimum charge 25 cents.

WANTED: Position as log culler or foreman in log camp, by experienced man. For further particulars apply Box 44, Orangeville, Ont. 16-19

WANTED, INTEREST OR POSITION with Manufacturing or Wholesale Lumber Company wanted by returned officer with fifteen years' lumber experience in large operations. Excellent references. Box 16, Canada Lumberman, Toronto. 17

Thoroughly experienced sawmill and lumberman as assistant manager or general superintendent of operations on coast or interior; age 36, married, an English Canadian and speaks French; satisfactory references. Write Box 988, Canada Lumberman, Toronto. 15-17

WANTED POSITION by representative and superintendent, still employed with wholesale firm, with twenty-five years' experience in the lumber business. Can give reference as to capabilities and take charge on a month's notice. Box 991, Canada Lumberman, Toronto. 18-

WANTED, POSITION AS LUMBER BUYER or Salesman, by experienced man, twenty-five years in retail and wholesale, four years travelling in province of Quebec as salesman for the sale of western and eastern lumber, good clientele; age forty-five; speaks both English and French. For further particulars apply Box 55, Canada Lumberman, Montreal. 17

Wanted—Employees

WANTED—Shingle Packer. Apply at once

St. Maurice Paper Co., Limited,
Montcalm Mills, P.Q.
17

WANTED—A number of experienced Hardwood Sawmill Operators to contract to take out large quantities of Hardwood during the coming winter. Stumpage can be furnished, if necessary, and the necessary cash advances to assist responsible operators. Address Box 10, Canada Lumberman, Toronto. 17-20

POSITION OPEN for a high-class man capable of organizing and assuming full management of all lumbering operations of a 500-mile timber limit for a Company operating a Saw-mill and a Pulp-mill. All replies will be treated confidentially. A permanent position with a good salary open for the right man. Box 993, Canada Lumberman, Toronto. 16-21

LUMBER EXPORT HOUSE has opening for intelligent young man, 18-23 years of age. Applicant must be ambitious, willing, and have a good education. Competent stenographer and typist, and be accurate at figures. Moderate salary to start, but good opportunity for advancement and to learn the business. Apply giving references, experience, etc., to Mr. S. Bick, P. O. Box 284, Montreal. 14-17

Business Chances

Wanted

Good reliable saw mill man with portable mill to cut two million feet or more Birch and Hemlock in Patterson Township. Warren Ross Lumber Co., Jamestown, N.Y. 14-19

FOR SALE

Saw, Heading and planing mill with electric light plant for lighting town. Will sell with or without electric light plant. Good supply of timber. For further information apply to Geo. Coultis & Son, Thedford, Ont. 16-17

Partnership

A returned officer who has an all round knowledge of lumber business acquired in Ontario and the West, is desirous of acquiring an interest in a concern where services and investment would show fair return. Replies with particulars treated confidentially. Box 23, Canada Lumberman, Toronto. 17-18

For Sale

Building and machinery of good Double Cut Band Sawmill, well equipped with steam feed, canter, loaders, etc.

Also two storey Brick Factory on large lot convenient to two railways; splendid location. Address Box 949, Owen Sound, Ont. 12-t.f.

Hardwood Bush Wanted

Good hardwood bush covering from 1000 to 5000 acres. State location, distance from railway and best cash price. Address Box 21, Canada Lumberman, Toronto. 17-18

FOR SALE

80 H.P. Circular Saw Mill with planer, shingle outfit. Plenty of timber can be procured reasonable. About 200 miles from Toronto. Might exchange for property in Toronto. Address Jas. Umpherson, 1000 Bathurst St., Toronto. 17

FOR SALE

On reasonable terms, a well established retail lumber business in a live and growing city, will be sold as a going concern, including central site, convenient to railway facilities. Apply Box 980, Sault Ste. Marie, Ont. 17-20

Timber Limit For Sale

Situated in Northern Ontario, 27¼ square miles. Estimated quantity of pine thereon upwards of 10,000,000 feet, as well as spruce and other timber. For full information apply to W. E. Bigwood, Bank of Hamilton Building, Toronto, or Byng Inlet, Ontario. 15-18

Timberlands For Sale

2¼ million ft. Birch and Maple.
½ million ft. Hemlock and Pine.
Situated 100 miles north of Toronto, 1 mile from railroad. For particulars write

E. J. WHITE,
15-18 — 15-16th St., Buffalo, N.Y.

For Sale

Hardwood Timber Limits of about seven million feet, with up-to-date sawmill.

BEDFORD MANUFACTURING CO.,
15-18 — Waterloo, Que.

Opportunity in Lumber Business

Will contract sell red cedar timber as cut—150,000,000-foot tract. Quality and accessibility good. Grand Trunk Railroad.

J. RANDALL BLACK,
14-17 — Edmonton, Alberta.

Saw Mill For Sale

Complete Saw Mill consisting of 16 x 20 Engine, Two Boilers, Board Mill, Log Jack, Slab Saw, Edger, Trimmer, Planer and miscellaneous equipment in good condition, immediately available.

THE HALL MACHINERY CO.,
17-18 — Sherbrooke, Que.

Timber Lands For Sale

in the Province of Quebec, on the South Shore of the St. Lawrence, on tide water. Freehold lands 35,000 acres, Crown lands 60,000 acres. An up-to-date sawmill is built, having a capacity of 40,000 to 50,000 feet of sawn lumber and 100,000 to 125,000 shingles.

For further information apply to the River Ouelle Pulp & Lumber Company, St. Pacome, Que. 17-20

Timber Limits at Pre-War Prices

61 Limits grouped as follows:
23 near Quatsino Sound, Vancouver Island.
6 adjacent to Cowichan Lake, Vancouver Island.
32 in the Lillooet River District, B.C.

Let us send you summary of Engineer's detailed reports of these offerings.

Each one is the very cream of Investment.

BEST BROS. COMPANY,
206-7 C. P. R. Building,
17 — Saskatoon, Sask.

Timber Limit For Sale

We have for sale a timber limit in Northern Ontario (near Sault Ste. Marie) comprising an area of some 28,000 acres and containing some 19,000,000 feet of timber as follows: Pine, Cedar, Hemlock, Spruce, Maple, Birch, Elm, Ash and 10,000 cords Pulpwood.

Easy of access. Can be bought on terms at a very attractive price. Logs can be driven on rivers running through the property.

Apply, British American Distributors,
Suite 48-49, 25 Toronto Street,
17-18 — Toronto, Ontario.

FOR SALE

Mixed Timber Limit, Lake Huron Front. Splendid portable mill proposition. Box 18, Canada Lumberman, Toronto. 17-18

For Sale

One Detroit Hot Blast, Dry Kiln System, complete with Fan and Engine, also 85 feet of 9" double leather belt, used two weeks.

Port Hope Veneer & Lumber Co.,
13-t.f. — Port Hope, Ont.

FOR SALE

1,000 acres standing hardwood timber. 8 miles from railroad. Good portable mill proposition (Deeded Land), $5.00 per 1,000 ft. For particulars write Box 214, Thessalon, Ont. 17-20

ATTRACTIVE TIMBER PROPOSITION

has been placed in my hands for immediate sale; an exceptional opportunity to secure excellent timber lands at a moderate price. Call at office for particulars. W. Cooke, 203 Stair Building, Toronto. 17

Saw Mill Plant For Sale

Practically new and modern Saw Mill Plant, capacity about 30 Million feet per annum, located in the Interior of British Columbia on a beautiful inland lake and on the main line of the Grand Trunk Pacific Railway. About 500 Million feet of timber on and adjacent to Lake (about 90% Spruce) and another Billion feet available at reasonable prices. Natural conditions ideal for economical logging, manufacturing, piling and shipping. An advantage of about $4 per thousand feet in freight rates to the Prairie Provinces over Coast shipments.

This property offers unlimited possibilities as a lumber, pulp and paper property. Would consider selling a half interest. Terms reasonable.

A. C. FROST COMPANY,
134 South LaSalle Street,
5-t.f. — Chicago, Ill.

Saw Mill Property FOR SALE

Picnic Island sawmill plant at Little Current, Georgian Bay, 37 acres, for sale or lease for a term of years, or might put it in a good sized company, part cash, part stock; cutting capacity 140 M. a day, two thousand feet stone-filled lumber docks, 16 ft. water, Algoma railway station less than a mile distant, log booming capacity 10 million, telegraph and telephone, school taxes only, title from Crown, no debts or disputes; one of the best mills on the Bay, selling cheap to wind up an estate. For further particulars as to the mill and about twenty other buildings, etc., apply to Thomas Conlon, 44 Church Street, St. Catharines, Ont. 13-16

Virgin Timber For Sale

I have for sale, on very easy terms, in Virginia, 3,000 acres of Virgin Timber, mostly Shortleaf Pine, with some Oak. It is estimated to cut about 17 million feet of pine and oak, with a percentage of white wood, cherry and ash. Railway runs through the centre of it. The land will be worth $50.00 an acre after it is cleared. Apply

DON. M. CAMPBELL,
15-18 — Preston, Ont.

1300 Acres of Standing Timber FOR SALE

It consists of Birch, Basswood, Ash, Maple, Pine, Spruce, Cedar, Hemlock. Camps, logging equipment and sawmill on the ground; owner not a lumberman, engaged in other business. The said lands are located right on C. P. R. and C. N. R. sidings, six miles west of North Bay, better known as the Indian Reserve. Apply to

P. ADAMS,
13-18 — North Bay, Ont.

Lumber Yard

Excellent place in Montreal, for sale or to let. Room 8, LaPresse Building, Main 6255. 16-19

The Forest Revenue of Ontario

During the year ending October 31, 1918, the Ontario Government derived a forest revenue of $1,756,085 from its crown lands. Of this nearly half was derived from timber dues and approximately $190,000 from the fire tax and one per cent. per acre per year for lands under license. The total revenue for the year is the largest since 1912-13 when the revenues closed approximately two million dollars. The area under license at the close of the fiscal year is reported at 16,888 square miles, or 574 square miles greater than on the previous year. These figures indicate the vital importance of Ontario's forest resources in furnishing revenue for the support of the provincial administration, as well as in furnishing supplies and raw materials for the hundreds of wood using industries of the province.

Used Machinery For Sale

6—Racine Power Hack Saws.
1—22" x 40" x 10' London Gap Lathe
1—20" x 10' Engine Lathe
1—36" x 16' Engine Lathe

CHARLES P. ARCHIBALD & CO.
164 St. James Street, Montreal

Cut Your Selling Costs

Use MacLean Daily Reports and know where the projects are that offer the most profitable business. Reduce the percentage of wasted time and lost orders by concentrating on the most likely opportunities.

Rates and Samples on Request.

MacLEAN DAILY REPORTS, Ltd.
345 Adelaide Street West, TORONTO

DR. BELL'S

Veterinary Wonder Remedies

10,000 one dollar ($1.00) bottles Free to horsemen who give the Wonder a fair trial. Guaranteed for Colic, Inflammation of the Lungs, Bowels, Kidneys, Fevers, Distemper, etc. Send 25c for Mailing Package, etc. Agents wanted. Write your address plainly. DR. BELL, V.S., Kingston, Ont.

Timber Estimates

Maps and Reports
Plans for Logging Operations

Coolidge & Carlisle
Forest Engineers
BANGOR · MAINE

J. C. BISAILLON

HAY

Baled - Prompt Delivery

Specialty—EXPORT

Correspondence Solicited

315 Board of Trade Bldg.
MONTREAL

Code: A.B.C. 5th Edition
Member National Hay Association

Chs. E. DUCLOS

54 Notre Dame East
MONTREAL, QUE.

Receiver Shipper Exporter
Hay, Straw and Grain

Special Facilities for Shipping Camps
Write for Quotations

HORSES

UNION STOCK YARDS
OF TORONTO, Limited

'Canada's Greatest Live Stock Market'
Capital, $1,500,000. Two Hundred Acres. Dundas St. cars to Keele St., West Toronto. Auction Sales every Wednesday. Private Sales Daily.

Correspondence Solicited.

WALTER HARLAND SMITH
Manager Horse Dept.

We offer you the Best Grades of

WHITE PINE, SPRUCE, HEMLOCK, HARDWOODS

"Will have 150,000 ft. 1 in. and 1¼ in. Basswood for shipment in August and September."

Write for quotations

OLIVER LUMBER COMPANY
of Toronto, Limited
6 King St. West — Toronto

Review of Current Trade Conditions

Ontario and the East

Building activity continues in all the cities and the number of permits show a decided gain. All woodworking establishments are busy and furniture manufacturers have not been as rushed for many months as they are at this particular juncture. The whole situation is steadying down just now and price advances have not been so marked as during the past few weeks. It is felt that on some lines the upward tendency has for the present been checked, but it is believed that lumber will go still higher next year when producing costs are taken into consideration. Lath of all kinds is still scarce and high in price and there is quite an active demand for spruce lath. Crating lumber is rather quiet at present but other stocks are moving freely.

There is not much change in the export situation. While there is some improvement in facilities rates are exceptionally high and there is not a great deal of shipment on private account. However, with the assurance of the British Ministry of Shipping which has been given the Canadian Pulp and Paper Association, and with other agencies at work, it is hoped that ocean tonnage will improve in the not far-distant future.

In hardwoods the prices are still climbing and buyers are bidding one against the other. As long as the present brisk demand keeps up quotations are likely to go higher. American buyers are taking considerable quantities of Canadian hardwoods but the situation in Ontario is not nearly as acute as across the line. Green stock is being purchased rapidly as there is very little dry material available. Automobile manufacturers are taking all the wood that they can command. While stocks cannot be said to be exhausted, yet they are low in comparison to the call that is being made for them.

It is interesting to note that the rates on lumber in carload lots have been reduced from Vancouver to Toronto by 2c per hundred. The former figure was 79c and this has now decreased to 77c.

Hemlock is very scarce at the present time and is in good demand. Requisitions for white pine are increasing all the time and shipments across the border are steady while the market is firm. As the time proceeds for the opening of camps there is every indication that the supply of men will be ample in certain communities but the cost of supplies will be high—in fact, many firms are estimating that it is costing 10 to 15 per cent. more to get out the timber this year than any previous season.

Recent returns show that the export of lumber from B. C. coast mills to the United States during July were: Logs 8,012,970 ft. B. M.; lumber, rough and dressed, 23,882,955 ft. B.M.; shingles, 163,925, M.; siding, 2,060,152 ft. B.M .;flooring, 354,052 ft. B.M.; lath, 1,360 M.; moulding, 428,221 lin. ft.

It is understood that an advance in B. C. timbers is looked for in the near future. The brisk demand for Coast products across the border continues actively. There has been a recent advance in logs and all the Coast mills are rushed. In the East there is a great scarcity of flat grain fir flooring and the heavy call cannot be met by the mills. Edge grain flooring is also scarce while shingles are still ascending in price as buyers find out every time that they make inquiries regarding the figure.

United States

There has been no material change in general conditions throughout the country during the past two weeks. A congestion of cars at several points has existed owing to the strike of the railway shop men but these have now returned to work and for the time being, at any rate, freight is moving more freely. The spirit of unrest is, however, in the air and where the next outbreak will occur only time will reveal.

There has been during the past few weeks a decrease in the demand from retail buyers in all sections of the producing markets. This has been caused by the movement of the harvest. While prices are on the upward grade there have been no sharp advances during the past few days. Better weather conditions have been prevailing in the south and labor has become more plentiful. These factors have helped to augment production.

The number of orders for hardwoods continues large and while the requisitions are not so numerous or insistent as they were, it is announced that the supply of dry lumber is not equal to the demand by a considerable extent. There is a shortage of cars in several sections.

The furniture factories are making up for the slack trade of war times and have more business on hand than they can readily handle. They are buying large amounts of birch and oak even though the prices for the latter wood have reached unprecedented heights. The advance in southern oak prices has been partially checked because the mills have resumed operations, but the supply is still inadequate.

An interesting factor in connection with the lumber industry is the request on the part of the Railroad Administration for the Department of Justice to investigate charges of profiteering. Advancing prices for lumber have led some people to the conclusion that the lumber manufacturers are making unwarranted profits. It may be true that some of them are making more than the average of the years before the war, but it must be remembered that during the war the majority of the manufacturers got very low prices for what they sold and did not sell enough to make it an object to continue in business, only that they had their investments and the skeletons of their organizations which had to be preserved.

Buying of hemlock has slackened up somewhat just as the buying of many other woods has slackened. However, while part of the slackening is due to lessening in demand, it is more largely accounted for because of the scarcity of hemlock stocks and the inability of manufacturers to supply lumber to satisfy the requirements of the most eager purchasers. Orders booked continue to exceed production. For examples, for the week ended Aug. 9, orders exceeded production by 25 per cent. in northern territory. Shipments and production almost balanced, the former being 3 per cent. less than the latter. Prices remain strong with an upward tendency.

The white pine manufacturers, both in the North and in the West, are able to secure all the business that can be taken care of and furthermore do not have to expend any great effort to secure this business. A number of the prominent manufacturers continue their policy of price stabilization and the result is that white pine price changes have not been so frequent as those of other woods.

Great Britain

Conditions are moving along steadily and in some centres with encouraging results. The labor troubles, however, and the general political unrest do not tend to stabilize matters or to send forward. with any amazing spirit, the various building enterprises. At this period of the year when importing should be at its zenith there is no special activity in this line. It is announced that the government pine imports are being distributed slowly among importers but many are waiting patiently for allocations to fill orders. There has been an active requisition for plywood recently and every liklihood exists of the market becoming stronger as ttime goes on. The cost of production today is very heavy, which fact will have a bearing on the prices in the future.

It is understood that freight has been secured for shipments of pine deals and sidings, wintered stock, apart from Government wood, and these goods are expected some time in August or early in September. Quebec birch boards have been offered at about £45 c.i.f. for merchantable quality, and several shipments are close to hand or loading. Birch logs are in demand, and offers have been requested for a stock for shipment, but the probable date of arrival is uncertain.

The position of the Scandinavian and Finnish trade has not improved. There is a good demand for deal sizes, and some recent c.i f. shipments have no doubt resulted well for the importers. But generally, until the freight controversy has been cleared up trading will be unsatisfactory. The importers who pledged themselves to hold off until shipowners saw the error of their ways are not well satisfied with their position.

To estimate the situation of the hardwood market, present and prospective, is not an easy matter today. One set of considerations appears to lead to one conclusion, another set to quite a different conclusion. If demand regulated supply by decreasing values when it diminished in force we might now look forward to easier prices, for the demand has certainly fallen off lately owing to various circumstances, chief of which is the strike or lock-out in the furniture trade.

An impartial inquirer, in endeavoring to form an opinion of market prospects from the views of experts, would naturally ask himself the question whether agents, importers, exporters, or consumers are the best judges, says the Timber Trades Journal in speaking on the question of prices decreasing. The point is particularly interesting just now, as diametrically opposite views are expressed on this most

View of Mills in Sarnia.

BUY THE BEST

Retailers and woodworking establishments who like to get A1 NORWAY and WHITE PINE LUMBER always buy their stocks from us because we can ship them on quick notice. It pays to have the goods, but it pays better to "deliver" them.

We also make a specialty of heavy timbers cut to order any length up to 60 feet from Pine or B. C. Fir.

"Rush Orders Rushed"

Cleveland-Sarnia Sawmills Co., Limited

SARNIA, ONTARIO

B. P. Bole, Pres. F. H. Goff, Vice-Pres. E. C. Barre, Gen. Mgr. W. A. Saurwein, Ass't. Mgr.

important subject. Agents seem fairly convinced that values will rise. Importers, on the whole, are also inclined to take this view, although it must be admitted they do not back up their conviction by their actions. Consumers, on the other hand, maintain that values must drop or trade cannot expand. Allowing for the bias of interest, let us examine very briefly the reasons given on both sides. Agents look at the question mainly from the shipping standpoint; they see no prospect of anything like the normal quantities of wood arriving this year, and they maintain, therefore, that stocks must be very low during next winter. Further, as there is apparently no prospect of labor and of costs generally being reduced, it is not reasonable to anticipate an exception in the case of timber. Importers were never before at this time of the year so free from future commitments; they have mostly sold their purchases on c.i.f. terms, and when they have not done so they have found little difficulty in placing the wood with inland yard-keepers who are still holding very light stocks. The consumers' standpoint is different. House-building, repairs, railway and road work, cases and crates for export, etc., are greatly needed. Ever since the armistice greater trade expansion has been the crying need of the country, and the consumers assert that high prices have been the main cause of the very curtailment in trade. It is, therefore, they state, essential for prices to drop; and if values do not come down, they believe that the Government will take the necessary measures to enforce a reduction.

Market Correspondence

SPECIAL REPORTS ON CONDITIONS AT HOME AND ABROAD

Conditions Remain Satisfactory in Montreal Circles

The Montreal lumber position has not materially changed. The demand for American account continues to be very good—it is the one strong feature of the general market. For a short period the railway situation interrupted business and restricted a slackening of orders, while an embargo caused shipments to be held up. This, however, was speedily rectified, and orders again came in freely. Reports from representatives of Canadian firms are favorable to a continuation of good business from the States. It is freely predicted that prices will go still higher.

Local trade is moderate. Building is now going on at an accelerated pace, and the demand for lumber is likely to continue steady until the end of the season. The industrial housing scheme will probably be delayed owing to a disagreement as to a tax on the loan for meeting the expenses of the Provincial Technical Commission. Local lumber dealers are only buying in a hand to mouth fashion, and the yards are poorly stocked. Firms will certainly have to pay more for the goods in the near future.

B. C. stocks continue to be very firm. Clears are difficult to secure. The very strong rise in Western products has tended to check business. An inquiry for B. C. ties for foreign account elicited practically no answer.

Exports to the United Kingdom are on a large scale, practically all for the British Government. So far as this port is concerned, the greater part of the lumber has been shipped; the goods will, however, be sent during the winter months from the lower ports. The reports that spruce prices in the United Kingdom have dropped has precluded any lumber to speak of being sent on commercial account. There is a belief that, with the government stock absorbed, the outlook for next season is very bright. The United Kingdom will continue to require immense quantities of lumber, as extensive housing schemes are being put in hand.

The pulp market has improved. The demand from Europe is excellent, and the Riordon Company has lately exported to six foreign countries. Some inquiries for pulp cannot be filled. The shipping situation is better, the Canadian government having responded to some extent to the requests of the pulp and paper companies that space be placed at their disposal.

Business Continues Firm in Ottawa Market

A strong steady demand, coupled with firm prices, was the best feature of the Ottawa lumber market during the closing period of August. The market as compared with the first part of the month did not show any marked change nor could it be fairly said that business on the whole increased. Instead it stayed steady, and the lumber trade generally expressed satisfaction with it.

August in other years has generally been looked on as one of the lean months when members of the trade were away on their vacation or otherwise letting things slide along, and evaiding the hot weather. This year it was different. Firms went out after business. If there was not any on the surface they dug it up, and with the demand from the United States keeping up the best since the pre-war years resulted.

Generally while trade was good and, in fact, the best for this time of year there has been since 1914 it was not up to the pre-war year demand. Export to South America showed an increase. The American demand remained as it was during the latter part of July and early August. The domestic turn-over also held firm if it did not actually show improvement all along the line.

Export business to European countries did not show any change. Considerable shipments continued to go across the ocean, but over ninety-five per cent of the amount shipped was on government account. It is not generally expected that any great amount of private shipments will go to European countries this fall or winter.

Wholesalers reported a good demand for nearly all grades of pine and also some spruce. The principal shipments went to the United States. Some reports indicate that the stocks in the American yards are low and that there should be a continued good demand into the fall months. The stock going to the United States was mostly of the thinner grades, inch and inch and a quarter.

With the manufacturers the labor situation remained about the same, with a growing tendency toward a slight scarcity of woods labor. As new and larger camps are being operated this season there is a greater demand for woods help than last season. All of the camps were not filled by the third week of August, at which time shipments of men into the bush were being made.

With the woodworking factories there was little change in the domestic demand but the demand for export in some plants picked up. James Davidson's Sons, for instance, secured an order for fifteen carloads of doors. Twelve of the carloads were for Great Britain and three for South Africa. This plant has also secured the contract for the doors to be used by the Toronto Housing Commission. Doors for export advanced 15 per cent. in price and for domestic consumption 10 per cent. This firm has already established two woods camps with seventy-five men each.

Shingles and lath continued to hold firm in price with a fair demand prevailing. There was no surplus stocks on hand. Some increase in business was reported for stocks for building purposes and repairs. Building operations at Ottawa continued to proceed satisfactorily. With rents of commercial buildings and offices going up with those of the apartment houses, many real estate dealers predict that building will have to take a big jump next year to keep up with the growing demand for more floor space in the business sections. The activities of the Ottawa Housing Commission will also have a stronger tendency to stimulate structural activity and bring about a greater consumption of lumber of the building grades.

Prices Firm and Stocks Scarce in St John

The mills at St. John still continue to saw to full capacity. Should not all the logs reach the boom limits during the next two weeks there must be quite a shortage of logs and some mills will be forced to close down in the early fall. Trade locally still continues good and the factories and yards are very busy, all the factories having from three to four months work ahead of them, with no relief in the labor situation as far as bench hands are concerned. Prices remain very firm and stocks are scarce. This applies to material at home as well as western goods, very litte of which is coming into the markets.

The American market still remains very firm and has no signs of weakening at the present moment, the base price still being $5[illegible] per M. Random 2 x 3, 2x 4, 3 x 4 size is bringing $40.00 on car St. John; 2 x 6, 2 x 7, $39.00 to $40.00; 2 x 8, $45.00, and 2 x 10-1[illegible] about $50,00. Laths are very firm and practically nothing to offer. The price at present is $4.50 per M., f.o.b. mills here.

Pine lumber is also very scarce and good qualities are hard to find; prices remain stiff. The West India market is now beginning to call for stocks of the usual shipper quality but will be forced to await the new cut before any shipments can be made. The larger boards are bringing from $50.00 to $52.000 and the smaller boards $40.00 to $45.00 per M., f.o.b. St. John.

Shingles are very scarce with prices of extras $6.00; clears $5.50; 2nd clears $5.00; Ex. No. 1 $3.50 and if a buyer is badly in need he will offer more money.

Food & Provisions

For The Lumber Camp

We make a specialty of Lumbermen's Supplies, also all kinds of Farm Produce in Car Lots, such as Hay, Oats, Beans, Peas, Potatoes, etc.

Write for quotations and save half of your present freight rates.

Prompt shipment is assured from our generous stocks. Our facilities for shipping are excellent.

Hunter & Co.

LIMITED

Wholesale Grocers

Pembroke, Ontario

The quality of our goods has established their popularity among the more discriminating lumbermen. Try Hunter's.

THE HARRIS ABATTOIR COMPANY, LIMITED

specialize in supplying lumber companies with camp requirements. All product shipped to lumber companies is specially selected, specially cured, and specially packed to withstand many handlings before reaching destination.

Every lumberman should ask the Harris Abattoir Company to figure on all requisitions before placing orders.

All H. A. Brand goods are fully guaranteed.

The Harris Abattoir Company, Limited, specialize on making shipment when promised and Refrigerator Car Service to all points obviates any delay.

LIST OF PRODUCTS INCLUDES—

FRESH BEEF	BUTTER	AMERICAN BARRELLED PORK	EGGS & EGG MELANGE
BARRELLED BEEF	PURE LARD	SAUSAGES OF ALL KINDS	POTATOES AND VEGETABLES
CANADIAN BARRELLED PORK	SMOKED MEATS	CHEESE	FLOUR & MILL FEEDS
LONG CLEAR BACON	DOMESTIC SHORTENING		

H. A. Brand Oleomargarine —the new product which will save thousands of dollars for lumber companies. H. A. Brand Oleomargarine is higher priced than some, but you cannot afford to experiment by using inferior product as the only result of so doing would be reversion to Butter.

THE HARRIS ABATTOIR COMPANY LIMITED - West Toronto, Canada

Branches at: SUDBURY and OTTAWA, ONT. HALIFAX and SYDNEY, N. S. MONTREAL and QUEBEC, QUE. ST. JOHN, N. B.

Canada Food Control—Blanket No: 165.

Musings on Matters of Passing Interest

Much has been written about the "cussedness" of human nature. In this world things often go by contraries. Just at the particular moment that the inventor wants to display the merit of his particular machine or the proud mother reveal to admiring friends the cleverness of her child—well, there is a balk on the part of both the machine and juvenile. How often do things happen at the wrong time? The auspicious moment never seems to arrive just when it is of the most importance that it should. An old song used to run "It is seldom if ever you get them together, the time, the place and the girl." It would seem, by an extraordinary combination of circumstances, that an experiment tried recently by a leading industrial concern, in the shape of a "no-accident week," went entirely askew. All calculations were badly upset. Although notices had been posted by the local Safety Committee requesting that employees co-operate in eliminating all mishaps in both the yard and mill, and the help entered enthusiastically into the spirit and purpose of the move, the results were anything but gratifying. During that particular week more mishaps transpired than during any other week of the year, and yet it was to have been a "no-accident week." Fortunately none of the injuries were severe, but they occurred, nevertheless. The interpretation of the idea by the men, insofar as could be learned from an outsider, was that not one of them should miss having an accident during that week. However, there is nothing like trying, and while the first attempt may not have been satisfactory in its outcome, it was certainly ideal in thought and conception. It is only by a series of successive, even if unfruitful, endeavors that a desired goal is reached or perfection achieved.

* * *

Lightning and forest fires are again reaping their usual harvest in Canada, and the month of July has come in for its fair share of destruction. Northern Ontario and the mountainous districts of British Columbia have suffered the most from forest fires, while in Alberta and Saskatchewan prairie fires have done a great deal of damage to the fertile land. Farmers in all parts of Canada have suffered from lightning, many barns, with their valuable contents, having been totally destroyed. Although no estimate has yet been made, the loss from these sources will be very heavy. The Monetary Times' estimate of Canada's fire losses during July, 1919, is $1,118,377, as compared with $3,337,530 in June, and $3,369,684 in July a year ago.

* * *

To prepare the cheaper kinds of woods by a patented method that makes them more durable is the purpose of the organization of the Scandinavian Pencil Wood Company, just organized in Köge, Denmark, according to the Commercial Attache in Copenhagen. The woods especially to be prepared are birch, ash and elm, all wood treated by this process being called teakin wood. Certain changes in the character of the wood that normally take place only after many years of drying are by this chemical process produced within twenty-four hours. Thereafter, when the moisture that may still be left has evaporated, the wood becomes harder and more durable than by the ageing process. Teakin birch is of a beautiful golden brown color and when polished with potash it takes on a mahogany red hue. Teakin ash is a substitute for teak. Teakin elm has none of the disadvantages of natural elm. Teakin fir is of a uniform color all through and is used for office fitting and furniture and for veneering.

* * *

One of the outward signs that reconstruction is going on rapidly and that much new business is expected to develop is evidenced in the number of incorporated companies, both federal and provincial, which are being formed. The organizations which are taking out letters patent, were never quite as numerous, covering all fields of activity and including lumber concerns, mining concerns, pulp and paper concerns, iron working and steel concerns, oil concerns, fuel concerns, supply houses, jobbing houses, etc.

So long as any organization has the necessary money to meet the small preliminary outlay it can become incorporated if five provisional directors consent to allow their names to be used. The Canada Gazette and the Gazettes of the various provinces come out with names and capital stock ranging in some instances up in the millions. Wide powers are conferred on each corporate body and provisional directors are named—often lawyers lawyers' clerks or stenographers.

It has been stated that these names are used for purposes of convenience and until such times as a new concern is ready to go ahead and reveal the identity of its officers and directors. Gazettes publish the style and title of the companies, the trade papers state that charters have been granted to So and So, with an authorized capital stock of so many thousand dollars, and headquarters in such and such a place. The result is that wide publicity is obtained for the Wear-Well Clothing Co., Limited, of Toronto; the Provincial Phonograph Co., Limited, of London; the Sterling Lumber Co., Limited, of Hamilton; the New Thought Publishing Co., Limited, of Ottawa, or the Commonwealth Auto Truck Co., of Montreal. Now, concerns bearing such artistic appellations as these have a capital stock ranging, possibly, from $40,000 to $1,000,000, and yet their provisional directors are furnished in the Gazette as lawyers and lawyer's clerks.

If a newspaper man makes application to know who is really at the back or financially interested in the newly chartered bodies he is generally met with a smile and politely told the time is not just "ripe" yet to give such information and that the personnel of the company is really a "private matter" and comes under the confidential relations of counsel and client. Then if application for information is made to the Provincial Secretary in each of the provinces the reply is forthcoming, that "we really cannot give you the personnel or street address and number of such and such a company; all we know is that their head office is in Ottawa, Montreal, Quebec, Hamilton or London."

Now, what is the result? Many supply houses, commercial agencies, travellers, jobbers and others would like to get in touch with the new concern and send in a letter, say, to the "Provincial Phonograph Co., Limited, London," or the "Sterling Lumber Co., Limited, of Hamilton." It is well known that such institutions have been created, but the postmaster of each city returns all letters of inquiry in a few days, requesting that the street address and number of the company be given, as such organization cannot be located. The trade papers are appealed to in vain and also the provincial treasurer.

The "Provincial Phonograph Co.," and the "Sterling Lumber Company" exist according to letters patent, but are not really get-at-able. Surely when a concern is ready to take out a charter it should be prepared to do business, or at least open an office. If some stringent regulations were passed making all organizations, as soon as incorporated, have definite headquarters and an identity, there would possibly be less flotation of companies, good, bad and indifferent, about which nothing is ever heard of after the publication of their notice of incorporation in the press. The sooner the postal law or the joint stock company legislation of Canada and of the various provinces is amended to compel new concerns to have a fixed location, a place that can be discovered by the public or those anxious to get in touch with them to do a legitimate business the better it will be all round.

* * *

A New Orleans news item says: A very much out-of-the-ordinary lumber movement created interest here the other day, when a carload of birch, designed for export, arrived here as an express shipment from the mills of the B. Heinman Lumber Co., Wausau, Wis. The express charges on the shipment amounted, it is said, to $1,800.

Handle it Mechanically

with

JEFFREY CONVEYERS

The Standard Equipment for Handling Mill Refuse, Logs, Lumber, Etc.

"V" SHAPED TROUGH for large capacities of Refuse, Blocks, Etc. An all-steel trough with re-enforcing angles on the top edges may be used in place of the wood trough with steel lining illustrated above.

JEFFREY GAPPED SHEAVE WHEELS with Solid Rim and Single Flexible Teeth. Also furnished in Adjustable Rim—Double Flexible Teeth.

Jeffrey Wire Cable Conveyers

are especially adapted to economical handling of large capacities and to long distance handling of Sawdust and Mill Refuse.

Long Link Coil Chain with U-Bolts and Cross Bars carrying Slabs from Mill to Fire Pot.

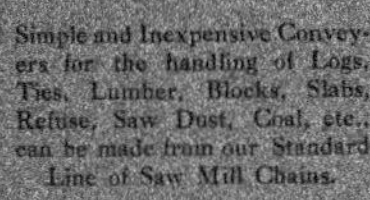

Simple and Inexpensive Conveyers for the handling of Logs, Ties, Lumber, Blocks, Slabs, Refuse, Saw Dust, Coal, etc., can be made from our Standard Line of Saw Mill Chains.

LET US FIGURE ON YOUR CONVEYING REQUIREMENTS

The Jeffrey Mfg. Co.

Canadian Branch and Warerooms

MONTREAL

Long Link Coil Chain with S-1½ Log Spur—handling Logs to Mill.

K-3 Attachment

Lumber Carrier between Mill and Yard Storage consisting of two strands of Jeffrey Plain Chain.

S1½ Log Spur

EDGINGS

Sandy Jarrick, Hydro Glen, intends erecting a sawmill at Ragged Rapids on the Severn River.

The Beaver Board Co. intend erecting a large addition to their plant at Thorold, Ont., in the near future.

Harry Alexander, Limited, Toronto, Ont., has been incorporated to carry on the business of woodworkers. Capital, $40,000.

A lumber warehouse at Hurdman's Bridge, near Ottawa, belonging to the McAuliffe-Davis Lumber Co., was recently visited by fire.

The sawmill at Gillies Bay, Ont., owned by Walter Wardrop, of Dyers Bay, Ont., was recently destroyed by fire. The mill will be rebuilt.

The Angle Canadian Construction Co., Limited, have been granted permission to change their name to the Anglo-Canadian Tie & Timber Co., Limited.

There is a great building campaign going on in the Oak Ridges district, near Toronto. Over 50 new houses and stores have already gone up this season.

Eureka Pattern Mfg. Co., Limited, Toronto, has been incorporated to do business as pattern-makers and to carry on woodworking in all its branches. Capital, $40,000.

A charter has been granted to Joseph Dolan & Sons, Limited, Ottawa, with a capital stock of $50,000. The company is empowered to buy, sell and deal in goods of all kinds, including the pulpwood, lumber, logging and timber business.

The Fibre Packing Co. of Canada, Limited, Walkerville, Ont., have been granted letters patent constituting them a private company for the purpose of manufacturing and dealing in fibres, fibre-board, fibre containers and other similar products. Capital, $100,000.

I. H. Weldon, president of the Provincial Paper Mills Co., Limited Toronto, recently spent a few days in Port Arthur on business. He states that if circumstances warrant it his company will erect a paper mill at Port Arthur early next spring.

The Seaman, Eaton Flooring Co., Limited, Toronto, Ont., have been incorporated to manufacture and deal in lumber, lumber products and builders' supplies. Capital, $40,000. The provisional directors are W. B. Seaman, M. H. Eaton, J. Seaman, A. Seaman and S. J. Arnott.

It is thought probable that Oakville Town Council will look with favor upon a proposition placed before it recently by a group of builders who plan to erect fifteen or more residences in the town, at a cost of from $5,000 to $8,000 each, and who are asking for exemption from taxes for one year.

The McDonald Lumber Co., who specialize in softwoods as well as in western stocks, have removed their offices from 193 Victoria St. to 34 Victoria St., Toronto, where they have larger and more commodious quarters. At the head of the company is Mr. N. L. McDonald, well known western lumberman, and associated with him is Mr. J. S. Knapman, formerly of Peterboro, who has spent many years in the timber business.

The Wattman-Kalbfleisch Car Body Company has begun in Stratford, and their plant is now in full operation. The company makes bodies for hearses, ambulances, sedans and service wagons. The new industry is an amalgamation of the Kalbfleisch Planing Mill, of Stratford, and the W. H. Wattman Car Body Co., of Toronto. One of the pieces of reconstruction recently undertaken by the firm was a body that was built in 1902, which was upset on the Hamilton highway and is now being remodelled on up-to-date lines.

The big paper plant at Espanola, owned by the Spanish River Pulp & Paper Mills, Limited, is being greatly extended. Construction started on a new addition on June 1st last, but this is now completed. A newsprint machine is being installed which will be in operation by Nov. 1st and will increase production by 50 tons a day. A second machine will be erected later on, and will be in operation early in the spring. The new units will enable the company to get the benefit of the favorable markets that are sure to prevail during the next few years in the United States.

Handley Page, Limited, with a capital stock of $2,500,000 and headquarters in Morrisburg, Ont., have been granted a federal charter to purchase, manufacture, build, erect, charter, operate, etc., aeroplanes of all kinds, including monoplanes, bi-planes, hydroplanes, flying-boats, seaplanes, aircrafts or other machines to navigate the air and for use in commercial, civil, naval and military aerial service. Among the incorporators of the company are Wm. H. Workman and Mark Kerr of London, Eng., Harry Clark of Montreal, Fred R. Chalmers and Wm. H. McGannon of Morrisburg.

Eastern Canada

The Three Rivers Shipyard Co., Three Rivers, are erecting an extension to their office.

The "Canadian Seigneur" sailed from Montreal on Aug. 21 for Liverpool. She is the first Canadian Government vessel to carry pulp to the Old Country.

Parker Creek Lumber Co., Montreal, have been granted a provincial charter to manufacture and deal in lumber, lath, shingles, and to operate paper and pulp mills. Also to manufacture any article made in whole or part of wood. Capital, $95,000.

The Smith Lumber Co., Limited, Woodstock, N. B., have completed their sawing of logs for the season, and have opened their cooperage plant. They recently received a carload of hoops from Indiana and will turn out 10,000 potato barrels.

The large stable of the St. Maurice Paper Co., Three Rivers, P.Q., containing twenty-four horses, fifty loads of hay and one carload of oats, was completely destroyed by fire recently. Nothing was saved. Loss about $20,000, partly covered by insurance.

Rimouski Fishing & Cold Storage Co., Limited, Montreal, P.Q., was recently incorporated. Wide powers have been granted this company under their charter, among which are to operate factories of all kinds and to build and operate ships and vessels. Capital $50,000.

The H. A. T. Lumber Co., Limited, Montreal, P.Q., have been incorporated to manufacture and deal in lumber and timber of all kinds and to erect and operate sawmills and factories and to manufacture any article made of wood. Capital, $100,000. The incorporators are J. M. A. Valois, L. J. Boileau, and J. R. Renaud.

The Cane Mola Co. of Canada, Limited, Montreal, P.Q., were recently incorporated. Among the powers granted this company under the charter were to manufacture and deal in barrels, boxes and other forms of packages and to operate sawmills, planing mills, box factories, and to deal in wood products of all kinds. Capital $100,000.

A federal charter has been granted to J. C. Nadeau, Limited, with headquarters in Montreal, and a capital stock of $50,000. The company is empowered to acquire the property and assets of the business now carried on in Montreal by J. C. Nadeau as a lumber merchant, and to conduct a general lumber and timber trade in all its branches. The incorporators are Joseph C. Nadeau, Louis J. Nadeau, Jean B. Tariff and others, all of Montreal.

The output of the Fraser Company, Limited, pulp mills at Edmundston, has reached 90 tons daily. The capacity for which the plant was constructed was 100 tons, but they do now expect to exceed this as a result of improvements which are being made. The Fraser Company are now shipping the 65 million feet of lumber which the British Government recently purchased from them.

The first shovelful of earth was removed from the future site of the mammoth plant of the International Paper Co., at Three Rivers, which will cost in the neighborhood of four million dollars. The International Paper Company has merged into its new venture the St. Maurice Lumber Co., already carrying on operations at Three Rivers. The excavation work will be rushed, and it is expected the structure of the mills proper will be up by December next. The plant will turn out pulp and finished paper of all grades.

A. R. Gould, of Presque Isle, Me., who is well known in New Brunswick through his connection with the St. John Valley Railway enterprise, is the president of a new company which has taken over the Aroostock Pulp & Paper Company's plant on the St. John River at Keegan, north of Van Buren, Me. Owing to difficulties the mill has been closed for some weeks, and now it is learned that Mr. Gould and H. B. Stebbings, of Boston, have purchased the stock interest of E. P. Lindsay and others in the enterprise and the plant will soon be in full operation once more and eventually on a larger scale than ever. The plant was built in 1917 and is thoroughly equipped, having a daily capacity of about 60 tons.

Western Canada

The Empire Timber Products, Limited, have been incorporated with registered office in Vancouver, B.C. Capital $100,000.

A big bush fire in the vicinity of the Vedder river, between Cultus Lake, B. C., and the river, recently destroyed a large amount of valuable timber.

A sawmill will shortly be in operation in the Burns Lake district, B. C. The man behind the enterprise is F. R. Keele, who is a Francois Lake rancher and has a big stand of fine timber.

After active service as major in the 10th Engineers (Forest) of the United States Army, Mr. Lafon, formerly assistant forester of British Columbia, has been appointed assistant chief forester under Chief Forester M. A. Grainger.

Among the recent incorporations are the following: Horne Lake Lumber Company, Ltd., $25,000, Murrayville; Kitselas Lumber Company, Ltd., $25,- ing Company. Ltd., $50,000, Vancouver; Glenwood Shingle, Tie and Lumber Company, Ltd., $25,000, Murrayville; Kitseleas Lumber Company, Ltd., $25,000, Usk.

The Beaver Cove Lumber and Pulp Co. will be in operation at Beaver Cove, B.C., in about six weeks. It is expected that the population of Beaver Cove will reach 10,000 before three years elapse. A number of returned men are working on the construction of the plant. The company will build a railway for hauling its timber.

B. R. Morton, superintendent of planting on the prairie forest reserves, with headquarters at Ottawa, is on the Coast to secure Sitka spruce and Douglas fir for reforestation in Scotland. The cones are sent to Kamloops, where a seed extracting plant is located. They are placed on trays and the room heated to 100 degrees. In from two to five hours the cones burst and the seeds drop to the floor. The cones of jack pine and lodgepole pine require up to twenty-four hours' heating.

Logs scaled by the provincial department in June amounted to 183,731,105 feet, compared with 171,640,268 feet in June, 1918. Log production for the first six months of the present year was 829,669,850 feet; for the corresponding period in 1918, 772,445,607 feet, an increase of 57,224,243 feet. The cut per species in June was: Douglas fir, 97,616,402 feet; red cedar, 39,391,614 feet; spruce, 15,943,754 feet; hemlock, 16,993,643 feet; balsam, 4,166,721 feet; yellow pine, 4,003,242 feet; white pine, 399,214 feet; jack pine, 160,426 feet; larch, 4,920,431 feet; cottonwood, 131,831 feet; maple, 2,165 feet; alder, 1,662 feet.

Eighty municipalities throughout Ontario have passed by-laws under the Housing Act, providing for appropriations ranging from $20,000 to $1,000,000, with Windsor providing the largest amount. Mr. J. A. Ellis, director of municipal affairs for the Ontario Government, gave this information, which shows that the Act is making headway throughout the province. Ottawa purchased land for $60,000, which has been divided into 160 lots, which became available about a week ago. Of the 160 lots, only 10 or 15 are still available. The Capital has since bought the Reid property for the same figure.

ONLY a few of the many lines of Van Supplies we have ready for immediate delivery, including Mackinaw Clothing, Black and Fancy; Ribbed Underwear, Wool Socks and Long Stockings, also Shanty Blankets.
Write or Wire for Prices and Samples
Our usual Standard of Quality—
The Best that Money can Buy

Is a most essential part of every lumber camp or mill equipment as it saves time and material and pays for itself in a very short time.

WILL PEEL AND WASH A BAG OF POTATOES IN FROM 3 TO 10 MINUTES ACCORDING TO SIZE OF MACHINE.

Now in use in the largest hotels, restaurants, clubs and lumber camps throughout Canada.

Made in three sizes for hand or power. Write for circular "L" for prices and particulars.

JOHN BURNS & CO. MONTREAL

Established 1865

Consult us About Your **HORSEFEED**

A part of our service is catering to the requirements of the lumbermen.

We can supply the first quality

HAY, GRAIN and FEED

at lowest market prices. Prompt delivery assured on all orders, large and small. Write or wire for prices.

James Scott & Co., Limited

651 St. James Street, MONTREAL

HAY GRAIN

Lumbermen!

Feeding Horses is a Problem!

Our figures will help you solve it. We solicit enquiries from the lumbermen. 30 years' experience. Write us to-day

Aime Guertin Ltd.

Farm Produce and Stable Supplies

534 Notre Dame St. W. Montreal

Machinery for Lumber and Logging Camps

QUICK SHIPMENT

Boilers, Locomotives, Locomotive Cranes, Travelling Derricks, Logging Cars, Flat Cars, Motors, Rails, Cable, Chains, Everything for Lumber and Logging Camps

T. J. McGOVERN

504 LUMSDEN BUILDINC

TORONTO

Railway and Track Supplies

For Lumber and Contractors' requirements

Rails, Locomotives, Accessories, Cars, Lion Brand Babbitt Metal

Correspondence solicited

Sessenwein Bros., Montreal

The Peter Hay Knife Co., Limited

GALT, ONTARIO

MANUFACTURING WOODWORKING

Machine Knives, Circular Cutters and Mortise Chisel

"HAMILTON" PRODUCTS

"Hamilton" Machinery is built in a plant that has been specializing in **High Grade Dependable Saw Mill, Pulp Mill and Hydraulic Equipment** for over sixty years. We guarantee our products in material, design and workmanship to be the equal of any on the market, and to give perfect satisfaction wherever used.

No. 2 Jack Works

"Quality First" Our Motto

SAW MILL

Boom Chains
Warping Anchors
Capstans for Warping
Log Jacks
Log Deck Equipment
Band Mills
Log Carriages
Set Works (steam & hand)
Edgers
Hush Frames
Live Rolls and Drives
Slashers
Trimmers
Cut-off Saws
Lath Mill Machinery
Shingle Mill Machinery
Filing Room Machinery
Resaws (circular)
Hogs
Drag Saws
Gang Circulars
Twin Circulars
Steam Feeds
Friction Feeds
Transmission Machinery
Haul-up and Transfer Chains

SAW MILL—Cont'd.

Refuse Burners
Conveyors
Engines (slide and piston valve)
Boilers
Feed Water Heaters

PULP MILL

Log Haul-Ups
Pulp Wood Slashers
Pulp Wood Conveyors
Barking Drums
Centrifugal Pulp Screens (horizontal and vertical)
Pulp Grinders
Centrifugal Pumps
Triplex Stuff Pumps
Slasher Tanks
Chippers
Chip Crushers
Chip Screens (rotary and flat)
Digester Fittings
Push Fans
Agitator Drives
Refuse Burners
Transmission machinery

HYDRAULIC POWER PLANT

Water Wheels
Water Wheel Governors
Head Gate Hoists
Stop Log Winches
Trash Racks
Butterfly Valves
Power Transmission
Hand Power Travelling Cranes
Steel Feeder Pipes
Surge Tanks

GENERAL

Gray Iron Castings
Brass Castings
Special Machines built to order
Patterns
Structural Steel Work
Transmission Machinery
Steel Plate Work
Tanks
Standpipes
Smoke Stacks
Boiler Breechings
Steel Pipe
Steel Bins and Hoppers

William Hamilton Co., Limited

Peterboro, Ontario

Agents: J. L. Neilson & Co., Winnipeg, Man.

Savings That Hold Good Wherever the Duplex Hauls

To lumbermen who have never owned the Duplex 4-wheel Drive, the simple facts must seem almost incredible.

Yet they **are** facts. And they are **conclusive.** They are based on ton-mile costs—the very bedrock of all hauling.

It is in ton-mile costs that Duplex savings average from 20 per cent. to as high as 60 per cent.

The figures leave no room for doubt; no room for argument.

They are quoted from the records of firms which operate a single Duplex, and those which operate whole fleets.

Whether these reports come from cities or small towns; from mining or lumber regions; from road-building operations, or wherever, the net result is the same.

The Duplex does make a **decided** and **definite** saving in the cost per ton-mile.

The comparison holds good in every case. Because that is true, the Duplex has repeatedly replaced horses, mules, and other trucks, in all kinds of hauling.

The reason, of course, is obviously sane and simple.

The Duplex drives with all four wheels. It always goes through—even where a team of horses would stall. And it always carries the load.

The Duplex wastes no power in spinning wheels. It saves itself from the damage of unequal strains. It requires only single rear tires instead of dual—a clear saving here of 30 per cent.

Duplex dealers always welcome a comparative demonstration. They are accustomed to regard the sale as good as closed when they are asked to compete in performance.

Business executives who have any hauling proposition, on any kind of road, will find it to their interest to inquire thoroughly into the Duplex facts.

Send for Booklet, "The Modern and Efficient Way to Haul Logs and Lumber."

Duplex Truck Company
2062 Washington Ave., Lansing, Mich.

Joseph Maw & Co., Winnipeg, Man. J. E. Ardell, Vancouver, B. C.
Reo Motor Sales Co., Toronto, Ont.

DUPLEX TRUCKS
Cost Less Per Ton-mile

FOR BOILERS — COME TO US!

Our shop practice is abreast of the world's best. Our workmanship is the kind you want. Horizontal Return Tubular, Vertical Tubular and Locomotive types. Refuse burners. Steel plate work, any kind. Correspondence invited.

Engineering & Machine Works,
of Canada, Limited

St. Catherines - - Ontario

Eastern Sales Office: Hall Machinery Co., Sherbrooke, Que.

Not altogether what we say, but what users say

"We have used the Alligator or Warping Tug manufactured by you for the last 7 or 8 years, and consider them indispensable to lumbermen on waters of French River or similar streams."

Will move a bag containing 60,000 logs in calm weather, 30,000 in a head wind

West & Peachey - Simcoe, Ont.

Montreal Toronto Winnipeg

The J. C. McLaren Belting Co.
Limited

General Mill Supplies MONTREAL

McKinnon Columbus Chain

LIMITED · ST. CATHARINES ONT.

Electric Welded and Fire Welded Chains – All kinds – All sizes

Coil Chain (All Sizes) Loading Chain
Logging Chain Boom Chain
Conveyor or Log Haul up Chain

CLIMAX Improved Geared LOCOMOTIVES FOR WOOD AND IRON RAILS

A [illegible] Climax Locomotive Designed Especially for Heavy Logging Work

Climax Locomotives are successfully operated on steep grades and sharp curves. Any weight or gauge. Locomotives in stock for immediate shipment. Get Catalog "[illegible]"

CLIMAX MANUFACTURING CO., 312 W. Main Street, CORRY, PA.
VANCOUVER MACHINERY DEPOT, LTD., VANCOUVER, B.C.

Peace Year 1919

Finds us optimistic for the future and well stocked with Horse Blankets, Feed Bags, Tarpaulins, Oil Clothing Tents, Flags, Straw Ticks and Grey Blankets

We Guarantee Prompt Shipment of Orders Entrusted to us

J. J. Turner & Sons Limited
PETERBOROUGH, ONT.

PUT YOUR PROBLEM UP TO US

We are specialists in building locomotives. We build all types and sizes, also all kinds of repair parts for locomotives and tenders.

Our experience puts us in a position to give you expert advice as to what particular type and size of locomotive is best suited to your needs.

Put your locomotive problem up to us.

MONTREAL LOCOMOTIVE WORKS, LIMITED

DOMINION EXPRESS BUILDING, MONTREAL, CANADA.

PRATT & WHITNEY CO.

OF CANADA, LIMITED

SMALL TOOLS

Taps — Dies — Reamers — Cutters — Drills

MADE IN CANADA

As good as money can buy—Guaranteed absolutely!

Head Office and Works, DUNDAS, ONT.

SALES OFFICES:
MONTREAL Drummond Bldg. | VANCOUVER | WINNIPEG Bank of Hamilton Bldg.

"Proctor" DRYERS

or Exacting Conditions

Your individual problems of veneer drying may be [illegible]ferent or the conditions more exacting. Because it is [illegible]dom that two drying problems are the same our engineers make a special study of your particular conditions, considering the relation of the drying to preceding and following operations, quantity to be dried, number of men employed, heat available, cost of power, etc.

ctor Veneer Dryers give a perfectly flat and pliable product without checks or splits

end for our practical Catalog—It will interest you

PHILADELPHIA TEXTILE MACHINERY CO.

SEVENTH STREET AND TABOR ROAD, PHILADELPHIA, PA., U.S.A.
Hamilton, Ont., Canada,—W. J. Westaway, 5 Sun Life Building.

Galvanizing Work

OF ALL CLASSES

Our galvanizing plant is the largest of its kind in Canada. All contracts, large and small, for Hot or Electro Galvanizing can be completed promptly. Satisfaction guaranteed.

Ask for quotation

ADDRESS

Ontario Wind Engine and Pump Company, Ltd.

TORONTO, ONTARIO

Branches: Montreal, Winnipeg, Regina, Calgary

A Requirement of Every Lumber Camp

The Desjardine Patent Log Sleigh

It facilitates speedy removal of lumber, and is easy to manipulate. Very strongly made, and is a great utility in lumber operations. Made in various sizes, and supplied with either short pole or rigged to receive cross chains

ALSO MAKE

MILL DUMP WAGONS,	LOG SLEIGH RUNNERS (Plain and Shaped)
STANDARD RAILROAD OR QUARRY CARTS,	LUMBERMEN'S DRIVING SLEIGHS
LUMBERMEN'S BUCK-BOARDS AND SLEIGHS	

Send for Catalogue

ALEXANDER BARR

PEMBROKE, ONT.

A WADE does 10 mens work Saws 25 cords a day!

A money-maker and hard work saver for land clearers and wood-cutting contractors. One man can move it from cut to cut. Simple and reliable. Hundreds in use all over the U. S. When not in use for wood cutting, the 4 H. P. motor will run mills, feed mills, feed cutters, pumps, etc.

Quick deliveries from over 100 points throughout the United States.

America must burn more wood for fuel. One Wade will do 10 men's work at one-tenth the cost. Write for free Book, "How Dan Ross cuts 40 cords a day," full details and special price.

Used and specified by the U. S. Government

The A. R. Williams Machinery & Supply Co., Ltd.

MONTREAL

Halifax, N. S. St. John, N. B.

Toronto, Ont. Winnipeg, Man.

HARNESS
for the heavy hauls

When the teams are sweating and straining up the hills or over the bad roads, you can depend on

Alligator Brand Harness

to stand the test.

Its strength and dependability make **Alligator Brand** the ideal harness for lumbering.

Handsome in appearance and easily handled it fills all the requirements of the lumberman

LAMONTAGNE LIMITED

338 Notre Dame St. W. MONTREAL — **85 Princess St. WINNIPEG**

52 Crown St., QUEBEC

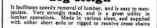

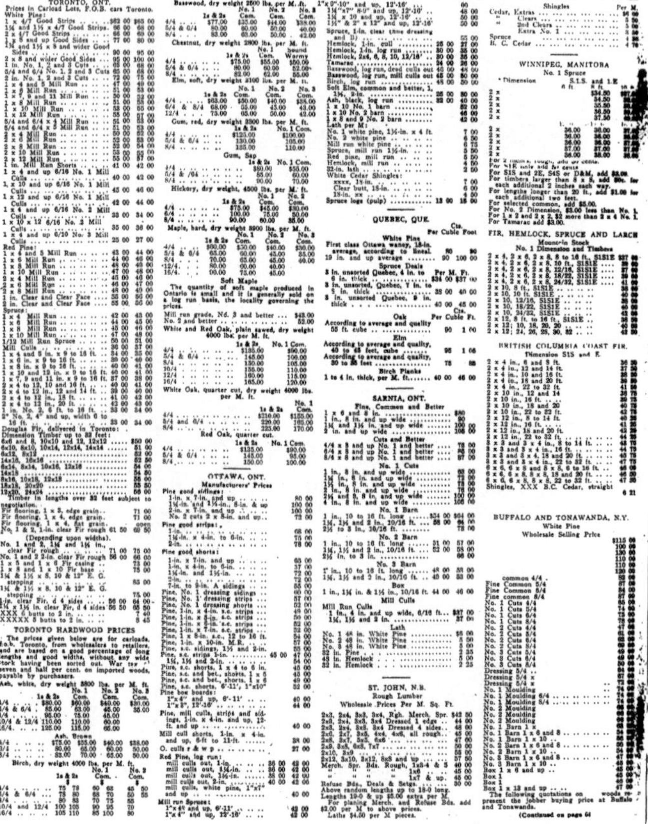

CURRENT LUMBER PRICES—WHOLESALE

TORONTO, ONT.

Prices in Carload Lots, F.O.B. cars Toronto.

White Pine:		
1 x 4/7 Good Strips	$62 00	$65 00
1¼ and 1½ x 4/7 Good Strips	66 00	68 00
2 x 4/7 Good Strips	66 00	69 00
1 x 8 and up Good Sides	77 00	80 00
1¼ and 1½ x 8 and wider Good Sides	90 00	95 00
2 x 8 and wider Good Sides	95 00	100 00
1 in. No. 1, 2 and 3 Cuts	65 00	68 00
5/4 and 6/4 No. 1, 2 and 3 Cuts	65 00	68 00
2 in. No. 1, 2 and 3 Cuts	72 00	75 00
1 x 4 and 5 Mill Run	47 00	49 00
1 x 6 Mill Run	51 00	53 00
1 x 7, 9 and 11 Mill Run	50 00	52 00
1 x 8 Mill Run	51 00	55 00
1 x 10 Mill Run	53 00	55 00
1 x 12 Mill Run	55 00	57 00
5/4 and 6/4 x 4 Mill Run	51 00	53 00
5/4 and 6/4 x 5 Mill Run	51 00	53 00
2 x 4 Mill Run	50 00	52 00
2 x 6 Mill Run	52 00	53 00
2 x 8 Mill Run	52 00	54 00
2 x 10 Mill Run	53 00	55 00
2 x 12 Mill Run	55 00	57 00
1 in. Mill Run Shorts	41 00	42 00
1 x 4 and up 6/16 No. 1 Mill Culls	40 00	42 00
1 x 10 and up 6/16 No. 1 Mill Culls	45 00	46 00
1 x 12 and up 6/16 No. 1 Mill Culls	42 00	44 00
1 x 4 and up 6/16 No. 2 Mill Culls	33 00	34 00
1 x 10 x 12 6/16 No. 2 Mill Culls	35 00	36 00
1 x 4 and up 6/10 No. 3 Mill Culls	25 00	27 00
Red Pine:		
1 x 4 and 5 Mill Run	43 00	44 00
1 x 6 Mill Run	44 00	46 00
1 x 8 Mill Run	48 00	49 00
1 x 10 Mill Run	47 00	48 00
2 x 4 Mill Run	45 00	46 00
2 x 6 Mill Run	46 00	47 00
2 x 8 Mill Run	48 00	49 00
1 in. Clear and Clear Face	55 00	56 00
2 in. Clear and Clear Face	55 00	56 00
Spruce:		
1 x 4 Mill Run	42 00	43 00
1 x 6 Mill Run	44 00	45 00
1 x 8 Mill Run	45 00	46 00
1 x 10 Mill Run	47 00	48 00
1/12 Mill Run Spruce	50 00	51 00
Mill Culls	36 00	37 00
1 x 4 and 5 in. x 9 to 16 ft.	34 00	35 00
1 x 6 in. x 9 to 16 ft.	39 00	40 00
1 x 8 in. x 9 to 16 ft.	40 00	41 00
1 x 10 and 12 in. x 9 to 16 ft.	40 00	41 00
1 x 7, 9 and 11 in. x 9 to 16 ft.	37 00	38 00
2 x 4 to 12, 10 and 16 ft.	40 00	41 00
2 x 4 to 12 in., 12 and 14 ft.	39 00	40 00
2 x 4 to 12 in., 18 ft.	41 00	42 00
2 x 4 to 12 in., 20 ft.	42 00	43 00
1 in. No. 2, 6 ft. to 16 ft.	33 00	34 00
2" No. 2, 4" and up, width 6 to 16 ft.	33 00	34 00

Douglas Fir, delivered in Toronto:
Dimension Timber up to 32 feet:

6x6 and 8, 10x10 and 12, 12x12	$50 00
6x10, 8x10, 10x14, 12x14, 14x14	51 00
6x12, 8x12	52 00
14x16, 16x16	52 50
6x14, 8x14, 10x16, 12x16	54 00
14x18	54 50
8x16, 10x18, 12x18	55 00
18x18, 20x20	55 50
12x20, 24x24	56 00

Timber in lengths over 32 feet subject to negotiation.

Fir flooring, 1 x 3, edge grain		71 00
Fir flooring, 1 x 4, edge grain		71 00
Fir flooring, 1 x 4, flat grain		open
No. 1 & 2, 1-in. clear Fir rough	61 50	69 50
(Depending upon widths).		
No. 1 and 2, 1¼ and 1½ in., clear Fir rough	71 00	75 00
No. 1 and 2 2-in. clear Fir rough	56 00	66 00
1 x 5 and 1 x 6 Fir casing		73 00
1 x 8 and 1 x 10 Fir base		75 00
1¼ & 1½ x 8, 10 & 12" E. G. stepping		85 00
1¼ & 1½ x 8, 10 & 12" E. G. stepping		75 00
1-in. clear Fir, d 4 sides	56 00	64 00
1¼ x 1½ in. clear Fir, d 4 sides	56 50	65 50
XXX 6 butts to 2 in.		7 40
XXXXX 5 butts to 2 in.		8 45

TORONTO HARDWOOD PRICES

The prices given below are for carloads, f.o.b. Toronto, from wholesalers to retailers, and are based on a good percentage of long lengths and good widths, without any wide stock having been sorted out. War tax of seven and half per cent. on imported woods, payable by purchasers.

Ash, white, dry weight 3800 lbs. per M. ft.

	1s & 2s	No. 1 Com.	No. 2 Com.	No. 3 Com.
4/4	$80.00	$60.00	$40.00	$30.00
5/4 & 6/4	85.00	63.00	45.00	35.00
8/4	95.00	75.00	45.00	
10/4 & 12/4	110.00	110.00	60.00	
16/4	125.00	115.00	65.00	

Ash, Brown

4/4	$75.00	$55.00	$40.00	$28.00
6/4	80.00	65.00	60.00	50.00
8/4	83.00	70.00	65.00	50.00

Birch, dry weight 4000 lbs. per M. ft.

	1s & 2s $		No. 1 Com. $		No. 2 Com. $	
4/4	75	78	60	63	45	50
5/4 & 6/4	78	80	68	70	50	55
8/4	80	83	70	75	55	
10/4 and 12/4	100	105	90	95	70	
16/4	105	110	85	100	80	

Basswood, dry weight 2600 lbs. per M. ft.

	1s & 2s	No. 1 Com.	No. 2 Com.	No. 3 Com.
4/4	$77.00	$55.00	$44.00	$38.00
5/4 & 6/4	80.00	60.00	50.00	40.00
8/4	83.00	65.00	50.00	42.00

Chestnut, dry weight 2800 lbs. per M. ft.

	1s & 2s	No. 1 Com.	Sound Wormy
4/4	$75.00	$55.00	$50.00
5/4 & 6/4	80.00	60.00	52.00
8/4	82.00	62.00	55.00

Elm, soft, dry weight 3100 lbs. per M. ft.

	1s & 2s	No. 1 Com.	No. 2 Com.	No. 3 Com.
4/4	$63.00	$50.00	$40.00	$38.00
6/4 & 8/4	68.00	55.00	45.00	43.00
12/4	75.00	65.00	50.00	42.00

Gum, red, dry weight 3300 lbs. per M. ft.

	1s & 2s	No. 1 Com.
4/4	$125.00	$100.00
5/4 & 6/4	130.00	105.00
8/4	135.00	110.00

Gum, Sap

	1s & 2s	No. 1 Com.
4/4	$80.00	$55.00
5/4 & /64	85.00	60.00
8/4	90.00	70.00

Hickory, dry weight, 4500 lbs. per M. ft.

	1s & 2s	No. 1 Com.	No. 2 Com.
4/4	$75.00	$45.00	$30.00
6/4	100.00	75.00	50.00
8/4	90.00	80.00	85.00

Maple, hard, dry weight 3900 lbs. per M. ft.

	1s & 2s	No. 1 Com.	No. 2 Com.	No. 3 Com.
4/4	$60.00	$50.00	$40.00	$30.00
5/4 & 6/4	65.00	60.00	45.00	35.00
8/4	70.00	65.00	45.00	40.00
12/4	80.00	60.00	40.00	
16/4	90.00	75.00	45.00	

Soft Maple

The quantity of soft maple produced in Ontario is small and it is generally sold on a log run basis, the locality governing the prices.

Mill run grade, Nd. 3 and better	$43.00
No. 2 and better	52.00

White and Red Oak, plain sawed, dry weight 4000 lbs. per M. ft.

	1s & 2s	No. 1 Com.
4/4	$135.00	$90.00
5/4 & 6/4	145.00	100.00
8/4	150.00	105.00
10/4	155.00	110.00
12/4	160.00	115.00
16/4	165.00	120.00

White Oak, quarter cut, dry weight 4000 lbs. per M. ft.

	1s & 2s	No. 1 Com.
4/4	$210.00	$155.00
5/4 and 6/4	220.00	165.00
8/4	225.00	170.00

Red Oak, quarter cut.

	1s & 2s	No. 1 Com.
4/4	$125.00	$90.00
5/4 & 6/4	145.00	95.00
8/4	150.00	100.00

OTTAWA, ONT.

Manufacturers' Prices

Pine good sidings:		
1-in. x 7-in. and up		80 00
1¼-in. and 1½-in., 8-in. & up		100 00
2-in. x 7-in. and up		100 00
No. 2 cuts 2 x 8-in. and up		72 00
Pine good strips:		
1-in.		68 00
1¼-in. x 4-in. to 6-in.		75 00
2-in.		78 00
Pine good shorts:		
1-in. x 7-in. and up		65 00
1-in. x 4-in. to 6-in.		37 00
1¼-in. and 1½-in.		72 00
2-in.		72 00
7-in. to 9-in. A sidings		55 00
Pine, No. 1 dressing sidings		60 00
Pine, No. 1 dressing strips		57 00
Pine, No. 1 dressing shorts		52 00
Pine, 1-in. x 4-in. s.c. strips		49 00
Pine, 1-in. x 5-in. s.c. strips		50 00
Pine, 1-in. x 6-in. s.c. strips		52 00
Pine, 1-in. x 7-in. s.c. strips		52 00
Pine, 1 x 8-in. s.c., 12 to 16 ft.		54 00
Pine, 1-in. x 10-in. M.R.		57 00
Pine, s.c. sidings, 1½ and 2-in.		55 00
Pine, s.c. strips 1-in.	45 00	47 00
1¼, 1½ and 2-in.		54 00
Pine, s.c. shorts, 1 x 4 to 6 in.		45 00
Pine, s.c. and bet., shorts, 1 x 5		45 00
Pine, s.c. and bet., shorts, 1 x 6		49 00
Pine, s.c. shorts, 6'-11', 1"x10"		52 00
Pine box boards:		
1"x4" and up, 6'-11'		40 00
1"x3", 12'-16'		44 00
Pine, mill culls, strips and sidings, 1-in. x 4-in. and up, 12-ft. and up		40 00
Mill cull shorts, 1-in. x 4-in. and up, 6-ft to 11-ft.		28 00
O. culls r & w p		27 00
Red Pine, log run:		
mill culls out, 1-in.	36 00	42 00
mill culls out, 1¼-in.	36 00	42 00
mill culls out, 1½-in.	35 00	42 00
mill culls out, 2-in.	40 00	42 00
mill culls, white pine, 1"x7" and up		40 00
Mill run Spruce:		
1"x4" and up, 6'-11'		42 00
1"x4" and up, 12'-16'		42 00
1"x9"-10" and up, 12'-16'		00
1¼"x7" 8-9" and up, 12'-10'		48 00
1¼ x 10 and up, 12'-16'		50 00
1½" & 2" x 12" and up, 12'-16'		50 00
Spruce, 1-in. clear (fine dressing and B)		55 00
Hemlock, 1-in. cull	26 00	27 00
Hemlock, 1-in. log run	30 00	35 00
Hemlock, 2x4, 6, 8, 10, 12/16'	30 00	35 00
Tamarac	24 00	26 00
Basswood, log run, dead culls out	40 00	48 00
Basswood, log run, mill culls out	45 00	50 00
Birch, log run	45 00	50 00
Soft Elm, common and better, 1, 1¼, 2-in.	25 00	30 00
Ash, black, log run	32 00	40 00
1 x 10 No. 1 barn		52 00
1 x 10 No. 2 barn		46 00
1 x 8 and 9 No. 2 barn		42 00
Lath per M:		
No. 1 white pine, 1½-in. x 4 ft.		7 00
No. 2 white pine		6 50
Mill run white pine		6 75
Spruce, mill run 1½-in.		5 50
Red pine, mill run		5 50
Hemlock, mill run		4 50
32-in. lath		2 50
White Cedar Shingles:		
xxxx, 18-in.		7 00
Clear butt, 18-in.		6 00
18-in. xx		4 50
Spruce logs (pulp)	13 00	15 00

QUEBEC, QUE.

	Cts. Per Cubic Foot	
White Pine		
First class Ottawa waney, 18-in. average, according to lineal	80	90
19 in. and up average	90	100 00
Spruce Deals	Per M. Ft.	
3 in. unsorted Quebec, 4 in. to 6 in. thick	$34 00	$37 00
3 in. unsorted, Quebec, 7 in. to 5 in. thick	38 00	40 00
3 in. unsorted Quebec, 9 in. thick	40 00	45 00
Oak	Cts. Per Cubic Ft.	
According to average and quality 55 ft. cube	90	1 00
Elm		
According to average and quality, 40 to 45 feet, cube	95	1 05
According to average and quality, 30 to 35 feet	75	85
Birch Planks		
1 to 4 in. thick, per M. ft.	40 00	45 00

SARNIA, ONT.

Pine, Common and Better		
1 x 6 and 8 in.		$80
1 in., 8 in. and up wide		90
1¼ and 1½ in. and up wide		100 00
2 in. and up wide		105 00
Cuts and Better		
4/4 x 8 and up No. 1 and better		78 00
6/4 x 8 and up No. 1 and better		85 00
8/4 x 8 and up No. 1 and better		87 00
No. 1 Cuts		
1 in., 8 in. and up wide		68 00
1¼ in., 8 in. and up wide		72 00
1½ in., 8 in. and up wide		73 00
2 in., 8 in. and up wide		76 00
2½ and 3, 8 in. and up wide		100 00
4 in., 8 in. and up wide		105 00
No. 1 Barn		
1 in., 10 to 16 ft. long	$54 00	$64 00
1¼, 1½ and 2 in., 10/16 ft.	58 00	64 00
2½ to 3 in., 10/16 ft.		78 00
No. 2 Barn		
1 in., 10 to 16 ft. long	51 00	57 00
1¼, 1½ and 2 in., 10/16 ft.	52 00	58 00
2½ in. to 3 in.		66 00
No. 3 Barn		
1" in., 10 to 16 ft. long	48 00	53 00
1¼, 1½ and 2 in., 10/16 ft.	40 00	53 00
Box		
1 in., 1¼ in. & 1½ in., 10/16 ft.	44 00	46 00
Mill Culls		
Mill Run Culls		
1 in., 4 in. and up wide, 6/16 ft.		$37 00
1¼, 1½ and 2 in.		37 00
Lath		
No. 1 48 in. White Pine		$6 00
No. 2 48 in. White Pine		5 50
No. 3 48 in. White Pine		5 00
32 in. Pine		2 25
48 in. Hemlock		5 00
32 in. Hemlock		2 25

ST. JOHN, N.B.

Rough Lumber

Wholesale Prices Per M. Sq. Ft.

2x3, 2x4, 3x3, 3x4, Rgh. Merch. Spr.	$42 50
2x3, 2x4, 3x3, 3x4 Dressed 1 edge	44 00
2x3, 2x4, 3x3, 3x4 Dressed 4 sides	48 00
2x6, 2x7, 3x5, 4x4, 4x6, all rough	45 00
2x8, 3x7, 5x5, 6x6	47 00
2x9, 3x8, 6x8, 7x7	50 00
2x10, 3x9	55 00
2x12, 3x10, 3x12, 8x8 and up	57 50
Merch. Spr. Bds. Rough, 1x3-4 & 5	40 00
" " " " 1x6	45 00
" " " " 1x7 & up.	48 00
Refuse Bds., Deals & Setgs.	30 00

Above random lengths up to 18-0 long.
Lengths 19-0 & up $5.00 extra per M.
For planing Merch. and Refuse Bds. add $2.00 per M to above prices.
Laths $4.50 per M pieces.

Shingles	Per M.
Cedar, Extras	$6 00
" Clears	5 50
" 2nd Clears	5 00
Extra No. 1	3 50
Spruce	4 [illegible]
B. C. Cedar	4 70

WINNIPEG, MANITOBA

No. 1 Spruce

Dimension	S.1.S. and 1.E 6 ft.	8 ft.	10 ft.
2 x		$34.50	[illegible]
2 x		34.50	[illegible]
2 x		35.50	[illegible]
2 x		36.50	[illegible]
2 x		37.50	[illegible]
2 x	36.00	36.00	[illegible]
2 x	36.00	38.00	[illegible]
2 x	36.00	38.00	[illegible]
2 x	37.00	37.00	[illegible]
2 x	38.00	38.00	[illegible]

For 2 inch, rough, add 50 cents.
For S1E only add 50 cents.
For S1S and 2E, S4S or D&M, add $3.00.
For timbers larger than 8 x 8, add 50c. for each additional 2 inches each way.
For lengths longer than 20 ft., add $1.00 for each additional two feet.
For selected common, add $5.00.
For No. 2 Dimension, $3.00 less than No. 1.
For 1 x 2 and 2 x 2, $2 more than 2 x 4 No. 1.
For Tamarac add $3.00.

FIR, HEMLOCK, SPRUCE AND LARCH

Mountain Stock

No. 1 Dimension and Timbers

2 x 4, 2 x 6, 2 x 8, 8 to 16 ft., S1S1E	$37 00
2 x 4, 2 x 6, 2 x 8, 10 ft., S1S1E	39 00
2 x 4, 2 x 6, 2 x 8, 12/16, S1S1E	37 00
2 x 4, 2 x 6, 2 x 8, 18/22, S1S1E	39 00
2 x 4, 2 x 6, 2 x 8, 24/32, S1S1E	41 00
2 x 10, 8 ft., S1S1E	38 00
2 x 10, 10 ft. S1S1E	40 00
2 x 10, 12/16, S1S1E	38 00
2 x 10, 18/22, S1S1E	40 00
2 x 10, 24/32, S1S1E	42 00
2 x 12, 8 ft. to 16 ft., S1S1E	38 50
2 x 12; 10, 18, 20, 20	40 50
2 x 12; 24, 26, 28, 30, 32	42 50

BRITISH COLUMBIA COAST FIR.

Dimension S1S and E.

2 x 4 in., 6 and 8 ft.	36 50
2 x 4 in., 12 and 14 ft.	37 50
2 x 4 in., 10 and 16 ft.	38 50
2 x 4 in., 18 and 20 ft.	39 50
2 x 4 in., 22 to 32 ft.	41 50
2 x 10 in., 12 and 14	38 75
2 x 10 in., 16 ft.	39 75
2 x 10 in., 18 and 20	40 75
2 x 10 in., 22 to 32 ft.	42 75
2 x 12 in., 8 to 14 ft.	40 25
2 x 12 in., 16 ft.	41 25
2 x 12 in., 18 and 20 ft.	42 25
2 x 12 in., 22 to 32 ft.	44 25
3 x 3 and 3 x 4 in., 8 to 14 ft.	43 75
3 x 3 and 3 x 4 in., 16 ft.	44 75
3 x 3 and 3 x 4, 18 and 20 ft.	45 75
3 x 3 and 3 x 4 in., 22 to 32 ft.	47 75
6 x 6, 6 x 8 and 8 x 8, 6 to 16 ft.	46 00
6 x 6, 6 x 8, 8 x 8, 18 and 20 ft.	46 50
6 x 6, 6 x 8, 8 x 8, 22 to 32 ft.	47 50
Shingles, XXX B.C. Cedar, straight	6 21

BUFFALO AND TONAWANDA, N.Y.

White Pine

Wholesale Selling Price

[illegible]	$115 00
[illegible]	100 00
[illegible]	130 00
[illegible]	110 00
[illegible]	110 00
[illegible]	120 00
common 4/4	52 [illegible]
Fine Common 5/4	57 [illegible]
Fine Common 6/4	54 00
Fine common 8/4	57 [illegible]
No. 1 Cuts 4/4	65 [illegible]
No. 1 Cuts 5/4	74 [illegible]
No. 1 Cuts 6/4	75 [illegible]
No. 1 Cuts 8/4	78 [illegible]
No. 2 Cuts 4/4	47 [illegible]
No. 2 Cuts 5/4	61 [illegible]
No. 2 Cuts 6/4	62 [illegible]
No. 2 Cuts 8/4	69 [illegible]
No. 3 Cuts 5/4	49 [illegible]
No. 3 Cuts 6/4	49 [illegible]
No. 3 Cuts 8/4	50 [illegible]
Dressing 5/4	64 [illegible]
Dressing 5/4 x	67 [illegible]
Dressing 5/4 x	73 [illegible]
No. 1 Moulding	74 [illegible]
No. 1 Moulding 6/4	74 [illegible]
No. 1 Moulding 8/4	76 [illegible]
No. 2 Moulding	[illegible]
No. 2 Moulding	[illegible]
No. 2 Moulding	[illegible]
No. 1 Barn 1 x	[illegible]
No. 1 Barn 1 x 6 and 8	54 [illegible]
No. 1 Barn 1 x 10	56 [illegible]
No. 2 Barn 1 x 6 and 8	50 [illegible]
No. 2 Barn 1 x 10	54 [illegible]
No. 3 Barn 1 x 6 and 8	47 [illegible]
No. 3 Barn 1 x 10	48 00
Box 1 x 6 and up	45 00
Box 1	45 00
Box 1	46 00
Box 1 x 13 and up	47 00

The following quotations on woods represent the jobber buying price at Buffalo and Tonawanda.

(Continued on page 64

How Dominion Rubber System Belting Service Helps Belt Users

For more than fifty years we have specialized in the making of belting and the solving of problems in transmitting power and conveying materials economically.

We maintain a staff of belting experts for the sole purpose of helping Canadian Manufacturers to "speed up" production by cutting belting costs and eliminating power wastage.

These experts will, without charge, analyze your transmission and conveying equipment in its entirety and will recommend changes only where they are necessary to increase the efficiency of that equipment.

You are under no obligation to us in availing yourself of this service—the only return that we request is that you purchase Dominion Rubber System Belting when you have been convinced that the changes recommended by our engineers will be beneficial. This special service is available through any of our branches.

Phone, wire or write the one nearest to you and let us prove to you that the kind of service we have given to Canada's largest industries and the kind we want to give to you, means more than just selling better belts.

Makers of

Dominion Hose, Packing and Industrial Rubber Goods and Dominion Tires, the GOOD Tires for every purpose.

Services Branches

Halifax,	Fort William,
St. John,	Winnipeg,
Quebec,	Brandon,
Montreal,	Regina,
Ottawa,	Saskatoon,
Toronto,	Edmonton,
Hamilton,	Calgary,
London,	Lethbridge,
Kitchener,	Vancouver,
North Bay,	Victoria.

Maple Leaf SAWS

Maple Leaf Circular Saws are made of Special High Grade Steel, accurately ground; have hard-tempered center which makes a stiff blade that will stand up under the most severe conditions, and is less liable to push over in case of accident.

Let us prove it to you if you have not discovered it already.

EVERY SAW GUARANTEED.

Cross-cuts, Band Saws, Shingle Saws, and Everything Pertaining to Saws for Lumbermen

The Largest ALL Canadian Saw Manufacturers

Shurly Dietrich Company

Limited

Ottawa Vancouver Galt

CURRENT LUMBER PRICES—Continued

MAPLE	1s & 2s	No. 1 Com.	No. 2 Com.
4/4	47 - 50	32 - 34	22 - 24
5/4 to 8/4	60 - 62	38 - 40	26 - 28
10/4 to 16/4	70 - 72	50 - 52	30 - 32
RED BIRCH			
4/4	62 - 64	42 - 44	26 - 28
5/4 to 8/4	64 - 66	44 - 46	28 - 30
SAP BIRCH			
4/4	58 - 62	36 - 38	22 - 24
5/4 and up	62 - 65	38 - 40	24 - 26
SOFT ELM			
4/4	47 - 49	32 - 34	24 - 26
5, 6 & 8/4	49 - 51	34 - 36	24 - 26
BASSWOOD			
4/4	52 - 54	42 - 44	20 - 21
Thicker	55 - 58	44 - 46	20 - 32
PLAIN OAK			
4/4	67 - 72	44 - 48	28 - 30
5/4 to 8/4	72 - 76	48 - 52	32 - 34
ASH, WHITE AND BROWN			
4/4	68 - 70	38 - 42	27 - 30
5/4 to 8/4	73 - 77	45 - 47	30 - 32
10/4 and up	100 - 90	60 - 63	31 - 33

BOSTON, MASS.

Quotations given below are for highest grades of Michigan and Canadian white pine and Eastern Canadian Spruce as required in the New England market in carloads.

White pine uppers, 1 to 2 in.		134 00
White pine uppers, 2½ and 3 in.		149 00
White pine uppers, 4 in.		160 00
Selects, 1 to 2 in.		125 00
Selects, 2½ and 3 in.		140 00
Selects, 4 in.		155 00
Fine common, 1 in., 30 per cent. 12 in. and up		92 00
Fine common, 1 x 8 to 11 in.		87 00
Fine Common, 1¼ to 2 in.		100 00
Fine Common, 2½ and 3 in.		136 00
Fine Common, 4 in.		148 00
1 in. shaky clear		72 00
1¼ to 2 in. shaky clear		76 00
1 in. No. 2 dressing		64 00
1¼ to 2 in. No. 2 dressing		68 00
No. 1 Cuts, 1 in.		80 00
No. 1 Cuts, 1¼ to 2 in.	85 00	87 00
No. 1 Cuts, 2½ and 3 in.		115 00
No. 2 Cuts, 1 in.		66 00
No. 2 Cuts, 1¼ to 2 in.	70 00	71 00

Barn Boards, No. 1, 1 x 12	[illegible]	[illegible]
No. 1, 1 x 10	[illegible]	[illegible]
No. 1, 1 x 8	[illegible]	[illegible]
No. 2, 1 x 12	[illegible]	[illegible]
No. 2, 1 x 10	[illegible]	[illegible]
No. 2, 1 x 8	[illegible]	[illegible]
No. 3, 1 x 12	[illegible]	[illegible]
No. 3, 1 x 10	[illegible]	[illegible]
No. 3, 1 x 8	[illegible]	[illegible]
Can. spruce, clear, 1 x 4 to 9 in.	[illegible]	[illegible]
1 x 10 in.	[illegible]	[illegible]
No. 1, 1 x 4 to 7 in.	[illegible]	[illegible]
No. 1, 1 x 8 & 9 in.	[illegible]	[illegible]
No. 1, 1 x 10 in.	[illegible]	[illegible]
No. 2, 1 x 4 & 5 in.	[illegible]	[illegible]
No. 2, 1 x 6 & 7 in.	[illegible]	[illegible]
No. 2, 1 x 8 & 9 in.	45 00	[illegible]
No. 2, 1 x 10 in.	[illegible]	[illegible]
No. 3 1 x 10 in.	[illegible]	[illegible]
Spruce, 12 in. dimension		[illegible]
Spruce, 10 in. dimension		[illegible]
Spruce, 9 in. dimension		[illegible]
Spruce, 8 in. dimension		[illegible]
2 x 10 in. random lengths, 8 ft. and up		[illegible]
2 x 12 in., random lengths		[illegible]

2 x 3, 2 x 4, 2 x 5, 2 x 6, 2 x 7	[illegible]
3 x 4 and 4 x 4 in.	[illegible]
2 x 8 in.	[illegible]
All other random lengths, 7-i and under, 8 ft. and up	[illegible]
5-inch and up merchantable boards, 8 ft. and up, p 1s	[illegible]
1-⅝ in. spruce lath	[illegible]
1-½ in. spruce lath	[illegible]

New Brunswick Cedar Shingles

Clears	[illegible]
Second Clears	[illegible]
Clear Whites	[illegible]
Extra 1s (Clear whites in)	[illegible]
Extra 1s (Clear whites out)	[illegible]
Red Cedar Extras, 16-in. 5 b to 2-in.	[illegible]
Red [illegible] 16-inch & butts to 2-in.	[illegible]
Red Cedar [illegible], 5 butts to 2¼	[illegible]
Washington 16-in. 5 butts to 2 in. extra red cedar	[illegible]

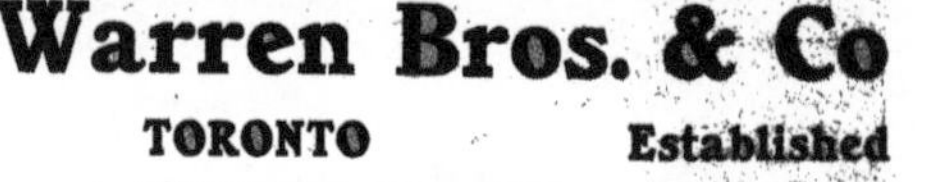

TORONTO Established

WHOLESALE GROCE

Special attention given to Lumber Trade

Write or wire us (at our expense) for quotations

Portable High Spar Overhead Skidder

Portable Ground Skidder

Tree Rig Ground Skidder

ALPHABETICAL INDEX TO ADVERTISERS

OXFORD
Saw Mill Machinery

20' Ordinary Frame Carriage

Heavy Carriage with Independent Set Works and Multi Hook Dogs

New Model Horizontal Engine, particularly adapted for portable mill work

Three Saw Gang Edger

Carriages with steel Logseats and Light Variable Feed Saw Husk, rope drive to suit light power. Edgers carrying from 2 to 7 saws to suit capacity of mill built in four sizes. Saw Husks with patented belted friction feed for ordinary size mills, also adapted for steam feed if desired. Lath Machines, capacity 40,000 in 10 hrs. Pole Road Trolleys, 8 to 10" flange.

OXFORD FOUNDRY & MACHINE
Company, Limited
OXFORD, - N.S.

LINK-BELT
Saw mill equipment is of the highest standard. Every piece can be distinguished by this trade mark
Look for it. It is your guarantee of quality, service and satisfaction. Write for our Saw Mill Book No. 260.
CANADIAN LINK-BELT CO. LTD.
WELLINGTON & PETER STS. TORONTO
Vancouver, B.C.—A. R. Williams Machinery Company, Limited.
Seattle, Wash.—Link-Belt Company of Washington, 576 First Avenue, S.
QUALITY---EFFICIENCY---RELIABILITY
Upon this foundation was built this, the Largest Saw Works in the World
Henry Disston & Sons, Inc.
PHILADELPHIA, U.S.A.

Bain Sleighs for Logging Operations

Logging is a severe test of a sleigh.

Therefore it pays to buy the best—one that has stood the test of time and hard usage—even though the first cost may be considerably more than one which may look just as good.

Bain Sleighs are Famous for Light Draft and Great Capacity

The Bain One-Beam Midland Sloop Sleigh

Clearance under Beam 7 in.

Steel shoes, short reach coupling; the blocks on runners give great strength; 2 ft. 10 in. or 3 ft. track.

The Bain Improved Sloop Sleigh

Clearance under Beam 7 in.

Steel shoes, short reach coupling, 3 ft. track.

The Bain One-Beam North Shore Bob Sleigh

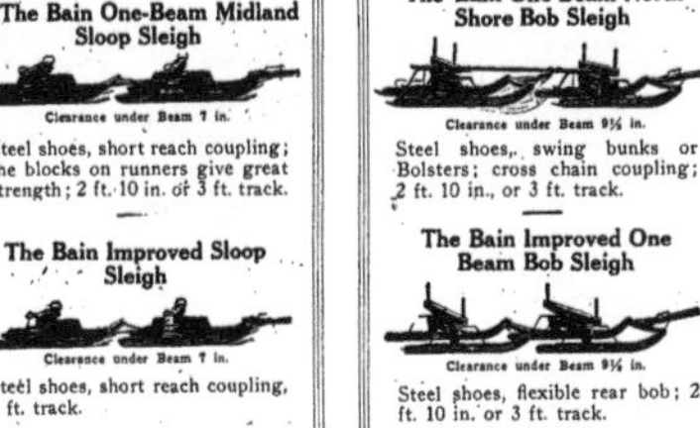

Clearance under Beam 9½ in.

Steel shoes, swing bunks or Bolsters; cross chain coupling; 2 ft. 10 in., or 3 ft. track.

The Bain Improved One Beam Bob Sleigh

Clearance under Beam 9½ in.

Steel shoes, flexible rear bob; 2 ft. 10 in. or 3 ft. track.

The Bain North Shore Sloop Sleigh

Clearance under Beam 7 in.

Steel shoes, cross chain coupling; 2 ft. 10 in. or 3 ft. track.

The Bain Heavy Sloop Sleigh

Clearance under Beam 7 in.

Steel shoes, short reach or cross chain coupling; 3 ft. 4 in., 4 ft. 4 in., or 4 ft. 8 in. track.

Massey-Harris Saw Outfits

Stationary or Portable, driven by the reliable Massey-Harris Gasoline Engine, for sawing Cordwood, Pulpwood, Poles, etc.

Massey-Harris Engines

Provide an Efficient and Economical Source of Power

Stationary, Portable or Semi-Portable, 1½ to 20 H.P.

Massey-Harris Co., Limited

HEAD OFFICES: TORONTO

Branches at—**Montreal, Moncton, Winnipeg, Regina, Saskatoon, Yorkton, Swift Current, Calgary, Edmonton.**

AGENCIES EVERYWHERE

CANADA LUMBERMAN BUYERS' DIRECTORY

The following regulations apply to all advertisers:—Eighth page, every issue, three headings; quarter page, six headings; half page, twelve headings; full page, twenty-four headings.

ACETYLENE PORTABLE LAMPS
Alexander Milburn Company

ASBESTOS GOODS
Atlas Asbestos Company, Ltd.

AXES
Canadian Warren Axe & Tool Co.

BABBITT METAL
Canada Metal Company.
General Supply Co. of Canada, Ltd.
Syracuse Smelting Works

BALE TIES
Laidlaw Bale Tie Company.

BALL BEARINGS
Chapman Double Ball Bearing Co.

BAND MILLS
Hamilton Company, William.
Waterous Engine Works Company.
Yates Machine Company, P. B.

BAND RESAWS
Mershon & Company, W. B.

BRAKING DEVICE
Ryther & Pringle Company

BELT CEMENT
Graton & Knight Mfg. Company.

BELT DRESSING
Atlas Asbestos Company, Ltd.
General Supply Co. of Canada, Ltd.
Graton & Knight Mfg. Company.

BELTING
Atlas Asbestos Company, Ltd.
Beardmore Belting Company
Canadian Consolidated Rubber Co.
General Supply Company
Goodhue & Co., J. L.
Goodyear Tire & Rubber Co.
Graton & Knight Mfg. Company.
Gutta Percha and Rubber Company.
Main Belting Company
Manhattan Rubber Mfg. Co.
D. K. McLaren Limited.
McLaren Belting Company, J. C.

BELTING (Transmission, Elevator, Conveyor, Rubber)
Dunlop Tire & Rubber Goods Co.

BIRCH, BASSWOOD
Clark & Sons, Edw.

BLOWERS
Sheldons Limited.
Toronto Blower Company.

BOILERS
Hamilton Company, William.
Jenckes Machine Company.
Marsh Engineering Works, Limited
Waterous Engine Works Company.

BOILER PRESERVATIVE
Beveridge Paper Company
International Chemical Company

BOX MACHINERY
Garlock-Walker Machinery Co.
Morgan Machine Company.
Yates Machine Company, P. B.

BOX SHOOKS
Davison Lumber & Mfg. Company

BUNKS (Steel)
Alaska Bedding Co. of Montreal.

CABLE CONVEYORS
Jeffrey Manufacturing Company.
Jenckes Machine Company, Ltd.
Waterous Engine Works Company.

CAMP SUPPLIES
Canadian Milk Products Limited.
Davies Company, William.
Dr. Bell Veterinary Wonder Co.
Gunns Limited
Harris Abattoir Company
Hunter & Company
Johnson, A. H.
Laporte Martin Limited
National Grocers, Limited
Peters Duncan Company
Turner & Sons, J. J.
Whitehead & Turner
Woods Manufacturing Company, Ltd.

CANT HOOKS
Canadian Warren Axe & Tool Co.
General Supply Co. of Canada, Ltd.
Pink Company, Thomas.

CARBIC FLARE LIGHTS
Foster, W. L.

CARS—STEEL BODY
Marsh Engineering Works, Limited

CAR WHEELS AND CASTINGS
Dominion Wheel & Foundries

CEDAR
Fesserton Timber Co.
Foss Lumber Company
Genoa Bay Lumber Company
Muir & Kirkpatrick.
Long Lumber Company.
Service Lumber Company
Terry & Gordon.
Thurston-Flavelle Lumber Company.
Vancouver Lumber Company.
Victoria Lumber and Mfg. Co.

CHAINS
Canadian Link-Belt Company, Ltd.
General Supply Co. of Canada, Ltd.
Hamilton Company, William.
Jeffrey Manufacturing Company.
Jenckes Machine Company, Ltd.
Pink & Co., Thomas.
Waterous Engine Works Company.
Williams Machinery Co., A. R., Vancouver.

CHINA CLAY
Bowater & Sons, W. V.

CHEMICAL PLANTS
Blair, Campbell & McLean, Ltd.

CLOTHING
Clarke & Company, A. R.
Grant, Holden & Graham.
Kitchen Overall & Shirt Company
McKenzie Limited
Woods Mfg. Company

COLLAR PADS
American Pad & Textile Co.

COLLARS (Shaft)
Bond Engineering Works

CONVEYOR MACHINERY
Canadian Link-Belt Company, Ltd.
Canadian Mathews Gravity Carrier Company.
General Supply Co. of Canada, Ltd.
Jeffrey Mfg. Co.
Waterous Engine Works Company.

CORDAGE
Consumers Cordage Company.

CORN SYRUP
Canada Starch Company.

COTTON GLOVES
American Pad & Textile Co.

COUNTERSHAFTS
Bond Engineering Works

COUPLINGS (Shaft)
Bond Engineering Works
Jenckes Machine Company, Ltd.

CRANES FOR SHIP YARDS
Canadian Link-Belt Company.

CROSS ARMS
Genoa Bay Lumber Company

CUTTER HEADS
Shimer Cutter Head Company.

CYPRESS
Blakeslee, Perrin & Darling
Chicago Lumber & Coal Company.
Long Lumber Company.
Wistar, Underhill & Nixon.

DERRICKS AND DERRICK FITTINGS
Marsh Engineering Works, Limited

DOORS
Genoa Bay Lumber Company
Harrington, E. I.
Long Lumber Company.
Mason, Gordon & Co.
Rutherford & Sons, Wm.
Terry & Gordon.

DRAG SAWS
Gerlach Company, Peter
Pennoyer & Company, J. C.
Williams Machinery Co., A. R.

DRY KILNS
Sheldons Limited.

DRYERS
Philadelphia Textile Mach. Company.

DUST COLLECTORS
Sheldons Limited.
Toronto Blower Company.

EDGERS
William Hamilton Company, Ltd.
Garlock-Walker Machinery Co.
Green Company, G. Walter
Haight, W. L.
Long Mfg. Company, E.
Waterous Engine Works Company.

ELEVATING AND CONVEYING MACHINERY
Canadian Link-Belt Company, Ltd.
Jeffrey Manufacturing Company.
Jenckes Machine Company, Ltd.
Waterous Engine Works Company.

ENGINES
Hamilton Company, William.
Jenckes Machine Company.
Waterous Engine Works Company.

EXCELSIOR MACHINERY
Elmira Machinery and Transmission Company.

EXHAUST FANS
Garlock-Walker Machinery Co.
Reed & Company, Geo. W.
Sheldons Limited.
Toronto Blower Company.

EXHAUST SYSTEMS
Reed & Company, Geo. W.
Sheldons Limited.
Toronto Blower Company.

FILES
Disston & Sons, Henry.
Simonds Canada Saw Company.

FIR
Associated Mills, Limited
Allan-Stoltze Lumber Co.
British American Mills & Timber Co.
Coal Creek Lumber Company.
Fesserton Timber Co.
Foss Lumber Company
Grier & Sons, Ltd., G. A.
Heeney, Percy E.
Knox Brothers.
Long Lumber Company.
Mason, Gordon & Co.
Reynolds Company, Limited
Service Lumber Company
Shearer Company, Jas.
Terry & Gordon.
Timberland Lumber Company.
Timms, Phillips & Co.
Vancouver Lumber Company.
Victoria Lumber and Mfg. Co.
Weller, J. B.

FIRE BRICK
Beveridge Paper Company
Elk Fire Brick Company of Canada.

FIRE FIGHTING APPARATUS
Dunlop Tire & Rubber Goods Co.
Pyrene Mfg. Company.
Waterous Engine Works Company

FIR FLOORING
Genoa Bay Lumber Company
Rutherford & Sons, Wm.

FLAG STAFFS
Ontario Wind Engine Company

FLOORING (Oak)
Long-Bell Lumber Company.

FLOUR
Western Canada Flour Mills Co., Ltd.

GALVANIZING
Ontario Wind Engine Company

GLOVES
Acme Glove Works
Eisendrath Glove Co.

GASOLINE ENGINES
Ontario Wind Engine Compan

GEARS (Cut)
Smart-Turner Machine Co.

GRATE BARS—Revolving
Beveridge Paper Company

GRAVITY LUMBER CARRIER
Can. Mathews Gravity Carrier Co.

GRINDERS (Bench)
Bond Engineering Works
Garlock-Walker Machinery Co.

HARDWOODS
Anderson Lumber Company, C. G.
Atlantic Lumber Co.
Bartram & Ball.
Bennett Lumber Company.
Blakeslee, Perrin & Darling
Cameron & Co.
Cardinal & Page
Davison Lumber & Mfg. Company
Dunfield & Company
Edwards & Co., W. C.
Fassett Lumber Company.
Fesserton Timber Co.
Fraser Limited.
Gillespie, James.
Gloucester Lumber Company
Grier & Son, G. A.
Heeney, Percy E.
Knox Brothers.
Long Lumber Company.
McLennan Lumber Company.
Moores, Jr., E. J.
Nicholson & Co., E. M.
Pedwell Hardwood Lumber Co.
Powell-Myers Lumber Co.
Russell, Chas. H.
Spencer Limited, C. A.
Stearns & Culver Lumber Co.
Summers, James R.
Taylor Lumber Company, S. K.
Webster & Brother, James.

HARDWOOD FLOORING MACHINERY
American Woodworking Machinery Company
Garlock-Walker Machinery Co.

HANGERS (Shaft)
Bond Engineering Works

HARDWOOD FLOORING
Grier & Son, G. A.
Long Lumber Company.

Graton & Knight Standardized Series Leather Belting

Tanned by us for belting use

Triple Insurance

A Belt is a beast of burden that can spill a large part of its load without your eye perceiving it.

Here is a belt travelling at a speed of more than a mile a minute. It operates completely around the pulleys 70 times every 60 seconds. At more than a revolution per second, think how even little leaks would foot up a big total if this were not the proper belt for the work to be done.

All Graton & Knight Standardized Series Leather Belts give triple insurance against power leaks because, first, they are made of leather, the one belting material that has the right degree of elasticity to give and take up its tension, and the best of pulley-gripping qualities. Second, this leather is tanned in our own tannery, specifically for belting purposes. Third, our belts are graded into a Standardized Series which includes belts built specifically for every power transmission need. Each is standardized in its manufacture and standardized for its work.

Selecting the proper belt and judging of its efficiency is not a job for guesswork or for the naked eye. It is a true engineering problem. Many of the best belted plants ask us to specify the belting for every pulley drive. Try the plan yourself. Then, when buying, call for "Graton & Knight——Brand or equal." This won't commit you to buying our belts. It will put your buying on the one basic consideration —the work to be done.

Write for Book, "Standardized Leather Belting."

Canadian Graton & Knight, Limited
MONTREAL, CANADA

Representatives in Canada:
THE CANADIAN FAIRBANKS-MORSE CO., LIMITED
St. John, Quebec, Montreal, Ottawa, Toronto, Hamilton, Vancouver, Victoria.

By means of standardized methods of grading and manufacture, together with extensive investigations in our Engineering Laboratory, our Engineers are able to specify the correct belt for a given drive. Tests show that a 14 to 16 ounce belt should be rated at not more than 80% of the capacity of a 16 to 18 ounce belt. Consult our Engineering Department.

Here is a 34" Gra-Knight 3-ply Belt 82½ feet long. It was installed in December, 1915, in the plant of The Powell Lumber Co., Lake Charles, La. 14 ft. Drive Pulley, 136 R. P. M. 52" Driven Pulley. Belt Speed 5900 F. P. M. 443 horse power. The cost per horse power per week to date is 1-1/3 cents with several more years service to come.

HARNESS
Beal Bros.

HEMLOCK
Anderson Lumber Company, C. G.
Bartram & Ball.
Bourgouin, H.
Callander Sawmills
Canadian General Lumber Company
Cane & Co., Jas. G.
Davison Lumber & Mfg. Company
Dunfield & Company
Edwards & Company, W. C.
Fesserton Timber Co.
Foss Lumber Company
Grier & Sons, Ltd., G. A.
Hart & McDonagh.
Long Lumber Company.
Mason, Gordon & Co.
Spencer Limited, C. A.
Terry & Gordon.
The Long Lumber Company.

HOISTING AND HAULING ENGINES
Garlock-Walker Machinery Co.
General Supply Co. of Canada, Ltd.
Marsh Engineering Works, Limited

HORSES
Union Stock Yards.

HOSE
Dunlop Tire & Rubber Goods Co.
General Supply Co. of Canada, Ltd.
Goodyear Tire & Rubber Co.
Gutta Percha and Rubber Company.

INDUSTRIAL CARS
Marsh Engineering Works, Limited

INSURANCE
Hardy & Co., E. D.
Rankin Benedict Underwriting Co.

INTERIOR FINISH
Eagle Lumber Company.
Hay & Co.
Mason, Gordon & Co.
Renfrew Planing Mills.
Terry & Gordon.

KNIVES
Disston & Sons, Henry.
Peter Hay Knife Company.
Simonds Canada Saw Company.
Waterous Engine Works Company.

LARCH
Otis Staples Lumber Co.

LATH
Austin & Nicholson.
Callander Sawmills
Canadian General Lumber Company
Cane & Co., Jas. G.
Carew Lumber Co., The John
Cardinal & Page
Dupuis Limited, J. P.
Eagle Lumber Company.
Fraser Limited.
Fraser-Bryson Lumber Company.
Genoa Bay Lumber Company
Gloucester Lumber Company
Grier & Sons, Ltd., G. A.
Harris Tie & Timber Company, Ltd.
Long Lumber Company.
McLennan Lumber Company.
New Ontario Colonization Company.
Otis Staples Lumber Co.
River Ouelle Pulp and Paper Co.
Spencer Limited, C. A.
Terry & Gordon.
Union Lumber Company.
Victoria Harbor Lumber Company.

LATH BOLTERS
Garlock-Walker Machinery Co.
General Supply Co. of Canada, Ltd.
Green Company, C. Walter.

LOCOMOTIVES
Bell Locomotive Works
General Supply Co. of Canada, Ltd.
Jeffrey Manufacturiing Company.
Jenckes Machine Company, Ltd.
Climax Manufacturing Company.
Montreal Locomotive Workks.

LATH TWINE
Consumers' Cordage Company.

LARRIGANS, SHOEPACKS
Palmer & Co., Ltd., John

LINK-BELT
Canadian Link-Belt Company
Canadian Mathews Gravity Carrier Company.
Jeffrey Mfg. Co.
Williams Machinery Co., A. R., Vancouver.

LOCOMOTIVE CRANES
Canadian Link-Belt Company, Ltd.

LOGGING ENGINES
Dunbar Engine and Foundry Co.
Jenckes Machine Company.
Marsh Engineering Works, Limited

LOG HAULER
Green Company, G. Walter
Jenckes Machine Company, Ltd.

LOGGING MACHINERY AND EQUIPMENT
General Supply Co. of Canada, Ltd.
Hamilton Company, William.
Jenckes Machine Company, Ltd.
Marsh Engineering Works, Limited
Waterous Engine Works Company.

LUMBER TRUCKS
Waterous Engine Works Company.

LUMBERMEN'S CLOTHING
Woods Manufacturing Company, Ltd.

MATCHES, FIRE BUCKETS
Eddy Company, E. B.

METAL REFINERS
Canada Metal Company.
Hoyt Metal Company.
Sessenwein Brothers.

MILLING IN TRANSIT
Renfrew Planing Mills.
Rutherford & Sons, Wm.

MOLDINGS
Genoa Bay Lumber Co.
Rutherford & Sons, Wm.

MOTOR TRUCKS
Duplex Truck Company

OAK
Chicago Lumber & Coal Company.
Long-Bell Lumber Company.
Sharpies, Reg., W. & J.
Weller, J. B.

OAKUM
Stratford Oakum Co., Geo.

OATS
National Elevator Company, Limited

OIL CLOTHING
Leckie, Limited, John.

OLD IRON AND BRASS
Sessenwein Brothers.

OVERALLS
Hamilton Carhartt Cotton Mills

PAPER
Bowater & Sons, W. V.
Riordon Pulp & Paper Company

PACKING
Atlas Asbestos Company, Ltd.
Consumers Cordage Co.
Dunlop Tire & Rubber Goods Co.
Gutta Percha and Rubber Company.

PAPER MILL MACHINERY
Bowater & Sons, W. V.

PILLOW BLOCKS
Bond Engineering Works

PINE
Anderson Lumber Company, C. G.
Atlantic Lumber Co.
Austin & Nicholson.
Bourgouin, H.
Callander Sawmills
Cameron & Co.
Canadian General Lumber Company
Cane & Co., Jas. G.
Cardinal & Page
Chicago Lumber & Coal Company.
Cleveland-Sarnia Sawmills Company
Colonial Lumber Company
Davison Lumber & Mfg. Co.
Donogh & Co., John.
Dudley, Arthur N.
Dunfield & Company
Eagle Lumber Company.
Edwards & Co., W. C.

Excelsior Lumber Company.
Fesserton Timber Company
Fraser-Bryson Lumber Company.
Fraser Limited.
Gillies Brothers Limited.
Gloucester Lumber Company
Gordon & Co., George.
Grier & Sons, Ltd., G. A.
Harris Tie & Timber Company, Ltd.
Hart & McDonagh.
Hettler Lumber Company, Herman H.
Long-Bell Lumber Company.
Long Lumber Company.
Mason, Gordon & Co.
McAuliffe Davis Lumber Company
McLennan Lumber Company.
Montreal Lumber Company.
Moores, Jr., E. J.
Muir & Kirkpatrick.
Otis Staples Lumber Co.
Parry Sound Lumber Company.
Russell, Chas. H.
Shearer Company, Jas.
Spencer Limited, C. A.
Summers, James R.
Terry & Gordon.
Union Lumber Company.
Watson & Todd, Limited.
Weller, J. B.
Williams Lumber Company
Wuichet, Louis.

PLANING MILL EXHAUSTERS
Garlock-Walker Machinery Co.
Reed & Company, Geo. W.
Sheldons Limited.
Toronto Blower Co.

PLANING MILL MACHINERY
American Woodworking Machinery Company
Garlock-Walker Machinery Co.
Mershon & Company, W. B.
Sheldons Limited.
Toronto Blower Co.
Yates Machine Company, P. B.

PORK PACKERS
Davies Company, William
Harris Abattoir Company

POSTS AND POLES
Auger & Company
Canadian Tie & Lumber Co.
Dupuis Limited, J. P.
Eagle Lumber Company
Harris Tie & Timber Company, Ltd.
Long-Bell Lumber Company.
Long Lumber Company.
Mason, Gordon & Co.
Terry & Gordon.

PULLEYS AND SHAFTING
Bond Engineering Works
Canadian Link-Belt Company
Garlock-Walker Machinery Co.
General Supply Co. of Canada, Ltd.
Green Company, G. Walter
Hamilton Company, William
Jeffrey Mfg. Co.
Jenckes Machine Company, Ltd.

PULP MILL MACHINERY
Canadian Link-Belt Company, Ltd.
Hamilton Company, William.
Jeffrey Manufacturing Company
Jenckes Machine Company, Ltd.
Waterous Engine Works Company

PUMPS
General Supply Co. of Canada, Ltd.
Hamilton Company, William
Jenckes Machine Company, Ltd.
Smart-Turner Machine Company
Waterous Engine Works Company

RAILS
Gartshore, John J.
Sessenwein Bros.

ROOFINGS
Reed & Company, Geo. W.

ROOFINGS
(Rubber, Plastic and Liquid)
Beveridge Paper Company
International Chemical Company

ROPE
Consumers Cordage Co.
Leckie, Limited, John

ROPE TRACES
Griffith & Son, G. L.

RUBBER GOODS
Atlas Asbestos Company
Dunlop Tire & Rubber Goods Co.
Goodyear Tire and Rubber Co.
Gutta Percha & Rubber Company

SASH
Genoa Bay Lumber Company
Renfrew Planing Mills.

SAWS
Atkins & Company, E. C.
Disston & Sons, Henry
General Supply Co. of Canada, Ltd.
Gerlach Company, Peter
Green Company, G. Walter
Hoe & Company, R.
Shurly-Dietrich Company
Shurly Co., Ltd., T. F.
Simonds Canada Saw Company

SASH, PORTABLE HOUSES
Davidson's Sons, James

SAW MILL LINK-BELT
Williams Machinery Co., A. R., Vancouver.

SAW MILL MACHINERY
Canadian Link-Belt Company, Ltd.
Dunbar Engine & Foundry Co.
Firstbrook Bros.
General Supply Co. of Canada, Ltd.
Haight, W. L.
Hamilton Company, William
Huther Bros. Saw Mfg. Company
Jeffrey Manufacturing Company
Long Manufacturing Company, E.
Mershon & Company, W. B.
Parry Sound Lumber Company
Payette Company, P.
Waterous Engine Works Company
Yates Machine Co., P. B.

SHEATHINGS
Beveridge Paper Company
Goodyear Tire & Rubber Co.

SHINGLE MACHINES
Marsh Engineering Works, Limited

SAW MANDRELS
Bond Engineering Works

SAW SHARPENERS
Garlock-Walker Machinery Co.
Waterous Engine Works Company.

SAW SLASHERS
Waterous Engine Works Company

SAWMILL LINK-BELT
Canadian Link-Belt Company

SHEET METALS
Syracuse Smelting Works

SHINGLES
Allan-Stoltze Lumber Co.
Associated Mills, Limited
Campbell-MacLaurin Lumber Co.
Cardinal & Page
Dominion Lumber & Timber Co.
Eagle Lumber Company
Foss Lumber Company
Fraser Limited.
Genoa Bay Lumber Company
Gillespie, James.
Gloucester Lumber Company
Grier & Sons, Ltd., G. A.
Harris Tie & Timber Company, Ltd.
Heeney, Percy E.
Long Lumber Company.
Mason, Gordon & Co.
McLennan Lumber Company.
Miller Company, Ltd., W. H.
Reynolds Company, Limited
Service Lumber Company
Shingle Agency of B. C.
Terry & Gordon.
Timms, Phillips & Co.
Vancouver Lumber Company.
Victoria Lumber and Mfg. Co.

SHINGLE & LATH MACHINERY
Dunbar Engine and Foundry Co.
Garlock-Walker Machinery Co.
Green Company, C. Walter
Hamilton Company, William.
Long Manufacturing Company, E.
Payette Company, P.

SHOEPACKS
Copeland Shoepack Co.
Gendron Penetang Shoepack Co.

SILENT CHAIN DRIVES
Canadian Link-Belt Company, Ltd.

SILOS
Ontario Wind Engine Company

SKIDDERS
Canadian Allis-Chalmers, Limited

SLEEPING ROBES
Woods Mfg. Company, Limited

SLEIGHS AND WAGONS
Barr, Alexander

SMOKESTACKS
Marsh Engineering Works, Limited
Waterous Engine Works Company.

SNOW PLOWS
Pink Company, Thomas.

SPARK ARRESTORS
Jenckes Machine Company, Ltd.
Reed & Company, Geo. W.
Waterous Engine Works Company.

SPRUCE
Bartram & Ball.
Bourgouin, H.
Cane & Co., Jas. G.
Cardinal & Page
Davison Lumber & Mfg. Company
Donogh & Co., John.
Dudley, Arthur N.
Dunfield & Company
Exchange Lumber Company.
Foss Lumber Company
Fraser Limited.
Fraser-Bryson Lumber Company.
Gillies Brothers.
Gloucester Lumber Company
Grant & Campbell.
Grier & Sons, Ltd., G. A.
Hart & McDonagh.
Lauder, Spears & Howland.
Long Lumber Company.
Mason, Gordon & Co.
McLennan Lumber Company.
Muir & Kirkpatrick.
New Ontario Colonization Company.
Nicholson & Co., E. M.
River Ouelle Pulp and Lumber Co.
Russell, Chas. H.
Service Lumber Company
Shearer Company, Jas.
Snowball Co., J. B.
Spencer Limited, C. A.
Terry & Gordon.
The Rideau Lumber Company

STEEL CASTINGS
Kennedy & Sons, Wm.

STEEL CHAIN
Canadian Link-Belt Company, Ltd.
Jeffrey Manufacturing Company.
Waterous Engine Works Company.

STEEL PLATE CONSTRUCTION
Marsh Engineering Works, Limited

STEAM PLANT ACCESSORIES
Waterous Engine Works Company.

STEEL BARRELS
Smart-Turner Machine Co.

STEEL DRUMS
Smart-Turner Machine Co.

STOVES AND RANGES
Davidson Company, Thos.
Enterprise Foundry Company

SWEAT PADS
American Pad & Textile Co.

SULPHITE PULP CHIPS
Davison Lumber & Mfg. Company

TANKS
Ontario Wind Engine Company

TARPAULINS
Turner & Sons, J. J.
Woods Manufacturing Company, Ltd.

TAPS AND DIES
Pratt & Whitney Company.

TENTS
Turner & Sons, J. J.
Woods Mfg. Company

TENTS, CLOTHING
Grant, Holden & Graham, Limited

TIES
Auger & Company
Austin & Nicholson.
Canadian Tie & Lumber Co.
Harris Tie & Timber Company, Ltd.
Long Lumber Company.
McLennan Lumber Company.
Terry & Gordon.

TIMBER BROKERS
Bradley, R. R.
Cant & Kemp.
Farnworth & Jardine.
Hillas & Co., W. N.
Hunter, Herbert F.
Smith & Tyrer, Limited

TIMBER CRUISERS AND ESTIMATORS
Sewall, James W.

TIMBER LANDS
Department of Lands and Forests.

TRACTORS
British War Mission

TRANSMISSION MACHINERY
Bond Engineering Works
Canadian Link-Belt Company, Ltd.
General Supply Co. of Canada, Ltd.
Jenckes Machine Company, Ltd.
Jeffrey Manufacturing Company.
Waterous Engine Works Company.

TRIMMERS
Garlock-Walker Machinery Co.
Green Company, C. Walter
Waterous Engine Works Company

TUGS
West & Peachey.

TURBINES
Hamilton Company, William.
Jenckes Machine Company, Ltd.

VALVES
Bay City Foundry & Machine Co.
Mason Regulator & Engineering Co.

VENEERS
Webster & Brother, James.

VENEER DRYERS
Coe Manufacturing Company
Philadelphia Textile Mach. Co.

VENEER MACHINERY
Coe Manufacturing Company
Garlock-Walker Machinery Co.
Philadelphia Textile Machinery Co.

VETERINARY REMEDIES
Dr. Bell Veterinary Wonder Co.
Johnson, A. H.

WATER HEATERS
Mason Regulator & Engineering Co.

WATERPROOFING
Beveridge Paper Company

WATER WHEELS
Hamilton Company, William.
Jenckes Machine Company, Ltd.

WIRE
Laidlaw Bale Tie Company.

WOOD DISTILLATION PLANTS
Blair, Campbell & McLean, Ltd.

WOODWORKING MACHINERY
American Woodworking Machy. Co.
Garlock-Walker Machinery Co.
General Supply Co. of Canada, Ltd.
Jeffrey Manufacturing Company.
Long Manufacturing Company, E.
Mershon & Company, W. B.
Waterous Engine Works Company.
Yates Machine Company, P. B.

WOOD PRESERVATIVES
International Chemical Company

WOOD PULP
Austin & Nicholson.
New Ontario Colonization Co.
River Ouelle Pulp and Lumber Co.

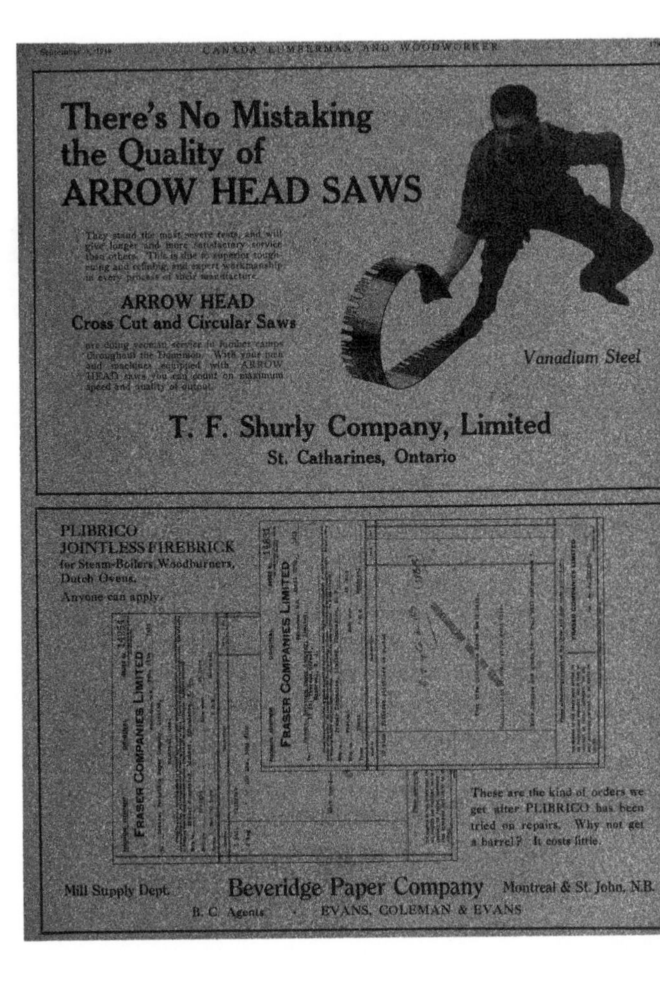
CANADA LUMBERMAN AND WOODWORKER
There's No Mistaking the Quality of ARROW HEAD SAWS
They stand the most severe tests, and will give longer and more satisfactory service than others. This is due to superior toughening and refining, and expert workmanship in every process of their manufacture.
ARROW HEAD
Cross Cut and Circular Saws
are doing yeoman service in lumber camps throughout the Dominion. With your men and machines equipped with ARROW HEAD saws you can count on maximum speed and quality of output.
Vanadium Steel
T. F. Shurly Company, Limited
St. Catharines, Ontario
PLIBRICO
JOINTLESS FIREBRICK
for Steam-Boilers, Woodburners, Dutch Ovens.
Anyone can apply.
FRASER COMPANIES LIMITED
FRASER COMPANIES LIMITED
These are the kind of orders we get after PLIBRICO has been tried on repairs. Why not get a barrel? It costs little.
Mill Supply Dept.
Beveridge Paper Company
Montreal & St. John, N.B.
B. C. Agents - EVANS, COLEMAN & EVANS

Serviceable Clothing
FOR LUMBERMEN

Clarke's Shirts and Mackinaws

Where the Work is Strenuous

is when Clarke's clothing is best appreciated. Our shirts and mackinaws are worn in great numbers throughout the lumber camps of Canada, and there are good reasons for their popularity. They are made to stand the strain of rough wear, are correctly proportioned to give the utmost comfort and are manufactured from materials that give warmth without undue weight.

See that you send your next order for clothing to Clarkes, the lumberman's outfitters.

Get prices and particulars in the meantime.

A. R. Clarke & Co. Limited

Montreal TORONTO Quebec

Vol. 39 Toronto, September 15, 1919 No. 18

Canada Lumberman & Wood Worker

Alphabetical Index to Advertisers, Page 60 Classified Directory to Advertisements, Page 76

DRY SPRUCE

MERCHANTABLE	
1 x 3	53,070
1 x 4	114,138
1 x 5	163,456
1 x 6	180,700
1 x 7	97,750
1 x 8	48,000
1 x 9	6,000
1" Shorts	48,000

5TH QUALITY	
1 x 4 and up	100,000
2 x 3 and up	27,231
3 x 4 and up	88,704
3 x 4/5	21,344
3 x 6	15,264
3 x 7/8	15,677
3 x 9/11	22,806

MILL CULL	
1 x 3	110,574
1 x 3 and up	51,067
1 x 4 and up	66,119
2 x 3 and up	114,605
3 x 4 and up	197,620

Merchantable Spruce

Our lines are now complete in 1 in., 2 in. and 3 in. from this year's cut.

Bartram & Ball Limited

Drummond Building, Montreal, Quebec.

KNOX BROTHERS LIMITED

MONTREAL

4th Quality and Better Quebec Spruce Especially Put Up for Export

1 x 5"	Merchantable	Spruce,	6/16	35,000'
1 x 6	"	"	"	65,000
1 x 7	"	"	"	20,000
1 x 8	"	"	"	35,000
1 x 9 and up	"	"	"	35,000
2 x 4 and up	"	"	6/9	40,000
2 x 5	"	"	10/16	15,000
2 x 6	"	"	"	130,000
2 x 7	"	"	"	90,000
2 x 8	"	"	"	38,000
2 x 9	"	"	"	10,000
2 x 12	"	"	"	8,000
4 x 6	"	"	"	28,000
6 x 6	"	"	12/16	24,000
3 x 6	"	"	6/16	41,000
3 x 7	"	"	"	76,000
3 x 8	"	"	"	275,000
3 x 9	"	"	"	113,000
3 x 10	"	"	"	144,000
3 x 11	"	"	"	170,000

B. C. Fir in Transit

4 cars ⅝ x 4 Ceiling.
4 cars 1 x 4 Ceiling.
1 car ⅜ x 3 Ceiling.
5 cars 1 x 4 Flooring.
1 car 12 x 12 Timbers, 24' to 48'.

Address

KNOX BROS., LTD., Drummond Bldg., MONTREAL

View of our Fir Mill from log pond, Vancouver, B.C.

Quick Action

You Can Have It

Try the Canada Lumberman Wanted and For Sale Department. Have you anything you wish to buy or sell in the Lumber Industry? You will find this department inexpensive, and a very effective business getter.

Our Classified Advertisers do not repeat the ad, often. They don't have to. They report immediate results. Use these columns to your own advantage.

CANADA LUMBERMAN and WOODWORKER
347 Adelaide St. W.
TORONTO

Frank H. Harris Lumber Company, Limited

Manufacturers and Wholesalers of

Yellow Pine and Southern Hardwoods

Yellow Pine in Transit at all Times

Mills: High Point, Miss. / Lake, Miss.

Office: 814 Excelsior Life Building, TORONTO, Canada.

"Horseshoe" Brand Red Cedar Shingles

Old Growth Fir Logs at Port Moody

Fir Timbers Our Specialty

"IT CAN'T BE DONE"—

You can't build a house on sandstone, neither can you make Quality Lumber out of poor logs. We are able through our own manufacturing facilities to offer the Eastern market the best in B.C. forest products. Send us your enquiries.

REYNOLDS COMPANY LIMITED

General Offices: VANCOUVER, B.C.

SAVOIE & CO. MANSEAU, QUE.

Lumber Dealers

Spruce, Hemlock, Hardwood, Lath, Cedar Posts, Pulp Wood

MILLING IN TRANSIT

We have facilities for milling lumber in transit. Manseau is on the Intercolonial Ry., 110 miles East of Montreal

---

QUICK ACTION

Can be assured if you will let the CANADA LUMBERMAN "Wanted and For Sale" department take care of your miscellaneous business needs.

We receive constant testimony from advertisers as to the value they have received from this far reaching and inexpensive method of publicity in the lumber trade and allied industries.

Try these columns. The result will surprise you.

CANADA LUMBERMAN

and WOODWORKER

347 Adelaide St. West - - TORONTO

Atlantic Lumber Company
HARDWOODS
WEST VIRGINIA SOFT RED AND WHITE OAK
Our Specialty: West Virginia and Pennsylvania Cherry
1055 Seneca Street

Standard Hardwood Lumber Co.
Hardwoods
Prompt Shipment { From Buffalo Yards or from Mill direct to you
8 Million Feet Dry Stock on Hand 1333 Clinton St.

Hugh McLean Lumber Co.
Hardwoods of All Kinds
Our Specialties—QUARTERED WHITE OAK SAP AND RED GUM
Established 25 Years 940 Elk Street

Miller, Sturm & Miller
1142 SENECA STREET
Hardwoods of All Kinds

G. Elias & Bro., Inc.
Established 1881
All Kinds of Hardwood Lumber
And in addition we carry a full line of White Pine, Yellow Pine, Spruce, Hemlock and Fir Timber, Lumber, Millwork and Boxes—Maple and Oak Flooring
CAREFUL ATTENTION TO MIXED CAR ORDERS

Taylor & Crate
Hardwoods of All Kinds
A stock of 18,000,000 to 20,000,000 feet of hardwoods carried at all times at our two big Buffalo Yards
Established 50 Years Rail or Cargo Shipments

T. Sullivan & Co.
HARDWOODS
We Specialize in Brown Ash and Elm
Car or Cargo Shipments Cor. Niagara and Arthur Sts.

Yeager Lumber Company, Inc.
SPECIALTIES
Oak, Poplar, Ash, Maple
932 Elk Street

B Buffa
U Hardw
F Lum
F Deal
A
L
O

Buffalo Hardwood Lumber Co.
940 Seneca St.
We Specialize in WHITE ASH
Anyone handling any of this stock, write us.
We also handle a complete stock of Plain Oak, Quar. Oak, Maple, Poplar, Red Cedar, etc.

Blakeslee, Perrin & Darling
A Complete Stock of Seasoned Hardwoods
including Ash, Basswood, Birch, Cherry, Chestnut, Cypress, Elm, Gum, Hickory, Maple, Plain and Quartered Oak, Poplar and Walnut.
1100 Seneca Street

New Ontario Colonization Co., Ltd.

MANUFACTURERS

Spruce, Tamarack, Whitewood, Poplar Lumber,
Rossed Spruce Pulpwood, Lath,

Full Planing Mill Facilities

Sales Office: BUFFALO, N. Y.
503 Niagara Life Bldg.

Mills: JACKSONBORO, ONT.
On Transcontinental Ry.

IMMEDIATE ORDERS TO PLACE

We have immediate orders to place for Box Boards and similar timber and are open to act as Agents in England for shippers exporting these goods. If quotation satisfactory very big business guaranteed.

REFERENCES ON APPLICATION.

Apply:

Timber Importers, Limited

GRACECHURCH BUILDINGS,
GRACECHURCH STREET, LONDON, E. C. 3.

Telegrams: Planchers, Grace, London. A B C Code, 5th Edition.

Standing Timber

in Large or Small Blocks

FOR SALE

THE undersigned offer for sale, in large or small blocks all their remaining timber lands and town property situated in the town of Parry Sound, Ont.

We have sold quite a number of timber parcels but still have some good bargains left in Townships of McDougall, Foley, McKellar, Monteith, Carling, Christie, McConkey, Mills, Allen, Secord, Falconbridge and Street.

Special Prices

Special bargains in the Townships of Falconbridge and Street for small mills.

The Parry Sound Lumber Co. Limited
26 Ernest Ave.
Toronto, Canada

QUALITY DRY STOCK

—and Immediate Shipment

A COMBINATION YOU CAN SECURE FROM US

ASH		
1"	FAS No. 1 & No. 2 Com..	26,000'
1½"	FAS No. 1 & No. 2 Com..	37,000'
2"	FAS & No. 1 Common ...	20,000'
2½"	FAS & No. 1 Common ...	6,000'
3"	FAS & No. 1 Common ...	5,000'
4"	FAS & No. 1 Common ...	5,400'
PLAIN OAK		
1"	FAS & No. 1 Common ...	41,200'
2"	FAS & No. 1 Common ...	27,000'
2½"	FAS & No. 1 Common ...	30,000'
3"	FAS & No. 1 Common ...	30,000'
4"	FAS & No. 1 Common ...	35,586'
PECAN		
2"	FAS No. 1 & No. 2 Com.	58,320'
2½"	FAS No. 1 & No. 2 Com.	27,910'
SOFT ELM		
¾"	FAS No. 1 & No. 2 Com.	16,400'
1"	FAS No. 1 & No. 2 Com.	13,200'
1½"	FAS & No. 1 Common	15,600'
2"	FAS & No. 1 Common ...	47,200'
2½"	FAS & No. 1 Common ...	28,700'
3"	FAS & No. 1 Common ...	48,000'
HARD MAPLE		
1½"	FAS & No. 1 Common ...	15,188'
1¼"	FAS & No. 1 Common ...	12,373'
2"	FAS & No. 1 Common ...	43,200'
2½"	FAS & No. 1 Common ...	240,000
3"	FAS & No. 1 Common ...	39,400'
HICKORY		
1"	FAS No. 1 & No. 2 Com..	13,000'
1½"	FAS & No. 1 Common ...	12,000'
2"	FAS & No. 1 Common ...	10,000'

John I. Shafer Hardwood Co., South Bend IND.

Trade (T) Mark
Reg. U. S. A.

ALABAMA HEWN OAK TIMBER—

HARDWOOD LOGS:—
Ash, Hickory, Poplar, Oak, Satin Walnut,
Mobile Bay Poplar, Dogwood

HARDWOOD LUMBER:—
Hewn Pitch Pine Timber, Pitch Pine Lumber

THE S. K. TAYLOR LUMBER COMPANY
Exporters Mobile, Alabama, U.S.A. Cables "Taylor, Mobile"

BRITISH COLUMBIA RED CEDAR SHINGLES

MADE UNDER PATENT RIGHTS TAKEN OUT BY NATURE

THE secret process whereby Nature stores in the Red Cedar of British Columbia the qualities which make it the ideal roofing product of the world, are beyond the ken of man.

EVERY other form of roofing aims to imitate—in quality—in appearance—the results attained by using Red Cedar Shingles.

LIKE all other imitations of Nature, these fall short. No man-made product—the result of quick manufacture—can approach Nature's laboratory methods, whereby the moisture and sunlight of a generation is utilized in the storm-defying weather-proof texture, and the storage of decay-resisting oils, permeating the entire shingle.

Nature Roofing is superior, and the best type of Nature Roofing is found in British Columbia Red Cedar Shingles.

Owing to the exceptionally strong demand, dealers are advised to place their orders with the British Columbia mills at the earliest possible date.

We are prepared to furnish dealers with supplies of our B. C. Red Cedar Shingle Booklets for distribution to your patrons. Write to-day, stating how many you can use.

SHINGLE AGENCY of B.C.
STANDARD BANK BUILDING
VANCOUVER, B. C.

Insuring Accurately Gummed Saws

SAW gumming wheels should hold their shape to insure accurately ground teeth. Aloxite saw gumming wheels do.

For years a great deal of brains and painstaking effort have gone into the making of these wheels. They are made right. They are made to perform one special duty—that of gumming saws.

Aloxite Saw Gumming Wheels cut clean—they free themselves without drag, without undue friction. They cut fast and cool without case hardening the saw teeth or drawing the temper.

Aloxite Wheels always insure better saw service

The Carborundum Company
Niagara Falls, N. Y.
New York Chicago Philadelphia Boston Cleveland
Cincinnati Pittsburgh Milwaukee Grand Rapids

Canada Lumberman and Woodworker

Issued on the 1st and 15th of every month by

HUGH C. MACLEAN, LIMITED, Publishers

HUGH C. MacLEAN, Winnipeg, President.

THOS. S. YOUNG, Toronto, General Manager.

OFFICES AND BRANCHES:

TORONTO - - Telephone A. 2700 - - 347 Adelaide Street West
VANCOUVER - - Telephone Seymour 2013 - - Winch Building
MONTREAL - - Telephone Main 2299 - - 119 Board of Trade
WINNIPEG - Telephone Garry 856 - Electric Railway Chambers
NEW YORK - - Telephone 3108 Beekman - - 1123 Tribune Building
CHICAGO - Telephone Harrison 5351 - 1413 Great Northern Building
LONDON, ENG. - - - - - - - - - - 16 Regent Street, S.W.

TERMS OF SUBSCRIPTION

Canada, United States and Great Britain, $2.00 per year, in advance; other foreign countries embraced in the General Postal Union, $3.00.

Single copies 15 cents.

"The Canada Lumberman and Woodworker" is published in the interest of, and reaches regularly, persons engaged in the lumber, woodworking and allied industries in every part of Canada. It aims at giving full and timely information on all subjects touching these interests, and invites free discussion by its readers.

Advertisers will receive careful attention and liberal treatment. For manufacturing and supply firms wishing to bring their goods to the attention of owners and operators of saw and planing mills, woodworking factories, pulp mills, etc., "The Canada Lumberman and Woodworker" is undoubtedly the most direct and profitable advertising medium. Special attention is directed to the "Wanted" and "For Sale" advertisements.

Authorized by the Postmaster-General for Canada, for transmission as second-class matter.

Entered as second-class matter July 18th, 1914, at the Postoffice at Buffalo, N.Y., under the Act of Congress of March 3, 1879.

Vol. 39 Toronto, September 15, 1919 No. 18

What Intensive Effort Can Achieve

Are we living in too great haste? The word goes round to "speed up" in all directions. The result is frequently carelessness, loss and shortsightedness. Pick up any daily journal and in glancing over its pages one cannot fail to observe the number of fatal accidents that occur in mill, factory, warehouse, street and rural road. Most of these might have been avoided with proper heed and less rush. According to the report of the Workmen's Compensation Board, the number of accidents in lumbering during the past year increased. With improved safety devices, the wide interest aroused in Safety campaigns and the propaganda which has been carried on for years, fatalities and mishaps should be reduced.

That it is possible to keep down hazards to the minimum is evidenced by a rather interesting experiment which has been carried out through the Ontario Pulp and Paper Makers' Safety Association, of which A. P. Costigane, of Toronto, is Safety Engineer. This association is particularly aggressive and has by various means driven home the conviction that something special should be done to check the ever-increasing toll of injuries. It was recently decided to fix a period during which, with the co-operation of all employees, a concentrated effort would be made to create a record. The experiment was tried in the three plants of the Spanish River Pulp & Paper Mills, Limited, on a certain week, and although some 1800 men are employed in the pulp and paper mills of the organization at Sturgeon Falls, Espanola and Sault Ste. Marie, there was only one mishap during "No Accident Week." This was through the foolhardiness of a youth who was playing ball in the board mill at the Soo. He reached his hand into the winders to recover the ball, which had lodged there, with the result that he had his fingers badly crushed and lost ten days.

Previous to entering upon the "No Accident Week" signs were placed in every department urging the men to be particularly careful, while red colored triangles were given the employees to wear on their overalls. Large cards were posted in prominent places with space left for the names of those who suffered accidents during the week, and, before the campaign, there was issued a statement to the effect that these cards would be printed with the names of any who were injured, when the period was over. There was also a large banner over the entrance gates with a reference to Safety Week and a request that the men help put it through without an accident.

In commenting upon the results of the experiment Mr. Costigane's report will be read with much interest by those engaged in the lumber and woodworking business. He states that one accident occurred, caused by pure carelessness, is most regrettable but much more to be deplored is the callous indifference of the injured youth toward the success of the campaign in which his fellow employees showed so much interest. The remarkable success of the experiment in the Spanish River Pulp & Paper Mills, he adds, shows what can be accomplished in preventing accidents when all pull together. The average accidents in these mills for the six months previous to the campaign works out at about seven per week, while during "No Accident Week" there was only one mishap, as already stated. If intensive efforts were made in all the mills of Canada the accident records would show a vast improvement, lost time would decrease in proportion, a large sum of money would be saved to employees and compensation payments would shrink within reasonable proportions. It is well worth the while for all mills to study this problem closely and emulate the example recently set at the big plants of this pulp and paper company by making a real attempt to reduce casualties.

Losing All Sense of Proportion

We are getting so that nothing staggers us. The terms millions and billions roll off the tongue of adults with the same ease and familiarity as one or two syllable words are pronounced in ordinary conversation. A few years ago when any organization was capitalized at $100,000, it was thought to be an exceptionally large sum, but now a company capitalization of a million does not arouse more than passing interest. The war has so increased our conception of figures that we do not marvel at the magnitude of any statistics presented in connection with our industrial, financial or commercial life.

Exaggeration is resorted to in story, in act, in speech and in conduct, no doubt to create an impression. We do not take time to familiarize ourselves with numbers. When an output is worth so many thousands we speak of it in terms of hundreds of thousands; hundreds of thousands are converted into millions, and millions trail off into billions. While the war brought about many changes, it also engendered recklessness and disregard in other respects. This is seen every day in the press; for instance, one weekly journal announced a few weeks ago that a small local sawmill had started up and that the cut for the season would be 300,000,000 feet. In a representative paper published in a prosperous city in the Maritime Provinces appears a paragraph that one lumber firm is shipping a large portion of the order which had been recently placed with it by the British government. It is stated that this is part of the 40,000,000,000 ft. order lately placed by the Imperial authorities in Canada. The term 40,000,000,000 is not a staggering one perhaps when applied to the national debt of the United States, Great Britain or France, but when it comes to a matter of the lumber production in Canada the phrase is, at least, mystifying. The annual cut of all kinds of lumber in Canada, according to returns compiled by the Ottawa Bureau of Statistics—and these are as nearly accurate as it is possible to get them—is between 4,000,000,000 and 5,000,000,000 ft. As the cut every year since the outbreak of hostilities in Europe has shown a decrease of 10 to 15 per cent., owing to a scarcity of men, high cost of operation, diminishing demand in many lines, etc., it may be stated that, with a generous increase in 1920, the total output in the Dominion during the coming season will not be over 6,000,000,000 feet.

If Great Britain had placed an order for 40,000,000,000 ft. as represented in the press despatch, it would mean that the entire output of all the Canadian mills would be taken up for the next six or seven years and not a board, plank or scantling be available for local builders. This would indeed be a distressing state of affairs, considering the active building campaign going on at the present juncture, and the other avenues for increased consumption of our wood goods such as the automobile industry, piano, phonograph, implement, carriage and furniture factories. The discrepancy in connection with the figure of 40,000,000,000 and the amount which has really been purchased in Canada—about 1,000,000,000 ft.—is not pointed out in any fault finding or critical spirit, but merely as revealing the trend of the age to magnify and exaggerate. It seems to take the colossal, gigantic or the stupendous in quantity, and, also in verbal terms, to arrest our attention in these days when there are so many distracting cares and rival interests.

Another shortcoming, too, is that in speaking of the timber holdings of lumber, pulp and paper companies. So many thousand acres are often referred to as so many thousand square miles. One enthusiast, when describing the immense timber berths of a Quebec concern lately, made the positive assertion that they were so many hundreds of thousands of square miles, whereas the term should have been acres. An authority who had given some particular attention to areas, declared that according to the rash statement made, the property of the company in question would cover nearly the whole surface of Canada or the United States. It is well to put the best foot forward in all our relations in life, but there is neither wisdom nor foresight in exploiting our national assets, production, etc., to the point of being ridiculous or romantic.

Reforestation as Good Investment

Explaining recent increases in manufacturers' prices, a furniture maker says that not only are wages higher and work hours shorter than they were before the war, but the cost of material has been increased to an extraordinary extent. Quartered oak, which formerly cost $78.00 per thousand feet, and which rose during the war to $92, is now quoted at $2.25. In England furniture manufacturers are said to be paying twice that price, which puts the cost of good oak lumber up to forty cents per square foot. The price of walnut is said to be advancing with equal rapidity.

There are many men still living who as boys took part in the destruction of the great hardwood forests of southwestern Ontario for the purpose of clearing the ground that crops might be planted. Had a tenth part of that forest wealth been spared the timber of Ontario's farms would to-day be one of the greatest sources of wealth in the province. The man who wants to leave something on the old homestead that will be of value to his children's children will make no mistake in setting out a plantation of hardwood trees. It may not yield any revenue in the lifetime of the present generation, but he who planteth a tree planteth hope.

Stiff Advance Made in Wharfage Rates

To the surprise of traders and shippers, the Montreal Harbor Commissioners gave notice of a stiff advance in wharfage rates. The lumber interests are naturally interested in the proposed new schedule, and the nature of the advance will be seen from the following comparison:—Timber and lumber, hewn or rough sawn, old rate 10c per 1,000 ft. b.m., or $1.50 per carload when handled by rail and measurement unknown; new rate 15c per 1,000 ft., or $2.50 per carload. Timber and lumber, planed or finished, old rate 10c per 1000 ft. or $1.50 per carload; new rate 20c per 1,000 ft., or $3.00 per carload. Under the new rate, timber and lumber has been classified into hewn or rough sawn and planed or finished, instead of being under one general classification, and it will be noted that the advances are very substantial. Railway ties, 8 feet lengths, have been boosted from 25c to 30c per 100 pieces, and 16 feet lengths from 50c to 60c. Shooks, shingles and staves go from 20c to 30c per ton, and wood pulp from 8c to 15c per ton.

Naturally there was a strong protest, not only against the increases, but against the suddenness with which the new tariff was issued. It was argued that the Harbor Commissioners, while perfectly within their rights as to issuing the schedule, should at least have consulted the trades interested. It was further asserted that the charges would militate against Montreal in competition with other ports, where there are no wharfage charges. Mr. Stanley Cook, the secretary of the Montreal Lumber Association, took a leading part in the representations made to the Commissioners, with the result that the Commissioners have agreed to postpone the coming into effect of the new tariff until January 1, 1920. This will enable the trades interested to base their contracts for next season on the new rates.

The main reason advanced by the Commissioners for the proposed changes is that more revenue is necessary to meet the general rise in labor and materials. The Commissioners have only advanced wharfage charges once since 1914. Besides, the government has raised the rate of interest on loans to the Commissioners from 3½ per cent. to 5 per cent., and in this connection it is understood that the Board of Trade will probably ask the government to consider the question of reverting to the former rate of interest, in order that the new wharfage rates may not be fully enforced. The government made an inquiry into the proposed new rates before sanctioning the issue of the schedule by the Commissioners.

Annual Grievance Looms Up Early

There are some things that always appear to be with us. The tariff question, the high cost of living, shorter hours of labor, the servant problem, women's franchise, the extravagance of governments, the mediocrity of statesmen, profiteering, and last, but not least, the high cost of transportation and shortage in the supply of cars.

The Canadian Manufacturers' Association and the Railway War Board have been sending out notices to leading lumber companies and other large shippers to the effect that it is advisable to move all supplies possible at the present time in order to avoid delay and congestion later on and also to facilitate the movement of western grain to the seaboard.

But before the western harvest gets under way there is a cry raised in parliament about the scarcity of cars. This complaint comes from Frank Cahill, M.P. for Pontiac, Que., who declared that it was impossible to secure cars for the shipment of lumber and pulpwood from his county to the United States. Mr. Cahill stated that he had made inquiries at the department of railways and was informed that the cause of the shortage was that so many Canadian cars were already across the line. He thought some action should be taken to secure their return at the earliest possible moment.

A rather startling statement was made by a cabinet minister when he affirmed that it was no easy matter to get Canadian cars returned from Uncle Sam's domain, and that some of them remained in the Republic as long as a year. If such a state of affairs as this exists there is certainly ample scope for investigation. It is high time that the Minister of Railways and Canals, the railway commission or some other judicial body gets busy in the matter of remedying this undesirable condition. Surely there is laxity somewhere or Canadian cars would never be permitted to remain across the line for months at a stretch, particularly when they are so urgently required at home. We have numerous governing and administrative bodies in Canada to look after every interest, individual and corporate, but no particular branch of the public service seems to afford lumbermen and other shippers such incessant worry as the car situation. No sooner does it improve in one particular than there is a drawback or barrier in some other. If matters in the transportation line were running smoothly and satisfactorily for any protracted period some Canadian concerns would mistake such a state of affairs for the millenium.

June exports of paper, pulp and pulpwood from Canada, totalled in value, $7,345,851, as compared with $9,120,262 in June last year. Paper shows a gain of $153,538, and mechanically ground pulp of $295,818, while chemically prepared pulp fell off $1,105,652, and unmanufactured pulpwood $1,118,114.

Exports for the first three months of the fiscal year show a decrease of $2,478,375 compared with last year and a gain of $4,702,547 compared with 1917.

Timber Wealth of Canada Seen at Great Fair

Keen Interest Aroused in the Magnificent Displays Made—Development of Lumber, Forestry, Pulp and Paper Activities Attractively Presented

The Canadian National Exhibition, Toronto, which has just closed its fortieth year, surpassed all records in the matter of attendance, exhibits and achievement. The big exposition has become national in character and representative of every art and enterprise in the Dominion. The attendance has reached nearly a million and a quarter and the educative, stimulating effect which the great annual spectacle and entertainment exerts upon the public mind cannot be measured in any community or financial sense.

The Canadian National as an institution has grown with each succeeding year and has kept step with every avenue of development and expansion that has characterized the onward march of the Dominion since the inauguration of Confederation.

There were a number of exhibits of special interest to lumbermen and among them were those of the Forest Branch of the Department of Lands of British Columbia, the Canadian Forestry Association and the Forest Products Laboratories, while woodworking firms also contributed to the interest and variety of the numerous splendid displays in all lines of industry, commerce, manufacture and invention.

One of the most spacious and attractive displays at the Canadian National Exhibition, Toronto, was that made by the Forestry Branch, Department of Lands of British Columbia. This was the first time in some years that an exhibit has been made of the wooded wealth of the Pacific Coast province and the results exceeded all previous undertakings. The space occupied in the Government Building was 12 x 55 feet. The walls were a natural finish of western pine, western spruce, western red cedar, Douglas fir, cottonwood, western hemlock and western larch.

The beauty and effectiveness of these woods were revealed in panels, pilasters, cornices, plate rails and newels. There were also samples of various woods displayed to good advantage, showing them finished in cherry, walnut, light and dark mahogany, fumed oak, antique oak, golden oak and various other woods. These artistic panels naturally aroused much admiration presenting the many pleasing finishes to which British Columbia forest products are capable of being turned. There were also seen in the booth two sample

Some of the many products made from B. C. woods showing everything from a berry box to a door

stands adorned with various mouldings, flooring, ceiling, siding and all exterior and interior trim, while on the walls were hung splendid photographs of typical British Columbia wood scenes illustrative of the giants of the forest and how they are converted to lumber.

Three centre tables added to the effectiveness of the exhibit. These were round and of an ornate pattern and finished in mahogany, oak and walnut. Another convenience was a Douglas fir settee, finished in oak, and what was of great interest to the ladies, proved to be a large red cedar chest.

On the back grounds of each of the different wood panels were the following in dull gilt letters, which drove home a striking message to the one million, two hundred thousand visitors at the fair: "B. C. woods are unexcelled for boats and canoes," "western pine for all finishes," "B. C. spruce for aeroplanes and finish," "B. C. red cedar for durability and elegance," "Douglas fir for strength and beauty," "cottonwood makes superb finish," "western larch is strong and durable," "B. C. woods for cottage and mansion; supply unlimited for quantity and quality."

The entire display was open and accessible. There were no side issues and the attention of callers was focused upon the natural and handsome appearance of the wealth of forest products.

At one end of the large space there was another department devoted to fir doors, finished in old English, golden oak, cherry and natural. A double panel of B. C. dimension shingles of diamond, octagonal, circular and other shapes, as well as Perfection and XXXXX was observed.

Other displays in the wood goods line were tight and slack cooperage in fir and spruce, a wound wire water pipe made of Douglas

A section of the B. C. exhibit showing variety of uses of western woods. Note the beautiful grain in the fir posts

fir; tin tipped spruce berry baskets; raspberry baskets of spruce enclosed in a spruce crate; fir heading; cottonwood egg cases; collapsible berry boxes—in fact, everything from the daintiest little box to the heaviest packing case, representing adequately the worth of Douglas fir, Sitka spruce and other species in the making of all boxes and cooperage.

At the front were four shields, bearing the Prince of Wales feathers, while there were also miniature flags and other attractive decorations making the space one of the most picturesque, instructive and unique in the building.

Several parts of an aeroplane were shown including an outer interplane strut of the Hoffer flying boat, forest patrol model, and a section of the front wing beam of the same boat made out of B. C. spruce.

Much interest was evinced by the public in the cottonwood exhibit. This material is excellent for veneer and plywood and the egg cases and similar packages made out of it called forth numerous inquiries. Another motto bore the announcement that B. C. spruce was the very thing for pails, tubs and boxes being light, strong and tasteless.

A distinct departure was made this year from the exhibit of former occasions. Instead of timber in the rough being featured, the exhibit consisted of the finished product which, needless to say, created a most favorable impression and aroused admiration for the representative woods from the dense forests of Canada's Sunset Province which is naturally proud of her forests of fir, cedar, hemlock and spruce. These were the woods used extensively during the war in the manufacture of aeroplanes for the British and Canadian flyers. During the European conflict 35,000,000 ft. of spruce were employed in aeroplane construction and 10,000,000 ft. of fir, while British Columbia placed at the disposal of the British Columbia government sufficient sawn lumber for the manufacture of 30,000 planes.

There were also displays of sulphite and sulphate pulp, as well [illegible] newsprint paper affording some conception of the wonderful possibilities of British Columbia in this direction.

The exhibit was in charge of Major James Brechin, British Columbia Lumber Commissioner for Eastern Ontario, whose offices are in the Kent Building, Toronto, and Mr. Wm. Robertson, of Victoria, B. C., who is in charge of trade extension work in connection with British Columbia forest products. It is probable that the exhibit at the Canadian National will be allowed to remain in Toronto and form a prominent feature in connection with the Lumber Commissioner's office.

Forestry, Woods, Pulp and Paper

Representative of the sylvan assets of the Dominion and the many useful products, industries, and operations arising out of this great national heritage, was the combined exhibit made at the Canadian National Exhibition by the Canadian Forestry Association whose headquarters are at Ottawa and the Forest Product Laboratories, Limited, of Montreal. The display, which was a striking one, was housed in the Railway Building and carried out under the auspices of the Canadian National Railways.

The pulp and paper industry of Canada is now forcing its way to the front and rapidly making of the Dominion the greatest newsprint country on earth. At one end of the booth was shown an immense roll of newsprint and on it were printed the words "The six Toronto daily newspapers require 1,000 spruce and balsam trees for each day's run." Then there were rolls of paper and spruce logs of various sizes all indicating the rapid growth of the newsprint industry. On the small roll, dated 1914, were the following figures: "Total number tons newsprint produced in 1914, 232,570—value, $11,386,845," on the 1919 roll, "800,000 tons newsprint—value $60,000,000." Nothing could be more expressive of the rapid expansion of this vast industry than the statistics covering a period of five years. The booth was adorned with several small spruce trees and one plant of interest was the Egyptian Papyrus on which the world once depended for its paper manufacture. Cards conveyed much timely information to passers-by and one of them stated that the export trade of Canadian newsprint paper last year was worth more money than all the other manufacturing exports in Canada in pre-war time. It is also stated that Canadian spruce is rapidly becoming the chief reliance for 40,000,000 newspapers issued daily in the United States and Canada.

The exhibit of Canadian Forestry Association and Wood Products Laboratories at Canadian National Exhibition

In three sections there were shown by the Forest Products Laboratory of Montreal the raw materials used in the conversion of wood to pulp by the sulphite, mechanical and sulphate processes together with an interesting description of each process. The descriptive nature of manufacture of pulp from the log to the finished bale aroused much interest. In the sulphite section there were the spruce log, barked log, chips, sulphur, limestone, cooking liquor, and the finished articles were washed pulp, screened pulp, pulp in sheets and in bales, bleached and unbleached. In the ground wood demonstration there were the logs, the barked log, the pulp as it came from the grinders, the screened pulp and the screenings, while in the sulphate division there was the barked log, chips, salt cake, fused salts, green and white liquor, lime and black ash, and black liquor, as well as the pulp back in sheets and baled. There was also exhibited sections of various trees, spruce, balsam, fir, hemlock, jack pine and poplar revealing the relative amount of wood used for pulp in the various processes, spruce heading by far the largest. Several discs of trees bearing the words "Can you guess the age of these logs?" were observed and the years ran from 39 to 1[illegible].

Next there were panels cut from the various trees of Canada, with the slogan "Learn to know the woods of Canada." White pine, cedar, tamarack, hemlock, poplar, basswood, chestnut, cypress, quarter-cut white oak, plain red oak, quarter-cut oak, plain white oak, maple, rock elm, walnut, birch, butternut, [illegible] ash, Douglas fir, western pine, spruce, B. C. cedar, Sitka spruce, etc., were presented. The story was told of how British Columbia played such an important part in the manufacture of aeroplanes during the war. British Columbia shipped in 1916 and 1917 sufficient wood for 30,000 aeroplanes.

In the hardwood department were three blocks—beech, birch and maple, and one of the statements was that 1,000,000 tons of these hardwoods are taken from the Canadian forests annually to supply the wood carbonizing and wood distilling industries of the country.

The Canadian Forestry exhibit was under the direction of Robson Black, of Ottawa, secretary of the association, while the display made by the Forest Products Laboratories of Canada was supervised by Wm. B. Stokes, who is in charge of the exhibit work of this institution. Various pulp and paper mills lent their assistance toward making the display interesting and instructive. There were also several large photographs in evidence depicting the interior of pulp mills and setting forth pictorially the various departments of the industry.

Imposing Display in Woodwork

An attractive display of doors, columns, newels, and [illegible] was made in the Process Building at the Canadian National Exhibition by Batts, Limited, of Toronto. Their space extended [illegible] ft. and attracted much favorable attention.

On one side was a pergola with Grecian columns, while next was a large and imposing entrance with Corinthian columns and on the right was a wide verandah with Ionic columns, while for interior decoration a number of columns and pedestals were shown in red, Georgia pine and chestnut. Many styles of doors were displayed. All exterior columns were of white pine and were exhibited in both fluted and plain effects. Doors were seen in solid and veneers of various patterns, the principal woods being Georgia pine, chestnut, B. C. fir and oak. Newel posts of various artistic types aroused interest, particularly those in chestnut and quarter-cut oak, while there was an inviting display of stairwork. Balustrades, shaped, octagonal, square and round formed the front of this representative exhibit. Batts, Limited, have been very busy for some time supplying the woodwork for military hospitals on Christie St., Toronto, Fredericton, N. B., and other large structures including Loew's theatres in London, Ottawa, and Brantford. The company are just now employing twenty-seven returned soldiers, nine of whom are taking vocational training and all the men are doing good work.

Artistic Effects in House Trim

The R. Laidlaw Lumber Co., of Toronto, had a striking presentation of various lines made by them in the way of doors, flooring, newels, verandah and interior columns, etc. Doors were shown in gum, mahogany, quarter-cut oak, plain oak, chestnut and birch; white oak, maple and birch flooring were much in evidence. The walls of the booth were adorned with beaver board and there was a fine array of newel posts and pedestals of every description, both fluted and plain. The entire frame work of a barn was shown in miniature, all being made out of 1 in. to 2 in. stock, while there was also a frame work of a garage. The barn model aroused much interest among farmers as in the structure the outside walls carry the roof so that no large timbers are required. There were also observed several Tennessee aromatic red cedar chests. The front entrance of a pretentious dwelling house was displayed showing some attractive effects. The exhibit was arranged by Mr. W. Warren, superintendent of the West End Yard of the Company, Toronto.

From Spruce Tree to Newsprint

The Spanish River Pulp & Paper Mills of Espanola and the Abitibi Power & Paper Co., of Iroquois Falls each made very creditable exhibits of newsprint and groundwood and sulphite pulp in the Government Building at the Canadian National Exhibition. Newsprint was displayed in large rolls, while pulp was shown both in sheets and bales. There were numerous photographs presented in connection with each display showing the various departments of the Espanola and Iroquois Falls plants, while by means of glass jars and other receptacles a representation of the conversion of spruce wood into the finished roll of paper was given. The exhibits were viewed with much interest by a large number of lumbermen, paper dealers, publishers and others.

Cooperage Business is Active in Canada

The Industry is an Ancient One and Method of Working the Stock is Interesting—Operation in Leading Canadian Plant Described.

The plant of the Sutherland, Innes Co., Limited, at Chatham, Ont.

The cooperage industry at present is enjoying an active market. Demand for tight and slack goods has sprung up on all sides and attention is being directed to the future development of this line owing to the large amount of export business being done in commodities requiring such containers.

It is true that the export of cooperage stock in the Dominion is at present not very large owing to high carriage rates to the seaboard and the excessive charges for ocean transportation. At one time about 10,000,000 slack barrel staves with heading to match were shipped annually to Great Britain, whereas to-day only a few cars are sent forward although the demand is heavy. It is expected that in time matters will adjust themselves and export will be resumed on a large scale.

There are in Canada large tracts of timber suitable for cooperage and where these are located within easy supply of water transportation they will be the source of keeping the industry going for many years to come.

It is interesting to study the history and development of the cooperage business. It is one of the oldest trades known and from time immemorial people have read about the barrel and the cask; in fact, the barrel is one of the oldest forms of containers as well as one of the most serviceable the world has ever known. In some Chinese manuscripts written as far back as 2000 B.C. there are to be found descriptions of the barrel. The cooperage industry is, therefore, one that has been with us almost since the commencement of things.

For many years the Sutherland, Innes Co., Limited, of Chatham, Ont., who have plants both in Canada and the United States, as well as offices in England, have occupied a premier position in turning out goods in the cooperage line. They manufacture slack cooperage stock for sugar, flour, apples and other dry materials, while tight barrel stock for wines, oils and other liquids is turned out at their plant across the border.

The raw material for the manufacture of slack cooperage stock is delivered to the mills in the form of logs or bolts. These are sections of trees, sawn the proper length and either in the round or, where of large diameter, split to convenient sizes for handling.

Logs Bolted to Proper Length

When the logs arrive at the mill, they are bolted to the proper length either with a swing circular saw or drag saw, they are then split on the bolting saw into quarter cut bolts, 5" to 6" wide. The bolts are then placed in steam boxes, and steamed at least twelve hours. This softens the wood and conditions it so that it will cut easily. After being taken out of the steam boxes the bolts are barked and go to the equalizing saws, which consists of two cross-cut circular saws, running on the same mandrel, so as to make all bolts exactly the same length. After being equalized the bolts are cut into staves, on a knife having a 30 in. circle and cutting 100 staves per minute, and are then piled in sheds for drying. When the staves are thoroughly seasoned, four to six weeks according to the weather, they are jointed on foot jointers to the bilge desired by the cooper, the bilge being of a suitable curve for the diameter of the barrel to be made.

For hoops the logs are sawn into plank 1½ in. thick, the planks are then boiled for 8 to 12 hours, and cut into beveled strips 5/16 x 3/16 x 13.8". The cutting is done on a knife cutting 140 to 150 strips per minute. These strips are planed on the edges, pointed at one end and thinned at the other on an automatic pointer and lapper, after which they are baled and coiled in coils of 10 hoops each, while hot. When dry they are ready to nail on the barrel.

The logs for heading are made into bolts by the same process as used for staves or bolts cut in the woods are used.

The Turning Out of Heading

The bolts are sawn on a swing saw into boards half an inch thick, then seasoned either in the open for a time, or piled direct in the kiln. All boards have to be thoroughly kiln-dried before being manufactured into heading. When thoroughly dry the boards are planed on one side, the edges jointed, the boards matched to the width of heading required, and turned round on a heading turner. Modern turners will turn from 2,500 to 3,900 sets of heading per day, depending on the diameter, and will make the heading with beveled edge, ready for the croze in the barrel, or a plain edge, the same as used in cheese boxes. The heading is packed in bundles, pressed in a heavy press and wired, after which it is ready to ship to the consumer.

Tight barrel staves are either split out of the bolts, with a froe, being made on the quarter, and then dressed to circle or flat, on a bucker or sawn on a drum saw. A bucker consists of two knives, between which the staves are forced by steam power, while a drum saw is a cylindrical saw, shaped like a drum, which saws the staves on a circle.

The staves are then jointed, sometimes kiln-dried, and finished into barrels by the cooper or machine shop. Tight barrel heading is made the same as slack barrel heading, but dowelled and flagged so as to be liquid proof. In this country steel hoops are used on tight barrels. In Europe, half round hickory, oak or chestnut hoops are used to a large extent.

Biggest Lumber Cut Ever in the East

New Brunswick will next winter have the greatest lumber cut in history, according to all present indications.

The Department of Lands and Mines is preparing for a historic unheard of sized cut of 250 million feet on the crown lands, and it is believed that the cut on privately owned lands will be equally as large.

Shipping is now being made available for lumber cargoes from New Brunswick to overseas points, and it is estimated that in one week more than twenty-five million feet of manufactured lumber has been shipped by New Brunswick firms across the Atlantic.

Recently when the general strike in the lumber industry on the Miramichi was called every mill with one exception had a steamer in the process of loading. The employees selected the psychological moment for their strike, but leading men in the lumber industry declare that the outlook for profitable operations were never better than to-day despite high prices for labor, supplies and everything that enters into production of manufactured lumber.

Returns have only just been completed for the last season's lumber operations on the crown lands of New Brunswick, and the figures have furnished some startling surprises. While the estimated cut of 200 million feet was said at the time to be extravagant, even the officials of the department have been surprised to find that complete returns show 210 million feet of lumber actually cut on the crown lands and stumpage charged upon it. Included in this gross amount are some five or six hundred thousand railway ties.

Meanwhile standing timber is being sold at unprecedented prices. One of the biggest deals of this kind closed for some time is just reported from Queen's county, and it is said that $15 per thousand is the price paid for the standing timber. Another case which illustrates the demand for timber lands is the recent sale by a York county farmer of the wooded part of his farm for $10,000.

When and Where is All This Going to End?

Retail Lumberman Acknowledges That He is Beaten When it Comes to Offering Definite Views on Higher Prices, Building Outlook and Market Tendency

"I went to my banker the other day," declared a Toronto retail lumberman, "to find out just how conditions stand. Some years ago when I started out in business I was told that when things were going awry, the future uncertain and no one seemed to be able to ferret out where we were at, that the proper person to consult was one's banker. Ostensibly he has a clear, unprejudiced vision and is able to weigh matters as calmly and carefully as any one. However, I am free to confess that my banker in the present instance did not shed much light upon the general situation. He acknowledged before I was through with my queries that he knew little or nothing more than I did and that all signs by which the times could be read in the past, had gone askew and, that one man's estimate or forecast was practically as good as another's.

"Not obtaining very much satisfaction from my financial friend I consulted another who is connected with a leading institution. He told me just as sure as to-morrow's sun was going to rise, that within a period of two years we would witness the most drastic times through which the country had ever passed. 'It is coming sure,' this pessimist declared. 'You cannot start an automobile down hill and expect that it will keep up its speed all the time; it is bound to strike the bottom sooner or later and when it does there is naturally a crash.' I walked away from this Jeremiah.

"I myself thought that I was somewhat of a seer and, on the day that the armistice was declared, I made the prediction that values in lumber would drop decidedly. I considered that the war had been responsible for the abnormal demand and so much material had been diverted into shipbuilding, shell boxes, ammunition waggons, transports, military camps, depots, etc., that with the necessity for these things removed and lumber reverting to its original and natural field, there would inevitably be a decline. You would think so to view the matter dispassionately. But, alas, something came along that we had not reckoned with and that was the house-building campaign. Returned men must have domiciles and, naturally, there is a shortage of dwellings in every centre, large and small. The demand started in with considerable rush. Dry stocks were low as the lumber operators had been decreasing their cut from year to year and knowing that the war would come to an end sooner or later they did not care to be caught with an unusual quantity on hand.

Uncertain As To The Direction

"Now, I do not know whether to be a pessimist or an optimist. The last two years I have been a pessimist and did not buy heavily. I wish that I had done so as I could have secured a number of snaps in January and February and, with advancing values, made a nice clean-up. Now I do not know what to do. We have been told that the expenses of getting out lumber are higher all the while; that wages are equal to last year and the outlay for camp maintenance is aviating. I noticed that one of the largest retail firms in the city of Toronto is advocating "now is the time to build a home" and intimating that it is utterly shortsighted to await until something drops. It is predicted that no omens are appearing of a change for the better and brick, paint, glass, lumber and everything that enters into the average dwelling continues to soar. One dealer points out that hemlock lumber was selling last spring at $35 per thousand and that the figure is now $50; white pine is selling at $60 to $65 and B. C. fir at $65 to $70. This may be timely advice and again it may not. I cannot say.

"I have always been inclined to look on the cheerful and promising side of each question but the present situation has me beaten at the start off. This one thing I do know, and that is there is an awful lot of cheap stuff being put into the class of houses that are going up at present, No. 3 hemlock, cedar culls and other materials that can not be covered up. Even the most uninitiated must see its flimsy character.

Building Boom Makes Good Times

"The disposition of many people is to adopt the motto of not "How good" but "How cheap." Comparatively few persons can really afford to build a house at present prices. Supposing they do go ahead and in six months from now it has been discovered that values have taken a decline and a dwelling may be put up $500 or $1,000 cheaper. What then? This is going to hit the real estate man or the speculative builder who is proceeding on the present basis. On the other hand, if values rise the fellow who builds now, is the one who will congratulate himself next spring that he did not delay matters.

"It is a difficult situation, indeed, for the average builder as well as the average lumberman to gauge himself with any degree of satisfaction. I realize that unless there is a lot of building going on in any town business generally is flat. Building activities put much money in circulation, not only in the ranks of labor but in the matter of general supplies and trade and the impetus is felt throughout the whole community. Let there be no building undertaken and times are generally stringent. A community must either grow or fall behind. There is no such a thing as marking time and while the prospects for structural work next year look bright I cannot tell you where we are at at the present juncture. If I knew I would only be too glad to pass along the information.

"I picked up a local paper the other day and this is what another retail lumberman says in regard to operating expenses. I think his figures are a little high so far as the cost of meals in the bush are concerned, otherwise he may be as correct in his estimate as I am. Here is the statement: 'We are away behind in the delivery of orders owing to the shortage of supplies. Mills are paying $65 to $70 per month to lumberjacks in the bush, while board for the men is costing 50 to 75c. a meal. Before the war bushmen could be secured for $30 per month and board cost about 15c. a meal per man. Horse feed also shows the same cost advancement, while increased freight rates also enter into the present high cost. Lumber will get dearer all the while and the longer you delay the more you will have to pay in putting up that new bungalow or apartment house."

General Activity in Lumber Industry

The Labor Gazette, Ottawa, gives in its current issue a general review of lumbering conditions in Canada during the past month which will be read with interest:

Westville reported that lumbering, though slightly in the previous month, continued to give considerable employment. Charlottetown reported that lumbermen were quiet. At St. John the saw and shingle mills were running steadily; Fredericton reported the lumber mills in full operation. Quebec reported that saw and shingle mills were working to capacity, and Sherbrooke reported that they were busy. Three Rivers reported that several hundred men were employed in the lumber mills and in the lumber department of the St. Maurice Paper Co. The sawmills at Ottawa and Hull was busy. Owen Sound reported that the saw and shingle mills were active. Calgary reported that there was still a demand for men in the lumber camps and sawmills. Fernie reported that employment in the lumbering industry was very seriously affected by disastrous fires which cleaned out considerable timber areas, including logging camps and sawmills, and it was feared that employment in this district would be affected for many seasons to come. Vancouver reported that the lumber camps of the district were fairly busy and that the saw and shingle mills were actively enagged. Victoria reported that the lumber and logging industry was active, large shipments of lumber and shingles being made to foreign ports. The Canadian Puget Sound lumber mill commenced operations after being closed for three years.

Exhibition Car Touring Northern Ontario

The railway exhibition car of the Canadian Forestry Association is making a decided hit all through Northern Ontario. As many as one thousand visitors a day have called to see the various displays which are attractively arranged. The car is exceptionally well fitted up for the purpose and contains a multitude of exhibits showing the manufacture of pulp and lumber. There is also a model forest nursery, model lookout towers, forest telephone equipment, a working wireless system, a maple sugar bush, as well as an exhibit of forest insects and their depredations. A motion picture lecture is given every evening in a local hall of each place visited and deals almost exclusively with the importance of the forest industries and the need of guarding their raw materials. Jas. Dickson, an experienced forester, is delivering the lectures in connection with the motion picture propaganda and is accompanying the railway exhibition car throughout Northern Ontario.

What Advertising Can Do For the Yardman

Retail Lumber Dealers Should Drive Home Facts Concerning Their Stock, Service and Facilities—How Business With Public May Be Increased and Quickened

Advertising is something which the retail lumberman has often thought of, but seldom puts into practice. He believes in a certain kind of publicity, realizes its value, has some conception of its potentialities and yet, for some reason or other, does not undertake it. He hesitates, perhaps, on account of no one to lead the way, at other times owing to doubt as to what mediums to employ, or the special means that he should avail himself of, sometimes due to the fact that business is too good and no artificial aid is necessary in order to cause the orders to come in satisfactory.

There are other yard men who now and then claim that advertising is not necessary in their particular case, because their's is a staple line. There is no use directing people's attention to articles as common as white pine, sash, doors, stairs, hardwood flooring, interior trim, newel posts, etc. They maintain that, like water, food, light and air, which are all around, there is no pressing necessity of drawing attention to them. And, of course, there is the man who, even against his own convictions, will exclaim that advertising don't pay, never did pay, and that the fellow, who makes use of printer's ink, has to increase the price of his merchandise to reimburse him for the outlay.

Again, there are a number who really cannot bear to part with the cash. They see in advertising an expenditure for something that is not immediately tangible. If the retail lumberman is being supplied with printed matter in the shape of envelopes, note heads, bill heads, booklets, leaflets, catalogues, folders, etc., he can see exactly what is being returned to him in concrete form for his outlay. In using newspaper space he does not get any evidence of bulk or quantity and circulation is, perhaps, to him unknown or uninteresting. He will be told by the publisher that so many copies of a daily or weekly paper are issued, but all that the advertiser sees is one or two. He cannot size up the quantity the same as when he goes out in his yard and makes an inventory of the number of thousand feet that he has in pile—either in his sheds or in the dry kiln. Thus it is difficult to gauge accurately what advertising will do for a man, not only in the immediate present but in the future.

Publicity as Wise Investment

There are a number of shortsighted individuals who want to see two dollars come in first for every one that goes out. They have no faith in the future and but little in themselves. They are not willing to look upon publicity as a wise investment that will yield, if properly directed and carefully supervised, adequate returns for any money spent in that direction. Of course, the retail lumberman cannot have bargain sales, great sacrifices, pre-inventory clean-ups, stock-taking and other kinds of sales, the same as the ordinary storekeeper, but he can direct attention to the facilities which his yard possesses, the representative stock he has in hand, and the service he renders. He can state that he will be glad to give any advice with respect to building, furnishing estimates, submitting plans, etc. In half a score of ways he can do something for his clients that will arouse appreciation and thus estabilsh a bond of union and connection that no competitor can break through and that time will strengthen and deepen.

There is another class of yardmen who feel that as they have been in business twenty, thirty or forty years, and their father was in business before them, and perhaps their grandfather, that is sufficient. Because Hammond, Edminson, Sellins, Walston or Ardley has been in the lumber line for years—in fact, born and brought up in the game, as the saying goes—there is no earthly necessity, they maintain, for seeking to make more widely known the name. One would think, to hear some of these people, that business was done on a name and a name alone. This is doubtless true to a certain extent, but no matter how historical, honored or esteemed a name may be, it will not do everything. At the back of it there must be seasonable goods, efficient delivery, correct estimating, a desire to serve and appreciation of favors extended as well as an idea of having every customer furnish repeat orders and not entirely cease connection with the lumber yard in one isolated transaction.

Make Them Think of Your Yard

The whole object of advertising is to emphasize the fact that when farmer Jenkins, contractor Meadows, citizen McVicar or the widow Harding wants anything in the line of lumber for extensions, renovations or any new structure such persons will immediately go to Weeks the lumberman. By his service, his attention to duty, his aggressiveness and judicious advertising he has impressed upon the community the thought that his name is indissolubly linked up with lumber. There is one form of advertising that even the printed page cannot surpass in benefits, and that is when a man is spoken of, not so much as Bill Kelly or Tom Carter, but as Kelly the lumberman, or Carter the lumberman.

The reputation of a retail man is, of course, like that of Rome, not built in a day, but if one's business name is carefully guarded it is an invaluable asset, the same as a man's honor, his character, his disposition, or his temperament. No one can adequately appraise the worth of these attributes. It is only in a crisis, in a period of stress and strain, promotion, sale or some other large transaction that the true value of such a man is known and recognized. In ordinary everyday affairs these qualities perhaps are not "cashed in" upon and too often are like good health, not appreciated until taken away or, in a measure, undermined. It is largely the same with advertising carried out in a thoughtful, earnest way and with

A home is always a good security

a sincere wish evidenced to live up to all promises made. Returns, while they may not be exactly keyed or tabulated, are such that, just like the business man with a good reputation, a name for fair dealing, and honest, open trading, they tally every time. No one can tell what these mean from a mere dollars and cents standpoint, because they cannot be given monetary measure, but, in the esteem of the community, the goodwill of men, the affection of the public and the high regard of neighbors, there is ample evidence that these qualities count for something, as fellows of loose morals, shady reputation, tricky habits, or shiftless methods must admit.

Emphasize the Home Building Idea

One good point for a retail lumberman to emphasize in all his publicity plans is that any man who builds a home, is a better and more substantial citizen than one who is a mere renter. A home-owning citizen has a real, personal stake in the community. He feels that he is part and parcel of the city or town in which he resides, and everything that makes for its uplift and welfare is shared by him to a certain extent. It has been aptly impressed that a man can borrow money on a home, which is splendid security, but he can not borrow heavily on oil stocks, mining shares, etc.

It has been declared that one can never tell when an emergency will arise that will make it necessary for an owner to get hold of some cash quickly. The query naturally comes up—where?—and, of course, this is a difficult question to answer unless one is able to offer some security. There is none better than a home for no man likes to see his residence slip out of his hands. Even if he does meet with a temporary reverse he will redouble his efforts to pay back whatever money he has borrowed and protect that which is vital to him and to the happiness and comfort of his family. A home is worth fighting for at any and all times for it stands for the best things on the earth today.

Mr. Petry Enters Upon New Duties

Geo. E. Petry, Toronto, Ont.

Geo. E. Petry, who has been associated for some time with R. G. Chesbro, of Toronto, in the sale of British Columbia forest products has been appointed Ontario representative for the Campbell-MacLaurin Lumber Co., Limited, of Montreal. Mr. Petry will have his headquarters in Toronto at 67 Winchester St. and will cover all parts of the Province. He is one of the best liked and aggressive of the younger salesmen in the lumber industry and has acquired an excellent insight in both the production and distribution end. Mr. Petry was born in Toronto where he received his educational and technical training. He spent some four years in the service of his father, W. F. Petry, who conducts a planing-mill and lumber yard at 25 St. Alban St. Later he was associated with other firms which served to broaden his experience and previous to going with Mr. Chesbro, he was identified with J. P. Johnson & Son, wholesale lumber dealers, Toronto. The Campbell, MacLaurin Co., who have mills at Drummondville and Ste. Joseph De Lepage, Quebec, specialize in spruce of all kinds, and also handle New Brunswick shingles, eastern hemlock and Ontario pine. Mr. Petry's many friends will wish him every success in his new sphere of operation.

Mr. Manbert Returns From Old Country

A. C. Manbert, of Toronto, lumber commissioner for Ontario, who has been spending several months in Great Britain, conducting propaganda work in the interest of white pine and other woods of the Province, sailed for Canada on the "Scotian," on September 3rd, and reached Toronto last week.

Mr. Manbert has done energetic and important work in the Old Land, and his letters, which have appeared from time to time in the "Canada Lumberman" have told of the favorable reception accorded him in all the leading cities by importers, timber merchants, and large consumers. There is an active requisition for white pine, but cargoes on commercial account cannot be shipped in quantities desired at the present time, owing to inadequate ocean tonnage and prevailing high rates of carriage. There is no doubt that Mr. Manbert's mission has served to place Ontario forest products in the forefront in Great Britain.

As soon as industrial, political and labor conditions in the Mother Country revert to normal direct results will, in all likelihood, follow the campaign carried on by Mr. Manbert, who is looking well after his extended trip abroad, and will resume his duties as president of the Canadian General Lumber Co. In a subsequent issue he will, at the request of the "Canada Lumberman," review the whole lumber and business situation abroad and present some interesting and timely observations.

Building Trades Demands Upset Many Plans

The prosperity of the lumber business is dependent upon the general commercial activity, good crops, exports, the building situation, etc. The last named is perhaps the most important single condition, as far as domestic business is concerned. The prolonged dullness in that section promised to give place to considerable activity, notwithstanding the rise in prices. Although there have been occasional strikes in the construction trades, there was nothing like an important disturbance of that branch of business.

Montreal, however, is now threatened with a serious upheaval, owing to the demands of the Building Trades Council for shorter hours and increased wages. Some men in all fourteen sections constituting the building trade, have gone on strike. The demands are in certain cases very high, ranging up to 50 per cent. increase. The contractors resist the claims of the men, mainly on the ground that it is impossible to complete the contracts without loss if the higher scales are conceded. These jobs have been based on old rates, and to add even 25 per cent. to the cost obviously involves a loss to the employers.

Apart from the effect upon the work in hand, the new scale will mean a serious check to the revival in building. Costs have already gone up to an extent which stopped construction for a time and it was only recently that work on a fair scale was commenced. If [illegible] extreme demands of the men are to be conceded, proprietors [illegible] think many times before they embark in building, and the contra[illegible] who are engaged in the speculative building of houses will [illegible] decline to go ahead, having regard to the fact that they will be [illegible] ing capital in putting up houses at a cost which precludes their [illegible] to possible buyers.

Pushed to their utmost, the claims of the men will stifle ent[illegible] prise, and will involve loss of trade to the lumber dealer and to oth[illegible] interested in the construction industry. There is a keen demand [illegible] houses in Montreal, and the public have been urged to "Build N[illegible] but such appeals will be in vain if men who are anxious to build [illegible] faced with a situation which will not allow of a profit upon [illegible] ment.

Spruce Bud Worms Do Much Destruction

Half of the balsam fir in New Brunswick has been destr[illegible] the spruce bud worm this year, according to a report by Pr[illegible] Graham, of the University of Minnesota, and Prof J. D. T[illegible] the Dominion Entomological Bureau, who have returned to F[illegible] icton after taking a trip of 125 miles through the crown timber [illegible] of the province in company with L. S. Webb, of the Forest [illegible]

They entered the woods about two weeks ago at Red Ban[illegible] Newcastle, and then went to the head waters of the little [illegible] Miramichi. They came south across the Renous, and out [illegible] woods at Boiestown. The trip was made on foot and practi[illegible] the balsam fir which has been very plentiful in that district, [illegible] destroyed. In some areas the pest attacked the spruce; and [illegible] Renous the damage to spruce has been quite serious.

The World Is So Small After All

Recently there came into the hands of W. Gerard Power, ma[illegible] ager of the River Ouelle Pulp & Lumber Co., St. Pacome, Que[illegible] rather interesting communication. The envelope bore the mark [illegible] the South American Mercantile Co., Uruguay, 828 Montevideo a[illegible] the inscription was River Ouelle Pulp & Lumber Co., Spruce, Ingl[illegible] terra. The last word had been crossed out by the postal authorit[illegible] and "Canada" substituted. That the letter reached its proper de[illegible] tination with apparently little loss of time, even though no pos[illegible] office address or province was furnished, is a tribute to the thorough[illegible] ness and foresight of the mail carriers. The River Ouelle Pulp [illegible] Lumber Co. believe that the South American Mercantile Co. mu[illegible] have seen their advertisement in the Export edition of the "Cana[illegible] Lumberman." From the meagre address the River Ouelle Co. co[illegible] sider it difficult to understand how the envelope should have reached them at all. This goes to show that the world is sometimes not a[illegible] large as we really think it is.

No Difficulty in Selling Lumber

Writing to the "Canada Lumberman" the manager of an Eas[illegible] ern Ontario lumber concern says "Business for this year has be[illegible] exceptionally good and there is not much difficulty in finding buye[illegible] for all our stock. Everything has been moving like hot cakes. [illegible] certainly does not look as if there would be any decrease in the figu[illegible] for wood goods during the next year at any rate. Production co[illegible] are high and the expense of feeding men in the bush is ascending [illegible] the while. Wages also remain at the top notch. Until there is som[illegible] evidence that the apex has been reached in matters of this kind, ther[illegible] certainly will not be any decrease in the price of lumber which h[illegible] not advanced as much in proportion as some other lines of building material."

Waterfront Workers Form Organization

The Long Shoremen on the Miramichi River who recently [illegible] on strike are now organized into a local of the International [illegible] Shoremen's Association. An agreement has been reached with [illegible] mill owners for all classes of work and this agreement will hold g[illegible] for the remainder of the year. The new scale of wages is, for [illegible] ship laborers, 65c an hour with a 9 hour day, all outside laborer[illegible] have an advance of 10c an hour. All mill men are to receive a [illegible] day with a 10 hour pay, as previously paid.

The agreement was reached at a public meeting which [illegible] representative of the workers on both sides of the river from Log[illegible] ville and Newcastle, as well as the operators. The agreement [illegible] unanimously adopted after some discussion. It was decided [illegible] ganize under the name of the Miramichi Waterfront Workers.

Douglas fir was discovered by Archibald Menzies at Noot[illegible] Sound, Vancouver Island, in 1792, during the voyage of Capta[illegible] Vancouver, who first explored the waters of the north Pacific coast.

How Some Mills Dispose of Waste Material

Means Adopted by Woodworking Plants to Convert Refuse to the Best Possible Use —Practical Outlets that the Future May Develop in This Line

Although there are not many saw mills in Ontario which as yet have electric drives, still there are a few, and this motive power is highly spoken of by its users as most satisfactory and economical. One mill owner in a town on the Georgian Bay who has instituted an electric drive, states that his saw dust is shipped by carload, and also all the other mill refuse, for which he finds a ready market.

The disposal of mill refuse has always been a live question with certain saw mill and woodworking operators, particularly those located a long way removed from wood-consuming centres or populous points where waste could be disposed of to advantage. The burner, the "hog" and the Dutch oven use up practically all waste material in the average steam saw mill that is not converted into lath or faggots. The city resident on paying a visit to some of these plants and seeing the amount of material being consumed in the engines and burners naturally exclaims "My, what a waste. Why, hundreds of families would give a great deal to have this stuff and look what it would be worth in K— or T—, etc." All this speculation is indulged in quite freely, but no thought is given to the fact that excessive freight charges would bring the cost of this material up to such an amount that its purchase would be practically prohibitive in the city.

Cheap wood is, of course, one of the economical conveniences of a saw mill town just the same as cheaper coal is the boon of those living near the mines, but all people cannot reside contiguous to the sources of supply or production of raw materials.

All these observations, naturally, bring up the question of what the majority of saw mill and woodworking plants do with their waste and how can it be most profitably or economically disposed of. Mills and woodworking plants that are run by electric power have to give considerable thought to disposing of saw dust, edgings, slabs and shavings, especially if the plants do not generate their own power. Those who do, naturally, burn up the material. Those concerns who do not, find it exceptionally difficult at times to get rid of the refuse. It accumulates and becomes a veritable nuisance, as well as increases the fire hazard of the plant.

Local Market Must be Found

The production of alcohol from sawdust or shavings can be accomplished by either hydrolysis or destructive distillation. After examining these two processes one is forced to the conclusion that owing to the high intial cost of equipment and the large scale on which the operations would have to be conducted, to be carried on profitably, this method of converting waste material cannot be considered by the small woodworker or even a group of factories.

Another possible outlet for this material might be to convert it into charcoal. This could be carried out on a much smaller scale and at much less expense than the production of alcohol. We have never heard of this method being tried and do not know whether it could be carried on profitably, or where a market could be found for the charcoal produced.

In practically all towns a limited market exists for sawdust and shavings. It has been demonstrated that they can be disposed of much more readily if they are kept separate from each other. The shavings can be used for bedding in stables, for packing crockery and other breakable commodities, and to a certain extent by gardeners and farmers for mulching around vines and shrubbery.

Again many firms have found it profitable to bale the shavings and in this way they can be shipped to a considerable distance. This offers an enlarged market. A few enquiries and perhaps a little judicious advertising might find a buyer who whould take all the shavings that your plant produces at a price that would more than pay for the labor envolved.

The owner of a plant in Vancouver, B.C., sold all his shavings to a firm of fish curers and smokers. They paid at the rate of 5c per bag for this material and did the filling of the bags, and the hauling, themselves. This is offered merely as an example, many opportunities of a like nature undoubtedly exist.

Sawdust Put to Many Uses

Sawdust has been put to a wide variety of uses, some of them, unfortunately, of very limited application. Its successful utilization depends largely upon the local market that may be found, as it is not a material that can be economically shipped to any distance.

As a suggestion, some of the uses to which sawdust has been put are as follows: Fuel in furnaces and stoves; fuel in gas producers; briquettes; fire lighters; fur dressing; meat smoking, absorbent on floors, in cuspidors, etc.; fire extinguishers; cleaning and drying agent for metals, machinery, etc.; bedding in stables; composition flooring, artificial wood, etc.; ethyl alcohol; distillation and extraction; hardening and annealing of metals; packing of all kinds, bottles, canned goods, etc.; heat insulation in cars, ice houses, etc.; sound deadening in floors, etc.; shipment of meats, shipments of grapes and other fruit; manufacture of soaps, manufacture of fertilizers; packing of ice cements, mortars and plasters; burning clay products; manufacture of wood flour; purification of gas; composition paving blocks; floor-sweeping compounds; manufacturing of oxalic acid; manufacture of carborundum and calcium carbide; protection of fresh concrete from too rapid drying; manufacture of illuminating gas; manufacture of wood meal fodder; manufacture of oatmeal wall papers; manufacture of velvet wall papers; lettering on floral emblems; manufacture of dyes; railroad signal rockets; medicinal purposes; stuffing pin cushions and dolls; manufacture of fireworks; circus rings; dressing wounds; moth preventive; coloring black clay pipes; drying ink; water-proofing mixtures; currying animals; tanning extrects; filtering meidum.

A large number of woodworking plants are equipped with blower exhaust systems that take the shavings and sawdust from the machines and deposit them in fire-proof vaults, usually at a distance from the factory. By having a separate vault for sawdust and one for shavings and having them elevated above the ground a suitable wagon can be driven under these vaults and loaded through a chute with a minimum of labor.

An Ontario manufacturer, who uses electric power, when asked how he disposed of his waste material, replied: The shavings we bale and dispose of wherever we can. Sometimes we find it necessary to advertise them.

We have a customer for all our sawdust. This we keep separate from the shavings by individual fans on rip and resaw, and blow it into a large bin overhead, so that it can be drawn off in sacks to haul to the customer. We find that small fans, driven from the counter shaft of the saws, work very satisfactorily, and have well paid for their cost and installation, and consume very little power,

The cuttings we sell for kindling wood. This is the best way we know of for disposing of planing mill waste.

In many centres where there are a number of factories using electric power it might be a good idea for them to get together and find some method of disposing of their waste collectively and at a profit. Through co-operation a market might be found or a method devised that would convert all waste material into a profit instead of losing it as at present.

If anyone, who has any suggestions to offer along this line, will communicate with the publishers of this journal their co-operation will be appreciated.

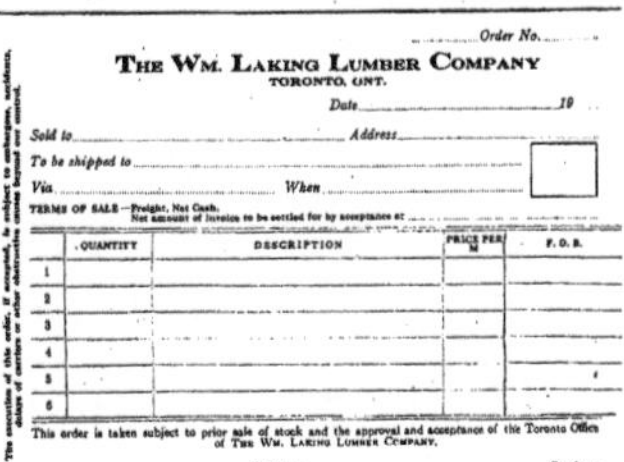

Order No.

THE WM. LAKING LUMBER COMPANY
TORONTO, ONT.

Date 19

Sold to Address

To be shipped to

Via When

TERMS OF SALE—Freight, Net Cash.
Net amount of invoice to be settled for by acceptance at

	QUANTITY	DESCRIPTION	PRICE PER M	F. O. B.
1				
2				
3				
4				
5				
6				

This order is taken subject to prior sale of stock and the approval and acceptance of the Toronto Office of THE WM. LAKING LUMBER COMPANY.

Salesman Purchaser

The execution of this order, if accepted, is subject to embargoes, accidents, delays of carriers or other obstructive causes beyond our control.

Convenient order form of Toronto wholesale lumber firm

How Logging Costs are Ascending

Word received from various lumber companies indicates that men are now being sent to the bush in large numbers and in most centres there is a larger available supply of help than last season. The prospects are that logging operations this fall and winter will be greater than any period since the outbreak of the war. Information comes to hand of the intention of not a few concerns to add to the number of their camps.

The Victoria Harbor Lumber Company, Victoria Harbor, Ont., will considerably increase their cut of logs during the coming season. The company have six camps in operation at the present time, which is double the number at this period last year.

The Pigeon River Lumber Co., Limited, of Port Arthur, report that in a general way the production of forest products in that district for the coming year will not be higher than a year ago, but they consider the cost will be considerably in excess of 1917-18. The company state they were in hopes that the labor market would be somewhat improved from conditions a year ago, although they expect wages to be as high, if not higher. The Pigeon River Lumber Company add that, in building their camps or making improvements to them, they consider the comfort of their men as far as possible and figure that it is a good investment to have lumberjacks well fed and well cared for. When woodsmen meet with such conditions they are more satisfied and do better work.

The Stone Lumber Company, Marksville, Ont., report that they are not yet sure how extensively they will undertake logging ,as prices of supplies and labor are such that profitable business appears impossible. They remark that, from the present outlook, it will take $10 more per M. to produce lumber than last year if an organization is to have an even interest on investment.

The Abbotsford Lumber, Mining & Development Co. of Abbotsford, B. C., assert that they cannot see much different conditions ahead unless it be that the eight hour day becomes general. The company expect to use, at least, as many men this year as last and if any change it will be an ancrease as they look to having as much business as in 1918 when the camp was barely able to keep the mill going. The company add: Camp supplies and provisions have gone up considerably, and in place of losing around $1,000.00 in feeding thirty men (we have a lot of married men who stay close to the camp and eat at home) we expect to have a deficit of over $1,500.00 this year. We are at present cutting over 120 M. per day, and while we have had a good many come and go, numerous old hands have stayed right with us, and taking everything into consideration, they have been very satisfactory. Our wages have increased 75c per M., and logs are costing to get out slightly over $1.00 more than last year.

Use of Electricity for Logging

The elimination of the fire hazard in the woods of the Pacific Coast is each year becoming more and more of a factor to be considered. As the lumber industry increases in volume the fire hazard, due to spark-emitting engines, increases.

The utilization of the electric donkey engine in place of steam has been given attention for several years. Some progress has been made. There were a good many obstacles to overcome. First a motor suited to this particular service had to be developed. The Snoqualmie Falls Lumber Co.,Snoqualmie Falls, Wash., is electrifying a logging operation. The company has installed 6,000 feet of transmission line and is successfully operating one of the electric units. Ultimately the entire camp will be electrified. The Snoqualmie Falls Lumber Co. generates its electric current at the mill from the refuse and returns the current to the woods.

One of the big Central Oregon pine lumber companies is considering the advisability of electrifying its logging railroads. There is no doubt that in the future electricity will play as large and important part in logging as it now does in the transformation of the log into lumber.

The subject of electricity in the logging camps is one of deep interest to the logging industry and will be discussed at the tenth session of the Pacific Logging Congress which will be held at Portland, Oregon, October 8 to 11. The headquarters of the congress will be at the Multnomah Hotel.

The officers of the congress are: W. W. Peed, president, Hammond Lumber Co., Eureka, Cal.; T. J. Humbird, vice-president, Humbird Lumber Co., Sandpoint, Idaho; George M. Cornwall, secretary-treasurer, editor, the Timberman, Portland, Oregon.

The executive committee consists of: British Columbia, J. M. Dempsey, British Columbia Loggers' Association, Vancouver; California, Donald Macdonald, the Pacific Lumber Co., Scotia; Idaho, H. M. Strathern, Post Falls Lumber & Mfg. Co., Post Falls; Montana, W. E. Ballord, Somers Lumber Co., Somers; Oregon, A. H. Powers, Smith-Powers Logging Co., Marshfield; Washington, Geo. W. Johnson, Admiralty Logging Co., Seattle.

What Spruce Forests Mean To Canada

"Mobilizing the Forests" was the subject of an address by Mr. Robson Black, secretary of the Canadian Forestry Association, at a meeting of the Bond Men's club, Montreal, on Sept. 3rd. He pointed out that pulp and paper exports from Canada had outstripped the record of all other manufactures of pre-war years, and that forest conservation had become the first storey of Canadian industry and finance.

There never has been any doubt that the development of agricultural crops and timber crops in Canada offers the line of least competitive resistance and most formidable promise, continued Mr. Black. Between the two activities existed no point of possible rivalry. Two-thirds of the Dominion of Canada is unfit for agriculture and can produce a profit to the state and private investor only when retained under growing timber. At this point of agreement, however, is encountered what has always been the millstone of forestry practice. Agricultural crops are annual and can be left to the business initiative of the individual. Forest crops repeat only in sixty to one hundred years. Agricultural planting is profitable within a twelvemonth; timber planting, for the ordinary human investor, defies most of the current business customs, for the dividends are never annual and may in some instances be centennial. These inherent peculiarities of conservative forest management outlaw private individuals as the dominant party and make forestry the natural function of the state.

Mr. Black emphasized that present deterioration of the forests in Canada was due to the continuation of a scheme of woodland exploitation that sufficed in an ancient day, but could not dovetail with modern industrial requirements or conceptions of government. Despite occasional claims, the main forest areas of Canada, east of British Columbia, the speaker claimed, were not reproducing their values. Studies of reproduction in New Brunswick had shown that on areas from which 9,000 feet per acre had been taken during the past thirty years, only enough trees were now growing to produce less than a thousand feet in the thirty years to come. In Mr. Black's view, any reform in the woods methods used by limit holders in Eastern Canada must of necessity be a compromise between ideal forestry and existing conditions. The first step must be a thorough survey of timber contents, rate of reproduction, best methods of removing all fire menaces such as lumbering slash, effective methods of logging so as to encourage growth of the best species, and this work called for friendly co-operation between limit holders and the provincial governments. Its obvious aim would be, not to increase immediate log supplies, but to put the prop of permanence beneath the wood-using industries of the Dominion.

"The spruce forests of Quebec and Ontario represent the country's most powerful magnet to those United States newsprint manufacturers who, self-robbed of their wood supplies by fire and poor management, are being forced to move equipment, lock, stock and barrel, to the source of forest materials over the Canadian border. Newsprint paper must continue to feed the huge maw of the American printing press, from which forty million papers proceed every week day," concluded Mr. Black.

Personal Paragraphs of Interest

James Innes of the Sutherland-Innes Co., Chatham, Ont., is on a business trip to England.

Alex. B. Lamont, of the C. G. Anderson Lumber Co., Ltd., Toronto, who has been spending the past few weeks at Midland and other points, has returned home.

F. L. Reed, of Toronto, late Ontario representative for the Campbell, MacLaurin Lumber Company, Montreal, has joined the selling staff of James G. Cane & Co., Toronto.

Oscar Thompson, of Syracuse, New York representative of the Union Lumber Co., spent a few days in Toronto recently on business.

D. C. Johnston, sales manager of the Union Lumber Co., Toronto, has returned after spending several weeks' holidays in an enjoyable automobile trip through the Adirondack Mountains.

A. L. Dawe, secretary of the Canadian Pulp & Paper Association, Montreal, is sailing for Canada from England on September 17th.

Geo. E. Lindsay, president of the Lindsay Factories, Limited, Toronto, who have disposed of their business, has been appointed manager for the J. C. Scott Co., Limited, who conduct a planing mill and lumber yard at 106 River St., Toronto.

J. L. MacFarlane, secretary of the Canadian General Lumber Company, who has been spending the past few weeks at his summer home ta Chemong near Peterboro, has resumed his duties and is much improved in health.

Geo. E. Petry, Toronto, Ontario representative of the Campbell-MacLaurin Lumber Company, Montreal, has returned from a business trip to Drummondville, Calumet, Ottawa, and other eastern points.

A. E. Masuret, Ontario representative of the "Service" Lumber Co., Vancouver, B.C., has removed his office from 30 King St. W., Toronto, to the Canada Permanent Trust Building, 18 Toronto St., where he has more commodious quarters.

L. C. Fisher, one of the Eastern representatives of the British Government Timber Buyer, Montreal, after a brief visit to the Pacific Coast, has returned to England. He was called home earlier than was expected. Mr. Denman is now in sole charge of the Montreal office.

Jasper Haines, familiarly known as "Jasper." of the McLennan Lumber Co., Montreal, is once more back on the job, after an absence due to illness. He underwent an operation in a Montreal hospital. Mr. Haines, who has been with the company for eight years, was formerly with the Bathurst Lumber Co.

A. J. Young, of the Young Lumber Co., North Bay and Toronto, has been appointed treasurer of the new provincial organization of Ontario Liberals. Z. Mageau, M.P.P. of Sturgeon Falls, who is a well known lumberman, has been elected an executive member of the Northern Ontario district.

A. N. Dudley, wholesale lumber dealer of Toronto, has returned from a visit to Duluth and other points. Mr. Dudley will spend several weeks on a hunting expedition and his many friends hope that by the time he has returned that he will have regained his customary good health. He has not been feeling up to the mark for some time past.

Douglas M. Read, who is a brother of Alex. P. and Alfred E. Read of Read Bros., Limited, wholesale lumbermen, Toronto, has entered the service of the firm. Mr. Read spent several years overseas, enlisting with the 198th Batt. and being later transferred to the 19th. He returned to Toronto in March last and has since been pursuing a business college course.

H. W. Larkin, son of C. A. Larkin, a former widely known lumberman, has entered the wholesale line and opened an office at 45 Canada Permanent Building, 18 Toronto St., Toronto, under the name of the Larkin Lumber Co. Mr. Larkin served for several years overseas and many friends are glad to see him back in the lumber industry once more.

Hon. Valentine Winkler, Minister of Agriculture and Immigration for Manitoba, has been seriously ill. Mr. Winkler was first elected to the legislature in 1892, and has been a member of that body practically ever since. For many years he was engaged in the lumber business. He was born in Neustadt, Ont., and his place of residence now is Morden, Man.

Major James Brechin of Toronto, B. C. lumber commissioner for the east, left a few days ago on an extended tirp to the Coast. On his return he will be accompanied by Mrs. Brechin and family. During his absence his duties are being looked after by Wm. Robertson of Victoria, B.C., who is in charge of trade extension in connection with the forestry branch of the Department of Lands.

C. C. Bockus has been appointed sales manager of the Edgecumbe-Newham Company, Ltd., with headquarters at Vancouver. Mr. Bockus was for three years with the Vancouver Lumber Company, and lately was the Eastern Canadian representative of the Allan-Stoltze Lumber Company, with his offices in Montreal. He has taken charge of the sales of the newly-formed Edgecumbe-Newham Company.

J. S. Knapman, of the McDonald Lumber Co., Toronto, recently returned from an extended business trip through Timmins, Porcupine and other points in Northern Ontario. He reports that the quantities of ties and pulpwood cut this season will be much larger than for many years and already there are huge piles of wood and ties along the railway tracks awaiting shipment.

Colonel Thos. Gibson, D.S.O., C.M.G., Deputy Overseas Minister of Militia for Canada, has returned to Toronto from London, England, and resumed his former duties as secretary of the Spanish River Pulp & Paper Mills. Colonel Gibson enlisted some four years ago with the 168th Oxford County Battalion, and crossed over as second in command. He spent about a year in France, where he was gassed and later returned to London, where he has ably filled leading administrative offices in miiltary circles.

Elijah Moore, one of the oldest and most respected residents of Thorold, Ont., pased away recently in his 76th year. He was engaged for a quarter of a century in the constructing business and was afterwards in charge of the millwright department of the Riordon pulp mill at Merritton and also represented this company during the erection of their plant at Hawkesbury. He was then invited to assume operating charge, but not caring to remove from his native town of Thorold, he returned there and was in charge of the millwright department of the Montrose Division of the Provincial Paper Mills Co. He is survived by four children.

Geo. H. Holt, of the Holt Timber Co., Chicago, spent a few days in Toronto recently and says that owing to the building trade strike there is a complete tie up of structural work in the Windy City. Carpenters are holding out for $1.00 an hour whereas the bosses have offered 92½c and there the matter has rested for some weeks. The retail lumbermen have also refused to sell any material to any contractors or private parties until after the labor trouble is over. This has been done to bring matters to a head and to clear the atmosphere. With a complete tie-up of men and materials it is expected that a settlement may be effected in the near future.

John B. Reid, of Toronto, vice-president of the Ontario Retail Lumber Dealers' Association, and Horace Boultbee, Toronto, secretary of the organization, were present at the annual convention of the National Retail Lumber Dealers' Association, which was held in Detroit, Mich., Sept. 11th-13th. There was a large and representative attendance and the gathering was marked by much enthusiasm and optimism. C. A. Bowen is the energetic secretary of the National Retail Lumber Dealers' Association and to him much credit is due for the splendid results of the great gathering.

John J. Miller, who for several years past has been inspector of the National Hardwood Lumber Association with headquarters in Toronto, has joined the staff of the C. G. Anderson Lumber Co., Toronto, and will manage the hardwood department. Mr. Miller entered upon his new duties at the first of the month. He has had a varied and thorough experience in hardwood lumber in all its activities and brings to bear upon his position expert knowledge and wide acquaintanceship of the trade. Mr. Miller succeeds H. A. Stewart, formerly of Buffalo, who recently left for Manilla, Philippine Islands, where he will supervise the mahogany department of Black & Yates, of New York City.

L. D. Barclay, of Toronto, eastern representative of Canadian Western Lumber Co. of Fraser Mills, B. C., returned recently after spending several weeks on a visit to Edmonton where his parents reside and on a trip to the Coast. He reports that the lumber business is very active in B. C. and that the American demand for Coast products is strong. Export trade is going on satisfactorily and all the mills are busy, some of them working overtime. Prices remain firm and regarding what trend they will take no one cares to predict. Shingle production is at its highest point in spite of the aviating values. Mr. Barclay says there is a great scarcity of houses not only in Vancouver but in nearly all the cities of the west and building operations are being rushed. Vancouver is enjoying much prosperity and has a bright future while the feeling of all the lumbermen in the province is optiimstic.

There has recently been concluded in Quebec a series of twenty-one meetings held under the auspices of the Canadian Forstry Association. The attendance of settlers was unusually excellent and the motion pictures shown were greatly enjoyed. A. H. Beaubien, who is employed by the Canadian Forestry Association, had charge of all the meetings.

Just Thirty Years Ago

Interesting items from the fyles of the September edition of the "Canada Lumberman" away back in 1889

It is reported that Messrs. J. B. and R. H. Klock have purchased Mr. James MacLaren's Bear Creek timber limit for $200,000.

* * *

Logs are being towed out of Lake Superior to the Bay City, Mich., mills. One raft of large dimensions passed Sault Ste. Marie last week.

* * *

The Longford Lumber Co.'s shingle mill at Orillia has been shut down for the season. The woodenware factory, however, has enough orders booked to keep the concern running for three or four months.

* * *

The Nassau mill, at Peterborough, closed Sept. 5th for the season, the supply of logs having been cut and the quantity of lumber in the yard being large, over twelve million feet. The steam mill will continue to run as usual.

* * *

Numerous gangs of men are being sent to the woods from Ottawa, Quebec and other points. Lumbermen are making preparations for the commencement of woods operations, and a lively winter's work in the woods is anticipated.

* * *

Mr. H. G. Buck of Norwood, is busily engaged in superintending the rafting of 50,000 feet of square timber at Belleville. It will be taken to Quebec, and on the arrival of the fall fleet will be shipped to Great Britain. This is the fourth raft Mr. Buck has shipped this year, making in all over 200,000 feet of square timber.

* * *

The mills of the Ontario Lumber Co., at French River, are run by steam, using a band saw, also a circular and gang saw. They cut on an average 100,000 feet of lumber per day, employing 100 men. This company load from 55 to 60 vessels with lumber for different ports each season. They are now engaged in making improvements in their mills.

* * *

A sawdust explosion took place in the Ottawa river, on the Hull side of the river, which threw water up some 15 feet high. There was luckily no boat in the vicinity at the time. The sawdust shoal in the Ottawa river just at the foot of the Government hill, is now fully a foot above the surface of the water. Recently several sawdust explosions have occurred in that vicinity which were big enough to swamp a small boat.

* * *

The sale of timber liimts and mills, at Oliver, Coate & Co.'s Mart, Toronto, was well attended on Sept. 5th. The attraction was the sale of the property of the R. C. Smith estate, Port Hope. Among those present were: Messrs. Conlen, St. Catharines; T. G. Hazlitt, Peterborough; Dalton Ullyot, Peterborough; J. B. Pearce, Norwood; Jno. D. Smith, Fenelon Falls; Alex. Campbell, Kinmount, and Wm. Boyd, Bobcaygeon.

* * *

Lumberers are rapidly sending men into the woods. Messrs. R. Hurdman & Co. of Ottawa, have three crews at work on their Magnicippi limits. Mr. A. Barnet has a crew at Barnet Lake; Mr. A. Fraser another at Misty Lake, Messrs. Chevrier & Whistle have two shanties running in full blast making logs for Messrs. Perley & Pattee. Mr. Louis Cheirier has a gang making improvements on the Nipissing branch of the Petawawa for Messrs. Booth & Co.

* * *

Complaints are again being heard from the various lumber quarters in Toronto regarding the snail pace adopted by the Grand Trunk railway in transmitting lumber from the various points of manufacture to the northern railway yard in that city. Ever since the Grand Trunk assumed control of the old Northern road there has been no end of bickering between the lumbermen and the railway officials, and a solution of the difficulty seems to be as far off as ever.

* * *

Mr. Robert Wilson, of Mr. J. R. Booth's firm, has returned to Ottawa after an extended tour through British Columbia. Mr. Wilson't object was to invest in the lumbering industry in that country, but owing to certain facts which he perceived on his trip he thought it advisable not to. He says that the mills there are of sufficient capacity to supply the local markets at present, and until the export trade is more developed there, and decreased in the eastern part of Canada, he is of the opinion that it would not be a wise investment.

* * *

A remarkable impetus has been given to the lumber industry of British Columbia within the past few months, and the next few years will witness a far greater development of the lumbering industry of that province. The facilities which British Columbia offers for the development of an export trade are such as to arrest the attention of capitalists. The Fraser River and its tributaries, which run through the vast timber regions of the northeast, offer exceptional advantages for floating the products of the forest to the sea coast for shipment.

* * *

The following are ruling prices at present for lumber at Vancouver: common S. I. S. do; on board cars, $13; 1 x 4 flooring; No. 1, $19; No. 2, $17; 1 x 6 flooring, No. 1, $18; do., No. 2, $16; ceiling, No. 1 S, 4 S, $19; No. 2, do, $17; common rough plank for sidewalks, delivered, $9, lath per M, $2, rough cedar, $10 to $12 per M. double dressed cedar, $35 per M; single dressed, do., $30 per M; shingles $2 per M; maple, $20 per M; curley do., $75; pickets, rough, $19 per M; dressed do., $20.

* * *

A deputation consisting of Messrs. Robert Innes, Thos. G. Hazlitt, A. P. Pousette, James M. Irwin, E. B. Edwards, of Peterboro, and R. C. Strickland, Lakefield, accompanied by Mr. Jas. Stevenosn, M.P., for Peterboro, visited Ottawa on the 18th, and waited on Hon. C. H. Tupper, minister of marine and fisheries, re the sawdust in the river question. The government have for some time been prosecuting offenders who have been using the river around Peterboro as a receptacle for their spare sawdust. The millmen cannot see why if a portion of the Ottawa river is exempted from this law their river should not be treated likewise. They asked Mr. Tupper to make some amicable arrangement.

* * *

The protection of our forests is a question of vast importance both to the national government and to the citizens, and a question which demands the consideration of the well-meaning citizen and the thinking men of the country. Our forests have been and still are. a great source of wealth, but the rapid rate at which they are being denuded by the woodman's axe, to say nothing of their destruction by immense fires, is sufficient to cause alarm. More care should be taken in the preservation of existing forests, and the sooner the people are educated to the importance and necessity of preserving them and the replanting of new ones the better. It is a matter of vital importance to the well-being of the nation.

* * *

A large and influential meeting of lumbermen and others who were interested, was recently held at Bridgewater, N.S., to consider the sawdust question. As is usually the case at such meetings, exemption from the operation of the law was claimed, and it was stated that practically little or no injury was done by throwing the saw dust into the streams. In this instance it was claimed that the river La Have should be exempted, upon the grounds of justice and reason, as it was shown by evidence, official and otherwise, that the navigation of the river is as good to-day as a quarter of a century ago, and that the idea that sawdust injured the fish was at best a mere conjecture, concerning which there has never been the slightest proof to back it up.

* * *

The E. B. Eddy Company have decided not to send any more men into the woods or make any more logs. The Eddy limits found employment for about 500 men yearly. The mills will close down unless sold. They employ a day gang of about 250. Unless the mills and limits are pnrchased before the logs are cut, several hundred men will be thrown out of employment.

* * *

A meeting of lumbermen operating timber limits in the Province of Quebec was held Sept. 5th, to consider the new regulations of the Crown Lands Department with respect to the prevetnion of destruction of timber by fire, and the tax imposed on limit holders for the purpose of enforcing such regulations. Mr. J. R. Booth presided. Under the new law the Government appoints fire rangers to enforce the regulations, and half the expense of maintaining these officials is paid by the Government, and the other half raised by assessment at the rate of ten cents per mile upon the limits under license.

* * *

At a recent sale of the Fredericton Boom Company, spruce logs brought $9.10 a thousand for merchantable, and two-thirds of that price for battens. White pine sold for $7.60, cedar $5, and hemlock $4.10.

* * *

During the month forest fires have done an immense amount of damage in New Brunsiwck; for miles the forest burned on each side of the tract on the Main Central Railroad. On the New Brunswick Railroad thousands of dollars of damage was done. The country roads were impassable on account of the heat. The towns of Fredericton and Moncton were surrounded by flames and the people had to fight hard to save their property.

* * *

There promises to be great activity in the woods in New Brunswick the coming winter, and the cut will be unusually heavy. Operators who have hitherto gone to Aroostook are seeking grounds on the Canadian side of the line in consequence of the trouble and expense arising out of the United States bonded system, and also on account of the extremely high rates charged by the Aroostook people for camp supplies.

* * *

Lumbering in Nova Scotia appears to have brightened up, and there is quite an active demand for milling property. J. E. Dickey Stewiacke, recently placed his saw mill and timber limits in Eastville on the market. They were at once taken up by a company from Amherst that intends to cut lumber on a large scale. This property is considered one of the finest water privileges in Nova Scotia.

* * *

The shingle mill, of Gilmour & Co., Trenton, Ont., was burned September 4th. Loss about $20,000; insured for $13,000. The mill had been partly shut down for some time.

* * *

Mr. L. H. Hillman's mill situated on the Ottawa, opposite Kettle Island, was burned Sept. 11th, and 1,500,000 feet of lumber. Loss nearly $200,000. The mill was valued at $22,000; insured for $8,000. The lumber was owned by the Rathbun Co., of Deseronto, and was principally this season's cut. It consisted of pine, ash, birch and basswood. It was valued at $175,000, and was partly insured. Fifty men are thrown out of employment.

Are You Really Making Profit in Business?

You May Think You Are — But You Had Better Keep an Eye on Those Insidious Leaks Whose Effect is Out of Proportion to Their Apparent Importance

By F. C. Belser

Although accounting has in the past been generally considered as an unproductive expense, and has therefore not been given the attention which it deserves, there has been in recent years a very general realization that, without accurate knowledge of the cost of production and the expenses of doing business, the manager of a business concern is as helpless as the pilot of an ocean liner without a compass. The progress of cost accounting is, therefore, now making rapid strides.

It is the aim of every merchant and manufacturer to dispose of his goods at a price which will return to him, first, the cost of the article, including his expense of doing business, and, secondly such a profit over and above the cost as will return to him a fair rate of return on the capital invested. Therefore, in fixing prices he starts, as a rule, with what he considers cost. The difficulty arises when his information regarding cost is inaccurate or misleading. In his effort to develop his business he undersells his competitors, and when these prices are met he shades them again, not knowing exactly when the point of danger is reached or passed.

Weaker Operators Drop Out

So, as competition increases and prices are reduced, the weaker operators perforce drop out. The demand presently exceeds the supply, the prices rise, thus rewarding with generous profits those who survive. This new condition attracts new enterprises. The supply increases and prices fall gain. The result is that in many industries extraordinarily prosperous periods alternate with exceptionally lean periods. These alternate periods of prosperity and depression are due partly, no doubt, to causes beyond the control of the particular industry, but it must be admitted that they are caused largely by faults and mistakes within the industry itself.

It is a remarkable fact that only relatively few enterprises become financially successful, and still fewer remain prosperous over long periods. Only occasionally is a business house encountered which has a history extending back over a generation, although there is no inherent reason why a business house, once established, should not go on indefinitely.

The profit factor is usually so small as compared with the cost of an article that any error in the costs, although the error may appear trifling in amount, must affect the profit factor by a very considerable percentage. For instance, suppose an article to cost $1.00 and to sell at a net profit at 5c; an error of 1c in the costs, or only 1 per cent. of the whole,would encroach upon the profit to the extent of 1c out of 5c, or 20 per cent. thereof. Thus it is seen that an error in the cost of an article has an effect on the net profit out of all proportion to its apparent importance.

A business may show a profit as a whole and yet it may not necessarily follow that profits have been earned on each item of merchandise, for losses on one class of goods may be more than offset by profits on other classes. The result of such a condition can only mean, in the long run, the loss of the profitable business to competitors, and the retention of the unprofitable business which no one else wants.

Price Cutting and the Public

No merchant knowingly sells an article below its actual cost, unless, perhaps, under very exceptional circumstances. It follows, therefore, that cutting of prices, resulting in keen competition, is generally the direct result of erroneous cost figures. If by cutting prices the merchant hurt only himself, there could perhaps be no vaild complaint, as he would very likely soon eliminate himself. But the effects of unsound competition must be considered in their relation not only to the individual, but as well to the industry as a whole, and to the consuming public.

By unsound business practices the individual ruins himself, brings down with him many of his competitors who must meet his competition, involving them all in losess for a time, and subjects the consuming public to erratic and violently fluctuating markets. If every member of an industry were fully informed as to his costs, the danger of underselling and price-cutting would be almost eliminated.

In recent years it has come to be recognized, therefore, that one of the most important activities of trade associations is to promote interest in accurate system of accounting and to aid every member of the association with the installation of such systems.

Fixing of Prices Prohibted

Thus, what is specifically prohibited by the Sherman Law, viz., the fixing of prices by agreement, is practically accomplished without effort and without direct design merely by making certain that every member of an industry knows his true costs, and then relying upon every indivdual to follow self-interest and fix prices based on sound economic principles.

Clear competition ought to centre around quality and service rather than price. It needs no salesman to secure orders at cut prices; anyone can do it. The variation in the market prices of articles of the same kind will tend to become of decreasing importance with the spread of more accurate cost accounts.

When a materially lower price does appear it will be the direct consequence of more efficient operation and it would be only fair that the efficient operator should reap the benefit of his enterprise. But efficient operation and the elimination of waste are themselves among the most important objects to be achieved with the aid of accurate accounts.

In speaking of the advantages of accurate knowledge of costs one is often met with the argument that the selling price is after all based upon the market made by other sellers, and that no individual merchant can exercise any control over the price. This argument is, of course, childish, for in the long run the cost of production plus a profit, must be recovered in any industry, and the sooner the real cost is known, the sooner will the price find its economic level. Moreover, the man who knows it first will be the one to profit by knowledge.

The surest way to prevent any article being held for sale at an economically unsound price is to have reliable data regarding its cost most widely disseminated.

Although business men may be in sharp competition with each other, they have in fact a very well defined community of interest. The unsound and uneconomic practices of an operator affect directly or indirectly every other operator in the same line. An enlightened self-interest, therefore, demands every effort on the part of all to prevent each indivdual from creating disturbed business conditions. No other one thing will so help to stabilize trading as full knowledge on the part of all as to the real cost of production and of distribution, and to secure this knowledge is a matter of comparative simplicity, if the problem is approached in the proper manner, and when the objects to be achieved are kept clearly in view.

Laurentide Enjoys Year of Prosperity

The Laurentide Co., whose mills are at Grand Mere, Que., had the best year on record for the twelve months ending June 30th last. The net revenue was $2,955,978 against $2,593,834. Of the former amount $232,651 came from lumber, a gain of $84,530. The amount available for dividends was $1,823,656 against $1,704,655. The directors made unusually large deductions for depreciation, these including $329,481 for paint, and $175,554 for the depletion of the timber limits. The sum of $150,000 is set apart for the pension fund. The surplus stands at $431,657, making a total surplus of $2,857,204.

In the balance sheet, timber lands are valued at $1,947,564, against $2,090,165 (less reserve for depletion—a total of $541,865 in 1919, and $366,311 in the previous year), and logs and supplies $2,533,912 as against $1,855,250, the total assets being $15,617,167, as compared with $14,805,905.

At the annual meeting George Chahoon, Jr., the president, referred to the question of reforestation, in which the company is a pioneer. He stated that approximately 1,000,000 young trees had been planted during the year, and that it was hoped that the nursery by the spring of next year, would be capable of producing sufficient to bring the annual planting up to 2,000,000 trees. The loss through fire during the past year had been practically nil, Mr. Chahoon paying tribute to the very wise and far-seeing policy of the province of Quebec regarding forest protection. The outlook for the current year was exceedingly bright. The consumption of newsprint paper, based largely as it is on the demand for advertising space, exceeded anything in the world's history.

Officers and directors were re-elected as follows: George Chahoon, Jr., president; Chas. R. Hosmer, vice-president; R. B. Angus, Edwin Hanson, F. A. Sabbaton, J. K. L. Ross, and Sir Thomas Skinner, Bart., Louis Armstrong was named treasurer; W. F. Robinson, secretary, and F. E. McNally, assistant secertary.

What Retail Lumberman is Up Against

"Honestly, I would hate to send a friend of mine a lumber bill for any small repair job or alterations," remarked a leading Hamilton, Ont., yard man the other day. "Not that I am ashamed of the prices that I am charging but any man not thoroughly familiar with the condition of the market, the scarcity of stock and trend of prices, would naturally conclude that I was holding him up or "sticking it into him" as the term is used. The fact is that quotations are now from 75 per cent. to 100 per cent. higher than they were before the war and unless a man has been undertaking some building or alterations no wand then requiring purchases from the yard he would naturally, come to the conclusion that, at the present levels, I was robbing him whereas I would only be getting a legitimate profit.

"It is utterly impossible now to build a few steps, lay a verandah floor, extend a platform, erect a sleeping porch or a new hen house, or do any small job without the cost appearing unreasonably high. I know of a customer who complained the other day about a bill that involved the making of only two flights of six steps, one flight four feet wide and the other two, and the cost was nearly $35. The carpenter's time alone—17 hours— was charged up at $15, and the material was put in at all the way from $75 to $90 per M. This citizen thought that the expenditure would only be about $15 or $20 at the most and when it ran to practically double this sum he naturally raised strenuous objections. On inquiry, however, he found that he had not been overcharged as the job was a small one and since he had some work done a couple of years ago a new price basis had been ushered in.

"It is really amusing to see the face that some customers will draw when they come in here and ask for a couple of white pine boards which at one time they could get for 75c or 90c and when they are told that the cost today is $2 to $3 they naturally think that we are profiteers or in the graft game. I assure you that we are not and that the retail lumberman, considering his heavy investment and service, is making less money to-day than at any previous period in his history. We do not like to charge the prices now prevailing but it is absolutely necessary to do so and there is seemingly little or no hope so far as I can see of values falling within the next twelve months at any rate."

Gillies Bros. Sell Lumber Depot

The purchase of the Gillies Lumber Mill property in Morristown, directly opposite Brockville, Ont., by interests said to be representing William Randolph Hearst, New York publisher, who, it is said, will erect a mammoth paper mill in the neighboring village, has given rise to much speculation. The site was formerly owned by Gillies Brothers, lumber manufacturers of Braeside, near Arnprior, who used the plant for their American depot.

The property has been sold by Gillies Brothers directly to a dummy party. They do not say who the purchaser is, but do state that in all probability a paper plant, employing many persons, will be erected on the site.

For a number of years Gillies Bros. conducted a successful lumber and building business at Morristown, but closed down when lumber went skyrocketing in prices.

Newsprint Companies Are Making Money

The pulp and paper companies have been making large earnings during the past three or four years owing to the abnormal demand for newsprint. In fact, the requisitions for this commodity are increasing all the while and tonnage coming on the market does not meet the increasing quantities called for. Several companies are adding new equipment and this will greatly augment production. Price Bros. & Co, of Quebec City, are installing a new unit at Kenogami; the Spanish River Pulp & Paper Mills are adding two machines at Espanola and the Abitibi Power & Paper Co. are preparing to place in position four additional machines at Iroquois Falls. Forty-seven freight cars arrived recently laden with parts of the new equipment in the shape of huge dryer rolls. An addition is being erected to the mill to accommodate the new machines.

In regard to the earnings of the companies it is interesting to note that the Laurentide Co., of Grand Mere, Que., has shown, with one or two exceptions, a steady gain during the past fourteen years and the following table will prove of interest:

Year	Net before divids.	P.C. earned
1919	$1,823,656	19.00
1918	1,704,655	17.75
1917	1,720,011	17.92
1916	917,822	10.92
1915	787,191	10.93
1914	730,774	10.14
1913	758,085	10.53
1912	753,572	10.45
1911	713,539	19.80
1910	216,305	23.20
1909	283,893	12.49
1908	251,459	9.02
1907	283,321	12.45
1906	271,846	11.74

The slight decrease in both net earnings and percentage earned in 1918, when compared to the previous year, are more nominal than real and due entirely to a change in bookkeeping practice.

Death of Mr. Joseph Chew

The death of Joseph Chew, 1195 Tenth Ave. W., Vancouver, took place recently following an operation. Deceased, who was 67 years of age, owned a shingle mill on False Creek and had been in business in the city for more than 15 years. He was born in Ontario and before going West, engaged in the lumber business around Midland and Georgian Bay. He was prominent in church circles having been a trustee of the Sixth Aveue Methodist Church. He leaves a wife and three children.

Ontario Legislators Who Will Once More Go to the Polls

Geo. C. Hurdman, M.L.A.,
West Ottawa

Udney Richardson, M.L.A.,
East Wellington

James Thompson, M.L.A.,
East Peterboro

Lumbermen Will Again be Candidates

Geo. C. Hurdman, M.L.A., of Ottawa, will once more be a candidate for the Ontario Legislature at the next provincial contest. He has been nominated by the Liberals of West Ottawa. In 1914 he was elected to that body and so energetic has he been on behalf of his constituents that his candidature has been well received by both political parties. Mr. Hurdman was born in the Capital City and comes of good United Empire Loyalist stock. He is president of the Hurdman Lumber Co., Limited, wholesale lumber dealers, and also president of the Canadian Quarries & Construction Co. He has always taken a deep interest in military matters.

Udney Richardson, M.L.A., of Elora, has again been nominated by the Liberals of East Wellington as their candidate at the next provincial election. Mr. Richardson was first elected to the Ontario House in 1911 and for many years has been engaged in the retail lumber business. He also handles grain. Mr. Richardson was born in West Garafraxa township, is of Scotch descent and previous to becoming a member of the legislature was Reeve of Elora for two years. He has always taken an active interest in the work of the Ontario Retail Lumber Dealers' Association, as well as district associations. Mr. Richardson has been particularly watchful of the progress of the Mechanics' Lien Act, which the association had amended a couple of years ago and is desirous of having a new bill introduced at the session next year.

Jas. Thompson, M.L.A., of Havelock, Ont., has been nominated as a candidate of the Conservative party in East Peterboro for the provincial field. He is widely known in the lumber arena and has represented East Peterboro in the Ontario House since 1908. Previous to receiving legislative honors he was warden of Peterboro county and also reeve of Havelock for several years. Mr. Thompson has always taken a deep interest in agricultural matters and is highly esteemed throughout his riding. He is also president of the Montieth Pulp & Timber Co., of Toronto, the Toronto Investment Co., the Thompson & Heyland Lumber Co., and other organizations. He resides in Havelock, Ont., but spends a great deal of his time in Toronto looking after his business interests.

Lumberman Left Large Estate

Property valued at $330,041 was left by Frank Hillock, a Toronto retail lumber dealer, who died June 10, 1918, and whose will made January 17, 1911, has been admitted to probate by Judge Morson, Toronto.

The personalty, valued at $230,861, is made up of $1,300 in household goods, $37,330 in stock-in-trade, horses, $380, book debts and promissory notes, $9,380, mortgages, $44,691, insurance, $13,929, of which $11,829 is payable to the widow; $16,352 cash, $2,268 paid on account of property bought at tax sales, which may be redeemed, $78,225 in stocks and bonds, and $106,380 in real estate. The realty consists of the lumber yards at 103 Albert Street, valued at $91,475; [illegible] street, $6,[illegible]; [illegible] Bower street, $2,747, and a lot in [illegible] township, $200.

Will Enlarge Pulpwood Operations

The Meigs Pulpwood Co., Inc., whose head office in New Brunswick is at Campbellton, with branches at Cascapedia, New Richmond, and other points, are conducting extensive pulpwood operations and during the coming season will carry on on a larger scale than ever.

The Meigs Company operate about 12 terminals and pulpwood propositions in Canada, and one of the terminals across the lake is at Oswego, N.Y. Four additional steamers will be put on the route carrying pulpwood from Quebec and New Brunswick to Oswego and other points. These steamers are now being loaded at Gaspe. Every cargo ranges from 1,000 to 1,500 cords of pulpwood. It is understood that the terminal at Oswego will have its present capacity increased.

Mr. Walter Meigs, president of the Meigs Pulpwood Co., Inc., recently paid a visit to Oswego and stated that not only would the storage facilities there be extended, but certain changes would be made in the conveyors and unloading devices at the plant.

Strike at Meaford Clears the Air

A strike of men employed in the yard of Seaman, Kent Co., at Meaford, Ont., took place recently. The men agreed to accept a sliding scale of 35c, 40c and 50c an hour for loading lumber at the dock, and from 35c to 40c an hour for piling lumber in the yards. The company are to have the right to employ what men they choose and to conduct piece work as heretofore. The men claim that the new scale will enable them to average from 45 to 50c an hour for day work. The company would not agree to dispense with piece work and the employees apparently are satisfied to forego this demand in consideration of an increase of from 5c to 10c an hour for work in the yards.

Empire Forestry Conference in London

An "Imperial Forestry Conference," which the British Government has definitely summoned to meet in London, England, next December or January at the same time as the Empire Timber Exhibit.

The scheme of this Imperial Forestry Conference was suggested by Robson Black, secretary of the Canadian Forestry Association, to Canadian, Scottish and English forestry leaders several months ago. It was taken up readily and advocated by Sir John Stirling-Maxwell to such good effect that the British Government's new Forestry Department is summoning representatives from all parts of the Empire.

The Conference will consider the forest conservation situation in Canada and other Dominions as well as the British Isles and will take up the question of forming a British Empire Forestry Association to act as a clearing house not only for information relative to Forestry problems and practices, but to promote inter-Imperial trade in forest products.

Building is Active in Canadian Cities

There has been no let-up in the value of building permits issued throughout Canada, and the total for the first seven months of this year is now nearly $11,000,000 ahead of the total for the same period last year. Permits issued in July totalled $8,132,278, a gain of $2,270,731 over last year's total of $5,861,547, and the largest amount of any month this year. These figures are for twenty-three Eastern cities and fourteen Western cities.

One of the most outstanding increases is shown by Windsor, which is now being invaded by numerous American firms seeking to manufacture their products in Canada. Last year permits were issued to the extent of $78,610 in July, and this year's total was $366,300, a gain of $281,690. The figures for the first seven months of the year have jumped in Windsor from $401,200 to $1,124,530.

Twenty-three Eastern cities show a gain of from $16,160,939 to $25,593,638 for the seven month period, and fourteen Western cities increased from $5,417,712 to $6,637,019 during the same time, the total increase for Canada being $10,652,006.

Spanish River Earnings are Large

Considerable progress toward putting the Spanish River Pulp and Paper Mills project upon a satisfactory working basis was made under the favorable conditions which prevailed in the paper industry during the year ending June 30, as indicated by the annual report which is now in the hands of the shareholders. Geo. H. Mead, of Dayton, Ohio, the president, refers to the completion of construction work and the proper balancing of the plants as referred to in the previous report as factors in giving the company its first annual opportunity to demonstarate its earning ability. The improvement shown and progress indicated does not, however, in the opinion of the board, yet represent an adequate return upon the very valuable resources of the company or the large amount of capital invested.

The total net revenue amounted to $2,757,964, compared with $1,729,231 in the previous year, and $2,117,734 for the period ending in 1917. Reserve for depreciation took $501,068, interest on funded debts $799,975, and $160,000 was appropriated for contingencies and taxes, leaving a balance of $1,296,921, which, added to $1,071,301 brought forward, makes a total balance of consolidated profit and loss accounts of $2,368,322.

Coast Shingle Mills Enjoy Big Boom

Operators of shingle mills in New Westminster, B. C., and valley generally are enjoying the biggest boom of their lives with but one trouble on their horizon, and not a labor trouble at that, for most of the workers in shingle mills are Orientals. The only little difficulty is the scarcity of raw material. First class red cedar is scarce, and as a result the mills are using stuff that would not have got by in the old days. Any old piece of cedar that will make a bolt is going to the mill, and there is little wasted, bolts being pretty well up to the tree tops among the knots.

But as long as a mill can get material, it is working to capacity, and shingles are fetching prices that compare favorably with other items in the H. C. of L. Ordinary good shingles of the XXX grade are now over $6 a thousand, and "perfections" have passed the $10 mark. This represents a lot of money flowing into British Cloumbia, for most of the product is going over the line. It is estimated that at least 75 per cent. is being exported.

This is not all velvet for the mill, for bolts are worth as high as $15 a cord, and there was a time when $3 was reckoned a good price.

More Lookout Towers to be Erected

Twenty-three candidates lately passed their examination for forest rangers in New Brunswick. At a recent meeting of the Forestry Advisory Board of the Department of Lands and Mines, the report of the building of lookout towers and the laying of telephone lines was approved. A telephone line will be built this fall from Bathurst to the head of the Nepisiguit River, a distance of about 60 miles. The line will be laid in co-operation with the Bathurst Lumber Company, each paying half the costs. Another line will be laid on the same basis in co-operation with the New Brunswick Railway Company and will be run into the forest about 30 miles from Deersdale, York Co., on the N. T. R. It is also expected that two more lookout towers will be completed in New Brunswick before the snow flies. One of these will be located on Bald Mountain, Northumberland County, and the other on Blue Mountain, Victoria County. The forest service intended to erect four lookouts in different parts of the province.

From the 1st of September all restrictions have been removed upon the importation of pulp and paper into Great Britain.

Getting After the Pulp Business

The Canadan Mission in London, Eng., is securing publicity for the development of the pulp and paper industry in Britain. Prominence is given to the fact that the Dominion is the second largest pulp and paper producing country in the world, and is rapidly overtaking the United States, which occupies the premier position. It is pointed out that Canada's preeminence as a paper producing country lies in the possession of hundreds of thousands of acres of pulpwood forests, and of conveniently located water powers. Not only has Canada the largest forest area in the British Empire, but it is also shown that the Dominion has developed water-power estimated at 1,941,700 horse-power, besides unlimited water powers yet undeveloped. The Mission is desirous of developing this branch of industry, in order that this important trade shall be kept within the Empire, instead of British users of paper having to rely on foreign importations. The Board of Trade statistics indicate that there is ample scope for the further development of this trade. At present the trade between the Old Country and Canada is hampered by lack of shipping facilities. In spite of these difficulties there has been a steady growth in this branch of commerce. During the fiscal year ended March 31st this year pulp and pulp-wood to the value of $99,259,166 were exported from Canada, compared with $52,975,457 and $63,486,222 in 1917 and 1918, respectively. Exports of mechanical and chemical pulp to the United Kingdom fell from 1,163,224 cwt. to 142,892 cwt. in the same period, owing to lack of shipping facilities. The Canadian printing paper imported in the United Kingdom for the fiscal year 1918-19 was valued at $38,484, as against the United States' import of $36.031,358 worth.

Death of Mr. Hiram Robinson

Many old friends in the lumber trade will regret to learn of the death of Hiram Robinson, who passed recently in Ottawa, in his eighty-eight year. The late Mr. Robinson who was born and educated in Hawkesbury, was for a long period connected with the firm of Hamilton Bros., lumber manufacturers, and for the past thirty years has been at the head of the Hawkesbury Lumber Co. He was also president of the Upper Ottawa Improvement Co., a director of the Ottawa and Hull Power Co. and other organizations. Mr. Robinson was for nearly forty years a school trustee in the Capital City and for half that time chairman of the Board and on his retisement from such long and faithful service was presented with a testimonial. The late Mr. Rboinson was also a former Mayor of Hawkesbury and chairman of the Board of Health there and some fifteen years ago was president of the Dominion Forestry Association in the affairs of which body he took a deep interest. He was also a promoter of the Consumers Electric Co. and of the Ottawa and Montreal Power Transmission Co. and a director of the local branch of the Ottawa General Trusts Corporation. In his passing a highly respected and venerable figure in the lumber business has gone to his reward. He played a most important part in the development of the lumber industry of the Ottawa Valley.

Wealthy Lumberman Leaves Generous Bequests

The will of the late Robt. Cox of Robt. Cox & Co., Ltd., widely known Canadian lumber exporters, has been filed for probate in the Surrogate Court, Ottawa.. The value of the estate is $1,780,543. There are some twenty bequests, legacies and annuities left to various relatives, friends and employees of the deceased lumberman. St. Luke's Hospital, Ottawa, and the Bootle Hospital, Bootle, England, will get a half a million each. They will receive half of total residue of the estate and it is estimated that the amounts of the legacies, annuities and bequests, as provided for by the wealthy testator, will aggregate about $400,000. The late Mr. Cox had financial holdings to the extent of between one-quarter and one-half million dollars in Canadian pulp and paper companies. The value of the estate held in the province of Ontario is set forth at $418,075. Lady Grey Hospital, Ottawa, is also given a legacy of five hundred pounds sterling.

Alarming Forest Fires in France

Forest fires, always at this season of the year prevalent in the south of France, have become more or less alarming along a 30-mile front between Toulon and Nice. Already about 20,000 acres of woodland have been consumed. The wind, unfortunately, continues to blow with violence. The hamlets in Fumas, Campaux and La Male were destroyed. In one night the Dum forest, with big reserves of cork, was wiped out.

The conflagration spread to the seashore, reaching Canadel, where ex-Premier Ribot has property. His park was destroyed. Visitors to his hotel got away by motor car and on a tug sent by the Maritime Prefecture.

Economy and Efficiency

In Barking Pulpwood with

The Moreau Barker

The Moreau Barker barks from two to three cords of wood per hour. Frozen logs in winter are handled as easily as dry wood in summer. Takes logs from 3" to 30" in diameter. Crooked logs are no objection to this machine. The Moreau Barker has a tension spring operated by the lever which controls the wheels according to the thickness of the bark and irregularity of the logs. This machine requires only 8 horse power to operate under all conditions.

Numbers of letters on our files testify the satisfaction the Moreau Barker has given many Canadian lumbermen.

We are prepared to prove the Moreau Barker equal to any work demanded of it.

Write us for further particulars

NOW MADE AND SOLD BY

La Compagnie Manufacturiers F. X. Bertrand

ST. HYACINTHE, QUE.

MANUFACTURERS OF STEAM ENGINES AND WOODWORKING MACHINES

The Plessisville Circular Resaw

Practice economy by making use of that last piece close to the bark. Our circular resaws will prove to you what you can save from your slabs.

Constructed on a strong solid base simple in operation and design, and manufactured from the best materials, our resaws give the maximum of output with economy in upkeep.

Write for particulars and specifications.

The PLESSISVILLE FOUNDRY

PLESSISVILLE, QUEBEC.

Quick Action Section

Special Lots Of Lumber— —Positions Wanted & Vacant

PUBLISHER'S NOTICE

Advertisements other than "Employment Wanted" or "Employees Wanted" will be inserted in this department at the rate of 20 cents per agate line (14 agate lines make one inch). $2.80 per inch, each insertion, payable in advance. Space measured from rule to rule. When four or more consecutive insertions of the same advertisement are ordered a discount of 25 per cent. will be allowed.

Advertisements of "Wanted Employment" will be inserted at the rate of one cent a word, net. Cash must accompany order. If Canada Lumberman box number is used, enclose ten cents extra for postage in forwarding replies. Minimum charge 25 cents.

Advertisements of "Wanted Employees" will be inserted at the rate of two cents a word, net. Cash must accompany the order. Minimum charge 50 cents.

Advertisements must be received not later than the 10th and 20th of each month to insure insertion in the subsequent issue.

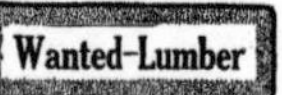

Basswood Wanted

No. 2 Common and Mill Cull. Winter cut preferred. Apply Firstbrook Brothers, Ltd., Toronto, Ont. 8-t.f.

Wanted Lumber

Hardwood Lumber wanted. Birch, Maple, Basswood and other Hardwoods. Dry or sawn to order. We send inspector. Box 14, Canada Lumberman, Toronto. 17-20

Rock Maple Blocks Wanted

Can use one million feet 13" to 16" in length, according to diameter, cut in bolts. Quote price per M. feet scale, loaded on cars. Box 13, Canada Lumberman, Toronto. 17-18

Wanted

10/4 and 12/4 No. 1 Common and Better Birch,

also

10/4 and 12/4 No. 1 Common and Better Soft Elm.

In quoting, state how the stock will run to 1st and 2nds and how long it has been cut. Box 996, Canada Lumberman, Toronto. 16-19

For Sale-Lumber

For Sale

30,000 setts Cheese Box Veneer. Apply C. A. Moses, Osgoode Station, Ont. 16-19

FOR SALE

100 pieces White Oak Piling, 30 to 60 ft. For particulars write

E. S. THOMPSON,
Appin, Ont.
16-t.f.

Wanted-Machinery

Wanted

Steel Refuse Burner—Second hand—20 to 25 feet diameter. Write stating size, condition and lowest price and where situated, to Refuse Burner, Box 23, Canada Lumberman, Toronto, Ont. 17-18

WANTED

1 2nd hand Pony Band Saw.
1 2nd hand Filing Machine for same.
Apply The Mageau Lumber Co. Ltd., Field, Ont. 18

WANTED

Second Hand Portable Saw Mill and Power Plant. Send particulars and prices to G. A. Keith, 27 Pinewood Road, Toronto. 18

For Sale-Machinery

FOR SALE

One second-hand 8" band saw, complete with saws; also circular resaw, with two inserted tooth saws, 42" dia. Keenan Bros., Ltd., Owen Sound, Ont. 16-19

Machinery For Sale

20 to 25 h.p. portable horizontal boiler and engine on skids, good condition. Easy terms to responsible party. Box 973, Canada Lumberman, Toronto. 18

FOR SALE

1 Steam Feed Carriage with Steam Set Works, "Waterous Model."
1 Nigger, complete, "Waterous Model."
1 Wicks Gang Saw, complete with saws and steam engine, "Midland," 60 H.P.
2 Shingle Machines, complete with saws.
11 Pulpwood Barkers.
For particulars apply to

CHICOUTIMI PULP CO.,
Chandler, Que.
17-20.

For Sale

1—17 x 24 Atlas Engine, with 36 in. x 10 ft. flywheel.
3—No. 94 Berlin Matchers, 15 in., fitted with hard steel knives on top and bottom cylinders—one pair shiplap, jointer and flooring heads with bits for each machine.
1—No. 182 Berlin Double Surfacer, 30 in. x 6 in.
1—No. 190 Berlin Buzz Planer.
1—No. 200 Berlin Picket Header.

The Otis Staples Lumber Company, Ltd.,
Wycliffe, B.C.
19-t.f.

FOR SALE—SAWMILL

25 H. P. Engine, 30 H. P. return tubular boiler. Three log seat carriage, overhead set, friction feed works, single edger and slab saw. All in fair order. Price $1,000. Box 915, Canada Lumberman, Toronto. 16-19

Used Saw Mill Machinery FOR SALE.

One McGregor & Gourlay endless bed Planer, knives 28" long, bed raises and lowers by power. Will plane 10" thick. In good condition. One B. F. Sturtevant Exhaust Fan, Intake 28" diameter, discharge 19" x 19" square; pulley 10" dia. x 8" face. In good working order, with an extra set of blades or fans. Also bonnet and piping for planer and discharge piping for fan.

Also two Moreau Rossers for peeling pulp wood. These are as good as new; used only one season. Will peel on an average 25 cords per day. Reason for selling, no more pulp wood to peel.

Complete Saw Mill for sale. Full particulars given on enquiry. All this machinery is at Kazubazua, Que., and belongs to Kazubazua Lumber Co. Any further information will be given by addressing

L. D. PHILIPS,
34 Thornton Ave.,
Ottawa, Ont.
16-19

FOR SALE
Saw Mill Machinery

Complete saw mill machinery; equipped with rotary, steam feed carriage, Gang Saw, Resaw, Edger, Butter, Lath Machine. Three Boilers and twin engine 300 H.P.; also saw gummers, filers and one shingle machine, with bolter and barker. For particulars apply:

CHICOUTIMI PULP CO.,
Chandler, Que.
16-19

Band Saw Mill Complete

Waterous 9 ft. Band Mill, Gunshot Feed Carriage, with extra Saws complete.

Filing Equipment

Three Saw Edger, lot of live Rolls, Engine, Shafting, Hangers, Pulleys, etc.

All of the above is Waterous equipment in good condition at a bargain.

The Geo. F. Foss Machinery & Supply Co., Limited,
305 St. James Street,
Montreal, Que.
17-t.f.

Wanted-Employment

Advertisements under this heading one cent a word per insertion. Box No. 10 cents extra. Minimum charge 25 cents.

WANTED: Position as log culler or foreman in log camp, by experienced man. For further particulars apply Box 44, Orangeville, Ont. 16-19

WANTED POSITION by representative and superintendent, still employed with large wholesale firm, with twenty-five years' experience in the lumber business. Can give reference as to capabilities and take charge on a month's notice. Box 901, Canada Lumberman, Toronto. 15-18

WANTED EMPLOYMENT—By married man, forty years of age; 25 years' experience, from swamping to managing, from stump to lumber pile, including office experience. Good reasons for having to look for employment. Will go any place. Hold Ontario Scaler's license.—Box 24 Canada Lumberman, Toronto. 18-19

Wanted-Employees

PLANING MAN WANTED—Good all-round man to work in planing mill; box factory; good opening for a man that can take charge of mill and yard; steady work. State experience and wages wanted. D. C. Baird, St. Mary's, Ont. 18-19

POSITION OPEN for a high-class man capable of organizing and assuming full management of all lumbering operations of a 500 mile timber limit for a Company operating a Saw-mill and a Pulp-mill. All replies will be treated confidentially. A permanent position with a good salary open for the right man. Box 903, Canada Lumberman, Toronto. 16-21

WANTED—A number of experienced Hardwood Sawmill Operators to contract to take out large quantities of Hardwood during the coming winter. Stumpage can be furnished if necessary, and the necessary cash advances to assist responsible operators. Address Box 19, Canada Lumberman, Toronto. 17-20

YOUNG MAN, experienced bookkeeper and stenographer, wanted, that will invest some money in limited company. Experienced in sash and door factory, planing mill and lumber business. Must be capable of taking full charge of office, and keeping all office work up to date. Opening on board of directors and secretary-treasurer for man with right qualifications. Apply to Box 26, Canada Lumberman, Toronto. 18-tf

We need at once a man who understands the grading and shipping of Hemlock, Spruce, and Hardwood lumber; also a man to grade on the Trimmers in our saw-mill at Huntsville.—The Muskoka Wood Mfg. Co. Ltd., Huntsville, Ont. 18

EXPERIENCED MAN to take charge of small Portable Saw-mill. Cutting operations in 100 acre bush near Toronto. Particulars and references to G. A. Keith, 27 Pinewood Road, Toronto. 18

Business Chances

Wanted

Good reliable saw mill man with portable mill to cut two million feet or more Birch and Hemlock in Patterson Township. Warren Ross Lumber Co., Jamestown, N.Y. 14-19

Partnership

A returned officer who has an all round knowledge of lumber business acquired in Ontario and the West, is desirous of acquiring an interest in a concern where services and investment would show fair return. Replies with particulars treated confidentially. Box 23, Canada Lumberman, Toronto. 17-18

For Sale

Building and machinery of good Double Cut Band Sawmill, well equipped with steam feed, canter, loaders, etc.

Also two storey Brick Factory on large lot convenient to two railways; splendid location. Address Box 949, Owen Sound, Ont. 12-t.f.

Hardwood Bush Wanted

Good hardwood bush covering from 1000 to 5000 acres. State location, distance from railway and best cash price. Address Box 21, Canada Lumberman, Toronto. 17-18

FOR SALE

On reasonable terms, a well established retail lumber business in a live and growing city, will be sold as a going concern, including central site, convenient to railway facilities. Apply Box 986, Sault Ste. Marie, Ont. 17-20

Timber Limit For Sale

Situated in Northern Ontario, 27¾ square miles. Estimated quantity of pine thereon upwards of 10,000,000 feet, as well as spruce and other timber. For full information apply to W. E. Bigwood, Bank of Hamilton Building, Toronto, or Byng Inlet, Ontario. 15-18

Timberlands For Sale

2¼ million ft. Birch and Maple.
¾ million ft. Hemlock and Pine.
Situated 100 miles north of Toronto, 1 mile from railroad. For particulars write

E. J. WHITE,
15-16th St., Buffalo, N.Y.
15-18

Timber Limit For Sale

We have for sale a timber limit in Northern Ontario (near Sault Ste. Marie) comprising an area of some 23,000 acres and containing some 19,000,000 feet of timber as follows: Pine, Cedar, Hemlock, Spruce, Maple, Birch, Elm, Ash and 10,000 cords Pulpwood.

Easy of access. Can be bought on terms at a very attractive price. Logs can be driven on rivers running through the property.

Apply, British American Distributors,
Suite 48-49, 25 Toronto Street,
Toronto, Ontario.
17-18

Lumber Yard

Excellent place in Montreal, for sale or to let. Room 8, LaPresse Building, Main 0985. 10-19

FOR SALE

Mixed Timber Limit, Lake Huron Front. Splendid portable mill proposition. Box 18, Canada Lumberman, Toronto. 17-18

For Sale.

One Detroit Hot Blast, Dry Kiln System, complete with Fan and Engine, also 35 feet of 9" double leather belt, used two weeks.

Port Hope Veneer & Lumber Co., Port Hope, Ont. 13-t.f.

FOR SALE

1,000 acres standing hardwood timber, 8 miles from railroad. Good portable mill proposition (Deeded Land), $5.00 per 1,000 ft. For particulars write Box 214, Thessalon, Ont. 17-20

ATTRACTIVE TIMBER PROPOSITION

has been placed in my hands for immediate sale; an exceptional opportunity to secure excellent timber lands at a moderate price. Call at office for particulars. W. Cooke, 208 Stair Building, Toronto. 18-19

For Sale

Hardwood Timber Limits of about seven million feet, with up-to-date sawmill.

BEDFORD MANUFACTURING CO., Waterloo, Que. 15-18

Saw Mill For Sale

Complete Saw Mill consisting of 16 x 20 Engine, Two Boilers, Board Mill, Log Jack, Slab Saw, Edger, Trimmer, Planer and miscellaneous equipment in good condition, immediately available.

THE HALL MACHINERY CO., Sherbrooke, Que. 17-18

Timber Lands For Sale

in the Province of Quebec, on the South Shore of the St. Lawrence, on tide water. Freehold lands 35,000 acres, Crown lands 60,000 acres.

An up-to-date sawmill is built, having a capacity of 40,000 to 50,000 feet of sawn lumber and 100,000 to 125,000 shingles.

For further information apply to the River Ouelle Pulp & Lumber Company, St. Pacome, Que. 17-20

Saw Mill Plant For Sale

Practically new and modern Saw Mill Plant, capacity about 30 Million feet per annum, located in the Interior of British Columbia on a beautiful Inland lake and on the main line of the Grand Trunk Pacific Railway. About 500 Million feet of timber on and adjacent to Lake (about 90% Spruce) and another Billion feet available at reasonable prices. Natural conditions ideal for economical logging, manufacturing, piling and shipping. An advantage of about $4 per thousand feet in freight rates to the Prairie Provinces over Coast shipments.

This property offers unlimited possibilities as a lumber, pulp and paper property. Would consider selling a half interest. Terms reasonable.

A. C. FROST COMPANY, 134 South LaSalle Street, Chicago, Ill. 5-t.f.

Virgin Timber For Sale

I have for sale, on very easy terms, in Virginia, 3,000 acres of Virgin Timber, mostly Shortleaf Pine, with some Oak. It is estimated to cut about 17 million feet of pine and oak, with a percentage of white wood, cherry and ash. Railway runs through the centre of it. The land will be worth $50.00 an acre after it is cleared. Apply

DON. M. CAMPBELL, Preston, Ont. 15-18

1300 Acres of Standing Timber FOR SALE.

It consists of Birch, Basswood, Ash, Maple, Pine, Spruce, Cedar, Hemlock. Camps, logging equipment and sawmill on the ground; owner not a lumberman, engaged in other business. The said lands are located right on C. P. R. and C. N. R. sidings, six miles west of North Bay, better known as the Indian Reserve. Apply to

P. ADAMS, North Bay, Ont. 15-18

Big Wood Ship Launching

With the launching of the Snoqualmie at the yards of the Puget Sound Bridge & Dredging Co., Seattle, Wash., one of the largest wood ships ever built slid down the ways. She is 330 feet long, 49 feet wide, 33 feet deep, and she has a tonnage of 5,000 deadweight. She was designed by E. P. Geary, known in local yachting circles as "Ted" Geary, whose plans have been approved by the United States Shipping Board. She was christened by Mrs. Kate Borst, 89 years old, daughter of a Snoqualmie Indian chief and wife of one of the first three white men to settle in the Snoqualmie Valley. More than a hundred Snoqualmie Indians executed a tribal dance as a part of the launching ceremony. There was also an historical pantomime depicting the development of the Snoqualmie tribe since the coming of the white man.

Five wood steamships each of 4,200 tons, built by the Patterson-MacDonald Shipbuilding Co., have been bought by British interests, at $520,000 for each ship, or a total of $2,600,000. The price approximates $124 a deadweight ton, as compared with $100 a ton for the Ferris type ships owned by the Shipping Board. The ships are the Bellata, Bundarra, Bethanga, Birriwa and Berringa. The first three are in Chilean waters, the fourth is now ready for delivery after her trial trip a few days ago, and the fifth is receiving the finishing touches at the Patterson-MacDonald plant. The ships were built for the Australian Government. Each of them has a lumber carrying capacity of 1,750,000 feet.

The permit system for regulating settlers' clearing fires is working out splendidly in Ontario. During 1918, 9,590 permits for the burning of slash by settlers were issued, as against 3,486 for the previous season. According to the report of the forest service the acreage covered by these permits amounted in 1918 to 39,683, as against 15,186 acres for the previous season. The permits are issued by the members of the fire ranging staff, and the Provincial Forester reports that generally speaking, the settlers co-operate heartily and appear to appreciate the wisdom of the new regulations.

The maximum number of rangers and supervisors was 1,190.

Timber Estimates

Maps and Reports
Plans for Logging Operations

Coolidge & Carlisle
Forest Engineers
BANGOR . . MAINE

Used Machinery For Sale

6—Racine Power Hack Saws.
1—22" x 40" x 10' London Gap Lathe
1—26" x 10' Engine Lathe
1—36" x 16' Engine Lathe

CHARLES P. ARCHIBALD & CO.
164 St. James Street, Montreal

Cut Your Selling Costs

Use MacLean Daily Reports and know where the projects are that offer the most profitable business. Reduce the percentage of wasted time and lost orders by concentrating on the most likely opportunities.

Rates and Samples on Request.

MacLEAN DAILY REPORTS, Ltd.
345 Adelaide Street West, TORONTO

DR. BELL'S
Veterinary Wonder Remedies

10,000 one dollar ($1.00) bottles Free to horsemen who give the Wonder a fair trial. Guaranteed for Colic, Inflammation of the Lungs, Bowels, Kidneys, Fevers, Distemper, etc. Send 25c for Mailing Package, etc. Agents wanted. Write your address plainly. DR. BELL, V.S., Kingston, Ont.

Code: A.B.C. 5th Edition
Member National Hay Association

Chs. E. DUCLOS
54 Notre Dame East
MONTREAL, QUE.

Receiver Shipper Exporter
Hay, Straw and Grain

Special Facilities for Shipping Camps
Write for Quotations

HORSES

UNION STOCK YARDS
OF TORONTO, Limited

"Canada's Greatest Live Stock Market" Capital, $1,500,000. Two Hundred Acres. Dundas St. cars to Keele St., West Toronto. Auction Sales every Wednesday. Private Sales Daily.

Correspondence Solicited.

WALTER HARLAND SMITH
Manager Horse Dept.

FOR SALE

About 200 M. 3 x 4 & up 4ths and better Pine
" 70 M. 2 in. Pine
" 25 M. 1 in. Pine
" 100 M. Cull Boards
" 100 M. 2 x 4 and up Culls
" 200 M. 3 x 4 and up Culls

With our resaw and planing plant we are prepared to manufacture any of this as may be required by buyers

J. B. Snowball Company
Limited
Chatham, - - New Brunswick

Review of Current Trade Conditions

Ontario and the East

The situation in the lumber arena remains steady and business is moving forward with considerable swing. All the wholesalers report that orders are coming in freely and that conditions are much more active during the present month than they were a year ago. Every grade of lumber is in active requisition, particularly hemlock and spruce, for house building purposes. There is still a great shortage in lath and dry stock is practically off the market, while green lath are being shipped in from various mills in Ontario as fast as they are cut. The market for shingles is exceptionally active, but the supply is short of the demand. The aviation of prices has for the time ceased, and it is thought that values have gone about as high as is possible. More carloads of shingles have been arriving of late than there have been for some weeks past. There is not much doing in the line of selling Coast or Mountain stocks in the East, owing to the abnormal call across the border and the high prices prevailing.

The export business is not particularly active at the present juncture, although space is more available. Exporters are inclined to the belief that before long rates will come down materially, and there is a disposition to go slow on the Old Country trade on the part of firms or other than those which have been doing an export business for years.

Building activity in some centres in the East has been interrupted by labor strikes just as things were getting under the full head of steam. There is still an uncertain atmosphere surrounding the whole lumber business. It is felt that 1920 costs will be higher than 1919, and all this means that the longer building is delayed the more expensive will be the structures put up. The outlay in building a home has now reached a figure that a few years ago would be counted as startling, but with lumber values practically doubled since the beginning of the war, the average builder thinks seriously before engaging in speculative undertakings. Not only in lumber but in everything else entering into the construction of dwellings prices have jumped enormously so that no one cares to make any predictions regarding the future. Everything in the shape of a forecast is likely to be upset by a shift in the labor, freight or cost of living situation.

Activity in building circles continues in Toronto and other leading cities. The value of permits issued in Toronto during August was $1,844,303, making the total for the past eight months of this year $10,362,590. An outstanding feature in connection with the permits is that the number of garages is increasing rapidly, no less than 185 being put up during the past month. There were also several additions to factories and warehouses. The increase in building permits in Toronto since the first of January shows nearly $5,000,000 over the corresponding period of last year, or in other words, a jump of practically 100 per cent.

All woodworking establishments are busy at the present time, and the longer builders delay the higher prices seem to go. Some two months ago the quotation on all lines of doors was increased by 15 per cent., and now another advance is going into effect, the most recent raise being 10 per cent. on pine doors and 20 per cent. on hardwood. There have also been sharp ascents in hardwood flooring, particularly oak; clear 3/8 in. quarter-cut oak is now quoted at about $190, while clear 3/8 in. plain oak is $140.

The manufacturer, the wholesaler, the retailer and the consumer of lumber are asking when and where it is all going to end, and echo alone answers where and when? It is beyond the ken of mortal man to solve the problem or furnish a satisfying and authoritative response.

Great Britain

Surveying the whole market it is rather difficult to accurately gauge conditions. While prices generally remain firm particularly on imported timbers, with the exception of one or two lines, such as red gum, sap gum and oak, of which there is a generous supply, there is considerable uncertainty regarding the whole industrial situation, due to labor disturbances, the national cry for rigid economy and the uncertain political outlook. August was a decidedly quiet month and merchants were engaged in making arrangements for reciving the wood purchased long before in the spring. Most of them found quite enough to do in storing or in delivering against outstanding orders.

Speaking of matters as it finds them, the "Timber Trades Journal" says: With prices at their present height, merchants will not accumulate stocks; and when the inducement to do so is only a saving of a couple of pounds per standard at the outside, business scarcely increases by such a concession. For instance, some of the Finnish specifications containing the proportionate 9 in. are offering on the basis of £29 for 7 in., and £29 for 3 x 9. These figures are cheap compared with Swedish at £33 and £35 respectively, but even £29 for Finnish 7 in. is felt to be a dangerous figure unless there is a good prospect of prompt sales.

Several other correspondents write this week that the market is decidedly weaker, and that spot prices are generally on a lower level. We believe this to be a fact; but we think it is merely a market fluctuation, and that the causes are easily discernible. The revival in trade continues slowly; but hitherto the consumption, small as it has been, has still been strong enough to absorb the meagre supplies which have been imported. But suddenly, towards the end of July, and during the first part of August, a stream of boats arrived almost simultaneously. Labor is difficult, barges are scarce, and there are no adequate facilities for dealing promptly with the wood. Parcels which arrived unsold, therefore, are being placed at the best prices obtainable, and those merchants who have held off until the last moment are enabled to do business at a very favorable juncture.

In regard to American hardwoods the conditions are stable and the market firm. While there has been a slackening up in a few lines owing to the strikes in the cabinet making trade it is felt that as soon as the industrial community begins to realize its responsibilities to the rest of mankind, business will take up a new lease of life. Much will depend upon the greatness or paucity of supplies in American hardwoods in regard to future prices:

The market for all kinds of mahogany is firm, and there is very little stock coming forward. The recent advance in freight rates from West African ports will no doubt prevent the importers from shipping as many logs as they would otherwise have done, because after all if the market was flooded with stock, values would certainly have the tendency to fall irrespective of freight rates and charges. The next mahogany auction sales will be held on September 11. The catalogues are not likely to be heavy; in fact, if they are on the same par as the previous sales, there will not be sufficient stock offering to meet all the requirements of the market. If this should prove the case, then values will not diminish, but are likely to advance still higher in view of the paucity of supplies, and the recent rise in freights.

In a recent edition a leading London paper says: "Looking ahead," said a high port official, "we think we can see daylight. The one danger point is in regard to the large timber consignments that are coming on the Government account for housing schemes. A million tons are to come from Canada. This will no doubt be distributed to various ports, near to the localities where it is needed, but we shall get our share. If it is shipped in steamers that do not require deep-water docks, it will not matter so much, but, otherwise, it will need lighters to move it to the places where it will be stored, and that will accentuate the shortage of lighters for general cargo."

In London the housing scheme is dragging on its way. If it ever gets into its stride huge quantities of battens chiefly 2 in. will be required. These are at the present time much neglected.

In floorings 7/8-in. is scarce, and merchants show no disposition to import any yet, this thickness should largely enter into the scheme for floors, etc. Laths, poles and putlogs are very limited, and a few good orders would clear all that are at present in stock.

United States

Firmness characterizes the general tendency of the lumber market. The upward tendency in prices still continues. In some centres building activities have ceased owing to strikes and lock-outs, but as time proceeds the general industrial situation is becoming more encouraging and the number of labor troubles lessening. One leading firm states that the railroads, labor demands and foreign exchange are the big problems of the day which must be settled before business can be expanded.

In the hardwood line the supply is still short of meeting the demand. Furniture and vehicle plants are doing an excellent trade, and it appears almost impossible to satisfy their wants. The general industrial demand is steady and operators need have no fear of the future, but can direct their attention along the line of increased production.

The car situation in the west is none too good, and many firms

View of Mills in Sarnia.

are behind in deliveries. It is feared by some that the conditions may become worse than a year ago on account of the general uneasiness in railway circles. The recent strikes put equipment in a bad way and the result is now being felt. The situation, however, is very uncertain and makes it a rather wild guess as to when business in the transportation line will become normal. The demands in the country lumber yards are growing faster than the dealers are able to get new orders filled or get shipment of old orders. The lumber market has steadied down to a considerable extent during the past few weeks. This may be due to the efforts on the part of the governmental authorities to reduce the cost of living. This has acted upon labor in such a manner that some of the radical demands for wage advances have ceased, and this, of course, eliminates the necessity on the part of the mill men to get more money to make ends meet.

But the excess of demand over supply will prevent any immediate drop in lumber prices, and, with the demand for housing facilities far from satisfied, and the certainty that the demand will not be met this year, it is hardly to be expected that there will be a decline in the market level during the coming winter, or next spring.

A continued heavy demand for practically all items is the feature of the southern pine market. There is an especially heavy run oh smáll dimension, coming from southern as well as from middle western consuming centres, which is taking up all such stock as rapidly as it can be manufactured under the present none too favorable circumstances. Heavy timbers are also moving in heavy volume and the demand for this class of material seems to be increasing daily. Large orders for sawn timbers from South America and other foreign markets are reported to have been received lately, and deals in 3x9 and 4x9 inch sizes are in heavy demand. A feature of last week was the leaping into the limelight of No. 2 common flooring, with offerings that have by far exceeded expectations and a call that is in excess of the supply. In fact for the higher grades of all dressed stock there is a very strong and healthy demand which exceeds the supply, with the result that there are no stocks worth mentioning left at the mills.

Some dulling of the sharp edge of quotations has been felt in the wholesale shingle market during the past week, though retail trade gave evidence that there are still many well filled private purses. The present inflated condition of the market would have given way to a more pronounced decline had the car supply been normal and the shipping facilities equal to production, which, while not large by any means, is fully equal to the demand. Consumers, rebellious at prices charged, are seeking and finding substitutes. This fact, well known to large producers, creates no present uneasiness since cedar logs are valued for their yield in sheathing lumber and siding, the latter being decidedly scarce with a rabid demand.

A recent despatch from Washington conveys the following interesting information with respect to export rates: Walker D. Hines, director general of railroads, has to-day issued instructions for the preparation of tariffs which will provide for class and commodity rates upon export traffic from points in Ohio, Indiana, Illinois, including cities located on both banks of the Mississippi River from Dubuque, Iowa, to St. Louis, inclusive, also from points in the southern peninsula of Michigan to south Atlantic and Gulf ports from Wilmington to New Orleans, inclusive.

When the tariffs have been prepared the matter will receive final consideration in Washington. The export rates to be established will be substantially the same as the rates which apply to New York on domestic freight from the same points of origin. The export rates to Key West will be the usual differential above the south Atlantic ports. Special consideration is to be given to export traffic when destined to Mexico and Central America, because of the generally low ocean rates from Gulf ports to those countries.

Market Correspondence

SPECIAL REPORTS ON CONDITIONS AT HOME AND ABROAD

Conditions in Ottawa Show Good, Steady Trade

Little by way of general change regarding prices, orders, or inquiries was shown in the Ottawa lumber market during the opening period of September. The noticeable feature of improvement was in the woods labor situation. Bushmen became more plentiful and the camps filled up well with prospects of a good season.

Orders and inquiries on the whole did not show much change, and remained steady as compared with the last two weeks of August. There was a fairly good demand (principally from the United States), the grades being mill run and better in pine and spruce. Spruce, if anything, showed some improvement, and the pine grades held firm.

Export business to points other than the United States did not alter. The shortage of bottoms handicapped to a certain extent shipments to South America. The South African demand and that to Europe remained stationary. Advices from exporters showed that the big majority of shipments going to European ports were still on Government account.

Lath and shingle continued in good demand and the market was not overcrowded with any surplus stocks. The sawmill cut of the Ottawa Valley this year, as was previously predicted, will hardly be as large as last year. There were fresh indications in support of this, as some of the mills already have closed down owing to shortage of logs occurring at the mill. The deficencies in supplies are attributed principally to two causes—one that low water has stranded many of the logs before they can reach the mill, and the other that the decline in the woods log output during the last two years is making itself felt. There are not as many logs in the streams to come down as during a pre-war normal season.

The sawmill cut for the valley is already pretty well sold, and indications are that with a light cut there is not going to be any surplus stocks of the staple grades on the market next spring. This would naturally have a tendency to sustain present prices, if they do not show a further advance before then. Some members of the trade believe that certain grades of stocks have not yet reached their highest levels.

Business on the whole was considered by lumbermen to be pretty fair and, while they generally agreed that no great boom was on, they felt that a steady trade was developing. The business which was dull during the war period, is gradually and steadily coming back. A fair amount of trade was done in the building grades with a good portion of the stock being used for repairs.

Reports concerning the woods camp operations were the principal features. Though the number of men offering to go to the woods was greater than during the closing period for August, it was problematical and difficult to judge if the quality or standard in woodsmen's efficiency was increased? Generally the reports to the "Canada Lumberman" were that camp operations were going ahead well, and given an even break with the weather and the health of the men in the bush the log output of the Valley should be considerably increased this season.

Outlook Good and Prices Holding Firm in Montreal

Speaking generally, Montreal lumber market conditions are satisfactory. Orders for the States are still good, the only difficulty being the scarcity of cars, and consequently slower deliveries. The outlook for further business is fine. Prices are holding very firm, and the chances are all in favor of a yet higher range of values.

B. C. lumber is not selling very freely, consequent on the very stiff advance in rates. An excellent market had been created for Western stocks, but the phenomenal rise in prices, owing to the demand for American account in the West, has tended to choke off Eastern buyers, who are not, as a rule, prepared to pay the heavy rates prevailing.

Local business has picked up. Unfortunately, however, a general strike of the building trades has been called, although the men have not fully complied with the order to quit. The reason for the strike is the usual demand for more money and shorter hours, some sections asking for an advance of 50 per cent. in wages. The demand for lumber in the province is very good.

Building permits for Montreal in August totalled $1,541,245, an increase of $482,981. For the year the value is $5,913,680, a gain of $2,205,790.

A large quantity of Government lumber continues to go forward to the United Kingdom. The shipments from this port will probably be completed by the end of this month and those from Quebec during October. Heavy shipments are also being made from the lower ports, notably from Campbellton, by means of tramps. During the winter, the lumber will be sent from Halifax and St. John. Practically all pine is shipped from Montreal and spruce from Quebec and the lower ports.

Exports of pulpwood show a decided declining tendency. For the month of June they were valued at $788,326, a falling off of $1,118,114; for the three months of the fiscal year they amounted to

Woods Manufacturing Co., Limited - Ottawa

Will give you prompt shipment and best prices on van supplies, of everything your men require from head to foot, consisting of **Mackinaw Clothing**, Underwear, Wool Socks and Mitts, Caps and Moccasins.

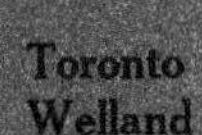

Toronto
Welland

Montreal
Winnipeg

THE HARRIS ABATTOIR COMPANY, LIMITED

specialize in supplying lumber companies with camp requirements. All product shipped to lumber companies is specially selected, specially cured, and specially packed to withstand many handlings before reaching destination.

Every lumberman should ask the Harris Abattoir Company to figure on all requisitions before placing orders.

All H. A. Brand goods are fully guaranteed.

The Harris Abattoir Company, Limited, specialize on making shipment when promised and Refrigerator Car Service to all points obviates any delay.

LIST OF PRODUCTS INCLUDES—

FRESH BEEF	BUTTER	AMERICAN BARRELLED PORK	EGGS & EGG MELANGE
BARRELLED BEEF	PURE LARD	SAUSAGES OF ALL KINDS	POTATOES AND VEGETABLES
CANADIAN BARRELLED PORK	SMOKED MEATS	CHEESE	FLOUR & MILL FEEDS
LONG CLEAR BACON	DOMESTIC SHORTENING		

H. A. Brand Oleomargarine—the new product which will save thousands of dollars for lumber companies. H. A. Brand Oleomargarine is higher priced than some, but you cannot afford to experiment by using inferior product as the only result of so doing would be reversion to Butter.

THE HARRIS ABATTOIR COMPANY LIMITED - West Toronto, Canada

Branches at: SUDBURY and OTTAWA, ONT. HALIFAX and SYDNEY, N. S. MONTREAL and QUEBEC, QUE. ST. JOHN, N. B.

$2,025,714, a decrease of $1,952,656. While newsprint exports grow, chemical and mechanical pulp have fallen back. Chemical pulp declined $1,105,652 in June, and $2,515,616 in the three months; mechanical increased $295,818 in June, but declined $47,308 in the three months.

St. John Complains of Slow Transportation

The last two weeks has seen no change in the lumber business at St. John excepting that the sawn lumber is not moving out as briskly as it was. Transportation both by water and rail is still the cause of this retrenchment, for if cars were available, fair sized orders have been sold to go forward to United States points and could be delivered but for the shortage in foreign cars as the Canadian Pacific and Canadian National roads still refuse to allow their cars to go out of Canada. The railways now claim that more foreign cars will be delivered over into Canada in the near future than has been the case during the last two months. Should St. John get its fair proportion of this amount then larger quantities of stock will move forward. Water transportation still continues scarce and hopes for immediate help are not good. Buyers are not as much in evidence as was the case a month ago and enquiries are also not as prevalent. This applies more to English cross water business as the exchange rate of the £ sterling being so low causes buyers on this side to hesitate as to future purchases. What the outcome may be remains to be seen. Certainly the lumber merchant who is a manufacturer, cannot go on and cut logs this coming winter and expect to sell sawn lumber at lesser prices than during the past few months. He will have to have them and more if wages advance. The possibilities of logs being cut at less than last winter's prices are very remote as logging contractors are asking higher figures than ever before.

Should nothing prevent it the mills at St. John expect to get only a normal cut of logs this winter as no one knows what is in the future. It is certainly too great a risk to take under present conditions. Local business is just fair, local prices remain unchanged and no great amount of house building has as yet been started but the future looks rather bright. American prices remain unchanged, laths and shingles being very much in demand at good quotations. All the St. John mills are still running but unless water comes within the near future some must shut down as between five and ten million feet of logs are still held from Grand Falls to the booms and heavy rains will be required to bring them out.

Commercial Aviation for Timber Surveys

As announced in a recent issue of the "Canada Lumberman" aerial surveys are making rapid progress and a leading concern in Annapolis, U. S., now announces that it is prepared to make photographs and survey timber, pulpwood, water areas, cities and towns by aeroplane, in Ontario, Quebec, eastern provinces and United States, and also to detect and report on forest fires. The company states that it will furnish aeroplanes for a number of other purposes including distribution of advertising of either a private or public character. Its equipment is complete and an efficient staff is maintained.

It is announced that members of a Boston expedition recently concluded cruising in aeroplanes over Labrador and that great timber lands were disclosed. From these lands millions of cords of pulpwood could be cut and rolled to streams for direct shipment. The extent of the discovery of the timber land was 2,000,000 acres and pictures taken from the air, numbering some 1,300, portray dense growths of pulp material in such a manner that the most available places can be readily located. The planes in their survey flew at a height from 2,000 to 9,000 ft. and sailed inland for more than 100 miles.

The success of the Labrador expedition is such as to justify the faith of aerial survey companies that commercial aviation by the use of aeroplanes is no longer regarded as a possibility but among the real accomplishments of the near future.

Erecting Many Houses for Their Men

The Spanish River Pulp & Paper Mills are erecting thirty new houses and two large boarding-houses at Espanola, Ont., in order to domicile the increased staff of the company, which now employs in all 6,750 men. Of these 5,000 are engaged in woods operations; 800 in the plant at Sault Ste. Marie; 500 at Espanola, and 450 at Sturgeon Falls. It is announced that the daily consumption of pulpwood by the industries of the Spanish River Pulp & Paper Mills is 750 cords and the output of the organization is 460 tons of newsprint, which will shortly be increased to 560; groundwood pulp, 400 tons; sulphite pulp, 220 tons, and board, 35 tons.

The Abitibi Power & Paper Co. are putting up fifty new houses for their workmen at Iroquois Falls, Ont., where large extensions to the plant will soon be carried out.

EDGINGS

Ontario

The McAuliffe Davis Lumber Co., Limited, Ottawa, recently sustained a small loss by fire. The amount of the damage was fully covered by insurance.

Brockville Paper Mfg. Co., Limited, Brockville, have been incorporated to manufacture and deal in paper, pulp, pulpwood, lumber and wood products. The capital stock is $250,000.

Joseph Dolan & Sons, Limited, Ottawa, Ont., have been incorporated to carry on in all its branches a general pulpwood, lumber, logging and timber business and to acquire and operate all the necessary mills and other plants. Capital $50,000.

Lewis & Turville, Limited, St. Thomas, Ont., have been incorporated to manufacture and deal in lumber, lath and building materials of all kinds. E. A. Lewis and B. C. Turville, both of St. Thomas, are among the incorporators. Capital, $40,000.

The Camden Paper Mills, Limited, of Camden East, Ont., are now in operation under the charge of E. S. Crabtree who is manager of the plant. The company are turning out some building paper but will be manufacturing kraft in the near future.

Canadian Sander Mfg. Co., Limited, Brockville, Ont., have been incorporated to manufacture and deal in all kinds of machinery, builders and mill supplies, patterns, lumber and building material and to carry on the business of pattern makers, mill workers and machinists. Capital $20,000.

The plant of the Bishopric Wallboard at Brookfield, Gloucester township, near Ottawa, was recently destroyed by fire. The industry was completely wiped out and the loss is about $200,000. Three freight cars, two C. P. R., and one G. T. R. on a siding at the factory, were also burned.

International Bushings, Limited, Toronto, Ont., have been incorporated to manufacture and deal in articles composed of or manufactured in whole or part from iron, steel, metal, wood or other combination of metals. Capital $25,000,000. R. P. Locke, barrister-at-law, is one of the incorporators.

The old Central Prison, Toronto, is being demolished by the Grand Trunk and Canadian Pacific Railways. The prison was built in 1873 and the railways will lay tracks where it now stands. The brick and stone work is being taken down and the lumber which is in good condition although 46 years old is being sold.

A new company, capitalized at $1,000,000, including 5,000 shares of 7 per cent. cumulative preferred and 5,000 common shares, has been incorporated under the laws of the Dominion and will be known as the Wendigo Power Company, with head office in Guelph. The company's plant will be located some 20 miles south of Larder Lake. The purpose of this company is the development of hydro-electric power on Wendigo Lake and certain parts of the Blanche River.

A provincial charter has been granted to Modern Dwellings, Limited, with a capital stock of $100,000 and head office in Oshawa. The new organization is empowered to erect dwelling houses of all kinds and deal in building material and to purchase, lease or take in exchange lands or interest therein and any buildings that may be on the said sites and sell, exchange, mortgage or otherwise dispose of the whole or any portion of the lands and all or any of the buildings.

A large and representative Industrial Conference was held this week in Ottawa. There were many delegates from the various industries. The lumber and timber interests were represented by Angus MacLean, Bathurst, N. B., J. Fraser Gregory, St. John, N. B., and Fred J. Booth, Ottawa. For the pulp and paper division F. A. Sabbaton, Grand Mere, Que. and P. B. Wilson, Sault Ste. Marie, Ont., and for the shipbuilding, H. B. Smith, Collingwood and R. W. Wilson, Halifax, attended.

The Galt Housing Commission have decided to build six houses. Action has been delayed owing to high tenders, but the commission has now succeeded in getting contracts within the $3,500 limit set by the Ontario Housing Act. Three of the houses to be built will be two-storey, brick veneer, while others will be a story and a half, stucco finish, and will sell at a lower figure. All houses, however, will have all conveniences, and it is expected when these are complete the Commission will soon sell others of the same style. Building operations to date in Galt show an increase of over $100,000 in value over last year.

Eastern Canada

The Duke and Duchess of Devonshire inspected the mills of the Laurentide Co., Ltd., while on a visit to Grand'Mere, P. Q.

The foundations for the new sulphate pulp mill which is being erected by Clarke Bros., Limited, at Bear River, N. S., have been completed.

H. Peladeau, Limited, 1311 Ontario St., E., Montreal, whose lumber yards were recently destroyed by fire announces that he will not rebuild on this particular site.

Omer Lamothe has begun the erection of a new saw mill at St. Louis de France, Champlain County, Que. The mill will be 53 ft. x 24 ft., 1½ storeys high.

The Foundries Building & Supplies Co. have been incorporated to acquire, develop and sell real estate, timber licenses, timber lands, standing timber and manufactured lumber. Capital $100,000.

J. P. Abel, Fortin, Limitee, Montreal, have been incorporated to take over and carry on as a going concern the business now conducted in Montreal under the name of J. P. Abel, Fortin & Cie, box manufacturers and lumber merchants. Capital stock $200,000.

The staff of the Canadian Export Paper Co., Montreal, spent Labor Day at Grand'Mere, P. Q., as the guests of the Laurentide Co., Ltd. The party visited the nurseries, were entertained at a lumberjack's dinner at the log sorting camp, and inspected the pulp and paper mills.

Shipbuilding is continuing active at various towns. In Parrsboro, N. S., W. R. Huntley & Son have laid the keel for a four masted 600 ton schooner and the Valley S. S. Co. have awarded a contract for a large schooner which will be built at Meteghan River, N. S.

The Parker Creek Lumber Co., Montreal, P. Q., have been incorporated to own and operate saw mills, shingle mills, lath mills and pulp and paper mills and to carry on the business of lumber merchants and manufacturers.

Notre Dame Lumber Co., Limited, Notre Dame du lac, P.Q., have been incorporated to manufacture and deal in lumber, wood, and all wood products. Capital $100,00. F. G. Quincey, Notre Damé du lac is one of the incorporators.

The Harbor Commissioners of Montreal have recently received tenders for timber for the construction of crib work. The quantity supplied will include crib work, construction timber, shipbuilding timber, B. C. timber and railway ties.

A launching took place recently from the shipyards of I. M. Comeau & Co., of Little Brooke, Digby, when the splendidly built four-masted schooner Charlotte Comeau was put afloat. The Charlotte Comeau is one of the largest schooners to be built in that section, measuring 172 feet over all, 156 ft. keel, 37.4 wide, 12.4 deep, 728 net and 799 gross tons.

A handsome four master vessel, Harry A. McLennan, was launched recently at Campbellton, N. B., at the McLennan ship yards. The name was given in honor of the eldest son of Mr. and Mrs. Alex McLennan who gave his life in the great war. The vessel is 186 ft. long, 35 ft. beam and net tonnage 719. It is nearly 60 years since a wooden vessel has been launched at Campbellton.

The Peaceland was recently launched at Annapolis Royal, N. S., by the Annapolis Shipping Co., being the smallest vessel built there in a number of years. The Peaceland, however, is a very pretty model and a handsome well built craft, her keel being 100 ft., beam 29 ft. and net tonnage 261. She has three masts and top masts complete. As soon as more timber can be accumulated another vessel of a larger type will be built at Annapolis Royal.

A new industry will shortly be in operation at Mullins Brook, York County, N. B., and will turn out hardwood last blocks. The promoter is H. Mobbs, of Kettering, England, one of the largest manufacturers of last blocks in the world. It is expected that 3,000,000 ft. or more of hardwood will be, manufactured by the end of the year. The newcomers have entered into an arrangment with the Nashwaak Pulp & Paper Co. to use that quantity.

Western Canada

Pitt River Shingle Mills, of Port Coquitlam, B. C., are planning the erection of $30,000 mill.

Lumber sold by the Canadian Western Lumber Company, Ltd., in June, was 11,217,000 board feet, valued at $303,437. The increase over last year's figures for June was $49,562.

H. D. Hyde, formerly manager of the Fraser River Shingle Co., has left Vancouver for Dallas, Texas, where he has been appointed manager for the south western branch office of Morse, Green, Limited.

The Pitt River Shingle Mill was burned to the ground recently. Dry kilns were saved. Alderman Wilson got the Port Coquitlam fire truck out and with a volunteer crew prevented the fire from spreading to the kilns.

The Georgetown Spruce & Cedar Co., Limited, Georgetown, B. C., have been incorporated to take over the business and assets of the Georgetown Spruce Co. and to continue a general lumber and manufacturing business.

Building permits issued in Winnipeg during July amounted to nearly $750,000. This is twice the value of the permits for the corresponding month of last year. The amount represented by building operations in Winnipeg since the first of the year is $1,500,000.

After having spent over three years on the battle front, some time as a private and the balance of the period as an officer, Ben. H. Babbitt is back in Canada again, and is now representing the "Service" Lumber Company of Vancouver, in Winnipeg.

Sir George Bury, president of the Whalen Pulp & Paper Mills, Limited, left recently for the north to inspect the company's large plants at Swanson Bay and Port Alice. He visited the Queen Charlotte Islands, where his company is taking out 60,000,000 feet of timber this season.

The scarcity of vacant houses in Victoria has caused many persons to repair old structures which have been unoccupied since the collapse of the industrial boom. As the result of building activities the mills have experienced an unusually big demand for lumber to be used locally.

An important addition to its plant, in the form of a spur track to connect its yards with the Esquimault and Nanaimo Railway system, will be installed shortly by the Canadian Puget Sound Lumber and Timber Company, Ltd., which recently commenced operations in Victoria.

The steel steamer "Canadian Trooper" recently loaded 806,000 ft. of lumber at Fraser Mills, B. C., this being another shipment of the big order of 70,000,000 ft. for the united Kingdom, on which practically all coast saw mills have been working. It is now estimated that about 12,000,000 or 15,000,000 ft. of the order has left Vancouver.

Loomis, McFee, Henry & McDonald, Limited, Vancouver, B. C., have been granted a Dominion charter. Wide powers were granted, such as to carry on the business of general contractors, to manufacture and deal in timber, lumber, sash and doors, portable houses, boxes and all articles made of wood. Capital $500,000. J. S. Pugh, barrister, Vancouver, is one of the incorporators.

Another mill will shortly be added to the list of the active lumber organizations in Greater Vancouver. This is the E. C. Walsh Lumber Company's new plant, which is to operate on the north shore of Burrard Inlet, just to the east of the Wallace shipyards. The mill, which is nearing completion, will cater chiefly to the export trade and has excellent facilities for shipping by water or by rail.

Canford is losing a sawmill and Merritt is gaining one. This is as a result of the determination of the management of the Nicola Pine Mills, Ltd., to remove from the first mentioned place to the latter, and work is proceeding rapidly to effect the change in the quickest possible time. The work of grading, track-laying, and construction has been going ahead as fast as it is possible for men to do it at what is known as the Central Yards, Merritt.

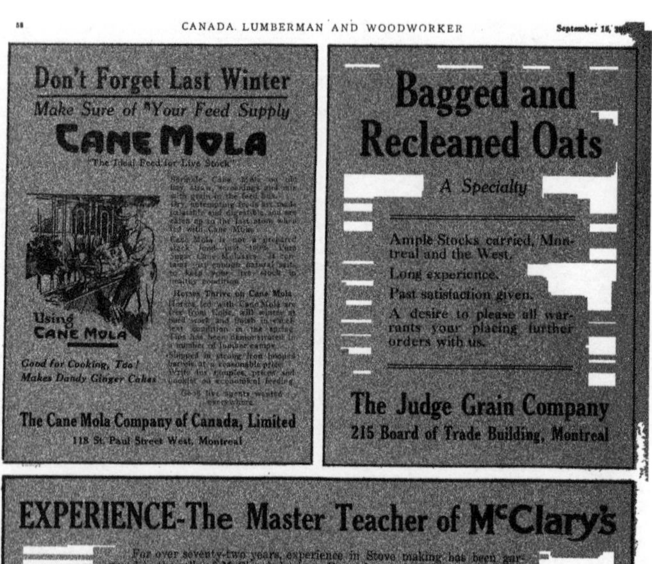
Don't Forget Last Winter
Make Sure of "Your Feed Supply
CANE MOLA
"The Ideal Feed for Live Stock"
Horses Thrive on Cane Mola
Using CANE MOLA
Good for Cooking, Too!
Makes Dandy Ginger Cakes
The Cane Mola Company of Canada, Limited
118 St. Paul Street West, Montreal
Bagged and Recleaned Oats
A Specialty
Ample Stocks carried, Montreal and the West.
Long experience.
Past satisfaction given.
A desire to please all warrants your placing further orders with us.
The Judge Grain Company
215 Board of Trade Building, Montreal

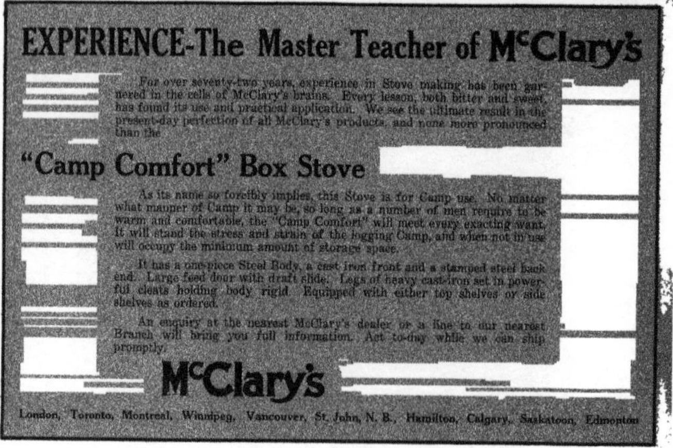
EXPERIENCE-The Master Teacher of McClary's
For over seventy-two years, experience in Stove making has been garnered in the cells of McClary's brains. Every lesson, both bitter and sweet, has found its use and practical application. We see the ultimate result in the present-day perfection of all McClary's products, and none more pronounced than the
"Camp Comfort" Box Stove
As its name so forcibly implies, this Stove is for Camp use. No matter what manner of Camp it may be, so long as a number of men require to be warm and comfortable, the "Camp Comfort" will meet every exacting want. It will stand the stress and strain of the logging Camp, and when not in use will occupy the minimum amount of storage space.
It has a one-piece Steel Body, a cast iron front and a stamped steel back end. Large feed door with draft slide. Legs of heavy cast-iron set in powerful cleats holding body rigid. Equipped with either top shelves or side shelves as ordered.
An enquiry at the nearest McClary's dealer or a line to our nearest Branch will bring you full information. Act to-day while we can ship promptly.
McClary's
London, Toronto, Montreal, Winnipeg, Vancouver, St. John, N. B., Hamilton, Calgary, Saskatoon, Edmonton

ALPHABETICAL INDEX TO ADVERTISERS

GOODHUE
BELTING
FACTORY TO YOUR MILL

CURRENT LUMBER PRICES—WHOLESALE

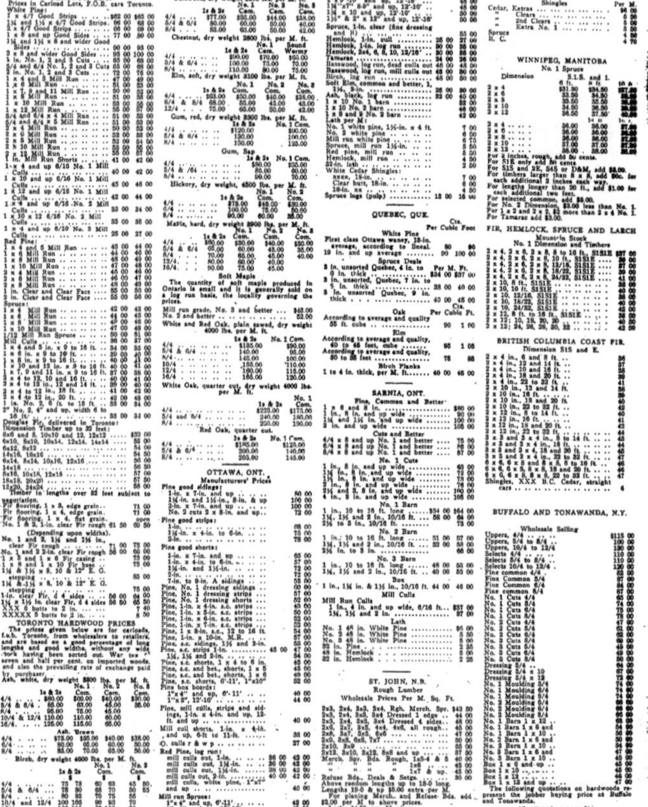

TORONTO, ONT.

Prices in Carload Lots, F.O.B. cars Toronto.

White Pine:

1 x 4/7 Good Strips	$62 00	$65 00
1¼ and 1½ x 4/7 Good Strips	66 00	68 00
2 x 4/7 Good Strips	68 00	69 00
1 x 8 and up Good Sides	77 00	80 00
1¼ and 1½ x 8 and wider Good Sides	90 00	95 00
2 x 8 and wider Good Sides	95 00	100 00
1 in. No. 1, 2 and 3 Cuts	65 00	68 00
5/4 and 6/4 No. 1, 2 and 3 Cuts	65 00	68 00
2 in. No. 1, 2 and 3 Cuts	72 00	76 00
1 x 4 and 5 Mill Run	47 00	49 00
1 x 6 Mill Run	51 00	53 00
1 x 7, 9 and 11 Mill Run	50 00	52 00
1 x 8 Mill Run	51 00	53 00
1 x 10 Mill Run	53 00	56 00
1 x 12 Mill Run	55 00	57 00
5/4 and 6/4 x 4 Mill Run	51 00	53 00
5/4 and 6/4 x 5 Mill Run	51 00	53 00
2 x 4 Mill Run	50 00	52 00
2 x 6 Mill Run	52 00	53 00
2 x 8 Mill Run	52 00	54 00
2 x 10 Mill Run	53 00	56 00
2 x 12 Mill Run	55 00	57 00
1 in. Mill Run Shorts	41 00	42 00
1 x 4 and up 6/16 No. 1 Mill Culls	40 00	42 00
1 x 10 and up 6/16 No. 1 Mill Culls	45 00	46 00
1 x 12 and up 6/16 No. 1 Mill Culls	42 00	44 00
1 x 4 and up 6/16 No. 2 Mill Culls	33 00	34 00
1 x 10 x 12 6/16 No. 2 Mill Culls	35 00	36 00
1 x 4 and up 6/10 No. 3 Mill Culls	25 00	27 00

Red Pine:

1 x 4 and 5 Mill Run	43 00	44 00
1 x 6 Mill Run	44 00	46 00
1 x 8 Mill Run	48 00	49 00
1 x 10 Mill Run	47 00	48 00
2 x 4 Mill Run	45 00	46 00
2 x 6 Mill Run	46 00	47 00
2 x 8 Mill Run	48 00	49 00
1 in. Clear and Clear Face	55 00	50 00
2 in. Clear and Clear Face	55 00	56 00

Spruce:

1 x 4 Mill Run	42 00	43 00
1 x 6 Mill Run	44 00	45 00
1 x 8 Mill Run	45 00	46 00
1 x 10 Mill Run	47 00	48 00
1/12 Mill Run Spruce	50 00	51 00
Mill Culls	36 00	37 00
1 x 4 and 5 in. x 9 to 16 ft.	34 00	35 00
1 x 6 in. x 9 to 19 ft.	39 00	40 00
1 x 8 in. x 9 to 16 ft.	40 00	41 00
1 x 10 and 12 in. x 9 to 16 ft.	40 00	41 00
1 x 7, 9 and 11 in. x 9 to 16 ft.	37 00	38 00
2 x 4 to 12, 10 and 16 ft.	40 00	41 00
2 x 4 to 12 in., 12 and 14 ft.	39 00	40 00
2 x 4 to 12 in., 18 ft.	41 00	42 00
2 x 4 to 12 in., 20 ft.	42 00	43 00
1 in. No. 2, 6 ft. to 16 ft.	33 00	34 00
2" No. 2, 4" and up, width 6 to 16 ft.	33 00	34 00

Douglas Fir, delivered in Toronto:

Dimension Timber up to 32 feet:

6x6 and 8, 10x10 and 12, 12x12	$52 00
6x10, 8x10, 10x14, 12x14, 14x14	53 00
6x12, 8x12	54 00
14x16, 16x16	54 50
6x14, 8x14, 10x16, 12x16	56 00
14x18	56 50
8x16, 10x18, 12x18	57 00
18x18, 20x20	57 50
12x20, 24x24	58 00

Timber in lengths over 32 feet subject to negotiation.

Fir flooring, 1 x 3, edge grain		71 00
Fir flooring, 1 x 4, edge grain		71 00
Fir flooring, 1 x 4, flat grain		open
No. 1 & 2, 1-in. clear Fir rough	61 50	60 50
(Depending upon widths).		
No. 1 and 2, 1¼ and 1½ in., clear Fir rough	71 00	75 00
No. 1 and 2 2-in. clear Fir rough	56 00	66 00
1 x 5 and 1 x 6 Fir casing		73 00
1 x 8 and 1 x 10 Fir base		75 00
1¼ & 1½ x 8, 10 & 12" E. G. stepping		85 00
1¼ & 1½ x 8, 10 & 12" E. G. stepping		75 00
1-in. clear Fir, d 4 sides	56 00	64 00
1¼ x 1½ in. clear Fir, d 4 sides	56 50	65 50
XXX 6 butts to 2 in.		7 40
XXXXX 5 butts to 2 in.		8 50

TORONTO HARDWOOD PRICES

The prices given below are for carloads, f.o.b. Toronto, from wholesalers to retailers, and are based on a good percentage of long lengths and good widths, without any wide stock having been sorted out. War tax of seven and half per cent. on imported woods, and also the prevailing rate of exchange paid by purchaser.

Ash, white, dry weight 3800 lbs. per M. ft.

	1s & 2s	No. 1 Com.	No. 2 Com.	No. 3 Com.
4/4	$80.00	$60.00	$40.00	$30.00
5/4 & 6/4	85.00	63.00	45.00	35.00
8/4	95.00	75.00	45.00	
10/4 & 12/4	110.00	110.00	60.00	
16/4	125.00	115.00	65.00	

Ash, Brown

4/4	$75.00	$55.00	$40.00	$38.00
6/4	80.00	65.00	60.00	50.00
8/4	83.00	70.00	65.00	50.00

Birch, dry weight 4000 lbs. per M. ft.

	1s & 2s $		No. 1 Com. $		No. 2 Com. $	
4/4	75	78	60	63	45	50
5/4 & 6/4	78	80	68	70	50	55
8/4	80	83	70	75	55	
10/4 and 12/4	100	105	90	95	70	
16/4	105	110	85	100	80	

Basswood, dry weight 2600 lbs. per M. ft.

	1s & 2s	No. 1 Com.	No. 2 Com.	No. 3 Com.
4/4	$77.00	$55.00	$44.00	$38.00
5/4 & 6/4	80.00	60.00	50.00	40.00
8/4	83.00	63.00	50.00	42.00

Chestnut, dry weight 2800 lbs. per M. ft.

	1s & 2s	No. 1 Com.	Sound Wormy
4/4	$90.00	$70.00	$65.00
5/4 & 6/4	100.00	75.00	70.00
8/4	110.00	80.00	75.00

Elm, soft, dry weight 3100 lbs. per M. ft.

	1s & 2s	No. 1 Com.	No. 2 Com.	No. 3 Com.
4/4	$63.00	$50.00	$40.00	$35.00
6/4 & 8/4	68.00	55.00	45.00	43.00
12/4	75.00	65.00	50.00	42.00

Gum, red, dry weight 3300 lbs. per M. ft.

	1s & 2s	No. 1 Com.
4/4	$120.00	$90.00
5/4 & 6/4	130.00	100.00
8/4	130.00	125.00

Gum, Sap

	1s & 2s	No. 1 Com.
4/4	$80.00	$55.00
5/4 & /64	85.00	60.00
8/4	90.00	70.00

Hickory, dry weight, 4500 lbs. per M. ft.

	1s & 2s	No. 1 Com.	No. 2 Com.
4/4	$75.00	$45.00	$30.00
6/4	100.00	75.00	50.00
8/4	90.00	60.00	35.00

Maple, hard, dry weight 3900 lbs. per M. ft.

	1s & 2s	No. 1 Com.	No. 2 Com.	No. 3 Com.
4/4	$60.00	$50.00	$40.00	$30.00
5/4 & 6/4	65.00	60.00	45.00	35.00
8/4	70.00	65.00	45.00	40.00
12/4	80.00	60.00	40.00	
16/4	90.00	75.00	45.00	

Soft Maple

The quantity of soft maple produced in Ontario is small and it is generally sold on a log run basis, the locality governing the prices.

Mill run grade, No. 3 and better	$43.00
No. 2 and better	52.00

White and Red Oak, plain sawed, dry weight 4000 lbs. per M. ft.

	1s & 2s	No. 1 Com.
4/4	$135.00	$90.00
5/4 & 6/4	140.00	95.00
8/4	145.00	100.00
10/4	155.00	110.00
12/4	160.00	115.00
16/4	165.00	120.00

White Oak, quarter cut, dry weight 4000 lbs. per M. ft.

	1s & 2s	No. 1 Com.
4/4	$225.00	$175.00
5/4 and 6/4	240.00	180.00
8/4	250.00	190.00

Red Oak, quarter cut.

	1s & 2s	No. 1 Com.
4/4	$185.00	$125.00
5/4 & 6/4	200.00	140.00
8/4	205.00	145.00

OTTAWA, ONT.

Manufacturers' Prices

Pine good sidings:		
1-in. x 7-in. and up		80 00
1¼-in. and 1½-in., 8-in. & up		100 00
2-in. x 7-in. and up		100 00
No. 2 cuts 2 x 8-in. and up		72 00
Pine good strips:		
1-in.		68 00
1¼-in. x 4-in. to 6-in.		75 00
2-in.		78 00
Pine good shorts:		
1-in. x 7-in. and up		65 00
1-in. x 4-in. to 6-in.		57 00
1¼-in. and 1½-in.		72 00
2-in.		72 00
7-in. to 9-in. A sidings		55 00
Pine, No. 1 dressing sidings		60 00
Pine, No. 1 dressing strips		57 00
Pine, No. 1 dressing shorts		52 00
Pine, 1-in. x 4-in. s.c. strips		49 00
Pine, 1-in. x 5-in. s.c. strips		50 00
Pine, 1-in. x 6-in. s.c. strips		52 00
Pine, 1-in. x 7-in. s.c. strips		52 00
Pine, 1 x 8-in. s.c., 12 to 16 ft.		54 00
Pine, 1-in. x 10-in. M.R.		57 00
Pine, s.c. sidings, 1½ and 2-in.		55 00
Pine, s.c. strips 1-in.	45 00	47 00
1¼, 1½ and 2-in.		54 00
Pine, s.c. shorts, 1 x 4 to 6 in.		45 00
Pine, s.c. and bet., shorts, 1 x 5		45 00
Pine, s.c. and bet., shorts, 1 x 6		49 00
Pine, s.c. shorts, 6'-11', 1"x10"		52 00
Pine box boards:		
1"x4" and up, 6'-11'		40 00
1"x8", 12'-16'		44 00
Pine, mill culls, strips and sidings, 1-in. x 4-in. and up, 12-ft. and up		40 00
Mill cull shorts, 1-in. x 4-in. and up, 6-ft to 11-ft.		38 00
O. culls r & w p		27 00
Red Pine, log run:		
mill culls out, 1-in.	36 00	42 00
mill culls out, 1¼-in.	36 00	42 00
mill culls out, 1½-in.	38 00	42 00
mill culls out, 2-in.	40 00	42 00
mill culls, white pine, 1"x7" and up		40 00
Mill run Spruce:		
1"x4" and up, 6'-11'		42 00
1"x4" and up, 12'-16'		42 00
1"x9"-10" and up, 12'-16'		48 00
1¼"x7" 8-9" and up, 12'-16'		48 00
1¼ x 10 and up, 12'-16'		50 00
1½" & 2" x 12" and up, 12'-16'		50 00
Spruce, 1-in. clear (fine dressing and B)		55 00
Hemlock, 1-in. cull	25 00	27 00
Hemlock, 1-in. log run	30 00	35 00
Hemlock, 2x4, 6, 8, 10, 12/16'	30 00	35 00
Tamarac	24 00	26 00
Basswood, log run, dead culls out	46 00	48 00
Basswood, log run, mill culls out	48 00	50 00
Birch, log run	48 00	50 00
Soft Elm, common and better, 1, 1¼, 2-in.	28 00	30 00
Ash, black, log run	32 00	40 00
1 x 10 No. 1 barn		52 00
1 x 10 No. 2 barn		46 00
1 x 8 and 9 No. 2 barn		42 00
Lath per M:		
No. 1 white pine, 1½-in. x 4 ft.		7 00
No. 2 white pine		6 50
Mill run white pine		6 75
Spruce, mill run 1½-in.		5 50
Red pine, mill run		5 50
Hemlock, mill run		4 50
32-in. lath		2 50
White Cedar Shingles:		
xxxx, 18-in.		7 00
Clear butt, 18-in.		6 00
18-in. xx		4 50
Spruce logs (pulp)	13 00	15 00

QUEBEC, QUE.

White Pine — Cts. Per Cubic Foot

First class Ottawa waney, 18-in. average, according to lineal	80	90
19 in. and up average	90	100 00

Spruce Deals — Per M. Ft.

3 in. unsorted Quebec, 4 in. to 6 in. thick	$34 00	$37 00
3 in. unsorted, Quebec, 7 in. to 9 in. thick	38 00	40 00
3 in. unsorted Quebec, 9 in. thick	40 00	45 00

Oak — Cts. Per Cubic Ft.

According to average and quality 55 ft. cube	90	1 00

Elm

According to average and quality, 40 to 45 feet, cube	95	1 05
According to average and quality, 30 to 35 feet	75	85

Birch Planks

1 to 4 in. thick, per M. ft.	40 00	45 00

SARNIA, ONT.

Fine, Common and Better

1 x 6 and 8 in.		$80 00
1 in., 8 in. and up wide		90 00
1¼ and 1½ in. and up wide		100 00
2 in. and up wide		105 00

Cuts and Better

4/4 x 8 and up No. 1 and better		75 00
6/4 x 8 and up No. 1 and better		85 00
8/4 x 8 and up No. 1 and better		87 00

No. 1 Cuts

1 in., 8 in. and up wide		63 00
1¼ in., 8 in. and up wide		72 00
1½ in., 8 in. and up wide		73 00
2 in., 8 in. and up wide		76 00
2½ and 3, 8 in. and up wide		100 00
4 in., 8 in. and up wide		105 00

No. 1 Barn

1 in., 10 to 16 ft. long	$54 00	$64 00
1¼, 1½ and 2 in., 10/16 ft.	58 00	64 00
2½ to 3 in., 10/16 ft.		73 00

No. 2 Barn

1 in., 10 to 16 ft. long	51 00	57 00
1¼, 1½ and 2 in., 10/16 ft.	52 00	58 00
2½ in. to 3 in.		66 00

No. 3 Barn

1 in., 10 to 16 ft. long	48 00	53 00
1¼, 1½ and 2 in., 10/16 ft.	40 00	53 00

Box

1 in., 1¼ in. & 1½ in., 10/16 ft.	44 00	46 00

Mill Culls

Mill Run Culls	
1 in., 4 in. and up wide, 6/16 ft.	$37 00
1¼, 1½ and 2 in.	37 00

Lath

No. 1 48 in. White Pine	$6 00
No. 2 48 in. White Pine	5 50
No. 3 48 in. White Pine	5 00
32 in. Pine	2 35
48 in. Hemlock	5 00
32 in. Hemlock	2 25

ST. JOHN, N.B.

Rough Lumber

Wholesale Prices Per M. Sq. Ft.

2x3, 2x4, 3x3, 3x4, Rgh. Merch. Spr.	$42 50
2x3, 2x4, 3x3, 3x4 Dressed 1 edge	44 00
2x3, 2x4, 3x3, 3x4 Dressed 4 sides	48 00
2x6, 2x7, 3x5, 4x4, 4x6, all rough	45 00
2x8, 3x7, 5x5, 6x6	47 00
2x9, 3x8, 6x8, 7x7	50 00
2x10, 3x9	55 00
2x12, 3x10, 3x12, 8x8 and up	57 50
Merch. Spr. Bds. Rough, 1x3-4 & 5	40 00
" " " " 1x6	45 00
" " " " 1x7 & up	45 00
Refuse Bds., Deals & Setgs.	30 00

Above random lengths up to 18-0 long.

Lengths 19-0 & up $5.00 extra per M.

For planing Merch. and Refuse Bds. add $2.00 per M to above prices.

Laths $4.50 per M pieces.

Shingles — Per M.

Cedar, Extras	$6 00
" Clears	5 50
" 2nd Clears	5 00
" Extra No. 1	3 50
Spruce	4 50
B. C.	4 70

WINNIPEG, MANITOBA

No. 1 Spruce

Dimension	S.1.S. and 1. 8 ft.	8 ft.	10 ft.
2 x 4	$31.50	$34.50	[illegible]
2 x 6	33.50	34.50	[illegible]
2 x 8	33.50	35.50	[illegible]
2 x 10	34.50	36.50	[illegible]
2 x 12	36.50	37.50	[illegible]
		14 ft.	16 ft.
2 x 4	36.00	36.00	[illegible]
2 x 6	36.00	36.00	[illegible]
2 x 8	36.00	36.00	[illegible]
2 x 10	37.00	37.00	[illegible]
2 x 12	38.00	38.00	[illegible]

For 2 inches, rough, add 50 cents.
For S1E only add 50 cents.
For S1S and 2E, S4S or D&M, add $3.00.
For timbers larger than 8 x 8, add 50c. for each additional 2 inches each way.
For lengths longer than 20 ft., add $1.00 for each additional two feet.
For selected common, add $5.00.
For No. 2 Dimension, $3.00 less than No. 1.
For 1 x 2 and 2 x 2, $2 more than 2 x 4 No. 1.
For Tamarac add $3.00.

FIR, HEMLOCK, SPRUCE AND LARCH

Mountain Stock

No. 1 Dimension and Timbers

2 x 4, 2 x 6, 2 x 8, 8 to 16 ft., S1S1E	$37 00
2 x 4, 2 x 6, 2 x 8, 10 ft., S1S1E	39 00
2 x 4, 2 x 6, 2 x 8, 12/16, S1S1E	37 00
2 x 4, 2 x 6, 2 x 8, 18/22, S1S1E	39 00
2 x 4, 2 x 6, 2 x 8, 24/32, S1S1E	41 00
2 x 10, 8 ft., S1S1E	38 00
2 x 10, 10 ft. S1S1E	40 00
2 x 10, 12/16, S1S1E	38 00
2 x 10, 18/22, S1S1E	40 00
2 x 10, 24/32, S1S1E	42 00
2 x 12, 8 ft. to 16 ft., S1S1E	38 50
2 x 12; 10, 18, 20, 20	40 50
2 x 12; 24, 26, 28, 30, 32	43 50

BRITISH COLUMBIA COAST FIR.

Dimension S1S and E.

2 x 4 in., 6 and 8 ft.	36
2 x 4 in., 12 and 14 ft.	37
2 x 4 in., 10 and 16 ft.	38
2 x 4 in., 18 and 20 ft.	39
2 x 4 in., 22 to 32 ft.	41
2 x 10 in., 12 and 14 ft.	38
2 x 10 in., 16 ft.	39
2 x 10 in., 18 and 20 ft.	40
2 x 10 in., 22 to 32 ft.	42
2 x 12 in., 8 to 14 ft.	40
2 x 12 in., 16 ft.	41
2 x 12 in., 18 and 20 ft.	42
2 x 12 in., 22 to 32 ft.	44
3 x 3 and 3 x 4 in., 8 to 14 ft.	43
3 x 3 and 3 x 4 in., 16 ft.	44
3 x 3 and 3 x 4, 18 and 20 ft.	45
3 x 3 and 3 x 4 in., 22 to 32 ft.	47
6 x 6, 6 x 8 and 8 x 8, 8 to 16 ft.	46
6 x 6, 6 x 8, 8 x 8, 18 and 20 ft.	46
6 x 6, 6 x 8, 8 x 8, 22 to 32 ft.	47
Shingles, XXX B.C. Cedar, straight cars	6

BUFFALO AND TONAWANDA, N.Y.

Wholesale Selling

Uppers, 4/4	$115 00
Uppers, 5/4 to 8/4	100 00
Uppers, 10/4 to 12/4	130 00
Selects 4/4	110 00
Selects 5/4 to 8/4	110 00
Selects 10/4 to 12/4	120 00
Fine common 4/4	82 00
Fine Common 5/4	87 00
Fine Common 6/4	84 00
Fine common 8/4	87 00
No. 1 Cuts 4/4	65 00
No. 1 Cuts 5/4	74 00
No. 1 Cuts 6/4	75 00
No. 1 Cuts 8/4	78 00
No. 2 Cuts 4/4	47 00
No. 2 Cuts 5/4	61 00
No. 2 Cuts 6/4	62 00
No. 2 Cuts 8/4	60 00
No. 3 Cuts 5/4	49 00
No. 3 Cuts 6/4	49 00
No. 3 Cuts 8/4	50 00
Dressing 5/4	64 00
Dressing 5/4 x 10	67 00
Dressing 5/4 x 12	72 00
No. 1 Moulding 5/4	74 00
No. 1 Moulding 6/4	74 00
No. 1 Moulding 8/4	74 00
No. 2 Moulding 5/4	66 00
No. 2 Moulding 6/4	66 00
No. 2 Moulding 8/4	66 00
No. 1 Barn 1 x 12	68 00
No. 1 Barn 1 x 6 and	54 00
No. 1 Barn 1 x 10	56 00
No. 2 Barn 1 x 6 and	50 00
No. 2 Barn 1 x 10	54 00
No. 3 Barn 1 x 6 and	47 00
No. 3 Barn 1 x 10	45 00
Box 1 x 6 and up	45 00
Box 1 x 10	45 00
Box 1 x 12	46 00
Box 1 x 13 and up	47 00

The following quotations on hardwoods represent the jobber buying price at Buffalo and Tonawanda.

(Continued on page 64

CURRENT LUMBER PRICES—Continued

MAPLE	1s & 2s	No. 1 Com.	No. 2 Com.
4/4	49 - 52	34 - 36	24 - 26
5/4 to 8/4	63 - 65	41 - 43	29 - 31
10/4 to 16/4	73 - 75	53 - 55	33 - 35
RED BIRCH			
4/4	61 - 66	44 - 46	28 - 30
5/4 to 8/4	67 - 69	47 - 49	31 - 33
SAP BIRCH			
4/4	60 - 64	38 - 40	24 - 26
5/4 and up	65 - 68	41 - 43	27 - 29
SOFT ELM			
4/4	49 - 51	34 - 36	26 - 28
5, 6 & 8/4	52 - 54	37 - 39	27 - 29
BASSWOOD			
4/4	54 - 56	44 - 46	31 - 33
Thicker	58 - 61	47 - 49	32 - 35
PLAIN OAK			
4/4	69 - 74	46 - 50	30 - 32
5/4 to 8/4	75 - 79	51 - 55	35 - 37
ASH, WHITE AND BROWN			
4/4	70 - 72	40 - 44	29 - 32
5/4 to 8/4	76 - 80	48 - 50	33 - 35
10/4 and up	108 - [illegible]	63 - 66	34 - 36

BOSTON, MASS.

Quotations given below are for highest grades of Michigan and Canadian white pine and Eastern Canadian Spruce as required in the New England market in carloads.

White pine uppers, s 1 to 2 in.		134 00
White pine uppers, 2½ and 3 in.		149 00
White pine uppers, 4 in.		160 00
Selects, 1 to 2 in.		125 00
Selects, 2½ and 3 in.		140 00
Selects, 4 in.		155 00
Fine common, 1 in., 30 per cent. 12 in. and up		92 00
Fine common, 1 x 8 to 11 in.		87 00
Fine Common, 1¼ to 2 in.		100 00
Fine Common, 2½ and 3 in.		130 00
Fine Common, 4 in.		145 00
1 in. shaky clear		72 00
1¼ to 2 in. shaky clear		75 00
1 in. No. 2 dressing		64 00
1¼ to 2 in. No. 2 dressing		68 00
No. 1 Cuts, 1 in.		80 00
No. 1 Cuts, 1¼ to 2 in.	85 00	87 00
No. 1 Cuts, 2½ and 3 in.		115 00
No. 2 Cuts, 1 in.		60 00
No. 2 Cuts, 1¼ to 2 in.	70 00	71 00

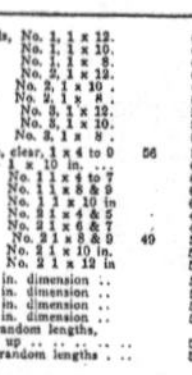

Barn Boards, No. 1, 1 x 12.		69 00
No. 1, 1 x 10.		64 00
No. 1, 1 x 8.		61 00
No. 2, 1 x 12.		64 00
No. 2, 1 x 10.		61 00
No. 2, 1 x 8.		58 00
No. 3, 1 x 12.		58 00
No. 3, 1 x 10.		57 00
No. 3, 1 x 8.		55 00
Can. spruce, clear, 1 x 4 to 9	56	58 00
1 x 10 in.		60 00
No. 1 1 x 4 to 7		63 00
No. 1 1 x 8 & 9		64 00
No. 1 1 x 10 in		65 00
No. 2 1 x 4 & 5		42 00
No. 2 1 x 6 & 7		49 00
No. 2 1 x 8 & 9	49	50 00
No. 2 1 x 10 in.		52 00
No. 2 1 x 12 in		56 00
Spruce, 12 in. dimension		50 00
Spruce, 10 in. dimension		57 00
Spruce, 9 in. dimension		56 00
Spruce, 8 in. dimension		55 00
2 x 10 in. random lengths, 8 ft. and up		53 00
2 x 12 in., random lengths		57 00

2 x 3, 2 x 4, 2 x 5, 2 x 6, 2 x 7	00
3 x 4 and 4 x 4 in.	00
2 x 8 in.	00
All other random lengths, 7-in. and under, 8 ft. and up	00
5-inch and up merchantable boards, 8 ft. and up, p 1s	00
1 x 2	00
1 x 3	00
1-⅜ in. spruce lath	00
1-½ in. spruce lath	00
New Brunswick Cedar Shingles	
	7 00
	6 50
	6 00
	5 50
	5 00
	4 50
	9 00
butts to 2-in.	5 00
Red Cedar Perfections, 5 butts to 2¼	5 75
Washington 16-in. 5 butts to 2-in. extra red cedar	6 55

Home in Kingston, Roofed with Brantford Asphalt Slates

Beauty, Fire Resistance, Economy Combined in this Roofing

The roofing that is being sold more and more throughout Canada not only for barns and small buildings, but for the most expensive homes, churches, golf clubs and public buildings, is Brantford Asphalt Slates.

Brantford Asphalt Slates are made from a special grade of long fibred felt which is exceedingly absorbent. This is thoroughly saturated and coated with Asphalt and surfaced with crushed slate, which is imbedded so firmly into the Asphalt that it cannot even be kicked off with the heel. This makes a splendid surface of beautiful reddish brown and dark green—a surface that never fades.

This grade of roofing is sold in three different forms. Brantford Asphalt Slates, Brantford Asphalt Slab Slates and Brantford Crystal Roofing.

The Slabs are really 4 slates in one and save time in roofing a large building.

Crystal Roofing is the same material as the Slates, only in roll form, and is especially adapted for barns and out-buildings requiring a permanent protective covering.

Asphalt is one of the most water-proof materials known, and Brantford Asphalt Slates being non-absorbent do not become water soaked or rot, neither do they crack nor fall off. They possess one great advantage over any other roofing made in that they cement together under the heat of the sun and form a solid, pavement-like surface on the roof, under which no rain or snow can drive, and no individual slates become loose or fall off. Highly recommended by prominent and experienced builders.

Brantford Asphalt Slates

will be used extensively in the future, and will play a big part in the great Period of Reconstruction which is just beginning.

Lumber dealers will find this a most profitable line to handle. Customers will buy it when ordering lumber, and it not only develops into a profitable sideline but also brings new customers and helps increase your lumber sales. At least put in a small stock of this roofing. You'll need no urging to send a large repeat order.

Let us send you full information, prices and samples.

Brantford Roofing Co. Limited

Head Office and Factory: BRANTFORD, ONT.

Branches at Toronto, Montreal, Halifax, Winnipeg

Yates
No. 281
Band
Rip Saw
As Installed in the Plant of
the Sawyer-Goodman Co.
Marinette, Wis.
Powerful Feedworks
of the "281"
Yates
The "Rip" With a "Rep"
Yates
Since the "281" was first built, 15 years ago, it has earned an enviable reputation as a band rip saw of exceptional durability and efficiency. The powerful feedworks, shown in section above, is but one of this machine's many strong features. It will stand up to the heaviest ripping at feeds up to 300 feet per minute.
Send today for our illustrated circular on this machine, and convince yourself as to its reputable excellence.
P. B. Yates Machine Company Ltd.
HAMILTON, ONT. CANADA
U.S.A. Plant, Beloit, Wisconsin, U.S.A.
The Invariable Choice of the Man Who Knows

Original "Dunbar" Machines

We are the original and the only makers of "Dunbar" Shingle Machines, Lath Machines, Clapboard Machines, Steam and Gasoline Logging Engines. Each is the best for its particular work. Are you using the best?

Lath Machine

From our many years of experience we evolved this "Dunbar" Original Lath Machine. Every improvement that could be suggested, every time-tested idea for the betterment of product and for greater speed, has been incorporated in this machine. We believe it has no equal, and there are a great number of mill men throughout Canada who share this belief with us. Carefully constructed of high grade materials and designed to work steadily under the hardest conditions.

Steam and Gasoline Logging Engines

Conditions in Canada necessitate an engine that will stand any amount of strain and hard work in the lumber industry. With this idea in mind we have brought out the "Dunbar" engines perhaps a little stronger than is really needed. They do their work easily and willingly, and stand a great amount of hard usage. Built entirely in Canada for the Canadian lumber trade.

Clapboard Mac[illegible]

You will need no excuse for the [illegible]ity of your product if you use [illegible]ginal "Dunbar" Clapboard [illegible] pert in every detail. This [illegible] give you the very best [illegible] most trying conditions. It [illegible] work without delays. It [illegible]tically no repairs and will [illegible] output. We cannot [illegible] highly because it is giving [illegible] vice to lumbermen in all [illegible] country.

Send for catalogues of any or all of these machines.

Dunbar Engine & Foundry Co.

WOODSTOCK, N.B.

ONTARIO

Canada's Banner Province

Ontario's timber production last year valued at $26,774,937 or 40% of Canada's total output.

Pine production, 905,442,000 ft. B.M.
Pulpwood, 246,282 cords.
Railway Ties, 5,704,459.

Ontario's woodworking industries, using 34 different kinds of wood, provide a ready market for the lumberman. Eighty-two per cent. of lumber used in Ontario's industries purchased within the Province.

Ontario's vast resources offer unsurpassed opportunities to the lumberman.

For maps and full information regarding Ontario, apply to

HON. G. HOWARD FERGUSON,
Minister of Lands, Forests and Mines.

GATES REFRACTORIES, LIMITED
382 St. James Street - - - MONTREAL

CANADA LUMBERMAN BUYERS' DIRECTORY

The following regulations apply to all advertisers:—Eighth page, every issue, three headings; quarter page, six headings; half page, twelve headings; full page, twenty-four headings.

ASBESTOS GOODS
Atlas Asbestos Company, Ltd.

AXES
Canadian Warren Axe & Tool Co.

BABBITT METAL
Canada Metal Company.
General Supply Co. of Canada, Ltd.
Syracuse Smelting Works

BALE TIES
Laidlaw Bale Tie Company.

BAND MILLS
Hamilton Company, William.
Waterous Engine Works Company.
Yates Machine Company, P. B.

BELT CEMENT
Graton & Knight Mfg. Company.

BELT DRESSING
Atlas Asbestos Company, Ltd.
General Supply Co. of Canada, Ltd.
Graton & Knight Mfg. Company.

BELTING
Atlas Asbestos Company, Ltd.
Beardmore Belting Company
Canadian Consolidated Rubber Co.
General Supply Company
Goodhue & Co., J. L.
Goodyear Tire & Rubber Co.
Graton & Knight Mfg. Company.
Gutta Percha and Rubber Company.
Main Belting Company
Manhattan Rubber Mfg. Co.
D. K. McLaren Limited.
McLaren Belting Company, J. C.

BELTING (Transmission, Elevator, Conveyor, Rubber)
Dunlop Tire & Rubber Goods Co.

BLOWERS
Toronto Blower Company.

BOILERS
Hamilton Company, William.
Jenckes Machine Company.
Marsh Engineering Works, Limited
Waterous Engine Works Company.

BOILER PRESERVATIVE
International Chemical Company

BOX MACHINERY
Garlock-Walker Machinery Co.
Morgan Machine Company.
Yates Machine Company, P. B.

BOX SHOOKS
Davison Lumber & Mfg. Company

BUNKS (Steel)
Alaska Bedding Co. of Montreal.

CABLE CONVEYORS
Jeffrey Manufacturing Company.
Jenckes Machine Company, Ltd.
Waterous Engine Works Company.

CAMP SUPPLIES
Canadian Milk Products Limited.
Davies Company, William.
Dr. Bell Veterinary Wonder Co.
Harris Abattoir Company
Johnson, A. H.
Turner & Sons, J. J.
Woods Manufacturing Company, Ltd.

CANT HOOKS
Canadian Warren Axe & Tool Co.
General Supply Co. of Canada, Ltd.
Pink Company, Thomas.

CARS—STEEL BODY
Marsh Engineering Works, Limited

CAR WHEELS AND CASTINGS
Dominion Wheel & Foundries

CEDAR
Fesserton Timber Co.
Foss Lumber Company
Genoa Bay Lumber Company
Muir & Kirkpatrick.
Long Lumber Company.
Service Lumber Company
Terry & Gordon.
Thurston-Flavelle Lumber Company.
Vancouver Lumber Company.
Victoria Lumber and Mfg. Co.

CHAINS
Canadian Link-Belt Company, Ltd.
General Supply Co. of Canada, Ltd.
Hamilton Company, William.
Hobbs Company, Clinton E.
Jeffrey Manufacturing Company.
Jenckes Machine Company, Ltd.
Pink & Co., Thomas.
Waterous Engine Works Company.
Williams Machinery Co., A. R., Vancouver.

CHAIN HOISTS
Hobbs Company, Clinton E.

CHINA CLAY
Bowater & Sons, W. V.

CHEMICAL PLANTS
Blair, Campbell & McLean, Ltd.

CLOTHING
Clarke & Company, A. R.
Grant, Holden & Graham.
Woods Mfg. Company

COLLAR PADS
American Pad & Textile Co.

CONVEYOR MACHINERY
Canadian Link-Belt Company, Ltd.
Canadian Mathews Gravity Carrier Company.
General Supply Co. of Canada, Ltd.
Jeffrey Mfg. Co.
Waterous Engine Works Company.

CORDAGE
Consumers Cordage Company.

CORN SYRUP
Canada Starch Company

COTTON GLOVES
American Pad & Textile Co.

COUPLINGS (Shaft)
Jenckes Machine Company, Ltd.

CRANES FOR SHIP YARDS
Canadian Link-Belt Company.

CROSS ARMS
Genoa Bay Lumber Company

CUTTER HEADS
Shimer Cutter Head Company.

CYPRESS
Chicago Lumber & Coal Company.
Long Lumber Company.
Wistar, Underhill & Nixon.

DERRICKS AND DERRICK FITTINGS
Marsh Engineering Works, Limited

DOORS
Genoa Bay Lumber Company
Long Lumber Company.
Mason, Gordon & Co.
Rutherford & Sons, Wm.
Terry & Gordon.

DRAG SAWS
Gerlach Company, Peter
Williams Machinery Co., A. R.

DRYERS
Philadelphia Textile Mach. Company.

DUST COLLECTORS
Toronto Blower Company.

EDGERS
William Hamilton Company, Ltd.
Garlock-Walker Machinery Co.
Green Company, G. Walter
Long Mfg. Company, E.
Waterous Engine Works Company.

ELEVATING AND CONVEYING MACHINERY
Canadian Link-Belt Company, Ltd.
Jeffrey Manufacturing Company.
Jenckes Machine Company, Ltd.
Waterous Engine Works Company.

ENGINES
Hamilton Company, William.
Jenckes Machine Company.
Waterous Engine Works Company.

EXCELSIOR MACHINERY
Elmira Machinery and Transmission Company.

EXHAUST FANS
Garlock-Walker Machinery Co.
Reed & Company, Geo. W.
Toronto Blower Company.

EXHAUST SYSTEMS
Reed & Company, Geo. W.
Toronto Blower Company.

FILES
Disston & Sons, Henry.
Simonds Canada Saw Company.

FIR
Associated Mills, Limited
Allan-Stoltze Lumber Co.
British American Mills & Timber Co.
Coal Creek Lumber Company.
Fesserton Timber Co.
Foss Lumber Company
Grier & Sons, Ltd., G. A.
Heeney, Percy E.
Knox Brothers.
Long Lumber Company.
Mason, Gordon & Co.
Reynolds Company, Limited
Service Lumber Company.
Shearer Company, Jas.
Terry & Gordon.
Timberland Lumber Company.
Timms, Phillips & Co.
Vancouver Lumber Company.
Victoria Lumber and Mfg. Co.
Weller, J. B.

FIRE BRICK
Beveridge Paper Company
Elk Fire Brick Company of Canada.

FIRE FIGHTING APPARATUS
Dunlop Tire & Rubber Goods Co.
Pyrene Mfg. Company.
Waterous Engine Works Company.

FIR FLOORING
Genoa Bay Lumber Company
Rutherford & Sons, Wm.

FLAG STAFFS
Ontario Wind Engine Company

FLOORING (Oak)
Long-Bell Lumber Company.

GALVANIZING
Ontario Wind Engine Company

GLOVES
Eisendrath Glove Co.

GASOLINE ENGINES
Ontario Wind Engine Company

GEARS (Cut)
Smart-Turner Machine Co.

GRAVITY LUMBER CARRIER
Can. Mathews Gravity Carrier Co.

GRINDERS (Bench)
Garlock-Walker Machinery Co.

HARDWOODS
Anderson Lumber Company, C.
Atlantic Lumber Co.
Bartram & Ball.
Bennett Lumber Company.
Blakeslee, Perrin & Darling
Cameron & Co.
Cardinal & Page
Davison Lumber & Mfg. Compa
Dunfield & Company
Edwards & Co., W. C.
Fassett Lumber Company.
Fesserton Timber Co.
Fraser Limited.
Gillespie, James.
Gloucester Lumber Compa
Grier & Son, G. A.
Heeney, Percy E.
Knox Brothers.
Long Lumber Company.
McLennan Lumber Company.
Moores, Jr., E. J.
Pedwell Hardwood Lumber Co.
Powell-Myers Lumber Co.
Russell, Chas. H.
Spencer Limited, C. A.
Stearns & Culver Lumber Co.
Summers, James R.
Taylor Lumber Company, S. K.
Webster & Brother, James.

HARDWOOD FLOORING MACHINERY
American Woodworking Machinery Company
Garlock-Walker Machinery Co.

HARDWOOD FLOORING
Grier & Son, G. A.
Long Lumber Company.

HEMLOCK
Anderson Lumber Company, C. G.
Bartram & Ball.
Bourgouin, H.
Canadian General Lumber Company
Cane & Co., Jas. G.
Davison Lumber & Mfg. Company
Dunfield & Company
Edwards & Company, W. C.
Fesserton Timber Co.
Foss Lumber Company
Grier & Sons, Ltd., G. A.
Hart & McDonagh.
Long Lumber Company.
Mason, Gordon & Co.
Spencer Limited, C. A.
Terry & Gordon.
The Long Lumber Company.

HOISTING AND HAULING ENGINES
Garlock-Walker Machinery Co.
General Supply Co. of Canada, Ltd.
Marsh Engineering Works, Limited

HORSES
Union Stock Yards.

HOSE
Dunlop Tire & Rubber Goods Co.
General Supply Co. of Canada, Ltd.
Goodyear Tire & Rubber Co.
Gutta Percha and Rubber Company.

INDUSTRIAL CARS
Marsh Engineering Works, Limited

INSURANCE
Hardy & Co., E. D.
Rankin Benedict Underwriting Co.

INTERIOR FINISH
Eagle Lumber Company.
Hay & Co.
Mason, Gordon & Co.
Renfrew Planing Mills.
Terry & Gordon.

KNIVES
Disston & Sons, Henry.
Peter Hay Knife Company.
Simonds Canada Saw Company.
Waterous Engine Works Company.

LARCH
Otis Staples Lumber Co.

LATH
Austin & Nicholson.
Canadian General Lumber Company
Cane & Co., Jas. G.
Cardinal & Page
Dupuis Limited, J. P.
Eagle Lumber Company.
Fraser Limited.
Fraser-Bryson Lumber Company.
Genoa Bay Lumber Company
Gloucester Lumber Company
Grier & Sons, Ltd., G. A.
Harris Tie & Timber Company, Ltd.
Long Lumber Company.
McLennan Lumber Company.
New Ontario Colonization Company
Otis Staples Lumber Co.
River Ouelle Pulp and Paper Co.
Spencer Limited, C. A.
Terry & Gordon.
Union Lumber Company.
Victoria Harbor Lumber Company.

LATH BOLTERS
Garlock-Walker Machinery Co.
General Supply Co. of Canada, Ltd.
Green Company, C. Walter.

LIGHTING APPLIANCES
Hobbs Company, Clinton E.

LOCOMOTIVES
Bell Locomotive Works
General Supply Co. of Canada, Ltd.
Jeffrey Manufacturiing Company.
Jenckes Machine Company, Ltd.
Climax Manufacturing Company.
Montreal Locomotive Workks.

LATH TWINE
Consumers' Cordage Company.

LINK-BELT
Canadian Link-Belt Company
Canadian Mathews Gravity Carrier Company.
Jeffrey Mfg. Co.
Williams Machinery Co., A. R., Vancouver.

LOCOMOTIVE CRANES
Canadian Link-Belt Company, Ltd.

LOGGING ENGINES
Dunbar Engine and Foundry Co.
Jenckes Machine Company.
Marsh Engineering Works, Limited

LOG HAULER
Green Company, G. Walter
Jenckes Machine Company, Ltd.

LOGGING MACHINERY AND EQUIPMENT
General Supply Co. of Canada, Ltd.
Hamilton Company, William.
Jenckes Machine Company, Ltd.
Marsh Engineering Works, Limited
Waterous Engine Works Company.

LUMBER TRUCKS
Waterous Engine Works Company.

LUMBERMEN'S CLOTHING
Woods Manufacturing Company, Ltd.

METAL REFINERS
Canada Metal Company.
Hoyt Metal Company.
Sessenwein Brothers.

MILLING IN TRANSIT
Renfrew Planing Mills.
Rutherford & Sons, Wm.

MOLDINGS
Genoa Bay Lumber Co,
Rutherford & Sons, Wm.

MOTOR TRUCKS
Duplex Truck Company

OAK
Chicago Lumber & Coal Comp
Long-Bell Lumber Company.

OAKUM
Stratford Oakum Co., Geo.

OIL CLOTHING
Leckie, Limited, John.

OLD IRON AND BRASS
Sessenwein Brothers.

OVERALLS
Hamilton Carhartt Cotton

PAPER
Bowater & Sons, W. V.

PACKING
Atlas Asbestos Company,
Consumers Cordage Co.
Dunlop Tire & Rubber
Gutta Percha and Rubber

PAPER MILL MACHINERY
Bowater & Sons, W. V.

PINE
Anderson Lumber Compan
Atlantic Lumber Co.
Austin & Nicholson.
Bourgouin, H.
Cameron & Co.
Canadian General Lumber
Cane & Co., Jas. G.
Cardinal & Page
Chicago Lumber & Coal
Cleveland-Sarnia Sawmills
Colonial Lumber Company
Davison Lumber & Mfg. Co.
Donogh & Co., John.
Dudley, Arthur N.
Dunfield & Company
Eagle Lumber Company.
Edwards & Co., W. C.

THREE LUMBERMEN SPECIALS

Harris Heavy Pressure
Best all round bearing metal made

Imperial Genuine Bearing Metal
For High Speed Engine Work

Aluminoid
For Light Countershaft Work

THE CANADA METAL COMPANY, Limited
Head Office and Factory, TORONTO
Branch Factories— HAMILTON MONTREAL WINNIPEG VANCOUVER

Excelsior Lumber Company.
Fesserton Timber Company
Fraser-Bryson Lumber Company.
Fraser Limited.
Gillies Brothers Limited.
Gloucester Lumber Company
Gordon & Co., George.
Grier & Sons, Ltd., G. A.
Harris Tie & Timber Company, Ltd.
Hart & McDonagh.
Hettler Lumber Company, Herman H.
Long-Bell Lumber Company.
Long Lumber Company.
Mason, Gordon & Co.
McLennan Lumber Company.
Montreal Lumber Company.
Moores, Jr., E. J.
Muir & Kirkpatrick.
Otis Staples Lumber Co.
Parry Sound Lumber Company.
Russell, Chas. H.
Shearer Company, Jas.
Spencer Limited, C. A.
Summers, James R.
Terry & Gordon.
Union Lumber Company.
Watson & Todd, Limited.
Williams Lumber Company
Wuichet, Louis.

PLANING MILL EXHAUSTERS
Garlock-Walker Machinery Co.
Reed & Company, Geo. W.
Toronto Blower Co.

PLANING MILL MACHINERY
American Woodworking Machinery Company
Garlock-Walker Machinery Co.
Mershon & Company, W. B.
Toronto Blower Co.
Yates Machine Company, P. B.

PORK PACKERS
Davies Company, William
Harris Abattoir Company

POSTS AND POLES
Auger & Company
Canadian Tie & Lumber Co.
Dupuis Limited, J. P.
Eagle Lumber Company
Harris Tie & Timber Company, Ltd.
Long-Bell Lumber Company.
Long Lumber Company.
Mason, Gordon & Co.
Terry & Gordon.

PULLEYS AND SHAFTING
Canadian Link-Belt Company
Garlock-Walker Machinery Co.
General Supply Co. of Canada, Ltd.
Green Company, G. Walter
Hamilton Company, William
Jeffrey Mfg. Co.
Jenckes Machine Company, Ltd.

PULP MILL MACHINERY
Canadian Link-Belt Company, Ltd.
Hamilton Company, William.
Jeffrey Manufacturing Company
Jenckes Machine Company, Ltd.
Waterous Engine Works Company

PUMPS
General Supply Co. of Canada, Ltd.
Hamilton Company, William
Jenckes Machine Company, Ltd.
Smart-Turner Machine Company
Waterous Engine Works Company.

RAILS
Gartshore, John J.
Sessenwein Bros.

ROOFINGS
Reed & Company, Geo. W.

ROOFINGS
(Rubber, Plastic and Liquid).
International Chemical Company

ROPE
Consumers Cordage Co.
Leckie, Limited, John

RUBBER GOODS
Atlas Asbestos Company
Dunlop Tire & Rubber Goods Co.
Goodyear Tire and Rubber Co.
Gutta Percha & Rubber Company.

SASH
Genoa Bay Lumber Company
Renfrew Planing Mills.

SAWS
Atkins & Company, E. C.
Disston & Sons, Henry
General Supply Co. of Canada, Ltd.
Gerlach Company, Peter
Green Company, G. Walter
Hoe & Company, R.
Shurly-Dietrich Company
Shurly Co., Ltd., T. F.
Simonds Canada Saw Company

SAW MILL LINK-BELT
Williams Machinery Co., A. R., Vancouver.

SAW MILL MACHINERY
Canadian Link-Belt Company, Ltd.
Dunbar Engine & Foundry Co.
Firstbrook Bros.
General Supply Co. of Canada, Ltd.
Hamilton Company, William
Huther Bros. Saw Mfg. Company
Jeffrey Manufacturing Company
Long Manufacturing Company, E.
Parry Sound Lumber Company
Payette Company, P.
Waterous Engine Works Company
Yates Machine Co., P. B.

SHEATHINGS
Goodyear Tire & Rubber Co.

SHINGLE MACHINES
Marsh Engineering Works, Limited

SAW SHARPENERS
Garlock-Walker Machinery Co.
Waterous Engine Works Company.

SAW SLASHERS
Waterous Engine-Works Company

SAWMILL LINK-BELT
Canadian Link-Belt Company

SHEET METALS
Syracuse Smelting Works

SHINGLES
Allan-Stoltze Lumber Co.
Associated Mills, Limited
Campbell-MacLaurin Lumber Co.
Cardinal & Page
Dominion Lumber & Timber Co.
Eagle Lumber Company
Foss Lumber Company
Fraser Limited.
Genoa Bay Lumber Company
Gillespie, James.
Gloucester Lumber Company
Grier & Sons, Ltd., G. A.
Harris Tie & Timber Company, Ltd.
Heeney, Percy E.
Long Lumber Company.
Mason, Gordon & Co.
McLennan Lumber Company.
Miller Company, Ltd., W. H.
Reynolds Company, Limited
Service Lumber Company
Shingle Agency of B. C.
Terry & Gordon.
Timms, Phillips & Co.
Vancouver Lumber Company.
Victoria Lumber and Mfg. Co.

SHINGLE & LATH MACHINERY
Dunbar Engine and Foundry Co.
Garlock-Walker Machinery Co.
Green Company, C. Walter
Hamilton Company, William.
Long Manufacturing Company, E.
Payette Company, P.

SILENT CHAIN DRIVES
Canadian Link-Belt Company, Ltd.

SILOS
Ontario Wind Engine Company

SLEEPING ROBES
Woods Mfg. Company, Limited

SMOKESTACKS
Marsh Engineering Works, Limited
Waterous Engine Works Company.

SNOW PLOWS
Pink Company, Thomas.

SPARK ARRESTORS
Jenckes Machine Company, Ltd.
Reed & Company, Geo. W.
Waterous Engine Works Company.

SPRUCE
Bartram & Ball.
Bourgouin, H.
Cane & Co., Jas. G.
Cardinal & Page
Davison Lumber & Mfg. Company
Donogh & Co., John.
Dudley, Arthur N.
Dunfield & Company
Exchange Lumber Company.
Foss Lumber Company
Fraser Limited.
Fraser-Bryson Lumber Company.
Gillies Brothers.
Gloucester Lumber Company
Grant & Campbell.
Grier & Sons, Ltd., G. A.
Hart & McDonagh.
Long Lumber Company.
Mason, Gordon & Co.
McLennan Lumber Company.
Muir & Kirkpatrick.
New Ontario Colonization Company.
River Ouelle Pulp and Lumber Co.
Russell, Chas. H.
Service Lumber Company
Shearer Company, Jas.
Snowball Co., J. B.
Spencer Limited, C. A.
Terry & Gordon.
The Rideau Lumber Company

STEEL CHAIN
Canadian Link-Belt Company, Ltd.
Jeffrey Manufacturing Company.
Waterous Engine Works Company.

STEEL PLATE CONSTRUCTION
Marsh Engineering Works, Limited

STEAM PLANT ACCESSORIES
Waterous Engine Works Company.

STEEL BARRELS
Smart-Turner Machine Co.

STEEL DRUMS
Smart-Turner Machine Co.

SWEAT PADS
American Pad & Textile Co.

SULPHITE PULP CHIPS
Davison Lumber & Mfg. Company

TANKS
Ontario Wind Engine Company

TARPAULINS
Turner & Sons, J. J.
Woods Manufacturing Company, Ltd.

TAPS AND DIES
Pratt & Whitney Company.

TENTS
Turner & Sons, J. J.
Woods Mfg. Company

TENTS, CLOTHING
Grant, Holden & Graham, Limited

TIES
Auger & Company
Austin & Nicholson.
Canadian Tie & Lumber Co.
Harris Tie & Timber Company, Ltd.
Long Lumber Company.
McLennan Lumber Company.
Terry & Gordon.

TIMBER BROKERS
Bradley, R. R.
Cant & Kemp.
Farnworth & Jardine.
Hunter, Herbert F.
Smith & Tyrer, Limited

TIMBER CRUISERS AND ESTIMATORS
Sewall, James W.

TIMBER LANDS
Department of Lands and Forests.

TRACTORS
British War Mission

TRANSMISSION MACHINERY
Canadian Link-Belt Company, Ltd.
General Supply Co. of Canada, Ltd.
Jenckes Machine Company, Ltd.
Jeffrey Manufacturing Company.
Waterous Engine Works Company.

TRIMMERS
Garlock-Walker Machinery Co.
Green Company, C. Walter
Waterous Engine Works Company

TUGS
West & Peachey.

TURBINES
Hamilton Company, William.
Jenckes Machine Company, Ltd.

VALVES
Bay City Foundry & Machine Co.

VENEERS
Webster & Brother, James.

VENEER DRYERS
Coe Manufacturing Company
Philadelphia Textile Mach. Co.

VENEER MACHINERY
Coe Manufacturing Company
Garlock-Walker Machinery Co.
Philadelphia Textile Machinery Co.

VETERINARY REMEDIES
Dr. Bell Veterinary Wonder Co.
Johnson, A. H.

WATER HEATERS
Mason Regulator & Engineering Co.

WATER WHEELS
Hamilton Company, William.
Jenckes Machine Company, Ltd.

WIRE
Laidlaw Bale Tie Company.

WOODWORKING MACHINERY
American Woodworking Machy. Co.
Garlock-Walker Machinery Co.
General Supply Co. of Canada, Ltd.
Jeffrey Manufacturing Company.
Long Manufacturing Company, E.
Mershon & Company, W. B.
Waterous Engine Works Company.
Yates Machine Company, P. B.

WOOD PRESERVATIVES
International Chemical Company

WOOD PULP
Austin & Nicholson.
New Ontario Colonization Co.
River Ouelle Pulp and Lumber Co.

The Home of "CONDOR" Belting

Made of 32 oz. duck and the best grade of rubber procurable.

Manufactured on giant presses weighing 550,000 pounds each, giving the greatest friction of any belt on the market.

The General Supply Company of Canada, Limited

OTTAWA MONTREAL TORONTO WINNIPEG VANCOUVER

Large Stocks Carried in Canada

Illustrating portable unit of Mathews Conveyor for unloading cars.

Photo by courtesy of [illegible] Lumber Co., Ltd., [illegible], Ont.

Illustrating permanent installation of Mathews Lumber Conveyor, between mill and shipping and distributing platform.

Photo by courtesy of [illegible] Cedar Mills, [illegible], B.C.

Write for Catalogue I.

CANADIAN MATHEWS GRAVITY CARRIER COMPANY, LIMITED

PORT HOPE - ONTARIO

The 1919 Model Kendall Circular Gang

A New Machine That IS New

This illustration shows the latest development of the Kendall Circular Gang.
It saws cants from 4 in. to 12 in. thickness at the rate of from 2500 to 8000 a day, will turn them into lumber, perfect in finish and cut evenly from end to end.
Big capacity on small logs, and lumber cut better than is possible on Band Saw, Circular or Vertical Gang, distinguish this machine.
It meets the demand for a machine that will turn small logs into merchantable lumber economically. Those already in use have proved their worth.

While all good points of previous models are retained, such weaknesses that use has made apparent have been eliminated. The new features and better construction of this 1919 Kendall Gang mean an appreciable increase in capacity, in [illegible] cutting ability, and in safety, convenience and sturdiness.

This latest development of the Kendall Gang patents is built in a shop that has specialized in high class machinery construction—that has built machinery for Canadian sawmills for more than seventy-five years. Our reputation is a guarantee that this New Model Kendall Gang is built as it should be.

When you investigate the Circular Gang question see that you get facts and figures of the "WATEROUS KENDALL GANG"—the New Machine that IS New.

MOLSONS BANK BUILDING VANCOUVER B. C. — WINNIPEG MAN.

Waterous

BRANTFORD, ONTARIO, CANADA

American Wood Working Machinery Co

Rochester, N. Y.

SALES OFFICE FOR BRITISH COLUMBIA, PORTLAND, OREGON
AGENTS FOR THE REST OF CANADA, GARLOCK-WALKER MACHINERY CO., TORONTO
AGENTS FOR GREAT BRITAIN, THE PROJECTILE CO., LONDON

American

features of an inside moulder and the slip-on head feature an outside moulder or profiler.

It is a high-duty machine with every convenience of adjustment at hand.

Get Circular of Garlock-Walker or write us direct—

Austin & Nicholson

CHAPLEAU, ONTARIO

Largest Producers of
RAILROAD TIES
in the Dominion

Pine and Spruce Lumber
Lath Piling
Railroad Ties
Pulpwood

First Class Planing-mill Equipment

Facilities for delivering Pulpwood to Michipicoten Harbour, Lake Superior

Splendid facilities for Dressing and Matching in straight car lots, one or more widths

Mills at NICHOLSON, ONTARIO, Main Line C.P.R.

Basswood

1 in., 1¼ in., 1½ in., 2 in., and 3 in., Dry Basswood

Dry Birch Stock

All thicknesses and grades in **Maple, Birch, Elm, Basswood** and **Brown Ash**
Also **Cottonwood, Tupelo, Gum, Magnolia** and **Buckeye**

Spruce, Hemlock and Pine

Can saw to order at MacDonald's Siding

Let us quote on your requirements

HART & McDONAGH

Temple Building, Cor. Bay and Richmond Streets
TORONTO, ONT.

We Handle Birch Also

Dry Stock on Hand for Quick Shipment

At Trout Creek, Ont.

60,000 ft. 4/4 No. 1 Com. & Bet. Birch.
66,000 " 5/4 " " " "
7,000 " 6/4 " " " "
26,000 " 8/4 " " " "
20,000 " 12/4 " " " "
14,000 " 16/4 " " " "
190,000 " 4/4 No. 2 & 3 Com. Birch.

At Lake Rosseau, Ont.

150,000 ft. 4/4 No. 3 Com. & Bet. Birch
45,000 " 5/4 No. 2 " " "
45,000 " 8/4 " " " "
15,000 " 10/4 No. 1 " " "
28,000 " 12/4 " " " "
15,000 " 16/4 " " " "

We advise Birch users to place their orders now. Immense quantities are being shipped to the United States and it is our opinion that prices will shortly advance from 10 to 25 per cent. in sympathy with American Hardwoods.

The Atlantic Lumber Company

310 Manning Chambers, TORONTO

Yards: BUFFALO, N.Y. **Mills: KNOXVILLE, Tenn.; FONDE, Kentucky.**

FOR SALE

500,000 ft. B.M.
3" SPRUCE
5" and up 8/16 feet

For particulars write—
THOS. HARLING & SON
(Lumber Dept.)
407 Board of Trade Building
MONTREAL

TIMBER LANDS

Bought and Sold

Timber and Pulp Wood Estimates

R. R. BRADLEY
Consulting Forester
58 Telegraph Building
Hospital St., MONTREAL

Manufacturers of
WIRE For TYING, BUNDLING and many other purposes. NAILS, Etc.
LAIDLAW BALE-TIE CO., Ltd.
HAMILTON, ONT.

USED SAW MILL MACHINERY

FOR SALE

Extra heavy log haul-up works with inch round and flat chain, 128 ft. centres.
2—Waterous log unloaders or kickers, 3 arms, 10 in. cylinders.
1—Waterous log loader, 3 arms, 10-in. cylinders.
1—Waterous right-hand double cutting band mill, 11 in. saws, 8 ft. wheel, with 8-block carriage; 24 in. opening; Payette set works and dogs; 8 in. x 36 ft. steam feed.
1—Waterous double edger for 20-inch saws, lever shifter.
1—Payette double edger for 18-in. saws, lever shifter.
48—live rolls about 8 ft. long by 10 in. dia.; extra heavy, sprocket drive.
1—Payette picket machine, made specially for shade roller stock, will feed pieces 16 in. long, also sorting table with chain top.
1—Payette edger for box and short stock.
1—Rogers twin circular or tie maker.
1—Payette lath bolter and lath machine.
1—Pair lath trimmers.
1—Picket trimmer (bunch trim),
—Pair Polson "Brown" type engines, coupled on quarters, 22 in. x 60 in., with 16 ft. x 48 in. belt, balance wheel. Excellent engines.
1—8 x 10 Centre Crank Engine.
1—10 x 14 Cowan Slide Valve Engine.
Pulleys, gears, heavy line shafting and countershafting with bearings.
Booms and boom chains, ½, ⅝ & ¾.
Winches and other mill supplies.
Prompt shipments and bargains for quick sale. Will send all particulars and prices on application.

Firstbrook Bros.
Limited
PENETANG

"WELL BOUGHT IS HALF SOLD"

We Have the Following Choice Hardwoods at One Point to Move Promptly

49M	4/4"	No. 2 Com. & Btr.	Birch
		About 15% No. 2 Common.	
16M	5/4"	No. 1 Com. & Btr.	Birch.
16M	6/4"	" "	" "
20M	8/4"	" "	" "
8½M	12/4"	" "	" "
7M	4/4"	No. 2 " "	Basswood
9½M	6/4"	No. 1 " "	"
11M	4/4"	No. 2 " "	Elm
4½M	6/4"	No. 1 " "	"

First Come

First Served

Canadian General Lumber Co.

Limited

FOREST PRODUCTS

TORONTO OFFICE:— 712-20 Bank of Hamilton Bldg.
Montreal Office:—203 McGill Bldg.
Mills: Byng Inlet, Ont.

PETRIE'S LIST

of
NEW and USED

WOOD TOOLS

for Immediate Delivery

Wood Lathes

20" Sidney, Famous
16" Cowan.
16" Sidney, Famous, patternmakers.

Band Saws

36" Sidney, Famous, pedestal.
32" Sidney, Famous, pedestal.
30" Cowan, bracket (2).
20" Sidney, Famous, pedestal.
60" Fay & Egan, band re-saw.

Saw Tables

No. 16 Sidney, Famous, variety.
No. 6 Sidney, Famous, variety.
No. 4 Sidney, Famous, combination.
Fisher, iron frame rip.
MacGregor-Gourlay power feed cut-off.
Greenlee automatic cut-off.
7' Williams, swing saw.
4' Sidney, Famous, swing saw.
Bench type, jig or scroll saw.

Wood Planers

26" double surfacer, with chip breaker.
24" Hermance, double surfacer.
24" Sidney, Famous, single surfacer.
24" Crescent, single surfacer.
24" MacGregor-Gourlay.
24" pony planer.
24" Champion planer and matcher, with moulding attachment.
24" Galt, planer and matcher.
18" Sidney Famous, single surfacer.
12" Buzz, with slotted head (2).
12" Petrie, buzz planers, safety heads (6)

Moulders

13" Clark-Demill four side.
12" Cowan four side.
12" Woods, four-side, inside.
8" Dundas four side.
6" Dundas sash sticker.

Mortisers

Cowan, upright power.
Galt, upright, compound table.
No. 1 Smart, foot power.
No. 2 Osborne, foot power.

Boring Machines

No. 7 Sidney, Famous, belt driven.
Gear driven, post borer.
Fay, single spindle, horizontal.
Jardine hub boring machine.

Clothespin Machinery

Humphrey automatic lathes (6).
Humphrey double slotters (3).

Miscellaneous

No. 30 Sidney, universal woodworker.
Vaughan, portable drag saw, power driven.
Champion, drag saw, friction feed.
Cowan moulder and panel raiser.
MacGregor Gourlay 12 spindle dovetailer.
Fay & Egan 12 spindle dovetailer.
No. 1 Ballantine dowel machine.
24" Fay, double drum sander.
M135 Cowan, sash and door relisher.
2-spindle Cant-Gourlay shaper.
No. 1 Defiance, axle shoulder shaper.
Superior saw arbors, 6"-30" saws (7).
M63 Cowan spindle carver.
Hall, automatic shingle machine.
Boss automatic shingle machine.
No. 2 Dominion, lath machine & bolter.
No. 3 Defiance, rim and felloe rounding machine.
24" Defiance shaft and pole tapering machine.
No. 1 Defiance, automatic, spoke driver.
8' Linderman, automatic, glue jointer.
8' McKeough & Trotter, hoop cutter.
No. 2 Reynolds, power screw driver.
Fal tenoner, double heads.
Dundas, wood frame tenoner.
6" American hardwood floor scraper.
3" x 7" universal wood trimmer.
20" American wood scraper.
Horizontal bracket carving machine.
No. 104 Covel, band saw roller.
No. 21 Covel, band saw filing clamp.

Ask to see our large stock of used supplies—belting, pulleys, machine shop equipment, mill supplies, pipe and fittings. Most of this material is as good as new and can be bought at greatly reduced prices.

H. W. PETRIE, LTD.
Front St. W., TORONTO, ONT.

SERVICE
Fir, Cedar and Spruce
LUMBER

"Service" Lumber Co.

Pacific Building, VANCOUVER, B.C.

Eastern Representative: A. W. BARNHILL, 20 St. James Street, Montreal.

Ontario Representative: A. E. MASURET, Canada Permanent Bldg., 18 Toronto St., Toronto. Telephone Main 2533

International Land & Lumber
Company, Limited

Lumber, Railway Ties Shims, Shingles, etc.

Head Offices, Ottawa, Ont.

Limits and Mills: ST. FELICIEN, LAKE ST. JOHN DISTRICT, QUEBEC

Our NEW TIMBER MILL

(Capacity 100,000 Feet Ten Hours.) NOW IN OPERATION

We solicit your enquiries for

Heavy Construction Material and Yard Stock

ANY SIZE TIMBERS UP TO 100 FT.

Give us an opportunity to prove to you that we have earned a reputation for Quality and Service.

Timberland Lumber Co., Limited

Head Office: Westminster Trust Bldg., NEW WESTMINSTER, B.C.

Mills at South Westminster, on B.C.E.R.

Shipments by C.P.R., C.N.R., G.N.R., N.P.R. and C.M. & St. P. Ry.

British Columbia Red Cedar Shingles

ARROW BRAND

XXX 6/2, Sixteen Inch All Clear and All Vertical Grain XXXXX 5/2

WHITE PINE

Cedar Spruce Hemlock Douglas Fir

Manufacturers and Wholesalers

Eastern Representative: R. G. CHESBRO, 1304 Bank of Hamilton Bldg., TORONTO, ONT.

Mills at Ruskin, Eburne, Nakusp, Summit, Vancouver.

ALLEN-STOLTZE LUMBER CO., LTD.

Vancouver, British Columbia

The Rat Portage Lumber Co., Limited, Vancouver

MANUFACTURERS OF

Douglas Fir, Spruce, Cedar and Hemlock Lumber

Rough Timbers, Dimension, Flooring, Ceiling, Siding, Interior and Exterior Finish of all kinds including Mouldings. Fir, Spruce and Cedar Lath

Prompt shipment of Fir timbers in all sizes and up to 100 feet in length

AIR DRIED CEDAR SHINGLES We specialize in supplying air dried Cedar Shingles, these cost more than kiln dried Shingles but make a better roof and last much longer

---

The following cars are now in transit:

Car No. 142081	8/4"	FAS Plain White Oak, good widths	13,000'
" " 70221	8/4"	FAS and Selects " " "	17,000'
" " 4517	5/4"	FAS Plain Red " " "	2,541'
	5/4"	Selects " " " "	4,000'
	6/4"	FAS " " " "	4,700'
	6/4"	Selects " " " "	1,470'
" " 33783	4/4"	FAS and Selects Plain White Oak, good widths	15,253'
" " 121307	4/4"	No. 1 Common Plain Red Oak	13,000'
" " 204782	8/4"	Sound Wormy Chestnut	10,000'
" " 18089	8/4"	" " "	20,000'
" " 17700	8/4"	" " "	15,434'
" " 6081	8/4"	" " "	16,700'
" " 91352	6/4"	" " "	13,000'
" " 120259	6/4"	" " "	17,500'
" " 79483	6/4"	" " "	18,000'
" " 40441	5/4"	" " "	14,000'
" " 74440	5/4"	" " "	13,000'
" " 21087	5/4"	" " "	13,000'
" " 504	4/4"	" " "	14,000'
" " 220817	4/4"	" " "	17,000'

Write, wire or phone for prices.

PERCY E. HEENEY, Wholesale Lumber
207 Weber Chambers, KITCHENER, Ont.

I HAVE IT

All Grades in White Pine
Lath A Specialty

Milling in Connection

E. J. MOOR
MIDLAND CANADA

LET'S GET ETHER

Planing Mill Stock

CYPRESS

Soft, Dry Stock, Finest Grades—
All Thicknesses— 4/4, 5/4, 6/4, 8/4, 10/4, 12/4

Yellow Pine Finish

Kiln Dried, Soft, Short Leaf Kind
Stock Widths 4/4, 5/4, 6/4, 8/4 by 4", 6", 8", 10", 12"

Also OAK, ASH, POPLAR, GUM

WISTAR, UNDERHILL & NIXON
Real Estate Trust Bldg., Philadelphia, Pa.

We Specialize in—

New Brunswick White Cedar Shingles

We also manufacture
Spruce and Pine Lumber, Lath, Cedar Ties, etc.

Shipments by Rail and Water.

W. H. MILLER CO., LTD.
Campbellton, N. B.

Consult us About Your **HORSEFEED**

A part of our service is catering to the requirements of the lumbermen.
We can supply the first quality

HAY, GRAIN and FEED

at lowest market prices. Prompt delivery assured on all orders, large and small. Write or wire for prices.

James Scott & Co., Limited
651 St. James Street, MONTREAL

QUALITY DRY STOCK

For Immedi Shipment

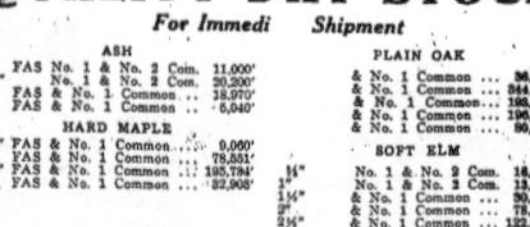

ASH

1"	FAS No. 1 & No. 2 Com.	11,000'
1¼"	No. 1 & No. 2 Com.	20,200'
2"	FAS & No. 1 Common ..	18,970'
4"	FAS & No. 1 Common ..	6,040'

HARD MAPLE

1¼"	FAS & No. 1 Common	9,060'
2"	FAS & No. 1 Common ...	78,551'
2½"	FAS & No. 1 Common ...	195,784'
3"	FAS & No. 1 Common ...	32,908'

PLAIN OAK

	& No. 1 Common ...	36,716'
	& No. 1 Common ...	344,387'
	& No. 1 Common ...	193,625'
	& No. 1 Common ...	196,222'
	& No. 1 Common ...	90,720'

SOFT ELM

¾"	No. 1 & No. 2 Com.	16,400'
1"	No. 1 & No. 2 Com.	13,460'
1½"	& No. 1 Common ...	30,380'
2"	& No. 1 Common ...	78,968'
2½"	& No. 1 Common ...	122,900'
3"	& No. 1 Common ...	141,149'

Service marks every order that we fill

John I. Shafer Hardwood Co., South Bend IND.

DOMINION LUMBER SALES LTD.

SUCCESSORS TO

Dominion Lumber and Timber Co., Limited

We control the output of two operating mills and are in a position to give immediate delivery

We specialize on timber orders **We can ship shingles immediately**

Enquiries solicited by letter or telegram at our expense

209 Winch Building, **VANCOUVER, B.C.**

L. N. GODFREY COMPANY

are in the

MARKET

for

Merchantable Spruce

by water or rail in the following sizes :

2 x 3 P1E	4 x 6 P1S
2 x 4 P1E	1½" x 4' No. 1 Lath
3 x 4 P1E	1⅝" x 4' " "
2 x 6 and wider	

Also Shingles, and Hemlock Boards, P1S random or stock lengths.

We will give prompt attention to quotations on these and other items.

In replying give description of lengths, state whether rough or dressed, etc.

60 Congress St., BOSTON, MASS.

51 EAST 42nd ST., NEW YORK CITY, N. Y

Pine Spruce Hemlock Ties

Always on hand ready to ship promptly

Send us your enquiries

BIRCH for Export

Our Specialty

ROCH JULIEN

76 St. Peter St. - QUEBEC

The Peter Hay Knife Co., Limited

GALT, ONTARIO

MANUFACTURING WOODWORKING

Machine Knives, Circular Cutters and Mortise Chisel

Emery and Corundum Wheels

You will find our product the best for quality and service in the lumber camp.

Send us your orders and we will ship promptly.

Vitrified Silicate

Brantford Emery Wheel Co. Limited

Brantford - Ontario

W. C. Edwards & Co. Limited

Wholesale Lumber

OTTAWA -:- CANADA

White and Red Pine, Spruce, Hemlock, Lath, Shingles, Bo
Box Shooks, Factory Material

Write us your requirements. **Planing Mill, Ottawa an Rockland**

DRESSING IN TRANSIT

Our new and efficient facilities make it possible to do your milling in transit quickly and at low cost. Prompt service is assured by three railway lines.

We are always glad to quote you very attractive prices and show you the quality of our work.

Ask Lumbermen who know and they will tell you to

TRY

Renfrew Planing Mill

Renfrew, Ontario

We offer the following stock for immediate delivery

2	cars	2"	Beech, No. 2 and Better.
10	"	1"	Beech, No. 2 and Better.
10	"	1"	Maple, No. 2 and Better.
1	"	1½"	Birch, F.A.S.
2	"	1"	Birch, F.A.S.
1	"	2"	Birch, F.A.S., 10" and up.
2	"	1½"	Soft Elm, No. 2 and Better.
10	"	1"	Soft Elm, No. 2 and Better.
2	"	1"	Soft Elm, No. 2 and No. 3 Common.
5	"		Cedar Posts, 4½" and up x 8 ft., Peeled.

Send us your enquiries

The Pedwell Hardwood Lumber Co.
79 Spadina Ave. - TORONTO

EXCELSIOR LUMBER CO.

33 RICHMOND ST. WEST, TORONTO

CAN SUPPLY YOU WITH

Spruce and Jack Pine Piling, 25 to 40 feet long.
Cedar Posts, 8 feet long.
2 cars 1½ inch Basswood, No. 2 Com. and Better.
100,000 feet 1 x 4 to 12 10/16 M.R. White Pine.
100,000 feet 2 x 4 to 12 10/16 M.R. White Pine.

The Fesserton Timber Company, Limited

Large Stock

White Pine-Red Pine-Spruce-Hemlock

Attractive Prices - Quick Shipment
Western Office - - Vancouver, B.C.

15 Toronto Street, MAIN 795-6 TORONTO

Putting Lumber Where It Belongs

Our Nationally Known Products--

Southern Pine Lumber
Oak, Oak Flooring, Gum,
Creosoted Posts,
Poles, Ties, Piling and
Wood Blocks
California White Pine

You buy and sell other trade-marked nationally advertised materials.

Comes now trade-marked, nationally advertised lumber--and Lumber is the biggest item you handle.

From actual experience you know the distinct advantage a nationally known branded product has over the unknown, unbranded, unadvertised product.

Consider lumber--

Isn't it, too, worthy of the good name of its manufacturer?
Wouldn't the name on lumber carry to the consumer and to you the same assurance of excellence that a good name does on paint, on hardware?

The Long-Bell Lumber Company

R. A. Long Bldg. Kansas City, Mo.

British Timber Importers and [illegible]

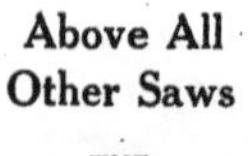

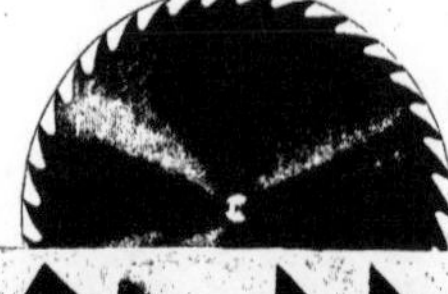

Quality,
Efficiency and
Power in

The Saws that have been made right since 1832 are standard of quality and are built on honor. They are dependable saws that cut smooth, saw fast, and are unusually successful on all kinds of cutting jobs. Whether it be a Solid Tooth Circular, Inserted Tooth Circular or Band Saw, you are assured of Quality and full value if you use a Simonds, the popular saw among Mill operators, Lumbermen and Sawyers, because it holds its tension and does not crack.

WRITE FOR PRICES.

Simond's Canada Saw Company, Limited

"The Saw Makers"

VANCOUVER, B.C. MONTREAL, Que. ST. JOHN, N.B.

In the United States—SIMONDS MANUFACTURING COMPANY

Feeding the Camp

IF that is your problem, remember that it is our business, too. We do a tremendous lumber camp trade and are fully acquainted with the food requirements of logging camps. We shall be glad to quote you on any lines you need this year, and will submit special quotations if you will drop us a card. We can supply you with all that's best in provisions and fresh meats, and give you a service you will appreciate.

WRITE OR WIRE US AT OUR EXPENSE—TODAY

LONG CLEAR BACON
BARRELED PORK
SAUSAGE
DAVIES PURE LARD
"PEERLESS" SHORTENING
MINCEMEAT, ETC.

THE WILLIAM **DAVIES** COMPANY LIMITED

MONTREAL TORONTO WINNIPEG

Canada Lumberman and Woodworker

Issued on the 1st and 15th of every month by
HUGH C. MACLEAN, LIMITED, Publishers
HUGH C. MacLEAN, Winnipeg, President.
THOS. S. YOUNG, Toronto, General Manager.

OFFICES AND BRANCHES:
TORONTO - - Telephone A. 2700 - - 347 Adelaide Street West
VANCOUVER - - Telephone Seymour 2013 - - Winch Building
MONTREAL - - Telephone Main 2299 - - 119 Board of Trade
WINNIPEG - Telephone Garry 856 - Electric Railway Chambers
NEW YORK - - - - - - - - - - - 309 Broadway
CHICAGO - Telephone Harrison 5351 - 1413 Great Northern Building
LONDON, ENG. - - - - - - - - - 16 Regent Street, S.W.

TERMS OF SUBSCRIPTION
Canada, United States and Great Britain, $2.00 per year, in advance; other foreign countries embraced in the General Postal Union, $3.00.
Single copies 15 cents.

"The Canada Lumberman and Woodworker" is published in the interest of, and reaches regularly, persons engaged in the lumber, woodworking and allied industries in every part of Canada. It aims at giving full and timely information on all subjects touching these interests, and invites free discussion by its readers.

Advertisers will receive careful attention and liberal treatment. For manufacturing and supply firms wishing to bring their goods to the attention of owners and operators of saw and planing mills, woodworking factories pulp mills, etc., "The Canada Lumberman and Woodworker" is undoubtedly the most direct and profitable advertising medium. Special attention is directed to the "Wanted" and "For Sale" advertisements.

Authorized by the Postmaster-General for Canada, for transmission as second-class matter.

Entered as second-class matter July 18th, 1914, at the Postoffice at Buffalo, N.Y., under the Act of Congress of March 3, 1879.

Vol. 39 Toronto, October 1, 1919 No. 19

The Significance of Fire Prevention Day

The Privy Council has appointed October 9 as "Fire Prevention Day," on which date the attention of the public will be specially directed to the extent of preventable losses of life and property by fire, and the best means of controlling it. The idea is that once every year the public should be forcibly reminded of the losses incurred by fire, and also instruction given as to how these can be avoided.

All sections of the lumber industry are greatly interested in this subject. The losses by the destruction of lumber yards and sash and door and other woodworking factories are enormous, and a considerable proportion of these can no doubt be eliminated if proper care be taken. We need not point out the immense destruction of timber limits—due to carelessness on the part of settlers, campers, fishermen, etc. In the St. Maurice district the railways have been the most prolific sources of fires. The Canadian Forestry Association, the St. Maurice Forest Protective Association, and other similar associations have done very valuable educational work through lectures and various forms of literature. Formerly, there was a feeling of antagonism to these efforts to lessen preventable losses, but the educational work has succeeded in convincing many of the settlers that the fires are an economic loss not only to the timber limit holders, but to the people who are dependent upon woods operations for at least a portion of their living.

Timber limit holders who neglect means to protect their forests not only endanger their own property, but those of the owners adjoining. Once a fire is started, there is no telling to what extent it will spread, unless means are at hand to check the outbreak. The Quebec Government recognized this, and last session introduced a Bill to compel holders of licenses who cut timber on Crown lands to patrol their limits, with rangers appointed by the government. If a license holder fails to employ the rangers, the Minister of Lands and Forests has power to employ them, and charge the cost to the license holder.

Canada has a very bad record in the matter of fires, not taking into account the forest fires. In 1918 over thirty million dollars were lost, competent authorities estimating that at least 75 per cent. of this was preventable. There is thus a large field for education on this subject, and the government is doing a real service to the country in trying to impress on the people the importance of preventing the loss of human life and the necessity of the conservation of material wealth. We are every day being reminded of the imperativeness of greater production—the preservation of existing wealth is equally urgent, especially when it is remembered that the destruction by fire is mainly due to preventable causes.

The Perplexing Problem of Existence

It is rather amusing to hear "the pot call the kettle black," yet this is what lessee and lessor are doing today. With a scarcity of houses in every town, and the mad rush to rent anything in the shape of a habitation, rentals have naturally climbed rapidly. It is the old law of supply and demand, and just now the demand happens to be much larger and more insistent than the supply. Landlords have been stigmatized by tenants as being profiteers, extortioners, tyrants and everything else that these terms imply. On the other hand, landlords are rejoining that there is very little money in leasing a dwelling, even at the present high values obtaining, as plumbing has increased more than 100 per cent., while a decorator asks from 75c to 80c an hour, and carpenters the same. Then taxes have taken a jump, while lumber, glass, paint and other things that go to keep a place in habitable condition have ascended so quickly that one is not aware of the sharp advance until rudely up against it. Real estate agents declare that there has been little profiteering among the landlords, and that the leased house is no gold-mine nowadays.

This brings up the whole question of the trend of people in general. Immediately after the outbreak of the war, when a panic seemed to seize the busines world, industries restricted operations, and many residents went to the front, there was a decided drop in rents in every large city. It was then that many possessors of homes thought they were making a mistake in carrying a house as it was much cheaper to live in a dwelling owned by someone else, pay a moderate rent and get rid of all the exactions entailed by a steadily ascending tax rate, local improvement levies and increased assessment.

Now the pendulum has swung the other way, and owing to the abnormal advances in rents, persons are rushing around in all directions to purchase houses, which, due to the heavy outlay of materials and labor, are commanding a greater figure than ever before. The whole question has been discussed in the press, and no satisfactory answer has been arrived at regarding the necessity of some restrictive legislation in the matter of rents. The solution of the problem to lease or to buy at the present time is perplexing, and as affording some light on the situation, one real estate agent said recently: "Let any man build a solid brick, eight roomed house today and attempt to rent it at $30 per month and he would not make 2 per cent. net profit on his investment." In years gone by 10 per cent. has been accounted a moderate return for house owners on their investment in property, but it is doubtful, even with rentals almost double to what they were, whether with the net income, when repairs, cost of materials, wages, etc., are taken into consideration, there is any short route to wealth in erecting and maintaining the ordinary six and eight roomed dwellings for tenants.

Landmarks in the Lumber Industry

We are becoming a nation with a past, and many of the institutions of the present are being linked up with historic interest. We speak of the Dominion as a young country—one with a great future before it—and seem to forget that our present status has been brought about through the heroic efforts and sturdy independence, splendid endurance and sustained self-denial of those who have gone before. Few of these pioneers are alive today to tell the tale of what they have accomplished, and leave only their records. Others are able, by means of the spoken word, to join in significant events which have been commemorated during the past few weeks.

Price Bros. & Company, of Quebec, have just celebrated the centennial of their existence, and the present head of this aggressive concern, Sir William Price, is a grandson of the doughty founder. At Rockland the other day the 50th anniversary of the building of the first sawmill in that progressive town was observed with enthusiasm and grateful appreciation of Hon. W. C. Edwards, of Ottawa, originator of the busy industries bearing his name. Mr. Edwards was present, and, after the long lapse of years since the inception of the mill, is in excellent health. He had the pleasure of being surrounded with a number of those who were co-laborers in early days in laying the foundation and erecting the timbers. The remarks made by the Senator on that occasion in reviewing his life history should prove an incentive to every worker of the present period.

Another lumberman who is still very much in the thick of the fray and has been a resident of the capital city of Ottawa for 62 years, where from a small shingle mill he has reared the vast enterprises that cover scores of acres at the Chaudiere, is the venerable J. R. Booth. Mr. Booth is never quite so happy as when supervising some construction work or going through the various departments of his great industries, seeing that everything is moving along with the utmost precision and maximum production of which modern machinery is capable.

Thus the lumber industry has attained an important and far-reaching development in Canada, and some of those associated with it over half a century ago, are still prominent figures in the business life of the day. All honor to them for the worth and work they have exemplified in careers that are outstanding, unique and inspiring in purpose and achievement.

Will Pulp Solve High Living Costs?

Sir George Bury is becoming equally as enthusiastic a pulp and paper man as he was a few months ago in railway affairs and administration. The former C. P. R. magnate is now president and executive head of the Whalen Pulp & Paper Mills, Vancouver, and foresees a great future for this industry. In fact, so optimistic is he that he believes pulp and its products will finally solve the high cost of living, and everybody hopes if this is the final solution of this perplexing problem that it may come speedily. The householder, the wage-earner, the buyer of wearing apparel and many other classes of citizens, will read with interest and satisfaction an interview which was recently had with Sir George. The only ones who will be alarmed by his prophetic utterance are the laundry proprietors and crockery manufacturers.

Here is the statement, and it shows that Sir George is not only a great booster for Canadian pulp, but also for the province of British Columbia:—"The pulp industry is in its infancy. It is in the same position as steel was twenty-five years ago. Paper made from pulp has been employed to make wheels on Pullman cars. In a few years everything we wear will be made of pulp. Five years from now the housekeeper will have all her kitchen utensils made of pulp. The laundry will largely disappear, because our underclothes, shirts, collars, tablecloths, napkins, etc., will be made from pulp.

British Columbia will produce the pulp for the world, because nowhere else in the world is there grown better wood than the Sitka spruce, found on the British Columbia Coast. Sitka spruce has the longest and strongest fibre of any wood, and was used exclusively in the manufacture of airplanes. It makes the strongest and whitest pulp, as strong as the pulp made by the Egyptians from linen in the form of papyrus. Nowhere in the world is there such a generous supply of pure water. One hundred thousand gallons is needed to make a ton of pulp. I believe that pulp will finally solve the high cost of living."

Editorial Short Lengths

The average wage of the United States railway employee now is $40 a week, or $2,000 a year. This is an increase of 100 per cent. Canadian railwaymen get about the same rate. The railways used to pay under rather than over the average commercial scale, but government operation has changed all that.

* * *

The late Hon. Peter Mitchell, a former Canadian politician, who used to style himself "the third party," had a favorite epigram to the effect that the best argument in the world is a bank account. Most sufferers from the high cost of living at the present day will agree that there is both point and wisdom in his observation.

* * *

Lumber and forest products form important items in our export trade. The figures for August show that they were in that month, as third on the list, ranking after animal products, with agricultural products in the first place. The total value was $20,982,228, against $14,790,014 in the corresponding month in 1918. The figures for July were about $2,000,000 better than for the same month in 1918.

* * *

The Montreal Board of Trade has decided to protest against the Bill providing that water carriers be placed under the control of the Railway Commissioner with regard to tolls and tariffs. It is contended that the jurisdiction which it would give the Board of Railway Commissioners over tolls and tariffs on freight traffic carried by water between ports in Canada, would tend to limit competition between the water carriers themselves, which in turn would tend to decrease the competition between water carriers and the railways, a condition which would almost invitably result in increased freight rates.

* * *

In reviewing conditions in the paper trade at the annual meeting of the association of wholesale dealers in that line, held lately in Montreal, President John F. Ellis, of Toronto, made some pointed observations in regard to the present position and future of Canada, which, he asserted, was in many ways tied up with the paper business. Mr. Ellis stated that the public debt of the Dominion is $1,800,000,000, an amount equal to the gross deposits of all the chartered banks in the land, as compared with $350,000,000 before the war. The reduction of this debt is a question in which every business man, individually, and every trade, collectively, is vitally interested. To pay this debt we must export more and import less. Not only must we seek to supply our own needs, but we must sell more and more of our products to the other nations of the world. The question of export trade is one which more closely affects the mill than it does the merchant, but in that of imports we have a lively interest. It is to the great credit of this young country that to-day our Canadian mills are manufacturing paper which is the equal of any in the world. There is no truer method of showing our Canadian patriotism, there is nothing we can do to help the industry in which we are so concerned, and the country which we so dearly love than to sell to our customers paper made in Canada by Canadian workmen.

It is gratifying to note in passing that imports of paper into Canada have been showing a steady decline, while exports have shown just as satisfactory an increase. During our last fiscal year, for instance, we exported approximately $100,000,000 worth of pulp, paper and pulp wood—truly a gigantic total, and a banner year for the industry. While the record for the past three months does not indicate that this figure will be reached this year, owing to the close of the war having created new conditions with our best customer, the United States, there is every reason to believe that Canada will continue in the front rank of the world's suppliers of pulp and paper. Dominion legislation prohibiting the export of pulp wood would go a long way toward still further enhancing this total in dollars. If our parliament could reach the conclusion that this country, which is blessed by nature with such a limitless store of raw material for paper, would export this material only in the form of the finished article a new chapter would be written in the history of the paper industry in Canada.

Britain Much Interested in Ontario Woods

Mr. Manbert Gives Vivid Impressions of General Conditions and Market Situation in Old Country—Recuperative Processes Not as Rapid as Expected

A. C. Manbert, Toronto, Ont.

After six months spent in Great Britain and on the Continent, Mr. A. C, Manbert, of Toronto, who has been doing effective propaganda work in England in the interest of Ontario forest products, has returned home and resumed his former duties as president of the Canadian General Lumber Co. Mr. Manbert was accorded a splendid reception in the Old Country and found all classes of people greatly interested in the Dominion while everywhere Canadians are enthusiastically received and the heroic part they played in the European conflict written large on the page of memory and gratitude.

Touching, upon conditions in the Mother Country Mr. Manbert, in conversation with the "Canada Lumberman," said: "The situation has been much more involved, and the process of turning over from the long concentration upon war business to peace times has been a much more difficult process than most men have imagined, and certainly more difficult than we all had hoped. The genesis of the matter is psychological, because you have to get out of the one mental attitude which developed great tensions and great concentrations, into an entirely different one; all of which is joined in an escape from a situation which was built upon conditions, so to speak, of Governmental direction and urge, and which now, in the liberation of the control of all men's minds and activities, finds in this readjustment great difficulty in accomplishing the new meshings of the cogs of the machinery.

"In concrete facts, it turns upon the attitudes of labor, the resulting costs of materials and the financial considerations which are embodied in exchange. Transportation also has played its tremendous, and for the time being its controlling part, because we were unable to take over to the people, as fast as they wanted it, the materials that they wanted, and now that transportation has somewhat improved, situations of port congestion and general unpreparedness of labor and facilities to carry the materials to their ulitmate places of consumption are creating great disarrangements and difficulties and blockades.

Cordial Attitude and Friendly Interest.

"The attitude of the British public is, as I have previously stated in my letters, most cordially directed towards this continent as a source of supply, so that fro mthe standpoint of friendly interest the trade instinct naturally runs this way. The two cotnrolling reasons which made me feel that it was desirable for me to return at this time were, that the general resumptive processes over there being so much slower and more difficult than we had hoped and desired, there was, from that point of view, less reason for me to remain, because the thing must work itself out in the development of time; and, on the other hand, the very marked change in conditions at home has undoubtedly tempered the acute interest which we had when I left here, in that market; so that, for the time being at least, we had lost the keen desire which we had for the European business. Whatever may be our ultimate purposes and expectations, for the immediate moment we are so overwhelmed and conecrned with the business which lies directly at hand here that I did not feel that we had either the material or the inclination to pursue the business with the ardor which was contemplated when I went over there."

The General Situation Summed Up.

Mr. Manbert's views in regard to the general situation in England are more completely outlined in a letter which he wrote before leaving the Old Country. This letter, which was diretced to the Minister of Lands, Forests and Mines and to the Chairman and Secretary of the Organization of Lumber Manufacturers who cooperated to send him on the mission, is, in part, as follows:

It is hard for us in Ontario to realize the degree to which some businesses have been suspended during the war, by reason both of absorption of their entire staff in war work, and also in some cases by the practical cessation of all opportunity for business. This necessitates the establishment of new relationships and has brought to me a number of people who are practically starting anew, and are anxious to learn about Ontario's sources of supply in timber and timber products.

Interviews of my soliciting have been intended to embrace every angle that is of particular interest, and have included Government and Shipping Officials, men of affairs who would be informed on British policies, agents and distributors in the timber trade, and merchants and manufacturers in whose business, timber figures either prominently or incidentally.

All of this has meant considerable travelling and I have covered England and Scotland quite thoroughly. In every case, have I received that courteous and enquiring consideration which has from the first marked the attitude of the people here, and which I feel that I can never quite adequately acknowledge.

I was, it is true, pleased to feel that, in some cases at least, my observations if not new, had an interest in coming from a fresh quarter, from the producer rather than the merchant. But always, and beyond this, I was made conscious of the magic potency of the name Canada. It was ever the "open sesame" that unlocked reserve and accredited my introduction. This sympathetic favour really amounts to a practical obsession "Canada has the preference" is the statement in variable forms which I continually hear.

Dissatisfaction Over White Pine Distribution.

When I wrote you last, I remarked that the local demand was generally good, and for White Pine, very keen. This condition still persists, and Idono t think it can be said as yet that the edge has been taken off the consumers' appretite. Indeed, in respect to White Pine, the method which the Timber Controller is taking of rationing his incoming stock, with selling prices stipulated, to certain distributors who have heretofore figured largely in the distribution of White Pine, has led to a good deal of dissatisfaction and criticism. Complaint has been bitterly made that the favoured ones have received an undue share of this much desired wood, to the serious disadvantage of others. So keen is the demand, it is probably true that but for the arrangement by the Controller, prices would have advanced considerably in excess of those named by him, and as it is. there are numerous charges of profiteering.

I can imagine it difficult to discuss food values or food discriminations with a hungry man. He wants any food rather than some particular variety. Perhaps, in this figure, you will understand my feeling that at the moment in the matter of Pine lumber, people are interested in getting any kind of Pine rather than some particular kind. And so, while they discuss earnestly questions of the future supply, it is the difficulties which lie in the way of resumption of business that so absorbingly engross them. In saying this, you will quite misunderstand my intention, if I seem to suggest that the discussions have had a limited scope. On the contrary, they have embraced a wide range of enquiry concerning both our immediate operating conditions and potential capacity for the future. The belief is general that the scene is laid for a great demand, but the immediate acute shortage overshadows this in present interest. terest.

In this matter of future business, I may here remark that when once time and untensioned restrictions give it free play to develop, I am satisfied it will have a broader range, both as to inquiry and personnel. The quickened interest of now engaged parties as well as the instinct of the less well established or unestablished, for new relationships guarantee this. Not all of these last named bear the hallmark of competence and promise, but their influence in stimulating salesmanship and practices is not to be overlooked.

Not Much Done Yet in Housing Line.

The housing programme I have followed with considerable interest. The complexities are many and I regret to report that progress is slow. While the Government has given some orders for bricks and doors in anticipation of their use, to satisfy the clamour of unemployed facilities, practically no real construction has begun, and it looks doubtful if very much will be accomplished this year.

The local factories are here again crying loudly against the importation of any manufactured articles, to appease which the Government has had to announce that all joinery will be of home manufacture. It is, however, pretty generally conceded that local facilities are quite inadequate to any extended consumption, and I am certain that a large market will exist for doors and sash when once building assumes substantial proportions. This is a matter that our Ontario factories should take cognisance of, and by keeping in touch with the situation prepare themselves to step in when the opportune moment arrives.

In respect to the use of Pine for doors and joinery work, while its superiority as a wood is well recognized here, I regret that familiarity with the Baltic Whitewood and Redwood has led people to be satisfied with the poorer qualities of these woods for this use, so that Pine does not enjoy the favour and vogue which is the case with us at home. On account of this, some of the specifications which have already been drawn for joinery work quite ignored our Canadian woods, and only specified Redwood and Whitewood from Scandinavia. I have promptly made this an occasion for protest, and am happy to say that these specifications have been changed so that our woods rank equally in the prescriptions.

The Smaller Lines of Wood Goods

Turned Goods, Small Wares and Miscellaneous Wood Manufacture.—In the past Britain has imported a vast amount of turned goods of all kinds, such as dowels, handles, pins, and so forth; likewise, various manufactures such as step-ladders, benches, drawing boards, and a host of articles of this sort. There are a number of concerns throughout the Kingdom who devote themselves largely to this class of business, and I have received many enquiries from parties who are anxious to get in touch with Canadian sources of supplies. Formerly, a considerable part of this business went to the States, but here again the import restrictions interfere, and quite apart from sympathetic considerations, Canada enjoys an unusual preference at this particular moment. One party, since calling on me has left for Canada and will visit the people to whom I have referred him. Others have expressed the same interest, and I have no doubt will follow the matter up exhaustively if they receive any reasonable inducement. It will, therefore, give me much satisfaction to lay this matter before our people who may be interested.

In all the foregoing I have attempted as briefly as possible, to summarize the subjects which I have followed up. There are others, but these are the chief ones. Some of the subjects are, of course, only indirectly of interest to our lumbermen, but they are directly of interest to the Province. Anything which came under the head of "Forest Products" has therefore received my careful attention.

Difficulties in Business Rehabilitation.

The interviews which I have had have been most interesting in throwing light upon the tremendous problems and difficulties that lie in the way of resumption and rehabilitation of business. I wish it were possible for me to give you some of the details of these various interviews, because it would bring to you more vividly the local atmosphere, and quite apart from information and intellectual interest, would help you to understand and appreciate perhaps more than you do, the distinct advantage which we, in our freer and less restrained situation, enjoy in the recovery of our normal and natural business life.

Shipping.—You are quite aware that this problem has not improved, as was hoped, and that the rates, instead of decreasing, have increased since I last wrote. As if this situatoin were not bad enough, port congestion is now becoming serious, and this again is going to affect both freights and quantities of imports, because the physical difficulty of handling the goods in the ports cuts both ways.

What, with labor difficulties, adverse exchange, and food and coal shortage, it is evident that the people of this country have got to put up with many inconveniences and disappointments for some time yet. To me, it becomes increasingly apparent that the signing of peace is only an incident and not an epoch in ending the effects of war, and that resumptions and recoveries here will unfortunately be much slower than we have so ardently desired. This is not to say that progress is not being made, nor that ultimately a tremendous business is not to result, because when once these many wrinkles in production are ironed out and processes attain their normal facility, the satisfying of the many deferred desires and needs is bound to create an activity that will probably last for several years.

In this, without attempting to prophesy, unavoidable changes in methods and relationships will work themselves out gradually with the readjustment, and with it all, to the extent that we are prepared to enter, we may share in this great business.

A Position of Favor and Promise

This brings me to the point which has given me much concern. If I have at all succeeded in making things appear to you as they do to me, you will agree that for the future we have a position of favors and promise in this market, but that at the immediate moment we have reached a sort of "impasse." The Timber Controller will not be successful in getting all his purchasers brought forward this season, and until controlled stocks are forwarded and distributed, new purchases and any real outlooking interest of private purchasers must be very limited. Any hopes that we had for new and unusual purchases by either private parties or the Government for the Housing programme have been resigned. In a word, recuperative processes, as I have already stated, are much slower than we commonly imagined they would be. The country is gropingly trying to "find itself." In a sense it is "marking time," and we must mark time with it.

All of this effectually, and for an indefinite period, limits my efforts in a way which I cannot complacently accept. Propaganda work of itself is only important when it leads to definitely productive results. My time is too valuable to spend on it alone. Besides, as an effort it canot endure without something to keep it vitalized—concrete results to give it life.

Conditions are also very different at home from what they were when I left. Recent advices from Ontario, Eastern Canada and the States indicate that for this year, at least, the market on the American Continent will qualify, for the time, the very acute interest we had in the export field, when I came over.

Upon my return I shall be prepared to report in detail upon all of the subjects upon which I have touched. I hope that the investigations I have made and the information acquired can be used to advantage to increase the trade with this great country, and to further the friendly interest in Canada which I have everywhere here found so abounding.

Lumbermen Gather at Festive Board

Stirring Addresses Delivered by Hon. Mr Ferguson, Mr. Manbert and Others on Export Trade Prospects

Representative lumbermen from various parts of Ontario assembled around the festive board at the King Edward hotel, Toronto, on Sept. 24th to listen to a most instructive, interesting and comprehensive address from A. C. Manbert, of Toronto, who recently returned from the Old Country where he spent several months as Ontario Timber Commissioner. Mr. Manbert who was engaged in propaganda work in the interest of forest products of the province, was cordially welcomed home by his confreres and was heard to splendid advantage in his remarks which, while covering to some extent matters that have already been outlined in able letters from his pen to the "Canada Lumberman" presented several new phases of the present situation with respect to industry, enterprise, reconstruction and national spirit and ideals as reflected in the British people.

After a full measure of justice had been done to the many attractive items on the bill-of-fare a toast to "The King" was honored.

W. E. Bigwood, chairman of the committee of the Ontario lumber manufacturers, who had the arrangements in hand, briefly but touchingly referred to the death of Hon. Frank Cochcrane, former Minister of Lands and Forests for the province of Ontario. "He was one of the big men in Canadian public life," declared the speaker, "a man of sterling qualities of character, who was loyal to the public interests and to his friends. The late Mr. Cochrane was always interested in the welfare and progress of the lumbermen and I would ask that you honor his memory by a silent toast." The members complied with the request of the chairman.

Mr. Manbert was then called upon by the chairman who stated that, when it was decided to send Mr. Manbert overseas in the interests of the timber trade of the province, it was understood that he was to stay away for a year or return in less time, if he deemed it advisable. He had come back at the end of six months "and he is here," added Mr. Bigwood, "to tell us why he is back and what he found out over there."

Mr. Manbert was given a most cordial reception as he rose to reply and spoke most interestingly of the work which he had carried out, a general outline of which is given in the interview with him on the preceding pages. He amplified this in not a few instances and dealt with some new phases of the problems, both present and prospective, which Canada and the Mother country would in the course of post-war development be called upon to solve. A more complete reference to these is held over until the next issue of the "Canada Lumberman."

At the close of Mr. Manbert's address, Walter M. Ross, Ottawa, proposed a hearty vote of thanks. He referred to the sacrifice that Mr. Manbert had made in giving up his extensive business connections to go abroad and carry on the splendid work which he had done. They all appreciated his industry and activity on behalf of the forest products of Ontario. He felt sure that, in selecting Mr. Manbert for this important work, the lumbermen had made no mistake, as a better representative could not possibly have been appointed. The resolution was carried amid applause.

Mr. Ferguson Announces Future Plans

Hon. G. Howard Ferguson, Minister of Lands, Forests and Mines, was next called upon by Mr. Bigwood who paid a warm tribute to the minister for his interest and activity in taking the initiative steps which lead to the sending of a representative of the lumbermen overseas. The speaker added that Mr. Ferguson had done everything possible to facilitate the work and to assist in making more widely known the merits of the forest products of the province.

In a short, stirring address Mr. Ferguson replied and expressed his pleasure listening to the interesting and vivid presentation by Mr. Manbert of conditions which had to be met in England at the present time. He was pleased with the selection made by the lumbermen when Mr. Manbert was appointed to go overseas and in him both the province and the lumbermen interested had found a most efficient and aggressive representative to carry on a propaganda campaign. Mr. Ferguson said he had received reports from many outside sources regarding what Mr. Manbert had done in the Old Country and it was a source of gratification to find that commendation of his work conducted over there came from all quarters. Mr. Manbert had put before the people of the Old Land the possibilities, qualities and manufacturing facilities of Ontario timber and he was sure that the province would benefit in the opportunities that would follow in the days to come. The Minister pointed out that he was revealing no secret when he announced that it was the intention of the Ontario Government to have qualified representatives in London, Eng., in practically every leading industry of the province and the move made in connection with the lumber industry was one of the first in the initiation of such practical work.

Ontario was the banner province of Canada and provided one-half of the lumber, as well as of all raw materials that was produced in the whole Dominion, and in the sending of men overseas to take part in the struggle for freedom and liberty her representation had also been equally as large. Mr. Manbert had referred to the unsatisfactory character of the office accommodation and equipment which the province had in London, but it was the intention of the provincial administration to provide in the near future more adequate and appropriate quarters that would be in keeping with the dignity, importance and business of the country. Every leading industry would be represented by a thoroughly qualified man who would have a full range of samples and be in a position to give the fullest information and advice. Mr. Ferguson said if he might use the term "expert" it would perhaps convey his meaning more clearly than any other. These men would represent every phase of the agricultural, industrial and productive life of Ontario and he felt sure that Ontario would thus get a fair share of the world's opportunities.

The mission of Mr. Manbert had amply justified itself and the Ontario Government was abundantly satisfied with the work that he had done. As Lumber Commissioner for Ontario Mr. Manbert had not gone overseas to sell forest products but to carry on an intelligent propaganda and secure intimate, first hand knowledge of market requirements in Great Britain during the period of readjustment and to convey authoritative information regarding what Ontario could supply, and how the producers here could best cater to the wants of the Old Land by adopting methods that were feasible and calculated to meet existing conditions. He believed the work done would commend itself to the province and hoped that it had not been completed, but that at a later date Mr. Manbert might be able to return overseas and finish the task so ably and well begun.

In closing Mr. Ferguson stated that, personally, he was much interested in the conservation and reproduction of Ontario woods.

Closing Remarks on the Work Done

Short addresses were also delivered by W. W. Humphreys, of Ottawa; W. J. Bell, of Sudbury; E. A. Dunlop, M.L.A. of Pembroke; Hon. Geo. Gordon of North Bay and Geo. H. Holt of Chicago. The latter read an original and catchy poem entitled "Well Done Manbert," which aroused much merriment. Hon. Mr. Gordon in his remarks stated that, owing to the rather poor health in which he had been during the past summer, he had not followed as closely as he would have liked the work which had been done, but after hearing the splendid address delivered by the Ontario Timber Commissioner, he was confident that his task had been performed in a manner satisfactory to the whole industry and that those with whom Mr. Manbert came in contact had only the best to say of him and his work. Mr. Gordon also commended Hon. Mr. Ferguson for his energy and foresight in arousing lumbermen of Ontario to take advantage of the overseas call for constructional material and for his co-operation in the matter of sending a commissioner to represent them so efficiently as Mr. Manbert had done.

Among the representatives of lumber manufacturing firms present were W. E. Bigwood (Graves, Bigwood & Co.) Byng Inlet, who presided; A. C. Manbert (Canadian General Lumber Co.) Toronto; W. M. Ross, (J. R. Booth), Ottawa; Hon. Geo. Gordon, (Geo. Gordon & Co.), Cache Bay; A. J. Young, (Young Lumber Co.), North Bay; W. J. Bell, (Spanish River Lumber Co.), Sudbury; F. N. Waldie, (Victoria Harbor Lumber Co.), Toronto; E. A. Dunlop, M.P.P., (Pembroke Lumber Co.), Pembroke; D. A. Gillies (Gillies Bros.), Braeside; J. J. McFadden, (McFadden & Malloy), Spragge; C. N. Carney, (Hope Lumber Co.), Thessalon; W. W. Humphreys, (W. C. Edwards & Co.), Ottawa; A. B. Gordon, (Tomiko Lumber Co.), Callender; D. C. Johnston, (Marshay Lumber Co.), Toronto; J. W. Slater (Hocken Lumber Co.), Toronto; A. E. Gordon, (Terry & Gordon), Toronto; J. McN. Austin, (Austin & Nicholson), Chapleau; H. G. McDermid, (Marshay Lumber Co.), Toronto; H. Shanacy, (Pratt & Shanacy), Midland; Henry I. George, (Graves, Bigwood & Co.), Buffalo; Geo. H. Holt (Holt Timber Co.), Chicago; Horace Boultbee, (Sec'y Wholesale Lumber Dealers' Ass'n, Inc.), Toronto; G. B. VanBlaricom (Canada Lumberman).

W. E. Bigwood, Toronto
Chairman of Ontario Lumber Manufacturers Committee

Hon. G. Howard Ferguson
Minister of Lands, Forests and Mines for the Province of Ontario

Walter M. Ross, Ottawa
Secretary of Ontario Lumber Manufacturers Committee

Mr. Manbert Says Farewell to British Friends

A. C. Manbert, of Toronto, Timber Commissioner for Ontario, in a letter to the trade press in England previous to his departure, says "farewell" and expresses his hearty appreciation of the many courtesies and kindness extended to him during his sojourn in the Old Country. In part he writes:

"While it has been delightful to receive these considerations personally, I have been pleased to understand that they arose out of a very genuine interest in the closer relationship with Canada which has been so quickened by the peculiar contact of the past five years.

"I would be very dull not to realise that the degree to which we may enter into the trade of this country really rests upon your grace. For while we must meet the demands of competition, in the last analysis the use of our goods is subject to your election. To possess your sympathetic interest gives then, to us, a great assurance. On the other hand, it is obvious that we must merit and inspire your enthusiasm, and it has been my keen purpose to study and attempt to understand your needs and convictions that I may interpret them to our people at home.

"I am sure all will agree as to the desirability of maintaining the interest of Canadian producers in the British market. To the extent that it exists, it will temper and qualify the attitudes of the producers in competing sources of supply. A considerable factor in accomplishing this is an alert understanding on your part of the conditions which affect our methods and administration, that is, the conflicting consideration of other markets, the characteristics of our timber, and the operating conditions which control the lengths, widths, and styles of manufacture. In doing this, and giving consideration to what we want to sell as well as what we want to buy, you will be obtaining access to larger reservoir of supply, with all the advantages which that implies.

"In Ontario we manufacture many sizes and kinds which you have not been importing. They are used elsewhere to advantage. Why not here?

"Operating conditions with us are of necessity changing. To produce the large quota of deals is no longer possible. With the very greatly increased cost of conversion here, perhaps other sizes can be used to advantage and profit. This is especially for agents and importers to consider—a matter of alert salesmanship. I hope I will not be misunderstood when I suggest that a sincere attempt to give effect to the idea will help to escape the restraints and limitations of old conventions, and invest the situation with more of freshness and adventure and less of the prosaic.

"We in Canada ardently desire, as do you, a return of full and free private trading. At the moment, conditions are not favourable to this, but ultimately the time will arrive. We, therefore, earnestly look forward for it to bring you into our midst with enlarged inquiry—for your good and for ours."

Nearly Million Ties Cut in Port Arthur District

J. A. Oliver, of Port Arthur, Ont., Crown Timber Agent, reports that during the season just closed a total of 989,865 ties were cut. Of this number 680,712 were cut on Crown lands and 299,153 were cut on private property.

Of pulpwood the cut amounted to 100,506 cords, of which 14,644 cords were taken from Crown lands, and 85,902 cords from private property.

From private property 1,068 cedar poles were cut during the season, and 10,387 cedar posts were cut from the same class of property.

Piles cut on Crown lands amounted to 1,762, and on private property 6,187, a total of 7,959.

Logs numbering 36,605, mostly of pine and measuring 1,599,168 feet board measure, were also cut.

Many Accidents in Western Lumber Industry

Statistics compiled by the Workmen's Compensation Board in British Columbia for the first half of the present year show that the lumber industry ranks, from a total wage basis, is the most important in the province, and at the same time from an accident standpoint, is the most hazardous. No less than 1,407 compensable accidents were filed during this period in the various branches of the manufacture of lumber. In addition to that number, there are also a considerable number of claims where the workmen are being paid on a monthly basis. These are not enumerated in the 1,407. The total cost to the industry of those claims finalled for the first six months period of this year is $185,601.47.

A glance at the statistics reveals some interesting facts in connection with the cost of accidents to this industry. Injured workmen receive under the act, fifty-five per cent. of their loss of wages through accident. For time lost alone $95,901.01 was paid to the workmen during the first six months of 1919. The average duration of incapacity due to accident was eighteen days. Of the total 1,407 cases reported, 980 of the workmen were sufficiently recovered to return to work within a month of the accident. Two hundred and fifty-two more recovered before the end of the second month, while 162 took a longer period.

For permanent partial disability, including awards for loss of limb and permanent injury not resulting in death, the sum of $47,687.36 was paid. Injuries to fingers and hands were the most common forms of accident coming under this heading. There were 304 accidents which resulted in loss or disuse of fingers, injuries to the hand, other than fingers numbered 103. The arm figured in 66 cases. The foot and ankle came in for 171 of the accidents, and the leg and knee for 204 more. Another very common accident was the breaking and injuring of ribs, 77 accidents to ribs being reported.

There has been a total number of fatal accidents of 39, or 47 per cent. of the total number of all fatal accidents in all industries in the province for the first six months of the year. This is most unfortunate. Some of these accidents could have been avoided, and it is hoped by the board that the employers will continue most actively the accident prevention campaign already started, and which has undoubtedly achieved great results in the last year and a half.

Well Done, Manbert!

By George H. Holt, Chicago

Who turned his back on New World charms
And dared the Ocean's hidden harms
To bear our tender in his arms?
'Twas Manbert.

Who loaded up with Lumber lore
And price temptations by the score
To plant them on a Foreign Shore?
'Twas Manbert.

Who challenged Norsk and Svensk and Finn
To help "Our Canada" to win
The markets they had gathered in?
'Twas Manbert.

Who juggled "Dollars," "Grades" and "Feet".
Till even Scotchmen on the street
Would sing the chorus, and repeat?
'Twas Manbert.

Who followed back the Frenchmen's trails
To lead the way to Lumber Sales
Through Calais, Paris and Marseilles?
'Twas Manbert.

Who faltered not at Trade entrenched.
Who prejudice with goodwill quenched.
Who ignorance with knowledge drenched.
'Twas Manbert.

To build the World the Allies won,
To cure the habit of the Hun,
This is the work so well begun
'By Manbert.

"To beard the lion in his den,
The Douglass in his hall,"
To court the 'Tiger' in his Fen
Nor hesitate at all,
Might quail the heart of other men
But Manbert
Did them all

National Retailers in Forward Movement

Great Gathering in Detroit Demonstrates Practical Benefits of Intelligent Co-operation and Adopts Progressive Measures for Better Business

The third annual meeting of the National Retail Lumber Dealers' Association of the United States, which was held at Detroit, Mich., on September 11th and 12th, marked an important epoch in the life of the Association. It can be confidently predicted that, as a result of this meeting and of the three years of serious and effective work which the Association has carried on, the National Retailers' Association is now firmly set upon its feet and its path of usefulness is clearly seen ahead.

There was a large attendance at the meeting, representing dealers from all parts of the United States. The interest taken in the discussion of the numerous important matters dealt with was indicative of definite purpose and determination to make the influence of the Association felt.

Broadly speaking, the meeting was divided into three elements. There was first of all a fine list of addresses. Secondly, there was keen discussion of many important association problems and, in the third place, there was a series of entertainment features which will make all the visitors hope that future meetings will also be held at Detroit.

Manufacturers Not to Blame for High Prices.

The addresses, which were comparatively few in number, were all on timely subjects. They commenced with the address of the president, Mr. J. J. Comerford, of Detroit. Mr. Comerford dealt with some of the retailers' problems in connection with which they could get best results through co-operation between retailers, wholesalers and manufacturers. Speaking of the present prices of lumber, he did not place the blame for their height upon the manufacturer, but upon some of the provisions of the Federal Income Tax which discourage production by the manufacturers. The manufacturer was not to blame for asking present prices, when more lumber was demanded by the consumer than the mills were able to turn out. Minimum service and maximum pay were now being given and demanded by labor, so that the producers were not able to meet the demands of the market. He wanted to see the laborer get good wages, but could not believe that shorter hours would be for the public good as they would result in reduced output and smaller earnings on the part of the workers.

Proper cost accounting methods were emphasized by Mr. Comerford as essential to modern retail lumber selling. Only through the adoption of scientific cost accounting could the retail lumber trade be made attractive enough to secure the services of young men of brains and executive ability. He also urged that manufacturers and retailers should co-operate in seeking to solve the problems of the employer and the employees. In conclusion, he suggested that the Association should hold a lumber conference every six months.

General L. C. Boyle, of Kansas City, Mo., attorney for the Association, delivered one of his invariably inspiring addresses, the subject being "The Past and Future of Lumber Dealers Associating Nationally." The retail lumber business, he said, could only be built up through intelligent co-operation between the dealers, consisting of the "elbow touch," and a courage born of mutual understanding. "There was a time," he said, "when you thought your business was your own affair, but to-day it is everybody's affair, and rightly so, because of the welfare of the whole community is linked up with what you do. You must let the public know and by so doing it will help instead of harm you."

Co-operation Urged in All Branches

A. L. Osborn, of Oshkosh, Wis., delivered an address upon "Closer Co-ordination of All Branches of the Lumber Industry." The key note of his address was contained in the following paragraph:

"Some of the great leaders in our industry have lately come to see that movements for keeping the public informed, for creating favorable sentiment and for securing fair legislative treatment can be best secured by the three branches uniting in a common way to furnish information and material for our common fight. If every retail dealer in the United States will become a militant knight in our fight to educate the public and to secure fair legislative treatment, our fight can easily be won. The exchange of information, the manufacturers taking the retailer and wholesaler into his confidence, and the joint assumption of responsibilities, mark a new and better era. Only a beginning has been had. No field for co-operation is so large or important as this. When we have no secrets from one an other and when representatives of all branches can sit in and listen to all discussions and know of all plans to better our industry, we will have taken the one biggest and most important step forward.

S. A. Linnekin, Commodity Expert of Babson's Statistical Organization, of Wellesley Hills, Mass., gave a fine review and forecast of business conditions, in which he explained the present trade and industrial situation. "As for commodity prices," he said, "the chances are that they are not far from the peak to-day. As with business, it is impossible, until commodities have been fully reapportioned among the consuming countries of the world, to expect any serious slump, at least, with any degree of permanency. These commodities, however, are fast being replenished in the hands of consumers and inside of six or eight months it seems reasonable to expect the beginning of the decline for the long pull downward. In some cases there may be further advances; but, in general, the safest buying policy seems to be to buy small lots frequently. With little to gain in the way of speculative profit the greatest stress should be placed on deliveries, which during the fall and winter may be a serious factor. We may not be so fortunate as to have a second successive open winter."

Regarding lumber, the speaker said that lower prices would be governed largely by the time that was required to put on the market lumber that cost less than it does to-day. It was not reasonable to expect any runaway advances from present levels. On the other hand, it was equally unreasonable to expect any immediate slump. In all probability, the conditions were such that a high average price would prevail well into next year. The general aspect would be firm.

A. C. Klumph, of Cleveland, Ohio, delivered an address, entitled: "Why the Retail Lumber Business"; during which he advocated strongly the more general support of lumber associations.

New Schedule of Fees Effective.

The busines end of the meeting included consideration of several important matters. A new schedule of fees was adopted ranging from $10.00 for members doing a business of $50,000 a year or less, up to $250.00 for members with an annual business of $900,000 or over.

A strong report against the abuse of the transit car privilege was presented by a special committee and adopted, but not without spirited dicussion and some opposition. A number of important resolutions were presented by a special committee for the purpose and were adopted. One of these instructed the secretary to secure copies of all State Lien Laws and city building codes and ordinances affecting the lumber business, to serve as a foundation for association work in the direction of securing a uniform standard of laws covering these subjects. Another resolution provided for the creation of an inter-insurance exchange in connection with the work of the Association.

Canadians Present at the Sessions.

The election of officers resulted in J. J. Comerford, of Detroit, being re-elected president. John E. Lloyd, of Philadelphia, was elected first vice-president; H. G. Foote, of Minneapolis, Minn., second vice-president; John Claney, of Chicago, was re-elected treasurer, and C. A. Bowen, of Detroit, was re-elected secretary.

The entertainment features of the meeting included a boat-ride and dance on the first evening, and a Jazz party, supper and dance on the second night. Special entertainment was provided for the ladies who attended the meeting.

Among the Canadians, who took part in the convention, were: J. B. Reid, Toronto, vice-president of the Ontario Retail Lumber Dealers' Association; J. C. Scofield, of the Windsor Lumber Company, Windsor, Ont.; Chester D. Belton, of the R. Laidlaw Lumber Company, Sarnia, Ont.; W. A. Hadley, of the S. Hadley Lumber Company, Chatham, Ont. ;E. C. Russell, Walkerville, and H. Boultbee, secretary of the Ontario Retail Lumber Dealers' Association, Toronto.

Home is the Surest Defence Against All Ills

For the Sake of Posterity, National Well Being and Progressive Civilization, Every Citizen Should Own His Abode—Its Power and Uplifting Influence

Much has been written and printed on the question of people owning their own homes—the advantage, benefit, wisdom, stability, economy, purpose, and strength of such a movement. One would think all these attributes or claims made on behalf of owning a home were sufficient in themselves to convince the ordinary individual, without being "fed up" on these truths or facts so many times. Nevertheless, it appears necessary to keep hammering away at things which all persons should know and appreciate. New converts of the home building plan are, of course, made by this method. The incessant presentation of a fact, the reiteration of a statement, the repetition of a mental picture or the recurrence of a thought will in time create an impression on most anyone and arouse conviction, courage or action.

The things to be remembered is that the ideas of every generation seem to change and young people are now brought up with conveniences, delights and attractions that were never possessed by their parents even at the close of life. To labor shorter hours, spend more money and have only one object in view, that of a rollicking good time, appears to be the animating motive in many careers, particularly in the urban centres. Of course, it is essential to counteract this baneful influence through the medium of publicity, in the hope that it may compel the thoughtless, frivolous and happy-go-lucky to pause and think.

Why Not Start Out Aright?

There is no valid reason why young men and young women should not begin life in homes, owned by them, rather than spend a decade or more paying rent to someone who has no interest in their welfare other than the receipt of the monthly cheque. It may require a little restraint, some measure of economy and self-control, as well as a vision and a purpose, but all these things are worth while and pay ample dividends later on. The "Retail Lumberman," of Kansas City, recently offered some valuable prizes for the best article on the subject "Why people should own their own homes"? The contest was limited to retail dealers or the members of their families or employees. The first prize was awarded to John P. Barton, manager of the Simpson Lumber Company, Stroud, Okla. After due consideration the judges awarded him the premium for not only having set forth the best arguments, but adhering most closely to the purpose outlined in the contest.

The points advanced by Mr. Barton are so pertinent, the facts so well arranged and the matter so logical that the "Canada Lumberman" believes his remarks which follow will be read with much interest and appreciation.

Economic Aspect of the Problem

There are three great reasons, or rather three great divisions of the many thousands of reasons, why people should own their own homes. These divisions I shall call the reasons of economy, the reasons of utility, and the reasons of Ethics.

Let us first consider the economic reasons—not because they are necessarily the most important, but because it usually comes natural for us to think of the things which affect our pocket-books first. The extravagance of being a perpetual payer of rent month after month and year after year, although an old argument in favor of building your own home, is, and always will be a mighty good one. The advantage of a warranty deed over a pile of rent receipts is one which cannot help to appeal to any thoughtful person.

Added to this there is that double source of expense and annoyance, the moving van, as the average renter moves, either through "beggar's choice" or downright compulsion, several times each year. A rented house almost never exactly suits the renter. As soon as he moves into it he begins to notice bad features and he looks forward to the day when he can move into a house which will suit him better. Unfortunately, after he makes a move to better himself, he finds other undesirable items about the new place which often make it even more unpleasant than the one he just moved from. If by a rare chance he is lucky enough to get a rented house which is about what he wants, the chances are that it will be sold by the time he gets settled down to enjoying life, and he is forced to make a hasty move on short notice into any vacant house there is available.

Besides the direct expense of these moves, there is always more or less furniture damaged and furniture sacrificed and discarded and new bought to fit the changes in the amount of room and the arrangement of each different house. The rugs which you bought for the rooms of the house you have just moved from are either too large or too small for the rooms of the house you move into. There is no suitable place for the book-case which you bought to fit a certain nook or corner in the other house. The window blinds are all the wrong size so they must all be scrapped and new ones bought. Every thing that was just a fit in the other house is now a hopeless misfit. For this reason it is not usually possible or practical for renters to own such attractive or comfortable furniture as the home owner of no greater income is able to afford.

Every Housewife Knows This

In practically every community in the United States it is now possible for thrifty people of moderate incomes to build or buy their own homes and pay for them in easy payments like rent. It is almost impossible to overestimate how much the renter adds to his financial and business chances by starting in to pay for his own home on this plan. He will automatically adopt new habits of thrift, and unconsciously he will strengthen his financial stability and gain increased respect and esteem in the eyes of his employer and business associates. The very act of making these regular payments on his home gives him the hopeful, confident feeling of a wise investor and encourages him to systematic saving and the accumulation of a bank account. If he needs additional capital to take advantage of a business opportunity, he can borrow money when credit would be refused to the less reliable rent payer. His employer will feel more inclined to give him the preference in any opening for advancement and his salary will grow as new responsibilities are trusted to him. When he started to buy this home he took a good long stride on the highway of achievement toward the goal of financial and business success.

From the standpoint of utility the rented house is almost never so useful to you as the house you build for yourself. Your rented house may be someone else's idea of a home, but too often it is not even this. If it was built for rental purposes in all likelihood utility, convenience and comfort had to sacrifice for economy and cheapness of construction. But perhaps the most numerous and least desirable type of rent house is the old home which the builder has outgrown and building himself a modern house rents out the old "shack." Such a house has the unpleasantness of a cast-off suit of clothes about it. It is generally the most uncomfortable and least useful kind of house which a renter is compelled to live, or rather to exist, in. However, at this time, the whole country is so under-built that renters are often forced to accept any kind of makeshift houses.

Another unfortunate condition which develops is the perpetual petty warfare of renter vs. landlord, on the subject of repairs, upkeep and improvements. If the renter takes a proper pride in the house he lives in he is liable to push the landlord a little too strong for expensive repairs and improvements. When these are refused the renter loses his pride and develops a hatred for all landlords and seeks revenge by abusing and often maliciously defacing the property which he rents. This unhappy condition causes renters, as a rule, to become shiftless and indifferent about the care of their premises, and this lack of pride becomes so habitual as to cheapen the quality of their work and to blunt their ambition, and is a great obstacle to their success in whatever line of work they may follow.

Ethical and Social Advantages

In what contrast is the more pleasant state of the man of grit and foresight who builds his own home! In the first place he can choose his building site in a congenial neighborhood. And then he and his good wife, for the good wife must always be a co-partner in the building of a real home, they two together create a home from their dreams. Each room they plan for their own special convenience and comfort. They have always wished for a certain arrangement of the rooms, or perhaps for special built-in features constructed according to their own particular ideas. It has been impossible for them to get these things in perhaps a dozen houses which they have rented, but now they are building their own and building it just like they want it. When the house is completed it is more than a mere house, it is truly their Home, a wonderful realization of their own individual hopes and aspirations!

Reducing Heavy Cost in Logging Operations

How the Employment of Modern Equipment Eliminates Work and Worry, Speeds up Production and Increases Efficiency—The Standard Steam Hoist

By "Woodsman"

This summer the writer had the privilege of assisting at the raising of a forty-eight feet long flag pole at the summer cottage. The pole was fresh cut, full of sap, and very heavy, and the man power available was, to say the least, inadequate for the job. We got it up eventually by the exercise of much muscular effort, also by the "sweat of the brow" and various other portions of the anatomy. But that experience impressed on all of us very forcibly the old, old lesson that green timber possesses great weight, and that it pays to use labor saving appliances if they can be procured. We knew it before, of course, but that one experience changed theoretical knowledge into practical knowledge, and we can now appreciate as never before the value of labor-saving tools to the men who are handling logs and heavy timbers every day, namely, the Canadian lumbermen.

Labor-saving methods for lumbermen are much better known in British Columbia and in the Pacific Coast States than in Ontario,

20 H.P. double drum, belt driven hoist for handling logs, made by Marsh Engineering Works, Belleville, and in operation in the bush in Ontario

Quebec, or the Maritime Provinces. The reason for this is easily found in the larger and heavier type of timber that is logged all along the Pacific Coast. Logs that run anywhere from five feet to nine feet in diameter cannot be handled readily by man and horse power alone, or by man and ox power. These nine-foot logs have, it is true, been moved in the early days of Pacific Coast lumbering by long strings of oxen, urged on by the whip lash, but it was a tremendous task, slow, tedious and costly in wages, even in those days of cheap labor. But necessity, that fertile mother of so many valuable inventions, forced the invention of better methods, and gradually through the years many types of special machines have been evolved to take care of these mammoth timbers at every stage of the journey from the stump to the saw. There are probably half a dozen firms in British Columbia and in the Western States who specialize in the designing and building of the large, powerful, complicated and costly skidding and loading machines that years of experience have proven to be necessary to the economical handling of the heavy western spruce, fir, cedar and red wood. There are probably as many methods of moving and transporting these logs as there are varieties of machines, each of these methods being claimed to be the very best for the particular locality and conditions where it was developed.

Cheapening the Cost of Production

Here in the East, however, conditions are entirely different. The logs are usually not too large to be moved by horse-power on sleigh or wheels. Moreover, they do not have to be transported up or down steep mountain sides, so the problem of getting them from the stump to the saw is very much simpler than it is in the West, in consequence of which necessity has not forced upon the lumberman the development and application of labor-saving methods. Nevertheless there are here and there a few of the larger and more progressive lumbermen in Ontario, Quebec and the Maritime Provinces who have made a beginning in the use of labor-saving machinery, not because of heavy timbers or unusually difficult surface conditions, but as a matter of deliberate choice and careful planning in order to cheapen the cost of production and thereby increase profits.

One large producer in the Ontario hinterland has for some ten or twelve years been using the standard steam hoisting engine which is in such general use by the larger builders and general contractors all over Canada. And it is only natural that he should take to the use of this engine in the woods, for the same engine that has been found so useful in the placing of heavy timbers in construction work should be equally as useful in the handling of these same timbers in the bush. Moreover, these machines are strongly built to withstand rough usage, are simple in operation so they do not require an expert engineer to run them, and are compact enough and light enough to be moved about from place to place as necessity arises, so they would appear to be eminently suitable for use in the woods. In fact, so useful has this particular lumberman found these standard steam hoists (of twenty or twenty-five horse-power) that he has gradually been adding one machine after another to his equipment year after year, until he now has at least seven of one make, and two more of other makes. Although these machines are incomparably cheaper than the ponderous and elaborate specially-designed machines necessary on the Pacific coast (the before-the-war price being in the neighborhood of eight hundred or ten hundred dollars according to size), yet all these machines that he has been accumulating from year to year represent a considerable investment of capital withdrawn from circulation and bringing in no interest. But this same lumberman is a shrewd, far-seeing financier, and knows well that these machines are earning him good dividends, even though he is able to use them for only two months in the year and they are idle for the remaining ten months of each year.

The Efficiency of the Hoists

Regarding the nature and quality of the work done by these engines, the writer was informed recently by one "in the know" that these engines are all used principally for loading on cars, and that the quantity loaded is only limited by the quantity furnished to the hoist, and that under favorable conditions one machine will load

Skidding logs in an Ontario lumber camp by modern methods. Only one man is required to operate the hoist

from 1,500 to 2,000 logs per day, either pine or pulp wood. The users of these hoists say that there is no comparison between hand work and engine work, so far as loading logs on cars is concerned. Some attempt has also been made during recent months to use these machines for taking logs out of water, but there are a number of improvements still to be effected in their operating methods to make this system as fully successful as the car loading system has proven to be. Moreover, although some of these engines have been in service for a number of years, very little repairs have been needed on any of them, showing that this type of machine is well adapted for use in the woods.

There are, of course, other lumbermen using this same type of machine, and this one lumberman is cited only as an instance of what is being done in Ontario, and of what could be done to a much larger extent in all of Eastern Canada only for the handicap of our inbred conservatism, which makes many of us satisfied with things as they are. But as labor costs continue to mount up the absolute necessity of adopting labor-saving machinery and methods will be forced upon the lumbermen until in time practically all except the very small producers will be using some form of labor-saving and profit-increasing machinery for piling, loading, skidding or hauling logs.

The photographs reproduced in this article were taken last winter in an Ontario lumber camp of medium capacity, and show how the gasoline engine is also being utilized by some progressive operators because of its lightness and the ease with which it can be moved about from place to place as required. The fire risk is also much less than with the steam-driven machines, as there is no smoke stack throwing out sparks to set fire to the immediate surroundings. The belt driven hoist which the gasoline engine is operating is exactly the same type as the steam-driven machines referred to above, but is a smaller size, being only ten-horse power rated capacity. It is also the standard two-drum contractors' and builders' hoist, and because it is a standard design and produced in quantities can be sold more cheaply than a machine of special design. This standard machine is built for either steam or electric or belt drive, and in a number of horse-power sizes, so that any lumberman can choose the right size for his work, and probably get delivery from stock.

Sawmills Use them for Loading Cars

The logs seen in the accompanying view, which were cut last winter in this particular camp, were about the average size of present-day Ontario logs, the largest measuring about thirty inches in diameter, and up to fourteen feet long. This little ten-horsepower machine was used for piling the logs in skidways, and also for loading the logs on cars. For piling on skidways it was found convenient to deck three or four skidways at each placing of the machine, thus saving time in moving the outfit. As used by this operator this little machine handled one thousand logs per day, piling them fourteen logs high, and worked right through the coldest weather, even when the mercury reached twenty below zero.

The officials in charge of the Canadian Forestry Battalions well knew the value of these hoists for logging purposes, and before they sailed from Canada purchased a number of these standard steam-driven machines from stock, of the twenty and twenty-five horse-power sizes, and took them with them overseas. These machines were used to such good advantage overseas, in both England and in France, that the British and French authorities were delighted with their performance, and the officers in charge of the Battalions, now returned to Canada, speak in the highest terms of the valuable assistance these Canadian-built machines rendered in expediting the production and delivery of the timbers so urgently needed in so many ways for the prosecution of the war. They speeded up operations over there as they had been doing here, and as they will continue to do in constantly increasing volume in Canada as Canadian lumbermen become better acquainted with their possibilities.

But it must not be thought that the lumberman is the only man in the lumber industry who is taking advantage of these labor-saving tools and making them earn money for him. The saw mills and the pulp mills are also finding uses for them, using their tremendous strength for lifting and placing logs, timbers and heavy sections, and also for moving loaded cars. For instance, one Quebec mill was confronted with the problem of placing loaded cars of lumber weighing up to eighteen or twenty tons. A small dinky locomotive would have done the work, but at considerable expense, and hand power was also too costly, but on investigation it was discovered that one of these little ten-horsepower standard hoisting engines, with only one drum, could easily do the work, and at much less cost, both for initial outlay and for operating expense. So one was bought and installed, taking steam from the power plant already in position, and did the work to the entire satisfaction of the mill operators. Other mills have installed the belt-driven machines, or the electric-driven, as suited their local conditions best, and for the same purpose, that is, for moving and placing loaded cars.

Economy and Service of Gasoline Tractor.

Another labor-saving tool used by a few of the wide-awake lumbermen of Ontario and East is the gasoline tractor with various forms of caterpillar tread. This will haul a regular train of wagons or sleighs loaded with logs, and under suitable local conditions is perhaps the best tool yet devised for the purpose for long hauls to the mills or to the railroad.

For the shorter distances, where the logs are being cut not too far from the track or the mill, it is possible that some of the various cableway systems that have been developed on the Pacific Coast and in the cypress swamps of the Southern States could be used to good advantage in Eastern Canada in place of the horses that are now used so commonly. The logs could be moved at much greater speed, and at a considerable saving in wages and other operating costs. For the small timbers now being cut in Ontario and East the standard hoisting engine as used by builders and contractors and referred to above could easily be utilized, and would do the work equally as well as the more elaborate and more expensive specially designed machines of the Pacific Coats.

Cableway Hauling of Logs

The writer knows of one Ontario lumberman who bought one of these expensively designed outfits from somewhere in the States. It was a large machine, occupying the whole floor of a flat car, and impossible to use except on its own car. It was probably all right for the heavy Western logs for which it had been designed, but according to common report was unsuited to our smaller logs and was soon dispensed with. If this machine had been desired (as is likely) to haul the logs from the stump to the track and then to load them on a car, the same work could have been done by one of the various cableway systems, using the standard hoists, at a much less expenditure of capital. It has been abundantly proven in practise that these standard machines are quite capable of operating almost any kind of cableway system of hauling logs, either for hauling them along the ground or suspended wholly or partly in the air, according to the distance and the nature of the ground to be traversed.

This cableway hauling of logs has not been practised as yet to any great extent in Ontario, Quebec, or the Eastern Provinces, but it is safe to say that the time is now far distant when it will largely supplant the more expensive horsepower hauling which is now in such common use.

More Aggressiveness in Pushing Coast Products

Logging operations on an extensive scale are being carried out on Toba Inlet, B.C., by the Canada Timber and Lands Company, of Toronto. Mr. E. Stewart, of Toronto, managing director and secretary-treasurer of the company, recently paid a business visit to the Coast, and, in an interview respecting conditions in the East, said that there was a splendid market for British Columbia forest products. Of course, there was always the question of freight rates to be considered, but, despite that, he was of the opinion that more and more B. C. lumber and timber would be used in eastern Canada as it became better known. In this connection, he said, a policy of more aggressiveness was needed to push the coast product, which was of such a quality that it could hold its own anywhere on the North American Continent. Mr. Stewart was highly optimistic of the future for B. C. lumber and said the demand for it in the east was becoming greater every day.

The fact that his company, which has its headquarters in the east, is pushing its logging operations ahead so rapidly is indicative of the demand that is being made for coast lumber. While there was some yellow pine coming from the United States, it was well known, said Mr. Stewart, that the supply of that commodity is being rapidly lessened and for that reason, he urged the trade out on the coast to bestir itself with a view to obtaining a firmer hold on the eastern Canadian market. That was the point that the B. C. lumber industry must ever keep before it, Mr. Stewart remarked, namely the securing of a better foothold in eastern Canada, and there was no reason, he added, why B. C. should not be the principal source of supply to that part of the Dominion.

Opens New Warehouse in Detroit

The Carborundum Company, of Niagara Falls, N.Y., announces the opening of branch offices and warehouse in Detroit, Mich. The new quarters will be located in the Burkhardt Building, at Second and Larned Streets, and under the management of Mr. Anthony Dobson, who is in charge of the Detroit sales district. The new offices and the warehouse are opened with a view to giving quicker and better service to the users of Carborundum products in the Detroit district, and to that end a complete stock of Carborundum and Aloxite grinding wheels, Carborundum and Aloxite paper and cloth and other Carborundum products will be carried. The opening of the Detroit branch is just another indication of the progressive policy of the Carborundum Company.

How Long Will the Timber of Canada Last?

If Proper Measures of Protection and Reproduction are Undertaken There is Little Danger of Famine — Improved Methods of Utilization Urged

With the conclusion of the war and the enormous possibilities of trade with devastated Europe in forest products, Canada is confronted by an amazing ignorance of the extent of her forest resources, says R. G. Lewis, in a timely and comprehensive article, which appears in a recent addition of the "By-water Magazine." Not so many years ago, adds the author, who is on the staff of the Forestry Branch, Department of the Interior, Ottawa, such expressions as "boundless forests," "unlimited forests," "unlimited timber wealth," and "inexhaustible supply of lumber," were commonly in use in describing these resources.

From this extreme we have passed to a temporary state of panic, when certain pessimistic individuals prophesied that our present supply of timber would not last more than 10, 20 or 30 years, depending on the depth to which the spirits of the respective prophets had fallen. While there is no doubt of the urgent necessity for better protection from forest fires, better administration of forests lands, improved methods of utilization, and, in some instances, actual reforestation, there is no immediate danger from a wood famine, and, if such measures are taken, no danger of such a famine in the near future.

Complete Stock Taking is Advocated

The first step necessary to provide for a future supply of forest products is a complete stock taking of our forest resources. It does not appear logical to make complicated plans for the administration of forests, the extent and nature of which are not accurately known, nor to build up an extensive export trade in a commodity in ignorance of the supply available, nor to encourage returned soldiers and other settlers to take up land, the suitability of which for agriculture is a doubtful question, yet all these things are being done with incomplete and inaccurate information.

Forest surveys, conducted by technically trained foresters, are designed to determine with reasonable accuracy the extent and nature of the existing forests, the quantities of the different forest products they contain at present, and what they can be relied upon to produce in future years, the area of land suitable for agriculture at present forested, and the area which is suitable only for forestry purposes.

Such surveys have been made and are being made at the present time in certain parts of Canada. Dr. B. E. Fernow, late Dean of the Faculty of Forestry at Toronto University, in 1909 and 1910, conducted a reconnaissance survey of the forests of Nova Scotia, the first provincial forest survey attempted in Canada. This survey was made by foresters with the idea of determining not only the present stand but the future possibilities of the province as a timber producer. It did not attempt to supply detail for commercial purposes. To quote from the report, "This fact will be appreciate dby practical men when it is stated that a reconnaissance and not a detail survey is involved, and that the total expenditure, including the compilation of data, map and report, did not exceed $6,000. The field work alone had, therefore, to be accomplished for the remarkably low cost of twenty-five cents per square mile of country, while any attempt at estimating the standing timber closely would have involved an expenditure of from $10 to $20 per square mile."

Valuable Facts Revealed by Survey

This survey established some interesting and valuable facts. Two-thirds of the area of the province consists of non-agricultural land covered with forest growth and not fit for any other use than timber growing. The actual green forest area consists of five million acres, to which is added recently-burned forest and better class barrens which can, eventually, be reforested. Ten per cent. is hopelessly barren. Less than 100,000 acres of virgin or semi-virgin timber remain. The quantity of coniferous timber was estimated at about ten billion feet.

The results of this survey were published by permission of the Department of Crown Lands of Nova Scotia by the Commission of Conservation.

A survey of Crown Lands in New Brunswick was begun in 1916 by a staff of foresters from the University of New Brunswick. Mr. G. H. Prince, the Provincial Forester, states that over a million and a half acres of Crown Lands have been covered by survey up to date, classifying the land of timber and the future possibilities of the land for producing timber. The work of surveying the seven and a half million acres of forest land belonging to the Crown has not proceeded far enough to warrant a definite estimate of the total stand of timber, but the information gathered up to the present would indicate something in the neighborhood of 13 billion feet of saw-timber. The privately owned timber land, about five million acres in extent, has been estimated to contain about the same quantity as the Crown Lands, making a total of, approximately, 25 billion feet of standing timber in New Brunswick.

An extensive study of the forest resources of British Columbia has been completed by Messrs. H. N. Whitford and R. D. Craig of the Commission of Conservation, and the complete report with maps is now available for distribution. This investigation is based on a large proportion of actual cruises (about 65 per cent.), the data being furnished by the British Columbia Forest Branch, the Dominion Forestry Branch, the timber owners, cruisers, surveyors, and others. In many cases more than one report for a single area was obtained and the estimates could thus be checked and, if necessary, revised. In addition to the estimates of standing timber, the report discusses geographical, physiographic, climatic, and soil relations, ownership of land, forest administration and policy, methods of logging and manufacture, descriptions of the tree species native to the province, and the insect injuries to the forest.

Divided Into Two Main Regions

In making up the total estimate of standing timber, the province has been divided into two main regions, the Coastal Belt and the Interior, separated by the axes of the Cascade and Coast Mountains.

The Interior has been divided into six regions and subdivided nto forty drainage basins. The Coastal Belt has been similarly divided into five regions and twenty-six drainage basins. A separate estimate of the timber by species, a classification of the land and a description of the geology, topography and transportation facilities for each of these sixty-six drainage basins is included in the report.

The estimate of standing timber in the Province of British Columbia is 350,835,000,000 board feet of saw material, and 15,465,000,00 board feet of pulpwood, piling, poles, and other small material. This total is made up of 136,534,700,000 board feet for the Interior and 214,299,460,000 board feet for the Coast region. This estimate includes with the total for the saw timber, 170 million feet of such species as spruce, hemlock, balsam, and cottonwood, which are suitable for pulp manufacture, and with the total for the smaller material, another nine million feet of pulpwood, which, together, would make a total of 255 million cords of pulpwood available in the province.

The forest land in the Prairie Provinces is under the administration of the Federal Government, together with that in the Railway Belt and the Peace River Block of British Columbia. This administration is divided among different branches of the Interior Department, and, while accurate information is available for certain areas, no survey covering all the forest land has yet been made.

An investigation of forest conditions in the Province of Saskatchewan was conducted by Mr. J. C. Bloomer of the Conservation Commission, but the final report is not yet available.

A preliminiary summary of the information gathered is as follows:

	Board Feet
Spruce saw timber	3,000,000,000
Poplar saw timber	4,000,000,000
Pine (jack pine) timber	800,000,000
Total saw timber	7,800,000,000
	Cords
Pulpwood (spruce, balsam, fir, and poplar)	55,000,000
Cordwood (jack pine)	78,000,000
Birch, tamarack and willow	17,000,000
Total	150,000,000
Total equivalent in board feet	83,000,000,000
	Acres
Approximate total forest area	98,200,000
Total wooded land area	73,000,000
Total area under present commercial spruce forest	750,000

The Stand in the Prairie Provinces

For the three Prairie Provinces of Manitoba, Saskatchewan and Alberta, the estimate is as follows:

	Board Feet
Spruce and tamarack	8,000,000,000
Poplar	12,000,000,000
Pine	3,000,000,000
	23,000,000,000

The statistical year book of Quebec for 1915 contains an estimate of the forest resources of the province. Neither a survey similar to that made in Nova Scotia nor an investigation of forest resources similar to that made in British Columbia has yet been made for the province, but the work of collecting data concerning the forest area is being carried on every year. The text of the year book does not state on what information the following estimate is made, but as it is the first official statement published, it must be accepted as such until confirmed by later information.

	Board Feet
Red and white pine	50,000,000,000
Spruce and balsam fir	125,000,000,000
Hardwood (birch, maple, etc.)	35,000,000,000
Cedar	20,000,000,000
Total saw timber	230,000,000,000
Pulpwood	100,000,000,000
Grand total	330,000,000,000

The Timber Possessions of Ontario

Up to the present time no official estimate of the forest resources of Ontario has been published. The lack of information has been more or less camouflage by conflicting and overlapping reports made by different authorities for different classes of resources in different regions, making any attempt at a general summing up impossible.

The present commercial forest is said to cover eighty million acres and to contain nine billion feet of pine on licensed lands, thirteen and a half billion on Crown lands, and 350 million cords of pulpwood of which 250 millions are tributary to railways and waterways. The potential forest area in the Laurentian region is estimated at fifty million acres. South of the Height of Land the pine belt is estimated as above at fifteen or twenty billion board feet and the pulpwood at 200 million cords. The forest area of the northern type is placed at fifty million acres and the southern hardwood type at three million, making a total of 103 million acres of potential forest area. The entire forest resources have been estimated at 100 billion feet, including spruce and balsam pulpwood.

This more or less confusing state of affairs is about to be remedied by an investigation similar to that recently completed in British Columbia. Mr. R. D. Craig of the Commission of Conservation has been given charge of the work of estimating the forest resources of Ontario. The work has been started and will probably be completed in two or three years' time. The size of the province, the comparative inaccessibility of much of its area and the diversities of climates and topography giving rise to diversities of forest types, make this a difficult undertaking, but one which will undoubtedly warrant the expenditure of time and labor involved.

On the completion of this study and the completion of the survey work being undertaken in Quebec and New Brunswick, it will be possible to make a reasonably accurate estimate of the total resources of the Dominion. With the information at present on hand, it is only possible to state that these resources represent a total area of about 250 million acres, containing from 500 to 800 billion feet board measure of merchantable saw timber and 800 million to one billion cords of pulpwood.

Lumber Priced by the Hundred

Material has advanced by leaps and bounds, and the price by the thousand seems almost prohibitive. Yet if we could educate our customers to buy by the piece, and not by the thousand, we would do away with much of the criticized "high prices."

We all know that the increase in price of material is getting unreasonable, and the market is such that we must get the advance in price in order to show any profit for ourselves—so we must seek some other method of doing business. The whole world is undergoing a change, and we feel that our business methods must likewise make a change or we will be holding the sock, and someone will come in and reap the reward. So we must educate the trade to buy by the foot and piece method, because of the many advantages in our favor.

We will admit that it will be inconvenient at first, but as soon as this method is adopted and used universally it will be a big improvement and will be a better method of handling our competitors, and will save much of the price cutting, as price cutting does not mean meeting competition, it simply means getting scared. You know better than your customer if your material is priced right, and we should also know why substituted articles are lower priced. If we make the difference clear in our own minds, we can make it clear to our customers.

One of the attractive newspaper advertisement series of the Shingle Agency of B. C.

If our competitor wishes to underprice an article, let him sell that particular article, but talk quality and service, and the majority of times you will make the sale. We must not cut our own throats for the sake of keeping company with our competitor.

Sears, Roebuck & Co., Montgomery Ward & Co., Chicago House Wrecking Co., and Gordon Van Tine are using the piece method and have been for years. We noticed in the latest catalogue of the Western Hardwood Lumber Co. all material is priced by the foot instead of by the thousand.

Ten dollars a thousand on lath is very high, but since we have been selling them at one cent each, we have had little criticism. 1-2 x 4-16 at $6.00 per thousand, we always figure eleven feet 66 cents and on selling 100 would amount to $66.00. Retailing 100 out at $60.00 per thousand, we would receive $64.02, or a loss of $1.98 on 100 pieces, and 66 cents does not seem nearly so high as $66.00 per thousand.

The majority of people that come to the yard are familiar with lumber sold by the thousand, but not by the piece, so there is a great help.

How many times in the last year have you heard this assertion? "What, lumber $60.00 per thousand." When I built my house two years ago, lumber was only $30.00. Now if we had quoted him by the piece, he might have thought it high, but probably would not have known if it was $30.00 or $60.00 per thousand.

I do not believe one person in ten coming to our places of business would stop to figure out the price per thousand if quoted by the piece, and the majority of people could not figure it out, and too, we forget the small things but never the large ones, so, by the piece we have the advantage, as they are not so apt to remember that a 2 x 4-12 cost 48 cents, as they would were it priced at $60.00 per thousand.

There is not a day we have not heard "Prices are too high." How are we to overcome this? I think the best solution will be to change our method of doing business, and quote by piece and foot.

I believe from personal observation that there is a certain amount of business that can be developed and handled by the right man and right methods. He must be a man of imagination and able to meet unfavorable conditions and unable to lay down on the job and say it can't be done. Are we that kind of men?—W. R. Coats before the recent Alberta Industrial Congress at Calgary.

Personal Paragraphs of Interest

R. S. Potter, of the R. S. Potter Lumber Co., Matheson, Ont., has been nominated by the Conservative party as its standard bearer in the Cochrane riding in the forthcoming provincial election.

Guy C. Long, of the Long Lumber Co., Hamilton, and wife are enjoying an extended holiday trip throughout the western provinces. They will visit several points on the Pacific Coast before their return.

Ed. Harper Wade, of Quebec, recently returned to his office after an attack of para-typhoid which is a most tedious illness. His many friends in the industry are pleased that he is now able to resume business.

J. C. Knight, managing director, Vancouver Lumber Co., Vancouver, who attended the recent National Industrial Conference in Ottawa, was in Toronto recently for a short time on his return to the West.

Brig.-Gen. J. B. White, of the Riordon Pulp & Paper Co., is on the general committee for the military ball to be given in Montreal by the G. O. C. and officers of District No. 1 in honour of the Prince of Wales. October 28 is the provisional date fixed.

Wm. Henderson, of Toronto, superintendent of the Shantymen's Christian Association, left recently on an extended trip to British Columbia, where he will spend a couple of months in the lumber camps, particularly in the inland district of the Province.

Alfred E. Clark, of Toronto, chairman of the Wholesale Lumber Dealers' Association, Quebec, has closed up his summer home at Grimsby Park where he spent the summer with his wife and family and is now at his Toronto residence, 17 St. Andrews Gardens.

L. G. Farr, general manager of the North Anson Manufacturing Co., North Anson, Me., and A. E. Hamilton, sales manager, have been on a buying trip to Montreal, Toronto and Ottawa, returning home by way of New Brunswick. They have made some large purchases of lumber.

Olivir Chenier passed away recently at the age of 70 years after an illness of several months, which developed into anaemia. Mr. Chenier, who was a resident of Buckingham, Que., was highly esteemed as a citizen and is survived by two daughters and one son. He has been engaged in lumbering all his life.

Among those who attended the annual conference of the National Retail Lumber Dealers' Association in Detroit recently were W. A. Hadley, of Chatham, president of the South-western Ontario Retail Lumber Dealers' Association; J. C. Scofield, of Windsor; E. C. Russell, of Walkerville and C. H. Belton, of Sarnia.

Joseph Oliver, of the Oliver Lumber Co., Limited, Toronto, who is Deputy Grand Sire of the Sovereign Grand Lodge, Independent Order of Oddfellows, attended the recent annual gathering in Baltimore, Md. It is expected that next year Mr. Oliver will be elevated to the highest position in the gift of the Order, that of Grand Sire.

Frank A. Kent, of the Seaman, Kent Co., Toronto, intends leaving toward the latter end of the month on a business trip to England. Mr. Kent reports that the plants of the company are very busy at the present time and are shipping large quantities of maple hardwood flooring to the Old Country. Mr. Kent expects to be absent on business for several weeks.

John J. Miller, who has been chief inspector for the National Hardwood Lumber Association at Toronto for the past seven or eight years, is now in charge of the hardwood department of the C. G. Anderson Lumber Co., Toronto. Mr. Miller was formerly deputy inspector of the Association at Buffalo and is well known to all the hardwood lumber manufacturers, wholesalers and dealers in Ontario.

A. P. Richards, who was for three years overseas and is a former resident of Burlington, Ont., has taken charge of the Sitka spruce end of the British Columbia business of Terry & Gordon, Toronto, and has his headquarters at Prince Rupert. Mr. Richards has been busy for some time in the shipment of Sitka spruce and a scow load of about 400,000 ft., principally of 2 in. stock has been going forward every week.

G. Brocklebank, representing C. V. Haerein, timber agent, Manchester, England, spent a few days in Toronto recently, calling upon the members of the trade. Mr. Haerein specializes in soft woods, and is particularly interested in British Columbia forest products. Mr. Brocklebank intends taking a trip to the Coast before his return home. This is his first visit to Canada and he speaks in appreciative terms of the reception accorded him.

Rev. Oswald J. Smith, 708 Dufferin Street, Toronto, who recently returned from spending several months in religious work among the logging camps in British Columbia, has been appointed secretary of the Shantymen's Christian Association and will make his headquarters in Toronto. R. D. Richardson, 103 St. Clair Ave., Toronto, has been secretary-treasurer of the Shantymen's Christian Association for some time, and retains the office of treasurer. The work has become so important and responsible that it was deemed advisable to divide the office of secretary-treasurer. Rev. Mr. Smith was formerly associate pastor of the Dale Presbyterian Church, Toronto.

J. J. Elliott, of the Elliott Woodworking Co., Toronto, recently returned from a successful business trip to Great Britain. While there he formed a company known as the Dominion Machinery Co. of Halifax, England, to manufacture and handle the Elliott combination woodworker for Great Britain and the Continent. He reports a strong demand for this machine and brought back orders for more than one hundred and fifty machines.

H. L. Hobard, who has been in the employ of the National Hardwood Lumber Association for many years in the New England district and latterly in Toronto, assisting J. J. Miller, inspector, who recently resigned, has been appointed as successor to Mr. Miller and has entered upon his new duties. The selection of Mr. Hobard is one that will prove acceptable to the members of the association and is another instance of a promotion well deserved.

Mrs. William Rutherford, wife of the founder of the firm of William Rutherford & Sons, Company, Ltd., Montreal, wholesale & retail lumber merchants, sash & door manufacturers, died on September 23, in Montreal, aged 83. The late William Rutherford predeceased her by sixteen years. She is survived by two daughters and five sons, three of the sons being connected with the firm: Mr. William Rutherford, president; Mr. Andrew Rutherford, vice-president; and Mr. Stewart F. Rutherford, secretary-treasurer. The last named is also managing director of the Dominion Box & Package Co., Ltd.

Lieut. Larkin Back in Lumber Game

Lieut. H. W. Larkin, M.C., Toronto

Lieut. H. W. Larkin, who returned several weeks ago from overseas, has embarked in the wholesale lumber business on his own account and opened an office in Canada Permanent Building, 18 Toronto St., Toronto, under the name of the Larkin Lumber Company. He was born in Brandon, Man., and is a son of C. A. Larkin, a former widely known lumberman of Toronto who retired at the commencement of the war. Lieut. Larkin was with his father and, after the business was incorporated in 1909, he was made secretary-treasurer of the company. He has had a wide experience in the industry, particularly in the selling and distribution ends. He took an active part in the management of the affairs of the Larkin Lumber Co. and when European hostilities broke out enlisted for overseas service. He left Canada in 1916 with the 48th Battery and in the spring of 1917 crossed to France where he was attached to the 13th Battery and 4th Brigade headquarters, being Adjutant of the latter from December, 1917. Lieut. Larkin participated in all the "shows" from Vimy Ridge until the signing of the armistice and, although in the thick of the fray at all times, managed to escape unscathed. He was awarded the M. C. for his splendid work. In the lumber line the Larkin Lumber Company specialize in softwoods and also B. C. forest products and shingles.

The Passing of Hon. Frank Cochrane

Many friends in the lumbering trade will regret to learn of the death of Hon. Frank Cochrane, who was a member of the Federal Cabinet. He had been in poor health for some time but the end came rather suddenly. For many years he was Minister of Lands, Forests and Mines in Ontario and his administration was characterized by firmness, foresight and aggressiveness.

A man of sound judgment, thorough business training, high ideals and devotion to duty he rose from being a lumberjack to occupying a foremost position in the public life of the Dominion. On the formation of the Borden ministry in 1911, Mr. Cochrane who had resigned his portfolio in Ontario, was given direction of Railways and Canals and during his regime demonstrated that he was efficient, energetic and broad-minded. In 1917 he resigned owing to continued ill health, but remained a member of the cabinet without portfolio.

Previous to entering upon political life he was a successful hardware merchant in Sudbury and had extensive business interests in Northern Ontario which country he knew and understood intimately.

Religious Instruction in All Logging Camps

What the Shantymen's Christian Association Has Done in Raising the Moral Status of Men and Banishing Menacing "Isms" from Ranks of Lumberjacks

Mr. Wm. Henderson, of Toronto, superintendent of the Shantymen's Christian Association, recently returned from an extended trip in the interest of the work throughout the Western States and Pacific Coast provinces. The labors of the Shantymen's Christian Association, organized by Mr. Henderson some eleven years ago, have extended in influence, usefulness and activity. In April of the present year work was started in the camps of British Columbia and there are now seven missionaries laboring in that province. During the winter of 1917-18 it was estimated that about 30,000 shantymen were ministered to in the camps of Ontario and those of Quebec as far east as the Laurentian Mountains and as far west as northern Saskatchewan and in Minnesota, Wisconsin and Michigan.

The Shantymen's Christian Association of the Unitetd States was organized about a year and a half ago to work in co-operation with the Canadian Association. Everywhere the Good Word is carried by the missionaries and the Gospels, in the various languages spoken by men in the camps, are given free distribution. No collection is taken up at any of the meetings and no general canvass of the big lumbermen employers has been made for funds for the important work. It is interesting to note that the greatest economy has been exercised in the administration of the affairs of the Association and there are no office expenses. The secretary-treasurer for Ontario, R. D. Richardson, 103 St. Clair Ave., Toronto, gives all his services free of charge and last year there were 18 missionaries engaged in the work. This year there have been a great deal more owing to the extension of activities to the camps in British Columbia. Mr. Henderson has pointed out that imparting the fundamental doctrines of the Christian religion has banished Bolshevism and the nefarious work of the I.W.W. and the living exponents of this non-denominational, non-sectarian work have done much to kill the propagation of various "isms" and "cetts" that of late have made serious inroads in labor's ranks in certain western districts, and particularly in mining and construction camps.

Extension of Work in the West

Discussing his recent trip to British Columbia, Mr. Henderson stated that until within the past few months no religious services had even been held in some of the camps of the Pacific Coast provinces. Everywhere the missionaries of the Shantymen's Christian Association have been received by the employees and logging superintendants with much favor and interest. The bearers of Glad Tidings go about their labors simply and quietly and have none of the clerical, starched-up or professional appearance of the fashionable city sky-pilot. The missionaries were taken from one camp to another in British Columbia free of charge by the steam tugs of the various logging companies, or if the destination was at some point which could not be reached by this means, then the journey was generally made in a gasoline launch.

To show the spirit exhibited, here is an exact copy of one of many letters received written by a large lumber concern and sent to their logging superintendant:

> "Mr. W. Henderson, superintendent of the Shantymen's Christian Association, and his associates are going north to visit the various camps in connection with the work of the Association, and we will be glad if you will show them any courtesy you can at our camps, as their mission is purely to preach the gospel at the camps, and we believe they are doing big work throughout Canada and the U. S. at such places as we have in the north. They intend going north tonight so that they will reach Rock Bay in the near future, and as above stated, kindly use them as well as you can while at our camps."

W. T. Overstall, 510 Hastings St., Vancouver, is secretary of the Association in Vancouver and in a recent interview with Mr. Henderson the Vancouver World said in part:

> "The idea of the Association, which has been operating in the east for a long time, is to send men into the logging camps who do not represent any particular church. The Association is endorsed by practically all of the churches.

Some Dangerous Doctrines Set Forth

That life is not all sunshine and that there is opposition in certain quarters to this non-sectarian, non-denominational Christian work, is evidenced by a bitter attack which was made upon it lately by the "Camp Worker," which describes itself as "the official organ of the British Columbia Loggers' and Camp Workers' Union." This eight page publication is printed in Vancouver and is evidently strongly Bolshevik in vision and surveillance. It announces, for instance, its constitution, as follows:

> "Modern society is divided into two classes: Capitalist and Wageworking, with interest entirely opposed to each other.
>
> "The present order gives to the capitalistic class an ever increasing supply of wealth and to the wageworker an ever increasing measure of degradation and misery.
>
> "Therefore, a struggle goes on between these two classes.
>
> "As sellers of labor, the workers are compelled to organize industrially, without regard to race, creed or color, not only in order to obtain better conditions, and to resist the ruthless exploitation by capital, but also to educate its members to their class position in society, so that they shall be able to take over the industries and to use them in the interests of the whole community instead of as at present for the benefit of a few."

An editorial entitled "A gospel of the free and easy" is intended to be ironical in tone and to cast ridicule and derision, not only upon the work of the Shantymen's Christian Association, but also on the religious instruction or efforts made by them and upon all organized moral movements to make the world a better and brighter place in which to live and move.

As a sample of the balderash ladled out in the columns of the "Camp Worker" the following is a fair specimen

> "It seems this society sends men into the camps (we

In the accompanying view, representative of British Columbia logging life and activity, the scenes depicted (from left to right) are—a logging camp; a logging train; when the logs come down the chute; a log chute, and a donkey engine and a boom of some of the finest logs in the province, giving som conception of the average large dimensions of B. C. trees.

In the above scenes, representative of British Columbia timber and logging life (reading from left to right) the views are a great rock cut for a lugging railway; the island highway, showing some of the monstrous trees of the coast; a night on the shore, depicting one of the missionaries of the Shantymen's Christian Association sleeping out in the open air; next comes the forest trail, showing a missionary on his route, and last, but not least, is a typical logging railway.

preamer to talk about Jesus, and give out books but does not make any collection.

"However, we have no particular desire to frown upon this work. If loggers in coast camps feel that they need their souls saved now and again, and Mr. Henderson and his association continues to provide them with the necessary weapons, free of charge, no doubt they will take advantage of the free and easy offer. But what struck us as pretty amusing was the statement, according to the Vancouver World, made by this Henderson person, to the effect that 'books are distributed but no money is taken for them.' (All the same Anyox leaflets.) This is followed by this peach: 'This policy has served to win the confidence of the men who for years had the idea drilled into them by I.W.W. and other radicals that preachers and Christian workers generally were nothing but a bunch of grafters who cared nothing for the workers but only wanted their money.'

"[illegible] Tut! We have preachers lining up with the boss during labor disputes, assisting in the work of misrepresentation and general vilification of men fighting for a mere advance in wages that may cover to some extent the advancing cost of living, while others express the fervent Christian hope that all Bolshies and other agitators should be placed on a ship of stone, flying sails of lead, with the wrath of God for a trade breeze and all the ship's passengers provided with non-stop tickets for Hell. Further, we know that the vulgar language and monkey pranks of Billy Sunday are not done for money and graft. No! No! He runs around like his lord and master in a female night shirt, with no place to lay his head, and when he wants the price of a drink of grape juice he sends his faithful partner, 'Ma,' down to the beach to see if God has put a dime in a red herring's mouth, or something of that kind. He follows his Master Billy does, even to the point of crucifixion. But it is the worker's crucifixion. These things can be multiplied indefinitely, and if the loggers in the coast camps tell some of these itinerating grafts a few home truths they can only thank themselves and the (profession?) they have chosen."

One of the strong points about the association is that it is enabled to carry on its work without any appeals to the men among whom the work is done for any financial assistance. Books are distributed but no money is taken for them. This policy has served to win the confidence of the men who for years had the idea drilled into them by I.W.W. and other radicals that preachers and Christian workers generally were nothing but a bunch of grafters who cared nothing for the workers but only wanted their money.

"We were everywhere received with the greatest kindness and consideration, both by the foremen and the men. We moved backwards and forwards on the logging trains in the camps and where water had to be crossed were supplied with boats free of charge.

"The men were generally very friendly," continued Mr. Henderson, "but many of them have their minds thoroughly poisoned by the Bolshevik teaching of the foreign element. Quite a number of English speaking men frankly admitted that they were Bolsheviks and held that the conditions under which they lived were little better than slave conditions, and this in spite of the fact that the meals to which they sat down could scarcely be bought in a city restaurant for less than a dollar. A Finlander said the working class were slaves, though it was later disclosed that he was earning $250 per month. The spirit of discontent is being industrially preached among these men, and cannot fail to do a great deal of harm unless something is done to counteract its influence."

Mr. Henderson states that this is the kind of criticism and discouragement which workers have run up against in certain sections of British Columbia, which appear to be hot-beds of anarchy, socialism and Bolshevism. However, the results on the whole have been most encouraging and opposition and censure of the character outlined in the "Camp Worker" only serve to inspire the missionaries to greater achievements and stimulate them with fresh zeal in the splendid work they are undertaking which has been growing from year to year in its results, benefits and efficiency.

"The best thing that ever happened," is the title of an article in the recent edition of the "American Lumberman" which was written by Mr. Henderson. As it sheds considerable light upon the progress of the work in the west, it is worthy of perusal:

The speaker was a member of the Northern Wisconsin Loggers' Association talking to the writer after their last Conference at Ashland, Wis.

By request Mr. John Miller, our assistant superintendent in Wisconsin and the writer, had laid before the Conference the methods of work and aims of the Shantymen's Christian Association in the United States and Canada.

The fact that the work was non-sectarian but carried on by good men of various churches, was emphasized and the advantage this was in the camps was pointed out. The reasons why all missionaries were pledged not to ask for collections in the camps was also explained and it was shown how this dispelled the principal charge made by I.W.W. and kindred trouble makers that all the interest any preacher had in them was to get money out of them was answered.

The history of the results of the work in the Canadian camps was outlined showing how quickly the men dropped their foolish fashion of blowing their stakes, and how the great majority had signed the prohibition petition a few years after this work was started among them. The absence of any I.W.W. troubles in the Ontario camps reached by our missionaries was also a striking testimony to what a little interest shown in the men would accomplish.

After the loggers had discussed the matter, a decision was arrived at expressing their confidence in Mr. Miller's work, and asking that he seek to secure enough assistance to provide, if possible, a monthly service in each of the camps represented by this Association. As a tangible evidence of their good will a small assessment was made on each member to raise a fund to be sent to Mr. H. Martin, the treasurer, 408 South Haynes Ave., Chicago, to help defray the expenses. They also promised that every member would assist the missionaries travelling to and fro to the camps.

This is what the speaker quoted as being "the best thing that ever happened."

The close of the first year of the United States' work shows that over 200 services had been held during the year and about 12,000 reached.

Britain Against Inporting Wooden Houses

The Daily News, of London, Eng., says the Standardization Committee of Inquiry into Health does not agree with the recent proposal of Agent-General Wade, of British Columbia, to solve the housing problems by the importation of wooden houses. The newspaper says that a London firm during the past twelve months approached the housing committees and commissioners with suggestions for building houses on the American colonial system. In no case had they been able to persuade the authorities to adopt the proposals despite the advantage in time and money saving. Wooden structures are considered unsuitable to the English climate, and the standardization committee is adverse to buildings of a temporary character.

New Eastern Representative Appointed

Joseph H. Poulin, Montreal

Joseph H. Poulin, Montreal, who has been appointed representative of Terry & Gordon, of Toronto, for Quebec, the Maritime provinces and the New England states, spent a few days in Toronto last week on business. Mr. Poulin has spent some fifteen years in the lumber business and is widely known in the East. Born in Albany, N. Y., he was educated there at the public school, business college and military academy and later took an advanced course under the regents of the University of the State of New York, graduating in 1903. He then spent two years in St. Laurent college, St. Laurent, Que., and was for three years active in railway work being connected with the freight tariff department of the New York Central Railway in Albany and Montreal. He was one of the organizers and first secretary-treasurer of the Eagle Lumber Co., Limited, Montreal, under the presidency of the late Leonidas Villeneuve, where he remained for several years being also the manager of the Montreal office. Mr. Poulin many times over has covered Quebec, the Maritime provinces and the Eastern States. Until quite recently he was Canadian manager for the Robert W. Hunt Co., of Chicago. As a member of the Terry & Gordon organization he is confidently looking forward to doing a record business for the firm.

Experimental Areas in Forestry Work

G. H. Prince, chief forester of New Brunswick, writes the "Canada Lumberman" as follows: In regard to the experimental plot of about 500 acres, which we are going to initiate this year by making experimental thinnings in several different methods, in co-operation with the Bathurst Lumber Company, good progress is being made. Mr. Angus McLean is very greatly interested in this proposition, and Dr. Howe, of Toronto, recently spent a week in Fredericton laying out the experimental areas. By mutual agreement the area will be reserved from further operation after this winter's cuts have been made for a period of twenty-five years and measurements will be made every few years to determine the results of the different methods of cutting. On some of it the slash will be burned, while on other parts it will be left, as is customary, on the usual logging operation.

Returned Soldiers in Forestry Line

C. E. Maimann, graduate of the University of New Brunswick, who recently returned from overseas and was engaged on the Crown Land Survey for New Brunswick, lately resigned, and has gone to Prince Albert to act as an assistant supervisor with the Dominion Forest Branch. H. C. Holman, B. Sc F., also a returned soldier, who has been engaged during the past season with the New Brunswick Forest Survey, has gone to take a position with the Dominion Forest Branch in Alberta. Both these men received substantial increases in salary and their many friends wish them continued success in their work in the west. R. D. Jago, formerly of the New Brunswick Forest Service, has returned from overseas, and has resumed work.

Want Quebec Timber Cutting Regulations Altered

At the summer meeting of the Woodlands Section of the Canadian Pulp and Paper Association the following resolution was passed: That in the opinion of this meeting certain changes in the regulations of the lands and forests governing the cutting of timber on Crown lands are essential to the preservation and perpetuation of the forests, and it is respectfully requested that the executive committee of the Canadian Pulp & Paper Association appoint a committee to co-operate with the existing committee of the province of Quebec Limit Holders' Association in waiting upon the Government with a view to urging the necessity of an early revision of these regulations in order to meet present day conditions.

This resolution was submitted to the executive committee of the Pulp and Paper Association, and met with their approval, Mr. J. A. Bothwell, the president, nominating the following committee: Messrs. Ellwood Wilson, Laurentide Company, Ltd., Grand'Mere, Que; R. P. Kernan, Donnacona Paper Company, Quebec.; W. Gerard Power, River Ouelle Pulp & Lumber Company, St. Pacome, Que.; P. W. Buchanan, Brompton Pulp & Paper Company, East Angus, Que.; Brig.-Gen. J. B. White, Riordon Pulp & Paper Co., Ltd., Montreal; Roy Campbell, Riordon Pulp & Paper Company, Ltd., Montreal; W. F. Clarke, Gulf Pulp & Paper Co., Clark City, Que; J. [illegible] Dalton, St. Maurice Paper Company, Cap Madeleine, Que.; R. Gautier, Bathurst Lumber Company, Ltd., Bonaventure, Que.; T. [illegible] Kenny, Jas. McLaren Company, Buckingham, Que.; M. H. Montgomery, Montgomery & Sons, Ltd., New Richmond, Que.; Arthur J. Price, Price Bros. and Company, Quebec; William Russell, [illegible] Richardson Co., Ltd., Matane, Que.; R. S. P. Smythe, St. Anne Lumber Co., Ltd., St. Anne des Monts, Gaspe Co., Que.; R. O. Sweezey, Royal Securities Corporation, Montreal; Anderson, Canada P[illegible] Company, Windsor Mills, Que.; A. L. Dawe, Canadian Pulp & Paper Association, Montreal

Mr. Ellwood Wilson has been appointed chairman of the committee and has addressed a letter to the various members outlining the principal objects of the proposed conference. The matter has also been taken up with Mr. P. G. Owen, secretary of the Quebec Limit Holders' Association, who has had informal conferences with the Deputy Minister of Lands and Forests, Quebec.

Prior to the deputation waiting upon the Hon. H. Mercier, the new Minister of Lands and Forests, at which it is hoped Sir [illegible] Gouin will be present, a meeting of the joint committees is [illegible] to be held, at which the entire subject will be discussed, so that the committee will be able to place before the Government [illegible] fined proposals.

How Fire Diminishes Timber in Rockies

In writing up his trip to the West a representative of a [illegible] Toronto paper speaks of the awful ravages of forest fires in [illegible] Columbia as follows: A trip through the Rocky Mountains [illegible] time serves to remind the traveller of the appalling waste of [illegible] natural heritage that occurs, with tragic precision, year after year. For the most part the public reads of the devastation being wrought in a certain area, utters a few explosive comments upon our [illegible] prodigality, and forgets about it—while the fire creeps on over the green-groved hill-side, leaving no trace but smoking ruin. I saw one big fire from the train window. It was several thousand feet up the mountain-side, but from the train the flames could be seen licking the very tops of tall trees that succumbed, with startling rapidity, to their fiery roaring onslaught. I have been told by one whose authority is, or should be, beyond question, that thus far this summer fires have destroyed fully five per cent. of the whole Rocky Mountain Forest Reserve. If that be the case (and I believe departmental officials will verify these figures), it is an easy matter for the reader to figure out the probable life of our priceless timbered areas on the Western coast.

Other things than trees are "going up in smoke" this rather ill-nurtured autumn. In its ability to spend money, and to provide for the spending of the money of others, the West has nothing to learn from the "oft-effeted" East. Not in a generation has there been such a passenger traffic as is moving this summer over these Western rails. Helping to restore the balance of an undoubtedly depleted crop, the money of thousands of United States tourists is being thankfully received by Canadian railroads, hotels, summer resorts and cities. I believe that I might say, without the slightest exaggeration, that from 50 to 70 per cent. of the people I meet on the main line trains are from "across the line." By that I do not refer to the ubiquitous American "drummer," who, like the poor, always is with us, and in goodly number. I am thinking solely of tourists—whole families of them, father, mother and four or five children, all "just having a real good time"—as they tell one—spending money, seeing Canada, "getting acquainted."

Gauging Aright Canada's Tree Growth

R. O. Sweezey, of Montreal, writes the "Canada Lumberman" as follows: "In noting your comments on page 86 of the September 1st issue of the 'Canada Lumberman' in regard to the growth of forest trees, I am inclined to think from my experience in the forests of Quebec and other Provinces that your figures do not represent the average growth of spruce and balsam. I quite appreciate the importance of impressing upon the public the fact that trees grow very slowly, but do not let us fool ourselves by under-estimating or under-valuing the assets which we possess. I find the fault of under-estimating is often as much to be deplored as that of over-estimating."

The Crompton Car Co., Limited, with headquarters in Toronto and a capital stock of $25,000, has been incorporated to manufacture, sell and deal in automobiles, vehicles and automobile parts and accessories. Among the incorporators are M. P. Vandervort and Murray H. Gillam.

Operates His Sawmill by Electricity

Mark Rogers of Parry Sound Says He Finds This Method Preferable to Steam in His Plant

Mark Rogers, of Parry Sound, Ont., is one of the best known lumbermen in that district, and in November last he purchased from Neibergall, Cook & Co., the saw and planing mills in Parry Sound. While these mills are not of large capacity, they are running satisfactorily this season. The sawmill had not been operating for several years but it was December last before Mr. Rogers was able to locate a stock of logs. This season he will have over a million feet of lumber cut as well as 5,000 railway ties. He stocks all kinds of logs. He finds that the planing mill business has been a great help in connection with his activities and during July trade was particularly good. Mr. Rogers makes his own flooring, siding, casings and all kinds of mouldings.

His saw mill is one of the very few electrically operated in Ontario. It is equipped with an inserted tooth Disston circular saw, double edger, trimmers and slash saw. The electric power is supplied by 100 h. p. slip ring C. G. E. motor, which stands up easily under the load. Mr. Rogers states that he finds electricity much more satisfactory than steam power. Parry Sound is building a new dam and power-house this year which will give the industry more current if it is needed.

In the planing mill Mr. Rogers has a three-sided planer and matcher made by Clark, Demill & Co. and a sticker made by the same people. He has also a rip saw and intends to install a resaw in the near future. These machines are driven by a 35 h. p. squirrel cage C. G. E. motor which gives splendid satisfaction. In the summer time Mr. Rogers employs about 25 men, which force is considerably smaller during the winter. He does not operate any camps but buys his logs or has choppers take them out. Two Canadian Northern spurs extend to his mill which facilitate quick delivery. Mr. Rogers handles shingles, flooring, siding, casings, base, sheeting, etc.—practically everything in the lumber and forest products line.

Mr. Rogers has had a rather interesting career, being born at Highgate, Kent. Co., in 1881. When very yougn his parents removed to a farm at Minden, in Haliburton Co. Here among the rugged hills and beautiful lakes he was reared, working hard on the farm in the summer time and attending school in winter. After securing his education he spent six years in the lumbering business—in the bush, on the river and in the sawmill.

At 24 years of age he started back to school again, getting his non-professional first-class teacher's certificate in 1909. The following year he attended the Faculty of Education in Toronto, securing his certificate which entitled him to teach in either public or high schools. He accepted a position on the staff of the Lindsay Collegiate Institute where he remained until 1911 when he resigned and went to Minden where, with his brother, E. A. Rogers, he leased the Minden mills from S. F. Stinson. They conducted a planing and chopping mill for five years and cut about one million feet of lumber annually, doing business under the firm name of Rogers Bros. Their stock consisted of hemlock, basswood, birch, elm, ash and spruce.

In 1916 the subject of this reference bought out E. A. Rogers' holdings but continued a year under the firm name and in 1917 he removed to Huntsville to look after his interests there. Some six years ago, with W. G. Holinshead as partner, Mr. Rogers purchased about 2,500 acres of timber in Sinclair and Brunel Tps. They built a little mill at Grassmere, six miles from Huntsville, and last year sold out their interest at this point and shortly after Mr. Rogers purchased the saw and planing mills of Neibergall, Cook & Co. in Parry Sound, as already stated and has been doing a thriving and prosperous business.

National Association Extends Work in Canada

The National Hardwood Lumber Association, whose headquarters are in Chicago, is enjoying a gratifying gain in membership. Mr. F. F. Fish, secretary-treasurer of the organization, recently paid a visit to Toronto, Montreal, and Quebec, and as a result fourteen membership applications were secured making the present representation from Canada stand at 39.

The association is extending its scope in the Dominion. It will be remembered that they placed an inspector in the Toronto district in 1911 and the work has grown so that they have two more engaged at present, and their time is entirely occupied in inspecting lumber under the bonded section of the National Hardwood Lumber Association.

It has been decided to place an inspector and open an office in Montreal. Several applications for the position have been received from inspectors of long experience in the Province of Quebec. The chief inspector of the association visited Montreal during the past month to consider the applications and select the best man fitted for the position, who, in addition to having a thorough knowledge of national railways, must be able to speak French as well as English.

John J. Miller, chief inspector of Toronto, has recently joined the staff of the C. G. Anderson Lumber Co., Toronto, and his successor will be named in a few days. The grading rules of the association have been adopted by practically every other association as being the most perfect for all practical purposes. Uniformity now prevails in the matter of grading rules and inspection. The only difference between the two associations—the National and the American Hardwood Manufacturers' Association—is that in grading rules and inspection the American Association confines the work of its inspection department to the settlement of disputes, while the National organization uses its department in the making of original inspections. That uniformity has been attained in the matter of grading rules which apply to the whole continent is a source of satisfaction in hardwood lumber circles.

The present membership of the association, so far as Canada is concerned, is as follows:

Toronto—C. G. Anderson Lumber Co. Atlantic Lumber Co. Robert Bury & Co. Edward Clark & Sons. Gall Lumber Co. Graves, Bigwood & Co. Hart & McDonagh. Johnston Lumber Co. Wm. Laking Lumber Co. McBean & Verrall. Oliver Lumber Co. Seaman, Kent Co. Pedwell Hardwood Lumber Co. Wilson Lumber Co. Frank H. Harris Lumber Co.

Montreal—Bennett Lumber Co. Geo. C. Goodfellow. E. M. Nicholson & Co. C. A. Spencer. Wm. Rutherford & Sons Co. Henri Peladeau. Eagle Lumber Co. Chas. H. Russell Co. Riordon Pulp & Paper Co. T. Prefontaine & Co. Geo. Kersley.

Quebec—Auger & Sons, Limited. W. & J. Sharples. Roch Julien.

Hamilton—Long Lumber Co.

Collingwood—A. G. McKean.

Huntsville—Muskoka Wood Mfg. Co. M. Martin.

Midland—Midland Woodworkers.

Owen Sound—John Harrison & Sons Co. Keenan Bros.

Wiarton—Geddes-Tyson Lumber Co.

Great Pulpwood Activities of Laurentide

Work in the logging department of the Laurentide Co., Grand Mere, P.Q., has been commenced. The company will this year operate twenty camps. There will be about a thousand men in these company camps. The rate of pay is $60 to $70 per month, with board, and a 10 per cent. bonus to every man who remains on the job for three months.

The department has had a great many applications from contractors, and will have no difficulty in securing the necessary cut. In all, about four thousand men and a thousand horses will be engaged in getting out wood for the Laurentide mill during the winter.

An innovation this year was the creation of a new district by the division of the old La Tuque District. This new district, the Ribbon River district, with headquarters at La Tuque, will be in charge of E. M. McLaren. The Mattawin district will be under B. C. McLaren, and St. Maurice under B. L. Butler. La Tuque district will be under B. L. Baxter, who was formerly a member of the logging office at Grand Mere.

Returned Soldiers Take Forestry Posts

S. M. Ritchie of Temple, N.B., a returned soldier and a scaler of some experience, has accepted the position of forest ranger for Albert Co. with headquarters at Hillsborough.

E. H. Lewis, a returned soldier, of Hillsborough, Albert Co., has secured a post as scaler's helper.

H. C. Lynn, of Campbellton, another returned soldier, has taken a position as forest ranger in Restigouche County. He will make his headquarters at Kedgwick and have charge of District No. 4.

Harvey Malcolm, of Flat Lands, Restigouche Co., also a returned soldier, has been appointed forest ranger in District No. 7, Restigouche County. His district will cover the watershed of the South East Upsalquitch River.

Britain Should Revert to Wooden Houses

In a recent editorial the Daily Mail, of London, Eng., says that as Britain has not got 335 million pounds to spend on the housing scheme, Britishers will have to go back to the simpler things. Thousands, it states, live in wooden houses in America, and they were common houses in England in old times. By using the material in hand in wooden huts the people will get good housing and pay their way while the taxpayer will be relieved.

River Drivers Must Complete Work

Cannot Quit in Midst of Operation and Collect Full Wages, According to Recent Decision in Quebec

It has been decided by the courts in Quebec city that river-drivers who contract to do certain work for the season cannot "jump their jobs" and collect full pay from their employers.

An important suit was tried before Chief Justice Sir F. X. Lemieux, in the Circuit Court, Quebec city, on Sept. 22, when seven river drivers entered action against the St. Anne Power Co. of Beaupre, Que., to recover alleged arrears of wages. Judgment was delivered in favor of the defendant company.

The particulars of the case are that the men (who were the plaintiffs in the action) were engaged to drive logs last spring for the St. Anne Power Co. and were to be paid $3.00 per day and the company paid them off at $2.50 per day.

The St. Anne Power Co. admitted that these men were employed at $3.00 per day, but stated that they did not finish the drive. They remained only 25 days and left without cause; consequently, by their course, the company did not complete the drive on the stream that these men were working on and the company was put to considerable expense and caused damage.

In delivering judgment in favor of the St. Anne Power Co. Chief Justice Lemieux spoke, in part, as follows:

His sympathy was with the laborer, but in future he would have to put that aside, for we had arrived at a time that all would have to be firmer with the laborer. The lumber industry was one of the principal industries in the province and the lumberman had as much right to protection as the employee. In this case these men left at a critical time for no reason whatever. Lumber companies were paying high wages and feeding the men well, and the men, in turn, had to give value for the amount they were paid; also that the young men in the country were worse than the young men in the city, in that they imagined that they were going to do as they pleased and work for a short time only, no matter what inconvenience they might cause a company. When they go on a drive they are supposed to remain until it is finished as it is only at a certain time in the spring that the logs can be conveniently floated. These men did not earn $1.00 a day for the company, therefore the Chief Justice stated he would dismiss the action with costs against the plaintiffs.

Valets and Private Secretaries for Lumberjacks?

Fear that the lumberjacks of Thompson Sound district might next ask the company to provide them with valets and private secretaries perhaps helped W. H. Higgins, one of British Columbia's oldest logging operators, to decide to close down the camps of Higgins & Company.

Mr. Higgins is 89 years of age and has bossed gangs of men in the woods in various parts of the North American Continent since 1847. He is, in spite of his years, physically fit and mentally alert.

"But I am a bit old fashioned may be," said the sturdy old Canadian, when he told friends recently in Vancouver of the circumstances leading to closing down the camp at Thompson Sound and putting the keys thereof in his pocket. "I for one cannot stand for the fanaticism which is sweeping the country and disturbing industry.

"I did not mind when the men gathered at the bunkhouse and organized a debating society. That was very well, and they had their meetings under a proper chairman and with parliamentary rules governing the proceedings. But organizers came to me and demanded that we install both shower and plunge baths, a change of sheets every day, brass bedsteads, box springs and hair mattresses for each man—well, that was going a bit too far.

"Soon we would have had to add other luxuries if we met such unusual demands," continued the veteran logger. He denied that the men had also applied to have tea and toast served to them in bed before undertaking the day's exercise in the sylvan glades of the North.

"But they desire to ape millionaires," said Mr. Higgins, with some heat, "and for my part I am through until this fanaticism passes. There is only one thing that I can do and that is to pay off all hands, and if they can live until we can reach a more sensible basis, I am sure I can."

Among the men at Mr. Higgins' camp were workers who had been engaged under him for many years. The cook had served with him for eleven years, he said, and one old New Brunswicker had worked with him for forty-five years. Some other men had been with him for from four to ten years. But the men who had carried on the agitation, which resulted in the closing of the camp, were newcomers.

"Well do I remember," said Capt. Higgins, "when we worked in the camps of New Brunswick for $9 a month. We used to spend the nights in a great big bunkhouse with a roaring fire in the middle of the room. One of the boys would fiddle and others would sing or dance or tell stories. We were happy in those days and worked hard all winter, and in the spring we would drive the rivers. We had salt pork and potatoes and Porto Rico molasses but not such a thing as sugar. In those days there was none of this high-sounding talk about proletariat dictatorship and such nonsense. And those camps produced the best men in Canada."

Mr. Higgins is apparently unable to solve present-day labor problems. But in his thirty-five years in the British Columbia forests he has solved many other problems. In the old days the man who "ran" the camp was the man who drove the oxen. The teamster, usually a profane and wicked co-worker, had the power of life and death over the day's work. Oldtimers will tell how the driver of oxen might sulk in his tent if a drizzle of rain appeared in the morning or might provide a partial holiday for all hands in the camp if one of his sturdy beasts suffered a scalded shoulder during the day.

It was this veteran who is credited with having first introduced the idea of steam power in logging operations, a departure which robbed the driver of oxen of his job for all time.

"Yes," said the logger, when he had paid his compliments further to the organizers who are spreading their propaganda among the lumber camps of the province, "I believe that I first introduced steam in logging. I did it to beat the oxen teamster, who was boss of the works always, until we got rid of him. We first tried steam on the side hills and the concentrated power worked splendidly. The late John Hendry was one of the first to recognize its merits."

"But let me say this," said he. "The lumber industry today can not see far into the future and is as uncertain as to what is before as during the war days. Labor unrest is the chief factor contributing to this condition. Unreasonable and unnecessary demands on the part of labor will mean that many a man in the business will be compelled to do as I have done—close down the camp and pay off the men and wait until there is a fair chance for all concerned. And I know that this will mean employment and all that goes therewith, but only suffering of some sort will bring about natural and normal relations in the industry between employer and employee."

Mr. Higgins worked for many years with the late James Ross, of Quebec, and the late James MacLaren, of Ottawa, in logging enterprises of various kinds. It was during the war that he created a record in outstanding accomplishments when in a serious emergency he rallied 800 men to a spruce camp in the Queen Charlotte Islands and organized them to carry out operations under the direction of the Imperial Munitions Board.

Cedars of Lebanon Made at Creation

The famous cedars of Lebanon, tradition says, were planted by God at the creation of the world and that they will endure until the last day. That there was a great grove of cedars of Lebanon in the days of King Solomon there can be no doubt, as it was from them that he obtained the wood for building the temple.

At the present day the grove contains 389 trees, of which only 15 are of large size. It is the centre of a great basin in the mountains 6,000 feet above the sea.

Mr. Booth Busy As Ever At 93

In the centre of the accompanying illustration is seen Mr. J. R. Booth, of Ottawa, Canada's oldest lumberman, who is now in his 93rd year and works harder and longer each succeeding month than he did the previous one.

Surrounding Mr. Booth are members of the Grenadier Guards Band, of London, England, who recently gave a concert in Ottawa and filled a two weeks' engagement at the Canadian National Exhibition, Toronto.

A rather interesting story is linked up with the taking of this picture. J. S. Knapman, of Toronto, purchasing agent of the McDonald Lumber Co., Toronto, happened to be in Ottawa during the engagement of the famous band. He was sitting in the rotunda of

J. R. Booth making a tour of his sawmill and other industries at Ottawa, in company with several members of the Grenadier Guards Band

the hotel when he overheard some of "the boys" remark that they would like to visit the industries at the Chaudiere.

"Would you care to see one of the largest operations in lumber, pulp and paper that there is in the British Empire?" inquired Mr. Knapman.

The musicians replied it would be a great pleasure and privilege for them. Accordingly Mr. Knapman called upon Mr. C. Jackson Booth and obtained the necessary permit for the men to be shown the teeming industrial activities of Mr. Booth at the Chaudiere Falls. As they were going through the plant they found Canada's veteran lumberman near a circular saw in the mill supervising the cutting up of an unusually large pine log. As Mr. Knapman entered the mill, Mr. J. R. Booth shook hands with him, saying: "Come over to the light, I want to see who you are," it being rather dark in the place where the "lumber king" was standing. As soon as they took a few steps, Mr. Booth mentioning the name of his visitor, remarked: "Yes, it is just twelve years since you used to come around here. You bought a good many thousand poles from me for the Bell Telephone Company, and I have not seen you since you went out of that business."

That a man of Mr. Booth's busy life and many important interests should recall the incident after a lapse of so many years shows what a remarkable keen and retentive memory he possesses.

Mr. Booth took particular delight in conducting the visiting bandsmen over the plant. The official photographer of the renowned musical organization being in the party, it was suggested that he secure a snapshot of Canada's most widely known lumberman, and that the picture is a good one all will readily acknowledge. Mr. Booth is never so happy as when supervising the many operations in connection with his mammoth enterprises in the Capital. It was said of him by a friend the other day that "the older he grows the more active he is."

Lumber Activities at Trout Creek

W. S. Kelly, manager of the Ballantyne Lumber Co., of Trout Creek, Ont., was in Toronto recently. The company have been busy shipping out white pine and spruce lumber during the past season and out of a stock of 2½ millions have only one quarter million yet to dispose of. They still have logs that will make about 300,000 ft. of lumber and these will be sawn in the spring.

Mr. Kelly reports that the Dominion Wood and Lumber Co. of Trout Creek will shortly put in operation their chemical plant which has been closed down for some time. This plant turns out acetate of lime, charcoal, alcohol, etc., from maple and birch. The sawmill of the Dominion Wood and Lumber Co. was operated for some months this spring and the company are now repairing and putting in good shape their ten miles of railway which extends from Trout Creek east through the limits of the company who several months ago acquired the holdings of Trussler Bros. in Laurier Tp.

The Ballantyne Lumber Co. whose limits are in Ballantyne township in Northern Ontario, have been shipping lumber during the past season to the Old Country, United States, Toronto and other Ontario points.

New Industry for Fort Frances

It is expected that a new industry in the shape of an insulite mill with a daily capacity of 50,000 feet will be launched in Fort Frances. The enterprise is likely to go ahead as soon as certain arrangements can be made concerning timber limits and waterpower. E. W. Backus is at the head of the new organization and the company is asking large limits from the Government and other concessions, the limits to include the territory drained by the Rainy Lake and its tributaries. The power has to be arranged for with the Minister of Public Works, who has intimated that no work will be done on Long Sault Rapids this year, the place from which the power is to be developed.

Pest Needs to be Stamped Out

John D. Tothill, who is in charge of the natural control investito make a number of trips into the woods this autumn and the reed from an investigation of the spruce budworm, which has been doing such damage to the balsam fir and also some of the spruce trees in New Brunswick, states that this bud worm question has become one of the most serious of the day. Mr. Tothill adds that one of the main things needed at the present time is publicity in regard to the depredations of the voracious pest. He is planning to make a number of trips into the woods this autumn and the results of his investigation will be followed with interest.

Lumberman Nominated for the Legislature

R. S. Potter, Matheson, Ont.

R. S. Potter, head of the R. S. Potter Lumber Co., Limited, Matheson, Ont., who has been nominated by the Conservative party as their standard bearer for the constituency of Cochrane at the forthcoming Provincial election, is a widely known resident of the North where he has lived for many years. Mr. Cochrane first went to New Ontario in 1898 as a time keeper in a lumber camp for J. R. Booth, of Ottawa, who was then operating at Haileybury. He spent two years at that work and then embarked into the prospecting and mining game, at which he passed most of his time until about four years ago when he re-entered the lumber arena. Mr. Potter, who is, as already stated, president of the R. S. Potter Lumber Co., has always taken a leading part in the development and expansion of New Ontario and has a wide circle of friends. The mill of his company is situated three miles north of Matheson, on the Watabeg River, mileage 208 on the T. & N. O. Ry. The lumber of the company consists mostly of jack pine and spruce. A large quantity of jack pine railway ties is turned out at the mill which has been very busy during the past season.

Little Foundation for Wide Report

Gillies Bros., who recently disposed of their plant in Morristown, N. Y., state that they cannot say what ultimate use will be made of the property. As to the probability of a large paper mill being erected there by Wm. Randolph Hearst, of New York, they are of the opinion that this is only a newspaper report. Gillies Bros. have not been using the property at Morristown for some years but have their own salesmen in northern New York district and distribute direct from their mill at Braeside, Ont.

Canadian Firm's Bow to British Trade

The September 6 issue of the Timber Trades Journal, of London, Eng., contains a full page advertisement of Terry & Gordon, Toronto, with cuts of the members of the firm. The announcement is inserted by their agents in Great Britain, Spencer, Lock & Co., 27 Clements Lane, London.

Mr Dunlop Once More Nominated

Edward A. Dunlop, M.L.A. Pembroke, Ont.

After the completion of four successive terms in the Ontario legislature E. A. Dunlop has again been nominated by the Conservative Association as its standard bearer in North Renfrew. There were a large number of women delegates at the convention who participated freely in the discussion and the business and Mr. Dunlop was accorded the nomination by a large majority over the only other nominee, which is a tribute to his personal popularity and the measure of esteem which he enjoys particularly among the fair sex of the riding. As is generally known, he has never met with defeat at the polls and he is always a welcome visitor to every lumbermen's gathering.

Mr. Dunlop is president of the Pembroke Lumber Company; a director of the Massey Lumber Company and vice-president of the Thos. Pink Company, Pembroke, manufacturers of lumbermen's tools. He is also brought in close contact with the lumbering business by reason of being president of Dunlop & Co. who specialize in hardware and cookery requirements for logging operations. Mr. Dunlop is associated with a number of other important organizations and is a former director of the Canadian Lumbermen's Association. Previous to entering upon his career in the Legislature he served in an aldermanic capacity in Pembroke for a number of years. One of the youngest members in the Ontario Legislature he will this month celebrate his 43rd birthday. His father, the late Arunah Dunlop, who passed away in 1892, represented North Renfrew in the Ontario Legislature at the time of his death and his son has proved a worthy successor.

Death of New Brunswick Lumberman

Daniel E. Richards, president of the Richards Mfg. Co., Campellton, died recently. He was one of the best known lumbermen in New Brunswick and in business circles was highly esteemed. He was 53 years of age, and some seven years ago when the Richards Mfg. Co. was organized he was elected president and carried on his duties until last spring when he was taken ill. He consulted many specialists in the hope of regaining his health and for a while appeared to be improving. Early last month his condition became serious and he gradually grew worse. The deceased was a son of the late Mr. and Mrs. David Richards, of Campbellton, and is survived by his wife, two sons and two daughters.

Progressive Lumber Co. Secures Charter

J. P. Abel, Fortin & Co., Limited, were recently incorporated and granted a charter to manufacture and deal in lumber and timber of all kinds and also to operate saw mills, box factories and to produce any articles made of wood. The new company have been empowered to acquire the property and assets of the business conducted in Montreal by J. P. Abel, Fortin & Co., box manufacturers and lumber dealers.

The incorporators are A. E. Fortin, Ernest Abel, Alphonse A. Paul, Ph. Trottier and J. H. Berard. The new company are capitalized at $200,000 and make a specialty of hardwood flooring. They also manufacture wooden boxes and excelsior and their place of business is at 379 Desjardins Ave., (Maisonneuve), Montreal, Que.

Hall Bros. in Larger Quarters

Hall Bros., Limited, wholesale lumber dealers, who recently removed their offices from 174 Mutual Street to 300 Crown Office Bldg., corner Queen and Victoria Streets, Toronto, where they have more convenient and commodious quarters, report business as being particularly active at the present time. The members of the firm are S. E. Hall, J. M. Hall and T. G. Hall, and they carry on extensive operations in all kinds of hardwoods. They own and operate a sawmill at Marlbank, Ont., where they cut mixed hardwoods and hemlock. They also furnish stock to several mills in the interest of their customers and operate a number of camps in Hastings County each winter. S. E. Hall is president and general manager of the company; J. M. is first vice-president and T. G. second vice-president.

Hall Bros. come of a family that has long been connected with lumber and timber; their father, the late Samuel Hall, being engaged in this line all his life. He carried on a square timber business throughout the white oak regions of the south and later operated a mill at Marmion, in Grey County, and then removed to Keady. His sons have had a practical insight from the logging to the distribution end. S. E. Hall, president of the company, after leaving home some fourteen years ago, was engaged for a considerable period with the Bradley Lumber Company, Hamilton. In 1908 he came to Toronto and launched out for himself, where he was afterwards joined by his brothers. During the war they did a large trade in supplying ship timbers and specialized in round and hewn stock, taking [illegible]ut lar[illegible] quantities of rock elm. The firm will ship this month t[illegible] the O[illegible] Country five hundred sticks of rock elm taken out some [illegible]ty mil[illegible] northwest of Toronto.

The Bolinder Crude Oil Engine

The "Canada Lumberman" has received from Swedish Steel [illegible] porting Co., Ltd., of Montreal, who are Canadian representat[illegible] the Bolinder Co. of Stockholm, Sweden, an attractive and [illegible] catalogue, illustrating the Bolinder heavy crude oil marine en[illegible] vessels equipped with the same. Varied and extensive use is [illegible] made of the crude oil engine. The Bolinder engine propels n[illegible] smaller craft, but also full-powered, ocean-going cargo car[illegible] four to five thousand tons capacity. It is predicted that this [illegible] and economical internal combustion engine will prove a serio[illegible] petitor to steam for propulsive powers.

Of special interest are a number of west coast vessels cons[illegible] particularly for the lumber carrying trade. Some of these a[illegible] powered motorships, equipped with 640 B.H.P. engines, whil[illegible] are auxiliary sailing vessels of 2,200 to 3,500 tons D.W., [illegible] with 320 to 640 B.H.P. engines. Other classes of vessels [illegible] to the lumberman are the oil-engined tow boats and the sel[illegible] ling barges. Of the latter class, especially, Great Britain [illegible] have a large number.

The aerial propelled barge is another kind of craft, which h[illegible] been found unexcelled for passage in very shallow or weed[illegible] where a marine propeller is impracticable. It is claimed [illegible] novel type of boat has proved highly satisfactory.

Many will probably be surprised to learn that quite a [illegible] of vessels in the British Navy are oil-engined. British A[illegible] ordered during the war not less than about [illegible] Bolinder [illegible] A number of Bolinder-engined motor-monitors [illegible]e launched in [illegible] and they have since done excellent work in m[illegible] waters.

Mr. Miller Joins Toronto Lumber Firm

Mr. Miller Joins Toronto Lumber Firm

John J. Miller, of Toronto, who has been appointed manager of the hardwood department of the C. G. Anderson Lumber Co., and has entered upon his new duties, is favorably known to the lumbering trade throughout Ontario. Mr. Miller has handled all ends of the business except the sawing, chopping and peeling of bark. He started his career with Wilson, Godfrey & Co., 63 Wall St., New York. Their yard was in Brooklyn, and after some time in the service they sent him on the road, buying and inspecting. He was with them ten years and covered the eastern section [illegible] Maine to Pennsylvania. Mr. [illegible]ler was next with H. H. S[illegible] & Co., 88 Wall St., New [illegible] for some nine years, [illegible] the major portion of the time in the south, looking after the [illegible]ritory from West Virginia to Louisiana. He thus got to kno[illegible] the leading lumber dealers in the east and south, and was [illegible] sociated with W. T. Hubbard, Toledo, Ohio. After being two y[illegible] there he made application for a position as inspector on the [illegible] of the National Hardwood Lumber Association, and passed the [illegible]amination, part of which was on Mr. Hubbard's yards. Mr. M[illegible] worked in the Detroit territory for about a year and then assist[illegible] in different markets. From the Buffalo market he came to Toronto, in 1910, where he has since carried out his duties as a faithful and earnest member of the inspecting staff of the National Hardwood Lumber Association.

Down the Arbor Walk to the Works

The accompanying picture shows a fine avenue of hardy Norway Maples on both sides of the long approach to the fifty-acre factory of Henry Disston & Sons, Inc., Philadelphia. The trees were planted some twenty-three years ago.

One of the long-time employes of the firm, when viewing this photograph, remarked: "Well, do I remember the old walk, and four times a day for many years I trod the path along with thousands of fellow-workers. It was of cinders, and in the summer this long, wide, deep bed of cinders seemed to absorb the sun's hot rays and

Rows of Norway Maples planted twenty-three years ago

throw them out with redoubled vigor as you walked along. The improvement is a lasting and beautiful memorial to the thoughtfulness of Samuel Disston, whom all the boys called 'Uncle,' for reaching the shade of the wide-spreading branches of the maple trees one enjoys the cool, delightful stroll along the smooth cement pavement to the entrance of the works."

It is peculiarly interesting and seemingly contrary that Disston, whose saws for years have been used in denuding many thousands upon thousands of acres of timber, should be planting, growing and preserving beautiful shade trees. Manufacturing plants in outlaying districts and municipalities may well take note of this as an example which will bear emulating.

Has Export Trade Been Overloaded?

The expected has happened. It was inevitable, judging from past experience.

The armistice had hardly been signed last fall when it at once became evident that a phenomenally large number of people were preparing to enter the lumber export business, a rather hazardous game at any time for those without experience and not even a hazard but substantially a sure-thing loss under the cataclysmal conditions for those witihout experience, says the "New York Lumber Trade Journal."

But did they know that or did it deter them if they did know? They did not, or it did not.

Being located in what is now probably the largest export and import market in the world, this paper, as soon as the armistice was signed, began to get all sorts of inquiries from would-be lumber exporters, many of whom obviously did not know the first rudiments or principles of the business, nor could they possibly command the means to that end. It was just a burning desire that obsessed them, as was perhaps but natural in the premises, to share in the phenomenal profits that by hearsay were presently to be realized in the export lumber business. The whole idea would have been comical had it not held so much that was obviously dangerous to all sound lumber business as well as to many, if not most of the newcomers, themselves. We regretfully so told some of them when we were able to get that far along with them in the discussion. But did they listen? They mostly did not. But probably and even obviously in some cases they attributed it to prejudice on our part.

A very few of the newcomers had a substantial foundation of the right character of lumber stocks, or at least a modicum of export lumber experience, or both, on which to trade. But the great mass of them were equipped apparently for this intricate export business only by more or less hazy knowledge or hearsay that big money was to be made therein and a burning desire as indicated to share in the golden opportunity with or without experience or perhaps even needed capacity to acquire it, and without even immediate availability of stocks. Later, when a tentative tour of some of the shrewdest wholesalers of the industry developed the undoubted fact that the much-heralded opportunities, on investigation, were for one cause or another mostly thin or hot air, even then these other would-be exporters were unterrified, but have rushed into what shrewder, more experienced heads were not willing to undertake.

Now comes the inevitable aftermath. There are numerous news items and personal comments from those in the know concerning the unsatisfactory lumber conditions abroad already. Where possible buyers abroad are not, as far as plants are concerned, physically as well as financially exhausted, or well nigh so, but even now ready to trade, word presently comes that they are "visiting to trade on concessions" for stock accumulated on consignment, as applied mostly to hardwoods. Oak has been very largely shipped even as compared with before the war. Oak and other hardwoods out of Baltimore, for example, we understand, constitute about two-thirds of the entire shipments, as borne out by the fact that the whole lumber list on the other side is a short one, and many other items are not at all represented in these consignments. High charges for storage bring such consignments out at a loss unless prompt and early absorptions on arrival have been provided for in advance. So nothing could be more foolish and futile than free consignments as such on a chance of getting orders on arrival. It would be well for the industry at large on both sides of the water, and especially for such consignors themselves, if they would consult such of the appointed means to the same end as, for example, the new overseas forwarding agency at Memphis, etc., before hasty action. It would not only redound to the interest of the industry at large, but would be money in their own pockets in the long run, even though the business were not alone quite so direct. In other words the consignment evil was perhaps never more an evil than now, from every point of view.

This subject matter perforce has been substantially a leading editorial at least about once a year for the last several decades in perhaps every standard lumber paper, and not by choice but by thrusting itself into view. Only, as indicated, this time the conditions seem worse than ever. So it may be added once again that the dangers of lumber exporting without right lines of experience as well as adequate available stocks, were never greater and soon or late, usually soon, are more than apt to spell disaster.

An Attractive Publication on "Belting"

The Main Belting Company of Canada, 10 St. Peter Street, Montreal, have just issued a most complete, attractive and comprehensive publication setting forth the quality and merits of Leviathan and Anconda belting. The illustrations, art work and letter press are decidedly pleasing, and the volume of 144 pages contains a mine of information with regard to power transmission, solution of modern belt problems, table of horse-power transmitted by various thicknesses of belts, belting in pulp and paper mills, rolling mill work, motor drives, machine shops, Canadian furniture factories, and other industries. Admirable illustrations are given of the Leviathan, which is a general purpose belting possessing extraordinary strength, toughness and flexibility and Anaconda belting, which is basically the same as Leviathan and possesses all the qualities which enable the latter to give highly satisfactory service, whether the problem be one of transmission, elevating or conveying.

A number of striking pictures are presented showing the strength, durability, economy, efficiency, etc., of the products of the Main Belting Co. of Canada. Users of belts in any ofrm will find in the new publication, entitled "Belting," a valuable and convenient work of reference. An index is given which readily indicates where the data on any power problems may be found. Special pages are devoted to the capacity of belt, elevators, centrifugal belt elevators, continuous belt elevators, etc., while timely particulars are furnished with respect to belt dressings, belt fasteners, clinching hooks, steel belt lacing, belt punches, cutting pliers, etc.

The new publication is so arranged that any additional printed matter issued by the Main Belting Company can be added by unloosening two or three paper fasteners which bnd the book firmly and, like a loose-leaf ledger, afford every facility for extension.

A total of 19,776,814 feet of lumber was shipped from British Columbia ports in August. Nearly seven and a half million feet was shipped on French vessels during the month. All these ships are being handled by the C. Gardner Johnson Agency, Vancouver. As soon as they are accepted by the Bureau Veritas and the French high commission the agency sends them to different mills to load. Nine of these wooden steamships, with a total tonnage of 18,900 d.w. tons, went to sea during the month, and it is expected that considerably more will be despatched in September.

Second Hand Machinery & Equipment Wanted & For Sale

PUBLISHER'S NOTICE

Advertisements other than "Employment Wanted" or "Employees Wanted" will be inserted in this department at the rate of 20 cents per agate line (14 agate lines make one inch). $2.80 per inch, each insertion, payable in advance. Space measured from rule to rule. When four or more consecutive insertions of the same advertisement are ordered a discount of 25 per cent. will be allowed.

Advertisements of "Wanted Employment" will be inserted at the rate of one cent a word, net. Cash must accompany order. If Canada Lumberman box number is used, enclose ten cents extra for postage in forwarding replies. Minimum charge 25 cents.

Advertisements of "Wanted Employees" will be inserted at the rate of two cents a word, net. Cash must accompany the order. Minimum charge 50 cents.

Advertisements must be received not later than the 10th and 20th of each month to insure insertion in the subsequent issue.

Wanted–Lumber

Basswood Wanted

No. 2 Common and Mill Cull. Winter cut preferred. Apply Firstbrook Brothers, Ltd., Toronto, Ont. 8-t.f.

Wanted Lumber

Hardwood Lumber wanted. Birch, Maple, Basswood and other Hardwoods. Dry or sawn to order. We send inspector. Box 14, Canada Lumberman, Toronto. 17-20

Wanted for Cuban Trade White Pine

Send lists and prices at once to

E. ANTONIO VAZQUEZ,
44 Whitehall Street,
10-22 New York City.

Wanted

10/4 and 12/4 No. 1 Common and Better Birch,

also

10/4 and 12/4 No. 1 Common and Better Soft Elm.

In quoting, state how the stock will run to 1st and 2nds and how long it has been cut. Box 996, Canada Lumberman, Toronto. 16-19

For Sale–Lumber

FOR SALE

30,000 feet 1" round edge Poplar.
25,000 feet 2" round edge Poplar.

Good widths and lengths. This stock is well dried out and ready for immediate shipment. J. B. Brand, Bank of British North America Bldg., St. John, N.B. 19-20

FOR SALE
Hickory Specials

100 M pcs. ¾" Dowels, 48" long.
20 M pcs. 1" Squares, 48" long.

Also some shorter stock. All high grade, second growth Hickory. Can ship immediately. Will sell cheap. Address Box 31, Canada Lumberman, Toronto. 19-20

For Sale

30,000 setts Cheese Box Veneer. Apply C. A. Muses, Osgoode Station, Ont. 16.19

Lumber For Sale

100 M. ft. 2 x 4"/up Merchantable Spruce.
200 M. ft. ¾" x 4"/up Cull Spruce.
50 M. ft. 1 x 4"/up Maple, No. 3 Com. and Bet.
80 M ft. Basswood, No. 3 Com. and Bet.
Also 1" Ash, Elm, and Beech, Red Oak.

Wire or write to

J. P. ABEL, FORTIN & CO.,
10 Maisonneuve, Montreal.

Wanted–Machinery

Wanted

Whitney No. 7 High Speed Double Spindle Shaper, with Countershaft complete. Must be in first class condition. Address Box 20, Canada Lumberman, Toronto. 19

Used Machinery Wanted

1 only gap lathe, 18 to 20 inch gap, 48 inch swing and 11 to 13 feet from centre to centre.
1 slide valve engine or Corliss Wheelock engine, 300 horse power.
1 lumber edger, 40 or 48 inches wide.
1 lath machine.
1 duplex cold water pump capable of pumping from 700 to 1,000 gallons per minute.

Send description and prices to

Searchmont Lumber Co., Limited,
10 Searchmont, Ont.

For Sale–Machinery

FOR SALE

One second-hand 8" band saw, complete with saws; also circular resaw, with two inserted tooth saws, 42" dia. Keenan Bros., Ltd., Owen Sound, Ont. 16-19

For Sale

Heavy Self-feed Rip Saw, carries a 22-inch saw and has Bevel Siding attachment. Photo, with description and price, on request. Box 28, Canada Lumberman, Toronto. 19

For Sale

One "S. A. Wood Matcher 24" fitted with 20 different sizes knives for top and bottom cylinders. Four pairs of heads with six sets of bits. Price $600, on cars. Savoie & Co., Manseau, Que. 19

For Sale

Portable mill of 40 h.p. edger, trimmers, butting saw and all machinery necessary for 12 M. feet daily, first class condition. Splendid site if wanted. Box 34, Canada Lumberman, Toronto. 19-20

FOR SALE—SAWMILL

25 H. P. Engine, 30 H. P. return tubular boiler. Three log seat carriage, overhead set, friction feed works, single edger and slab saw. All in fair order. Price $1,000. Box 915, Canada Lumberman, Toronto. 16-19

For Sale

1—17 x 24 Atlas Engine, with 36 in. x 10 ft. flywheel.
3—No. 94 Berlin Matchers, 15 in., fitted with hard steel knives on top and bottom cylinders—one pair shiplap, jointer and flooring heads with bits for each machine.
1—No. 182 Berlin Double Surfacer, 30 in. x 6 in.
1—No. 190 Berlin Buzz Planer.
1—No. 290 Berlin Picket Header.

The Otis Staples Lumber Company, Ltd.,
19-t.f. Wycliffe, B.C.

FOR SALE

1 Steam Feed Carriage with Steam Set Works, "Waterous Model."
1 Nigger, complete, "Waterous Model."
1 Wicks Gang Saw, complete with saws and steam engine, "Midland," 60 H.P.
2 Shingle Machines, complete with saws.
11 Pulpwood Barkers.

For particulars apply to

CHICOUTIMI PULP CO.,
17-20 Chandler, Que.

FOR SALE
Saw Mill Machinery

Complete saw mill machinery; equipped with rotary, steam feed carriage, Gang Saw, Resaw, Edger, Butter, Lath Machine. Three Boilers and twin engine 300 H.P.; also saw gummers, filers and one shingle machine, with boiler and barker. For particulars apply:

CHICOUTIMI PULP CO.,
16-10 Chandler, Que.

Band Saw Mill Complete

Waterous 9 ft. Band Mill, Gunshot Feed Carriage, with extra Saws complete.

Filing Equipment

Three Saw Edger, lot of live rolls, Engine, Shafting, Hangers, Pulleys, etc.

All of the above is Waterous equipment in good condition at a bargain.

The Geo. F. Foss Machinery & Supply Co., Limited,
305 St. James Street,
17-t.f. Montreal, Que.

Used Saw Mill Machinery FOR SALE

One McGregor & Gourlay endless bed Planer, knives 28" long, bed raises and lowers by power. Will plane 10" thick. In good condition. One B. F. Sturtevant Exhaust Fan, Intake 23" diameter, discharge 10" x 19" square, pulley 10" dia. x 8" face. In good working order, with an extra set of blades or fans. Also bonnet and piping for planer and discharge piping for fan.

Also two Moreau Rossers for peeling pulp wood. These are as good as new; used only one season. Will peel on an average 25 cords per day. Reason for selling, no more pulp wood to peel.

Complete Saw Mill for sale. Full particulars given on enquiry. All this machinery is at Kazubazua, Que., and belongs to Kazubazua Lumber Co. Any further information will be given by addressing

L. D. PHILIPS,
24 Thornton Ave.,
16-19 Ottawa, Ont.

Wanted–Employment

Advertisements under this heading one cent a word per insertion. Box No. 10 cents extra. Minimum charge 25 cents.

WANTED POSITION by representative and superintendent, still employed with large wholesale firm, with twenty-five years' experience in the lumber business. Can give reference as to capabilities and take charge on a month's notice. Box 901, Canada Lumberman, Toronto. 10-20

WANTED EMPLOYMENT—By married man, forty years of age; 26 years' experience, from swamping to managing, from stump to lumber pile, including office experience. Good reasons for having to look for employment. Will go any place. Hold Ontario Scaler's license.—Box 24 Canada Lumberman, Toronto. 18-19

WANTED: Position as log culler or foreman in log camp, by experienced man. For further particulars apply Box 44, Orangeville, Ont. 16-19

LUMBERMAN, 30 years of age, having sold lumber throughout New York and New England States, wishes to represent a Canadian firm in the same territory, excellent recommendations. Box 30, Canada Lumberman, Toronto. 19-20

Wanted–Employees

WANTED, FOREMAN FOR CIRCULAR SAWMILL cutting thirty-five thousand feet, steady job year round. Box 32, Canada Lumberman, Toronto. 19

YARD MAN WANTED for inspecting and looking after yard of hardwood lumber.

MERRITT & COMPANY,
Chatham, Ont.

PLANING MAN WANTED—Good all-round man to work in planing mill; box factory; good opening for a man that can take charge of mill and yard; steady work. State experience and wages wanted. D. C. Baird, St. Mary's, Ont. 18-19

YOUNG MAN FOR GENERAL OFFICE WORK, experienced in ledger, trial balance, etc. Must be a good writer and accurate. Some experience in lumber business preferred. Excellent prospects for right man. Apply by letter, giving age, references, and salary, to The Seaman Kent Co., Ltd., Toronto. 19

POSITION OPEN for a high-class man capable of organising and assuming full management of all lumbering operations of a 500 mile timber limit for a Company operating a Saw-mill and a Pulp-mill. All replies will be treated confidentially. A permanent position with a good salary open for the right man. Box 963, Canada Lumberman, Toronto.

WANTED—A number of experienced Hardwood Sawmill Operators to contract to take out large quantities of Hardwood during the coming winter. Stumpage can be furnished if necessary, and the necessary cash advances to assist responsible operators. Address Box 19, Canada Lumberman, Toronto. 17-20

YOUNG MAN, experienced bookkeeper and stenographer, wanted, that will invest some money in limited company. Experienced in sash and door factory, planing mill and lumber business. Must be capable of taking full charge of office, and keeping all office work up to date. Opening on board of directors and secretary-treasurer for man with right qualifications. Apply to Box 25, Canada Lumberman, Toronto. 18-tf

Business Chances

For Sale

1,880 ACRES OF TIMBER, estimated to cut 25,000 ft. per acre, $9,500. Box 654, Nelson, B.C. 19-22

Lumber Yard and Planing Mill

City, Niagara district; yard and mill fully equipped; ten thousand; might rent. Twenty thousand dollar stock; turnover fifty thousand yearly; easily financed. J. P. Lawrason, Business Broker, 25 Toronto St., Toronto. 19

For Sale

500 acres timber, Parry Sound, close to lake, river and water-power sawmill; water-power furnishing seventy-five horsepower on river, where logs can be towed down stream; power may be developed to furnish light and power to adjacent village by completing natural dam; twelve thousand five hundred dollars. John Fisher & Co., Lumsden Building, Toronto. 19

A Good Word for the Wholesaler

We hold no brief for the wholesaler. He's human, and he wants to get rich. We have a hunch that he has not been nor is he at present always above getting something for nothing when the opportunity presents itself. But the retailer who is without sin, let him cast the first stone! The wholesaler has his troubles and his weak spots; he isn't any saint, not if we know what a saint is. But he is offering us a vital kind of service, and in more than one instance he has looked out for our interests. Of course, he did this mainly because his own interests depended upon the conserving of ours, but none the less he has done us good service; and the future of the business, the interests of wholesaler and retailer and customer, depend upon our having a good human understanding of each other so that we can fit our work into the whole fabric of lumber handling in such a way as to cut out the most waste and the most lost motion and the most useless expense. We're not going to get anywhere in realizing the full possibilities of business by looking exclusively to our own little corner. The man who does that is likely to have the experience of the amateur carpenter who was building a hen house. He got so interested in lining it up that the first thing he knew he had himself nailed in with no doors nor windows from which he could emerge. — American Lumberman.

On Last Quarter of Their Shipbuilding Contract

With the launching of the Wilfrid Laurier on August 23, the Foundation Company of B. C., Limited, completed three-quarters of its contract for twenty 3,000-ton wooden steamships to be built at Victoria for the French Government. As a result, three ways at the time of writing are empty, and are not likely to be filled again unless the company manages to secure further contracts.

The La Salle, the fourteenth ship of the contract to take the water, was launched from the Point Ellis Yard of the Foundation Company on August 14.

Trials of several of the Foundation ships made recently have upheld the reputation of the local yards. The Ontario, which was tried out on August 1, averaged 12.38 knots, while the Ottawa registered 12.56 knots. The Ottawa was the second ship of the contract powered with engines built by the Victoria firm of Hutchison Brothers. The Winnipeg, the other ship so powered, averaged 13.52 knots. The Canada was tried out on August 28, and averaged 12.13 knots, exceeding its contract speed by 1.13 knots. Fuel tests made during the trial run showed that the Canada burned 16 tons during twenty-four hours.

Lumber Company Will Have Switch Line Installed

To facilitate the loading of its lumber shipments to eastern Canada and the United States, the Moore-Whittington Lumber Co. is making arrangements with the Canadian National Railway whereby it will have a switch line of its own on the new terminals which are being established on the old Indian Reserve.

At present lumber from the Moore-Whittington mill has been carted in wagons to the Esquimalt and Nanaimo line, which is a considerable distance away, or to the old terminal of the C.N.R. When the new C. N. R. terminal is established, however, it will be necessary to cart the lumber only across the Point Ellis bridge and on to the Reserve, a short haul. Here the company will have a siding of its own where it can load into freight cars. The lumber will be shipped, of course, to Patricia Bay, whence it will be ferried to the mainland and on to the C. N. R. transcontinental system. Officials of the mill have conferred with officials of the railway company and they feel that the C. N. R. is out to get the lumberman's business.

Worst Forest Fires for the Last Nine Years

After a 750 mile trip through the Interior on horse back, M. A. Grainger, Chief Provincial Forester and head of the Forest Branch, returned to his desk at the Parliament Buildings late in August. Mr. Grainger started from Vancouver and proceeded eastward, spending five weeks in travelling the Hope to Princeton Trail, through the Douglas Lake country and various other points in the Interior. Later he headed north and rode into the North Thompson country. His mission was not so much in connection with forestry work as in looking over grazing areas and sizing up crop conditions. While it had undoubtedly been a very bad year in many localities, Mr. Grainger found that the crops were, generally speaking, not as bad as he had anticipated. Forest fires in the Kootenay country, he stated, had been probably worse than in any year since 1910.

Plans whereby British Columbia forest products will be exhibited in different points in the United Kingdom are being promoted by the provincial authorities. The exhibition will include samples of timber, lumber, farm produce, fruits, minerals, etc. The Department of Agriculture, which is collecting the exhibit, is informed by Agent General F. C. Wade, K.C., that arrangements for the display of the exhibit can be made through the Victoria League of Great Britain, an organization which conducts lectures and exhibitions to show people in the Old Country the inducements for settlement offered by different parts of the Empire. The exhibit will be just as complete as it is possible to make it, and it will be replenished regularly with new articles as they are required.

Review of Current Trade Conditions

Ontario

Business in the lumber line continues brisk although some wholesalers report a shortening up in requisitions during the past week. All the lumber companies are preparing to undertake logging operations on a scale that has outclassed anything in that direction since the outbreak of the war. Some firms have doubted the number of their camps and the limit of their logging operations is only restricted by the forces of men available. The demand for lumber of all kinds is good particularly in the west and north and it is interesting to note the predictions that are made in various quarters. One wholesaler remarked recently that lumber would not only be scarce within the next six months but that there would be a regular famine in a number of lines, while the sales manager of another concern stated that they had the largest order book filled out that had ever been known in the history of the firm.

In the retail yards there is a considerable movement of stock and not a few lines are depleted. Many dealers have allowed their grades to run low and are getting anxious about obtaining fresh supplies. Shipments in some cases are reported rather uncertain owing to car delays at certain points. The mills report that wholesalers are looking up stocks of white pine to replace those which they have recently disposed of but that they find it difficult to lay hands on any large blocks.

Hemlock is very scarce and there is an excellent demand for this lumber in house construction. In hardwood there is a decided shortage of the thicker ends of birch and elm. The makers of hardwood flooring are using all the thinner stuff that they can possibly get their hands on in order to satisfy the demand of construction companies, house builders and contractors for all kinds of structures. Furniture factories are rushed at present and there has been many buyers from automobile concerns across the border visiting Ontario in search of birch. The prospects for business this fall are particularly bright and the country is being scoured for many lines of hardwood.

In British Columbia stocks trade is rather quiet and no one is in a position to predict what shape matters will take. There has been a slight easing up in the price of shingles but this always occurs in the fall of the year owing to the diminished demand. Laths are practically off the market. It is predicted that the base price of B. C. timbers will take an advance of from $4 to $5 owing to the large export trade which has been done from the Pacific Coast province. There has been a pretty active call for timbers for some time and it is felt that there may be a scarcity of them in the near future.

In Toronto it is expected that the number of brick dwellings erected in 1919 will exceed the total number of erections for 1916-17-18. To September 15th there have been 1,843 constructions and they total $700,000.

"There has been an increase of 125 per cent. in the erection of brick dwelliings this year," stated an official.

There is comparatively little southern pine coming in at the present time except 2 x 4, which is used for studding. There is, however, a fair importation of chestnut, gum and cypress. A large quantity of the former is being used for interior trim in houses and comes in in No. 1 common & better in 1 and 1½ inch. There is a fair quantity of cypress being imported in shop and better and this material is used for tank work and some sash and door construction. Gum is commanding a decidedly high price, the prevailing figure for 1st and 2nds being around $110, exclusive of duty and exchange. Chestnut in 1st and 2nds in 1½ inch is bringing $105 and in 1 inch $100, with values constantly stiffening. In most all southern woods, the supply is far short of the demand and, while there has been a scarcity of labor, there was until recently no strikes, but during the past few days some mills in the south have had trouble in this direction which all adds to the gravity of the situation.

Great Britain

Conditions abroad are comprehensively reviewed in an interview which appears in another column with A. C. Manbert, of Toronto, lumber commissioner from Ontario, who recently returned from overseas. English trade journals bear out exactly what he says in regard to tonnage outlook and port congestion.

There is still great difficulty experienced in getting tonnage for timber cargoes. Business with Canada and America is more or less at a standstill for this reason. There is only a poor chance of getting shippers to make quotations on a c.i.f. basis, and, on the other hand, buyers are by no means ready to make purchases on free-on-board lines. There is a deadlock, therefore, and the position unfortunately is not likely to improve until more tonnage becomes available. A lot of steamers are still being used in connection with the war, and it will be some time before they are set free for commercial purposes. Some shipbuilding is going on, it is true, though a good lot of speeding up is also required in this direction.

Business is fairly good and the market is firm so far as American hardwoods are concerned. There is still considerable delays in obtaining parcels of timber arriving in the Port. The congestion at the docks has now reached enormous proportions, and many week's delay often occurs before timber can be got out of the incoming vessel. There are now some indications that these delays will be modified in the near future, through the introduction of motor lorries to clear away the essential imports, such as foodstuffs and perishable goods, which under ordinary circumstances, have preference over timber and cotton, etc. In the meantime, the demand for all kinds of hardwoods is growing stronger week by week. The supplies coming forward are on a considerable scale, especially plain oak; there appears to be an abundance offering on the market. With regard to quartered oak, this is extremely scarce, and some difficulty is experienced in obtaining anything approaching moderate quantities at the moment. Red gum and sap gum are to be obtained in fair quantities, so that the market generally is in a healthy state.

In regard to the unberthed ships at Liverpool the Timber Trades Journal says:

What has really happened is that since the armistice our shipping has increased far more rapidly than has the inland distributing power of the country, and we have now come to the point where twelve or fifteen large ships are waiting berths at London, and fifty at Liverpool. That is absolute waste of ship-carrying power, as merely bringing a cargo into a port is useless unless it can be distributed. The solution lies in making the most of the existing facilities and in supplementing them. We are putting forward proposals with regard to the possibility of increasing facilities for road transport. The establishment of a mobile fleet of lorries capable of carrying goods for distribution over short distances was undertaken some time ago, and numbers of lorries have been working quite successfully, while we have had put at our disposal a certain number of battalions of the transport workers for the purpose of supplementing proved deficiencies. The idea is not to compete with civilian labor, and we have the cordial support of labor and of the employers. These men have put in six million days' work, and they have shifted 27,000,000 tons weight of stuff to prevent blocks arising in the docks.

The Government Buyer has promised, or threatened, that very large shipments from Canada will be made this autumn. There is now rather more sign of his activities. All the pine that has been shipped could have been sold over and over again, and there is not the least fear of any scarcity of this particular wood. But with regard to spruce the case is rather different. Spruce competes with Swedish and Finnish productions, and although most of the Scandinavian shipments have come to the East Coast, it has often been possible hitherto to send the wood across the country at a profit, owing to the bare state of the importers' yards on the South and West Coast. With the advent of more spruce cargoes this trade will either cease or gradually diminish. At the present time, the prices for good average specifications of spruce are about £34 or £34 10s. c.i.f. to the West Coast, a much cheaper figure than that at which the East Coast importers can supply Swedish whitewood. It need scarcely be pointed out that the volume of spruce shipments during the next couple of months will have a very strong effect on the prices of Scandinavian wood, and the fear of a rush of cargoes is undoubtedly making all business rather slow and difficult. Probably the Government Buyer wishes to reduce the price of timber—it will be to his credit with the authorities if he can do so—but if his intention is to flood the country with spruce he will merely congest our ports, find himself unable to sell the wood promptly, and bring about a state of confusion. In a falling market, merchants are always very shy of purchasing; and if in the present circumstances values begin to fall no one can predict the result. The Government methods of dealing with the hardwood trade at the beginning of the year will not soon be forgotten. The market was a falling one, and the Government's experiments in getting rid of their stock involved some heavy and quite unlooked-for losses on the part of merchants who relied on the situa-

tion being dealt with in a business-like manner. As long as the Government holds large stocks of timber, and has the power to alter its policy, and make experiments there can be no stable market. However, as we have before pointed out, there is little likelihood of the Shipping Controller permitting the valuable time of ships to be wasted in delays at the ports when there is no urgent need for further supplies of timber from abroad.

United States

There is not much change in general conditions so far as the main features of the market are concerned. Generally speaking, a good tone prevails in trade circles, but whether this will continue in view of the strike of the steel workers and the shutting down of many large plants it is not as yet definitely known. Building permits awarded during August fell off considerably below those of July, but still the returns for the month were away ahead of what they have been in any corresponding period during the past five years. The first eight months of the present year have been outstanding in the matter of structural undertakings, the crest of the curve being passed in July. It is believed that actual construction work has not yet reached its minimum and the building season will be prolonged to the end of the year, provided good weather prevails. It is stated that during the past two months there has been less of building in the repair and alteration line and more in the shape of new and large structures.

The southern pine market shows great stability and while matters have been a little quieter during the past few days, there is practically no lull in the market, and it is thought that manufacturers may in time catch up with their orders. There has been a slight increase in production in some districts brought about by a better supply of labor; on the other hand, some districts report a decided shortage in help. Stocks of flooring, finish and ceiling are still being heavily drawn on and production remains under the demand, indicating that there is much building activity in the country. There is, however, an apparent exception in the case of the Georgia-Florida mills, which report a slight falling off in the call for dressed stock, regarded by them as unusual at this time in view of the fact that for a year previously no let up in this demand has been in evidence. The planing mill market has been extremely busy for some weeks and has been realizing good prices—which, it might be mentioned, are no weaker now because of the present, and likely only temporary, lull in the demand. The tendency toward price stabilization is steadily extending throughout the South, as the manufacturers are beginning to realize more and more that something must be done to assure future prosperity for the industry rather than present profits. Logging operations are beginning to progress more actively, now that most parts of the South have enjoyed some days of fair weather, and the manufacturers are planning to make the most of every opportunity to insure an adequate supply of logs next season.

There are numerous foreign inquiries for hardwood, but almost the entire production is being bought up by home buyers. Prices are firm with the outlook, on the whole, very favorable. It has been noted by economists that people nowadays buy goods of a good deal higher quality than ever before; and this is illustrated in the lumber market. It is the best grades that are wanted, and they consequently are becoming harder and harder to find. It has been remarked that never before has the demand been so one sided as now, running so heavily toward the high grades. That does not mean that the common grades are being neglected; there is a market for them too, although it must be admitted that many purchasers of them are forced because the better stuff is not available. Flooring and finish are the scarcest items on the whole hardwood list, according to most reports; and prices are well maintained on everything. In this connection it is well to note the growing belief that the crest of the price movement has now been reached, although no recession this season is expected. Many retailers have given this matter of price much thought and have decided against stocking up against the future on the ground that prices can go no higher and are more likely to go down with the next season. They argue this way: Last winter there was an abnormally small cut of logs. The sharp price advances of this year were not on account of heavy consumption or buying, but because the supply was small. The next logging season will soon open, and the log cut will be materially increased over that of last year, which will alter the situation.

The situation in cypress is very active and there has been a decided upward tendency in prices. Producers have been doing everything in their power to stabilize the market and prevent any radical alteration in values. Production remains close to normal, but it is very difficult to replenish the low and badly broken stocks in view of the great demand. The country trade in the middle West especially is growing impatient for supplies for fall and early winter construction, particularly for fencing, and is willing to pay premiums on bookings if quick shipments could be obtained. Millwork manufacturers are preparing for an active business next season, confident of a great building volume next spring, and their demands are already beginning to be felt.

Market Correspondence

SPECIAL REPORTS ON CONDITIONS AT HOME AND ABROAD

St. John Reports Little Quieter Conditions

Conditions in the market at St. John are not quite so good as two weeks ago. The American buyers are not disposed to purchase at the present asking prices of the manufacturers and certainly the manufacturers cannot take any less money for their product and make any profit at all, so they are compelled to hold their sawn material.

What the outcome may be no one can tell; certainly the prices which are being offered here to-day are not profitable and if the stocks are sold on existing figures no one can go out and manufacture them and produce them again at the same prices. The costs of doing business this year have certainly been enormous, far beyond the expectations of the operators and, unless there is a great margin between the log price and the manufacturer's lumber price no producer of lumber can get out without a loss. No mills are producing up to normal and costs of handling far exceed expectations. Stocks are now at their highest and will begin to recede as the mills begin shutting down for the season, which some mills at St. John will be forced to do very soon as they will have cut out their supply of logs.

No shipments by water are taking place at the present time from St. John; also the car shortage is even more stringent than ever before and the C. P. R. will not even allow loading of foreign box cars, giving only flat cars for lumber. These are very expensive to load as it is costing $12.00 to $15.00 per car to stake them and oftimes this is the profit on a car of lumber. The buyers of the lumber refuse to pay for the stakes, even though they take them at their destination. This is a hardship which the manufacturer is up against; he must pay the freight and also provide part of the equipment to carry the freight. Certainly something must be done to remedy the transportation question and it cannot come too quickly. The railroads must build more cars as quickly as possible and the lumber shipper should be placed on an equal footing with all other trades, but under present conditions they are called upon to bear untold hardships.

Local business remains good, the country districts are doing considerable fall repair work. All the factories are busy. The St. John river has risen during the past week and it is hoped that the drive being up within forty miles of the booms will reach the booming limits and can be rafted out this fall. The drive contains from five to ten million feet of logs for the different mills at St. John.

Operators are now preparing for the woods and will make a normal cut on the St. John waters, but will not cut more than needed for next year's operations.

Good Demand and Higher Prices in Ottawa

Another advance in manufacturers prices, a good demand, coupled with an all around tendency toward absolute firmness, were the features of the Ottawa lumber market as shown, in the last week of September. Practically every grade in pine from old culls to good sidings advanced in price. Pine inch and a quarter, good siding, reached the top notch price of $102 per M. and old culls advanced to twenty-eight dollars.

The advance in nearly every instance was in the pine grades. No. 1 White pine lath went to $7.50 per M. and No. 2 of the same grade went to $7. All sidings, strips, and practically every grade of pine "shorts" advanced. The jump in the market in the last week of September came as a surprise to some of the trade, for though advances had been prophesied a month or so ago, it was not expected the aviation would take place so soon.

The correspondent of the "Canada Lumberman" has information that even considering the latest increases that the market is going to

Woods Manufacturing Co., Limited - Ottawa

Will give you prompt shipment and best prices on van supplies, of everything your men require from head to foot, consisting of **Mackinaw Clothing**, Underwear, Wool Socks and Mitts, Caps and Moccasins.

Toronto
Welland

Montreal
Winnipeg

QUALITY

SERVICE

We are Specialists in Catering to "The Lumber Camp Trade"

REFRIGERATOR CAR SERVICE TO ALL POINTS.

Before placing orders be sure to get our quotations on—

FRESH BEEF	BUTTER	AMERICAN BARRELLED PORK	EGGS & EGG MELANGE
BARRELLED BEEF	PURE LARD	SAUSAGES OF ALL KINDS	POTATOES AND VEGETABLES
CANADIAN BARRELLED PORK	SMOKED MEATS	CHEESE	FLOUR & MILL FEEDS
LONG CLEAR BACON	DOMESTIC SHORTENING		

H. A. BRAND OLEOMARGARINE—Has saved Lumber Companies thousands of dollars—The only substitute for Butter is THE BEST OLEOMARGARINE. You are sure of THE BEST when you buy H. A. BRAND.

THE HARRIS ABATTOIR COMPANY LIMITED, West Toronto, Canada

Branches at SUDBURY and OTTAWA, ONT. MONTREAL and QUEBEC, QUE.
HALIFAX and SYDNEY, N. S. ST. JOHN, N. B.

advance still more before the end of the year. The ratio is that the demand against existing stocks, warrants it. It is a case of the visible supply as compared with requisitions. The augmented prices are the real feature of the market.

Outside of prices there was a continuous flow of inquiries and a nice business in export orders. The most of the export stock shipped went to the United States and was from mill run up to better. As compared with the late August and early September business the tendency in this regard was toward an increased demand for the better grades. South American and South African business remained about normal. A few white pine shipments went forth to each country.

The movement in buildings grades did not show much change. A confident feeling existed that these grades next spring will fetch more money than they do now. There is not yet a shortage. Dealers believe the demand now is not what it is going to be.

Retail yards were pretty well filled up. Wholesalers were fairly busy shipping to the U. S. On the other hand there may be what to the trade is known as a "shuffle" take place between the wholesalers during the winter months. This, of course, is problematical. It is subjected largely to the demand and nobody, however, in the wholesale lines showed any signs of worry.

A damper to the ardor of enthusiasm, which was showed some months ago about the opening up of the European export trade was spread late in September. The "Canada Lumberman" is reliably informed that the stocks purchased on Government account by Sir James Ball during his visit to Canada this summer, are not getting across as fast as some of the trade expected. Consequently a new order of things presents itself. The belief was current in many lumbering circles throughout the Dominion that the purchases made by the British Timber Controller in Canada would get over to Europe about the end of August. This is now upset. Stocks were shipped on Government account during September. According to a private forecast made there is not much chance of getting the remaining government stocks out of the country and overseas much before winter if not later. It is a hard thing to say but it seems to be the best informed advice on the situation at Ottawa. Any lumberman can see that, with Government stocks getting preference with ocean tonnage that, in a trade sense, it follows the fellow or firm which is not exporting to England on other than Government account, has to further sit back and await developments. Besides he holds his lumber and his money is tied up.

The labor situation for the woods remained reasonably good. Wet weather in the north country hindered the establishment of camps and the starting of actual cutting operations. In the transportation situation foreign cars showed symptoms of growing scarce. The movement of the grain crop in the United States is the probable cause. Lath and shingles were in strong demand and both remained scarce.

Conditions with woodworking factories and allied operations did not show much change.

Conditions in Montreal Are Not So Brisk

Building conditions in Montreal have caused a slackening in local requirements. Many men are out on strike, particularly carpenters and plumbers, holding up many jobs and causing an easing off in others. The masters and men are dead-locked on the question of hours and labor, and in view of the near close of the season employers are not inclined to give way, especially as the demands, if conceded, will involve a loss on existing contracts. A considerable amount of work is in hand, and there is likely to be a satisfactory addition to the jobs to be figured on providing the men are reasonable in their requirements. Should the unions succeed in forcing the abnormal rates, then construction will be restricted.

The Industrial Housing Scheme for Montreal has been dropped for the present year, owing to the difference of opinion between the Commission and Dr. Nadeau, the Provincial director, as to imposing a tax of 2½ per cent. on the loan. In other parts of the province progress is reported with schemes; for instance, St. Lambert will borrow $750,000 and Sherbrooke proposes to form a housing company. Building generally in the province is going ahead at a good rate, and lumber is in fair request.

Orders for the United States continue to come in freely, but unfortunately foreign cars are scarce.

Pacific Coast stocks are moving rather slowly, consequent on the abnormal prices.

There is considerable activity in the sash and door section, notwithstanding the recent advances in prices. The outlook is stated to be excellent.

Export business to the United Kingdom has slowed down, nearly all the Government stock having been shipped. A fair amount of lumber is being sent on commercial account; liner freights, although cheaper than before, are still too high to permit of large quantities being shipped. Some spruce is going forward on tramps. A large quantity of timber for shipbuilding is being shipped from Quebec, which port has still an appreciable quantity of spruce to be sent to the United Kingdom.

An Aggressive Wholesale Lumberman

Roch Julien, wholesale lumber merchant, 7 St. Peter Street, Quebec, has been connected with the lumber trade during his business life. He has had a wide practical experience, being engaged in his earlier years in the building of mills and as a sawyer. In 19[illegible] he succeeded H. Dupre & Co., with mills and limits at Lac aux Sables, P. Q., and in 1917 opened in the city of Quebec, as a wholesale lumber merchant. He also does an export business with the U. S. and Europe, specialising in birch. Mr. Julien is president of Julien & Julien, lumber manufacturers, Festubert, and of La Reine Lumber Co., Ltd., La Reine. The mills are at Lac Chat, Festubert and La Reine. Mr. Julien has made a great success, and is regarded in Quebec as likely to figure more prominently in the lumber trade.

Roch Julien, Quebec, P.Q.

The Increasing Call For Flooring

The almost universal replacement of carpets by rugs in the homes of this country makes a beautiful and durable floor an important part of a house and the production of high-grade flooring is one of the notable developments of modern lumber manufacturing, according to the Architectural and Building Code Service of the National Lumber Manufacturers Association.

Flooring of high quality is made from maple, birch, beech, oak, yellow pine, Douglas fir, and other woods; it is manufactured to exact standard sizes, of selected thoroughly seasoned stock and is as carefully handled as is interior finish.

Every detail has been considered to make a perfect floor, even to the recommendation of steel cut nails, driven at an angle of 45 degrees, with no nails placed wiithin six inches of the ends of the flooring pieces.

The grain of woods is carefully studied. Maple, beech and birch are close grain woods which give equally good appearance and service for floors, whether slashed or quarter-sawed, and red and white oak floorings are popular.

Strictly speaking, yellow pine and Douglas fir are softwoods, but edge grain flooring made of them gives such good service that it is widely used.

Arrivals of wood goods to the Coast ports and London have been very numerous during the month of August, says an English Exchange, but it is curious to observe that the percentage of planed stocks arriving is comparatively small. Canadian spruce and Finnish red and whitewood have come forward in plenty, also Sweden has been to the fore with her sawn wood, but not overmuch planed.

Rock elm is the strongest and most valuable of the elms cut in Canada, as stated in a report on the Forest Products of Canada, issued by the Forestry Branch, Department of Interior. Red elm is at the opposite extreme, while white elm, the most abundant of the three species, has qualities between the other two. Most of the elm cut is used in the slack cooperage industry. It is also used in the manufacture of agricultural implements, boats and vehicles, and for building purposes.

Steady Demand for Pitwood in Wales

Importers are Desirous of Doing Business with Canada — Prospects of the Market Reviewed

Norman D. Johnston, Canadian Government Trade Commissioner of the United Kingdom, in a recent report to the Department of Trade and Commerce, Ottawa, says that in South Wales there is a good demand for pit wood or pit props and if Canada can compete with other countries there importers are very desirous of doing business.

Surveying the whole situation present and prospective, Mr. Johnston says:

The principal sources of supply for pitwood previous to the war, when the total importation into the United Kingdom amounted to almost three and a half million loads, were Russia, France, Sweden, Portugal, Norway and Spain. During the war supplies from Russia declined from 1,538,714 loads in 1913 to 55,304 loads in 1917, from Sweden 359,988 loads in 1913 to 76,253 loads in 1917, from Portugal 315,538 to 74,814, from Norway 114,777 to 81,273 loads, and from Spain 103,123 to 961 loads during the same period. France maintained the best position in this trade, and from 1914 to 1917 was the largest supplier to this market, her exports of pitwood to Great Britain being 984,331 loads in 1913 and 706,263 loads in 1917.

In 1913 practically no pitwood was imported from Canada or Newfoundland. On the advent of war when supplies were curtailed from the accustomed sources importers began to get some of their requirements across the Atlantic, and this trade showed signs of greatly increasing, the imports from Canada in 1915 and 1916 being 12,383 loads and 21,545 loads respectively, and from Newfoundland 86,404 loads and 81,148 loads during these two years respectively, but principally on account of the shortage of freight space the imports from Canada in 1917 declined to 1,280 loads and from Newfoundland to nil.

In South Wales very large quantities of pitwood or pitprops are used, and if Canada can compete with other countries importers are very desirous of doing business. It remains to be seen when conditions become normal whether Canadians will be able to sell their pitwood in South Wales as cheaply as those countries whose proximity gives them an advantage in shipping. A good deal of attention has also been given to home supplies of pitwood from their own forests, but transportation has been difficult.

Sizes and Kinds in Demand

In order to give an idea of the sizes in demand, one firm in South Wales is desirous of having a cargo 75 per cent 6½ feet lengths, 2½ inches to 5½ inches top, and 25 per cent 9 feet lengths, 3 inches to 7 inches top.

Another concern mentions lengths from 6½ feet to 9 feet, which are the sizes they usually import from France and Spain.

A third firm requires pitprops in 6½ feet lengths, with diameters of 4 inches minimum at tops and up to 7 inches maximum, and in 9 feet lengths with diameters of 5 inches minimum at tops up to 10 inches maximum.

A fourth house states that the cargoes they desire should consist of about 50 per cent 6½ feet lengths, 3½ inches to 7 inches diameter at the small end, and 50 per cent 9 feet lengths 4½ inches to 10 inches at the small end.

It will therefore be seen that all of these specifications vary only slightly and can very well be taken as indicative of the sizes required in South Wales.

The inquiries which have been received at this office from Canadian firms wishing to sell pitwood have been mostly of spruce and fir. Although spruce is used, firwood is preferable as collieries do not seem to care for spruce, it being stated that as spruce is brittle by nature it gives no warning when subjected to a sudden squeeze.

The trade in pitwood is at present partially under Government control, and the Coal Controller has placed a maximum price for pitprops to the collieries. The maximum price at which firwood is allowed to be sold on this market is 65s. per ton ex ship Cardiff. If Canadians could deliver c.i.f. Bristol Channel ports at about 55s. to 60s. per ton on delivered weights a good trade could probably be done. The Government is taking a great many of the ships that are available for this trade to bring sawn woods to this country, and with the high freight rates now ruling it is more difficult to do a trade. The present ruling price for French pitwood is 65c. per ton net f.o.b. Bristol channel.

One firm has a buyer who would probably be willing to send out their own vessel for a cargo of about 2,000 cords fresh cut spruce props of the specifications first mentioned in the above paragraph on the sizes in demand if they could obtain a quotation of about $10 per cord loaded and stowed free of cost in the steamer. The importer's remuneration in the event of business would be 2½ per cent payable by the shippers.

A great many Canadian firms quote a price per cord f.o.b. Canadian port. This is very unsatisfactory, as all business is done at price per ton and quotations are received from other countries at price per English ton of 20 cwts. (1 cwt.=112 pounds) c.i.f. Bristol Channel port, and Canadians who wish to do a busienss should quote in this manner as it is practically impossible to ascertain the freight rates on this side. It is necessary that the importer should know the landed costs in order to compare Canadian prices with these from other countries.

In making quotations it should also be stated whether the wood is stripped of the bark or not and whether the weight would be free from bark.

Major Hartt Again in the [illegible]

Major J. I. Hartt, M.L.A., Orillia, Ont.

Major J. I. Hartt, M.L.A., of Orillia, who will once more be the standard bearer of the Conservative party in East Simcoe at the next provincial election, is a widely known lumberman, and for some years has been prominent in the Orange Order and the Canadian Forestry Corps. Born in 1867 in Ireland he came to Canada in 1884. Previous to entering the larger areas of public service, in 1911, he represented Orillia in the municipal council for some years. Major Hartt has long been identified with the lumber industry, and was with the Gilmour Co. in Trenton in their palmy days, remaining with that firm thirteen years. Later he took a position with the Fesserton Timber Co., after which he formed the firm of Hartt & Steele, and for a number of years has carried on business for himself. At the annual meeting of the Orange Order, held two years ago, Major Hartt was elected Grand-master of the Grand Orange Lodge, Ontario West; he has also been Supreme Grand Master of the Loyal True Blue Association. The Major spent a considerable period overseas in Forestry work and one of the achievements of the Canadian boys under him was the erection of a saw mill of 35,000 ft. daily cutting capacity, in the south of France. The work in connection with building the mill, erecting the machinery and getting it in operation was all accomplished within nine days—a remarkable record.

Lumbermen Do Not Want Limited Hours

At the National Industrial Conference recently held in Ottawa, J. Fraser Gregory, of Murray & Gregory, Limited, lumber manufacturers, of St. John, N.B., made an interesting and forcible address in which he declared that industry would collapse if the demands made upon it were too heavy. Consideration should be given the fact that the government took all excess profits, and apart from capital and labor the consuming public should be taken into account. Mr. Gregory spoke particularly on seasonable occupations—agriculture, building, a large part of lumbering, and other industries, were peculiar to summer, conditions making it impossible to do the work in the winter. "We should not be hampered by limiting hours," proceeded Mr. Gregory, "if the logs are not hauled to the rivers when the snow is on the ground, they have to lie there for another year. The export trade of Canada is largely made up of lumber. If we cannot produce as cheaply as other countries, we will lose the market." Mr. Gregory said that machinery had been so highly perfected that there was little manual laobr in manufacturing lumber.

Association of Construction Industries

A federal charter has been granted to the Association of Canadian Building and Construction Industries, with headquarters in Ottawa. Wide powers are conferred upon the company, among them being to promote better relations between its members and owners, architects and engineers, and to establish and maintain methods of practice by the members and the industry, to disseminate useful information, extend construction and improve conditions, etc. The incorporators of the company are Jas. P. Anglin and W. E. Ramsay of Montreal, Fred Armstrong and Arthur H. Dancy, of Toronto, George A. Crane, Alex. I. Garvock, and W. A. Mattes, of Ottawa.

EDGINGS

Ontario

The sawmill of Herman Goutz, Maynooth, Hastings Co., Ont., which was burned some time ago, has been rebuilt, and is once more in operation.

The recently formed Woodworkers and Carpenters' Union are asking from the various companies in Woodstock, Ont., unionized shops, a 44-hour week, and a minimum wage of 55 cents an hour.

Hart & McDonagh, wholesale lumber dealers, of Toronto, have removed their office to 311 Temple Bldg., corner Bay and Temperance Sts., Toronto, where they have commodious and attractive quarters.

John Harrison & Sons Co., Owen Sound, Ont., are now operating four camps on Fitzwilliam Island, and intend to take out about 150,000 cedar ties this season, as well as a quantity of oak, pine and spruce logs. They have just brought down a sample of oak logs and find the timber of excellent quality.

The King Edward Construction Co. with a capital stock of $2,350,000 and headquarters in Toronto, has been granted a charter to construct and erect hotels, apartments, dwelling houses, shops, factories, boarding houses, etc. Among the incorporators of the company are Russell P. Locke, Frederick H. McCallum and others.

Ruttan & Ellis' planing mill and factory in Belleville was badly damaged by fire recently. The blaze, when first seen, was at the doors of the boiler room, and spread rapidly until the upper part of the mill was in flames. After several hours' work the firemen extinguished the blaze. The loss was about four thousand dollars.

F. F. Fry, Limited, with head office in Toronto, and a capital stock of $40,000, is a new organization empowdered to carry on the business of general contractors, for the construction and equipment of public and private works, etc. Among the incorporators are J. G. Carroll, F. F. Fry and Geo. W. Sharp, contractors of Toronto.

The civic woodyard has opened in Ottawa. Deliveries are made one week after orders are received. The price is $13 a cord for cut hardwood and $12 for uncut hardwood. This consists of birch, beech and maple in excellent condition. Last year the price was $13.75 a cord. Mill wood is sold for $7.75. The city has 3,500 cords on hand.

The mill of Halton Sawmill Co., managed by J. E. Carson of Hamilton, and located near Georgetown, was burned recently. The mill had been sawing lumber for the past two years for H. G. Cockburn & Son of Guelph, in Nassagaweya and Esquesing townships, and had recently been removed to a 75 acre piece of timber near Georgetown.

J. J. McFadden, of McFadden & Mulloy, Spragge, Ont., who spent a few days in Toronto, recently, on business, states that his company have now in operation seven camps, whereas last year at this particular time they had only four. Men are more plentiful than they have been for some time and good progress is being made in logging operations.

The United Home Builders, Limited, with a capital stock of $50,000, and headquarters in Windsor, has been incorporated, to carry on the business of contractors and builders to deal in builders and contractors' supplies, and to purchase real estate, etc. The incorporators are John G. Coleridge, Alexander Simmons, B. R. McKenzie, M.C., A. A. Smith and others.

A large real estate deal has just been completed, whereby the Canadian Aeroplane, Ltd., plant, on Dufferin street, Toronto, has been sold by the Imperial Munitions Board to the Columbia Graphaphone Co. for $600,000. The building is a two-storey structure, containing 250,000 square feet of floor space, and is the second largest plant in Toronto under one roof.

The Belt Grip Pulley Co. of Canada, Limited, with a capital stock of $200,000, and head office in Toronto, is a newly-chartered concern to manufacture, buy, sell and deal in all kinds of pulleys, castors, trucks, and carriage wheels, and to operate factories and warehouses in connection with the same. Among the incoroporators are Hugh J. Harkins, John J. Coffey, and Thos. R. McNair.

Peter S. McLaren passed away recently at his home in Tiverton, Ont. He had attained the advanced age of 90 years and was a pioneer in Bruce county. The late Mr. McLaren was born in Prescott County, locating in Bruce in 1852 and becoming one of the leading men of the district. took a prominent part in all its activities. He was a contractor and lumberman, and leaves two sons and one daughter.

The W. A. Kribs Co., Limited, has been incorporated with a capital stock of $250,000 and head office in Hespeler, Ont. The incorporators are Gordon Kribs, R. L. Kribs, L. A. Kribs and others. The company is empowered to manufacture, buy sell and deal in all kinds of merchandise, to lease, sell and convey timber limits, to construct dwelling houses, to operate saw mills and carry on a wholesale and retail lumbering business.

The by-law to grant a free site to the Brockville Paper Mfg. Co. was submitted to the ratepayers of Brockville, recently, and carried by a large majority. 878 ratepayers voted for and only one against the measure. The site selected is the W. H. Woods property on Park St. north. On the location will be built a large building, two storeys high with basement. The dimensions will be 425 x 65 ft., and the industry will employ 150 hands.

The Canada Creosoting Co., Limited, with a capital stock of $100,000 and chief place of business in Toronto, has been granted a federal charter to manufacture, sell and deal in all kinds of timber, lumber, wood and wood products; wood preservatives. oils and chemical materials and compounds, and also all appliances and machinery connected with or incidental to, the operation of the company. Among the provisional incorporators are Wm. A. J. Case, solicitor, and Jas. B. Taylor, and Geo. E. Atwood, accountants, and Clifford G. Lynch, secretary, all of Toronto.

A federal charter has just been granted to the Alf. McDonald Lumber Co., Limited, of Peterborough, with a capital stock of $200,000. The company is empowered to take over the business and assets of the estate of the late Alf. McDonald, and to carry on a general lumber business in all its branches, including logging, driving, sawing, manufacturing, etc. The incorporators of the company are Mrs. Margaret McDonald, John R. McDonald, Alf. D. McDonald, Clarence McDonald and Dennis Gleeson, all of Peterboro.

Eastern Canada

J. & W. Duncan, 1801 Ontario St. E., Montreal, have started the work of rebuilding their woodworking factory and office which was destroyed by fire some time ago.

The Riordon Pulp & Paper Co. are erecting a number of workmen's houses at Hawkesbury, Ontario. A contract for just over 30 has been let; other houses will be built next year.

By order of the Court, the assets of Mr. Paul Demers, Sash & Door manufacturer, Montreal, are to be sold by auction. These comprise the sash and door factory and a large amount of real estate in Montreal.

John Sullivan and Frank McCormick have formed a partnership, under the name of Sullivan and McCormick, and will operate for Murray & Gregory Ltd. of St. John, N. B., in the State of Maine along the Tulandic stream. They have been acting as foreman for that firm for the last two years, supervising lumber cutting along that stream.

Hugh G. Watson of St. John, N.B., a well-known lumberman, died recently in Moncton, N.B., from injuries sustained at the speedway. He was knocked down by one of the horses, which ran away. Mr. Watson was forty-four years of age and is survived by three brothers.

E. M. McLaren of the Logging Division of the Laurentide Co., Ltd., Grand Mere, P. Q., made a flight with Lieut. Graham, over some limits to the north of Lake St. John, which he wished to explore. The flight from Grand Mere to Lake St. John took two hours, but owing to a very bad head wind the return trip took four and one-half-hours.

The Laurentide Co. Ltd., Grand Mere, P.Q., will install three additional grinder units, each consisting of one 2,800 horse-power motor direct connected to two magazine grinders. The new grinders will increase the capacity of the groundwood department to a total of about 400 tons, air-dry weight, of groundwood pulp per day.

Speaking at a meeting of the Quebec Manufacturers and Merchants' Association, held in Quebec, the Hon. Dr. Pelletier urged the development of trade between the Province of Quebec and Europe. As a result of his eight years' experience in England, he believed there were splendid openings for this trade, and he mentioned in particular that there was a great demand for lumber, toys and various descriptions of articles in wood. It was essential, however, that an office be opened in London with a special representative.

Considerable interest has been aroused by the formation of a company which will use aeroplanes and dirigibles to explore and exploit the hitherto practically untouched forest, mineral and fur resources of that vast stretch of territory known as Ungava. The company has just been incorporated and is composed of the following Ottawa men: Capt. E. L. Janney, late of the Royal Air Force, president; Charles Hopewell, ex-mayor of Ottawa, vice-president; Capt. J. Hedley Cameron, late of the Royal Air Force, secretary; H. C. Sherwood, treasurer, and Major William Black, late of the Canadian Army Medical Corps. The company has an authorized capital of $75,000. The territory which is to be explored by the new company comprises tbout 700,000 square miles. Ths winter activities will be centered on a stretch of interior Ungava, lying to the north of the village of Seven Islands, 320 miles below the city of Quebec on the north shore of the St. Lawrence river. Trading posts will be established at various points of the interior of Ungava.

Western Canada

The Pitt River Shingle Mill of Port Coquitlam, B. C., was recently burned to the ground. The los sis about $30,000.

J. C. McNabb & Son, Limited, with headquarters in Vancouver, and a capital stock of $100,000, has been incorporated to manufacture, sell and deal in all kinds of builders' supplies, including lumber.

That more than one man should be employed in yarding logs is the recommendation of a coroner's jury which investigated the death of C. G. Storrick, a logging foreman at Haslam Lake, who was accidentally killed.

More than 12,000,000 feet of the British order of 70,500,000 feet of British Columbia lumber is now enroute to England. The representative of the British Government hopes to have 40,000,000 feet on the way over by the end of the year.

The O. I. M. Lumber Co. Limited, with headquarters in Nelson, B.C., and a capital stock of $50,000, has been incorporated. Another concern, which has been granted letters patent is the Charles W. Johnson Lumber Co., Limited, of Vancouver, with a capital of $30,000.

The Cochrane-Annable Company has opened up yards in Trail, having leased the limits of the G. M. Annable Company on Violin mountain, near Rossland. Mr. Cochrane is a recent arrival from Minnesota, while Mr. Annable has been in the Kootenay for some years.

To secure the co-operation of the forertsy officials in B. C. province, Dr. J. W. Swaine, chief of the division of forest insects, entomological branch of the federal service, was in the West recently from Ottawa. Yellow pine has suffered in the interior, but it is hoped by proper logging operations to keep the pest out of the green timber.

One thousand mne are being sought by the Finger Lumber Company to work in their lumbering camps surrounding The Pas., Man. The camps will open on the Carrot and further up the Saskatchewan river towards Cumberland. It is proposed to cut between 50 and 60 million feet of logs. To produce this into sawn lumber, the mill at The Pas is having its machinery doubled.

Sir George Bury, head of the Whalen Pulp and Paper Company, is an enthusiast on the future of the pulp industry, and in a recent interview, said that British Columbia will produce the pulp for the world, because nowhere else in the world is there grown better wood than the Sitka spruce, found on the British Columbia Coast. Sitka spruce has the longest and strongest fibre of any wood, and was used extensively in the manufacture of airplanes. It makes the strongest and whitest pulp, as strong as the pulp made by the Egyptians from linen in the form of papyrus. Nowhere in the world is there such a generous supply of pure water. One hundred thousand gallons is needed to make a ton of pulp.

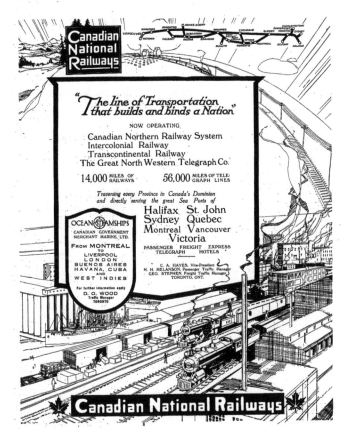

USE YOUR MOTOR TRUCK

Erect gin poles where logs are to be stored and let your truck do all the stacking at these locations.

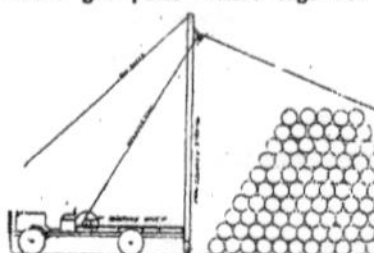

BAY CITY WINCHES

will meet your needs better than any other equipment on the market. Other designs made for loading trucks and trailers. Write for pamphlets on this equipment.

Bay City Foundry & Machine Co.
1601 Water Street · BAY CITY, MICH.

The Bertrand Circular Sawmill

All our mills are built on the latest improved machinery by the most skilled workmen, from the best obtainable materials—to meet the requirements of our customers.

We manufacture all kinds of sawmill and woodworking machinery.

Put your saw mill problems up to us.

The above illustration portrays our circular saw mill. We manufacture this model on 12 and 16 foot carriages.

La Compagnie Manufacturiere F
ST. HYACINTHE, QUE.

MANUFACTURERS OF STEAM ENGINES AND WOODWORKING MACHINES

Pink's Lumbering Tools

The Standard Tools in every province of the Dominion, New Zealand, Australia, etc.
We manufacture all kinds of lumber tools. Light and Durable.

Long Distance Phone, No. 87

Send for Catalogue and Price List.

Sold throughout the Dominion by all Wholesale and Retail Hardware Merchants.

MADE IN CANADA

It's a Pink anyway, you take it, and it's the best Peavey

The Thomas Pink Company, Limited

Manufacturers of Lumber Tools

PEMBROKE . . . . ONTARIO

CRACKED!
Question No. 4
Why did
this bearing crack?
ANSWER
SYRACUSE
BABBITTS
Syracuse Smelting
Works
Brooklyn, N.Y.
THERE are buyers of babbitt who understand that a saving of a cent or two a pound on the price is not warranted when the ultimate cost is considered.

CURRENT LUMBER PRICES—WHOLESALE

TORONTO, ONT.

Prices in Carload Lots, F.O.B. cars Toronto.

White Pine:

1 x 4/7 Good Strips	$62 00	$65 00
1¼ and 1½ x 4/7 Good Strips	66 00	68 00
2 x 4/7 Good Strips	66 00	69 00
1 x 8 and up Good Sides	79 00	82 00
1¼ and 1½ x 8 and wider Good Sides	93 00	98 00
2 x 8 and wider Good Sides	95 00	100 00
1 in. No. 1, 2 and 3 Cuts	65 00	68 00
5/4 and 6/4 No. 1, 2 and 3 Cuts	68 00	70 00
2 in. No. 1, 2 and 3 Cuts	72 00	75 00
1 x 4 and 5 Mill Run	48 00	50 00
1 x 6 Mill Run	51 00	53 00
1 x 7, 9 and 11 Mill Run	50 00	52 00
1 x 8 Mill Run	52 00	54 00
1 x 10 Mill Run	55 00	57 00
1 x 12 Mill Run	57 00	59 00
5/4 and 6/4 x 4 Mill Run	51 00	53 00
5/4 and 6/4 x 5 Mill Run	51 00	53 00
2 x 4 Mill Run	50 00	52 00
2 x 6 Mill Run	52 00	53 00
2 x 8 Mill Run	53 00	55 00
2 x 10 Mill Run	56 00	58 00
2 x 12 Mill Run	57 00	59 00
1 in. Mill Run Shorts	41 00	42 00
1 x 4 and up 6/16 No. 1 Mill Culls	40 00	42 00
1 x 10 and up 6/16 No. 1 Mill Culls	45 00	46 00
1 x 12 and up 6/16 No. 1 Mill Culls	45 00	46 00
1 x 4 and up 6/16 No. 2 Mill Culls	33 00	34 00
1 x 10 x 12 6/16 No. 2 Mill Culls	35 00	36 00
1 x 4 and up 6/10 No. 3 Mill Culls	25 00	27 00

Red Pine:

1 x 4 and 5 Mill Run	43 00	44 00
1 x 6 Mill Run	44 00	46 00
1 x 8 Mill Run	47 00	48 00
1 x 10 Mill Run	48 00	49 00
2 x 4 Mill Run	45 00	46 00
2 x 6 Mill Run	46 00	47 00
2 x 8 Mill Run	48 00	49 00
1 in. Clear and Clear Face	60 00	62 00
2 in. Clear and Clear Face	60 00	62 00

Spruce:

1 x 4 Mill Run	42 00	43 00
1 x 6 Mill Run	44 00	45 00
1 x 8 Mill Run	45 00	46 00
1 x 10 Mill Run	48 00	49 00
1/12 Mill Run Spruce	50 00	51 00
Mill Culls	36 00	37 00
1 x 4 and 5 in. x 9 to 16 ft.	36 00	38 00
1 x 6 in. x 9 to 16 ft.	39 00	40 00
1 x 8 in. x 9 to 16 ft.	40 00	41 00
1 x 10 and 12 in. x 9 to 16 ft.	40 00	41 00
1 x 7, 9 and 11 in. x 9 to 10 ft.	37 00	38 00
2 x 4 to 12, 10 and 16 ft.	40 00	41 00
2 x 4 to 12 in., 12 and 14 ft.	39 00	40 00
2 x 4 to 12 in., 18 ft.	41 00	42 00
2 x 4 to 12 in., 20 ft.	42 00	43 00
1 in. No. 2, 6 ft. to 16 ft.	33 00	34 00
2" No. 2, 4" and up, width 6 to 16 ft.	33 00	34 00

Douglas Fir, delivered in Toronto:

Dimension Timber up to 32 feet:

6x6 and 8, 10x10 and 12, 12x12	$52 00
6x10, 8x10, 10x14, 12x14, 14x14	53 00
6x12, 8x12	54 00
14x16, 16x16	54 50
6x14, 8x14, 10x16, 12x16	56 00
14x18	56 50
8x16, 10x18, 12x18	57 00
18x18, 20x20	57 50
12x20, 24x24	58 00

Timber in lengths over 32 feet subject to negotiation.

Fir flooring, 1 x 3, edge grain		71 00
Fir flooring, 1 x 4, edge grain		71 00
Fir flooring, 1 x 4, flat grain		open
No. 1 & 2, 1-in. clear Fir rough	61 50	69 50

(Depending upon widths).

No. 1 and 2, 1¼ and 1½ in., clear Fir rough	71 00	75 00
No. 1 and 2 2-in. clear Fir rough	56 00	66 00
1 x 5 and 1 x 6 Fir casing		73 00
1 x 8 and 1 x 10 Fir base		75 00
1¼ & 1½ x 8, 10 & 12" E. G. stepping		85 00
1¼ & 1½ x 8, 10 & 12" F. G. stepping		75 00
1-in. clear Fir, d 4 sides	56 00	64 00
1¼ x 1½ in. clear Fir, d 4 sides	56 50	65 50
XXX 6 butts to 2 in.		7 40
XXXXX 5 butts to 2 in.		8 50

TORONTO HARDWOOD PRICES

The prices given below are for carloads, f.o.b. Toronto, from wholesalers to retailers, and are based on a good percentage of long lengths and good widths, without any wide stock having been sorted out. War tax of seven and half per cent. on imported woods, and also the prevailing rate of exchange paid by purchaser.

Ash, white, dry weight 3800 lbs. per M. ft.

	1s & 2s	No. 1 Com.	No. 2 Com.	No. 3 Com.
4/4	$80.00	$60.00	$40.00	$30.00
5/4 & 6/4	85.00	68.00	45.00	35.00
8/4	95.00	75.00	45.00	
10/4 & 12/4	110.00	110.00	60.00	
16/4	125.00	115.00	65.00	

Ash, Brown

4/4	$75.00	$55.00	$40.00	$38.00
6/4	80.00	65.00	60.00	50.00
8/4	83.00	70.00	65.00	50.00

Birch, dry weight 4000 lbs. per M. ft.

	1s & 2s $		No. 1 Com. $		No. 2 Com. $	
4/4	75	78	60	63	45	50
5/4 & 6/4	78	80	68	70	50	55
8/4	80	83	70	75	55	
10/4 and 12/4	100	105	90	95	70	
16/4	105	110	85	100	80	

Basswood, dry weight 2500 lbs. per M. ft.

	1s & 2s	No. 1 Com.	No. 2 Com.	No. 3 Com.
4/4	$77.00	$55.00	$44.00	$38.00
5/4 & 6/4	80.00	60.00	50.00	40.00
8/4	85.00	63.00	50.00	42.00

Chestnut, dry weight 2800 lbs. per M. ft.

	1s & 2s	No. 1 Com.	Sound Wormy
4/4	$90.00	$70.00	$65.00
5/4 & 6/4	100.00	75.00	70.00
8/4	110.00	80.00	75.00

Elm, soft, dry weight 3100 lbs. per M. ft.

	1s & 2s	No. 1 Com.	No. 2 Com.	No. 3 Com.
4/4	$63.00	$50.00	$40.00	$38.00
6/4 & 8/4	68.00	55.00	45.00	43.00
12/4	75.00	65.00	50.00	42.00

Gum, red, dry weight 3300 lbs. per M. ft.

	1s & 2s	No. 1 Com.
4/4	$120.00	$90.00
5/4 & 6/4	130.00	100.00
8/4	150.00	125.00

Gum, Sap

	1s & 2s	No. 1 Com.
4/4	$80.00	$55.00
5/4 & 6/4	85.00	60.00
8/4	90.00	70.00

Hickory, dry weight, 4500 lbs. per M. ft.

	1s & 2s	No. 1 Com.	No. 2 Com.
4/4	$75.00	$45.00	$30.00
6/4	100.00	75.00	50.00
8/4	90.00	60.00	35.00

Maple, hard, dry weight 3900 lbs. per M. ft.

	1s & 2s	No. 1 Com.	No. 2 Com.	No. 3 Com.
4/4	$60.00	$50.00	$40.00	$30.00
5/4 & 6/4	65.00	60.00	45.00	35.00
8/4	70.00	65.00	45.00	40.00
12/4	80.00	60.00	40.00	
16/4	90.00	75.00	45.00	

Soft Maple

The quantity of soft maple produced in Ontario is small and it is generally sold on a log run basis, the locality governing the prices.

Mill run grade, No. 3 and better	$43.00
No. 2 and better	52.00

White and Red Oak, plain sawed, dry weight 4000 lbs. per M. ft.

	1s & 2s	No. 1 Com.
4/4	$135.00	$90.00
5/4 & 6/4	140.00	95.00
8/4	145.00	100.00
10/4	155.00	110.00
12/4	160.00	115.00
16/4	165.00	120.00

White Oak, quarter cut, dry weight 4000 lbs. per M. ft.

	1s & 2s	No. 1 Com.
4/4	$225.00	$175.00
5/4 and 6/4	240.00	190.00
8/4	250.00	190.00

Red Oak, quarter cut.

	1s & 2s	No. 1 Com.
4/4	$185.00	$125.00
5/4 & 6/4	200.00	140.00
8/4	205.00	145.00

OTTAWA, ONT.

Manufacturers' Prices

Pine good sidings:		
1-in. x 7-in. and up		84 00
1¼-in. and 1½-in., 8-in. & up		102 00
2-in. x 7-in. and up		102 00
No. 2 cuts 2 x 8-in. and up		70 00
Pine good strips:		
1-in.		70 00
1¼-in. and 1½-in.		75 00
2-in.		80 00
Pine good shorts:		
1-in. x 7-in. and up		65 00
1-in. x 4-in. to 6-in.		57 00
1¼-in. and 1½-in.		70 00
2-in.		72 00
7-in. to 9-in. A sidings		56 00
Pine, No. 1 dressing sidings		62 00
Pine, No. 1 dressing strips		58 00
Pine, No. 1 dressing shorts		52 00
Pine, 1-in. x 4-in. s.c. strips		51 00
Pine, 1-in. x 5-in. s.c. strips		52 00
Pine, 1-in. x 6-in. s.c. strips		54 00
Pine, 1-in. x 7-in. s.c. strips		54 00
Pine, 1 x 8-in. s.c., 12 to 16 ft.	48 00	56 00
Pine, 1-in. x 10-in. M.R.		58 00
Pine, s.c. sidings, 1½ and 2-in.		55 00
Pine, s.c. strips, 1-in.	45 00	49 00
1¼, 1½ and 2-in.		56 00
Pine, s.c. shorts, 1 x 4 to 6 in.		45 00
Pine, s.c. and bet., shorts, 1 x 5		45 00
Pine, s.c. and bet., shorts, 1 x 6		47 00
Pine, s.c. shorts, 6'-11', 1"x10"		52 00
Pine box boards:		
1"x4" and up, 6'-11'		40 00
1"x3", 12'-16'		44 00
Pine, mill culls, strips and sidings, 1-in. x 4-in. and up, 12-ft. and up		40 00
Mill cull shorts, 1-in. x 4-in. and up, 6-ft to 11-ft.		38 00
O. culls r & w p		29 00
Red Pine, log run:		
mill culls out, 1-in.	36 00	42
mill culls out, 1¼-in.	36 00	42
mill culls out, 1½-in.	38 00	42 00
mill culls out, 2-in.	40 00	42 00
mill culls, white pine, 1"x7" and up		40 00
Mill run Spruce:		
1"x4" and up, 6'-11'		42 00
1"x4" and up, 12'-16'		42 00
1"x9"-10" and up, 12'-16'		48 00
1¼"x7" 8-9" and up, 12'-16'		48 00
1¼ x 10 and up, 12'-16'		50 00
1½" & 2" x 12" and up, 12'-16'		50 00
Spruce, 1-in. clear (fine dressing and B)		55 00
Hemlock, 1-in. cull	25 00	27 00
Hemlock, 1-in. log run	30 00	35 00
Hemlock, 2x4, 6, 8, 10, 12/16'	30 00	35 00
Tamarac	24 00	26 00
Basswood, log run, dead culls out	46 00	48 00
Basswood, log run, mill culls out	48 00	50 00
Birch, log run	48 00	50 00
Soft Elm, common and better, 1, 1½, 2-in.	25 00	30 00
Ash, black, log run	32 00	40 00
1 x 10 No. 1 barn		52 00
1 x 10 No. 2 barn		45 00
1 x 8 and 9 No. 2 barn		42 00
Lath per M:		
No. 1 white pine, 1½-in. x 4 ft.		7 50
No. 2 white pine		7 00
Mill run white pine		7 25
Spruce, mill run 1½-in.		6 75
Red pine, mill run		6 75
Hemlock, mill run		6 00
32-in. lath		3 50
White Cedar Shingles:		
xxxx, 18-in.		7 00
Clear butt, 18-in.		6 00
18-in. xx		4 50
Spruce logs (pulp)	18 00	18 00

QUEBEC, QUE.

	Cts. Per Cubic Foot.	
White Pine		
First class Ottawa waney, 18-in. average, according to lineal	80	90
19 in. and up average	90	100 00
Spruce Deals	Per M. Ft.	
3 in. unsorted Quebec, 4 in. to 6 in. thick	$34 00	$37 00
3 in. unsorted, Quebec, 7 in. to 9 in. thick	38 00	40 00
3 in. unsorted Quebec, 9 in. thick	40 00	45 00
Oak	Cts. Per Cubic Ft.	
According to average and quality 55 ft. cube	90	1 00
Elm		
According to average and quality, 40 to 45 feet, cube	95	1 05
According to average and quality, 30 to 35 feet	75	85
Birch Planks		
1 to 4 in. thick, per M. ft.	40 00	45 00

SARNIA, ONT.

Fine, Common and Better		
1 x 6 and 8 in.		$80 00
1 in., 8 in. and up wide		90 00
1¼ and 1½ in. and up wide		100 00
2 in. and up wide		105 00
Cuts and Better		
4/4 x 8 and up No. 1 and better		75 00
6/4 x 8 and up No. 1 and better		85 00
8/4 x 8 and up No. 1 and better		87 00
No. 1 Cuts		
1 in., 8 in. and up wide		63 00
1¼ in., 8 in. and up wide		72 00
1½ in., 8 in. and up wide		73 00
2 in., 8 in. and up wide		75 00
2½ and 3, 8 in. and up wide		100 00
4 in., 8 in. and up wide		105 00
No. 1 Barn		
1 in., 10 to 16 ft. long	$54 00	$64 00
1¼, 1½ and 2 in., 10/16 ft.	58 00	64 00
2½ to 3 in., 10/16 ft.		73 00
No. 2 Barn		
1 in., 10 to 16 ft. long	51 00	57 00
1¼, 1½ and 2 in., 10/16 ft.	52 00	58 00
2½ in. to 3 in.		66 00
No. 3 Barn		
1 in., 10 to 16 ft. long	48 00	53 00
1¼, 1½ and 2 in., 10/16 ft.	49 00	53 00
Box		
1 in., 1¼ in. & 1½ in., 10/16 ft.	44 00	46 00
Mill Culls		
Mill Run Culls		
1 in., 4 in. and up wide, 6/16 ft.		$37 00
1¼, 1½ and 2 in.		37 00
Lath		
No. 1 48 in. White Pine		$6 00
No. 2 48 in. White Pine		5 50
No. 3 48 in. White Pine		5 00
32 in. Pine		2 35
48 in. Hemlock		5 00
32 in. Hemlock		2 25

ST. JOHN, N.B.

Rough Lumber

Wholesale Prices Per M. Sq. Ft.

2x3, 2x4, 3x3, 3x4, Rgh. Merch. Spr.	$42
2x3, 2x4, 3x3, 3x4 Dressed 1 edge	
2x3, 2x4, 3x3, 3x4 Dressed 4 sides	
2x6, 2x7, 3x5, 4x4, 4x6, all rough	
2x8, 3x7, 5x5, 6x6	
2x9, 3x8, 6x8, 7x7	
2x10, 3x9	
2x12, 3x10, 3x12, 8x8 and up	
Merch. Spr. Bds. Rough, 1x3-4 & 5	
" " " " 1x6	
" " " " 1x7 & up	44 50
Refuse Bds., Deals & Setgs.	44 00

Above random lengths up to 18-0 long.

Lengths 19-0 & up $5.00 extra per M.

For planing Merch. and Refuse Bds. add $2.00 per M to above prices.

Laths $4.50 per M pieces.

Shingles

	Per M.
Cedar, Extras	$6 00
" Clears	5 50
" 2nd Clears	5 00
" Extra No. 1	3 50
Spruce	4 50
B. C. Cedar	4 70

WINNIPEG, MANITOBA

No. 1 Spruce

Dimension	S.1.S and 1.E 6 ft.	8 ft.	10 ft.
2 x 4	$35 50	$38 50	[illegible]
2 x 6	37 50	38 50	[illegible]
2 x 8	37 50	39 50	[illegible]
2 x 10	38 50	40 50	[illegible]
2 x 12	40 50	41 50	[illegible]
	12 ft.	14 ft.	16 ft.
2 x 4	40 00	40 00	[illegible]
2 x 6	40 00	40 00	[illegible]
2 x 8	40 00	40 00	[illegible]
2 x 10	41 00	41 00	[illegible]
2 x 12	42 00	42 00	[illegible]

For 2 inches, rough, add 50 cents.

For S1E only add 50 cents.

For S1S and 2E, S4S or D&M, add $3.00.

For timbers larger than 8 x 8, add 50c. for each additional 2 inches each way.

For lengths longer than 20 ft., add $1.00 for each additional two feet.

For selected common, add $5.00.

For No. 2 Dimension, $3.00 less than No. 1.

For 1 x 2 and 2 x 2, $2 more than 2 x 4 No. 1.

For Tamarac add $3.00.

FIR, HEMLOCK, SPRUCE AND LARCH

Mountain Stock

No. 1 Dimension and Timbers

2 x 4, 2 x 6, 2 x 8, 8 to 16 ft., S1S1E	$39 00
2 x 4, 2 x 6, 2 x 8, 10 ft., S1S1E	41 00
2 x 4, 2 x 6, 2 x 8, 12/16, S1S1E	39 00
2 x 4, 2 x 6, 2 x 8, 18/22, S1S1E	41 00
2 x 4, 2 x 6, 2 x 8, 24/32, S1S1E	43 00
2 x 10, 8 ft. to 16 ft., S1S1E	40 00
2 x 10, 10 ft. S1S1E	42 00
2 x 10, 18/22, S1S1E	42 00
2 x 10, 24/32, S1S1E	44 00
2 x 12, 8 ft. to 16 ft., S1S1E	41 50
2 x 12; 10, 18, 20	43 50
2 x 12; 24, 26, 28, 30, 32	45 50

BRITISH COLUMBIA COAST FIR.

Dimension S1S a

2 x 4 in., 6 ft.	30
2 x 4 in., 8, 12 and 14 ft.	30
2 x 4 in., 16 ft.	30
2 x 4 in., 18 and 20 ft.	30
2 x 4 in., 22 to 32 ft.	30
2 x 10 in., 8, 12 and 14	41 75
2 x 10 in., 16 ft.	42 75
2 x 10 in., 18 and 20 ft.	43 75
2 x 10 in., 22 to 32 ft.	45 75
2 x 12 in., 8 to 14 ft.	43 25
2 x 12 in., 16 ft.	25
2 x 12 in., 18 and 20 ft.	45 25
2 x 12 in., 22 to 32 ft.	47 25
3 x 3 and 3 x 4 in., 8 to 14 ft.	46 75
3 x 3 and 3 x 4 in., 16 ft.	47 75
3 x 3 and 3 x 4, 18 and 20 ft.	48 75
3 x 3 and 3 x 4 in., 22 to 32 ft.	50 75
6 x 6, 6 x 8, 8 x 8, 6 to 16 ft.	49 00
6 x 6, 6 x 8 and 8 x 8, 18 and 20 ft.	49 50
6 x 6, 6 x 8, 8 x 8, 22 to 32 ft.	50 50
Shingles, XXX B. C. Cedar, straight cars on 69c rate	6 08

BUFFALO AND TONAWANDA, N.Y.

White Pine

Wholesale Selling Price

Uppers, 4/4	$115 00
Uppers, 5/4 to 8/4	100 00
Uppers, 10/4 to 12/4	130 00
Selects 4/4	110 00
Selects 5/4 to 8/4	110 00
Selects 10/4 to 12/4	120 00
Fine common 4/4	82 00
Fine Common 5/4	87 00
Fine Common 6/4	84 00
Fine common 8/4	87 00
No. 1 Cuts 4/4	68 00
No. 1 Cuts 5/4	74 00
No. 1 Cuts 6/4	75 00
No. 1 Cuts 8/4	78 00
No. 2 Cuts 4/4	47 00
No. 2 Cuts 5/4	61 00
No. 2 Cuts 6/4	62 00
No. 2 Cuts 8/4	60 00
No. 3 Cuts 5/4	49 00
No. 3 Cuts 6/4	49 00
No. 3 Cuts 8/4	50 00
Dressing 5/4	64 00
Dressing 5/4 x 10	67 00
Dressing 5/4 x 12	73 00
No. 1 Moulding 5/4	74 00
No. 1 Moulding 6/4	74 00
No. 1 Moulding 8/4	74 00
No. 2 Moulding 5/4	66 00
No. 2 Moulding 6/4	66 00
No. 2 Moulding 8/4	66 00
No. 1 Barn 1 x 12	62 00
No. 1 Barn 1 x 6 and 8	54 00
No. 1 Barn 1 x 10	56 00
No. 2 Barn 1 x 6 and 8	50 00
No. 2 Barn 1 x 10	54 00
No. 3 Barn 1 x 6 and 8	47 00
No. 3 Barn 1 x 10	45 00
Box 1 x 6 and up	45 00
Box 1 x 10	45 00
Box 1 x 12	46 00
Box 1 x 13 and up	47 00

The following quotations on hardwoods represent the jobber buying price at Buffalo and Tonawanda.

(Continued on page 77)

CURRENT LUMBER PRICES—Continued

MAPLE	1s & 2s	No. 1 Com.	No. 2 Com.
4/4	49 - 52	34 - 36	24 - 26
5/4 to 8/4	62 - 65	41 - 43	29 - 31
10/4 to 16/4	73 - 75	53 - 55	33 - 35
RED BIRCH			
4/4	64 - 66	44 - 46	28 - 30
5/4 to 8/4	67 - 69	47 - 49	31 - 33
SAP BIRCH			
4/4	60 - 64	38 - 40	24 - 26
5/4 and up	66 - 68	41 - 43	27 - 29
SOFT ELM			
4/4	49 - 51	34 - 36	26 - 28
5, 6 & 8/4	52 - 54	37 - 39	27 - 29
BASSWOOD			
4/4	54 - 56	44 - 46	31 - 33
Thicker	58 - 61	47 - 49	33 - 35
PLAIN OAK			
4/4	69 - 74	49 - 50	30 - 32
5/4 to 8/4	75 - 79	51 - 55	35 - 37
ASH, WHITE AND BROWN			
4/4	70 - 72	40 - 44	29 - 32
5/4 to 8/4	76 - 80	48 - 50	33 - 35
10/4 and up	103 - 93	63 - 66	34 - 36

BOSTON, MASS.

Quotations given below are for highest grades of Michigan and Canadian white pine and Eastern Canadian Spruce as required in the New England market in carloads.

White pine uppers, 1 to 2 in.		134 00
White pine uppers, 2½ and 3 in.		149 00
White pine uppers, 4 in.		169 00
Selects, 1 to 2 in.		125 00
Selects, 2½ and 3 in.		140 00
Selects, 4 in.		155 00
Fine common, 1 in., 30 per cent. 12 in. and up		92 00
Fine common, 1 x 8 to 11 in.		87 00
Fine Common, 1¼ to 2 in.		100 00
Fine Common, 2½ and 3 in.		130 00
Fine Common, 4 in.		143 00
1 in. shaky clear		72 00
1¼ to 2 in. shaky clear		75 00
1 in. No. 2 dressing		64 00
1¼ to 2 in. No. 2 dressing		68 00
No. 1 Cuts, 1 in.		80 00
No. 1 Cuts, 1¼ to 2 in.	85 00	87 00
No. 1 Cuts, 2½ and 3 in.		115 00
No. 2 Cuts, 1 in.		60 00
No. 2 Cuts, 1¼ to 2 in.	70 00	71 00

Barn Boards, No. 1, 1 x 12		60 00
No. 1, 1 x 10		64 00
No. 1, 1 x 8		61 00
No. 2, 1 x 12		64 00
No. 2, 1 x 10		61 00
No. 2, 1 x 8		58 00
No. 3, 1 x 12		58 00
No. 3, 1 x 10		57 00
No. 3, 1 x 8		55 00
Can. spruce, clear, 1 x 4 to 9 in.	55 00	58 00
1 x 10 in.		60 00
No. 1 1 x 4 to 7 in.		[illegible]
No. 1 1 x 8 & 9 in.		64 00
No. 1 1 x 10 in.		65 00
No. 2 1 x 4 & 5 in.		42 00
No. 2 1 x 6 & 7 in.		[illegible]
No. 2 1 x 8 & 9 in.	40 00	[illegible]
No. 2 1 x 10 in.		[illegible]
No. 2 1 x 12 in.		[illegible]
Spruce, 12 in. dimension		[illegible]
Spruce, 10 in. dimension		[illegible]
Spruce, 9 in. dimension		[illegible]
Spruce, 8 in. dimension		[illegible]
2 x 10 in. random lengths, 8 ft. and up		52 00
2 x 12 in., random lengths		54 00

2 x 3, 2 x 4, 2 x 5, 2 x 6, 2 x 7	[illegible]	[illegible]
3 x 4 and 4 x 4 in.	[illegible]	[illegible]
2 x 8 in.	[illegible]	[illegible]
All other random lengths, 7-in. and under, 8 ft. and up	40 00	[illegible]
5-inch and up, merchantable boards, 8 ft. and up, p 1s	[illegible]	[illegible]
1 x 2		[illegible]
1 x 3		[illegible]
1-⅜ in. spruce lath		[illegible]
1-½ in. spruce lath		[illegible]
New Brunswick Cedar Shingles		
Extras		[illegible]
Clears		[illegible]
Second Clears		[illegible]
Clear Whites		[illegible]
Extra 1s (Clear whites in)		[illegible]
Extra 1s (Clear whites out)		[illegible]
Red Cedar Extras, 16-in. 5 butts to 2-in.		[illegible]
Red Cedar Eurekas, 18-inch 5 butts to 2-in.		[illegible]
Red Cedar Perfections, 5 butts to 2¼		[illegible]
Washington 16-in. 5 butts to 2-in. extra red cedar		[illegible]

ALPHABETICAL INDEX TO ADVERTISERS

DOMINION
RUBBER
SYSTEM
AND ASSOCIATED COMPANIES

Lumbermen's Tents and Clothing

Pure wool, Waterproof Mackinaw Coats, Pants and Shirts, the kind you have been looking for.

Repellant Brand Army Duck Tents

The best duck that money can buy. We can equip your van complete.

Pure wool Blankets, Sweaters, Underwear. Hand Knit Mitts and Socks. Palmer's Shoe Packs, Buck and horse hide Moccasins, etc.

Grant-Holden-Graham, Limited

Factory and Warehouse

147 to 151 Albert Street, Ottawa, Can.

The Mark of Dependability

See that the cordage transmission, rope or lath yarn on your hauls bears this stamp of reliability.

LION BRAND

CORDAGE

Wherever the strain is severe and a rope is required to resist unusual tension—you'll find LION BRAND giving faithful service.

PLAY SAFE - SPECIFY LION BRAND

CONSUMERS CORDAGE CO., LIMITED, 285 St. Patrick Street MONTREAL, QUE.

Montreal · Halifax · St. John, N.B. · Toronto, 11 Church St.

Agents and Stocks at

Tees & Persse, Ltd., Winnipeg, Regina, Saskatoon, Moose Jaw, Calgary, Edmonton, Fort William. James Bisset & Co., Quebec. Macgowan & Co., Vancouver.

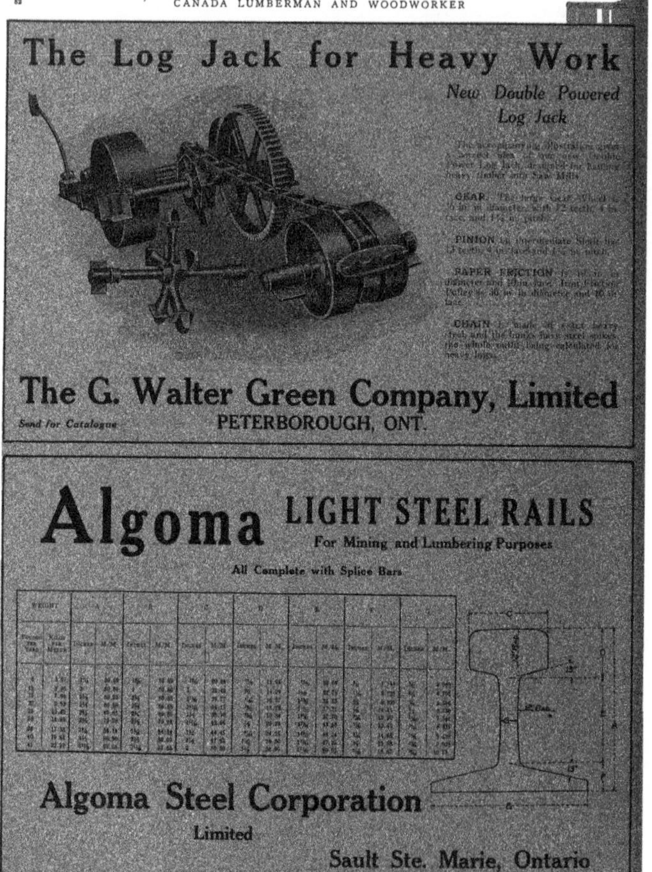
The Log Jack for Heavy Work
New Double Powered Log Jack
GEAR.
PINION
PAPER FRICTION
CHAIN
The G. Walter Green Company, Limited
Send for Catalogue
PETERBOROUGH, ONT.
Algoma LIGHT STEEL RAILS
For Mining and Lumbering Purposes
All Complete with Splice Bars
Algoma Steel Corporation
Limited
Sault Ste. Marie, Ontario

CANADA LUMBERMAN BUYERS' DIRECTORY

The following regulations apply to all advertisers:—Eighth page, every issue, three headings; quarter page, six headings; half page, twelve headings; full page, twenty-four headings.

ASBESTOS GOODS
Atlas Asbestos Company, Ltd.

AXES
Canadian Warren Axe & Tool Co.

BABBITT METAL
Canada Metal Company.
General Supply Co. of Canada, Ltd.
Syracuse Smelting Works

BALE TIES
Laidlaw Bale Tie Company.

BAND MILLS
Hamilton Company, William.
Waterous Engine Works Company.
Yates-Machine Company, P. B.

BELT CEMENT
Graton & Knight Mfg. Company.

BELT DRESSING
Atlas Asbestos Company, Ltd.
General Supply Co. of Canada, Ltd.
Graton & Knight Mfg. Company.

BELTING
Atlas Asbestos Company, Ltd.
Beardmore Belting Company
Canadian Consolidated Rubber Co.
General Supply Company
Goodhue & Co., J. L.
Goodyear Tire & Rubber Co.
Graton & Knight Mfg. Company.
Gutta Percha and Rubber Company.
Main Belting Company
Manhattan Rubber Mfg. Co.
D. K. McLaren Limited.
McLaren Belting Company, J. C.

BELTING (Transmission, Elevator, Conveyor, Rubber)
Dunlop Tire & Rubber Goods Co.

BLOWERS
Toronto Blower Company.

BOILERS
Hamilton Company, William.
Jenckes Machine Company.
Marsh Engineering Works, Limited
Waterous Engine Works Company.

BOILER PRESERVATIVE
International Chemical Company

BOX MACHINERY
Garlock-Walker Machinery Co.
Morgan Machine Company.
Yates Machine Company, P. B.

BOX SHOOKS
Davison Lumber & Mfg. Company

BUNKS (Steel)
Alaska Bedding Co. of Montreal.

CABLE CONVEYORS
Jeffrey Manufacturing Company.
Jenckes Machine Company, Ltd.
Waterous Engine Works Company.

CAMP SUPPLIES
Canadian Milk Products Limited.
Davies Company, William.
Dr. Bell Veterinary Wonder Co.
Eckardt & Co.
Harris Abattoir Company
Johnson, A. H.
Turner & Sons, J. J.
Woods Manufacturing Company, Ltd.

CANT HOOKS
Canadian Warren Axe & Tool Co.
General Supply Co. of Canada, Ltd.
Pink Company, Thomas.

CARS—STEEL BODY
Marsh Engineering Works, Limited

CAR WHEELS AND CASTINGS
Dominion Wheel & Foundries

CEDAR
Fesserton Timber Co.
Foss Lumber Company
Genoa Bay Lumber Company
Muir & Kirkpatrick.
Long Lumber Company.
Service Lumber Company
Terry & Gordon.
Thurston-Flavelle Lumber Company.
Vancouver Lumber Company.
Victoria Lumber and Mfg. Co.

CHAINS
Canadian Link-Belt Company, Ltd.
General Supply Co. of Canada, Ltd.
Hamilton Company, William.
Hobbs Company, Clinton E.
Jeffrey Manufacturing Company.
Jenckes Machine Company, Ltd.
Pink & Co., Thomas.
Waterous Engine Works Company.
Williams Machinery Co., A. R., Vancouver.

CHAIN HOISTS
Hobbs Company, Clinton E.

CHINA CLAY
Bowater & Sons, W. V.

CHEMICAL PLANTS
Blair, Campbell & McLean, Ltd.

CLOTHING
Acme Glove Works
Clarke & Company, A. R.
Grant, Holden & Graham.
Woods Mfg. Company

COLLAR PADS
American Pad & Textile Co.

CONVEYOR MACHINERY
Canadian Link-Belt Company, Ltd.
Canadian Mathews Gravity Carrier Company.
General Supply Co. of Canada, Ltd.
Jeffrey Mfg. Co.
Waterous Engine Works Company.

CORDAGE
Consumers Cordage Company.

CORN SYRUP
Canada Starch Company

COTTON GLOVES
American Pad & Textile Co.

COUPLINGS (Shaft)
Jenckes Machine Company, Ltd.

CRANES FOR SHIP YARDS
Canadian Link-Belt Company.

CROSS ARMS
Genoa Bay Lumber Company

CUTTER HEADS
Shimer Cutter Head Company.

CYPRESS
Chicago Lumber & Coal Company.
Long Lumber Company.
Wistar, Underhill & Nixon.

DERRICKS AND DERRICK FITTINGS
Marsh Engineering Works, Limited

DOORS
Genoa Bay Lumber Company
Long Lumber Company.
Mason, Gordon & Co.
Rutherford & Sons, Wm.
Terry & Gordon.

DRAG SAWS
Gerlach Company, Peter
Williams Machinery Co., A. R.

DRIVING BOOTS
Acme Glove Works

DRYERS
Philadelphia Textile Mach. Company.

DUST COLLECTORS
Toronto Blower Company.

EDGERS
William Hamilton Company, Ltd.
Garlock-Walker Machinery Co.
Green Company, G. Walter
Long Mfg. Company, E.
Waterous Engine Works Company.

ELEVATING AND CONVEYING MACHINERY
Canadian Link-Belt Company, Ltd.
Jeffrey Manufacturing Company.
Jenckes Machine Company, Ltd.
Waterous Engine Works Company.

ENGINES
Hamilton Company, William.
Jenckes Machine Company.
Waterous Engine Works Company.

EXCELSIOR MACHINERY
Elmira Machinery and Transmission Company.

EXHAUST FANS
Garlock-Walker Machinery Co.
Reed & Company, Geo. W.
Toronto Blower Company.

EXHAUST SYSTEMS
Reed & Company, Geo. W.
Toronto Blower Company.

FILES
Disston & Sons, Henry.
Simonds Canada Saw Company.

FIR
Associated Mills, Limited
Allan-Stoltze Lumber Co.
British American Mills & Timber Co.
Coal Creek Lumber Company.
Fesserton Timber Co.
Foss Lumber Company
Grier & Sons, Ltd., G. A.
Heeney, Percy E.
Knox Brothers.
Long Lumber Company.
Mason, Gordon & Co
Reynolds Company, Limited
Service Lumber Company
Shearer Company, Jas.
Terry & Gordon.
Timberland Lumber Company.
Timms, Phillips & Co.
Vancouver Lumber Company.
Victoria Lumber and Mfg. Co.
Weller, J. B.

FIRE BRICK
Beveridge Paper Company
Elk Fire Brick Company of Canada.

FIRE FIGHTING APPARATUS
Dunlop Tire & Rubber Goods Co.
Pyrene Mfg. Company.
Waterous Engine Works Company.

FIR FLOORING
Genoa Bay Lumber Company
Rutherford & Sons, Wm.

FLAG STAFFS
Ontario Wind Engine Company

FLOORING (Oak)
Long-Bell Lumber Company.

GALVANIZING
Ontario Wind Engine Company

GLOVES
ACme Glove Works
Eisendrath Glove Co.

GASOLINE ENGINES
Ontario Wind Engine Company

GEARS (Cut)
Smart-Turner Machine Co.

GRAIN
Dwyer Company, W. H.

GRAVITY LUMBER CARRIER
Can. Mathews Gravity Carrier Co.

GRINDERS (Bench)
Garlock-Walker Machinery Co.

HARDWOODS
Anderson Lumber Company, C. G.
Atlantic Lumber Co.
Bartram & Ball.
Bennett Lumber Company.
Blakeslee, Perrin & Darling
Cameron & Co.
Cardinal & Page
Davison Lumber & Mfg. Company
Dunfield & Company
Edwards & Co., W. C.
Fassett Lumber Company.
Fesserton Timber Co.
Fraser Limited.
Gillespie, James.
Gloucester Lumber Company
Grier & Son, G. A.
Heeney, Percy E.
Knox Brothers.
Long Lumber Company.
McLennan Lumber Company.
Moores, Jr., E. J.
Pedwell Hardwood Lumber Co.
Powell-Myers Lumber Co.
Russell, Chas. H.
Spencer Limited, C. A.
Stearns & Culver Lumber Co.
Summers, James R.
Taylor Lumber Company, S. K.
Webster & Brother, James.

HARDWOOD FLOORING MACHINERY
American Woodworking Machinery Company
Garlock-Walker Machinery Co.

HARDWOOD FLOORING
Grier & Son, G. A.
Long Lumber Company.

HAY
Dwyer & Company, W. H.

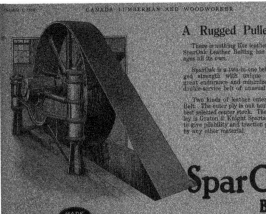

A Rugged Pulley-Gripper

There is nothing like leather for belting, and SparOak Leather Belting has peculiar advantages all its own.

SparOak is a two-in-one belt combining rugged strength with unique pulley-grip. Its great endurance and minimized slip make it a double-service belt of unusual qualities.

Two kinds of leather enter into a SparOak Belt. The outer ply is oak tanned, cut from the best selected center stock. The ply next the pulley is Graton & Knight Spartan leather, tanned to give pliability and traction power unequalled by any other material.

SparOak
Belting

MADE IN CANADA

SparOak Belts grip from the start. During the weeks most new belts take to "work in," a SparOak Belt is giving full power and keeping production up to normal. And SparOak Belts keep on gripping for years under adverse conditions. They withstand repeated shifting, and the wear against step cone or flange pulleys. They render efficient service on drives with high speeds, small pulleys, and heavy loads. In short, any of the factors that quickly wear out ordinary belts affect SparOak belting amazingly little.

Canadian Graton & Knight Limited
MONTREAL, CANADA

Representatives in Canada:
THE CANADIAN FAIRBANKS-MORSE CO., LIMITED
St. John, Quebec, Montreal, Ottawa, Toronto, Hamilton, Vancouver, Victoria

Graton & Knight
Standardized Series
Leather Belting

Tanned by us for belting use

HARNESS
Padgitt Company, Tom

HEMLOCK
Anderson Lumber Company, C. G.
Bartram & Ball.
Bourgouin, H.
Canadian General Lumber Company
Cane & Co., Jas. G.
Davison Lumber & Mfg. Company
Dunfield & Company
Edwards & Company, W. C.
Fesserton Timber Co.
Foss Lumber Company
Grier & Sons, Ltd., G. A.
Hart & McDonagh.
Long Lumber Company.
Mason, Gordon & Co.
Roch, Julien
Spencer Limited, C. A.
Terry & Gordon.
The Long Lumber Company.

HOISTING AND HAULING ENGINES
Garlock-Walker Machinery Co.
General Supply Co. of Canada, Ltd.
Marsh Engineering Works, Limited

HORSES
Union Stock Yards.

HOSE
Dunlop Tire & Rubber Goods Co.
General Supply Co. of Canada, Ltd.
Goodyear Tire & Rubber Co.
Gutta Percha and Rubber Company.

INDUSTRIAL CARS
Marsh Engineering Works, Limited

INSURANCE
Hardy & Co., E. D.
Rankin Benedict Underwriting Co.

INTERIOR FINISH
Eagle Lumber Company.
Hay & Co.
Mason, Gordon & Co.
Renfrew Planing Mills.
Terry & Gordon.

KNIVES
Disston & Sons, Henry.
Peter Hay Knife Company.
Simonds Canada Saw Company.
Waterous Engine Works Company.

LARCH
Otis Staples Lumber Co.

LATH
Austin & Nicholson.
Canadian General Lumber Company
Cane & Co., Jas. G.
Cardinal & Page
Dupuis Limited, J. P.
Eagle Lumber Company.
Fraser Limited.
Fraser-Bryson Lumber Company.
Genoa Bay Lumber Company
Gloucester Lumber Company
Grier & Sons, Ltd., G. A.
Harris Tie & Timber Company, Ltd.
Long Lumber Company.
McLennan Lumber Company.
New Ontario Colonization Company.
Otis Staples Lumber Co.
River Ouelle Pulp and Paper Co.
Spencer Limited, C. A.
Terry & Gordon.
Union Lumber Company.
Victoria Harbor Lumber Company.

LATH BOLTERS
Garlock-Walker Machinery Co.
General Supply Co. of Canada, Ltd.
Green Company, C. Walter.

LIGHTING APPLIANCES
Hobbs Company, Clinton E.

LOCOMOTIVES
Bell Locomotive Works
General Supply Co. of Canada, Ltd.
Jeffrey Manufacturing Company.
Jenckes Machine Company, Ltd.
Climax Manufacturing Company.
Montreal Locomotive Workks.

LATH TWINE
Consumers' Cordage Company.

LINK-BELT
Canadian Link-Belt Company
Canadian Mathews Gravity Carrier Company.
Jeffrey Mfg. Co.
Williams Machinery Co., A. R., Vancouver.

LOGGING COLLARS
Padgitt Company, Tom

LOCOMOTIVE CRANES
Canadian Link-Belt Company, Ltd.

LOGGING ENGINES
Dunbar Engine and Foundry Co.
Jenckes Machine Company.
Marsh Engineering Works, Limited

LOG HAULER
Green Company, G. Walter
Jenckes Machine Company, Ltd.

LOGGING MACHINERY AND EQUIPMENT
General Supply Co. of Canada, Ltd.
Hamilton Company, William.
Jenckes Machine Company, Ltd.
Marsh Engineering Works, Limited
Waterous Engine Works Company.

LUMBER TRUCKS
Waterous Engine Works Company.

LUMBERMEN'S CLOTHING
Woods Manufacturing Company, Ltd.

METAL REFINERS
Canada Metal Company.
Hoyt Metal Company.
Sessenwein Brothers.

MILLING IN TRANSIT
Renfrew Planing Mills.
Rutherford & Sons, Wm.

MOLDINGS
Genoa Bay Lumber Co.
Rutherford & Sons, Wm.

MOTOR TRUCKS
Duplex Truck Company

OAK
Chicago Lumber & Coal Company.
Long-Bell Lumber Company.

OAKUM
Stratford Oakum Co., Geo.

OIL CLOTHING
Leckie, Limited, John.

OIL ENGINES
Swedish Steel & Importing Co.

OLD IRON AND BRASS
Sessenwein Brothers.

OVERALLS
Hamilton Carhartt Cotton Mills

PAPER
Bowater & Sons, W. V.

PACKING
Atlas Asbestos Company, Ltd.
Consumers Cordage Co.
Dunlop Tire & Rubber Goods Co.
Gutta Percha and Rubber Company.

PAPER MILL MACHINERY
Bowater & Sons, W. V.

PINE
Anderson Lumber Company, C. G.
Atlantic Lumber Co.
Austin & Nicholson.
Bourgouin, H.
Cameron & Co.
Canadian General Lumber Company
Cane & Co., Jas. G.
Cardinal & Page
Chicago Lumber & Coal Company.
Cleveland-Sarnia Sawmills Company.
Colonial Lumber Company
Davison Lumber & Mfg. Co.
Donogh & Co., John.
Dudley, Arthur N.
Dunfield & Company
Eagle Lumber Company.
Edwards & Co., W. C.

Excelsior Lumber Company.
Fesserton Timber Company
Fraser-Bryson Lumber Company.
Fraser Limited.
Gillies Brothers Limited.
Gloucester Lumber Company
Gordon & Co., George.
Grier & Sons, Ltd., G. A.
Harris Tie & Timber Company, Ltd.
Hart & McDonagh.
Hettler Lumber Company, Herman H.
Long-Bell Lumber Company.
Long Lumber Company.
Mason, Gordon & Co.
McLennan Lumber Company.
Montreal Lumber Company.
Moores, Jr., E. J.
Muir & Kirkpatrick.
Otis Staples Lumber Co.
Parry Sound Lumber Company.
Roch, Julien
Russell, Chas. H.
Shearer Company, Jas.
Spencer Limited, C. A.
Summers, James R.
Terry & Gordon.
Union Lumber Company.
Watson & Todd. Limited.
Williams Lumber Company
Wuichet, Louis.

PLANING MILL EXHAUSTERS
Garlock-Walker Machinery Co.
Reed & Company, Geo. W.
Toronto Blower Co.

PLANING MILL MACHINERY
American Woodworking Machinery Company
Garlock-Walker Machinery Co.
Mershon & Company, W. B.
Toronto Blower Co.
Yates Machine Company. P. B.

PORK PACKERS
Davies Company, William
Harris Abattoir Company

POSTS AND POLES
Auger & Company
Canadian Tie & Lumber Co.
Dupuis Limited, J. P.
Eagle Lumber Company
Harris Tie & Timber Company, Ltd.
Long-Bell Lumber Company.
Long Lumber Company.
Mason, Gordon & Co.
Terry & Gordon.

PULLEYS AND SHAFTING
Canadian Link-Belt Company
Garlock-Walker Machinery Co.
General Supply Co. of Canada, Ltd.
Green Company, G. Walter
Hamilton Company, William
Jeffrey Mfg. Co.
Jenckes Machine Company, Ltd.

PULP MILL MACHINERY
Canadian Link-Belt Company, Ltd.
Hamilton Company, William.
Jeffrey Manufacturing Company
Jenckes Machine Company, Ltd.
Waterous Engine Works Company

PUMPS
General Supply Co. of Canada, Ltd.
Hamilton Company, William
Jenckes Machine Company, Ltd.
Smart-Turner Machine Company
Waterous Engine Works Company

RAILS
Gartshore, John J.
Sessenwein Bros.

ROOFINGS
Reed & Company, Geo. W.

ROOFINGS
(Rubber, Plastic and Liquid)
International Chemical Company

ROPE
Consumers Cordage Co.
Leckie, Limited, John

RUBBER GOODS
Atlas Asbestos Company
Dunlop Tire & Rubber Goods Co.
Goodyear Tire and Rubber Co.
Gutta Percha & Rubber Company

SASH
Genoa Bay Lumber Company
Renfrew Planing Mills.

SAWS
Atkins & Company, E. C.
Disston & Sons, Henry
General Supply Co. of Canada, Ltd.
Gerlach Company, Peter
Green Company, G. Walter
Hoe & Company, R.
Shurly-Dietrich Company
Shurly Co., Ltd., T. F.
Simonds Canada Saw Company.

SAW MILL LINK-BELT
Williams Machinery Co., A. R., Vancouver.

SAW MILL MACHINERY
Canadian Link-Belt Company, Ltd.
Dunbar Engine & Foundry Co.
Firstbrook Bros.
General Supply Co. of Canada, Ltd.
Hamilton Company, William
Huther Bros. Saw Mfg. Company
Jeffrey Manufacturing Company
Long Manufacturing Company, E.
Parry Sound Lumber Company
Payette Company, P.
Waterous Engine Works Company
Yates Machine Co., P. B.

SHEATHINGS
Goodyear Tire & Rubber Co.

SHINGLE MACHINES
Marsh Engineering Works, Limited

SAW SHARPENERS
Garlock-Walker Machinery Co.
Waterous Engine Works Company.

SAW SLASHERS
Waterous Engine Works Company

SAWMILL LINK-BELT
Canadian Link-Belt Company

SHEET METALS
Syracuse Smelting Works

SHINGLES
Allan-Stoltze Lumber Co.
Associated Mills, Limited
Campbell-MacLaurin Lumber Co.
Cardinal & Page
Dominion Lumber & Timber Co.
Eagle Lumber Company
Foss Lumber Company
Fraser Limited.
Genoa Bay Lumber Company
Gillespie, James.
Gloucester Lumber Company
Grier & Sons, Ltd., G. A.
Harris Tie & Timber Company, Ltd.
Heeney, Percy E.
Long Lumber Company.
Mason, Gordon & Co.
McLennan Lumber Company.
Miller Company, Ltd., W. H.
Reynolds Company, Limited
Service Lumber Company
Shingle Agency of B. C.
Terry & Gordon.
Timms, Phillips & Co.
Vancouver Lumber Company.
Victoria Lumber and Mfg. Co.

SHINGLE & LATH MACHINERY
Dunbar Engine and Foundry Co.
Garlock-Walker Machinery Co.
Green Company, C. Walter
Hamilton Company, William.
Long Manufacturing Company, E.
Payette Company, P.

SHOEPACKS
Acme Glove Works

SILENT CHAIN DRIVES
Canadian Link-Belt Company, Ltd.

SILOS
Ontario Wind Engine Company

SLEEPING ROBES
Woods Mfg. Company, Limited

SMOKESTACKS
Marsh Engineering Works, Limited
Waterous Engine Works Company.

SNOW PLOWS
Bateman-Wilkinson Company
Fink Company, Thomas.

SPARK ARRESTORS
Jenckes Machine Company, Ltd.
Reed & Company, Geo. W.
Waterous Engine Works Company.

SPRUCE
Bartram & Ball.
Bourgouin, H.
Cane & Co., Jas. G.
Cardinal & Page
Davison Lumber & Mfg. Company
Donogh & Co., John.
Dudley, Arthur N.
Dunfield & Company
Exchange Lumber Company.
Foss Lumber Company
Fraser Limited.
Fraser-Bryson Lumber Company.
Gillies Brothers.
Gloucester Lumber Company
Grant & Campbell.
Grier & Sons, Ltd., G. A.
Hart & McDonagh.
Long Lumber Company.
Mason, Gordon & Co.
McLennan Lumber Company.
Muir & Kirkpatrick.
New Ontario Colonization Company.
River Ouelle Pulp and Lumber Co.
Roch, Julien
Russell, Chas. H.
Service Lumber Company
Shearer Company, Jas.
Snowball Co., J. B.
Spencer Limited, C. A.
Terry & Gordon.
The Rideau Lumber Company

STEEL CHAIN
Canadian Link-Belt Company, Ltd.
Jeffrey Manufacturing Company.
Waterous Engine Works Company.

STEEL PLATE CONSTRUCTION
Marsh Engineering Works, Limited

STEAM PLANT ACCESSORIES
Waterous Engine Works Company.

STEEL BARRELS
Smart-Turner Machine Co.

STEEL DRUMS
Smart-Turner Machine Co.

SWEAT PADS
American Pad & Textile Co.

SULPHITE PULP CHIPS
Davison Lumber & Mfg. Company

TANKS
Ontario Wind Engine Company

TARPAULINS
Turner & Sons, J. J.
Woods Manufacturing Company, Ltd.

TAPS AND DIES
Pratt & Whitney Company.

TENTS
Turner & Sons, J. J.
Woods Mfg. Company

TENTS, CLOTHING
Grant, Holden & Graham, Limited

TIES
Auger & Company
Austin & Nicholson.
Canadian Tie & Lumber Co.
Harris Tie & Timber Company, Ltd.
Long Lumber Company.
McLennan Lumber Company.
Terry & Gordon.

TIMBER BROKERS
Bradley, R. R.
Cant & Kemp.
Farnworth & Jardine.
Hunter, Herbert F.
Smith & Tyrer, Limited

TIMBER CRUISERS AND ESTIMATORS
Sewall, James W.

TIMBER LANDS
Department of Lands and Forests.

TRACTORS
British War Mission

TRANSMISSION MACHINERY
Canadian Link-Belt Company, Ltd.
General Supply Co. of Canada, Ltd.
Jenckes Machine Company, Ltd.
Jeffrey Manufacturing Company.
Waterous Engine Works Company.

TRIMMERS
Garlock-Walker Machinery Co.
Green Company, C. Walter
Waterous Engine Works Com

TUGS
West & Peachey.

TURBINES
Hamilton Company, William.
Jenckes Machine Company, Ltd.

VALVES
Bay City Foundry & Machine Co.

VENEERS
Webster & Brother, James.

VENEER DRYERS
Coe Manufacturing Company
Philadelphia Textile Mach. Co.

VENEER MACHINERY
Coe Manufacturing Company
Garlock-Walker Machinery Co.
Philadelphia Textile Machinery Co.

VETERINARY REMEDIES
Dr. Bell Veterinary Wonder Co.
Johnson, A. H.

WATER HEATERS
Mason Regulator & Engineering

WATER WHEELS
Hamilton Company, William.
Jenckes Machine Company, Ltd.

WIRE
Laidlaw Bale Tie Company.

WIRE ROPE
Canada Wire & Cable Co.

WOODWORKING MACHINERY
American Woodworking Machy. Co.
Garlock-Walker Machinery Co.
General Supply Co. of Canada, Ltd.
Jeffrey Manufacturing Company.
Long Manufacturing Company, E.
Mershon & Company, W. B.
Waterous Engine Works Company.
Yates Machine Company, P. B.

WOOD PRESERVATIVES
International Chemical Company

WOOD PULP
Austin & Nicholson.
New Ontario Colonization Co.
River Ouelle Pulp and Lumber Co.

CANADA LUMBERMAN AND WOODWORKER
Beardmore Extra Quality Waterproof
Cement Leather Belting
For the Wet Place
Tell us your belting troubles and we can help you.
The General Supply Company of Canada, Limited
OTTAWA MONTREAL TORONTO WINNIPEG VANCOUVER
Large stocks available for immediate shipment
RELIABLE WIRE ROPE
MADE IN CANADA
S.M.S., Crucible Steel, Plough Steel or Extra Plough Steel
Galvanized or Plain
Large Stocks
Prompt Shipments
Transmission and Haulage Rope, Hoisting Rope, Flexible Hoisting Rope Mooring Lines, Drilling Cables, Sash, Cord, Tiller Rope, Rope Slings, etc.
CANADA
WIRE & CABLE
CO. LTD.
District Offices and Warehouses
HALIFAX, N.S.
MONTREAL
W., WINNIPEG
CALGARY, ALTA.
VANCOUVER
TORONTO
Phone Belmont 2500
CANADA

Alphabetical Index to Advertisers, Page 64 — Classified Directory to Advertisements, Page 80

American Wood Working Machinery Co.

Rochester, N. Y.

SALES OFFICE FOR BRITISH COLUMBIA, PORTLAND, OREGON
AGENTS FOR THE REST OF CANADA, GARLOCK-WALKER MACHINERY CO., TORONTO
AGENTS FOR GREAT BRITAIN, THE PROJECTILE CO., LONDON

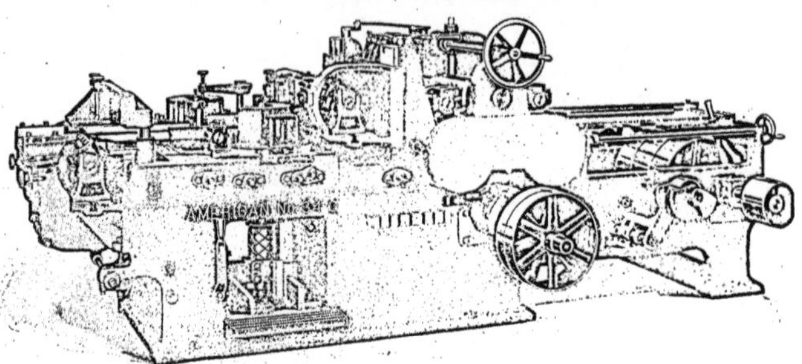

American 34-C Fast ou

This Machine has all the good features of an inside moulder and the slip-on head feature of an outside moulder or profiler.

It is a high-duty machine with every convenience of adjustment at hand.

Get Circular of Garlock-Walker or write

CANADIAN SALES AGENTS:

Garlock-Walker M Ltd.

32-34 Front Street West, Toronto

TORONTO WINNIPEG

For Prompt Delivery of 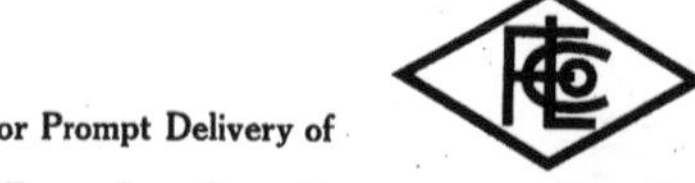

Hemlock, Spruce, Lath, Pulpwood and ds

The Year Round----In Any
Dressed and Ripped to Your Orders

We specialize in Hemlock and Spruce Timbers. Let us know your requirements. We can assure you of immediate shipment through our splendid transportation facilities. Rail and water del

Fassett Lumber Company, QUEBEC

OFFERS WAN

For Whole or Part

100,000 P

Birch Veneer 19 x 19 stock

The Wm. Rutherford & S Ltd.

425 Atwater Ave. - MONTREAL

TERRY & GORDON

Manufacturers and Wholesalers

of the

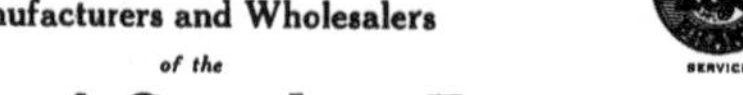

Head Office—703 and 704 CONFEDERATION LIFE BUILD
TORONTO, ONTARIO

Branch Office—VANCOUVER, B.C.
A. S. NICHOLSON, Manager

Representatives in Ontario of

The British Columbia Mills Timber Trading Company

Vancouver B.C.

Export Agents—SPENCER, LOCK & COMPANY,
London, England

The Quality of Our Product is Our Best Advertisement

We Solicit Your Enquiries for Lumber in Any Quantities

Let us quote you on your requirements in

WHITE PINE

You will find our prices low considering the quality of our goods.

We offer specially the following

75,000 feet 2 x 4—10/16 Mill Run White
100,000 " 2 x 6—10/16 " " "
80,000 " 2 x 8—10/16 " " "
100,000 " 1 x 4—8/16 Barky Strips White

HOCKEN LUMBER CO., LIMITED

630 Confederation Life Building PHONE MAIN 3153 **TORONTO**

Manufacturers of

WIRE For TYING, BUNDLING and m ny other purposes. NAILS, Etc.

LAIDLAW BALE-TIE CO., Ltd.
HAMILTON, ONT.

Timber Estimates

James W. Sewall
OLD TOWN, - MAINE

TIMBER LANDS
Bought and Sold

Timber and Pulp Wood Estimates

R. R. BRADLEY
Consulting Forester
58 Telegraph Building
Hospital St., MONTREAL

USED SAW MILL
MACHINERY
FOR SALE

Extra heavy log haul-up works with inch round and flat chain, 128 ft. centres.
2—Waterous log unloaders or kickers, 3 arms, 10 in. cylinders.
1—Waterous log loader, 3 arms, 10-in. cylinders.
1—Waterous right-hand double cutting band mill, 11 in. saws, 8 ft. wheel, with 3-block carriage; 24 in. opening; Payette set works and dogs; 8 in. x 36 ft. steam feed.
1—Waterous double edger for 20-inch saws, lever shifter.
1—Payette double edger for 18-in. saws, lever shifter.
48—live rolls about 8 ft. long by 10 in. dia.; extra heavy, sprocket drive.
1—Payette picket machine, made specially for shade roller stock, will feed pieces 16 in. long, also sorting table with chain top.
1—Payette edger for box and short stock.
1—Rogers twin circular or tie maker.
1—Payette lath bolter and lath machine.
1—Pair lath trimmers.
1—Picket trimmer (bunch trim).
—Pair Polson "Brown" type engines, coupled on quarters, 22 in. x 50 in., with 16 ft. x 48 in. belt, balance wheel. Excellent engines.
1—8 x 10 Centre Crank Engine.
1—10 x 14 Cowan Slide Valve Engine.
Pulleys, gears, heavy line shafting and countershafting with bearings.
Booms and boom chains, ½, ⅝ & ¾.
Winches and other mill supplies.
Prompt shipments and bargains for quick sale. Will send all particulars and prices on application.

Firstbrook Bros.
Limited
PENETANG

"WELL BOUGHT IS HALF SOLD"

We Have the Following Choice Hardwoods at One Point to Move Promptly

49M	4/4" No. 2 Com. & Btr. Birch				
	About 15% No. 2 Common.				
16M	5/4" No. 1 Com. & Btr. Birch.				
16M	6/4"	"	"	"	"
20M	8/4"	"	"	"	"
8½M	12/4"	"	"	"	"
7M	4/4" No. 2	"	"	Basswood	
9½M	6/4" No. 1	"	"	"	
11M	4/4" No. 2	"	"	Elm	
4½M	6/4" No. 1	"	"	"	

First Come

First Served

Canadian General Lumber Co.
Limited

FOREST PRODUCTS

TORONTO OFFICE :— 712-20 Bank of Hamilton Bldg.
Montreal Office :—203 McGill Bldg.
Mills : Byng Inlet, Ont.

Quick Action

You Can Have It

Try the Canada Lumberman Wanted and For Sale Department. Have you anything you wish to buy or sell in the Lumber Industry? You will find this department inexpensive, and a very effective business getter.

Our Classified Advertisers do not repeat the ad, often. They don't have to. They report immediate results. Use these columns to your own advantage.

CANADA LUMBERMAN and WOODWORKER
347 Adelaide St. W.
TORONTO

Frank H. Harris Lumber Company, Limited

Manufacturers and Wholesalers of

Yellow Pine and Southern Hardwoods

Yellow Pine in Transit at all Times

Mills: High Point, Miss. / Lake, Miss.

Office: 814 Excelsior Life Building, TORONTO, Canada.

"Horseshoe" Brand Red Cedar Shingles

Old Growth Fir Logs at Port Moody

Fir Timbers Our Specialty

"IT CAN'T BE DONE"—

You can't build a house on sandstone, neither can you make Quality Lumber out of poor logs. We are able through our own manufacturing facilities to offer the Eastern market the best in B.C. forest products. Send us your enquiries.

REYNOLDS COMPANY LIMITED

General Offices: VANCOUVER, B.C.

SERVICE

Fir, Cedar and Spruce

LUMBER

"Service" Lumber Co.

Pacific Building, VANCOUVER, B.C.

Eastern Representative: A. W. BARNHILL, 26 St. James Street, Montreal.

Ontario Representative: A. E. MASURET
Canada Permanent Bldg., 18 Toronto St., Toronto.
Telephone Main 3833

QUICK ACTION

Can be assured if you will let the CANADA LUMBERMAN "Wanted and For Sale" department take care of your miscellaneous business needs.

We receive constant testimony from advertisers as to the value they have received from this far reaching and inexpensive method of publicity in the lumber trade and allied industries.

Try these columns. The result will surprise you.

CANADA LUMBERMAN

and WOODWORKER

347 Adelaide St. West - - TORONTO

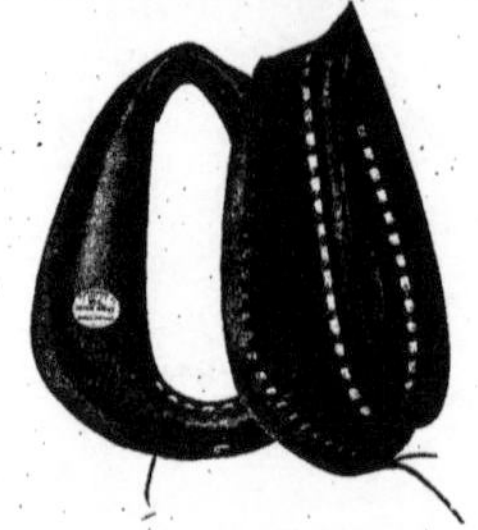

FEDERAL
QUALITY

Canada Lumberman and Woodworker

Issued on the 1st and 15th of every month by

HUGH C. MACLEAN, LIMITED, Publishers

HUGH C. MacLEAN, Winnipeg, President.
THOS. S. YOUNG, Toronto, General Manager.

OFFICES AND BRANCHES:

TORONTO - - Telephone A. 2700 - - 347 Adelaide Street West
VANCOUVER - - Telephone Seymour 2013 - - Winch Building
MONTREAL - - Telephone Main 2299 - - 119 Board of Trade
WINNIPEG - Telephone Garry 856 - Electric Railway Chambers
NEW YORK - - - - - - - - - - - 309 Broadway
CHICAGO - Telephone Harrison 5351 - 1413 Great Northern Building
LONDON, ENG. - - - - - - - 16 Regent Street, S. W.

TERMS OF SUBSCRIPTION

Canada, United States and Great Britain, $2.00 per year, in advance; other foreign countries embraced in the General Postal Union, $3.00.

Single copies 15 cents.

"The Canada Lumberman and Woodworker" is published in the interest of, and reaches regularly, persons engaged in the lumber, woodworking and allied industries in every part of Canada. It aims at giving full and timely information on all subjects touching these interests, and invites free discussion by its readers.

Advertisers will receive careful attention and liberal treatment. For manufacturing and supply firms wishing to bring their goods to the attention of owners and operators of saw and planing mills, woodworking factories, pulp mills, etc., "The Canada Lumberman and Woodworker" is undoubtedly the most direct and profitable advertising medium. Special attention is directed to the "Wanted" and "For Sale" advertisements.

Authorized by the Postmaster-General for Canada, for transmission as second-class matter.

Entered as second-class matter July 18th, 1914, at the Postoffice, at Buffalo, N. Y., under the Act of Congress of March 3rd, 1879.

Vol. 39 Toronto, October 15, 1919 No. 20

False Ideals and Economic Losses

"Not how good, but how cheap," seems to be the animating motive of no small proportion of the populace at the present time. Owing to the high cost of material there is a disposition on the part of certain speculative builders and others to erect dwellings that are showy and attractive rather than those which are substantial and permanent. What the purchase of a house "don't know won't hurt him," appears to be the structural philosophy of these gentlemen who are buying up cull lumber, cheap shingles, No. 3 lath, and everything else that is far from possessing strength, endurance or reliability.

Attention has been called to this phase of the situation several times, but still the work of sacrificing quality goes steadily on. In the long run neither the purchaser nor the contractor is satisfied, and experiments in most cases prove very costly and create heart burnings and bitter misgivings. Any workman knows there is no satisfaction in cheap tools, that their purchase is a dissipation of money and their use a waste of effort and the same observation applies with respect to incorporating in a home material that will not withstand the test of time and use. The home is the strength and bulwark of the nation, and if it will not endure, then our communities will savor of the nature of the mushroom towns and mining centres of the west where existence is generally brief and cosmopolitan birds of passage predominate. In the older centres, however, the home is supposed to represent fixity of purpose, stability of interest, and solidity of effort. It should be erected so that it will not be a handicap to industry or enterprise. It is part of the national machinery, the machinery that produces Canadian cities, and in this connection the "Contract Record" asks, "is it logical to suppose that a poor type of house will turn out on the average a high type of citizen"?

Canada needs good buildings. That is a fact that cannot be too strongly emphasized. We have a severe climate, and we must erect buildings of a type that will protect our workers both in home and factory from the extremes of heat and cold. Then there is the question of fire waste, about which too much cannot be said. We must allow the erection of no more flimsy fire-traps. Fireproof or fire-resistant structures, we must have, and it is encouraging to note that the majority of manufacturers and municipalities are beginning to realize this fact. It would indeed be cheaper to pull down dangerous structures right now and re-build them in a safe type of construction, rather than to wait until they burn down, with the resultant danger to the lives of the occupants, and the destruction of the goods and equipment contained, as well as the endangering of life and property in the surrounding commuity.

From another viewpoint, the folly of using poor materials and "cheap" construction is evident. Wages are now higher than they ever were before, and labor constitutes about 40 per cent. of the cost in building work. Is it wise, therefore, to throw away high-priced labor on cheap buildings that will not stand the test of time and climate? Surely not. The best material is generally the cheapest in the long run, because it lasts longer and gives better service in every way. Cheap lumber or cheap shingles are a poor investment, and concrete lacking the proper proportion of cement is no economy, except for the speculative builder who isn't permanently in the contracting business. Neither is a flimsy lath and plaster or frame shack the proper type of dwelling for the Canadian climate. But it's not against the type, so much as the quality, that objection is raised. Excellent houses can be built, using stucco, hardwall plaster, or frame construction, but, in the effort to cut down costs, some houses are being put up at the present time which, to use the expression of a critic, have walls that one "could whistle through." This is sheer waste of money. Good citizens won't live in them unless they are forced to, and to be forced to live in them will make them poorer citizens. In the name of common sense and humanity, let us build solid houses. The children of the poor should have protection against heat and cold, and room to breathe, just as much as the children of our millionaire profiteers.

Housing Fiasco in the Metropolis

Lumbermen throughout the Dominion are interested in the Federal Government scheme for erecting workingmen's houses to meet the pressing demands in every part of the country. It involves the expenditure of $25,000,000, a considerable portion of which would necessarily be spent in lumber. We may assume that in houses of this description lumber to the value of $5,000,000 would be used. The Quebec Legislature last session passed a special Act dealing with the subject and regulating the conditions, financial and otherwise, under which the scheme, so far as it affects the province, is to be carried out; a technical commission has also been appointed to develop the scheme and to supervise the work in a general way.

Progress, however, has been slow, and in the case of Montreal the plan has been a fiasco. Hull, Sherbrooke, St. Anne de Bellevue, Quebec, Three Rivers, St. Jerome and St. Lambert are all negotiating for loans, but whereas the province's quota of the $25,000,000 set aside is $7,000,000, the applications for loans to date total $16,000,000; an evidence that the need is far greater than the possible supply of houses, with the money available. This does not take into consideration the city of Montreal, where the scheme is hung up. The scarcity of housing accommodation there is very acute, yet practically no steps have been taken to put the Act into operation.

There are two main reasons for this lamentable lack of enterprise. The Administrative Commissioners, after consulting various bodies, appointed a Housing Commission of five members—eminent citizens, but with no experience in the work, and with not a single representative of the constructional interests. To begin with, two members resigned almost immediately, and now a third has dropped out after a short experience. Various reasons are given for these departures, but the explanation given by a former member is that the scheme is unworkable. The work can be carried out either by the cities or towns, by individuals, or by companies, borrowing the money from the province at 5 per cent. There are certain other expenses which are inevitable, and the interest ultimately to be paid will more likely be in the neighborhood of 8 or 9 per cent., as 2½ per cent has to be paid for the expenses of the Technical Commission. It is unlikely that any city or town will embark on any building operations, and housing companies will not be attracted by the proposition, owing to the amount of dividend being limited. These are the objections to two of the methods for carrying out the Act, although it may be pointed out that in the cities and towns, which have applied for loans it is proposed to form companies for this purpose. As to individual loans, the objection is that the Housing Commission cannot properly supervise the construction, that the estimates are likely to be exceeded, and that in fact the chances are all in favor of the municipalities having to bear the burden of uncompleted houses.

Considerations of this character weighed with the men who have declined to remain members of the Montreal Commission. But beyond this, there is a very marked difference of opinion as to Montreal contributing 2½ per cent. of its share of the loan, for the expenses of the Technical Commission. Mr. Alf. Lambert, who has just resigned from the chairmanship, strongly opposed what he regarded as an unjustifiable tax and as an endeavor to make Montreal bear the greater share of the expenses of the Commission. There is thus a deadlock. While a certain amount of advancement has been made in other parts of the province, Montreal, the most important factor in the general scheme, is for the present to be counted out. If anything practical is to be done to meet the housing requirements of the city quick action is required. Already too much time has been wasted, and if Montreal is to benefit, preparations must be made during the winter for work to commence in the spring.

Mr. Lambert complains that the Administrative Commissioners have not backed up his efforts to get something effective done. The Commissioners failed to pass a by-law defining the duties and powers of the Housing Commission—although one was submitted—and also give authority for borrowing money for the work. The consequence is that men who offered to organize housing companies have not been able to go ahead. The whole affair apparently is an example of how not to adminster the Act.

Why Woodsmen Really Leave Home

The life of a bushman is both rugged and picturesque. It partakes of the romantic and the practical, and much depends upon the viewpoint. In the days before the war there was little need of advertising in order to secure a sufficient number of strong, stalwart, sturdy chaps for logging operations, but, like many other avenues of industrial endeavor and achievement, there has been a marked change in the method of operation and the personnel of the working force.

The average worker apparently believes that the great panacea for all economic ills is shorter hours and higher wages, and if these are not secured then an ultimatum is frequently launched in the shape of a strike. In the realm of commercial affairs, advertising is supposed to solve many difficulties and make smooth the pathway to any desired goal. The whole social order of things was upset by the recent European conflict, and events, customs and practices that would have staggered us in the days of old are accepted at the present juncture with an equanimity and sang-froid that is almost startling. We have ceased to be aroused by the ordinary and even the extraordinary and the exaggerated do not create more than a passing interest, all of which leads up to the observation that the lumber industry, from its open air, primeval character, will always enlist the attention of various nationalities the world over.

In a recent issue of a Toronto paper one employment concern advertised for fifty bushmen, and in order to induce a large influx of applicants stated that in this particular camp in North Ontario mostly Britishers were employed. It was also pointed out that an Irishman was the foreman, which means that his name must carry weight and influence with the rank and file of lumberjacks, but for real attractiveness, originality, diversity, effectiveness and attention compelling details, a refreshing announcement lately appeared in the "Want Columns." In it are touches of the sublime and the ridiculous, the grave and the gay, the stirring and the tender, self-reliance and human weakness, mountain peaks of contentment and vales of despair—but why go on in this strain?

Read the advertisement and learn all these particulars first hand. In some instances the clarion call and seductive appeal beats any recruiting rally ever held during military campaigning days.

> 2,000 Bushmen—We send men every morning and every night to the camps. Rail fares are paid by the lumber companies, and not deducted if stay from three to six months. Present wages $60 to $65 month with board and lodgings free. It is usual to work ten hours daily. No Sunday work. These camps are run by large and responsible lumbering companies. The work is cutting down trees, mostly pine trees, chopping off the branches and sawing up into logs, making temporary roads through the bush, rolling and skidding the logs to the main roads, etc., good healthy work for able bodied, full blooded men of any nationality, willing to do an honest day's work. The work is easier and healthier than concrete or pick and shovel work, and working among the pines in the bracing northern atmosphere makes flesh and bone that cannot be beat; always provided you keep your feet dry and your nose clean and tidy. Men who have not been in the bush before need not expect to find palaces. The life is rough and ready, but there is usually more and better food served than can be bought here for fifty cents a meal, and there are lots of good warm blankets. The camps have stores where all necessary supplies may be had, tobacco included, these you can have charged against your wages after you have worked a while. Many men who cannot save money here do so in the bush when they stay through the season, about six months, coming out in the spring with $300 to $400 in their jeans. Don't go to the bush unless you have made up your mind to rough it, and don't go unless you intend to stay at least three months. When ready call on us with one dollar fee and we will do the rest. Remember, shipping every night and every morning for Massey, Cartier, Thor Lake, Nairn Centre, Milnet, Collins Inlet, Foots Bay, Shawanaga, Sturgeon Falls, Mac-Tier, Hanover, Bolger, Ravensworth, Lake Bolkaw and Nicholson.

Editorial Short Lengths

Business failures in Canada to-day are the lowest on record. Last year, out of thousands and thousands of manufacturing and financial concerns, storekeepers and others doing business, only 873 had to close their doors. In 1917 the number was only 1,097. These are phenomenal figures and indicate a state of prosperity never before approached.

To find a year when failures were as few as in 1918, we have to go back 36 years, to 1882, when business concerns were not half as numerous as they are to-day.

* * *

Speaking of trade opportunities in Great Britain for the Canadian manufacturer, A. L. Dawe, of Montreal, secretary of the Canadian Pulp and Paper Association, who spent several months overseas, surveying the field for that particular industry, says, "the opportunities in the Mother Country are just what Canadian manufacturers desire to make them. The business is there waiting for them. I found that many of the larger Canadian firms had already sent representatives to England, with a view to turning the present trade into a permanent market. But my experience has been that the only way to get this trade which is waiting, is to send over expert men, and look after it, just as firms here do for the home trade in Canada. If our manufacturers do this, I see no reason why a large and profitable export trade to Great Britain should not be built up."

WORK OR WANT

Production is a world necessity.
Cost of living is increased by empty shelves and idle plants.
Decreased output means increased selling price.
Greater production alone can assure the safety of our nation.
Be a Peace Patriot!
PRODUCE!

Lumber Price Levels Will Be Maintained

Unlikely That There Will Be Any Radical Changes Until Next Season's Cut Comes on Market and Value Thereafter Will Depend Upon Various Factors

There is much discussion among lumbermen to-day regarding the future course of the market. While this is natural enough at any time, it is of special importance to-day for a number of reasons. With a few minor interruptions, the market for lumber in Ontario has been good, ever since the extreme demands arising out of the war brought to an end the period of inactivity following the collapse of the real estate and building booms of 1912 and 1913. The market for lumber from that date to the present has been characterized, to a very extent, by two outstanding features, namely: Reduction in output at an increase in cost, and a strong demand. There have been times when the demand, shifting from one use to another, has been less active, but in a general way, during the period of war use, and now during the period of reconstruction, there has been a strong demand of a fairly general nature, throughout the last few years. These conditions should be borne in mind by anyone who tries to develop a workable theory of market changes for the immediate future.

How General Stocks are Depleted.

Growing out of the conditions outlined above, the trade is approaching the coming winter with certain strongly defined features. In the first place, the result of the reduced output for several years is that there may be said to be a famine in lumber to-day. Last year's stocks had been practically eliminated before those which the mills produced this year came on the market. What the mills will have produced this year has been subjected to keen demand and will be used up more rapidly even than was last year's production; so that the trade will enter next Spring with an even greater shortage than existed in the Spring of 1919. These conditions, and the high cost of labor and materials, are responsible for the increasing price which lumber has brought during the past year. The question upon which the whole situation seems to rest is how soon these conditions may be expected to give place to others which will make for lower prices.

Much the same problem has confronted lumbermen annually as each year's operations got underway. During the last few years there has been increasing uncertainty as to what changes might be expected; but during the continuance of the war the uncertainty was increased by the impossibility of foretelling what the effect of the end of the war would be upon industrial conditions. Each Fall, retailers have been in doubt about the buying policy for the Winter months, and each Spring they have been much in the dark about the conditions that could be expected during the approaching Summer. Each succeeding year's problem seemed to be more difficult to deal with during the continuance of the war, until, at the end of the winter of 1918-19 there were many retailers who had given up the attempt and had become pessimistic enough to assert, much too publicly, that the bottom had fallen out of the market and we were in for a bad Summer. This attitude of depression was unreasonable, and there were a few who predicted an exceptionally active Summer. The course of events during the year has more than justified the latter prediction.

Why Changes Have Been Wrought.

Looking back upon the Summer months of 1919, it is easy enough to see what has brought about the change. The lumber requirements of the people of Canada for industrial expansion and house building had been neglected for so long that they became an important element in the demand. This applied not only to Canada but to the whole of North America and the manufacturers of lumber found their market extended in nearly every direction, until a "runaway market" developed, with lumber, as it has often been said, "auctioned off to the highest bidder."

Anyone who makes a hobby of prophesying should be able, by considering these points, to see with some degree of exactness, what is ahead of the trade during the coming Winter and part of next year. Conditions such as those which have prevailed during the past year can reasonably be expected to continue until the logs that are taken out of the woods during the coming Winter reach the market in the form of lumber during 1920. Lumber consumers will have to get along until that time with the meagre supplies that are now available.

Next Summer will be the testing time for the trade. Operators are to-day planning far more production than for many years past. Woods labor is more plentiful, though still very high in price and inefficient. With good operating conditions during the coming Winter, there should be a larger output of logs than has been the case for many years past.

What capacity will the market have for absorbing the increased output next year? Barring social and industrial upheavals which must be left out of consideration because they cannot be foretold, it is more than probable that even an abnormally large production of lumber next year will find a hungry market waiting for it. It will have been produced at a comparatively high cost, if present labor conditions continue. If the demand continues strong it may be expected that lumber will hold its own fairly well.

Present Firmness Likely to Continue.

These are the conditions which would lead most smoothly to a satisfactory return to normal trade. While the wish may be, to a considerable extent, father to the thought, these conditions are being predicted by manufacturers and wholesalers. They are being anticipated also by many retailers. If these conclusions are not seriously at fault, the trade may look forward to a fairly good Winter's business, depending, of course, upon the severity of the weather, and to good Spring and Summer business to follow. The present firmness of the price situation is likely to continue until next year's cut comes on the market and the course of the prices thereafter will depend upon factors which lie in the future, such as the extent of the Winter's cut, the possibility of resuming the export trade, the cost of the stock that has been produced during the Winter and the existing labor situation.

There is no question but that, with reasonable encouragement, the demand for lumber will be sufficient to offset any unsettled market conditions which might conduce to rapid price decline. The natural conclusion to reach, with such information as is now available, is that the decline in price, which seems to be fairly generally expected, will come about gradually, commencing possibly towards the middle or the end of next Summer and that it will be so gently tempered as to involve no real cause for anxiety about next year's trade.

Uprooting The Wooden House Prejudice

In the last issue of the "Canada Lumberman" reference was made to a proposal by Mr. F. C. Wade, Agent General for B. C. in London, Eng., that Great Britain should meet the housing difficulty there by the importation of wooden houses. Although there was at first opposition to this proposal, the Ministry of Health seems to have been won over, and to have taken steps to remove restrictions in the building laws which will make for the construction of this class of house. The Englishman has been prejudiced in favor of the brick house, but under the stress of a famine in dwellings, opinion has changed, and there is now a demand for the cheaper and more quickly constructed wooden house. Whatever their defects, they cannot be worse than the thousands of jerry built houses constructed in Great Britain.

Canadian firms have not been slow in getting after this business, and negotiations are proceeding for the supply of a large number of houses. According to a cable, inquiries have been received for Canadian houses for France, Belgium and the Mediterranean. Our readers are acquainted with the difficulties which faced the Canadian Timber Products Association early this year in the matter of a large order for portable houses for France. The shipping freights proved a bar to the closing of this business, and it is to be hoped that there will be no repetition of this handicap. Canadian woodworking interests want all the work possible, and it would be a matter for regret if after all the spadework put in by Canadians the order for houses for Great Britain should be diverted to other countries.

It is understood that the designs and specifications submitted by the Ministry of Health did not meet with the approval of the Canadian firms interested, and that alterations, the result of experience on this side, have been suggested.

Mr. Wade, in an interview in London, naturally boosted B. C. fir; it was the "best wood in the world," he declared. Mr. Wade also said many good words for the wooden house. "These wooden houses," he stated, "are more damp-proof than the average brick house. The wooden house is general all over Canada, the United States, and South America, and is satisfactory in every way. There is no need to worry about any danger of fire." Why Englishmen like to live in brick houses Mr. Wade cannot understand. Brick, he said, is not damp-proof, is not good to look at, and is not cheap. Though he could not say what they would cost in England, he was sure they would be much cheaper, even adding the cost of freightage, than the conventional house of brick.

Some Practical Plans in the Cutting of Timber

Experimental Work to be Conducted by Leading Lumber and Paper Companies— What the Investigations Will Include—Visits to the Areas

Propaganda for the better treatment of our woodlands has always carried a prominent and noteworthy characteristic in the sympathy and co-operation of the lumbermen. The meeting of foresters and lumbermen in frank and open discussion of their problems invariably incites comment of admiration and envy from the visiting foresters from other countries. A striking characteristic has been friendly co-operation—in discussion.

Foresters and lumbermen have met and talked and made resolutions on the advisability of doing certain things for the benefit of the forest. They have separated to meet again next year to talk and make more resolutions. They have been doing this for thirty years and they have accomplished much in an educational way. But in reality the forests can be improved only by action in the forest, not in the office chair, not in the hotel corridor, not even at the banquet table. However, the more progressive lumbermen and foresters have realized this and so it has come to pass that theories are to be put into practice. Indeed, the only way to determine whether or not a theory will work is to try it—a self-evident fact lost sight of by other men than those interested in the welfare of the forests.

Experimental Cutting of Spruce Limits.

The Bathurst Lumber Company, in co-operation with the New Brunswick Forest Service is carrying on experimental cuttings on 500 acres of under-sized spruce on the Nipisguit River. A portion of the area is being cut under the strip system. Strips from one chain wide to three chains wide are cut clean, with strips two chains wide each uncut or lightly culled. A portion is being cut clean in more or less circular patches of various sizes, comprising one-quarter acre to two acres in extent. Other portions are being thinned by cutting to 10, 8 and 6-inch diameter limits respectively. The slash on one-half the area of each cutting system is to be burned and on the other half unburned. The Provincial Forest Service furnishes a forest engineer who, in cooperation with Mr. Lordon, of the Bathurst Lumber Company, will carry out the plans of the cutting.

The Laurentide Company, in co-operation with the Quebec Forest Service, will undertake similar experimental cutting in a stand of 300 acres, mostly culled only for pine on Cache Lake, whose waters reach the St. Maurice River at Rapid Blanc. The area contains a peat bog, a merchantable black spruce swamp, balsam and spruce ridges, a merchantable stand arising from an old burn, and mature spruce and balsam in various degrees of mixture with hardwoods, so that most of the types in which logging operations are being conducted in Quebec are represented on this comparatively small area. The Logging Department and the Forestry Division of the Laurentide Company and the Provincial Forest Service will co-operate in carrying out details of the cutting.

On both areas a careful record will be made of the cost of slash burning.

Keeping Tab on the Growth.

The Commission of Conservation at Ottawa has the task of measuring and recording the results on each of these experimental areas. Sample acres will be laid off and the volume of wood fibre and rate of growth under the present and past conditions will be ascertained and will be used as the standard to measure the results of the various methods of cutting in terms of future growth.

The investigations will include the effect of cutting to various diameter limits upon windfall, upon diameter increment, volume accretion, upon the growth of the young trees already established in the stands, and the reproduction of the commercial species after the cutting. The areas upon which the slash is burned and those upon which it is unburned will be used for a comparative study of the effects of these two conditions upon reproduction and, in co-operation with the Dominion Entomological Branch, upon prevalence of insect diseases. These areas (burned and unburned) will also be studied in a comparative way by an expert from the standpoint of breeding ground for the various heart rot diseases of spruce and balsam.

This work will be carried on during the logging operations and will doubtless occupy a small investigation party during the coming summer. After that, it is planned to visit the areas periodically for a number of years to measure and record results. In this way only can accurate and useable data be obtained from the experimental cuttings.

Special Study of Spruce Budworm.

Negotiations are on the way between the Fisheries Branch at Ottawa, the Provincial Forest Service of New Brunswick and the Commission of Conservation to establish an experiment station on 240 acres belonging to the Mirimachi Fish Hatchery of South Esk, New Brunswick. The area is badly infected by spruce budworm, and a special study will be made of this disease on the area of the Dominion Entomological Branch. The area is being cruised and plans drawn up for regulated cutting.

In this connection, it might be mentioned that the Commission of Conservation and the Entomological Branch, in co-operation with the respective companies have already established some 25 acres of permanent sample plots on the Laurentide Company limits at Lake Edward and on the Riordon Pulp and Paper Company limits on Lac Tremblant, where a detailed study is being made of forest insect and fungus diseases; of the effects of the various degrees of cutting on the regeneration and growth of spruce and balsam; and particularly experiments are being inaugurated to determine the conditions for a more abundant natural reproduction of spruce after logging.

Forest Problems of Economic Bearing.

It is reported that the Riordon Pulp and Paper Company has under way plans for the establishment of an extensive experimental area, some 5,000 acres, it is said, where not only different cutting methods will be tried but also experiments in broadcast seeding and in underplanting in the various conditions usually presented by logged-over and burned-over lands. Detailed and expert studies like those outlined above for the other cutting eas will be encouraged and facilities supplied fos them. In fact, the plan is apparently to develop a forest experiment station where any investigator or investigate body of proved achievement may attempt to solve forest problems of economic bearing.

Making Food Palatable for the Equine

For many years breeders of thoroughbred horses in England have realized the value of using molasses for conditioning. In Canada there have been various prepared stock foods in which molasses were used; for these prepared foods the user paid a fancy penny. The Cane Mola Company of Montreal are going after stock owners to use the straight unprepared sugar cane molasses which they import in large quantities, and which is marketed at a very reasonable price.

While there are different kinds of molasses, authorities are agreed that the safest variety is the original sugar cane molasses, and that its effect on horses and other stock is highly beneficial.

One of the most important uses of sugar cane molasses is for the disposal of poor quality hay and feed which would ordinarily be left uneaten. It is usually the most practical way of making feeds palatable and digestible. The usual method is to thin the molasses with water so that it runs as freely as cream and to pour it over dry corn fodder straw or old hay. A sprinkling can with the hose enlarged often proves very handy. Some find it well to grind up their roughage and mix the molasses with roughage and grains. This is the best method, for besides the grain which may be substituted pound for pound to that of molasses the roughage also replaces much of the grain. Horses are ordinarily fed from two to six pounds per day, according to teh amount of work required from them. In the lumber camp the use of molasses might be studied to advantage.

Canadian Timber Will Have to Wait

As a result of the congestion at British ports, the bulk of the Britsh Government's large purchase of timber from Canada will have to wait for shipment until 1920. There has been much criticism, especially on the part of the British timber trade, of the method of Government importation. One prominent trader stated recently that "huge quantities of spruce and other Canadian goods have been purchased, partial shipment of which has added to the dock congestion, conditions being now at such a pass that the shipping department is at wits end to know where to find a dumping ground for the vast quantities remaining unshipped.

From Farmer Youth To Captain of Industry

How J. D. Irving, New Brunswick Lumberman, Has Developed Business From Small Sawmill into Large, Prosperous Activities with Wide Markets

General view of the busy waterfront

The Irving Sawmill at Buctouche, N.B.

Sawmill Waste is Really Appalling

Angus McLean Says That it is Great Economic Loss Which Should be Corrected Speedily

We must be satisfied with nothing less than absolute safety from fire in our forests.

Our waste and unproductive forest lands should be reclaimed and set to growing timber.

Our cutting should be so regulated that there would be no usable material whatever left in the woods when cutting is done.

Our waste in the saw milling eliminated until not even a grain of saw dust will be burned for naught. All material at the saw mills that is not usable in some form may be used as fuel to create power.

This is the summing up of a general lumbering review of New Brunswick and Nova Scotia by Angus McLean, general manager of the Bathurst Lumber Co., Bathurst, N.B., in a recent article in the "Busy East," in which he contends that forest fires should be stamped out, waste lands reclaimed for tree growing, extravagant practices of sawmills discouraged, and the establishment of pulp and paper mills fostered, in order that the maximum values from the forests may be secured.

Mr. McLean says: I am, of course, familiar with conditions prevailing on the north shore of New Brunswick, but conditions vary but very little in the whole of this province and they are also very similar to conditions prevailing in Nova Scotia.

In this country we are not subject to any serious forest fire hazard and with any kind of ordinary care we should completely abolish this hazard. This condition is due to the fact that we have a heavy precipitation here during the periods that are usually dangerous for fires. Then we invariably get early snows and they cover the ground in the woods usually up to the 1st of May, and in the thick forests very often up to the early part of June. By that time the green undergrowth in the woods is up and covers the ground so that fires do not run. Our experience of ten years here has been so uniformly satisfactory in this respect that we are quite satisfied we are practically at the point where we will absolutely eliminate this hazard. We have had a few minor fires in our woodlands, but they have always been extinguished before much if any damage was done, so that our loss from bush fires covering this ten year period has been practically nil. What fires have taken place were invariably started by some settler burning up his slash without proper supervision. Our Minister of Crown Lands, Dr. Smith, has taken the necessary and proper steps to stop this hazard and regulate the burning of all slash in the future, and we are convinced he will succeed.

Most of our woodlands have a thriving growth of young timber on them, but we have some areas of bog and burned-over territory which should be receiving attention and prepared to produce timber, as most of our lands are not fit for farming and are only suitable for growing trees. The bog lands ought to be drained and the old burned-over lands, of many years standing, put into shape that young trees could grow on them. This requires some attention from a practiced forester. Apart from these above-named lands our timber reproduces itself without any artificial effort whatever. Please remember that these burned-over areas are of long standing, and they were largely caused by hunters who claimed they needed open areas in the forest in order to get game as the moose and deer could not be successfully hunted in the dense growth.

Next and one of the most important matters is the cutting of timber. This, of course, is done under government regulations when cutting timber in our forests. There has, however, been very great loss caused in cutting timber in our forests here in the past, owing to the small trees cut in yarding and making roads being allowed to remain in the woods to rot and also when trees are felled too much timber is left at the stump in way of butting and large tops. Am quite sure fully one quarter of the trees has been wasted in this way in the past. Of course in the ordinary course of lumbering for sawn lumber only, it is not feasible to take out the defective butts and small tops profitably, but these can all be used profitably in the pulp and paper industry and this is in the line our Provincial Government should devote some time to, and encourage these establishments in every possible way.

Next, the waste at the sawmills in New Brunswick and also in Nova Scotia is really appalling. Every mill in the land has either a steel incinerator or an open burner, into which thousands of cords of good material are being dumped and burned up annually, causing a serious loss of good raw material which should be utilized, and depriving many men of work to fit this material for the market. This is a great economic loss which should be very speedily corrected. In New Brunswick alone, hundreds of thousands of dollars are lost in this operation annually.

Another matter that is worthy of serious consideration is the manufacturing of our lumber and other products from wood into [illegible] near as possible the finished products at home. Too much unfinished raw material is being shipped out of the country on which needless cost is entailed in the way of freight charges and our country is deprived of the expenditure of labor to convert.

Winnipeg Wholesalers Elect Officers

G. U. Bacon, of the Great West Lumber Co., was elected president at the recent annual meeting of the Winnipeg Wholesale Lumbermen's Association; R. Westcott was appointed vice-president, and A. Scoville, sec.y-treas. The directors elected were: B. B. Sprague, M[illegible] Watson, W. B. Tomlinson, W. E. Allan, F. J. Chapman.

A number of important matters were considered at the gathering, and a hearty vote of thanks accorded E. C. Carter, the retiring president, and the other officers for their faithful and efficient services. It is expected that considerable new work will be carried out by the new officers and there is no doubt the Association has been of much practical benefit and help to the industry.

G. U. Bacon, Winnipeg,
Newly-elected President of the Association

Among the matters discussed during the past year were a uniform set of purchase terms and also the effort to have an inspector appointed at Winnipeg for adjustments of claims and shortages so that these matters would not have to be attended to by anybody except an independent party acting in the best interest of all concerned. This inspector has not yet been appointed but the matter is still being negotiated. A sales department was operated for some time during the past year with the idea of moving surplus stock but owing to the very unsettled conditions the department was discontinued for the time being.

There was a good attendance of members at the annual meeting of the Western Retail Dealers' Association at Calgary, and a great deal of good work was accomplished at this convention.

A credit rating department was established to give members first hand information regarding credit matters they were interested in and this department is conceded by all who make use of it to be a great help along the lines for which it is intended.

The past year was a hard one on the different members of the association. At the time of the influenza epidemic, while the association did not lose any members, several of them lost relatives and the association did whatever it could to express their sympathy in these sad cases. Later on in the year the notorious strike caused considerable disruption in business when all the members put business in second place and did everything to help support constituted authority to the best of their ability.

Erection of Mill Cut Houses in England

According to recent press advices from England regulations are soon to be issued by the Ministry of Health to overrule the local building by-laws, and will open her new field for Canadian enterprise, permitting the erection of mill-cut houses. This step is taken to relieve the housing situation. A Canadian timber man here says that the transport of mill-cut houses from Canada to Britain is too expensive, but is a large possibility. A Canadian firm which manufactures from Canadian finer timbers, is using the Baltic woods for rougher parts and accessories. It is also purchasable cheaper here. He believes this plan will allow manufacturers to cost little in excess of the Canadian price.

How Transit Car Problem is Viewed by Trade

The Practice is Growing Rapidly and Said to be Responsible for Transportation Congestion—Pros and Cons of Perplexing Question Presented

For many years it has been the practice for individuals or companies to load up lumber or shingles and start them en route to some railroad centre with the hope and expectation of being able to sell the material before it reached its destination. There is no topic of conversation over which there has been so much animated argument or so radically different views expressed as this so-called transit car problem, declares the "Mississippi Valley Lumberman."

A few manufacturers make a specialty of marketing the output of their mills through this method. As a rule, however, a great majority of the cars sent in transit are owned or controlled by wholesalers, brokers, or jobbers,who guess or gamble that prices will be higher at the time their material is ready to be delivered than they paid for it. Some of this class are mere middlemen who are used by certain manufacturers to secure the advantage of current market prices by putting stock in transit.

Some Stoutly Champion the Method

Those who make a specialty of buying, handling or selling transit cars stoutly champion this method of supplying the trade, claiming that it is more satisfactory, economical and praferable than the slow method of waiting for mill shipments. They further claim that by inducing or forcing the trade to take what the producer has, rather than what the retail distributor wants, constitutes good salesmanship. They defend the liberal bonus which they sometimes extort from those in urgent need of stock, by pointing to the chances they are taking and the loss they must assume on certain other transactions. The champions of the transit car take the position that those who own or control any forest product have a legal and a moral right to do as they please with it. The manufacturer having sold it has no further interest in it; the retail lumbermen or consuming trade do not have to buy it unless they want to. They insist that orders which they place with the manufacturer should be given the same consideration as that received from any other buyer. Further, that if they are willing to take such stock as the manufacturer has available and pay him a hundred per cent. of the invoice on receipt of bill-of-lading, the manufacturer would be very short-sighted and they would be unjustly treated if the material was not turned over to them. One reason they claim why they get the stock is that the dealers are not willing to do business on the same terms as they do.

On the other hand, the large majority of manufacturers condemn the shipping of material in transit. From undisputed records they show that the principal reason why periods of prosperity and high prices for forest products have been suddenly or gradually changed to conditions of depression and low prices was due, almost entirely to dumping of material on the market in excess of what the trade could assimilate. They claim that the radical fluctuation in the prices of material in transit has a tendency to encourage the dealer to hold off placing his order for future requirements. This often results in a congestion of business which is not desifable from the standpoint of the producer, and exceedingly detrimental to that of the retail distributor; that the whole tendency of sending material in transit is to keep the market constantly upset and prevent a normal, steady demand, and a stabilizing of prices which is to the best interests of both the manufacturer and retail distributor.

Strong Condemnation of Transit Cars

The retail lumbermen generally are inclined to side with the views of the manufacturer. The realize that, if rightly controlled, a certain amount of forest products, especially shingles, might be kept in transit so as to supply unexpected and urgent demands. The dealers, however, point out that, as a rule, the character of the lumber included in a transit car seldom meets their needs or requirements. In a large majority of cases where they are compelled to resort to transit cars, they are forced to buy as much or more undesirable or unsaleable stock than they get of the material they must have. They admit that occasionally they do get some bargains, but that more often their urgent necessities are taken advantage of by those who have cars in transit; that prices are not regulated so much by the charcater of the stock as by the proximity of the car to its destination.

The retail lumbermen generally are disposed to credit the transit cars with being largely responsible for delayed shipments. They openly accuse the manufacturer of taking the material which should be used in filling orders accepted weeks or months ago to use in making attractive cars of lumber which are sent forward in transit. Through this means they secure the benefit of the high prices, while the dealer not only is deprived of the material which belongs to him, but, in addition thereto, forced to take a lot of unsalable stock.

The practical railway operators bitterly denounce any system which will permit the dumping on them of an unlimited number of cars of forest products, without any definite information as to what disposition is to be made of this property. Just now there is a shortage of cars for definite business, and the transit car practice prevents the use of equipment for this purpose.

On an average, fifty cars of so-called transit material was received at the Minnesota Transfer each day during the month of September. These cars are shuffled back and forth in the switching yards in order to get out, and send on to their destination, those cars which have been re-consigned. On the average, these cars will remain in the possession of the transfer companies for six or seven days. Some of them, however, remain on demurrage several weeks. To-day there is one car which was received the 25th of August, while there are at least a dozen which came in all the way from the first to the fifth of September. The railroad regulations provide that the consignee has two days' free time to unload. A demurrage charge of $2.00 is assessed for each of the next succeeding four days, and a heavy penalty of $5.00 for each and every one of the days thereafter, where the car is undiverted or unloaded.

Information received from railroads and other sources indicates that the number of transit cars which are leaving the coast and are passing through certain gateways on the transcontinental lines is more for the last week than for any similar period for months. This is surprising considering the fact that there is supposed to be a pronounced car shortage on the Pacific Coast.

Would Stop Indiscriminate Practice.

In regard to the use and abuse of cars in transit, Horace F. Taylor, of Buffalo, N. Y., president of the National Wholesale Lumber Dealers' Association, whose headquarters are in New York, has sent to the members the following letter which will be read with interest, particularly at this juncture when the annual congestion of traffic at termial points and the shortage of cars is looming up:

This important matter will shortly be taken up at a conference between the Railroad Administration and wholesalers, manufacturers and retailers with the purpose of cutting out such abuse of the privilege as exists. Our association has an unusual opportunity to be of service to all concerned if we can be successful in proposing a restriction which will preserve the trade necessity of diversion and prohibit its abuse.

You are urgently requested, therefore, to promptly submit your definite views (1) as to retention of present regulations, (2) prohibition of the privilege, or (3) such modification as you would recommend. If time permits before the date of conference, these views will be summarized by your Trustees or Executive Committee for the use of our Railroad and Transportation Committee, to whom the matter has been referred.

This is not a new matter to our association; for six months or more, it has been the subject of conference and correspondence with the authorities, and at our March meeting, the following resolution to which your attention is again called, was unanimously adopted by vote of wholesalers and manufacturers alike.

> "RESOLVED: That we condemn the practice of making indiscriminate transit car shipments of unsold lumber and other forest products, as tending to the demoralization of market conditions, it being understood that this resolution shall not be construed as opposing a proper use of the reconsignment privilege."

"If we should begin to-day to protect our cut-over land from fire and to use wholly practical methods of forestry to secure reproduction after logging, we could secure in the next 50 or 60 years an annual production of over 60,000,000,000 feet a year without lessening our forest capital. And this would be done without devoting to tree growth land that is not chiefly valuable for that purpose," declared Henry S. Graves of the United States Forestry Service, in a recent address.

Price Brothers Celebrate Centenary

Historic Quebec Firm Has Made Splendid Progress in Lumber, Pulp and Paper Activities

Sir William Price,
Head of the present large organization

The nationally known firm of Price Bros. & Co., Limited, of Quebec, who have pulp and paper mills at Kenogami, Jonquière and Rimouski, and saw mills at more than half a dozen points in Quebec, recently celebrated the one hundredth anniversary of the founding of their business.

The company are large manufacturers of spruce lumber, lath, cedar shingles, ties, pulpwood, sulphite, and groundwood pulp, newsprint, cardboard, etc., and are one of the most prosperous and progressive organizations on the continent.

The significant and historic event was commemorated by a private gathering held at Kenogami where the big paper mills of the company are situated. About 150 old employees of the firm were invited to attend and it would have afforded Sir Wm. Price, head of the concern, much delight to have included many more but lack of accommodation made it necessary to limit the number. A special train on which were the invited guests left Quebec on August 26 and all the establishments of Price Bros. were represented. At Kenogami the party were joined by representatives of that busy centre and from Jonquiere. The trip was a most interesting and impressive one and many were the happy incidents recalled, the historic associations revived and hearty well wishes showered upon the head of the firm for the continued success and expansion of the aggressive company.

The company are now installing a new newsprint unit at Kenogami and erecting a new saw mill at Matane. Since 1900 the industrial operations of Price Bros. have increased fivefold and before another ten years elapse, it is predicted that they will be among the largest, if not the largest, producers on the continent of newsprint, groundwood pulp and lumber. The founder of the business was the late Wm. Price, grandfather of Sir William of the present day, and the year was 1817.

This young man arrived in Quebec in 1810 from Elstree, Hertfordshire, England, at the age of twenty-one years. Europe was then in the midst of the wars of the Empire and under the shock of the decree of Berlin issued by Napoleon establishing the continental blockade. Some time afterwards the United States issued the decree of the Embargo prohibiting American vessels from leaving their ports and communicating with England and France.

Access to the Scandinavian countries interdicted and the United States refusing to trade with her, England decided to send a representative to Canada to purchase wood for masts which the Admiralty required.

After having fulfilled his mission William Price started on his own account a lumber business. His first operations were made on the Ottawa and the St. Maurice, but he principally applied himself to develop his industry on the south side of the St. Lawrence, from Riviere Du Loup to Matane, and afterwards to the Saguenay.

About 1850 he covered the region of Quebec with his saw mills and hundreds of vessels traversed the seas of the world loaded with products from the William Price Quebec industry. He had then industrial establishments at the following places:

Hadlow, Batiscan, Riviere du Loup, Isle Verte, Bic, Rimouski, Metis, Tartigou, Riviere Blanche, Matane, Cap Chat, Papinachois or Bersimis, Sault au Cochon, Escoumains, Bergeronnes, Moulin Baude, Tadousac, Baie des Rochers, Riviere Noire, Petites Isles, Petit Saguenay, Anse St. Jean, Anse a Pelletier, Grand Baie, Chicoutimi, Riviere du Moulin.

From his marriage with Jane Evan there were 14 children, seven boys and seven girls. He died on the 14th of March, 1867, at his residence "Wolfesfield," St. Louis Road, Quebec, at the age of 78 years surrounded by his children and enjoying the respect of his fellow-citizens.

At this time his three sons, William, David and John, were his partners and practically managed the business. William died on the 12th of June, 1880, at the age of 53 years, while he was a member of the Quebec Legislative Assembly. David died in 1883. He was senator for the Laurentide Division. Before Confederation he had been elected Legislative Councillor for the same Division. The Honorable John succeeded his brother in the Senate and died in the month of August, 1899.

The estate of William Price, Sr., as well as the estates of his three sons, David, William and John, became the property of William (Sir William), younger son of Henry, by the will of his uncle, Honorable John Price.

Apart from large cash bequests that he directed his legatee to pay, the Honorable John Price, by his last will and testament, wished to keep intact under one head the large estate of Price Brothers, following therein the policy of his father and brothers who predeceased him, with the evident intention of more effectively continuing the work begun in 1817 in the Province of Quebec.

Sir William inherited the estate of his uncle at a relatively early age and assisted by his brothers Henry and Arthur undertook the heavy burden of directing a large firm which experienced hands had hitherto managed.

He renewed the mills which had somewhat deteriorated in nearly all the establishments and about 1900 launched into the new pulp and paper industry without, however, neglecting the old industry of sawn timber. From 1900 until now the industrial operations of Price Brothers under the inspiration of the young heir have increased five-fold. Not only has Sir William maintained in the commercial world the name of his ancestors as lumber merchants; but he has put his Company in the foremost place of the country's great paper manufacturers.

With the new developments which are being provided the Price Company will attain in the manufacture of paper, before ten years have elapsed, first place on the continent. People asked with anxiety after the death of John Price what would become of the Price fortune amassed from father to son in the hands of the young man then called Willie Price.

His uncle had prudently trained him to the work, it is true, for close onto ten years under his supervision and direction, but what would this young man full of life do with these estates that sudden fortune invited to dissipation? Would he take the profits only with the pleasures without also assuming at the same time the heavy moral responsibilities of his new position?

A great many young men would have succumbed to the temptations of the easy life with its pernicious influence under like circumstances.

The young man did not lose his head, he remained steadfast at his post and showed himself worthy of the confidences of his uncle and the intrusted deposit has been kept with the greatest care.

Statistical Returns Make Fair Progress

In regard to the members of the Canadian Lumbermen's Association furnishing statistics of lumber production, sales and shipments, etc., each month and sending the same to the Secretary of the C. L. A. for tabulation in order that a better estimate of trade activities in general might prevail, it is learned that the process of carrying this out has been a little slower and more tedious than at first anticipated, when such a step was decided upon at the annual meeting of the C. L. A. held last February in St. John, N. B. Like the current of a river, this movement is expected to gather strength as it flows, and it may be necessary to carry on an education campaign for some time, such as was conducted in the Southern Pine trade for several years, before the statistical department of the Canadian Lumbermen's Association can accomplish much in the way of practical results. The Association is determined to "carry on" in this regard and believes that each month will see greater co-operation and united effort.

An Employment Bureau For Loggers

Recent advices received from B. C. state that prominent employers in the logging and timber camps of the Province have decided to open an employment bureau in Vancouver where men will be given work without having to pay a fee. There will be a job for every man, and if at the time of his application there is not a position available, one will be found for him. The employers intend in the first place to look after the interests of Canadian and British-born loggers, especially the returned lumbermen who are anxious to take up their former occupation. Recently there were eleven camps in the Province closed down, six through strikes and the remainder from other causes. It is estimated that there are approximately 1,200 loggers affected by reason of the strikes and the shutting down of the various camps in B. C.

John Readhead died recently at his home in Lowville, Ont., at the advanced age of 85 years. Mr. Readhead followed the lumber business for a long period and was well known.

Should View Present Conditions as Normal

Unbiased Study of Whole Lumber Situation Convinces Representative Committee Prices Will Not Fall—Structural Undertakings Should Not be Delayed

Some exceptionally thorough investigations into the lumber price situation in the United States have been undertaken of late, with results that are of much importance to the trade. It was to be expected that the public would harbor doubts about the necessity for increased lumber prices under conditions which have recently developed, similar to the doubts that have arisen regarding advances in many other lines. The result has been several government enquiries.

Probably the most unbiased study of the siutation, so far as lumber is concerned, has been made in the State of Illinois. A few months ago, when the State of Illinois was considering the construction of many needed buildings, and how to promote the erection of much important and necessary private construction, there was a general contention that the prices of building materials were too high. Those who were not connected with the manufacture of building materials had an idea that prices would greatly decline during 1919, and that those who spent money on building operations would be losers. The State, therefore, decided to appoint a disinterested body of public men to investigate the situation and make the facts known. A committee was appointed, consisting of ten lawyers and prominent business men. They investigated and heard evidence for two months, prying into building material prices, production costs and the conditions of supply and demand. Their conclusions are very striking and important.

The Relative Value of Lumber

The following extracts from their report are interesting to the lumber trade:

"The public mind, in starting building and construction operations, is influenced almost solely by prices of what may be termed the basic building materials to wit: Steel, lumber, cement and brick.

"This committee attempts to analyze the price of lumber not alone from the standpoint of cost as represented by several constituent parts, but from the standpoint of its relative value."

"The price of one thousand feet of lumber purchased

In 1913		In 1917
23.4	bushels of wheat	12.4
35	bushels of corn	16.3
290	pounds of hogs	180
201	pounds of bacon	109
10	barrels of apples	8.5
190	pounds of cotton	133
328	yards cotton sheeting	216
1949	pounds of steel	1725

"It must be remembered that the price of these other commodities continued to soar higher through 1918, while the price of lumber was not only held down, but reduced by the Government.

"Stumpage and timber values in this country will, in the opinion of the commission, increase materially, not alone because of the great demand for lumber, but because of the fast diminishing supply.

"The lumber situation is international in its scope. There is a world-wide demand, but only limited fields of production.

"With over twenty million acres of timber destroyed by artillery fire, or burned for strategic purposes during the world war; with Russian sawmills dismantled, stripped of all machinery which the Bolsheviks sold to the Germans, and with general industrial chaos throughout Russia, Canada and the United States will be called upon to supply most of the lumber used through the construction period.

"With the demand far greater than ever before, it is the opinion of this commission, that lumber prices will go up rather than down.

Engalnd's Guarantee Against Lower Prices

"Roger E. Simmons, of the U. S. Trade Commission, Department of Commerce, who recently returned from an investigation for the Government of the timber and lumber conditions in Russia and England, testified to the fact that England was so sure that lumber prices would increase that the Government is making a guarantee to private builders, if they go ahead and build now, that if in five years the price of lumber, material and construction has come down, the Government will pay 75 per cent. of the difference to the builder and investor. He further testified London trade papers, as well as the general press, already are printing articles concerning what they call a timber famine.

"On account of this world demand for lumber, there will be many attempts, no doubt, to encroach upon the Forest Preserves of this country. Such an encroachment, unless limited, would rob the future generations of their rightful heritage. It would be a public menace. It would endanger our entire national conservation policy.

"The commission is unable to see how the cost of labor in the manufacturing of lumber can be materially lowered so long as the cost of living remains at its present level.

"The commission is obliged to report that the record contains no evidence showing that illegal agreements for the reason of profiteering exist in any of the businesses investigated by the commission, subject to certain observations regarding cement."

Advises That Building Should Go On.

Among the recommendations made by the committee to the public is the following:

> **"In view of opinions expressed in this report, we believe it to be our duty as public officials, to advise the public not to delay building projects in the hope that prices will come down materially. We do not believe they will. We deem it the part of wisdom to accept present conditions as normal and that building operations should be based upon that principle. All contemplated buildings, homes, and improvements should be started now. Reconstruction can only be accomplished in its real sense by every citizen subscribing to the doctrine 'buy now, 'build now!'."**

The important fact to bear in mind in connection with the above report is that after the expenditure of several thousand dollars and two months' time, this body of intelligent, able men have become informed, have reversed their former opinions and have been convinced. Their advice means much to those contemplating construction.

Small Export Trade in Lumber

Only 3.1 per cent. of the total lumber production of the United States was exported in 1918, according to recent Government figures, which prove how unfounded is the statement reported to have been made by a prominent forester that "the forests are being drained to support foreign factories."

In 1918, the Government figures give somewhat more than one billion three hundred million feet of lumber as exported out of an estimated production of 32 billion feet. Of these exports about 110 million feet was in railroad ties, not quite as much in hewn and sawed timber while over one billion feet was in the form of boards, planks and deals.

Figures for the first three months of 1919 show only a slight increase in value of lumber exports over the monthly figures of the last half of 1918. For April, May and June, 1919, the exports are greater, the increase in value being about 40 per cent over the average value of 1918 months. But even if the entire year of 1919 shows an increase of 40 per cent., which is extremely unlikely—June, 1919, exports of merchandise were the peak and July figures were 30 per cent. lower—but even on this extreme supposition, the total lumber exports for 1919 would be less than two billion feet out of a total predicted production of 32,000,000,000 feet or about the equivalent of the 1918 yield.

Want Some Return From Timber Dues

A well-attended meeting of the Huntsville Board of Trade and the residents of Dwight and vicinity, was held recently to discuss the possible method of improving the roads. The fact that the Ontario Government has secured hundreds of thousands of dollars from the district in timber dues, it seems only just that some return should be given this locality. Petitions were therefore prepared asking the Colonization Department to appropriate a sufficient sum for road improvements, especially on this much travelled highway.

Progressive Lumber Co. Expanding

Live Prairie Province Organization Will Greatly Increase Output and Install New Equipment

The Finger Lumber Co., Limited, of The Pas, Manitoba, intend putting in four logging camps during the coming winter and will employ about six hundred men. The company state that wages are running from $55 to $75 per month and help is hard to get even at this figure while camp supplies are costing from 100 to 150 per cent. more than they did before the war. The company will increase their mill capacity and are installing a new band resaw and trimmer and also a new band mill.

The Finger Lumber Company, of which H. Finger is president, H. S. Smith vice-president, and W. H. Miner, secretary-treasurer,

General view of the Finger Company's plant

commenced operations in the Spring of 1912, and own extensive timber limits along the Saskatchewan and the Carrot rivers.

Their logging thus far has ben conducted on the limits along the Carrot river, where a number of camps last winter were operated. The logs are driven down the Carrot river into a storage boom located where the river empties into the Saskatchewan. They are then towed from this storage boom to the saw mill by the company's own tugs.

The company are the pioneers in the lumber industry in Northern Manitoba, that vast strentch of land hitherto considered as the

Tugs of Finger Lumber Company at work on the river

frozen hinterland. With the advent of the Hudson Bay Railway the so-called frozen waste is now considered the richest part of Manitoba.

The capacity of the plant now is 25,000,000 feet annually and the output is mostly spruce, there being only a sprinkling of cottonwood and tamarac. Carrot River spruce is considered high quality; has fine texture and compares favorably with white pine. The lumber is hauled from the sorting works to the yard by rail, and the planing mill is equipped with modern fast-feed machines and resaws.

The company operate their own electric light plant, and the motive power for both the sawmill and the planing mill is steam. Most of the company's product is marketed in the Prairie Provinces, but during the last few years it has developed a market in the United States. The Pas is the western terminus of the Hudson Bay Railway in Manitoba.

Retailers Resent High Cost Allegations

At a recent meeting of the Chamber of Commerce in Sarnia, Ont., one of the speakers was James Dunn, a contracto from the neighboring city of Port Huron, Mich., and, in the course of his remarks, he is reported to have said that the high prices of lumber in Sarnia had kept building back. This statement has not been well received by the retail lumbermen of Sarnia, who naturally are indignant at the observation and have not been backward in letting their opinion be known, for the impression was conveyed that the public had been "held up."

C. H. Belton, of the R. Laidlaw Lumber Co., remarked that the assertion was absurd and utterly uncalled for, and, according to a recent press despatch, intimated that a suit for damages might be heard in the near future.

John McGibbon of McGibbon, Limited, also entered a protest at the figure quoted by the Port Huron contractor, and stated that all the season lumber had been from five to twenty-five dollars per M. cheaper in Sarnia than in adjoining centres. It is said that the last has not been heard of the allegation and the question will be taken up at the next meeting of the Board of Commerce.

Schroeder Co. Buy Lauder-Spears Mill

The Schroeder Mills and Timber Co., Pakesley, Ont., have bought the Lauder, Spears and Howland sawmill which is located on the Lost Channel at the foot of the Pickerel River and intend operating the plant next season. The mill has direct connection with the C. P. R. at Pakesley by means of the Key Valley Railway, which is a standard gauge road, twelve miles long. Pakesley Station is located 206 miles north of Toronto. The Lauder, Spears & Howland plant, when fully completed and the second unit installed, will have a sawing capacity of 100,000 feet to 125,000 feet a day. The lumber as it is cut will be brought to Pakesley to dry.

In speaking of logging operations for the coming season James Ludgate, Ontario manager of the Schroeder Mills and Timber Co., says that in camp supplies the prices are about the same as last season. Beef is cheaper but dried fruits are dearer. Feed for horses is ten per cent. above what it was a year ago. Labor is more plentiful but not as sufficient as it might be, and many young lads, that should be at school, are roaming around looking for work. Mr. Ludgate states that the returned soldiers are in evidence everywhere and just like they were before the war—nearly all good men—a little more reckless perhaps than they were but this, he believes, is natural, as economy was not one of the things practiced to excess during the European conflict.

The Schroeder Co., who contemplated paying their men by the day system and inaugurating it this fall, have not done so owing to the fact that there appears to be a great deal of labor unrest in the country. They consider it an inopportune time to enter upon anything new.

Rock Creek Co. Get Timber Limits

The Rock Creek Lumber Co., of Flagstone, B. C., have bought the timber holdings located at Crow's Nest from Malcolm McInnes, of Calgary. It is said that the consideration was around $200,000. The limits comprise twelve sections of valuable saw timber and large quantities of mining props and poles. The estimated cruise of the timber runs well up into the millions of feet exclusive of the smaller timber, which can be manufactured into props, etc. The Rock Creek Lumber Co., intend to operate very extensively and are already engaged in reconstructing the sawmill, which has been idle for some time, so that when completed it will have a capacity of about 50,000 feet B.M. per day. They are also constructing a large flume which will be supplied with water from Alexander Creek, formerly known as the North Fork of Michel Creek, and by this means the logs will be conveyed from the limits to the mill during practically any season of the year, and thus insure a permanent supply of saw timber for the mill. Camps as well are being built in the limits and roads laid out.

An Echo of the Election Contest

Major Hartt, lumberman of Orillia, who was M.P.P. for East Simcoe, has issued a writ against R. H. Halbert, president of the U. F. O., claiming $10,000 damages because defendant on Aug. 14, at a farmers' meeting at Barrie, "recklessly, falsely and maliciously" charged Hartt with having said at a meeting in North Bay, that "farmers remind me of a lot of hogs feeding at a trough, and, after they are full, still squealing for more." Major Hartt asks for an injunction to restrain Halbert from repeating the statement.

Personal Paragraphs of Interest

York Long, managing director of Chas. Long & Co., Liverpool, is on a business visit to Canada.

John H. Cole, of Knight Bros. Co., Ltd., Burk's Falls, Ont., spent a few days in Toronto recently calling upon the lumber trade.

Frank W. Gordon, manager of the B. C. forest products department of Terry & Gordon, Toronto, left recently on an extended business trip to the Coast, where he will spend several weeks.

L. D. Barclay, of Toronto, eastern manager of the Canadian Western Lumber Co., Fraser Mills, B.C., who was confined to his home for several days with illness, is once more at his desk.

J. B. Knox of Knox Bros., Montreal, has returned from a brief visit to the Pacific Coast. He reports that business continues very good, with a strong market.

H. J. Terry, of Terry & Gordon, Toronto, has returned from a holiday trip to Winnipeg, Minneapolis and Chicago. He has not been feeling up to the mark for some time, but as a result of his outing is much improved.

R. McDonagh, of the firm of Hart & McDonagh, wholesale lumber dealers, Toronto, who has been confined to his home for some time owing to an attack of inflammatory rheumatism, is able to be at his office again.

The name of the British Government Timber Buyer has been changed to that of the Imported Lumber Disposal Section, Board of Trade, London, England. Mr. S. C. Denman, Montreal, is the representative in Eastern Canada.

Sidney R. Anderson, of Toronto, who is a well known lumber salesman, has opened an office in the Manning Chambers, Queen St. West, Toronto, and embarked in the wholesale lumber line. He will handle both hard and softwoods.

A. G. Richardson, the chief of the plant Safety First department of the Laurentide Co., Grand'Mere, P. Q., represented that company at the annual congress of the National Safety Council held in Cleveland, Ohio. At the same congress, G. W. Dickson, of the Riordon Pulp & Paper Co., Hawkesbury, read a paper on "How to use Danger Signals in a Paper Mill."

Captain R. J. Graham, who recently returned from overseas, has purchased a mill site in Wiarton. He has a large quantity of standing timber on Great LaCloche Island and also on Manitoulin Island and it is his intention to cut and manufacture it at Wiarton. Operations will commence in the near future but much will depend on the available labor supply.

William Robertson, of Victoria, B. C., who has been in Toronto for several weeks assisting Major James Brechin, B. C. Lumber Commissioner, left recently for the West where he will resume his duties in connection with trade extension work in the Forestry Branch of the Department of Lands. Major Brechin has returned from a trip to the Coast accompanied by his wife and family and has taken up his residence in Toronto. He reports the lumber business in the West as being very active with a strong market and all the mills busy.

Will Build Thousands of Houses

While the Dominion Government passed legislation to assist in meeting the house shortage in Canada, the Ontario Government has been the only Provincial administration that has put the Federal scheme into practical effect, Mr. J. A. Ellis, of the Bureau of Municipal Affairs, Toronto, said recently. With the exception of Alberta and Saskatchewan the other provinces had merely appointed committees for the purposes of investigation. In the case of Saskatchewan and Alberta letters had been received by Mr. Ellis from Edmonton and Regina asking for particulars of what had been done in Ontario.

Mr. Ellis asserted that there would be 1,200 houses, built with Provincial assistance, completed by the end of October, and that they would all be occupied before the end of October. "There is no fear of any of the municipalities having houses on their hands under the Ontario scheme," he said. "Our architects draw the plans and if they do not quite satisfy the prospective tenant or purchaser, any necessary alterations are made. In that way we eliminate any cause for future complaint, and that is perhaps why we have not the slightest trouble obtaining tenants. Next year 4,000 more houses will be built."

Another Advance in Industrial Progress

Owing to the rapid development and extension of the pulp and paper industry in Canada, the Dominion Bridge Co., of Montreal have made arrangements for the establishment of an entire plant which will be devoted to the production of paper making machinery and accessories. The company have already built a number of machines for paper mills which have been designed by their own engineers, and the equipment has met with a most favorable reception. While various lines of pulp and paper-making installations have been manufactured in the Dominion, large machines such as Fourdriniers for the big newsprint and book paper plants of the Dominion have been built in either the United States or England.

Artistic display of doors, columns, newels and stairwork by Batts Limited, of Toronto, at recent Canadian National Exhibition

The announcement that these will now be turned out in Montreal is a distinct step in advance in the way of industrial achievement and an augury of the status which the pulp and paper industry is assuming in Canada. It is asserted that the strides in this field during the past two years have been greater than in any other line of activity.

Good Opportunities for Canadian Firms

"Opportunities await the Canadian manufacturers of pulp and paper in the British market, according to A. L. Dawe, Secretary of the Canadian Pulp and Paper Association, Montreal, who has recently returned from a three months' trip to Great Britain.

"I found a large and increasing demand for all classes of Canadian-made paper," stated Mr. Dawe. "Publishers, box makers, and other users of paper products are eager to get their supplies from Canada. They realize that in the past they have relied too much on alien countries, such as the Scandinavian countries and Germany. The opportunities for the Canadian manufacturers in England are just what our producers wish to make them. The business is there waiting for them. The only way to get this trade is to send over expert men and look after it, just as firms here do for the home trade in Canada. If our manufacturers do this, I see no reason why a large and profitable export trade to Great Britain should not be built up."

Timber Exchange Opens in London

The Timber Exchange will shortly be opened in London, Eng., by the Right Honorable Sir Auckland Geddes, M. P., president of the Board of Trade. That the timber trade should have an exchange in the city of London where agents, brokers, importers, merchants and others interested can get together and transact their business has long been felt and recognized. It is announced by the exchange that the formation of such an organization is a definite step in the scheme of national reconstruction, and this is attested by the fact that the president of the Board of Trade will perform the opening ceremony on October 8th. Many leading firms have already joined the exchange and it is prophesied that such a body will be both useful and influential.

Improved Automatic Roller Dryer

An attractive bulletin has been issued by the Coe Mfg. Company, of Painesville, Ohio, which illustrates and describes their automatic progressive roller veneer dryer, which is the result of sixty-seven years' experience. The Coe Mfg. Co. state they are the oldest and largest manufacturers in the world of veneer cutting and drying equipment.

Their automatic progressive roller veneer dryer is an improved apparatus which dries green veneer and thin wood products within a fraction of an hour after being cut ready for the glue room or crating. Owing to the scientific control of the drying factors the veneer is not only dried flat but uniformly seasoned without internal stresses, marking, splitting, checking, case-hardening or other defects.

Just Thirty Years Ago

Interesting items from the fyles of the October edition of the "Canada Lumberman" away back in 1889

The Georgian Bay Lumber Co. recently filled a contract for square timber for England, consisting of 837,071 feet.

* * *

A timber limit located on the Assiniboine river, near Fort Pelly, was recently sold at auction in Winnipeg. It brought $3,000.

* * *

It is announced that the Department of Crown Lands at Quebec will hold a large public sale of timber limits some time during the month of December.

* * *

The Thunder Bay River Boom Company has rafted to the various lumber and shingle mills at Alpena, Mich., this season, 1,115,104 logs, which scaled 111,848,640 feet.

* * *

Another large lumber mill may be built on the Fraser River, B. C., next spring. It will be nearly opposite the Ross-McLaren mills and will be as large as any in the province.

* * *

The Brunette Sawmill Company (Ltd.), New Westminster, is cutting 8,000,000 to 10,000,000 feet, in addition to which they are turning out large quantities of shingles, lath and pickets.

* * *

Wages for work in the woods in the Ottawa district are, for scorers, from $35 to $37 a month; liners, $40 to $42, while a number of hewers have been engaged at $60. General hands are offered $20 to $25.

* * *

The Rathbun Company have recently secured about eighty-five square miles of valuable timber limits on the head waters of the River Trent. The company have also made purchases of large quantities of wood and other material along the extension of the N. T. and Q. railway.

* * *

The Wm. Hamilton Manufacturing Company of Peterboro are busily engaged in turning out orders for mill machinery. They have orders ahead for ten boilers and three engines, with accompanying sawmill machinery.

* * *

The Ottawa lumbermen have undertaken the task of clearing the entrance to the canal of sawdust. In two days 400 feet square by 5 feet deep, or, in other words, 30,000 yards of sawdust were scooped into the main channel.

* * *

Davidson & Hay's new sawmill at Cache Bay has commenced operations. It is beautifully situated on an arm of Lake Nipissing, and is one of the best equipped in Canada, being fitted up with the most approved machinery.

* * *

The Grand Trunk Railway Co. has contracted for 1,000 new cars to facilitate the lumber and grain shipments. It is to be hoped that ere very long the complaints of the lumbermen on the car question will be found no longer necessary.

* * *

Messrs. W. R. Thirstle & Co., Pembroke, Ont., in order to wind up their business, are offering for sale their saw milling properties, timber limits, etc. The milling property consists of the Pembroke mill, with lath and shingle mills, boomage and piling grounds.

* * *

Experts in forestry, as a rule, have intimated, if not asserted directly in their discussions, that the supply of choice lumber in the United States is nearer exhaustion than the Canadian stock. This view is broadly controverted by Consul Hotchkiss, of Ottawa, who says that if he were asked whether Canada or the United States would probably be the first to reach the end of supply of marketable commercial woods, he would reply unhesitatingly, that Canada must first face these conditions. Mr. Hotchkiss believes that it is "safe to say" that the encroachments upon the Canadian pine, in particular, are serious, and that by the process of culling, in order to meet the English demand for clear lumber, the forests of the Dominion have become so reduced that the greater part of the output hereafter will be found available for the markets of the United States only. The English market maintains a peculiar demand for quality and shape, and takes only the product of the choicest trees.

* * *

The lumber export trade during the past season has been very good, especially during the mid-summer months. One of the causes of the heavy shipments during these months was the unusually large demand for square timber, of which a great deal was shipped. The export trade to South America is not a steady business as it varies according to tonnage.

* * *

Messrs. McCuaig & Morehead, of Ottawa, have purchased Mr. E. B. Eddy's limits, with plant, etc., at the head of Lake Temiscamingue, comprising about 135 square miles of territory, situated partly in Ontario and partly in Quebec. They will commence at once the work of taking out square timber. The price paid for the limit is in the neighborhood of $40,000 cash.

* * *

The Big Mill of the Rathbun Company, Deseronto, recently cut in six days 609,000 pieces of lath, an average of 101,500 pieces a day. The largest cut made in one day was 109,000 pieces. All previous records were broken by cutting 49,000 pieces on a single machine in one day. The largest output in six days last year was 409,000 pieces, being an average of 83,166 pieces.

* * *

A monster raft, consisting of 559,000 feet of timber, owned by Mr. J. G. Grier, of Ottawa, was recently shipped from that city to Kingston, viz. the Rideau canal. The raft was principally composed of hemlock, and will be used in the construction of the dry dock being built at Kingston. The trip occupied five weeks' time, and the raft was the largest that ever went through the canal.

* * *

The rise in the rivers has given a new impetus to lumbering in the Province along the Nashwaak, in New Brunswick, and the logs are getting down in fine style. The Marysville sawmills are again at work and will continue sawing the balance of the season. The demand for lumber is strong with a rising market. The St. John Gazette announces that Mr. Alex. Gibson recently paid $12 a thousand for 120,000 piled at Pleasant Point. No man in the Province better knows the value of lumber.

* * *

Exports of lumber, deals, etc., from St. John, N.B., during September, show an increase of from $147,843 to $250,302, as compared with the corresponding month of 1888. The shipments were: Scantling and boards, 2,715,392 feet; deals, 17,095,717 feet; deal ends, 738,133 feet; birch timber, 610 tons; pine timber, 7,200 tons; palings, 38,285; lath, 8,170,300; piling, 1,637 pieces; shingles, 2,909,576; spruce timber 7,502 feet, and clapboards, 13,425 feet.

* * *

Last year the cut of logs in British Columbia was estimated at 100,000,000. The estimated output for this year is placed at 125,000,000 feet. Along the coast between the Fraser river and Port Neville there are now twenty camps, and two on Howe Sound. The number of men employed in connection with the camps is placed at 600, which with the same loggers scattered along the coast will probably make a total of 700 men who are cutting logs for various lumber companies in that province.

* * *

A leading feature of the Toronto Exhibition was a band sawmill, cutting lumber from oak, ash, hemlock and pine saw logs. By the use of this mill six boards are sawed where five were only got by a circular mill. This mill is very simple, easy to run, while the power required is fully one-half less than a circular. The lumber is better cut, and in cutting one million feet of lumber 163,000 feet is saved in sawdust alone. The mill was shown by the Waterous Engine Works Co. and is the outcome of many years experience.

* * *

The Dominion Government has refused the petition of Peterborough saw mill owners in regard to throwing sawdust in the Otonabee river. Inspector Gilchrist, of Peterborough, has received fresh instruction from the department of Marine and Fisheries to see that the fines imposed by the magistrates are collected, and also to continue prosecutions as long as the mill owners violate the law. The Government is evidently determined to enforce the law regarding sawdust in streams, so far at least as it refers to the Otonabee river.

* * *

In view of the high prices for square timber at Quebec, last summer there will probably be a large increase in the quantity made the coming winter as compared with last year. It does not follow, however, that the high prices obtained this summer will be maintained next year. An increase of 50 per cent. in the output would necessarily have a great tendency to weaken prices unless there there should be an unusually large demand, and those who base their calculations for next season upon the high figures obtained this year are likely to find out that they have committed a grave mistake. That a large amount of money will be made out of the winter's cut, when disposed of next year, there is no doubt, providing the market is not glutted. The indications are, judging from the preparations being made, that the winter's cut will be a large one.

* * *

The necessity of devising some means to prevent the accumulation of sawdust and mill refuse in the navigable streams is apparent, as is evidenced by the enormous banks of sawdust which are now obstructing the navigation of the Ottawa river, between Ottawa and Hull. With reference to Mr. Sandford Fleming's report on sawdust in the Ottawa river, an Ottawa despatch says: "It is understood that the statement published as to the river channel being clear does not refer to the soundings from the Chandiere down to the Rideau locks. With regard to this part of the river, it is learned that by a recent survey and soundings made, by order of the Department of Railways and Canals, at the foot of the locks of Rideau Canal, that the accumulation of sawdust and slabs is very large and increasing daily. There are now only between one and two feet of water in the mid-channel over the surface of the sawdust, where there formerly was from eight feet at the sill to thirty feet in the river channel. Had the river been usually low this fall it would have been impossible for the boats to enter the locks and, consequently, navigation would have been closed. There is a probability of the channel being dredged this fall. A report on the subject has been prepared, and will be submitted to the Government, when it is expected the necessary orders to set about the work forthwith will be given.

Heavy Export Business Will Come in Time

Conditions in Old Land Will Readjust Themselves So That Canadian Forest Products Will Get to the Forefront—Survey of the Future

At the gathering of Ontario lumber manufacturers, held in Toronto on September 24th, Mr. A. C. Manbert, Ontario Timber Commissioner, who returned recently, after spending several months in Great Britain, conducting propaganda work in the interest of Ontario forest products and more particularly white pine, touched upon a number of phases and incidents in connection with the overseas situation, to which only brief reference was made in the last issue of the "Canada Lumberman." In his introductory remarks he drew a graphic, present-day picture of the great city of London with its teeming millions, all animated by good nature and buoyant spirits. The whole interest of the people and their activities had been concentrated on the winning of the war and the sense of freedom and relief from artificial control to one of unrestrained action and movement was everywhere noticeable. They seemed to have a good time in "finding themselves," so to speak, after the deprivations through which they had passed during the last four years. Mr. Manbert said that we knew something of the war in Canada, but comparatively little compared to what the Mother Country had experienced in the way of restrictions and restraint. He spoke of the new atmosphere prevailing in the Old Land, and how many problems were viewed, from interesting and hitherto unapproached angles, by reason of altered conditions.

Coming down to the commercial and industrial affairs Mr. Manbert said that in his communications to the lumbermen's committee in the Province and also in his articles that appeared in the press, he had not concerned himself much with statistics under war conditions or pre-war conditions, as, arising out of the changed relations and circumstances, he considered these as possessing little more than historic or sign-post value and not calculated to meet the present situation.

He referred to the warmth of welcome accorded him in all quarters, and added that the average Canadian could scarcely realize how keen the interest was in Canada, which is regarded as the premier colony, and great things were expected from her. It might be that Great Britain and Canada understood each other a little better than any of the other dominions in matters of policy and general attitude and approach. Mr. Manbert said that he had arrived in the Old Country at a time when there was a great feeling of relief at timber control being removed, with all its attendant restraints. When the controller ceased official supervision of the timber, he really continued his perpetual control by buying up large quantities of wood products and the people wondered why the thing was done, whether it was for fear that prices would rise or heavy stocks were required for the housing campaign or if the policy was really the same as before, but operating under another name. A great deal of uncertainty and dissatisfaction had been created in the trade. The timber controller proceeded to dispose of the old stock of pine by allocating it to certain persons who were to see that the stock was not sold above a stipulated price. Spruce from the Baltic regions was also auctioned off and those who were disappointed in not being able to buy at auction, were naturally much aroused and charged the controller with favoritism.

When the government auctioned off the stocks the charge was made that the government was profiteering. The government was evidently feeling its way and did not know how to travel or how its actions would work out. Individual operation is the best method of governing the control of timber and bringing matters back to normal basis. Control had been an impediment in the way of free business. Any remarks that he had to make, Mr. Manbert said, were not delivered in a critical spirit, but simply observations in the nature of things and he was setting forth matters exactly as he found them.

The Baltic Competition is Keen

In regard to the timber situation, Mr. Manbert believed that the timber controller would get over all the pine this year that he had purchased in Canada, but that 100,000 standards of spruce would remain here over winter. Great Britain had used, before the war, about 4,000,000,000 standards of forest products and with the interruptions brought about by the European conflict there had of late been about 50 per cent. of the importations coming from Scandinavia. The Baltic countries competed with the woods from Canada. Their white fir, which was really spruce, and red fir, which was really a pine, were put up in splendid shape, and in a way calculated to meet the exact needs of the English buyer. The white wood was a little softer than our Ontario spruce, but not softer, however, than the Quebec spruce, and the red fir was very much like our own red pine, but carried a little less clear and was sounder knotted. In texture he did not see much difference from our red pine. Mr. Manbert referred to the splendid way in which the Swedish exporters put up their product, all the lumber being stamped and branded while the cutting was even and square. The result was that the Scandinavian product had won an enviable reputation in the Old Country and enjoyed a splendid market by reason of its high standard and careful markings. Taking a long range view it might be admitted that the Scandinavians were perhaps a little better salesmen and catered to the trade in general and to the individual in particular in a manner that suited his whims for the British buyer who was often exacting and, perhaps at times, hypercritical. Of course, Scandinavia did not bestow all these extra attentions without making the purchaser pay for them. The British buyer was apt to think, in a case of Canadian timber, because there was a little wane on the edge or a slight discoloration which in no way impaired its strength or durability, that the product was not quite as good as that more carefully prepared by the Baltic manufacturers.

It was little things like these which were considered important over in the Old Land and Mr. Manbert thought that more detailed and careful attention might be given to methods of sawing in Canada. Here logs were taken out and brought down in good shape, but were too often butchered in converting them into lumber. Canadian white pine was a preferred wood over in Great Britain and the way we use it in the Dominion would be regarded by the Englishman as a sacrilege. Here the wood is employed in erecting fences, outbuildings, etc., but in the Mother Country it is regarded as being in a class by itself and among the aristocrats in forest products.

Stocks Low and Distribution Slow

On his arrival in the Old Country Mr. Manbert stated that he found general stocks of lumber very low. Ordinary packing boxes were used for making furniture—not the kind that the good housewife covers over with drapery, but regular household articles which were painted. There were only a few thousand feet of Ontario white pine on hand and for everything that dealers had the demand was most urgent.

Touching upon the seriousness of port congestion the speaker said that it was desperate and in London vessels waited as long as two weeks in order to get a berth and even then there were inordinate delays in unloading stocks, owing to the extreme shortage of labor, lack of storage facilities, space accommodation, etc. The same state of affairs prevailed at Bristol, Manchester and other ports. So many handlings of cargoes impeded deliveries and naturally had their effect on the return use of wood. In speaking of the English methods of resawing spruce and pine deals some startling figures were presented, one instance being furnished where it had cost a firm $25.90 per M. to resaw three inch deals into inch stock, and dress it on four sides. Thirteen to fourteen shillings a day was being paid for common labor, which was not any too efficient and eight hours constituted a day's work. When questioned regarding this heavy outlay of converting deals into the finished product the reply was forthcoming from one operator, the less we do the higher the price of working and the higher the price of working the less we do.

In turned goods, joinery, box shooks, etc., which he had referred to in his reports, Mr. Manbert said there was a great and growing opportunity if Canada was prepared to enter largely in this line, and the interest in our own local market did not make us unmindful of the openings existing over there. "The keen interest and anxiety of every one to talk to me was the basis of a lot of inquiries regarding Canada, and in me getting and giving much general information," continued the speaker, "I endeavored in all my interviews and investigations in connection with propaganda work to make perfectly clear the conditions under which I was sent over by the lumber manufacturers and the province of Ontario. I informed them frankly that I was not there to infringe but to bring back intelligent word to the people here of how we could, as far as possible, meet British requirements in the supply of, and demand for, forest products. The nature of my mission was, I believe, thoroughly understood and appreciated. I sought to impress upon importers and consumers that our timber was different from their home-grown product, and that we had not a sufficient supply to produce it all in eleven inch deals, and that, by insisting in having it that width the available quantity would be greatly reduced, and by shutting out the six, eight and ten inch widths they were penalizing themselves. I found that there was a growing impression in the trade that it was not absolutely necessary to have deals in all the wider widths and informed them that it was advisable in the general scheme of things to take sizes which are provided in other markets for our forest products."

"Some merchants informed me that it was largely a lack of mutual understanding and that the changes brought about by the war and other contributing factors would tend to make them amenable to new conditions. The absence of entire confidence in our manufacturing methods is, I am firmly convinced, due to want of information, and remoteness from the points of supply makes it difficult for the British buyer to give close study to the situation. One man told me that he could use lumber for the making of patterns of greater thickness than he had been doing. Certain routines have been established in the past and the natural and inevitable way has been to travel in that direction. I had many inquiries from all classes of people regarding Canada and the conditions under which we operate here in producing lumber. Many wished to learn how to form closer connections with the industry in the Dominion, how they could get good substantial lines, etc., and it was my business to tell them that I posibly could and give all the information desired."

Work Can Go So Far and No Farther

Mr. Manbert said that it might be asked why he had returned at this particular juncture. Aside from the mark-time period through which the Old Country was passing and that a position had been reached where the recuperative processes in industrial and national life were generally working themselves out to a stable and normal state of things, there was a limit to which propaganda work could be carried. It must be linked to something concrete to give it life and action, as people after all were most vitally interested in the man who delivered the goods. A propaganda campaign could not of itself endure without something to keep it vitalized and visualized. It must be connected up with a selling programme and tangible results follow. Then interest at home was not as alert in the export situation as some months ago, owing to numerous requisitions for our lumber across the border and by reason of building activity and other local demands.

In closing, Mr. Manbert paid a warm tribute to the efficiency and courtesy of the officials of the Ontario Government office in England and the many kindnesses and assistance he had received from the staff. He thought the people of the banner province of the Dominion should feel proud of the representative which they had in the Agent-General of Ontario, and suggested that larger and more commodious quarters and better equipment—quite apart from the timber business altogether—might well be provided for by the provincial administration.

With respect to future developments in our forests products and how rapidly expansion would ensue in this direction he could not foretell. Owing to the complex industrial and economic situation overseas, with its many currents and cross-currents, any one who would prophesy would be either a mountebank or an idiot. There was bound to be a great demand but just when that would eventuate it was not easy to say. Turning over the page from war conditions to a peace basis was not a simple, easy problem, as many had imagined. It would require time, patience and perseverance, and if results were not as promising and achievements as prompt as had been predicted, it was due, in no small measure, to the fact that our expectations had been too great and our hopes too ardently conceived.

Prince of Wales Visits Sawmill

On the occasion of his recent visit to the Pacific Coast His Royal Highness the Prince of Wales was enthusiastically received. The prince paid a visit to the Hastings saw mill of the British-Columbia Mills Timber and Trading Co., Vancouver, and took much interest in the conversion of B. C. giant trees into lumber. The entrances and the mill offices were all draped in bunting and decked with evergreens, while His Royal Highness had the pleasure of entering the mill premises under a beautiful arch of forest greenery, with the words emblazoned above: "Welcome to the Hastings Sawmills. Established 1865."

Shortly before noon the prince arrived, accompanied by members of his staff, and though little notice had been given of the exact time of his arrival a large crowd gathered along Dunlevy Avenue leading from Hastings Street down to the mill. Among other visitors on hand was the Hon. Martin Burrell. The Prince on alighting from his auto was welcomed by Mr. Eric W. Hamber, Mr. Arthur Hendry and Mr. Alex. Hendry, who showed him around the mill.

His Royal Highness was initiated by his guides into the whole process by which a huge and shaggy log is converted into an orderly pile of lumber. In the booming ground of the mill he was shown three logs lying on end varying from 74 to 92 inches in diameter. Then the boom men guided a big stick to the dogged chain of the log slip that dragged it up into the mill. Three huge iron cants worked automatically grasped it with human precision and rolled it into place. At the touch of a lever the carriage on which it rested rolled it into the revolving saws and huge planks were sliced off as one would cut off a piece of cheese.

An instance of the thoughfulness of the mill officials was shown in the tastefully arranged programmes of the visit, which were distributed as souvenirs among the visitors. In addition to this, as a closing touch, Mr. Hamber presented His Royal Highness with a series of photographs bound in a volume and representing a log in the whole process of its manufacture into lumber. The prince acknowledged the gift gracefully, and then, led by Mr. Hamber, all present united in three cheers and a "tiger," the mill hands joining not less heartily than the rest.

Big Forestry Campaign in Britain

That England, with an area of less than the State of New York, is planning to invest $17,000,000 in a ten-year campaign to reforest 250,000 acres of land, inspires Dean Hugh P. Baker, of the New York State College of Forestry, at Syracuse, to comment on the need in New York State of particularly noting England's condition and her plans. Great Britain will replace for future commercial use the timber used in France during the war by this expenditure of many millions, while, Dean Baker points out, New York has difficulty even in putting through a plan of co-operation with lumbermen and other private holders for steps toward the growth of timber for the future. He sees in all this a need for a definite forest policy for his state as well as for the nation.

Spruce Mill Plant Busy at Seal Cove

Active Demand for High Class Factory and General Purpose Spruce of Progressive Organization

One of the most complete and modern sawmills is that erected at Seal Cove, B.C., which is operated by the Prince Rupert Spruce Mills, Limited. This company is aggressive and alert and has a large force of men engaged in the industry. The men behind the enterprise are all practical and thoroughly experienced in lumbering operations. The president of the Prince Rupert Spruce Mills is A. E. Munn, who will be remembered by many old friends in Ontario, particularly in the Georgian Bay district, where he was interested for a number of years in sawmilling and logging. The vice-president is N. S. Lougheed of Abernethy & Lougheed, while the general manager and treasurer is A. A. Ewart of Dempsey-Ewart, Limited, Drury Inlet, B.C.

The mill at Seale Cove was built by J. S. Emerson of Vancouver, under the management of E. F. Duby, now of Portland, Oregon, and the plant was leased to the present company some time ago. In 1918 the mill was operated for six months under a contract for the Imperial Munitions Board for the recovery of aeroplane stock. The present output of the plant is 100,000 ft. per day in rough lumber, and in manufactured lumber about 50,000 ft. The principal product is band sawed Queen Charlotte Sitka spruce, while the company specialize in clear, rough spruce and aeroplane spruce.

The incorporators of the Spruce Mills Company had each carried on logging contracts with the Imperial Munitions Board and their camps at Skidegate Inlet and Cumshewa Inlet in the Queen Charlotte Islands contributed largely to the input of spruce logs for the British government. When the war suddenly terminated there were many million of feet of these logs on hand. The operators are now converting these overplus spruce logs into a product that is meeting with a ready sale in the present active market, much of which is finding favor in the east. The company have supplied a large quantity of lumber for the new dry dock which is under construction in Prince Rupert. Mr. Ewart, the general manager of the mill, has taken up his residence in Prince Rupert. The superintendent of the plant is David Lougheed, and the assistant superintendent, A. H. Gee, and both are well qualified for their respective positions. It is understood that the company have in view plans for extensions in the shape of the erection of a second storage or dry shed of the capacity of the present one—2,500,000 feet—and a finished lumber factory. The material is all on the ground, ready for these additions.

With an unlimited supply of the best kind of virgin spruce near at hand, the ample log storage, the splendid mechanical facilities for manufacturing, handling and shipping direct by rail or water, having the sea in front and the G.P.T. railway in the rear, the Prince Rupert Spruce Mills have entered upon a successful career.

Port Congestions Hold Up English Imports

An interesting report on conditions in the British timber market has been issued by Alfred Dobell & Co., of Liverpool, who state: The arrivals of New Brunswick and Nova Scotia spruce deals were again light, but stocks have increased as deliveries have been delayed by difficulties at the ports of discharge. The demand continues satisfactory. There has been very little change in the position of Douglas fir since our last report. A considerable increase is reported in f.o.b. values. In Scandinavian deals, boards, etc., the arrivals of flooring boards were moderate and insufficient to keep pace with the consumption. Values are very firm. Deals arrived in fair quantities, but port congestion has held up deliveries. In pitch pine forward business has been quiet. C.i.f. quotations remain very firm, and there has been a further advance in f.o.b. values. Several steamers with cargoes, consisting largely of pitch pine, have arrived, but owing to port congestion it will be some time before discharging berths can be allocated, thus holding up deliveries.

The position in American hardwoods has not materially altered since our last report. Consignment parcels are still arriving freely, with the result that stocks are accumulating, and forward business, in view of the unsettled conditions, is difficult to arrange.

New Lumber Company Will Build Mill

Lumber and Pulpwood of British Columbia, Ltd., with a capital stock of $1,000,000, headquarters in Toronto, has been incorporated to manufacture, buy, sell, import, export and deal in timber, lumber, wood, pulpwood, fibreboard, pulpboard, etc. The organization is also empowered to buy, sell and develop timber limits. It is understood that Ontario capital is largely interested in the new concern which owns 49 square miles of timber limits near Fort George, B. C. It is the intention of the company to develop these limits and erect a sawmill on the property in the near future. The timber consists principally of spruce and the capacity of the contemplated mill will be 100.000 ft. a day.

Davis Rafts of Munition Spruce

The first Davis rafts of cut lumber that entered Vancouver harbor were recently at the government wharf awaiting shipment east. The tugboat Coutli made the long haul from Masset Inlet to Vancouver without incident. There are 2,500,000 feet in the two big rafts, which draw fourteen feet. This lumber was cut at the Masset Timber Company mills at Buckley, on Masset Inlet. It consists entirely of spruce lumber, part of the production of the war-time airplane spruce campaign. The Masset Company bought it from the Imperial Munitions Board.

Splendid view of the well-equipped Prince Rupert Spruce Mills at Seal Cove, B.C., which specialize in band-sawed Sitka Spruce

Present Value of a "Lumber Dollar"

As Compared With Other Building Materials, The Increase in Lumber Has Been Modest

At a most successful gathering of the Northern Lumbermen Salesmanship Congress held in Antigo, Wis., a stirring and timely address on "The Value of a Lumber Dollar" was given by Dr. Wilson Compton, secy.-manager of the National Lumber Manufacturers' Association. The lumber price level may sag sometimes in the future but it is unlikely that it will drop declared Dr. Compton who said:

Roughly speaking the prices of lumber today are twice as high as they were before the war. This means that the purchasing power of each dollar spent for lumber is only half its former purchasing power. There are several reasons for this. Some are relatively permanent and basic; others are superficial and temporary. In looking to the future of the lumber market we should especially give heed to the fundamental conditions. The superficial causes of present prices may quickly vanish.

At the signing of the armistice last November hemlock prices at the mill were 66 per cent. higher than they had been during the twelve months before the outbreak of the war; southern pine prices 85 per cent. higher; Douglas fir 93 per cent; and the average price for all softwoods 75 per cent. Among the hardwoods plain oak was 38 per cent. higher; hard maple 46 per cent; birch 58 per cent; poplar 61 per cent; basswood 69 per cent, and all lumber taken together, both hardwood and softwood, 65 per cent. higher than during the twelve months ended June 30, 1914.

As against the 65 per cent. increase in lumber prices were increases in average prices of other building materials of 94 per cent., including sand and gravel which had increased 91 per cent., lime 95 per cent, cement 73 per cent. common brick 105 per cent., steel 129 per cent. and building tile 108 per cent. During the same period anthracite coal prices had increased 88 per cent., bituminous coal 111 per cent., coke 188 per cent. and fuel oil 92 per cent.

Obviously the increase in lumber prices during this period was modest in comparison with the increases in prices of other commodities with which lumber usually competes.

But let us carry the comparison back over a longer and more representative period. The year immediately prior to the outbreak of the war in 1914 was one of rather unusual depression in the lumber industry and in some other industries also. To use that period therefore as a standard of comparison does not show the whole truth. During that period lumber prices generally were substantially lower than they had been eight years before, namely, in 1906 and 1907.

The year 1906 and the first nine months of 1907 were generally prosperous ones for industry, commerce and agriculture in this country. Let us therefore use the prices of that period as a standard of comparison of lumber prices with the prices of other commodities. Between the first nine months of 1907 and the time of the signing of the armistice in 1918, a span of nearly twelve years, the net increase in average prices of lumber, including all major hardwoods and softwoods, was 56 per cent.

During this period of nearly twelve years prices of hemlock increased 60 per cent., of southern yellow pine 61 per cent., of plain oak 74 per cent., of Douglas fir 41 per cent. as compared with the net average for all lumber, of 56 per cent. During the same period the prices of Portland cement increased 71 per cent., of common brick 98 per cent., of lime 115 per cent., of bituminous coal 119 per cent., of anthracite coal 101 per cent., of coke 123 per cent., of fuel oil 151 per cent.

As compared with the advances in prices of these other building materials and fuels picked at random the 56 per cent. increase in lumber during the 12-year period ending with the signing of the armistice was exceedingly modest. Certain it is that the dollar had at the end of the period a greater relative purchasing power over lumber than it had over any of the other groups of necessaries, foods, fuels and other building materials.

France Will Have Many New Forests

Except in the Vosges and the Pyrenees the forests of France were carefully guarded. Each big woodland was named "foret," each little grove was a designated "bois." The State was careful that these fragments of woodland be not destroyed. Humble people gathered firewood from the ground, but the trees were not cut.

It has been held by military experts that the "forests" and "bois" of northern France won the war for democracy. In the final rush of the Germans toward Paris the woodlands were the points of vantage which the defenders most stubbornly held and which the aggressors most diligently sought to capture. It was in the Belleau Woods that American valor first made itself vitally felt as a determining factor in the world war. It was in St. Gobain forest that the Germans made their most determined effort to check the tide of the allies' advance, and it was in the great forest of the Argonne that the German retreat was most stubbornly contested by the beaten enemy of civilization.

Now many of the forests of northern France are a memory. Where the war swept, the forests vanished. Worse than this, the French willingly sacrificed the far greater forests of the Vosges and the Pyrenees and the great pine groves of the southern coast. Wood was a great necessity for the winning of the war, and France gladly accepted the services of experienced Canadian and American foresters who comprised special forestry regiments, and whose sole duty was to transform French forests into war material. Though these regiments seldom came within range of German bullets, they did an important work.

Now France is confronted with the problem of reforestation. And she is going about the work in the characteristic systematic French manner. When it was a question of a war to be won the French gave their lives and fortunes without question and without repining. Now that the war has been won they are displaying the same spirit in the work of repairing war's ravages. Wherever there was a forest before the war there is to be a new forest. The French may be mercurial and effervescent, but when it comes to a matter of the motherland's welfare there is no more practical people on the surface of the earth.

Mr. Hebard is Appointed Inspector

H. L. Hebard has been appointed inspector for Toronto and district for the National Hardwood Lumber Association, whose headquarters are in Chicago. Mr. Hebard succeeds John J. Miller, who is now identified with the C. G. Anderson Lumber Co. Mr. Hebard has been in the employ of the N. H. L. A. for a number of years, leaving in 1917 to serve the Government during the war and immediately on his discharge he was re-engaged by the Association. He has had experience that will enable him to handle the Toronto district in a satisfactory manner and the officers of the National Hardwood Lumber Association say they consider themselves quite fortunate in being able to secure so competent a man without delay.

B. C. Fir Makes Tallest Flag Pole

British Columbia's gift, the mammoth flag mast, is now in Kew Gardens and is the tallest flag pole in Europe. The huge pole reached England four years ago and its size has delayed its speedy erection, for it was no easy matter to lift a spar of the length of 250 feet. The spar, which replaces the present flag staff at Kew Gardens, London, which was also from British Columbia, is the finest sample of Douglas fir that the B. C. Forestry department could find. Their best men roamed the forest slopes of the Pacific for a long time, and twelve giants were felled to find this particular spar. Some of the twelve were fully 250 feet high, but a slight warp or defect condemned all except this one, which is a perfect spar 220 feet high.

Mr. Meyer Organizes New Company

The many friends of Montague L. Meyer, British timber purchaser, who visited Canada some months ago in company with Sir James Ball, British Timber Controller, will be interested in learning that he has formed a new company in London, Eng. Montague L. Meyer, Limited, has been registered as a private company, with a capital stock of £100,000, to take over the business of timber merchants, carried on formerly under the style of Montague L. Meyer. The offices of the company are at Pelmerston House, London, E. C.

Find Shortage of Help in North

Austin & Nicholson, of Chapleau, stated that they are operating approximately the same number of camps this year as last. Up to the present men have been more plentiful, although during the last month there was a definite shortage of labor, which the firm believe will improve when the saw-mills close down. Camp supplies are on the average about 10 per cent. to 15 per cent. more costly than last year. Austin & Nicholson are not taking out any pulpwood at all this season.

Wall Board Men Take Pulp Plant

The Niagara Wall Board Co., Inc., Buffalo, N.Y., have acquired the pulp mill of the Moore Paper Co. at Penn Yan, N.Y. By acquiring this mill the Niagara Company, which was recently organized by Buffalo men who have grown up with the wallboard industry, control their own supply of semi-manufactured fibre used in the production of wall board. In addition to the pulp plant a factory building has been acquired a short distance from the mill for a finishing plant. By locating both plants in the same city a practical arrangement has been effected. The president of the company is J. B. O'Brien, and C. C. Hullinger is secretary-treasurer.

MORE LUMBERMEN CANDIDATES IN THE ONTARIO CONTEST

R. E. Butler, Woodstock, Ont., who is Conservative Standard Bearer in North Oxford

Zotique Mageau, Sturgeon Falls, Late Representative, who is again running in Liberal Interests

James G. Cane, Toronto, Liberal Standard Bearer, who is Candidate in Northwest Toronto

Good Luck to the "Boys of the Bush"

James G. Cane, of Jas. G. Cane and Co., wholesale lumber merchants, Toronto, has been nominated by the Liberals of Northwest Toronto as their candidate for seat "B" in the Ontario provincial elections. His running mate is Lieut.-Col. H. S. Cooper, M.C. Mr. Cane is putting up a vigorous campaign.

Zotique Mageau, who has represented the riding of Sturgeon Falls in the Ontario Legislature in the Liberal interests since 1911, has again been nominated as the standard bearer of the party in the forthcoming provincial elections. Mr. Mageau is a well known lumberman.

R. E. Butler, head of the R. E. Butler Lumber Co., Woodstock, Ont., has been unanimously nominated by the Conservatives of North Oxford as their standard-bearer in the coming provincial elections. In accepting, he stated that as he contested the riding on four different occasions, he had about decided to make way for someone else. He had, however, been approached by so many electors from different parts that he had consented to allow his name to go before the convention.

Senators Visit Mills and Nurseries

At the invitation of Senator Smeaton White, of Montreal, several members of the Senate have visited Shawinigan and Grand Mere, P. Q., for the purpose of inspecting the industries of those places. The party was met on their arrival at Shawinigan Falls from Ottawa by Mr. H. Biermans, general manager of the Belgo Canadian Pulp & Paper Co., Ltd., and afterwards visited the mills of that company, in addition to inspecting the plants of the Shawinigan Water & Power Co. and allied concerns. At a luncheon Mr. Biermans took occasion to refer to the action of the Government in fixing the price of paper, which he considered was detrimental to business interests.

Dinner at the Laurentide Inn, Grand Mere, with Mr. George Chahoon, Jr., president, provided an opportunity for many of the senators in short speeches to express to him their appreciation of the national work he and his company were performing in welding into one harmonious whole a community of working people free from labor troubles. In this fact alone it provided an object lesson for the rest of the Dominion. The company's policy of re-afforestation was also highly commended, and the support of the visiting senators pledged to such a work.

In reply, Mr. Chahoon briefly sketched the history of his company for the last seventeen years, and modestly disclaimed any credit for the position the company now occupied in the manufacturing world or for the model living conditions of the town of Grand Mere. He admitted, however, that the ideal relations existing between its employees were in a great measure responsible for the prosperity of the company. He dwelt at considerable length upon the necessity of a reafforestation policy for the whole Dominion, pointing out the grave position that the United States now finds itself in, owing to the depletion of its forests. His own company had entered into an extensive scheme of reafforestation, and would plant 2,000,000 trees next year, but he felt that the Government should compel timber operators to plant one tree for every one cut down, and the Provincial Government should at the same time co-operate in the way of exemption of taxation for such lands as were being replanted.

Mr. Guy Tombs, traffic manager of the Canadian Export Paper Co., Mr. L. Armstrong, secretary-treasurer of the Laurentide Co., and Mr. F. A. Sabbaton also made short speeches.

Activity in Lumbering is General

Reviewing general conditions in the lumber arena the Labor Gazette, of Ottawa, in its last issue, says: Westville reported that lumbering operations showed a further slight decline. Charlottetown reported quietness. The saw and shingle mills at St. John were operating steadily. Fredericton reported that the lumber mills and booms were very busy and that preparations were being made for the season's operations in the woods. Quebec reported the sawmills of the district still working at full capacity except in a few cases where the last season's cut was limited through failure to obtain men and through the epidemic. The saw and shingle mills at Sherbrooke were well employed. The sawmills at Ottawa and Hull were rather busy. Peterborough reported quietness. Owen Sound reported that the sawmills continued to be active. Sault Ste. Marie reported that the lumber yards were very active and that lumbermen were experiencing difficulty in securing the right class of men for their operations. Calgary reported that men were being sought for the lumber camps and sawmills. Following the severe bush fires in July, Fernie reported further fires in August which resulted in a serious curtailment in the amount of logs taken out, so that in some instances mills were forced to close down, while others operated only at limited capacity. Despite this, however, lumbermen in nearly all cases were actively engaged in making preparations for logging operations on a very large scale. Vancouver reported the saw and shingle mills busy. Victoria reported the lumber trade very active on foreign shipments.

Death of Public Spirited Lumberman

In speaking of the death of Daniel E. Richards, which was referred to in the last issue of the "Canada Lumberman," the press of his native town, Campbellton, N.B., pays the departed lumberman and captain of industry a well merited tribute. "The Graphic" says:

Deceased, who was 52 years of age, was the eldest son of the late Mr. and Mrs. David Richards, and was born here. Early in his life he went into the lumber business with his father, and to his careful study of that business is no doubt due the great success of the various enterprises with which he was connected. He was president of the following companies: Richards Manufacturing Co. Ltd., Continental Lumber Co., Restigouche Lumber Co., Restigouche Log Driving & Boom Co., Tobique Lumber Co.

He always took a deep interest in the welfare of Campbellton and for a number of years represented Ward [illegible] on the council board. The various enterprises with which he was connected contributed much to the prosperity of Campbellton.

Logging Operations and Legal Decision

The Quebec Compensation law applies to lumbering in connection with a mill. An interesting legal decision was rendered recently in Quebec in the case of Perron vs. Veillette, and judgment was given in favor of the plaintiff for $370. The particulars of the suit are as follows:

An axeman employed at a lumber shanty was severely hurt by a fellow workman through being struck on the foot by his axe. He brought action against his employer under the Workmen's Compensation Act of Quebec, claiming $162.50 for temporary incapacity, estimated at 10 per cent. The defendant, who was under contract as a jobber to cut wood for the Belgo-Canadian Pulp and Paper Company from its own timber limits, claimed that the nature of this work was agricultural, not industrial, and, consequently, the law did not apply. The defendant proved that he was a farmer and that, like all the farmers in that neighborhood, he cultivated his own land in the summer and in the winter took small contracts for cutting wood. The law of France, upon which the Quebec law was based, and which declares that forestry operations are agricultural, was also quoted in support of his contention.

It was held by the Court, in accordance with a recent judgment of the Court of Appeal, that lumbering operations carried on in connection with a particular mill cannot be separated from the actual work of the mill and are therefore industrial. It was further held that it made no difference whether the lumbering was carried on directly by the industrial company operating with the company. Neither did the fact that the defendant was a farmer make all the work performed by him agricultural. The Court, therefore, ruled that the law of industrial accidents applied to this case and judgment was given in favor of the plaintiff for $370.

Finds Big Improvement in Camps

Rev. Thomas M. Joplin, field secretary of the Shantymen's Christian Association, is in Montreal on his annual visit. He represents an association that works in the lumber camps of Canada from the Atlantic to the Pacific. Its eleven missionaries visited some two hundred and seventy camps in the year that ended March 31 last, and addressed over 13,000 men. Dog trains and sledges were requisitioned to carry the missionaries to some of the remote spots where the camps were situated. In the past year the Shantymen's Christian Association has extended its activities to British Columbia.

Mr. Joplin reports that conditions in the shanties in British Columbia are by no means as crude as they were ten years ago. Bunk houses are well lighted and heated and fitted with iron beds. Running water and shower baths are provided and a large reading room is included in the camp. Excellent food is provided. The men work eight hours a day for $90 a month and up, and the work is far less difficult than it formerly was, all the heavy lifting being done by donkey engines.

According to Mr. Joplin there is a Bolshevik element among the foreign-born lumbermen, which the missionaries have been able to fight successfully. "In the present condition of unrest one good missionary makes more for the safety of the country than a regiment of soldiers," is a statement of William Henderson, of Toronto, superintendent of the Shantymen's Christian Association.

Mr. Joplin is spending a month in Montreal and will endeavor to raise the sum of $5,000, which the executive of the Association has decided is Montreal's share towards the work. Mr. Joplin hopes to obtain French-speaking workers in Montreal in the interest of the work which is undenominational in character.

Preventing Track Creeping on Grades

On the logging railroads of the Smith-Powers Logging Co. we have in the past tried various methods for preventing rails from running or "creeping." We have tried tying them down with cable, putting in switch points and letting the rail run, and various other schemes.

The best results we have obtained have been by placing a heavy piece of timber under the rails as a "dead man," preferably a timber 8 x 16 inches, and 10 to 16 feet long, which offers a 16-inch bearing surface for the rail. This timber is firmly embedded and tamped tightly to the rail with proper grade and is secured by bracing it from the banks, or anchoring it in rock or concrete bed.

If it is on a bridge we bolt the "dead man" through the stringers with machine bolts. We then slot each rail three times on each side with slots large enough to fit a track spike. These slots are cut about three inches apart and the spikes driven into them just as into an ordinary tie.

The number of "dead men" necessary, we find, varies according to the grade, amount of traffic, weight of steel and condition of the road bed. On some of our 6 per cent. grades we place these timbers every few hundred feet and we have found them quite successful in holding our tracks in place.

It has been suggested that I say something about our method of shooting the tops off high lead trees. We shoot them at a height where the diameter of the tree is from 20 to 24 inches, providing the tree is sound and reasonably straight. The most successful way in which we have been doing this is to cut in a square notch, on the leaning side of the tree, to a depth of six to 10 inches. The height of the notch will average about the same. We use on an average 22 stocks of 20 per cent. stumping powder and tamp it in with about two gallons of wet clay. We take the powder out of the sticks so as to make a paste of it, put the cap in the middle of the charge and use about 12 feet of fuse.

We hang a strap and climber's block two feet below the notch in which the powder is placed. Sometimes we attach a light rope or a piece of whistle wire to the lower end of the fuse, running from there to the ground. This is an extra safety precaution so that in case the climber has trouble in getting down the tree the cap can be pulled out of the charge from the ground.

We use a single three-quarter-inch manila rope, or a 3/8-6/19 steel cable, which is preferable for hoisting rigging to the top of the tree. We leave this line in the tree so as to use it for raising the men to oil the block after the tree is rigged. When there is a wind blowing, or when a tree top has considerable lean to it, our climbers invariably prefer to shoot the tops rather than to cut them off. On calm days and with straight standing trees the usual way is to chop off the tops with an axe.

Another thing we are doing is using large clevises on the end of the main line for the high lead yarders. The advantage over the old style rigging plate is that two tag lines can be hung to it and several smaller clevices dispensed with. This has a particular advantage in small logs, enabling a yarder to handle several of them rather than one, as is only possible with the single tag line method.

We have a hole punched in the side of this clevise and a light link and a swivel put in for the trip line. This clevise is never used for ground haul, or in pulling through a tommey, as it is too cumbersome. It is only adaptable to the high lead.—By Fred W. Powers, superintendent of Smith-Powers Logging Co., of Powers, Ore., delivered at the tenth session of the Pacific Logging Congress at Portland, Ore., Oct. 8 to 11.

Missing Bushmen Returned

The three bushmen reported lost for the past ten days in the Stockpool district reported at Biscotasing safe and sound. They were out for ten days without shelter of any kind, and subsisted on berries and boughs. Their only regret is that the fourteen men who have been searching so industriously for them since their disappearance had to suffer the hardships of a hard and fruitless hunt.

Archambault, an experienced bushman, found that his party had travelled farther than expected the first day out, and as they were in virgin bush he lost his bearings. He landed at Biscotasing Lake the following day, and by following the chain of lakes came out on the C. P. R. Instead of attempting to retrace his steps, he came through the bush to the lumber office at Stockpool.

They travelled more than seventy miles, and incidentally cruised a large timber area.

The Why? of Another Victory Loan

WHEN, on the morning of November 11th, 1918, the guns were hushed and glad tidings flashed across the world, there followed with the Nation's Prayer of Thanksgiving, one yearning query, which found echo in the faster beating hearts of wives, mothers, fathers, brothers, sisters and sweethearts. That query was "How soon will our boys be home?" And from France and Flanders, from Italy and Egypt, from Palestine and from far-off Siberia, there came an answering echo, "How soon, how soon, may we go home?"

CANADA caught the spirit of these longings, and at once resolved to satisfy them. It was an appalling task. Shipping was tragically scarce. The composition of the Army of Occupation had not then been settled. And other parts of the Empire as well as Canada were looking for the speedy return of their men.

THE problem was this. The half-million men that Canada had overseas had taken more than four years to transport to the field of battle. To bring them home in a few months was a gigantic undertaking—one to tax all Canada's ingenuity and resources. Canada solved the problem, but it meant crowding into a few short months, an expense for demobilization which it was impossible to foresee.

THEN, too, besides the sentimental aspect of the necessity for bringing the men home quickly the economic side could not be overlooked. That was, to transform efficiently and speedily the nation's army of fighters into a national army of workers.

* * *

Need Divides Itself in Two Parts The answer to the question "Why does Canada need another Victory Loan?" divides itself into two parts. (a) To finish paying the expenses of demobilization, and the obligations we still owe to our soldiers. (b) To provide national working capital.

Obligations to Soldiers The obligations to soldiers include:
That already incurred cost of bringing home troops from overseas.
The payment of all soldiers still undemobilized. This includes more than 20,000 sick and wounded who are still in hospital, and who of course remain on the Army payroll till discharged.
The upkeep of hospitals, and their medical and nursing staffs, until the need for them is ended.
These three items alone will use up at least $200,000,000 of the Victory Loan 1919.

Gratuities There is also the gratuity which has been authorized, and has been and is being paid to assist soldiers to tide over the period between discharge and their re-adjustment to civil life. For this purpose alone, $61,000,000 must be provided out of the Victory Loan 1919, in addition to the $59,000,000 already paid out of the proceeds of the Victory Loan 1918.

Land Settlement Furthermore, soldiers who desire to become farmers may, under the Soldiers' Land Settlement Act, be loaned money by Canada with which to purchase land, stock and implements. The money so advanced will be paid back; meantime each loan is secured by a first mortgage. Up to August 15th, 29,495 soldiers had applied for land under the terms of this Act; and 22,281 applications had been investigated, and the qualifications of the applicant approved. For this purpose Canada this year requires $24,000,000.

Vocational Training For this work which, with the Vocational Training and Soldiers' Service Departments, embraces the major activities of the Department of Soldiers' Civil Re-establishment, an appropriation of $57,000,000 is necessary.

These national expenditures are war expenses. They will be accepted readily by every citizen who gives thought to the task which Canada faced following the Armistice, and to the success with which she has met it.

National Working Capital Canada needs national working capital, so that she may be able to sell on credit to Great Britain and our Allies the products of our farms, forests, fisheries, mines and factories.

You may ask "Why sell to them if they can't pay Cash?" The answer is, "Their orders are absolutely essential to the continuance of our agricultural and industrial prosperity."

The magnitude of these orders and the amount of employment thus created, will depend upon the success of the Victory Loan 1919.

The "Why" of Credit Loans Farmers and manufacturers (and that includes the workers on these orders) must be paid cash for their products. Therefore, Canada must borrow money from her citizens to give credit, temporarily, to Great Britain and our Allies. Actually, no money will pass out of Canada. If Canada does not give credit, other countries will; and they will get the trade, and have the employment that should be ours, to distribute amongst their workers. And remember, we absolutely need these orders to maintain employment. If we don't finance them business will feel the depression, employment will not be as plentiful, and conditions everywhere will be adversely affected.

For Transportation Money must also be available to carry on the nation's shipbuilding programme, and other transportation development work.

For loans to Provincial Housing Commissions who are building moderate priced houses.

These, then, are some of the things for which Canada needs national working capital. She is in the position of a great trading company, and her citizens who buy Victory Bonds are the shareholders.

Those who give thought to our outstanding obligations to soldiers, and to our need for national working capital, cannot fail to be impressed with the absolute necessity for the

Victory Loan 1919

"Every Dollar Spent in Canada"

Issued by Canada's Victory Loan Committee
in co-operation with the Minister of Finance
of the Dominion of Canada.

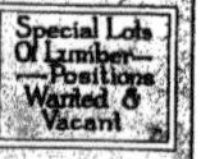

PUBLISHER'S NOTICE

Advertisements other than "Employment Wanted" or "Employees Wanted" will be inserted in this department at the rate of 20 cents per agate line (14 agate lines make one inch). $2.80 per inch, each insertion, payable in advance. Space measured from rule to rule. When four or more consecutive insertions of the same advertisement are ordered a discount of 25 per cent. will be allowed.

Advertisements of "Wanted Employment" will be inserted at the rate of one cent a word, net. Cash must accompany order. If Canada Lumberman box number is used, enclose ten cents extra for postage in forwarding replies. Minimum charge 25 cents.

Advertisements of "Wanted Employees" will be inserted at the rate of two cents a word, net. Cash must accompany the order. Minimum charge 50 cents.

Advertisements must be received not later than the 10th and 20th of each month to insure insertion in the subsequent issue.

Wanted—Lumber

Basswood Wanted

No. 2 Common and Mill Cull. Winter cut preferred. Apply Firstbrook Brothers, Ltd., Toronto, Ont. 8-t.f.

Wanted Lumber

Hardwood Lumber wanted. Birch, Maple, Basswood and other Hardwoods. Dry or sawn to order. We send inspector. Box 14, Canada Lumberman, Toronto. 17-20

Wanted for Cuban Trade White Pine

Send lists and prices at once to

E. ANTONIO VAZQUEZ,
44 Whitehall Street,
10-22 New York City.

Wanted To Buy LATH

We are in the market for large quantities of Lath; all grades, including No. 3 and 32". Paying good prices and cash on receipt of B.L.

What have you to offer? Send good description, lowest price F.O.B. Chicago, stating quantity offered.

COVEY DURHAM COMPANY,
431 S. Dearborn St.,
20-21 Chicago, Ill., U.S.A.

For Sale—Lumber

FOR SALE

50,000 feet 1" round edge Poplar.
25,000 feet 2" round edge Poplar.

Good, widths and lengths. This stock is well dried out and ready for immediate shipment. J. B. Brand, Bank of British North America Bldg., St. John, N.B. 19-20

FOR SALE Hickory Specials

100 M pcs. ¾" Dowels, 48" long.
20 M pcs. 1" Squares, 48" long.

Also some shorter stock. All high grade, second growth Hickory. Can ship immediately. Will sell cheap. Address Box 31, Canada Lumberman, Toronto. 19-20

For Sale—Machinery

For Sale

Portable mill of 40 h.p. edger, trimmers, butting saw and all machinery necessary for 12 M. feet daily, first class condition. Splendid site if wanted. Box 34, Canada Lumberman, Toronto. 19-20

For Sale

1—17 x 24 Atlas Engine, with 36 in. x 10 ft. flywheel.
3—No. 94 Berlin Matchers, 15 in., fitted with hard steel knives on top and bottom cylinders—one pair shiplap, jointer and flooring heads with bits for each machine.
1—No. 182 Berlin Double Surfacer, 30 in. x 6 in.
1—No. 199 Berlin Buzz Planer.
1—No. 290 Berlin Picket Header.

The Otis Staples Lumber Company, Ltd.,
19-t.f. Wycliffe, B.C.

FOR SALE

1 Steam Feed Carriage with Steam Set Works, "Waterous Model."
1 Nigger, complete, "Waterous Model."
1 Wicks Gang Saw, complete with saws and steam engine, "Midland," 60 H.P.
2 Shingle Machines, complete with saws.
11 Pulpwood Barkers.

For particulars apply to

CHICOUTIMI PULP CO.,
17-20 Chandler, Que.

Band Saw Mill Complete

Waterous 9 ft. Band Mill, Gunshot Feed Carriage, with extra Saws complete.

Filing Equipment

Three Saw Edger, lot of live rolls, Engine, Shafting, Hangers, Pulleys, etc.

All of the above is Waterous equipment in good condition at a bargain.

The Geo. F. Foss Machinery & Supply Co., Limited,
305 St. James Street,
17-t.f. Montreal, Que.

Wanted—Employment

Advertisements under this heading one cent a word per insertion. Box No. 10 cents extra. Minimum charge 25 cents.

LUMBERMAN, 30 years of age, having sold lumber throughout New York and New England States, wishes to represent a Canadian firm in the same territory, excellent recommendations. Box 30, Canada Lumberman, Toronto. 19-20

OFFICE POSITION WANTED in lumber company. Five years' practical experience. Pay Rolls, Specifications, Bookkeeping, etc., etc. Quebec province preferred. No objection to northern location. Box 39, "Canada Lumberman," Toronto. 20

WANTED POSITION by representative and superintendent, still employed with large wholesale firm, with twenty-five years' experience in the lumber business. Can give reference as to capabilities and take charge on a month's notice. Box 991, Canada Lumberman, Toronto. 19-20

WANTED OFFICE POSITION by Clerk with good experience in lumber office work, Bookkeeping, etc., general assistant to manager, or charge of small office. Preferably North Shore, or Gaspe coast in Quebec province. References from former employers. H., Box 41, Canada Lumberman, Toronto, 20

Wanted—Employees

YARD MAN WANTED for inspecting and looking after yard of hardwood lumber.

MERRITT & COMPANY,
tf Chatham, Ont.

POSITION OPEN for a high-class man capable of organizing and assuming full management of all lumbering operations of a 500 mile timber limit for a Company operating a Saw-mill and a Pulp-mill. All replies will be treated confidentially. A permanent position with a good salary open for the right man. Box 993, Canada Lumberman, Toronto. 16-21

WANTED—A number of experienced Hardwood Sawmill Operators to contract to take out large quantities of Hardwood during the coming winter. Stumpage can be furnished if necessary, and the necessary cash advances to assist responsible operators. Address Box 19, Canada Lumberman, Toronto. 17-20

YOUNG MAN, experienced bookkeeper and stenographer, wanted, that will invest some money in limited company. Experienced in sash and door factory, planing mill and lumber business. Must be capable of taking full charge of office, and keeping all office work up to date. Opening on board of directors and secretary-treasurer for man with right qualifications. Apply to Box 25, Canada Lumberman, Toronto. 18-tf

Business Chances

For Sale

1,280 ACRES OF TIMBER, estimated to cut 23,000 ft. per acre, $9,500. Box 654, Nelson, B.C. 10-22

For Sale

Building and machinery of good Double Cut Band Sawmill, well equipped with steam feed, canter, loaders, etc.

Also two storey Brick Factory on large lot convenient to two railways; splendid location. Address Box 949, Owen Sound, Ont. 12-t.f.

FOR SALE

On reasonable terms, a well established retail lumber business in a live and growing city, will be sold as a going concern, including central site, convenient to railway facilities. Apply Box 980, Sault Ste. Marie, Ont. 17-20

For Sale

One Detroit Hot Blast, Dry Kiln System, complete with Fan and Engine, also 35 feet of 9" double leather belt, used two weeks.

Port Hope Veneer & Lumber Co.,
13-t.f. Port Hope, Ont.

FOR SALE

1,000 acres standing hardwood timber. 8 miles from railroad. Good portable mill proposition (Deeded Land), $5.00 per 1,000 ft. For particulars write Box 214, Thessalon, Ont. 17-20

Timber Lands For Sale

in the Province of Quebec, on the South Shore of the St. Lawrence, on tide water. Freehold lands 85,000 acres, Crown lands 60,000 acres.

An up-to-date sawmill is built, having a capacity of 40,000 to 80,000 feet of sawn lumber and 100,000 to 125,000 shingles.

For further information apply to the River Ouelle Pulp & Lumber Company, St. Pacome, Que. 17-20

TIMBER LIMITS

I have a number of good Timber Limits for sale. Particulars, Wm. Cooke, State Building, Toronto. 20-t.f.

Saw Mill Plant For Sale

Practically new and modern Saw Mill Plant, capacity about 30 Million feet per annum, located in the Interior of British Columbia on a beautiful inland lake and on the main line of the Grand Trunk Pacific Railway. About 500 Million feet of timber on and adjacent to Lake (about 90% Spruce) and another Billion feet available at reasonable prices. Natural conditions ideal for economical logging, manufacturing, piling and shipping. An advantage of about $4 per thousand feet in freight rates to the Prairie Provinces over Coast shipments.

This property offers unlimited possibilities as a lumber, pulp and paper property. Would consider selling a half interest. Terms reasonable.

A. C. FROST COMPANY,
134 South LaSalle Street,
5-t.f. Chicago, Ill.

Sale of Valuable Timber Limits

Situated on Lake Keinawisick, Amadamika and Long Lake, tributaries to the Harricanaw River, in the County of Timiskaming, P.Q.:

Berth 676, S. ½ No. 16-4, Range Block A, 25 sq. m.; berth 677, No. 14-5, Range Block A, 17½ sq. m.; berth 678, S. ½ of N. ½ 16-4, Range Block A, 12½ sq. m.; berth 679, 16-3, Range Block A, 12 sq. m.; berth 680, 15-3, Range Block A, 15½ sq. m.; berth 681, S. ¾ 17-5, Range Block A, 25 sq. m.; berth 682, N. ½ 17-5, Range Block A, 25 sq. m.; berth 683, S.E. corner of S. ½ 15-4, Range Block A, 6¼ sq. m.; berth 996, N. ½ 17-4, Range Block A, 25 sq. m.

Tenders will be received at the office of the Company, Room 65, Banque Nationale Building, Ottawa, until November 1st, 1919, each tender to be accompanied by certified cheque for 10% of amount tendering.

20 LUMSDEN LUMBER CO., LIMITED.

Miscellaneous

Wanted 4-foot LATH

Charles H. Stewart,
691 Lothrop Avenue,
Detroit, Michigan
20-23

Car Wheels For Sale

125 pairs 18" chilled cast iron wheels, fitted to axles with roller bearing. Suitable for piling cars or tram line.

JNO. J. GARTSHORE,
58 Front Street W.,
20-21 Toronto, Ontario.

Perpetuating Supply of Pulpwood

Canada produces annually about $100,000,000 worth of pulp and paper products During the past ten years, especially, the industry has made rapid progress, until it is now one of the most important in the country. The three outstanding requisites for the maintenance of the industry are large accessible forest areas, particularly of spruce and balsam, adequate cheap power, preferably water-power, and a plentiful supply of labor. As to the two former, nature has been prodigal in her gifts to Canada. Water-power is not only abundant but is widely distributed. The virgin coniferous forests of Eastern Canada were of vast extent, and it is perhaps not entirely surprising that the early settlers and explorers considered them to be all but illimitable.

But, for at least thirty years, keen observers have foreseen the possibility and, indeed, the probability, of exhausting the natural supply of pulpwood. The rapid growth of the paper industry has brought the time within measurable distance. The larger producers of paper, particularly in Quebec and Northern Ontario, where the industry is mainly centred, have scented the danger and have taken initial steps to put the pulpwood forests on a permanent basis. It goes without saying that it is a great advantage to have an adequate supply of pulpwood forests at the "back door" of the mills. Consequently, extensive planting of cut-over lands has already been undertaken.

Not Sowing Seeds of Business

Are you sowing seeds of business? Or do you depend on a "volunteer" crop ?

What would you think of a farmer who, after harvesting a crop left the ground untilled on the theory that without any effort on his part he would get a good volunteer crop the following year ? asks the "Retail Lumberman."

You'd decide that he was a pretty shiftless fellow, wouldn't you ?

All right, then, how about your fields; the territory upon which you depend for your crop of orders? Are you tillng them, cultivating them, harvesting them continually, persistently, properly and profitably ?

In this connection we want to tell our readers about a little news item that appeared in one of the local papers published in a certain Western town. The item said: "Lumber prices continue to climb, according to contractors, who say there is no telling where the prices will stop. Ordinary dimension lumber is retailing from $55 to $60 per thousand feet. Shingles too, have taken a big jump."

We haven't investigated yet, but we'll bet a new fall hat against your laundry bill that the dealers in that town are NOT advertising in their local papers. We'll also bet that they have neglected to establish the proper personal relations with the publishers of those papers. Also, they have failed to tell their publishers just what is happening in all the lumber producing sections to cause lumber prices to advance, and it is very evident that they have not informed those papers as to the comparative advances in prices of other commodities which would, of course, show that the advances in lumber are still short of reaching the same percentage as in the case of other staples.

Those dealers have NOT sown the seeds of business diligently.

Trees as Every Day Environment

Trees not less than architecture determine the beauty of the city. Trees proved certain factors in the life of cities which, form the sanitary standpoint, are invaluable. For example, the Commissioner of Health of the City of New York some years ago investigated the cause of the high death rate in that city and found that the extreme heat was one of the main causes. It was, therefore, resolved that "one of the most effective means for mitigating the intense heat of the summer months and diminishing the death rate amongst children is the cultivation of an adequate number of trees in the streets." The 81,000 trees in the City of Paris are an example of what can be done when tree planting is undertaken by the city as a businesslike proposition.

The economic value of shade trees, both to the city and to the indivdual home, is also inestimable. A certain farm in Ontario possesed a fine avenue of pine trees leading to the house. For some reason these trees were cut down and it is vouched by first-hand authority that when the farm was sold a few years later its value had depreciated $5,000 owing to this one factor.

Trees, as one of Nature's finest products, which constitute an environment to our everyday life, are not appreciated as they should be. Remove the trees and place humanity under desert conditions and its life would be lowered in morale. It is reasonable to expect, therefore, that one of the ways many individuals will wish to commemorate the great war will be by planting trees. Fortunately the choice of suitable trees is large, but, owing to that very fact, sometimes trees of an unsuitable type are planted through ignorance.

Review of Current Trade Conditions

Ontario and the East

Generally speaking, business continues brisk and the whole outlook is favorable. Nearly every wholesale firm reports that buying has been proceeding freely on the part of the retail yardmen and there is a decided scarcity of stock in some lines, particularly in hemlock, which has been in most active requisition. Preparations are going on on the part of most of the larger firms to greatly increase their cut in the woods during the coming winter and the extent of operations will be determined by the amount of help available. Different reports come from various centres and it is interesting to note that, while men are plentiful in certain sections, there is a decided shortage in others. It is felt, however, that when the saw-mills close down a certain percentage of labor will be released for woods operation. A number of mills have finished their cut for this year and are looking forward to increased production during 1920. Other plants will be busy up till the end of the present month or until streams freeze up. The reports, that have been circulated in some newspapers to the effect that, owing to the high cost of production, the log cut this season would be smaller than usual, is misleading, as not a few concerns are doubling the number of their camps while others are materially increasing them. Building continues quite active in the various cities, but prices have again taken a jump which has caused a slight setback in certain quarters.

During the past month white pine doors have advanced 50c each and chestnut doors $1.00 each, while oak doors have ascended 20 per cent. It is the same with all other building materials, and flooring is "out of sight," as one saleman expresses it. The prevailing quotation on clear, quartered, 3/8 oak is now $225 per M, whereas not so long ago it was selling at $150 per M. Select No. 1 3/8 is now $165 and only a few weeks ago was $125. Clear plain red and white oak flooring is now $150 while selects bring $125. Birch, selected red, has jumped from $120 per M. and clears to $95. The only item of flooring in which no aviation has taken place is maple, which is not in as active demand as other lines of hardwoods. Recently white pine sash and window frames have gone up from 15 to 20 per cent., while there are similar advances in many other items. Hemlock is now selling at $52 per M. for plank, sized, and boards, dressed, 1 x 4 to 1 x 12, are up to $55. Spruce flooring, 1 x 4, strips, is quoted at $58, which is an advance of $4, and pine flooring, 1 x 4, is $68. Every other line shows a raise from $2 to $4 and in some instances more.

It would appear that the large builders defer action, the more their structural undertakings are going to cost. As to when the present ascending values will cease, this is largely a matter of conjecture and will be determined by the cut in the woods this winter, the relative cost of living, wages, export demand, etc.

Hardwoods of all kinds are in active demand, particularly birch and elm. Furniture factories, automobile concerns, gramophone plants and others are all doing a rushing business and increasing costs seem in no way to deter the number of inquiries coming to hand from every quarter. The people have money and are evidently determined to buy a good article in either the furniture or the musical instrument line. Quality is the watchword in most of the purchases.

In regard to British Columbia stocks, there is a fair demand at the present juncture, but some complaints are made regarding delayed shipments and car shortage. There has been some drop in shingles, as is usual at this period of the year when the "peak of the load," so to speak, is over. Some predict that prices will fall considerably, while others expect a reduction of only 50 or 75 cents. Lath of all kinds are still very scarce and high in price.

It may be added that B. C. timber prices are somewhat firmer and there is a fair call for the goods. Flat grain flooring from the Coast is difficult to get in straight car load lots and there is a lively call for the same.

Summing up the whole situation, a leading wholesaler declared that business was never better, but stocks are getting lower all the while, and there is no evidence of prices showing any tendency to recede. Collections are satisfactory and shipments for the most part are good, although some firms report difficulties owing to Canadian roads refusing to allow their cars any longer to go across the border with lumber consignments as many thousands of Canadian cars not being returned promptly.

It is interesting to note that at a large gathering of retail dealers recently held in Detroit one of the best authorities of he trade, who has carefully canvassed the situation, advised his hearers to buy lumber steadily for the next seven months as, in his opinion, there was no possibility of any reduction in values before that period. Except in Montreal, where a strike of the building trades has held up many contracts, the number of building permits in all the larger centres of population continue to show a gratifying gain. There is still an abnormal demend for houses in most eastern cities and towns, and rents are continually advancing, while prices for all sorts of dwellings have gone up amazingly, and were never as high as at present.

One item of interest to the Canadian lumber trade in general is that the railroad administration in the U. S. will make no increase in freight rates before the return of the roads to private operation, in January next. Canadian carriage charges have ascended in every instance, and recently they have been augmented on the other side of the line, and it was freely predicted that another advance would be put into effect this fall, but the latest intelligence that tariffs wil remain as they are for some months, is most welcome.

Several consumers and others are complaining of getting worked lumber from the mills in Northern On due to the fact that planing mills are so busy that it to secure car loads dressed in transit, with any degree Every dressing plant is pushed to capacity.

Great Britain

Trade in general is slowing improving but th are so many disturging factors and cross currents that no on an gauge the general situation. In the meantime, the present chaotic state of affairs is accepted with equanimity and there is a quiet confidence that all will come out right in the end. The excrescences are largely on the surface and it is believed that the heart of the nation is sound and true. English trade papers are not disposed to be pessimistic over the situation, and, while admitting that business is dull, there is a hopeful note pervading their utterances. Trade on the Continent is marking time and the revolutionary spirit seems to be sweeping over Europe, retarding construction and extinguishing the spirit of enterprise.

In regard to the future, the "Timber Trades Journal" says: "We are not optimistic enough to think that labor troubles are over, or even on the wane, but provide the only revolution preached is revolution of the peaceable order, we need not despair because of the growing power of the working classes. House-building still lags behind other trades, and consequently the demand for timber is only moderate, but in the meantime there are many other industries which are consuming large quantities of wood, and which are experiencing a very busy time. Unfortunately, it is just house-building timber which is so plentiful, while Archangel wood for shipbuilding, yellow pine for engineering, etc., are extremely scarce and dear. Sawmills are pretty fully employed owing to the growing demand for cases and boxes; for whitewood in the broader dimensions there is an active inquiry. Whitewood deals are particularly scarce. . .

The Government Timber Buyer's Department will in future be known as the Imported Timber Disposal Section, Board of Trade, and we understand that the selling of the Government stocks will be carried on as hitherto at Salisbury House. Since March, when Government buying ceased, it has been a misnomer to speak of a Government timber buyer, and it will be satisfactory to the trade to observe the first signs of the demobilisation of the of the Timber Supplies Department, and to realise that the hold exercised by the State over the timber trade is on the wane.

The needs of Europe for timber are more urgent than ever, and Continental importers are on the qui vive in order to be ready to take advantage of opportunities as they arise. During the coming winter the Continent will not be so well supplied as Great Britain with imported timber; but on the other hand, she is less ready for the material. Holland and Denmark overrated the position in the early days of the season, and had to unload a good part of their purchases on other markets. France and Belgium have bought sparingly, and unless depression in trade is very severe next winter there will be a good outlet in 1920 for imported timber in these countries.

In regard to market prices and prospects, it is interesting to read the following from an exchange: "In the timber trade especially—a trade in which long views must be taken—doubt as to the

future makes the business of the merchant most harassing. It is not that merchants have suddenly lost their faculty of foresight or of judging of such matters as the probable supplies of timber in the future, the probable extent of the consumption, etc. All this to the experienced merchants is more or less plain sailing; and in any case most established firms would be quite willing to use their business instinct and back their considered opinions. But when they have to take into account political factors, their confidence fails them, and most feel that their only refuge is in a policy of masterly inactivity. A fortnight ago we referred to the fact that the usual autumn negotiations for the ensuing season had not commenced, and we have not yet heard of any pourparlers for 1920 goods. And yet in Great Britain many merchants speak as if it were a matter of course that free-on-board prices in Scandinavia would remain absolutely firm, and in all probability advance. Swedish exporters openly state that they expect to make in 1920 at least another £2 per standard on this year's top figures, and the arguments they use to support their view seem prety conclusive—the world-shortage of timber, the growing consumption, the urgent ned for sawn wood after the war of destruction, the elimination of Russia as an exporting country for another two years, the extraordinary high cost of production, etc.—all these are very strong reasons for the maintenance of sawn wood at at least its present level of values in the exporting countries. Leaving the question of freights out of accounts for the moment, as we are dealing with free-on-board values, why then, we may ask, should there be such an absolute lack of interest shown in forward contracts? The explanation, we believe, is political rather than commercial; and we fear that uncertainty in political matters will remain with us for some time."

United States

During the past few days interest has been largely centred upon the steel strike and the outcome of the railwaymen's strike in Great Britain. This has naturally detracted somewhat from the even, steady tone of business, and in various cities too there have been labor troubles, which have interfered to some extent with ordinary merchandising and distribution. Different reports come to hand, depending very much upon the localities from which they emanate. In Buffalo it is declared that trade has been very brisk for the last two or three weeks, while in Boston there were practically nothing doing at all owing to the policemen's strike.

Writing to the "Canada Lumberman" regarding conditions at the Hub, a leading firm says: "The strike of the police, together with the upheaval in labor all over the world, has put a check on business. We look for a proper solution of the labor situation in the near future, after which we expect to see a good market for commodities and a general improvement in business. We might mention there have been some shipments of spruce in this market within the last two or three weeks which have been sold at considerable concessions. This naturally hurts the market temporarily. The same situation has affected hemlock boards and other kinds of lumber"

As the Fall months advance building naturally becomes quieter and fewer permits are taken out. There is plenty of work still to do, however, in finishing the work that has started, and the prospects are that work will be resumed next year on an even larger scale. The country is still way short of adequate housing facilities, and it is quite likely that there will be more than usual activity in the cities where building operations are carried on throughout the colder months. Country building will probably drop off with the first appearance of severe weather.

Some building has been deferred because the projectors believe that construction work will be cheaper. Some has been put off because builders could not get materials. But the outlook is not especially good for any great change in either respect.

High wages for labor have come to stay. There may be some recession from the present high level, but there will not be a return to the level which prevailed before the war. Labor, in the manufacture of the raw material, in the production of finished goods and in actual construction work, is the chief item of cost, and while labor remains high little drop in prices can be expected.

As for supplies, the outlook is no better. The lumber industry never before faced a winter with as little surplus. In no producing districts and at no individual mill is there the usual supply of stock for this season of the year. Manufacturers will make an effort during the coming winter to prepare for an active sawing season next year, but scarcity of labor will interfere with their plans, and the supply of lumber next season is also likely to be inadequate to supply the demand.

Supply and demand govern the material market, and if the matter of production costs did not enter into the question, prices would still be strong. But with a shortage of labor, and with high wages paid to labors cost will be a factor in the lumber markets which cannot be escaped.

Distribution centers for hardwoods report that the demand is not as strong as recently, a condition undoubtedly due to the steel strike and other labor disorders. The unsatisfactory outlook in the labor world brings a marked degree of caution, which, together with the falling off in exports, is expected by many dealers to bring an early recession in prices. But such a development appears very unlikely when the situation surrounding the production and marketing of hardwoods is viewed in its true light. As indicated, there has been a slight recession in the demand, yet it remains very active and more than enough to cover everything produced with large-scale industrial consumption the largest factor. Quartered and plain white oak is the market feature, with red gum and poplar also moving especially rapidly. There is a very active demand for veneers; likewise for box boards. Flooring and interior trim mills are running full time, with enough orders right now to cover several months' production; and sash and door plants are also very busy. Reports from furniture manufacturing centers state that extensive additions and new plants are being erected with all possible speed and that other arrangements to facilitate a speedier and larger production are under way. The manufacturers expect a large volume of future business, and are preparing for it. Agricultural implement and vehicle manufacturers have the same prospects, and the automobile plants report an unprecedented demand for cars of all descriptions. Industries, taken all together, report orders ahead for four to six months, and in some cases a year, with plenty of business in sight after that. The hardwood situation is strong in view of the present and prospective demand alone, and additionally so in view of the curtailed production.

Market Correspondence

SPECIAL REPORTS ON CONDITIONS AT HOME AND ABROAD

Good Steady Demand Reported at Ottawa

Continued firm prices, a steady demand with orders keeping up and stocks remaining about the same were the feature of the Ottawa lumber market during the opening period of October. As compared with the latter part of September the market showed little or no general charge locally. Lath and shingles continued to remain scarce and both advanced in price. No. 1 white pine lath went to $8 per thousand and all grades of shingles showed a general advance of about fifty cents for the same quantity.

Taken all around the market was good for this time of year and though the general volume of business transacted was not as large as that done during the pre-war years, manufacturers and others of the trade were optimistic and looked for a "fairly good" business, even into the winter months. The pricipal reason given for the volume of business not being as great was on account of the cutting off of the war demand for shell box and other stocks for war purposes and because existing stocks are not proportionately as great as in 1914-15 and years before. Consequently, it could hardly be expected that with lowered stocks the manufacturers and others could dispose of or turn over as great a quantity.

Of the factors effecting the market little could be determined but taken all around the situation appeared satisfactory to the lumbermen. The export situation to Great Britain and Europe was, of course; the most interesting. This did not show any improvement but rather if anything became less favorable on account of the British railway strike.

"During the strike ships reached British ports and were tied up. There were few ships coming back. Consequently there was so much less available cargo space for lumber shipments or anything else," was the terse summary of Mr. P. C. Walker, of the Shepard and Morse Lumber Co.

Outside of the British export situation, transportation of lumber shipments to South America or South Africa showed no change. A difference of opinion existed about the number of foreign cars available. Some shippers were of the opinion that the situation taken all around was better in this regard than what it had been last year

at this time or the year before. Others mentioned that foreign cars wer beginning to grow short.

"The cars may be getting a little scarcer all right but they are a great deal more plentiful than they were this time two years ago or last year," commented another shipper. There the situation stands.

The woods reports indicate that operations with some companies and camps are only getting on moderately well, on account of there not being all the labor that is required. "The thing is that that there is lots of labor to go to the bush. It is a question of keeping them there after they arrive," commented Mr. Walter Ross, of the John R. Booth firm, Ottawa. The "Canada Lumberman" was informed that the great trouble being exercised in the camps this year is what is known in lumbering or camp parlance as "transients"—i.e., men who shift quickly from one camp to another.

This shifting on analysis has a serious effect on production as well as being very costly to the companies or operators who send the men into the woods.

With the latest advance in lumber prices as contained in the last issue of the "Canada Lumberman," some comment arose at Ottawa to whether or not it was the high price of lumber which was retarding building operations. Lumbermen pointed out that this could hardly be the case, as lumber was one of the last commodities to increase with the war. It was further stated that even supposing ten thousand feet of lumber was used in the erection of a house and the advance had been $20 per M., that would only mean an increased item of cost of $200. Again it was mentioned that lumber was only one of several commodities that enter into the present day or modern structure. Heating, plumbing and steamfitting was cited as an instance by a lumberman who stated that including the cost for installing had advanced six hundred per cent against lumber's estimated $20 per M. increase.

The situation with the sawmills remained pretty much unchanged. The majority of mills in the valley will run as late as they can this season or so long as their supplies of logs hold out. So far there has only been two mills reported closed down, they being the Shepard and Morse mill and that of McLachlin Bros., at Arnprior. The Gillies Bros. mill, at Braeside, which was destroyed by fire some time ago is, of course, out of operation and steps are now being taken to reconstruct it. Mill and factory labor remained good.

With the woodworking plants and factories business kept up well, and no serious signs presented themselves to indicate that a general slump in business was to occur soon.

Montreal Business Shows No Material Change

On the whole, business in Montreal is slower. Local trade is dull, owing to building conditions; the orders for the U. S. show signs of falling away; and the B. C. market is quiet except for dimension stock. Prices, however, are very firm. Despite the lull in business, the general outlook is regarded as satisfactory. The commercial position is sound, and there is no indication of any fall in prices; on the contrary, the opinion is that we shall see a higher range of values.

The easing off in the U. S. demand is probably due to the rather unsettled conditions due to the labor troubles. These are calculated to interfere with building, and with the buying of lumber.

The B. C. market is adversely influenced by the dearness of stock. The mills in the West are very busy, filling orders for American account, and prices are exceptionally stiff.

Local trade continues to be more or less hampered by the strike in the building industry, particularly as the carpenters are mostly affected. Many of the men have returned to work, but at the time of writing a considerable number are holding out. These want an advance from 60c to 75c an hour, with an eight-hour day. In spite of this handicap the building permits continue satisfactory. For September the total was $1,050,976, an increase of $770,651; for the year to date the total was $6,964,644, a gain of $2,976,441.

Box makers are tied up owing to a strike, and many of the factories are closed. The men demanded an increase of 20 per cent. in wages, an eight-hour day, and union recognition. As these requirements were not immediately met, the men walked out.

The pulpwood section shows a hardening tendency. For a time American mills bought in very small quantities, believing that prices would fall. This was due, according to a dealer, to offers of large quantities of wood by irresponsible brokers, who failed to deliver anything like the amounts specified. The prices quoted were comparatively low. The general impression given was that there was planty of wood, whereas the quantity is limited, as little was taken out by farmers last season. The mills are now coming more freely into the market and prices are improving.

The lumber export position is about the same,except that freights are inclined to be easier and more space is available. Very little Government lumber remains to be sent from this port. The stocks to be lifted in the Maritime Provinces are very heavy, and this will be shipped during the winter.

The exports of pulpwood continue to decline. During July the total was $1,234,527, a decrease of $1,019,357; while for the four months of the fiscal year the total was $3,260,241, a falling off of $2,972,013. In July exports of paper were substantially higher, but chemical pulp was $100,000 lower at $2,654,333, and mechanical pulp $26,000 down at $435,604. During the four months, chemical pulp declined $5,225,530 and mechanical $70,572. Paper, however, was $3,045,299 to the good.

Norweigan Wood Trade Faces Difficulties

In regard to the Norweigan wood trade C. E. Sontum, Canadian Commercial Agent at Christiania, Norway, says: "Business in the export market is still dominated by the dearth of tonnage, and substantial quantities sold for shipment May and June are still left to wait for shipping opportunity. This belated delivery of sold goods is mainly caused by delays of the boats owing to strikes and slow forwarding at the places of discharge, supplementary tonnage being difficult to procure. Prices are maintained firm with a rising tendency. With shorter working hours and diminished output the mills are also by necessity in want of higher prices, as the cost of raw materials is showing no decrease. The demand, mainly from England, is well maintained and the competition from Finland, however, especially in sawn goods, appears to make itself felt in some quarters, buyers keeping back in expectation of a more plentiful supply from that country, but as shipping accommodation will hardly prove easier to obtain in those waters, the importance attached to the supply from Finland may turn out to be illusory. The Belgian market, of which much was expected, has not yet developed to anything important. Holland at present is also lifeless. Some few feelers are sent out, but as a rule the orders are being covered more cheaply from stocks within the country. Australia meanwhile has appeared as a buyer on quite a fair scale, and several transactions have been made in planed goods at prices of about £28 10s. to £29 per standard basis f.o.b.

"Owing to the difficult shipping conditions and the slow clearing of stocks consequent thereon, there is no business to speak of in the battens market. Prices are, however, maintained at about the former level."

The Moral Fibre of the Lumber Man

All lines of business at times offer temptations and afford opportunities for crooked dealing. Perhaps the lumber business offers its full share of such; but it is believed that the buying and selling of lumber in general are done honestly. At any rate, association membership, systematic grading and official inspection are designed not only to sanction honestly but to eliminate temptations to crookedness. The so-called lumberman who violates the ethics of the trade is soon made to feel very lonesome in his isolation, says the "American Lumberman."

However, there are two conditions of the lumber market that tempt the buyer in one case and the seller in another and bring about practices that are not sanctioned by the better class of lumbermen in any branch of the industry. When the market is falling it is temptingly easy for the buyer to cancel contract orders; and it is temptingly convenient when conditions are reversed for the seller to delay or divert deliveries on such orders. With demand as it has been in recent months and with supply not within hailing distance of demand the eager buyer is likely to be suspicious of delays in delivery. On the other hand, if the market should decline reluctance on the part of the buyer to accept delivery might cause similar suspicions in the mind of the seller.

Nobody really wishes to put the lumber business on this "catch-as-catch-can" basis, and the suspicions developed by such practices are demoralizing to the trade. Plain speaking would demand the application to them of terms that require no explanation or definition. The lumber industry as a whole is above sanctioning them, for when a balance is struck for the whole industry they leave no profit in money but a big loss in character. A few buyers and a few sellers make a little money at the expense of a few other buyers and sellers, and to the discredit of the whole trade.

The chief end and aim of all forms of organization and of all education are to bring about fairer dealings among men, to inspire loftier ideals and to raise all human relations to a higher level. This is only a manifestation of foresight, real wisdom; for the true interests of every person engaged in industry are best served by the enforcement of ethical laws. With the lumber industry in an unstable condition the moral fibre of the individuals engaged in it is being put to a test. Evidence is plentiful of a desire to meet that test by the fulfillment of every moral obligation, cost what it will. The few exceptions to the rule merely serve to mark defects that the industry will find means to cure in due time.

EDGINGS

Ontario

The Dominion Lumber & Coal Co. will shortly erect a planing mill on Rosslyn Ave., Hamilton.

Several young men from Toronto and vicinity, who were attracted by the high wages offered in the lumber camps and went north for a few weeks to engage in logging operations, have returned. They report the work heavy—a real man's job.

The will of the late Hiram Robinson, well-known lumber man, of Ottawa, who died recently, bequeathed $100,000 to the city for the new hospital. The stipulation is made that the grant is to be used within a specified time for the children'e ward.

An examination of candidates desiring to be licensed as saw-log cullers was held recently in Kenora. It was announced that there would be no further examinations this season and only British subjects and bonafide residents of Canada were examined for licenses.

The many friends of W. D. Cargill, M.L.A., one of the lumber legislators of Ontario, will sympathize with him in the loss of his home, in Cargill, which was recently destroyed by fire. The residence was one of the finest in Western Ontario and the loss is estimated at $30,000.

The Conger Lumber Co., Parry Sound, Ont., have finished sawing for the present season and are now operating several camps in connection with their logging operations. The company cut about 5,000,000 feet of hemlock this year, which is an increase of about 23 per cent. over the production in 1918.

Fire broke out in the dry kiln of the large planing mill of Philip Ament, Brussels, Ont. The fact that the kiln was completely filled with heading made the work of fighting the flames more difficult. Assistance was sought from outside towns and the fire was kept confined entirely to the dry kiln. The loss is covered by insurance.

The Wagar Furniture Co., Limited, with headquarters at North Bay, and capital stock of $40,000, has been incorporated to manufacture all kinds of furniture, wood, tin and metal wares and to conduct a general furniture business. Among the incorporators are Walter S. Wagar, Harvey A. Heavener, John Blanchet, all of North Bay.

The Marshay Lumber Co., of Toronto, have bought the saw mill and limits of La Forest and Clemow at La Forest on the Canadian National Railways, about fifty miles north of Sudbury, Ont. The mill was erected last year, and is equipped with a double cutting band and has a capacity of about 50,000 feet a day. The timber on the limits is principally white pine with a sprinkling of jack pine.

Lumber and Pulpwood of British Columbia, Limited, with a capital stock of $1,000,000, and head office in Toronto, has been granted a charter to manufacture, buy, sell, import, export and deal in timber, lumber, wood, pulpwood, fibreboard, pulpwood, etc., and to buy, sell and develop timber limits. The incorporators of the Company are given as Frederick H. McCallum, F. M. Squires and Russell P. Locke, Toronto.

A federal charter has been granted to Telbax of Canada, Limited, with headquarters in Windsor and capital stock of $300,000. The company is empowered to originate, compose and advise forms of advertising, and to conduct any other business pertaining to printing, lithographing, stationery, account book making and to carry on the business of importers, dealers and manufacturers in paper, pulp and paper substitutes of all kinds. Among the incorporators of the company are J. C. Scofield of the Windsor Lumber Co., Limited, Windsor, Ont.

A large number of sawmills have already closed down for the season, some of them a few days earlier than usual. McLachlin Bros., Arnprior, have found that owning to the low water in the Ottawa River it was impossible to bring down a further supply of logs to the sorting booms, and every foot of the vast quantity of timber in the booms had been cut up. McLachlin Bros. intend making a number of changes during the coming winter in their sorting tables and installing more modern methods with a view to economy of time and labor.

G. Kastner, J. E. Murphy and others have made a proposition to the council of Wiarton, Ont., with a view to purchasing the flooring factory and operating it to full capacity as soon as arrangements can be completed. The casket factory, which has long been vacant, may also be converted into a furniture manufacturing plant in the near future. Capt. R. L. Graham, who returned recently from overseas, has purchased the site of the Johnson, Hunter, Crawford mill, and it is possible will erect early next year a sawmill and woodworking plant on the property.

The Fesserton Timber Co. of Toronto have finished their cutting operations for the season at Monteith and Haliburton. At the mill operated by them at Montreal on the Driftwood river, about 4,000,000 feet of spruce was sawed and considerable pulpwood taken out. At Haliburton, where Austin & Roberts' mill sawed 1,500,000 ft. for the company, the bulk of the output was hemlock, although there was a fair sprinkling of hardwood. The Fesserton Timber Co. report the lumber situation as very strong at the present time, and they are looking for a continuance of the present high prices for, at least, a considerable time.

A charter has been granted to the Triangle Lumber Co., Limited, with headquarters in Toronto, and a capital stock of $300,000. The company is empowered to manufacture, sell and deal in lumber and sawmill products of all kinds, acquire timber limits and standing timber and to manufacture pulp and paper, etc. The company will acquire the limits and camps of Boivin, Black and Jemmett of Haileybury, as well as a controlling interest in the business of James Kingston. The officers of the Triangle Lumber Co. are: President, J. H. Black, Toronto, Vice President, Matthew Boivin, Haileybury; Secy.-Treas., D. L. Jemmett, Haileybury.

Tenders were recently received in Ottawa for the pine, spruce, cedar and tamarac timber on the Indian Reserve at Lac La Croix in the Rainy

River district. The successful tenderer was required to deposit a sum of $5,000 as a guarantee for the proper carrying out of the undertaking and a sworn return by a licensed culler of the material cut each season. Seven years are allowed for the removal of the timber under an annual license, and all brush, treetops and other debris resulting from lumbering operations must be piled and burned during the winter months. Tenderers had to state the price they would offer for the merchantable pine, spruce, cedar and tamarac on a stumpage basis per M feet, B.M., over and above the Crown dues at the usual tariff.

Eastern Canada

The Canada Fibreboard Co. was recently registered at Quebec, P. Q.

J. A. Culligan, lumber manufacturer, of Benjamin Mills, N.B., was on a business visit to Montreal, recently.

The sawmill of the River Valley Lumber Co., Ltd., Oromocto, N.B., was totally destroyed by fire. The loss is partially covered by insurance.

The St. Maurice Lumber Co., Three Rivers, Que., intend erecting a two-storey office building at a cost of $20,000. The plans for the structure have been prepared.

The Kipawa Fibre Co. Limited, will erect thirty new houses on the townsite of their new sulphite pulp plant at Temiskaming, Que. The dwellings will be for the employees of the mill.

The assets of Paul Demers, sash and door manufacturer, Montreal, were sold by auction on October 3. The factory, machinery and other property were bought by Mr. E. Guiment, Montreal.

The Wayagamack Pulp and Paper Co. Three Rivers, Que., intend installing additional machinery and will increase their output of kraft paper by about thirty per cent. Orders for the equipment were recently placed in England.

The Canada Paper Co., Limited, of Windsor Mills, Que., who several months ago purchased the St. Anne river limits, now have forestry parties out surveying the timber and laying out working plans, but do not expect to start cutting operations until next season.

The Brompton Lumber Mfg. Co., Bromptonville, Que., has been incorporated with a capital stock of $49,000, to carry on a lumber business, and to manufacture and deal in wood products of all kinds. Antoine Fournier, mill manager, of Bromptonville, is one of the incorporators.

The Laurentide Co. of Grand Mere, Que., have awarded the contract for two paper machines each of 166 inches width. The machines will be built by the Dominion Bridge Co., Montreal, and when in operation, will increase the newsprint output of the Laurentide Co. to 360 tons a day. An extension of 320 x 90 feet, two storeys high, will be built to the present plant to house the additional equipment.

Fire broke out recently in the sash and door factory of the Kent Lumber Co. at Granby, Que. The loss was about $10,000, and the insurance $6,300. The cause of the blaze is believed to be due to spontaneous combustion. The plant was completely destroyed, but it is understood that Mr. Solomon, the proprietor, intends to rebuild. In rescuing his books from the office he had a narrow escape and received some painful bruises about the hands and face.

The new Kipawa sulphite pulp plant of the Riordon Pulp & Paper Co., which is being erected at Temiskaming, Que., is rapidly nearing completion. Construction work is practically finished and the machinery is now being installed. The power house and power development should be in operation in a few weeks' time. The Kipawa mill will be turning out 30,000 tons of bleached sulphite per annum, and will be running early in the new year. This is the first unit of 100 tons, and it is understood that a second unit will be proceeded with early next year.

Western Canada

The Haywood Lumber Co. is erecting sheds and offices at Radway Centre, Alta.

Laden with 1,250,000 feet of lumber for South Africa, the American barquentine, Conqueror, recently left Victoria.

The C. E. Walsh Lumber Co., of Vancouver, is now in operation and has already cut a large amount of lumber. A new engine and boiler room was recently completed.

Among recent incorporations in British Columbia are the Coast Box Co. Limited, the Kelly Lake Lumber Co., Limited, the Thomas Gwilt Shingle Co. Limited, and Western Hemlock Mills, Limited.

Fire believed to have been due to spontaneous combustion broke out recently in the sawdust storage building of the Vancouver Lumber Co., Ltd., Vancouver. Damage was done to the extent of about $10,000, and at one time the blaze threatened to spread throughout the yards.

The Tait Lumber Co., Langley, B.C., have received an order for a large quantity of B. C. maple, which will be used in the manufacture of furniture. British Columbia maple differs in a marked degree from the Eastern product, it being softer and much shorter in the grain.

A total of 19,776,814 feet of lumber was shipped from British Columbia ports in August. Nearly seven and one-half millions of this amount was forwarded in French vessels. Nine of the wooden ships built at Victoria for the French Government assisted in this work. Large consignments will also be sent to France.

The A. A. Rerrie lumber mill, north of Shortreed, B.C., on the G. N. R., are adding improvements to their plant and building and a light logging railway to the nearby timber limits. The mill is cutting about 26,000 feet per day, but the shortage of cars is proving a drawback to their operations. The mill is run by electric motive power.

It is believed that great quantities of lumber now being forwarded from British Columbia ports will go toward reconstruction undertakings in Egypt. The revolt there resulted in a tremendous amount of destruction to railway buildings and equipment, station houses being burned, bridges destroyed, tracks torn up and ties ruined.

Major Cowper-Young, who was formerly connected with the Dominion Spruce Board in aeroplane construction, will establish a shingle and planing mill at Prince Rupert, B. C. Major Young has let the contrct for the dry kilns and refuse burners, and says he hopes to show the world that on Queen Charlotte Islands they have better pine than anywhere else where pine is grown and cut.

Camp Comfort and Convenience Assured when McClary's Stoves are Installed
McClary's Camp Comfort Stove fulfils all the exacting requirements of the Camp with ease. They are built of durable materials only. The Stove can be readily assembled as all parts are subject to a minute and careful inspection before shipment.
The Body is made of one piece of heavy sheet steel—cast-iron front and stamped steel back end. Large feed door with draft slide. Legs of heavy cast-iron set in powerful cleats hold body rigid. Equipped with either top or side shelves as ordered. Throws off a powerful heat.
WRITE US SO THAT YOU MAY USE US
Our nearest Branch, on receipt of your request, will forward all the necessary information.
McClary's
London, Toronto, Montreal, Winnipeg, Vancouver, St. John, N. B., Hamilton, Calgary, Saskatoon, Edmonton

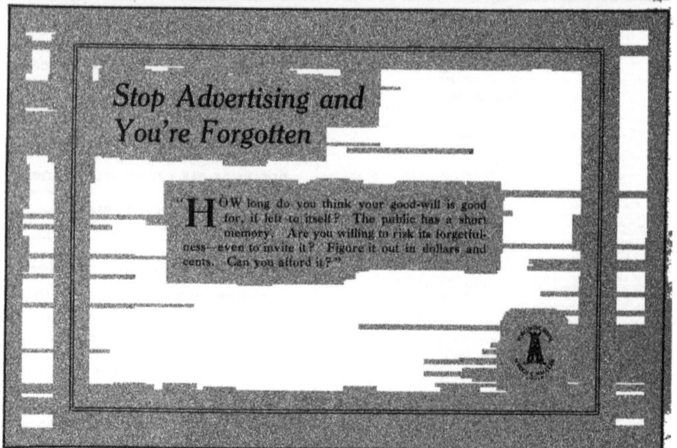
Stop Advertising and You're Forgotten
"HOW long do you think your good-will is good for, if left to itself? The public has a short memory. Are you willing to risk its forgetfulness—even to invite it? Figure it out in dollars and cents. Can you afford it?"

ALPHABETICAL INDEX TO ADVERTISERS

When
You
Overhaul
Install

"Acme Waterproof"
Leather Belting

This brand is especially well suited to the wet places in a saw or pulp mill and will run true as long as it is in service. When you are overhauling your mill equip it with "Goodhue Belts" and you will never regret it. They are honestly made of solid leather—every inch a good belt and they won't stretch.

Get our details and prices

J. L. Goodhue & Company, Limited

DANVILLE - QUEBEC

WINNIPEG AGENTS—Bissett & Webb, Ltd., 151 Notre Dame Ave., East, Winnipeg, Man.
VANCOUVER AGENTS—Fleck Bros., Ltd., 1142 Homer St., Vancouver, B.C.

Standard Machinery & Supplies, Ltd., Bank of Toronto Bldg., St. James St., Montreal, Que., agents for the Island of Montreal.

AN "ALL DISSTON" MILL.

Ask any Filer about the quality of Disston Crucible Steel—made in the Disston Works since 1855.

It is very frequently found that every saw in use in a modern, efficient mill is a Disston.

In fact, after Disston's 80 years of leadership, it could not well be otherwise.

Wherever lumber is produced, it is known and acknowledged that Disston Saws represent the maximum in quality and in true-cutting, profitable service.

HENRY DISSTON & SONS, Ltd.

"The Largest and Longest Established Makers of Hand Saws, Cross-Cut Saws, Band Saws, Circular Saws and Tools."

TORONTO, CANADA

BRANCH: VANCOUVER, B.C.

DISSTON-SAWS

CURRENT LUMBER PRICES—WHOLESALE

TORONTO, ONT.

Prices in Carload Lots, F.O.B. cars Toronto

White Pine:

1 x 4/7 Good Strips	$62 00	$65 00
1¼ and 1½ x 4/7 Good Strips	66 00	68 00
2 x 4/7 Good Strips	66 00	69 00
1 x 8 and up Good Sides	70 00	82 00
1¼ and 1½ x 8 and wider Good Sides	93 00	98 00
2 x 8 and wider Good Sides	95 00	100 00
1 in. No. 1, 2 and 3 Cuts	65 00	68 00
5/4 and 6/4 No. 1, 2 and 3 Cuts	68 00	70 00
2 in. No. 1, 2 and 3 Cuts	72 00	75 00
1 x 4 and 5 Mill Run	48 00	50 00
1 x 6 Mill Run	51 00	53 00
1 x 7, 9 and 11 Mill Run	50 00	52 00
1 x 8 Mill Run	52 00	54 00
1 x 10 Mill Run	55 00	57 00
1 x 12 Mill Run	57 00	59 00
5/4 and 6/4 x 4 Mill Run	51 00	53 00
5/4 and 6/4 x 5 Mill Run	51 00	53 00
2 x 4 Mill Run	50 00	52 00
2 x 6 Mill Run	52 00	53 00
2 x 8 Mill Run	53 00	55 00
2 x 10 Mill Run	56 00	58 00
2 x 12 Mill Run	57 00	59 00
1 in. Mill Run Shorts	41 00	42 00
1 x 4 and up 6/16 No. 1 Mill Culls	40 00	42 00
1 x 10 and up 6/16 No. 1 Mill Culls	45 00	40 00
1 x 12 and up 6/16 No. 1 Mill Culls	45 00	46 00
1 x 4 and up 6/16 No. 2 Mill Culls	33 00	34 00
1 x 10 x 12 6/16 No. 2 Mill Culls	35.00	36 00
1 x 4 and up 6/10 No. 3 Mill Culls	25 00	27 00

Red Pine:

1 x 4 and 5 Mill Run	43 00	44 00
1 x 6 Mill Run	44 00	46 00
1 x 8 Mill Run	47 00	48 00
1 x 10 Mill Run	48 00	49 00
2 x 4 Mill Run	45 00	46 00
2 x 6 Mill Run	46 00	47 00
2 x 8 Mill Run	48 00	49 00
1 in. Clear and Clear Face	60 00	62 00
2 in. Clear and Clear Face	60 00	62 00

Spruce:

1 x 4 Mill Run	42 00	43 00
1 x 6 Mill Run	44 00	45 00
1 x 8 Mill Run	45 00	46 00
1 x 10 Mill Run	48 00	49 00
1/12 Mill Run Spruce	50 00	51 00
Mill Culls	36 00	37 00
1 x 4 and 5 in. x 9 to 16 ft.	36 00	38 00
1 x 6 in. x 9 to 16 ft.	39 00	40 00
1 x 8 in. x 9 to 16 ft.	40 00	41 00
1 x 10 and 12 in. x 9 to 16 ft.	40 00	41 00
1 x 7, 9 and 11 in. x 9 to 16 ft.	37 00	38 00
2 x 4 to 12, 10 and 16 ft.	40 00	41 00
2 x 4 to 12 in., 12 and 14 ft.	39 00	40 00
2 x 4 to 12 in., 18 ft.	41 00	42 00
2 x 4 to 12 in., 20 ft.	42 00	43 00
1 in. No. 2, 6 ft. to 16 ft.	33 00	34 00
2" No. 2, 4" and up, width 8 to 18 ft.	33 00	34 00

DOUGLAS FIR

(Delivered in Toronto)

Dimension Timber up to 32 feet:

6x6 and 8, 10x10 and 12, 12x12	$52 00
6x10, 8x10, 10x14, 12x14, 14x14	53 00
6x12, 8x12	54 00
14x16, 16x16	54 50
6x14, 8x14, 10x16, 12x16	56 00
14x18	56 50
8x16, 10x18, 12x18	57 00
18x18, 20x20	57 50
12x20, 24x24	58 00

Timber in lengths over 32 feet subject to negotiation.

Fir flooring, 1 x 3, edge grain		71 00
Fir flooring, 1 x 4, edge grain		71 00
Fir flooring, 1 x 4, flat grain		open
No. 1 & 2, 1-in. clear Fir rough	61 50	69 50

(Depending upon widths).

No. 1 and 2, 1¼ and 1½ in., clear Fir rough	71 00	75 00
No. 1 and 2 2-in. clear Fir rough	56 00	66 00
1 x 5 and 1 x 6 Fir casing		73 00
1 x 8 and 1 x 10 Fir base		75 00
1¼ & 1½ x 8, 10 & 12" E. G. stepping		85 00
1¼ & 1½ x 8" 10 & 12" E. G. stepping		75 00
1-in. clear Fir, d 4 sides	56 00	64 00
1¼ x 1½ in. clear Fir, d 4 sides	56 50	65 50
XXX 6 butts to 2 in.		7 00
XXXXX 5 butts to 2 in.		8 40

LATH

		Red Pine
No. 1 White Pine, 4 ft.	$8 00	$7 75
No. 2 White Pine, 4 ft.	7 50	7 25
No. 3 White Pine, 4 ft.	7 00	6 75
Mill run white pine, 32 in.	4 00	3 50
Merchantable spruce lath, 4 ft.	7 50	

TORONTO HARDWOOD PRICES

The prices given below are for carloads f.o.b. Toronto, from wholesalers to retailers, and are based on a good percentage of long lengths and good widths, without any wide stock having been sorted out. War tax of seven and half per cent. on imported woods, and also the prevailing rate of exchange paid by purchaser.

ASH, WHITE

(Dry weight 3800 lbs. per M. ft.)

	1s & 2s	No. 1 Com.	No. 2 Com.	No. 3 Com.
4/4	$125.00	$80.00	$50.00	$35.00
5/4 & 6/4	135.00	90.00	53.00	40.00
8/4	190.00	100.00	60.00	40.00
10/4 & 12/4	200.00	150.00	80.00	.....
16/4	220.00	100.00	90.00	.....

ASH, BROWN

4/4	$75.00	$55.00	$40.00	$38.00
6/4	80.00	65.00	60.00	50.00
8/4	83.00	70.00	65.00	50.00

BIRCH

(Dry weight 4000 lbs. per M. ft.)

	1s & 2s		No. 1 Com.		No. 2 Com.	
	$		$		$	
4/4	75	78	60	63	45	50
5/4 & 6/4	78	80	68	70	50	55
8/4	80	83	70	75	55	
10/4 and 12/4	100	105	90	95	70	
16/4	105	110	85	100	80	

BASSWOOD

(Dry weight 2500 lbs. per M. ft.)

	1s & 2s	No. 1 Com.	No. 2 Com.	No. 3 Com.
4/4	$77.00	$55.00	$44.00	$38.00
5/4 & 6/4	80.00	60.00	50.00	40.00
8/4	83.00	63.00	50.00	42.00

CHESTNUT

(Dry weight 2800 lbs. per M. ft.)

	1s & 2s	No. 1 Com.	Sound Wormy
4/4	$95.00	$80.00	$50.00
5/4 & 6/4	105.00	85.00	55.00
8/4	115.00	85.00	55.00

ELM, SOFT

(Dry weight 3100 lbs. per M. ft.)

4/4	$63.00	$50.00	$40.00	$38.00
6/4 & 8/4	68.00	55.00	45.00	43.00
12/4	75.00	65.00	50.00	42.00

GUM, RED

(Dry weight 3300 lbs. per M. ft.)

	Plain 1s & 2s	Plain No. 1 Com.	Quartered 1s & 2s	Quartered No. 1 Com.
4/4	$120.00	$90.00	$130.00	$105.00
5/4	125.00	95.00	135.00	110.00
6/4	130.00	100.00	140.00	115.00
8/4	150.00	125.00	150.00	125.00

Figured Gum, $10 per M. extra, in both plain and quartered.

GUM, SAP

	1s & 2s	No. 1 Com.
4/4	$70.00	$55.00
5/4 & 6/4	75.00	60.00
8/4	85.00	70.00

HICKORY

(Dry weight 4500 lbs. per M. ft.)

	1s & 2s	No. 1 Com.	No. 2 Com.
4/4	$100.00	$70.00	$45.00
5/4	120.00	85.00	53.00
6/4	125.00	85.00	53.00
8/4	135.00	95.00	60.00

MAPLE, HARD

(Dry weight 3900 lbs. per M. ft.)

	1s & 2s	Com. No. 1	Com. No. 2	Com. No. 3
4/4	$60.00	$50.00	$40.00	$30.00
5/4 & 6/4	65.00	60.00	45.00	35.00
8/4	70.00	65.00	45.00	40.00
12/4	80.00	90.00	40.00	
16/4	90.00	75.00	45.00	

SOFT MAPLE

The quantity of soft maple produced in Ontario is small and it is generally sold on a log run basis, the locality governing the prices.

WHITE AND RED OAK

(Plain sawed. Dry weight 4000 lbs. per M. ft.)

	1s & 2s	No. 1 Com.
4/4	$130.00	$90.00
5/4 & 6/4	135.00	95.00
8/4	140.00	100.00
10/4	150.00	110.00
12/4	150.00	110.00
16/4	165.00	120.00

WHITE OAK, Quarter Cut

(Dry weight 4000 lbs. per M. ft.)

	1s & 2s	No. 1 Com.
4/4	$230.00	$175.00
5/4 and 6/4	250.00	180.00
8/4	260.00	

RED OAK, Quarter Cut

	1s & 2s	No. 1 Com.
4/4	$185.00	$125.00
5/4 and 6/4	200.00	140.00
8/4	205.00	140.00

OTTAWA, ONT.

Manufacturers' Prices

Pine good sidings:		
1-in. x 7-in. and up		84 00
1¼-in. and 1½-in., 8-in. & up		102 00
2-in. x 7-in. and up		102 00
No. 2 cuts 2 x 8-in. and up		70 00
Pine good strips:		
1-in.		70 00
1¼-in. and 1½-in.		75 00
2-in.		80 00
Pine good shorts:		
1-in. x 7-in. and up		65 00
1-in. x 4-in. to 6-in.		57 00
1¼-in. and 1½-in.		70 00
2-in.		72 00
7-in. to 9-in. A sidings		56 00
Pine, No. 1 dressing sidings		62 00
Pine, No. 1 dressing strips		58 00
Pine, No. 1 dressing shorts		52 00
Pine, 1-in. x 4-in. s.c. strips		51 00
Pine, 1-in. x 5-in. s.c. strips		52 00
Pine, 1-in. x 6-in. s.c. strips		54 00
Pine, 1-in. x 7-in. s.c. strips		54 00
Pine, 1 x 8-in. s.c., 12 to 16 ft.	48 00	56 00
Pine, 1-in. x 10-in. M.R.		58 00
Pine, s.c. sidings, 1½ and 2-in.		55 00
Pine, s.c. strips, 1-in.	45 00	40 00
1¼, 1½ and 2-in.		56 00
Pine, s.c. shorts, 1 x 4 to 6 in.		45 00
Pine, s.c. and bet., shorts, 1 x 5		45 00
Pine, s.c. and bet., shorts, 1 x 6		47 00
Pine, s.c. shorts, 6'-11', 1"x10"		52 00
Pine box boards:		
1"x4" and up, 6'-11'		40 00
1"x3", 12'-16'		44 00
Pine, mill culls, strips and sidings, 1-in. x 4-in. and up, 12-ft. and up		40 00
Mill cull shorts, 1-in. x 4-in. and up, 6-ft to 11-ft.		38 00
O. culls r & w p		28 00

RED PINE, LOG RUN

mill culls out, 1-in.	36 00	42
mill culls out, 1¼-in.	36 00	42
mill culls out, 1½-in.	38 00	42
mill culls out, 2-in.	40 00	42
mill culls, white pine, 1"x7" and up		40 00

MILL RUN SPRUCE

1"x4" and up, 6'-11'		42 00
1"x4" and up, 12'-16'		42 00
1"x9"-10" and up, 12'-16'		48 00
1¼"x7" 8-9" and up, 12'-16'		48 00
1¼ x 10 and up, 12'-16'		50 00
1½" & 2" x 12" and up, 12'-16'		50 00
Spruce, 1-in. clear (fine dressing and B)		55 00
Hemlock, 1-in. cull	25 00	27 00
Hemlock, 1-in. log run	30 00	35 00
Hemlock, 2x4, 6, 8, 10, 12/16'	30 00	35 00
Tamarac	24 00	26 00
Basswood, log run, dead culls out	46 00	48 00
Basswood, log run, mill culls out	43 00	50 00
Birch, log run	48 00	50 00
Soft Elm, common and better, 1, 1¼, 2-in.	25 00	30 00
Ash, black, log run	32 00	40 00
1 x 10 No. 1 barn		52 00
1 x 10 No. 2 barn		48 00
1 x 8 and 9 No. 2 barn		42 00
Lath per M:		
No. 1 white pine, 1½-in. x 4 ft.		7
No. 2 white pine		7
Mill run white pine		7
Spruce, mill run 1½-in.		6
Red pine, mill run		6
Hemlock, mill run		6 50
32-in. lath		3 00
White Cedar Shingles:		
xxxx, 18-in.		7 00
Clear butt, 18-in.		6 00
18-in. xx		4 50
Spruce logs (pulp)	18 00	18 00

QUEBEC, QUE.

WHITE PINE

	Cts. Per Cubic Foot	
First class Ottawa waney, 18-in. average, according to lineal	80	90
19 in. and up average	90	100 00

SPRUCE DEALS

	Per M. Ft.	
3 in. unsorted Quebec, 4 in. to 6 in. thick	$34 00	$37 00
3 in. unsorted, Quebec, 7 in. to		

	00	40 00
	00	45 00

OAK

	Cts. Per Cubic Ft.	
	90	1 00

ELM

According to average and quality, 40 to 45 feet, cube	1 05
According to average and quality, 30 to 35 feet	85

BIRCH PLANKS

1 to 4 in. thick, per M. ft.	40 00	45 00

SARNIA, ONT.

FINE, COMMON AND BETTER

1 x 6 and 8 in.	$85 00
1 in., 8 in. and up wide	90 00
1¼ and 1½ in. and up wide	106 00
2 in. and up wide	108 00

CUTS AND BETTER

4/4 x 8 and up No. 1 and better	82 00
6/4 x 8 and up No. 1 and better	82 00
8/4 x 8 and up No. 1 and better	97 00

No. 1 CUTS

1 in., 8 in. and up	72 00
1¼ in., 8 in. and up	82 00
1½ in., 8 in. and up	82 00
2 in., 8 in. and up	87 00
2½ and 3 in., 8 in.	107 00
4 in., 8 in. and up	112 00

No. 1 BARN

1 in., 10 to 16 ft. long	$69 00
1¼, 1½ and 2 in., 10/16 ft.	72 00
2½ to 3 in., 10/10 ft.	

No. 2 BARN

1 in., 10 to	62 00
1¼, 1½ and	63 00
2½ in. to 3	

No. 3 BARN

1 in., 10 to 16 ft. long	52 00	62 00
1¼, 1½ and 2 in., 10/16 ft.	58 00	67 00

1 in., 1¼ in. & 1½ in., 10/16 ft.	47 00	49

Mill Run Culls

No. 1 48 in. White Pine	$7 00
No. 2 48 in. White Pine	6 50
No. 3 48 in. White Pine	6 00
32 in.	3 00
48 in.	6 00
32 in.	2 95

ST. JOHN, N.B.

ROUGH LUMBER

Wholesale Prices Per M. Sq. Ft.

2x3, 2x4, 3x3, 3x4, Rgh. Merch. Spr.	$42
2x3, 2x4, 3x3, 3x4 Dressed 1 edge	44
2x3, 2x4, 3x3, 3x4 Dressed 4 sides	48
2x6, 2x7, 3x5, 4x4, 4x6, all rough	45
2x8, 3x7, 5x5, 6x6	47
2x9, 3x8, 6x8, 7x7	50
2x10, 3x9	55
2x12, 3x10, 3x12, 8x8 and up	57
Merch. Spr. Bds. Rough, 1x3.4 & 5	40
" " " " 1x6	45
" " " " 1x7 & up.	45
Refuse Bds., Deals & Setgs.	30

Above random lengths up to 18-0 long.
Lengths 19-0 & up $5.00 extra per M.
For planing Merch. and Refuse $2.00 per M to above prices.
Laths $4.50 per M pieces.

SHINGLES

Cedar, Extras ...
" Clears ...
" 2nd Clears ...
" Extra No. 1 ...
Spruce ...
B. C. Cedar ...

WINNIP

No.

Dimension

2 x 4 ...
2
2
2
2

Sturtevant
SYSTEMS
Sturtevant Supremacy
Quality—Efficiency—Economy
ANNOUNCING A
NEW DRY KILN
WHICH PREVENTS
Casehardening
Checking
Splitting
Honeycombing
MINIMIZES SPOILAGE!
SAVES TIME!
With practically no spoilage—the new Sturtevant kiln dries wood in a few weeks where old, crude, inefficient methods consumed months and even years.
Rugged construction insures reliable, continuous service. Compartment type design permits easy and frequent tests and individual treatments. Temperature and humidity automatically controlled. Circulation of air positive. Built to your specifications. Without obligation—our engineering and kiln experts will advise you.
B. F. STURTEVANT CO. of Canada, Ltd.
Sturtevant
PRODUCTS

CURRENT LUMBER PRICES—Continued

2 x 12	40 50	41 50	44 00
	12 ft.	14 ft.	16 ft.
2 x 4	40 00	40 00	41 00
2 x 6	40 00	40 00	41 00
2 x 8	40 00	40 00	41 00
2 x 10	41 00	41 00	42 00
2 x 12	42 00	42 00	43 00

For 2 inches, rough, add 50 cents.
For S1E only add 50 cents.
For S1S and 2E, S4S or D&M, add $3.00.
For timbers larger than 8 x 8, add 50c. for each additional 2 inches each way.
For lengths longer than 20 ft., add $1.00 for each additional two feet.
For selected common, add $5.00.
For No. 2 Dimension, $3.00 less than No. 1.
For 1 x 2 and 2 x 2, $2 more than 2 x 4 No. 1.
For Tamarac add $3.00.

FIR, HEMLOCK, SPRUCE AND LARCH

Mountain Stock

No. 1 Dimension and Timbers

2 x 4, 2 x 6, 2 x 8, 8 to 16 ft., S1S1E	$39 00
2 x 4, 2 x 6, 2 x 8, 10 ft., S1S1E	41 00
2 x 4, 2 x 6, 2 x 8, 12/16, S1S1E	39 00
2 x 4, 2 x 6, 2 x 8, 18/22, S1S1E	41 00
2 x 4, 2 x 6, 2 x 8, 24/32, S1S1E	48 00
2 x 10, 8 ft. to 16 ft., S1S1E	40 00
2 x 10, 10 ft. S1S1E	42 00
2 x 10, 18/22, S1S1E	42 00
2 x 10, 24/32, S1S1E	44 00
2 x 12, 8 ft. to 16 ft., S1S1E	41 50
2 x 12; 10, 18, 20,	43 50
2 x 12; 24, 26, 28, 30, 32	45 50

BRITISH COLUMBIA COAST FIR.

Dimension S1S and E.

2 x 4 in., 6 ft.	$39 50
2 x 4 in., 8, 12 and 14 ft.	40 50
2 x 4 in., 10 ft.	41 50
2 x 4 in., 18 and 20 ft.	42 50
2 x 4 in., 22 to 32 ft.	44 50
2 x 10 in., 8, 12 and 14 ft.	41 75
2 x 10 in., 16 ft.	42 75
2 x 10 in., 18 and 20 ft.	43 75
2 x 10 in., 22 to 32 ft.	45 75
2 x 12 in., 8 to 14 ft.	43 25
2 x 12 in., 16 ft.	44 25
2 x 12 in., 18 and 20 ft.	45 25
2 x 12 in., 22 to 32 ft.	47 25
3 x 3 and 3 x 4 in., 8 to 14 ft.	46 75
3 x 3 and 3 x 4 in., 16 ft.	47 75
3 x 3 and 3 x 4, 18 and 20 ft.	48 75
3 x 3 and 3 x 4 in., 22 to 32 ft.	50 75
6 x 6, 6 x 8, 8 x 8, 6 to 16 ft.	49 90
6 x 6, 6 x 8 and 8 x 8, 18 and 20 ft.	49 90
6 x 6, 6 x 8, 8 x 8, 22 to 32 ft.	50 50
Shingles, XXX B. C. Cedar, straight cars on 60c rate	6 96

BUFFALO AND TONAWANDA, N.Y.

WHITE PINE
Wholesale Selling Price

Uppers, 4/4	$115 00
Uppers, 5/4 to 8/4	[illegible]
Uppers, 10/4 to 12/4	[illegible]
Selects 4/4	110 00
Selects 5/4 to 8/4	[illegible]
Selects 10/4 to 12/4	[illegible]
Fine common 4/4	[illegible]
Fine Common 5/4	87 00
Fine Common 6/4	[illegible]
Fine common 8/4	[illegible]
No. 1 Cuts 4/4	[illegible]
No. 1 Cuts 5/4	74 00
Cuts 6/4	[illegible]
Cuts 8/4	[illegible]
Cuts 4/4	[illegible]
Cuts 5/4	[illegible]
Cuts 6/4	[illegible]
Cuts 8/4	[illegible]
Cuts 5/4	[illegible]
Cuts 6/4	[illegible]
Cuts 8/4	[illegible]
ng 5/4	[illegible]
ng 5/4 x 10	67 00
ng 5/4 x 12	73 00
Moulding 5/4	74 00
Moulding 6/4	74 00
Moulding 8/4	74 00
Moulding 5/4	[illegible]
Moulding 6/4	[illegible]
Moulding 8/4	[illegible]
Barn 1 x 12	[illegible]
Barn 1 x 6 and 8	[illegible]
Barn 1 x 10	[illegible]
Barn 1 x 6 and 8	[illegible]
Barn 1 x 10	[illegible]
Barn 1 x 6 and 8	47 00
Barn 1 x 10	45 00
x 6 and up	45 00
x 10	[illegible]
x 12	46 00
x 13 and up	47 00

The following quotations on hardwoods represent the jobber buying price at Buffalo and Tonawanda.

	1s & 2s	No. 1 Com.	No. 2 Com.
MAPLE			
4/4	49 - 52	34 - 36	24 - 26
5/4 to 8/4	63 - 65	41 - 43	29 - 31
10/4 to 16/4	73 - 75	53 - 55	33 - 35
RED BIRCH			
4/4	64 - 66	44 - 46	[illegible]
5/4 to 8/4	67 - 69	47 - 49	[illegible]
SAP BIRCH			
4/4	60 - 64	[illegible]	[illegible]
5/4 and up	[illegible]	[illegible]	[illegible]
SOFT ELM			
4/4	49 - 51	[illegible]	[illegible]
5, 6 & 8/4	[illegible]	[illegible]	[illegible]
BASSWOOD			
4/4	[illegible]	[illegible]	[illegible]
Thicker	58 - 61	[illegible]	[illegible]
PLAIN OAK			
4/4	[illegible]	[illegible]	[illegible]
5/4 to 8/4	75 - 79	[illegible]	[illegible]
ASH, WHITE AND BROWN			
4/4	70 - 72	[illegible]	[illegible]
5/4 to 8/4	[illegible]	[illegible]	[illegible]
10/4 and up	[illegible]	[illegible]	[illegible]

BOSTON, MASS.

Quotations given below are for highest grades of Michigan and Canadian white pine and Eastern Canadian Spruce as required in the New England market in carloads.

White pine uppers, 1 in.		$140 00
White pine uppers, 1¼, 2 in.		[illegible]
White pine uppers, 2½, 3 in.		[illegible]
White pine uppers, 4 in.		[illegible]
Selects, 1 in.		[illegible]
Selects, 1¼, 2 in.		[illegible]
Selects, 2½, 3 in.		145 00
Selects, 4 in.		155 00
Fine common, 1 in., 30 per cent. 12 in. and up		[illegible]
Fine common, 1 x 8 and up		[illegible]
Fine common, 1¼ to 2 in.		[illegible]
Fine common, 2½ and 3 in.		[illegible]
Fine Common, 4 in.		[illegible]
1 in. shaky clear		[illegible]
1¼ to 2 in. shaky clear		[illegible]
1 in. No. 2 dressing		[illegible]
1¼ to 2 in. No. 2 dressing		[illegible]
No. 1 Cuts, 1 in.		[illegible]
No. 1 Cuts, 1¼ to 2 in.	[illegible]	[illegible]
No. 1 Cuts, 2½ and 3 in.		[illegible]
No. 2 Cuts, 1 in.		[illegible]
No. 2 Cuts, 1¼ to 2 in.	[illegible]	[illegible]

Barn Boards, No. 1, 1 x 12	[illegible]
No. 1, 1 x 10	[illegible]
No. 1, 1 x 8	[illegible]
No. 2, 1 x 12	[illegible]
No. 2, 1 x 10	[illegible]
No. 2, 1 x 8	[illegible]
No. 3, 1 x 12	[illegible]
No. 3, 1 x 10	[illegible]
No. 3, 1 x 8	[illegible]
Can. spruce, clear, 1 x 4 to 9 in.	[illegible]
1 x 10 in.	[illegible]
No. 1, 1 x 4 to 7 in.	[illegible]
No. 1, 1 x 8 & 9 in.	[illegible]
No. 1, 1 x 10 in.	[illegible]
No. 2, 1 x 4 & 5 in.	[illegible]
No. 2, 1 x 6 & 7 in.	[illegible]
No. 2, 1 x 8 & 9 in.	[illegible]
No. 2, 1 x 10 in.	[illegible]
No. 2, 1 x 12 in.	[illegible]
Spruce, 12 in. dimension	[illegible]
Spruce, 10 in. dimension	[illegible]
Spruce, [illegible]	[illegible]
Spruce, [illegible]	[illegible]
2 x 10 [illegible]	[illegible]
[illegible] 9 ft.	[illegible]
2 x 12 [illegible]	[illegible]
2 x 3, 2 x 4, 2 x 5, 2 x 6, 2 x 7	[illegible]
3 x 4 and 4 x 4 in.	[illegible]
2 x 8 in.	[illegible]
All other random lengths, and under, 8 ft. and up	[illegible]
inch and up merchantable boards, 8 ft. and up, p 1s	[illegible]
x 2	[illegible]
1 x 3	[illegible]
1-⅝ in. spruce lath	[illegible]
1-½ in. spruce lath	[illegible]

New Brunswick Cedar Shingles

Extras	[illegible]
Clears	[illegible]
Second Clears	[illegible]
Clear Whites	[illegible]
Extra 1s (Clear whites in)	[illegible]
Extra 1s (Clear whites out)	[illegible]
Red Cedar Extras, 16-in. 5 butts to 2-in.	[illegible]
Red Cedar Eurekas, 18-inch, 5-butts to 2-in.	[illegible]
Red Cedar Perfections, 5 butts to 2¼	[illegible]
Washington 16-in. 5 butts to 2 in. extra red cedar	[illegible]

BELL

Oil Burning Geared Locomotives

The Ideal Tractive Power for Timber and Lumber Loads

Compact and Efficient

This type of Bell locomotive has been doing splendid service in timber hauling in Ontario. It is simple to operate, and can be easily handled by one man. Compare the first cost, the fuel cost, and length of service with any other type of locomotive, and comparison will prove the superior adaptability of these splendid engines for the lumber industry.

Bell Locomotive Works Inc.

Founded 1908

11 Pine Street, NEW YORK, N.Y.

THE GENERAL SUPPLY COMPANY OF CANADA

LIMITED

356-360 Sparks St, OTTAWA Can.

Also at

MONTREAL, TORONTO, WINNIPEG, VANCOUVER

A Boon to Lumbermen

Payette's Famous Patent Mill Dogs

650 Sets already sold

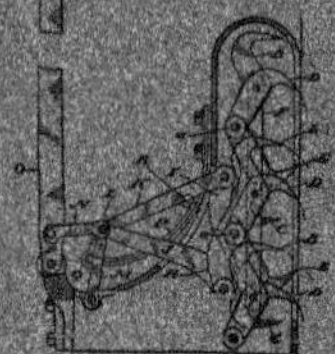

BECAUSE

(1) They will dog with perfect ease and safety in any class of timber.
(2) Will dog just as easily frozen maple or hardwoods of any description.
(3) Will dog the last board, just as easily as they dogged the first one.
(4) They do not tear the board or stock.
(5) Many other reasons, too numerous to mention here.

Write us for full particulars and booklet on same.

We also manufacture the following High-Grade Saw-Mill Machinery:—New Modern Saw-Mill Carriages, with either three or two head blocks; P. Payette's New Patent Saw-Mill Dog, for use in either winter or summer. P. Payette's Grip Set Works; Steam Feed Valves, Steam Lifter and Loaders, Valves. Five different classes and styles of Edgers, for either light or heavy duty. Combined Gang-Circulars and Edgers, or Independent Gang Circulars.
Steam Canters, Steam Lifters and Loaders, and a general line of saw-mill machinery. Detachable Chain-Sprockets, Castings of Gray Iron, Semi-Cast Steel, and brass castings for general use.
Descriptive Booklet and prices mailed free upon request.

P. Payette & Company

Engineers and Machinists

Penetanguishene, Ontario

J. T. PAYETTE, Proprietor

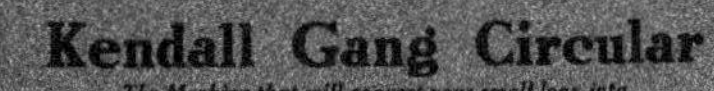

The Machine that will convert your small logs into more and better lumber, quicker than ever before.

The illustration shows one of the latest designs of gang circular patented by Mr. [illegible] Kendall, the well-known millwright of [illegible]. This machine takes [illegible] to gang saws—will cut cants up to [illegible] inches in thickness, and we furnish with it necessary saw collars for any thickness of lumber desired. It has a hollow mandrel, water cooled saws; each saw has a separate guide, easily accessible and readily adjustable, and the bridge tree is so designed that it can be removed, the saws taken off and a new set put on in [illegible] minutes. Safety fingers hung just inside the front press roll prevent a cant flying back off the saws. Lumber cut on these machines is guaranteed to come out absolutely true in size from end to end, and so smooth that 1/16 in. over size is all the allowance necessary for finish.

Read what one user says about it:—

"The machine has given every satisfaction and in many cases far exceeded my idea of sawing lumber; the proof of this being that our customers are paying me $1.00 to $1.50 per thousand more for certain classes of lumber than they can purchase same quality elsewhere—this advantage being purely on account of the uniform and smooth sawing this saw is capable of doing."

We are the original manufacturers of these machines

We have been manufacturing them for the past fourteen years, and the experience gained in all those years is at your disposal. We make these machines in three sizes, as follows, using

[illegible] saws for 8-in. cants as illustrated.
[illegible] saws for 10-in. cants.
[illegible] saws for 12-in. cants.

Each size is of the very latest design and up-to-date in every improvement.

May we send you a list of satisfied users?

We also make a complete line of [illegible] circulars with chain or [illegible] feed for slabbing logs for these machines.

William Hamilton Co., Limited

PETERBORO - - ONTARIO

CANADA LUMBERMAN AND WOODWORKER
Pride of the Mill
Yates
No. 91 Planer and Matcher
makes good wherever it is installed. When you tell your customers you are equipped to make better lumber than your competitors, and fill orders quicker, you naturally want a machine that can be depended upon to do it. In other words you want a Yates No. 91.
From the cast in one piece base to the improved grinding and jointing attachments this machine is the best that correct design and careful construction can produce.
Drop us a card asking for our "Matcher Book."
Sent free on request.
Yates
P. B. Yates Machine Company Ltd.
HAMILTON, ONT. CANADA
U. S. Plant, with Offices, BELOIT, WISCONSIN

Original "Dunbar" Machines

We are the original and the only makers of "Dunbar" Shingle Machines, Lath Machines, Clapboard Machines, Steam and Gasoline Logging Engines. Each is the best for its particular work. Are you using the best?

Lath Machine

From our many years of experience we evolved this "Dunbar" Original Lath Machine. Every improvement that could be suggested, every time-tested idea for the betterment of product and for greater speed, has been incorporated in this machine. We believe it has no equal, and there are a great number of mill men throughout Canada who share this belief with us. Carefully constructed of high grade materials and designed to work steadily under the hardest conditions.

Steam and Gasoline Logging Engines

Conditions in Canada necessitate an engine that will stand any amount of strain and hard work in the lumber industry. With this idea in mind we have brought out the "Dunbar" engines perhaps a little stronger than is really needed. They do their work easily and willingly, and stand a great amount of hard usage. Built entirely in Canada for the Canadian lumber trade.

Clapboard Machine

You will need no excuse for the quality of your product if you use the original "Dunbar" Clapboard Machine. Expert in every detail. This machine will give you the very best service under most trying conditions. It will turn out work without delays. It will need practically no repairs and will increase your output. We cannot recommend it too highly because it is giving this very service to lumbermen in all parts of this country.

Send for catalogues of any or all of these machines.

Dunbar Engine & Foundry Co.

WOODSTOCK, N.B.

ONTARIO

Canada's Banner Province

Ontario's timber production last year valued at $26,774,937 or 40% of Canada's total output.

Pine production, 905,442,000 ft. B.M.
Pulpwood, 246,282 cords.
Railway Ties, 5,704,459.

Ontario's woodworking industries, using 34 different kinds of wood, provide a ready market for the lumberman. Eighty-two per cent. of lumber used in Ontario's industries purchased within the Province.

Ontario's vast resources offer unsurpassed opportunities to the lumberman.

For maps and full information regarding Ontario, apply to

HON. G. HOWARD FERGUSON,
Minister of Lands, Forests and Mines.

GATES REFRACTORIES, LIMITED

382 St. James Street - - - MONTREAL

CANADA LUMBERMAN BUYERS' DIRECTORY

The following regulations apply to all advertisers:—Eighth page, every issue, three headings; quarter page, six headings; half page, twelve headings; full page, twenty-four headings.

ASBESTOS GOODS
Atlas Asbestos Company, Ltd.

AXES
Canadian Warren Axe & Tool Co.

BABBITT METAL
Canada Metal Company
General Supply Co. of Canada, Ltd.
Syracuse Smelting Works

Bale Ties
Laidlaw Bale Tie Company

BAND MILLS
Hamilton Company, William
Waterous Engine Works Company
Yates Machine Company, P. B.

BELT CEMENT
Graton & Knight Mfg. Company

BELT DRESSING
Atlas Asbestos Company, Ltd.
General Supply Co. of Canada, Ltd.
Graton & Knight Mfg. Company

BELTING
Atlas Asbestos Company, Ltd.
Beardmore Belting Company
Canadian Consolidated Rubber Co.
General Supply Company
Goodhue & Co., J. L.
Goodyear Tire & Rubber Co.
Graton & Knight Mfg. Company
Gutta Percha and Rubber Company
Main Belting Company
Manhattan Rubber Mfg. Co.
D. K. McLaren Limited
McLaren Belting Company, J. C.

BELTING (Transmission, Elevator, Conveyor, Rubber)
Dunlop Tire & Rubber Goods Co.

BLOWERS
Toronto Blower Company

BOILERS
Hamilton Company, William
Jenckes Machine Company
Marsh Engineering Works, Limited
Waterous Engine Works Company

BOILER PRESERVATIVE
International Chemical Company

BOX MACHINERY
Garlock-Walker Machinery Co.
Morgan Machine Company
Yates Machine Company, P. B.

BOX SHOOKS
Davison Lumber & Mfg. Company

BUNKS (Steel)
Alaska Bedding Co. of Montreal

CABLE CONVEYORS
Jeffrey Manufacturing Company
Jenckes Machine Company, Ltd.
Waterous Engine Works Company

CAMP SUPPLIES
Burns & Company, John
Canadian Milk Products Limited
Davies Company, William
Dr. Bell Veterinary Wonder Co.
Eckardt & Co.
Harris Abattoir Company
Johnson, A. H.
Turner & Sons, J. J.
Woods Manufacturing Company, Ltd.

CANT HOOKS
Canadian Warren Axe & Tool Co.
General Supply Co. of Canada, Ltd.
Pink Company, Thomas

CARS—STEEL BODY
Marsh Engineering Works, Limited

CAR WHEELS AND CASTINGS
Dominion Wheel & Foundries

CEDAR
Fesserton Timber Co.
Foss Lumber Company
Genoa Bay Lumber Company
Muir & Kirkpatrick
Long Lumber Company
Service Lumber Company
Terry & Gordon
Thurston-Flavelle Lumber Company
Vancouver Lumber Company
Victoria Lumber and Mfg. Co.

CHAINS
Canadian Link-Belt Company, Ltd.
General Supply Co. of Canada, Ltd.
Hamilton Company, William
Hobbs Company, Clinton E.
Jeffrey Manufacturing Company
Jenckes Machine Company, Ltd.
Pink & Co., Thomas
Waterous Engine Works Company
Williams Machinery Co., A. R. Vancouver

CHAIN HOISTS
Hobbs Company, Clinton E.

CHINA CLAY
Bowater & Sons, W. V.

CHEMICAL PLANTS
Blair, Campbell & McLean, Ltd.

CLOTHING
Acme Glove Works
Clarke & Company, A. R.
Grant, Holden & Graham
Woods Mfg. Company

COLLAR PADS
American Pad & Textile Co.

CONVEYOR MACHINERY
Canadian Link-Belt Company, Ltd.
Canadian Mathews Gravity Carrier Company
General Supply Co. of Canada, Ltd.
Jeffrey Mfg. Co.
Waterous Engine Works Company

CORDAGE
Consumers Cordage Company

CORN SYRUP
Canada Starch Company

COTTON GLOVES
American Pad & Textile Co.

COUPLING (Shaft)
Jenckes Machine Company, Ltd.

CRANES FOR SHIP YARDS
Canadian Link-Belt Company

CROSS ARMS
Genoa Bay Lumber Company

CUTTER HEADS
Shimer Cutter Head Company

CYPRESS
Chicago Lumber & Coal Company
Long Lumber Company
Wistar, Underhill & Nixon.

DERRICKS AND DERRICK FITTINGS
Marsh Engineering Works, Limited

DOORS
Genoa Bay Lumber Company
Long Lumber Co.
Mason, Gordon & Co.
Rutherford & Sons, Wm.
Terry & Gordon

DRAG SAWS
Gerlach Company, Peter
Williams Machinery Co., A. R.

DRIVING BOOTS
Acme Glove Works

DRYERS
Philadelphia Textile Mach. Company

DUST COLLECTORS
Toronto Blower Company

EDGERS
William Hamilton Company, Ltd.
Garlock-Walker Machinery Co.
Green Company, G. Walter
Long Mfg. Company, E.
Waterous Engine Works Company

ELEVATING AND CONVEYING MACHINERY
Canadian Link-Belt Comptny, Ltd.
Jeffery Manufacturing Company
Jenckes Machine Company, Ltd.
Waterous Engine Works Company

ENGINES
Hamilton Company, William
Jenckes Machine Company
Waterous Engine Works, Company

EXCELSIOR MACHINERY
Elmira Machinery and Transmission Company

EXHAUST FANS
Garlock-Walker Machinery Co.
Reed & Company, Geo. W.
Toronto Blower Company

EXHAUST SYSTEMS
Reed & Company, Geo. W.
Toronto Blower Company

FILES
Disston & Sons, Henry
Simonds Canada Saw Company

FIR
Associated Mills, Limited
Allan-Stoltze Lumber Co.
British American Mills & Timber Co.
Coal Creek Lumber Company
Fesserton Timber Co.
Foss Lumber Company
Grier & Sons, Ltd., G. A.
Heeney, Percy E.
Knox Brothers
Long Lumber Company
Mason, Gordon & Co.
Reynolds Company, Limited
Service Lumber Company
Shearer Company, Jas.
Terry & Gordon
Timberland Lumber Company
Timms, Phillips & Co.
Vancouver Lumber Company
Victoria Lumber and Mfg. Co.
Weller, J. B.

FIRE BRICK
Beveridge Paper Company
Elk Fire Brick Company of Canada

FIRE FIGHTING APPARATUS
Dunlop Tire & Rubber Goods Co.
Pyrene Mfg. Company
Waterous Engine Works Company

FIR FLOORING
Genoa Bay Lumber Company
Rutherford & Sons, Wm.

FLAG STAFFS
Ontario Wind Engine Company

FLOORING (Oak)
Long-Bell Lumber Company

GALVANIZING
Ontario Wind Engine Company

GLOVES
Acme Glove Works
Eisendrath Glove Co.

GASOLINE ENGINES
Ontario Wind Engine Company

GEARS (Cut)
Smart-Turner Machine Co.

GRAIN
Dwyer Company, W. H.

GRAVITY LUMBER CARRIER
Can. Mathews Gravity Carrier Co.

GRINDERS (Bench)
Garlock-Walker Machinery Co.

HARDWOODS
Anderson Lumber Company, C. G.
Atlantic Lumber Co.
Bartram & Ball
Bennett Lumber Company
Blakeslee, Perrin & Darling
Cameron & Co.
Cardinal & Page
Davison Lumber & Mfg. Company
Dunfield & Company
Edwards & Co., W. C.
Fassett Lumber Company
Fesserton Timber Co.
Fraser Limited
Gillespie, James
Gloucester Lumber Company
Grier & Son, G. A.
Harris Lumber Co., Frank H
Heeney, Percy E.
Knox Brothers
Long Lumber Company
McLennan Lumber Company
Moores, Jr., E. J.
Pedwell Hardwod Lumber Co.
Powell-Myers Lumber Co.
Russell, Chas. H.
Spencer Limited, C. A.
Stearns & Culver Lumber Co.
Summers, James R.
Taylor Lumber Company, S. K.
Webster & Brother, James

HARDWOOD FLOORING MACHINERY
American Woodworking Machinery Company
Garlock-Walker Machinery Co.

HARDWOOD FLOORING
Grier & Son, G. A.
Long Lumber Company

HAY
Dwyer & Company, W. H.

Alaska Double-Deck Bunk

When You Use "ALASKA" Double-Deck Bunks

YOUR men work harder and more steadily, because at the end of the day they can utterly relax with entire comfort on these sanitary steel bunks. The twisted link fabric springs have just the proper amount of tension to "give" without sagging. They support the body in a perfectly normal position, and when overlaid with an Alaska mattress they supply all the rest the most exacting workmen could demand.

They are noiseless under pressure, and because of their all-steel construction are not only durable and rigid, but entirely vermin proof.

Finished in black japan. Elevation of lower spring, 19 inches; of upper spring, 50 inches.

Shipping Weight, 118 lbs.

Alaska on an article means high-grade, every particle

ALASKA BEDDING OF MONTREAL LIMITED

400 St. Ambroise St., MONTREAL

Associated with
SIMMONS COMPANY
KENOSHA, Wis., U.S.A.

Write us for quotations
Sending full particulars of your needs

HARNESS
Padgitt Company, Tom

HEMLOCK
Anderson Lumber Company, C. G.
Bartram & Ball
Bourgouin, H.
Canadian General Lumber Company
Cane & Co., Jas. G.
Davison Lumber & Mfg. Company
Dunfield & Company
Edwards & Company, W. C.
Fesserton Timber Co.
Foss Lumber Company
Grier & Sons, Ltd., G. A.
Harris Lumber Co., Frank H
Hart & McDonagh
Long Lumber Company
Mason, Gordon & Co.
Roch, Julien
Spencer Limited, C. A.
Terry & Gordon

HOISTING AND HAULING ENGINES
Garlock-Walker Machinery Co.
General Supply Co. of Canada, Ltd.
Marsh Engineering Works, Limited

HORSES
Union Stock Yards

HOSE
Dunlop Tire & Rubber Goods Co.
General Supply Co. of Canada, Ltd.
Goodyear Tire & Rubber Co.
Gutta Percha and Rubber Company

INDUSTRIAL CARS
Marsh Engineering Works, Limited

INSURANCE
Hardy & Co., E. D.
Rankin Benedict Underwriting Co.

INTERIOR FINISH
Eagle Lumber Company
Hay & Co.
Mason, Gordon & Co.
Renfrew Planing Mills
Terry & Gordon

KNIVES
Disston & Sons, Henry
Peter Hay Knife Company
Simonds Canada Saw Company
Waterous Engine Works Company

LARCH
Otis Staples Lumber Co.

LATH
Austin & Nicholson
Canadian General Lumber Company
Cane & Co., Jas. G.
Cardinal & Page
Dupuis Limited, J. P.
Eagle Lumber Company
Fraser Limited
Fraser-Bryson Lumber Company
Genoa Bay Lumber Company
Gloucester Lumber Company
Grier & Sons, Ltd., G. A.
Harris Tie & Timber Company, Ltd.
Long Lumber Company
McLennan Lumber Company
New Ontario Colonization Company
Otis Staples Lumber Co.
River Ouelle Pulp and Lumber Co.
Spencer Limited, C. A.
Terry & Gordon
Union Lumber Company
Victoria Harbor Lumber Company

LATH BOLTERS
Garlock-Walker Machinery Co.
General Supply Co. of Canada, Ltd.
Green Company, C. Walter

LIGHTING APPLIANCES
Hobbs Company, Clinton E.

LOCOMOTIVES
Bell Locomotive Works
General Supply Co. of Canada, Ltd.
Jeffrey Manufacturing Company
Jenckes Machine Company, Ltd.
Climax Manufacturing Company
Montreal Locomotive Works

LATH TWINE
Consumers' Cordage Company

LINK-BELT
Canadian Link-Belt Company
Canadian Mathews Gravity Carrier Company
Jeffrey Mfg. Co.
Williams Machinery Co., A. R., Vancouver

LOGGING COLLARS
Padgitt Company, Tom

LOCOMOTIVE CRANES
Canadian Link-Belt Company, Ltd.

LOGGING ENGINES
Dunbar Engine and Foundry Co.
Jenckes Machine Company
Marsh Engineering Works, Limited

LOG HAULER
Green Company, G. Walter
Jenckes Machine Company, Ltd.

LOGGING MACHINERY AND EQUIPMENT
General Supply Co. of Canada, Ltd.
Hamilton Company, William
Jenckes Machine Company, Ltd.
Marsh Engineering Works, Limited
Waterous Engine Works Company

LUMBER TRUCKS
Waterous Engine Works Company

LUMBERMEN'S CLOTHING
Woods Manufacturing Company, Ltd.

METAL REFINERS
Canada Metal Company
Hoyt Metal Company
Sessenwein Brothers

MILLING IN TRANSIT
Renfrew Planing Mills
Rutherford & Sons, Wm.

MOLDINGS
Genoa Bay Lumber Co.
Rutherford & Sons, Wm.

MOTOR TRUCKS
Duplex Truck Company

OAK
Chicago Lumber & Coal Com
Long-Bell Lumber Company

OAKUM
Stratford Oakum Co., Geo.

OIL CLOTHING
Leckie Limited, John

OIL ENGINES
Swedish Steel & Importing Co.

OLD IRON AND BRASS
Sessenwein Brothers

OVERALLS
Hamilton Carhartt Cotton [illegible]

PAPER
Bowater & Sons, W. V.

PACKING
Atlas Asbestos Company, Ltd
Consumers Cordage Co.
Dunlop Tire & Rubber Goods Co.
Gutta Percha and Rubber Company

PAPER MILL MACHINERY
Bowater & Sons, W. V.

PINE
Anderson Lumber Compan
Atlantic Lumber Co.
Austin & Nicholson
Bourgouin, H.
Cameron & Co.
Canadian General Lumber Company
Cane & Co., Jas. G.
Cardinal & Page
Chicago Lumber & Coal Company
Cleveland-Sarnia Sawmills Compan
Colonial Lumber Company
Davison Lumber & Mfg. Co.
Dudley, Arthur N.
Dunfield & Company
Eagle Lumber Company
Edwards & Co., W. C.

Excelsior Lumber Company
Fesserton Timber Company
Fraser-Bryson Lumber Company
Fraser Limited
Gillies Brothers Limited
Gloucester Lumber Company
Gordon & Co., George
Grier & Sons, Ltd., G. A.
Harris Lumber Co., Frank H
Harris Tie & Timber Company, Ltd.
Hart & McDonagh
Hettler Lumber Company, Herman H.
Long-Bell Lumber Company
Long Lumber Company
Mason, Gordon & Co.
McLennan Lumber Company
Montreal Lumber Company
Moores, Jr., E. J.
Muir & Kirkpatrick
Otis Staples Lumber Co.
Parry Sound Lumber Company
Roch, Julien
Russell, Chas. H.
Shearer Company, Pas.
Spencer Limited, C. A.
Summers, James R.
Terry & Gordon
Union Lumber Company
Watson & Todd, Limited
Williams Lumber Company
Wuichet, Louis

PLANING MILL EXHAUSTERS
Garlock-Walker Machinery Co.
Reed & Company, Geo. W.
Toronto Blower Co.

PLANING MILL MACHINERY
American Woodworking Machinery Company
Garlock-Walker Machinery Co.
Mershon & Company, W. B.
Toronto Blower Co.
Yates Machine Company, P. B.

PORK PACKERS
Davies Company, William
Harris Abattoir Company

POSTS AND POLES
Auger & Company
Canadian Tie & Lumber Co.
Dupuis Limited, J. P.
Eagle Lumber Company
Harris Tie & Timber Company, Ltd.
Long-Bell Lumber Company
Long Lumber Company
Mason, Gordon & Co.
Terry & Gordon

PULLEYS AND SHAFTING
Canadian Link-Belt Company
Garlock-Walker Machinery Co.
General Supply Co. of Canada, Ltd.
Green Company, G. Walter
Hamilton Company, William
Jeffrey Mfg. Co.
Jenckes Machine Company, Ltd.

PULP MILL MACHINERY
Canadian Link-Belt Company, Ltd.
Hamilton Company, William
Jeffrey Manufacturing Company
Jenckes Machine Company, Ltd.
Waterous Engine Works Company

PUMPS
General Supply Co. of Canada, Ltd.
Hamilton Company, William
Jenckes Machine Company, Ltd.
Smart-Turner Machine Company
Waterous Engine Company

RAILS
Gartshore, John J.
Sessenwein Bros.

ROOFING
Reed & Company, Geo. W.

ROOFINGS
(Rubber, Plastic and Liquid)
International Chemical Company

ROPE
Consumers Cordage Co.
Leckie, Limited, John

RUBBER GOODS
Atlas Asbestos Company
Dunlop Tire & Rubber Goods Co.
Goodyear Tire and Rubber Co.
Gutta Percha & Rubber Company

SASH
Genoa Bay Lumber Company
Renfrew Planing Mills

SAWS
Atkins & Company, E. C.
Disston & Sons, Henry
General Supply Co. of Canada, Ltd.
Gerlach Company, Peter
Green Company, G. Walter
Hoe & Company, R.
Shurly Co., Ltd., T. F.
Shurly-Dietrich Company
Simonds Canada Saw Company

SAW MILL LINK-BELT
Williams Machinery Co., A. R., Vancouver

SAW MILL MACHINERY
Canadian Link-Belt Comptny, Ltd.
Dunbar Engine & Foundry Co.
Firstbrook Bros.
General Supply Co. of Canada, Ltd.
Hamilton Company, William
Huther Bros. Saw Mfg. Company
Jeffrey Manufacturing Company
Long Manufacturing Company, E.
Parry Sound Lumber Company
Payete Company, P.
Waterous Engine Works Company
Yates Machine Co., P. B.

SHEATHINGS
Goodyear Tire & Rubber Co.

SHINGLE MACHINES
Marsh Engineering Works, Limited

SAW SHARPENERS
Garlock-Walker Machinery Co.
Waterous Engine Works Company

SAW SLASHERS
Waterous Engine Works Company

SAWMILL LINK-BELT
Canadian Link-Belt Company

SHEET METALS
Syracuse Smelting Works

SHINGLES
Allan-Stoltze Lumber Co.
Associated Mills, Limited
Campbell-MacLaurin Lumber Co.
Cardinal & Page
Dominion Lumber & Timber Co.
Eagle Lumber Company
Foss Lumber Company
Fraser Limited
Genoa Bay Lumber Company
Gillespie, James
Gloucester Lumber Company
Grier & Sons, Limited, G. A.
Harris Lumber Co., Frank H
Harris Tie & Timber Company, Ltd.
Heeney, Percy E.
Long Lumber Company
Mason, Gordon & Co.
McLennan Lumber Company
Miller Company, Ltd., W. H.
Reynolds Company, Limited
Service Lumber Company
Shingle Agency of B. C.
Terry & Gordon
Timms, Phillips & Co.
Vancouver Lumber Company
Victoria Lumber and Mfg. Co.

SHINGLE & LATH MACHINERY
Dunbar Engine and Foundry Co.
Garlock-Walker Machinery Co.
Green Company, C. Walter
Hamilton Company, William
Long Manufacturing Company, E.
Payette Company, P.

SHOEPACKS
Acme Glove Works

SILENT CHAIN DRIVES
Canadian Link-Belt Company, Ltd.

SILOS
Ontario Wind Engine Company

SLEEPING ROBES
Woods Mfg. Company, Limited

SMOKESTACKS
Marsh Enginering Works, Limited
Waterous Engine Works Company

SNOW PLOWS
Bateman-Wilkinson Company
Pink Company, Thomas

SPARK ARRESTORS
Jenckes Machine Company, Ltd.
Reed & Company, Geo. W.
Waterous Engine Works Company

SPRUCE
Bartram & Ball
Bourgouin, H.
Cane & Co., Jas. G.
Cardinal & Page
Davison Lumber & Mfg. Company
Donogh & Co., John
Dudley, Arthur N.
Dunfield & Company
Exchange Lumber Company
Foss Lumber Company
Fraser Limited
Fraser-Bryson Lumber Company
Gillies Brothers
Gloucester Lumber Company
Grant & Campbell
Grier & Sons, Ltd., G. A.
Harris Lumber Co., Frank H.
Hart & McDonagh
Long Lumber Company
Mason, Gordon & Co.
McLennan Lumber Company
Muir & Kirpatrick
New Ontario Colonization Company
River Ouelle Pulp and Lumber Co.
Roch, Julien
Russell, Chas. H.
Service Lumber Company
Shearer Company, Jas.
Snowball Co., J. B.
Spencer Limited, C. A.
Terry & Gordon
Rideau Lumber Company

STEEL CHAIN
Canadian Link-Belt Company, Ltd.
Jeffrey Manufacturing Company
Waterous Engine Works Company

STEEL PLATE CONSTRUCTION
Marsh Engineering Works, Limited

STEAM PLANT ACCESSORIES
Waterous Engine Works Company

STEEL BARRELS
Smart-Turner Machine Co.

STEEL DRUMS
Smart-Turner Machine Co.

STOVES
Burns & Company, John

SWEAT PADS
American Pad & Textile Co.

SULPHITE PULP CHIPS
Davison Lumber & Mfg. Company

TANKS
Ontario Wind Engine Company

TARPAULINS
Turner & Sons, J. J.
Woods Manufacturing Company, Ltd.

TAPS AND DIES
Pratt & Whitney Company

TENTS
Turner & Sons, J. J.
Woods Mfg. Company

TENTS, CLOTHING
Grant, Holden & Graham, Limited

TIES
Auger & Company
Austin & Nicholson
Canadian Tie & Lumber Co.
Harris Tie & Timber Company, Ltd.
Long Lumber Company
McLennan Lumber Company
Terry & Gordon

TIMBER BROKERS
Bradley, R. R.
Cant & Kemp
Farnworth & Jardine
Hunter, Herbert F.
Smith & Tyrer, Limited

TIMBER CRUISERS ESTIMATORS
Sewall, James W.

TIMBER LANDS
Department of Lands and Forests

TRACTORS
British War Mision

TRANSMISSION MACHINERY
Canadian Link-Belt Company, Ltd.
General Supply Co. of Canada, Ltd.
Jenckes Machine Company, Ltd.
Jeffrey Manufacturing Company
Waterous Engine Works Company

TRIMMERS
Garlock-Walker Machinery Co.
Green Company, C. Walter
Waterous Engine Works Compan

TUGS
West & Peachey

TURBINES
Hamilton Company, William
Jenckes Machine Company, Ltd.

VALVES
Bay City Foundry & Machine Co.

VENEERS
Webster & Brother, James

VENEER DRYERS
Coe Manufacturing Company
Philadelphia Textile Mach. Co.

VENEER MACHINERY
Coe Machinery Company
Garlock-Walker Machinery Co.
Philadelphia Textile Machinery

VETERINARY REMEDIES
Dr. Bell Veterinary Wonder Co.
Johnson, A. H.

WATER HEATERS
Mason Regulator & Engineering

WATER WHEELS
Hamilton Company, William
Jenckes Machine Company, Ltd.

WIRE
Laidlaw Bale Tie Company

WIRE ROPE
Canada Wire & Cable Co.

WOODWORKING MACHINERY
American Woodworking Machy. Co.
Garlock-Walker Machinery Co.
General Supply Co. of Canada, Ltd.
Jeffrey Manufacturing Company
Long Manufacturing Company, E.
Mershon & Company, W. B.
Waterous Engine Works Company
Yates Machine Company, P. B.

WOOD PRESERVATIVES
International Chemical Company

WOOD PULP
Austin & Nicholson
New Ontario Colonization Co.
River Ouelle Pulp and Lumber Co.

Canada Lumberman & Wood Worker

Write or wire for prices on
mixed cars containing

ROBIN HOOD FLOUR

Feed Oats, Bran, Shorts & Cereals

Our products will please you better

ROBIN HOOD MILLS LIMITED

Board of Trade Building
MONTREAL

BUY VICTORY BONDS

E. D. HARDY & CO., OTTAWA

Shimer Circular Bit Jointing Heads

A circular shear cut head that is unsurpassed as a Jointing Head for stock from 1" to 3"; always ready for the job without a set up, saving you money, and assuring a perfect square joint. Made in four, six or eight bits with or without Self Centering Colet.

Write for Prices

SHIMER CUTTER HEAD CO. OF CANADA, LTD., GALT, ONTARIO

Successors to Samuel J. Shimer & Sons

ASBESTOS

We manufacture practically every article
that can be made of Asbestos—including

Asbestos { Packings
Boiler Gaskets
Pipe and Boiler
Coverings

Atlas Asbestos Co., Limited, Montreal

**SMART
TURNER
Steam and
Power Pumps**

The Pumps for Long, Hard Service

The Smart-Turner Machine Company, Limited

HAMILTON CANADA

Soo Line Pike Poles, Peavies, Cant Hooks and Sager Axes

in the hands of your woodsmen will give you satisfaction and save your money.

Ask your dealer or order direct.

Made by
Canadian Warren Axe & Tool Co.
ST. CATHARINES, ONT.

Atlantic Lumber Company
HARDWOODS
WEST VIRGINIA SOFT RED AND WHITE OAK
Our Specialty: West Virginia and Pennsylvania Cherry
1055 Seneca Street

Standard Hardwood Lumber Co.
Hardwoods
Prompt Shipment { From Buffalo Yards or from Mill direct to you
8 Million Feet Dry Stock on Hand 1333 Clinton St.

Hugh McLean Lumber Co.
Hardwoods of All Kinds
Our Specialties—QUARTERED WHITE OAK SAP AND RED GUM
Established 25 Years 940 Elk Street

Miller, Sturm & Miller
1142 SENECA STREET
Hardwoods of All Kinds

G. Elias & Bro., Inc.
Established 1881
All Kinds of Hardwood Lumber
And in addition we carry a full line of White Pine, Yellow Pine, Spruce, Hemlock and Fir Timber, Lumber, Millwork and Boxes—Maple and Oak Flooring
CAREFUL ATTENTION TO MIXED CAR ORDERS

Taylor & Crate
Hardwoods of All Kinds
A stock of 18,000,000 to 20,000,000 feet of hardwoods carried at all times at our two big Buffalo Yards
Established 80 Years Rail or Cargo Shipments

T. Sullivan & Co.
HARDWOODS
We Specialize in Brown Ash and Elm
Car or Cargo Shipments Cor. Niagara and Arthur Sts.

Yeager Lumber Company, Inc.
SPECIALTIES
Oak, Poplar, Ash, Maple
932 Elk Street

BUFFALO

Buffalo Hardwood Lumber Dealers

Buffalo Hardwood Lumber Co.
940 Seneca St.
We Specialize in
WHITE ASH
Anyone handling any of this stock, write us.
We also handle a complete stock of Plain Oak, Quar. Oak, Maple, Poplar, Red Cedar, etc.

Blakeslee, Perrin & Darling
A Complete Stock of Seasoned Hardwoods
including Ash, Basswood, Birch, Cherry, Chestnut, Cypress, Elm, Gum, Hickory, Maple, Plain and Quartered Oak, Poplar and Walnut.
1100 Seneca Street

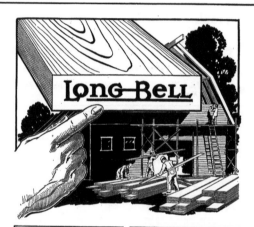

British Timber Importers and [illegible]

BROWNING & COMPANY

(Established over a Century)

IMPORTERS of and AGENTS for

ALL KINDS OF

CANADIAN WOOD GOODS

22/3 LAURENCE POUNTNEY LANE, CANNON STREET,

LONDON, E.C.4.

OFFERS OF AGENCIES INVITED

BRITISH IMPORTERS

CANADA CAN SUPPLY YOU

Britain's greatest store-house of timber, Canada, offers the logical market for British importers. The "Canada Lumberman" is the medium through which British importers can reach the complete lumber and timber industry of the Dominion in all its phases. The "Canada Lumberman" will, through the use of its advertising columns, bring you into close touch with the whole trade, which can only be reached by the nationally read lumber journal of Canada.

The Canada Lumberman and Woodworker

347 Adelaide Street West, - TORONTO, CANADA

Sample copies, detailed information, advertising rates, will be gladly supplied. Address the Publishers direct, 347 Adelaide Street West, Toronto, Canada, or

Our London Office—16 Regent St. S. W. 1,

NEW ZEBRA, WOOD, WESTERN UNION, and PRIVATE CODES USED.

Telephones:
1391 Long Distance.
400 Private Branch Exchange.

Cables:
"HILLAS," HULL

W. N. HILLAS & COMPANY

WOOD BROKERS

FOR EVERY CLASS OF TIMBER

***Head Office:* HULL, England**

To the Lumber Companies of Canada:

You have the Goods. Place your Lists with full particulars in our hands. We are in daily touch with all the Buyers in the United Kingdom.

PLEASE NOTE. We pay cash against all documents, and take the whole of the Delcredere risk on Buyers.

Canada Lumberman
and Woodworker

Issued on the 1st and 15th of every month by
HUGH C. MACLEAN, LIMITED, Publishers
HUGH C. MacLEAN, Winnipeg, President.
THOS. S. YOUNG, Toronto, General Manager.

OFFICES AND BRANCHES:

TORONTO - - Telephone A. 2700 - - 347 Adelaide Street West
VANCOUVER - - Telephone Seymour 2013 - - Winch Building
MONTREAL - - Telephone Main 2299 - - 119 Board of Trade
WINNIPEG - Telephone Garry 856 - Electric Railway Chambers
NEW YORK - - - - - - - - - - - 309 Broadway
CHICAGO - Telephone Harrison 5351 - 1413 Great Northern Building
LONDON, ENG. - - - - - - - 16 Regent Street, S. W.

TERMS OF SUBSCRIPTION

Canada, United States and Great Britain, $2.00 per year, in advance; other foreign countries embraced in the General Postal Union, $3.00.
Single copies 15 cents.

"The Canada Lumberman and Woodworker" is published in the interest of, and reaches regularly, persons engaged in the lumber, woodworking and allied industries in every part of Canada. It aims at giving full and timely information on all subjects touching these interests, and invites free discussion by its readers.

Advertisers will receive careful attention and liberal treatment. For manufacturing and supply firms wishing to bring their goods to the attention of owners and operators of saw and planing mills, woodworking factories, pulp mills, etc., "The Canada Lumberman and Woodworker" is undoubtedly the most direct and profitable advertising medium. Special attention is directed to the "Wanted" and "For Sale" advertisements.

Authorized by the Postmaster-General for Canada, for transmission as second-class matter.

Entered as second-class matter July 18th, 1914, at the Postoffice, at Buffalo, N. Y., under the Act of Congress of March 3rd, 1879.

Vol. 39 Toronto, November 1, 1919 No. 21

The Lumberman and His Problems

In the ups and downs of business it is not an unusual experience for one who has enjoyed a moderate measure of prosperity or even scored a decided success in a financial way, to sit back occasionally and ruminate whether he might not have done better had he entered, at the outset of his career, some other sphere of activity. After an insight of twenty-five or thirty years one is inclined to review the past with considerable interest and raise an interrogation to the effect that, had he his life to live over again, would he follow the same course.

It is a peculiar characteristic of human nature that it never seems exactly satisfied. We are all prone to observe the snags and pitfalls which beset our own road, but the route of the other fellow resembles a primrose path leading down a pleasant vale to the borderland of happiness and content. We see too much of our own difficulties and obstacles, but have not the same broad vision or perspective regarding the perplexities of the other fellow. This may be accunted for quite easily when we remember that those on the outside seldom see what is going on in the inside, and in respect to our own particular vocation we are all on the inside and know comparatively little of what is transpiring on the outside. Lack of intimate acquaintance and daily association makes us think that the other fellow always has the best proposition, that his customers are more easily satisfied, that his manufacturing and selling conditions are more pleasant and agreeable and generally the whole of his organization conducted with less worry and disappointment, less labor and other deterrents than our own.

Reverting to the lumber business, too often the contractor wishes he were a retail lumberman and the retail lumberman believes that had he started into the wholesale business he would have ere this earned a sufficient reward, as the result of his foresight and devotion to duty, to enable him to live in comparative luxury for the rest of his natural days. The wholesaler thinks that had he gone into the manufacturing line and dealt with the conversion of the raw material into the finished product, instead of acting as a large distributor, he would have cleaned up and, to use a colloquial expression, been on "Easy Street" by this time. The manufacturer will tell of his troubles with labor, production, raw materials and delivery, and wish that he were rid of them all and had simply to buy the stock and turn it over; then he would be comparatively happy.

Thus the flame of human interest and desire plays upon many scenes. Each one of which looks more alluring than the other, but when the other is reached then there seems to be a spot just beyond where all worries cease and satisfaction prevails. It all makes an interesting commentary upon the aims and desires, the pursuits and the pleasures, the ambitions and disappointments of the average man and few seem thoroughly content with their lot. Now and then one will admit that he has selected the right course and will be frank enough to acknowledge that the business he is in is not bad, yet adds a proviso that he would like to be in some other end of it; and so the ripples on the stream are seen on every hand. It is well summed up in the viewpoint of a leading lumberman who is recognized as one of the shrewdest and most successful of sawmill operators in the Dominion, yet the other day he declared seriously that he wished he had gone into the wholesale end of the business. He added: "The lot of the sawmill men is the most uncertain of any. There are so many 'ifs' about it. If we can get the men we can cut the logs; if we get the snow, we can haul them to the stream; if we get the rain we can float them to the mills; if we get them to the mills there is the question of labor; if labor is available, there is another 'if' in the way of the transportation, etc. Thus the whole circuit is one of 'ifs'. We send our men to the woods in August or September and the lumber made from the timber then cut is not sold or distributed until practically a year after. Thus we have to finance twelve months ahead or behind, which ever you like to call it. Now, with the wholesaler, matters are entirely different. He can go out and buy a block of stock, pay for it and sell the whole thing within a week or a month, collect his money and make a nice clean-up without any of the overhead worries that we have to go through for several months. If a fire should visit his lumber, why it is no doubt well insured, and he has not to wrestle with the labor problem, the weather, cutting, hauling, driving, sorting and manufacturing. The wholesaler should be a happy man to-day during this period of unrest, agitation and strife."

The Future of the Wooden House

The cabled reports from London give confused accounts of the wooden house situation. One clear fact, however, emerges from these reports—that a vigorous agitation has been waged in favor of wooden houses being erected to meet the very acute housing problem. The Ministry of Health was at first hostile, as the result of investigations into the suitability of the houses for Great Britain, and also on the assumption that the cost would be nearly as large as for brick dwellings. But the pressure of public opinion was too strong, and the department issued a series of regulations governing the construction of wooden houses. These involved considerable expenditure, due to elaborations deemed necesary to conform with British conditions. For instance, the lumber required by the regulations was larger in amount than in a typical Canadian wooden house. The result was strong criticism of the regulations, as being calculated to deter the building of the houses. The regulations did not survive the criticism; they were withdrawn, and the responsibility for the houses thrown upon the various municipal authorities, it being stipulated that the materials must be sufficiently strong to stand the inclement weather.

The wooden houses have found a backer in Sir Charles Ruthen, a member of the Council of the Society of Architects. He pointed out the pressing need for houses, and stated that if the output of bricks increased two hundred and fifty per cent. it would be some fifteen or twenty years before the present shortage would be overtaken. At the present time seven million people were improperly housed. The facts, he stated, showed the impossibility of production of brick houses and the crying need of the immediate use of wood in building.

He estimated that if the housing problem is to be handled in any degree satisfactorily during the next five years a grand total of 1,044,000 houses must be erected or well over 200,000 each year. Calculating twenty-five thousand bricks to each house this would mean that five thousand million bricks would be required each year. To secure this amount two and a half times the number of workmen engaged in this industry before the war must be found to meet the demand.

The British Columbia representatives in London are hotfoot after the business for supplying wooden houses, and it is stated in a cable that some orders have already been given out. Three sample houses of different types have been sent from B. C. to London, and there is a probability of very extensive contracts resulting. Eastern Canadian firms have also gone after the trade very strenuously, the Canadian Timber Products Association, in conjunction with the Export Association Co. of Canada, having taken up the matter with the Ministry of Health. There are now several sample houses in France, where there is said to be a demand for these buildings, while Belgium is also in the market for some thousands of houses.

There would thus appear to be a very promising field for Canadian enterprise, provided always that sufficient shipping facilities and fair shipping rates can be obtained. The steamship companies are now charging very high rates, and these make it very difficult to compete with Scandinavian countries, where the freights are considerably lower.

The Many Recompenses of Courtesy

Courtesy costs nothing, yet is a valuable asset in all sections of business and social life. This is a truism which is not always recognized in a practical form. There is no class of men who appreciate courtesy more than the travellers of business houses. They are away from home, often for weeks together, in all seasons; have to encounter all classes and preserve a tactful and cheerful manner under all conditions.

"From a considerable experience on the road," remarked the head of a wholesale lumber firm, "I have a strong appreciation of the difficulties of travellers. Travellers are entitled to every courtesy from firms, and personally I am a believer in giving every representative at least a brief interview. Regarded even from the selfish point, such interviews are of value to those who are buyers of lumber. Travellers know general conditions in the lumber business far better than a man who sits in the office, and are able to give one much information of value, as they necessarily cover a very wide area. Naturally a busy man does not want his time taken up in the discussion of irrelevant topics, but any traveller worth his salt soon realizes the situation and does not waste time.

"In the lumber trade, at any rate, a refusal to see a traveller may mean the loss of stock worth while buying. To draw on my own experience, I always, in my younger days, used to call on one man—not because he bought from me, but because of the encouragement I received from the few words I had with him. I came away, perhaps at the end of a disappointing day, with a fresh stock of energy. He was, in a word, courteous. We sometimes hear of men who, although rough in speech and of a sour disposition, have yet kindly natures; but as a rule we avoid these prickly thorns. We are naturally attracted to men with courteous dispositions, and travellers are quick to size up a man's characteristics."

Editorial Short Lengths

In the Abitibi, P.Q., region there are now fifty sawmills completed and another four are in course of construction. At La Reine 6 mills are completed; Dupuy, 3; La Sarre, 6; Macanic, 6; Aulhier, 2; Privat, 4; Launay, 1; Trecesson, 2; Dalquier, 1; Figuery, 1; La Motte, 1; Amos, 5; Landrienne, 2; Barraute, 2; Courville, 1; Senneterre, 2; Doucet, 2. It is estimated that during next season 60,000,000 feet of lumber will be produced in this region. The Quebec Government has spent large sums in developing the district.

Although comparatively little lumber has been sent to the United Kingdom on liners this season, a fair quantity has gone on tramps. The steamship lines have had such large quantities of ordinary cargo offered, that they have been able to ask very high rates, with the result that lumber could not be shipped except on a speculative basis. Room, too, is restricted, and the steamship lines are not anxious for lumber. The Government Timber Buyer is rushing all the lumber that can be sent, and the port of Montreal is loaded up with cars awaiting to be placed on board. The Liverpool strike interferred somewhat with shipments, but it is hoped to have the great bulk of the lumber shipped by the end of this month.

The Commissioner inquiring into the high cost of living has addressed a questionnaire to all manufacturers of lumber in Canada. The lumbermen are asked to give information about cost of production, and the reason for the price advances since 1914. A statement issued by the Cost of Living Commissioner is to the following effect: "Since the housing problem is one of the most serious in the country at present, lumber is one of the necessities which come within the scope of this investigation. The present high price of building materials is having a deterrent effect on building operations. There is a tendency to consider these prices abnormal and temporary. This inquiry aims to find out what increase has taken place.

In regard to logging operations during the coming season it is rather difficult to gauge conditions accurately at the present juncture. There will be a much larger cut in many centres, particularly in the Ottawa Valley and Northern Ontario, but advices regarding the availability of help differ widely. At some points bush workers are reported as numerous and the camps well filled up, while in others there is a shortage of man power. A large number of foreigners, now that the war is over, have returned home laden with cash-filled wallets by reason of the high wages received, and this effluxion has materially lessened the number of lumberjacks in various districts. It is generally conceded that labor is not as efficient as it was before the war, and that it now requires three men to accomplish what was formerly carried out by two. In the production of timber during 1920 labor will play an important factor, and just how it will shape up eventually cannot be stated as yet. It is too early to read conditions aright or make any predictions, but a number of operators are hoping that, with the closing of a large number of sawmills at the end of the present month, there will be an improvement in those parts of the country which now complain of a dearth of help.

The following statement given out in a recent interview with Mr. Wharton Clay, Commissioner of the Associated Metal Lath Manufacturers of Chicago, covers very fully the present building situation:

Those who are holding off from building at the present time will be sadly left. The general public already understand that prices on building materials are not going to be any lower. The Trade Associations now have the problem of convincing the public that the number of mechanics available in the United States for building construction is far below the normal requirements. This is due to many reasons, chief of which are the natural death rate in the past few years, with practically no addition of apprentices to fill up the depleted ranks. This was particularly intensified by the influenza epidemic of last year. The death rate among building mechanics was very high, due to the exposed conditions under which they are required to work.

Further, thousands have left the building trade and gone into other occupations which have offered them steady employment, and hundreds will never return.

It is entirely possible that the great building boom will bring a shortage of material, and the difficulty of transportation will be greatly magnified, and on the whole, conditions are better for the economical construction of building at the present time than they are likely to be for many years to come.

Lumber Stocks In West Are Greatly Reduced

Major-General McRae Tells Wholesale Lumbermen That Costs Are Mounting Rapidly, But Good Market Is Assured For The Next Two Years

Major-General A. D. McRae, Vancouver, B.C.

The Wholesale Lumber Dealers' Association, Inc., resumed its monthly meetings after the summer recess, on October 17, at one of the best meetings that they have yet held. Thirty members of the association attended the dinner which was held at the Albany Club, Toronto.

At the conclusion of the dinner, Mr. A. E. Clark, who occupied the chair, spoke for a few minutes about the work of the association. He welcomed the members back to their duties as members of the association, ing the forthcoming association and suggested strongly that duryear they should give as much attention as possible to promoting its interests.

The business end of the meeting consisted of a discussion of a few matters of routine, after which addresses were delivered by Major-General A. D. McRae of Vancouver, B. C., Mr. A. C. Manbert of Toronto, and Mr. John Pearson, who spoke on behalf of the Navy League of Canada.

Major-General A. D. McRae was a guest at the meeting having been in Toronto on a business visit. Lumbermen in all parts of Canada are intimately acquainted with General McRae's splendid record, both as the head of the Canadian Western Lumber Company, B. C., and as one of the most important Canadian officers who went overseas during the war. General McRae's wide business and organizing experience led to his services being utilized in connection with some of the most important purchasing and organization work of the Canadian forces, and finally he occupied a leading position in connection with the British Department of Propaganda.

After referring to a few matters relating to the war, General McRae described conditions in B. C. as they are to-day, chiefly in connection with lumber industry. He stated that the lumber manufacturing business on the coast presented many startling contrasts from that of five years ago. Practically the whole of the trouble facing them to-day was the outcome of labor conditions. While the general situation on its face appeared excellent, it was evident to the close observer that they were going to have considerable difficulty during the approaching winter. In preceding winters they always counted upon a good deal of unemployment at the coast. This year they were going to have a great deal more. Under the demobilization scheme of the Canadian forces, the boys were given the opportunity of taking their discharges wherever they liked in Canada, and many of them had decided in favor of going to the west coast. The unemployment situation on this account would be greatly aggravated and would become acute during winter.

Western Log Supply is Limited

The labor situation was the regulating factor in connection with the production of lumber, as the latter depended entirely upon the supply of logs. They could, therefore, anticipate a rather long shutdown of all the Pacific Coast mills during the winter as the log supply would be very limited.

Speaking of the situation in the woods, General McRae again laid emphasis upon the influence of the labor situation in British Columbia to-day. They had an eight-hour day for labor. The efficiency of woods labor had fallen off from 30 to 33 per cent. so that they were only getting about 50 per cent. of their former output. On a logging chance which used to cost from $3.35 to $4.00 per thousand, to put in the logs, the cost to-day was $14. Wages were from $4.50 to $12 per day, and when he left the coast the men had been on strike for a $5.00 minimum, with the eight-hour day lasting from the time when the man started from the camp until they arrived back. Many other demands were made, some of which were not only impossible, but utterly fantastic. They simply meant that the men wanted in future to be boss. He understood that some sort of a settlement had now been reached, giving the men certain concessions.

It was quite impossible to satisfy labor at the coast to-day. Organization in the woods was under the O. B. U., and that meant I. W. W., whose doctrine it was to break the employer. They advocated that the men should lie down on the job. General McRae urged the manufacturers of Eastern Canada, if they were faced with organized labor in the wods or mills, to get it under the American Confederation of Labor or some other responsible body which would ilve up to its agreements.

Should Eject All Strike Leaders

The strike in B. C. had actually been brought about by a small minority of the employes. Quite 80 per cent. of their men had been all right. Probably not over 10 per cent. of them wanted to strike, while 80 per cent. wanted to stay. In most comps it had been 2, 3, or 4 men who had drawn out all the rest. Investigation showed that these strike leaders were men who had been driven out of Spokane, Seattle and other United States Pacific coast cities. If the Canadian Government would only take these men by the back of the neck and put them out of the country much of the labor trouble in Canada would be eliminated.

Discussing the situation in the Pacific Coast mills, General McRae said that conditions were improving, but the output was regulated almost entirely by the supply of logs they could get in the water. The cost of logs had gone up rapidly, and the result was that they were "up in the air". How long they would stay up nobody could say. Of course it was going to come down some time. But purchasers were afraid lest they should be caught in the avalanche.

Between 75 and 85 per cent. of the B. C. Coast lumber business to-day was with the United States. But a good many of the Coast mills, appreciating the fact that their bread and butter business was at home, had endeavored to take care of the home trade, as well as they could.

General McRae referred also to the situation in connection with available lumber stocks. When he went overseas, about the beginning of the war, they had about 100,000,000 feet on sticks. To-day they had about 28,000,000 to 29,000,000 feet, so that it appeared certain that stocks were going to be very low for some time. The building programme in the Western States was going to be larger next year than this year, so that he thought the market for British Columbia lumber was well assured for perhaps another couple of years in the United States. At the same time the output in British Columbia was going to be very limited. That was the situation as it appeared to him.

Mr. Manbert Reviews Conditions Overseas

Mr. A. C. Manbert, of the Canadian General Lumber Co., Toronto, who recently returned from Great Britain, where he had conducted propaganda work on behalf of Ontario lumber manufacturers, also addressed the meeting, giving a very interesting description of some of the conditions, both social and industrial, which he found in England during his six months' stay. Much that Mr. Manbert had to say has already been reported in the "Canada Lumberman," both in his correspondence from abroad and in personal reports upon his return.

Mr. John Pearson, representing the Navy League of Canada, also addressed the meeting to urge the Wholesale Lumber Dealers to take an active part in the forthcoming Navy League campaign to raise funds for its various activities in Canada. At the close of his address, on the chairman's suggestion, practically every member promised that his firm would furnish, at least, one man to help in making up the Wholesale Lumber Dealers' team to take part in the campaign on October 21st, 22nd, and 23rd.

A few further remarks were made by the chairman, and by Mr. Manbert, regarding the activities of the association during the coming months. The meeting then adjourned.

A federal charter has been granted to the Edmonton Lumber Exchange with a capital stock of $200,000 and headquarters in Edmonton. The new organization is empowered to carry on in all its branches a lumber, timber and pulpwood business and to manufacture, sell and deal in timber, logs, lumber and wood of all kinds, pulp, paper, etc., and to acquire timber limits, water lots, etc. Among the incorporators are J. W. S. Chappelle, W. F. Cavanagh, J. J. Nierengarten and Benjamin Shore, all of Edmonton.

Educating England To Use Wooden Houses

Canadian Mission in London is Conducting Live Propaganda Campaign and Seeking to Dispel Many False Misconceptions Prevailing in Old Land

"The housing situation in England is, as you know, serious, and requires prompt and expeditious attention, and one of the difficulties is material," says a representative of the Canadian Mission in London in a letter to the "Canada Lumberman."

"We have been doing everything in this office to advance the cause of the lumber-built house, because we know, if we can overcome the official prejudice and the general feeling here that the lumber-built house is a temporary domicile, that Canada and Canadian lumber can take care of itself once the public are sufficiently educated in this country to accept the idea that a well-built, properly planned house of lumber is a suitable place of abode in this country."

"We have been endeavoring to get pictures of Canadian houses in the press, and have partially succeeded, but owing to the great strike and trouble through which this country is now passing, and the cutting down of newspapers it is almost impossible to get space at the present time, but as soon as the situation is relieved we will continue the propaganda."

The following articles have been sent out from the Canadian Mission, London, the first one going to the Canadian press and the second one to the British press. They are well worth perusing:

Canadian Timber for British Houses

During the last few weeks there has been a great controversy in the British press as to the prompt solution of the housing question in England. Much has been written relative to the wooden house. The general idea seems to be that it most be something of the up-ended packing case or rabbit hutch, and many ridiculous reasons are assigned as to why a house built of wood is not suitable for the United Kingdom.

Some say that, owing to the climate, people could not live in them. Canadians will smile at this when they think of the comparative mildness of the British climate to some winters they have passed comfortably in their wooden homes of Canada.

Another statement is made that a house built of wood will not last, yet there are many contradictions of this fallacy in houses built of wood in England that were in existence before Queen Elizabeth's time. Some say that a wooden house is hard to paint. Others contend that they have wooden houses in Canada because there is no brick or stone to build others.

The sum total of the situation is that the people of Great Britain have got to be educated to the fact that a properly and economically planned and well built house of wood, either plastered or finished in panel, is a warm, durable, economical and comfortable place to live in. To this end the people of Canada, and particularly the women of Canada, can do a great service to the lumber industry by making it their personal duty to write to any friends they may have in England, explaining to them the advantages and comfort of a wooden house. Personal letters of this kind will have a most beneficial effect upon the situation.

Although the shortage of houses and the housing question is a very acute one here, yet in the city of London alone at the present time there are over 60,000 substantially built stone and brick houses empty and to let. In the year 1903, which was considered a slack time, there were only 15,791.

The reason of this extraordinary state of affairs is, that, owing to the obsolete, inconvenient and unworkable plans of these houses, it is almost impossible for people to get domestic servants to go into them, where such things as water and coal have to be carried up many flights of stairs, etc.

One of the difficulties of the situation will be to induce the architects of this country to adopt new ideas and new systems. Although the great inventor, Edison, has said that in the last five years, owing to the exigencies of the war, civilization has advanced 250 years, yet it will be exceedingly difficult to overcome prejudices of architects and contractors in this country, and the only way to do it will be by demonstrating to the private individual in the way that has been already outlined by a method of correspondence, pictures, etc., to personal friends in this country.

Quickest Solution of the Housing Problem

To-day there are over 60,000 houses in London empty. In the year 1903 there were 15,791, yet we are told on every hand the shortage in housing accommodation is acute. What is the reason of this? The reason for this can only be attributed to the obsolete, inconvenient and economically unworkable plan and construction of the present London house.

On the basic principle of the present great reconstruction [of] the world that "old things have passed away and all things have become new" we must look for a more speedy and practical solution of the present difficulty than by continuing to build the rows of uninteresting, badly arranged brick houses that one sees in most of our large cities. The prompt solution of the trouble is houses built of wood. Judging from the press, the general impression seems to be that a house of this nature is a sort of rabbit hutch or up-turned packing case or army hut. Anyone who has visited Canada and seen the well planned, economically worked, comfortable and cheerful residences of the people constructed of wood will at once appreciate the absurdity and fallacy of these ideas. Some have gone so far as to say that owing to climatic reasons houses built of wood are not suitable for this country. A properly constructed wooden house plastered in the ordinary way on the inside is just as warm and comfortable as any more solid structure of stone or brick, and the rigours of the winter climate in many parts of Canada have no terrors for the people on the score of comfortable homes.

A steam-heated Canadian house, with an open fireplace, where, for cheerful reasons, wood or coal fires can be burned, are far more comfortable than the average English house with the small, smoky coal grate, where one can roast one's front whilst one's back is shivering in the Arctic regions of the atmosphere of the room.

In building groups of wooden houses central heating can easily be established and an enormous economy in coal could be effected.

One amusing reason assigned by a prominent person was as follows: Oh, yes, they certainly have to build houses of wood in Canada as they have no brick or stone. This, to the average Canadian, is more than amusing. Another reason assigned is that a house built of wood is difficult to paint. It is unnecessary to say this difficulty can easily be got over. The question of durability of a wooden house has also been brought up, but looking around England one can see wooden structures dating from the time of Elizabeth and further back the evidence is before those who wish to prove the durability of this class of structure. A properly constructed, well taken care of house, built of wood, will last at any rate one hundred years, and will always be a far more cheerful and comfortable home and less expensive than the present method of building in this country.

For artistic effect, economy and comfort, those who have experienced living in well constructed Canadian houses, built of wood, can readily testify to their suitability for the British Isles. The Eastern Canadian hardwoods are well fitted for flooring and panelling, and the far-famed Douglas fir and cedar of British Columbia cannot be excelled for the outside work, also supplying the durable, light, and serviceable cedar shingles for the roofs. Those who have seen the beautifuly finished and grained panelling of the Douglas fir and cedar for interior decorations all testify to its suitablity for inside lining, finishing and decorative purposes.

What Canada Could Supply Abroad

In regard to the prospect of the Canadian Timber Products Association supplying the Old Country with portable or ready-made houses, A. G. Rose, of Ottawa, who spent several months abroad last winter, investigating requirements and conditions, in the interest of the Canadian Timber Products Association, writes the "Canada Lumberman" as follows:—

"I do not think that the wooden house proposition will be acceptable in Breat Britain; at least, from my experience of three months' work over there, this is the conclusion I arrived at. In fact, the British Government refused to allow the erection of wooden houses in the country. I understand the Canadian Mission in London recently have asked for films showing examples of Canadian frame houses for advertising purposes. The house they want would have to be in the British style of architecture, and, of course, this is entirely different to the house we concluded to build for France. but this is a matter that the Canadian Timber Products Association would have to look into. The freight rates now are very high, and we do not see how we could ship ready-cut houses to England at the present rates. I feel that the factory men at the present time are crowded and are not in a position to take up the available export business."

New Timber Cutting Regulations in Quebec

Deputation Urges Upon the Government Necessity of Several Changes in Lumbering Operations—Reforestation of Lands Held Under Licenses

A deputation of the Woodlands Section of the Canadian Pulp & Paper Association and of the province of Quebec Limit Holders' Association on October 15th at Quebec interviewed the Hon. H. Mercier, the Minister of Lands and Forests, on the subject of the cutting of timber on crown lands. This was following up the resolution passed at the summer meeting of the Woodlands Section of of the first named association—"That in the opinion of this meeting certain changes in the regulations of lands and forests governing the cutting of timber on crown lands are essential to the preservation and perpetuation of the forests, and it is respectfully requested that the Executive Committee of the Canadian Pulp and Paper Association appoint a committee to co-operate with the existing committee of the province of Quebec Limit Holders' Association in waiting upon the Government with a view to urging the necessity of an early revision of these regulations in order to meet present day conditions."

On the previous day a conference between members of the committee of the section and the Limit Holders' Association was held at which, in an informal way, the proposed changes were discussed. The following were present: Messrs. Ellwood Wilson, Laurentide Co., Ltd., (chairman); R. P. Kernan, Donnacona Paper Co.; W. Gerard Power, River Ouelle Pulp & Lumber Co., (pres. of the Canadian Lumbermen's Association); Brig.-Gen. J. B. White, Riordon Pulp & Paper Co., Ltd.; J. M. Dalton, St. Maurice Paper Co.; T. F. Kenny, Jas. Maclaren Co.; M. H. Montgomery, Montgomery & Sons, Ltd.; William Russell, Jas. Richardson Co., A. L. Dawe, secretary of the Canadian Pulp and Paper Association, and Paul G. Owen, secretary of the Limit Holders' Association.

The Future Supply of Lumber

The members, in discussing the various points of the proposed changes, insisted upon the necessity of a change in the regulations so as to insure a good supply of lumber in the future. The question of waste was also touched on, it being urged that it was imperative to take steps to prevent this. The co-operation of the Government and the licensees was necessary to this end.

The subject of hardwoods was also brought up, particularly in relation to their utilization and logging. Some experiments are being conducted, which it was said gave promise of very satisfactory results. It was also pointed out that hardwoods had been used successfully for pulpwood purposes in some mills.

In connection with the general subject the following recommendations were submitted by Mr. Wilson:—All stumps should be cut not over one foot in height. All material down to three and one-half inches at the small end should be cut from the tops, where it is necessary to accomplish this, pieces down to four feet in length should be taken. All branches burnt and blown down and those attacked by insects or fungi, should be taken. All roads should be made with hardwoods. So far as possible all camps should be made of hardwood. All logging debris should be burnt to prevent the spread of disease, to eliminate the fire hazard, and to improve conditions for reproduction. Wherever hardwood is accessible to the mills it should be utilized. In the sulphate and soda processes this is now done, and while it cannot be utilized with the sulphite process, up to fifteen per cent. of hardwood ground wood pulp can be used in making newsprint. It takes less power to grind, the yield is about 25 per cent. more than for spruce and balsam and the quality of pulp is good. It does not bark easily in the knife barkers but does bark without difficulty in the tumbling barrels, and less of it needs rebarking than with spruce and balsam. In regard to driving, hardwood, cut and barked in the fall, is said to drive better than softwood. Cut in the spring and left with the branches on till fall, the hardwood logs float the whole season without difficulty. Mills which do not use balsam fir should do so, as there is no objection to its use whatever.

The Hon. H. Mercier gave the deputation a very cordial reception. The case for the deputation was presented by Mr. W. Gerard Power, who submitted the following draft for a Bill, embodying the changes desired. These changes were the result of the discussion at the conference held the previous day.

Par. 7.—Reforestation of the Lands Held Under Licenses to Cut Timber

1669a. When, on public lands held under license to cut timber, there are areas of more than one hundred acres deprived of coniferous timber, if the person or company holding such license wishes to plant forest trees thereon they may apply to the Minister and ask for a special license. for this purpose

The Minister shall obtain from the applicant, or, if the applicant be a company or corporation, from its president, manager, secretary, treasurer or officer duly authorized an affidavit stating: 1, that such area of land is deprived of coniferous timber and advantageous for reforestation; 2, that the applicant is in good faith and really intends planting the land applied for.

If the Minister is satisfied with the truth and sufficiency of the facts set forth in the affidavit, he may, under his hand and seal, issue to such applicant a special license, containing a description of the land and allowing its occupation for planting purposes.

1669b. Planting of such area shall be made within four years of the issuing of the license, and it shall be performed in accordance with the requirements of the present law as well as with the conditions of the license.

Not less than twelve hundred trees per acre shall be planted, except where the nature of the soil, mountains, rocks, rivers and other natural obstacles render such planting impossible.

If the land is already timbered with other than coniferous trees, sufficient of these must be removed to ensure the growth of the planted trees, and in such removal the Government cutting regulations shall not apply and no stumpage dues shall be collected.

1669c. Holders of licenses under the present law shall have such licenses registered in the register kept by the Crown lands' agent, in accordance with the terms of article -563.

1669d. If the planting license contains any clerical error ,misnomer or misdescription of the land, the Minister may annul such license and order a new and corrected one to be issued, which shall take effect from the date of the first one.

1669e. The planting license may be transferred, and then shall be subject to the rules and restrictions contained in article 1562, 1563, 1564, 1568 and 1569, mutatis mutandis.

1669f. Four years after the planting, if the conditions of the license have been fulfilled and if the planted trees are in growing condition, the Lieutenant-Governor, on payment of the sum of $1.00 per square mile or portion thereof shall vest the lessee with the absolute property of the land occupied under said license for 99 years, subject to a renewal of the lease for a further like period, and one-half the cost of said planting shall be refunded to the lessee by the Government on production of proper vouchers.

1669g. All land occupied or patented under the present law shall be free from all provincial, municipal and school taxes of any kind, during the existence of the planting license.

1669h. The cost of fire protection on the territory planted as above shall be divided between the Government and the lessee.

1669i. When the trees so planted shall have reached sufficient size to warrant thinning, such thinning shall be made at the cost of the lessee and he shall pay to the Government a stumpage tax not to exceed one dollar and a half per cord or 128 cubic feet stacked.

1669j. At any time after the trees as planted above shall have reached a diameter of six inches at four and one-half feet from the ground the lessee may cut any or all of said trees, and shall pay to the Government a stumpage tax not to exceed one dollar and a half per cord of 128 cubic feet stacked.

One point brought out was that the limit holders had no intention to encroach on the rights of the settlers, but that it was desired to co-operate so that the natural resources of the province could be developed.

Lumbermen Are Active in Fire Protection

New Brunswick Speaks Appreciatively of Their Assistance During the Past Season —Province Had 342 Fires With Total Damage of $154,000—The Causes

G. H. Prince, provincial forester of New Brunswick, has issued an interesting report giving a summary of the forest fires in that province during the season of 1919. The total number from April to September (both months inclusive) was 342, of which 240 were caused by the railways, and 102 from other causes, as follows: Fishermen, campers, travellers, hunters and smokers, 25; settlers, neglecting clearing fires, 38; industrial operations and careless use of fire, 13; accidental, 4; incendiary, 7; unknown, 15.

The total area burned was 11,326 acres, or about 17¾ square miles, and the total damage done was $154,155.

The damage resulting from the fires through each cause was:

Railroads	$5,400.00	or 3.5%	of total damage
Fishermen, campers, travellers, smokers, etc.	48,870.00	or 31.7%	"
Settlers	67,985.00	or 44.1	"
Industrial	11,000.00	or 7.1	"
Accidental	1,100.00	or .7	"
Incendiary	12,700.00	or 8.2	"
Unknown	7,100.00	or 4.7	"
Totals	$154,155.00	or 100%	

The number of fires occurring each month was:

	Railway Fires	Other Fires	Total
April	2	2	4
May	26	40	66
June	129	45	174
July	54	11	65
August	28	4	32
September	1	—	1
Totals	240	102	342

The total number of locomotive inspections made was 275; of these 202 were found satisfactory and 73 had defective appliances. In the 75 locomotives with defective appliances these were found to have 88 defects in the front ends and 40 defects in the ashpans.

Co-operation of the Lumbermen

Great credit is due the lumbermen and lumber companies throughout the province for their earnest co-operation in forest fire protection. About 60 of their chief woodsmen were appointed co-operative fire wardens during the dry season of the year. They assisted materially in keeping down the fire danger. It is to be hoped that this will be carried on and extended next year.

Through an agreement with the Public Works Department of the Province about 500 road supervisors co-operated with the Forest Service in reporting and putting out forest fires in the vicinity of their work. These arrangements worked very well and did much to keep down the numerous small fires occurring along our highways. Thanks to Hon. P. J. Venoit, the Minister of Public Works, for his interest and co-operation in this work.

There were 36 prosecutions for violation of the Forest Fire Act of New Brunswick. These were principally for burning slash without a fire permit or neglecting to attend to clearing fires. Twenty-nine convictions were obtained, two cases were withdrawn and five cases dismissed.

Settlers Careless in Clearing Land

With the exception of about six weeks of extra dry weather during May and June, the past fire season was an average one as regards weather conditions in New Brunswick.

The most disastrous fire of the year was caused by carelessness of settlers clearing land and not taking the proper precautions against their clearing fire spreading. At Kedgwick, in Restigouche County, on June 12th and 13th, several of these fires got beyond control and caused enormous damage, especially to lumber and property. In this county alone there were 22 fires burning over 8,180 acres or about 13 square miles, and doing about $126,000 damage, most of which was to ties, logs, saw-mills and settlers' houses.

During the past season the Provincial Forest Service, through the co-operation of the Canadian Forestry Association, has carried on a rather extensive campaign to educate the public on the importance of better forest fire protection in New Brunswick.

This was done principally by the distribution of posters, circulars, and through newspapers, motion pictures houses, schools, Boy Scouts, exhibitions and exhibition car.

About 10,000 instructive and attractive fire posters in French and English were distributed by the Forest Rangers throughout the Province.

Educating the Public on Fire Prevention

About 3,000 circulars on fire protection and slash burning were distributed to the citizens of New Brunswick, as well as 500 circulars on "How to Burn Your Slash" were distributed to the settlers by the rangers.

The newspapers were used extensively and to good advantage in advertising the importance of the work the Forest Service was doing in New Brunswick, and in advertising prosecutions and violations of the Forest Fire Act.

Several good reels of moving pictures on Fire Protection have been shown, and through the co-operation of the owners of moving picture houses numerous instructive and warning slides have been shown during the dry season of the year. Two lectures with motion pictures were given by Mr. Robson Black at the Provincial Normal School, which should have good results in educating our coming school teachers on this big subject.

An interesting letter for the school teachers and school children, with 12,000 booklets "About Camp Fires" was distributed and read throughout the schools of the Province on June 4th. Interesting literature on fire protection was sent to the camp meetings of the Boy Scouts and two of our rangers attended their meeting and gave the boys talks on fire protection and "How to Make a Camp Fire," etc.

An interesting fire protection and pulp exhibit was displayed at the Fredericton and Chatham exhibitions.

The fire protection display was represented in four scenes—one scene the year of the fire, another, two years after the fire, another, five or ten years after the fire, and another, twenty years after the fire. Each of these scenes represented the conditions as they actually were in the forest. In the twenty-year growth were two small live deer, which added much to the attractiveness of the booth. Numerous moose, deer and bear heads, with mounted wildcat, beaver and owls formed a good background.

Through the co-operation and assistance of Mr. Stokes of the Forest Products Laboratory, Montreal, a good pulp exhibit was displayed. The whole was surrounded with white birch railing, which added much to the rustic effect of the booth. The booth, as a whole, attracted a great deal of attention and met with approval and commendation on all sides. Here the members of the Forest Service met many people who were interested in forest fire protection and distributed considerable good literature.

Will Wooden Houses Solve the Problem?

A controversy on the subject of wooden houses has been raging for some time in the British press, and its outcome will be awaited with much interest by Canadians. Wooden houses on the American plan have been suggested as a means of solving the acute housing problem, and if adopted under the Government housing scheme will probably lead to a very large trade in portable houses from Canada.

F. C. Wade, agent-general for British Columbia, has offered to have 500 wooden houses delivered in Britain so as to be available for occupation by Christmas. He states that such structures can be imported and erected at a cost of fifteen hundred dollars and upwards. The British Ministry of Health, however, is not yet convinced of the superior merits of wood as opposed to brick or stone, doubt being held as to whether it would stand the damp island climate of more than fifty years. The opinion has also been expressed that the necessity of frequent repainting makes the wooden house expensive. A third objection is the shipping shortage on the Atlantic,, and a fourth is the expected hostilities of labor unions to the importation of such finished material.

There are few wooden houses in Britain, the reason being the by-laws against their erection. The Ministry of Health is now drawing new regulations to permit the building of such structures. There are other signs that public opinion is veering round in the direction of wood, and further education as to its advantages will be of great benefit to the Canadian timber trade.

His Royal Highness Pays Visit to Leading Coast Sawmill

The royal party returning from the mill. In the front row, reading from left to right are: Mayor Gale (in silk hat), Major-General Sir Henry Burstall, Alderman Woodside, Rear-Admiral Sir Lionel Halsey, Mr. J. Alex. Hendry, the Prince, Mr. Hamber, Mr. Arthur Hendry, Sir Godfrey Thomas, Alderman Owen

ON September 23 the British Columbia Mills Timber & Trading Company was honored by a visit from His Royal Highness the Prince of Wales to the Hastings Saw Mill. The large plant presented a gay appearance, an arch of forest greenery and maple leaves with the words "Welcome to the Hastings Saw Mill" was placed over the entrance, and other parts of the plant were profusely decorated with evergreen trees, flags, bunting and appropriate emblems, which received added effect from the serenely beautiful weather.

His Royal Highness, who was accompanied by Rear-Admiral Sir Lionel Halsey and Major-General Sir Henry Burstall, arrived about 11 o'clock. He was received by Mr. Eric W. Hamber, the president, Mr. Arthur E. Hendry, general superintendent, and Mr. J. Alex. Hendry, secretary. With the party were the Hon. Martin Burrell, His Worship Mayor Gale, the aldermen, and many others.

Immediately after the welcome the royal party, under the guidance of Mr. Hamber and Mr. Arthur E. Hendry, proceeded to the mill. Cards giving some facts concerning the Hastings Saw Mill, and information relating to the departments to be visited, were distributed amongst the guests. The route was marked out by a line of bunting, along which were stationed at intervals members of the Royal Northwest Mounted Police. In order that no part of the route would have to be duplicated, the dry kilns and planing departments, where ceiling, flooring, siding and several varieties of mouldings were being manufactured, were first visited.

Next came the log pond, where several booms were to be seen, and the log slip. His Royal Highness was much interested in watching the huge logs being drawn up from the water, one of which he followed to the log deck. The log deck is always an interesting part of a sawmill to one strange to it, especially when the logs are of the size seen at the Hastings Saw Mill, the largest on this occasion being 8½ feet in diameter and 95 feet long. His Royal Highness was much impressed by the demonstration of mechanical power, and he stood for a considerable time watching the 60 inch circular saws "break down" the big logs. Passing to the opposite side of the mill he watched the 14 inch band saw sawing timbers 24 inches square and over 100 feet long, and their being carried away by the live rollers. Passing successively the second band saw, the edgers and through the grading, measuring and tallying departments, the royal party proceeded along the electric railway to the wharves and export sheds, where piles of lumber were lying ready for shipment abroad. There were some fine Douglas fir timbers and spars up to 24 inches square and 100 feet in length for shipment to the United Kingdom, Australia, Japan and China, Douglas fir flitches of the best grade for Japan, and rough dressed lumber of smaller dimensions for Australia, the Fiji Islands and other countries. Nearby were some fine timbers from 12 to 24 inches square and from 60 to 90 feet long, ready for shipment to the Atlantic seaboard.

Too much time having been taken up, up to this point, His Royal Highness was unable to visit the picket, lath and broom handle plant, and filing room. The party therefore returned to the administrative building where His Royal Highness was presented with a souvenir of his visit in the form of an illuminated album of photographs, bound in morocco, of the great trees of British Columbia, the processes by which the logs are manufactured into lumber, and its being loaded on ships for transport to all parts of the world. The presentation was made by little Master Eric C. Hamber, nephew of Mr. Eric W. Hamber, and son of the late Captain H. B. Hamber, who was killed on active service with the Royal Air Force. The page opposite the presentation words was the interesting photograph of the Duke and Duchess of Cornwall and York, now Their Majesties King George V. and Queen Mary, the parents of the Prince, which was taken on the occasion of their visit to the Hastings Saw Mill on September 30, 1901.

On leaving His Royal Highness expressed himself to Mr. Hamber as being much pleased to have the opportunity of seeing a large modern sawmill in operation, and he thanked him for all the arrangements that had been made for his visit.

The departure of the royal visitor was made amid three rousing cheers and a tiger, led by Mr. Hamber, from the hundreds of employees, invited guests and spectators. The Prince during his tour of the Pacific Coast province was given a most enthusiastic welcome at every point and completely captured the hearts of all by his cheery smile, unaffected manner and unfeigned interest in all that he saw and heard on his trip.

His Royal Highness being received by the president, Mr. Eric W. Hamber

Urge Improvements in Logging Operations

Woodlands Section Says Level of Intelligence and Training of Men Directing Work in the Woods Must Be Raised—Changes in Methods Outlined

In general, there are three ways which could be used to improve and cheapen logging operations.

First, to ascertain where timber is located and its amount, lumbermen cannot cut logs without maps any more than a general can fight battles. If the amount of timber on a given area is not known accurately no accurate estimate of costs can be made, nor intelligent operating plans.

Second, the level of intelligence and training of the men directing woods' operations on the ground must be raised. Logging is a branch of engineering, and engineering training is essential if methods are to be cheapened and improved. In the West, the schools are giving courses in logging engineering with success. It cannot be expected that untrained, uneducated men can run logging operations well, any more than such men could be expected to handle mill operations.

Third, a much greater degree of co-operation between firms operating in the same territory is necessary.. Co-operation in making road and stream improvements, in hiring labor and buying provisions, in hauling, driving and all other woods' operations.. The woods' managers of various companies aand operators in the same territory are still far too suspicions of one another, are continually trying to take advantage and "put one over" on the other fellow, and are still constantly making and breaking agreements in regard to the scale of wages to be paid.. Wherever co-operation of any kind has been tried, it has proved successful, and a much greater measure is necessary in the future of logging operations.

The foregoing constitutes the recommendations made by the Woodlands Section of the Canadian Pulp and Paper Association in regard to improvements in logging operations. A committee was appointed by the section two years ago to go thoroughly into the whole subject. The members presented a report at the last annual meeting held at the beginning of 1919. The report which was referred back for further consideration, is as follows:

In considering any possible improvements in logging operations it is necessary first to have some clear idea of conditions in the forests in order to discuss the question intelligently.

Roughly our forests in Eastern Canada consist of the following types, practically pure stands of red pine or jack pine or black spruce, and mixed stands of spruce, balsam and hardwood, the latter covering the largest percentage of area.

Taking the latter type as the most common and the most important, the average number of spruce and balsam trees per acre, 4 in. and up, in the St. Maurice Valley is about 159.5, which, if these were evenly spaced, would mean that on an average acre the trees would be 16.5 apart each way, so that it is readily seen that the cost of cutting and skidding these trees is much more than it would be if the trees were spaced say six feet apart. The hardwoods compose quite a large percentage of the stand and as they are not utilized are only an obstruction to logging operations, as is the small hardwood brush. Then, too, the softwood is likely to be in clumps which are rather widely scattered, making logging difficult and expensive, or sometimes fine large trees stand alone, and as it is difficult to go far from a road for them they are often left by the jobbers.

The highest number of cords per acre 6 in. and up at breast height in the St. Maurice Valley was 19.2, the lowest 11.8 spruce and balsam combined. The figures for Government diameter limit were 16.2 and 6.1, or an average of virgin country well timbered of 12.7 cords 6 in. and up 10.2 cords cut to Government limit.

The highest percentage of balsam was 82.2 per cent. of the softwood stand and the lowest amount was 43.5 per cent. The grand average was: balsam, 64.2 per cent.; red spruce and black spruce, 20.2 per cent., and white spruce, 15.6 per cent. Taking all the trees in a fairly average mixed stand we get the following percentages:

Total stand, 244.9 trees per acre.

Above Government diameter limit, 190 trees per acre.

	% of total stand	% merchantable stand
Under diameter limit	22.42	....
White Spruce	1.70	2.27
Black and Red Spruce	1.84	2.38
Balsam	64.04	82.54
Spruce and Balsam, combined	67.64	87.18
White Pine	.04	.05
Cedar	.23	.30
White Birch	9.27	11.95
Maple	.24	.31
Ash	.007	.009
Other Hardwoods	.15	.20
All Hardwoods	9.67	12.47

General Picture of the Woods

The general composition of the country is roughly: water, 6.1 per cent.; good merchantable timber, 33.8 per cent.; poor merchantable timber, 6.3 per cent.; black spruce, 1.1 per cent.; burnt, not reproducing, 5.29 per cent.; swamp, 42 per cent.; burnt, reproducing 23.3 per cent.; burnt, reproducing in jack pine, 5.32 per cent.; lumbered, 13.0 per cent.; and settled, 5.22 per cent.

Classified by percentage of total species above Government diameter limit, we have white spruce 28.57 per cent. black spruce, 31. per cent., 9 in. and up, and balsam 75.1 per cent. 7 in. and up.

The above gives a rough general picture of the woods we have to operate and show that the quantities of timber are low, making logging more expensive than if the forests were well stocked. We might say that if we called a fully softwood stand 100 per cent our forests run about 14 per cent. stocked.

As giving some idea of how our logging operations are carried on, an investigation of an average operation carried out in extremely good territory where the stand of softwood was estimated at ten cords per acre, the amount actually cut was 6.4 cords. The balance was not all left standing, but much was wasted in high stumps, long tops, wood used for skids, and roads and lodged trees left.

Now, in order to discuss improvements in logging intelligently it is necessary to run over various wood's operations and describe them briefly as now carried on and to suggest possible improvements.

The first step is exploring; that is, locating the locality to be cut. This is usually done by some foreman who goes into the woods, picks out the territory to be cut over, and estimates how much he thinks can be cut, and who then takes some jobbers up and bargains with them for the price per thousand and the locality. Some firms have their timber mapped and estimated several years in advance and this locating of and bargaining with jobbers can be done by some higher official in the office. In the latter case, the amounts are known with much more accuracy than in the former, and the cut can be more closely predicted. In the former case, the jobber usually gets a territory with a good deal more timber than he needs and he generally cuts the best and leaves a good deal which is very expensive to get at a later date.

Cutting Plan for Series of Years

It would seem that an improvement in procedure would be to have a map and reasonably close estimate made of the whole territory of an owner; then for the logging manager in consultation with the general management and the superintendent of manufacturing, or the head of the sawmill in the case of a lumbering concern, to make out a cutting plan for a series of years, taking into consideration all of the factors. If a firm did not care to spend the money to map all of its territory at once, it could make maps for one or two years in advance. Knowing just how much timber was in each section and the amount required each year, plans could be accurately made which would get the timber out in the cheapest way; camps could be located for several years, as could roads, stream improvements could be made and the district progressively logged until cut out. Knowing how much timber there was in each tract, the jobbers could be more intelligently handled, and if the amount cut fell below the estimate the blame could be accurately placed.

In examining cut-over territory, it has always been noticed that much less has been cut than it was possible to get, and, as no enough is left to make it worth while to go back, this timber is entirely wasted.

The next operation is taking in provisions. This is usually done in summer by rail, boat or wagon to the main depots at the end of the summer roads and then the provisions are taken in on "jumpers" or by canoes and the men to the new camps. Sometimes, provisions are taken in the winter previous to cutting and left in caches till the next year in care of a keeper. In hauling from railhead to main depots and from there into the woods two horses, or one horse, waggons, the latter more usually, are used. The only improvement that could probably be made here would be the hauling by small tractors and trailer waggons or sleighs, but this cannot be done until some of the almost impossible grades on the country roads have been materially reduced, as one bad hill in a long haul will determine the maximum load to be hauled, no matter what the length of road. Where portaging must be done over a series of years, the saving to be effected by increasing the size of the average load should be calculated and the road work done to that amount.

Reducing Waste in Camp Building

At present, camps are built of spruce and balsam with pole or tar paper roofs and much good timber is wasted. The average jobbers' camp contains 2,618 bd. ft. and stable 1,700 bd. ft. A camp seldom lasts more than two years, and as an average company operation calls for 347 camps and stables this means 1,300,000 bd. ft. per annum. Camps could be built of hardwood, especially birch and poplar, which would reduce this waste, or camps could be taken down and made into logs when finished with. Some experiments have been made with portable camps made in small sections which bolt together; these have been quite successful and will last for four or five years, especially if painted. The jobbers, on leaving their camps, usually break all the windows and smash things up generally, thus adding to the waste.

Better Methods in Felling Trees

Felling is now generally done with the saw and the days of wasteful chopping with the axe are about over. The principal improvements which can be made in felling are, better laying out of work by the camp foreman, cutting of lower stumps, cutting further into the tops, taking branched trees, taking everything that can be gotten out of a tree, that is, leaving only the part that is actually rotten instead of leaving the whole tree, and cutting all the trees which the law allows instead of leaving isolated trees or those a little difficult to get at uncut. Time studies should also be made so that a foreman should know just what constituted a day's work for a crew. Some idea of the wastes in the above respects can be gained by actual figures covering 347 jobbers for one winter. 6,314 stumps were cut over two feet high, the highest being 3.0 ft. If these stumps had been cut 1 ft. high, by no means a difficult operation, there would have been a great saving of the best wood in the tree. A careful estimate over a large area showed that by high stumps, 4,496 cords were wasted annually. That this waste is due to carelessness was shown by the fact that of all the stumps measured seven per cent. were cut under one foot, many of them down to six inches, and this without any orders to do so. It was also shown that there was a tendency on the part of the fellers to increase the height of stumps as the diameter of the trees increased. The earlier the cutting is commenced in the fall, the easier it will be to cut low stumps. One great source of waste in the St. Maurice Valley is the custom of cutting logs thirteen and one-half feet in length. Trees should be cut so as to get the greatest amount of good timber out of them, regardless of the length of the log. By measuring trees as ordinarily cut it was found that the average length of the top left was 20.1 ft., and that if one piece was taken out of each top, varying from four to 16 ft. in length and 4 in. in diameter at the small end, a saving in one year's cut of 3,000,000 ft. board measure would result. Such pieces cut from the tops would cost no more to haul or drive but would cost more to handle at the mill owing to their small size, but wood smaller than this is being bought from the farmers, and from the Abitibi region as a regular thing. Some other items of waste as shown by records are branched trees left in a winter's operations of cutting about 46,500,000 feet, 276; good logs cut and left in the woods, 2,453; logs 6 in. and up left in tops, 2,441.

Company camps have been tried in years past and were practically forced on some of the operators by the shortage of labor during the past season. So far as is known they have never delivered logs as cheaply as the jobbers could. The Companies usually have to pay more and feed better than the jobbers and cannot get so much work out of the men. Then, too, the camp foremen are not sufficiently are not sufficiently intelligent to plan out their work, make time studies and use their heads for the improvement of the work.

Some sort of light portable saw should be developed, run by gasoline engine which would reduce the number of men necessary in the woods and increase the output. Several types have been invented but, so far, none that is practical for this country.

Skidding, Hauling and Culling

It is hard to think of any improvements which can be made in skidding, except to begin work earlier in the fall and get the logging finished before the snow becomes deep enough to seriously impede the work.

Hauling is done almost entirely today by one-horse sleds. Using double teams increases the cost of the roads and makes snow sheds and ice roads often necessary. It is thought that by using small tractors, hauling say five or six cords to a load, the work can be materially cheapened. Such machines do not need very much work done on the roads and can manoeuvre easily in the woods. By having two sets of sleighs for each tractor, they can be kept running steadily. In their use it pays to have a skilled mechanic to keep them always in good order. An extra machine, or a good upply of repair parts, should be always on hand. As the cost of the machines is low, this is quite feasible.

Culling is one branch of logging which needs a thorough overhauling. The present methods of measurement which have been handed down are neither practical nor scientiific. The cullers have not sufficient education to do the work intelligently; they are underpaid and too much work is expected of them. The result is that they often estimate when they should measure. The custom of measuring by the board foot unit should be abandoned and the cord or cubic foot substituted. Many logging superintendents think they are getting the best of the jobber by using the board foot scale, which they think gives them a large over run, but even in the case of saw timber the mill men seldom know accurately just what the over run is. By using the cubic foot , buyer would know just what he was getting. The change would be of great value to the paper and pulp mill, which carries out all its other measures in cords. As there is no possible means of exactly changing amounts in board feet to amounts in cords, the mills are at a disadvantage. If the whole subject of logging measurement were put into the hands of an expert for development, many improvements could be made. A self registering caliper for measuring logs has been developed and a model made by one of the instrument-making houses.

Reducing the Cost in Driving

The great importance of river driving and the length of time it has been used should have greatly increased the efficiency of it, but so far as can be seen this is not the case. The work has been left to men without engineering experience or education and is apparently run more by tradition than anything else. As the amount of water is the principal determining factor, and as this is at its maximum only for a short period in the spring, there should be a large enough force on hand to see that the drive starts promptly and that the stream is kept continually full of logs. The number of men required on a drive should not be computed by the number of logs but by the difficulty of the stream; there should always be sufficient to keep the logs moving. Most of a crew's time is spent in breaking jams which should never be allowed to occur. Leaky dams are another factor of waste as these take longer to fill up than tight ones and the crews are often idle while dams are filling up. If accurate estimates of the amount of timber to come on a given stream were available the amount to be spent in improvements could be accurately gauged, and these could often be done co-operatively when a new territory was opened up, thus cheapening the drive for years to come. Short booms placed at sharp ends and dangerous points in a river would often reduce the danger of jams materially, at a low cost. Plenty of men should be used at dangerous points instead of being strung along the course of a creek or river. The number of drowning accidents is far too large. This could be decreased by furnishing the men with light life belts which would not impede their work. One company has already purchased some of these. There should be more co-operation in driving the small streams than at present.

Abolish Present System of Sorting

Sorting is part of the lumbering operation which should be given up altogether in its present form. All the logs put into any certain stream by the operators upon it should be pooled, and a man placed at the log haul of each operator on the river to measure the logs taken up. In this way the enormous number of men now used at the sorting gaps on rivers where the same logs are often gone over two or three times would be eliminated, and adjustments could easily be made between the cullers' sheets for logs delivered on the streams and those taken out at the log hauls. The only obstacle to this scheme is that each operator insists that his logs are bigger than anyone's, without really knowing anything about it. Even if this were so, it could easily be adjusted.

New Position for Mr. C. J. Brooks

Charles J. Brooks, Toronto

Chas. J Brooks, who for the past two years and a half has been Eastern representative of the Vancouver Lumber Co., with headquarters in Toronto, is leaving in the near future for Vancouver, where he has been appointed to a responsible position with E. C. Walsh Lumber Co. of that city, who are wholesalers and manufacturers, with mills at North Vancouver, having a capacity of about 50,000 feet a day, sawing principally fir. The many friends, which Mr. Brooks has made during his residence in Toronto, while regretting his departure, will join in expressions of hearty well wishes for his continued success in the lumber arena. Mr. Brooks, who was born in Prince Edward Island, has had a thorough experience and insight into all branches of the business, and is, therefore, well equipped for the new duties which he is undertaking. His first position was with Chappell Bros. & Co., of Sydney, N. B., where he spent four years in their factory. He was next engaged in logging work in New Brunswick and then joined the staff of Murray & Gregory, Ltd., of St. John, being first in the shipping department and later in the office. Going west, Mr. Brooks took a postion with the Moose Jaw Sash & Door Co. as shipper and foreman of their stock-cutting departments. He spent three years with this organization and then was with the Rat Portage Lumber Co. in their plant at Norwood, Man., in which he devoted his attention particularly to machine work. Nine years ago Mr. Brooks went to the Coast and joined the Vancouver Lumber Co., where he was first in the shipping department and subsequently on the selling staff. He came East nearly three years ago to assist Mr. C. J. Plant (now sales manager of the company) in his work in Toront, and on the departure of the latter for the West, Mr. Brooks was appointed manager of the company's interests in the East. He has always taken an active interest in the welfare of the industry in general and has been aggressive in looking after sales of B. C. forest products for his firm.

K. M. Brown of Vancouver, who succeeds Mr. Brooks as Eastern representative of the Vancouver Lumber Co., has arrived in Toronto and is assuming his new duties. Mr. Brown has been for some time on the head office staff of the company and is thoroughly familiar with the industry as a whole.

Export Outlook for B. C. Timber

Speaking of the export lumber trade a leading paper of Vancouver says: If lumber shipments to Great Britain from this province continue at their present rate during the next month or so, at the end of that period the mills of the coast will have completed the large order placed with them by the British government, and must turn their attention to securing orders elsewhere. According to statements made recently by several prominent lumbermen of this city, it is hardly probable further orders will be given out by the government, and it will, therefore, be left to private enterprise to shoulder the responsibility of providing export markets for one of British Columbia's most important industries. With the exception of the Hastings Mill and the Dollar Mill, which have been giving serious attention to export trade for some time, very few of the mills oof British Columbia had gven much thought to securng trade across the seas. One or two of the mills had been shipping to the Orient and to Australia, but the trouble with this trade was that when the demands of the Canadian prairies became more insistent, export business was allowed to go by the board, being picked up again only when the need for greater scope in marketing made itself felt.

Like every other industry, the export trade to the lumbering industry is one of the most vital factors to its development. It is true that the trade of the prairies has furnished reason for extension of some of the plants on the coast, but the market there is limited, is canvassed by competitors from Eastern Canada, and to a very great extent depends upon the crop conditions.

The tremendous importance of export business and how it should be vigorously pursued, as a source of expansion, achievement and inspiration, is conceded by all. But so far, as has already been mentioned, with the exception of occasional efforts to establish a footing abroaed, no really consistent attempt has been made by [illegible] lumbermen of this province to capture the great market that is [illegible]er to them, not only in Europe, but in the Far East, in Australia [illegible] in South America. In Japan and China there is a market for [illegible] lumber that will absorb the entire output of British Columbia [illegible] many years to come, if it can only be secured. In China, more [illegible]ticularly, opportunities are offered that do not exist elsewhere.

Opens Lumber Market and Exchange

A. T. Smith, who for some time has been selling lumber, has [illegible]ed the Lumber Market and Exchange, Toronto, with offices at 3[illegible] [illegible]toria Street. The object of the new organization is to render [illegible] service both to wholesalers and retailers in the matter of stock [illegible] all business is done on a two per cent. commission basis. The [illegible]change has lists of various kinds of lumber that are availab[illegible] when a purchaser is in need of any material of whatever kind, [illegible]ness or grade, informaton will be readily furnished where it can [illegible] tained, where located, price, shipping facilities, etc. Mr. Smith [illegible] that, by his new system, he is able at all time to give quotation[illegible] place orders with any of the reliable wholesale merchants in [illegible] or Hamilton with whom he has made arrangements to sell their [illegible] at rock bottom prices and this convenience eliminates the [illegible] method of telephoning or writing several firms. Both hard and [illegible] woods are being handled.

Paper Company Adopts Forestry Branch

The Abitibi Pulp & Paper Co., whose plant is at Iroquois [illegible] have organized a Forestry Department. The scope of the Depart[illegible]ment is a large one and has been concentrated under the [illegible] heads of Nursery, Engineering, Protection and Investigation. [illegible] splendid site has been selected adjacent to Twin Falls and 10 acre[illegible] of land have been cleared and prepared ready for actual operation[illegible] in the spring of next year. It is proposed to clear and prepare [illegible] similar 10 acres annually until a maximum of 50 acres is reached. Here will be developed the stores of supply for the Reforestatio[illegible] branch. The nursery will be placed on such a basis as to give [illegible] annual yield of from 1,000,000 to 2,00,000 4-year-old trees. As [illegible] first stock grown from seed will not be available to the Reforesta[illegible]tion branch until 1922 and 1923, the company will purchase plant[illegible]able stock of from 3 to 4 years in age in order that the Reforestatio[illegible] department may commence operations in 1920.

Will Build New Mill at Oromocto

Robert B. Smith, M.L.A., of Oromocto, N.B., manager of th[illegible] River Valley Lumber Company, Ltd., was in St. John, recentl[illegible] arranging for the purchase of the Flewelling mill at Hampton, King[illegible] County.

It is the intention to take the machinery from this mill, whic[illegible] was completely equipped with gang and rotary systems, and remov[illegible] it to Oromocto, where it will be used in the new mill which the Rive[illegible] Valley Lumber Company will erect to replace that which was de[illegible]stroyed in the recent fire which almost swept all of Oromocto of[illegible] the map.

The Flewelling mill was formerly used in the manufacture o[illegible] lumber, from which the wood for the old-fashioned matches, mad[illegible] at Hampton in large quantities, was supplied and the mach[illegible]inery is said to be in excellent condition.

It was said that Mr. Smith plans to start immediate operation[illegible] to dismantle the Flewelling mill and thus be able to have the machin[illegible]ery towed to Oromocto before the close of navigation, which woul[illegible] make it possible to have the new mill built and ready to commenc[illegible] sawing in the early spring.

New Lumber Company Obtains Charter

A provincial charter has been granted the Empire Timber, Lum[illegible]ber & Tie Co., Ltd., with headquarters in Toronto and a capital stock of $85,000. The company is empowered to carry on the business [illegible] lumbermen and saw and planing millers and to buy, hold and [illegible] in timber limits, timber lands, logs, etc., as well as to manufac[illegible] ties and all articles made of wood. R. H. McKee, who is at the [illegible] of the Ontario Lumber and Supply Co., Limited, with offices at [illegible] Tyrell Building, Kng Street West, Toronto, is president and manag[illegible] of the Empire Timber, Lumber and Tie Co., Limited, which, it [illegible] understood, will embark in the retail line and has acquired suitab[illegible] premises at 358 Greenwood Ave., Toronto. The Ontario Lumbe[illegible] and Supply Co. will devote its entire attention to the wholesale line

A charter has been granted to the Economy Timber Co., Limited, o[illegible] Courtenay, B. C., with a capital stock of $25,000.

What Wholesaler Does for Lumber Business

An Indispensable Link in the Chain of Distribution who Stimulates Production and Sales and Increases Purchasing Power of the Consumer

By Louis Germain, Jr.

This need for economic lumber distribution developed the wholesaler, who by reason of his knowledge of the various kinds of lumber manufactured in all sections of the country, required by the consuming public, and his ability to handle these various kinds and species of lumber in different places, and in large quantities, has for forty years made it possible for the wholesaler to serve the consuming public by supplying any or all species needed at a minimum cost of distribution.

The term "wholesaler" has often been misapplied and confused with the commission agent, the jobber or the broker, none of whom perform his function, so in referring to the wholesaler we should clearly recognize that in distributing the manufacturer's product in carload lots of lumber to either the indivdual consumer or to the retail yard, he acts independent of either, or both, he is engaged in buying and selling lumber at wholesale for and on his own acount, advances money in payment therefor, takes title to the lumber at point of production, assumes transportation hazard and risk and customarily extends credit to his purchasers, thus carrying the burden of finance and credit risks with resultant necessary services to both of his clients.

Naturally, considering the many classes of lumber distributed, the types of wholesale organizations are many and varied, but the legitimate wholesaler will be found as performing necessary functions in the industry.

Having defined the wholesaler, it is interesting to note that of the total mills in the United States, only about three per cent of the mills who produce about forty-seven per cent of the total, distribute their own product either through their own selling organization or through mill selling agencies; the remaining ninety-seven per cent of the mills being dependent upon the wholesaler to a greater or less extent for the disposal of their product. There are approximately three thousand five hundred wholesalers serving approximately twenty-five thousand retailers and wholesale consumers of lumber the country over. The capital investment in the wholesale lumber business undoubtedly amounts to more than one billion dollars, and the organization of especially trained experts employed by wholesale firms has been estimated at approximately one hundred thousand persons.

These facts lead to the consideration of what functions the wholesaler performs, and whether or not he is an economic necessity in service to the consuming public, to the mills large and small, and in the scheme of democratic industrial order which the policy of our government has fostered.

Indispensable Sales Force

The wholesaler furnishes an absolutely indispensable sales force to the small mill operator. He is the agent through which the smaller manufacturers have been and are enabled to effectively and vigorously compete in the sale of their product.

He places at the disposal of each mill an efficient sales organization which it would be impossible for a single small mill to maintain independently. The mills can be divided into two classes—timber or dimension mills and board mills. To the former the wholesaler is indispensable. He furnishes special cutting to suit available timber. Most mills in the Eastern and Southeastern states are of this character.

Not only does he save the small mill and the capital investment necessary to maintain a sales organization, but he also actually helps to finance most mills, both large and small, by paying cash, or from 75 to 90 per cent. of the mill value, for lumber at the time of shipment. Among many mills he makes cash advances to enable such mills to buy additional timber or equipment, to meet pay rolls or to finance surplus lumber stocks, which would otherwise be dumped upon the markets at times when they could not be absorbed.

He is also the agency through which odd lots of stock are efficintly marketed, where they can be used to the best advantage or in substitution for other kinds of lumber, to very material saving for the mills.

The wholesaler purchases generally at the mill, assuming the responsibility of risk, damage or delays in transportation or losses due to railroad overcharges on both weight and freight rates. He asumes the sales credit risk and conserves to many mills their limited capital for increased production, at all times guaranteeing a market for his goods without usual sales worries, thus permitting the manufacturer to give his entire time to the details of production.

To the consumer the wholesaler supplies varied services.

Adjusts Market Demands to Supply

Through his efficient sales organization, with direct personal contact with indivdual buyers, the wholesaler is able to give information to the consuming public as to the most acceptable kind of lumber available at lowest market prices suitable to each buyer's use, and by substituting, at times, lumber from one territory, in place of another, supplies the consumer with the most efficient character of lumber suited to his use at the lowest available market price, thus helping to adjust to the public demand with resultant conservation in the industry.

This same constant contact with the consumer together with the wholesaler's knowledge of available stock at various mills, permits delivery from points taking the most advantageous freight rate to the benefit of the consumer, since on many classes of lumber the freight is from 25 per cent to 45 per cent. of the total delivered selling price and a big factor in establishing market values at points of consumption.

Shipments from points of production where stocks are most available and obtainable at the lowest freight cost consequently permit the wholesaler to equalize conditions in various manufacturing sections as well as to stabilize market prices to the consumer at delivery point.

Effects Economy of Service

In meeting the requirements of the large consuming trade, more particularly the industrial trade and manufacturers, who require lumber in large quantities for remanufacture, or in the handling of large orders of all one size or quality or orders of very difficult character or mixed orders covering various kinds of lumber, the wholesaler, having at his disposal the product of many mills located in different sections, can meet this greater variety of demand more promptly and efficiently and by handling same through the one selling organization can more efficiently serve the consumer at a lower cost for such service than could any one individual or group of manufacturers seeking such trade in competition from various sections of the country.

Large contracts of all one class of size of material that could not be handled by any one manufacturer, are distributed through the wholesaler to many mills whose timber is especially suitable for such special cutting, thus giving the buyer the benefit of securing production from many sources of supply at competitive cost prices, but with the saving in energy and time to the consumer in having to deal with one agency.

Consumers Depend on Wholesalers

Acting as he does, for a large number of industrial and consuming users of lumber, notably the railroads, large industrial plants who require lumber in large quantities for their own products, the expert knowledge of the wholesaler with his intimate acquaintance with the grades and classes of lumber produced in various sections provides to such buyers services that they could not secure unless they organized individual departments to purchase requirements at much higher cost to themselves than the service charge paid by them to the wholesaler.

Many such buyers are entirely dependent upon the wholesaler's knowledge, as the same market would not be available to them except at a greater cost and loss of energy to themselves were it not for the organization of the wholesale distributor whose services to them are indispensable.

While in a geenral way the wholesaler finances most of the manufacturers, he at the same time assists all commercial buyers in their financing by extending terms of payment to the consumer that permits him the option of either paying cash on delivery or settling by note or trade acceptance. This, in many cases, especially among the small retail yards, small industrial plants and in large building contracts, allows renewals of these notes from time to time

*Address delivered before the recent Northern Lumbermen's Salesmanship Conference at Antigo, Wis.

with a considerable assistance to the purchaser in carrying the burden of his own financial requirements.

The wholesaler, in all cases, carries the financial burden, and in many cases, makes it possible for the consumer to take orders which he otherwise could not handle with his own restricted banking facilities. In this way it is estimated that the wholesaler more than doubles the consumer's purchasing power and banking credit, and in that way performs an especial service to the general public, keeping in the industry many small operators, both manufacturers and retailers of a competitive nature who would otherwise be unable to function, and who at all times tend to level market values.

In addition to stimulating retail sales of lumber by reason of extension of credit, in turn the wholesaler, especially during present abnormal times, performs a special service to the extent of stimulating production at the sources of supply by financing mills in the production of small bodies of timber that could not be handled by the large mills, and in that way materially assist the public in conserving to their use timber that could not otherwise be placed upon the market. This function of the wholesaler is more especially appreciated at the present time when stimulation of production is needed to meet the enormous present demand.

Function for Public Benefit

In many other ways, various types of wholesalers function for the benefit of the public, such as guaranteeing to the small buyer delivery of material at a fixed price, f.o.b. destination, establishing a fixed cost of the lumber delivered at his plant and protecting him against the usual transportation hazard, risk or overcharge. Also, through their buying organizations many wholesalers supervise the manufacture, inspection and shipment of lumber at the mills, saving to the consumer at the cost of sending his own inspector to the mill and saving losses to the mills in supervising their grades to meet the qualities required by the consuming public.

Adjustment of claims, due to mismanufactured stock, damage in transit, re-inspection, through personal contact of the wholesaler, permits of fair and equitable adjustment to the mutual protection of both manufacturer and consumer. This is a service much needed but very often misjudged.

Securing empty cars for loading at points where cars are needed, tracing shipments in transit, diverting lumber that is needed to markets in dire need, re-routing of cars to avoid embargoes or congestion, shipping by water to sections of the country where water delivery can be accomplished, and looking after the many other intricate details of transportation that are most necessary to the distribution of lumber, and burdensome to the consumer, are services to both other branches of the industry which are performed daily by the wholesale distributor.

Wholesaler Has Won Place

In conclusion, it is found that the wholesale distributor has won his place and is an indispensable economic necessity, due entirely to the functions and services he performs and due to the absolutely competitive and independent factors that prevail in industry in keeping with the principles of business freedom assured us under our democratic form of government.

The war has given a great impetus to socialism. The present labor unrest is due to this influence. Socialism means Government ownership, not only of the telephones and railroads, raw materials and manufacturing plants, with centralization of power and finance, and with the entire loss of personal initiative so productive under our present order of business democracy.

The greatest enemy that socialism has to-day is democracy. The greatest saviour of civilization and independence to-day is democracy.

Business Can Preserve Democracy

You can best preserve democracy how ? By preserving business and industrial democracy, by conserving competition, by conserving potential but fair and honest competition. By preserving individual initiative, individual opportunity; by preventing monopolies by law, as the Sherman law has done. I do not mean that there should not be great units and large organizations of capital or industry, as a great saving can be accomplished to the general public by economies of such organizations, and the benefits of large scale productions with reduction of overhead cost both in manufacturing and distribution, but these organizations should not be of such character as to become monopolistic in control.

Co-operation, but independence of the various branches in industry, is the salvation to business democracy.

Co-operation in our industry of all three branches—the manufacturer, the wholesaler, the retailer—is necessary, but it must be of such character as to preserve competition. The competition must be clean, fair and honest, and of such character that men can grow, no matter how small their beginnings may be, so long as they have the ability, the energy, the enterprise and the courage to do honestly and to do successfully. There is room with ample return for both capital and energy for the prosperous growth of all three branches of our industry and through honest co-operation their interests can be so united to better educate the public as to the services and functions performed by each and by preserving fair competition in the industry, a greater service can be rendered by all to the public in general in keeping with the wonderful opportunity of our great business democracy.

How Far Does Your Trade Extend?

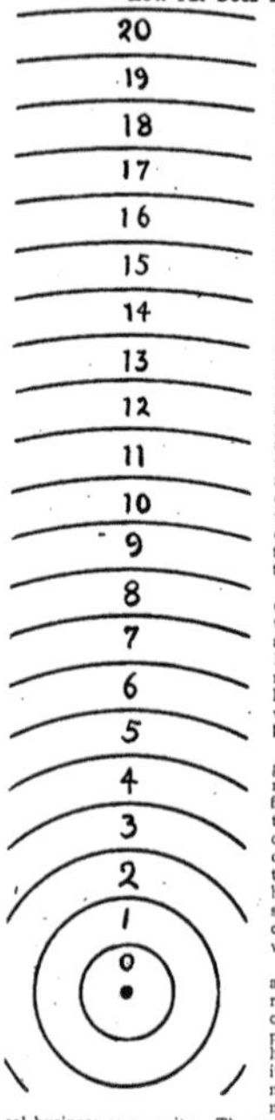

The retailer's local community, as shown by the accompanying diagram, may be confined to the area of the inner circle, designated "0," or it may overflow into the surrounding territory designated "1," "2," "3" and so on.

In the diagram, "0" represents a territory two miles in diameter, containing 3.14 square miles, or 2,010 acres. A town occupying this area may have a population of from 3,000 to 5,000, or from 600 to 1,000 families—say, on an average, 750 families.

The belts of territory surrounding "0" have a breadth of one mile. In the case of cities, their area will take in one or more of these belts. The acreage of each belt is indicated in the accompanying table. Allowing 4 to 5 families per acre, on an average, the approximate urban population of each belt in the city area can be computed. In the table following a town of 750 families is assumed, all contained within the circle designated "0." The rural territory begins with belt No. 1, and extends, in the diagram, to a distance of 21 miles out from the retailer's place.

The retailer's field, before serious competition from other neighboring towns or cities is encountered, will almost certainly take in Belts Nos. 1, 2, 3, 4 and 5, and may take in a number more. Each retailer will know just how many of these mile-wide belts he can fairly count as his own field.

The accompanying table will suggest to each retailer the approximate number of families residing in his field; and suggests the amount of their probable annual consumption of the particular class of merchandise sold by the retailer. It is for the retailer himself to ascertain just how many families in his field he is serving regularly, and how close he comes to doing all the business which his field is able to yield him.

The significance of the accompanying diagram is interpreted in the reading matter above. The centre of the inner circle, marked "0," represents the retailer's store, or the heart of the local business community. The circular strips or belts marked 1, 2, 3 and so on, represent mile-wide areas surrounding the local business community. The area of each of these belts, expressed in square miles and acres, is given in the table accompanying, as is also the probable population by families. The amount of business which the retailer's field should yield is likewise indicated.

James R. Summers, wholesale lumber merchant, Toronto, and wife have returned from an extended motor tour through Northern Ontario, going as far north as Sturgeon Falls. Mr. Summers managed to do some duck hunting while away and had good luck. He reports that the roads for the most part were in good condition and that many improvements are being made to the highways.

Cut on Ontario Crown Lands Will be Large

Reports from Various Timber Districts in Province Generally Reveal Extension in Operation—Increasing Costs Will Make Lumber Sell for Higher Figures

It is interesting to review conditions and activities in various parts of Ontario during the past season so far as they pertain to crown lands. For the information presented in this article the "Canada Lumberman" is indebted to the Crown Timber Agents of the province, who are closely in touch with the progress and development of the lumber, tie and pulpwood industry.

Everyone is looking for a large timber cut in the Port Arthur district during the coming season. It is too early yet to give data, because none of the tie contractors have closed or signed up contracts for this season's output, according to J. A. Oliver, Crown Timber Agent. Everyone is, however, expecting a record production. The tie contractors, so far, are holding out for a raise in price over last season, while the railways are holding out for a lower figure. In connection with pulpwood for export, the pulp companies are offering a slight raise over last winter, while the contractors are anticipating the same. Generally, conditions are about identical with those of last year. Some classes of labor are demanding higher wages than last spring and, in addition, supplies are more expensive, particularly hay and oats. It is too soon to speak with any assurance regarding the supply of labor. The Port Arthur district generally gets some benefit from the harvesters returning from the West, and also from the dock employees and elevator employees who quit when the shipping season is over on the Great Lakes. At present, there is not sufficient bush labor. No new saw mills are going up in the Port Arthur district, although some small settlers' mills have been put in.

A report received from Crown Timber sources in the Thessalon district states there will be about 100 per cent. increase this season in the output of logs. Wages of lumberjacks run from $65.00 to $70.00 per month, with board, while camp supplies are very high. Hay and potatoes are some 40 per cent. above last year's quotations, and it is believed that it will cost 10 per cent. to 15 per cent. more this season to get out logs than it did last year. There will not be many ties taken out in Algoma and the total amount will not exceed 5,000, while the production of pulpwood will be limited—about 5,000 cords in all.

W. P. Christie, of Parry Sound, who is the Crown Timber Agent in that district, remarks: The outlook for the coming season in this agency looks better than the past few years, and the prospects for an enlarged cut this winter appear bright at present. The operators in this district find men more plentiful and wages and other expenses compare well with last season. For the past few years the output of ties and pulpwood has been small. The Schroeder Mills and Timber Company, who are heavy operators in Mowat and Blair townships, have purchased the mills formerly owned by Lauder, Spears and Howland, situated in the township of Mowat, and will cut part of the output at that mill and the balance of their logs will be put on the market for sale. In all their operations in past years the Schroeder Co. sold their stock of logs to other lumber companies in Ontario

P. J. Whelan, Crown Timber Agent of Arnprior, says: As far as I know at the present time there will be taken out in this district during the present season, around sixty million ft. B.M. of lumber, and about twenty thousand cords of pulpwood, and two hundred thousand ties, on crown lands under license. On settlers' lots and lands, on which there is no crown dues, there will be around twenty million ft. B.M. of lumber, and thirty thousand cords of pulpwood, and one hundred thousand railway ties. Men seem to be fairly plentiful, and wages run from $55 to $65 per month, but experienced bushmen like we used to have in the days gone past, are scarce.

George Bremner, Crown Timber Agent of Cochrane, gives the following summary of the timber situation in his district: Men seem to be quite plentiful, only the lumbermen have difficulty in holding them. Wages are about $65.00 per month with board and other expenses a little higher than last year. The output in pulpwood last year would be somewhere near 250,000 cords. The tie production in this district is not large, perhaps about 200,000 ties. There is only one new sawmill being erected so far and it is at the crossing of the Driftwood River on the Canadian Government Railway. It is being built by the Carol C. Critsinger Corporation.

Wm. Margach, the Crown Timber Agent at Kenora, observes that it is too early in the season to give definite data regarding the timber cut in 1919, the season for which the Agency prepares reports really beginning about October 1 and ending about April 30 or May. Mr. Margach adds: Hardly any camps are operating as yet, there being practically no summer cutting, and the camps will really not be in operation for, at least, another month or six weeks. I might say that men seem a little more plentiful and really a better class of men, this being the second and third year for some of them. No new sawmills are being built in and around Kenora.

Another representative of the Crown Lands Department, writing from New Liskeard, Ont., states that he does not expect lumbering operations will be very much changed from last season. Men are scarce and hard to keep, and wages are much the same as last year.

In regard to the timber operations in the Sault Ste. Marie district, A. H. Huckson, Crown Timber Agent, believes there will be a slightly larger cut this season than last. Two firms are taking out waney timber and there will be an increase in pine operations owing to the fires last summer. Labor conditions are a little easier than last season but wages are slightly higher and other items of expenditure about the same. Last season there was a cut of about 6,000,000 feet of pine saw logs, 125,000 cubic feet of waney timber, 75,000 railway ties and 160,000 cords of pulpwood but this season there will be a larger increase in all these lines with the exception of pulpwood.

A new sawmill is being erected at Searchmont by the Searchmont Lumber Co. (of which Hon. George Gordon, A. B. Gordon and others are members) who have six townships in the district. A new company formed in the United States is opening up an operation in the township of Pennyfeather and intend erecting mills for the cutting of hardwood and other timber. The township of Whitman has been acquired by the Horner Lumber Co., of Reed City, Mich., who intend building a sawmill for hardwood at Glendale.

S. J. Hawkins, Ontario Timber Agent at Webbwood, asserts that there are about forty-six camps in that district, which is double of what there were last year. Men have become more plentiful during the past few days and some of the camps are about filled up. Wages run from $60 to $65 per month while other items are about the same as last year with a few higher in price. In regard to the output of 1919, Mr. Hawkins states that he cannot give any estimate as yet but last year it was very small. Very little pulp wood and ties are being cut in the Webbwood district; only what the farmers get out.

Next Logging Congress in Vancouver

The annual meeting of the Pacific Coast Logging Congress which was held in Portland, Ore., was one of the largest ever and the 1920 gathering will meet in Vancouver.

The new president is Arthur Hendry, of the British Columbia Mills Timber and Trading Co., Vancouver. The papers read at the sessions were all of a practical and helpful character and among the delegates from B. C. were W. R. W. Armstrong, secretary of the B. C. Loggers' Association; J. Garrett, of the Munn & Kerr Co.; F. R. Pendleton, Wm. Hanson, F. Wilkinson and J. W. Wilkinson, of the Wilkinson Co., Vancouver; E. J. Palmer, Victoria Lumber and Manufacturing Co.; J. M. Dempsey, of the Dempsey Logging Co.; G. G. Johnson, Capilano Timber Co., North Vancouver; H. B. Gilmour, B. C. Workmen's Compensation Board and W. Rae

One feature of the congress was the introduction of movies and slides of equipment that was handled by those who read papers.

The list of officers for the coming year is: Pres., Arthur Hendry, Vancouver; vice-president, Joseph Irving, Everett, Wash; secretary, George M. Cornwall, Portland, Oregon; Executive: Oregon, A. S. Kerry; Washington, Wm. Chisholm; British Columbia, W. W. Johnston; California, W. W. Peed (retiring president); Idaho, W. D. Humston; Montana, E. H. Pallies.

November 11 has been definitely set as the date for the holding of the Forestry Conference in Syracuse, N. Y., at which Col. H. S. Graves, Chief of the United States Forest Service will come to New York state to discuss with all interested organizations his proposed National Forest Policy. This date has been set, with the consent of Col. Graves, so as to make it possible for the manufacturers, retailers and dealers in lumber, foresters, those interested in all phases of conservation, to attend and hear Col Graves explain his proposed program.

Canada's Great Forests Are Extolled

But Time is Not Far Distant When Spruce May be Exhausted, Says Leading Authority

C. Price-Green, Toronto

In a comprehensive address delivered recently by Mr. C. Price-Green, of Toronto, Commissioner, Industrial and Resources Department, Canadian National Railways, at the National Chemical Exposition in Chicago, the speaker said:

One of the important phenomena of this progressive age is that business men, as a result of the war, have become more or less practical economists. Though they may never have read a word on the subject, they have come to regard their business in its relation to world trade. One hears the question of the balance of trade, exchange, the labor situation and kindred topics discussed by the man on the street as common topics of conversation. In like manner the manufacturers now see the creative value of the chemist and the wonderful work he has wrought in industrial development and his place in finding a use for the raw products of mine, field, water powers, forest and fisheries.

Referring to the timber wealth of the Dominion, Mr. Price-Green remarked:

Canada has the largest forest area within the British Empire, and its pre-eminence as a paper-producing country lies in its possession of 350,000 square miles of pulpwood forest which, it is estimated, will yield over a thousand million cords of pulpwood. Upon these forests America is largely dependant for her news print. The more important of these forest areas lie along the line of the Canadian National Railways, in the provinces of Ontario, Quebec, New Brunswick, Nova Scotia and British Columbia, and support the leading manufacturing industry of the Dominion of Canada. In 1890 Canada's export of pulp and paper products amounted to but a hundred and twenty dollars; in 1918 they reached a total of over 71 million dollars.

Considering the huge demand and rapid consumption of paper, these resources afford attractive openings for pulp and paper mills for the manufacture of sulphite, sulphate, mechanical pulp and news print. As there are throughout these areas, many important water powers, the economic value of these forests can readily be recognized. A few facts regarding the consumption of pulpwood for newsprint will give some realization of the rapid rate at which the forest products of the world are being consumed. The newspapers of Chicago alone, consume daily equal to more than 5,000 average size spruce trees, and one edition of Chicago's largest newspaper requires the spruce of 30 acres of forest. With but one-fifteenth of the world's population the United States consumes one-half of the world's production of paper. At the present rate of consumption and destruction by fire, insects and fungus growth, one is forced to the conclusion that the time is not far distant when a substitute will have to be found for spruce, in the making of news print, and one of the most likely sources of supply is to be found in the vast quantities of straw from the grain growing area, which, at the present time, is being wasted.

The most valuable stands of timber remaining in Canada lie in British Columbia, tributary to the line of the Canadian National Railways. It is estimated by the government that these contain no less than 52 thousand million feet of merchantable timber, including such varieties as Douglas fir and silver spruce; from the latter, during the war, the stock for no less than 35,000 aeroplanes was taken out. * * * * When one considers its vast undeveloped areas, with its known resources, one must be convinced that Canada is on the eve of a period of great activity, for it is only since the war that the people of the world at large have awakened to its wonderful possibilities.

The question naturally suggests itself, if Canada has all this material wealth, why does she not develop it herself? The answer is that Canada needs men and money more than anything else to support increased production. She has only eight million people and they have accomplished perhaps more than any other eight million in history. Her war record is sufficient in support of this statement.

Four Billion Dollar Sale of Lumber

The largest lumber transaction in the history of the world h[illegible] just been completed by the sale of all the surplus lumber and timb[illegible] belonging to the Emergency Fleet Corporation to the Americ[illegible] Lumber Sales Co., with headquarters on the 12th floor of the Co[illegible]onial Trust Building, Philadelphia.

The American Lumber Sales Company is a corporation form[illegible] for the purpose of purchasing this material from the Fleet Corpo[illegible]tion.

Mr. Walker, the president and executive head of the new c[illegible]pany, is well known to the lumber trade. He is the president of [illegible] Lumbermen's Bureau and of the American Woods Export Asso[illegible]tion, with headquarters at Washington, D. C., and recently comp[illegible] a two years' investigation of the European lumber markets o[illegible] half of the Department of Commerce and of the National L[illegible] Manufacturer's Asociation.

Through its contract with the Emergency Fleet Corpora[illegible] new company comes into posession of approximately 100,000,[illegible] of lumber, located in forty-five shipbuilding and storage yards [illegible] the Atlantic and Gulf Coasts. This is the largest stock of [illegible] in the world, and as 50 per cent, of it is located in the large [illegible]ing markets of the East, it is thought that the placing of this [illegible]ial on the market will relieve, to a considerable degree, th[illegible] shortage of lumber which has existed in these markets f[illegible] months. Thirten months' time is allowed in which to mark[illegible] stock. The American Lumber Sales Co. is planning to export [illegible]siderable quantities of this material to be used in the rebuild[illegible] the devastated areas of Europe.

The lumber involved in this sale is largely long leaf yello[illegible] although there are also considerable quantities of Douglas [illegible]ress and oak. This material was got out during the war in conn[illegible] with the wooden shipbuilding program, which was terminated [illegible] the coming of the Armistice, and the forests of the country [illegible] culled over to secure the finest timber available for this purp[illegible]

The prices at which this material was purchased have not be[illegible] announced, but it is understood that the total transaction invol[illegible] approximately $4,000,000.00.

Included among the various yards which are being taken o[illegible] by the American Lumber Sales Company in connec with th[illegible] transaction, is the rail and water yard and complete milling p[illegible] of the Edward F. Henson Company at Philadelphia. This yard h[illegible] been under lease to the Emergency Fleet Corporation this le[illegible] is being assumed by the new company.

Recent Timber Arrivals in Liverpool

The timber report of a leading Liverpool timber broker furnishes the following information:

Imports during August were larger than for some time past a[illegible] deliveries, though hampered by congestion at the docks and ra[illegible]way depots, have been fairly satisfactory. Stocks, almost with[illegible] exception, are within moderate compass. There has been no mate[illegible] change in the business of the past month, although with the la[illegible] outlook becoming more settled the future is regarded with more co[illegible]fidence. Until the freight position improves and the foreign ex[illegible]changes become more stibilized, business will continue difficult.

The following table shows imports on timber into Liverpo[illegible] during August, and total stocks on August 31:

Commodity	Import	Stock	Price, September [illegible]
Quebec waney boards	50,000 c. ft.	50,000 c. ft.	6s. 9d. to 10s. per c[illegible]
British Columbia & Oregon pine logs and planks	Nil	136,000 "	Logs—6s. 6d. to [illegible] 6 d. per c. ft. Planks—£38 to [illegible] per std.
Oak planks, Canadian and American	150,000 c. ft.	100,000 "	6s. per c. ft.
Birch logs	35,000 "	18,000 "	5s. to 7 s. per c. [illegible]
Birch planks	40,000 "	47,000 "	4s. to 8s. per c[illegible]
Quebec pine deals	1,950 stds.	3,000 std	£43 to £55 pe[illegible]
Quebec Red pine deals ...	770 "	1,085 "	"
Quebec Spruce deals	1,150 "	900 "	"
New Brunswick and Nova Scotia Spruce and pine deals	4,320 "	6,900 "	Spruce—£[illegible] per std.
Sleepers and crossing, Canadian and United States	610 "		

Good Progress Made on New Mills

Clarke Bros., Limited, of Bear River, N. S., report tha[illegible] construction is being carried on with satisfactory progress in conne[illegible] with their new sawmill and new sulphate pulp plant, and that [illegible] are also making readjustments and extensions to their woodwor[illegible] establishment at Lake Jolly. Clarke Bros. will be operating a[illegible] the usual number of lumber camps during the coming winter seas[illegible] The labor situation is somewhat difficult, wages and the cost [illegible] camp supplies all being higher than in 1918. The work in loggi[illegible] operations is just starting.

The busy waterfront at Buctouche, N.B., showing sailing vessels laden with lumber and other products from the industries of J. D. Irving, Ltd., whose factories and buildings cover a floor area of over 135,000 square feet. The storage sheds and warehouses are seen in the background.

Some of the splendid logs owned by the Finger Lumber Co., Ltd., of The Pas, Man. The logs are driven down the Carrot river into a storage boom, located where the stream empties into the Saskatchewan. The company are the pioneers in the lumber industry in Northern Manitoba.

Western Provinces Adapted to Tree Growth

During a recent address Robson Black, of Ottawa, secretary of the Canadian Forestry Association, in speaking before a gathering of financial men in Winnipeg said:

"Forestry is the science of obtaining maximum profits from a great natural resource. It is concerned with growing repeated crops of timber on non-agricultural soils. 75 per cent of Manitoba is under the growth and not more than 35 per cent. of the whole provincial area will ever pay a profit to the farmers' plow. One half of Saskatchewan and two-thirds of Alberta are adapted by nature for the growing of profitable crops of timber. The timber is the largest crop in point of acreage, and in view of the experience of such provinces as Quebec and New Brunswick and nations like Sweden, it offers possibilities that some day may rival the profits from grain.

"Since confederation the forest areas of Canada have been responsible for over 1,500 million dollars of export trade as compared with 2,000 million dollars received for cereal crops. This year pulp and paper exports alone from the spruce growing sections of Quebec, Ontario and to a smaller extent from British Columbia have jumped to 120 million as against 120 dollars in 1890—a million times as great."

Mr. Black told how spruce areas in United States and Canada were making enormous rises in value. 40 million newspapers a day are produced on this continent and this publishing industry alone makes increditable demands upon the very limited sources of spruce wood supply. Several American newspapers stripped from 15 to 30 acres of forest for each Sunday edition turned out. The Winnipeg daily papers were consuming probably 250 spruce and balsam trees with each day's run. Coupled with the lumbering industry the pulp and paper industry had shown the old time phrase of "exhaustless forests" to be nothing short of undiluted moonshine. These industries in the eastern states and Canada were now coming forward with schemes which approximated scientific forest management. The day of forest butchery must end or the country ceases to be an international competitor. The history of the lumbering industry has been one of continuous chase of virgin timber supplies from county to county and north to south. President Dodge, of the International Paper Company, recently declared that there were not today two stands of spruce in eastern America that would justify the erection of two fifty-ton pulp mills. In eastern United States the last stand of the great American lumber industry was now being made in the south after stripping Maine, Wisconsin, Michigan and other lake states. The president of the Southern Pine Manufacturers has declared that 3,000 mills under his jurisdiction will go out of business in ten years because of exhausted forests.

Turning to Canada, the speaker showed that the forest resources in the three prairie provinces except for the areas in the forest reserves, are in a state of progressive deterioration; 80 per cent. of the west's original inheritance of splendid forests has been destroyed by forest fires. On the most valuable portions of what now remains, said the speaker, the methods of commercial operating under sanction of the Dominion government were leaving the forest properties continually poor. Mr. Black declared that few, if any, lumbermen and pulp company executives in eastern America were any longer deluded by the old fiction that unregulated logging at present in vogue throughout the Dominion will do anything but destroy the capital values of our timber area. European practice now centuries old which looked upon a timber tract as a source of permanent timber crops was now being adapted to American and Canadian conditions. As far as the three western provinces are concerned, this calls emphatically for the handling of the public-owned timber berths of over 6,000 square miles by the Dominion forestry branch, which is the government's only technically qualified department. The United States government has had its entire area of national forests lands under strict regulation by the U. S. Forest Service for many years past and with uniformly satisfactory results to the American people and the commercial operator.

The speaker made clear that in the truest sense the most valuable and indispensable timber areas in the prairie provinces are not "alienated" as people commonly suppose. The Dominion government representing the interests of the west, is absolute master of the methods of handling such timber berths and can at any time establish on these areas such constructive forestry practice as is in the true interests of the community. Mr. Black explained that the quarrel as to the ownership of the forest resources in the west was not the conservationist's business, his only concern is to see that no matter who owns the western forests they are administered in the interests of the greatest number of people over longest possible period of time. In any event, ownership of the prairie province forests does not constitute an immediate financial asset, looked at from the point of view of relieving other forms of taxation. The Dominion government spends more than 200 thousand dollars annually on the Western forests for protection and administration over and above what comes to the federal treasury as revenues.

"Forest is state business. A corner grocery, a broker, a farmer, follow the individualist's law of business, by which for a given investment he expects and must have a fairly immediate return. This natural factor removes the practice of forestry from the sphere of private effort because the forest is a long time proposition maturing its crops only in cycles of 60 to 100 years. Forestry therefore is community insurance for the community has a vastly more considerable interest in perpetuating the forest estate than has the commercial timber land operator. Only the state with its self-perpetuating life can afford to enter upon a policy that will ensure the continuance to posterity of the public-owned forest inheritance."

When Lumbermen Get on the Job

In the recent Navy League campaign, when over $150,000 was raised in Toronto, the wholesale lumbermen played an important part in the canvass and also subscribed liberally to the fund. A. E. Clark was captain of the team, which consisted of about fifteen representatives of various firms. The block bounded by Yonge St. on the west, Toronto St. on the east, King St. on the south and Adelaide St. on the north was taken over entirely by the lumbermen who conducted their work thoroughly and met on the whole with a generous response. The members devoted three days to the subscription campaign and their labors were highly praised by the central committee.

The lumbermen's team collected in the neighborhood of $10,000 and the following constituted the members of the canvassing committee: Messrs. Wilson, (Canadian General Lumber Co.); George, (R. Laidlaw Lumber Co.); Hardy, (Union Lumber Co.); Spragge, (Victoria Harbor Lumber Co.); Findlay, (Long Lumber Co.); Greene, (Terry & Gordon); Howes, (Campbell, Welsh & Paynes); J. R. Carter, (Fesserton Timber Co.); Barclay, (Canadian Western Lumber Co.); Lamont, (C. G. Anderson Lumber Co.); Alex Read, (Read Bros.); Armstrong, (Seaman, Kent Co.); Jarvis, (Elgie & Jarvis Co.); A. C. Gordon, (Edward Clark & Sons). The captain, A. E. Clark, has written a letter of thanks to each of the firms represented, expressing his gratification at the active work done by them individually and collectively

Hardwood Limits and Plant Change Hands

The Jones-Webster Corporation of Wenlock, Vermont, in which Edward Clark & Sons, of Toronto, have a controlling interest, have disposed of their saw-mill, logging equipment and timber-cutting rights on 70,000 acres of limits to the Warner Sugar Refining Co., Wall St., New York. It is the intention of the purchasers to continue operating the sawmill and to erect a large stave plant at Wenlock for the manufacture of their own barrels. The sawmill has a cutting capacity of 30,000 ft. a day and the timber of the holdings consist principally of birch and maple. The Jones-Webster Corporation retain the present stock of lumber and will finish cutting this year's allottment of logs in about six weeks. They have on hand some 4,000,000 ft. of lumber, which has practically all been sold, but has yet to be shipped out. Edward Clark & Sons will still maintain their selling organization in the Eastern states and will devote their attention more exclusively to the wholesale line. They have been engaged in the manufacturing end in Vermont for about two years.

Good Market for Maple Flooring

J. Forsyth Smith, Trade Commissioner, Liverpool, sends an interesting report to the Department of Trades and Commence at Ottawa in regard to the market for maple flooring in England. He says that the general outlook for this commodity at the present time is excellent, as there is a good demand, and with the large amount of building in prospect, this should steadily increase, as industrial conditions become more settled. The sizes most in demand are 1-inch and 1½-inch by 4-inch and 4½-inch. Wholesale prices at various dates during the past few years have been as follows:

December 31, 1917,	30 to	40	per standard
June 1, 1918,	35 to	45	per standard
December 31, 1918,	35 to	45	per standard
February 1, 1919,	30 to	37	10s. per standard
May 1, 1919,	25 to	35	per standard
August 1, 1919,	55 to	65	per standard
September 1, 1919,	55 to	65	per standard

Forest Fires Sweep Valuable Timber

A bush fire, about seven miles west of Fernie, did damage to the estimated extent of $5,000 to A. J. Farquharson, cedar dealer, operating a camp in that locality. Between 12,000 and 15,000 manufactured cedar fence posts were destroyed, also a large quantity of mining props and poles, together with bush equipment, chutes, roads and landings. The limits were also badly fire-swept. Mr. Farquharson managed to save his camps, which are located on the opposite side of the railway, from the fire.

It is very exceptional at this season of the year for fires to be considered dangerous, but the past season has been the most disastrous in the history of this district. Millions upon millions of feet of merchantable standing timber have been swept over by fire, and huge quantities of the same fire-killed, which unless logged and manufactured within a short time, will be a total loss. The rain precipitation this season has been practically nil, and consequently the condition in the woods is excedingly favorable to fires rapidly spreading once they have started.

Many Hungry Souls With But Single Thought

There is nothing like the open air to give one a healthy, keen appetite, and the accompanying picture shows a boat-load of hungry sorters at the dinner-shack. The picture was taken some time ago at the sorting camp of the Laurentide Co., Grand Mere, Que., and the scow is seen approaching the dock. One can almost picture the effectiveness of the attack of the boys upon a ton or two of pork and beans, as determination is written in every lineament of their countenances. Some of the expectant ones seem to have visions of an unusually good meal, for the company is particularly happy, and after a busy morning's work no five o'clock tea morsels are required to tempt their voracious appetites. After the fray is over, one can picture the outcome as something in the nature of a massacre. The Laurentide boys are, to use a terse term, good feeders, and, incidentally, good workers. The camps of the Laurentide Co. are well managed, and the town of Grand Mere is a model one in many respects, with every modern convenience and facility for education, relaxation, entertainment or healthy sport.

Laurentide workers arriving at sorting camp for noon-day meal

New Company Has Big Plans Ahead

As stated recently a federal charter has been granted to Lumber and Pulpwood of British Columbia, Limited, with a capital stock of $1,000,000, and headquarters at 120 Bay St., Toronto. The officers of the company are: President, Joseph Oliver (Oliver Lumber Co.), Toronto; Vice-President, E. V. Tillson, (The Tillson Co.), Tillsonburg; Sec.-Treas., John W. Gordon, 120 Bay St., Toronto; Directors, James A. Thomson, (Gartshore-Thomson Co.), Hamilton; George C. Goodfellow, (Wholesale Lumber), Montreal.

The distribution of the products in Ontario will be taken care of by the Oliver Lumber Co. of Toronto, who have been over forty years in business, while the requirements of the Maritime Provinces and Quebec will be looked after by George C. Goodfellow, wholesale lumberman of Montreal, who has five lumber yards in that city.

The company have been incorporated for the purpose of manufacturing lumber and cutting pulpwood from the valuable timber limits secured in 1908 at a low cost by the Willow River Timber Co., which was organized as strictly a timber holding and not a lumber manufacturing company. The limits are situated on the watershed of Ahbau Lake and Willow River, Caribou District, B.C., and consist of forty-nine square miles of standing timber. It is estimated that the limits will produce over 500,000,000 feet, board measure, of good, general-purpose lumber, and 250,000 cords of the finest pulpwood. About 80 per cent. of the timber is white spruce, 10 per cent. white or balsam fir, with a small stand of red fir. The company propose to erect a complete sawmill plant with a capacity of 100,000 feet in ten hours, and to install the most up-to-date machinery.

In regard to pulpwood, the company state that this industry is merely in its infancy in the Pacific Coast Province, and they point out that one ton of B. C. spruce will produce 2305 lbs. of ground pulpwood. The company add that should it be considered desirable when conditions warrant, the organization will be recapitalized or a subsidiary company formed to manufacture both pulp and paper, and if a sulphite mill were erected, all edging, slabs and other mill waste could be utilized.

An Attractive Business Calendar

The E. Long Manufacturing Co. of Orillia, Ont., have issued a large and decidedly attractive calendar, which is one of the finest productions ih that line. Upon a buff background is shown a birdseye view of the company's large factories, and at the foot of each sheet are seen splendid cuts of the representative lines made by this enterprising firm. These include log jacks, log deck equipment, portable sawmills, semi-portable and heavy duty mills, saw frames, edgers, Pacific Coast mill equipment, saw mill repairs and supplies, lath machines, lath bolters and other information. The whole calendar is a work of art and beauty and contains much useful and valuable information.

More Power for Bathurst Lumber Co.

Plans have been prepared for a hydro-electric power development at Grand Falls, on the Nepisiguit River, for supplying power to the Bathurst Lumber Co., Bathurst, N.B., in connection with their lumber mills and pulp plant. The current will be transmitted over a transmission line, with steel piles, to Bathurst, a distance of 19 miles. Two units will be installed, provision being made for a third unit. Each unit will be 4,500 h.p. The turbines will be of the vertical, umbrella type, direct connected to generators, and will work under a head of 100 feet. The dam and power-house—the former 450 feet long—will be constructed of concrete. Mr. William Kennedy, Jr., of Montreal, is the hydraulic engineer, and Dr. L. A. Herdt, Montreal, the electrical engineer.

Wooden Shipbuilding Under Community Plan

Continuance of the wooden shipbuilding industry on the Pacific coast depends on the success of a scheme for community building and operation. The last of the twenty wooden cargo carriers built by the Foundation Company for the French government has been launched, and unless further business is forthcoming from another direction the industry will have ceased. The work of outfitting the hulls is being proceeded with at present. Several hundreds of workmen employed at the Point Ellice and Point Hope yards have been paid off. The last launching took place at Point Ellice, B. C., on October 10. This marked the completion of the largest shipbuilding contract ever awarded in British Columbia.

The plan of building wooden vessels under a community plan has received the endorsation of the Foundation Company, according to an announcement by Bayly Hipkins, vice-president and Pacific Coast manager of the company, after a conference in New York, with the directors of his company. Definite plans have not yet been made public. The company is understood to be willing to assist in financing the scheme by purchasing stock and by contributing its plant and organization to Victoria. The management points to the urgent need for tonnage and the high freight rates which show no sign of diminishing in the near future. The vessels will pay for themselves in a comparatively short time, company officials state and will help to transport British Columbia products to overseas markets. The building of four wooden vessels at a cost of $500,000 each has been proposed, involving the raising of funds to the extent of $2,000,000.

The death of Frank Skinner White ocurred recently in St. John. He was a higly esteemed citizen and a popular business man. Mr. White was manager and a member of the firm of W. Malcolm Mackay Ltd., lumber merchants, and was well known throughout the country. He is survived by his wife and one son.

The Passing of Pioneer Lumberman

John Headhead, who recently passed away at Lowville, Ont., was a widely known lumberman and actively connected with the industry up to his death. He was born in Peterboro in 1835 and, when twelve years of age, started rafting down the Trent Canal, and then on the St. Lawrence river to Quebec, which work he continued for some years. Later he followed millwrighting and started operating plants of his own, sawing by the thousand feet at Stone Bridge on the Welland Canal, Ancaster, Carlisle, Freelton and other places. In 1868 he purchased from James Hadden, another pioneer, a lbolck of timber in Nelson township, Halton County, where he operated continuously till his death, cutting several large stocks. He had no less than four sawmills burned, the last one when he was nearing his 70th year, but his courage never failed and he quickly set about rebuilding. He still owned a mill at the time of his death which he ran last Spring for several weeks, doing all his own saw-filing and setting. The late Mr. Readhead was for several years a member of the municipal council and held other public positions. Walter Readhead, of Milton, a director of the Canadan Hereford Breeders' Association, in which the late Mr. Readhead also took much interest, is a son of the deceased, who was well known in Halton, Wentworth, and Welland counties, where he enjoyed a wide measure of esteem.

How Canada's Lumber May Reach Foreign Ports

This is a picture showing Benson log rafts moored at San Diego Harbor after a journey of 1,200 miles by ocean from the Columbia River. It affords a good idea of how Canada's timber may reach foreign ports in future, thereby ameliorating the shipping problem. The cut is kindly loaned to the "Canada Lumberman" through the courtesy of the Intelligence Branch of the Department of Trade & Commerce, Ottawa, and affords some conception how rapidly transportation systems, and means are changing to meet present-day requirements regarding bulk, service and delivery. In connection with the numerous big rafts now seen on the Pacific Coast it may be stated that the first Davis rafts of cut lumber that entered Vancouver harbor were recently at the government wharf awaiting shipment east. The tugboat Contli made the long haul from Masset Inlet to Vancouver without incident. There are 2,500,000 feet in the two big rafts, which draw fourteen feet. This lumber was cut at the Masset Timber Company's mills at Buckley, on Masset Inlet. It consists of spruce lumber, part of the production of the war-time airplane spruce campaign. The Masset Company bought it from the Imperial Munitions Board.

Help is Scarce in the North

F. E. Hawkes, who operates a saw and planing mill at South Gillies, Ont., in the Thunder Bay District, reports that during the past season he cut about ,0000 feet per day. The timber was mostly small, consisting of balsam and spruce. His cut during the past summer was around 300,000 feet. Mr. Hawkes says that he finds labor the hardest problem to deal with and it is difficult at times to get sufficient help. He does a lot of custom work for farmers and others, in both sawing and planing, but does not operate any camps, buying most of his logs from outsiders. Lumber is ruling high in the Port Arthur district at the present time, and the prospects are evceedingly good for next season's activities.

Timber Operations Extending in England

A new organization for the development of Canadian export trade has been launched in London in the formation of Shawinigan, Ltd. The corporation which is financed by Montreal and English interests, has as chairman and managing director H. T. Meldrum of Montreal. The vice-chairman is S. Ray Marshall of London, and the directors are: Edmond J. Boake, London, John Dawbarn, Liverpool, and Howard Murray, Montreal. It will deal in the products of the greatest electro-chemical centre in the Empire, Shawinigan Falls. They will have the sole right to sell products in the United Kingdom and Europe.

Timber Operators & Contractors, which was formed in Britain by demobilized officers and men of the Canadian Forestry Corps, at present are logging and sawing at seven different British centres, and are launching out into Siberia and Europe, as well as acting as British agents for Canadian timber firms. They have acquired one of the best re-saw plants in the United Kingdom, the Priddy and Hale plant, at Rotherhithe, Surrey docks, are erecting a creosoting plant, and will build a sash and door factory. The firm is capitalized at $2,500,000 and is headed by Major-General Alexander McDougall, former general officer commanding the Canadian Forestry Corps.

Pembroke Sawmills Have Busy Season

Pembroke is one of the busy town in Eastern Ontario and has long been a prosperous and thriving community. As a lumber centre it is well known and possesses two large concerns, both of which have had a good season. These are the Pembroke Lumber Co., Limited, and the Colonial Lumber Co., Limited, the products of which are shipped to many points. The output of these two companies is about 40 million feet annually.

The Pembroke Lumber Company, which has been one of the town's leading industries for over 25 years, was founded by the Hon. Peter White, Mr. A. T. White, Arunah Dunlop, Cornelius Chapman, Thomas Deacon and John Bromley, and has always been a going concern. It has increased its plant from time to time.

At present the Company employs about 250 men in its mills, and manufactures about 20,000,000 feet of lumber per year. Besides its ordinary log cutting equipment it operates a lath and picket mill, its planing being done by the recently erected planing mill of Mr. L. S. Barrand. The company is operating six logging camps this year with a staff of about six hundred men. Two of these camps are on the Big Jocko river, two on the Little Jocko, one near Kenny's Siding and another near Diver on the C. N. R.. The officers of the company are President, Mr. E. A. Dunlop; Treasurer, Dr. J. D. Deacon, and Manager, Mr. Arthur Eastcott.

The Colonial Lumber Company, which was originally founded by Messrs. Robert Booth, Robert Gordon, E. F. and G. F. Faquier,

Transportation of Canadian timber by log rafts

E. J. Chamberlin, and J. W. Smith, about twelve years ago, these gentlemen taking over the plant of Messrs. A. and P. White, has prospered exceedingly. The Colonial Lumber Company suffered a number of reverses through fire, but even that did not impede its progress, and to-day its plant is up-to-date in every respect. It employs about 250 men about its mills, and some 600 in its logging camps, seven of which it is operating this year, two on the Kippewa River, three on the Deux Rivieres, and two on Deep River. Its average yearly output is about 20,000,000 feet, while it operates both a lath and picket mill. The officers of the Company are: President, Mr. E. J. Chamberlin; Vice-President, Mr. J. W. Smith; and Secretary-Treasurer, W. R. Beatty, Mayor of Pembroke.

Eastern Concern is Rushing Business

The Davison Lumber & Manufacturing Co., of Bridgewater, N. S., say that during the past summer they have found market conditions better than they have been for many years. Both the local and export demand for lumber was exceptionally good and the selling prices allowed of a respectable margin of profit. The sales of the company were limited by their output, which, for the past two years, has been only about 50 per cent. of normal, but they are making preparations to log to normal capacity this winter. While at present the labor to do this does not appear available locally, they hope to find sufficient help through the medium of labor bureaus and by other means.

The Davison Lumber & Manufacturing Company report that the demand for hardwood flooring is decidedly active, and they are booked up for, at least, three months ahead to the full capacity of their mill, and the same observation may be made with regard to box shooks. For several months their planing mill, box factory and hardwood flooring departments have been working time and a half. Between the company's mills at Bridgewater, Sprinfield and Mill Village, the Davison organization hope to have available for next season's cutting about 40,000,000 feet spruce, pine, hemlock and hardwood. The lumber market for next year appears promising and good hopes are held out for its stability if operators will come up to the demand and not adopt the old idea of "any old price but we must have the order."

proper count, scale and return of all material cut from these lands each year. He is furnished with an assistant or counter, who assists him during the scaling season. About 5,000,000 feet is considered sufficient work for any scaler. Each camp is visited every two weeks and the yards of logs counted and scaled, marked and numbered. A report is furnished the Crown Land Office every two weeks on the logs scaled and counted at each of the 700 or 800 camps in operation. This report is checked and a duplicate mailed at once to the licensees, so that he is properly informed of any infractions of cutting regulations, such as cutting undersized timber, too high stumps. If the licensee disputes the scale the logs are still there and a check scaler is put on and the dispute immediately settled. This system, tried out last season, has given very satisfactory results, and will be in use again this year, with only slight modifications.

Beck Company Buys Little Current Mills

The C. Beck Mfg. Co., Limited, of Penetanguishene, Ont., who operate two saw mills as well as extensive woodworking plants in that town, have purchased the mills and timber of the Little Current Lumber Co., Little Current, in the Algoma district of Ontario. The Beck Co. are now operating their camps.

The Little Current Lumber Company's mill is built upon solid rock, which resulted in securing for its machinery its excellent smoothness of operation. The machinery of the sawmill consists of a double-cutting band saw and a gang-saw in addition to the full equipment of edgers, trimmers, etc. The capacity of the plant is about 140,000 ft. in twenty hours when the mill is operated night and day. The plant of the Little Current Lumber Co. was formerly owned by W & A. McArthur, Cheboygan, Mich., and it was taken over by Mr. Geo. T. Jackson (then interested in that company), along with the others. There is a well-equipped lath department, and the number of men employed in the plant is from 150 to 200

What the conditions will be during the coming season the Beck Co. say that it is dfficult to determine at present owing to the unsteadiness of labor. Men are going out from the camps now faster than they can be put in and the situation is most discouraging and unsatisfactory. Those who shift at short notice or no notice at all, are mostly foreigners and by their frequent migrations not only interrupt business but cause an enormous amount of trouble and loss both of time and money to the lumbermen. It was thought when the war was over that conditions would settle down somewhat but the "travelers" from one camp to another appear to be as numerous as ever.

Will Use Both Wood and Concrete

A recent despatch from London, Eng., says: The Ministry of Health anounces that with a view of securing more rapid erection of houses, it is negotiating with a number of firms for the erection of buildings of other materials than brick or stone. These materials will include wood, reinforced concrete and asbestos sheeting. as well as interlocking and hollow terra cotta bricks. Messrs. Boulton and Hall are prepared to erect a large number of one-storey wooden bungalows on a plan approved by the Ministry of Health. The approximate cost of each bungalow is to be about $3,000. This firm has stated that it hopes to build about a thousand of these houses each year.

Lumber Piled High Awaits Shipment

While the winter port season draws near the problem of lumber merchants in New Brunswick becomes more involved for they have still many millions of feet of lumber belonging to the British government piled high in their yards and on every available space near their mills. In addition, they have the vast majority of this year's cut on hand. and the question which is causing them no small concern is where they are going to find room for it all. Some of the mills have runs a long distance for their mills, and the pilers have to carry the deals etc., three and four times as far as would be necessary if that already sold was disposed of. With the approach of the winter port season the chances of getting cargo space become more remote, and the real problem will be in the spring. The merchants are making every effort to better conditions and are hoping against hope that steamers will be released to carry away the supply, which has been left too long on their hands.

Rafting operations at the Douglas booms. Fredericton, which had been suspended for some time on account of lack of water, have been resumed. Between one and two million feet of lumber were at the booms. The corporation drive at Grand Falls, N.B., was estimated to be about two million feet. but by the time it reached Bristol it was said to be four million feet. The St. John River Log Driving Company were all through their sorting at Van Buran, early in July, but their logs were held up there by lack of water.

The Forestry Corps Knew No Failure

Only Now is Magnitude of Task Performed by Sturdy Canadians Being Fully Appreciated

The Canadian Government was asked by the Imperial authorities to supply, if possible, fifteen hundred men for lumbering operations in Britain. This was in February, 1916, after the war had been going on a year and a half. The conditions under which the war was being waged had created an enormous and ever-increasing demand for timber for use in a great variety of ways. It was required in the construction of the endless lines of trenches, in the walling and roofing of dugouts, in the building of military roads and railways, in the strengthening of wire entanglements, in the building of huts, and in a hundred other ways.

During the first eighteen months of the war an attempt had been made to supply this demand by increased production in Great Britain and by heavy imports from this country. It was found, however, that the movement of this timber drew heavily upon the tonnage, which was urgently needed for the transportation of foodstuffs, munitions, and other essentials. The British Government having decided to rely upon the home timber industry, a practical difficulty presented itself; it was found impossible to procure an adequate supply of the right kind of labor. It was then that an appeal was made to the Canadian Goevrnmetn. Six weeks saw sixteen hundred men of the first Forestry Battalion (the 224th) mobilized at Quebec, drawn from all parts of Canada. This battalion took to England its own equipment, including mills, lorries, etc., valued at a quarter of a million. By May 13th sawn lumber was being produced in England by this battalion.

Of the work done by the Canadian Forestry Corps, much has been said and written, but relatively few people in Canada have anything approaching an adequate conception of the service which this corps rendered in the war. The first draft which crossed the ocean under Lieut.-Col. Alexander McDougall (now Major-General McDougall, C.B.), was followed by a steady stream of foresters. The initial experiment, if it can be so called, was successful from the beginning. The work of the first battalion revealed the possibilities of more extended operations, and the Canadian Forestry Corps came into being. The Canadian lumbermen, as has been stated, took with them their own mills and machinery. What was equally, or more important, they took with them their own methods, and they worked under the direction of officers who understood thoroughly the business of lumbering. Beginning with the forests of the south of England, the operations of the Corps were soon extended across the Channel into France, and northward into the Highlands of Scotland. Major-General McDougall, who became the Director-General of Timber Operations in Great Britain and France, provided at an early stage for a great expansion of the service by the advance purchase of equipment sufficient for a force of ten thousand men. The wisdom of this step was fully demonstrated by subsequent events. It meant a great saving of time during a period when time was everything. The working conditions in Britain differed radically from those prevailing in Canada, but the Canadian machinery was adaptetd to these conditions with very little change, and, under the direction of practical lumbermen, Colonel Gerald V. White, C. B. E., in Great Britain, and Brigadier- General J. B. White, D. S. O., in France, the field operations of the corps were conducted upon a scale of production which was a revelation to the governments and people of both France and England.

One example of this will serve as an illustration. In February of 1918, when important events were anticipated on the western front, an emergency call was made for forty thousand tons of timber to be sent to the front. The mills were running day and night, the men voluntarily working for long hours, without extra pay or other inducement, and by the tenth of February shipments had commenced. By March 20 the whole order had been filled, eleven days before the expiration of the time set.

The work of the Canadian Forestry Corps is deserving of a specially written history, and it is satisfactory to learn that something has been done in that direction by the publication of a book entitled "The Canadian Forestry Corps, Its Inception, Development and Achievements." The work has been prepared at the request of Sir Albert Stanley, the President of the Board of Trade, and is written by Mr. C. W. Bird, of the Timber Supply Department, and Lieutenant J. B. Davies, of the Forestry Corps. What is contained in this book conveys a much better idea of the magnitude of the task performed than could be gathered from previous contributions dealing only with special phases. It pays to the Corps and its officers no tribute which they do not well deserve.

Timber Wealth of Western Canada

Timber has always played an important part in assisting in the development of new countries. This is particularly true of the prairie portions of Western America, where the first need of every settler is lumber. In this particular, nature has been exceptionally kind to the four Western provinces of Canada, for while the prairie provinces of Manitoba, Saskatchewan and Alberta produce a certain amount of lumber, the lumber needs of the prairie districts of these provinces could not be filled were it not for the vast timbered areas of the province of British Columbia. This province differs from its three sister provinces to the east in that it is more or less mountainous throughout, and only in the valleys is there opportunity offered for agriculture, horticulture, and animal industry, but the province possesses one of the great undeveloped timber areas of the world. Conservative estimates indicate that the commercial standing timber in the province of British Columbia amounts to 366,000,000,000 feet. This timber comprises cedar, Douglas fir, spruce, hemlock, white fir, lodgepole pine, western yellow pine, yellow cypress, western larch, western white pine and cottonwood.

This vast timbered area has already been developed to a certain extent through the medium of sawmills and allied woodworking industries, but the extension of this portion of our industrial activity will offer opportunities for a further investment of capital coincident with our extension of agricultural settlement east of the mountains and of our overseas export lumber business. There would also seem to be an opening for the extension of our wood pulp and paper making industry in view of the vast quantities of suitable pulpwood to be found in all these four Western Provinces, and in this connection it is noted that we must endeavor to correct the situation which occurred last year in which Canada exported pulpwood to the value of $15,000,000, whereas this pulpwood manufactured into paper at home, at the then existing prices, would have realized the sum of $79,000,000.—Col. J. S. Dennis, Chief Commissioner, Department of Development, C. P. R., before recent Alberta Industrial Congress at Calgary.

The Safety Speed of Circular Saws

The National Safety Council recommends the speed of circular saws corresponding to rim velocity of 9425 feet per minute.

Diam. of Circular Saw	R. P. M.
12 inch	3,000
14 inch	2,570
16 inch	2,245
18 inch	2,000
20 inch	1,800
22 inch	1,635
24 inch	1,500
26 inch	1,385
28 inch	1,285
30 inch	1,200
32 inch	1,120
34 inch	1,055
36 inch	1,000
60 inch	600
72 inch	500

Some manufacturers recommend somewhat higher speeds than here given; however, more than a 20 per-cent. increase is inadvisable.

Band saws are operated at speeds of from 3,500 to 8,000 feet per minute, the heavier saws running at the higher speeds.

Grinding of Wood from Young and Old Trees

Green or freshly cut wood is known to yield a more desirable ground wood pulp than seasoned wood. It is not unnatural to assume, therefore, that a similar difference might occur in the grinding of wood from very small trees which contain a large proportion of heartwood, and smaller trees of the same species. This assumption has been verified by the Forest Products Laboratory, at Madison, Wis.; in a series of commercial grinding experiments on wood from large and small white fir (Abies concolor), grown in Plumas County, California. Paper was afterwards made from the pulp on the laboratory machine, and tested for strength and color.

The small or young wood was cut from trees 18 inches or less in diameter, and the large or old wood was split from a single tree 40 inches in diameter and 130 feet high. Under like grinding conditions, the actual solid volume of old wood ground was, in every instance, appreciably less than the volume of young wood ground in the same time.

In brief, the tests demonstrate that (1) there is a considerable difference in the quality of pulp produced from white fir, depending upon whether the wood is taken from old or from young trees, and (2) the advantages as regard production, power consumption, strength, and color are all in favor of young wood.

J. A. Mathieu, Rainy River,
Returned in recent Ontario elections in Conservative interests

John Carew, South Victoria,
late Conservative Member, who did not seek re-election

Chas. M. Bowman, West Bruce,
Veteran Liberal representative, who recently retired

W. D. Cargill, South Bruce,
who put up strong fight but lost the battle

Lumbermen Candidates are Defeated

Only Two Were Returned at the Polls in the Recent Ontario Campaign—Mageau and Mathieu Win

In the recent Ontario elections the lumbermen legislators did not fare very well at the polls and went down in the general upheaval. There were ten members identified with the industry who sat in the last provincial parliament—four Liberals and six Conservatives. The Liberals were Charles M. Bowman, West Bruce; Zotique Mageau, Sturgeon Falls; Udney Richardson, East Wellington; George C. Hurdman, Ottawa West. The Conservatives were John Carew, South Victoria; W. D. Cargill, South Bruce; Edward A. Dunlop, North Renfrew; James I. Hartt, East Simcoe; James A. Mathieu, Rainy River; James Thompson, East Peterborough.

All of the foregoing sought re-election with the exception of Charles M. Bowman and John Carew, who withdrew from political life. This left eight lumbermen legislators in the field and in addition there were three other lumbermen who sought parliamentary honors in the persons of R. S. Potter, of Matheson, who ran in the Liberal interests in Cochrane, R. E. Butler, of Woodstock, who contested North Oxford in the Conservative cause and James G. Cane, of Toronto, who was the Liberal standard bearer for seat "A" in Northwest Toronto. This made eleven lumbermen who went to the polls, five in the Liberal interests and six in the Conservative ranks. The late Sir John A. Macdonald once remarked that there was nothing quite so uncertain in this life as a horse race or an election. Out of the eleven lumbermen contestants, only two were returned by the people. They were Zotique Mageau, Liberal, Sturgeon Falls and James A. Mathieu, Conservative, Rainy River.

Mr. Richardson was defeated by a United Farmer candidate in East Wellington; George C. Hurdman by a Conservative in Ottawa West; W. D. Cargill by a Liberal in South Bruce; James I. Hartt by an Independent Liberal in East Simcoe; James Thompson by a United Farmer in East Peterborough; R. S. Potter, by a Liberal in Cochrane; R. E. Butler by a United Farmer in North Oxford; J. G. Cane by a Conservative in Northwest Toronto, and Edward A. Dunlop by a United Farmer in North Renfrew.

There will thus be only two lumbermen legislators in the new House, one Conservative, Mr. Mathieu of Rainy River, and one Liberal, Mr. Mageau of Sturgeon Falls.

J. A. Mathieu was re-elected for Rainy River in the Conservative interests and has been a member of the Ontario house for the past seven years. He spent a long period in the lumber arena in Wisconsin and Minnesota and knows the business in all departments. He is a public-spirited and enterprising citizen and is vice-president of the Shevlin-Clark Lumber Co. and also vice-president and director of the Shevlin-Mathieu Lumber Co., as well as manager of other concerns. He has resided in Rainy River for the past seventeen years.

W. D. Cargill, who was defeated in the recent election as the Conservative standard bearer for South Bruce, has been a member of the Ontario Legislature since 1914 and his father represented East Bruce in the House of Commons for several years. Mr. Cargill is president of Cargill's Ltd., who operate a large woodworking plant, and also is a director of the Hepworth Mfg. Co., Hepworth, Ont., and president of several other organizations. Previous to becoming a member of the Ontario Legislature, he contested South Bruce in the Conservative interests for the Federal house n 1913.

John Carew, who was not a candidate in the present election, having retired on his own account, is a progressive lumberman from Lindsay and his withdrawal from the political arena will be much regretted by many friends. Mr. Carew was first elected to the Ontario Legislature in 1914 in the Conservative interests as a representative of South Victoria. He was well liked on both sides of the House. Not only does Mr. Carew conduct a busy sawmill at Lindsay but he also runs a planing mill and retail lumber yard. He has always taken a deep interest in the advancement of the town and is a useful and progressive citizen.

Chas. M. Bowman of West Bruce is another member of the late House who did not seek re-election. He had been Liberal whip for the past sixteen years and will be greatly missed by many old friends. He came through six elections without a defeat, which is a unique record. Mr. Bowman is actively engaged in several woodworking industries and was for a number of years president of the Southampton Lumber Co., Ltd., operating in the Bruce Peninsula for ten years. He has always taken an active interest in the development of Southampton where he is a director of a number of live, go-ahead concerns not only in that town but in Port Elgin and Durham. He is a former president of Southampton Board of Trade and a former reeve of that town.

References to the careers of other Ontario lumbermen legislators who were members of the late House have been made in the last two issues of the "Canada Lumberman."

Eastern Lumber Plant Changes Hands

The Brompton Lumber & Mfg. Co., Bromptonville, Que., has purchased the plant of the Tobin Mfg. Co., and will operate the same in all its departments, which include wholesale lumber, hardwood flooring, planing mill and woodworking factory. The officers of the company are: President, E. W. Tobin, M.P., Vice-President, P. Alegre, Managing-Director, U. E. Germain; Directors—A. Fournier and J. P. Mullins. It is the intention of the Brompton Lumber & Mfg. Co. to cater to the retail yards in the provinces of Quebec and Ontario, and also to carry a full stock of B. C. fir, which can be shipped mixed with eastern products. The company are very busy at the present time and are having a remarkably good season.

Manitoba Has Small Forest Fires

Manitoba had by far the lowest forest fire losses of the prairie provinces this year largely because of a vigorous enforcement of the system of supervising settlers' fires says the Winnipeg "Free Press. Exactly the same law is in force in Saskatchewan, but was left a dead letter by the provincial authorities, with the result that Saskatchewan lost an incredibly large share of its timber properties. Alberta has not yet taken provincial action in curbing the forest evil, although to it belongs the primary responsibility. Alberta's losses in timber have been enormous and the evil effects upon the provincial water supply, for power and irrigation, are among the serious consequences.

A Busy Sawmill in Nipissing District

Denison & Gunter, of Porterville, Ont., expect to operate their sawmill until about the close of the present year and have had a very satisfactory season. They started sawing on June 1st and up to the first week in September has cut over a million and half feet mostly hardwoods. The firm are now trucking logs from the bush. Their mill is located in Sabine township, Nipissing district, on the portion of the Canadian National Railway formerly known as the Central Ontario running from Picton through Prince Edward and Hastings county and terminating at Wallace in the Nipissing district, some four miles north of the northern boundary of Hastings county.

The mill has a double cut band saw put out by the Breeze Deni-

Glimpse of the mill and logs along the track

sion Co., of Newburgh and a cutting capacity of about twenty thousand feet daily in hardwoods on an ordinary run of logs, and is driven by a fifty horsepower engine and boiler carrying only eighty pounds of steam. The boiler is fired entirely by sawdust.

The band wheels of the mill are six feet in diameter and take an eight inch saw, which when properly fitted, cuts a kerf only seven-sixty-fourths of an inch. The saving against an average circular saw, which cuts a kerf of about seventeen sixty-fourths of an inch wide, can be readily seen.

The lumber from the band saw can be cut thinner and still equal the strength of the circular saw in asmuch as the band sawn lumber is smooth and the fibre of the timber not bruised or broken.

Newsy Happenings of Much Interest

J. M. Berry of the Berry Lumber Co., New York City, spent a few days in Toronto recently, calling upon the members of the trade.

A barge carrying 200,000 laths and 616,821 feet of lumber cleared from St. John, October 10th, for Boston. It was shipped by the Pjepscot Company.

C. C. Schreiber, of Sudbury, Ont., who for twelve years was inspector of ties and buyer of construction material for Mackenzie & Mann, has joined the selling staff of the Hocken Lumber Co., Toronto, and has entered upon his new duties.

C. G. Anderson of the C. G. Anderson Lumber Co., Toronto, severely wrenched his right hand while cranking his Reo car, which back fired. He was laid up a few days, but is able to attend to business, although the disabled member is, at times, painful.

A serious fire broke out in Oromocto, N.B., recently and wiped out nearly the entire village as well as the sawmill and lumberyard of the River Valley Lumber Company, which was the chief industry of the village. R. B. Smith, M.P.P., manager of the company, estimater their loss at $200,000. The fire was discovered in the saw mill underneath the engine room, and a few minutes later had spread, and the mill was soon a mass of flames. A high westerly wind was blowing at the time and soon the blaze spread to the offices, mill yard and lumber piles. There were four million feet of manufactured lumber in the yard and two cars on the railway siding.

William Robertson, forester for the commission of conservation, was in St. John, recently, while en route to Northumberland County, to make a preliminary examination of Dominion lands on which timber had ben destroyed by the spruce bud worm. The utilization of the lumber killed will depend upon the result of his investigations.

Lively Briefs From the East

The Bonny River Lumber Company of St. George will cut two million feet of lumber on the Brine property about Mill Lake this winter. Roscoe Burgess and Matt. McKay have contracted for one million each. The mill now operating in St. George will be moved into the woods and the lumber manufactured there. The company has also put a crew in at Piskegan. Their output will be rafted and towed to St. George for manufacture.

Twenty-two young men, eighteen of whom were returned soldiers, took examinations last week for forest rangers. They were taken to Victoria Mills, near Fredericton, where they were given an examination on scaling. The remainder of the examinations were written in the parliament buildings.

Two schooners, the E. M. Roberts and the Maplefield sailed within the past few days for Barbadoes, lumber laden. The former took away 209,383 feet of lumber and 6,196,001 shingles, while the latter carried 3,405,000 cedar shingles.

The American Consul in St. John gave out the following account of lumber shipments to the United States for the t ree months ending September 30. The report shows a considerable increase over the corresponding months last year:

Laths..		
Lumber	12,510,000 ft.	
Pine boards	82,000 ft.	
Pulpwood cords	4,457	
Shingles..	340,000	
Spruce piling	2,492 pcs.	
Wood pulp	6,255,000 lbs.	322,667.41
Total..		
Total for the same period 1918		652,607.97

Returned Men on Field Work

H. S. Laughlin, forester of the J. B. Snowball Co., ham, N. B., in reviewing the summer field activities, says that the work was started June 24th and completed Sept. 15th. 50 sq. miles was surveyed into blocks 2½ miles square and cruised. The line work was started with a crew of five men and one crew of four men cruising, but after about three weeks three of the returned men on the party had a return of their disabilities and the party was shortened to six men all doing line work. When the line was finished only one cruising crew of four men was retained. The cost of the work, line and cruise (5½) was about $.07 per acre. Of the original party seven were ex-service-men.

The new terminals of Halifax harbor showing the Olympic in the dock.

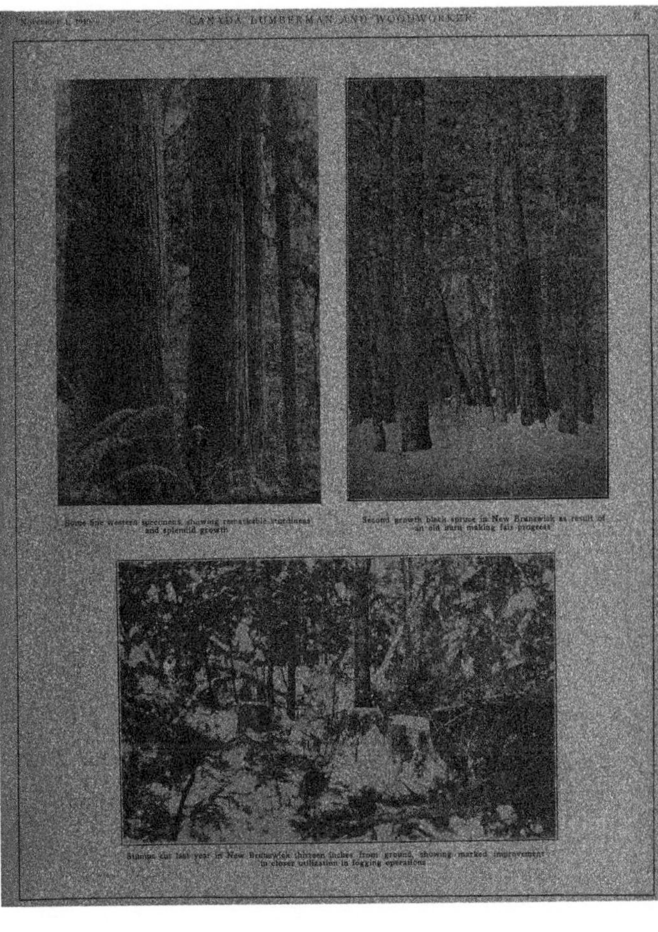

Some fine western specimens showing remarkable sturdiness and splendid growth

Second growth black spruce in New Brunswick as result of an old burn making fair progress

Stumps cut last year in New Brunswick thirteen inches from ground, showing marked improvement in closer utilization in logging operations

Quick Action Section

Special Lots Of Lumber—Positions Wanted & Vacant

PUBLISHER'S NOTICE

Advertisements other than "Employment Wanted" or "Employees Wanted" will be inserted in this department at the rate of 20 cents per agate line (14 agate lines make one inch). $2.80 per inch, each insertion, payable in advance. Space measured from rule to rule. When four or more consecutive insertions of the same advertisement are ordered a discount of 25 per cent. will be allowed.

Advertisements of "Wanted Employment" will be inserted at the rate of one cent a word, net. Cash must accompany order. If Canada Lumberman box number is used, enclose ten cents extra for postage in forwarding replies. Minimum charge 25 cents.

Advertisements of "Wanted Employees" will be inserted at the rate of two cents a word, net. Cash must accompany the order. Minimum charge 50 cents.

Advertisements must be received not later than the 10th and 20th of each month to insure insertion in the subsequent issue.

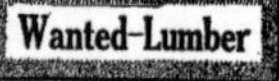

Basswood Wanted

No. 2 Common and Mill Cull. Winter cut preferred. Apply Firstbrook Brothers, Ltd., Toronto, Ont. 8-t.f.

Wanted Lumber

Hardwood Lumber wanted. Birch, Maple, Basswood and other Hardwoods. Dry or sawn to order. We send inspector. Box 14, Canada Lumberman, Toronto. 21-24

WANTED—Plastering Lath

1,000,000 Spruce or Hemlock, Spruce preferred. Quote delivered here and when can ship. Terms: 80 per cent. sight draft, balance on arrival.

THE BILLMEYER LUMBER CO.,
21-22 Cumberland, Md.

Wanted for Cuban Trade
White Pine

Send lists and prices at once to

E. ANTONIO VAZQUEZ,
44 Whitehall Street,
19-22 New York City.

Wanted To Buy
LATH

We are in the market for large quantities of Lath; all grades, including No. 3 and 32". Paying good prices and cash on receipt of B.L.

What have you to offer? Send good description, lowest price F.O.B. Chicago, stating quantity offered.

COVEY DURHAM COMPANY,
431 S. Dearborn St.,
20-21 Chicago, Ill., U.S.A.

FOR SALE
Hickory Specials

100 M pcs. ¾" Dowels, 48" long.
20 M pcs. 1" Squares, 48" long.

Also some shorter stock. All high grade, second growth Hickory. Can ship immediately. Will sell cheap. Address Box 81, Canada Lumberman, Toronto. 21-22

FOR SALE

About 300 M. ft. Birch, Red Oak, Beech and Elm, ready for immediate shipment. Also ¾" Crating Spruce, 1", 2" and 3".

Apply: J. P. ABEL FORTIN LTD.,
379 Desjardins Avenue,
21 Maisonneuve, Montreal.

Wanted-Machinery

Wanted

Small second hand twin screw alligator with cable. State price and condition. P. & J. Shannon, Biscotasing, Ont. 21

Wanted

1 Pony Double Cut Band, 1 Heavy Edger, 1 Log Jack with chains complete, 10 Live Rollers, Trimmer and Slab Slash. Give description and condition, also prices.

HUBBEL BROS.,
21 Bancroft, Ont.

Double Surfacer Wanted

Yates No. 177 Double Surfacer or other similar machine wanted at once. Sectional rolls, infeed rolls, and chip breaker, sectional pressure bar and round cylinders. Must be in first class condition.

Canadian Box & Shook Mills Limited,
21 Sherbrooke, Que.

For Sale-Machinery

For Sale Cheap

One full front 80 H.P. Tubular Steam Boiler, Goldie & McCulloch make. One 65 H.P. Steam Engine, Wheelock's newest type, Goldie & McCulloch make. All as good as new, only used a short time. Move quick for bargain. Apply to Gordon Lumber Co., Stratford, Ont. 21-22

FOR SALE

One Brown type engine, first class condition, 10" x 24" all fittings, ready to set up, 16" x 7' belt wheel.

One Belt, 70' 6" x 44" 3 ply leather endless, scarcely soiled. Two Belts, 60' 6" x 20" double leather, scarcely soiled. Two inserted tooth lumber saws, one 56" practically new, one 52", in good condition. W. H. Cook, Box 356, Orillia, Ont. 21

Band Saw Mill Complete

Waterous 9 ft. Band Mill, Gunshot Feed Carriage, with extra Saws complete.

Filing Equipment

Three Saw Edger, lot of live rolls, Engine, Shafting, Hangers, Pulleys, etc.

All of the above is Waterous equipment in good condition at a bargain.

The Geo. F. Foss Machinery & Supply Co., Limited,
805 St. James Street,
17-t.f. Montreal, Que.

For Sale

1—17 x 24 Atlas Engine, with 36 in. x 10 ft. flywheel.
3—No. 94 Berlin Matchers, 15 in., fitted with hard steel knives on top and bottom cylinders—one pair shiplap, jointer and flooring heads with bits for each machine.
1—No. 182 Berlin Double Surfacer, 30 in. x 6 in.
1—No. 190 Berlin Buzz Planer.
1—No. 290 Berlin Picket Header.

The Otis Staples Lumber Company, Ltd.,
19-t.f. Wycliffe, B.C.

For Sale

One "S. A. Wood Matcher 24" fitted with 20 different sizes knives for top and bottom cylinders. Four pairs of heads with six sets of bits. Price $800, on cars. Savoie & Co., Manseau, Que. 21

Wanted-Employment

Advertisements under this heading one cent a word per insertion. Box No. 10 cents extra. Minimum charge 25 cents.

YOUNG MAN, experienced in all branches of lumber trade, open for position as sales man or manager of manufacturing plant or yard. Box 52, Canada Lumberman, Toronto. 21-22

OFFICE POSITION WANTED in lumber company. Five years' practical experience. Pay Rolls, Specifications, Bookkeeping, etc., etc. Quebec province preferred. No objection to northern location. Box 39, "Canada Lumberman," Toronto. 21

WANTED EMPLOYMENT—By practical Lumberman capable of organizing and taking full charge of lumbering operations, no matter how large. Plenty of experience; good references. Box 42, Canada Lumberman, Toronto. 21-22

WANTED OFFICE POSITION by Clerk with good experience in lumber office work. Bookkeeping, etc., general assistant to manager; or charge of small office. Preferably North Shore, or Gaspe coast in Quebec province. References from former employers. H., Box 41, Canada Lumberman, Toronto. 21

SCOTCHMAN, 29 years of age, wishes position in lumber office, any part of Canada or States. Salary $160 per month and prospects. Has had 15 years office experience, banking 3 years, paper and pulp office 4 years, lumber office 5 years. Has had experience in all branches of lumber office work—accounting, surveying, etc. Inside post wanted. Willing to work to gain good position and can guarantee satisfactory work and trustworthiness; is shorthand typist. Apply Box 48, Canada Lumberman, Toronto. 21

Wanted-Employees

WANTED AT ONCE, fifteen first class construction millwrights. Wire or write the Finger Lumber Co., Ltd., The Pas, Manitoba. 21

WANTED: — PRACTICAL SAW-MILL MAN with portable mill to manufacture hardwood lumber, commencing first of January. Convenient location. Southern Ontario. Bradley Co., Hamilton, Ont. 21

WANTED HARDWOOD INSPECTOR at Montreal, familiar with National Hardwood Lumber Association grading rules. Permanent position at good salary. Must speak French. Box 53, Canadian Lumberman, Toronto. 21-22

POSITION OPEN for a high-class man capable of organizing and assuming full management of all lumbering operations of a 500 mile timber limit for a Company operating a Saw-mill and a Pulp-mill. All replies will be treated confidentially. A permanent position with a good salary open for the right man. Box 983, Canada Lumberman, Toronto. 16-21

Business Chances

For Sale

1,980 ACRES OF TIMBER, estimated to cut 25,000 ft. per acre, $9,500. Box 654, Nelson, B.C. 19-22

To:
Lumbermen—
Trust Companies—
Banks—
Executors of Estates—
Or Private Owners of
Timber and Pulp Lands.

If you are contemplating offering your Limits for sale by Auction, bear in mind that the Capital of the Dominion the greatest lumber centre in America and the place to hold your sale.

Will be pleased to give you all information as to details, etc.

WM. A. COLE,

OFFICES:
63 Sparks Street, Ottawa, Ont.
Established—1895.
References—Any Bank.

Planing Mill Wanted

Will buy planing mill in Ottawa Valley or Central Ontario. Must have siding and yard room. Give price and full description. Box 50, Canada Lumberman, Toronto. 21-22

One Detroit Hot Blast, Dry Kiln System, complete with Fan and Engine, also 35 feet of 9" double leather belt, used two weeks.

Port Hope Veneer & Lumber Co.,
18-t.f. Port Hope, Ont.

Bargain—Must be sold quick, two side mill, both double cut bands; one Band Re-Saw, two Edgers, Lath Mill, Filing equipment, Engines, Boilers, Belting and Shafting all complete. Apply Box 43, Canada Lumberman, Toronto. 21

TIMBER LIMITS

I have a number of good Timber Limits for sale. Particulars, Wm. Cooke, Stair Building, Toronto.

CAPABLE MAN WITH EXPERIENCE IN WOODWORKING BUSINESS.

One who could manage practical end of business. Good prospects with interest in business to right party. Address P. O. Box 416 Carleton Place, Ont.

Saw Mill Plant For Sale

Practically new and modern Saw Mill Plant, capacity about 30 Million feet per annum, located in the Interior of British Columbia on a beautiful inland lake and on the main line of the Grand Trunk Pacific Railway. About 500 Million feet of timber on and adjacent to Lake (about 90% Spruce) and another Billion feet available at reasonable prices. Natural conditions ideal for economical logging, manufacturing, piling and shipping. An advantage of about $4 per thousand feet in freight rates to the Prairie Provinces over Coast shipments.

This property offers unlimited possibilities as a lumber, pulp and paper property. Would consider selling a half interest. Terms reasonable.

A. C. FROST COMPANY,
134 South LaSalle Street,
5-t.f. Chicago, Ill.

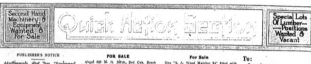

Big Lumber Cut Promised

New Brunswick will this winter have the greatest lumber cut in history, according to all present indications.

The Department of Lands and Mines is preparing for a hitherto unheard of size cut of 250 million feet on the crown lands, and it is believed that the cut on privately owned lands will be equally large.

Shipping is now being made available for lumber cargoes from New Brunswick to overseas points, and it is estimated that in one week more than twenty-five million feet of manufactured lumber has been shipped by New Brunswick firms across the Atlantic.

Recently when the general strike in the lumber industry on the Miramichi was called every mill with one exception had a steamer in the process of loading. The employees selected the psychological moment for their strike, but leading men in the lumber industry declare that the outlook for profitable operation was never better than to-day, despite high prices for labor, supplies, and everything that enters into production of manufactured lumber.

Returns have only just been completed for the last season's lumber operations on the crown lands of New Brunswick, and the figures have furnished some startling surprises. While the estimated cut of 200 million feet was said at the time to be extravagant, even the officials of the department have been surprised to find that complete returns show 210 million feet of lumber actually cut on the crown lands and stumpage charged upon it. Included in this gross amount are some five or six hundred thousand railway ties.

Meanwhile standing timber is being sold at unprecedented prices. One of the biggest deals of this kind closed for some time is just reported from Queen's county, and it is said $15 per thousand is the price paid for the standing timber. Another case which illustrates the demand for timber is the recent sale by a York county farmer of the wooded part of his farm for $10,000.

Canada's Shipping Rapidly Expands

The program of ship construction undertaken by the Dominion Government early in 1918 has yielded substantial results. To date, fifteen ships have ben delivered, and are already in service under the direction of the Canadian National Railways. There have been 25 sailings, aggregating 116,000 tons of traffic. Voyages have been completed betwen the Atlantic seaboard and the United Kingdom, and from the Pacific Coast to Great Britain. Thirteen voyages have been completed between Canada and the West Indies and Cuba to South America, and one to Newfoundland. A service is already under way to Australia and New Zealand, and it is possible that the first ship will be available at Vancouver on or about Dec. 1. Additional sailings will be inaugurated in London, Glasgow, Avonmouth and St. John's.

When the present government ship-building program is completed, 60 vessels will be in service. These will have a deadweight tonnage of about 325,000 tons.

The Dominion of Canada ships have brought some 35,000 tons of raw sugar from Cuba. A real shortage was averted by the national ships, as no privately-owned ships were available for the service.

McGibbon Sawmill Burned to Ground

The saw-mill of the McGibbon Lumber Co., Limited, was burned to the ground recently at Penetanguishene, Ont. The blaze broke out shortly before noon, and, fanned by a high wind, the mill was soon a mass of flames. The loss is estimated at $25,000, partly covered by insurance. The mill was equipped with a circular saw and had a cutting capacity of 40,000 ft. per day, the product being white pine, hemlock, hardwood, lath and shingles. The industry was run for many years by the late Chas. McGibbon, and since his death, by his sons. The plant was one of those visited by the Ontario Retail Lumber Dealers' Association on the occasion of their annual outing in July last to the Georgian Bay, and had been very busy during the past season.

Why is Bird's-Eye Maple?

What makes the bird's-eye maple? That is the question which is often asked when a beautiful piece of furniture made of this wood is displayed. There have been a number of theories, but the real reason is simple.

The favorite theory has been that sapsuckers by pecking holes through the bark of young maples make scars wihch produce the bird's eye figure in the wood during the successive years. Bird-pecked hickory is often cited as an analogous case, yet who ever saw bird's eye figures in hickory, though the bark may have been perforated like a collender by the bills of energetic sapsuckers? Some attribute it to the action of frost, but no such connection between cause and effect has been shown to exist.

The explanation of the phenomenon is simple, and a person can work it out for himself. The bird's-eye figure is produced by casual or abnormal buds which have their origin under the bark of the trunk. The first buds of that kind may develop when the tree is quite small. They are rarely able to force their way through the bark and become branches, but they may live many years just under the bark, growing in length as the trunk increases in size, but seldom appearing on the outside of the bark. If one such bud dies another will likely rise near it and conduce the fantastic growth known as bird's-eye.

It is said the Japanese produce artificial bird's-eye growth in certain trees by inserting buds beneath the mark. The Field Museum, Chicago, has a sample of what is claimed to be artificially produced bird's-eye wood from Japan.

Review of Current Trade Conditions

Ontario and the East

The situation during the past two weeks has not materially changed, and business on the whole is reported good. Now and then one runs across a wholesaler or manufacturer who states that things have dropped off a bit, but, on the other hand, the bulk of the trade are exceptionally well satisfied with what they have been able to accomplish during the past few months. The most striking phase of the whole situation is that the mills are endeavoring to ship out as much lumber as possible in order to have their yards as clear as they can before the snow flies and the usual fall congestion of traffic sets in. The result has been that many retailers have been busy unloading cars, and their stocks, which were low, have been replenished to quite an unexpected extent. This has caused buying to fall off somewhat, but it has not materially altered the general state of affairs. The eyes of the trade are naturally being turned on what will eventuate next year. The mills have advanced white pine $3.00 per M. on all stuff that is now being bought, and, one wholesaler stated that if a man required a carload of material, he would quote him a certain price, but if he wanted half a million feet, the figure was raised accordingly as the delivery of this quantity could not be made within a short time. Prices were liable to take jumps and it was necessary to protect himself against such contingencies.

There is quite an active demand for 1 in. 1½ in. and 2 in. mill run white pine in the Buffalo and Tonawanda markets The outcome is that stocks with the majority of Ontario wholesalers and mills are lower than they have been at any time during the past four or five years. Hemlock is particularly scarce.

B. C. shingles have taken a drop and are now selling around $6.90 and $7.00. The demand has fallen off and further declines in prices are expected. The result of the recent aviation in shingles has been that some dealers do not care to touch them at all. There has been little stability to the whole market and the patent roofing man has taken advantage of the situation and has enjoyed a record business. Lath are still very scarce and almost any price can be obtained for them. No one ever dreamed that lath, which a year ago were a drug on the market and could not be moved at any figure, would have developed such an abnormal demand, but it is one of the peculiar characteristics of the building and general market situation. There is not much material from the Coast coming in at the present time. Orders of various lines are taken and some Easterners are figuring on scoring his business in a Western Ontario town, where, it is rumored, 500 houses will be put up by a construction company in order to meet the demands occasioned by industrial expansion, particularly in the automobile line. At least five million feet of Douglas fir, dimension and shiplap, will be required. If this order of 200 cars goes through, it will give much activity to Western wood goods.

So far as the labor situation and logging progress is concerned, these are covered in special reports presented in another column from the Ontario crown timber agents and other companies in the East.

In summing up the whole matter it would seem that the labor situation has been very little improved from last Fall, and there is still much restlessness and jumping of jobs. The one hope is that matters may steady down and a larger supply of men be available as soon as the sawmills close down, which the majority of them will do at the end of October or by the middle of November This has been a particularly fine Fall for operating, and those who had a supply of logs, have taken full advantage of the opportunity.

The main topic of conversation is the price of lumber for next year, which some predict will show an increase of $5.00 per M. on all kinds of softwoods, whereas in regard to the hardwoods there is no foretelling how exalted quotations may be. Cost of production climbs all the while. It is interesting to know that before the war the wholesale cost of white pine for box and better was $20.00 to $22.50, and today the figure is from $45.00 up. In hemlock, the prewar quotation for No. 1 was $14.00 to $17.00 wholesale, and today the figure is $32.00 to $35.00. In merchantable spruce the figure before the European conflict was $16.00 to $18.00 and today it is just double, $35.00 to $37.00 being the reigning quotation. In Western woods the advances have been particularly striking and the market from the other side has been decidedly brisk. A graphic description of Western conditions, so far as the lumbering situation, present and prospective, is concerned, was furnished by Maj.-Gen. A. D. Rae at the recent meeting of the Wholesale Lumber Dealers' Association, a full report of which will be found in another column.

In hardwoods there is a scarcity of all kinds of thick stock. Many inquiries are being received for two and three inch birch which cannot be filled. Three inch soft elm for automobile manufacturing is also being called for but the supply is very limited, while agricultural implement men are asking for two, three and four inch maple and can get only small quantities.

The lumber trade has informed the Ottawa government that 44,000 Canadian cars are withheld in the United States as against 23,250 American cars in Canada. It is hoped that things will be evened up in the near future.

Announcement was made at the City Architect's office, Toronto, recently that the end of 1919 will see approximately 2,300 new houses occupied or ready for occupation in Toronto. This is a larger number than was built in all the cities of Ontario put together in 1918. Permits have already been issued for 2,400 brick houses in Toronto this year, and 2,200 of these with about 100 frame and roughcast dwellings, will be finished by the year's end. Building permits in Toronto so far this year represent some $ 14,000.000 which is reported to be nearly three times the value of the permits issued in Montreal where progress was checked for a considerable period by the building trades strike. All over Ontario the end of the war has been followed by building activities, despite the high cost of material and labor.

The housing problem is a serious one all over the country. There are not enough houses for the people to live in, and they are not being built fast enough to meet the demand. This makes a rather good outlook for the lumber industry for next year, but there is some doubt whether production will be advanced so that full advantage can be taken of the demand. Labor is in smaller supply than it should be, but even worse than this is the disposition of labor to loaf on the job or to refuse to labor at all. It is quite probable that were every laborer disposed to exert himself, production in all lines could be speeded up to a point where supplies would be nearly, if not quite, adequate

United States

The brisk demand, which has been in evidence for all kinds of lumber, has fallen off to a certain extent. This is caused owing to the approaching Fall months and the subsidence of building activity and, to a certain extent, by the car congestion at various points. Another contributing factor has been the steel strike and the industrial unrest which has characterized many cities and towns. In some lines there is a softening of prices, partcularly in Southern pine, but even with the decreased demand, it will take the mills a long time to catch up with production. Prices are changing rapidly on a number of other lines, rising and falling, so that it is almost impossible to keep tab on the general situation.

The first recession in 1919 building activity as indicated by building permits issued, is manifest in the September returns. Official reports from 160 cities give a total estimated valuation for September of somewhat over $137 million as against an estimated valuation of about $161 million from 153 cities for August—which was the biggest month of the year. Seventy-eight cities show a decrease in September, 67 show a gain over August. The general outlook is not at all reassuring owing to the continued demands of labor, and if trouble does not break out in one trade, it seems to find an opening in another. The steel strike is petering out, but there looms ahead the possibility that the production of a large part of the output of fuel will be stopped the first of next month by a strike of soft coal miners because exorbitant demands have not been met. In fact, in most lines of staple production, labor troubles, past, present or prospective, make the future very uncertain.

The lumber industry has not been entirely free of trouble of this character. Strikes or threats of strikes have handicapped the manufacturers, while building operations in many places have been hampered by the demands of workmen. Another thing which has militated against successful operation in the lumber industry is the difficulty of getting supplies to market. Car shortage, or a shortage of motive power, is prevalent all over the country where lumber is produced. The effect just at the present is not as bad as it has been in the immediate past, for building operations, particularly in the country districts, is less pronounced during the cold weather.

Production has nowhere been up to normal, because of labor

shortage and indisposition on the part of labor to produce. This takes the form of less work during working hours, and refusal to work at all while the laborer has enough money to pay for the next meal and the next night's bed.

There is a steady demand for hardwoods and the factory demand keeps up well although building requirements have fallen off a bit. Offerings in many centres are limited. Production at several of the important hardwood centres during the last few weeks has increased, but this has brought no increase in unsold stocks as the output has been fully covered by demand. Supplies of quartered white and red oak are at rock bottom and the market is strong at the highest prices ever quoted. Plain oak also is in an exceptionally good position; in fact, in all the woods unsold stocks are extremely light as compared with normal for this time of year. The hardwood industry, in the South especially, is experiencing a car shortage that is retarding shipments.

There has been a falling off in the demand for southern pine and prices are somewhat weaker. The decline in the demand for southern pine, in common with most other building woods, seems largely confined to the cities, and should this situation continue the manufacturers have hopes for at least a brisk country trade during the late fall and early winter to support the market in the meanwhile. However, any real period of trade dullness seems out of the question, especially for the reason that a great building season is expected next spring and the retailers are likely to start their buying for spring requirements early to make sure that they are under cover. Heavy rains in some producing sections have interfered with operations considerably during the past few days. A considerable decrease in demand is reported in Douglas fir and there is none too good conditions prevailing in regard to transportation and distributing.

Great Britain

It is interesting to note in connection with the British market that, according to a letter recently sent out by one Liverpool firm, the arrivals of New Brunswick and Nova Scotia spruce deals at Liverpool and Manchester during the month of September amounted to 14,000 standards, and the stocks now total over 22,000 standards. It is stated that the consumption was disappointing, largely due to the goods already sold being held up owing to transportation difficulties.

The arrivals of Douglas fir at Liverpool consisted of 85,000 feet, and the consumption was light. Continuing, the report says, in respect to Scandinavian deals and boards, that there were no arrivals of flooring boards to Liverpool, and only a small quantity to Manchester. The consumption was satisfactory. Stocks are light and values firm and deals arrived in fair quantities.

The import of pitch pine consisted mainly of pitch pine lumber. There was a fair consumtion, but stocks at Manchester and Liverpool now amount to nearly 1¼ million feet. Congestion and lack of distributing facilties curtailed deliveries, so that the stock includes timber that would otherwise have gone into consumption. C. I. F. quotations are at present somewhat easier.

The demand for hardwoods during the past month, especially the latter part of the month, on account of the railway strike, was very dull and inactive. Consignments still arrive freely and owing to the poor consumption, aggravated by transport difficulties and labor unrest, the major portion has gone into store.

The government auction sale of hardwoods sold without reserve, held on Sept. 25, was well attended. The bidding was brisk throughout and the quantity offered was cleared at satisfactory prices. The auction sales of mahogany held during September were well attended, and the moderate quantities offered were cleared at prices which show an advance upon the preceding sales. Sound, well-squared logs of cedar are in demand, but there is no enquiry for round logs.

Lately the inquiry for fresh goods was a little more active, probably on account of the short period which now remains for shipping. Many firms have this season endeavored to put off buying in the hope of obtaining autumn bargains, as they often did in pre-war days, but the sudden strike has now upset all their calculations. It is principally Swedish stocks which are inquired for, and especially the Gefle and Soderhamn makes. For even if the price of common wood should fall, it is not impossible that the value of prime productions, and especially of larger sizes, can be reduced. The import cost at the present time is so heavy that there is only a moderate profit on the present selling prices, and the supply in proportion to the demand is very short.

There is anxiety in all the ports as to coming timber arrivals. Surrey Commercial Docks, the largest wood depot in the world, are already congested. The 200 acres of piling grounds are becoming crowded, especially those close to the six miles of quays.

Mr. Montague L. Meyer, who is disposing of the Government timber stocks, of which he was the official buyer during the war, says: "There is timber congestion in every large port in the country. This is due first to the shortage of small timber ships that could enter the smaller ports and so distribute the arrivals; secondly, the shorter day, slacker labor, and shortage of barges and transport. Large quantities of Government timber are already here from Scandinavia, and have been sold to the trade in addition to what has come on private account. But the congestion at the ports is aggravated by the difficulty of getting it inland, to Birmingham and elsewhere, where it is wanted. It must be remembered that timber is a seasonable trade. Most places of origin close in October because of the frozen waters, and do not open again until May. We have to get the wood in for the coming reconstruction schemes or there would be a shortage that would be worse than a temporary congestion. The congestion will be worse before it becomes better, which should be by Christmas. By then I expect we shall have in about 150 more cargoes from Scandinavia, Canada and America—in all 150,000 to 200,000 standards (each standard 165 cubic ft.). All departments are working to distribute it to ports where the congestion is least pressing at the time and the ships can be accommodated."

Among the many lessons of the war is that home-grown timber, when graded and properly seasoned, is in no respect inferior to imported wood for most purposes, says "Timber". The problem of encouraging the use of home-grown timber is engaging serious attention inside and outside the trade, and the growing number of merchants interesting themselves practically with the exploiting of English-grown trees is a remarkable sign of the times.

It is asserted that the Government is not the best agent for the manufacture of timber, and that the latter should be in the hands of the trade. As regards sources of supply, it is urged by the friends of home-grown tmber that the United States may in the future be ignored as a regular source of supply, as the American market is unable to do more than supply its own requirements. In Canada it is asserted that, although things have not yet touched the same low level, they are tending in the direction of depletion, a somewhat remarkable statement in view of the existing conditions of demand and supply.

Market Correspondence

SPECIAL REPORTS ON CONDITIONS AT HOME AND ABROAD

Local Business at St. John Good—Export Fair

During the past month business at St. John has been, locally, very good. Prices have kept up and consumption has also kept stocks moving in good volume. The general building trade has been active, and a large amount of remodelling of buildings, both exterior and interior has taken place. A considerable number of old structures of quite a large size have changed hands and are being converted into apartment houses. These are in good demand at reasonable rentals, which are leaving the owner a fair return on his investment.

The St. John Housing Commission have let a contract for twelve houses, some being self-contained and some semi-detached, which are being erected in Lancaster, near the C. P. R. elevators and within sight of the St. John winter port, on good high land affording a fine view of the harbor. These dwellings will cost about $4,000 each, including land. The demand for all kinds of finish for houses is very heavy, showing very little signs of abatement. Stocks are very scarce, B. C. products being especially so, and also very high in price. This, of course, is helping the Eastern manufacturer sell his own native stocks, such as spruce and pine, at prices about same as B. C. products, but his opportunity to get deliveries to his works are much better than if B. C. products were supplied.

The factories are all busy and will continue so for at least some months, largely on interior finish for construction now being carried on.

Refuse lumber is in fair demand and bringing good prices in the local market.

Laths, locally, are almost impossible to find and prices range

about $6.00 per M and upwards. There are practically no laths at St. John to-day for local consumption.

The English market for foreign shipment still remains in fair condition. Freights are not quite so firm, around 225 shillings being the offered price of steamer charters for the British ports. Of course, some vessels are getting somewhat greater freights, but on a whole it is felt that conditions will weaken in freight charges. Prices are fair and it is felt that they will continue so. Any manufacturer with a good specification of 7 x 3 and up deals, carrying a good percentage of 9 inch and up, can get a good price.

The American market is weaker than a while ago, and shows no signs of improvement. With winter coming on and business in building slowing down, not as much demand will take place; also many portable mills are sawing this winter. What effect this will have remains to be seen. If the winter is severe, not as much lumber will be cut, as is anticipated, and is supplies are cut down and the present demand keeps up, a good price will be realized.

Two St. John mills have ceased operations for the season, the Randolph mill, and one of the Murray & Gregory mills below the Falls. All others are operating and will continue to do so until the closing of navigation.

Logging crews are now in the woods. Men are scarce, wages in some localities being $75.00 to $80.00 per month with board. With high supplies and higher wages than a year ago, as cheap a log as in 1919 certainly cannot be expected.

Business in Montreal Moving Along Well

Business in Montreal has picked up all along the line. There was a lull for a short time, but orders are now coming in more freely, and prospects are cheerful. Locally, the demand is better, due to more building coming out, while the sash and door factories and the box makers are doing a satisfactory turnover. Lath is firm and difficult to obtain. A considerable amount has been sold from the saw. The chances are that next spring it will be almost unobtainable. The orders from over the border, which dropped for a time, are now picking up, although on some lines foreign cars are in very short supply Hardwoods are very firm, with a fair business passing. In B. C. stocks, the chief demand is for timber, other descriptions being slow on account of the high prices ruling. Shipments are none too brisk.

Building is undoubtedly improving. The permits taken out last month reach a high total, the records showing considerable additional constructional activity, notwithstanding some labor disturbances. There are two very large buildings included in last month's permits, although the chief new work is an apartment and other houses. Montreal is very short of dwelling accommodation and unless there is still more progress in building, the famine will become very acute.

The labor situation is more settled. The strike of the employees in the box-making factories was short-lived, the men going back on the old conditions. A dispute at St. Therese, near Montreal, involving a strike at three piano factories has gone before a board of conciliation. The strike in the Montreal building trade is gradually dying out. Many men are now back at work, although the unions claim that it is at higher wages. It is certain, however, that men are now employed under the old conditions, despite the pressure of the unions.

The export season is now drawing to a close. Practically all the Government lumber has been shipped from this port, and the greater bulk from Quebec; it is probable that a small amount in the latter port will be left over until next season. There is promise of great activity at the winter ports, but it is certain that a considerable stock in the Maritime Provinces will not be lifted until 1920

A further decline in the exports of pulpwood has to be recorded. For the month of August the total of $944,877, was $1,033,135 below that of the corresponding month in 1918. The aggregate for five months of the fiscal year is $4,.05,118, a falling off of $3.905,148. During August paper substantially advanced, while chemical pulp gained $73,000 and mechanical pulp $3,000. For the five months chemical pulp decreased $7,562,000, and mechanical pulp increased $67,500.

The Market at Ottawa Slackens up Somewhat

A slackening of demand, coupled with confidence that a fair winter's business would be done, were the features of the Ottawa lumber market, during the closing period of October. A decline in orders and inquiries were noted, especially from the United States, but at this season of the year trade reports indicated that such was to be expected. Business, in the general opinion of lumbermen, was better than for a corresponding period a year ago, even if somewhat quieter than during the preceding two weeks.

That there is no tendency toward the market weakening was indicated by prices, which remained absolutely firm, and in three of the better pine grades advanced. The top notch figure for good pine, inch and inch and a quarter siding, was reached when the manufacturers' prices took an eight dollar jump and went to $110 per M. The reason given for the increase in these particularly fine grades is that stocks was low and the demand is fairly heavy. Some lumbermen looked at it as a matter of replacement of stock and if the purchaser did not want to pay the new price, they did not seem much worried, consoling themselves that before the winter months were through their stocks would bring more money.

Local, domestic, and foreign business outside of the United States remained just about the same as it was during the two preceding weeks.

For ocean export "bottoms" were the whole thing and they continued scarce. Reports at Ottawa were that with the settlement of the British railway strike, shipping was getting back to where it had been before, with the result that the orders on Government account to the Old Country were beginning to move more freely. Patience seemed to be the virtue of most shippers to the Old Country, they expressing their contentment with the procedure of affairs by remarking, the stock was purchased by the British Goverment. It is going out of the country, which lessens existing stocks here. And the sooner it gets across the more opportunity there is for ocean space to ship on our own account.

The car situation to the United States became a little more acute than it had been. A few orders were delayed. Some shippers prophesied that it could be expected as the beginning of one of the worst car shortages that the local trade had ever experienced. Various reasons were given for holding this view. Some took the position that during the war fewer cars had been built by American roads for use in the United States than during the pre-war years. To further add to the troubles of the retail situation there had been a big increase in commercial shipments since the armistice was signed, which taxed the railways to handle the business. Now comes the movement of the western grain crop, and there is not the usual number of cars available which are in first-class condition.

Another point in support of this was that railway reports to the shippers intimated that there were more Canadian cars on American roads than there were American cars on Canadian rails, hence a shortage in car space could be easily noted.

The labor situation so far as the woods were concerned, began to tighten up a little. Reports from manufacturers and operators indicated that while there was still a pretty good general offering of bushmen, their numbers were not as great as they had been. All the help that is needed for the woods camps has not yet been obtained. Even when labor is obtained and shipped to the woods, the seemingly ever prevalent problem of the "transients" throws a monkey wrench in the machinery, so far as production is concerned. Woods operators, even in spite of the obstacles before them, are setting their backs, and believe the timber output of the Ottawa Valley for the 1919-20 season will establish a high record over the war years.

The sawmill season neared its close, but if logs and labor hold out it is the intention of the mill heads to cut well up till the ice begins to form.

Conditions with the woodworking plants and factories remained about the same, there being enough business in sight to keep them busy. There was a good demand for furniture and, in some circles, there was a shortage of cabinet makers' labor. One plant was working fifty hours per week and paying forty-five cents an hour, and reported it could use more hands.

Shingles and lath, though they did not advance further in price, remained scarce, and reports agreed that stocks of both were low and hard to get.

Big Schooner for Carrying Timber

Mr. Alexander Livventaal, Montreal, has designed a four-masted schooner for the purpose of carrying lumber. The idea is to build the vessel mainly from the lumber to be carried, the ship to be dismantled at the end of the voyage; certain parts of the vessel, including the rigging and the internal combustion engine for steering, would be shipped back to Canada. He estimates the construction of these ships at about twenty dollars, plus fifteen dollars for sailing, a total of thirty-five dollars per standard, to which would be added a royalty to the owner. The ship would be manned by twelve men, comprising the captain, mate, second mate, cook, wireless operator, engineer and six men. Mr. Livventaal, who was born in Switzerland, is a naturalized Englishman, and now proposes to settle in Canada. He states that he was connected as a consulting engineer, with Sir William Armstrong, and the late Count Zeppelin. We hope to be able, at a later date, to give full particulars of his lumber ship, which differs in essential particulars from the Davis raft, which will convey B. C. lumber, bought by the British Government, to England.

In the accompanying views, looking from left to right, the first shows two black spruce (left of centre) attacked by Bud Worm. The next scene shows young trees in the foreground entirely denuded and the larger trees badly damaged. The last view shows a dead fir after an operation.

The Spruce Bud Worm Ravages

By H. S. Laughlin, Chatham, N.B.

The Spruce Bud Worm is reported as having done considerable damage in the province of New Brunswick and during the present years its ravages have supassed anything previously reported.

Loggers state that there was no evident sign of the worm in the Tabucintao watershed last year, but this summer the stand in places had the appearance of being fire swept.

On investigation it was found that the last five years' growth of the trees affected had been suppresed, so much so, in fact, that the total growth for these five years was no more than the one year's growth just previous. This seems to be sufficient evidence to prove that the bud worm has been affecting the timber for the last five years, and, no doubt, gradually increasing in number and its ravages increasing in proportion.

Balsam Fire has suffered the most. In the areas affected this tree has been absolutely denuded and there is very little or no chance for its recovery. This is more especially true in areas where fir has been left standing after logging.

Black Spruce has been damaged to considerable extent too but not so much as the Fir. In mixed stands of Black Spruce and Fire the worm seemed to attack the Fir in preference to the spruce. But in the pure stands of Black Spruce the tree has been greatly damaged. Some of the younger trees have been entirely denuded and will not recover. The larger, sturdier trees are still green, though the terminals of the branches and twigs are denuded, yet early in September a few of the dormant secondary buds burst, sending out their tender light green shoots. It is feared that these shoots will be too tender for the early frosts but there is not a great abundance of them. The belief is that the greater proportion of these buds will hold over the winter and that bursting forth next spring will aid the tree in recovering. But next spring will have its own story to tell.

The White Spruce seems to have escaped so far from the ravages. Several instances were noted where this tree had a healthy crown, even in the midst of attacked trees.

Personal Paragraphs of Interest

W. T. Mason, of Mason, Gordon & Co., Montreal, was in Toronto lately on business.

J. B. Knox of Knox Bros., Limited, Montreal, spent a few days in Toronto recently calling upon the trade.

J. L. Campbell of Campbell, Welsh and Paynes, Toronto, and daughter, have been spending a few weeks' holidays at Atlantic City, N.J.

F. A. Kirkpatrick, of Muir and Kirkpatrick, Toronto, who was confined to his home with illness for several days, is able to resume his duties.

Hugh A. Rose, of Toronto, who represents Mason, Gordon & Co., left lately on a business trip throughout the Maritime Provinces.

J. H. Lefebvre, of Howick Station, P.Q., died in Montreal on October 13, after a brief illness. He was largely interested in lumber operations in the Province of Quebec.

M. C. Foley has embarked in the wholesale lumber business under the name of the Foley Lumber Co., and has opened an office in Room No. 31, Canada Permanent Building, Toronto St., Toronto.

James W. Sewall of Old Town, Maine, reports that there seems to be considerable increased activity in timber circles in the northeast. His business of estimating and valuing timber reflects such activity to a marked degree and forms a fairly good barometer of conditions. His office is engaged in surveying, and estimating the pulpwood and lumber on over 700,000 acres of land scattered from New York through New England to the very northern end of New Brunswick. Ordinarily at this time of year timber cruising work becomes quiet.

O. A. Gignac, of J. H. Gignac Ltd., lumber merchants, Quebec, has been elected a member of the executive committee of the newly formed Quebec division of the Canadian Manufacturers' Association.

H. Brown, of the Atlantic Lumber Co., Toronto, will leave next month on an extended trip to the Old Country. Since his return from overseas last spring he has been actively engaged as a lumber salesman, assisting J. W. Jacobson, local manager of the Atlantic Lumber Co.

S. G. Denman, Montreal, the Eastern Canada representative of the Import Lumber Section of the Board of Trade, London, has sailed for England to confer with the department as to the shipping during the winter of the Government bought stocks in Canada, from Halifax and St. John.

Lieut.-Col. R. H. Webb, formerly of the Webb Lumber Co., Toronto, has returned after having been in service overseas for more than five years. He was one of the First Canadians to enlist in service and was wounded several times, being unfortunate enough to have his leg shot off by a shrapnel shell, which killed fourteen men behind him.

Sidney R. Anderson, wholesale lumber dealer, who recently opened an office in the Manning Chambers, Toronto, intends leaving on a trip to the Old Country about the middle of the present month and will be accompanied by Mrs. Anderson. He received the sad intelligence a few days ago that his mother has passed away at Hull, England.

Brig.-General W. B. R. Hepburn, C.M.G., M.P., of Picton, Ont., has arrived in Canada, after three and a half years' active service with the Canadian Foresters. He went overseas in April, 1916, with the rank of major, and after sometime on the headquarters staff in London, was appointed deputy director general and second in command of timber operations. O. M. F. C. During his absence overseas Brigadier-General Hepburn was re-elected to Parliament by his division, Prince Edward County.

Know Your Costs When Estimating

Once upon a time (that is the way all stories should begin) two retail dealers figured against each other on a bill of material for a building to be erected on a farm. Before going any further, we will say that this is a true story, says the "Mississippi Valley Lumberman." One of these dealers was the manager of a yard belonging to a line yard concern, and his figures had to be confirmed and approved by the headquarters office. His estimate came to just an even thousand dollars. The other dealer cut his figures to the bone—and then some—and his estimate was more than three hundred dollars less than the yard manager's total.

He had been so afraid that he would be too high that he had cut all the profit, and more than that, out of his estimate.

But he learned what the yard manager had bid, and immediately tried to recoup. He went to the customer and told him that he had made a bad mistake, and that he could not sell the material for so little. He then named a new price which was thirty-five dollars below the figures of the yard manager.

Meanwhile, the estimate had gone in to headquarters, where an error of seventy-five dollars was found, and the manager was immediately notified.

This left the other dealer the higher bidder by forty dollars, and he wondered why he did not get the order.

The moral to this story is that every dealer should know what it costs him to do business; then he should figure every bill at a fair profit and then adhere to his estimate.

EDGINGS

Wm. Bonter & Sons, Marmora, Ont., contemplate building a saw and grist mill.

D. J. MacDonald is erecting a new sawmill on Turner St., Ottawa. The building is one storey high, 36 x 40 ft.

The C. Beck Mfg. Co., of Penetanguishene, have bought the mills and timber of the Little Current Lumber Co., Little Current, Ont.

The offices of the Canadian Pulp & Paper Association have been removed to 701-2 Drummond Building, St. Catherine St. West, Montreal.

A provincial charter has been granted the Empire Timber, Lumber & Tie Co., Ltd., with headquarters in Toronto and a capital stock of $85,000.

The Alfred McDonald Lumber Co., of Peterboro, intend erecting a new box factory and will also further develop their sash, door and planing mill business.

A provincial charter was recently granted to the Laoc Coal & Lumber Co., Limited, Hamilton, to manufacture and deal in lumber and other wood products.

Victor Attridge, who for many years has conducted a planing mill and lumber yard in Schomberg, Ont., has disposed of his business to Burnel Graham of that place. Mr. Attridge is now building several houses in Schomberg.

Manufacture of tone arms, motors and accessories for phonographs is being undertaken in Kitchener by the General Phonograph Corporation of New York, which has purchased the Pollock Manufacturing Company's plant, according to an announcement by Mr. A. B. Pollock.

The Elliot Woodworker Company, of Toronto, have secured the plant in Belleville formerly occupied by the Burril Rock Drill Co., and expect to commence operations in a few weeks. The new plant is well equipped with metal-working tools. The Toronto plant will be continued for a time at least.

Marks-Hanley, Limited, has been granted a charter to carry on the business of lumbering, planing mills and to manufacture woodenware of all kinds as well as deal in timber, lumber, etc. The capital stock of the company is $15,000 and the headquarters in the city of Ottawa. The provisional directors are Edward Marks, E. A. Hanley, Wm. H. Hanley.

A charter has been granted to the Partridge Lumber Co., Limited, with headquarters in Rainy River and a capital stock of $100,000 to carry on the business of timber merchants, sawmill proprietors and timber growers and to buy, sell and deal in timber and wood of all kinds. The incorporators are Thomas M. Partridge, Harry F. Partridge, of Minneapolis, Minn., and Wm. J. Moran and Charles W. Chappell, of Winnipeg.

J. E. L. Streight, of Islington, Ont., has completed a new office and stables in his lumber yard and hopes to have his new sheds ready by the year. It is Major Streight's intention to build a new planing mill in Spring. It will be a two-storey brick structure of the latest type and embody all modern ideas. Business has been good during the past season and is continuing active right along. Major Streight says that one difficulty during the summer was a shortage in help.

It is understood that M. J. O'Brien, Limited, a $20,000,000 corporation, will erect a large pulp and paper mill at the north end of Lake Temiskaming. During the past year preliminary survey has been carried on and with reasonable assurance of an adequate labor supply, the big project is expected to be launched next year. Waters tributary to the Quinze River and the Quinze Lake flow through territory containing vast pulpwood resources which, with care, appear to be practically unlimited for several generations. The company own and control part of the great water-power of the Quinze River, the whole of which would make it possible to generate 100,000 horsepower or double that amount, according to some authorities.

A new company, with the title of the Judge, Jones Milling Company, of Belleville, has been formed, and comprises of the firms of Grahams, Ltd., Belleville, and the Judge Grain Company, Montreal. The new concern is building at a Belleville a mill to manufacture about 250 barrels of flour, 250 barrels of cornflour, one hundred barrels of rolled oats, three hundred barrels of corn meal, and one thousand sacks of feed per day, in addition to an elevator to handle oats and a quantity of grain, for cleaning and bagging in transit. Mr. Geo. B. Jones, of the Judge Grain Company, Montreal, is removing to Belleville to look after the Judge, Jones Milling Company's interests there. Mr. Jones is a miller of several years' experience.

A controlling interest in the Toronto Paper Mfg. Co., Ltd., has been sold to the Howard Smith Paper Mills, Ltd., of Montreal, the figure for the stock being $138. a share. The company's authorized capital is $1,000,000, of which $750,000 has been issued. Under the terms agreed upon every shareholder has the right to dispose of his stock at the figure named, and the Howard Smith Paper Mills is prepared to pay more than $1,000,000 to secure control. As soon as sufficient stock has been turned over to insure the consummation of the undertaking, the officers of the Toronto Paper Mfg. Co. will step out. The president of the Toronto Paper Co. is R. S. Waldie and vice-president, W. J. Sheppard, of Waubaushene. Both are widely known in lumbering circles, the former being vice-president of the Victoria Harbor Lumber Co. and the latter president of the Georgian Bay Lumber Co. The Toronto Paper Mfg. Co. has a large plant at Cornwall, which was established a number of years abo by the late John R. Barber, M.P.P., and others.

Eastern Canada

A large vessel, the "Illmanau," of London, called recently at Rimouski and loaded 2,500,000 feet of lumber for Price Bros & Co.

John D. Walker, of Rexton, N. B., is starting a winter operation at that place and expects to take out between four and five million feet. Part of this timber will be for winter sawing and the remainder for next summer's cut.

The Grand River Co., Montreal, P. Q., has been incorporated to manufacture and deal in lumber, pulp, paper and similar products. Capital $50,000. E. E. Howard and W. H. Howard, barristers, of Montreal, are two of the incorporators.

Ewart C. Atkinson, of Fredericton, Peter Mahoney, of Gagetown and Abner B. Belyea, of Fredericton, have been incorporated as E. C. Atkinson Lumber Company, Limited, with head office at Gagetown and capital stock of forty-eight thousand dollars. The company' is authorized to transact a general lumbering business.

La Compagnie Saguenay Limitee, Chicoutimi, P. Q., has been incorporated to manufacture and deal in lumber, wood products and pulpwood. Capital $25,000. W. Blanchette and J. B. Claveau, lumber merchants of Chicoutimi, are among the incorporators.

The Walter Walton Co., Ltd., insurance specialists, recently opened an office at 310 Coristine Building, Montreal, with Mr. H. B. Warren as manager. The parent company's offices are in New York. The company do a general insurance business, but specialise on lumber, mills and woodworking plants.

The St. Anne Lumber Co., Montreal, P. Q., have been incorporated to own and operate mills, factories, etc., for the manufacture of timber, lumber, pulpwood and other articles made of wood, and to manufacture and deal in lumber and wood products. Capital $500,000. L. H. Ballantyne and F. G. Bush, Montreal, are two of the incorporators.

The total cut of wood expected during the coming lumbering season in the Abitibi region will reach seventy million feet of cut and prepared lumber. This is unprecedented in bulk totals. There are at present in the Abitibi region, fifty-five sawmills in operation and they work almost the whole year round. The coming season's cut is under way with excellent prospects.

The Davison Lumber & Mfg. Co., Ltd., of Bridgewater, N. S., who were manufacturing specially prepared, dry, pressed baled sulphate and sulphite pulp chips, closed down their plant some months ago when ground wood pulp took a slump, and have since not operated owing to being so busy in their lumbering, hardwood flooring, planing mill and box factory departments, in all of which they have orders to last for several months.

Speaking at a meeting of the Quebec Manufacturers' and Merchants Association held in Quebec, the Hon. D. Pelletier urged the development of trade between the province of Quebec and Europe. As a result of his eight years' experience in England, he believed there were splendid openings for this trade and he mentioned in particular that there was a great demand for lumber, toys and articles of various descriptions in wood. It was essential, however, that an office be opened in London, with a special representative.

The forests belonging to the late E. Stebelin, of Weymouth, N. S., were recently cruised by a party of surveyors, who have found in the property 48 million superior feet of merchantable spruce and pine, 70,000 cords of pulp wood, 200,000 feet of hemlock, three million superior feet of merchantable hardwood timber and a large quantity of hardwood. The surveyors have allowed for farms, burned, etc., 1,000 acres, leaving a solid block of 8,500 acres of green timber. This land, situated on the Tusket River, constitutes the largest block of timber in the west side of lower Nova Scotia.

Capt. Daniel Owen, who has just returned from an exploration by aeroplane, is to be president of a company formed to develop the pulp areas he discovered. The capital will be $10,000,000. Capt. Owen, before going on active service, practiced law in Annapolis. A large banking syndicate, headed by the Greene interests, is said to be behind this project. In speaking of the Labrador Pulp Company, Capt. Owen said that this was unquestionably one of the finest pulp properties in the world, for not only are the million and a half acres owned by the company exceptionally heavily covered with spruce, but the property is magnificently watered.

Western Canada

Richard Arthur Trethewey, formerly head of the Abbotsford Timber & Trading Company, died at the family residence in Matsqui municipality, just outside of Abbotsford, B. C. recently. He was fifty-one years of age.

Fire recently visited the British Columbia Fir & Cedar Lumber Company's mill which was destroyed along with dry kilns, over half a million feet of lumber and also a storage shed of the Alberta Lumber Co. The loss is estimated at $200,000.

A charter has been granted to the Elk Valley Lumber Co. with headquarters in Winnipeg. The company is empowered to purchase timber lands of all kinds and to manufacture, buy and sell saw logs, timber products, lumber, pulpwood, railway ties, etc., and to carry on the business of lumbering and pulp-making in all their branches as well as other woodworking activities. The capital stock is $200,000.

Thirteen carloads of paper consigned to the New York Times are on their way east from Prince Rupert. This paper was made from pulp furnished by spruce logs felled on the Queen Charlotte Islands during the airplane wood-cutting industry which concluded with the signing of the armistice. Large amounts of spruce left over were sold to the Pacific Mills at Ocean Falls for the making of news-print.

The B. C. supreme court has decided that one company cannot buy shares from another company, the case in point being the action of Neil McKinnon, lumberman of Vancouver, who sued for $108,941, the defendant being G. D. Brymer, assignee of the Campbell River Lumber Company. In 1914, Albert McKillop sold to the Campbell River Lumber Company 800 shares in the North American Lumber Company, and in May, 1916, assigned his interest to McKinnon, who endeavored to secure judgment, but failed.

Several new mills are reported in the northern and southeastern parts of British Columbia. At Boulder Creek, near Nelson, Mr. O'Neil and associates are to build a plant. Another is proposed west of that city by Basking & Stedman, and machinery has arrived for A. S. Horswill's plant at Nelson. At Kelly Lake on the Pacific Great Eastern, Munro & Morrison will erect a 40,000-foot capacity mill. The Nicola Pine Mills (Ltd.), which had its plant at Canford, Nicola Valley, burned a few months ago, plans to replace the mill. R. P. Shannon and other Vancouver lumbermen have rebuilt the mill on the north arm of the Fraser south of Vancouver and will cut hemlock exclusively, with an output of between 50,000 and 60,000 feet. This is the first mill in the province planned to cut hemlock only.

Lumbermen's Tents and Clothing

Pure wool, Waterproof Mackinaw Coats, Pants and Shirts, the kind you have been looking for.

Repellant Brand Army Duck Tents

The best duck that money can buy.
We can equip your van complete.

Pure wool Blankets, Sweaters, Underwear. Hand Knit Mitts and Socks. Palmer's Shoe Packs, Buck and horse hide Moccasins, etc.

Grant-Holden-Graham, Limited

Factory and Warehouse

147 to 151 Albert Street, Ottawa, Can.

When rope is exposed to rough usage

you can rely on LION BRAND

Anywhere a rope is required to resist unusual strain, Lion Brand cordage gives faithful and dependable service.

Lion Brand Transmission Rope and Lath Yarn are the result of years of experience and we stand behind our product.

Our service extends from Coast to Coast

THE LION IS A SYMBOL OF STRENGTH

CONSUMERS CORDAGE CO., LIMITED, 285 St. Patrick Street MONTREAL, QUE.

Montreal Halifax St. John, N.B. Toronto, 11 Church St.

Agents and Stocks at

Tees & Persse, Ltd., Winnipeg, Regina, Saskatoon, Moose Jaw, Calgary, Edmonton, Fort William.
James Bisset & Co., Quebec. Macgowan & Co., Vancouver.

Under the

Exacting Conditions

of the high-grade material and workmanship that enters into their manufacture, Arrow Head Saws can always be relied upon to give consistently good

T. F. Shur

CANADA LUMBERMAN AND WOODWORKER
"60" Vessels
Canada's Commerce Carriers
"Total" Tonnage 325,000
Canadian Government Merchant Marine, Limited
ASIA
CANADA
PACIFIC OCEAN
UNITED STATES
PANAMA CANAL
AFRICA
ATLANTIC OCEAN
SOUTH AMERICA
AUSTRALIA
NEW ZEALAND
The Canadian Government in order to assist in the establishment of direct trade connections with other countries, is now engaged in completing a programme of building cargo steamers, comprising 60 vessels with a total tonnage of 325,000 tons.
Information relative to marine freights and towards assisting the development of direct trade connections with overseas countries will be gladly furnished on application to:
"The Line of Transportation that builds and binds a Nation."
14,000
56,000
HALIFAX ST. JOHN SYDNEY QUEBEC MONTREAL VANCOUVER VICTORIA
PRINCE ALBERT
EDMONTON
VANCOUVER
KAMLOOPS
VICTORIA
CALGARY
SASKATOON
REGINA
BRANDON
WINNIPEG
PORT WILLIAM
PORT ARTHUR
DULUTH
COCHRANE
OTTAWA
TORONTO
MONTREAL
QUEBEC
CHARLOTTETOWN
SUMMERSIDE
MONCTON
SYDNEY
ST. JOHN
HALIFAX
Canadian National Railways

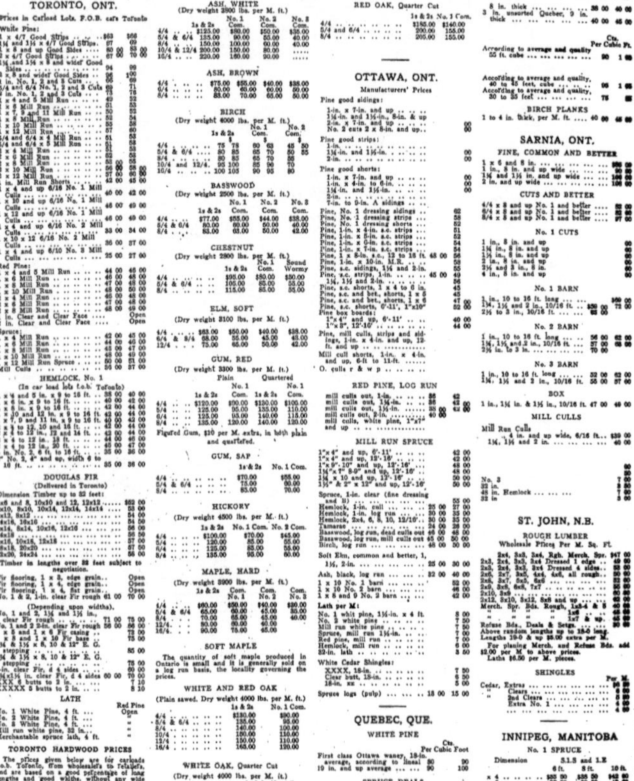

CURRENT LUMBER PRICES—WHOLESALE

TORONTO, ONT.

Prices in Carload Lots, F.O.B. cars Toronto

White Pine:

1 x 4/7 Good Strips	$63	$66
1¼ and 1½ x 4/7 Good Strips	67	69
1 x 8 and up Good Sides	80 00	83 00
2 x 4/7 Good Strips	67 00	70 00
1¼ and 1½ x 8 and wider Good Sides	94	99
2 x 8 and wider Good Sides	96	100
1 in. No. 1, 2 and 3 Cuts	66	69
5/4 and 6/4 No. 1, 2 and 3 Cuts	69	71
2 in. No. 1, 2 and 3 Cuts	73	78
1 x 4 and 5 Mill Run	49	52
1 x 6 Mill Run	51	53
1 x 7, 9 and 11 Mill Run	50	52
1 x 8 Mill Run	52	54
1 x 10 Mill Run	55	58
1 x 12 Mill Run	57	60
5/4 and 6/4 x 4 Mill Run	51	53
5/4 and 6/4 x 5 Mill Run	51	53
2 x 4 Mill Run	51	53
2 x 6 Mill Run	52	53
2 x 8 Mill Run	53 00	55
2 x 10 Mill Run	56 00	58 00
2 x 12 Mill Run	57 00	60 00
1 in. Mill Run Shorts	42 00	45 00
1 x 4 and up 6/16 No. 1 Mill Culls	40 00	42 00
1 x 10 and up 6/16 No. 1 Mill Culls	46 00	49 00
1 x 12 and up 6/16 No. 1 Mill Culls	46 00	49 00
1 x 4 and up 6/16 No. 2 Mill Culls	33 00	34 00
1 x 10 x 12 6/16 No. 2 Mill Culls	36 00	37 00
1 x 4 and up 6/10 No. 3 Mill Culls	25 00	27 00

Red Pine:

1 x 4 and 5 Mill Run	44 00	46 00
1 x 6 Mill Run	46 00	48 00
1 x 8 Mill Run	47 00	48 00
1 x 10 Mill Run	48 00	50 00
2 x 4 Mill Run	46 00	48 00
2 x 6 Mill Run	47 00	48 00
2 x 8 Mill Run	48 00	49 00
1 in. Clear and Clear Face		Open
2 in. Clear and Clear Face		Open

Spruce:

1 x 4 Mill Run	42 00	45 00
1 x 6 Mill Run	44 00	46 00
1 x 8 Mill Run	45 00	47 00
1 x 10 Mill Run	48 00	49 00
1 x 12 Mill Run Spruce	50 00	51 00
Mill Culls	36 00	37 00

HEMLOCK, No. 1

(In car load lots f.o.b. Toronto)

1 x 4 and 5 in. x 9 to 16 ft.	38 00	40 00
1 x 6 in. x 9 to 16 ft.	40 00	42 00
1 x 8 in. x 9 to 16 ft.	42 00	44 00
1 x 10 and 12 in. x 9 to 16 ft.	42 00	44 00
1 x 7, 9 and 11 in. x 9 to 16 ft.	40 00	42 00
2 x 4 to 12, 10 and 16 ft.	42 00	44 00
2 x 4 to 12 in., 12 and 14 ft.	42 00	44 00
2 x 4 to 12 in., 18 ft.	44 00	46 00
2 x 4 to 12 in., 20 ft.	45 00	47 00
1 in. No. 2, 6 ft. to 16 ft.	35 00	36 00
2" No. 2, 4" and up, width 6 to 16 ft.	35 00	36 00

DOUGLAS FIR

(Delivered in Toronto)

Dimension Timber up to 32 feet:

6x6 and 8, 10x10 and 12, 12x12	$52 00
6x10, 8x10, 10x14, 12x14, 14x14	53 00
6x12, 8x12	54 00
14x16, 16x16	54 50
6x14, 8x14, 10x16, 12x16	56 00
14x18	56 50
8x16, 10x18, 12x18	57 00
18x18, 20x20	57 50
12x20, 24x24	58 00

Timber in lengths over 32 feet subject to negotiation.

Fir flooring, 1 x 3, edge grain..		Open
Fir flooring, 1 x 4, edge grain..		Open
Fir flooring, 1 x 4, flat grain..		Open
No. 1 & 2, 1-in. clear Fir rough	61 00	70 00

(Depending upon widths).

No. 1 and 2, 1¼ and 1½ in., clear Fir rough	71 00	75 00
No. 1 and 2 2-in. clear Fir rough	56 00	66 00
1 x 5 and 1 x 6 Fir casing		72 00
1 x 8 and 1 x 10 Fir base		75 00
1¼ & 1½ x 6, 10 & 12" E. G. stepping		85 00
1¼ & 1½ x 8, 10 & 12" E. G. stepping		75 00
1-in. clear Fir, d 4 sides		60 00
1¼x1¼ in. clear Fir, d 4 sides	60 00	70 00
XXX 6 butts to 2 in.		7 10
XXXXX 5 butts to 2 in.		8 10

LATH

	Red Pine
No. 1 White Pine, 4 ft.	Open
No. 2 White Pine, 4 ft.	"
No. 3 White Pine, 4 ft.	"
Mill run white pine, 32 in.	"
Merchantable spruce lath, 4 ft.	"

TORONTO HARDWOOD PRICES

The prices given below are for carloads f.o.b. Toronto, from wholesalers to retailers, and are based on a good percentage of long lengths and good widths, without any wide stock having been sorted out. War tax of seven and half per cent. on imported woods, and also the prevailing rate of exchange paid by purchaser.

ASH, WHITE

(Dry weight 3800 lbs. per M. ft.)

	1s & 2s	No. 1 Com.	No. 2 Com.	No. 3 Com.
4/4	$125.00	$80.00	$50.00	$35.00
5/4 & 6/4	135.00	90.00	55.00	40.00
8/4	150.00	100.00	60.00	40.00
10/4 & 12/4	200.00	150.00	80.00	.....
16/4	220.00	160.00	90.00	.....

ASH, BROWN

4/4	$75.00	$55.00	$40.00	$38.00
6/4	80.00	65.00	60.00	50.00
8/4	83.00	70.00	65.00	50.00

BIRCH

(Dry weight 4000 lbs. per M. ft.)

	1s & 2s $		No. 1 Com. $		No. 2 Com. $	
4/4	75	78	60	63	45	50
5/4 & 6/4	80	85	65	70	50	55
8/4	80	85	65	70	55	
10/4 and 12/4	95	100	85	90	70	
16/4	100	105	90	95	80	

BASSWOOD

(Dry weight 2500 lbs. per M. ft.)

	1s & 2s	No. 1 Com.	No. 2 Com.	No. 3 Com.
4/4	$77.00	$55.00	$44.00	$38.00
5/4 & 6/4	80.00	60.00	50.00	40.00
8/4	83.00	63.00	50.00	42.00

CHESTNUT

(Dry weight 2800 lbs. per M. ft.)

	1s & 2s	No. 1 Com.	Sound Wormy
4/4	$95.00	$80.00	$50.00
5/4 & 6/4	105.00	85.00	55.00
8/4	115.00	85.00	55.00

ELM, SOFT

(Dry weight 3100 lbs. per M. ft.)

4/4	$63.00	$50.00	$40.00	$38.00
6/4 & 8/4	68.00	55.00	45.00	43.00
12/4	75.00	65.00	50.00	42.00

GUM, RED

(Dry weight 3300 lbs. per M. ft.)

	Plain 1s & 2s	Plain No. 1 Com.	Quartered 1s & 2s	Quartered No. 1 Com.
4/4	$120.00	$90.00	$130.00	$105.00
5/4	125.00	95.00	135.00	110.00
6/4	125.00	95.00	140.00	115.00
8/4	135.00	120.00	140.00	120.00

Figured Gum, $10 per M. extra, in both plain and quartered.

GUM, SAP

	1s & 2s	No. 1 Com.
4/4	$70.00	$55.00
5/4 & 6/4	75.00	60.00
8/4	85.00	70.00

HICKORY

(Dry weight 4500 lbs. per M. ft.)

	1s & 2s	No. 1 Com.	No. 2 Com.
4/4	$100.00	$70.00	$45.00
5/4	120.00	85.00	55.00
6/4	125.00	85.00	55.00
8/4	135.00	95.00	60.00

MAPLE, HARD

(Dry weight 3900 lbs. per M. ft.)

	1s & 2s	Com. No. 1	Com. No. 2	Com. No. 3
4/4	$60.00	$50.00	$40.00	$30.00
5/4 & 6/4	65.00	60.00	45.00	35.00
8/4	70.00	65.00	45.00	40.00
12/4	80.00	80.00	40.00	
16/4	90.00	75.00	45.00	

SOFT MAPLE

The quantity of soft maple produced in Ontario is small and it is generally sold on a log run basis, the locality governing the prices.

WHITE AND RED OAK

(Plain sawed. Dry weight 4000 lbs. per M. ft.)

	1s & 2s	No. 1 Com.
4/4	$130.00	$90.00
5/4 & 6/4	135.00	95.00
8/4	140.00	100.00
10/4	150.00	110.00
12/4	150.00	110.00
16/4	165.00	120.00

WHITE OAK, Quarter Cut

(Dry weight 4000 lbs. per M. ft.)

	1s & 2s	No. 1 Com.
4/4	$230.00	$175.00
5/4 and 6/4	250.00	180.00
8/4	260.00	

RED OAK, Quarter Cut

	1s & 2s	No. 1 Com.
4/4	$185.00	$140.00
5/4 and 6/4	200.00	155.00
8/4	205.00	155.00

OTTAWA, ONT.

Manufacturers' Prices

Pine good sidings:

1-in. x 7-in. and up		
1¼-in. and 1½-in., 8-in. & up		
2-in. x 7-in. and up		00
No. 2 cuts 2 x 8-in. and up..		00

Pine good strips:

1-in.		
1¼-in. and 1½-in.		00
2-in.		00

Pine good shorts:

1-in. x 7-in. and up		00
1-in. x 4-in. to 6-in.		00
1¼-in. and 1½-in.		00
2-in.		
7-in. to 9-in. A sidings		
Pine, No. 1 dressing sidings		62
Pine, No. 1 dressing strips		58
Pine, No. 1 dressing shorts		52
Pine, 1-in. x 4-in. s.c. strips		51
Pine, 1-in. x 5-in. s.c. strips		52
Pine, 1-in. x 6-in. s.c. strips		54
Pine, 1-in. x 7-in. s.c. strips		54
Pine, 1 x 8-in. s.c., 12 to 16 ft.	48 00	56
Pine, 1-in. x 10-in. M.R.		58
Pine, s.c. sidings, 1½ and 2-in.		55
Pine, s.c. strips, 1-in.	45 00	49
1¼, 1½ and 2-in.		56
Pine, s.c. shorts, 1 x 4 to 6 in.		45
Pine, s.c. and bet., shorts, 1 x 5		45
Pine, s.c. and bet., shorts, 1 x 6		47 00
Pine, s.c. shorts, 6'-11', 1"x10"		52 00

Pine box boards:

1"x4" and up, 6'-11'		40 00
1"x3", 12'-16'		44 00
Pine, mill culls, strips and sidings, 1-in. x 4-in. and up, 12 ft. and up		
Mill cull shorts, 1-in. x 4-in. and up, 6-ft to 11-ft.		
O. culls r & w p		

RED PINE, LOG RUN

mill culls out, 1-in.	36	42
mill culls out, 1¼-in.	36	42 00
mill culls out, 1½-in.	38 00	42 00
mill culls out, 2-in.	40 00	
mill culls, white pine, 1"x7" and up		

MILL RUN SPRUCE

1"x4" and up, 6'-11'		42 00
1"x4" and up, 12'-16'		42 00
1"x9"-10" and up, 12'-16'		48 00
1¼"x7" 8-9" and up, 12'-16'		48 00
1¼ x 10 and up, 12'-16'		50 00
1½" & 2" x 12" and up, 12'-16'		50 00
Spruce, 1-in. clear (fine dressing and B)		55 00
Hemlock, 1-in. cull	25 00	27 00
Hemlock, 1-in. log run	30 00	35 00
Hemlock, 2x4, 6, 8, 10, 12/16'	30 00	35 00
Tamarac	24 00	26 00
Basswood, log run, dead culls out	46 00	48 00
Basswood, log run, mill culls out	45 00	50 00
Birch, log run	48 00	50 00
Soft Elm, common and better, 1, 1½, 2-in.	25 00	30 00
Ash, black, log run	32 00	40 00
1 x 10 No. 1 barn		52 00
1 x 10 No. 2 barn		46 00
1 x 8 and 9 No. 2 barn		42 00

Lath per M:

No. 1 whit pine, 1½-in. x 4 ft.	8 00
No. 2 white pine	7 50
Mill run white pine	7 50
Spruce, mill run 1½-in.	7 00
Red pine, mill run	7 00
Hemlock, mill run	6 00
32-in. lath	3 50

White Cedar Shingles:

XXXX, 18-in.		7 50
Clear butt, 18-in.		6 50
18-in. xx		5 00
Spruce logs (pulp)	18 00	15 00

QUEBEC, QUE.

WHITE PINE

	Cts. Per Cubic Foot	
First class Ottawa waney, 18-in. average, according to lineal	80	90
19 in. and up average	90	100

SPRUCE DEALS

	Per M. Ft.	
3 in. unsorted Quebec, 4 in. to 6 in. thick	$34 00	$37 00
3 in. unsorted, Quebec, 7 in. to 8 in. thick	38 00	40 00
3 in. unsorted Quebec, 9 in. thick	40 00	45 00

	Cts. Per Cubic Ft.	
According to average and quality 55 ft. cube	90	1 00
According to average and quality, 40 to 45 feet, cube	95	1 05
According to average and quality, 30 to 35 feet	75	85

BIRCH PLANKS

1 to 4 in. thick, per M. ft.	40 00	45 00

SARNIA, ONT.

FINE, COMMON AND BETTER

1 x 6 and 8 in.	$86 00
1 in., 8 in. and up wide	90 00
1¼ and 1½ in. and up wide	106 00
2 in. and up wide	106 00

CUTS AND BETTER

4/4 x 8 and up No. 1 and better	82 00
6/4 x 8 and up No. 1 and better	82 00
8/4 x 8 and up No. 1 and better	97 00

No. 1 CUTS

1 in., 8 in. and up	00
1¼ in., 8 in. and up	00
1½ in., 8 in. and up	00
2 in., 8 in. and up	00
2½ and 3 in., 8 in.	00
4 in., 8 in. and up	00

No. 1 BARN

1 in., 10 to 16 ft. long		$69 00
1¼, 1½ and 2 in., 10/16 ft.	$59 00	72 00
2½ to 3 in., 10/16 ft.	65 00	

No. 2 BARN

1 in., 10 to 16 ft. long	56 00	62 00
1¼, 1½ and 2 in., 10/16 ft.	57 00	68 00
2½ in. to 3 in.	70 00	

No. 3 BARN

1 in., 10 to 16 ft. long	52 00	62 00
1¼, 1½ and 2 in., 10/16 ft.	55 00	57 00

BOX

1 in., 1¼ in. & 1½ in., 10/16 ft.	47 00	49 00

MILL CULLS

Mill Run Culls

4 in. and up wide, 6/16 ft..	$39 00
1¼, 1½ and 2 in.	40 00
	00
	50
No. 3	7 00
32 in.	3 50
48 in. Hemlock	7 00
32 in	3 00

ST. JOHN, N.B.

ROUGH LUMBER

Wholesale Prices Per M. Sq. Ft.

2x4, 3x3, 3x4, Rgh. Merch. Spr.	$47 00
2x3, 2x4, 3x3, 3x4 Dressed 1 edge ..	49 00
2x3, 2x4, 3x3, 3x4 Dressed 4 sides..	52 00
2x6, 2x7, 3x5, 4x4, 4x6, all rough..	50 00
2x8, 3x7, 5x5, 6x6	52 00
2x9, 3x8, 6x8, 7x7	55 00
2x10, 3x9	60 00
2x12, 3x10, 3x12, 8x8 and up	62 00
Merch. Spr. Bds. Rough, 1x3-4 & 5	40 00
" " " " 1x6	45 00
" " " " 1x7 & up.	45 00
Refuse Bds., Deals & Setgs.	30 00

Above random lengths up to 18-0 long.
Lengths 19-0 & up $5.00 extra per M.
For planing Merch. and Refuse Bds. add $2.00 per M to above prices.
Laths $6.50 per M. pieces.

SHINGLES

	Per M.
Cedar, Extras	$6 00
" Clears	6 00
" 2nd Clears	5 00
Extra No. 1	4 00
	4 00

INNIPEG, MANITOBA

No. 1 SPRUCE

Dimension	S.1.S and 1.E 6 ft.	8 ft.	10 ft.
x 4	$35 50	$35 50	$42 00
x 6	37 50	38 50	42 00
x 8	37 50	39 50	42 00
x 10	38 50	40 50	43 00

(Continued on page

CURRENT LUMBER PRICES—Continued

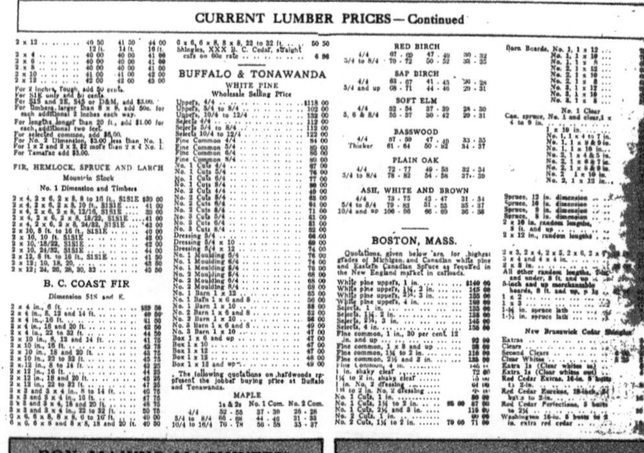

2 x 12	40 50	41 50	44 00
	12 ft.	14 ft.	16 ft.
2 x 4	40 00	40 00	41 00
2 x 6	40 00	40 00	41 00
2 x 8	40 00	40 00	41 00
2 x 10	41 00	41 00	42 00
2 x 12	42 00	42 00	43 00

For 2 inches, rough, add 50 cents.
For S1E only add 50 cents.
For S1S and 2E, S4S or D&M, add $3.00.
For timbers, larger than 8 x 8, add 50c. for each additional 2 inches each way.
For lengths longer than 20 ft., add $1.00 for each additional two feet.
For selected common, add $6.00.
For No. 2 Dimension, $3.00 less than No. 1.
For 1 x 2 and 2 x 2, $2 more than 2 x 4 No. 1.
For Tamarac add $3.00.

FIR, HEMLOCK, SPRUCE AND LARCH

Mountain Stock

No. 1 Dimension and Timbers

2 x 4, 2 x 6, 2 x 8, 8 to 10 ft., S1S1E	$30 00
2 x 4, 2 x 6, 2 x 8, 10 ft., S1S1E	41 00
2 x 4, 2 x 6, 2 x 8, 12/16, S1S1E	39 00
2 x 4, 2 x 6, 2 x 8, 18/22, S1S1E	41 00
2 x 4, 2 x 6, 2 x 8, 24/32, S1S1E	43 00
2 x 10, 8 ft. to 16 ft., S1S1E	40 00
2 x 10, 10 ft. S1S1E	42 00
2 x 10, 18/22, S1S1E	42 00
2 x 10, 24/32, S1S1E	44 00
2 x 12, 8 ft. to 16 ft., S1S1E	41 50
2 x 12; 10, 18, 20,	43 50
2 x 12; 24, 26, 28, 30, 32	40 50

B. C. COAST FIR

Dimension S1S and E.

2 x 4 in., 6 ft.	$39 50
2 x 4 in., 8, 12 and 14 ft.	40 50
2 x 4 in., 10 ft.	41 50
2 x 4 in., 18 and 20 ft.	42 50
2 x 4 in., 22 to 32 ft.	44 50
2 x 10 in., 8, 12 and 14 ft.	41 75
2 x 10 in., 16 ft.	42 75
2 x 10 in., 18 and 20 ft.	43 75
2 x 10 in., 22 to 32 ft.	45 75
2 x 12 in., 8 to 14 ft.	43 25
2 x 12 in., 16 ft.	44 25
2 x 12 in., 18 and 20 ft.	45 25
2 x 12 in., 22 to 32 ft.	47 25
3 x 3 and 3 x 4 in., 8 to 14 ft.	46 75
3 x 3 and 3 x 4 in., 16 ft.	47 75
3 x 3 and 3 x 4, 18 and 20 ft.	48 75
3 x 3 and 3 x 4 in., 22 to 32 ft.	50 75
6 x 6, 6 x 8, 8 x 8, 6 to 16 ft.	40 00
6 x 6, 6 x 8 and 8 x 8, 18 and 20 ft.	40 50
6 x 6, 6 x 8, 8 x 8, 22 to 32 ft.	50 50
Shingles, XXX B. C. Cedar, straight cuts on 60c rate	4 96

BUFFALO & TONAWANDA

WHITE PINE

Wholesale Selling Price

Uppers, 4/4	$118 00
Uppers, 5/4 to 8/4	102 00
Uppers, 10/4 to 12/4	132 00
Selects 4/4	112 00
Selects 5/4 to 8/4	112 00
Selects 10/4 to 12/4	122 00
Fine Common 4/4	84 00
Fine Common 5/4	80 00
Fine Common 6/4	90 00
Fine Common 8/4	90 00
No. 1 Cuts 4/4	67 00
No. 1 Cuts 5/4	76 00
No. 1 Cuts 6/4	77 00
No. 1 Cuts 8/4	80 00
No. 2 Cuts 4/4	49 00
No. 2 Cuts 5/4	63 00
No. 2 Cuts 6/4	64 00
No. 2 Cuts 8/4	71 00
No. 3 Cuts 5/4	61 00
No. 3 Cuts 6/4	61 00
No. 3 Cuts 8/4	62 00
Dressing 5/4	66 00
Dressing 5/4 x 10	69 00
Dressing 5/4 x 12	74 00
No. 1 Moulding 5/4	76 00
No. 1 Moulding 6/4	74 00
No. 1 Moulding 8/4	76 00
No. 2 Moulding 5/4	68 00
No. 2 Moulding 6/4	68 00
No. 2 Moulding 8/4	68 00
No. 1 Barn 1 x 12	65 00
No. 1 Barn 1 x 6 and 8	56 00
No. 1 Barn 1 x 10	58 00
No. 2 Barn 1 x 6 and 8	52 00
No. 2 Barn 1 x 10	56 00
No. 3 Barn 1 x 6 and 8	49 00
No. 3 Barn 1 x 10	47 00
Box 1 x 6 and up	47 00
Box 1 x 10	47 00
Box 1 x 12	47 00
Box 1 x 13	48 00
Box 1 x 13 and up	49 00

The following quotations on hardwoods represent the jobber buying price at Buffalo and Tonawanda.

	1s & 2s	No. 1 Com.	No. 2 Com.
MAPLE			
4/4	52 - 55	37 - 39	26 - 28
5/4 to 8/4	66 - 68	44 - 46	31 - 33
10/4 to 16/4	76 - 78	56 - 58	33 - 37
RED BIRCH			
4/4	67 - 69	47 - 49	30 - 32
5/4 to 8/4	70 - 72	50 - 52	33 - 35
SAP BIRCH			
4/4	63 - 67	41 - 43	26 - 28
5/4 and up	68 - 71	44 - 46	29 - 31
SOFT ELM			
4/4	52 - 54	37 - 39	28 - 30
5, 6 & 8/4	55 - 57	39 - 42	29 - 31
BASSWOOD			
4/4	57 - 59	47 - 49	33 - 35
Thicker	61 - 64	50 - 52	34 - 37
PLAIN OAK			
4/4	72 - 77	49 - 53	32 - 34
5/4 to 8/4	78 - 82	54 - 58	37 - 39
ASH, WHITE AND BROWN			
4/4	73 - 75	43 - 47	31 - 34
5/4 to 8/4	79 - 83	51 - 53	35 - 37
10/4 and up	106 - 08	66 - 69	36 - 38

BOSTON, MASS.

Quotations given below are for highest grades of Michigan and Canadian white pine and Eastern Canadian Spruce as required in the New England market in carloads.

White pine uppers, 1 in.		$140 00
White pine uppers, 1¼, 2 in.		145 00
White pine uppers, 2½, 3 in.		155 00
White pine uppers, 4 in.		160 00
Selects, 1 in.		135 00
Selects, 1¼, 2 in.		138 00
Selects, 2½, 3 in.		145 00
Selects, 4 in.		155 00
Fine common, 1 in., 30 per cent. 12 in. and up		92 00
Fine common, 1 x 8 and up		98 00
Fine common, 1¼ to 2 in.		116 00
Fine common, 2½ and 3 in.		135 00
Fine Common, 4 in.		146 [illegible]
1 in. shaky clear		72 00
1¼ to 2 in. shaky clear		[illegible]
1 in. No. 2 dressing		64 00
1¼ to 2 in. No. 2 dressing		[illegible]
No. 1 Cuts, 1 in.		80 00
No. 1 Cuts, 1¼ to 2 in.	85 00	87 00
No. 1 Cuts, 2½ and 3 in.		116 00
No. 2 Cuts, 1 in.		[illegible]
No. 2 Cuts, 1¼ to 2 in.	70 00	71 00

Barn Boards, No. 1, 1 x 12	[illegible]
No. 1, 1 x 10	[illegible]
No. 1, 1 x 8	[illegible]
No. 2, 1 x 12	[illegible]
No. 2, 1 x 10	[illegible]
No. 2, 1 x 8	[illegible]
No. 3, 1 x 12	[illegible]
No. 3, 1 x 10	[illegible]
No. 3, 1 x 8	[illegible]
No. 1 Clear	
Can. spruce, No. 1 and clear, 1 x 4 to 9 in.	[illegible]
1 x 10 in.	[illegible]
No. 1, 1 x 4 to 7 in.	[illegible]
No. 1, 1 x 8 & 9 in.	[illegible]
No. 1, 1 x 10 in.	[illegible]
No. 2, 1 x 4 & 5 in.	[illegible]
No. 2, 1 x 6 & 7 in.	[illegible]
No. 2, 1 x 8 & 9 in.	[illegible]
No. 2, 1 x 10 in.	[illegible]
No. 2, 1 x 12 in.	[illegible]
Spruce, 12 in. dimension	[illegible]
Spruce, 10 in. dimension	[illegible]
Spruce, 9 in. dimension	[illegible]
Spruce, 8 in. dimension	[illegible]
2 x 10 in., random lengths, 8 ft. and up	[illegible]
2 x 12 in., random lengths	[illegible]
2 x 3, 2 x 4, 2 x 5, 2 x 6, 2 x 7	[illegible]
3 x 4 and 4 x 4 in.	[illegible]
2 x 8 in.	[illegible]
All other random lengths, 7-in. and under, 8 ft. and up	[illegible]
5-inch and up merchantable boards, 8 ft. and up, p 1s	[illegible]
1 x 2	[illegible]
1 x 3	[illegible]
1-⅝ in. spruce lath	[illegible]
1-½ in. spruce lath	[illegible]

New Brunswick Cedar Shingles

Extras	[illegible]
Clears	[illegible]
Second Clears	[illegible]
Clear Whites	[illegible]
Extra 1s (Clear whites in)	[illegible]
Extra 1s (Clear whites out)	[illegible]
Red Cedar Extras, 16-in. 5 butts to 2-in.	[illegible]
Red Cedar Eurekas, 18-inch, 5 butts to 2-in.	[illegible]
Red Cedar Perfections, 5 butts to 2¼	[illegible]
Washington 16-in. 5 butts to 2 in. extra red cedar	[illegible]

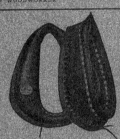

ALPHABETICAL INDEX TO ADVERTISERS

Reasons Why You Should Use

ATKINS STERLING QUALITY SAWS

Reason No. 1—ATKINS STEEL

Reason No. 2 -- Atkins Workmanship

WORKMANSHIP in saw making is a matter of experience. The Atkins name has been closely connected with the making of saws for nearly Three Hundred Years.

We believe we understand the science of saw making to the highest degree, and it is strictly upon the ground of superior workmanship we solicit the patronage of discriminating users of saws. Examine an Atkins with the greatest care and note with what unvarying accuracy the silver-like blade is shaped and finished. Care in workmanship is here carried to the utmost by skilled artisans whose purpose it is to keep "Atkins Always Ahead".

Watch for Reason No. 3

Send for Free Catalogue.

E. C. ATKINS & CO.

Factory: HAMILTON, ONT. Branch: 109 Powell St., VANCOUVER, B.C.

Clarke's Mackinaws, Moccasins, Shirts, Socks, Gloves and Mitts are well known to lumbermen for their satisfactory qualities.

A. R. CLARKE & CO.
LIMITED
Montreal Toronto Vancouver Quebec

Don't miss seeing our travellers with these goods. They are now on the road.

BELTING STABILITY

There has been such uniformity of satisfaction following the selection of

DUNLOP
"Gibraltar RedSpecial"

—"THE ORIGINAL RED RUBBER BELT"—

that we feel our quarter-century policy of "Keep the Quality Up as Well as the Production" is being amply rewarded.

"Gibraltar RedSpecial" faces any kind of a test unflinchingly. The man who wishes to talk power, "duck," or elasticity can find ample sway for his talents in a comparison of "Gibraltar RedSpecial" with any other belting.

Minimum loss of power. Mastery of heavy loads and jerky strains. Highest quality of friction uniting the plies. Adequate weight, No Stretching—these are some of the virtues of Dunlop "Gibraltar RedSpecial" Belting, proven in thousands of cases of actual use in Pulp and Paper Mills, on Main Drives in Saw and Lumber Mills, Mines, Steel Plants, etc.; in fact, in any and every kind of transmission work.

THE DUNLOP UNRESERVED GUARANTEE

If you have a difficult drive anywhere in your factory drop a line to our Head Office, or to our nearest branch, and we will send a man experienced in belt engineering to consider your requirements. If it is an instance where "Gibraltar RedSpecial" Belting may be suitably employed we will recommend its use; and we will stand behind our recommendation with the fullest guarantee ever issued by a firm producing rubber products.

Dunlop Tire & Rubber Goods Co., Limited

Head Office and Factories - - - TORONTO

BRANCHES IN THE LEADING CITIES

Makers of Tires for all purposes, Mechanical Rubber Products of all kinds, and General Rubber Specialties

"HAMILTON" CIRCULAR RE-SAWS

Here is a strong, rigid, well-designed machine, specially gotten up for resawing slabs. The feed rolls are carried on a sliding frame that is easily adjustable to cut lumber any desired thickness. The binding or press roll is 18 in. diam., fitted with saw discs and power driven. The saw used is 42 in. diam., driving pulley 18 in. diam. x 12 in. face. Cut shows Left-Hand Machine.

We also make this machine with wooden frame, having the mandrel and saw carried on an adjustable sliding frame.

Descriptive circular sent upon request.

"HAMILTON" HUSK FRAMES

Made in different sizes to suit all requirements. Frames are all of cast iron, of heavy section throughout, planed on top and bottom, with mandrel boxes lined with high grade babbitt. Mandrels are exceptionally large, of forged steel with forged collar, and the guide is the famous Parkhurst steel saw guide with steel splitter.

We manufacture a complete line of up-to-date Sawmill Machinery for either Band or Circular Mills.

William Hamilton Co., Limited

Peterboro, Ontario

Agents—J. L. Neilson & Co., Winnipeg, Man.

Lumbermen Should Duplex Savings

In the forests and in the towns, Duplex 4-Wheel Drive Trucks are hauling logs and lumber at a lower cost per ton mile.

The facts reported to us by Duplex operators seem almost incredible at times.

But we know they are true, because the testimony is unanimous—everywhere the Duplex is hauling for less.

Comparisons are made with horses and mules, with other trucks, and even with narrow-gauge railroads.

In every case, the Duplex shows definite savings

These decided savings are due to the principle of construction of the Duplex. It drives with all four wheel *all the time.*

The Duplex always goes through with its load—even where other trucks would stall light.

Single tires only are required for the rear wheels, which alone means a saving of 30 per cent.

In total, Duplex savings run from 20 to 60 per cent. And it *always saves.*

Comparative tests are welcomed by Duplex dealers.

They know the Duplex will demonstrate its lower per ton-mile, beyond any question or doubt.

Lumbermen who study the Duplex will see how it saves.

Send for Booklet — "The Modern and Efficient Way to Haul Logs and Lumber"

Duplex Truck Company

2062 Washington Avenue Lansing,

Joseph Maw & Co., Winnipeg, Man.

Reo Motor Sales Co., Toronto, Ont.

DUPLEX TRU

Cost Less Per Ton-mile

Oldest and Best

Chisel Tooth Saws

Choice of Lumbermen Everywhere

The even temper of these saws and the fine quality of steel from which they are made have proved Hoe saws reliable for nearly one hundred years.

More than one hundred thousand "Hoes" are to-day successfully sawing lumber in all parts of the globe. The Hoe Chisel Tooth Saw, invented 40 years ago, is still the best for cutting hardwood.

Special Flanged Shanks and Superior Bits Supplied

R. HOE & CO. 504-520 Grand Street **New York City**

America's Oldest Saw Manufacturers

Rubber Goods
FOR LUMBERMEN

Belting Our long experience in the making of Rubber Belts enables us to specialize on this line. "P.M.S.," "Special Drive" and "Lion" are our leading brands for power transmission.

Packings "Redstone" High Pressure Sheet Packing has proved by test that it will outlast any other similar packing on the market. We make Spiral and Ring Packings, etc., that are equally reliable.

Hose for Steam, Water, etc., in various grades, made especially to give satisfactory and economical service under different conditions.

Fire Hose One or more of our twenty brands of Fire Hose will be found, not only in the best equipped Factories, Mills, etc., but in almost every Fire Department in the Dominion.

Gutta Percha & Rubber, Limited

TORONTO MONTREAL WINNIPEG REGINA SASKATOON CALGARY EDMONTON VANCOUVER

D.K.McLaren's

Genuine British Oak Tanned

Leather Belting

Genuine Oak

Genuine Oak

We stand behind all we say about every inch of—

D. K. McLaren

LIMITED

Genuine Oak Tanned

Leather Belting

The force from mighty machinery is being transmitted silently, swiftly, smoothly by D. K. McLaren's Belting.—A vast amount of power efficiently delivered without waste.

Implicit trust is placed in D. K. McLaren Belting by engineers everywhere; because they are firmly convinced that their confidence is well founded.

"That they can rely on D. K. McLaren Belting to consistently uphold its reputation at all times"—the answer to all Belting problems.

A Guarantee that is on every piece of D.K.McLaren's High Grade Belting.

SPECIAL BELTS

D·K·McLAREN LIMITED

Head Office and Factory
351 St. James St.
Montreal

ST. JOHN, N.B.
90 Germain St.

TORONTO, ONT.
194 King St. W.

VANCOUVER, B. C.
849 Beatty St.

CANADA LUMBERMAN BUYERS' DIRECTORY

The following regulations apply to all advertisers:—Eighth page, every issue, three headings; quarter page, six headings; half page, twelve headings; full page, twenty-four headings.

ASBESTOS GOODS
Atlas Asbestos Company, Ltd.

AXES
Canadian Warren Axe & Tool Co.

BABBITT METAL
Canada Metal Company
General Supply Co. of Canada, Ltd.
United American Metals Corporation

Bale Ties
Laidlaw Bale Tie Company

BAND MILLS
Hamilton Company, William
Waterous Engine Works Company
Yates Machine Company, P. B.

BAND RESAWS
Mershon & Company, W. B.

BELT CEMENT
Graton & Knight Mfg. Company

BELT DRESSING
Atlas Asbestos Company, Ltd.
General Supply Co. of Canada, Ltd.
Graton & Knight Mfg. Company

BELTING
Atlas Asbestos Company, Ltd.
Beardmore Belting Company
Canadian Consolidated Rubber Co.
General Supply Company
Goodhue & Co., J. L.
Goodyear Tire & Rubber Co.
Graton & Knight Mfg. Company
Gutta Percha and Rubber Company
Main Belting Company
Manhattan Rubber Mfg. Co.
D. K. McLaren Limited
McLaren Belting Company, J. C.

BELTING (Transmission, Elevator, Conveyor, Rubber)
Dunlop Tire & Rubber Goods Co.

BLOWERS
Toronto Blower Company
Sturtevant Company, B. F.

BOILERS
Hamilton Company, William
Jenckes Machine Company
Marsh Engineering Works, Limited
Waterous Engine Works Company

BOILER PRESERVATIVE
International Chemical Company

BOX MACHINERY
Garlock-Walker Machinery Co.
Morgan Machine Company
Yates Machine Company, P. B.

BOX SHOOKS
Davison Lumber & Mfg. Company

BUNKS (Steel)
Alaska Bedding Co. of Montreal

CABLE CONVEYORS
Jeffrey Manufacturing Company
Jenckes Machine Company, Ltd.
Waterous Engine Works Company

CAMP SUPPLIES
Burns & Company, John
Canadian Milk Products Limited
Davies Company, William
Dr. Bell Veterinary Wonder Co.
Eckardt & Co.
Gunns Limited
Harris Abattoir Company
Johnson, A. H.
Turner & Sons, J. J.
Woods Manufacturing Company, Ltd.

CANT HOOKS
Canadian Warren Axe & Tool Co.
General Supply Co. of Canada, Ltd.
Pink Company, Thomas

CARS—STEEL BODY
Marsh Engineering Works, Limited

CAR WHEELS AND CASTINGS
Dominion Wheel & Foundries

CEDAR
Fesserton Timber Co.
Foss Lumber Company
Genoa Bay Lumber Company
Muir & Kirkpatrick
Long Lumber Company
Service Lumber Company
Terry & Gordon
Thurston-Flavelle Lumber Company
Vancouver Lumber Company
Victoria Lumber and Mfg. Co.

CHAINS
Canadian Link-Belt Company, Ltd.
General Supply Co. of Canada, Ltd.
Hamilton Company, William
Hobbs Company, Clinton E.
Jeffrey Manufacturing Company
Jenckes Machine Company, Ltd.
Pink & Co., Thomas
Waterous Engine Works Company
Williams Machinery Co., A. R. Vancouver

CHAIN HOISTS
Hobbs Company, Clinton E.

CHINA CLAY
Bowater & Sons, W. V.

CHEMICAL PLANTS
Blair, Campbell & McLean, Ltd.

CLOTHING
Acme Glove Works
Clarke & Company, A. R.
Grant, Holden & Graham
Woods Mfg. Company

COLLAR PADS
American Pad & Textile Co.

CONVEYOR MACHINERY
Canadian Link-Belt Company, Ltd.
Canadian Mathews Gravity Carrier Company
General Supply Co. of Canada, Ltd.
Jeffrey Mfg. Co.
Waterous Engine Works Company

CORDAGE
Consumers Cordage Company

CORN SYRUP
Canada Starch Company

COTTON GLOVES
American Pad & Textile Co.

COUPLING (Shaft)
Jenckes Machine Company, Ltd.

CRANES FOR SHIP YARDS
Canadian Link-Belt Company

CROSS ARMS
Genoa Bay Lumber Company

CUTTER HEADS
Shimer Cutter Head Company

CYPRESS
Chicago Lumber & Coal Company
Long Lumber Company
Wistar, Underhill & Nixon

DERRICKS AND DERRICK FITTINGS
Marsh Engineering Works, Limited

DOORS
Genoa Bay Lumber Company
Long Lumber Co.
Mason, Gordon & Co.
Rutherford & Sons, Wm.
Terry & Gordon

DRAG SAWS
Gerlach Company, Peter
Williams Machinery Co., A. R.

DRIVING BOOTS
Acme Glove Works

DRYERS
Philadelphia Textile Mach. Company

DUST COLLECTORS
Sturtevant Company, B. F.
Toronto Blower Company

EDGERS
William Hamilton Company, Ltd.
Garlock-Walker Machinery Co.
Green Company, G. Walter
Long Mfg. Company, E.
Waterous Engine Works Company

ELEVATING AND CONVEYING MACHINERY
Canadian Link-Belt Comptny, Ltd.
Jeffery Manufacturing Company
Jenckes Machine Company, Ltd.
Waterous Engine Works Company

ENGINES
Hamilton Company, William
Jenckes Machine Company
Waterous Engine Works, Company

EXCELSIOR MACHINERY
Elmira Machinery and Transmission Company

EXHAUST FANS
Garlock-Walker Machinery Co.
Sturtevant Company, B. F.
Reed & Company, Geo. W.
Toronto Blower Company

EXHAUST SYSTEMS
Reed & Company, Geo. W.
Toronto Blower Company

FILES
Disston & Sons, Henry
Simonds Canada Saw Company

FIR
Associated Mills, Limited
Allan-Stoltze Lumber Co.
British American Mills & Timber Co.
Coal Creek Lumber Compeny
Fesserton Timber Co.
Foss Lumber Company
Grier & Sons, Ltd., G. A.
Heeney, Percy E.
Knox Brothers
Long Lumber Company
Mason, Gordon & Co.
Reynolds Company, Limited
Service Lumber Company
Shearer Company, Jas.
Terry & Gordon
Timberland Lumber Company
Timms, Phillips & Co.
Vancouver Lumber Company
Victoria Lumber and Mfg. Co.
Weller, J. B.

FIRE BRICK
Beveridge Paper Company
Elk Fire Brick Company of Canada

FIRE FIGHTING APPARATUS
Dunlop Tire & Rubber Goods Co.
Pyrene Mfg. Company
Waterous Engine Works Company

FIR FLOORING
Genoa Bay Lumber Company
Rutherford & Sons, Wm.

FLAG STAFFS
Ontario Wind Engine Company

FLOORING (Oak)
Long-Bell Lumber Company

GALVANIZING
Ontario Wind Engine Company

GLOVES
Acme Glove Works
Eisendrath Glove Co.

GASOLINE ENGINES
Ontario Wind Engine Company

GEARS (Cut)
Smart-Turner Machine Co.

GRAIN
Dwyer Company, W. H.

GRAVITY LUMBER CARRIER
Can. Mathews Gravity Carrier Co.

GRINDERS (Bench)
Garlock-Walker Machinery Co.

HARDWOODS
Anderson Lumber Company, C. G.
Atlantic Lumber Co.
Bartram & Ball
Bennett Lumber Company
Blakeslee, Perrin & Darling
Cameron & Co.
Cardinal & Page
Cox, Long & Company
Davison Lumber & Mfg. Company
Dunfield & Company
Edwards & Co., W. C.
Fassett Lumber Company
Fesserton Timber Co.
Fraser Limited
Gall Lumber Company
Gillespie, James
Gloucester Lumber Company
Grier & Son, G. A.
Harris Lumber Co., Frank H
Heeney, Percy E.
Knox Brothers
Long Lumber Company
McLennan Lumber Company
Moores, Jr., E. J.
Pedwell Hardwod Lumber Co.
Powell-Myers Lumber Co.
Russell, Chas. H.
Spencer Limited, C. A.
Stearns & Culver Lumber Co.
Summers, James R.
Taylor Lumber Company, S. K.
Webster & Brother, James

HARDWOOD FLOORING MACHINERY
American Woodworking Machinery Company
Garlock-Walker Machinery Co.

HARDWOOD FLOORING
Grier & Son, G. A.
Long Lumber Company

HAY
Dwyer & Company, W. H.

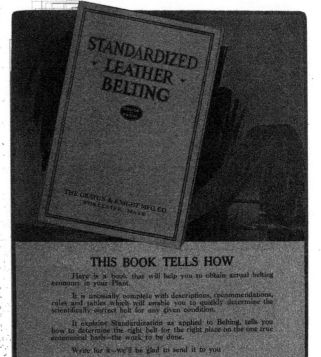

HARNESS
Padgitt Company, Tom

HEMLOCK
Anderson Lumber Company, C. G.
Bartram & Ball
Bourgouin, H.
Canadian General Lumber Company
Cane & Co., Jas. G.
Davison Lumber & Mfg. Company
Dunfield & Company
Edwards & Company, W. C.
Fesserton Timber Co.
Foss Lumber Company
Grier & Sons, Ltd., G. A.
Harris Lumber Co., Frank H
Hart & McDonagh
Long Lumber Company
Mason, Gordon & Co.
Roch, Julien
Spencer Limited, C. A.
Terry & Gordon

HOISTING AND HAULING ENGINES
Garlock-Walker Machinery Co.
General Supply Co. of Canada, Ltd.
Marsh Engineering Works, Limited

HORSES
Union Stock Yards

HOSE
Dunlop Tire & Rubber Goods Co.
General Supply Co. of Canada, Ltd.
Goodyear Tire & Rubber Co.
Gutta Percha and Rubber Company

INDUSTRIAL CARS
Marsh Engineering Works, Limited

INSURANCE
Hardy & Co., E. D.

INTERIOR FINISH
Eagle Lumber Company
Hay & Co.
Mason, Gordon & Co.
Renfrew Planing Mills
Terry & Gordon

KNIVES
Disston & Sons, Henry
Peter Hay Knife Company
Simonds Canada Saw Company
Waterous Engine Works Company

LARCH
Otis Staples Lumber Co.

LATH
Austin & Nicholson
Canadian General Lumber Company
Cane & Co., Jas. G.
Cardinal & Page
Dupuis Limited, J. P.
Eagle Lumber Company
Fraser Limited
Fraser-Bryson Lumber Company
Genoa Bay Lumber Company
Gloucester Lumber Company
Grier & Sons, Ltd., G. A.
Harris Tie & Timber Company, Ltd.
Long Lumber Company
McLennan Lumber Company
New Ontario Colonization Company
Otis Staples Lumber Co.
River Ouelle Pulp and Lumber Co.
Spencer Limited, C. A.
Terry & Gordon
Union Lumber Company
Victoria Harbor Lumber Company

LATH BOLTERS
Garlock-Walker Machinery Co.
General Supply Co. of Canada, Ltd.
Green Company, C. Walter

LIGHTING APPLIANCES
Hobbs Company, Clinton E.

LOCOMOTIVES
Bell Locomotive Works
General Supply Co. of Canada, Ltd.
Jeffrey Manufacturing Company
Jenckes Machine Company, Ltd.
Climax Manufacturing Company
Montreal Locomotive Works

LATH TWINE
Consumers' Cordage Company

LINK-BELT
Canadian Link-Belt Company

Canadian Mathews Gravity Carrier Company
Jeffrey Mfg. Co.
Williams Machinery Co., A. R., Vancouver

LOGGING COLLARS
Padgitt Company, Tom

LOCOMOTIVE CRANES
Canadian Link-Belt Company, Ltd.

LOGGING ENGINES
Dunbar Engine and Foundry Co.
Jenckes Machine Company
Marsh Engineering Works, Limited

LOG HAULER
Green Company, G. Walter
Jenckes Machine Company, Ltd.

LOGGING MACHINERY AND EQUIPMENT
General Supply Co. of Canada, Ltd.
Hamilton Company, William
Jenckes Machine Company, Ltd.
Marsh Engineering Works, Limited
Waterous Engine Works Company

LOG STAMPS
Superior Mfg. Company

LUMBER TRUCKS
Waterous Engine Works Company

LUMBERMEN'S CLOTHING
Woods Manufacturing Company, Ltd.

METAL REFINERS
Canada Metal Company
Hoyt Metal Company
Sessenwein Brothers

MILLING IN TRANSIT
Renfrew Planing Mills
Rutherford & Sons, Wm.

MOLDINGS
Genoa Bay Lumber Co.
Rutherford & Sons, Wm.

MOTOR TRUCKS
Duplex Truck Company

OAK
Chicago Lumber & Coal Comp
Long-Bell Lumber Company

OAKUM
Stratford Oakum Co., Geo.

OIL CLOTHING
Leckie Limited, John

OIL ENGINES
Swedish Steel & Importing Co.

OLD IRON AND BRASS
Sessenwein Brothers

OVERALLS
Hamilton Carhartt Cotton Mills

PAPER
Bowater & Sons, W. V.

PACKING
Atlas-Asbestos Company, Ltd.
Consumers Cordage Co.
Dunlop Tire & Rubber Goods Co.
Gutta Percha and Rubber Compan

PAPER MILL MACHINERY
Bowater & Sons, W. V.

PINE
Anderson Lumber Company, C. G.
Atlantic Lumber Co.
Austin & Nicholson
Bourgouin, H.
Cameron & Co.
Canadian General Lumber Company
Cane & Co., Jas. G.
Cardinal & Page
Chicago Lumber & Coal Company
Cleveland-Sarnia Sawmills Compan
Colonial Lumber Company
Cox, Long & Company
Davison Lumber & Mfg. Co.
Dudley, Arthur N.
Dunfield & Company
Eagle Lumber Company
Edwards & Co., W. C.

CLIMAX Improved Geared LOCOMOTIVES FOR WOOD AND IRON RAILS

A Climax Locomotive Designed Especially for Heavy Logging Work

Climax Locomotives are successfully operated on steep grades and sharp curves. Any weight or gauge. Locomotives in stock for immediate shipment. Get Catalog "H."

CLIMAX MANUFACTURING CO., 313 W. Main Street, CORRY, PA.
VANCOUVER MACHINERY DEPOT, LTD. VANCOUVER, B.C.

Manufactured by
J. J. TURNER & SONS, LIMITED, Peterborough, Ont.

PUT YOUR PROBLEM UP TO US

We are specialists in building locomotives. We build all types and sizes, also all kinds of repair parts for locomotives and tenders.

Our experience puts us in a position to give you expert advice as to what particular type and size of locomotive is best suited to your needs.

Put your locomotive problem up to us.

MONTREAL LOCOMOTIVE WORKS, LIMITED

DOMINION EXPRESS BUILDING, MONTREAL, CANADA.

PRATT & WHITNEY CO.

OF CANADA, LIMITED

SMALL TOOLS

Taps — Dies — Reamers — Cutters — Drills

MADE IN CANADA

As good as money can buy—Guaranteed absolutely!

Head Office and Works, DUNDAS, ONT.

SALES OFFICES:

MONTREAL VANCOUVER WINNIPEG

"ABOVE ALL THE OTHERS"

[illegible]

Proctor DRYERS for VENEERS

give a perfectly flat and pliable product without checks or splits

Made by the oldest and largest builders of dryers.
Ask for Proctor Dryer Catalog for your material.

PHILADELPHIA TEXTILE MACHINERY CO.

Drying Machine Specialists

[illegible] STREET AND TABOR ROAD, PHILADELPHIA, PA., U.S.A.

Excelsior Lumber Company
Fesserton Timber Company
Fraser-Bryson Lumber Company
Fraser Limited
Gillies Brothers Limited
Gloucester Lumber Company
Gordon & Co., George
Grier & Sons, Ltd., G. A.
Harris Lumber Co., Frank H
Harris Tie & Timber Company, Ltd.
Hart & McDonagh
Hettler Lumber Company, Herman H.
Long-Bell Lumber Company
Long Lumber Company
Mason, Gordon & Co.
McLennan Lumber Company
Montreal Lumber Company
Moores, Jr., E. J.
Muir & Kirkpatrick
Otis Staples Lumber Co.
Parry Sound Lumber Company
Roch, Julien
Russell, Chas. H.
Shearer Company, Pas.
Spencer Limited, C. A.
Summers, James R.
Terry & Gordon
Union Lumber Company
Watson & Todd, Limited
Williams Lumber Company
Wuichet, Louis

PLANING MILL EXHAUSTERS
Garlock-Walker Machinery Co.
Reed & Company, Geo. W.
Toronto Blower Co.

PLANING MILL MACHINERY
American Woodworking Machinery Company
Garlock-Walker Machinery Co.
Mershon & Company, W. B.
Toronto Blower Co.
Yates Machine Company, P. B.

PORK PACKERS
Davies Company, William
Gunns Limited
Harris Abattoir Company

POSTS AND POLES
Auger & Company
Canadian Tie & Lumber Co.
Dupuis Limited, J. P.
Eagle Lumber Company
Harris Tie & Timber Company, Ltd.
Long-Bell Lumber Company
Long Lumber Company
Mason, Gordon & Co.
Terry & Gordon

PULLEYS AND SHAFTING
Canadian Link-Belt Company
Garlock-Walker Machinery Co.
General Supply Co. of Canada, Ltd.
Green Company, G. Walter
Hamilton Company, William
Jeffrey Mfg. Co.
Jenckes Machine Company, Ltd.

PULP MILL MACHINERY
Canadian Link-Belt Company, Ltd.
Hamilton Company, William
Jeffrey Manufacturing Company
Jenckes Machine Company, Ltd.
Waterous Engine Works Company

PUMPS
General Supply Co. of Canada, Ltd.
Hamilton Company, William
Jenckes Machine Company, Ltd.
Smart-Turner Machine Company
Waterous Engine Company

RAILS
Gartshore, John J.
Sessenwein Bros.

ROOFING
Reed & Company, Geo. W.

ROOFINGS
(Rubber, Plastic and Liquid)
International Chemical Company

ROPE
Consumers Cordage Co.
Leckie, Limited, John

RUBBER GOODS
Atlas Asbestos Company
Dunlop Tire & Rubber Goods Co.
Goodyear Tire and Rubber Co.
Gutta Percha & Rubber Company

SASH
Genoa Bay Lumber Company
Renfrew Planing Mills

SAWS
Atkins & Company, E. C.,
Disston & Sons, Henry
General Supply Co. of Canada, Ltd.
Gerlach Company, Peter
Green Company, G. Walter
Hoe & Company, R.
Shurly Co., Ltd., T. F.
Shurly-Dietrich Company
Simonds Canada Saw Company

SAW MILL LINK-BELT
Williams Machinery Co., A. R., Vancouver

SAW MILL MACHINERY
Canadian Link-Belt Comptny, Ltd.
Dunbar Engine & Foundry Co.
Firstbrook Bros.
General Supply Co. of Canada, Ltd.
Hamilton Company, William
Huther Bros. Saw Mfg. Company
Jeffrey Manufacturing Company
Long Manufacturing Company, E.
Mershon & Company, W. B.
Parry Sound Lumber Company
Payete Company, P.
Waterous Engine Works Company
Yates Machine Co., P. B.

SHEATHINGS
Goodyear, Tire & Rubber Co.

SHINGLE MACHINES
Marsh Engineering Works, Limited

SAW SHARPENERS
Garlock-Walker Machinery Co.
Waterous Engine Works Company

SAW SLASHERS
Waterous Engine Works Company

SAWMILL LINK-BELT
Canadian Link-Belt Company

SHEET METALS
United American Metals Corp'n.

SHINGLES
Allan-Stoltze Lumber Co.
Associated Mills, Limited
Campbell-MacLaurin Lumber Co.
Cardinal & Page
Dominion Lumber & Timber Co.
Eagle Lumber Company
Foss Lumber Company
Fraser Limited
Genoa Bay Lumber Company
Gillespie, James
Gloucester Lumber Company
Grier & Sons, Limited, G. A.
Harris Lumber Co., Frank H
Harris Tie & Timber Company, Ltd.
Heeney, Percy E.
Long Lumber Company
Mason, Gordon & Co.
McLennan Lumber Company
Miller Company, Ltd., W. H.
Reynolds Company, Limited
Service Lumber Company
Shingle Agency of B. C.
Terry & Gordon
Timms, Phillips & Co.
Vancouver Lumber Company
Victoria Lumber and Mfg. Co.

SHINGLE & LATH MACHINERY
Dunbar Engine and Foundry Co.
Garlock-Walker Machinery Co.
Green Company, C. Walter
Hamilton Company, William
Long Manufacturing Company, E.
Payette Company, P.

SHOEPACKS
Acme Glove Works

SILENT CHAIN DRIVES
Canadian Link-Belt Company, Ltd.

SILOS
Ontario Wind Engine Company

SLEEPING ROBES
Woods Mfg. Company, Limited

SLEIGHS
Bateman-Wilkinson Company

SMOKESTACKS
Marsh Enginering Works, Limited
Waterous Engine Works Company

SNOW PLOWS
Bateman-Wilkinson Company
Pink Company, Thomas

SPARK ARRESTORS
Jenckes Machine Company, Ltd.
Reed & Company, Geo. W.
Waterous Engine Works Company

SPRUCE
Bartram & Ball
Bourgouin, H.
Cane & Co., Jas. G.
Cardinal & Page
Cox, Long & Company
Davison Lumber & Mfg. Company
Donogh & Co., John
Dudley, Arthur N.
Dunfield & Company
Exchange Lumber Company
Foss Lumber Company
Fraser Limited
Fraser-Bryson Lumber Company
Gillies Brothers
Gloucester Lumber Company
Grant & Campbell
Grier & Sons, Ltd., G. A.
Harris Lumber Co., Frank H
Hart & McDonagh
Long Lumber Company
Mason, Gordon & Co.
McLennan Lumber Company
Muir & Kirpatrick
New Ontario Colonization Company
River Ouelle Pulp and Lumber Co.
Roch, Julien
Russell, Chas. H.
Service Lumber Company
Shearer Company, Jas.
Snowball Co., J. B.
Spencer Limited, C. A.
Terry & Gordon
Rideau Lumber Company

STEEL CHAIN
Canadian Link-Belt Company, Ltd.
Jeffrey Manufacturing Company
Waterous Engine Works Company

STEEL PLATE CONSTRUCTION
Marsh Engineering Works, Limited

STEAM PLANT ACCESSORIES
Waterous Engine Works Company

STEEL BARRELS
Smart-Turner Machine Co.

STEEL DRUMS
Smart-Turner Machine Co.

STOVES
Burns & Company, John

SWEAT PADS
American Pad & Textile Co.

SULPHITE PULP CHIPS
Davison Lumber & Mfg. Company

TANKS
Ontario Wind Engine Company

TARPAULINS
Turner & Sons, J. J.
Woods Manufacturing Company, Ltd.

TAPS AND DIES
Pratt & Whitney Company

TENTS
Turner & Sons, J. J.
Woods Mfg. Company

TENTS, CLOTHING
Grant, Holden & Graham, Limited

TIES
Auger & Company
Austin & Nicholson
Canadian Tie & Lumber Co.
Harris Tie & Timber Company, Ltd.
Long Lumber Company
McLennan Lumber Company
Terry & Gordon

TIMBER BROKERS
Bradley, R. R.
Cant & Kemp
Farnworth & Jardine
Hunter, Herbert F.
Smith & Tyrer, Limited

TIMBER CRUISERS AND ESTIMATORS
Sewall, James W.

TIMBER LANDS
Department of Lands and Forests

TRACTORS
British War Mision

TRANSMISSION MACHINERY
Canadian Link-Belt Company, Ltd.
General Supply Co. of Canada, Ltd.
Jenckes Machine Company, Ltd.
Jeffrey Manufacturing Company
Waterous Engine Works Company

TRIMMERS
Garlock-Walker Machinery Co.
Green Company, C. Walter
Waterous Engine Works Company

TUGS
West & Peachey

TURBINES
Hamilton Company, William
Jenckes Machine Company, Ltd.

VALVES
Bay City Foundry & Machine Co.

VENEERS
Webster & Brother, James

VENEER DRYERS
Coe Manufacturing Company
Philadelphia Textile Mach. Co.

VENEER MACHINERY
Coe Machinery Company
Garlock-Walker Machinery Co.
Philadelphia Textile Machinery Co.

VETERINARY REMEDIES
Dr. Bell Veterinary Wonder Co.
Johnson, A. H.

WATER HEATERS
Mason Regulator & Engineering Co.

WATER WHEELS
Hamilton Company, William
Jenckes Machine Company, Ltd.

WIRE
Laidlaw Bale Tie Company

WIRE ROPE
Canada Wire & Cable Co.

WOODWORKING MACHINERY
American Woodworking Machy. Co.
Garlock-Walker Machinery Co.
General Supply Co. of Canada, Ltd.
Jeffrey Manufacturing Company
Long Manufacturing Company, E.
Mershon & Company, W. B.
Waterous Engine Works Company
Yates Machine Company, P. B.

WOOD PRESERVATIVES
International Chemical Company

WOOD PULP
Austin & Nicholson
New Ontario Colonization Co.
River Ouelle Pulp and Lumber Co.

Beardmore Extra Quality Waterproof
Cement Leather Belting
For the Wet Place
Tell us your belting troubles and we can help you.
The General Supply Company of Canada, Limited
OTTAWA MONTREAL TORONTO WINNIPEG VANCOUVER
Large stocks available for immediate shipment

CANADA
WIRE & CABLE
CO. LTD.

WATEROUS
BRANTFORD
CANADA
GRAND

Vol. 39 Toronto, November 15, 1919

Alphabetical Index to Advertisers, Page 68 Classified Directory to Advertisements, Page 84

AMERICAN WOOD WORKING MACHINERY

ROCHESTER, N. Y.

SALES OFFICE FOR BRITISH COLUMBIA, PORTLAND, OREGON
AGENTS FOR THE REST OF CANADA, GARLOCK-WALKER MACHINERY CO., TORONTO
AGENTS FOR GREAT BRITAIN, THE PROJECTILE CO., LONDON

FIRST IN QUALITY

The Complete Matcher

Our No. 77A—Model 5

A Supreme Achievement

This matchless machine embodies everything that makes for a thoroughly efficient and desirable Matcher and Planer. It is the last word in modern woodworking machinery in design and equipment. Its work is as perfect as it is possible for human achievement and present-day machinery to produce and its capacity is far greater than any other machine on the market.

Automatic Belt Release and Tighteners; built-in Head Knife Jointers for both top and bottom heads; a Feed Roll Gearing that eliminates all chains and sprockets; Matcher Logs quickly and easily adjusted; micrometer adjustment of Feed Rolls and Platen; these are a few of its desirable features.

Its capacity for an increased output in all patterns of siding, ceiling, flooring, etc., makes it an all round superior machine.

CANADIAN SALES AGENTS

Garlock-Walker Machiner

32-34 FRONT STREET WEST, TORONTO

TORONTO MONTREAL WINNIPEG

Hemlock, Spruce, Lath, Pulpwood and Hardwoods

The Year Round----In Any Quantity
Dressed and Ripped to Your Orders

We specialize in Hemlock and Spruce Timbers. Let us know your requirements. We can assure you of immediate shipment through our splendid transportation facilities. Rail and water delivery.

Fassett Lumber Company, Limited

FASSETT
QUEBEC

OFFERS WANTED

For Whole or Part of

100,000 Pieces

Birch Veneer 19 x 19 x 1/4" stock

The Wm. Rutherford & Sons Co Ltd.

425 Atwater Ave. - MONTREAL

TERRY & GORDON

Manufacturers and Wholesalers

of the

Products of Canadian Forests

Head Office—703 and 704 CONFEDERATION LIFE BUILDING,
TORONTO, ONTARIO

Branch Office—VANCOUVER, B.C.
A. S. NICHOLSON, Manager

Representatives in Ontario of

The British Columbia Mills Timber and Trading Company

Vancouver, B.C.

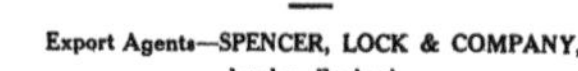

Export Agents—SPENCER, LOCK & COMPANY,
London, England

The Quality of Our Product is Our Best Advertisement

We Solicit Your Enquiries for Lumber in Any Quantities

"What you get for what you pay" in buying lumber was ne more important than it is today. Make your slacking dollar its full duty in buying reliable quality only.

Hocken Lumber Company's limits in the famous La Cloche hills produce medium size, tight knotted, close grained White and Red Pine trees—straight, smooth and unblemished. Nature made them, and our up-to-the minute mill is turning them into lumber so nearly perfect that we are proud to recommend it to the trade. It is our mark of accomplishment. It is the consumer's mark of assurance.

HOCKEN LUMBER CO., LIMIT

630 Confederation Life Building PHONE MAIN 3153 **TORON**

Manufacturers of
WIRE For TYING, BUNDLING and many other purposes.
NAILS, Etc.

LAIDLAW BALE-TIE CO., Ltd.
HAMILTON, ONT.

Timber Estimates

James W. Sewall
OLD TOWN, - MAINE

TIMBER LANDS

Bought and Sold

Timber and Pulp Wood Estimates

R. R. BRADLEY
Consulting Forester
58 Telegraph Building
Hospital St., MONTREAL

USED SAW MILL
MACHINERY
FOR SALE

Extra heavy log haul-up works with inch round and flat chain, 128 ft. centres.
2—Waterous log unloaders or kickers, 3 arms, 10 in. cylinders.
1—Waterous log loader, 3 arms, 10-in. cylinders.
1—Waterous right-hand double cutting band mill, 11 in. saws, 8 ft. wheel, with 3-block carriage; 24 in. opening; Payette set works and dogs; 8 in. x 36 ft. steam feed.
1—Waterous double edger for 20-inch saws, lever shifter.
1—Payette double edger for 18-in. saws, lever shifter.
48—live rolls about 8 ft. long by 10 in. dia.; extra heavy, sprocket drive.
1—Payette picket machine, made specially for shade roller stock, will feed pieces 16 in. long, also sorting table with chain top.
1—Payette edger for box and short stock.
1—Rogers twin circular or tie maker.
1—Payette lath bolter and lath machine.
1—Pair lath trimmers.
1—Picket trimmer (bunch trim).
—Pair Polson "Brown" type engines, coupled on quarters, 22 in. x 50 in., with 16 ft. x 48 in. belt, balance wheel. Excellent engines.
1—8 x 10 Centre Crank Engine.
1—10 x 14 Cowan Slide Valve Engine.
Pulleys, gears, heavy line shafting and countershafting with bearings.
Booms and boom chains, ½, ⅝ & ¾.
Winches and other mill supplies.
Prompt shipments and bargains for quick sale. Will send all particulars and prices on application.

Firstbrook Bros.
Limited
PENETANG

"WELL BOUGHT IS HALF SOLD"

Spruce Users
We Offer the Following

200M' 5/8 x 3—6/16'
17M' 5/8 x 4— "
40M' 5/8 x 5— "
8M' 5/8 x 6— "
29M' 5/4 x 5—12' and 13'
5M' 5/4 x 6— "
17M' 2 x 7—12'
17M' 2 x 7—13'
5M' 2 x 8—6/9'
7M' 2 x 8—13'
7M' 2 x 9—6/9'
32M' 2 x 9—10' and 11'
37M' 2 x 9—12'
100M' 2 x 9—13'
8M' 2 x 10—6/9'
19M' 2 x 10—10' and 11'
33M' 2 x 10—12'
100M' 2 x 10—13'

5/4 and 2" 1918 cut

Manufacture High Class
Grade - - Good

Canadian General Lumber Co.
Limited

FOREST PRODUCTS

TORONTO OFFICE :— 712-20 Bank of Hamilton Bldg.
Montreal Office :—203 McGill Bldg.
Mills : Byng Inlet, Ont.

Quick Action

You Can Have It

Try the Canada Lumberman Wanted and For Sale Department. Have you anything you wish to buy or sell in the Lumber Industry? You will find this department inexpensive, and a very effective business getter.

Our Classified Advertisers do not repeat the ad, often. They don't have to. They report immediate results. Use these columns to your own advantage.

CANADA LUMBERMAN
and WOODWORKER
347 Adelaide St. W.
TORONTO

The Rat Portage Lumber Co., Limited, Vancouver

MANUFACTURERS OF

Douglas Fir, Spruce, Cedar and Hemlock Lumber

Rough Timbers, Dimension, Flooring, Ceiling, Siding, Interior and Exterior Finish of all kinds including Mouldings. Fir, Spruce and Cedar Lath

Prompt shipment of Fir timbers in all sizes and up to 100 feet in length

AIR DRIED CEDAR SHINGLES We specialize in supplying air dried Cedar Shingles, these cost more than kiln dried Shingles but make a better roof and last much longer

---

I offer the following West Virginia stock for immediate shipment:

100,000 Ft. 4/4 Sound Wormy Chestnut
100,000 " 5/4 " " "
75,000 " 6/4 " " "
70,000 " 8/4 " " "

No. 1 Common and Better Chestnut

100,000 Ft. 4/4
100,000 " 6/4
100,000 " 8/4, 60% 14 and 16 feet long, 50% to 60% 10 ft. and wider.
15,000 " 4/4 FAS Plain White Oak.
75,000 " 4/4 No. 1 Common Plain White Oak.
100,000 " 6/4 No. 1 Common Plain White Oak.
I also have a car of 4/4 No. 1 Com. and Btr. Tennessee Red Cedar in Transit.

Write, wire or phone for prices.

PERCY E. HEENEY, Wholesale Lumber
207 Weber Chambers, KITCHENER, Ont.

I HAVE IT

All Grades in White Pine
Lath A Specialty

Milling in Connection

E. J. MOORES, J
MIDLAND

LET'S GET ETHER

Planing Mill Stock

CYPRESS

Soft, Dry Stock, Finest Grades—
All Thicknesses— 4/4, 5/4, 6/4, 8/4, 10/4, 12/4

Yellow Pine Finish

Kiln Dried, Soft, Short Leaf Kind
Stock Widths 4/4 5/4 6/4 8/4 by 4", 6", 8", 10", 12"

Also OAK, ASH, POPLAR, GUM

WISTAR, UNDERHILL & NIXON
Real Estate Trust Bldg., Philadelphia, Pa.

We Specialize in—

New Brunswick White Cedar Shingles

We also manufacture
Spruce and Pine Lumber, Lath, Cedar Ties, etc.

Shipments by Rail and Water.

W. H. MILLER CO., LTD.
Campbellton, N. B.

International Land & Lumber
Company, Limited

Lumber, Railway Ties Shims, Shingles, etc.

Head Offices, Ottawa, Ont.

Limits and Mills: ST. FELICIEN, LAKE ST. JOHN DISTRICT, QUEBEC

Island Soft Douglas Fir

well manufactured into

TIMBERS of any size or any kind.
SAWN CLEARS (kiln dried) for factory purposes.
FINISHED CLEARS or COMMONS for yard trade
(made to special sizes when desired)

Carefully graded and shipped under P.C.L.I. certificate.

CEDAR, HEMLOCK, SPRUCE, SHINGLES

McELROY LUMBER COMPANY Limited
redit Foncier Building • • VANCOUVER, B.C.

SPEND YOUR "ROOFING DOLLARS" IN CANADA

National economics and the spirit of patriotism demand today—as never before—that Canadians should buy Canadian products.

British Columbia
Red Cedar
SHINGLES

—are "Made in Canada"—they come from Canadian forests—are made by Canadian labor.

—are a standard for roofing which knows no superior in the world—for service—for satisfaction—for economy.

In advising your patrons to use British Columbia Red Cedar Shingles you are not only asking them to act in the best interests of Canada but also giving them a roofing product that cannot be excelled.

Trade-marks Carried by

B. C. Red Cedar Shingles

Send to us for Dealers' Booklets—they give your patrons valuable information about roofing—We'll send you a package on postcard request.

SHINGLE AGENCY OF B. C.
STANDARD BANK BUILDING
VANCOUVER, B. C.

QUALITY *PLUS* SERVICE

Our right to advertise Quality plus Service has been won by our practice of never failing to give Quality plus Service—and that, because our customers must be satisfied. The following is Quality Hardwood, with which goes real Service.

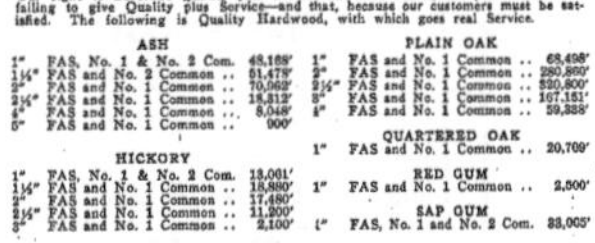

ASH		
1"	FAS, No. 1 & No. 2 Com.	48,168'
1½"	FAS and No. 2 Common ..	61,478'
2"	FAS and No. 1 Common ..	70,062'
2½"	FAS and No. 1 Common ..	18,812'
4"	FAS and No. 1 Common ..	8,048'
5"	FAS and No. 1 Common ..	900'

HICKORY		
1"	FAS, No. 1 & No. 2 Com.	13,061'
1½"	FAS and No. 1 Common ..	18,880'
2"	FAS and No. 1 Common ..	17,480'
2½"	FAS and No. 1 Common ..	11,200'
3"	FAS and No. 1 Common ..	2,100'

PLAIN OAK		
1"	FAS and No. 1 Common ..	68,498'
2"	FAS and No. 1 Common ..	280,860'
2½"	FAS and No. 1 Common ..	320,800'
3"	FAS and No. 1 Common ..	167,151'
4"	FAS and No. 1 Common ..	59,388'

QUARTERED OAK		
1"	FAS and No. 1 Common ..	20,709'

RED GUM		
1"	FAS and No. 1 Common ..	2,500'

SAP GUM		
1"	FAS, No. 1 and No. 2 Com.	83,005'

John I. Shafer Hardwood Co., South Bend IND.

Standing Timber

in Large or Small Blocks

FOR SALE

Special Prices

THE undersigned offer for sale, in large or small blocks all their remaining timber lands and town property situated in the town of Parry Sound, Ont.

We have sold quite a number of timber parcels but still have some good bargains left in Townships of McDougall, Foley, McKellar, Monteith, Carling, Christie, McConkey, Mills, Allen, Secord, Falconbridge and Street.

Special bargains in the Townships of Falconbridge and Street for small mills.

The Parry Sound Lumber Co. Limited
26 Ernest Ave.
Toronto, Canada

ALABAMA HEWN OAK TIMBER:—
HARDWOOD LOGS:—

Trade  Mark

Reg. U. S. A.

THE S. K. TAYLOR LUMBER COMPANY
Exporters **Mobile, Alabama, U.S.A.** Cables "Taylor, Mobi"

Barometer of Prices

Our Monthly Price List especially published for the Buyers of Foodstuffs for Lumber Camps is a veritable Barometer of Prices.

ASK FOR IT!

SPECIAL DEPARTMENT

Your enquiries and orders will be looked after by a Director of the firm in personal charge of this department. You will receive prompt and courteous service.

TRY IT!

100 PER CENT. VALUE

Are you buying at the right price or paying too much? There is only one price to pay. **The Fair Market Price.** That is the one we charge for **100% Value.**

Send a Trial Order

WE'LL PROVE THIS

Fifty years of Experience and Service is the Bond we furnish with each transaction.

LAPORTE, MARTIN LIMITEE

Wholesale Grocers

584 St. Paul Street West - Montreal

Canada Lumberman and Woodworker

Issued on the 1st and 15th of every month by
HUGH C. MACLEAN, LIMITED, Publishers
THOS. S. YOUNG, Toronto, General Manager.

OFFICES AND BRANCHES:
TORONTO - - Telephone A. 2700 - - 347 Adelaide Street West
VANCOUVER - - Telephone Seymour 2013 - - Winch Building
MONTREAL - - Telephone Main 2299 - - 119 Board of Trade
WINNIPEG - Telephone Garry 856 - Electric Railway Chambers
NEW YORK - - - - - - - - - - - 309 Broadway
CHICAGO - Telephone Harrison 5351 - 1413 Great Northern Building
LONDON, ENG. - - - - - - - 16 Regent Street, S. W.

TERMS OF SUBSCRIPTION
Canada, United States and Great Britain, $2.00 per year, in advance; other foreign countries embraced in the General Postal Union, $3.00.
Single copies 15 cents.

"The Canada Lumberman and Woodworker" is published in the interest of, and reaches regularly, persons engaged in the lumber, woodworking and allied industries in every part of Canada. It aims at giving full and timely information on all subjects touching these interests, and invites free discussion by its readers.

Advertisers will receive careful attention and liberal treatment. For manufacturing and supply firms wishing to bring their goods to the attention of owners and operators of saw and planing mills, woodworking factories, pulp mills, etc., "The Canada Lumberman and Woodworker" is undoubtedly the most direct and profitable advertising medium. Special attention is directed to the "Wanted" and "For Sale" advertisements.

Authorized by the Postmaster-General for Canada, for transmission as second-class matter.
Entered as second-class matter July 18th, 1914, at the Postoffice, at Buffalo, N. Y., under the Act of Congress of March 3rd, 1879.

Vol. 39 Toronto, November 15, 1919 No. 22

Giving Stability to the Lumber Industry

A move was begun at the last annual meeting of the Canadian Lumbermen's Association to inaugurate a statistical department by which the members of the organization would make regular returns to the secretary of the amount of lumber cut, sold, shipped and in stock. The returns would be totalled up and sent out in the aggregate to all who co-operated in the plan.

It was pointed out at the time that such figures if available would afford a ready reference and authentic guide regarding the state of the market, manufacture and distribution and thus impart stability and strength to conditions generally, guarding against overproduction on the one hand and underproduction on the other as well as affording a mass of information that would be otherwise valuable and instructive. Various lumbermen's associations on the other side of the line have for some years followed this procedure from week to week and, while progress was at first slow and many held back from joining in the move, there is now a general compliance with the programme and the old order of things would not be reverted to under any circumstances.

Thus far as great progress as is desired has not been made by the Canadian Lumbermen's Association in this step but it is hoped that further encouragement and assistance will be lent to the project. No one member will have access to the figures of another as only the aggregates are available and thus all share alike in the benefit and results.

One of the most vital elements in the production, sale and handling of lumber is to secure a clear, concise and comprehensive review of economic conditions in the trade and this is particularly important with respect to export and the domestic supply and demand. The Association, if such data as outlined was available, would be in a position to state what it could furnish, when, in what quantities, grades, thicknesses, widths, delivery points, etc. A forward movement of this character would be in line with the advancement of the times and the larger and broader fields of activity. Expansion and greater production are the watchwords of the hour and on all sides one hears of low stocks, the increasing uses and larger calls for forest products. To secure an intelligent grasp of the whole situation, a statistical department can render great help and prove to be of much use and advantage to all concerned. Lumbermen, individually and collectively, would know where they are at and matters would proceed on a more even keel. If the Canadian Lumbermen's Association was in receipt of detailed reports with reference to leading woods—such as are supplied by associations across the border,—it would be a source of much gratification all around.

Subjoined is a review for one week furnished by a leading western lumbermen's organization and it shows at a glance the how, why, when and where of trade conditions in short, condensed form. It is hoped the day is not far distant when somewhat similar service may be presented to the members of the industry in Canada. The benefits accruing from such a convenience would be practical, timely and cumulative.

Here is the statement in question, and its various aspects and features are worth study on the part of lumbermen on this side of the forty-ninth parallel:—

"A distinct advance in the volume of orders is reported by lumber manufacturers in the last week or 10 days. Total new business at 123 mills contributing to the report last week was 62,609,000 feet —a gain of more than 3,500,000 feet over the previous week. At the same time the mills are getting a steady run of inquiries indicating that buying for the spring trade will start much earlier this year than usual. The prevailing car shortage alone prevents the manufacturers from taking on a heavier run of orders, and all advices point to a continuation of the short car supply."

"The industry as a whole still is 30 per cent. short of stocks and with a brisk buying movement opening up it is hardly expected that stocks will get back to normal this winter. While the mills last week cut 87,491,000 feet, shipments aggregated 67,809,248 feet—an excess of cut over shipments of 19,681,752 feet. At this rate it will take the mills a long time to make up the existing shortage, but with a normal car supply the surplus production soon will be overcome entirely. Rail shipments last week were 1643 cars, leaving an aggregate of 7168 cars of unfilled orders on the books of the mills. Building operations in cities in the North-west where strikes had been in progress, are getting back to normal and local orders are increasing accordingly. The total for the week was 5,611,100 feet. Export orders were 5,510,822 feet and domestic cargo orders 7,177,226 feet—a total of 12,688,048 feet of waterborne business."

The World-Wide Demand for Lumber

It is not easy in the present disturbing and abnormal situation to forecast what will prevail in the lumber industry next year, so far as demand and supply are concerned. Under ordinary circumstances, members of the industry have, by reason of conditions present and past, been able to gauge the future with a certain amount of assurance and confidence. In these days many well-timed calculations are, however, upset, whether of a political or trade character. The result of the recent elections in Ontario has demonstrated how far astray predictions may be in the realm of party politics. Still, in commercial matters, signs are not generally as wide of the mark as in parliamentary prognostications. Barring fresh labor troubles and exactions, and, anticipating the subsidence of the general unrest which has been predominant for some time, the coming season should be a banner one in the production and distribution of forest products.

There is evidence on every side that stocks are low and the number of requisitions in structural and other lines of consumption are constantly increasing, all of which will tend to speed up operation. Prices will, according to present indications, be well maintained and are likely to ascend owing to a world-wide shortage of lumber. It requires no great economic foresight to predict what will develop in this state of affairs. On the Canadian side of the border conditions are analogous to those prevailing in the United States and the observations of a leading sales manager of one of the largest firms in America, who recently visited all their eastern offices, are timely and pertinent. It is pointed out by him that stocks are much below normal. In their own case the amount of lumber available for shipment within the next thirty days is only one-third of what their monthly average offering has been for the past five years and their stock is in no wise different from that of other manufacturers as a whole. Other observations worthy of note which reflect a careful review of the whole situation are to the effect that according to information sent out by the Department of Labor, the actual present day housing requirements of the United States is more than one million houses; four hundred and fifty thousand factories; more than six hundred thousand hotels; nearly five hundred thousand schools and public institutions; about fifty-five thousand apartments; fourteen thousand railroad stations and freight sheds, and twenty thousand theatres and churches.

The Government's estimate also is that the biggest building year the United States ever had was in 1916. It developed about one and a half billion dollars' worth of construction. The greatest volume of building material of all kinds that all the building manufacturers of the country turned out in a single year totaled in value barely two billion dollars. That was at the time when labor was plentiful and friendly to capital. To-day it is estimated that all the manufacturers of about three thousand kinds of building material and equipment which enters into the construction of modern build ing, cannot turn out a billion dollars worth of material, while the volume of business required at the present time would total four and a half billion dollars.

The pre-war dollar will to-day go further in producing buildings than will the same dollar expended in commodities in general. Although general commodities have been advanced 116 per cent. of what they were in the days before the war, construction costs have advanced only 60 to 100 per cent. over what they were prior to 1917. This in spite of the greatly increased freight rates since 1916.

Wages are higher than ever before. Rents have advanced throughout the country, so that buildings are a remunerative investment at present rentals, when they would not have been on the basis which obtained the early part of the year. There is little doubt but what ships will be much more plentiful next year than they have in the past, which will give China, Japan, Australia and the East and West Coast of South America, to say nothing of Europe, an opportunity to get lumber which they so urgently need.

Growth of Industrial Housing Scheme

Although Montreal has done little towards bringing into force the provisions of the Provincial Housing Act, other cities and towns in the province have taken preliminary action which should result in industrial housing schemes materializing next season. If these plans are carried into effect it will mean a considerable expenditure for lumber. From all parts of Canada come reports of a shortage of houses, due partly to the demand of our men coming home from the front, and partly to a disinclination to build, owing to the high cost of construction. Efforts are no doubt being made to meet these demands, but they are quite inadequate, and we must look to the provincial housing schemes, aided by the Federal grant, to supplement private enterprise. Even then, there will be a serious shortage of accommodation. As showing the urgent need of houses, it may be stated that the applications under the Act are nearly three times the amount available in the Province of Quebec, and that others have yet to come in. But, if anything substantial is to be done, quick action is necessary.

The city of Sherbrooke has been granted $500,000 toward a model garden suburb to accommodate 200 families. The money is to be expended through a housing company, which will commence operations in the spring. The city of Quebec is also getting in line, the proposal being to build a model garden suburb of 500 homes, to be known as the Confederation Garden Suburb. This project again will be handled through a housing company. At Ste. Anne de Bellevue, Hull, St. Lambert, St. Jerome and Three Rivers, schemes are under consideration, the first steps having been taken towards erecting a large number of houses. Quebec will want at least $1,250,000 and Three Rivers $1,000,000. In the latter place the need of houses is particularly pressing, owing to the industrial expansion there.

The pulp and paper companies have already done much in the way of providing suitable accommodation, believing that the schemes are of benefit to the companies as well as to the men. Laurentide, Ltd., the Abitibi Co., the Stadacona Paper Co., and St. Maurice Paper Company are a few names that occur to us, while the Riordon Pulp & Paper Co. and Kipawa Fibre Co. Ltd., have schemes, which will shortly go into effect, for erecting houses at Hawkesbury and Temiskaming respectively.

Possibilities of the British Market

At the request of the Canadian Trade Mission to England, the Canadian Pulp and Paper Association in June last decided to send Mr. A. L. Dawe, the secretary, to England to assist the mission in stimulating interest among the British importers of pulp and paper in Canada's production of these commodities. Mr. Dawe remained in England for three months, and the result of his study of the British markets is embodied in a bulletin issued by the Association. This deals very thoroughly with the situation, and gives some very pertinent pointers which apply to trades other than those specially studied. It is a well-written report, which is especially valuable at a time when Canada is making serious efforts to cultivate export business.

Mr. Dawe treats at length with the chaotic conditions in the paper business which followed the declaration of war, and also with the reimposition in April last of restrictions on imports from all countries except Canada and Newfoundland. The result of the restrictions was beneficial to this country, the lack of shipping facilities being the bar that prevented Canada from taking fuller advantage of her preferred position. In September the position was again changed by the removal of all trade restrictions. To quote Mr. Dawe: "Thus, the entire burden of retaining British business secured under the former favorable conditions and of making Great Britain a permanent market for their products, is placed upon the Canadian manufacturers. We have, unfortunately, the reputation of being opportunists in trade. This can be overcome if those firms who have already secured a footing in Great Britain will formulate for themselves and their representatives a definite trade policy which they are willing to maintain at all costs, remembering that export business is like advertising in that success lies in continuity of effort, the practice of keeping everlastingly at it. The British market is no place for weaklings or quitters. Unless a manufacturer is prepared to stick it out at all hazards, he had better not make a beginning. Even in the short time that I have been in England, the Canadian domestic markets recovered to such an extent that orders for overseas export, eagerly sought and thankfully received three months ago, no longer occupy such a favored position. It is open to question whether such a policy is fair to our accredited agents abroad or to the overseas consumer. The present partiality of British buyers towards products of the Empire is very real and may easily be turned into a valuable asset by the exercise of the same policy of fair play and courtesy that Canadian manufacturers extend to their domestic customers. Without it, the opportunity will be lost." The report refers in detail to the papers used in Great Britain, and expresses the opinion that the British market for newsprint should prove of prime importance in the near future.

On the subject of pulp, Mr. Dawe points out that the imports and general pulp business of Great Britain are closely associated with the British and Scandinavian Woodpulp Association, which consists of bona fide manufacturers of pulp as well as agents and merchants in the same commodity. One of the purposes of Mr. Dawe's visit was to endeavor to assist the Canadian Trade Mission in securing additional freight space for the large volume of pulp which was then ready to be shipped to England, but for which it had been impossible to obtain space. Mechanical pulp, necessarily, received the first attention as being the most urgent. As a result of the courtesy extended by the Shipping Controller, Mr. Dawe is able to report that the bulk of the mechanical pulp that was lying in Canada last May is now on its way to Great Britain. These shipments included pulp from the Chicoutimi Company and the Gulf Pulp & Paper Company of Clark City. Talks and correspondence with the leading British manufacturers indicate that there is every possibility of substantially increasing the quantity of Canadian easy bleaching sulphite pulp of good quality and not requiring more than 6-8 per cent. of bleach. The entire market in Great Britain of bleached sulphite is said not to exceed 30,000 tons per annum.

Splendid Work of Canadian Mission

Lloyd Harris of Brantford, who is returning to Canada after acting as Chairman of the Canadian Mission in London, Eng., for a considerable period, is a splendid type of a public spirited Canadian business man, who has devoted his best energies, talent and thought to the advancement of Canadian trade and the expansion of the overseas activities of the Dominion. This work has been one of faithfulness, foresight and devotion on the part of Mr. Harris who has been arduous in season and out of season in doing all that was possible to strengthen the commercial and industrial ties which bind Canada to the Mother Country. During the war and subsequently Mr. Harris has served the interests of the Empire in extending trade in all directions and fostering stronger and more vital business relations between Canada and Great Britain.

No greater tribute could be paid to the worth and high character of his labors than that which appeared recently in the London "Times," which stated that Mr. Harris had carried the Canadian trade banner and hoisted it in places where hitherto Canada had been but a name. The "Times" thinks that the work of Mr. Harris and the Canadian Mission points a moral to the British Government, its results being precisely those which the Department of Overseas Trade should achieve. Concluding it says,—"The Government would do well to study the methods of the Canadian Mission, and even better, to call some great business men of the dominions with their virility, energy and enterprise, to assist in a consultative capacity in the vitally important task of developing British trade in fields where they themselves have prospered."

Editorial Short Lengths

One billion feet of timber killed by 1445 fires is the estimate given for Montana's tremendous forest fire losses for the season just closed. Half of the fires were started by human agency and were preventable. The fires burned over 570,000 acres of land and were suppressed at a cost of $1,200,000, according to figures compiled by the forestry office at Missoula.

The construction of the World's Fair buildings in Chicago in the early nineties afforded the first large northern market for southern yellow pine, according to R. C. Bryant, Industrial Examiner for the Forest Service," its use being due to its relative cheapness. A great impetus was given the yellow pine trade in the Chicago and other northern markets by this development, the demand for the product rapidly increased and it is now marketed over a wide territory extending from coast to coast."

Canada is a young country and has not many of the traditions of the older countries of Europe and Great Britain where businesses of certain characters are handed down from father to son and have been in the family for many generations or centuries. It is, therefore, unique to find in the Dominion a lumber industry that has been conducted by one family for a hundred years. The story in the news columns of the "Canada Lumberman" regarding the history of the Johnston saw mill enterprise reverting from father to son for three generations is out-of-the-ordinary and especially in connection with lumbering, which business, from its nature, is regarded as evenascent or, more properly speaking extending over a few years at the most in any location. The name of Johnston in connection with timber operations in York county has long been an honorable one and the members have served the community well and faithfully. Its founders have been men of purpose and steadfastness, who played an important part in the settlement and development of the district.

Bad luck in business lies not so much in the stars as in the business man himself according to business statisticians. Eighty-six per cent. of the business failures in 1918 were classed as due to the individual, while only fourteen per cent. were assigned to outside causes. Among the factors of the eighty-six per cent. of failures, compilers of figures numbered extravagance, lack of capital, and speculation outside regular business.

Lack of capital is holding up thousands of enterprises which would go far toward meeting lack of employment and scarcity of production.

Thrift and rigid economy, both business and personal, must replace extravagance if the crisis engendered by the high cost of necessities is to be met. New capital can be produced most easily and most certainly through saving. Safe investment will add to instead of detract from the business assets of the nation.

"Lack of character is one of the chief contributing causes to commercial failure," according to a leading authority. Thrift, saving and safe investment not only are proofs of character, but developers of character.

Errors will happen in the best regulated business and the newspaper is not exempt from lapses of this kind. There is just this difference that when a private individual or corporation makes a mistake comparatively few know about it—in many cases only the seller and the buyer, the general public remaining in blissful ignorance. When an error finds its way into the public press or a trade journal there are hundreds who immediately spot it and wonder how such an inconceivable "bull" could be made. The critics forget that such inaccuracies occur every day in ordinary commercial life but are known only to a few while in the press, which reaches out in all directions, they are open and wide yet there are scores of people who imagine the oversight should never have occurred. There were until a few days age two reputable citizens of somewhat similar names residing in Toronto in the persons of Lieut.-Col. Robert Watson of the Hart House medical staff and Lieut.-Col. Robert S. Wilson, head of the Wilson Lumber Co. The former passed away and in publishing a picture a Toronto journal unfortunately used a cut of Lieut.-Col. Robert S. Wilson as being that of the departed gentleman. Of course, the latter is very much alive. The edition had been printed before the mistaken identity was discovered and there was no redress, except to make an apology and explanation the next day. Lieut.-Col. Wilson has naturally been the subject of many jocular references during the past few days. As a military man he has managed to survive the "attacks" and can be found every day at his office in the Confederation Life Building instead of at the cemetery or mausoleum.

The Timber Age is Coming—Not Going

It is a common error to suppose that timber is gradually being displaced by other materials and is constantly becoming less important economically. On the contrary, the new uses which are constantly being found for wood more than counterbalance the substitution of other materials. The per capita consumption of timber is increasing, not decreasing, and it is fair to state that, outside of food products, no material is so universally used and so indispensable in human economy as wood. Furthermore, it is a material which beyond question, can be and is being made very much more valuable to the community at large as a result of the timber research which is always going on.—W. Kynoch, Acting Supt. Wood Products Laboratories of Canada, Montreal.

One Hundred Years in the Sawmill Business

Outstanding Record of Historic Johnston Family, of Pefferlaw, Pioneers in Lumber Industry of Ontario—Early Days in Bush of York County

W. H. Johnston, Pefferlaw, Ont.
Third generation in sawmill family

"Here's your overcoat, Johnston! Now get! You're the biggest fibber in the party."

This was the injunction to W. H. Johnston, lumberman, of Pefferlaw, Ont., when returning from Toronto on one occasion. A company of lumbermen were assembled in the smoking car and began discussing who had seen the greatest number of logs cut from any one tree. Mr. Johnston had listened with interest to the conversation in which he had taken no part, but was finally compelled to participate in order to give his experience. When he replied that he had seen twenty-eight logs taken from one tree in Ontario, the others looked up in amazement, and one big operator handed the Pefferlaw man his coat and told him to clear out.

"Hold on!" said Mr. Johnston, "This tree was a most peculiarly shaped one. It was a white pine with a heavy trunk, and from that trunk there grew five large branches. It was the most unique tree that I had ever seen and was practically five trees in one. Nevertheless, we got twenty-eight logs from it which were sawed at my mill."

Talking about sawmills, the Johnston plant at Pefferlaw, a pretty village located some fifty-five miles north of Toronto, on the Canadian National Railways, is possibly the most historic institution of its kind in Canada, and the Johnston family has a record in the lumber industry that is not surpassed in longevity so far as the "Canada Lumberman" has been able to learn.

It was in 1906 when the C. N. R. was being built from Toronto to Sudbury, that the survey carried the line directly through a white pine bush which was on the farm of John Johnston, a cousin of Mr. W. H. Johnston. There were thirty-five pine trees which were sawn at the Johnston mill and they made 120,000 feet of 1", 2" and 3" lumber, which was sold to the R. Laidlaw Lumber Company, of Toronto. Mr. Johnston received one cheque from them for $2,884.61, which, considering the price that lumber was bringing in those days, was certainly a handsome return. In addition to the material sold to the Laidlaw Co., Mr. Johnston disposed of about $400 worth of stuff to other parties, and the total income from this grove, located along the bank of the Black River, which contained some of the finest pine trees ever seen by any lumberman, was over $3,000. The trees were possibly the largest of any ever sawn in this part of Ontario.

The Johnston family have been in the sawmill and lumbering game for practically one hundred years, and the mill has never changed hands, descending from father to son and then to grandson. True, the mill was burned a couple of times, but this did not deter the owner from going to the bush the next day and cutting timber to begin at once rebuilding operations. One hundred years is a long time in the life of any individual or institution, and that one sawmill should be operated for a century by three generations of Johnstons, is an outstanding event in the annals of the timber industry of the province.

In order that one may gain some idea of the early methods followed as contrasted with those of the present day, it is only necessary to recall that the founder of the business was Capt. Wm. Johnston, who was a native of Berwick-on-Tweed, Scotland. He followed a naval career and was captain of the "Blake," a British man-of-war, during the time that Napoleon was endeavoring to bring all Europe to his feet. The battle of Waterloo, fought one hundred and four years ago, practically terminated the military career of the little Corsican corporal. Then a large number of members of the army and navy got their discharge, and among them was Capt. Wm. Johnston, who was the grandfather of W. H. Johnston, the present proprietor of the business. Capt. Johnston came to Canada on a sailing vessel. The trip was tiresome and long, requiring three months to cross the ocean. He finally arrived in Montreal, and transportation by land in those days was about as slow as by water, and the retired naval officer decided to hoof it from the commercial metropolis to Toronto. He sent his luggage along by batteau, while he himself travelled afoot. En route he faithfully recorded each day's transactions in a diary. This was in 1816, and the entries afford a mass of information about the life and habits of the people of that period, and also gave a vivid description of the character of the country through which he passed. Some years ago the Department of Archives, Ottawa, learned of this most unique volume, and sent an officer to Pefferlaw to interview W. H. Johnston. The representative requested the loan of the diary and took it to Ottawa, and there it remains in the Archives, although Mr. Johnston, if possible, intends to secure it as a family heirloom.

Pte. Geo. K. Johnston,
"Princess Pats"
Fourth generation in sawmill family

From Toronto Capt. Wm. Johnston went up to Jackson's Point, on Lake Simcoe, where he took up land in Georgina Township. He was in receipt of a generous pension from the British Government, and, surveying the natural wooded resources on all sides, concluded that it would be a wise project to build a sawmill. Construction was begun on a dam at Baldwin, on the west Black River, four miles south of where he resided. Before the work was completed, the water was raised one night and the workmen informed Mr. Johnston that the dam and all material on hand had been swept away. Mr. Johnston never bothered going to see how great was the havoc wrought.

It was some time after this that the Captain was looking for his cow one morning as "bossie" had disappeared during the night. In following the trail, he met an Indian and asked him if he had seen anything of the missing animal. The Indian replied that there was no use of looking any further east as the river flowed on that side and the cow would not be able to ford the stream, and he had, therefore, better betake his steps in another direction. This led the pioneer to come and take up land at lot 23, concession 5, in the township of Georgina, where he soon discovered the lumber potentialities of the surrounding country. He

The sawmill of W. H. Johnston, Pefferlaw, Ont., which has been in the one family for a century. This is the third mill erected, two former ones having been burned

wanted some money to carry on construction work, and wrote to a brother in Scotland, telling him of the splendid location so far as water-power and the varied character of the timber were concerned. The brother forwarded a generous sum and suggested that he call the place "Pefferlaw," which was the name of a field on the old homestead among the heather-clad hills, and means a beautiful greensward.

Began Work of Erecting Mills

Capt. Johnston proceeded in 1823 to erect a sawmill, grist mill and woollen mill at Pefferlaw. The stones for the grist mill were imported from France and drawn from Toronto to Holland Landing by ox-team. They were then placed on rafts and poled along the shore to the mouth of the Black River, then drawn by oxen to their final destination. The Black River or Muckatoo, which is the Indian term for the stream, flows through Pefferlaw and empties into Lake Simcoe at Port Bolster, some four or five miles below the village. Just in front of Mr. W. H. Johnston's residence the Black River and Corner's Creek unite, and the location of the mill as well as the Johnston home is most attractive. It was necessary for Capt. Johnston to secure adequate water-power as soon as possible, and he began by building a dam on the river and connected the two streams with a race-way. Later he had one race-way built on the west side for the grist mill and another on the east side for the saw and woollen mills. It required the efforts of a neighbor one whole summer and fall to dig each of these ditches by the slow process of hand-labor. This man with a shovel, working many long hours a day, finally accomplished the task, and for each race-way, the excavator received his pay in one hundred acres of land, which was handed over to him by Capt. Johnston.

In viewing these water-courses to-day, the visitor can hardly conceive that such a large undertaking was successfully carried out by one lone hand. Capt. Johnston died on the 28th of March, 1851, and was succeeded by his son, George Johnston, who ran the mills and a general store as well. George Johnston died on March 6th, 1896, and was succeeded in the business by his son, W. H. Johnston, who was born July 19th, 1861, and is still at the helm. W. H. Johnston is one of the leading residents of York County, and, apart from the historic association of his family in the history of the county and the part they played in the development of the lumber business, he has always evinced much concern in the progress and welfare of the community in which he resides. Capt. Wm. Johnston had nine children, his son, George Johnston, the same number, and his grandson, W. H. Johnston is also the father of nine, seven of whom are living.

What Present Owner Has Done

W. H. Johnston has been running the sawmill and lumber business for himself since 1888 and previous to that conducted it for six years for his father, so that he has been practically identified with the operations for nearly forty years.

Capt. Wm. Johnston had three sons. He left the grist mill to James, the woollen mill to William, and the sawmill to George, the father of the present owner. The woollen mill was burned down some years ago, the grist mill passed into other hands, but the sawmill is still there by the dam and has cut as much as 2,000,000 feet during one season, which is a pretty good output considering its equipment.

In 1900 a planing mill was put up a little south of the sawmill by W. W. Corner, and in order to acquire full possession of the water-power and build a suitable concrete dam, Mr. Johnston bought Mr. Corner out in 1906 and erected one of the best dams to be found in any part of Ontario. There is 10 ft. head of water and an ample supply at all times. Mr. Johnston owns considerable deeded land in Brock and Georgina Townships and on it has yet 1,000,000 feet of timber to cut, consisting of pine, hemlock, cedar, maple, tamarac beech and basswood. The capacity of the sawmill is about 12,000 feet a day and it operates for a considerable period in the spring, and occasionally in the fall, as business requires. A considerable trade has been built up in custom sawing for the farmers and in supplying bill stuff for those who require it.

Both the planing mill and the sawmill are operated by water-power and the latter is well equipped, has concrete floors, a matcher, sticker, planer, rip-table, buzz planer, tennoner, etc. Here any kind of dressing can be done, moulding turned out and a certain amount of manufacturing of window sash and frames, as well as outside and odd-sized doors is carried on. A large business has been established with not only the surrounding country, but in connection with the summer homes built at Jackson's Point, Sutton and other points on Lake Simcoe. Mr. Johnston not only deals in all kinds of rough and dressed lumber, but in shingles, poles, posts, lath, lime and cement; in fact there is scarcely anything in structural requirements which he cannot supply.

The Black River furnishes abundant power for both the planing and saw mills. From the raceway a concrete flume leads to the planing mill, and from the penstock the water drops on a 32-inch Lafelle water wheel, developing about thirty-five horse power. At the back of the planing mill there has been built a solid wall of concrete to prevent the premises being flooded in the spring. At the sawmill, power is furnished in a similar way, the Lafelle turbine being 56 inches in diameter, furnishing seventy-five horse power. The logs are floated to the mill and from the log pond to a flat car which runs on a railway track down into the water and has spikes at one end to catch the timber. The car is hauled up into the mill by means of a bull wheel operated by a lever and chain pull.

Every spring the adjoining yard is filled with logs drawn in by farmers and others. These are rolled from the bank to the saw carriage. The equipment of the mill, while not modern, answers the purpose very well. The circular saw is 56 inches in diameter, with inserted teeth, and the carriage is 36 feet long, but, by means of an extension, timber up to 50 feet in length have been cut. The carriage is a hand feed one and after a slab has been taken off each side of the log the setting is done by a ratchet device. The slabs are cut into firewood by means of a butting saw, and the wood drops down into a hopper, from where it is drawn out into the yard. The edging is done by hand on a small circular saw. The bulk of the logs sawn during the past season were hemlock, cedar, spruce and pine. The saw carriage and saw jack were made by Paxton, Tate & Co., of Port Perry, Ont., when that firm was in business.

Public Spirited and Progressive Citizen

As already stated, Mr. Johnston built a fine concrete dam above the planing mill in 1906, and in 1913 constructed another concrete dam at the mill site, so that he is assured of ample power. He also owns a fine farm of over one hundred acres, and, outside of his business interests, is fond of motoring, both by land and water, and as a huntsman has managed for many years to secure his full quota of deer. He is a member of the Round Lake Hunt Club, which goes in search of the fleet footed animals every fall in the Nipissing district. The walls of his office are decorated with many spoils of the chase, suitably mounted, and his rifles are encased in a gun cabinet made from the wood of the first piano that ever came into Georgina Township. Another curio is an oak pulley, taken from the flagstaff of old Fort Garry, Winnipeg. Many other objects of interest are also seen.

Mr. Johnston has always been a public spirited citizen and served as deputy reeve of Georgina Township. He was also a member of the York County Council for some years, and was warden of the county in 1908, and, on the occasion of his retirement, was presented by his colleagues with a handsome gold headed cane. Some years ago Mr. Johnston was the standard bearer of the Liberal party in North York against the present member, T. Herbert Lennox, and conducted a spirited campaign, being defeated by only a few hundred votes. He is a member of the York Pioneers, having many Indian and other historic relics in his home, and also belongs to Malone Lodge, A. F. and A. M., Sutton, and Sharon Lodge, Queensville. In patriotic and other work he took a leading part during the war.

His eldest son, George K. Johnston, who is now associated with him in business, served overseas as a member of the Princess Pats, enlisting in September, 1915, and receiving his discharge in March last. He was severely wounded at Courcelette, a bullet going through his left arm and chest. This resulted in his being confined to the hospitals in France and England for some fourteen months. After his recovery he rejoined his corps and was in every fight in which they were engaged from Amiens to the capture of Mons. Another son, Robert, is in charge of the planing mill, while Mr. Johnston has two other boys, who will no doubt become lumbermen when they attain manhood's estate.

Changes Wrought by Father Time

Naturally Mr. Johnston has witnessed much development in the lumber business, and he well remembers as a boy when the Black River was filled with hewn timber on its way to the eastern markets. He has seen hemlock lumber sold at the mill for five dollars per M, and today it is nine or ten times that figure. He is an ardent supporter of afforestation, which, he believes, should be vigorously prosecuted by the government to ensure the perpetuity of our forest wealth, and as a measure of national conservation and thrift. It takes too long for coniferous trees to reproduce themselves in the lifetime of the ordinary individual, and as succeeding generations will reap the benefit of a progressive forestry programme, such work should be conducted in their behalf. In front of his home Mr. Johnston has a fine row of spruce trees, which he planted twenty years ago, thus giving practical evidence of the faith that is in him in the matter of silviculture.

How Workmen's Compensation Act Applies

Satisfactory Results That Have Been Brought About Through Its Administration in Sawmill and Logging Activities of Ontario—Safety Work Progress

By Frank Hawkins, Ottawa, Secretary of Lumbermen's Safety Association*

Frank Hawkins, Ottawa, Ont.

It is no longer necessary to apologize for safety work nor to explain what safety work means. It not only counts for the amelioration of suffering—the humanitarian bond of sympathy between the injured and those in a position to help—it counts for increased efficiency in the workshop or mill, and efficiency means increased production of better goods for less money, which in the last analysis means a larger opportunity to compete in the world's markets, in other words that "Safety is a paying proposition."

I think every one will concede this to be the case.

The question, therefore, resolves itself merely into one of method: that is of law and its administration.

When Mr. Price invited me to address you he suggested the subject: "Accident Prevention in Canadian Woodworking Plants."

In Canada we have our Provincial Workmen's Compensation laws just as you have here in the United States. The Association with which I am connected is the Lumbermen's Safety Association of Ontario. I therefore speak only from the point of view of that Province, and of our particular group. Class 1, which embraces lumbering, sawmills, manufacture of veneer, excelsior and cooperage stock. lumber yards in connection with mills, creosoting of timber, and kiln drying of lumber.

A further explanation is due to you in that our group does not take in woodworking factories. We have 34 classes or groups of industries operating under the Workmen's Compensation Act of Ontario.

It is reasonable to believe that comparison of laws and their administration adopted by various states and provinces may be of practical value. This is my apology then for referring only to the Ontario Workmen's Compensation Act and to Class 1 thereunder, in the hope that other papers presented at this Conference may, by inviting comparison and discussion lead to betterment in law and administration.

The Workmen's Compensation Act of Ontario came into effect the first of January, 1915, and at that time could only be regarded as legislation of the most advanced type. It completely abolished common law rights in so far as damage suits for accidents are concerned; it vested arbitrary powers in a commission appointed by the provincial government from whose ruling there is absolutely no appeal. It exempted railways from the operation of the act under schedule one, putting them in a separate class, together with Dominion Telephone, Telegraph and Express companies, Municipalities, etc. The whole cost of awards made by the Commission is payable out of the group funds contributed by each industry. The industries also pay a large proportion of the expenses of administration. Whether or not this whole subject of compensating the injured is a matter for Federal rather than State or Provincial legislation is a subject which might easily be considered in the near future.

The Protection of the Bread Winner

It is to be conceded that where the bread winner is incapacitated through accident some form of compensation is due not only for the injured himself, but in order to relieve suffering and want on the part of his wife and children or other dependents. From the point of view of the workmen, legislation of this character is much to be desired because under the old law he had to prove negligence on the part of his employer, otherwise he had no right to recover damages. If through negligence he contributed to the accident or if he were injured through the negligence of a fellow employee, or if he assumed the risk of the employment he was barred.

Under the old law if the employer and employee did not agree upon a settlement the remedy was an action in court. This meant long delay, annoyance, and great expense to one, or both of the parties, and, with the technicality and complication that prevailed, much uncertainty as to the result. The ordinary workman or his dependent widow shrank from such a proceeding or feared the danger of an appeal, or perhaps had not the money with which to proceed. [illegible] the other hand employers often suffered from vexatious litigation by irresponsible claimants. Under the new law, with its simple provisions and methods of procedure, settlements are made expeditiously and without expense to either party, and payments go direct to the person entitled.

On the other hand the employer was forced to defend all suits, with the possibility of a court judgment that might mean practically ruination and the consequent ill-will of both employer and employee. The employer is now relieved from all anxiety on this score as he can neither sue nor be sued for damages.

Representations made by the Lumbermen's Safety Association with regard to the Safety Associations being recognized by the Board as representing the respective groups of employers have been acknowledged, and favorably considered.

Adoption of Current Cost Plan

The Association has also urged the necessity that an appeal to some judicial tribunal should be had on certain general principles. We do not seek to appeal to such tribunal on the matter of awards made by the Board. This suggestion, however, is opposed by the Board as they are not prepared to recommend legislation of this character.

A recent amendment to the Act includes clerical employees, and on and after January 1, 1920, their salaries will be assessed just in the same way that the workmen are included. In similar fashion an employer or partner, or executive officer of any company, or a member of his family, if employed by the company, may be covered in precisely the same way as the workman by including a reasonable amount as salary in the pay roll, and so notifying the Board.

Another recent amendment increases pensions for widows and children. On April 24, 1919, a widow's pension was increased from $20.00 to $30.00, with an increase from $5.00 to $7.00 for a child, the maximum for all dependents being from $40.00 to $60.00 per month.

We have persistently urged against the building up of large reserves to provide for deferred liabilities and the Board has abandoned their former position in this regard. In other words, the Current Cost plan is now practically adopted by the Board. When it is considered that under the Act the Board may assess upon all industries or any one industry for any amount, and as often as the Board may deem fit, the necessity of building up large reserves is not apparent

Merit rating also is a settled policy of the Board. A workman cannot contract himself out of the operations of the Act.

Medical aid must be provided for as long as is necessary and an employer is prohibted from collecting any sum from any employee in any way toward medical aid; nor can any doctor collect anything from the workman for services covered by the Act. The employer must also furnish the necessary transportation for an injured employee to the doctor, the hospital, or the man's home. The cost of medical aid has added practically 15 per cent. to the amount of the assessments.

The gross revenue for the year (all classes) in schedule I amounted to	$4,319,439.98
Expenditures	3,474,769.09
Leaving a provisional balance of	$ 844,670.89

The various classes may appoint inspectors to examine and report on industries within their group, and persistent failure to carry out the betterments suggested by the Inspector renders that industry liable to pay individually the whole amount of any damages awarded, at the discretion of the Board.

Last winter our Inspector visited a number of camps and, in addition to ordinary safety work, his inspection covered hygienic and

*Paper read before Annual Congress of National Safety Association held recently in Cleveland, Ohio.

sanitary conditions, also first aid to the injured. It is proposed to extend this feature during the coming winter.

The Average Rate and Disabilities

In the year 1918, owing no doubt to inexperienced labor, the number of accidents in Class 1, increased to 1,160 as against 975 in 1917. But the number of permanent disability cases was reduced in 1918 by seven, and of deaths by four, as compared with 1917; leaving 1,069 temporary disability cases in 1918 as against 873 in 1917. The year 1918 was the first full year where medical aid was in operation. there being 212 that received medical aid only—i. e., there was no compensation paid—so that it was impossible to compare this with only part of 1917, when there were only 63 cases in which medical aid only was given.

The average rate (over all industries) per $100 of pay roll for the first year's operations in 1915 was $1.64, subsequently adjusted to $1.27; for 1916 the average rate was $1.09; for 1917, 98 cents, which is expected to be still further reduced for 1918. The rates charged for lumbering operations are per $100 of pay roll.

Sawmills $1.60
Logging or lumbering 1.20

It is claimed by the Board that a full measure of compensation has been provided and every reasonable effort has been made to avoid imposition.

Where work is sub-let the principal is responsible for reporting to the Board and is to see that all assessments are paid, and all returns made to the Board.

In this condensed fashion I have endeavored to carry out Mr. Price's suggestion to give you some idea of the operation and also some of the results obtained in the application of the Workmen's Compensation in the Province of Ontario, Canada.

While industries do not agree with the commissioners on all points it is only simple justice to say that the Board has administered the Act in a fair and impartial manner.

Labor, Capital and Public Service

We are finding out that the safeguarding of machinery, printing of bulletins, the holding of safety conferences, and indemnifying the injured is not the sum total of safety work. However estimable and just these things may be we must henceforth take a larger view of the human being. Our intercourse with one another now must be on the basis of "man to man." The old order has passed away or is rapidly passing. No longer may the arbitrary and overbearing manner of the capitalistic employer or the equally intolerant attitude of the labor agitator be able to hoodwink and deecive. An intelligent and fearless public opinion must enforce the rights of both capital and labor—it will supply the necessary ingredients whereby the wheels of progress may be efficiently lubricated and the great public service be uninterruptedly maintained. This is a great triumvirate: Labor—Capital—Public Service; and we must fully appreciate that what injures or affects one injures or affects all. We shall learn presently that a closed factory is a public loss, and the employer who interferes with public service by closing his factory must open it again at the public demand; and similarly the human factor must be brought to realize that the threat, "We will get 'ours'—or quit work"—will have to be replaced by something that will keep the workman at his bench, while at the same time giving him a contented mind and a fat pay envelope.

We must cultivate a community spirit between employer and employee—a spirit founded upon the rock of mutual confidence and esteem—every one must feel that the new order of things means justice and the square deal. This, I conceive to be a work for wich the National Safety Council is eminently manned and equipped to perform.

Improving and Elevating Lumber Business

Reforms Which Have Been Brought About Through Branding and the Progress Achieved by Means of United Action of the Manufactures

However harsh it may seem to say it, there can be no doubt that less average efficiency in advance is shown in modern politics than can justly be said of the conduct of other or private departments of modern affairs. Another curious aspect may be noted in the fact that the industries in spite of the habitually obstructive attitude, meanwhile, of the government toward them, even to the extremity of menacing public safety, private affairs have sustained themselves with wonderful vigor, resultant profit and progress, says a writer in "Lumber." It means comparatively less average capacity and honesty in public than in private life. It ought to be "the other way round," but however humiliating the confession, that is not so. Guile, in other words is in larger degree an attribute of the legislator than of the average citizen in a position to contribute strength, character and stability to the industrial community than legislation, with all its defects, has made it possible to prevent or rob it of. This is not saying that all politicians are bad or that all business men are good. It probably is a fact that there are more bad men in both departments of life than they individually realize or appreciate.

Very few persons, men or women, physically repulsive know it; the same is true morally of men who, evidently, cannot see what makes them unattractive, or "as others see them." The mere presence of men of this latter ilk creates an atmosphere that no matter how adroitly concealed, to the man of the world is not hidden, but betrays itself. By the same token, it, too, is equally within the power of the discerning to detect the presence of the traits that beget confidence and attract, not repel, even strangers. Often when one encounters a man essentially base and accordingly also repellant, one asks himself if such a man can have any real sense of his true character, or how other men regard him? It is then that one judges that the man does not know because if he did he never would be guilty of thus consciously making himself so—his instinct of self preservation against inevitable personal injury would settle that.

Lumber Industry an Example of Advancement

The point sought now to be raised is that of showing, for example, how the lumber industry as a result of the leadership, without which co-ordination can avail nothing, has passed from a state of primitive crudity to its present highly developed, more refined eminence in point of efficiency and its success—compelling powers of achievemnnt. The latter may have derived some part of its inspiration from a sense of needed self-protection against aggressive, competitive service, but, if so, very good. This department of "Lumber" has more than once held and sought to prove that service is the best attribute of competition, because a form of rivalry infinitely better than mere slaughter of prices. The latter is like bloodletting; it weakens, strangles and, carried far enough, would plunge the whole fabric of business into a state, more or less, of bankruptcy. Prosperity derives its sustaining vitality from but one all essential fountain of energy, and that, as everybody with a spark of conscious acumen in his make-up knows, is profit. Take away or seriously impair profits and with the same certainty that disease depletes physical strength, business is impaired and prosperity droops. This is one of the self-evidently enduring because changeless business principles that even that vaunted aggregation of purity and wisdom, the Congress of the United States, has never yet discovered; plain and unmistakable as it is, this is the gospel of a truth members of Congress have yet to learn. Why? There can be no other reason than that they are less concerned about the welfare of the country than anxiety about the security of their own tenures of office, their privileges, "honors" and emoluments. It would be idle to attempt even an ample epitome of the processes and agencies by which the lumber industry has attained to its present status among the major industries of this country. For the purposes of this article and wihin the space available to that end, to trace a single example of progression and its companion refinements should suffice.

The Advent of Branded Lumber

The advent of lumber branding reform about three years ago at a meeting at Jacksonville, Fla., of the Southern Cypress Manufacturers' Association, has been called epochal until the phrase has become trite. But after all, a form of expression become trite is its own sufficient certificate of charcter—it has withstood the wear and tear of time and repetition. I don't know the extent to which the country over, branded lumber is to-day a full-fledged vogue, but while not the only available means of either gaining or keeping a reputation in need of no special certificate, it not the less on that account is a thing that, whether adapted or neglected by the individual, nobody has had the temerity to object to or seriously or consistently find fault with it.

Upon his introduction of the measure, J. F. Wiggington, as chairman of the committee in charge of the preliminaries, in speaking of the motive prompting its purposes, or the sentiment that had inspired the movement, said in effect that there was not a member of the association who did not then know that cypress lumber occupied a particularly fortunate position in the lumber world, or one who did not feel that such position had its roots in the sincerity of purpose of members to harmonize their efforts in a manner to secure the best results consistent with the highest business principles. That was historical; a later declaration of principle was that the theory of the trade-mark brand is to build up a preferential demand based upon the collateral principle that its use would be that of "identifying it to the consumer." Right there is a kind of service that whether wholly competitive or partly altruistic signifies a refinement of business reciprocity than which it would be hard to imagine a policy or sentiment more salutary. Many a time, as the association records show, with some question of grading under discussion, the final vote would be determined by, not considerations of convenience, expediency or advantage, but the known wishes of consumers.

In the succeeding interval not only has the trade-mark with its attendant guarantees been perfected and, even by certain very large individual producers, but hand in hand with it have come other similarly judicious and public-spirited reforms now in force and effect in producing circles to a gratifying and supposedly a growing extent throughout the country.

Strongly Endorsed by Retail Trade

The whole subject, as now universally understood, has not only been endorsed by strong retail organizations, but by the same token manufacturers adopting it claim and no doubt believe that thereby to a very considerable extent, they have capitalized an asset consisting of well-earned reputations and by the same token serving to not only swell dividends, but a means of making business life morally worth living besides. It, more particularly, is held by adherents of the branding policy that there is no more doubt about the advantages of branding flour or any other commodity of high advertised standing than in branding lumber under like conditions. As already intimated, anybody can think of this proposition as he pleases; it is hardly thinkable that such or any other person would dispute the validity of it. Nobody has probably ever thought the operation of the protective principle involved would interest small purchasers, but apply only to sales and contracts too large to admit of personal selection or inspection. It, too, has been held a valid conclusion that objection to the theory wholly or in part, so far as its intrinsic merits are concerned, or without regard to possibly adverse individual interests, would, of necessity come from a class of competition unwilling from some cause to be bound by any such uniform code of self-imposed restrictions. It can be seen how an operator from any cause himself destitute of recognized standing or known to be in the habit of fraudulently mixing or otherwise arbitrarily lowering regular grades, could hardly be expected to take kindly to the restrictions under review. As declared by Mr. Wigginton at Jacksonville, the consumer, as a matter of equitable security of protection, is made a participating beneficiary, and in that particular factor, a spirit of comity is set up in the highest degree, commendatory.

Other Reforms Incidentally Akin

Simultaneously with the advent of, and in consonance with, the branding theory as against "anonymous lumber," other reforms have included sales of lumber to consumers, adulterating or lowerering standard grades and other ethical or moral restrictions of abuses in earliest days rife throughout the trade. As, in some part, an epitome of the whole subject, a formal declaration by the National Retail Lumber Dealers' Association, adopted several years ago, will, in conclusion, not be amiss, as follows:

"This association hereby endorses and will support the efforts of all associations of lumber manufacturers which are devising ways and means for the branding of the product of their members and thereby assuring within a reasonable variation, the integrity of the grade as well as making possible the identification of the stock with consequent protection to the retail dealer and the consuming public.

"Be it, therefore, resolved that we stamp withour approval the efforts being made by the various associations of lumber manufacturers to improve and elevate the lumber business by more careful grading and manufacture and that we in particular recommend the movement to hereafter brand all stock with the kind and grade."

Many More Houses Will Go Up Next Year

Altogether 93 municipalities have come under the Ontario Housing Act, including 18 cities, 43 towns, 18 villages, and 14 townships, while about 10 other cities and towns contemplate following their example. This means that all the cities in the province, with the exception of two, will take advantage of the Provincial Housing Commission's scheme and practically all the towns.

Appropriations aggregating $10,620,000 have been granted to 83 of the municipalites, and 70 of them are actually building. The others are developing their schemes and will put them into effect next year.

Windsor heads every place in the province with a building programme for 1919 of about 150 houses, while Hamilton, Oshawa and Niagara Falls are each constructing approximately 100 houses. Approximate figures for other municipalities are: Brantford, 30; New Toronto, 60; the Soo, 60; Ford City, 30; London, 20; Ottawa, 50; Paris, 20; Port Colborne, 30; Sarnia, 20; St. Catharines, 25; Sudbury, 30; York Township, 50; Iroquois Falls, 50; Hawkesbury, 50; Port Credit, 30. The whole of the houses at Port Credit are for returned soldiers.

"Next year," said J. A. Ellis, of Toronto, the director of the Provincial Housing Commission, "the municipalities contemplate erecting 4,000 houses at least. None of the other provinces, with the exception of British Columbia, has yet started actual building, so that Ontario is again the first province in the Dominion."

Windsor has the most ambitious scheme for 1920, planning to put up between 600 and 700 houses. Ottawa has already mapped out a scheme for the construction of 300 houses in the spring, every one of which is already taken. Niagara Falls contemplates erecting 300, while Hamilton can easily do the same.

The general average cost of the houses being erected in the province runs between $1,000 and $4,000 each.

Many New Uses for the Aeroplane

The Department of Agriculture at Ottawa has discovered a new use for the aeroplane. The Entomological Branch is investigating the mosquito in the Lower Fraser Valley in British Columbia. By using the aeroplane, the country can be surveyed in order to map out the swampy areas and other breeding places that are readily located in photographs taken from over head, according to a statement by Dr. C. Gordon Hewitt, Dominion Entomologist, that appears in the October Agricultural Gazette. The aeroplane was used in making a comprehensive survey of the complicated water system of the Fraser River and the adjacent bodies of permanent and temporary water in that district. A flight reported by Dr. Hewitt has demonstrated the possibility of using this machine also for making surveys of timber that is being killed or has already been destroyed by various insects. Its use, it is believed, will help very greatly in the entomological work with various insects being carried on by the Federal Department of Agriculture.

Veteran Lumberman Celebrates Golden Wedding

Mr. R. E. Jameson, who spent many years in the lumber business, and his wife recently celebrated the 50th anniversary of their wedding at the home of their daughter, Mrs. J. E. Davis, 845 Logan Ave., Toronto. The venerable couple are still in excellent health and were the recipients of many tangible tokens of esteem. Mr. Jameson is 80 years of age and was born in Waterloo County, while his wife (Miss Charlotte Eakins) was born in Oxford County 72 years ago. They were married at Eastwood October 27th, 1869. Mr. and Mrs. Jameson have a family of three children and two grandchildren.

Mr. Jameson, who retired from active work about ten years ago, is still a man of abounding good health considering his advanced age. He operated a saw-mill ot Lynden, Wentworth County, and afterwards in Culross Township, Bruce County. Later he conducted a planing-mill in Blythe. He then came East and resided in Trenton for many years and ran saw-mills at Bannockburn and Gilmour as well as conducting extensive timber operations in Hastings County along the Central Ontario Railway. Subsequently he owned a number of portable mills in that section of the Province until his retirement. Mr. and Mrs. Jameson have been residing with their daughter, Mrs. J. E. Davis in Toronto during the winters and spend each summer at Oakville, Ont.

Mr. Jackson Will Remain in Bay City

George D. Jackson of the Little Current Lumber Co., who has been manager of the Little Current Lumber Co., Little Current, Ont., whose mills and timber have been sold to the C. Beck Mfg. Co. of Penetanguishene, will not be connected with the new organization in any way. Mr. Jackson will devote all his time and attention to the Little Current Lumber Co.'s interests in Bay City, Mich., of which he is sec'y.-treas., and many Canadian friends will regret his absence from operations in Ontario. The Little Current Lumber Co.'s equipment consists of a double-cutting band saw, Wickes Bros. gang-saw, together with a full complement of edgers and trimmers. About three years ago the Little Current Lumber Co. built a new lath mill and it is a very nice plant.

Character and Not Money Builds Business

Senator Edwards Declares Every Successful Lumberman of Ottawa River Started with no Capital Except Courage, Honesty, Industry and Endurance

Hon. W. C. Edwards, Ottawa, Ont.

Hon. W. C. Edwards, head of W. C. Edwards & Co., the widely known lumber and woodworking firm of Ottawa and Rockland, Ont., was recently honored by the residents of the latter prosperous community on the occasion of the golden anniversary of the establishment of the Edwards mill in that town of which the veteran Senator is the father.

The occasion was a significant and memorable one from various standpoints and the tributes paid to Mr. Edwards were warm and sincere. He was presented with a handsome oil portrait of himself accompanied by an appreciative address which said in part:

"It is interesting to note that many old employees, some of whom came as mere lads when the business was first started, still remain in the service of the company, a silent tribute of their belief and faith in you, sir, and the other members of your firm. While we stand today among surroundings which are largely the outcome of your perseverance and ability, we recognize the fact that such results were not gained easily, but only after many reverses, which might have discouraged most men, were overcome."

The recipient was deeply touched by the evidences of affection and esteem in which he is held by the four thousand residents of Rockland and in his reply, gave a graphic and interesting sketch of his early struggles and the remarkable expansion of the industry of which for over half a century he has been the guiding spirit. The Senator, who is in his seventy-sixth year, has risen from the ranks in the lumber industry in which he has spent all his life. He recounted many amusing and timely incidents in his career and referred to the cordial relations which had always existed between his employees and the firm. Mr. Edwards has courage, optimism, perseverance and energy. These were his great outstanding assets and how he overcame many barriers and won his way to the front is narrated in his story which follows:

November 8, 1918, marked the fiftieth anniversary of the commencement of operations of the firm here, for it was on the 8th day of November, 1868, a cold, bleak morning, that I embarked on the old steamer Caroline of the Ottawa Forwarding Company at Thurso, where I had been formerly employed, and debarked at what is now the town of Rockland. You have today, I understand, a population of about 4,000 with well maintained streets, concrete sidewalks, three churches, three school houses, one of them a High School, numerous stores and shops and many comfortable homes, the greater number of which are the private properties of the employees of the firm. This is a result arising from the fact that several years ago the firm made a survey of a considerable portion of its property and building lots were sold to the employees at nominal prices, and lumber was supplied at a low cost and on easy payment to facilitate houses being built.

The firm also built a very considerable number of houses, which have always been supplied to actual employees at a nominal rental. So that with the two sawmills of existing proportions and the number of men employed not only here, but in Ottawa and other places, it must be admitted that great progress and development have been made, for the contrast is very considerable.

On a Bleak November Morn

To illustrate, I arrived at McCaul's Point, which is now Rockland, that bleak November morning alone. Two families were the only occupants at the time, the James McCaul and the Way families. These two small families composed the entire population of the immediate locality. The tools I carried with me on the steamer Caroline were two pick axes and three spades. The first employees were William Way and Magloire Lariviere, and with my own hands and their assistance I dug and prepared the foundation for the first mill erected in Rockland. The erection of the frame of the mill was carried out by contract with James Erskine. The machinery was obtained in Montreal and Ottawa, and the mill went into operation in May, 1869. The total quantity of lumber cut that season was 3,000,000 feet—a very small quantity as compared with the production for many years past. The results of the operations of the company have placed it among the very limited few who have succeeded in the lumber business on the Ottawa, as compared with the very large number who have failed of success. The fact is that only from three to five per cent. of those who engaged in lumbering on the Ottawa have been successful.

None of those who have succeeded began with what is popularly known as capital, namely, money. In every instance the successful

General view of the lower mill of W. C. Edwards & Co. at Rockland, Ont., affording some idea of the extensive character of the industry founded fifty years ago. This is known as mill No. 1, and in the distance can be seen Mill No. 2.

lumbermen of the Ottawa river, past and present, embarked in the undertaking possessed of no capital whatever, excepting their individuality, composed in greater or less degree of physical and mental capacity, courage, determination, industry, endurance and economy; together with a practical knowledge of the business; and, last but not least, the quality which brings confidence and credit, namely, character and honesty of purpose. For, after all, these are the qualities which are the basis and mainspring in all the business of the world, and are the major portion of the capitalization of the industry.

More Than Mere Money Required

So-called capital, composed of an article popularly called money, cuts but a very small figure, relatively; and no amount of it will ensure success in lumbering on the Ottawa without the vital qualities I have named.

I think that I may fairly claim that the general testimony would be that I possessed in greater or lesser degree the essential qualities

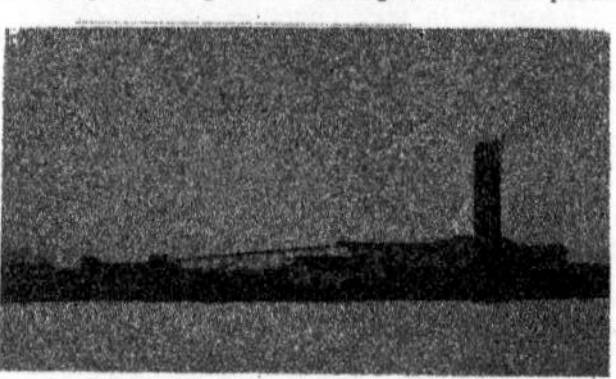

View of Mill No. 2 of W. C. Edwards & Co. at Rockland, Ont. This is sometimes known as the Upper Mill

for success which I have named, and that to my efforts and constant hard work is due a reasonable share of the success of the company.

But, no matter how constant, energetic and skilful I might have been, how helpless I would have proved in my efforts toward what has been attained without the helpers and the laborers who have been my constant aid in each department of the undertaking.

For many years I worked side by side with the employees of the firm, for there was no department of the work in which I could not and did not engage with my own hands, from the cutting and hauling of the logs in the woods to driving the streams and manufacturing and shipping the lumber, and there was no employee in any single operation of the business in the woods, on the river, in the mills, boiler houses or engines, whose place I could not fill, and did not fill for days and weeks at a time on very many occasions. At no time in my business career have I ever asked an employee to do anything whatsoever that I would not do myself.

This very close intimacy with the working man and his work instilled in me the greatest possible regard for honest labor, and throughout my life there never has been a time I would not go farther to take off my hat to greet an honest conscientious workman than any other class of any community, from the highest dignitaries in the land downwards, and none it gives me greater pleasure to meet than a worthy old employee.

Sixteen Hours a Day for Him

Changes that have taken place are in the reduction of hours of work, which have been greatly lessened. No lessening of hours could take place in the operations in the woods, for the reason that in the northern latitude in winter we have but a few hours of daylight each day. It was not 10 or 12 hours a day that I worked, but, for the greater part of my life, 14 to 16 hours.

The war is over so far as the destruction of human kind is concerned, and the world will recover. But certainly not on the basis on which it is now operating. Now, what is the remedy? None but the following—to labor, produce, economize and trade. In due course, and before we are much older, the world will starve for both food and clothing if present conditions continue. The former wealth of the world was made by producing and trading, and the remedy for the present most unfortunate condition cannot be accomplished by any other means. Two further factors for the enrichment of the world would be disarmament and general prohibition, and, if, in addition, world free trade were proclaimed and put into effect, mankind would prosper as never before, and the peace of the world be guaranteed.

The unfortunate popular idea that there are amassed enormous fortunes, in an article called money, that can and ought to be distributed among mankind, is a most unhappy fallacy and delusion. The property and labor of the world constitute its wealth, and with [illegible] normal cessation of labor, property soon loses its value.

Labor is Great World Wide Factor

Actual money cuts a very small figure in the world's affairs. Labor is the great factor in the production of the world's necessities and confidence and credit are the mainspring and primary foundations. The present aspect of the world's affairs is all in the direction of a most serious limitation of production, and the positive destruction of confidence and credit; and with the wheels of production [illegible] commerce thus clogged there can be but one outcome, starvation.

It is true that this very unhappy condition is greatly more [illegible]gravated in Europe than in the United States and Canada, but th[illegible] [illegible]sidious impression has been transported and permeates this side [illegible] the water, to a certain extent, but perhaps less in Canada than [illegible] United States, and certainly less on the Ottawa river than in [illegible] parts of Canada. It is remarkably absent as between your[illegible]selves and the firm of W. C. Edwards and Company. For here [illegible] are today giving testimony of the fact that for a period of over [illegible] the best of cordial and amicable relations have existed between [illegible] and your employers in a most singular and exceptional manner.

The portrait in oil, which was presented to Mr. Edwards, was painted by G. Horn Russell. It is a head and shoulders picture splendidly executed and attractively framed, and Mr. Edwards has the appreciated gift hung up in his beautiful home in Ottawa.

The reference to the jubilee of the Rockland mills has been held over for some time by the "Canada Lumberman" in order that illustrations might be presented of the historic plants. It took several days to secure these and it is a pleasure to present in this number views of the busy industries which have been built up through the energy, foresight and vision of Hon. W. C. Edwards and his associates.

Company to Specialize in Railroad Supplies

A charter was recently granted to the T. M. Partridge Lumber Co. Limited, Rainy River, Ont., which was formed for the purpose of taking over the interests of T. M. Partridge of Minneapolis, Minn., who has operated in the Rainy River district for several years. The officers of the new company are President, T. M. Partridge and Secy.-Treas.; H. F. Partridge, Minneapolis. The timber limits of the organization are situated in the wild land Indian reserve and also on the Lake of the Woods in the vicinity of Rainy River. The company propose to produce white cedar poles, posts, piling, tamarac ties and piling and other railroad supplies. The output will be marketed in the western provinces of the Dominion where an extensive business has already been developed. The company anticipate selling the saw timber produced from their lands for the present, although there is a probability of constructing a mill at Rainy River if conditions in the future warrant doing so.

Heavy Lumber Imports from B.C.

During the first eight months of the present year an aggregate of 760,554,000 board feet of lumber has been imported into the United States, duty free, from various foreign countries. Nearly all this comes from British Columbia. This is an average of approximately 95,000,000 feet per month.

The volume of lumber imports, according to the monthly reports of the bureau of foreign and domestic commerce, has been increasing from month to month, since the first of the year.

For the month of January the volume of boards, plank and other sawed lumber imported into the United States was 54,241,000 feet, besides 10,688,000 pieces of lath and 137,818,000 shingles.

By March the lumber imports had increased to 66,362,000 feet and lath to 15,480,000 pieces while shingle imports had dropped for that month to 97,843,000.

In May the lumber imports went up to 155,644,000 feet, lath to 46,124,000 pieces and shingles to 229,271,000.

The August imports were 139,742,000 feet of lumber, [illegible] lath and 194,548,000 shingles.

The average monthly imports of lumber during 1918 were approximately 100,000,000 feet, of lath 50,000,000 and of shingles 140,000,000. All came in duty free.

A district logging engineer with headquarters at Missoula reports that he has seen cedar trees more than 2,000 years old, still alive and growing in the Kaniksu forest which is in the extreme northeastern corner of Washington. "These trees," says the engineer, "varied in size from a foot to ten feet in diameter. I used a boring instrument on them and found that the trees were in all cases 2,000 years old and some of them nearly 3,000. The wood is firm and is a potential source of high grade timber."

Reducing Accidents in Logging Operations

The One Remedy that is Certain Preventative is Carefulness—Specific Instructions on Various Methods of Work and Use of Equipment

By James Boyd*

Logging operations procure the source of supply for the lumber manufacturing plants. Accidents happen, but in most instances they result in minor injuries. It is rare that many men suffer injury at one time, because as a rule they work in groups of two or three. Still, one operation reports 183 personal injury cases in 1918.

The best statistics on the subject have been propared by Henry Burr, Vice-President of T. H. Mastin and Company, Kansas City. The experiences of this organization over a series of years, which insures lumber companies only against liability and workmen's compensation, is that 39 per cent. of all accidents in lumber operations are in the logging department of which 21 per cent. are in the woods and 18 per cent. on the logging railroads. The cost of the accidents in the logging department is 21 per cent. of the cost of all the claims in the lumber industry and that in the railroad department is 20 per cent., or a total of 41 per cent. of the entire cost of personal injury.

Mr. Burr has prepared the following figures showing causes of accidents in percentage to the total number of accidents reported:

	Per cent.
Log cutting	45
Skidding by power	15
Loading by power	18
Skidding by animals	2
Loading by animals	3
Hauling by animals	8
Swamping	4
Unclassified	5

In the operation of the logging railroads the following causes contribute in the percentage shown:

	Per cent.
Operation of cars	26
Maintenance of way	46
Unloading logs	8
Accidents in pond	5
Coupling cars	4
Boarding and alighting	4
Unclassified	3

Bulletins of the National Safety Council have done good work in lessening the number of accidents in operations where they have been used. A company began posting bulletins in 1916; that year it had 272 accidents; in 1917 the number was 225, and in 1918, 183.

Those companies which do not change men often have few accidents. Some of them avoid putting green men in places where there is a possibility or likelihood of an accident, using the new men in places where there is not a great deal to be done, and practically no risk, until they become sufficiently acquainted with the requirements of the work so they can throw around themselves the necessary precaution. Others employ only competent men, and require those in charge of operations to keep a careful watch over their men and see that they take no unnecessary risks.

The Choctaw Lumber Company, Broken Bow, Okla., maintains a Welfare Department under the direction of J. W. Clark. Part of the duties of this department relate to a reduction of accidents. Each employee is given a small book which gives directions for the prevention of accedents. Here are the instructions for the Woods Operations:

Open Letter to Woods Foremen

1. Instruct every man who is new in your crew regarding his duties and point out to him where he may meet with danger. New men are more liable to accident.
2. The axe and the saw teeth are the cause of most minor injuries to logging men. Keep this idea before your men.
3. Falling trees with the cutters is the cause of most all deaths from accidents in the woods. Keep the men on the lookout.
4. Catching logs on the move injures men and may cause death if the cant hook should fail. Stop this practice; some one on POLLY the year 'round from this carelessness, two at the present.
5. Keep the safety idea before your men all the time and make a record for your crew.
6. Co-operation among the men in the woods, as the swampers and the teams, the saws and the haulers, and the men and the foremen, is of absolute importance; foremen see that this condition is maintained.
7. Men who refuse to use ordinary precaution among their fellow workmen will have to be replaced.
8. Keep the women and children in mind when you think of Safety First and it will be easier.

Open Letter to Workmen in Woods

1. We have a desire to see every man on his feet and making his own way in the world and wish to help you.
2. Carelessness causes 90 per cent. of the accidents of industry. Cut out your part of the carelessness and you have done your part.
3. The axe, the saw, and the falling tree are the arch enemies of the woods department.
4. Always strike with the axe aimed out and from the body and there can be no injury with the axe.
5. Don't treat the Safety idea lightly; it may save your life and keep your children from being orphans.
6. A crippled man is not a man; he is only part of a man. Be a whole man.
7. Industry needs every man of us. Let's work together that all may be happy.
8. We have SAFETY FIRST rules now and I am asking every one of you to co-operate with each other and with the foreman to make your department free from injury. We should all be better for the rule.

Mr. Clark publishes a monthly paper as part of his work. Following is the "Safety First Department" from a recent issue:

The Safety First Department

The accident record for the month is very good. One hand badly hurt in the Bismarck planer mill, due to "carelessness and awkwardness," as the injured man puts it. It might have been a wrist as well as the two leaders in the hand. Be on the lookout at all times and stay away from danger.

The new floor in the machine shop is a much needed improvement and will aid in preventing accident. Uneven floors are dangerous.

W. L. Douglas was hit by a falling limb at Broken Bow camp. This is a type of injury that can't well be avoided at times. Eternal vigilance will help.

One man injured at each camp by axe cuts. These appear too frequently. The foreman should point out this danger and then the men should quit chopping toward the feet; chop out from the body and you can't cut your foot. It will take more time to do this, but it will save you a foot, perhaps.

The cleanest place on the job is the car shed of the Bismarck car repair men. These men could keep a house neat and orderly.

A health pamphlet and a safety first pamphlet will be sent to each working hand this week. Read these and then take them home and keep them. I have done several weeks of hard work in preparing them and I know the material they contain is authoritative. We mean to send much of this to your home and ask you to keep it and try to get good from it.

The one remedy that is a certain preventative of all accidents is carefulness.

*Paper read before National Safety Council at eighth annual Congress held recently in Cleveland, Ohio.

Louisville is After New Industries

The town of Louiseville, P.Q., is anxious to secure additional industries. The Tourville Lumber Mills Co. have a very fine sawmill in the town, manufacturing over 20 millions feet of lumber, mainly for export. The town offers a bonus to any company which will locate there and which can offer guarantees. The population is 2,000, with 1500 in the vicinity, and a good supply of labor is, we are informed, available. The town is on the C.P.R., 20 miles west of Three Rivers, and is situated on a navigable river. All particulars can be obtained from the mayor.

What Aggressive Yardmen Are Saying, Doing and Planning

Progressive Retail Lumber Merchant of Quebec

L. Hamel, Quebec City, Que.

L. Hamel, who was recently elected Vice-President of the Quebec Retail Lumber Dealers' Association, is General Manager of the E. T. Nesbitt Regd. and is one of the most progressive citizens in the ancient capital. Mr. Hamel spent some twenty-two years in the employ of the late Mr. Nesbitt, who died two years ago, and became proprietor of the business in May last. Born in Quebec in 1875 he showed an aptitude for business at an early age. After completing his education, he entered the service of E. T. Nesbitt, and the expansion of the business of late years has been very satisfactory. The capital stock has been increased many times and the annual turn-over is now exceptionally large. The company employ about one hundred men and has shown initiative, courage and aggressiveness. Mr. Hamel was elected a director of the Association of Contractors at the beginning of the present year and has always taken a deep interest in the welfare and uplift of similar organizations. At the last municipal elections he was made a member of the city council, representing Limoilou district, and, possessing public spirit, business ability and thorough knowledge of the needs of the community, Mr. Hamel has proven himself to be a live representative. He is a member of St. Jean Baptiste Society and interested in several benevolent bodies. Of an agreeable personality and pleasant manner, he makes friends on all sides.

The planing mill and factory of the company, of which he is at the head, are located on the 10th Ave. Limoilou Ward. The company manufacture sash, doors, mouldings, boxes, etc., as well as deal in lumber and also carry on considerable construction work making a specialty of wooden buildings. Mr. Hamel has always been an ardent supporter of organization and all get-together movements and is enthusiastic over what has been accomplished by the Quebec Retail Lumber Dealers' Association since its inception nearly three years ago.

Effective Advertisements for Retail Lumbermen

The Long-Bell Lumber Co. of Kansas City, Mo., who are wide advertisers of trade-marked lumber, not only believe in live publicity for their own product but also in co-operating with the buyers of Long-Bell lumber in making the demand for this line more active and aggressive. The latest move on the part of the Long-Bell Lumber Co. is to institute an attractive advertising service for retail lumber dealers and circulate several thousand copies of a neat booklet containing striking advertisements. These are gotten up in convenient sheet form and the one, two or three column cuts are supplied by the company free of charge. All that the advertiser has to do is to write away for the cuts and hand them over to the local newspaper publisher along with the accompanying reading matter, which may be changed to suit the particular needs or special purposes of any retail lumberman.

In connection with this service the Long-Bell Lumber Co. sample advertisements which have been prepared by their advertising department will be found of much interest.

One paragraph alone sets forth the object of this new feature and here are the words:—"Every lumberman is well aware of the wonderful power of advertising. It is the most stimulating element in business to-day and there never was a time like the present to put the merits of one's goods before the buying public. These are prosperous times. "Build Now" campaigns, "Home Owning" campaigns, reasons for the necessity of better farm equipment, etc., have covered the nation. The building idea is strong and growing and a little local boost to the movement on your part is bound to show real and tangible results."

How Retailer Should Write His Ads.

A lot of you are going to stop right here and say that this is a foolish thing to write about because you have nothing to sell.

Grant that—just to avoid argument—but this title still holds good. Note that it is on the writing of ads., says J. C. Dionne in the "Lumber Co-operator."

Perhaps it hasn't struck some of you that the first step in writing an ad is to have something to write.

Many of you have filled newspaper space with words—but how many ads did you ever write?

Olendorff could converse in French about the straw colored [illegible] of his aunt, but that wasn't a particularly interesting subject for many people.

You can mention "Wood, Cement, Lime and Coal," but that doesn't give much food for thought to man who has a [illegible] floor or a hen house in mind. Chances are he doesn't even think of what those things he wants are made of.

Before you write "an ad" you should know thoroughly two things—at least—and those are 1st, what you have to sell, and 2nd, how that thing will benefit your reader.

And if your ad doesn't contain the answers to these two points, your ad is worse than wasted.

So then, when we speak of the "writing of ads," we speak of the preliminary work of "getting ready to write the ad."

Just go over what you have to sell; even if you don't write a single ad, that investigation will be of value to you, for it will show you a lot of things you didn't know you had.

How about stock? Plenty? What kinds and amounts? What sorts of things can be made from that stock? How about prices? How about conditions? Any special grades or species or materials?

Then how about Service? Deliveries? Accounting? Credits? Plan-book services? Information? Construction aids?

How about your office? Pleasant? Clean? Suggestive Displays?

These are a few of the first and main things to consider.

List them—answer them—and the first thing you know you'll find the best ads you ever wrote lying on the paper in front of you.

It's a great indoor sport these days. Give it a whirl.

New Retail Firm Starts Operations

Carl Sorensen & Co. of Port Arthur, have begun operations in the logging line in the vicinity of Fort Frances, where the firm have a large block of timber land, which is adjacent to the Canadian National Railway. It is the intention of Mr. Sorensen to erect a sawmill at a convenient point for the purpose of cutting the logs, which will be shipped to Fort William. The company will also take out large quantities of cedar posts, for which an unlimited market exists in Western Canada.

Mr. Sorensen was for many years connected with the Shevlin interests in Minnesota and Dakota, coming to Port Arthur some eight years ago and establishing the Lakeside Lumber Company, which he disposed of when the war broke out. During the past two years or so he has been secretary-treasurer of the Terminal Land and Investments, Limited, owners of large real estate holdings in Fort William and Port Arthur.

It is the intention of the firm of Carl Sorensen & Co. to establish a lumber yard at Fort William and find a market for their lumber in both cities. In addition to cutting on their own behalf, they have placed contracts for large quantities of lumber with contractors, so that when they are ready to begin business in the two cities next spring, they will have full stocks of building material.

Lumbermen's Organizations Will Hold Annuals

Arrangements are being made for the annual meetings of the various Lumbermen's Associations. That of Wholesale Lumber Dealers' Association, Inc., will be held in Toronto on January 9th, and the Lumbermen's Credit Bureau annual will be on the same day. The Lumbermen's section of the Board of Trade will meet and elect officers for the coming year on January 2nd. The annual convention of the Ontario Retail Lumber Dealers' Association will be held in Hamilton during the early part of February. It is likely that a two days' convention will take place and the dates will be announced later.

The Busy Retailer and Some of His Present Day Problems

Selling Lumber by Use of Telephone

Do you make good use of your telephone in getting after new business or simply wait until you hear it jingle, and then take what ever orders come in over the line. There is no reason why the instrument should not be made to do service for the retail lumberman for, by its use, he can get in touch with many customers and prospects, not only in his home town but in the surrounding country.

The telephone opens up numerous avenues of new business when rightly employed and should prove a splendid result producer. Its possibilities are almost unlimited and yet, in many offices it is a thing quite outside the actual reception of orders or listening to inquiries. It should serve as a salesman and can be used to advantage on divers occasions and with effective results. The best way to find this out is to make a systematic and persistent effort and see what business can be brought in through its agency, intelligently directed.

It is especially important that telephone selling be done at opportune times.

Take the case of the dealer who goes after farmers' trade. Any old time of day is not always a good time to call up a farmer—as illustrated by the dealer who called a farmer at ten o'clock one forenoon. The farmer was not very far away from the house—but he was very busy in the field. When he finally came to the telephone, Mr. Dealer got an eye-opener.

"Do you realize," said Mr. Farmer, "that farmers are mighty busy in the fields this time of year and a half hour in the field at this time of day is worth a whole lot more to me than coming to this telephone and chewing the rag with you about my future lumber requirements or building intentions."

That wasn't all that Mr. Farmer said but when he had finished, the dealer had learned that noon, night or stormy days are surely the best times to telephone farmers about goods you do not definitely know they are in the market for.

It is a good plan to study your customers and time your calls. Decide when they are most likely to be in need of your merchandise, then call them where there is the least chance of their being busy. Results are apt to be especially good on rainy days, when outside farm work is slack.

A dealer once figured that before he placed his orders for fence posts, it would be a good scheme to get a line on the probable requirements of his trade as this might allow him to buy enough posts to get a quantity price. So he called up a list of forty or fifty farmers one day, told his proposition and was happily surprised to get enough orders to make two carloads.

This instance points out another very important requirement in telephone salesmanship.

Always have a good reason for calling up.

It is not wise to call up in a general way and merely ask a party if he wants anything in your line. Have one or more definite items to suggest or offer.

Sometimes it is best, of course, to offer the conversation along general lines to warm up a customer—like the dealer who called up the farmer who was road commissioner in the town. He first asked him for some road information and complimented him on a new piece of road. Finally the object of the call was stated and a sale was made easily.

The average lumberman constantly has numerous opportunities to make his telephone one of his best business builders. Besides making direct sales, it affords him a wonderfully efficient way to keep in close touch with the building intentions of his trade—and that is the best developer of new business.

Of course there is nothing equal to the personal call to convince a customer of the merchant's real interest. But the telephone is the best substitute.

Business Good in Georgetown District

J. B. Mackenzie of Georgetown, Ont., who is secretary of the local retail lumbermen's association, states the annual meeting will be held about the middle of December for the election of officers and for a review of the business of the past session. It is also expected that problems arising for the coming year will be discussed and considered. Mr. Mackenzie reports that the building trade has been good in his district and that the prospects for its continuance are bright as should building operations ease up in towns, farmers have a great many repairs to make which have been deferred by lack of skilled help.

Public Spirited Lumberman Who Gets There

R. H. Spencer, Trenton, Ont.

R. H. Spencer of Trenton, Ont., is a gentleman widely known, not only in lumber circles but also in the ranks of Masonry particularly in the Eastern part of Ontario. He has been associated with Gill & Fortune, lumber, merchants of Trenton, ever since they bought out Messrs. Gilmour & Co., nearly fifteen years ago, and has had full charge of their accounting. Before that he was with the Gilmour firm and previous to that was chief accountant of the Central Ontario Railway for seventeen years. This line is now part of the Canadian National system. Mr. Spencer is a progressive citizen and finds time, outside of his active business duties, to serve his fellows as a member of the Town Council, and as secretary-treasurer of Board of Education.

In Masonry he has always been a leading light and his record in the craft has been one of advancement and devotion to duty. This was recognized at the annual meeting of the Grand Chapter, R. A. M. in Toronto in June last when he was elected Grand J. He made his first acquaintance with the craft in 1893 when he was initiated into Trent Lodge No. 38 of which he became Worshipful Master four years later. He was D. D. G. M. of Prince Edward District No. 13 in 1909-10, and was exalted in St. Marks Chapter, R. A. M. No. 26 in 1895, becoming Z of the Chapter in 1903. R. W. Bro. Spencer was Grand Superintendent of Prince Edward District No. 11 in 1905 and for many years has been on the Executive Committee of the Grand Chapter. He is also a member of King Baldwin Preceptory, Knights Templar, No. 6, Belleville, and during the past year was Grand Constable of the Sovereign Great Priory of Canada. A member of Remeses Temple Mystic Shriners of Toronto, he is an indefatigable worker in any line to which he directs attention. Mr. Spencer was born in Camden Township, Addington County, and was educated in Newburgh and Napanee, and started his career by teaching a rural school.

Eastern Company Had Good Season

A charter has been granted the E. C. Atkinson Lumber Co. Limited, with headquarters at Gagetown, N.B. The officers are: President and Treasurer, E. C. Atkinson; Vice-Pres., Peter Mahoney; Secretary, Abner B. Belyea. The extent of the company's operations include a cut this year of 4,000,000 feet of lumber, 2,000,000 feet in the parish of Southampton, York County, and 2,000,000 feet in and around Gagetown, Queen's County.

The Atkinson Lumber Co. are also operating one stationary mill at Southampton, and a portable mill near Gagetown. They have timber limits, leased and soil right, and also standing timber to the extent of 1,000,000 feet, and have about 25,000,000 feet more under option. The company are associated through their sales end of the business with W. Malcolm McKay, Limited, lumber exporters, St. John, N.B., and are just closing a satisfactory season.

Lumber Stocks Will Cost More

Writing to the "Canada Lumberman" a leading lumber firm in the Muskoka district says:—We have two camps in but the number of pieces on skids is away short compared with the same date last year when we had only one camp. Men have been very hard to get.. However we expect to get fairly well filled up between now and December 1st. Wages are about the same as last year, $70.00 per month being the rule, while camp supplies in most lines are higher. As far as we can learn the stock being taken out in our vicinity will not be any greater than that of last year but will cost more per thousand feet. Our mill started cutting about the middle of last April and closed down on September 9th, cutting out a stock of about 4,000,000 feet.

Interested in European Operations

Brig.-General W. B. R. Hepburn, C.M.G., M.P., Picton, Ont.

Brig.-General W. B. R. Hepburn, C.M.G., M.P., Picton, Ont., who recently arrived in Canada after a three and a half years' active service with the Canadian Forestry Corps, has been at Ottawa during the past few days attending to his legislative duties. He was warmly welcomed back to the capital after an absence of several years. Brigadier-General Hepburn was re-elected representative for Prince Edward County while he was overseas. Major-General Alex. McDougall, who was in charge of the operations of the Canadian Forestry Corps in Great Britain and Brig.-General Hepburn have started business in London, England, under the title of Timber Operations & Contractors Ltd. Their headquarters are at 11-12 Pall Mall, London. They expect to carry on business generally throughout Europe. Gen. Hepburn will return to England at an early date in connection with his interests but does not expect to reside there permanently. His native town is Picton, Ont., where he is well known and for many years was connected with steamship companies, beginning his career as a purser and becoming President and General Manager of the Ontario & Quebec Navigation Co., and also President of Hepburn Bros., Ltd. He has sat in the House of Commons, representing Prince Edward County since 1911 and politically is a Conservative Unionist.

Price Bros. Erecting New Sawmills

Price Bros. & Co., of Quebec, are erecting several new sawmills, which will add greatly to their production of lumber. They have commenced to knock down the old mill at Matane and will build a new one which it is hoped to have completed by May 1st. The equipment will consist of one double-cutting band saw, one single-cutting band saw, two horizontal band re-saws, two Champion Waterous edgers, lath mill, etc., in fact the whole equipment for this thoroughly modern plant is being supplied by the Waterous Engine Works Co., Limited, of Brantford. Price Bros. & Co. are also erecting a duplicate sawmill at Rimouski and at Metis, as well as a smaller mill at St. Juste, besides making drastic changes in their St. Marguerite mill.

In regard to logging operations, Price Bros. do not expect to have more than five camps of their own, as most of their logs are supplied by contractors. The company expect to cut about 200,000,000 ft. this winter if they have a favorable season for woods operations. They do not find the labor situation at all satisfactory as help is hard to get and wages very high and men are independent. The company are installing a new paper machine at Kenogami, which will be in operation some time during the winter. It is the same width as their present machines and will add about fifty tons a day to their output of newsprint.

The Passing of Veteran Shipbuilder

John B. Young died recently at Lunenburg, N. S. He was with the old firm of J. D. Eisenhauer & Co. for many years, but in 1894 started out for himself and built a number of vessels in the shipyard on his own premises, for his own banking and freighting trade. For several years Mr. Young gave up building schooners, but, in response to the great call for tonnage, he installed up-to-date machinery last year and produced a number of fine ships. The salt bulk and frozen herring trade always interested Mr. Young and his schooners have gone to Newfoundland in the business for many years. He also operated a large store and was a successful business man.

Kraft Pulp Producers Handicapped

The demand for high-grade sulphite is exceptionally active at the present time and the prospects are very bright. In regard to sulphate or kraft pulp, the market is somewhat quieter owing to the fact that there is more or less Scandinavian kraft coming into the United States market recently and is being sold at cut prices, in fact the Scandinavian pulp is being sold at a figure under the cost of production. It is understood that the mills, who are holding some of this kraft pulp in Scandinavia, are being forced by their banks to realize, and as they have special freight rates coming to the American side, they can bring their pulp over for very low carrying charges. It has been stated that the freight on pulp from the Scandinavian mills to the United States is only about 25 per cent of what it costs Canadian manufacturers to ship their kraft pulp from Canada to the British market. The Canadian manufacturers feel this is rather a bad handicap, and it is seriously interfering with the call for kraft pulp from the Canadian mills to the United States.

School on Wheels Teaching Forestry

During November a carload of information on forests and their products will visit many centres in the Prairie Provinces. For the past few months the car has visited the forested sections of Eastern Canada and attracted much interest and attention. The exhibits in the car were brought together and arranged by Mr. Robson Black of the Canadian Forestry Association. The car is the property of the Canadian Government Railways and will be moved from point to point over the lines of the several railway companies operating in the western provinces, and will be under the supervision of an official of the Dominion Forestry Branch.

The exhibits have been drawn from many different countries, including Canada, the United States, Great Britain, Germany, France, Scandinavia, Egypt and Japan. Lectures will be given by the men in charge of the car in the car itself and also in halls in the towns visited, where every phase of the timber industry, from the planting of seedlings to the manufacture of all manner of wood products, will be explained and as far as possible demonstrated. The car contains a miniature nursery of spruce and Scotch pine seedlings.

Big Paper Plant for Port Arthur

The Great Lakes Paper Company will commence immediately the erection of a huge plant costing between $[illegible] and $[illegible] just east of Port Arthur city limits. The plant will consist of a groundwood mill with an annual output of [illegible] tons, a sulphite mill, annual capacity 7,500 tons, and a newsprint paper mill of [illegible] to 35,000 tons annual output. Power from the Hydro-electric plant at Nipigon will be used, from 12,000 to 16,000 h.p. being contracted for delivery at the plant at a cost of $17.50 per h.p., by Dec. 31, 1921.

Engineers, headed by Hardy Ferguson, of New York, are to be on the ground within a few days. Foundations will be commenced at once if weather permits. The plant is to be in full operation by June, 1921.

The personnel of the company is Lewis L. Alsted, President Combined Locks Paper Co., Wis.; George Seaman, President Seaman Paper Company, Chicago, and James Whalen, President, Port Arthur Shipbuilding Company.

The firm will employ thousands of men in construction and operation. A site of 100 acres has been given free by J. J. Carrick out of his 600-acre holdings immediately east of Port Arthur.

Demountable Ships for Australia

Announcement was made in New York that the Pacheco Lumber Company, a New York concern, controlled by British capital, this winter will ship 50,000,000 feet of Douglas fir from Seattle to points in the British Empire in the form of demountable ships.

About 500,000 feet of timber will be used in the hulls of the ships. When they reach their destinations these hulls will be dismantled and delivered as lumber. The hulls and cargo of each ship will represent about 5,000,000 feet, it was said. Admiral Robert E. Peary's famous old exploring ship, the Roosevelt, now owned in New York, will tow the first of the demountable ships to Australia.

The Market for Woodenware in Cuba

In response to inquiries the Acting Trade Commissioner in Havana, Cuba, writes respecting the market for small woodenware in Cuba:—

Wholesale druggists in Havana state that wooden containers for pharmaceutical products are now being used on account of the scarcity of tinned trays. They state that most of those goods are brought from the United States, but think that Canada could compete in this market. Different sizes of wooden pill-boxes are used, but not for pills but for different kinds of ointments. Pills for the most part are put up in cardboard boxes, as these are much cheaper. They also make a quantity of wooden bottles for putting up homeopathic remedies and for sending fragile articles by mail.

Large quantities of handles for carrying parcels are also sold. They are made with a round piece of wood for the hand, wire run through and doubled down with a hook at each end to fasten on the parcel. Many dealers have their firm name and some kind of small advertisement stamped on these wooden handles, which they say they would require to have done where they are manufactured.

There is a large market here for broom handles, also handles for different kinds of tools, such as pick-axes, axes, hammers, etc. There is a limited quantity of wooden faucets for wine and beer barrels used.

Canadian Firm Rushed on Lumbermen's Clothing

Griffith B. Clarke's Leopard III. setting the pace in motor boat races at Toronto

Griffith B. Clarke, president of A. R. Clarke & Co., Limited, the widely known manufacturers of lumbermen's clothing of all kinds, has outside of the large and important business which he directs, always been interested in recreation and organized baseball and hockey teams teams among the big staff of employees of the company. Mr. Clarke has one particular hobby and that is motoring both on water and land. He possesses two of the fastest speed boats on Lake Ontario, Leopard I. and Leopard III. The former won the Prince of Wales Gold Medal, and the latter the Gold Challenge Cup, the Great Lakes International $1,000 trophy, on September 9th at the Canadian National Exhibition. Leopard III. which is a remarkably speedy craft covered a course of thirty miles in admirable shape, averaging 46 miles an hour. Leopard I. is another lightning craft and, with Mr. Clarke at the wheel, the Prince of Wales Gold Medal was captured on Labor Day. The journey of twenty miles was made in less than forty-two minutes. The accompanying illustration shows Leopard III. setting a pace of mile a minute with Mr. Clarke at the helm. The "Leopards" have been for some years a leading feature in the Canadian National Exhibition motor boat races, which invariably attract much interest and create keen enthusiasm. That "Griff" Clark has been able to carry off the premiums is a matter of gratification to his many friends.

A. R. Clarke & Co., Limited, report that there has been a greatly increased demand this fall for all kinds of lumbermen's clothing and particularly for their well known line of mackinaw coats. The call for work shirts, sheep lined coats, moccasins, gloves and other A. R. C. brand garments has been the greatest in the history of the firm which indicates big activity in woods operations all over the Dominion. The company state that they have never been as busy in the matter of lumbermen's clothing as at present and in many lines there has been an increase of fifty per cent.

The present business was founded in Peterboro in 1852 by John Clarke, father of the late A. R. Clarke, moving in 1882 to Toronto, where they located on their present site, the firm being styled A. R. Clarke & Co. In 1896 the firm was reorganized and became A. R. Clarke & Company Limited. At that time they employed about fifty or sixty men and were capitalized at $25,000.

In 1902 they started to manufacture patent leather and were, as far as we can learn, the first firm in Canada to do so. Later other lines were added. The glove department alone has an output of approximately 1000 dozen pairs a week. Some three hundred are on the payroll and the total production for this year will be well over $3,000,000.

Mr. Griffith B. Clarke, head of the company, came into the firm in 1906, after completing his education at St. Andrew's College, Toronto. Unlike many other young fellows, who doubtless would have ridiculed the idea, Mr. Clarke donned overalls and went to work in the beam house—the most disagreeable task in the whole process of tanning, but one which the successful tanner must be intimately acquainted with, since it underlies the ultimate quality of the leather. As vice-president of the company later on Mr. Clarke had much to do with the buying of materials and the sale of patent leather and has made several trips to Europe in this connection.

Readers will recall the unfortunate death of Mr. A. R. Clarke, president of the company, who was one of the victims of German "kultur" on the ill-fated Lusitania.

Some years previous to this Messrs. C. E. and F. G. Clarke who had been in the business with the late Mr. A. R. Clarke when the tannery was moved from Peterboro to Toronto, started another tannery in Toronto for the purpose of specializing on sheepskins. These two younger brothers passed away within a couple of months of each other—Mr. Charles E. Clarke on Christmas Day, 1917, and Mr. F. G. Clarke on February 18th, 1918.

Following the death of his father, Mr. Griffith B. Clarke became president of A. R. Clarke & Co., Ltd., and has combined new blood and enterprise with the rigid principles laid down by the founder of the business.

Part of the glove stitching department of A. R. Clarke & Co., Toronto

Scene in the cutting room in the Clarke glove department

Veteran Northern Lumberman Passes Away

One of the best-known lumbermen in Northern Ontario passed away recently in the person of Wm. Turnbull, who was one of the pioneer citizens of Huntsville, Ont. He had been ailing for some months. Mr. Turnbull had been a resident of Huntsville for the past thirty-three years, being at first a partner in the lumbering firm of Heath, Tait & Turnbull. Some years later, upon the retirement of Mr. Heath the Huntsville Lumber Co. was organized with Andrew Tait, now of Toronto, as president, and Mr. Turnbull as secretary. The latter continued his active management of this company until two years ago, when he retired.

Mr. Turnbull who was born in Glasgow, Scotland, enjoyed the

The late William Turnbull, Huntsville, Ont.

confidence of his associates in the lumber industry and his passing marks the severance of another link connecting the present with the past. He is survived by his wife (formerly Miss Elizabeth M. Lightbody of Glasgow) and three children. They are Harry Turnbull of Sarnia, Ont., Mrs. McCloskey of Powasson, Ont., and Mrs. Cameron of Chicago. John Turnbull, President of the Nasmith Company, Toronto, is a nephew. Previous to taking up his abode in Huntsville in 1886 the late Mr. Turnbull was a resident of Toronto for a short time and later lived in Orillia.

The remains were interred in St. Andrew's cemetery, Huntsville, and the last sad rites were attended by a large concourse of people evidencing the esteem and respect in which he was held.

Lumber Industry Active Around Nelson

That the lumber industry in and around Nelson is booming and that the interior is experiencing prosperity such as not been known since the war is the encouraging information given F. F. Payne of Nelson who was recently in Vancouver on business. He says that practically every stick of timber that can be sawed is being placed on the market, all the yards being cleaned up. New mills are being built at Boulder Creek just north of Nelson by Mr. O'Neil and associates. Seventy-five men are employed and 200 in the mill and limits. Baskin and Stedman have erected a new mill just west of Nelson and are cutting poles, posts and timber.

Machinery has been received by A. S. Horswill for a new mill at Nelson and in a few weeks this plant will be in operation. Kreyscher and Kenny have a portable mill on Groohman Creek and are cutting timber for the flume and bringing down logs to cut at the plant at Nelson. This plant which has been engaged for the most part in box making, is being extended.

Should Encourage Wooden Shipbuilding

Shipbuilding in Nova Scotia is in a very unsettled state at the present time, although the best authorities maintain that if all the shipbuilding plants in the world kept in full swing for the next ten years they could not supply the demands for ships, says the Yarmouth "Times." Still the industry for this province does not offer to the builder a sufficient inducement to justify him in continuing his operations and in as much as the shipbuilders have gone to such an expense as to equip their various plants, and many thousands of workmen are being thrown out of employment just at this season of the year, when all the returned soldiers are looking for work, it is at this time the Nova Scotia government should make a special effort to offer immediate assistance to encourage this very important industry.

The government of Nova Scotia some two years ago passed an act, authorizing this government to borrow on the credit of the province, two millions of dollars to stimulate the shipbuilding movement.

A commission was appointed with a person of reputed importance as chairman, to investigate the needs of this industry and recommend a course of action to the government. Aside from the fact of the chairman taking a trip to England and Europe, at the expense of the government, absolutely nothing was done.

The report of the commission was to the effect that the shipbuilding industry in Nova Scotia was sufficiently flourishing and did not need any government assistance.

Neighboring Dominions, much smaller in size and population, foster the shipbuilding industry to the extent of guaranteeing a dividend of 5 per cent. on the stock of a company that would incorporate to build wooden vessels. In addition to this, they offered a bonus of as high as twenty dollars a ton for every vessel that is built.

With our knowledge of the industry, the report, to our mind, was not based on good judgment and foresight. Its authors did not realize that, though the industry appeared to be booming at the time, double the quantity of ships would have been built and more if it were not for the uncertainty as to the duration of the war.

Many more yards would have been opened, and many more ships built if the people had the assurance that the shipbuilding business would not terminate with the end of the war, or before they had time to get under full operation.

There is no desire on our part to criticize the incapacity of the commission, but our remarks on the question are made with a view to getting the government to again take up this very important subject and have the commission take such steps as are necessary to offer assistance to re-establish this fast fading industry and offer inducements which will justify builders to resume their operations and thus keep up this very important industry which has made such headway and created such a boom in shipbuilding in Nova Scotia.

If the Dominion of Canada considers it advisable to spend sixty millions of dollars to create employment for returned soldiers, etc., our government should at least spend a little effort and money in fostering this very important industry.

Develop Pulp Business with Orient

Sir George Bury, who is head of the Whalen Pulp and Paper Co. of Vancouver, has sailed for the Orient and will be absent for several months in connection with the development of the pulp trade with the East. Sir George is of the opinion that there is a great future for British Columbia pulp in China and Japan and says that several large deals are pending and that the Coast needs the business. The output of the Whalen Co. has lately been increased from 56,000 to 75,000 tons annually. The President of the Company stated before his departure that trade and commerce is best provided by the managers first visiting new markets personally and establishing a connection so that future dealings are of a more friendly character. For this reason Sir George will spend several months in the East.

Would Defer Wharfage Rates Increase

The committee of the Montreal Board of Trade Transportation Bureau on November 6 discussed the increase in wharfage rates which the Montreal Harbor Commissioners propose to make effective on January 1st next. It was stated that these increases involve a considerable amount, and will seriously add to the cost of doing business through the port of Montreal, which would to that extent hamper the business of the port as compared with that of competitive ports. It was decided to ask the council of the Board of Trade to interview the Harbor Commissioners for the purpose of ascertaining if it is not possible, from the standpoint of the Harbor Commissioners, to avoid the necessity of increasing the wharfage rates in the manner proposed. Should this not be found feasible it was decided to urge a further postponement of the proposed increases in order to afford the council of the Board of Trade time to bring the whole matter to the attention of the Dominion Government.

The British Columbia Government has inherited a ready-made town—Thurston Harbor, Queen Charlotte Island. It is a munition town, erected at a time when production of spruce for airplanes was a matter of life and death for the Empire.

With the ending of the spruce industry came the end of business life in the town, so Major A. C. Taylor, Director of the Department of Air Supplies for the Imperial Munitions Board, offered the entire establishment to the Provincial Forestry Department. The offer has been accepted.

Market For Wooden Turnings in Australia

In response to inquiries, Mr. C. Harlett, Acting Canadian Trade Commissioner in Melbourne, writes:

Parts for piano-players, rolls, for typewriters and skewers for cotton mills are not marketable here. Piano-players are not made here, and spare parts are supplied by the makers of the players. Typewriter rolls are also supplied by the makers of the various machines on the market, as the outside rubber vulcanizing process cannot be done here. There are no cotton mills in Australia and therefore no call for skewers.

Pill boxes are made locally but of poor quality and finish compared with the imported articles, the trade in which is largely confined to the products of one United States house. If Canadian products can compete in quality and factory price with the product of this firm, there is a prospect of good business, but this can only be definitely determined by the production of samples.

Draw pulls, rollingpins, rack pins, and, to some extent, floats for fish nets, hubs for carts and short handles for tools (not hickory), are made locally. Hickory handles are the most popular and are mostly imported from the United States.

Turnings for baby carriages, croquet mallets and stakes, hickory handles, wood faucets, pill boxes, and hubs for carts are the articles for which there is a market in Australia, provided Canadian quality and price (f.o.b. ocean port) are competitive with those of United States manufacturers.

If Canadian manufacturers will supply particulars of quality and prices of the lines above indicated, this office would be in a position to approach dealers and definitely ascertain their selling possibilities.

New Power Plant of Bathurst Company

The Bathurst Lumber Co. of Bathurst, N. B., report that good progress has been made in connection with their logging operations, as, owing to the exceptionally fine Fall, work has been carried on in the woods expeditiously. It looks as if the company are going to have a very much larger cut of logs than a year ago.

In regard to labor, they say that men are not too plentiful. Wages run from $10.00 to $15.00 a month higher than last year and the costs of all supplies are practically the same, so that as far as can be judged at present, the costs of lumber for 1920 will be considerably higher than it was for 1919. One of the large saw-mills of the Bathurst Lumber Co. at Bathurst, has closed down while the other is still being operated and will be kept going until the freeze-up takes place, which is usually about December 1st.

The company are now proceeding to develop their water-power on the Nepisiquit River at the Grand Falls, twenty miles from Bathurst. They are putting in two units of 4500 horse power each, and this power will be transferred to Bathurst for running the pulp-mills, saw-mills and other industries of the company, who hope to have it going in a year from now.

With respect to the building of a paper mill in connection with their plant, Angus McLean, General Manager of the Bathurst Company, states that nothing has finally been determined as yet and that no decision will be made until some time next year.

Wooden House Campaign in Britain

The latest cable information from London as to wooden houses bears out the news given in our issue of November 1st regarding the difficulty of the Canadian type being accepted in England. Not only is there a certain amount of prejudice to be overcome, but it is asserted that the cost, including the freight, will bring it up to something near that of brick houses.

A recent message states that a "wooden frame house from British Columbia, with accommodation, fittings and conveniences for domestic use approximately to those now required in Government assisted schemes, is not likely to be completed for much less than $3,500 and the cost may not improbably be even more. The Canadian wooden house commonly referred to differs in many respects from the house which a tenant in this country expects to obtain." continues the official announcement from the Ministry of Health. "These wooden houses, for instance, have as a rule a basement containing a stove for central heating of the whole house. This method of heating differs entirely from that to which the English housekeeper is accustomed, and if the English prejudice in favor of the open fire is to be respected, considerable modifications in internal design and construction are inevitable."

Sir Charles T. Ruthen, an eminent British architect, has built three wooden houses at Newton, near Swansea, at a cost of $725 less than a brick house of the same size, and Sir Charles claims that it will be more damp proof, and will last at least 200 years.

The walls of these experimental houses are covered both inside and out with cement stucco. A bitumen sheet makes them vermin and damp proof. Strength is obtained by a scientific system of lacing with wooden laths. The roof is tiled. As far as appearance is concerned, there is no reason, in Sir Charles' opinion, why a house built on such a system should not be quite as attractive as a brick house.

There can be no doubt, judging from reports in English papers, that wooden houses would meet with considerable favour, providing the cost is reasonable. Those British firms manufacturing wooden houses have been overwhelmed with inquiries, and one London firm has sold large quantities at prices ranging from $410 for a two room house to $2,075 for a six-roomed bungalow. These houses have felt-covered roofs and asbestos-lined walls. Mr. Wade, the Agent General of B. C. in London, has received thousands of inquiries.

Sir Kingsley Wood, M. P., Parliamentary Secretary to the Ministry of Health, in an interview, stated that the Ministry fully recognized the necessity of making what housing provision is possible for the winter months. "I have seen the proposals for wooden houses," he said. "Many, I understand, have been successfully built in Canada and the U. S. A., but judging from the facts before us, they do not meet with enthusiasm from the workers of this country. The Ministry have formed the opinion that the workers would not accept such houses in lieu of brick. It is considered, too, that they would not be so inhabitable or durable as to make them a possible alternative to the present Government scheme. We recognize, however, the plight in which so many thousands of people find themselves to-day, and the public may be sure that if some more speedy and cheaper method of building can be found we shall not hesitate to make use of it."

Mr. W. F. Regan has offered to import 60,000 houses from the United States in 12 months, and he suggests that the Government should order the houses.

Canada's Opportunity in Wood Supplies

Mr. Harrison Watson, Government Trade Commissioner in London, who is on a visit to Canada, in an interview declared that in the matter of wood supplies of all kinds there is a splendid opportunity in the United Kingdom for export.

To give an instance of the quantities in which these people order Mr. Watson said he was talking to one U. K. buyer who had returned from a business visit to Canada who informed him that he had placed one order for $200,000 worth of wooden pegs, used for the manufacture of furniture. An insignificant article like a wooden peg therefore mean the necessity of a great production and output if the Old Country market is to be met and satisfied.

The mills in the United States on the other hand are in most cases equipped to handle large quantities at a small margin of profit and in many instances the English buyer comes to Canada, finds he cannot get his demands satisfied here, buys all the Canadian goods that are offered, but is finally forced to place the bulk of his orders in the United States.

Canadian export firms also suffer by the lack of direct representation in the United Kingdom. The buyer over there on enquiry for a certain article finds that Canada produces it but has no official representative or agents for that particular article in the United Kingdom. He finds that the United States produces the same article and producers have their direct agents in London and Glasgow, or some other large centre, and the importer is not obliged to do his business by the correspondence route.

Seventy-five million boxes are used in the United Kingdom every year and about nine tenths of these are imported. In this line Mr. Watson said there were vast possibilities in the export of box shooks from Canada.

McGibbon Lumber Co. Will Rebuild Mill

The McGibbon Lumber Co. of Penetanguishene, Ont., whose mill was recently destroyed by fire, report that their loss is $30,000.00 and fairly well covered by insurance. It is understood that the company will rebuild as soon as insurance and other matters are adjusted, and that a new and larger plant will likely be ready for operation next season.

In speaking of the fire a local paper says: The blaze broke out at the noon hour when all the men were at home for dinner and in a few hours the mill, one of the old landmarks in the town, was burnt to the ground. Fanned by a high wind it was only a few minutes till the whole structure was a mass of flames. When the firemen arrived on the scene they directed their attention towards saving the adjoining buildings and keeping the fire from spreading. Thanks to the rain falling in the forenoon, they were successful. Had the shingles on some of the old frame buildings in that vicinity been dry there is no telling where the fire would have been stopped.

When President Beatty was an Urchin

There was taken at Thorold, Ont., some thirty-four years ago on the occasion of a Trades Celebration, an interesting picture, showing some timber which formed a feature of the procession. This timber was exhibited by McCleary & McLean, who conducted a sawmill and yard at Thorold for many years. In connection with the illustration presented one can never foretell to what height the small boy, ever present when anything unusual is going on, will rise in the esteem of his fellows and the service of his country.

In the photograph are noticed three lads, standing near the front and to the rear of the log. There is one little chap scarcely

A parade in Thorold which Mr. E. W. Beatty saw in 1885

noticeable, his head just appearing over the side of the obstruction. He was of miniature proportions physically in 1885 but to-day he is a nationally-known figure and leader. His name is Edward Wentworth Beatty, K.C., President of the Canadian Pacific Railway.

L. B. E. McCleary, to whom the "Canada Lumberman" is indebted for the picture, showed it to T. L. Church, Mayor of Toronto, not long ago. Toronto's Chief Magistrate is a personal friend of the C. P. R. magnate, and when told who the boy was, said "Oh yes, Eddie, as usual, trying to get out of sight! He always did hide his light under a bushel." The lad in the centre of the group of the three boys is A. A. Ewart, Secretary and General Manager of the Prince Rupert Spruce Mills Co., Ltd., of Prince Rupert, B. C., and the boy to the reader's left is Dr. Harry Beatty, now of Toronto, Chief Surgeon of the Canadian Pacific Railway and brother of the C. P. R. President.

West Keenly Alive to Forest Problems

Taking advantage of the growing interest in public affairs throughout the Prairie Provinces, Mr. Robson Black, Ottawa, Secretary of the Canadian Forestry Association, accompanied by a motion picture operator, addressed thirty public meetings between October 14th and November 1st. Mr. Black found the public interest in questions related to provincial forest management strikingly intensified as compared with four or five years ago. Western Canadian Clubs, Boards of Trade, Bankers and Mortgage Loans Associations and other representative bodies held luncheons and dinners in nearly all large cities in order to provide an opportunity to hear forest conservation addresses. At some of the evening meetings in places like Calgary, Prince Albert and Winnipeg, the attendance of men ran as high as 600.

The chief point in the addresses was an outline of the extent of the prairie province forests and their present wretched condition owing mostly to unrestricted forest fires. Instead of an increasing variety of wood-using industries, the larger mills were giving up operations and enormous areas—as, for example, 40,000,000 non-agricultural acres in Saskatchewan—were being turned into permanent wildernesses. The effect of burned forests upon irrigation was also discussed in detail and proved one of the hardest hitting points in the whole conservation argument. The industrial potentialities of spruce-growing lands, the need of provincial and Dominion co-operation in debarring the annual fire plague, the value of tree-planting to crop production were other points treated by Mr. Black. The Forestry Association is endeavoring to establish a resident Western propagandist and to engage a Children's Lecturer. The latter would give his entire time to school addresses in all parts of Canada and would make generous use of motion pictures. In this way, scores of thousands of young men and women annually would become personally acquainted with the interesting truths of forest protection and the constructive handling of the natural resources. An appeal will be made for better financial support of the Forestry Association which has a slight government revenue and a national membership of ten thousand.

Real Possibilities of Lumber Ship

Commenting on the proposed Livventaal lumber schooner, and a suggestion that salt water will injure lumber, Captain Midford, of Ottawa, writes:—

When the export of lumber was so desperately required in England for war purposes, the writer brought to the attention of lumber exporters here and in London the real possibilities of lumber-ship. He was met by some of the objections mentioned in the item cited—the Pacific Coast and Nova Scotia experiments, etc. In 1915 the Timber Trade Journal, London, cited the answers to these objections and said "until the strains to which any ship and floating structure is subjected and provided for upon the same scientific lines necessary and imperative to meet and overcome these strains, no timber raft would ever become a success." From Joggings raft to the latest by Vickers, of Pacific Coast failure, no one has provided for this condition, hence these failures.

It was clearly shown to exporters here and in London that a lumber-ship could be designed from five to fifty million feet B. M. capacity, and the freight would be a very considerable below 8.80.

For goodness sake don't let any shipbuilder see or read this next objection made by Montreal lumber exporters, viz.: "Salt water would have a detrimental action upon the lumber, it being pointed out that wooden vessels invariably had their bottoms copper sheathed in order to protect the timber from the salt water." Wooden ships were never coppered for the purpose cited, but to prevent the terredo worm boring into the ship's bottom. When we were building Brooklyn Bridge, the Navy Yard gave us timber sunk in salt water in 1774. These timbers were successfully used to build 40-ton derricks. It may be interesting to Montreal lumber exporters to know that while the terredo worm will bore and travel all through a timber any dimensions, it will never bore through two pieces of lumber no matter how thin.

Great Cedar Shingle Congress in Seattle

The red letter days on the shingle manufacturers' calendar this winter will be December 10 and 11 on which dates will be held the third annual session of the Red Cedar Shingle congress.

On account of its location in the centre of the shingle producing industry, Seattle again will be the meeting place. Sessions will be held in the Washington hotel.

An interesting feature of this year's congress will be a "service exhibit" of what the shingle manufacturers are doing in the way of intensive merchandising.

A special invitation is being extended to lumber dealers everywhere and to eastern shingle distributors, thus providing an opportunity for manufacturers, wholesalers and retailers to get together on common ground and discuss ways and means of bettering the shingle industry. The detailed program, in charge of J. S. Williams, secretary of the Shingle Branch of the West Coast Lumbermen's Association, probably will be completed in the next few days.

How Canadian Timber Ascends in Value

"I am interested in a large estate of some thousands of acres in Canada," said G. St. Lawrence Mowbray, chairman of the Anglo-Belgian corporation at the annual meeting in London, Eng. "Three years ago it was proposed to clear a considerable area for agriculture. There was a considerable amount of timber but we were advised it was unsaleable and would cost between £5 and £15 per acre to have it felled and burned. As the war was on we did not proceed with the project, but we have now received an offer of £10,000 from a large lumber firm in Canada for the right to go and cut such timber as they saw fit." Mr. Mowbray added that the erection of wooden dwellings and factories now being advocated in England would add greatly to the demand for Canadian timber.

Pulp and Sawmills for Labrador

Major Daniel Owen recently spent a few days at his home in Annapolis Royal, Nova Scotia. He is President and Treasurer of the North American Corporation, Limited, with head offices in Boston, and says that branches will shortly be opened throughout Canada and the United States. The first securities to be offered the public will be the South Labrador Pulp & Lumber Co. with a capital stock of $10,000,000, of which Major Owen is also President. This company will exploit the timber limits recently explored in British Columbia by the aerial expedition, which sailed from Annapolis Royal. A large staff of hydraulic engineers, pulpmen and lumbermen has been retained. The lumber mills will be in active operation next year and it is hoped by the end of the season a large pulp plant will also be located on the property. Several thousand tons of machinery and supplies will go out at the opening of navigation.

Scarcity of Help in Bush Operations

Reports received by the Government Employment Bureau at Ottawa from all parts of Canada indicate that there is great difficulty in getting men to go to the lumber camps this season, or to remain when they get there. One large operator is asking for a thousand additional men; others are in a like predicament.

The situation is made worse in the eyes of lumbermen in that of the shantymen who have returned from overseas ten thousand have drifted into other occupations. After their martial experiences abroad and fleeting glimpses of life in many old world centres these lads seem to have gained a thirst for city life, which they are now trying to quench. Even the fact that wages paid in the camps have doubled since the old days does not draw them from the lure of the big city.

It is true that a small proportion of men who lived originally in the city are going to outside occupations, and some of them to the bush, attracted by the healthy open-air life, the rude comfort, and the bountiful food which are the rule there. But these do not begin to make up for the loss of the shantymen.

But the lumbermen are willing to take a number of greenhorns to work in with what experienced men they get, and to teach those who are quick and adaptable whatever there is to learn.

How Logging Costs Keep Going Skywards

It is interesting to note what it costs to board men in the lumber camps to-day. In most operating centres wages are about the same this year as last although there is a tendency on the part of men to demand a higher figure in some districts. Operators have not yet ascertained this season what it is costing them to board the men for any definite length of time, but report on the whole that supplies are about the same in figure as last year, although hay and oats are much higher. Here is how costs have ascended during the past four years in the matter of rationing men, feeding teams and wages in the bush.

One of the largest operators in Ontario, who employed about four hundred men in his camps during 1918-19, has just been furnished by the Auditing Dept. with a complete statement of what the outlay has been during the past four years. Each season covers about seven months and the costs are arrived at on the basis of twenty-six working days to the month.

Subjoined is a comparative statement of expenditures, which shows that, while men were boarded for about 50c a day in 1914-15, the disbursement last Winter was about $1.11. Feeding teams, which in 1914-15 cost less than $2.00 a day, now runs about $3.25, and wages have aviated from $27.00 per month to $65.00. Thus it will be seen why the quotations for lumber are constantly augmented and, judging from present indications, forest products will go considerably higher by the time that next season's cut comes on the market.

Here is a table of interest:

	Per Month, 26 Working Days		
	Boarding Men	Feeding Teams	Wages
1914/15	$13.73	$49.40	$26.98
1915/16	15.17	51.61	24.54
1917/18	26.06	69.83	54.09
1918/19	29.04	84.59	64.52

Experimental Cutting By Eastern Lumber Co.

The work on the permanent experimental plot which has been laid out on the Nepisiguit River through the co-operation of the Bathurst Lumber Company, the Conservation Commission and the Crown Land Department of New Brunswick, is progressing very favorably.

An area of 490 acres of forest land has been set aside for 25 years by mutual agreement and the Bathurst Lumber Company is cutting this area according to many various regulations and systems laid down by Dr. C. D. Howe of the Conservation Commission with a view to finding out what change may be made in the rate of growth and nature of the reproduction resulting from each of the various methods of cutting. On some of the area all the slash and brush is being burned and all material in the tops suitable for pulpwood is being taken out.

Mr. Angus McLean, General Manager of the Bathurst Lumber Company, is taking a keen interest in this experimental cutting and thinning and deserves much credit for making possible this valuable experiment even with increased cost for logging, it being one of the first and most extensive experimental thinnings being undertaken in Canada.

Mr. John Lordon, Superintendent for the Bathurst Lumber Company, has been in charge of the logging for the Bathurst Lumber Company, and R. D. Jago, of the Forest Service, laid the plot out and has been in charge of the cutting for the Conservation Commission. Mr. Hermann Good, a returned soldier who won the Victoria Cross, has filled the position of camp foreman over the 50 men employed in a very satisfactory manner.

Dr. C. D. Howe, of the Conservation Commission, picked out the side for the plot and expects to visit the area for the third time in December, after most of the cutting has been completed.

W. M. Robertson, B.Sc.F., of the Conservation Commission, is in charge of the plot at the present, having relieved Mr. R. D. Jago recently, who had to return to Fredericton.

Wages Are Higher and Men Scarce

W. Gerard Power, Manager of the River Ouelle Pulp & Lumber Co., St. Pacome, Que., says in regard to logging in the Eastern part of the Province that wages are very much higher than last year and men are none too plentiful. It is difficult to get any idea at the present time just what the log crop will be during the present Autumn and coming Winter. Much will depend on what kind of a winter Quebec has in the matter of snow, cold weather, etc. The River Ouelle Pulp & Lumber Co. had a very satisfactory season when everything is taken into consideration but has been hampered for several months now by car shortage. As large a quantity of lumber has not been moved as there would have been, had shipping arrangements been normal..

Shortage of Loggers is Experienced

There is practically not a lumber company in the mountains that could not use more men at bush work, states I. R. Poole, secretary of the Mountain Lumber Manufacturers' Association, and unless the influx, now overdue, of harvesters from the prairie helps out the situation the log cut this coming winter and the lumber cut the following summer will be seriously curtailed. This year's lumber cut is shorter than last year's because of the labor shortage, which so far has not shown any improvement.

Lumbermen Responsible for Employees

A recent despatch from Fredericton, N. B., says:—Chief Game Warden L. A. Gagnon, returned from Albert County lately where he had three cases of violations of the game act before Justice of the Peace A. A. Reid, of Harvey, all of which resulted in conviction.

One of the charges was against a lumberman under the new amendment to the game act which holds a lumberman liable for violations of the act by men in his camps. Some of the lumberman's employes were found in the woods with rifles but without having a license. The lumberman was fined $50 and costs. These were the first cases coming under the recent amendment.

Pit Props for Steel Corporation

It may not be generally known that the Dominion Steel Corporation own 50,000 acres of timber limits in Cumberland, N. S. From these the company secure all their pit props. Sufficient timber is contained in these limits to take care of the company's needs for an indefinite period, besides which they have a certain quantity for sale for commercial purposes.

Quick Action Section

Special Lots Of Lumber—Positions Wanted & Vacant

PUBLISHER'S NOTICE

Advertisements other than "Employment Wanted" or "Employees Wanted" will be inserted in this department at the rate of 20 cents per agate line (14 agate lines make one inch). $2.80 per inch, each insertion, payable in advance. Space measured from rule to rule. When four or more consecutive insertions of the same advertisement are ordered a discount of 25 per cent will be allowed.

Advertisements of "Wanted Employment" will be inserted at the rate of one cent a word, net. Cash must accompany order. If Canada Lumberman box number is used, enclose ten cents extra for postage in forwarding replies. Minimum charge 25 cents.

Advertisements of "Wanted Employees" will be inserted at the rate of two cents a word, net. Cash must accompany the order. Minimum charge 50 cents.

Advertisements must be received not later than the 10th and 20th of each month to insure insertion in the subsequent issue.

Wanted-Lumber

Basswood Wanted

No. 2 Common and Mill Cull. Winter cut preferred. Apply Firstbrook Brothers, Ltd., Toronto, Ont. 8-t.f.

Wanted Lumber

Hardwood Lumber wanted. Birch, Maple, Basswood and other Hardwoods. Dry or sawn to order. We send inspector. Box 14, Canada Lumberman, Toronto. 21-24

WANTED—Plastering Lath

1,000,000 Spruce, or Hemlock, Spruce preferred. Quote delivered here and when can ship. Terms: 80 per cent. sight draft, balance on arrival.

THE BILLMEYER LUMBER CO.,
21-22 Cumberland, Md.

Wanted for Cuban Trade White Pine

Send lists and prices at once to

E. ANTONIO VAZQUEZ,
44 Whitehall Street,
19-22 New York City.

Wanted To Buy LATH

We are in the market for large quantities of Lath; all grades, including No. 3 and 32". Paying good prices and cash on receipt of B.L.

What have you to offer? Send good description, lowest price F.O.B. Chicago, stating quantity offered.

COVEY DURHAM COMPANY,
431 S. Dearborn St.,
20-23 Chicago, Ill., U.S.A.

For Sale-Lumber

FOR SALE Hickory Specials

100 M pcs. ¾" Dowels, 48" long.
20 M pcs. 1" Squares, 48" long.

Also some shorter stock. All high grade, second growth Hickory. Can ship immediately. Will sell cheap. Address Box 31, Canada Lumberman, Toronto. 21-22

PULPWOOD FOR SALE

Ten thousand cords of pulpwood for sale; next summer delivery. Shipping point, Blue River, Canadian National Railway. Apply to

QUEBEC LUMBER CO.,
Phone 329 98 St. Peter Street,
22-23 Quebec, Que.

Wanted-Machinery

Wanted

Barlenger Braking Device, six blocks, with or without cable. Apply Bishop Lumber Co., Ltd., Nesterville, Ont. 22-23

For Sale-Machinery

For Sale Cheap

One full front 80 H.P. Tubular Steam Boiler, Goldie & McCulloch make. One 65 H.P. Steam Engine, Wheelock's newest type, Goldie & McCulloch make. All as good as new, only used a short time. Move quick for bargain. Apply to Gordon Lumber Co., Stratford, Ont. 21-22

FOR SALE

One, Brown type engine, first class condition, 10" x 24", all fittings, ready to set up, 16" x 7' belt wheel.

One Belt, 70' 6" x 44", 3 ply leather endless, scarcely soiled. Two Belts, 60' 6" x 20" double leather, scarcely soiled. Two inserted tooth lumber saws, one 56" practically new, one 52" in good condition. 1 Leonard-Ball centre crank high speed engine, 14" x 14", 12½" x 30" belt wheels. 1 belt, 72' 36", double leather, scarcely soiled. 1 belt, 66' 8", 28" double leather, scarcely soiled. W. H. Cook, Box 356, Orillia, Ont. 23

Band Saw Mill Complete

Waterous 9 ft. Band Mill, Gunshot Feed Carriage, with extra Saws complete.

Filing Equipment

Three Saw Edger, lot of live rolls, Engine, Shafting, Hangers, Pulleys, etc.

All of the above is Waterous equipment in good condition at a bargain.

The Geo. F. Foss Machinery & Supply Co., Limited,
305 St. James Street,
17-t.f. Montreal, Que.

For Sale

1—17 x 24 Atlas Engine, with 86 in. x 10 ft. flywheel.
3—No. 94 Berlin Matchers, 15 in., fitted with hard steel knives on top and bottom cylinders—one pair shiplap, jointer and flooring heads with bits for each machine.
1—No. 182 Berlin Double Surfacer, 30 in. x 6 in.
1—No. 199 Berlin Buzz Planer.
1—No. 290 Berlin Picket Header.

The Otis Staples Lumber Company, Ltd.,
19-t.f. Wycliffe, B.C.

Band Mill For Sale

One Band Mill complete for sale, consisting of two 12" double-cut Band Saws, one Band Resaw, four Engines, five Boilers, two large Smoke Stacks, one complete Electric Light Outfit, steam feed and steam set steel Carriages, Dump Carts, etc. Situated at Midland, Ont. A bargain for quick sale. The Mageau Lumber Co., Ltd., Field, Ont. 22

For Sale

One "S. A. Wood Matcher 24" fitted with 20 different sizes knives for top and bottom cylinders. Four pairs of heads with six sets of bits. Price $800, on cars. Savoie & Co., Manseau, Que. 21-t.f.

Wanted-Employment

Advertisements under this heading one cent a word per insertion. Box No. 10 cents extra. Minimum charge 25 cents.

YOUNG MAN, experienced in all branches of lumber trade, open for position as salesman or manager of manufacturing plant or yard. Box 52, Canada Lumberman, Toronto. 21-22

LUMBER SALESMAN with established connection among first credit rating clients only, wishes to secure a manufacturers line of matched Spruce boards, and Hemlock lumber, on a percentage basis. Can place large orders from A1 firms. Apply Box 54, Canada Lumberman, Toronto. 22

LUMBERMAN OF EXPERIENCE in all branches of the business, will shortly be open for engagement of responsibility, or as salesman. Have several years' experience and first class connection with the best trade in the Maritime Provinces, Quebec, Ontario and Eastern States. This is an opportunity for a firm to secure a highly recommended man able to produce results. Apply Box 56, Canada Lumberman, Toronto. 22

Wanted-Employees

WANTED FIRST CLASS INSPECTOR experienced in both hard and soft woods. J. R. Eaton & Sons, Limited, Orillia, Ont. 22

WANTED HARDWOOD INSPECTOR at Montreal, familiar with National Hardwood Lumber Association grading rules. Permanent position at good salary. Must speak French. Box 53, Canadian Lumberman, Toronto. 21-22

Business Chances

Planing Mill Wanted

Will buy planing mill in Ottawa Valley or Central Ontario. Must have siding and yard room. Give price and full description. Box 50, Canada Lumberman, Toronto. 21-22

For Sale

Bargain—Must be sold quick, two side mill, both double cut bands; one Band Re-Saw, two Edgers, Lath Mill, Filing equipment, Engines, Boilers, Belting and Shafting all complete. Apply Box 48, Canada Lumberman, Toronto. 22

Saw Mill Plant For Sale

Practically new and modern Saw Mill Plant, capacity about 30 Million feet per annum, located in the Interior of British Columbia on a beautiful inland lake and on the main line of the Grand Trunk Pacific Railway. About 500 Million feet of timber on and adjacent to Lake (about 90% Spruce) and another Billion feet available at reasonable prices. Natural conditions ideal for economical logging, manufacturing, piling and shipping. An advantage of about $4 per thousand feet in freight rates to the Prairie Provinces over Coast shipments.

This property offers unlimited possibilities as a lumber, pulp and paper property. Would consider selling a half interest. Terms reasonable.

A. C. FROST COMPANY,
134 South LaSalle Street,
5-t.f. Chicago, Ill.

Auction Sale of Valuable Quebec Timber Limits

R. H. Klock & Co., through W. A. Cole, Auctioneer, on the Nineteenth day of February, 1920, at the hour of three o'clock p.m., subject to one reserve bid, will offer for sale by Public Auction at the Russell House in the City of Ottawa, in the Province of Ontario, timber berths numbers 176 and 177, Kipawa, are 100 sq. miles more or less. These timber limits contain large quantities of pine, spruce, and other wood goods. For further particulars apply to James B. Klock, 70 St. Matthew St., Montreal; Errol M. McDougall, K.C., Royal Trust Building, Montreal; D. B. Rochester, 145 James Street, Ottawa, and W. A. Cole, Hope Chambers, 63 Sparks Street, Ottawa, Auctioneer.

To:
Lumbermen—
Trust Companies—
Banks—
Executors of Estates—
Or Private Owners of Timber and Pulp Lands.

If you are contemplating offeri your Limits for sale by Auction, bear in mind that the Capital of the Dominion is the greatest lumber centre in America and the place to hold your sale.

Will be pleased to give you all information as to details, etc.

WM. A. COLE,

OFFICES:
63 Sparks Street, Ottawa, Ont.
Established—1895.
References—Any Bank.

For Sale

1,280 ACRES OF TIMBER, estimated to cut 25,000 ft. per acre, $9,500. Box 654, Nelson, B.C. 19-22

Standing Timber For Sale

300 M. Standing Timber. Going to cut this winter. Half Pine, balance Oak, Chestnut, Maple, Ash. This could be cut to order, if sold before it is cut. Thos. Leedham, St. Williams, Ont. 22-23

TIMBER LIMITS

I have a number of good Timber Limits for sale. Particulars, Wm. Cooke, Stair Building, Toronto.

For Sale

Fine industrial site, situated near western boundary of Ottawa, Ont. Good property for almost any industry. Mill and storage buildings almost new, with some shafting erected. Five hundred feet siding on C. P. R. If interested apply Box 55, Canada Lumberman, Toronto. 22

Canadian Timber for Europe

Canada's position as a candidate for part of the tremendous overseas trade that is expected to accompany the rebuilding of devastated Europe is carefully expounded in the export edition of the Canada Lumberman and Woodworker. This contains a shadow map of the European markets in which Canada hopes to sell some of her merchantable timber. There are startling figures, but they are quoted by the Canada Lumberman from a census taken by the Dominion Bureau of Statistics. The pulpwood is estimated at about one billion cords. It is stated that the timber wealth of British Columbia alone amounted in 1908 to 300 billion feet. Up to 1917 only about 30 million feet board measure had been cut. Canada's unsurpassed opportunity in world markets created by the necessity for rebuilding Europe's ruined farms and cities is dealt with in a leading article. The structural material each country requires, how it should be cut, graded and delivered, is tersely told, with the admonition that "Canada should bid for a large share of this business, because she has the foretss, the mills and the labor necessary to produce large quantities of timber to suit all markets."—Timber Trades Journal of London, Eng.

General Activity in Lumber Trade

The last edition of the Labor Gazette, Ottawa, says:

Charlottetown reported dullness in the lumber industry. The saw and shingle mills at St. John were busy. Fredericton reported that the lumber mills of the district continued to operate at full capacity and that preparations were being made for the winter bush work. Quebec reported that most of the sawmills in the district were still operating, but that river driving was confined to the floating of grounded logs. The lumber camps had not yet opened up. Sherbrooke reported that the lumber camp was fairly active and that the saw and shingle mills were busy. The sawmills at Ottawa and Hull were in full operation. Peterborough reported that the lumbering industry was very active and that there was some difficulty in getting men for the woods. Owen Sound reported that the sawmills were fairly active, but that the tie and shingle mills were rather quiet. Sault Ste. Marie reported a demand for men.

Fire Fighting or Prevention?

Except London, Paris and Berlin, European cities have paid little attention to modern fire protective equipment. They have directed their chief energies to fire prevention. Municipal expenditures have been devoted to the control of building construction and maintenance. On the contrary, Canada has developed very elaborate and efficient fire-fighting facilities. As regards appliances, methods and personnel, the fire brigades of large Canadian and American cities are incomparably superior to those of other countries. In this course of action lies one of the essential differences between the respective policies of Canadian municipalities and those of Europe. To prevent rather than to extinguish fires has not impressed public bodies in Canada as being a part of their functions. Consequently, the annual maintenance costs of city fire departments average $1.43 per capita, fire losses $2.96 per capita, and insurance rates $1.18 per capita in Canada as compared with 21 cents, 71 cents and 26 cents, respectively, in Europe.

Review of Current Trade Conditions

Ontario and the East

The lumber situation as a whole continues brisk but the outlook is somewhat perplexing and there is considerable speculation being indulged in regarding production for next year, where the desired quantities are going to come from and what the prices will be. Shipments are going ahead in a satisfactory manner and there is little complaint heard regarding car congestion. Now that all the mills have practically closed down, they will catch up in the matter of sending out their stock. More men will be available for shipping purposes and it is hoped that the woods labor will be replenished at many centres. Dressing mills which have been literally flooded with orders for planing and matching lumber, have now caught up and are accepting business so that factories requiring work lumber will be able to secure their requirements much more readily.

An example of the shortage in white pine is furnished in a statement by a leading Ontario organization which this year took the output of five mills, all of which sawed considerably more than last year, yet this company had 5,000,000 feet of lumber less to sell during the first week in November than it had on January 1st last year. This is a surprising state of affairs showing how low available stocks are in many districts; in other words production has been greater and sales far heavier than usual. In fact, ever since the 1st of April business with most lumber concerns has been the best on record. November and December are usually counted rather quiet months and it is not out of the ordinary that matters should slow down somewhat. Shipments of white pine to the other side of the line still continue actively.

In regard to hardwoods, there is a shortage in all lines, particularly in maple, elm, ash and birch, in both the thin and thick ends, and within the past few days a marked improvement has taken place in the demand for basswood. Prices are very firm and it is more a question of trying to get the stock than to get a price. The latter takes care of itself if the wholesaler and manufacturer has the goods required by automobile concerns, implement men, furniture manufacturers and others. Never were so many inquiries received for any "old thing at all."

It is reported that some of the logging jobbers in Quebec Province are paying their bushmen as high as $100 a month and board, and if this is the case one can form some conception of the price that hardwoods will likely go next season. It means that manufacturers will, in all likelihood, be asking as much for their stocks as the wholesalers are receiving to-day for whatever quantities they have on hand.

A careful study of the whole situation reveals the fact that it is decidedly difficult to get any desired quantity of hardwood in a certain grade or thickness and carloads are mostly of the mixed variety. Some firms intend taking their price list off the market as they have not the stock to sell and they realize that, under no circumstances, can values descend. The outlook, so far in forest products, is strong and healthy and there is little fear with the improved shipping facilities for next season, the bright prospects for building and the increased use of wood in many directions, but quotations will go higher.

There will be no new stocks of dry lumber coming on the market before June 1st next and what will happen between now and that date it is impossible to foretell. Hardwood flooring companies are very busy, having more business than they can attend to or can secure stock for, and every woodworking establishment is running pretty well to capacity.

Retail lumbermen state that fall repairs have loomed up briskly in the country and the trade is naturally pleased at the Farmers' party coming into power at Queen's Park, Toronto. This all means better business for the communities in which they reside as there will be a general brightening up of farm premises, out-buildings and other structures.

The demand for Coast products is only fair and not a great deal of stuff is coming through owing to the activity of the United States market. There has been an increase in the base price of timber and shingles are a little easier. Laths are still very scare and command any old price,—in fact it would be a shame to state what some of the holders of lath have been receiving for whatever consignments they can get their hands on.

Building continues actively and Toronto still leads the way. The City Architect reports the total value of permits issued in October to be $2,400,000, or an increase of $1,623,799 over October, 1918. There have been $434,000 worth of factories erected this month and 400 garages valued at $160,090.

The totals for October, rated as one of the biggest building months of the year, for the past eight years in Toronto are as follows:—1912, $1,573,620; 1913, $1,987,027; 1914, $814,468; 1915, $413,756; 1916, $496,184; 1917, $786,225; 1918, $776,201; 1919, $2,400,000.

Great Britain

No important change in the trading aspect during the past few days has taken place. The dominating feature of the market is the volume of stock that has arrived lately. Most of it has gone into store either on account of importers or shippers. The latter are holding out firmly for their valuations, and if these are not forthcoming the stock is yarded until such time as the demand becomes more active. The shippers' agents are confident that the demand will become active enough to absorb all their stocks of hardwood at advanced prices, and that before very long. Not while supplies are pouring in, of course, but when the import begins to tail off as it is expected soon to do. The position is interesting, if somewhat complex.

Whether it be due to the accumulation of arrivals, or simply that members of the London trade are inclined to take a "breather," it must be admitted that but slow progress has been made in buying and selling during the past week.

However, the certain knowledge that only a little more than a month remains within which to get goods forward from the Baltic ports will assuredly act as a stimulant during the last weeks, and those firms whose stock lists are somewhat "scrappy affairs" will seek to improve them by further purchases.

The announcement of the coming softwood sales has been received in London with a curious admixture of regrets and pleasure. The leading importers do not hesitate to condemn the action of the brokers, in scarcely polite terms, whereas the old habitues of the sale rooms, who depended largely upon the catalogues for their requirements, are looking forward, with the utmost keenness, to the approaching sale.

To many members of the London trade, the coming of the timber exchange was looked upon as a useful foil to the auctions, because it was believed that constant contact between members of each branch of the trade would have led to greater freedom, and the necessity for public auctions would not have been urgent.

"It is, therefore, difficult to forecast the future of softwood sales and a timber exchange. Very frankly, we do not think the trade can regularly support a weekly auction and a weekly exchange," says a correspondent of the "Timber News," which, in reference to the Swedish market, says:

One of the most curious features of the soft-wood market today is the strong upward tendency of f.o.b. values. Wholy undeterred by the rivalry of the Finnish exporters, the Swedish shippers have steadily plodded along all through the summer, never yielding to pressure, and now, as the season draws to its close, f.o.b quotations are advanced.

The late entry of French and Spanish buyers served to strengthen the shippers' hands, and now the Cape buyers are in the field, paying prices for deals which appear incredibly high for South Swedish productions.

The exporters have ideas regarding next f.o.w. values which will yet surprise the importers in this country.

Needless to say, the buyers in the United Kingdom will not be led astray by the undue optimism of the Swedish shippers, and it will therefore mean that a few months will elapse before negotiations are seriously entered into for f.o.w. cargoes.

It is, from many points of view, regrettable that quotations are soaring, because the markets are already difficult, even with values at their present level, and enhanced prices will only serve to complicate matters in the future.

Slowly but surely more boats are becoming available for wood cargoes. During the last few days the change has been quite noticeable, though for how long it is going to last is another matter. As the winter months approach an increased supply of tonnage naturally comes about owing to so many ports being closed to navigation. The offering of more boats may therefore be only temporary.

The best chance of getting lower rates is for competition to take place between the great English and American shipping companies. There has already been a whisper of something of the sort coming

about in the future. The sooner it takes place the better, from the charterer's point of view. The timber trade, at any rate, has had quite enough of exorbitant freights.

The export season has practically closed. All the lumber bought for Government account has been shipped from this port, while there is a comparatively small amount to go from Quebec, but this will be sent next season. A considerable amount is being exported from Halifax and St. John.

The pulp markets are very firm, mechanical is selling freely, and sulphite is also in demand. Newsprint is very scarce, with signs that prices will go considerably higher.

United States

Business has slowed down somewhat in many of the leading cities owing to the coal strike and labor unrest, as well as the falling off in the building line at this season of the year. There has also been considerable upsetting of market conditions owing to the $10,00 penalty assessed against cars held for demurrage. The result is that numerous cars, which were in transit, were hastened to their destination, and, speaking of the recent action of the United States Railroad Administration in imposing this penalty, a leading paper says: There still continues to be something of a hysterical feeling in transit car circles, reflected in substantial concessions from market prices for cars which are near or at transfer points. For some reason which has not been clearly explained dimension constitutes a very large proportion of all transit shipments. A month ago many transit cars did not have 50 pieces each of 14, 16, or 18 foot lengths. In some cases these very desirable lengths were entirely omitted. Now a good share of the cars are very evenly balanced.

It is particularly noticeable that both in assortment and quality the consignments included in transit car shipments are much better than before the announcement that a severe penalty would be imposed.

During the week there has been a very material reduction in the number of transit cars loaded with lumber being offered to the trade in many commercial centres. There seems to be quite a radical difference of opinion among jobbers as to the reason for this substantial shutting off of the supply. Some of the brokers insist that this is the off season for transit cars, as shippers do not care to run the risk of having material come into the market after winter has set in, because the chances are that it will have to be unloaded and remain in storage until next spring. Other handlers of transit cars insist that there are still at least 30 days remaining, during which time the dealers could take on a reasonable amount of transit material, due to the fact that there has been no perceptible let-up in the consumers' trade. This latter class of jobbers frankly state that the $10.00 penalty for holding cars at transfer points is the real cause why many concerns on the coast have discontinued putting lumber in transit and others have cut in two the number of cars they had been sending on.

Scarcity of stocks at the mills and inadequacy of railroad service are large contributors to the present low volume of lumber movement. Of course, retail yards are not buying a great deal of lumber with winter at hand, but there is some disposition to look ahead, as next year promises to be even more active in building circles. Many wise buyers are placing orders for stock now, and are willing to take it as soon as it can be shipped. Millmen are not inclined to take business at the present market level for shipment after first of the year. They got their fill of that kind of business this year and have been shipping lumber at a loss for months.

Some mills in various parts of the country report enough business on hand to keep them busy for the remainder of the year. The chief obstacle at present is the car shortage. Only about thirty to fifty per cent. of required equipment is being supplied by the railroads, and the coal emergency is reducing the percentage. There was some softening in both the southern pine and the western markets a few weeks ago, but that period has apparently passed, and quotations for mill shipment are approaching the highest level known this year.

The hardwood market shows even greater activity than heretofore, and while transactions have been curtailed somewhat by the car shortage the week has been an excellent one for sellers. Price adcanves, particularly on the better grades, are reported from the majority of the large buying centres. With stocks scarce and production barely keeping up to previous levels the future will undoubtedly see a continuation of the present situation. Factory buyers are the most active and lumber is being sought especially by the flooring manufacturers, who are unable to supply the demand.

So far this year production of southern pine has exceeded orders booked by less than normal production for two weeks, while the mills still have on hand unfilled orders which it will take at least six weeks to fill. Consequently, it is not surprising that the market shows a firmer tendency with the belief becoming general that the low point of the recent softening has been reached. Manufacturers in all sincerity believe that because of conditions which are outside of their control production can not be greatly stimulated and that the demand will equal, if it does not exceed, the supply, and consequently are not worrying about getting business. Weather conditions have improved and as a result the production outlook is better, but log supplies are low at many mills. The car situation is by no means the best and this is hindering business to a considerable extent.

Market Correspondence

SPECIAL REPORTS ON CONDITIONS AT HOME AND ABROAD

Conditions Remain Unchanged on St. John Market

The last two weeks has seen little if any change in the lumber situation at St. John. The mills are still sawing on old contracts. No shipments from the city mills are taking place, and when the season closes they will all have a very large stock of sawn lumber piled on their wharves, mostly all of which had been sold in the early Spring to the British Government and is being paid for as sawn to date.

No new contracts or sales for deals to be sawn in 1920 have been made, and evidently no one wishes to speculate in buying for 1920 delivery. The mills are all arranging to have normal cuts in 1920, and have crews in the woods getting out logs The cut on the Upper St. John will be for St. John mills, the same as in 1919, about 40 million feet. The balance of the cut will be made on the lower reaches of the St. John.

Prices for logging have been arranged for at about same as paid in 1918-19, and, as men are becoming more plentiful, it looks as if the operators will not have to pay as high wages as in 1918. This, of course, will be offset by increases in provisions for man and beast, which are higher than a year ago. Many of the rotary mills which arranged to go in for full cuts during the early Fall have cut down their quantities and will, therefore, not take out as much sawn lumber as was anticipated. This is caused by the stand taken by the deal buyers in which they refuse to speculate in contracts at any set price for next year's cut.

Local business remains good and the factories have orders for some time to come and should be busier than last winter. Prices locally remain unchanged. Local business at St. John should be better than for some years past, and the future holds a bright outlook. Numerous plans are in progress for building during 1920. Many houses are needed and with the municipal and city commission housing schemes being now arranged for, it certainly looks as if the Spring and Summer of 1920 should find a large amount of work.

Laths are impossible to find at any price. Shingles are also very scarce, especially in the higher grades.

Montreal Business is Steady—Good Outlook

Montreal lumber market conditions continue to be satisfactory taken as a whole. Here and there it is reported that trade has slackened, but this is only natural at this season, when yards are not inclined to order in any large quantities in view of the lull that takes place in building during the winter.

Indications are that next year's cut in the province will be on a larger scale, providing that the labor is available. That will be the important factor. One manufacturer states that he sees little improvement in this respect. Men have not yet settled down, and the tendency is still to jump from job to job.

American orders have declined. Advices from the New England States are to the effect that the yards have large stocks on hand, that shipments are still arriving, and that for the time being there is no inclination to do further buying. The season for sending large shipments via the canals is now closed.

B. C. stocks are selling slowly, except timber, for which the base price has been again advanced. Shingles are dull and cheaper.

Hardwoods are a better market, with limited supplies. Pulpwood is being bought, but prices are uncertain.

Local sash and door firms are well supplied with orders, and the box-makers are fairly busy.

The outlook in the building trade is very good, and with the settlement of labor troubles there should be an excellent opening in

the spring. A committee of the Builders' Exchange has been appointed to stabilize conditions next season. Architects have a considerable amount of work in hand, and if the provincial housing schemes materialize, the demand for lumber next season will be on a large scale. The public has evidently come to the conclusion that costs will not come down, and that there is no use waiting for cheaper production. The Montreal permits for last month totalled $1,519,892, an increase of $1,140,842,—this, following on a number of previous substantial increases, indicates that the revival is no mere flash in the pan. For the ten months the permits amounted to $8,484,636, a gain of $4,117,283.

Purchases Playfair Mill at Midland

Z. Mageau, M.L.A., of Sturgeon Falls, has purchased the old Playfair & White mill at Midland, Ont. This mill has not been in operation for some time. Some of the equipment, such as band saw, steel carriage, band re-saw, 400 h.p. engine and a boiler or two, will be used in the mill of the Field Lumber Co. at Field, Ont., on the C. N. R. main line. The name of the latter concern has just been changed to the Mageau Lumber Co. Limited, and the capacity of the plant will be increased to 50,000 feet a day.

New Sawmill Going Up at Douglastown

The Miramichi Lumber Co., Chatham, N. B., are erecting a new mill at Douglastown on the site of the old Hutchison mill. The equipment consists of a double cutting band and a Yates re-saw, and everything will be entirely new. The company expect to saw about 75,000 feet per day.

In regard to logging operations, the company state they are not cutting as much as usual, only about 30,000,000 feet. They are not ating three camps of their own, and the balance is being carried out by jobbers. The cost of the logging will run from 10 per cent. to 15 per cent. more than last year. The officers of the Miramichi Lumber Co. are G. F. Underwood, President; J. P. Riley, Vice-President; J. W. Brankley, General Manager; W. P. Eaton, Resident Manager.

Managers Visit the Government Nursery

The managers of the Province of Quebec Fire Protective Associations were recently the guests of Mr. G. C. Piche, Chief Forester, at the Government Nursery of Berthierville. They inspected the nursery, visited the experimental cuttings, and discussed various subjects. The following day they visited Lachute and inspected some plantings of spruce and Scotch pine made on the drifting sands.

The Laurentide Co., Ltd., Grand 'Mere, and the Wayagamack Pulp & Paper Co., Three Rivers, P. Q., have each purchased three Cleveland tractors. Heretofore all the logging work of the companies has been done by men and horses in the woods.

Messrs. Hanssen and Faulkner, of the Forestry Division of the Laurentide Co., Grand 'Mere, Que., have made an intensive timber survey of the Mekinac limit and report some good reproductions of the old burns.

C. A. Moyle, chief engineer of the Riordon Pulp & Paper Co., recently visited the plant of the Laurentide Co., Grand 'Mere.

Activities of National Lumber Dealers

A meeting of the Executive Committee of the National Wholesale Lumber Dealers Association was held at No. 66 Broadway recently in New York, the following being present: H. F. Taylor, President, Buffalo, N. Y., J. W. McClure, Memphis, Tenn., F. R. Babcock, Pittsburg, Pa., H. W. McDonough, Boston, Mass., W. G. Power, St. Pacome, Que., C. A. Goodman, Marinette, Wis., Trustees, E. F. Perry, Secretary, W. W. Schupner, Department Manager, W. S. Phippen, Traffic Manager.

A number of matters were considered, among the most important being that in connection with the transit car situation. The reports of J. W. McClure, C. A. Goodman and Secretary Perry of the Committee appointed to represent the Association at the International Trade Conference at Atlantic City, were most interesting, and action was taken with a view of emphasizing the desirability of a closer relation on the part of the lumber industry in the work of the Chamber of Commerce of the United States. This will be conducted in co-operation with other lumber associations. The reports of special committees carrying out the provisions of Referendum No. 28 of the Chamber of Commerce of the United States showed progress and of the "Our Country First" conference at Chicago by H. H. Hettler and the National Retail Lumber Dealers Association at Detroit were received. The Executive Committee also endorsed the action of the National Lumber Manufacturers Association requesting an appropriation from Congress for the housing and maintenance of the Forest Products Laboratory of the United States Department of Agriculture. The Committee on union with the National Bureau of Wholesale Lumber Distributors reported progress.

The departmental activities of the Association through the Bureau of Information and Transportation Bureau were fully covered and indicated a large amount of important work handled for members. A substantial gain in membership is reported, the total now reaching 461, the largest in the history of the Association.

Personal Paragraphs of Interest

S. Bick of the Bennett Lumber Co., Limited, Montreal, is on a visit to England.

G. I. Jones of the Jones Hardwood Co., Boston, spent a few days in Toronto recently on business.

F. C. Hooton, Manager of the Strahle Lumber & Salt Co., Saginaw, Mich., spent a few days in Toronto calling upon the trade.

Mrs. Firstbrook, wife of Mr. John Firstbrook, President of Firstbrook Bros. Limited, box manufacturers, Toronto, passed away recently.

A. N. Dudley of Toronto, Secretary-Treasurer of the Hobel Hunt Club, has been spending the past few weeks on a deer-hunting expedition north of Spragge, Ont.

J. P. Johnson, W. J. Lovering and Dr. Kemp of Toronto, have been enjoying a successful deer-hunting expedition at Swamp Lake, near Mount Irwin, Peterboro County.

Gilbert Brocklebank, representing C. V. Haerem, Manchester, Eng., was in Toronto recently on his way to the Pacific Coast where he will look into the lumber export situation.

Mrs. Frank Pauze, wife of Mr. Frank Pauze, of U. Pauze and Fils, lumber merchants and manufacturers of interior trim, Montreal, died on October 31, aged 51. She leaves four children.

Frank J. Hathway, President of the French Bay Lumber Co., Limited, Sault Ste. Marie, Ont., who are manufacturers of hardwood lumber, was in Toronto recently calling upon the trade.

A. E. Gordon of Terry & Gordon, Toronto, and Arthur Eastcott, Manager of the Pembroke Lumber Co., Pembroke, have returned from a successful deer-hunting expedition near Mattawa.

H. J. Plunkett of the Plunkett-Webster Lumber Co., wholesale lumber merchants, New York, spent a few days in Toronto lately on business in connection with the purchase of Canadian hardwoods.

E. Roberge, manager of the Exchange Lumber Co., Montreal, has been on a selling trip to Boston, and Leon Gagne, jr., of the same company, has visited New York, Philadelphia and other points in the U. S.

The many friends of W. C. Thuerck, of Haileybury, Ont., will sympathize with him in the death of his little daughter from diphtheria. Mr. Thuerck has for some years been a member of the staff of Terry & Gordon, Toronto.

Hon. Beniah Bowman, who was elected as a U. F. O. member of the Ontario Legislature for Manitoulin Island, is the new Minister of Lands, Forests and Mines in the cabinet of Premier E. C. Drury and succeeds Hon. G. Howard Ferguson who will be the leader of the Conservatives in the Legislative Assembly.

F. H. Pont, of the firm of Wm. Pont, lumber merchants, Zaandam, Holland, who was in Toronto recently on his way home from a trip through the timber belts of the Dominion, stated that his firm were contemplating entering the lumber business in Canada if conditions in Russia, where it had previously had large interests, did not soon improve.

G. W. White of G. W. White & Son, Watertown, J. S. Caldwell, Syracuse, James B. Cleveland of Johnston & Murray, Watertown, and O. M. Thomson, Syracuse, N. Y. state representative of the Union Lumber Co., Toronto, were in Toronto recently on their return from a deer-shooting expedition at Mileage 44 on the T. & N. O. Ry. The party had a splendid time and report fairly good luck. There was about four inches of snow on the ground in that section early in November.

Herbert L. Hebard, who has been appointed Inspector of the National Hardwood Lumber Association for Toronto and district, succeeding John J. Miller, is already well known to a large number of lumbermen, and during the comparatively short period that he was assisting Mr. Miller, made a large number of friends. Mr. Hebard was born in Boston, Mass., and up to the time of coming to Toronto had always been a resident in that city. He was educated at the public schools of Boston, being graduated from the High School in 1906. Mr. Hebard then went to work for J. M. Woods & Co., East Cambridge, Mass., and was with them as an inspector up to the time that he entered the service of the National Hardwood Lumber Association.

Advertising is Business Insurance

A large manufacturer who, during the war, devoted his entire plant to war-work, kept his advertising running continuously, although he could not fill a single order. When asked why he did it, he said that he was insuring a market for his product when he returned to his regular lines. He has since reverted to his pre-war products and his plant is running to full capacity with more business in sight than he can handle.

Advertising was business insurance for him.

Logging Regulations on Crown Lands

Hon. E. A. Smith, Minister of Lands and Mines for New Brunswick, has issued the following logging regulations with respect to the cutting of timber on Crown lands of the province:

Diameter Limit—

No sound butted tree smaller than the following diameters measured inside the bark at a point not less than twelve inches from the ground shall be cut:—Spruce, white and red pine, twelve inches; princess or jack pine, ten inches. (Penalty fifty cents per tree in addition to regular stumpage.)

No Undersized Cutting on Spruce Barrens and Slow Growing Thickets—

shall take place without written permission from the Crown Land Office. A charge not exceeding fifty cents per thousand in addition to stumpage will be made to cover cost of supervision.

Stump Height—

All sound butted trees must be cut as low as possible and never higher than sixteen inches regardless of snow conditions. (Penalty twenty-five cents per tree.)

Saw to be Used—

The saw shall be used in felling trees and cutting them into logs; if the axe is used the length for scaling shall be taken from point to point being the extreme length of the log.

Trimming Allowance on Logs—

Six inches over-run in the length of a log shall be the maximum allowance made for trimming; if this is exceeded the log will be scaled as one foot longer.

Size of Tops—

All tops shall be taken out to as low a diameter as possible. Spruce tops 6 inches in diameter is the maximum allowed except in case of very bushy top when 7 inches will be allowed. Fir 6 inch top is the maximum allowed. White and red pine 7 inch top is the maximum allowed. (Penalty $7.50 per thousand feet.)

Mixing Logs—

Logs cut on Crown Lands shall be placed in separate brows from those cut on Granted Lands and shall be marked with a different mark.

Skids, Roads, Bridges, Camps, Hovels—

No spruce, white or red pine shall be used as skids or in the building of roads or bridges where other species are available. Where soft wood must be used fir must be taken in preference to spruce. (Penalty $7.50 per thousand feet.)

Trees Wholly Killed by Spruce Bud Worm or Fire—

must be yarded and browed separately from living trees in order to obtain the two-thirds rate of stumpage; otherwise the full rate will be charged.

Lodged and Burned Trees and Windfalls—

All lodged trees, all spruce and white and red pine necessarily cut out of roads, yards, landings, etc., and any dead, burnt or blown down trees suitable for lumber shall be taken out. (Penalty $7.50 per thousand feet.)

Protect Young Growth—

All reasonable care must be taken to prevent injury to young spruce trees below the diameter limit.

Scalers are sworn to report all violations of the Game Laws coming under their notice.

Many Activities of the Busy East

The Boony River Lumber Company intend to cut two million of lumber on property about Mill Lake, N. B this winter. Roscoe Burgess and Matt McKay have taken contracts for one million each. The mill now operated in St. George, N. B., will be moved into the woods and the lumber will be manufactured there. Sawing operations will be in charge of George Patterson. who owns the mill. The company also have a crew in at Piskechegan. This output will be brought down the river and manufactured at St. George.

W. H. Harrison, Gladys Leslie Welsford and Leah Edna Gaskin of St. John, have been incorporated to carry on a general lumber and pulp wood business with head office in Fredericton, N. B., and a total capital stock of $24,500, under the name of the United Lumber, Limited. These same persons have also been authorized to carry on lumber business under the name of the Atlas Lumber Company Limited.

The New Brunswick department of Lands and Mines has received from the Laurentide Pulp and Paper Company of Quebec information concerning the results of experiments carried on by it in the use of hard woods in the manufacture of pulp-wood. Hardwoods, such as birch, beech, maple, etc, were experimented with and contrary to the general opinion were found to be suitable for the manufacture of excellent grades of pulp. The information has been received with great interest as hardwoods constitute some thirty per cent. of the forest growth of New Brunswick. Hon. E. A. Smith, minister of Lands and Mines, is much interested in the matter and it will be followed up with a view to having hardwoods utilized in the province for the making of pulp.

Four vacant lots of crown lands were sold at the Crown Lands office, Fredericton, a few days ago. In the county of Gloucester twenty-five acres at the northern end of Miscou Island was bid in by George Vibert at $1.60 per acre. There was some keen bidding on this lot. In Northumberland County sixty-two acres on the southern side of Allanville Settlement was bid in by trustees of the school district at $1.00 per acre. Three acres on the road from Chatham to Burnt Church at Grand Dune was bid in by Jules Gouvereau at the upset price of $2.00 per acre. In Kent forty-two acres north of west branch of St. Nicholas river was bid in by Robert M. Mundle at the upset price of $4.00 per acre

---

Lumber shipments from St. John have been comparatively small for some time only sailing vessels occasionally taking away cargos. A few days ago the Barque Montrose, 984 tons, sailed for London, England, with 854,304 feet of deals valued at $33,826. The lumber was shipped by George McKean & Company Ltd.

Word was received in St. John by the Furness Withy Steamship Line that the S. S. Cape Premier has sailed from Glasgow on November 5. She is enroute to St. John to carry a carge of lumber overseas for Stetson, Cutler & Company.

Indications point to a very heavy cut of lumber in New Brunswick this winter. It will be heavy on both crown lands and private owned lands. The decision to cut more lumber is said to be the result of indications in the world market that there will be a tremendous demand next year. France and Belgium are expected to have requirements for reconstruction and the United States and British markets are expected to be under supplied.

During the last season there has been a steady movement of manufactured lumber overseas from various New Brunswick ports, but scarcity of shipping retards that movement to quite an extent. The shipping situation will gradually improve and the expectation is that the huge quantities of manufactured lumber, which has been piled on the mill-yards all over the province, some of it for more than one season, will be cleared in 1920. The labor situation as far as the lumber woods is concerned is said to be satisfactory.

Col. T. G. Loggie, Deputy Minister of Lands and Mines for New Brunswick, announces that the construction of the telephone line up the Nepisiguit River from Bathurst, which has been delayed by the non-arrival of the wire until a few days ago, has now been commenced and several miles of line have already been strung. This line will penetrate about 70 miles from Bathurst into the very centre of the province and is part of the policy of constructing woods telephone lines and lookouts in the interests of better fire protection in New Brunswick.

The construction is being carried out by the Bathurst Lumber Company according to a standard agreed on, and the cost is equally divided between the Forest Service and the Bathurst Lumber Company. The actual work is under the supervision of Mr. Mathias Cloutier, of St. Eugene, Que., who has had extensive experience in the construction of tree telephone lines, and who has been loaned to New Brunswick for this purpose.

Mr. H. C. Kinghorn, of the Forest Service, and Mr. D. R. Morrison, an experienced lineman from St. John, left recently to work on the line a few days to familiarize themselves with the method of construction. They will then start the construction of a 40 mile line in the centre of Northumberland Couty which is designed to connect with a new lookout to be constructed in Bald Mountain. This is expected to be one of the best lookouts in the Province, a very extensive area being visible from it. It is hoped to finish this line and also a line in Victoria County to connect with a new lookout to be placed on Blue Mountain.

Big Shipyard Plant is on the Market

After erecting a six-way shipyard with all necessary mechanical appliances and factories, spending $2,500,000 in wages and utilizing 22,000,000 feet of British Columbia fir in wooden ship-building in twenty-seven months, the William Lyall shipyards plant of North Vancouver, B. C., has completed its work, finds no more contracts available and is now advertised for sale. A great wartime industry has come to an end after producing over 40,000 tons of wooden shipping most of the vessels being now at sea.

EDGINGS

Ontario

E. H. Mann & Co. of Peterboro will erect a new saw-mill on Otonabee St., Peterboro.

The Kelly Lumber Co. of Bridgenorth, Ont., intend erecting a saw mill in Lakefield, Ont.

Chas. Boaz of Clayton, Ont., has built a cement flume under his saw-mill and carried out other improvements to the plant.

John McLellan, a well-known lumberman, has purchased the planing mill property in Harriston, Ont., belonging to the estate of the late George Gray & Co., and will operate the same. The industry is one of the oldest in Harriston.

The Fesserton Timber Co. of Toronto, recently purchased 2,000,000 feet of jack pine and spruce from the International Land & Lumber Co., Ottawa. About 75 per cent. of the quantity secured is jack pine and the remainder spruce. The lumber was sawn at St. Felicien, Lake St. John District, Que.

The Victoria Harbor Lumber Co. of Victoria Harbor, Ont., recently finished sawing for the season and had a very good operating year although the cut was not as large as in 1918. The company are conducting six camps this season, and will take out considerably more timber than last winter.

Handsomely-framed certificates of the membership of the Lumbermen's Credit Bureau, Inc. of Toronto, have been sent out to the members and now adorn the walls of their respective offices. The Lumbermen's Credit Bureau is in a flourishing condition at the present time and has forty-three members, the largest in its history.

A charter has been granted to the La Sarre Lumber Co., Limited, with a capital stock of $75,000 and headquarters in Toronto. The company is empowered to buy, sell and deal in timber and wood and to conduct the business of timbermen, sawmillers and lumbermen and operate saw and planing mills. Among the provisional incorporators are James M. Forgie, C. A. St. C. McKay, W. B. Sturrup and T. S. H. Giles of Toronto.

A charter has been granted to the Kenora Lumber Co. with a capital stock of $200,000 and headquarters in the town of Kenora. The company is empowered to carry on in all its branches a lumber, timber and pulpwood business, and to manufacture, buy, sell and deal in timber, logs, lumber and wood of all kinds. The provisional directors are Henry P. Cook and Rupert H. Moore of Kenora.

Seaman, Kent Co., Limited, of Toronto, have purchased the large factory formerly owned by the West Lorne Wagon Works at West Lorne, Ont. and will convert the building into a plant for turning out oak flooring exclusively. This will make five plants, the output of which is controlled by Seaman, Kent Co. They are very busy at all their factories and have been doing considerable export trade, although owing to the scarcity of hardwoods, they have turned down a number of orders from the Old Country.

A charter has been granted to Thomson Bros. Limited, with a capital stock of $60,000 and headquarters in Toronto, to carry on a general contracting and construction business and also to manufacture and deal in building materials and to conduct the business of a lumber, saw and planing miller and manufacturer of lumber and woodenware. The incorporators are,—James Bruce Thomson, Thomas Thomson, Wm. R. Thomson, Allan G. Thomson and James G. Thomson, all of Toronto.

The Parkdale Lumber Co., with a capital stock of $20,000, has been granted a charter to carry on the business of timber merchants, saw-mill proprietors and timber growers, and to import, export and deal in timber and wood of all kinds. The headquarters of the company are at Dunchurch, District of Parry Sound, Ont., and the provisional directors are,—John H. Hosick, Dunchurch, James Hall, Toronto, James Hosick, Vernon E. Steele and James F. Ross of Port Colborne.

A provincial charter has been granted the Lakefield Canoe & Boat Club. The headquarters of the company are at Lakefield, Ont., and the capital stock is $50,000. The company is empowered to manufacture, buy, sell and deal in canoes and boats of every kind and to buy, sell and generally deal in wood, timber and lumber. It is understood that the Lakefield Canoe & Boat Club will take over the assets and business formerly carried on by the Lakefield Canoe Co. The incorporators of the company are,—Wm. J. Rooney, Douglas T. Chamberlain, Chas. H. Manaton of Lakefield.

Eastern Canada

The Kipawa Fibre plant at Temiskaming is expected to be in operation making pulp next month. The company have just awarded a contract for several houses as part of an industrial housing scheme.

A provincial charter has been granted to Gagnon & Fils & Cie, Ltee., with headquarters at Saint George in the county of Beauce, Que., and a capital stock of $99,500. Among the powers conferred on the company is to deal in pulp, paper and wood and the general manufacture and production of lumber. Sir Joseph Gagnon it at the head of the company.

The Ste. Anne Lumber Co., with a capital stock of five hundred thousand dollars and head offices in Montreal, has been incorporated to buy, sell and deal in timber, lumber, paper and pulp wood and to operate mills in this line. Among the provisional incorporators are Linton Hossie Ballantyne, Francis George Bush, and Herbert W. Jackson of Montreal.

La Compagnie de Meubles de Matane, Limitee, has been granted a charter with a capital stock of $49,000 to deal in lumber, timber limits, etc., as well as operate planing mills, saw mills, etc. The provisional directors are Joseph A. Malenfant, H. Charest, P. Bouffard, and Hector Gagnon, all of Matane, Que., where the headquarters of the company are located.

The Federal Lumber Co., Limited, with headquarters at Sherbrooke, Que., and a capital stock of $95,000 has been incorporated to manufacture, sell and deal in all kinds of pulp, paper, lumber and to own, hold and operate timber limits and to conduct the business of lumbering in all its branches. Among the provisional directors are R. A. Oughtred, John P. Wells, Charles D. White and Walter H. Lynch, all of Sherbrooke.

A charter has been granted to the Great Eastern Paper Co. Limited, Montreal, with a capital stock of $5,000,000 to carry on the business of lumbering and the lumber trade in all its branches and all other business incidental thereto, and to manufacture and deal in logs, lumber, timber, pulp, pulpwood, paper, etc. The incorporators are John W. Cook, K.C., Allen A. Magee, T. B. Heney and M. Goudrault and others.

Men are going to the lumber camps daily, and are getting from $75 to $90 a month. Men are coming out daily also. Having earned a month's pay they feel rich enough and come out of the woods to spend their wealth. Woodsmen demand higher wages from jobbers who contract to get out lumber by the thousand than they do from the lumber firms, as they say that they have to work harder for contractors than for the big concerns.

It is the intention of the Quebec Provincial Government carefully to survey the cutting of timber throughout the lumber camps of the province. A large number of inspectors from the Department of Lands and Forests under the direction of Mr. G. C. Piche, chief of the forestry service, have started their organization and will visit more than two thousand of these camps during the coming winter. Infractions of the law will be severely dealt with.

Annie Frances Coughlan, J. D. Pollard Lewin and James J. Stothart, all of St. John, have been incorporated to carry on a shipbuilding business under the name of New Brunswick Shipbuilding Co., Ltd., with capital stock of $320,000, and head office in St. John. The same three persons have been authorized to carry on shipbuilding under the name of St. Martins Shipbuilding Company, Limited, with capital stock of $140,000, and head office at St. Martins.

Elwood Burtt, lumberman, has paid $50,000 for a block of approximately 9,000 acres in the Keswich district, N. B. The owner of the property has been John A. Weatherbee, of Bangor, Maine, and the block adjoins another that is also owned by Maine interests. As well as the standing lumber on the property there are some 5,000 cords of pulpwood. It is Mr. Burtt's intention to carry on lumbering operations on his new property for his mill at Cardigan, N. B.

Natagan Lumber Co. Limited, has been incorporated with a capital stock of $49,900 and chief place of business at Barraute, Que. The company is empowered to buy, sell and deal in all kinds of wood, and to conduct business as saw-mill operators, planing mill, shingle mills, etc., and also logging operations. The incorporators are,—Henri Grandbois of St. Casimir, Albert Lainesse of Lemieux and P. D. Cloutier, J. Alfred Gagnon, J. A. Mireault of St. Prosper de Champlain.

Western Canada

The Cameron Lumber Co. of Garbelly Road, Vancouver, are erecting a new drying kiln.

The Haywood Lumber Co. of Edmonton have had plans drawn up for the erection of offices and the laying out of a lumber yard at Bellis, Alta.

January 28-30 are the dates on which it has been arranged to hold the 1920 convention of the Western Retail Lumbermen's Association in Winnipeg.

Shipbuilding continues active at Prince Rupert. The keel of the first steamer to be built has been completed and the keel of the second half finished.

The head office of Canadian Lumber Yards, Limited, so it has been decided by the directors, will be in Vancouver, B. C. This decision was arrived at at a meeting held recently in Montreal.

Mr. Hudson of Everett, Wash., was recently in British Columbia looking to the establishment of a pulp and paper mill at Squamish, the coast terminal of the Pacific Great Eastern Railway Company.

It is reported that the Dominion Government plans to place contracts for fifty wooden schooners with British Columbia shipyards. According to the report, twenty-six of the ships will be constructed at Victoria, and the others will be turned out by yards on the mainland.

The Imperial Lumber Co. are making great alterations to their Wawanesa yards which are nearing completion. A long new coal shed has been built and a new office and timber shed are in course of erection. H. E. Mitchell is the manager of the Wawanesa yards and reports business as good in his section of Manitoba.

More than 12,000,000 feet of the British order of 70,500,000 feet of British Columbia lumber is now en route to England. The representative of the British government hopes to have 40,000,000 feet on the way over by the end of the year, according to information received by the department of immigration and colonization.

The number of local industries in Prince Rupert will shortly be augmented by a new saw mill which is being erected for Olaf Hanson and R. E. Allen. Mr. Hanson is an experienced lumberman and Mr. Allen was for several years at Hazelton as chief forester in the Forestry Department. The mill is being equipped with a box factory in addition to the ordinary plant for producing commercial lumber from their own timber limits.

The Canada Timber and Land Co., of Toronto, of which E. Stewart is manager, have been busy cutting logs on their limits on the Tobin river, 120 miles north of Vancouver and have already taken out about two million feet of cedar logs and this quantity will be greatly increased. Difficulty has been experienced in getting the logs to the mills owing to the low water which prevails in many parts of the Pacific Coast province due to the dry season.

Announcement was made recently by H. H. Elliott of the White Shore Chemical Co., that active work would be started very soon on the development of the sodium sulphate deposits on the shore of Lake White Shore. This is the largest deposit in the Dominion and according to Mr. Elliott its use will revolutionize the pulp making industry in Canada. It will increase the output of bye-products of the pulp mills from 12 as at present to more than 40, it is stated, most important of these being artificial silk, which can be manufactured from the pulp. The mine is situated northwest of Biggar, west of Oban and close to both the G. T. P. and C. P. R. Shipments will commence early next year.

GATES REFRACTORIES, LIMITED

382 St. James Street - - - MONTREAL

Reasons Why You Should Use

ATKINS STERLING QUALITY SAWS

Reason No. 1—ATKINS STEEL
Reason No. 2—ATKINS WORKMANSHIP

Reason No. 3 -- The Temper

"DRAWING THE TEMPER" of an Atkins' Saw is a study in itself. Experts who have made this particular work their life-long practise give direct personal supervision, and the final touch which could make or mar the steel is given with that exacting care characteristic of the complete manufacture.

It is the Atkins' method of tempering that gives the stamina to the steel and adds a toughness to its Sterling Quality, which makes Atkins' Saws second to none when put to the real test for cutting power and length of service. You will always find the temper of an Atkins' just right.

Watch for Reason No. 4

Send for Free Catalogue.

E. C. ATKINS & CO.

Factory: HAMILTON, ONT. Branch: 109 Powell St., VANCOUVER, B.C.

ALPHABETICAL INDEX TO ADVERTISERS

Why pay good money to generate power and then employ a poor belt that will only transmit a fraction of that power.

If you equip your mill with Goodhue Belts you can transmit 100% of the power generated.

Goodhue Belts stretch 15% to 25% less than other belts and have just the right amount of "cling" on the pulley.

Write us for particulars and prices

YOU CAN DO IT WITH A— **GOODHUE BELT**

Winnipeg Agents: Bissett & Webb, Limited, 181 Notre Dame Ave. East, Winnipeg, Man.

Standard Machinery & Supplies, Limited, Bank of Toronto Building, St. James Street, Montreal, Que.—Agents for the Island of Montreal.

Vancouver Agents: Fleck Bros., Limited, 1142 Homer St., Vancouver, B. C.

J. L. GOODHUE & COMPANY, LIMITED

DANVILLE, QUEBEC CANADA.

Stop Advertising and You're Forgotten

"HOW long do you think your good-will is good for, if left to itself? The public has a short memory. Are you willing to risk its forgetfulness—even to invite it? Figure it out in dollars and cents. Can you afford it?"

CURRENT LUMBER PRICES—WHOLESALE

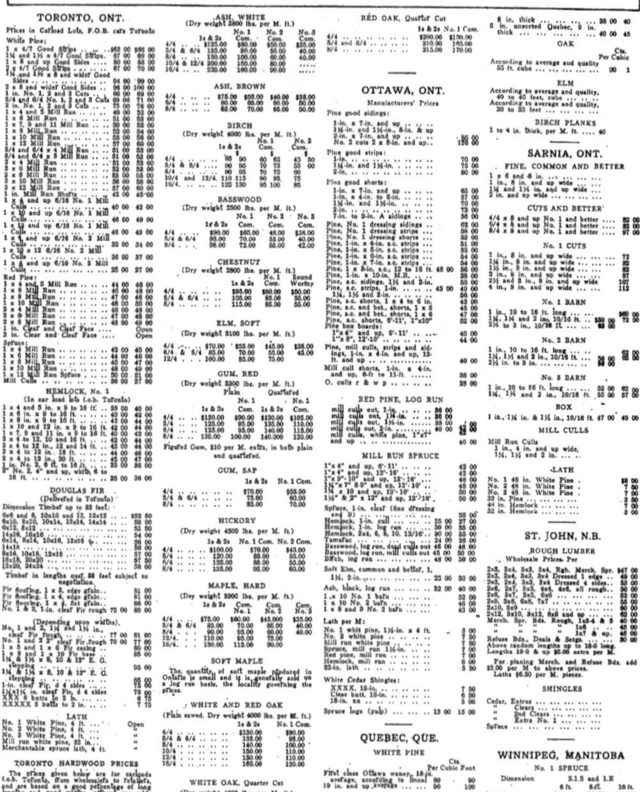

TORONTO, ONT.

Prices in Carload Lots, F.O.B. cars Toronto

White Pine:

1 x 4/7 Good Strips	$63 00	$66 00
1¼ and 1½ x 4/7 Good Strips	67 00	69 00
1 x 8 and up Good Sides	80 00	83 00
2 x 4/7 Good Strips	67 00	70 00
1¼ and 1½ x 8 and wider Good Sides	94 00	99 00
2 x 8 and wider Good Sides	96 00	100 00
1 in. No. 1, 2 and 3 Cuts	66 00	69 00
5/4 and 6/4 No. 1, 2 and 3 Cuts	69 00	71 00
2 in. No. 1, 2 and 3 Cuts	73 00	76 00
1 x 4 and 5 Mill Run	49 00	52 00
1 x 6 Mill Run	51 00	53 00
1 x 7, 9 and 11 Mill Run	50 00	52 00
1 x 8 Mill Run	52 00	54 00
1 x 10 Mill Run	55 00	58 00
1 x 12 Mill Run	57 00	60 00
5/4 and 6/4 x 4 Mill Run	51 00	53 00
5/4 and 6/4 x 5 Mill Run	51 00	53 00
2 x 4 Mill Run	51 00	53 00
2 x 6 Mill Run	52 00	53 00
2 x 8 Mill Run	53 00	55 00
2 x 10 Mill Run	56 00	58 00
2 x 12 Mill Run	57 00	60 00
1 in. Mill Run Shorts	42 00	45 00
1 x 4 and up 6/16 No. 1 Mill Culls	40 00	42 00
1 x 10 and up 6/16 No. 1 Mill Culls	46 00	49 00
1 x 12 and up 6/16 No. 1 Mill Culls	46 00	49 00
1 x 4 and up 6/16 No. 2 Mill Culls	33 00	34 00
1 x 10 x 12 6/16 No. 2 Mill Culls	36 00	37 00
1 x 4 and up 6/10 No. 3 Mill Culls	25 00	27 00

Red Pine:

1 x 4 and 5 Mill Run	44 00	46 00
1 x 6 Mill Run	46 00	48 00
1 x 8 Mill Run	47 00	48 00
1 x 10 Mill Run	48 00	50 00
2 x 4 Mill Run	46 00	48 00
2 x 6 Mill Run	47 00	48 00
2 x 8 Mill Run	48 00	49 00
1 in. Clear and Clear Face		Open
2 in. Clear and Clear Face		Open

Spruce:

1 x 4 Mill Run	42 00	45 00
1 x 6 Mill Run	44 00	46 00
1 x 8 Mill Run	45 00	47 00
1 x 10 Mill Run	48 00	49 00
1 x 12 Mill Run Spruce	50 00	51 00
Mill Culls	36 00	37 00

HEMLOCK, No. 1

(In car load lots f.o.b. Toronto)

1 x 4 and 5 in. x 9 to 16 ft.	38 00	40 00
1 x 6 in. x 9 to 16 ft.	40 00	42 00
1 x 8 in. x 9 to 16 ft.	42 00	44 00
1 x 10 and 12 in. x 9 to 16 ft.	42 00	44 00
1 x 7, 9 and 11 in. x 9 to 16 ft.	40 00	42 00
2 x 4 to 12, 10 and 16 ft.	42 00	44 00
2 x 4 to 12 in., 12 and 14 ft.	42 00	44 00
2 x 4 to 12 in., 18 ft.	44 00	46 00
2 x 4 to 12 in., 20 ft.	45 00	47 00
1 in. No. 2, 6 ft. to 16 ft.	35 00	36 00
2" No. 2, 4" and up, width 6 to 16 ft.	35 00	36 00

DOUGLAS FIR

(Delivered in Toronto)

Dimension Timber up to 32 feet:

6x6 and 8, 10x10 and 12, 12x12	$52 50
6x10, 8x10, 10x14, 12x14, 14x14	53 00
6x12, 8x12	53 50
14x16, 16x16	54 00
6x14, 8x14, 10x16, 12x16	56 00
14x18	56 00
8x16, 10x18, 12x18	57 00
18x18, 20x20	57 50
12x20, 24x24	58 00

Timber in lengths over 32 feet subject to negotiation.

Fir flooring, 1 x 3, edge grain		81 00
Fir flooring, 1 x 4, edge grain		81 00
Fir flooring, 1 x 4, flat grain		66 00
No. 1 & 2, 1-in. clear Fir rough	75 00	80 00

(Depending upon widths).

No. 1 and 2, 1¼ and 1½ in., clear Fir rough	77 00	81 00
No. 1 and 2 2" clear Fir rough	70 00	77 00
1 x 5 and 1 x 6 Fir casing		80 00
1 x 8 and 1 x 10 Fir base		85 00
1¼ & 1½ x 8, 10 & 12" E. G. stepping		95 00
1¼ & 1½ x 8, 10 & 12" E. G. stepping		85 00
1-in. clear Fir, d 4 sides		75 00
1¼x1¼ in. clear Fir, d 4 sides		78 00
XXX 6 butts to 2 in.		6 75
XXXXX 5 butts to 2 in.		7 75

LATH

No. 1 White Pine, 4 ft.	Open
No. 2 White Pine, 4 ft.	"
No. 3 White Pine, 4 ft.	"
Mill run white pine, 32 in.	"
Merchantable spruce lath, 4 ft.	"

TORONTO HARDWOOD PRICES

The prices given below are for carloads f.o.b. Toronto, from wholesalers to retailers, and are based on a good percentage of long lengths and good widths, without any wide stock having been sorted out. War tax of seven and half per cent. on imported woods, and also the prevailing rate of exchange paid by purchaser.

ASH, WHITE

(Dry weight 3800 lbs. per M. ft.)

	1s & 2s	No. 1 Com.	No. 2 Com.	No. 3 Com.
4/4	$125.00	$80.00	$50.00	$35.00
5/4 & 6/4	135.00	90.00	55.00	40.00
8/4	150.00	100.00	60.00	40.00
10/4 & 12/4	200.00	150.00	80.00	.....
16/4	220.00	160.00	90.00	.....

ASH, BROWN

4/4	$75.00	$55.00	$40.00	$38.00
6/4	80.00	65.00	60.00	50.00
8/4	83.00	70.00	65.00	50.00

BIRCH

(Dry weight 4000 lbs. per M. ft.)

	1s & 2s $		No. 1 Com. $		No. 2 Com. $	
4/4	85	90	60	65	45	50
5/4 & 6/4	90	95	70	75	55	60
8/4	90	95	70	75	60	
10/4 and 12/4	110	115	90	95	75	
16/4	125	130	95	100	85	

BASSWOOD

(Dry weight 2500 lbs. per M. ft.)

	1s & 2s	No. 1 Com.	No. 2 Com.	No. 3 Com.
4/4	$90.00	$65.00	48.00	$38.00
5/4 & 6/4	95.00	70.00	55.00	40.00
8/4	98.00	72.00	55.00	42.00

CHESTNUT

(Dry weight 2800 lbs. per M. ft.)

	1s & 2s	No. 1 Com.	Sound Wormy
4/4	$95.00	$80.00	$50.00
5/4 & 6/4	105.00	85.00	55.00
8/4	115.00	85.00	55.00

ELM, SOFT

(Dry weight 3100 lbs. per M. ft.)

4/4	$70.00	$55.00	$45.00	$38.00
6/4 & 8/4	85.00	70.00	55.00	45.00
12/4	100.00	85.00	75.00	

GUM, RED

(Dry weight 3300 lbs. per M. ft.)

	Plain 1s & 2s	Plain No. 1 Com.	Quartered 1s & 2s	Quartered No. 1 Com.
4/4	$120.00	$90.00	$130.00	$105.00
5/4	125.00	95.00	135.00	110.00
6/4	125.00	95.00	140.00	115.00
8/4	135.00	100.00	140.000	120.00

Figured Gum, $10 per M. extra, in both plain and quartered.

GUM, SAP

	1s & 2s	No. 1 Com.
4/4	$70.00	$55.00
5/4 & 6/4	75.00	60.00
8/4	85.00	70.00

HICKORY

(Dry weight 4500 lbs. per M. ft.)

	1s & 2s	No. 1 Com.	No. 2 Com.
4/4	$100.00	$70.00	$45.00
5/4	120.00	85.00	55.00
6/4	125.00	85.00	55.00
8/4	135.00	95.00	60.00

MAPLE, HARD

(Dry weight 3900 lbs. per M. ft.)

	1s & 2s	Com. No. 1	Com. No. 2	Com. No. 3
4/4	$75.00	$60.00	$45.000	$35.00
5/4 & 6/4	85.00	70.00	55.00	40.00
8/4	90.00	95.00	60.00	40.00
12/4	110.00	95.00	75.00	
16/4	130.00	115.00	90.00	

SOFT MAPLE

The quantity of soft maple produced in Ontario is small and it is generally sold on a log run basis, the locality governing the prices.

WHITE AND RED OAK

(Plain sawed. Dry weight 4000 lbs. per M. ft.)

	1s & 2s	No. 1 Com.
4/4	$130.00	$90.00
5/4 & 6/4	135.00	95.00
8/4	140.00	100.00
10/4	150.00	110.00
12/4	150.00	110.00
16/4	165.00	120.00

WHITE OAK, Quarter Cut

(Dry weight 4000 lbs. per M. ft.)

	1s & 2s	No. 1 Com.
4/4	$230.00	$175.00
5/4 and 6/4	250.00	180.00
8/4	260.00	

RED OAK, Quarter Cut

	1s & 2s	No. 1 Com.
4/4	$200.00	$150.00
5/4 and 6/4	210.00	165.00
8/4	215.00	170.00

OTTAWA, ONT.

Manufacturers' Prices

Pine good sidings:

1-in. x 7-in. and up		
1¼-in. and 1½-in., 8-in. & up		
2-in. x 7-in. and up		95 00
No. 2 cuts 2 x 8-in. and up		170 00

Pine good strips:

1-in.		70 00
1¼-in. and 1½-in.		75 00
2-in.		80 00

Pine good shorts:

1-in. x 7-in. and up		65 00
1-in. x 4-in. to 6-in.		57 00
1¼-in. and 1½-in.		70 00
2-in.		72 00
7-in. to 9-in. A sidings		56 00
Pine, No. 1 dressing sidings		62 00
Pine, No. 1 dressing strips		58 00
Pine, No. 1 dressing shorts		52 00
Pine, 1-in. x 4-in. s.c. strips		51 00
Pine, 1-in. x 5-in. s.c. strips		52 00
Pine, 1-in. x 6-in. s.c. strips		54 00
Pine, 1-in. x 7-in. s.c. strips		54 00
Pine, 1 x 8-in. s.c., 12 to 16 ft.	48 00	56 00
Pine, 1-in. x 10-in. M.R.		58 00
Pine, s.c. sidings, 1½ and 2-in.		55 00
Pine, s.c. strips, 1-in.	45 00	49 00
1¼, 1½ and 2-in.		56 00
Pine, s.c. shorts, 1 x 4 to 6 in.		43 00
Pine, s.c. and bet., shorts, 1 x 5		45 00
Pine, s.c. and bet., shorts, 1 x 6		47 00
Pine, s.c. shorts, 6'-11', 1"x10"		52 00

Pine box boards:

1"x4" and up, 6'-11'		40 00
1"x3", 12'-16'		44 00
Pine, mill culls, strips and sidings, 1-in. x 4-in. and up, 12-ft. and up		40 00
Mill cull shorts, 1-in. x 4-in. and up, 6-ft to 11-ft.		38 00
O. culls r & w p		28 00

RED PINE, LOG RUN

mill culls out, 1-in.	36 00	
mill culls out, 1¼-in.	36 00	
mill culls out, 1½-in.	38 00	
mill culls out, 2-in.	40 00	42 00
mill culls, white pine, 1"x7" and up		40 00

MILL RUN SPRUCE

1"x4" and up, 6'-11'		42 00
1"x4" and up, 12'-16'		42 00
1"x9"-10" and up, 12'-16'		48 00
1¼"x7" 8-9" and up, 12'-16'		48 00
1¼ x 10 and up, 12'-16'		50 00
1½" & 2" x 12" and up, 12'-16'		50 00
Spruce, 1-in. clear (fine dressing and B)		55 00
Hemlock, 1-in. cull	25 00	27 00
Hemlock, 1-in. log run	30 00	35 00
Hemlock, 2x4, 6, 8, 10, 12/16'	30 00	35 00
Tamarac	24 00	26 00
Basswood, log run, dead culls out	46 00	48 00
Basswood, log run, mill culls out	45 00	50 00
Birch, log run	48 00	50 00
Soft Elm, common and better, 1, 1½, 2-in.	25 00	30 00
Ash, black, log run	32 00	40 00
1 x 10 No. 1 barn		52 00
1 x 10 No. 2 barn		46 00
1 x 8 and 9 No. 2 barn		42 00

Lath per M:

No. 1 whit pine, 1½-in. x 4 ft.	8 00
No. 2 white pine	7 50
Mill run white pine	7 50
Spruce, mill run 1½-in.	7 00
Red pine, mill run	7 00
Hemlock, mill run	6 00
32-in. lath	3 50

White Cedar Shingles:

XXXX, 18-in.		7 50
Clear butt, 18-in.		6 50
18-in. xx		5 00
Spruce logs (pulp)	13 00	15 00

QUEBEC, QUE.

WHITE PINE

	Cts. Per Cubic Foot	
First class Ottawa waney, 18-in. average, according to lineal	80	90
19 in. and up average	90	100

SPRUCE DEALS

	Per M. Ft.	
3 in. unsorted Quebec, 4 in. to 6 in. thick	$34 00	$37 00
3 in. unsorted, Quebec, 7 in. to 8 in. thick	38 00	40
3 in. unsorted Quebec, 9 in. thick	40 00	45

OAK

	Cts. Per Cubic	
According to average and quality 55 ft. cube	90	1

ELM

According to average and quality, 40 to 45 feet, cube

According to average and quality, 30 to 35 feet

BIRCH PLANKS

1 to 4 in. thick, per M. ft. 40

SARNIA, ONT.

FINE, COMMON AND BETTER

1 x 6 and 8 in.

1 in., 8 in. and up wide

1¼ and 1½ in. and up wide

2 in. and up wide

CUTS AND BETTER

4/4 x 8 and up No. 1 and better	82 00
6/4 x 8 and up No. 1 and better	82 00
8/4 x 8 and up No. 1 and better	97 00

No. 1 CUTS

1 in., 8 in. and up wide	72
1¼ in., 8 in. and up wide	82
1½ in., 8 in. and up wide	82
2 in., 8 in. and up wide	87
2½ and 3 in., 8 in. and up wide	107
4 in., 8 in. and up wide	112

No. 1 BARN

1 in., 10 to 16 ft. long		$60 00
1¼, 1½ and 2 in., 10/16 ft.	$50 00	72 00
2½ to 3 in., 10/16 ft.	85 00	

No. 2 BARN

1 in., 10 to 16 ft. long		62 00
1¼, 1½ and 2 in., 10/16 ft.	56 00	65 00
2½ in. to 3 in.	59 00	

No. 3 BARN

1 in., 10 to 16 ft. long	52 00	62 00
1¼, 1½ and 2 in., 10/16 ft.	55 00	57 00

BOX

1 in., 1¼ in. & 1½ in., 10/16 ft.	47 00	49 00

MILL CULLS

Mill Run Culls

1 in., 4 in. and up wide, 1¼, 1½ and 2 in.

LATH

No. 1 48 in. White Pine	$8 00
No. 2 48 in. White Pine	7 50
No. 3 48 in. White Pine	7 00
32 in. Pine	3 50
48 in. Hemlock	7 00
32 in. Hemlock	3 00

ST. JOHN, N.B.

ROUGH LUMBER

Wholesale Prices. Per

2x3, 2x4, 3x3, 3x4, Rgh. Merch. Spr.	$47 00
2x3, 2x4, 3x3, 3x4 Dressed 1 edge	49 00
2x3, 2x4, 3x3, 3x4 Dressed 4 sides	53 00
2x6, 2x7, 3x5, 4x4, 4x6, all rough	50 00
2x8, 3x7, 5x5, 6x6	52 00
2x9, 3x8, 6x8, 7x7	55 00
2x10, 3x9	60 00
2x12, 3x10, 3x12, 8x8 and up	62 00
Merch. Spr. Bds. Rough, 1x2-4 & 5	40 00
" " " " 1x6	45 00
" " " " 1x7 & up	46 00
Refuse Bds., Deals & Setgs.	30 00

Above random lengths up to 18-0 long.
Lengths 19-0 & up $5.00 extra per M.

For planing Merch. and Refuse Bds. add $2.00 per M to above prices.
Laths $6.50 per M. pieces.

SHINGLES

Cedar, Extras
" Clears
" 2nd Clears
" Extra No. 1
Spruce

WINNIPEG, MANITOBA

No. 1 SPRUCE

Dimension	S.1.S and 1.E 6 ft.	8 ft.	10 ft.
2 x 4	$35 50	$38 50	$42 00
2 x 6	37 50	38 50	42 00
2 x 8	37 50	39 50	42 00
2 x 10	38 50	40 50	43 00

(Continued on page 72)

CURRENT LUMBER PRICES—Continued

2 x 12	40 50	41 50	44 00
	12 ft.	14 ft.	16 ft.
2 x 4	40 00	40 00	41 00
2 x 6	40 00	40 00	41 00
2 x 8	40 00	40 00	41 00
2 x 10	41 00	41 00	42 00
2 x 12	42 00	42 00	43 00

For 2 inches, rough, add 50 cents.
For S1E only add 50 cents.
For S1S and 2E, S4S or D&M, add $3.00.
For timbers larger than 8 x 8, add 50c. for each additional 2 inches each way.
For lengths longer than 20 ft., add $1.00 for each additional two feet.
For selected common, add $5.00.
For No. 2 Dimension, $3.00 less than No. 1.
For 1 x 2 and 2 x 2, $2 more than 2 x 4 No. 1.
For Tamarac add $3.00.

FIR, HEMLOCK, SPRUCE AND LARCH
Mountain Stock

No. 1 Dimension and Timbers

2 x 4, 2 x 6, 2 x 8, 8 to 16 ft., S1S1E	$39 00
2 x 4, 2 x 6, 2 x 8, 10 ft., S1S1E	41 00
2 x 4, 2 x 6, 2 x 8, 12/16, S1S1E	39 00
2 x 4, 2 x 6, 2 x 8, 18/22, S1S1E	41 00
2 x 4, 2 x 6, 2 x 8, 24/32, S1S1E ...	43 00
2 x 10, 8 ft. to 16 ft., S1S1E	40 00
2 x 10, 10 ft. S1S1E	42 00
2 x 10, 18/22, S1S1E	42 00
2 x 10, 24/32, S1S1E	44 00
2 x 12, 8 ft. to 16 ft., S1S1E	41 50
2 x 12; 10, 18, 20, ...	43 50
2 x 12; 24, 26, 28, 30, 32	45 50

B. C. COAST FIR
Dimension S1S and E.

2 x 4 in., 6 ft.	$39 50
2 x 4 in., 8, 12 and 14 ft.	40 50
2 x 4 in., 16 ft.	41 50
2 x 4 in., 18 and 20 ft.	42 50
2 x 4 in., 22 to 32 ft.	44 50
2 x 10 in., 8, 12 and 14 ft.	41 75
2 x 10 in., 16 ft.	42 75
2 x 10 in., 18 and 20 ft.	43 75
2 x 10 in., 22 to 32 ft.	45 75
2 x 12 in., 8 to 14 ft.	43 25
2 x 12 in., 16 ft.	44 25
2 x 12 in., 18 and 20 ft.	45 25
2 x 12 in., 22 to 32 ft.	47 25
3 x 3 and 3 x 4 in., 8 to 14 ft.	46 75
3 x 3 and 3 x 4 in., 16 ft.	47 75
3 x 3 and 3 x 4, 18 and 20 ft.	48 75
3 x 3 and 3 x 4 in., 22 to 32 ft.	50 75
6 x 6, 6 x 8, 8 x 8, 6 to 16 ft.	49 00
6 x 6, 6 x 8 and 8 x 8, 18 and 20 ft.	49 50
6 x 6, 6 x 8, 8 x 8, 22 to 32 ft.	50 50
Shingles, XXX B. C. Cedar, straight cars on 60c rate	6 96

BUFFALO & TONAWANDA
WHITE PINE

Wholesale Selling Price

Uppers, 4/4	$118 00
Uppers, 5/4 to 8/4	102 00
Uppers, 10/4 to 12/4	132 00
Selects 4/4	112 00
Selects 5/4 to 8/4	112 00
Selects 10/4 to 12/4	122 00
Fine Common 4/4	84 00
Fine Common 5/4	89 00
Fine Common 6/4	88 00
Fine Common 8/4	89 00
No. 1 Cuts 4/4	67 00
No. 1 Cuts 5/4	76 00
No. 1 Cuts 6/4	77 00
No. 1 Cuts 8/4	80 00
No. 2 Cuts 4/4	49 00
No. 2 Cuts 5/4	63 00
No. 2 Cuts 6/4	64 00
No. 2 Cuts 8/4	71 00
No. 3 Cuts 5/4	51 00
No. 3 Cuts 6/4	51 00
No. 3 Cuts 8/4	52 00
Dressing 5/4	66 00
Dressing 5/4 x 10	60 00
Dressing 5/4 x 12	74 00
No. 1 Moulding 5/4	76 00
No. 1 Moulding 6/4	74 00
No. 1 Moulding 8/4	76 00
No. 2 Moulding 5/4	68 00
No. 2 Moulding 6/4	68 00
No. 2 Moulding 8/4	68 00
No. 1 Barn 1 x 12	65 00
No. 1 Barn 1 x 6 and 8	56 00
No. 1 Barn 1 x 10	58 00
No. 2 Barn 1 x 6 and 8	52 00
No. 2 Barn 1 x 10	56 00
No. 3 Barn 1 x 6 and 8	49 00
No. 3 Barn 1 x 10	47 00
Box 1 x 6 and up	47 00
Box 1 x 10	47 00
Box 1 x 12	47 00
Box 1 x 12	48 00
Box 1 x 13 and up	49 00

The following quotations on hardwoods represent the jobber buying price at Buffalo and Tonawanda.

	1s & 2s	No. 1 Com.	No. 2 Com.
MAPLE			
4/4	52 - 55	37 - 39	26 - 28
5/4 to 8/4	66 - 68	44 - 46	31 - 33
10/4 to 16/4	76 - 78	56 - 58	35 - 37
RED BIRCH			
4/4	72 - 74	52 - 54	35 - 37
5/4 to 8/4	75 - 77	55 - 57	38 - 40
SAP BIRCH			
4/4	68 - 72	46 - 48	31 - 33
5/4 and up	73 - 76	49 - 51	34 - 36
SOFT ELM			
4/4	57 - 59	42 - 44	33 - 35
5, 6 & 8/4	60 - 62	35 - 47	34 - 36
BASSWOOD			
4/4	62 - 64	52 - 44	38 - 40
Thicker	61 - 60	50 - 57	39 - 42
PLAIN OAK			
4/4	74 - 79	51 - 55	34 - 36
5/4 to 8/4	80 - 84	56 - 60	39 - 41
ASH, WHITE AND BROWN			
4/4	75 - 77	45 - 49	33 - 36
5/4 to 8/4	81 - 85	53 - 55	37 - 39
10/4 and up	108 - 110	68 - 71	38 - 40

BOSTON, MASS.

Quotations given below are for highest grades of Michigan and Canadian white pine and Eastern Canadian Spruce as required in the New England market in carloads.

White pine uppers, 1 in.		$140 00
White pine uppers, 1¼, 2 in.		145 00
White pine uppers, 2½, 3 in.		156 00
White pine uppers, 4 in.		160 00
Selects, 1 in.		135 00
Selects, 1¼, 2 in.		135 00
Selects, 2½, 3 in.		145 00
Selects, 4 in.		155 00
Fine common, 1 in., 30 per cent. 12 in. and up		92 00
Fine common, 1 x 8 and up		95 00
Fine common, 1¼ to 2 in.		110 00
Fine common, 2½ and 3 in.		135 00
Fine Common, 4 in.		145 00
1 in. shaky clear		72 00
1¼ to 2 in. shaky clear		75 00
1 in. No. 2 dressing		64 00
1¼ to 2 in. No. 2 dressing		68 00
No. 1 Cuts, 1 in.		80 00
No. 1 Cuts, 1¼ to 2 in.	85 00	87 00
No. 1 Cuts, 2½ and 3 in.		115 00
No. 2 Cuts, 1 in.		60 00
No. 2 Cuts, 1¼ to 2 in.	70 00	71 00

Barn Boards, No. 1, 1 x 12 ...		75 00
No. 1, 1 x 10 ...		70 00
No. 1, 1 x 8 ...		65 00
No. 2, 1 x 12 ...		[illegible]
No. 2, 1 x 10 ...		[illegible]
No. 2, 1 x 8 ...		[illegible]
No. 3, 1 x 12 ...		[illegible]
No. 3, 1 x 10 ...		[illegible]
No. 3, 1 x 8 ...		57 [illegible]
No. 1 Clear		
Can. spruce, No. 1 and clear, 1 x 4 to 9 in.		[illegible]
1 x 10 in.		[illegible]
No. 1, 1 x 4 to 7 in.		[illegible]
No. 1, 1 x 8 & 9 in.		[illegible]
No. 1, 1 x 10 in...		[illegible]
No. 2, 1 x 4 & 5 in.		[illegible]
No. 2, 1 x 6 & 7 in.		[illegible]
No. 2, 1 x 8 & 9 in.		[illegible]
No. 2, 1 x 10 in.		[illegible]
No. 2, 1 x 12 in..		[illegible]
Spruce, 12 in. dimension		[illegible]
Spruce, 10 in. dimension		[illegible]
Spruce, 9 in. dimension		[illegible]
Spruce, 8 in. dimension		[illegible]
2 x 10 in., random lengths, 8 ft. and up		[illegible]
2 x 12 in., random lengths		[illegible]
2 x 3, 2 x 4, 2 x 5, 2 x 6, 2 x 7	45 00	46 00
3 x 4 and 4 x 4 in.		47 00
2 x 8 in.		[illegible]
All other random lengths, 7-in. and under, 8 ft. and up		45 00
8-inch and up merchantable boards, 8 ft. and up, p 1s ..	42 00	43 00
1 x 2		[illegible]
1 x 3		47 00
1-⅝ in. spruce lath		[illegible]
1-½ in. spruce lath		[illegible]

New Brunswick Cedar Shingles

Extras		[illegible]
Clears		[illegible]
Second Clears	[illegible]	[illegible]
Clear Whites	[illegible]	[illegible]
Extra 1s (Clear whites in) ..		5 00
Extra 1s (Clear whites out) ..		4 50
Red Cedar Extras, 16-in. 5 butts to 2-in.		7 50
Red Cedar Eurekas, 18-inch, 5 butts to 2-in.		10 00
Red Cedar Perfections, 5 butts to 2¼		12 00
Washington 16-in. 5 butts to 2 in. extra red cedar		7 25

A dry powder is most convenient

Use Klim

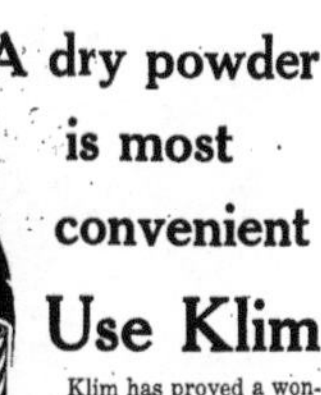

Klim has proved a wonderful convenience and economy in homes, hotels, lumber camps, boarding houses, and on ships—in fact everywhere that milk is used regularly. This powdered separated milk is especially valuable in lumber camps where large quantities are needed and shipping and storage are factors to be considered.

It is no problem to get Klim into camp. Ship it by freight as you would any other imperishable food. Klim will arrive as fresh and sweet as when it left our plants in the country and will remain so until the last fine particle is used.

In camp, Klim is your cook's own milk supply. He regulates it to his daily needs, restoring to liquid form the exact quantity of Klim required. It is so easy for him to dip a cupful from the tin and whip it into a quart of water. Thus he has "under his thumb" a constant, unfailing supply of purest separated milk; never so much that part is left over to spoil, never so little as to occasion a shortage. He is not annoyed with sour or frozen milk, he is able to eliminate all waste, and he gets the genuine flavor into his cooking. Your men will be enthusiastic over the varied menu and delicious foods Klim makes possible.

If you appreciate the part good food plays in getting full value from your payroll, you will not hesitate to order at least one case of Klim, Hotel size (equal to 240 quarts) from your wholesale grocer.

CANADIAN MILK PRODUCTS LIMITED

TORONTO

WINNIPEG MONTREAL ST. JOHN

Plants at Brownsville, Belmont, Burford, Glanworth and Hickson, Ontario.

"The Original Red Belt"

"The Long-Grain Friction Belt"

¶ Dunlop "Gibraltar RedSpecial" is the proven benefactor of many an industry in this country which has felt the need of offsetting rising costs by speeding up production and by the elimination of belt trouble.

* * *

¶ "Gibraltar RedSpecial" is a real rubber belt. It may be compared to other brands of belts only as a powerful magnifying glass might be compared with the object whose imperfections it brings into the limelight.

* * *

¶ The first belts of this brand sold have been in use for years and have proven that scientific research—combined with approximately one quarter of a century's experience in the rubber goods manufacturing industry—could offer no more in belt merits than those features for which this Dunlop Product is so well and favorably known.

* * *

¶ We believe Dunlop "Gibraltar RedSpecial" cannot be made better. It is a red, frictioned-surface belt, constructed of the highest grade rubber, and specially-woven duck of tremendous tensile strength. This accounts for its great tenacity, its enduring flexibility and its absolute uniformity throughout.

* * *

¶ Provision has been made in "Gibraltar RedSpecial" against drying out and rotting. The richness of the rubber—compounded to retain its pliability indefinitely—waterprooofs the duck as well as holds the plies securely together. It also serves to minimize internal chafing due to the constant bending of the belt. All unnecessary stretch is taken out in the manufacturing process.

* * *

¶ You will find Dunlop "Gibraltar RedSpecial" Frictioned-Surface Belting doing daily duty the year round in Pulp and Paper Mills, Iron Foundries, Steel and Rolling Mills, Saw and Lumber Mills, Mines, etc., in a truly efficient manner.

* * *

¶ We also specialize on Conveyor and Elevator Belts to meet every need.

The Dunlop Unreserved Guarantee

If you have a difficult drive anywhere in your factory drop a line to our Head Office, or to our nearest branch, and we will send a man experienced in belt engineering to consider your requirements. If it is an instance where "Gibraltar RedSpecial" Belting may be suitably employed we will recommend its use; and we will stand behind our recommendation with the fullest guarantee ever issued by a firm producing rubber products.

Dunlop Tire & Rubber Goods Co., Limited

Head Office and Factories - - - TORONTO

BRANCHES IN THE LEADING CITIES

Makers of Tires for all Purposes, Mechanical Rubber Products of all kinds, and General Rubber Specialties

D 36

FIRE BRICK

We make several brands of fire brick made by every known process of manufacture from a selection of various high grade Pennsylvania clays. This enables us to furnish the best adapted fire brick for your boilers, dutch ovens, refuse burners, kilns, etc.

We specialize in fire brick for power plants and if you will advise us whether your boilers are hand fired or stoker fired and kind of fuel used we can then give you the proper brick for your work.

We manufacture the following well-known brands:

"Elkco Special," "Elk Steel," 'St. Marys," "Keystone" and "Rotex"

Write for copy of our catalogue, "Refractory Efficiency Engineering."

Elk Fire Brick Co. of Canada, Ltd.

HIGH GRADE FIRE BRICK and CLAY

Sun Life Bldg., Hamilton, Canada

Representatives for Maritime Provinces:
RHODES, CURRY COMPANY, LTD., Head Office, AMHERST, N.S.
Branches at Halifax, Sydney and New Glasgow, N.S.

Gerlach Machinery

PRODUCES THE BEST as Well as the Cheapest

Tight or Slack Staves, Headings, Kegs, Barrels and Short Box Shooks

100% to 400% profit in Cooperage Stock today. Be wise and purchase the best Machinery.

DIXIE PORTABLE GASOLINE DRAG SAW

Present Price $225.00 with 1 Blade

Circular, Drag and Cylinder Saws made since 1854

The Peter Gerlach Co.

Established [illegible]

Cleveland, Ohio

The Log Jack for Heavy Work

New Double Powered Log Jack

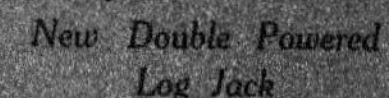

The accompanying illustration gives a correct idea of our new Double Power Log Jack designed for hauling heavy timber into Saw Mills.

GEAR—The large Gear Wheel is [illegible] in. in diameter, with [illegible] teeth, 4 in. face, and [illegible] in. pitch.

PINION on intermediate Shaft has 13 teeth, 4 in. face and [illegible] in. pitch.

PAPER FRICTION is 30 in. in diameter and 10 in. face. Iron Friction Pulley is 30 in. in diameter and 16 in. face.

CHAIN is made of extra heavy steel, and the hooks have steel spikes, the whole outfit being calculated for heavy logs.

The G. Walter Green Company, Limited

Send for Catalogue PETERBOROUGH, ONT.

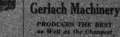

"Brazel Patent" SNOW PL

Known in every Camp from the Atlantic to the Pacific as the most satisfactory Snow Plow made.

Combination Model, Lumberman's Snow Plow, can be

or without Rut Cutter.

One man to operate. Adjusting wheels close together make change for light or heavy work in an instant. Wings placed to throw snow 9 ft. wider than sleigh track or narrower if desired. Height of mouldboards prevent snow falling back on track. BRAZEL PLOWS cut 6 in. wider than logging sleighs, roll snow outside track and away from roadway. Cut off knolls, fill up holes and leave a perfectly level road. Cut off dirt and manure heaps from an ice road, leaving a clean roadbed. Roll and push entirely away from the road, 12 inches of loose snow each time the plow passes over.

THE BATEMAN-WILKINSON CO., LIMITED
300 Symington Ave., Toronto

Successors to the WILKINSON PLOW CO., LIMITED
Catalogue and prices on application.

TORONTO, CANADA

The Bertrand Circular Sawmill

All our mills are built on the latest improved machinery by the most skilled workmen, from the best obtainable materials—to meet the requirements of our customers.

We manufacture all kinds of sawmill and woodworking machinery.

Put your saw mill problem up to us.

The above illustration portrays our circular saw mill. We manufacture this model on 12 and 16 foot carriages.

La Compagnie Manufacturiere F. X. Bertrand
ST. HYACINTHE, QUE.

MANUFACTURERS OF STEAM ENGINES AND WOODWORKING MACHINES

Good Will

—a mighty valuable asset to your business and something that cannot be built up in a few days. It is the result of painstaking efforts to give the customer just a little more than he expects—keeping the quality of your products standard—and backing up every word of your advertisements. In short, it's Service — Real Service — that builds Good Will.

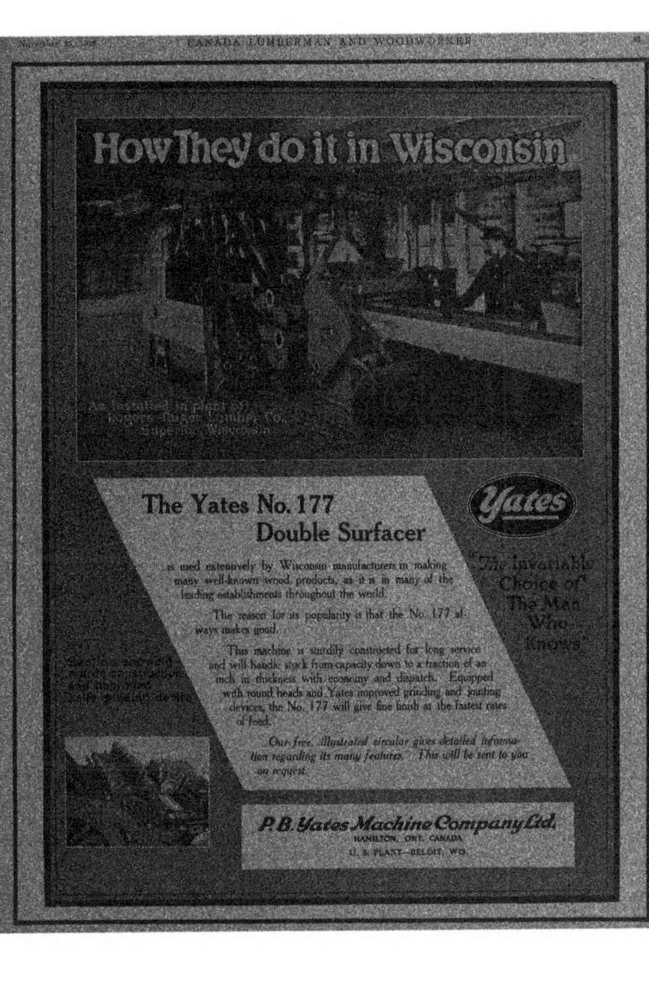
How They do it in Wisconsin
As installed in plant of
Superior, Wisconsin
The Yates No. 177
Double Surfacer
is used extensively by Wisconsin manufacturers in making many well-known wood products, as it is in many of the leading establishments throughout the world.
The reason for its popularity is that the No. 177 always makes good.
This machine is sturdily constructed for long service and will handle stock from capacity down to a fraction of an inch in thickness with economy and dispatch. Equipped with round heads and Yates improved grinding and jointing devices, the No. 177 will give fine finish at the fastest rates of feed.
Our free, illustrated circular gives detailed information regarding its many features. This will be sent to you on request.
Yates
"The Invariable Choice of The Man Who Knows"
P. B. Yates Machine Company Ltd.
HAMILTON, ONT. CANADA
U. S. PLANT—BELOIT, WIS.

CANADA LUMBERMAN BUYERS' DIRECTORY

The following regulations apply to all advertisers:—Eighth page, every issue, three headings; quarter page, six headings; half page, twelve headings; full page, twenty-four headings.

AIR CONDITIONING
Sturtevant Company, B. F.

ASBESTOS GOODS
Atlas Asbestos Company, Ltd.

AXES
Canadian Warren Axe & Tool Co.

BABBITT METAL
Canada Metal Company
General Supply Co. of Canada, Ltd.
United American Metals Corporation

Bale Ties
Laidlaw Bale Tie Company

BAND MILLS
Hamilton Company, William
Waterous Engine Works Company
Yates Machine Company, P. B.

BAND RESAWS
Mershon & Company, W. B.

BELT CEMENT
Graton & Knight Mfg. Company

BELT DRESSING
Atlas Asbestos Company, Ltd.
General Supply Co. of Canada, Ltd.
Graton & Knight Mfg. Company

BELTING
Atlas Asbestos Company, Ltd.
Beardmore Belting Company
Canadian Consolidated Rubber Co.
General Supply Company
Goodhue & Co., J. L.
Goodyear Tire & Rubber Co.
Graton & Knight Mfg. Company
Gutta Percha and Rubber Company
Main Belting Company
Manhattan Rubber Mfg. Co.
D. K. McLaren Limited
McLaren Belting Company, J. C.

BELTING (Transmission, Elevator, Conveyor, Rubber)
Dunlop Tire & Rubber Goods Co.

BLOWERS
Toronto Blower Company
Sturtevant Company, B. F.

BOILERS
Hamilton Company, William
Jenckes Machine Company
Marsh Engineering Works, Limited
Waterous Engine Works Company

BOILER PRESERVATIVE
International Chemical Company

BOX MACHINERY
Garlock-Walker Machinery Co.
Morgan Machine Company
Yates Machine Company, P. B.

BOX SHOOKS
Davison Lumber & Mfg. Company

BUNKS (Steel)
Alaska Bedding Co. of Montreal

CABLE CONVEYORS
Jeffrey Manufacturing Company
Jenckes Machine Company, Ltd.
Waterous Engine Works Company

CAMP SUPPLIES
Burns & Company, John
Canadian Milk Products Limited
Davies Company, William
Dr. Bell Veterinary Wonder Co.
Eckardt & Co.
Gunns Limited
Harris Abattoir Company
Johnson, A. H.
Turner & Sons, J. J.
Woods Manufacturing Company, Ltd.

CANT HOOKS
Canadian Warren Axe & Tool Co.
General Supply Co. of Canada, Ltd.
Pink Company, Thomas

CARS—STEEL BODY
Marsh Engineering Works, Limited

CAR WHEELS AND CASTINGS
Dominion Wheel & Foundries

CEDAR
Fesserton Timber Co.
Foss Lumber Company
Genoa Bay Lumber Company
Muir & Kirkpatrick
Long Lumber Company
Service Lumber Company
Terry & Gordon
Thurston-Flavelle Lumber Company
Vancouver Lumber Company
Victoria Lumber and Mfg. Co.

CHAINS
Canadian Link-Belt Company, Ltd.
General Supply Co. of Canada, Ltd.
Hamilton Company, William
Hobbs Company, Clinton E.
Jeffrey Manufacturing Company
Jenckes Machine Company, Ltd.
Pink & Co., Thomas
Waterous Engine Works Company
Williams Machinery Co., A. R. Vancouver

CHAIN HOISTS
Hobbs Company, Clinton E.

CHINA CLAY
Bowater & Sons, W. V.

CHEMICAL PLANTS
Blair, Campbell & McLean, Ltd.

CLOTHING
Acme Glove Works
Clarke & Company, A. R.
Grant, Holden & Graham
Woods Mfg. Company

COLLAR PADS
American Pad & Textile Co.

CONVEYOR MACHINERY
Canadian Link-Belt Company, Ltd.
Canadian Mathews Gravity Carrier Company
General Supply Co. of Canada, Ltd.
Jeffrey Mfg. Co.
Waterous Engine Works Company

CORDAGE
Consumers Cordage Company

CORN SYRUP
Canada Starch Company

COTTON GLOVES
American Pad & Textile Co.

COUPLING (Shaft)
Jenckes Machine Company, Ltd.

CRANES FOR SHIP YARDS
Canadian Link-Belt Company

CROSS ARMS
Genoa Bay Lumber Company

CUTTER HEADS
Shimer Cutter Head Company

CYPRESS
Chicago Lumber & Coal Company.
Long Lumber Company
Wistar, Underhill & Nixon

DERRICKS AND DERRICK FITTINGS
Marsh Engineering Works, Limited

DOORS
Genoa Bay Lumber Company
Long Lumber Co.
Mason, Gordon & Co.
Rutherford & Sons, Wm.
Terry & Gordon

DRAG SAWS
Gerlach Company, Peter
Williams Machinery Co., A. R.

DRIVING BOOTS
Acme Glove Works

DRYERS
Philadelphia Textile Mach. Company

DRY KILNS
Sturtevant Company, B. F.

DUST COLLECTORS
Sturtevant Company, B. F.
Toronto Blower Company

EDGERS
William Hamilton Company, Ltd.
Garlock-Walker Machinery Co.
Green Company, G. Walter
Long Mfg. Company, E.
Waterous Engine Works Company

ELEVATING AND CONVEYING MACHINERY
Canadian Link-Belt Comptny, Ltd.
Jeffery Manufacturing Company
Jenckes Machine Company, Ltd.
Waterous Engine Works Company

ENGINES
Hamilton Company, William
Jenckes Machine Company
Waterous Engine Works, Company

EXCELSIOR MACHINERY
Elmira Machinery and Transmission Company

EXHAUST FANS
Garlock-Walker Machinery Co.
Sturtevant Company, B. F.
Reed & Company, Geo. W.
Toronto Blower Company

EXHAUST SYSTEMS
Reed & Company, Geo. W.
Sturtevant Company, B. F.
Toronto Blower Company

FILES
Disston & Sons, Henry
Simonds Canada Saw Company

FIR
Associated Mills, Limited
Allan-Stoltze Lumber Co.
British American Mills & Timber Co.
Coal Creek Lumber Company
Fesserton Timber Co.
Foss Lumber Company
Grier & Sons, Ltd., G. A.
Heeney, Percy E.
Knox Brothers
Long Lumber Company
Mason, Gordon & Co.
Reynolds Company, Limited
Service Lumber Company
Shearer Company, Jas.
Terry & Gordon
Timberland Lumber Company
Timms, Phillips & Co.
Vancouver Lumber Company
Victoria Lumber and Mfg. Co.
Weller, J. B.

FIRE BRICK
Beveridge Paper Company
Elk Fire Brick Company of Canada

FIRE FIGHTING APPARATUS
Dunlop Tire & Rubber Goods Co.
Pyrene Mfg. Company
Waterous Engine Works Company

FIR FLOORING
Genoa Bay Lumber Company
Rutherford & Sons, Wm.

FLAG STAFFS
Ontario Wind Engine Company

FLOORING (Oak)
Long-Bell Lumber Company

GALVANIZING
Ontario Wind Engine Company

GLOVES
Acme Glove Works
Eisendrath Glove Co.

GASOLINE ENGINES
Ontario Wind Engine Company

GEARS (Cut)
Smart-Turner Machine Co.

GRAIN
Dwyer Company, W. H.

GRAVITY LUMBER CARRIER
Can. Mathews Gravity Carrier Co.

GRINDERS (Bench)
Garlock-Walker Machinery Co.

HARDWOODS
Anderson Lumber Company, C. G.
Atlantic Lumber Co.
Bartram & Ball
Bennett Lumber Company
Blakeslee, Perrin & Darling
Cameron & Co.
Cardinal & Page
Cox, Long & Company
Davison Lumber & Mfg. Company
Dunfield & Company
Edwards & Co., W. C.
Fassett Lumber Company
Fesserton Timber Co.
Fraser Limited
Gall Lumber Company
Gillespie, James
Gloucester Lumber Company
Grier & Son, G. A.
Harris Lumber Co., Frank H
Heeney, Percy E.
Knox Brothers
Long Lumber Company
McLennan Lumber Company
Moores, Jr., E. J.
Pedwell Hardwod Lumber Co.
Powell-Myers Lumber Co.
Russell, Chas. H.
Spencer Limited, C. A.
Stearns & Culver Lumber Co.
Summers, James R.
Taylor Lumber Company, S. K.
Webster & Brother, James

HARDWOOD FLOORING MACHINERY
American Woodworking Machinery Company
Garlock-Walker Machinery Co.

HARDWOOD FLOORING
Grier & Son, G. A.
Long Lumber Company

HAY
Dwyer & Company, W. H.

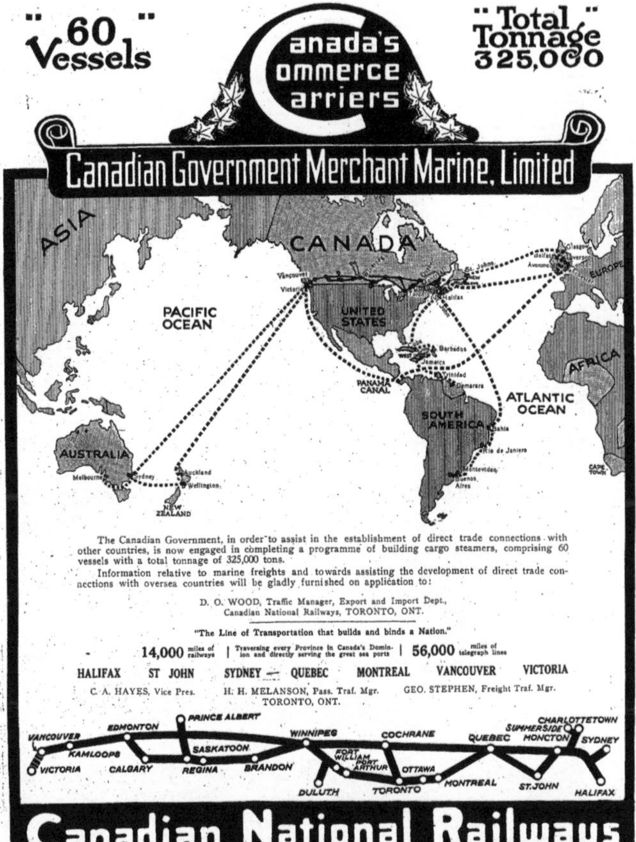

"60" Vessels
Canada's Commerce Carriers
"Total" Tonnage 325,000
Canadian Government Merchant Marine, Limited
ASIA
CANADA
PACIFIC OCEAN
UNITED STATES
EUROPE
AFRICA
ATLANTIC OCEAN
SOUTH AMERICA
AUSTRALIA
NEW ZEALAND
PANAMA CANAL
Vancouver
Victoria
Halifax
Barbados
Jamaica
Trinidad
Demarara
Bahia
Rio de Janiero
Montevideo
Buenos Aires
Melbourne
Sydney
Auckland
Wellington
Glasgow
Liverpool
Avonmouth
CAPE TOWN
The Canadian Government, in order to assist in the establishment of direct trade connections with other countries, is now engaged in completing a programme of building cargo steamers, comprising 60 vessels with a total tonnage of 325,000 tons.
Information relative to marine freights and towards assisting the development of direct trade connections with oversea countries will be gladly furnished on application to:
D. O. WOOD, Traffic Manager, Export and Import Dept., Canadian National Railways, TORONTO, ONT.
"The Line of Transportation that builds and binds a Nation."
14,000 miles of railways | Traversing every Province in Canada's Dominion and directly serving the great sea ports | 56,000 miles of telegraph lines
HALIFAX ST JOHN SYDNEY QUEBEC MONTREAL VANCOUVER VICTORIA
C. A. HAYES, Vice Pres. H. H. MELANSON, Pass. Traf. Mgr. GEO. STEPHEN, Freight Traf. Mgr.
TORONTO, ONT.
PRINCE ALBERT
EDMONTON
VANCOUVER
KAMLOOPS
VICTORIA
CALGARY
SASKATOON
REGINA
BRANDON
WINNIPEG
FORT WILLIAM
PORT ARTHUR
DULUTH
COCHRANE
TORONTO
OTTAWA
MONTREAL
QUEBEC
ST. JOHN
SUMMERSIDE
CHARLOTTETOWN
MONCTON
SYDNEY
HALIFAX
Canadian National Railways

HARNESS
Padgitt Company, Tom

HEMLOCK
Anderson Lumber Company, C. G.
Bartram & Ball
Bourgouin, H.
Canadian General Lumber Company
Cane & Co., Jas. G.
Davison Lumber & Mfg. Company
Dunfield & Company
Edwards & Company, W. C.
Fesserton Timber Co.
Foss Lumber Company
Grier & Sons, Ltd., G. A.
Harris Lumber Co., Frank H
Hart & McDonagh
Long Lumber Company
Mason, Gordon & Co.
Roch, Julien
Spencer Limited, C. A.
Terry & Gordon

HOISTING AND HAULING ENGINES
Garlock-Walker Machinery Co.
General Supply Co. of Canada, Ltd.
Marsh Engineering Works, Limited

HORSES
Union Stock Yards

HOSE
Dunlop Tire & Rubber Goods Co.
General Supply Co. of Canada, Ltd.
Goodyear Tire & Rubber Co.
Gutta Percha and Rubber Company

HUMIDIFIERS
Sturtevant Company, B. F.

INDUSTRIAL CARS
Marsh Engineering Works, Limited

INSURANCE
Hardy & Co., E. D.

INTERIOR FINISH
Eagle Lumber Company
Hay & Co.
Mason, Gordon & Co.
Renfrew Planing Mills
Terry & Gordon

KNIVES
Disston & Sons, Henry
Peter Hay Knife Company
Simonds Canada Saw Company
Waterous Engine Works Company

LARCH
Otis Staples Lumber Co.

LATH
Austin & Nicholson
Canadian General Lumber Company
Cane & Co., Jas. G.
Cardinal & Page
Dupuis Limited, J. P.
Eagle Lumber Company
Fraser Limited
Fraser-Bryson Lumber Company
Genoa Bay Lumber Company
Gloucester Lumber Company
Grier & Sons, Ltd., G. A.
Harris Tie & Timber Company, Ltd.
Long Lumber Company
McLennan Lumber Company
New Ontario Colonization Company
Otis Staples Lumber Co.
River Ouelle Pulp and Lumber Co.
Spencer Limited, C. A.
Terry & Gordon
Union Lumber Company
Victoria Harbor Lumber Company

LATH BOLTERS
Garlock-Walker Machinery Co.
General Supply Co. of Canada, Ltd.
Green Company, C. Walter

LIGHTING APPLIANCES
Hobbs Company, Clinton E.

LOCOMOTIVES
Bell Locomotive Works
General Supply Co. of Canada, Ltd.
Jeffrey Manufacturing Company
Jenckes Machine Company, Ltd.
Climax Manufacturing Company
Montreal Locomotive Works

LATH TWINE
Consumers' Cordage Company

LINK-BELT
Canadian Link-Belt Company
Canadian Mathews Gravity Carrier Company
Jeffrey Mfg. Co.
Williams Machinery Co., A. R., Vancouver

LOGGING COLLARS
Padgitt Company, Tom

LOCOMOTIVE CRANES
Canadian Link-Belt Company, Ltd.

LOGGING ENGINES
Dunbar Engine and Foundry Co.
Jenckes Machine Company
Marsh Engineering Works, Limited

LOG HAULER
Green Company, G. Walter
Jenckes Machine Company, Ltd.

LOGGING MACHINERY AND EQUIPMENT
General Supply Co. of Canada, Ltd.
Hamilton Company, William
Jenckes Machine Company, Ltd.
Marsh Engineering Works, Limited
Waterous Engine Works Company

LOG STAMPS
Superior Mfg. Company

LUMBER TRUCKS
Waterous Engine Works Company

LUMBERMEN'S CLOTHING
Woods Manufacturing Company, Ltd.

METAL REFINERS
Canada Metal Company
Hoyt Metal Company
Sessenwein Brothers

MILLING IN TRANSIT
Renfrew Planing Mills
Rutherford & Sons, Wm.

MOLDINGS
Genoa Bay Lumber Co.
Rutherford & Sons, Wm.

MOTOR TRUCKS
Duplex Truck Company

MOTORS
Sturtevant Company, B. F.

OAK
Chicago Lumber & Coal Comp
Long-Bell Lumber Company

OAKUM
Stratford Oakum Co., Geo.

OIL CLOTHING
Leckie Limited, John

OIL ENGINES
Swedish Steel & Importing Co.

OLD IRON AND BRASS
Sessenwein Brothers

OVERALLS
Hamilton Carhartt Cotton

PAPER
Bowater & Sons, W. V.

PACKING
Atlas Asbestos Company, Ltd.
Consumers Cordage Co.
Dunlop Tire & Rubber Goods Co.
Gutta Percha and Rubber Company

PAPER MILL MACHINERY
Bowater & Sons, W. V.

PINE
Anderson Lumber Company, C. G.
Atlantic Lumber Co.
Austin & Nicholson
Bourgouin, H.
Cameron & Co.
Canadian General Lumber Company
Cane & Co., Jas. G.
Cardinal & Page
Chicago Lumber & Coal Company
Cleveland-Sarnia Sawmills Company
Colonial Lumber Company
Cox, Long & Company
Davison Lumber & Mfg. Co.
Dudley, Arthur N.
Dunfield & Company
Eagle Lumber Company
Edwards & Co., W. C.

CLIMAX Improved Geared LOCOMOTIVES FOR WOOD AND IRON RAILS

A 62-ton Climax Locomotive Designed Especially for Heavy Logging Work.

Climax Locomotives are successfully operated on steep grades and sharp curves. Any weight or gauge. Locomotives in stock for immediate shipment. Get Catalog "H."

CLIMAX MANUFACTURING CO., 313 W. Main Street, CORRY, PA.
VANCOUVER MACHINERY DEPOT, LTD., VANCOUVER, B. C.

FOR SALE EVERYWHERE
Manufactured by
J. J. TURNER & SONS, LIMITED, Peterborough, Ont.

PUT YOUR PROBLEM UP TO US

We are specialists in building locomotives. We build all types and sizes, also all kinds of repair parts for locomotives and tenders.

Our experience puts us in a position to give you expert advice as to what particular type and size of locomotive is best suited to your needs.

Put your locomotive problem up to us.

MONTREAL LOCOMOTIVE WORKS, LIMITED

DOMINION EXPRESS BUILDING, MONTREAL, CANADA.

PRATT & WHITNEY CO.

OF CANADA, LIMITED

SMALL TOOLS

Taps — Dies — Reamers — Cutters — Drills

MADE IN CANADA

As good as money can buy—Guaranteed absolutely!

Head Office and Works, DUNDAS, ONT.

SALES OFFICES:
MONTREAL, Drummond Bldg. — VANCOUVER — WINNIPEG, Bank of Hamilton Bldg.

IMPROVING YOUR PRODUCT

The engineering experience of 35 years has made it possible for the Proctor Organization to build dryers for every individual drying need. The usual results are an improved product and improved working conditions. That's why users of Proctor Dryers are always ready to recommend and demonstrate their dryers.

"Proctor" DRYERS for VENEERS

give a perfectly flat and pliable product without checks or splits

Made by the oldest and largest builders of dryers.
Ask for Proctor Dryer Catalog for your materials.

PHILADELPHIA TEXTILE MACHINERY CO.

Drying Machine Specialists

SEVENTH STREET AND TABOR ROAD, PHILADELPHIA, PA., U.S.A.
Hamilton, Ont., Canada,—W. J. Westaway, 5 Sun Life Building.

Excelsior Lumber Company
Fesserton Timber Company
Fraser-Bryson Lumber Company
Fraser Limited
Gillies Brothers Limited
Gloucester Lumber Company
Gordon & Co., George
Grier & Sons, Ltd., G. A.
Harris Lumber Co., Frank H
Harris Tie & Timber Company, Ltd.
Hart & McDonagh
Hettler Lumber Company, Herman H.
Lloyd, W. Y.
Long-Bell Lumber Company
Long Lumber Company
Mason, Gordon & Co.
McLennan Lumber Company
Montreal Lumber Company
Moores, Jr., E. J.
Muir & Kirkpatrick
Otis Staples Lumber Co.
Parry Sound Lumber Company
Roch, Julien
Russell, Chas. H.
Shearer Company, Pas.
Spencer Limited, C. A.
Summers, James R.
Terry & Gordon
Union Lumber Company
Watson & Todd, Limited
Williams Lumber Company
Wuichet, Louis

PLANING MILL EXHAUSTERS
Garlock-Walker Machinery Co.
Reed & Company, Geo. W.
Toronto Blower Co.

PLANING MILL MACHINERY
American Woodworking Machinery Company
Garlock-Walker Machinery Co.
Mershon & Company, W. B.
Toronto Blower Co.
Yates Machine Company, P. B.

PORK PACKERS
Davies Company, William
Gunns Limited
Harris Abattoir Company

POSTS AND POLES
Auger & Company
Canadian Tie & Lumber Co.
Dupuis Limited, J. P.
Eagle Lumber Company
Harris Tie & Timber Company, Ltd.
Long-Bell Lumber Company
Long Lumber Company
Mason, Gordon & Co.
Terry & Gordon

PULLEYS AND SHAFTING
Canadian Link-Belt Company
Garlock-Walker Machinery Co.
General Supply Co. of Canada, Ltd.
Green Company, G. Walter
Hamilton Company, William
Jeffrey Mfg. Co.
Jenckes Machine Company, Ltd.

PULP MILL MACHINERY
Canadian Link-Belt Company, Ltd.
Hamilton Company, William
Jeffrey Manufacturing Company
Jenckes Machine Company, Ltd.
Waterous Engine Works Company

PUMPS
General Supply Co. of Canada, Ltd.
Hamilton Company, William
Jenckes Machine Company, Ltd.
Smart-Turner Machine Company
Waterous Engine Company

RAILS
Gartshore, John J.
Sessenwein Bros.

ROOFING
Reed & Company, Geo. W.

ROOFINGS
(Rubber, Plastic and Liquid)
International Chemical Company

ROPE
Consumers Cordage Co.
Leckie, Limited, John

RUBBER GOODS
Atlas Asbestos Company
Dunlop Tire & Rubber Goods Co.
Goodyear Tire and Rubber Co.
Gutta Percha & Rubber Company

SASH
Genoa Bay Lumber Company
Renfrew Planing Mills

SAWS
Atkins & Company, E. C.
Disston & Sons, Henry
General Supply Co. of Canada, Ltd.
Gerlach Company, Peter
Green Company, G. Walter
Hoe & Company, R.
Shurly Co., Ltd., T. F.
Shurly-Dietrich Company
Simonds Canada Saw Company

SAW MILL LINK-BELT
Williams Machinery Co., A. R., Vancouver

SAW MILL MACHINERY
Canadian Link-Belt Comptny, Ltd.
Dunbar Engine & Foundry Co.
Firstbrook Bros.
General Supply Co. of Canada, Ltd.
Hamilton Company, William
Huther Bros. Saw Mfg. Company
Jeffrey Manufacturing Company
Long Manufacturing Company, E.
Mershon & Company, W. B.
Parry Sound Lumber Company
Payete Company, P.
Waterous Engine Works Company
Yates Machine Co., P. B.

SHEATHINGS
Goodyear Tire & Rubber Co.

SHINGLE MACHINES
Marsh Engineering Works, Limited

SAW SHARPENERS
Garlock-Walker Machinery Co.
Waterous Engine Works Company

SAW SLASHERS
Waterous Engine Works Company

SAWMILL LINK-BELT
Canadian Link-Belt Company

SHEET METALS
United American Metals Corp'n.

SHINGLES
Allan-Stoltze Lumber Co.
Associated Mills, Limited
Campbell-MacLaurin Lumber Co.
Cardinal & Page
Dominion Lumber & Timber Co.
Eagle Lumber Company
Foss Lumber Company
Fraser Limited
Genoa Bay Lumber Company
Gillespie, James
Gloucester Lumber Company
Grier & Sons, Limited, G. A.
Harris Lumber Co., Frank H
Harris Tie & Timber Company, Ltd.
Heeney, Percy E.
Long Lumber Company
Mason, Gordon & Co.
McLennan Lumber Company
Miller Company, Ltd., W. H.
Reynolds Company, Limited
Service Lumber Company
Shingle Agency of B. C.
Terry & Gordon
Timms, Phillips & Co.
Vancouver Lumber Company
Victoria Lumber and Mfg. Co.

SHINGLE & LATH MACHINERY
Dunbar Engine and Foundry Co.
Garlock-Walker Machinery Co.
Green Company, C. Walter
Hamilton Company, William
Long Manufacturing Company, E.
Payette Company, P.

SHOEPACKS
Acme Glove Works

SILENT CHAIN DRIVES
Canadian Link-Belt Company, Ltd.

SILOS
Ontario Wind Engine Company

SLEEPING ROBES
Woods Mfg. Company, Limited

SLEIGHS
Bateman-Wilkinson Company

SMOKESTACKS
Marsh Enginering Works, Limited
Waterous Engine Works Company

SNOW PLOWS
Bateman-Wilkinson Company
Pink Company, Thomas

SPARK ARRESTORS
Jenckes Machine Company, Ltd.
Reed & Company, Geo. W.
Waterous Engine Works Company

SPRUCE
Bartram & Ball
Bourgouin, H.
Cane & Co., Jas. G.
Cardinal & Page
Cox, Long & Company
Davison Lumber & Mfg. Company
Donogh & Co., John
Dudley, Arthur N.
Dunfield & Company
Exchange Lumber Company
Foss Lumber Company
Fraser Limited
Fraser-Bryson Lumber Company
Gillies Brothers
Gloucester Lumber Company
Grant & Campbell
Grier & Sons, Ltd., G. A.
Harris Lumber Co., Frank H
Hart & McDonagh
Lloyd, W. Y.
Long Lumber Company
Mason, Gordon & Co.
McLennan Lumber Company
Muir & Kirpatrick
New Ontario Colonization Company
River Ouelle Pulp and Lumber Co.
Roch, Julien
Russell, Chas. H.
Service Lumber Company
Shearer Company, Jas.
Snowball Co., J. B.
Spencer Limited, C. A.
Terry & Gordon
Rideau Lumber Company

STEEL CHAIN
Canadian Link-Belt Company, Ltd.
Jeffrey Manufacturing Company
Waterous Engine Works Company

STEEL PLATE CONSTRUCTION
Marsh Engineering Works, Limited

STEAM PLANT ACCESSORIES
Waterous Engine Works Company

STEEL BARRELS
Smart-Turner Machine Co.

STEEL DRUMS
Smart-Turner Machine Co.

STOVES
Burns & Company, John

SWEAT PADS
American Pad & Textile Co.

SULPHITE PULP CHIPS
Davison Lumber & Mfg. Company

TANKS
Ontario Wind Engine Company

TARPAULINS
Turner & Sons, J. J.
Woods Manufacturing Company, Ltd.

TAPS AND DIES
Pratt & Whitney Company

TENTS
Turner & Sons, J. J.
Woods Mfg. Company

TENTS, CLOTHING
Grant, Holden & Graham, Limited

TIES
Auger & Company
Austin & Nicholson
Canadian Tie & Lumber Co.
Harris Tie & Timber Company, Ltd.
Long Lumber Company
McLennan Lumber Company
Terry & Gordon

TIMBER BROKERS
Bradley, R. R.
Cant & Kemp
Farnworth & Jardine
Hunter, Herbert F.
Smith & Tyrer, Limited

TIMBER CRUISERS AND ESTIMATORS
Sewall, James W.

TIMBER LANDS
Department of Lands and Forests

TRACTORS
British War Mision

TRANSMISSION MACHINERY
Canadian Link-Belt Company, Ltd.
General Supply Co. of Canada, Ltd.
Jenckes Machine Company, Ltd.
Jeffrey Manufacturing Company
Waterous Engine Works Company

TRIMMERS
Garlock-Walker Machinery Co.
Green Company, C. Walter
Waterous Engine Works Company

TUGS
West & Peachey

TURBINES
Hamilton Company, William
Jenckes Machine Company, Ltd.

VALVES
Bay City Foundry & Machine Co.

VENEERS
Webster & Brother, James

VENEER DRYERS
Coe Manufacturing Company
Philadelphia Textile Mach. Co.

VENEER MACHINERY
Coe Machinery Company
Garlock-Walker Machinery Co.
Philadelphia Textile Machinery Co.

VETERINARY REMEDIES
Dr. Bell Veterinary Wonder Co.
Johnson, A. H.

WATER HEATERS
Mason Regulator & Engineering Co.

WATER WHEELS
Hamilton Company, William
Jenckes Machine Company, Ltd.

WIRE
Laidlaw Bale Tie Company

WIRE ROPE
Canada Wire & Cable Co.

WOODWORKING MACHINERY
American Woodworking Machy. Co.
Garlock-Walker Machinery Co.
General Supply Co. of Canada, Ltd.
Jeffrey Manufacturing Company
Long Manufacturing Company, E.
Mershon & Company, W. B.
Waterous Engine Works Company
Yates Machine Company, P. B.

WOOD PRESERVATIVES
International Chemical Company

WOOD PULP
Austin & Nicholson
New Ontario Colonization Co.
River Ouelle Pulp and Lumber Co.

For the Small Tract of Timber Put in a Portable Saw Mill

For working up isolated tracts of timber many large lumber firms are making good, effective, and profitable use of Portable Saw Mills. Long's Portable Saw Mill machinery features many improvements for the rapid, economical, and efficient output of lumber on the small tract, and we have received many expressions of approval on the accomplishment of this machinery.

Long's Portable Saw Mills are built according to the best principles of workmanship for durability, and reliable service. Send for our catalogue, illustrating Portable Saw Mills.

The E. Long Manufacturing Co., Limited

Orillia Canada

Robert Hamilton & Co., Vancouver.
Gorman, Clancey & Grindley, Ltd., Calgary & Edmonton

A. R. Williams Machy. Co. of Winnipeg Ltd., Winnipeg
Williams and Wilson, Ltd., Montreal.

Vol. 39 Toronto, December 1, 1919 No. 23

Alphabetical Index to Advertisers, Page 80 Classified Directory to Advertisements, Page 86

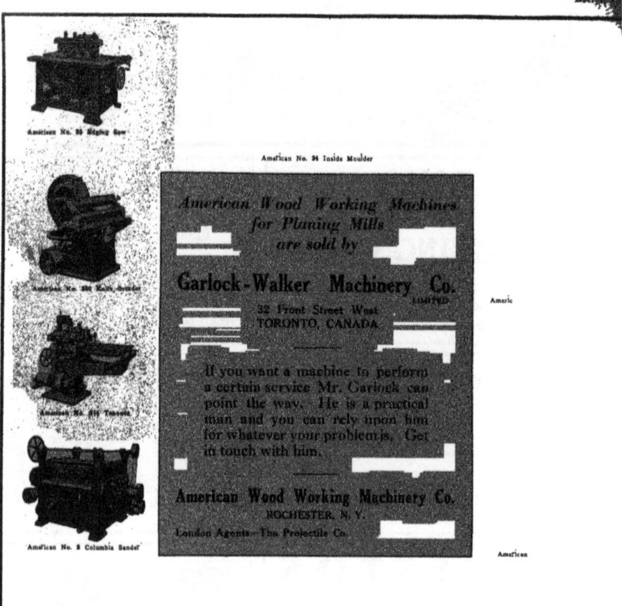

American Six Roll "Boss" Timber Sizer

American No. 65 Planer and Matcher

American No. 505 Fast Feed Moulder

American No. 49 Double Surfacer

American No. 339 Hardwood Matcher

Davison Lumber & Manufacturing Co., Ltd.

Bridgewater, N. S.

THE LARGEST LUMBERING INDUSTRY IN NOVA SCOTIA PRODUCTION 40 MILLION FEET PER ANNUM

Send us your enquiries for

Spruce, Pine, Hemlock or Hardwood Lumber
Box Shooks and
Dry Pressed Baled Sulphite and Sulphate Pulp Chips

OUR SPECIALTIES:

Nova Scotia White Spruce and Hardwood Flooring

We are equipped with everything appertaining to Modern Saw Milling and operate from the Woods to the finished product.
If you want something special quickly, try us. We will cut, dry, work and ship within a few days from receipt of order.
We are located on the main line of the Halifax and South Western Railway and on Tidewater.

We Operate:

A Double Band Mill at Springfield, N.S., Capacity 120,000 ft. per day
A Rotary and Gang at Mill Village, N.S. " 40,000 ft. per day
A Rotary and Gang at Bridgewater, N.S., " 80,000 ft. per day
A Planing Mill at Bridgewater, N.S., " 100,000 ft. per day
A Box Shook Factory at Bridgewater, N.S., Capacity 50,000 ft. per day
A Dry Kiln at Bridgewater, N.S., " 100,000 ft. per day
A Chipping Mill at Bridgewater, N.S., " 100 cords per day
A Ground Wood Pulp Mill at Charleston, N.S., Capacity 40 tons Spruce Pulp per day.

PHONE: BRIDGEWATER 74

DUNFIELD & CO., Limited

Exporters of Nova Scotia and New Brunswick

Spruce, Pine, Hemlock and Hardwood

in 1 in., 2 in., 3 in., 4 in.

Spruce Laths and Railway Ties

Head Office: **8 Prince St., Halifax, N.S.** ***Branch Office:*** **8 Market Square, St. John, N.B.**

U. K. Brokers: Duncan, Ewing & Co., K21 Exchange Bldg., Liverpool. Telegraphic Address: Dunfield, Halifax. Codes: ABC 5th Ed. Western Union

Austin & Nicholson

CHAPLEAU, ONTRIO

Largest Producers of
RAILROAD TIES
in the Dominion

Pine and Spruce Lumber
Lath Piling
Railroad Ties
Pulpwood

First Class Planing-mill Equipment

Facilities for delivering Pulpwood to Michipicoten Harbour, Lake Superior

Splendid facilities for Dressing and Matching in straight car lots, one or more widths

Mills at NICHOLSON, ONTARIO, Main Line C.P.R.

Basswood

1 in., 1¼ in., 1½ in., 2 in., and 3 in., Dry Basswood

Dry Birch Stock

All thicknesses and grades in
Maple, Birch, Elm, Basswood and **Brown Ash**
Also **Cottonwood, Tupelo, Gum, Magnolia** and **Buckeye**

Spruce, Hemlock and Pine

Can saw to order at MacDonald's Siding

Let us quote on your requirements

HART & McDONAGH

Temple Building, Cor. Bay and Richmond Streets
TORONTO, ONT.

SOUTHERN HARDWOODS Dry Stock at Buffalo for Quick Shipment

WHITE ASH

	1 & 2	Clear Strips	No. 1 Com.	No. 2 Com.
1 in.	.....	800	36,000	75,000
1¼ in.	60,000	15,500	.....	4,000
1½ in.	33,900	5,200	51,000	26,100
2 in.	82,800	500	119,000	30,000
2½ in.	6,500	.....	2,000	1,500
3 in.	10,500	.....	5,800	2,500
4 in.	4,500	.....	300	500

BASSWOOD

	1 & 2	Clear Strips	No. 1 Com.	No. 2 Com.
1 in.	16,700	2,200	201,000	105,000
1¼ in.	220,300	17,000	199,500	115,800
1½ in.	102,600	.....	86,800	35,000
2 in.	20,900	.....	9,000	4,500
2½ in.	87,000	.....	24,900	13,000
3 in.	19,550	.....	8,500	3,900
4 in.	1,300	.....	.....	.....

BUTTERNUT

	1 & 2	No. 1 Com.	No. 2 Com.
1 in.	17,300	45,800	23,600
2 in.	8,400	17,000	10,000
2½ in.	3,000	3,000	.....

CHERRY

	1 & 2	Clear Strips	No. 1 Com.	No. 2 Com.
1 in.	177,000	8,000	139,200	64,500
1¼ in.	11,500	.....	8,600	2,000
1½ in.	41,000	.....	31,700	70,300
2 in.	10,100	.....	16,200	31,900
2½ in.	2,500	.....	1,100	1,200
3 in.	17,700	.....	500	3,300
4 in.	9,900	.....	2,200	1,600

CHESTNUT

	1 & 2	Clear Strips	No. 1 Com.	S.W. & No. 2 Com.
¾ in.	.....	.....	6,500	.....
1 in.	70,000	.....	33,300	140,500
1¼ in.	125,800	1,900	58,200	155,200
1½ in.	90,500	.....	55,000	20,000
2 in.	29,200	.....	65,300	107,200
2½ in.	4,000	.....	1,100	.....
3 in.	2,800	.....	1,300	.....
4 in.	1,500	.....	300	.....

CYPRESS

	1 & 2	Select	No. 1 Shop	No. 2 Shop
1 in.	.....	.....	45,000	8,200
1¼ in.	.....	3,400	10,800	.....
1½ in.	.....	44,100	10,200	13,000
2 in.	.....	13,000	19,200	6,600
2½ in.	.....	8,000	.....	.....
3 in.	.....	62,400	25,100	5,000
4 in.	.....	10,300	.....	.....

PLAIN RED GUM

	1 & 2	No. 1 Com.	No. 2 Com.
1 in.	21,300	12,200	.....
1¼ in.	3,200	200	.....
1½ in.	9,000	11,300	.....
2 in.	.....	1,800	.....

FIGURED RED GUM

	1 & 2	No. 1 C.
1 in.	6,000	.....

QUARTERED RED GUM

	1 & 2	No. 1 Com.
4/4	1,000	6,000
5/4	4,100	.....
6/4	2,900	2,500
8/4		

SAP GUM

	1 & 2	No. 1 Com.	No. 2 Com.	No. 3 Com.
1 in.	101,400	47,000	4,500	.....
1¼ in.	3,000	8,000	2,100	4,000
1½ in.	300	1,000	2,500	500
2 in.	2,700	32,100	7,700	4,800

QUARTERED SAP GUM

	1 & 2	No. 1 C.
5/4	14,500	.....

HICKORY

	1 & 2	No. 1 Com.	No. 2 Com.	No. 3 Com.
1 in.	2,200	3,300	1,600	.....
1¼ in.	300	700	650	.....
1½ in.	4,000	1,300	.....	1,000
2 in.	3,400	4,200	1,200	300
2½ in.	11,000	9,000	3,700	500
3 in.	1,400	5,580	.....	.....
4 in.	400	200	.....	.....

PLAIN RED OAK

	1 & 2	Clear Strips	No. 1 Com.	No. 2 Com.
½ in.	30,200	.....	.....	.....
⅝ in.	131,000	.....	44,400	29,200
¾ in.	10,300	.....	87,000	48,000
1 in.	243,200	.....	21,000	47,400
1¼ in.	107,700	2,400	.....	13,200
1½ in.	117,100	4,300	15,200	30,000
2 in.	53,100	.....	84,800	12,000
2½ in.	46,100	.....	8,000	1,100
3 in.	28,800	.....	12,800	3,000
4 in.	13,000	.....	7,900	.....

PLAIN WHITE OAK

	1 & 2	Clear Strips	No. 1 Com.	No. 2 Com.
⅜ in.	.....	.....	....	.....
½ in.	.....	.....	.....	.....
⅝ in.	20,150	.....	.....	16,900
¾ in.	80,900	.....	115,000	28,000
1 in.	38,300	.....	80,000	50,200
1¼ in.	73,300	.....	10,000	8,000
1½ in.	37,800	.....	20,000	12,000
2 in.	21,000	.....	50,000	23,000
2½ in.	146,800	.....	47,500	1,000
3 in.	75,800	.....	45,800	4,400
3½ in.	5,500	.....	3,000	1,500
4 in.	60,000	.....	13,500	15,000

QUARTERED RED OAK

	1 & 2	Clear Strips	No. 1 Com.	No. 2 Com.
¾ in.	300	.....	1,700	.....
1 in.	20,200	2,300	.....	.....
1¼ in.	2,000	.....	.....	.....
1½ in.	.....	.....	.....	.....
2 in.	1,000	.....	7,400	.....

QUARTERED WHITE OAK

	1 & 2	Clear Strips	No. 1 Com.	No. 2 Com.
½ in.	5,500	.....	.....	.....
⅝ in.	30,500	.....	40,600	3,000
¾ in.	.....	.....	.....	.....
1 in.	10,400	.....	2,400	8,000
1¼ in.	17,000	.....	3,400	1,300
1½ in.	13,300	.....	8,000	.....
2 in.	31,500	.....	21,100	4,700
2½ in.	1,000	.....	.....	.....

POPLAR

	1 & 2 18 in. & up	1 & 2	Box Boards 13 in. & up	Bright Seps
⅝ in.	8,800	20,600	.....	4,600
1 in.	1,200	45,000	10,600	24,200
1¼ in.	2,800	1,900	.....	2,000
1½ in.	4,300	300	.....	12,000
2 in.	.....	16,600	.....	16,000
2½ in.	.....	25,800	.....	28,000
3 in.	.....	7,000	.....	38,600
4 in.	.....	6,000	.....	6,800

POPLOR (Continued)

	Stained Saps	Clear Strips	No. 1 Com.	No. 2 Com.
⅝ in.	13,800	.....	22,300	2,600
1 in.	32,000	.....	56,900	97,300
1¼ in.	2,600	.....	15,600	8,000
1½ in.	13,700	.....	32,000	.....
2 in.	7,000	.....	141,300	27,500
2½ in.	3,700	.....	1,000	.....
3 in.	1,500	.....	17,000	32,000
4 in.	700	.....	750	.....

BLACK WALNUT

	1 & 2	No. 1 Com.	No. 2 Com.	No. 3 Com.
1 in.	700	21,000	23,100	1,000
1¼ in.	100	1,300	1,200	.....
1½ in.	250	8,500	3,200	.....
2 in.	500	12,500	4,500	.....
3 in.	110	.....	250	.....
4 in.	...	500	1,200	.....

Also Large Stock of BEECH, BIRCH and MAPLE

THE ATLANTIC LUMBER CO., Inc., 310 MANNING CHAMBERS TORONTO

MANUFACTURERS SOUTHERN HARDWOOD LUMBER

Head Office: BOSTON, MASS. **Yards: BUFFALO, N.Y.** **Mills: KNOXVILLE, TENN.; FONDE, KENTUCKY**

FRASER COMPANIES, Limited

Bleached Sulphite Pulp Mill. Saw Mills (all Band Saw Mills). Shingle Mills.

HERE THEY ARE ON THE MAP

Mills and Railway Connections

Saw and Shingle Mills.	Railway Connections.
Cabano, Que.	Temiscouata Ry.
Glendyne, Que.	C. N. Ry.
Estcourt, Que.	C. N. Ry.
Edmundston, N.B. ...	C.P.R.; C.N.R. and Temiscouata Ry.
Magaguadavic, N.B.	C. P. R.

Saw and Shingle Mills.	Railway Connections.
Baker Brook, N.B. ...	C. N. Ry., Temiscouata Ry.
Plaster Rock, N. B. ...	C. P. Ry.
Fredericton, N. B. ...	C. P. Ry. and C. N. Ry.
Nelson, N.B. ...	C. N. Ry.
Campbellton, N. B. ...	C. N. Ry.

Bleached Sulphite Mill, Edmundston, N. B. ... ... Railway Connection, C.P.R., C.N.R. and Temiscouata Ry.

Bleached Sulphite. Rough and Dressed Spruce. White Cedar Shingles. Railway Ties

Piano Sounding Board Stock a Specialty.

Selling and Purchasing Offices :-- EDMUNDSTON, N. B.

Atlantic Lumber Company
HARDWOODS
WEST VIRGINIA SOFT RED AND WHITE OAK
Our Specialty: West Virginia and Pennsylvania Cherry
1055 Seneca Street

Standard Hardwood Lumber Co.
Hardwoods
Prompt Shipment { From Buffalo Yards or from Mill direct to you
8 Million Feet Dry Stock on Hand 1333 Clinton St.

Hugh McLean Lumber Co.
Hardwoods of All Kinds
Our Specialties—QUARTERED WHITE OAK SAP AND RED GUM
Established 25 Years 940 Elk Street

Miller, Sturm & Miller
1142 SENECA STREET
Hardwoods of All Kinds

G. Elias & Bro., Inc.
Established 1881
All Kinds of Hardwood Lumber
And in addition we carry a full line of White Pine, Yellow Pine, Spruce, Hemlock and Fir Timber, Lumber, Millwork and Boxes—Maple and Oak Flooring
CAREFUL ATTENTION TO MIXED CAR ORDERS

Taylor & Crate
Hardwoods of All Kinds
A stock of 18,000,000 to 20,000,000 feet of hardwoods carried at all times at our two big Buffalo Yards
Established 50 Years Rail or Cargo Shipments

T. Sullivan & Co.
HARDWOODS
We Specialize in Brown Ash and Elm
Car or Cargo Shipments Cor. Niagara and Arthur Sts.

Yeager Lumber Company, Inc.
SPECIALTIES
Oak, Poplar, Ash, Maple
932 Elk Street

B Buff
U Hard
F Lumb
F Deale
A
L
O

Buffalo Hardwood Lumber Co.
940 Seneca St.
We Specialize in WHITE ASH
Anyone handling any of this stock, write us.
We also handle a complete stock of Plain Oak, Quar. Oak, Maple, Poplar, Red Cedar, etc.

Blakeslee, Perrin & Darling
A Complete Stock of Seasoned Hardwoods
including Ash, Basswood, Birch, Cherry, Chestnut, Cypress, Elm, Gum, Hickory, Maple, Plain and Quartered Oak, Poplar and Walnut.
1100 Seneca Street

Checking Up Long-Bell Grades

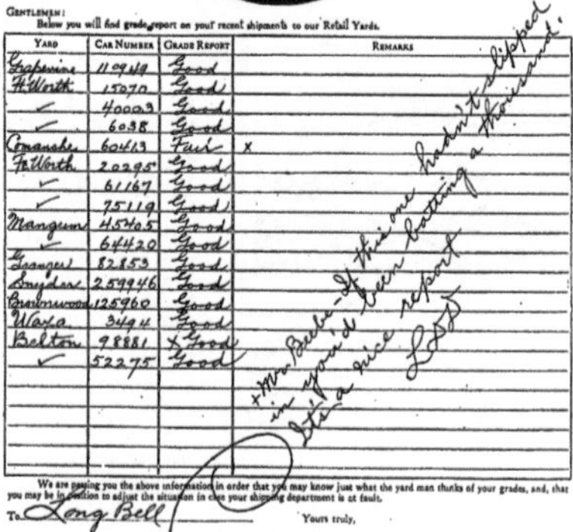

GENTLEMEN:
Below you will find grade report on your recent shipments to our Retail Yards.

YARD	CAR NUMBER	GRADE REPORT	REMARKS
Grapevine	110940	Good	
Ft. Worth	15070	Good	
✓	40003	Good	
✓	6038	Good	
Comanche	60413	Fair	x
Ft. Worth	20295	Good	
✓	61167	Good	
✓	75119	Good	
Mangum	45405	Good	
✓	64420	Good	
Granger	82853	Good	
Snyder	259946	Good	
Brownwood	125960	Good	
Waco	3494	Good	
Belton	98881	x Good	
✓	52275	Good	

x Mr. Beebe—If this one hadn't slipped in you'd been batting a thousand. It's a nice report. L.S.S.

We are passing you the above information in order that you may know just what the yard man thinks of your grades, and, that you may be in position to adjust the situation in case your shipping department is at fault.

To Long Bell

Yours truly,

W.M. CAMERON & CO., INC.
Purchasing Department

(Facsimile of a grade report received at our office)

Quality lumber means first of all lumber that is up to grade. To this end unusual caution is exercised by all our graders. This trade-mark on our products is an assurance to both dealer and consumer that he is obtaining the very best lumber we know how to make:

LONG-BELL
The Mark on Quality Lumber

The above grade report on shipments to Wm. Cameron & Co. is typical and further proves that our extra efforts to provide quality lumber are not in vain.

OUR NATIONALLY KNOWN PRODUCTS

Southern Pine Lumber
Oak, Oak Flooring, Gum
California White Pine
California White Pine Sash and Doors
Screen Doors, 3-ply Veneers
Creosoted Lumber and Timbers
Posts, Poles, Ties,
Piling and Wood Blocks

The Long-Bell Lumber Company

R. A. Long Bldg. Kansas City, Mo.

British Timber Importers and Merchants

BROWNING & COMPANY

(Established over a Century)

IMPORTERS of and AGENTS for

ALL KINDS OF

CANADIAN WOOD GOODS

22/3 LAURENCE POUNTNEY LANE, CANNON STREET,
LONDON, E.C. 4.

OFFERS OF AGENCIES INVITED

BRITISH IMPORTERS

CANADA CAN SUPPLY YOU

Britain's greatest store-house of timber, Canada, offers the logical market for British importers. The "Canada Lumberman" is the medium through which British importers can reach the complete lumber and timber industry of the Dominion in all its phases. The "Canada Lumberman" will, through the use of its advertising columns, bring you into close touch with the whole trade, which can only be reached by the nationally read lumber journal of Canada.

The Canada Lumberman and Woodworker
347 Adelaide Street West, - TORONTO, CANADA

Sample copies, detailed information, advertising rates, will be gladly supplied. Address the Publishers direct, 347 Adelaide Street West, Toronto, Canada, or

Our London Office—16 Regent St. S.W. 1.

NEW ZEBRA, WOOD, WESTERN UNION, and PRIVATE CODES USED.

Telephones:
1391 Long Distance.
400 Private Branch Exchange.

Cables:
"HILLAS," HULL

W. N. HILLAS & COMPANY

WOOD BROKERS

FOR EVERY CLASS OF TIMBER

***Head Office:* HULL, England**

To the Lumber Companies of Canada:

You have the Goods. Place your Lists with full particulars in our hands. We are in daily touch with all the Buyers in the United Kingdom.

PLEASE NOTE. We pay cash against all documents, and take the whole of the Delcredere risk on Buyers.

The Ideal Edger for Light Mills

Specifications

Our new Double Edger is built on entirely new lines, and possesses many features that commend it to mill men. The saving in material alone will soon pay for the machine. The output of a mill with this machine can be increased by one-third. It is best adapted for medium-sized or portable mills that cut from 5,000 to 25,000 feet of lumber per day.

SAWS—This Edger is fitted with either two or three saws as required. The saws are 16 in. in diameter, and 10 in. gauge. The greatest distance between saws is:—Two saw machines, 24 in.; three saw machine, 20 in.; the least distance between saws, 2 in.

DRIVE PULLEY—The Drive Pulley is 9 in. x 8 in., affording a good belt grip, and is supported by an outside bearing.

SAW ARBOR—The Saw Arbor is made of 2½ in. steel, and has very wide bearings.

For Shingle, Lath and Portable Saw Mill Machinery
write the well known manufacturers

The G. Walter Green Co.
Limited
PETERBOROUGH, ONT.

Send for Catalogue

We Invite Your Special Inquiries

for

CAMP SUPPLIES

Address them to our Director, Mr. J. Laporte:-
Special Sales Department

LAPORTE, MARTIN LIMITEE

Wholesale Grocers

584 St. Paul Street West - Montreal

Canada Lumberman and Woodworker

For Forty Years Canada's National Journal

Issued on the 1st and 15th of every month by
HUGH C. MACLEAN, LIMITED, Publishers
THOS. S. YOUNG, Toronto, General Manager.

OFFICES AND BRANCHES:

TORONTO - - Telephone A. 2700 - - 347 Adelaide Street West
VANCOUVER - - Telephone Seymour 2013 - - Winch Building
MONTREAL - - Telephone Main 2299 - - 119 Board of Trade
WINNIPEG - Telephone Garry 856 - Electric Railway Chambers
NEW YORK - - - - - - - - - - - - 309 Broadway
CHICAGO - Telephone Harrison 5351 - 1413 Great Northern Building
LONDON, ENG. - - - - - - - 16 Regent Street, S. W.

TERMS OF SUBSCRIPTION
Canada, United States and Great Britain, $2.00 per year, in advance; other foreign countries embraced in the General Postal Union, $3.00.
Single copies 15 cents.

"The Canada Lumberman and Woodworker" is published in the interest of, and reaches regularly, persons engaged in the lumber, woodworking and allied industries in every part of Canada. It aims at giving full and timely information on all subjects touching these interests, and invites free discussion by its readers.

Advertisers will receive careful attention and liberal treatment. For manufacturing and supply firms wishing to bring their goods to the attention of owners and operators of saw and planing mills, woodworking factories, pulp mills, etc., "The Canada Lumberman and Woodworker" is undoubtedly the most direct and profitable advertising medium. Special attention is directed to the "Wanted" and "For Sale" advertisements.

Authorized by the Postmaster-General for Canada, for transmission as second-class matter.

Entered as second-class matter July 18th, 1914, at the Postoffice, at Buffalo, N. Y., under the Act of Congress of March 3rd, 1879.

Vol. 39 Toronto, December 1, 1919 No. 23

Expanding Factors in Lumber Trade

This is the age of expansion. Progress is evidenced all along the line. A fair index of the trend of the times is the number of new companies which are being incorporated. Each week sees many industrial and commercial organizations which have been granted charters. These newly-formed concerns represent every line of business, and more particularly lumber, pulp and paper.

In the lumber arena there is a feeling of optimism and confidence prevailing, not only with respect to the future demand, but regarding the stability of conditions in general. It will be a question next year of where the requisite stocks can be obtained. There is already a dearth of supplies in many kinds of wood. Should building activity keep up in 1920—and there is no reason why it should not—there is likely to be a decided shortage of material, and those who have postponed structural operations this season in the hope that 1920 would usher in larger supplies and lower prices, may find themselves sadly astray in their calculations and predictions.

The lumber business is growing wider in its activities and its exponents have become more numerous. Within the last three months there have been probably two score companies incorporated and fully a score of new wholesale firms have been established in Toronto, Montreal and other cities to embark in the handling of forest products. During the war there were comparatively few new lumber syndicates organized and several wholesale firms went out of business owing to the stringency of conditions and the gradual shifting of the demand from the ordinary channels of distribution to meet the unusual demands created. The whole complexion of things was changed, but now the pendulum has swung in the other direction and a large percentage of lumber, which formerly went into shipbuilding, aeroplanes, shell boxes, gun carriages, gun stocks, cantonments, saddle trees, cots, etc., has reverted to the usual lines.

So far as manufacture and distribution are concerned, everything is now back to where it was, but the question, bound to loom large in the near future, is where can sufficient lumber be obtained? Stocks are low, production will not increase a great deal, and the demand has, for many weeks, been most insistent and widespread. It requires little or no selling ability to dispose of wood goods to-day, but it does require a careful study of the situation, a thorough knowledge of conditions and not a little foresight and perception to secure the lines that are in urgent requisition. Much will depend upon the attitude of labor during the next few weeks, the character of the winter and the cost of supplies, etc., as to whether the volume of woods operations of 1919-20 will exceed in the aggregate that of 1918-19.

* * *

Another Evidence of National Stability

The recent success of the Victory Loan portrayed the faith and confidence which the Canadian people as a whole have in the solidity of the Dominion and its future welfare. The splendid response which attended the floating of the bonds is an object lesson of the optimism and assurance with which Canadians view their country's weal. They have demonstrated that they are self-reliant, far sighted, enthusiastic and aggressive. It is these qualities in a people or a firm which make for stability and permanence, progress and expansion.

Canada played a heroic part during the war. She never fell down on the job, and in a similar sense she is making good with her industrial problems and the rehabilitation of conditions displaced during the five years of the European conflict, in which the whole current of events was changed. Now the old problems have to be taken up again, and many new ones as well, and it is interesting to record the prophetic words of Sir Henry Drayton, the new Finance Minister of Canada, who proclaimed that the success of the recent loan was the final making of Canada's pledges—the final chapter in the war efforts. He stated that our dollars are going to be doubled and the world's markets were at our doors. To-day is Canada's, and we can make to-morrow Canada's, too.

The fact that practically every centre in the Dominion exceeded its objective, and that so many firms won the Prince of Wales flag shows that, individually and collectively, much can be accomplished if a high standard is set and every effort bent in the direction of its achievement. For anyone to have stated five years ago that it would be possible to raise a popular loan in Canada of nearly seven hundred million dollars would be tantamont to the observer inviting an investigation of the workings of his mental machinery, but great things are being done and there will be greater things yet accomplished.

The credit of the country has been preserved, her enterprises will be fostered, her foreign trade extended, her processes in military re-establishment adjusted and her export outlets afforded every facility. The last chapter of Canada's war effort has been in keeping with her marvellous war record.

Much that was accomplished was done through the energy, activity and devotion of a number of self-sacrificing and public spirited business men who did all in their power to see that the success of the loan was assured. It is gratifying that their efforts were so richly rewarded, not from dollars and cents standpoint, but in the carrying out of a duty well and nobly done. There is no doubt that these men put forth greater endeavors on behalf of their country than they usually do in their own private business, and the people generously responded. The support came from all classes and was one united, whole-hearted, aggressive effort, showing that even with the absence of a patriotic appeal or war urge, really big things can be realized. The press also played its part and the whole principle underlying the loan was "Canada First."

Apart altogether from financial considerations, the sixth Victory Loan was a splendid advertisement for the country, revealing the financial strength of the Dominion, the energy of her people, the spirit of the times and confidence in the future. With such a sentiment manifesting itself on every side and with a co-operative, good-natured effort there is little to fear regarding the days to come.

It has been pointed out that the spirit exhibited during the recent campaign should continue to manifest itself by subscribers holding their bonds. In doing this they will help greatly to advance the value of the security, with the resultant benefit to the subscriber and to still further confirm the credit of Canada.

With work and thrift, greater production and the practice of economy, there is no doubt that the Dominion will weather any post-war storm and sail triumphantly into the port of prosperity, efficiency and expansion.

* * *

The Ebb and Flow of the Lumberjack

Everywhere there is restlessness in the ranks of the ordinary lumberjack, especially the foreigner. He seems imbued with a spirit of moving here and moving there and getting nowhere. How to correct this tendency to travel and to make these men remain in camps after their transportation has been paid to the destination, is one of the big problems that lumbermen have to face. The constant shifting is getting to be a matter so serious as to call for legislative or other restrictive action. The camps are comfortable, the food substantial and varied, and wages the highest ever known for this class of work, yet the practice of "jumping" is as pronounced as ever.

The country is crying out for more lumber and larger production. Operators are willing to open up more camps. They have the virgin material, but if they cannot get someone to fell the standing timber the quantities available are of no use for constructional or manufacturing purposes. Increased output simply resolves itself into getting the men, and in some centres help is reported as being decidedly scarce. But everywhere there is one general grievance, and that is, the elusiveness of certain types of woodsmen which seriously impedes operations, disarranges internal administration and general efficiency in the camps.

The situation now and then has its amusing side. One lumber company applied recently to an immigration centre for assistants in the bush. Back same the reply:—"We have no one that we can recommend. All around here now are either thieves or thugs." One manufacturer, whose mills are still busy, inserted advertisements in the country newspapers to the effect that he required men for the woods and was willing to give them $70 a month, with board and transportation, and if they remain three months, to pay their fare back home. This has resulted in calling forth a representative class of young farmers who are expert at handling a team, and, while they may not know all about bush work, still they readily learn. They are content to receive this liberal wage and come out in the spring with several hundred dollars to their credit, eager to assume the work on the farm again. This plan is eliminating the foreigner and resulting in greater efficiency and augmented production.

* * *

Use of Tractors in Woods Operations

The purchase of six tractors for log hauling by the Wayagamack Pulp & Paper Company and Laurentide Limited, reported in our last issue, is worthy of comment, as evidence of the tendency to adopt mechanical devices in woods operations. In Quebec, at any rate, the use of tractors is rare, the River Ouelle Pulp & Lumber Company being one conspicuous instance where these machines have been successfully tried. Mr. W. G. Power, of that company, at a meeting of the Woodlands section of the Pulp & Paper Association, in January last year, gave some details of the operation by his company, emphasizing the point that the tractors must be properly handled if good results are to be secured. In other words, lumber and pulp companies must be prepared to make the necessary capital outlay—not to cut down here and there with a view to saving expense. That way lies failure. To secure the full benefits of tractors, arrangements must be made to ensure continuous operation during the season; a breakdown might entail the holding up of the entire hauling.

The Laurentide and Wayagamack Companies apparently intend to thoroughly test out these machines, particularly in connection with pulpwood. These efforts will be following up the recommendation of the Woodlands Section Committee on Logging Improvements, which suggested that by the use of small tractors, hauling say five or six cords to a load, the work can be materially cheapened. Such machines do not need very much work done on the roads and can manoeuvre easily in the woods. By having two sets of sleighs for each tractor, they can be kept running steadily. In their use it pays to have a skilled mechanic to keep them always in good order. An extra machine, or a good supply of repair parts, should always be on hand. As the cost of the machines is low, this is quite feasible.

On the Pacific Coast the use of tractors is more general. At the last convention of the Pacific Coast Logging Association four papers on this subject were read, three of them dealing with Western problems. The tractors used are of the caterpillar type, and the writers of the papers expressed the opinion that the machines are economical and efficient. In one instance the total cost was figured at $4.25 per thousand logs, and in another at $30 per day per unit, this allowing for two men, and also for the cost of depreciation. Up to 30,000 feet are moved per day per caterpillar machine by one company, while another company's average is 36,000 feet per day, on a three round trip schedule.

The increased cost of manual labor, combined with the decrease in the productive capacity of the men, has naturally directed attention to the employment of more mechanical devices for logging operations, not only with the view to decreasing costs, but also with the object of putting the companies in a position where they will not be subject to the vagaries of many of their employees. It was stated at one conference of the Woodlands Section that in woods operations very little improvement, from the mechanical side, has been made in recent years, although from the mill end there has been great progress. While tractors, of course, will not suit every condition, there is evidently, in the opinion of the officials of the Laurentide and Wayagamack Companies, a sphere of usefulness for them in that particular branch of the lumber business with which they are identified.

* * *

Editorial Short Lengths

Efficiency and greater production, thrift and economy are the characteristics, both national and individual, which will re-establish Canadian industry on a sound peace footing.

* * *

A leading business man said the other day there was nothing more discouraging than a competitor financially embarrassed—no, nothing, except being financially embarrassed yourself.

* * *

Gentlemen, the demands that some of the radicals are making cannot be satisfied with increased wages, for they demand nothing less than turning industry over to them. There is no justification for that kind of partnership, for the only kind that is successful in business is that which is earned and paid for.—Chas. Piez, President of Link-Belt Co.

* * *

The Associated Boards of Trade, at a recent convention in Toronto carried a resolution in favor of daylight saving by a majority of one. Strange what an important figure this is getting to be. The new coalition government in Ontario had a majority of one, and the average individual in these days of stress and strain and the high cost of living has to look out for Number one if he wants to keep from the reach of the bailiff and the sheriff.

* * *

President Beatty, of the Canadian Pacific Railway, intimated in an address before the Canadian Club of Toronto that another increase in freight and passenger rates was not one of the improbable happenings of the future. There is really nothing startlingly new in this announcement, as the frequency of advances is almost as common a subject of conversation in transportation circles as the weather, the political situation and the success of the U. F. O. movement.

* * *

From the reports received throughout the Sudbury district a large number of new sawmills are being erected and woods operations, particularly, will be carried on more extensively than ever before, especially with regard to the taking out of ties and pulpwood, of which the call has been unusually active during the past few months. The prospects for an increased demand in these lines are exceptionally strong, and there is no doubt all that can be produced will find a ready market.

* * *

It has been said "The East is East and the West is West, never the twain shall meet." A despatch from the prairie provinces states that owing to the scarcity of coal some of the rural residents are burning up lumber, which costs $40 to $50 per thousand, and in the East there is reported to be a decided shortage of lumber, with the call in many lines unusually insitent and only diminishing stocks in sight. Two great contrasts are thus brought out,—in the East greatly depleted stocks of lumber, while in the West there is lumber to burn.

* * *

The head of a leading industrial organization, the name of which is known all over the American continent, stated in a recent address before the Associated Business Papers Congress that he had always believed in technical and trade papers and that they had exercised and are still exerting a powerful and beneficial influence in advancing the status and progress of industry. He was of the opinion that they had a large mission still ahead of them and a mission that would call for every bit of energy and intelligence that the publishers and editors were capable of bringing into play.

* * *

It used to be an uneventful week in Canada when a new breakfast cereal was not placed on the market. This gave rise to a jocular saying that even sawdust was being dished up for the delectation of appetites at the morning meal. The next development was in the line of gramophones, and scarcely a week passed without some new brand being placed before the public, and all proclaimed the latest achievement in beauty, art and tone. Now another epoch has arrived, and it is a quiet week when no new organization is announced in the pulp and paper line or some extension to the output of the present large companies. The activity in pulp and paper stocks has of late been particularly marked, and the securities have been eagerly seized upon whenever offered to the public.

* * *

The Imperial Department of Overseas Trade in London is organizing an exhibition of timbers grown within the British Empire, to take place from July 5th to 17th, 1920. It is proposed that the exhibition shoud include: (a) Speciments of timber (polished and unpolished); (b) Timbers used as flooring, panelling, etc., furniture, ply wood and woodenware generally; (c) Wood pulp. The principal object of the exhibition is to bring prominently before users of timbers the full range of those grown within the British Empire, and to demonstrate the chief uses to which they may be put. Canada will be represented by a large variety of lumber. On this side the arrangements are in the hands of Mr. Stokes, of the Forest Products Laboratories, University Street, Montreal, who is still collecting specimens and data.

* * *

Says a leading Canadian manufacturing firm in a line closely allied to the lumber business:—It is seemingly useless to agitate for lower prices until the world's starved condition is remedied and the productive capacity of the world catches up with the needs of the consumer. This can never be as long as the present labor unrest exists and the only satisfactory solution of the problem appears to lie in industrial peace and increased production. We urge our customers and friends to eliminate all possible wasteful methods, purchasing only such goods as will take care of their present needs and those of the immediate future. By all assisting in this, more rapid recovery to a sensible level of trade conditions can be made and the present spasmodic, chaotic and disproportionate conditions will give way to a conservative and sound basis of doing business.

* * *

The Federal Government recently advertised for a superintendent of the Forest Products Laboratories, Montreal, to succeed Dr Bates. The applicants were required to have high technical qualifications and business abilities, but unfortunately the salary offered was not commensurate with the necessary qualifications. The result was as might have been expected. The salary was not sufficient to attract men of the high standard required, and the Government is now about to offer an appreciable increase in the remuneration. The Government has not been generous in its support of an institution which has done good work for the country. The consequence is dissatisfaction, and the gradual loss of officials to pulp and paper companies, who are prepared to pay for the qualifications possessed by men who have made a study of important problems connected with the lumber and pulp and paper industries. Indications point to a very large expansion of these industries, particularly in the province of Quebec, and the Government cannot expect to retain members of the staff when companies are willing to offer them salaries substantially higher than those paid by the federal administration.

* * *

The sawmills of Canada are gradually disappearing through the clearing up of limits in the various sections, and rarely is there an operating location where more timber exists than will supply the requirements for a comparatively few years. It is a sad story to publish in nearly every edition of the "Canada Lumberman" the destruction of several plants by fire. In spite of the utmost precautions, the best fire-fighting appliances, stand-pipe installations, water mains, sprinkling systems and other usually effective safeguards, there is no appreciable diminution in the number of mills wiped out by the devouring element. This is all the more regrettable at this particular period of industrial expansion and greater production. The output of every mill in Canada running at full capacity can be sold at profitable prices for many months to come. The situation grows serious, and anything that can be done to stamp out the ravages of the fiend not only in the timber areas of each province, but also in lumbering towns, should receive strong encouragement and support. No matter how heavy an insurance is carried there is bound to be a decided loss to the sufferer, owing to the fact that no building of any kind can be replaced to-day within fifty per cent. to one hundred per cent. over and above what it would cost three or four years ago.

* * *

"I notice that a number of American firms buying Canadian lumber are insisting in their agreements that they be paid on the basis of American funds, the exchange running against Canada to the extent of about four per cent. just now. I hope, when the balance of trade has readjusted itself—as it will some time in the future—that Canadians will return the compliment. I have known American funds to be at a premium in Canada especially in the fall when the grain shipments are heavy and that state of affairs may roll around again. Then Canadian wholesalers and manufacturers should see that they are paid in par value by their American customers. It is 'a poor rule that will not work both ways' and 'a turn about is fair play' in matters financial," declared a leading wholesale lumber merchant of Toronto recently.

* * *

The Montreal Board of Trade have had under consideration the proposed increase in wharfage charges, and have passed the following resolution—"That while the Board of Trade fully appreciate the necessity that the Harbor Commissioners are under of securing adequate revenue, it, as representing those from whom said revenue is collected, holds that it is entitled to have some voice in the adjustment of the charges that produce it, so that they may be fair to all concerned, and it would, therefore, seem reasonable that the commissioners should agree to discuss the new tariff of wharfage charges with representatives of the board and other organizations interested." The Commissioners will be asked to receive a deputation on the subject.

* * *

The overwhelming prominence of wood in the construction of dwellings in New Zealand is shown by the fact that of the 229,423 private dwellings erected in 1916, 219,000 were of wood, 7,000 of brick, 1,280 of stone and 1,680 of concrete, says the Vice Consul at Auckland in a recent consular report. In many counties, he adds, there is not a single dwelling built of brick or stone.

A Progressive Lumber Manufacturer

Frank Blais Has Built Several Sawmills in Quebec and Directs Many Other Activities

Frank Blais, Amos, Que.

With twelve dollars of borrowed money in his pocket Frank Blais went to Boston some twenty-five years ago to work in a brick yard. To-day he is a prosperous wholesale lumber merchant and manufacturer in the province of Quebec and owns and operates four saw mills, extensive timber limits, a general store and a flourishing pulpwood and hay and grain business. His life story is one of push, purpose and achievement. He is a progressive French-Canadian citizen, of whom the province of Quebec has many, not only in the lumber business but in other lines of achievement. Mr. Blais' first job was, as stated, in a brick yard in Boston. He then drifted into bush work and went to New York state to cut logs and get a practical acquaintance with woods operations. His next move was into the state of Connecticut where he secured a position with a man named C. B. Terrell, who was a lumberman and contractor. Mr. Blais stayed with him for seven years doing all kinds of work from cutting poles to running portable sawmills. Seventeen years ago he returned to Canada and opened a general store at St. Thecle, Que. This village is located in Champlain county, on the Canadian Government Railways. About this time he began to buy pulpwood for the Riordon Pulp and Paper Co., of Montreal, and still continues this work, along with his many other activities. In 1904 he built two sawmills, one at St. Thecle and the other at Hervey Junction, and for several years supplied railway contractors with all their requirements in forest products and also feed for their horses. He furnished about 400 cars of hay and 25

Mr. Blais' boat conveying logs to the mill at Amos, Que.

cars of oats annually until construction on the railway was completed and the business in this line ran about $200,000 a year.

In 1912 Mr. Blais built another sawmill at Doheny station, 25 miles east of LaTuque on the Transcontinental railway to Quebec, which has a cutting capacity of 40,000 feet a day. He has there 20,000 acres of patented land covered with a splendid growth of red birch and spruce. Two years later he erected a fourth sawmill at Amos of equal capacity to the one at Doheny and has since purchased sixty square miles of timberland consisting principally of spruce. There is about a million feet of pine on the land, the remainder being black spruce, the stand of this being estimated at 30,000,000 feet.

The subject of this reference conducts a planing mill and a shop for mill repairs. He also manufactures shingles and, in his planing mill, during the past summer, dressed three quarters of a million feet of lumber. He also owns a large general store for supplying the many workpeople that he employs with the necessities of food and raiment.

All logs are hauled by an alligator, a steam boat and two gasoline launches and are driven by booms to the various mills. His output of spruce, pine and birch is marketed chiefly in New York state, since the work on the Canadian Government Railways was completed. The accompanying view shows one of Mr. Blais' boats drawing logs. Mr. Blais is a busy man conducting all these operations alone but he has a large number of competent employees, who have co-operated with him in building up his business to its present gratifying proportions.

Northern Spruce Mills Sold Up To Saw

Frank W. Gordon of Terry & Gordon, Toronto, who visited all the producing centres in the Sunset Province during October and November, returned home recently and gives some interesting information regarding lumbering and logging conditions in B. C.

Stocks at all Northern British Columbia Spruce Mills are sold right up to the saw, all of this moving readily to New York and other Eastern American points. The larger mills in this district are closed down for the winter, the smaller ones continuing to operate into the winter, as far as possible. The majority of plants in the Southern interior of the province were closed down at least a month earlier than usual, owing to a log shortage. This combined with an unprecedented demand for all classes of lumber has reduced stocks to a point where the situation becomes serious, particularly to the consumers of the Western provinces. However, a kernel of reassurance may be extracted from the programme for next year's production by the Mountain millmen who are exercising their resources unsparingly to make production sufficient to take care of a widening demand. New operations will tend to increase the production of Western soft pine and spruce. Coast loggers and millmen are struggling valiantly to cope with prevailing conditions. A serious situation is developing in the shortage of logs, with possibilities of Coast logging camps closing down until spring, which leaves no alternative for ninety per cent. of the tidewater mills but to discontinue operations until logs are available. While prices embracing all B. C. lumber seem high and appear to the lay mind to be a lucrative proposition for the lumbermen, Mr. Gordon is of the opinion that the majority of mills throughout B. C. have not been able to pay usual interest rates on their capital investment. Production costs were always in advance of raises in selling prices. Coast fir logs cost the millmen on an average of $18.00 per M. Manufacturing costs are not less than $10.00 per M., and the present selling price on fir timbers is less than $26.00 F.O.B. cars B. C. mill points.

As is usual at this time of year, requisitions from the natural markets are not at all brisk, except for clears and factory stock of all kinds. There is an insistent demand from Western and Eastern Canadian provinces for clear and factory cedar, pine and fir, which must remain unsatisfied until next year's cut comes to the market. At present it looks as if the American buyer will continue to take upwards of 75 per cent. of B. C.'s production for next year. There is a strong movement among the large distributors in Seattle, Minneapolis, Chicago and other American centres to get protection in prices and secure as much stock for next year as possible.

British Columbia mill men, however, are loathe to assume any obligations for next year's production. Any stock which they are offering now is for immediate movement only.

Prices On Southern Woods Keep Soaring

W. H. Harris, of the Frank H. Harris Lumber Co., Toronto, returned recently from spending six weeks in the Soutth on a purchasing trip to cover the requirements of the firm for the next few weeks. He bought large quantities of yellow pine, cypress, red and sap gum and quarter-cut oak. The company operate two mills at High Point, Miss. Mr. Harris reports that the recent oil boom in Texas and Oklahoma is causing a pressing demand for yellow pine, both dimension and timbers, all the way from 4 x 4 up to 16 x 16 inches of varying lengths. These are used for the erection of derricks and there has been a recent advance from $2.00 to $4.00. The rains in the South have been heavy and continuous, interfering seriously with logging operations, and the help problem is growing more acute all the time with the demand for higher wages and shorter hours.

Mr. Harris visited all parts of Alabama, Tennessee, Mississippi and Louisiana, and says that the feeling throughout these states is an optimistic one in regard to the future demand and prices of lumber. All hardwoods have recently advanced from $10 to $20 per M. owing to the increased cost of production, and yellow pine, which underwent a decline at the time the $10 a day demurrage was placed on cars in transit, has now passed over and quotations are back to practically where they were some weeks ago, with the number of requisitions increasing all the while.

The Frank H. Harris Lumber Co. report that there is a good demand in Canada for yellow pine, interior finish and trim and also for southern hardwoods, and shipments, considering the congested car situation in some districts, are coming through satisfactorily.

Lumbermen Discuss Freight Rate Problem

Many Instances of Inequalities Pointed Out—Shippers Always Seem to be on the Defensive and Never on the Aggressive—Group Ratings

The Wholesale Lumber Dealers' Association held their monthly meeting on November 21st at the Albany Club, Toronto. Mr. A. E. Clark occupied the chair, and there was a very representative attendance.

The first matter of business, after the members had dined, was a report presented by the chairman relating to the recent Navy League campaign. A team representing the wholesale lumbermen of Toronto had been appointed by the chairman, as a result of a decision reached at the October meeting, and the report of the work done by the team showed that it had made the best record of any of the various teams engaged in the campaign. The total collected by the lumbermen, exclusive of "specials," was $9,453.25, while the next highest team total was $5,329.75. The lumbermen's team, moreover, collected three times as much as any other team working in a similar section of the city. The chairman read a most appreciative letter of thanks from the Navy League for the work the lumbermen had done. Considering the fact that this was the first time that the lumbermen had worked in a campaign of this kind and that they were opposed by some teams which had had considerable experience in work of this nature, their record was a fine one.

Some Work for Transportation Committee

Railway freight rates were the subject of a long discussion introduced as the result of a reference to the subject by the Fesserton Timber Company. In southwestern Ontario, the Fesserton Timber Company frequently met with difficulty arising out of the fact that no freight rates are published to Canadian Northern Railway points in this territory. Frequently a representative of the railway would make a mistake in figuring a rate and the result would be that the freight charges were higher than those upon which the wholesaler had based his quotation. It was suggested by the Fesserton Timber Company that the transportation committee of the association should take this matter up with the Canadian National Railways.

Mr. A. C. Manbert mentioned the inequalities between the rates on lumber from Georgian Bay points into the eastern States, as compared with those from some other Canadian producing points, which resulted in discrimination against the Georgian Bay producers. He also pointed out that the rates from Ontario points to some points in the eastern States were higher than those from points in the United States in Wisconsin and upper Michigan, in spite of the fact that the haul from the latter point was longer. In the past it had been difficult to get the railway companies to take these matters into consideration, as railway conditions had not been favorable. Now that the roads in the United States were to be returned to their original owners, however, and some orderly arrangement of these matters seemed to be probable, while at the same time there was a prospect of a national system of railroads being developed in Canada, it seemed that the opportunity might be here to press upon the C. P. R. and upon the Canadian National Railways the necessity for establishing arrangements with the roads in the United States which would give us rates such as we were entitled to have.

The Advantage of Group Rates

Mr. A. E. Eckardt spoke of the grouping privilege whereby railways on the other side were able to get group rates to points in a district, such for instance as "Toronto and West," in Ontario. If the railways here could give the United States railways these grouping privileges, it was only right that the railways on the other side should grant us similar privileges, such as group rates into Pennsylvania, New York, etc. His own experience had been that the shippers were always on the defensive with the railway companies, instead of being aggressive. Everything brought up before the Board of Railway Commissioners seemed to be presented from a railway standpoint, and the shippers were not prepared with the data necessary to oppose them. He referred, for instance, to the matter of minimum weights, and suggested that the Wholesale Lumber Dealers' Association should start a propaganda for the simplification of freight tariffs. He urged that each member should keep on file, in a readily available manner, all information regarding the trouble he was experiencing in connection with minimum weights.

Mr. Eckardt also referred to a standard form for the presentation of overcharge claims, copies of which he had received from the C.P.R. These he exhibited to the members and suggested that they were a good thing, as claims presented in this manner would be more promptly attended to by the railway.

The Chairman, Mr. A. E. Clark, also pointed out a number of inequalities in rates, and said that the association would do well to memorialize the railways and the government on the subject at once.

Declares Charges are Exorbitant

Mr. J. H. Duthie, of the McDonald Lumber Company, Toronto, who was a guest at the meeting, and who has had extensive experience with the railway companies of the United States and Canada in connection with freight rates, both as a shipper and as an employee of the railways, was asked by the chairman to speak on the subject. He expressed the opinion that it would be possible for the shippers, now that the Canadian Government was taking over the Grand Trunk, to insist on dealing directly with the officials of the government roads, instead of having to deal with the Car Service Bureau. He discussed the question arising out of the appointment of a commission to operate the government railroads and asked whether the government would also be justified in appointing another commission to watch over the operating commission. If the men appointed to the operating commission were competent there would be no use for another commission, such as the Dominion Railway Board, to watch over them.

Mr. Duthie stated that the present freight rates were exorbitantly high. The main thing needed in Canada to-day was restoration of railway competition. If we obtained that we would get a reduction of 25 per cent. in freight rates within six months, notwithstanding the statements recently made by some of the railway company representatives that they would soon need higher rates.

There was only one way to get what they wanted from the railway companies. That was to know exactly what was wanted before appearing before them. Most of the railway company officials were fair-minded men and would give you what was right. Unfortunately, many of the railway men were not acquainted intimately with the requirements of business. If they were, the shippers would be treated very differently. He believed, however that if they were to go before the Canadian National Railways with a well-prepared case, pointing out the desirability for establishing through rates, they would get them. It was a very simple matter for the railway companies to arrange rates, and if they could be shown that existing rates were unfair they would change them.

The discussion resulted in the matter being left in the hands of the transportation committee with the understanding that they would study the subject closely and take such steps as are necessary.

Some Ideals in Public Service

Mr. W. H. Alderson, of Gutta Percha & Rubber Limited, Toronto, who attended the meeting as a guest of the association, was then introduced. Mr. Alderson is second vice-president of the Toronto Board of Trade, and he delivered an address upon public service ideals and upon the work which is being carried out by the Toronto Board of Trade. He outlined a large number of questions which the Public Affairs Committee of the Board had dealt with during the past year and urged the members of the Association to give the Board their heartiest co-operation.

Mr. K. M. Brown, the new representative in Eastern Canada of the Vancouver Lumber Company, Vancouver, B.C., was introduced to the members present and addressed them briefly. Mr. Brown, who made a most favorable impression upon his future confreres, spoke of conditions in the West, laying particular emphasis upon the fact that many of the western mills are operating double shifts and are still unable to keep up with the orders they are receiving.

On motion of Mr. W. E. Bigwood, seconded by Mr. W. J. Lovering, it was decided that a letter should be written by the secretary to the new Minister of Lands and Forests for Ontario, congraulating him upon his appointment to this important department, offering him the co-operation and services of the association and requesting him to be the guest of the Association at its next monthly dinner.

The meeting then adjourned.

R. McDonagh, of Hart & McDonagh, wholesale lumber merchants, Toronto, has now quite recovered from his long and painful attack of rheumatism and is able to attend to his regular duties again.

The Qualities of a Good Lumber Salesman

Red Blooded, Hard Working, Smiling Salesman Radiating Optimism From Every Pore is One of Best Advertisements that Any Firm Can Have

"Several years ago the cypress people saw the necessity of advertising and boosting the sale of their 'wood eternal,' as they are pleased to call it. They spent thousands on top of thousands of dollars advertising in the highest class trade papers and leading magazines of the country," said V. M. Lacey, of St. Louis, Mo., who is President of the Lumber Salesmen's Association, in that city, in a recent address.

"I don't think their salesmen thought so much of their wood until they began to see its praises sung on a page or two of every trade paper they picked up, and in almost every good magazine in the country. Then these salesmen reached the conclusion that they had something to sell of unusual merit, and wherever you meet a cypress salesman you will meet an individual filled with confidence and optimism because he has read everywhere that he is selling a 'wood eternal,' a wood that will last forever.

"All this time we boys who were selling southern pine had an article to sell that filled ten regirements where cypress filled one. We had and have an article that will construct complete everything from a chicken coop to a giant warehouse, but I wonder just how many of use realized what a wonderful wood we had to sell.

"I am strongly of the opinion that boosting and advertising southern pine has had as much to do with our position to-day as any natural cause such as supply and demand. Everywhere we go the slogan "Own Your Own Home" stares us in the face. Everywhere we go we hear the hammer and the saw, and every salesman radiates optimism, and in my opinion boosting and advertising has had as much to do with our present prosperity as anything else. We salesmen are not advertisers in printed form, but every one of us is an advertiser of the lumber we sell, and I am going to say, without equivocation, that a red-blooded, hard-working, smiling salesman radiating optimism from every pore of his skin, is the best advertisement any firm ever had, or ever will have.

"However, we southern pine salesmen have our weak points, and, taking myself as just a fair average, I want to say a few words about our common weakness.

Know Good Points of What You Sell

"I do not believe we know anything near enough about the good points of the wood we are selling, and the Lord knows we, as a class, hardly know anything about the wood our competitors are selling.

"We all know that when an adding machine salesmen comes to us with a machine to sell that he can explain every point of that machine, every reason why it is better than the other fellow's machine in the points that he wants to bring out, and you can't ask him a thing about the machine that he cannot answer instantly, and if most of us will be frank and admit it, nearly anybody can ask us questions about the merits or demerits of our southern pine that we cannot answer intelligently.

"I remember quite well a number of years ago of selling a bill for two million feet of crating stock at a certain price. Business was terribly dull and the firm I was with was very hard up for orders. This was a very sharp buyer. I do not mean sharp in the ordinarily accepted term, but I mean he was shrewd and keen, and if a salesman escaped with his pants he was a bird. Well, to make a long story very short, this buyer told me he could not buy southern pine from me because he could buy hardwood at a much cheaper price, so the result was he showed me his price on hardwood, and, like the sucker I was, I took the order, and all the time he was laughing in his sleeve because the southern pine was worth, on account of the easiness of working, saving in freight in the re-shipping, etc., three or four dollars more than the hardwood. Well, I'll admit I was a cub salesman, but a lot of us are cubs sometimes even though we have been in harness all our lives, and get caught up on things we should know. But it is not so much the mistakes that we make that I am driving at. I guess none of you has gotten stung on one so simple as I was hooked on; the thing is, however, that every one of us should endeavor, if he wants to be an expert salesman, to first learn as much as possible about the true merits of his own wood, and, secondly, learn all he possibly can about the wood his competitors are selling. I do not mean that he should try to become an expert in the knowledge of all woods, but we surely should try to learn as much as possible about our principal competing woods.

"I wish to speak just a few words here as to the service we may render our customers.

"It seems to me that during these strenuous days about the best service we can render is the service of honesty and truthfulness. Ous customers are looking to us to do all we can for them in the way of getting stocks for them to do business on, and while we are apparently almost helpless along that line, there are many little things we can do that will help and be appreciated. Some of us, at times, permit ourselves to be persuaded to take orders for something that does not show on the stock sheet, thinking, that we are helping our customers. I think you will agree with me that we are not helping our customer when we do this, but are rather hindering him, so let's be honest and tell him so.

"Another thing we all should do, and I believe most of us already do, and that is, tell our competitors that a customer is in the market for this or that, but that our firm hasn't the stock, and in that way gain the good will of both the customer and some other salesman. I believe in fighting fairly for every thing I can get, but if I haven't the stock why keep the knowledge that my customer wants certain items to myself, when I know that one of my competitors has it? I am afraid we do not get close enough together; we don't meet often enough to discuss conditions that are prevailing. Believe me when I say that when you get a few fellow salesmen boosting you along as an honest, square competitor, willing to give and take honest information, you have added an asset to yourself as a salesman that nothing can take away.

Helping the Customer to Get Lumber

"I knew the time when it just naturally hurt a salesman to see a competitor in a customer's office; I have had salesmen slip out and call my customers up and tell them not to place an order with Lacey until he could see him. That was the custom, almost, although, I now look back and see what a despicable custom it was. I don't think those things are done any more. We have got to keep the trade supplied with our lumber ,and a mighty good way to do so is to help your customer get our lumber somewhere, if you can't furnish it yourself.

"Another mighty good thing for all of us to do is to keep posted as to production and supply of competitive woods.

"I am perfectly aware of the fact that most of us are old salesmen who have been in harness a long number of years, and doubtless have a good working knowledge of our business, but what our employers want us to do is to grasp the finer and better points of our business. They want us to become experts; they want us to become men who can discuss our lumber in a frank, intelligent way, and to be able to convince our customers and prospective customers that we really know what we are talking about, and want us to be able to explain why we know what we are talking about. Any man here who is willing to admit the truth frankly (and I know we are all willing to do this), will admit that many a sale has been lost by a hesitating reply. It isn't that we don't know how to sell our lumber, and it isn't that we are not good salesmen, but it is because we must put more expert knowledge into our work; we must know more of our own wood, and we must learn more about our competitive woods."

Public Ownership of Timberland Advocated

Public ownership of timberland, national or state—with private cutting and marketing—was advocated by the Paper and Pulp Association's committee on forest conservation, in a report submitted to the Association conference held recently in New York city. Such ownership was said to be essential for the growing of the older and larger sizes of timber, its production being too long and hazardous an undertaking, with too little earnings to attract private capital in adequate amounts.

In line with this opinion, speedy adoption and executive of national and state forest policies, co-ordinated and co-operative, was urged. Forest surveys and land classification as first steps were declared necessary.

Public purchase of cutover lands by nation and states should be enlarged and extended to all parts of the country, the report said. It also advocated the vigorous and general extension of fire prevention co-operation between the nation and the states, state adoption of uniformly fair forest taxation laws, estimate of forest nurseries and the preparation of forest working plans. A large programme of forest planting on denuded lands which show little promise of new natural crops was urged.

The Present Selling Price Next Year's Cost

Lumber Stocks are Low, Producing Expenses High and the Demand May be Difficult to Meet—The General Outlook Reviewed in Some Details

Everything betokens stiff increases in the price of lumber next season in all parts of Canada and this observation is not made without due consideration and a general survey of conditions which are and will contribute to the ascension in values.

Labor is scarce at many points, restless and excessive in its demands. The general efficiency of a woodsman is only about 66 per cent. of what he was before the war, and it takes three men to do what two men formerly carried out. Stocks of lumber in all lines, both hard and softwoods, are low and never did wholesalers have less available quantities to dispose of than at the present time. There will be no dry lumber coming on the market until May or June next, and during the past season more lumber was sold and shipped green from the saw than was ever known in the history of the industry in the East. Some of the mills did not take the trouble to put the lumber on stick at all, but sent it out in carload lots to customers who demanded the product in any shape.

The increase in wages, the higher cost of camp supplies, particularly horse feed, and the general inefficiency of men will make logging costs from 10 per cent. to 15 per cent. higher than during the season of 1918-19. It, therefore, looks as if this year's selling price will be next year's cost price. The demand for lumber is bound to be large, not only for export purposes, but for home consumption, while there is an insistent call for white pine, hemlock, birch and maple from the other side of the line, where a tremendous building boom is foreshadowed.

In no product does the outlay for labor play as important integral a part as in lumber. Wages and the expenditure for feeding men, constitute about 70 per cent. of the total cost of the product. In many parts of the country lumberjacks are getting $70.00 to $75.00 a month with board. which means a disbursement of $110 to $115 in order to keep a man on the job, and in some cases the bushwhacker is hardly worth his board let alone the wages, but the industry has to put up with this indifference and incompetence simply because sufficient help is not available in order to make a discriminating choice.

Everything being considered, lumber has not advanced as much in price as has hardware, glass, plumbing, brick, tile and other articles so universally used by the building trade. A general estimate, based on an accurate survey of all kinds of woods, places the advance around 65 per cent. The heaviest increases have been on the cheaper grades owing to the excessive call for them, as many builders have been proceeding on the principle of not how good, but how cheap can they erect houses. The better grades of lumber have not gone up anything in like proportion to the cost of production.

A well-known manufacturer estimated the other day that it was costing nearly 200 per cent. more to get out logs and drive them to the mill and convert them into the finished product than it did before the war, when wages were $40.00 to $45.00 a month, and good board could be supplied for 40c to 50c a day. Then the cost of all supplies was about 100 to 125 per cent. less that at to-day's market figures.

A cry has been heard about building operations likely to stagnate owing to the high cost of lumber, and that if there was only a drop there would be much structural activity. When it is considered that the expenditure for wood products, which includes joist, studding. flooring, ceiling, casing—in fact general interior and exterior trim—is on the average only one-fifth of the total cost of a house, it will be realized that the price of lumber does not play such a relatively important part. In building a house, costing anywhere from $8,000 to $15,000 not more than ten to fifteen thousand feet of wood goods would be used in its erection, and even if the price is from $30 to $60 per M higher, this is comparatively small when contrasted with the wages of carpenters, bricklayers and other trades now receiving $1.00 an hour on numerous jobs.

Some manufacturers of hardwoods have withdrawn their price lists altogether. They have only odds and ends to sell and will not be in a position to furnish anything in quantities until early next year. The call has gone forth from automobile concerns, implement men, gramophone and piano makers, furniture producers and flooring manufacturers for birch, maple, oak and other allied lines, but the sources of supply are limited and practically any figure, no matter how exorbitant. can be secured. It is not now a question of price, but of getting the goods.

The situation is, not to speak of the probable demands from abroad, one that is causing much anxiety, and, while some are predicting a famine in lumber, it may not reach that acute stage, but may become neighborly near the mark. While the supply may not be "broken," it will be "badly bent," and reminds one of the rustic who went down to New York City with quite a large roll of bills and had a gala time. On his return home, somewhat saddened and impoverished, an acquaintance enquired concerning his experiences in the metropolis. The youth told him down to the minutest detail.

"You must have come home dead broke after all that," remarked his friend,

"No," mused the bucolic sojourner, "not broke exactly, but to tell the honest truth, I'm badly bent."

Smaller Lumber Production Across Border

On the basis of partial returns received by the Forest Service, United States Department of Agriculture, from 731 saw mills in all parts of the country, each of which cut in both 1917 and 1918 more than 5,000,000 board feet of lumber, the estimated total production of lumber in the United States in 1918 was 32,760,000,000 feet, as compared with a production of approximately 36,000,000,000 feet in 1917. The decrease in 1918 was general, not being confined to any one region; but it was greatest in the southern and eastern states and smallest in the western states. The chief producing states in 1918 were: Washington, with a total cut of 3,250,000,000 feet; Oregon, with 2,000,000,000 feet, and Louisiana, with more than 1,500,000,000 feet. More than 500,000,000 feet was produced in each of the following states: Mississippi, California and Nevada (the two in one division), Wisconsin, Arkansas, Texas and Idaho.

Making permanent records of forest growth.

The man in the picture is determining the position of the trees by means of an alidade attached to a plane-table. Each tree has a number painted on its trunk and corresponding numbers are placed on the map. This is a material assistance in keeping a permanent record of the trees and simplifies the study of the progress made by them under different conditions from year to year. The portion of the plot shown in the picture has been slashed and the slash burned. For purposes of comparison the remainder of the plot has only been slashed.

CANADA'S COAL

There is much concern in Canada, particularly in Ontario, which province depends largely upon imported coal, over the source of coal supply for the present winter, because of the strike situation in the United States.

Just why this worry should make itself manifest seems somewhat of a mystery, when one stops for a moment to consider and investigate the situation. In Alberta we have 16 per cent. of the total supply of coal in the whole world. The heating value of Western coal has been tested by householders, manufacturers, railways, and power plants throughout Western Canada, and all concerned have found Western coal an economical and efficient fuel. Steam coal produced in the Crow's Nest Pass district compares very favorably with the very best United States steam coal, and big concerns like the Canadian Pacific Railway, the T. Eaton Company and the Winnipeg Electric Railway Company have adopted the use of this coal because of its qualities as an efficient fuel, linked up with a big saving in the annual coal bill. In Alberta we have over 300 mines, many of which are equipped with the most modern equipment, costing millions of dollars, and yet the annual production of these mines is only 40 per cent. of what could actually be produced. This is because of a lack of a market that can take all the coal mined. At present Western Canada imports about 3,000,000 tons of coal annually, valued at $18,000,000. This huge sum of money is sent to the United States to pay for coal imported into this country. That money assists to develop United States industry. It helps to keep the overhead expenses of the mines low because of the fact that the more coal produced means less overhead expense. Again, by sending this $18,000,000 out of Canada we are very materially affecting our already heavy adverse trade balance. The fact should not be lost sight of, too, that on this $18,000,000 we must pay $720,000 in exchange alone.

The whole trouble why Western coal operators have not made more headway in marketing their product is owing to a lack of educational propaganda—as it were, to a lack of pep. They have the product, the men, the equipment, and the market. But the operators must be assisted in their problems by everybody concerned in the welfare of the future of Canada. Daily and trade papers, boards of trade, wholesale and retail coal dealers, all must spread the propaganda that we have in Western Canada coal that has been tested and found to be equal to that which has been imported for so long. Emphasis should be laid on the following facts: one of Canada's principal industries will be materially assisted to develop; millions of money will be kept in the country and so help our adverse trade balance; equally as good heating values can be obtained from Western coal as from imported coal; the more Western coal used, the lower the overhead at the mines, and consequently the lower the price to the consumer.

Alberta operators complain, and justly too, that their overhead expenses are very high through their inability to secure a market for slack coal, which is now merely thrown away. For instance, smaller mines in the Lethbridge field waste 50,000 tons of this product annually. Slack coal can be utilized to advantage in power plants. Such plants at Regina, Saskatoon and Winnipeg have burned this fuel with great success.

Another factor that is keeping back the development of the coal mining industry of the West is the high freight rate applied to the shipment of all grades of coal, especially on slack coal.

* * *

The "Western Canada Coal Review" in a recent editorial criticized very severely the actions of the Dominion Government and the Provincial Government of Manitoba in asking for bids for coal specifying that only United States coal was required. Why this discrimination? Why this encouragement to buy in foreign markets when an equal product is at our own doorstep? Why this apathy to our severe adverse trade balance? Why this discouragement of the development of our natural resources? Why this apathy towards assisting the employment problem in Canada? Perhaps the Government officials can answer.

As an instance of ignorance of even many Winnipeg manufacturers of the burning qualities of Western coal, a certain representative of a large coal mine visited Winnipeg in the Fall of 1918, and found a manufacturer was contemplating placing a big order for the best American steam coal to heat his power plant, not giving any consideration whatever to Canadian coal. After talking over the possibilities of burning Alberta coal in his plant, he decided to give it a trial. This year, the same manufacturer without any hesitation whatever, promptly gave this same mine another big order for his coal supply for the winter of 1919, saying only one word in reply to the mine's representative of what he thought of the coal: "WONDERFUL."

* * *

At present Ontario is faced with what looks like a fuel famine. Why should this be? At the moment of writing there are stored at the head of the lakes 250,000 tons of soft coal and 324,000 tons of anthracite, with additional shipments arriving as lake steamers arrive. Now, why should there be a shortage in Ontario when this supply is lying at the lakes ready for shipment into Western Canada? Does not this importation seem like "Carrying Coals to Newcastle"? Why should the Ontario Fuel Commissioner not commandeer all of this coal and divert it to Ontario and so help the serious fuel situation in this province?

Are we to sit still and smile, or act? Which is it to be?

Bolshevik Exponents Told to "Move Along"

Have Made Appearance in Eastern Logging Camps and Seek to Gain Recruits for One Big Union—How their Sinister Appeals are Made

The exponents of I. W. W. Bolshevism, Socialism, Soviet Government, One Big Union and all the other isms are making their appearance in Ontario and Quebec, and are beginning to get in their nefarious work. They are doing this secretly, quietly, but most persistently in the lumber camps of the eastern provinces. So smooth have been their methods of procedure and so insidious their practice that in not a few cases these exponents have worked for several days before their mission has been discovered by the operators and secured a number of subscribers to the One Big Union, known as The Lumberworkers' Industrial Union of the One Big Union. The appeal is made alluringly, the tone used is confidential and the general attitude of the agent invites confidence. The representative of the I. W. W. or Bolshevism comes into camp as an ordinary lumberjack, remains a few days and mingles among the men, talking on various subjects at first and gradually leading up to the main idea in view; then at the proper time a document is handed to those whom it is desired to enlist and they are asked to read it over. They are told in a suggestive way that what has been accomplished in the West can, with equal success, be carried out in Ontario, if the co-operation of loggers is secured, individually and collectively.

The entrance fee is only $1.00 and what manner of men is there who would not put up this small initiation charge if he could obtain one tithe of the benefits and emoluments so enticingly presented by the glib-tongued, suave individual who can picture things in their most serene condition. In some cases where the listener is particularly easy, he is induced to pay not only the entrance fee of $1.00, but also to hand over $4.00 or $5.00 extra in the shape of monthly dues, which are $1.00 a month. In not a few cases this has been done in several camps where a fairly large sum of money was collected before the exponent of Bolshevism or I. W. W. was spotted, and told to move along.

The plan of campaign on the part of the Bolshevists is as deliberate and far-seeing as would be conducted by a well-organized political party in order to win an election or carry a certain cause to victory.

General Warning Sent to Operators

All the lumber camps of Ontario and Quebec have been warned and their managers and foremen will be on the look-out for the lurking individuals who are seeking to spread a dangerous industrial doctrine and striving to build up their cause by a tissue of falsehoods and misrepresentation that could only find lodgment in the minds of the illiterate and those unacquainted with the actual condition of affairs. This class consists principally of foreigners who are working in the camps and know little about Canadian state of affairs.

It is the object of the Bolsheviki and I. W. W. agents to appeal to the discontented, the indolent, the ignorant, the grouchy and the easily-swayed members of any camp. However, it is thought, now that the lumber camps have been warned, there will be little or no difficulty in keeping a close watch on developments and inviting these "gentlemen," who come in to scatter such dangerous creeds, to proceed on their way.

Following is a copy of the leaflet that has been placed in the hands of a number of workers in camps. It purports to present what has been accomplished in British Columbia through the agency of the Lumberworkers' Industrial Union, and while some of the exactions have been met there is much of that outlined which has not been granted. The literature sets forth the demands of the men rather than what they have been successful in securing.

Road Between Desire and Realization

There is a long road between desire and realization, between planning and achievement, and when the loggers say they have obtained all that is portrayed in the leaflet, they are not only sadly misrepresenting affairs, but will stop at no end in the way of distorted statement and seductive appeal to gain their objective in the shape of the One Big Union.

Any other movement that seeks to cripple the lumbering industry, increase restlessness and discontent, hamper production and stamp out contentment and generally break down customs and institutions that have been tried and, after years of experience and insight, found not to be defective, should be promptly suppressed.

The attached circular, therefore, should not be taken too seriously in view of the foregoing explanation, and it is given space merely to show how far some mistaken individuals will go in presenting a movement that has to be bolstered up by deceit, dishonesty, selfishness and greed:

What the Workers of British Columbia Have Done!

In January last, a number of lumber-workers on the Coast who realized that only in unity was there strength, got together and formed what was known as the B. C. Loggers Union, an organization embracing all camp workers.

The growth of the organization was marvellous; in fact there is not another labour organization that has increased its membership at the rate that this did. In nine months it exceeded eleven thousand paid-up members, and extended its activities over the whole of the Province of B. C. At the general convention held in Vancouver last July it was decided to affiliate with the One Big Union, and to change the name to the Lumberworers Industrial Union of the One Big Union, and to extend its activities throughout the Dominion.

Since the organization came into existence the living and working conditions of the logger have improved tremendously; in many cases it has not been necessary for the men to take further action to secure the improvements, the existence of the organization being sufficient to cause the boss to come through, for he realized that the organized logger would not continue to accept those conditions which the unorganized worker was compelled to endure.

In the past, when the workers did not like a camp, they quit individually, and in a few days there were other men on the job, living under the same conditions, until they in turn quit in disgust, and another crew took their place. It was a common occurrence for a camp to have three crews, one going, one working, one coming; but now, instead of leaving the job and permitting such conditions to continue, the workers stay right there and see that the boss provides conditions fit for human beings.

The following schedule of camp conditions was drafted by the B. C. loggers at their recent convention, and is now in operation in the majority of the camps, particularly on the coast, where the camps are practically one hundred per cent. organized;

A minimum wage of $5 a day. A strictly 8-hour day, camp to camp, with time and one-half for overtime, legal holidays and Sundays. Semi-monthly pay day. No contract, piece-work or bonus system. The employer to pay transportation to the job, but if the worker is not put to work, or is discharged before having earned twenty-five dollars over and above all expenses, including fare back to town, then transportation both ways to be provided by the employer. At boat landings proper landing facilities to be provided, with house adjoining, supplied with stove and wood. Transportation from boat or railroad to camp. No bunkhouse shall be less than 18 x 24, and not contain more than six single iron beds, each with springs, mattress, two double blankets, sheets, pillows and slips, and kept in sanitary condition; the sheets and pillow slips to be washed once a week, blankets once a month, and every time bedding is changed from one person to another; the employer to bear the cost of same. A stove to be placed in the centre of the bunk house. A wash-house, dry-rack and bath-house to be installed in all camps. The bath-house to be partitioned from the dry-house. Antiseptic soap and towels to be provided free. Hot and cold water to be provided. Toilets with light, 300 feet from all buildings. Kitchen staff to be provided with sleeping quarters separate from the kitchen. A sanitary store-room in connection with the kitchen. Meat houses not closer than 15 feet from kitchen. Earthenware to be used in place of enamelware; forks, knives and spoons to be of nickel silver. Dining room tables to be covered with oil cloth. Six men only to a table. Kitchen utensils to be of copper, aluminum or pressed steel. Dish-up table and sink to be lined with zinc. Buildings for blacksmith and filer to be built suitable for this work. A reading room to be provided in all camps. The Health Act, in respect to camp sanitation, to be rigidly enforced. All complaints to be dealt with through the camp committee. Every employer who is situated more than 5 miles from the office of a medical practitioner, and employing one or more men, shall at all times maintain in or about such place of employment satisfactory means of transportation to carry all injured workmen to the nearest hospital. A licensed "First-aid" man shall be employed in camps where there are 10 to 25 men, and an additional one for every 25 thereafter.

Are you living and working under these conditions? If not! Why not?

Is it because you are not organized? If so the immediate remedy is right at your hand. **There are organizers in your district, ready to assist you to organize.** Campworkers like yourself, and men who have proven the value of organization. Join up with them and immediately you cease to be an insignificant individual camp-worker, drifting aimlessly along at the mercy of the boss,, and become instead a vital part of that mighty driving force—organized labor—which is powerful enough to improve the working and living conditions of all workers in industry. The organization is entirely in the hands of the members on the job. The members in a camp control their own activities. In each camp a delegate is elected. He signs up new members, collects dues, remits all moneys to and keeps in constant touch with. the district headquarters, and generally looks after the business of the organization on the job.

Every man who has the desire to improve his conditions and with the initiative and back-bone to act for himself is urged to become a delegate. Men are wanted who are not afraid to do a little work; men who have the courage of their convictions; men who consider that they have the right to say under what conditions they will work and live. Are you that man? Are you willing to assist in improving the conditions of yourself and your fellow-workers, irrespective of what the boss may say or think? Do you consider that you have the right to organize with your fellow-workers? Or are you willing to drift along in the same old rut that your grandfathers did, ignorant of the fact that the world has changed since they trod the earth? Do you realize that changing conditions require new methods, and that if you want anything better in the shape of living and working conditions, and wages, that you must organize, must combine and co-operate with your fellow-workers, in order to get them? Have you a mind of your own, or do you let someone else think for you, and meekly do as you are told?

Prove your manhood! Think for yourself! Investigate the aims and objects o,ncstitution and laws of the Lumberworkers Industrial Union of the One Big Union, and you will then do as 11,000 other camp-workers have done before you, JOIN IT.

Do it now. Entrance fee $1. Monthly dues $1.

Make your aim to equal that of B. C. A 100 per cent camp. A 100 per cent. Province. A 100 per cent. Dominion. It's up to you!

If you desire further information write the District headquarters at Prince Albert, Cranbrook, Kamloops, Nelson, Princeton, Prince George, Prince Rupert, or the general headquarters at 61 Cordova St. W., Vancouver, B. C.

Pulp Prices Continue to Advance

There is great activity in pulp and paper securities and the latest company to make a public offering is the Saguenay Pulp and Power Co., which controls the Chicoutimi Pulp Co. (the largest producer of wood pulp in the world), the St. Lawrence Pulp and Lumber Corporation, the Saguenay Light and Power Co., the Roberval-Saguenay Railway Co., and the Chicoutimi Port Co. The Saguenay Pulp and Power Co. are now offering $1,500,000 serial, gold bonds, bearing interest at six and a half per cent.

Hon. F. L. Beique is president of the company and, in a récent letter, he gives some interesting information regarding the activities of the organization and the steadily increasing price of ground wood pulp. Senator Beique says that the mills at Chicoutimi and Val-Jalbert have been running to capacity since the first of the year. Stocks of mechanical pulp, which had grown to over 60,000 tons, in the early months of 1919, have all been sold and shipped. It is understood that the bulk of the pulp has been disposed of in the Old Country. Steadily higher figures are now being secured for the output. The pulp, which the company sold last year and during the first six months of the present year, brought from $26 to $29 per ton but quotations have now advanced to over $40. The last sales were made at $42.50.

In regard to chemical pulp the capacity of the plant at Chandler has been increased by forty tons a day and the output is now averaging 112 tons. Operating costs have been reduced by over $10 per ton.

Sawmill and Much Lumber Burned

The smaller one of the two sawmills of the Brown Corporation near Trois Pistoles, Que., was recently destroyed by fire and several million feet of lumber were burned as well as about a hundred thousand cords of pulpwood. The damage is estimated at over a million dollars. The flames were particularly difficult to fight. The blaze started late in the afternoon and was fanned by a high wind, the mill being first wiped out and then the yard. The flames were kept from the larger of the two mills. A. Keens is the manager of the Brown Corporation for the district and the headquarters of the company are at Berlin, N. H. The company operate pulp mills at La Tuque, Que.

Mr. Thuerck Reviews Northern Activities

W. C. Thuerck, Haileybury, Ont.

W. C. Thuerck, Haileybury, Ont., who has charge of the northern interests of Terry & Gordon, of Toronto, has had a wide and varied experience in the lumber business, starting at the age of 14 with Noyes & Sawyer, of Buffalo, N. Y., first as tally boy in the yards, then in the planing mill, and finally in the head office.

After having served six years with the above mentioned firm, he severed his connection and entered the employ of Smith, Fassett & Co., of North Tonawanda, in the capacity of shipper and inspector, serving six years in this capacity. and obtaining a thorough knowledge of the grading of lumber, especially pine.

In November, 1911, Mr. Thuerck took charge of the Canadian operations of Smith, Fassett & Co., at Charlton, Ont., where he had full charge of the plant, yard and bush operations, increasing the capacity of the mill from 20,000 ft. per day of ten hours to a capacity of 40,000 ft., and a season's production of 9,250,000 ft. In November, 1916, Smith, Fassett & Co. sold their Charlton plant to the Beaver Board Co., of Buffalo, who are operating a barking drum on the saw mill site. Mr. Thuerck was engaged from November, 1916, till March, 1917, in making final disposition of Smith, Fassett & Co.'s stock at Charlton, and entered the employ of Terry & Gordon on April 1st, 1917, as their representative in northern Ontario.

Writing to the "Canada Lumberman" on November 1st, Mr. Thuerck states that they then had about three inches of snow and a wet fall which had delayed all bush operations. The high price being paid to settlers for pulpwood and ties has had the effect of turning operators to these lines rather than the production of logs. Present indications point to a cut about equal to last year's with less operators.

Terry & Gordon expect to produce about 2,000,000 ft. of spruce at Charlton, and had about one quarter of this quantity on skids on November 1st. They will also have about three-quarters of a million feet of Jack pine. They have a like quantity at Kenebeek on the Elk Lake branch; also about 300,000 feet of white pine of good quality at Osseo, which is also on the Elk Lake branch of the T. & N. O. railroad. They have started to cut about 500,000 ft. of Jack pine. These operations, including the sawing of the logs, will all be in personal charge of W. C. Thuerck. Terry & Gordon will also produce upwards of 100,000 ties during the coming winter and spring.

Mr. Thuerck was born in Buffalo in 1886, but became a naturalized Canadian five years ago. He is well-known and highly regarded in the North country.

Z. Mayhew, representing Simpson, Clapp & Co., wholesale lumber merchants, New York, was in Toronto recently. This firm specializes in Eastern spruce and B. C. products, lath, shingles, staves, etc.

High Lead Logging System in Eastern Canada

Skidders Are Now Being Put on the Market for This Modern Service—How Cost of Woods Operations May Be Greatly Reduced

By "Woodsman"

A general idea of the high-lead system of yarding logs, or bringing the logs from the stump to the loading ground, as practised and developed on the Pacific Coast, is presented in the accompanying crude sketch. Many systems have been tested in that country of large and heavy logs, and this high-lead system has been found the most satisfactory of all for general work under ordinary conditions. For special conditions such as extra steep mountain sides, ravines, or for distances too great to be reached by the high-lead line, various other cable way systems are to be preferred; but these unusually difficult surface conditions are not found to such an extent east of the Rockies, and it is, therefore, believed by those who have studied the matter thoroughly that the high-lead system is the best one for general use all through Eastern Canada.

It is also thought that the time is not far distant when this system will be brought into use in most of the lumber camps of Ontario and the East by reason of the increasing cost of labor and supplies, and the generally poor quality of labor now available. It is simply a matter of getting better acquainted with the method and its advantages, including the low cost of installation and operation, and as soon as this knowledge becomes better disseminated, the lumbermen will be eager enough to avail themselves of the method.

Briefly stated, this high-lead system is simply a means of dragging the logs quickly along the ground, but with the forward end raised off the ground sufficiently to lead it safely around or over all obstructions. Thus only the one end of the log really drags the ground, and all the rest of the log is in the air. By this means the log arrives at its destination clean, and free of mud or pebbles, which are so apt to be forced into its surface by any of the ground haulage systems.

How the System is Operated

To secure this high-lead sufficiently high to thus hold the forward end of the log in the air in transit, the highest tree in the vicinity is selected, limbed and topped, and a block attached near the top, as shown. The skidding machine is then located near the base of the tree; the cable is run from the drum up through the block on the tree and out to the log, the hooks are attached and the log hauled in to the tree, and the hooks sent out for another log. In some camps the hooks are sent out by horse power, in others the line passes over a block at the far end of the course, and thence on to another block at the far end of the course, and thence back to another block on the spar tree, and down to a second drum on the skidder, which second drum and line returns the empty hooks to the far end of the run much quicker than a horse.

This return line is usually of smaller diameter than the mainhaul line, as the strain on it is much less. This return line has to be twice the length of the mainhaul line, or a trifle more—that is, if the extreme length of the log haul is 600 feet the return line should be from 1200 to 1300 feet long. Some camps let this return line run along the ground, but at a sufficient distance from the path of the logs in coming in to avoid fouling. As this tends to wear the return line out quickly many operators attach the block for this return line high up on the spar tree to keep the line off the ground, which makes the line last from two to three times as long. Both of these methods are in daily use, and the choice depends largely on personal preference.

The need of this system all over Canada is great, but so far practically no effort has been made by any manufacturer of skidding machinery to supply this need except for the handling of the extremely heavy timber of the Pacific Coast, and the rest of Canada has either had to use the extremely heavy machinery designed for the Pacific coast—or go without. One Eastern logging company were so anxious to make use of this system, with light machinery properly designed for use with the general run of logs found in Eastern Canada that they sent a representative recently to tour the United States and inspect the best equipment manufactured and used in that country, but to their great disappointment, the representative returned with a report that all the United States machinery was too heavy for use in Eastern Canada.

Skidders Adapted for Eastern Use

To remedy this condition, and meet the demand for this class of machinery of the proper size, weight and price for use in Canada, the enterprising firm of Marsh Engineering Works, Limited, of Belleville, Ont., have recently designed and are now putting on the market a number of sizes of skidders adapted for use with this high-lead system. These skidders are offered in both gasoline and steam drives, and the large range of sizes makes it possible for any operator in any section east of the Rockies to select from the list just the right size for his particular kind of timber and the distance to be traversed.

Regarding the distance from the spar tree up to which it is possible to clear the ground by this high-lead system, on the Pacific Coast it is customary to clear up to one thousand feet from the tree in all directions, avoiding where possible the necessity of dragging the logs across the railroad track. But with the shorter types of trees found in Eastern Canada about six hundred feet from the spar tree would be the maximum distance that could be properly

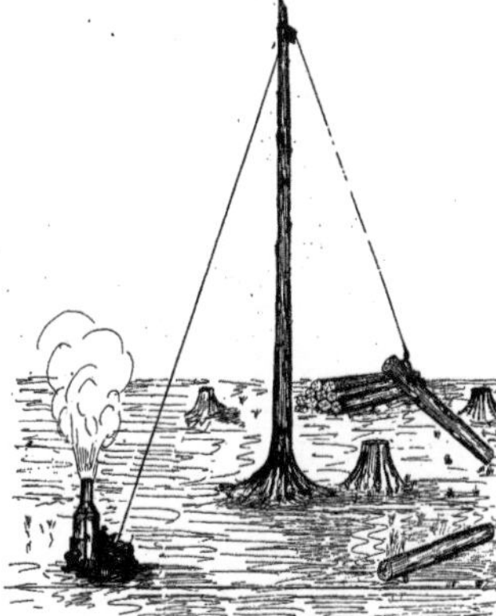

The high-lead method which may be brought into use in Ontario and Quebec Lumber Camps.

worked, as at a greater distance than this the forward end of the log would not be lifted off the ground high enough to clear obstructions. With the smaller and lighter type of machines now available for this work it is possible to move the outfit often at a minimum outlay of energy and money, which overcomes the difficulty.

As one operator says "Modern costs of labor and horse feed will help to introduce skidding machinery, which the East has been very slow to adopt." It is an old saying that "it is an ill wind that blows nobody any good," and this apparently ill wind of high labor costs is going to compel many lumbermen to adopt skidding and loading machinery to their own financial profit, for they will speedily find their operating expenses so much reduced by the use of this modern machinery that they will make more money than ever in spite of the increased costs of labor and all kinds of supplies.

Personal Paragraphs of Interest

C. M. Bartram, of Bartram & Ball, Montreal, is recovering from an attack of typhoid fever.

E. M. Bliss, President of the Bliss Lumber Co., Detroit, was in Toronto recently on business.

Leon Gagne, representing the Exchange Lumber Co., Montreal, was a recent caller on the Toronto trade.

John J. Miller, of the C. G. Anderson Lumber Co., Toronto, left recently on a business visit to the Maritime Provinces.

J. W. Mosher, of the L. N. Godfrey Co., Boston, has been on a buying trip to St. John, N. B., Montreal and Toronto.

W. C. Gall of the Gall Lumber Co., Toronto, who was laid up for several days with sciatica, is once more able to be at his desk.

Horace Hartley of Montreal, representing J. and D. A. Harquail Co., Limited, Campbellton, N. B., was in Toronto recently on a business visit.

J. A. McFadgen, President of the Manufacturers Lumber Co., Limited, Stratford, Ont., has returned from a successful deer-hunting expedition.

Chas. Pedwell, of McVicar, Ont., was in Toronto recently on business. He operated two mills during the past season, at McVicar and Lion's Head.

G. H. Askwith, assistant sales manager of the Riordon Pulp and Paper Company, Montreal, has been operated on for appendicitis. He is on the road to recovery.

G. C. Hurdman of the Hurdman Lumber Co., Ottawa, former representative of Ottawa West in the Ontario Legislature, spent a few days in Toronto recently.

J. L. Macfarlane, of the Canadian General Lumber Co., Toronto, who has not been feeling well for some time, is now improving steadily and able to attend to his duties.

M. McKinnon of Knight Bros. & McKinnon, Limited, manufacturers and dealers in lumber and builders' supplies, Cobalt, Ont., was in Toronto recently calling upon the trade.

J. W. Smith and W. R. Beatty of the Colonial Lumber Co., Limited, Pembroke, Ont., were in Toronto recently attending the annual meeting of the Canada Lumber Co. of Weston.

It has been arranged that C. A. Govan, of the Montreal office of the Imperial Timber Disposal Section, Board of Trade, London, shall sail for England by the "Carmania," leaving New York on December 17.

C. W. Wilkinson, General Manager of the Union Lumber Co., Toronto, is in Great Britain on a business trip and will look into the export situation. Before returning he intends to visit some of the battlefields of France and Flanders.

W. C. Laidlaw of the R. Laidlaw Lumber Co., has returned from Nairn Centre, Ont., where he spent a couple of weeks in deer-hunting. The party with which he was connected had rather indifferent luck, deer in that district being very scarce.

Keith Davidson, formerly a Lieutenant in the Royal Air Force, and partner in the plant of James Davidson's Sons, Ottawa, has after an absence of many months, resumed his activities in connection with the opertion and administration of the big woodworking plant.

W. G. Paynes and Maurice Welsh of Campbell, Welsh and Paynes, wholesale lumber merchants, Toronto, returned recently after a successful deer hunting trip to Bass Lake in the Bobcaygeon district. The party, of which they were members, secured their full complement of deer.

Word has been received that F. V. Wyckoff of A. Wyckoff & Sons Co., Elmira, N. Y., manufacturers of wooden water pipe, passed away recently in the Johns Hopkins hospital in Baltimore. Mr. Wyckoff was very well known to the lumber trade in Ontario in connection with purchases which his firm have made for years,

C. G. Anderson of the C. G. Anderson Lumber Co., Toronto, and Norman C. Hocken, of the Hocken Lumber Co., Toronto, who were members of a hunting party which went to West River, near Little Current, Ont., have returned, having remarkably good luck. There were nine in the company and the full complement of deer was secured.

Lieut. Thomas A. Williams, Second Brigade, C. F. A., who recently returned from the front where he spent three and a half years on active service, has been admitted into the firm of the Williams Lumber Co., wholesalers and exporters, Ottawa. Lieut. Williams graduated from McGill as an electrical engineer just before going overseas.

J. D. McCormack, of Vancouver, General Manager of the Canadian Western Lumber Co., spent a few days in Toronto recently, calling upon members of the industry. He reports an active demand for B. C. products with stocks very low. His own company has only about one-third of the lumber on stick, which it usually has at this season of the year and the market is very strong, particularly from across the border.

F. J. Niven, who for several years has been employed in the timber license department of the Ontario Government, has been appointed Secretary of the department of Lands, Forests & Mines, succeeding C. C. Hele, who has taken a responsible position with a financial concern in Toronto. Mr. Niven is thoroughly familiar with the work of the Department and should prove a valuable and faithful official in his new and responsible post.

John B. Reid, of Toronto, vice-president of the Ontario Retail Lumber Dealers' Association, and former chairman of the Lumbermen's Section of the Toronto Board of Trade, has retired from the active management of Reid & Company, his son, Capt. George T. Reid, now being in charge of the business. Mr. Reid, Sr., has not been feeling up to the mark of late, and has been ordered by his physicians to take a needed rest and conserve his strength as much as possible.

Major-General A. D. McRae, of Vancouver, spent a few days in Toronto recently on the way to visit his mother in Glencoe. It will be remembered that a few weeks ago General McRae addressed the Wholesale Lumber Dealers' Association on lumber conditions in the Pacific Coast Province. He has been carrying his right arm in a sling for the past few weeks, having been thrown from his horse while riding and sustaining a fracture at the wrist. The bone was knitting very well when he had the misfortune to fall in Winnipeg and break his arm a second time.

Hon. T. D. Pattullo, of Victoria, Minister of Lands for British Columbia, was in Toronto recently on his return from a business trip to Ottawa. He spent some time with Major James Brechin, B. C. Lumber Commissioner for eastern Canada. The latter will soon move into larger premises on the sixth floor of the Kent building, corner Yonge and Richmond streets, where he will have double the office space, part of which will be used for the display of British Columbia forest products. Major Brechin recently spent several days in western Ontario in propaganda work.

New Wholesale Lumber Firm Organized

Anderson, Shreiner & Mawson have embarked in the wholesale lumber business and opened offices in Rooms 5 and 6, Phoenix Bldg., 43 Victoria St., Toronto. They will deal in all kinds of Ontario woods, and the firm are S. R. Anderson, who is widely known as a lumber salesman from his long connection with the industry, W. C. Shreiner, President of the Eagle Lake Lumber Co., Limited, and Harry (Pink) Mawson, Secretary-Treasurer of the Eagle Lake Lumber Co. All the members of the new organization have had wide practical experience in the lumber business and for many years were engaged with the C. G. Anderson Lumber Co. They will sell the output of the Eagle Lake Lumber Co., consisting of birch, hemlock and spruce, and will also handle other woods. Mr. Anderson recently left on a trip to Great Britain and will not be back until the end of January. Mr. Mawson is in charge of the office and has taken up his residence in Toronto. He recently joined the ranks of the benedicts and is receiving the congratulations of many friends.

Anderson, Shreiner & Mawson expect to develop a large business and have already established favorable connections. The Eagle Lake Lumber Co. operate two mills at Eagle Lake and King Lake in the district of Parry Sound, and cut nearly a million feet during the past season which will be shipped out during the coming winter.

New Operating Company Organized

The Elk Valley Lumber Co. has been organized and the purpose is to operate the timber limits of the Seippel Timber Co., better known as the Cedar Valley Timber, and the saw-mill plant of the Elk Lumber Co. of Fernie, B. C. J. S. Hough of Winnipeg, is President of the new company and also President of the Elk Lumber Co. H. D. Campbell of Stillwater, Man., is General Manager. The company intend to carry on a large operation, and new camps have been constructed on the limits, about four miles from Fernie, and sufficient logs will be taken out for a mill cut of many feet. The logs will be brought down from the limits to the mill by means of a standard gauge railway about four and a half miles in length, which is being built at the present time. The new company will also operate the camps of the Elk Lumber Co. in West Fernie, B. C. The company has its headquarters in Winnipeg. The Seippel limits upon which the major part of the operations will take place, contain sufficient merchantable saw timber to insure at least a ten years' operation.

Hauling Heavy Ship Timbers by Motor Truck

Toronto Firm Specialize in Handling Rock Elm Trees for Export—How the Wood is Bought, Cut and Hauled to Cars—Its Characteristics

S. E. Hall, Toronto.

Hall Bros. Limited, of Toronto, have built up a large lumber business by means of specialization, and one of the particular things to which they devote attention is getting out Rock Elm for shipbuilding. Their operation in this line is, possibly, the only one of its character in the Dominion, and is, therefore, worth more than passing notice. It is a fact that Rock Elm is not an abundant wood in Ontario and its characteristics are little known.

In addition to conducting two sawmills near Marlbank in Hastings County and carrying on lumber camps, Hall Bros. keep up with their activity in Rock Elm the year round. Before the war they worked up a large trade in hewn Rock Elm timber. Rock Elm is purchased in whatever section the firm are able to locate it. The timber is somewhat widely scattered, but Hall Bros. have men constantly on the search for this particular wood and they generally know from the topography of the country where such timber abounds. There is no great quantity of Rock Elm in Ontario but in certain districts quite a sprinkling can be found. Rock Elm generally grows in clusters from twenty-five to one hundred trees on high ground either of a rocky or sandy character. The timber is particularly strong, tough and durable and is in every way well adapted for shipbuilding purposes whether used above or below water, for ships' decking, timbering, flooring, etc. There is no wood quite as well liked in the Old Country for this work as the Canadian Rock Elm. It is for the most part straight grain and will last an indefinite period. It will also bend and possesses other advantages that need not be enumerated.

Taking Out Shipbuilding Timber

In 1917 Hall Bros. took out about 2,500 sticks of Rock Elm, both square and round, or some seventy-five carloads, and last year their business was over double that. Most of this wood is placed on the cars and shipped to Quebec for the Old Country. Before the war Hall Bros. conducted their own negotiations direct with Old Country firms, but of late have been doing business through Canadian organizations who maintain offices and have permanent representatives in Britain. It is interesting to note that the timber now being shipped is largely in the round log.

Hall Bros. have gangs of men cutting down the trees during the Fall, Spring and Winter, and this year have shipped about seventy-five cars from certain districts within 60 miles of Toronto. The timber is inspected at the loading point for export. The standing trees are bought from farmers and others at $30.00 per 1000 ft. log measurement, and Hall Bros. dispose of the product on a cubic foot basis. The difference in price between square and round timber is about 25c per cubic foot. The trees cut range in length from twenty to fifty feet and the average is about thirty-five feet. Each log, when sawn into lumber, would make, probably, from three hundred to one thousand feet. The logs, or, more properly speaking, trees, are shipped on flat single and double cars about twenty-five to thirty trees being on each car. A gang of three men will cut and fell about thirty to thirty-five trees a day.

Motor Truck Does Good Work

The hauling is done to the nearest railway station by means of teams and also by a heavy five-ton motor truck, which the firm have been using with considerable success during the last few months. They contend that it does as much work as four teams and thus effects a material saving not only in cutting down time and distance but in outlay as well. The truck used is an Acason, manufactured by the Acason Motor Truck Co., Detroit, is a forty-five horse power machine, with four cylinders, four gears ahead, and has a capacity of five tons. Not only will the truck itself carry short timbers but it hauls wagon trucks or trailers attached by means of a pole and chain. The wagon trailers, the reach of which can be lengthened to fifty feet or more so as to take on the longest trees as possible, carry from two to five and six round sticks of timber. With this load the heavy truck travels along the highways at ten to twelve miles an hour without any difficulty, whereas an ordinary team of horses will not make more than four miles an hour on the average and cannot pull nearly as heavy a load. Hall Bros. maintain that the use of a heavy duty truck largely solves their rural transportation problem and has enabled them to conduct operations much more expeditiously and economically than they have been able to achieve heretofore. The outlay for oil and gasoline averages $5.00 a day

Heavy duty motor truck of Hall Bros., Toronto, conveying rock elm logs from the bush to the point of shipment.

and then there are wages of a driver and a helper. All the other men are kept in the woods drawing the fallen trees to one loading spot. The round sticks of timber are then deposited on the trucks, which are hauled to the edge of the bush by horses so that a motor truck can be readily attached to the wagons and the timber hustled out without any delay or obstruction. It is easy to make four trips a day from six to eight miles each way, and if the roads are good, as many as five trips can be accomplished.

Does as Much as Four Teams

Hall Bros. compute that the motor truck will do as much as four teams of horses,—not taking into consideration operation in the bush but merely the hauling of the timber. They believe that the saving can be reckoned on the following basis, not counting, or course, depreciation, but merely the cost of each day's operation.

Motor Truck, Oil and Gas	$ 5.00
Wages of a Driver and a Helper	7.00
	$12.00

Four teams of horses and drivers at $8.00 each—$32.00, thus a saving of $20.00 is actually effected in hauling timber by the motor method. Of course, there has to be made a certain allowance for wear and tear, but it will be seen that the difference is one worth while, considering in the log problem in the Summer and Fall months. It would be impossible to operate successfully and economically during the Winter season or when the rains have been exceptionally heavy. Under fair normal conditions, however, Hall Bros. are convinced that the truck is the proper thing in their business, and next season its use will enable them to further extend their operations in handling Rock Elm from the bush to the shipping point.

Rock Elm is used for garbage stringers and planking in shipbuilding, and, as stated, the trees are from twenty to fifty feet and varying in diameter at the point from fourteen to twenty-two inches.

Hall Bros. have just concluded drawing in the district referred to some fifteen carloads of sticks, which have been handled in remarkably quick time considering the weight and size of the timber.

S. E. Hall is president of Hall Bros. Limited, J. M. Hall first vice-president and T. G. Hall second vice-president and they all come of a family that has been in the lumbering industry for many years in Bruce and Grey counties.

Loading a trailer in rock elm bush preparatory to an eight mile haul.

Fraser Companies Building Two New Mills

The Fraser Companies, Limited, of Edmundston. N.B., are erecting a new saw and shingle mill at Campbellton, with a capacity of 150,000 ft. a day of lumber, and 125,000 shingles for the sawing season. The mill will be equipped with two double-cut band saws. They are also building a small double-cut band saw mill at Magaguadavic. The Fraser Companies will have, when these latest additions are completed, no less than twelve saw-mills located at Edmundston, Magaguadavic, Baker Brook, Plaster Rock, Fredericton, Nelson and Campbellton, N. B. and Cabano, Glendyne and Estcourt in Quebec. The company also operate a large bleached sulphite mill at Edmundston. The principal products of the Fraser Companies are rough and dressed spruce, white cedar shingles and railway ties. They make a specialty of piano sounding board stock. All the mills of the company are equipped with band-saws and the installation at the plants is of the very latest type.

More Squabbling on Wooden House Problem

An explanation of the attitude of the British Ministry of Health towards wooden houses was given last week in the House of Commons by Dr. Addison, the Minister of Health. Canada is interested to the extent that Great Britain is looking to this country to supply whatever houses are required. The action of the Ministry has been strongly criticized by what Dr. Addison termed "freak newspapers," but he refuses to be stampeded into urging local authorities to build dwellings which may prove unsuitable for English conditions. The Ministry do not condemn wooden houses—the point made against them is that houses of the Canadian type will have to be altered if they are to be made suitable and that the cost will be almost as large as brick dwellings.

There is a movement to convert army huts into dwellings to meet the emergency, but experiments show that these are cold. "We knew that all along," the Minister said. Even so, there was a considerable amount of extravagant building. The Government proposal to give a subsidy of 150 pounds sterling per house was limited to a certain number of houses to be built within a limited time. "The Government," he added, "would be no party to delivering the country again to the sporadic system of house building, which has given us slums in every town."

In the present condition of the woodworking industry of B. C. and in the East it may be questioned whether Canada is in a position to deliver a large number of houses very promptly. Advices from the Pacific Coast are to the effect that the firms making these houses are exceptionally busy.

Big Exhibition of Empire Grown Timber

The British Trade Commissioners in Canada have been notified by the Department of Overseas Trade of the British Government that the Department are organizing an exhibition of timbers grown within the British Empire to take place in London from the 5th July to 17th July, 1920.

The classification embraces—

(a) Specimens of Timber (polished and unpolished);
(b) Exhibits demonstrating the various uses to which timbers are put, viz., floors, panelling, staircases, furni ply wood, and articles of everyday use;
(c) Wood pulp.

A committee has been formed to arrange all details con [illegible] with the Exhibition, and includes representatives of—

Colonial Office.
Crown Agents for the Colonies.
Government of India.
Self-Governing Dominions.
Forestry Authority.
British Societies interested in the production [illegible] ization of timber.

The main object of the Exhibition is to bring [illegible] fore architects, inspectors, firms who have to specify imbers [illegible] contracts, as well as the users and consumers of timbers, [illegible] range of Imperial grown timbers and especially those timbe[illegible] up to the present are only very slightly, if at all, known in [illegible] try, and at the same time to demonstrate the chief uses [illegible] such timbers are suitable.

The building in which the Exhibition will be held has [illegible] area of 40,000 square feet, and it is felt that this Exhibition [illegible] afford a most favorable opportunity for displaying the various [illegible] of timber produced in the British Empire.

A catalogue will be issued giving full particulars of all exhibits displayed, and in order to arrive at uniformity in the compilation of this work it is suggested that at least the following information should be inserted:—

(a) A short concise statement regarding each kind of timber exhibited, showing the size in which it is usually obtainable, and the purpose for which it is specially suited; also giving the following particulars, viz
1. Weight in lbs. per cubic foot.
2. The result of tests carried out with regard to
Tension,
Compression, both with and across the grain,
Detrusion,
Modulus of Rupture,
Modulus of Elasticity,
Fire Resistence.
(b) A list of the shippers of the various kinds of timber in each of the Dominions.
(c- A list of importers and large timber merchants in the United Kingdom who would be prepared to supply the various timbers to users in this country.

It is hoped that the Catalogue will not only be useful to visitors to the Exhibition but will in future serve as a book of reference on all commercial timbers grown within the British Empire.

The British Trade Commissioners in Canada are as follows:—G. T. Milne, O.B.E., 367 Beaver Hall Square, Montreal; F. W. Field, 260 Confederation Life Building, Toronto; and L. B. Beale, 610 Electric Railway Chambers, Winnipeg.

The North Wants More Consideration

Once more the talk is heard of a probable secession of the Northern part of Ontario from the South. This movement it is said, is gaining ground, the discontent arising owing to alleged lack of proper recognition for the mining and lumbering districts. It is rumored that a monster convention is being planned and will be held during January, to give expression to the feelings which prevail in certain quarters. This agitation is no new thing and may not be very deep rooted or firmly entrenched if the new Provincial Government gives adequate consideration to the mining and lumbering activities of the North and to their importance, requirements and development.

Italy needs immense quantities of lumber. Before the war about 75 per cent. of Italian lumber imports were drawn from Austria; it is now conceded that Switzerland, Canada and the United States are the only sources of supply. North America can ship all the lumber that can be spared, according to the statements of an Italian Government official. A great area, estimated at over 1,000,000 acres, was completely destroyed along the Italian front during the war. This waste calls for a very large reforestration policy being adopted.

Wood Preservation Means Much to Industry

Reduces Cost of Upkeep Where Timber is Used in Exposed Service—Combatting the Principal Agencies Which Bring About Deterioration

By W. Kynoch, B. Sc. F., F. E. (Tor.), Acting Supt. Forest Products Laboratories of Canada, Montreal.

W. Kynoch, Montreal, Acting Supt. Forest Products Laboratories

I have no doubt that many of your readers are aware that the preservative treatment of timber is a fairly wide subject. It is not my intention this time to attempt a detailed discussion of any one of the many phases of the question. I shall endeavor merely to deal with it briefly and in a more or less general way going a little into detail, perhaps on some points.

The advancing cost of timber generally and the increasing difficulty in obtaining supplies of naturally durable woods have brought home to the consumer the fact that wood preservation is an effective means of prolonging the life of timber. and thus of materially reducing cost of upkeep where timber is used in exposed service. An important consideration also is that efficient preservative treatment enables woods of poor natural durability, but which otherwise may be excellently adapted for certain purposes, to be used for such purposes.

The very important influence which it is posible to exert in the direction of conserving forest resources by means of the preservative treatment of timber should certainly not be overlooked. It has been estimated that if all the railway ties, poles, mine timber and other products adapted for treatment in the United States actually received such treatment an anual saving of some 6,000,000,000 board feet, representing a monetary saving of some $72,000,000, could be effected.

Perhaps some idea of the extent of the wood preserving industry in the United States may be conveyed by the statement that every year somewhere about 140,000,000 cu. ft. of timber receive preservative treatment. This includes some 35,000,000 ties, almost twice the total yearly tie consumption of Canada in the years immediately preceding the war. This figure is a fairly conservative one. It has been considerably exceeded in some years.

Timber Treatment on Large Scale

In Great Britain timber preservation is practised on an extensive scale .The treatment of railway ties, telegraph poles, piling, wood paving blocks, etc., is standard practice. In France, Germany and some other European countries we have practically the same condition of affairs. In Canada there have been certain conditions which have delayed the adoption of timber treatment on a large scale, but the indications are that we may expect a rapid expansion of the wood preserving industry in the near future. I believe it is not more than some 13 or 14 years ago since treated railway ties were first used in this country. Since that time a small number have been used each year, this number, however never exceeding 10 per cent, of the annual consumption, and usually being considerably lower than that. A rapid increase in the number of ties treated yearly will without doubt take place in the next few years.

Wood preservation has been defined as "the art of protecting structural timber from deterioration by destructive agents." The principal agencies which bring about such deterioration are decay, wood boring insects and marine borers and, of these, decay is by far the most important.

If we are going to take intelligent measures to guard against the decay of timber, the first thing to consider or to find out is what causes the disease. If we know or can determine this and if we also inform ourselves as to the character of the tissues which are open to attack, we have taken the initial step in the direction of preventive measures.

It is certainly time that widespread misconceptions are current regarding the decay of wood. It is a very common occurrence to find people who have been dealing with timber all their lives and who are continually being confronted with the phenomenon of decay, entertaining totally erroneous ideas about it and citing many merely contributory factors or chance circumstances as causes.

The decay of timber is due to the action upon it of low forms of plants known as wood-destroying fungi and bacteria, and is practically wholly brought about by the former. This conclusion has been reached as a result of exhaustive scientific research and thousands of carefully conducted tests, carried out in the various civilized countries of the world. Incidentally, decay of wood can now be induced or prevented at will in the laboratory.

How Decay in Timber is Caused

In the case of an ordinary "green" plant, food materials are drawn chiefly from the soil. A wood-destroying fungal plant, however, derives its nutriment directly from wood substance. The fungus chemically decomposes certain constituents of the cell walls of the timber, converts them into assimilable substances and utilizes these for further growth and development. The active part of the plant consists of a number of minute thread-like filaments, which perforate the walls of the wood cells. break them down chemically, and ramify through and through the timber. Under certain circumstances these filaments grow out to the surface of the wood, where aggregations of them give rise to structures known as fruiting bodies, which, for every species of fungus are of characteristic shape, color, etc. When present these provide a ready means of ascertaining what species of fungus is growing within the wood. The function of the fruiting body is to produce spores, extremely minute and light structures which correspond to the seeds of higher plants. Spores are formed in enormous numbers, are released into the air when ripe, and are widely distributed by air currents.

Infection of sound timber is brought about in two ways, namely by contact either with spores or with living fungal filaments under favorable conditions. The popular idea that the "germs of decay" are inherent in timber per se is entirely erroneous.

Certain conditions are essential to the growth of these fungi. There must be food material (i.e. wood), a suitable percentage of moisture therein, a favorable temperature and a certain amount of air within the wood.

Prevention of Fungi Growth

Note, therefore, that there are four essentials for the action of fungi. It is obvious then that if fungal growth is to be prevented at least one of these four essentials must be so modified or controlled as to become unfavorable to fungal growth. Timber continually completely submerged in water is deprived of air, so lasts for thousands of years in some cases. Wood kept very dry does not contain enough moisture to permit fungi to grow, so may remain sound almost indefinitely. Under ordinary circumstances one cannot by any easy means prevent the ingress of air into timber. Nor can one control the temperature of the outdoor air. To prevent moisture from getting into wood in outdoor service is also extremely difficult, although some processes aiming at this have been devised. There is still one factor, the wood itself.

It will be readily perceived that the simplest way to prevent decay is to impregnate the timber with some material which is poisonous to wood-destroying fungi; in other words to poison the food supply of the plants. If this is efficiently done it becomes chemically impossible for the fungi to act upon the timber.

The very first requirement for a wood preservative, therefore, is that it be strongly toxic to wood-destroying fungi. All materials which do not possess this essential property may be immediately dismissed from serious consideration as preservatives. Toxicity is usually tested by determining the smallest quantity of preservative which will inhibit the growth of a known fungus. Toxicity, however, is not the only requirement; a good preservative should also be:—

(a) Permanent—Therefore must be a reasonably stable substance; must not be dissociated under the temperature and other conditions necessary for its application; must not be volatile or highly soluble in water.

(b) Readily and cheaply obtainable in large quantities.

(c) Non-corrosive of iron, steel, etc.

(d) Non-injurious to wood—must not act chemically upon

the wood substance so as to reduce its mechanical strength.

(e) Non-injurious to health of workmen.
(f) Easily applied.
(g) Able to penetrate wood easily.
(h) In case of use for ties must not short-circuit electric currents.

In some cases odor is important and also the question whether or not the preserved wood can be painted.

Probably hundreds of materials have been proposed for use as wood preservatives, but the great majority of these fail to fulfil or even approach the fulfilment of the requirements just stated. Those which have been most successful in this respect may be divided into three classes:

1. Water-soluble preservatives.
2. Crude oils.
3. Creosote oils.

Water-Soluble Preservatives

A large number of this class of materials has been tested at various times, but many are either of too low toxicity against fungi or react chemically with wood substance, reducing its mechanical strength. The best results obtained with this class of preservative have been secured with several metallic salts, namely mercuric chloride, copper sulphate and zinc chloride. Sodium flouride and some other flourine compounds have been more recently used, especially in Austria and Germany, with promising indications.

One of the most serious drawbacks to the use of all these materials for the impregnation of timber for outdoor service is the fact that they are more or less readily soluble in water and, therefore, while they are easily applied are liable also to be easily removed or leached from the wood. They are most valuable therefore in localities where the annual precipitation is low. It appears to be true of these water-soluble preservatives that when injected into timber, a certain amount of the injected material is permanently combined with, or at least permanently held, in the wood substance. Leaching tests show that prolonged soaking or washing fails to extract from the wood all that was put into it. It has never been shown, however that the material thus fixed in the wood is sufficient to protect it against fungal attack. The proportion thus retained evidently undergoes some physical or chemical change, and this change may impair or destroy its toxic properties, so that the fact that such a phenomenon occurs may or may not be of any significance. A great deal remains to be found out regarding questions of this kind. Of the salts mentioned a few moments ago, namely copper sulphate, mercuric chloride and zinc chloride, the latter has proved to be the best, all things considered.

Copper Sulphate, which was first used about 1840 in England and France, is cheap and initially of fairly high toxicity against wood-destroying fungi. It is readily leached from the wood. The chief drawback in its use is its action on iron and steel. As you know copper is immediately deposited when a piece of iron is brought into contact with a solution of copper sulphate. This makes it impossible to use it in the ordinary type of wood-preserving plant.

Mercuric Chloride, whilst very strongly toxic against wood-destroying fungi (in fact it is the most toxic preservative used) and much less easily soluble in water than either copper sulphate or zinc chloride, is very expensive and has a strong corrosive action on iron. It, therefore, cannot be used in the ordinary type of wood preserving plant. An interesting point in this connection is the use, in Germany, of treating cylinders, with the necessary piping, etc., built of reinforced concrete.

Sodium Flouride is more toxic than zinc chloride, is less easily leached from the wood, is less corrosive on iron than zinc chlorde, and very much less than mercuric chloride. It has been subjected to exhaustive tests by Malenkovic, in Austria, with very promising results. It is a comparatively new preservative, however, and at present cannot be readily and cheaply obtained in large quantities in Canada or the United States.

Zinc chloride is the most widely used water-soluble preservative It has been in continuous use since 1838, when it was first employed for the purpose in England. At the present time its use in Great Britain is extremely limited, but it is still extensively used in France, Germany, Holland and other European countries, largely for the treatment of railway sleepers. In the States about 20,000,000 pounds of this material are annually used, chiefly for tie treatment. It is cheap and strongly toxic against fungi. It has several drawbacks, perhaps the most serious being its very easy solubility in water, which, of course means leaching in exposed service. It is only slightly corrosive on iron at the concentrations used in treating timber, but it is usual in commercial practice to make a higher allowance for depreciation on a plant operating with zinc chloride than where creosote oil is used. Zinc chloride solution at high concentrations attacks wood substance, but at strengths used in their preservation (1½ to 3½ per cent.) does not appear to be injurious at ordinary temperatures.

A feature common to these water-soluble preservatives (except copper sulphate) and which is advantageous for some uses of treated timber, is that they do not import any color or odor to wood, and that they do not act on paint; so that the treated wood can be painted. A disadvantage (a serious one in the case of ties), is that the treated timber should be piled for drying subsequent to treatment, thus necessitating a second seasoning period. This is, of course, not the case with creosote oil.

Crude Oils

Little need be said about this class of materials. As a rule their toxicity to wood-destroying fungi is practically nil. The object aimed at in using them is to water-proof timber that has been thoroughly dried and by preventing re-absorption of water to keep the wood below the moisture content necessary for fungal growth. It is very difficult to secure any appreciable depth of penetration with these oils, so that in practice we get a mere surface coating which is readily pierced or broken in use, (say for ties), and moisture thus admitted. This, together with their non-toxic character, constitutes a serious objection to their use. They are very little used commercially. Perhaps it may be of some interest to mention the McMullen process, invented by the late Mr. McMullen of Picton, Ontario, which consisted in drying ties or other timber in a special kiln, subsequently dipping them into a petroleum residue and finally applying fine gravel to facilitate handling and prevent the ties from adhering to one another when piled.

Creosote Oil

The creosote oils are the most widely used and most generally efficient materials at present in commercial use for the preservation of timber. Creosote has been in continuous use since 1838 (about 80 years) when it was first employed in England for the purpose by John Bethell. It is strongly toxic to fungi (being about equal to zinc chloride in this respect), has a considerable water-proofing effect on timber, is fairly cheap, readily obtainable in large quantities, penetrates timber fairly easily, consists largely of practically insoluble substances and, in short, conforms more nearly to the requirements of a good preservative, as stated a few minutes ago, than any other material at present known. It is not without objectionable features, not by any means an ideal wood preservative, but all things considered, is the best in sight at present.

The subject of creosote oils alone is quite an extensive one and would be well worth going into in detail. We might just glance for a few minutes at this subject in a general way, mainly in order to note that creosote oils may vary widely in composition, and in value as preservatives of timber.

The term "creosote oil" or "creosote" as now understood, has been defined as "a distillate heavier than water, obtained by the distillation of a tar or a tar-like substance." The most important commercial tars from which creosote oils may be obtained are three in number—Coal-tars, oil-tars, and wood-tars.

Coal-Tars—Obtainable chiefly in:—

(a) Destructive distillation of bituminous coal at high temperatures (1500 to 3000°F) as carried out in the manufacture of illuminating gas and coke in gas house plants and by-product retorts.

The tars obtained vary considerably according to the coal, retorts, temperature, etc., but the main features are—presence of tar acids and hydrocarbons of the aromatic series.

These Features are Characteristic of Coal-tar Creosotes

(b) Combined distillation and combustion of bituminous coal at lower temperatures.

Tar acids are present but hydrocarbons are mainly of paraffin series. These tars are not important to us just now.

Oil-Tars—Obtained in:—

(a) Manufacture of water gas in which petroleum "gas-oil" together with coke or anthracite coal is employed. Main features are absence of tar acids, and presence (in small quantity) of hydrocarbons of paraffin series.

(b) Destructive distillation of crude petroleum in the manufacture of oil gas. Main features are absence of tar acids and presence (in much greater quantity than in (a) of hydro-carbons of the paraffin series.

These Features are Characteristic of Oil-tar Creosotes

Wood Tars—Obtained in:—

(a) Destructive distillation of coniferous or deciduous woods (chiefly coniferous). Main features are presence of tar acids and volatile constituents in large proportion (much larger than in coal tar creosotes) and small proportion of naphthalene and anthracene.

These Features are Characteristic of Wood-Tar Creosotes

(Wood-tar creosotes are more corrosive on iron than coal-tar creosotes because of high proportion of tar acids—these could be removed, however.)

The most valuable of these materials for wood preserving is coal-tar creosote and its value appears to be largely due to the high proportion of aromatic hydrocarbons or their derivatives present—it consists almost wholly of these.

Adding Tar to Creosote Oil

In practice creosote is often mixed with refined tar of various kinds or coal,tar creosote may be mixed with water-gas tar creosote, and so on. The question of adding refined or unrefined tar to creosote oil has given rise to a great deal of discussion and there is much to be said on both sides. The addition of tar tends to lower the cost of the preservative and may be of some advantage in increasing the water-proofing effect of the treatment. Adding tar, which contains much free carbon, tends to decrease the power of the preservative to penetrate timber. but refined or filtered tar may be open to this objection to the same extent. However, any addition of tar, whether refined or not, increases the viscosity of the preservative and decreases its power to penetrate—although this difficulty may perhaps be partly overcome by raising the temperature of the preservative during treatment. Again, the addition to creosote of anything servative. Any increase which can be made in the water-proofing series, such as oil-tar, will probably reduce the toxicity of the preservatice. Any increase which can be made in the water-proofing power of the preservative is of particular value in the case of wood paving blocks.

More Research Work in Creosotes

There is considerable difference of opinion as to the character of creosote oil best suited for the treatment of timber for various purposes. The lighter constituents are apparently the more toxic, but are also the more soluble in water, whilst the heavier ones, whilst less toxic to fungi, are practically insoluble. Obviously creosotes can be manufactured to conform to various specifications, and there is still a need for more research into this subject. Many of the proprietory preservatives on the market are special creosotes, and some of these possess certain advantages on account of uniformity of product and for other reasons. It is highly questionable, however, whether there is any justification for the high prices charged for these materials in some instances.

Standard specifications for creosote oil for the treatment of ties and paving blocks, etc., have ben developed and adopted by the American Wood Preservers Association, The American Railway Engineering Association, The United States Forest Service, and others.

I think it will be clear from what has been said that this subject of creosote oils is a fairly extensive and important one.

A word now as to the method by which preservatives are applied to wood. These may be divided into two classes:

(1) Non-pressure processes.
(2) Pressure processes.

Non-pressure processes include the application of the preservative with a brush, dipping the timber, and more or less prolonged soaking in the preservative. These methods, especially the soaking, are of considerable value for the treatment of timber for certain purposes. Pressure processes are those which involve the use of higher than atmospheric pressures in order to force the preservative into the wood. Where timber is subject to mechanical wear and abrasion, as in the case of railway ties, paving blocks, piling, etc., it is absolutely essential that a deep penetration of the preservative into the timber be secured. A surface coating, or a very shallow penetration (say a sixteenth or an eighth of an inch), which can easily be pierced or broken, is of practically no value.

Forcing the Preservative Into the Wood

The obtaining of this essential feature, deep penetration, involves the employment of pressure to force the preservative into the wood. Some of those present are, I believe, familiar with the modern wood preserving plant, but for those who are not I may sap that such a plant consists essentially of one or more steel cylinders with a capacity of say 500 to 800 ties each, together with the necessary pumping and vacuum machinery, boilers, gauges, thermometers. working and storage tanks, etc. A large and well-drained seasoning or storage yard for the accommodation of ties and timber is also an important adjunct to the modern treating plant.

There are a dozen or more pressure processes in use which differ in various particulars. I do not propose to describe these in detail. Pressure processes, in which creosote oil is used, are sometimes differentiated into "full cell" processes, in which the object is practically to force as much preservative into the timber as possible, and "empty cell" processes, in which the object is to saturate the cell walls of the wood without leaving any free oil in the cavities of the cells. Empty-cell processes aim at decreasing the cost of treatment by using less preservative, while at the same time securing deep penetration.

The maximum temperatures and pressures employed commercially are 200°F and 200 lbs. per square inch respectively, and in all processes means are provided for controlling the temperature of the preservative and the pressure applied to it at all stages of the operation. In some processes the timber is subjected to a preliminary vacuum, which is broken by the admission of the preservative, after which pressure is applied, the object being to do away with any resistance to the entrance of the preservative which might be offered by the air in the wood cells and thus to secure a deep penetration. In at least one process the timber is subjected to a preliminary air pressure, preservative is then forced in under a slightly higher pressure, the pressure is then considerably raised and finally, when pressure is released, the compressed air in the wood cells expands and forces out the surplus preservative. In some cases a final vacuum is drawn for the same purpose.

Extracting the Moisture from the Wood

The drier the timber the more easily will the preservative penetrate it, so that wood should be thoroughly air-dry when it is treated. Where it is necessary to treat green, or unseasoned timber, however, direct steaming with saturated steam, followed by vacuum, is resorted to chiefly for the purpose of extracting as much moisture from the wood as possible before treatment. Some important considerations are involved in connection with steaming, into which it is unnecessary to enter here. The use of steam, however, is fraught with considerable danger of serious damage to the timber unless care be taken to employ relatively low temperatures and short steaming periods only. A knowledge of the effect, upon the particular species of timber concerned of steaming for various periods and at various temperatures should be possessed before timber is subjected to steaming. Otherwise serious damage may result.

It will be seen then when variations within a considerable range can be made in temperature, pressure, rate of increase or decrease of these, duration of pressure or temperature periods, vacuum (and the stage or stages of the process at which it can be applied), etc., a very large number of combinations is possible and the details of treatment may vary considerably.

In every case, however, and whatever preservative is used, the object in view is to establish a protective zone of treated timber extending inwards from the surface of the wood to the minimum depth of from ½ to ¾ in.

The basic essential requirement then is a fairly deep and uniform penetration. I want to draw special attention to this because in present commercial practice specifications are always based on the injection of so many pounds of preservative per cubic foot of wood. It is well recognized by wood preservers and others familiar with the treatment of timber that this is an extremely unsatisfactory basis. It is true of almost all our timbers that sapwood is more readily penetrable than heartwood of the same species. It is quite obvious then that a pole tie, for example, might conform strictly with a specification calling for the injection of 8 lbs. of creosote oil per cubic foot, and still be very inefficiently treated, because the oil might be practically all in the sapwood, the heartwood exposed on the face of the tie receiving merely a surface coating. Again, penetration may be ¼ in. deep in some places, and 1 in. in others. Excellent results are, of course. very frequently obtained in commercial practice, but the fact remains that compliance with the ordinary specification, as is well recognized, does not constitute any guarantee that a tie is properly protected. It may or may not be.

Creosotic Treatment of Railway Ties

What is needed, therefore, is some means by which a uniform penetration of known depth can be ensured in every tie treated. Now I want to guard particularly against exaggeration, but I will venture so far as to say that I believe we have, at our laboratories, approached this desideratum more nearly than has yet been done elsewhere, and that in a very simple, if somewhat revolutionary manner. We completed some year or so ago, in our experimental plant, an investigation of the creosote treatment of Jack-pine and Eastern Hemlock for railway ties. We found hemlock an extremely refractory wood to deal with. In fact, we were unable to secure a satisfactory penetration by any ordinary process, even when the timber was air-dry. By the method developed we were able to secure a satisfactory penetration in air-dry hemlock heartwood with a pressure period of two hours, while air-dry jack-pine heartwood (which we found could be efficiently treated by several processes in commercial use in about two hours) we found could be more efficiently treated in less than one hour when this method was used. The method consisted in producing in the surfaces of the timber, lengthwise with the grain, incisions of a special character. These incisions are very narrow in proportion to their length, and are so made that the disturbance to the fibres of the timber is very slight, the incisions closing up after treatment so as to be barely noticeable. The timber thus incised was then pressure treated in the ordinary way with creosote. Any other preservative could, of course, be used.

How Theory of Thing Works Out

The theory of the thing is as follows: First there are provided in the outer layers of the timber a number of centres, from each of which the preservative, under the action of the pressure, is simultaneously distributed. These centres (i. e. incisions) are of any reasonable depth desired—say from ¼ to ¾ in. When the preservative distributed from one centre meets that distributed from adjacent centres the treatment is complete. Wood, however, is much more easily penetrable lengthwise with, than across the grain.

It is necessary to compensate for this feature and this was accomplished by using an incision of the character indicated and thus presenting to the action of the preservative a much larger surface for penetration across than with the grain. The type of incision used has some other special features, which need not be described here.

I should like to go into this matter at length, because there are special features connected with it which do not at first appear However, I think it can be seen that the depth of the penetration is dependent on the depth of the incisions so that a means of ensuring penetration to the desired depth is provided. Uniformity of penetration is further secured by proper spacing and arrangement of the incisions (which we found to be very important). The time necessary for the preservative distributed from adjacent incisions to meet is affected also by the spacing and arrangement and, of course, by the species and character of the wood also.

Too Little Attention to Timber Study

Although a great deal of attention has been given, and rightly and necessarily given, to the mechanical equipment by means of which preservatives are injected into wood and also to the chemistry of wood preservatives, when we come to the wood itself it is often an entirely different story. There are, of course, notable exceptions, but it is a very frequent occurrence for statements to be made both verbally and in the literature of wood preservation, which appear to indicate that little or no intelligent attenion has been given to the study of timber. (Incidentally it is a common error to suppose that timber is gradually being displaced by other materials, and is continually becoming less important economically. On the contrary, the new uses which are constantly being found for wood more than counterbalance the substitution of other materials. The per capita consumption of timber is increasing, not decreasing, and it is fair to state that outside of food products no material is so universally used and so indispensable in human economy as wood. Furthermore it is a material which beyond question can be and is being made very much more valuable to the community at large as a result of the timber research which is always going on). However, to return to my subject—

A well-known engineer in a recent treatise on wood preservation, made a number of statements of the kind I have in mind. In speaking of a certain method of felling oaks he says that it is claimed to improve the timber and to render the sapwood as strong as the heartwood. It has been proved by thousands of careful tests on a number of species that there is no difference in strength between sapwood and heartwood of equal moisture content. The idea that sapwood is weaker than heartwood of the same tree or species is entirely wrong. The same writer, in dealing with the decay of timber, states that under certain circumstances gases are evolved which "enter into combinations and produce fungi." Fungi could, of course, no more be produced thus than could an apple tree, or any other plant.

The Albuminous Matter in Wood

In a booklet issued not long ago, which deals with a certain patented process, there appears a report by a gentleman—whose name I will refrain from quoting, but who is, or was, connected with a well-known institution of learning. This gentleman is careful to explain that timber treatment is a subject to which he has given attention for many years. He concludes his report with the statement that a certain metallic salt protects timber from decay by coagulating the albuminous matter in "the cells of wood and the interstices of the fibres" thus forming a material which is strongly resistant to the action of enzymes and which coats the cell and the fibre surfaces. I wish to draw particular attention to the alleged effect of "coagulating the albuminous matter" in wood, because this expression has been used from time to time in writings on timber preservation for the last 80 years or so, and it is still turning up, like the proverbial bad penny. It is important then to try to ascertain how much "albuminous matter" there is in wood and where it is to be found.

Albumins are essentially nitrogenous substances. The cellulose complex and the lignin complex, which constitute the bulk of the wood are certainly not albuminous matter, neither are the starches and sugars which are present in relatively small quantity. The dilute solutions of various salts which ascend from the roots to the leaves by way of the sapwood are not albuminous. In short, such materials appear to be of possible occurrence only in those cells of the wood which in life, that is in their functional condition, are characterized by the presence of protoplasm. Elements of this kind exhibit certain distinctive anatomical features and form only a small percentage of the wood. Further, as soon as they cease to function, becoming part of the heartwood, their contents undergo certain chemical changes and, in some cases, actually give rise to antiseptic materials, so that living protoplasm is confined to the sapwood. This being the case the quantity of "albuminous matter" in the average piece of timber is so small as to be entirely negligible, and in any case, does not form an actual part of the wood substance any more than the contents of a box form part of the box. For practical purposes it is not of the slightest significance whether the albuminous matter is coagulated or not since even if it were entirely removed the decay of timber could proceed just the same.

Instances of this kind could be multiplied almost indefinitely, but I think enough has been said to indicate that it is well to pay some attention to the timber itself when dealing with preservative measures.

Company is Held Liable on Notes

A judgment of special commercial interest is contained in a judgment of the Superior Court, rendered recently in Montreal by Mr. Justice Demers, in which the Compagnie Generale l'Entreprises Publiques, Limitee, is condemned on two actions to pay to Paul Galibert a sum of $20,000, found to be due on notes.

The factum on which the case was presented for adjudication was a voluminous one, and the plea of the defence raised an important point of law respecting the obligations of a principal towards a third party.

The Etienne Dussault Company, Limited, contractors, of Quebec, had a contract with one Gagnon, of Arthabasca, for the supply of lumber for certain works being carried out by Dussault. The contract, which was for $30,000, was signed "Horace Dussault, president." From time to time the Dussault Company made advances to Gagnon in relation to his contract, giving him notes, which were likewise signed, "Horace Dussault, president." These notes were discounted by Gagnon with Paul Galibert.

It was stated that the Dussault Company knew of the manner in which the contract and the notes were signed by the president, and all notes were duly honored up to the ones at issue in the present action in regard to which contestation was entered on the main plea of change of company and that, according to the by-laws of the company, the president was not authorized to sign alone, but that contracts and notes must be countersigned by Mrs. Dussault.

In 1912, the Dussault Company, by letters-patent, changed their name to the Compagnie Generale d'Entreprises Publique, and after the change Paul Galibert, who did not then know of the change, discounted other notes, which are signed in the same way as the others. It was these, amounting to $20,000, which the company refused to pay. Hence the present action.

"The question for the court to decide," said Mr. Justice Demers in his judgment recently, "is whether the Compagnie Generale d'Enterprises Publique, the defendants, should be condemned in the two actions for the amount sued for?

"The court finds (1) that although Horace Dussault had no express mandate to sign these notes he had a tacit mandate; (2) that the change in the name Etienne Dussault Company to the name of the company defendant does not change the liability, as the company is composed of the same persons; (3) that even if the new company (the company defendant) were successors to the Dussault Company, they would still be liable in the light of the law of Article 1728 of the Civil Code, which provides that the principal or his legal representative are responsible towards third parties for all acts made by their mandatory in the execution and within the limits of the mandate after dissolution if the third party did not know of the dissolution. In this instance the plaintiff did not know of the change the company made, and it follows that the article quoted applies. (4) Even if the company defendant advanced too much money to Gagnon, it was through their own imprudence, and it cannot prejudice the holder of the notes in due course.

For these reasons judgment was given for plaintiff for the sum of $20,000 as claimed in his two actions against the company defendant, with costs. (944 and 3717, S.C.M.)

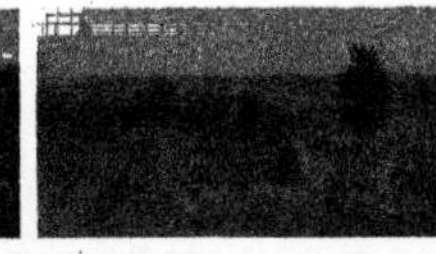

The first view on the left shows an area repeatedly burned near Madawaska, Ont. This area was once heavily timbered with pine. The next view is that of rocky land near Turriff, Ont., repeatedly burned. It is of no use for agriculture and very little hope for a new forest crop. The thick growth seen in the picture on the right illustrates a dense stand of young white and red pine of 30 years' growth, located near Mattawa, Ont., which has enjoyed protection from forest fires.

Ontario Timber Survey Making Headway

Roland D. Craig, Forest Engineer, of the Commission of Conservation, Ottawa, who is in charge of the timber survey now being made in the province of Ontario, writes to the "Canada Lumberman" that he and his staff are making satisfactory progress on the survey of the timber resources. They have now practically completed the reconnaissance work for the Ottawa river drainage area. Mr. Craig adds:—Though as yet we have not been able to personally see all the timber owners in this district, those whom we have seen, including most of the large operators, have furnished us with estimates of the timber on their holdings. We have found them anxious to have the survey completed and to make it as reliable as possible in order that reasonably accurate information as to the actual timber situation may be available.

Owing to the fact that many of the licenses were granted for only certain kinds of timber the owners frequently have very little information as to the other kinds not included in their cutting rights. This makes it necessary for us to do more field work than would have been required if they had complete cruises of their holdings. The rapidly increasing value of the hardwoods makes it imperative that we should not overlook them in our estimates. Now that the white pine is being cut off, the spruce, hemlock and even jack pine are becoming important species in regions where formerly they were considered of negligible value.

We find that very extensive areas have been destroyed by fire and that on the whole the reproduction of coniferous species is far from satisfactory from the standpoint of sustained yields. In many areas, however, where fire has been kept out, excellent stands of white and red pine are coming up.

In view of the progressive forest policy in the platform of the United Farmers of Ontario we do not anticipate any change in our co-operative arrangement with the Ontario Government as a result of the change in administration.

New Plant for Making Furnace Fire Brick

Gates Refractories, Ltd., Montreal, are now operating their own plant for the production of furnace fire brick. The plant is at Montreal East, and consists of buildings containing 12,000 feet of floor space. Two large crushers, one dry and one wet, have been installed with the necessary conveyors for carrying the crushed and ground clay from the dry to the wet machine. The storage of the materials and the molding operations are carried out in this department, and to the rear of this building is a drying room, 60 by 60 ft. The floor of this section is of tile, under which the steam piping is located for the drying of the bricks after they come from the molds. The baking and burning kilns are located near the drying room. At present two are in operation, one of 50 tons and one of 60 tons capacity. Two others of 60 tons capacity each will be completed and in operation before the close of the year. The present output of the factory is about 300 tons per month, but this will probably be doubled within the next few months. Efficiency tests have been made at the McGill University on these bricks, and the fusing point has been determined, officially, at approximately 1750 degrees C., or 3200 degrees F. A railway siding is provided at one side of the plant, and there are also facilities for shipping by lake or ocean vessels.

Gates Refractories Ltd. were recently reorganized, with larger capital, in order to extend the business and acquire the factory referred to, so that the company could be in a better position to produce bricks for their own requirements, and in fact, to manufacture all special shaped high grade fire brick for every industrial purpose. The company also specialize on power plant brick-work, such as furnace building and boiler setting, and carry out contracts in all parts of Canada.

Too Much Sawmill Waste Burned Up

Hundreds of tons of sawmill waste which could be used for newsprint and other coarse paper are being burned every day, and there are millions of feet of stumps and small timber in southern cut-over lands which could be used for the same purpose, J. F. Kidd of Lake, Miss., told the annual convention of the Southern Logging association at New Orleans.

"I understand," said Mr. Kidd, "that many small town weekly and semi-weekly newspapers have been forced to suspend publication because of the high cost of newsprint, and even some of the city dailies are having a rocky road to travel, but it seems that there is inefficiency and neglect of opportunity somewhere when raw material is being wasted in quantities with a market crying for the products which could be manufactured from this waste."

He advocated establishment through the southern timber belt of either pulp or paper mills to convert into paper what "now goes up in smoke."

Passing of Mr. Hiram McLean

Hiram McLean died recently in Truro, N.S., from the effects of typhoid fever. He came to Truro in 1900 from Scotsburn, Pictou County, and worked as a master builder on different contracts in Truro. In a few years he branched out into the lumber business and latterly had been associated with his brother-in-law, Mr. Harry McKay, as large lumber manufacturers and dealers, and shipbuilders in Economy and other districts in western Colchester.

This firm had built the large vessels the "Truro Queen" and "Acadian Queen" at Central Economy, and at the present time have another vessel in the stocks, besides extensive lumber operations at Economy and Five Islands; and now from this busy hive the senior partner has been taken away by the hand of death. Mr. McLean, who is survived by his wife, one son and one daughter, was an honorable man and a good citizen.

Sprinkler System Saved Big Factory

Had it not been for the effective sprinkler system, the James Davidson's Sons lumber factory, Wellington and Rochester streets, Ottawa, would have been destroyed by fire recently.

Fire of unknown origin broke out in the ceiling of the factory, but the sprinklers succeeded in confining the flame to narrow limits, it only penetrating the roof. When the firemen arrived, they were confronted with the task of extinguishing a cupola in the roof.

Fire Chief Graham of Ottawa spoke very enthusiastically of the sprinkler system, and stated that if it had not been installed the entire plant would have been destroyed owing to the highly inflammable nature of the material stored in the factory.

Ontario Lumberman Leaves Large Estate

In the will of the late Senator Peter McLaren, lumberman, of Perth, Ont., which has been filed for probate, an estate valued at $1,092,182.78 is disposed of. Much of the estate is made up of lumbering interests in the Canadian West and timber areas and iron lands in the West, while a large portion, approximately $100,000, is investments in banks and other stocks.

By the will, to which there are three codicils, the estate is divided among the Senator's widow, two sons, James and William, and three daughters, Kathleen, Margaret Hall and Mary Benedict. To his wife is left his residence, together with twenty-five acres of land, and the income from $100,000, which on her demise is to pass to her daughters. To his son, William, is left a farm of 600 acres, and to each of the three daughters the sum of $50,000, together with 15 per cent. of the residuary real estate when sold. The residue of the estate is equally shared by the two sons.

Busy Eastern Lumber Company

The Pontiac Lumber & Pulp Co., whose headquarters are at St. Tite, Que., make a specialty of dressed lumber. Their sawmill is located at Macamic (Abitibi), Que., and has a sawing capacity of 70,000 ft. a day, while the output of their planing mill is one carload a day. The company cut during a season about 6,000,000 ft.,

Sawmill of Pontiac Lumber and Pulp Co., located at Macamic, Que.

but intend, in the near future, to increase the output to 10,000,000 ft. Their limits are located in the township of Aiguebelle, situated some twenty-eight miles from the mill, and for several years the company have not been obliged to cut much timber on their own lands as they buy a great deal from the farmers in the surrounding country.

The Varnish Tree Grows in China

Varnish is produced in China from a tree commonly spoken of as the varnish tree, but known botanically as rhus vernicifera, which is found in abundance in the mountains of Hupeh, Kweichew and Szechwan.

The varnish is taken from the tree after it is about six inches in diameter by tapping at intervals of from five to seven years, until the tree is 50 or 60 years years of age. A good sized tree will yield from five to seven pounds of varnish.

The natural color of the crude varnish as applied is black. It is considered the most indestructible varnish known. One peculiarity is that it hardens only in a moist atmosphere.

Demand for Box Boards in Bristol Market

Canadian Trade Commissioner Norman D. Johnston, of Bristol, Eng., says mention was recently made of the fact that a firm which has obtained their box boards from Sweden would be prepared and would like to buy from Canada, providing Canadian manufacturers can compete in price. This firm is a large branch of a very important concern, and if a Canadian manufacturer can supply their requirements satisfactorily other business would no doubt result. They generally purchase certain box parts which enable them to make up cases of varying sizes. These parts are cut to accurate dimensions, being smooth sawn and are usually formed of two pieces, tongued, grooved, glued, and smooth on one side so as to take a good impression when put through the two-color printing machine. The following specifications were given as indicating a very considerable part of the normal requirements of this firm:—

23¼ x 13½ x 5/16 inch.
23¼ x 12 x "
21⅞ x 13½ x "
21⅞ x 12 x "
19⅝ x 8 x "
17 x 8¼ x "

They also purchase boards cut to certain lengths, but varying as regards widths. The widths would be from 4-inch upwards in steps of ½-inch and the size—

21⅞ x 5/16 inch
17 x "
13 x 5/8 inch
15 x 5/8 inch

All the quotations received so far from Canada have been much too high, and in order to give some idea of the prices which would have to be equalled, if not bettered, the following are the Swedish quotations on certain sizes:—

23¼"x13½"x5/16"—25s. 10d. per 100 pcs., f.o.b., Gothenburg, Sweden.
21⅞"x13½"x5/16"—24s. 0d. " " " " " "
17" x 8¼"x5/16"—21s. 3d. " " " " " "

The freight from Gothenburg to this country is about £6 per standard.

Timber in varying widths averaging 5-inch, not tongued and grooved, lengths from 16-inch to 23¼ by 5/16-inch in thickness, average £30 per standard f.o.b. Gothenburg, while the prices delivered to the works in Bristol average £38 10s. 0d.

The kind of wood usually supplied from Sweden has been white and red fir, but the former is preferred. The timber is usually cut some months previous to shipment and air-dried. It is doubtful whether steam or kiln-dried wood could stand the damp climate of this country. The boards are generally imported in bundles of 25 pieces bound by wire.

If any Canadian firm can compete with these Swedish prices they are asked to communicate with this office.

Scotland Desires Ready-Made Houses

Acting Trade Commissioner J. Forsyth Smith, of Glasgow, Scotland, sends some interesting information to the Department of Trade and Commerce, Ottawa, on the types of ready-made wooden houses which are wanted in Scotland. Mr. Smith says: Considerable interest is being manifested in Scotland in the possibility of securing from Canada ready-made wooden houses to meet the great demand created by the present abnormal shortage in house accommodation, especially for the artisan classes.

The following types are suggested as those for which there would be a considerable demand:—

Two-room house, i.e., one bedroom, one living-room, with scullery, bath-room, cellar and larder.

Three-room house, i.e., two bedrooms, one living-room, with adjuncts as above.

Four-room house, i.e., three bedrooms, one living-room (or two bedrooms, one living-room and one kitchen), with adjuncts as above.

It is considered that delivered prices from £200 to £300 would prove very attractive.

Manufacturers in a position to offer ready-made houses of these or other types are asked to communicate with Mr. Smith.

Paper Mill Ordered to Pay Damages

The strong smell emanating from paper mills has been a long-standing cause of complaint on the part of residents living close to such plants, but never before had a paper manufacturer been called upon to pay damages on this claim.

Such was the occurrence in the civil courts at Three Rivers, Que., where Mr. Willie Cyr of Cap de la Madeleine, Que., claimed $250 damages from the Wayagamack Pulp & Paper Co., of Three Rivers, Que., which, he said, caused him prejudice in his property, through the bad smell emanating from the plant.

Judge Drouin, after hearing testimony in the case, decided that the plaintiff was entitled to the full amount claimed. The case has an important bearing, owing to the large number of such mills throughout Quebec Province, and the possibility of other identical claims being filed as a consequence of this decision.

Industrial Increase in Saguenay District

Extensive improvements in connection with the pulp and paper industries are being carried out in the Saguenay district, P. Q. Fraser, Brace & Co. are engaged in constructing a dam and other works for the development of a power on the Shipshaw River, which will supply current for a new power mill at Saguenay for Price Bros. The Chicoutimi Pulp Company are adding to their power development of Chicoutimi, not only for power purposes for the ground wood mill, but for extra lighting for the town. J. G. White & Co., New York, are building extensive wharves at Ha! Ha! Bay, which will probably be electrified. At Kenogami, Price Bros. have erected a theatre and club house for the men at a cost of $50,000.

The Passing of Veteran Engineer

Barnabas F. Ward passed away recently at the age of 81 years. In 1883 he entered the employ of the Waterous Engine Works Co., of Brantford, as travelling engineer and held that position continuously up to the time of his death. Mr. Ward was highly respected by all the customers of the firm and the news of his death will be learned with sincere regret throughout a wide territory. The deceased came originally from Barrie, Ont., and during the early years of his connection with the Waterous Company covered the territory north of Toronto and more latterly looked after the Province of Quebec. Owing to ill health Mr. Ward retired a few years ago to his farm at Highland Grove, Ont.

New Sawmills in Sudbury District

Experiments Being Made in Cutting Up Fire Killed Jack Pine—Increased Logging Output

"Lumberjack" writing to the "Canada Lumberman" from Sudbury, Ont. says: The prospect for a fairly successful season of lumbering is better than a year ago. The supply of men is improving but not up to expectations. They are like migratory birds, constantly on the move and operators are anxiously waiting for them to settle down. Notwithstanding the high rate of wages which are from $55 to $70 per month and board, they keep shifting. From present appearances the output of saw logs will be 25 per cent. over last season; railway ties about 15 per cent. greater and pulpwood 10 per cent. On the Canadian National Railway north of Sudbury there is a hive of industry. 75 camps are in operation cutting logs, pulpwood and railway ties, employing some 3,000 men. Two camps are making board timber which is unusual for some years past.

Numerous portable saw mills have been engaged in sawing railway ties from timber too large to make axe ties.

From Mile C. N. R. to Mile 125 there are some 10 tie mills and at Gogama, Laforest and Co. are erecting a mill with a capacity of 40,000 ft. per day.

At Mile 93 Haight & Dickson have erected a fine mill to manufacture timber from their limits.

At mile 96, McCreary and Son have built a good mill and will experiment with fire killed Jack pine. They have 40,000 such logs on skids at this date. If this venture proves profitable it will be a source of revenue to the province and other firms will no doubt follow in cutting Jack pine killed by fire which has been in the past a total loss.

At Mile 125 Tionaga Siding, R. B. Herron & Co. have erected a large mill and are now engaged in sawing. They have three camps cutting logs for next season's cut. Most of the men employed at this point are returned soldiers.

Representative Canadian Lumber Firm

Under this heading "Timber" of London, Eng., in a recent edition, says: Terry & Gordon, of Toronto, are two outstanding representatives of the Transatlantic timber trade. To those in Great Britain who have regard to the wholesale expansion of the woodgoods industry in the Dominion, an introduction of Messrs. Terry & Gordon is superfluous. They are widely known and everywhere appreciated. But for the few who may not enjoy the personal or abstract acquaintance of the popular "T. and G.," it may be said that Mr. Terry and Mr. Gordon have been in trade for a considerable period in the East of Canada, doing a large business in East and States Canadian woods. They have extensive offices in Vancouver, and do a huge volume of traffic in British Columbia pine, cedar, etc., in which latter centre of the Canadian lumber world they possess a large, if not the largest, representation.

Terry & Gordon specialize in Eastern woods, including pine and red pine, spruce and hemlock. They are equally interested in Western woods. As an example of push and progress, it may be said that these gentlemen have more than doubled their business within the last few years, and they now desire to effect a worldwide export traffic. To that end they have given their agency in Great Britain to Spencer, Lock & Co., 27, Clementslane, E.C., who themselves have established a "front rank" reputation in successful trading, and whose connection with Terry & Gordon will make for the good of all concerned.

Associated with Terry & Gordon is Mr. Frank Gordon, who spent some years in charge of the firm's branch at Vancouver, and who is now located at Toronto, where the central depot is situated, and who, it may be mentioned, has been succeeded in the Vancouver branch by Mr. Allan Nicholson. Not less important of the Terry & Gordon branches are the agencies at New York and Montreal, where a growing and influential circle of commerce has been welded. As may be seen from the photographs referred to, Messrs. Terry & Gordon are by no means in the "sere and yellow leaf." They are, however, fully representative of the "Maple Leaf," and as examples of "get on" in contradistinction to "get off," one would have to travel far to find a more fitting combination of ability coupled wih experience.

That Terry & Gordon are not "letting the grass grow under their feet" is evidenced by the arrival at Liverpool of three ships, which have been discharging at the Mersey. They are the "Lake Glebe," "Lake Frohna," and "Lake Furlough," from each of which a valuable timber cargo has been satisfactorily transhipped. Another vessel, the "Lake Fibre," is now unloading at the same port of arrival. Further shipments of pine have been arranged for the immediate future, the ports of arrival being Liverpood, Belfast and Glasgow. The s.s. "Scotian" and the m.s. "Holbrook" have reached the Scottish port, and the "Midmore Head" and "Fanad Head" have been berthed at the Ulster port. Messrs. Terry and Gordon are to be congratulated on the flowing tide of prosperity attending their exports. The trade knows and appreciates their enterprise, and is prepared to meet it half-way. The extension of shipments to the Lagan and the Clyde will be welcomed by Hibernia and Caledonia, the former with a "cead mille failthe." and the latter by the vernacular, "Mon, but it's guide!"

Presentation to Sir James Ball

Sir James Ball, London, Eng.

The Home-Grown Timber Merchants' Advisory Committee of the United Kingdom held a dinner at the Grosvenor Hotel, London, S.W., recently, in honor of Sir James Ball, when they presented him with his portrait in oils, painted by Mr. Stanhope Forbes. Mr. Donald Munro, O. B. E., occupied the chair.

A presentation was made to Sir James Ball by Sir John Maxwell. The portrait bore the following inscription: "Presented by the Home Timber Trade Advisory Committee of the United Kingdom to Sir James Ball as a mark of respect and esteem and in recognition of his successful work as Controller of Timber Supplies during the great war."

In the course of his remarks, Sir John said the perfect chief must have a precise knowledge of the subject with which he is dealing, and devote himself to the problems which came before him. He should see that those who worked with him were the right men, and that they were capable of doing their work, and he should have a real and genuine enthusiasm in his work. Sir James Ball answered all those qualifications. The future of the home-grown timber trade was somewhat uncertain, and one of the most important uncertainties was the question of transport.

Sir James Ball, in reply, said that, with the exception of the general engineer's knowledge of how to use timber, he came into the work without any special qualification. There were two sides to the timber control—the home timber trade and the imported timber trade—but he always looked upon the home timber trade as the more difficult of the two. They were cut off from imported timber, and had to rely upon the home-grown trade. In less than twelve months they got to work with the right men at the head of affairs, with the result that they more than doubled their output. He should look upon the portrait as one of the greatest gifts he had ever received, and it would be treasured by his family long after he had passed away.

Mr. Horton presented a silver rose bowl to Mr. Calder, which bore the following inscription: "Presented to James W. Calder, Esq., Acting Controller of Timber Supplies, by the members of the Home-Grown Timber Trade Advisory Committee as a token of esteem and regard, and in recognition of valuable services rendered during the great war."

Last of Timber Limits Disposed Of

The last of the McMullen timber limits has just been sold to Ernest Chisholm, owner of the Kemptown Mines, and H. McK. McCallum, Truro, N. S. These lands consist of fifty-five hundred acres of virgin timber three miles from Mulgrave and one mile from railway, and are estimated to contain over twenty million feet of merchantable timber. These lands holdings, combined with the present contiguous holdings of Chisholm and McCallum, make one solid block of ten thousand acres, one of the largest single timber lots in Nova Scotia. T. G. McMullen was at one time the lumber king of Nova Scotia, and since his retirement from active business has thus finished selling his entire holdings of over three hundred thousand acres.

Link-Belt Co., of Chicago, Ill., are completing a new addition to their Belmont factory at Indianapolis. The extension consists in completing their new furnace buildings Nos. 7 and 8, but for the present the company will install only furnace No. 7, which will be fifteen-ton capacity instead of ten-ton like the present furnaces. The company are also purchasing the necessary machinery such as rolling mills, sand blast and other foundry equipment.

Breezy Paragraphs from the East

William Murray & Sons of York Mills. N. B., have purchased a piece of property near Hervey Station for the purpose of erecting a planing mill in the spring. They have also purchased the Swan sawmill at Tweedside and intend to manufacture lumber and shingles there.

Although the highest wages ever in the history of lumbering in New Brunswick are being paid, operators report that men are scarce. except on the North Shore. As high as $70 per month is being paid to lumbermen and in some cases $125 and even $150 per month is being offered to cooks to take charge of large camps.

A saw mill and box factory, owned and operated by Moirs Limited, was destroyed by fire on November 14. The buildings, which were fully equipped with modern machinery, were insured for $50,000. An estimate of the loss exceeds this amount. Fire apparatus was dispatched from Halifax, but arrived too late to save the buildings, although they prevented the blaze from spreading to the large lumber piles.

The Nashwaak Pulp & Paper Company have concluded the purchase of a new pulp and paper mill site at South Devon, N. B. The property consists of twenty acres located near the mouth of the Nashwaak river and is tapped by both the Canadian National and Canadian Pacific railwys. Hon. N. M. Jones, mnaging director of the company, says he is not as yet in a position to make any announcement concerning the erection of a pulp mill.

Shipping is beginning to pick up at this port and already large lumber shipments are being recorded. The C. P. O. S. liner Batsford sailed from St. John, November 21, with a large cargo of deals for Browhead, Ireland, for orders. The S. S. Cape Premier, another large liner, is now in port, loading lumber for Stetson, Cutler & Company. The schooner Abbie C. Stubbs recently sailed for Bridgetown, British West Indies, with 337,633 feet of pine boards, valued at $13,505.32.

Announcement was made that the sale of stumpage on the Christie Murray property in the upper end of the parish of Dumfries, York County, has been completed. The property consists of 450 acres land, on which it has been estimated that there are over two and a half million feet of spruce, as well as more than three-quarters of a million feet of birch and maple, the purchaser having until 1924 to remove the lumber. The purchaser is Henry Swim of Doaktown, who secured the lumber for $23,000.

An unusual large cut of lumber, as previously predicted, is expected in New Brunswick this winter, according to an announcement of Col. T. G. Loggie, Dputy Minister of Lands and Mines. If the snow fall is not to heavy the cut may be the largest on record. On the area in which the spruce bud worm did so much damage this summer a great deal of the lumber will be lost as it will be impossible to spare the time to cut it. Most of the spruce, which was destroyed, is of an inferior quality, while the pest did its greatest work of destruction to the balsam fir.

The large corporation drive on the St. John river reached the booms in Fredericton recently and the crews were paid off. Oldtime river men say that this was the latest date for the drive to reach the booms in thirty years. At that time the drive was in charge of Walter Jackson, who is now manager of the St. John Log Driving Company, who was also in charge of this drive. In spite of the late arrival of the corporation drive the St. John River Log Driving Company, by carrying on rafting operations until November 3 have cleaned up the supply of logs so that only between one and two million feet will be carried over winter in the booms.

Newsy Briefs from the West

The B. C. Fir and Cedar Lumber Company, which had its plant wiped out by fire some weeks ago, has announced the decision to reconstruct. The new plant will have a nine-hour capacity of 75,000'.

It is reported that the Dominion Government plans to place contracts for fifty schooners with British Columbia shipyards. According to report 25 of the ships will be constructed at Victoria and the other half will be turned out by yards on the mainland.

Prices of lumber in Vancouver were raised recently $2 per thousand in all classes. Lumbermen are looking for higher prices in the spring. It is freely predicted that there will be a jump of from ten to eleven dollars before April because of the unprecedented demand for lumber from all parts of the United States.

The Forest Mills, Ltd., have let logging contracts on the Kettle River, B.C., and work has already been commenced and will be continued all winter. It is expected the company's big mill at Cascade will commence sawing in April. It will have a capacity of 85,000 feet per day, and give steady employment to 75 men.

Frank Buckley, manager of an extensive lumber and logging plant at Buckley, B. C., on Massett Inlet, Queen Charlotte Island, is on his way back from England, with, it is understood, sufficient capital to carry out large developments. Much of his holdings contain spruce, and it is believed the manufacture of wood pulp will be part of the new undertakings.

A federal charter has been granted the Western Spruce & Cedar Co., Ltd., with a capital stock of $100,000 and headquarters in Vancouver, to carry on the business of timber merchants, sawmill, shingle mill and pulp mill proprietors, loggers, etc. The incorporators are Thomas T. Howland, of Minneapolis, Minn., Wm. E. Burns, Robert K. Walkem and George J. Thomson, of Vancouver.

The lumber mills in the district of Langley, B. C., are keeping very busy, although experiencing a shortage of cars. Rennie's mill at War Hoop is operating steadily. A large number of ties are being taken out and also shingle bolts, which is a source of revenue to the farmers. Altogether the prosperity of the Fraser Valley is considerably enhanced by the active logging operations throughout all wooded sections along the B. C. E. Railway.

An informal dinner was held recently in Vancouver by the B. C. Loggers' Association, who were the hosts of the B. C. lumber merchants. About one hundred attended the function, F. C. Riley, of the firm of Bloedel, Stewart & Welch, President of the Association, presided, and was assisted by W. B. W. Armstrong, Secretary of the Loggers' Association. Various topics of interest were discussed and the get-together movement was given considerable impetus. Many expressions were voiced on the need of a spirit of co-operation.

A whirlwind of buying, both domestic and export, to the United States, of lumber through the west has advanced the wholesale price of lumber from five to seven dollars per thousand, according to recent advices from Winnipeg. American buyers are held chiefly responsible. Even common lumber base price is now wholesale at mills $42.30 per M with a spread of at least seven dollars. Previously it was three dollars below list price. Many large dealers have been caught, having sold hundreds of cars at list price two weeks ago without getting their orders for delivery accepted by Pacific Coast mills.

Mechanics' Lien Act Will be Revised

It will be good news to retail lumbermen and others to learn that the new Ontario Government intends making certain revisions to the Mechanics and Wage Earners Lien Act which move has been urged by the Ontario Retail Lumber Dealers' Association for some time. At the last session of the Ontario Legislature, a committee of the House was appointed to undertake the work of revision and, if thought advisable, to bring in an entirely new act as the present one is obsolete and defective in many respects. Many members of that committee were defeated at the polls but it is understood that the work will go on. Hon. Walter Rollo, Minister of Labor, has announced this fact but until the international labor convention at Washington is over and a consultation has been held with Dr. Riddell of the Trades and Labor Department, it is impossible to give out the details of procedure.

Death of Veteran Yardman

Walter Beatty, a resident of Pembroke, Ont., for 56 years and a former Mayor of that town, died recently. He was born in the township of Young, County of Leeds, twelve miles from the present city of Brockville in 1841, and was educated there, going afterwards to Pakenham. From there he came to Pembroke to enter the emplcy of the late Lawrence Naismith. He proved himself so efficient that in 1871 Mr. Naismith took him as a partner in his planing mill and contracting business. Upon Mr. Naismith's death Mr. Beatty took over the business himself, and it has flourished under his proprietorship until now it is one of the largest of its kind in the Ottawa Valley. Many large carpentering contracts will be memorials to Mr. Beatty for his field in that capacity was large. He had contracts on the Post Office, the Presbyterian Church, the General Hospital, the West Ward School, the Bishop's Palace, and many more of the larger buildings in town.

Mr. Beatty took great pride in the fact that he was active at his advanced years and it was inspiring to see a man of 78 working so hard and moving about so quickly. A few years ago there was a banquet given in Pembroke to all the old men who had been in business in Pembroke for 50 years or more. Mr. Beatty was there.

Work has been commenced on a very extensive match splint factory at Berthierville, P.Q.. for the Log Supply Company. The cost is estimated at about $2,000,000. The factory will comprise a log haul and machine shop, boiler house, and masher house, and will be 533 x 320 feet. The building will have a concrete foundation, and will be constructed of steel and brick. The engineers and contractors are the Austin Co., New York.

Many Coast Logging Camps Shut Down

That shipbuilding operations at Prince Rupert are going ahead full blast with the prospects of the continuation of activities for some time to come, was the impression which N. S. Lougheed, of the Abernethy & Lougheed Lumber Co., who returned recently to Vancouver from an inspection trip in the north, received when he visited the northern town.

"The keel for the second steamer for the Canadian Government was laid a few days ago," explained Mr. Lougheed, "and it looks as if the industry will have smooth sailing for the next few months. Several hundred men are being given employment and the industry means a great deal to Prince Rupert."

Mr. Lougheed was questioned as to the logging industry along the coast, especially with regard to the campaign to root out the I.W.W. element in the logging camps. He explained that practically all the camps have been shut down, a few are being operated at the present time and in these the I.W.W. element is being reduced to a minimum. No trouble, he believed, was being experienced now with this element, although he only visited one camp on his trip and could not speak authoritatively.

As far as his concern is concerned, Mr. Lougheed explained, the operations were confined to cleaning up the surplus stock of logs which were cut for the Imperial Munitions Board order. These, of course, are being handled through Prince Rupert. He did not visit Vancouver Island, but stated that one big camp was being operated, that being the Kelly camp. He anticipated much activity in the logging industry on the Island during the next few years. He visited Ocean Falls but all camps are shut down in that vicinity.

Another well-known lumberman who returned recently to Vancouver is A. B. Martin, of the Pacific Mills, Ltd. He was as far north as Ocean Falls. He states that the outlook for the logging business next year is exceptionally bright.

Many Opportunities for Work in Bush

Latest reports from all employment offices of the information and service branch of the Department of Soldiers' Civil Re-Establishment, Ottawa, show there is considerable opportunity for employment for large numbers of men, in the bush, at mining and lumber centres. During last week, 2,505 ex-members of the forces were found employment. This brings the total placements to date to 95,819, being 95.1 per cent. of the applications made to the Information and Service branch. In the lumber camps better meals and accommodations are being provided for the workers than in the past years, and wages are high. Nova Scotia and New Brunswick are asking for men for outdoor work. Returned men who are skilled workers would find opportunities throughout Ontario, particularly in Kitchener, where the factories are reported to be short in their output owing to lack of sufficient workers.

Wilful Waste in Logging Methods

Major A. Barclay, of Montreal, a civil engineer, who went down the North Shore of the St. Lawrence accompanied by Mr. W. D. Sweezy, of Quebec, in the beginning of September last to explore the country inland from Matane, Que., for Ontario capitalists interested in the pulp and paper business, returned recently. Major Barclay stated that his principals were anxious to learn the value and condition of the forest properties in the section that he visited. He said that the pulp and paper business was destined to become an important industry in the Province, and that it would eventually assume large proportions.

Relating his experience during his trip of exploration, Major Barclay said: Mr. Sweezy and myself went down the river as far as Matane, and from north of that point went into the woods. In our tour of exploration we covered nearly 2,000 square miles of ground. Shortly after we started on our tour the weather became cold and the lakes froze over, so that we had to abandon our canoe and continue our work on foot.

It is an immense silent country; even the birds that flit from tree to tree do so noiselessly. The only sound is the roar of the water-falls. The country is rich in its water powers, large streams with high falls, that find their way into the St. Lawrence, from the height of land 300 miles from the shore.

We came across a tremendous lot of birch, as well as spruce, cedar and Jack-pine. We saw no fur-bearing animals, but came across their tracks. As for flies, all I can say is that it is an ideal country for them.

We travelled past magnificent spots for the establishment of villages, and found trees of great age, among them black spruce fully 200 years old. Timber we met with in other sections showed age from 80 to 90 years, which went to demonstrate that this part of the country had been swept by fire and the growth of timber all destroyed.

Major Barclay spoke in severe terms of the manner in which logging has been carried on in that country by the jobber, who only thought of the easy dollars he was making, and who carried on a destruction that the Government should not allow. He said: "Everywhere we went in close proximity to the river, we saw signs of wilful destruction in the manner in which logging has been carried on by the jobber. We came to numerous places where trees had been cut near the shore, or in other places near an easy road to haul the logs to the river. A jump had then been made to other sections where the work of logging could be carried on as easily as possible, while timber in small areas more difficult to reach was left, and thus the cutting commercially ruined. As a matter of course the further you have to go after the timber the greater the expense, and when the shore timber is depleted and the jobber called to go further inland, he is compelled to ask a higher price for his product. On the other hand, if he cut the timber as he reached it, without making a choice in his cut, he would preserve the material instead of carrying on uncalled for destruction.

There is another feature connected with careless logging that the Government should see to and arrest. That is the conditions created by the loggers who pick out their cuts from easy pockets, and allow an accumulation of brush to catch fire, burning down miles and miles of valuable timber. These timber limits are filled with Indian and French-Canadian trappers after fur-bearing animals, who make their camp near such brush, and, in my opinion, are responsible for many of the forest fires that take place. We came into contact with a great many such traps on our tour of exploration that indicated the large number of trappers who crowded into the woods after the fur-bearing animals.

Major Barclay said it was the same old story of neglect on the part of the Government not to learn the importance of the country's forest resources and its protection. This thing was not alone confined to the Province of Quebec, it existed in Ontario and in British Columbia. To his mind it was like wild-catting in gold mines.

"As it is," said Major Barclay, "it is a great waste, throwing away the 95 per cent. of the cut for the sake of getting the remaining 5 per cent., that costs the least money to produce. We came across a fine lot of timber, and if the areas worked very properly cleared, you would get the hunters off and then secure better fire protection. It is a great country in its wealth of timber and its enormous water powers. I am not finished with my exploration and am coming back again to continue the work."

In view of the tone of the inquiries from France and the United Kingdom for timber, the Pacific Coast lumber interests expect to ship huge quantities during 1910 and 1920, according to G. Loken, manager for G. W. McNear, Inc., the well-known San Francisco house, and junior member of that firm. Mr. Loken, who is now in New York, stated that one French inquiry had been for 60,000,000 lineal feet, and that Great Britain and Italy also indicated that they would depend upon the Pacific Coast for building materials to be used in reconstruction work.

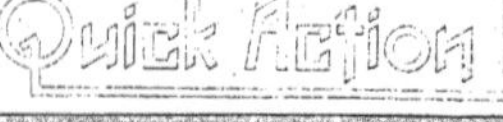

PUBLISHER'S NOTICE

Advertisements other than "Employment Wanted" or "Employees Wanted" will be inserted in this department at the rate of 20 cents per agate line (14 agate lines make one inch). $2.80 per inch, each insertion, payable in advance. Space measured from rule to rule. When four or more consecutive insertions of the same advertisement are ordered a discount of 25 per cent. will be allowed.

Advertisements of "Wanted Employment" will be inserted at the rate of one cent a word, net. Cash must accompany order. If Canada Lumberman box number is used, enclose ten cents extra for postage in forwarding replies. Minimum charge 25 cents.

Advertisements of "Wanted Employees" will be inserted at the rate of two cents a word, net. Cash must accompany the order. Minimum charge 50 cents.

Advertisements must be received not later than the 10th and 20th of each month to insure insertion in the subsequent issue.

Wanted–Lumber

Basswood Wanted

No. 2 Common and Mill Cull. Winter cut preferred. Apply Firstbrook Brothers, Ltd., Toronto, Ont. 8-t.f.

Wanted Lumber

Hardwood Lumber wanted. Birch, Maple, Basswood and other Hardwoods. Dry or sawn to order. We send inspector. Box 14, Canada Lumberman, Toronto. 21-24

LUMBER WANTED

500M ft. or more 1 x 4" and up, Cull Spruce.
500M ft. or more 2 x 6" and 7", Merchantable Spruce.

Give description as to grade, widths and lengths.

Edward W. Parkhill & Co., Inc.,
23 Burlington, Vt., U.S.A.

Maple and Spruce

Wanted stock lists and quotations on end dried, white quartered and straight grained action Maple, four and five quarter, also Spruce Lath and Furring, bundled. Box 70, Canada Lumberman, Toronto. 23-2

Wanted To Buy LATH

We are in the market for large quantities of Lath; all grades, including No. 3 and 32", Paying good prices and cash on receipt of B.L.

What have you to offer? Send good description, lowest price F.O.B. Chicago, stating quantity offered.

COVEY DURHAM COMPANY,
481 S. Dearborn St.,
20-23 Chicago, Ill., U.S.A.

For Sale–Lumber

FOR SALE
Hickory Specials

100 M pcs. ¾" Dowels, 48" long.
20 M pcs. 1" Squares, 48" long.

Also some shorter stock. All high grade, second growth Hickory. Can ship immediately. Will sell cheap. Address Box 31, Canada Lumberman, Toronto. 23-24

LATH FOR SALE

Will contract to supply during December, January, February and March, two to four million. For particulars apply Box 76, Canada Lumberman, Toronto. 23

Piling

We can furnish Piling, any length or size, on short notice.

WM. POLLOCK & SON,
23-2 Englehart, Ont.

PULPWOOD FOR SALE

Ten thousand cords of pulpwood for sale; next summer delivery. Shipping point, Blue River, Canadian National Railway. Apply to

QUEBEC LUMBER CO.,
Phone 320 98 St. Peter Street,
22-25 Quebec, Que.

For Sale

Delivered in log at Berkeley C. P. R. station, 100 miles north of Toronto—(estimated), 75,000 ft. large, clear virgin white pine; 200,000 ft. spruce and balsam; large quantity cedar telegraph poles, fence posts, ties; dry, sound tamarac piles, and ties; and a quantity maple and other hardwoods.

J. RITCHIE,
23 Port Arthur, Ont.

For Sale

Five to ten cars Selected White Pine Trimmer Ends; 1 x 4 and wider; 1" thick and thicker; 10" long and longer.

JOHN B. SMITH & SONS,
23-24 Toronto, Ont.

Wanted–Machinery

Wanted

Barienger Braking Device, six blocks, with or without cable. Apply Bishop Lumber Co., Ltd., Nesterville, Ont. 22-23

Wanted

Barienger brake, either 4 or 6 drum type. Apply Bishop Lumber Co., Ltd., Nesterville, Ont. 23-24

Wanted

To purchase, upright Gang, 44" to 40" wide, 18" stroke. Communicate with The Pembroke Lumber Co., Pembroke, Ont. 23-24

Machinery Wanted

1 Reshw, 48 to 54" wheels.
1 8 or 10" Sticker, 4 sides.
1 Iron Planer, 14 to 16" x 5 to 7' long.
1 Left Hand Carriage, complete with 8" steam feed.
1 6 and 8 Steam Nigger.
1 Shaving Separator.
Quantity of 16' Galvanized Shaving Pipe.

Would entertain good second-hand equipment. Full particulars to Box 77, Canada Lumberman, Toronto. 23

For Sale–Machinery

For Sale

1—17 x 24 Atlas Engine, with 86 in. x 10 ft. flywheel.
1—No. 182 Berlin Double Surfacer, 30 in. x 6 in.
1—No. 199 Berlin Buzz Planer.
1—No. 290 Berlin Picket Header.

The Otis Staples Lumber Company, Ltd.,
19-t.f. Wycliffe, B.C.

Good second-hand Hockey Stick Bending Machine for sale. Apply J. H. Still Mfg. Co., St. Thomas, Ont. 23-2

For Sale

Quantity of Planer Knives.
Two expansion Shimer Heads and Cutters.
One Sticker Cylinder Arbor.

MAASS BROS.,
23 Ottawa, Ont.

FOR SALE

One Waterous double truck Band Mill Complete.
One steam Log Loader.
One steam Ticker.
One Waterous Nigger, 10 and 8" cylinders.
Two Air Cushions.
One 10" Steam Feed, 40 ft. cylinders.
One steam set works, Carriage Wheels and Track. Also a number of steel and wood pulleys, live rolls, etc.

For full information apply Box 74, Canada Lumberman, Toronto. 23-2

Wanted–Employment

Advertisements under this heading one cent a word per insertion. Box No. 10 cents extra. Minimum charge 25 cents.

STEADY YOUNG MAN, retail experience, wishes position with wholesale firm, with chance of getting on road. Box 65, Canada Lumberman, Toronto. 23

WANTED EMPLOYMENT—By practical Lumberman capable of organizing and taking full charge of lumbering operations, no matter how large. Plenty of experience; good references. Box 42, Canada Lumberman, Toronto. 23

YOUNG MARRIED MAN anxious to secure position giving opportunity of advancement in lumber business. Have already had some experience. Can furnish the best references as to character, etc. First class education. Box 505, Canada Lumberman, Montreal, Que. 23-24

RETURNED SOLDIER, single, 28, correct French and English, fair knowledge of Spanish and Italian; full business education, eight years' experience in lumber trade, four as local manager of sawmills, one year as spare foreman in sulphite plant testing and shipping department. Open for engagement in any capacity if prospects of advancement on merit. Would quickly qualify as foreign representative, South America or Europe. Apply Box 73, Canada Lumberman, Toronto. 23

Wanted–Employees

EXPERIENCED SALESMAN—Salesman for well established lumber firm, state experience and salary. Box 67, Canada Lumberman, Toronto. 23

WANTED—Concern operating in Northern Ontario has opening for active, energetic man to assist in woods operations. Permanent position and advancement for man possessing right qualifications. Address Box 60, Canada Lumberman, Toronto. 23-24

Business Chances

For Sale

Fine industrial site, situated near western boundary of Ottawa, Ont. Good property for almost any industry. Mill and storage buildings almost new, with some shafting erected. Five hundred feet siding on C. P. R. If interested apply Box 55, Canada Lumberman, Toronto. 22-1

Auction Sale
of Valuable
Quebec Timber Limits

R. H. Klock & Co., through W. A. Cole, Auctioneer, on the Nineteenth day of February, 1920, at the hour of three o'clock p.m., subject to one reserve bid; will offer for sale by Public Auction at the Russell House in the City of Ottawa, in the Province of Ontario, timber berths numbers 176 and 177, Kipawa, are 100 sq. miles more or less. These timber limits contain large quantities of pine, spruce, and other wood goods. For further particulars apply to James B. Klock, 70 St. Matthew St., Montreal; Errol M. McDougall, K.C., Royal Trust Building, Montreal; D. B. Rochester, 145 James Street, Ottawa, and W. A. Cole, Hope Chambers, 63 Sparks Street, Ottawa, Auctioneer.

Saw Mill Plant For Sale

Practically new and modern Saw Mill Plant, capacity about 30 Million feet per annum, located in the Interior of British Columbia on a beautiful inland lake and on the main line of the Grand Trunk Pacific Railway. About 500 Million feet of timber on and adjacent to Lake (about 90% Spruce) and another Billion feet available at reasonable prices. Natural conditions ideal for economical logging, manufacturing, piling and shipping. An advantage of about $4 per thousand feet in freight rates to the Prairie Provinces over Coast shipments.

This property offers unlimited possibilities as a lumber, pulp and paper property. Would consider selling a half interest. Terms reasonable.

A. C. FROST COMPANY,
134 South LaSalle Street,
8-t.f. Chicago, Ill.

To:
Lumbermen—
Trust Companies—
Banks—
Executors of Estates—
Or Private Owners of
Timber and Pulp Lands.

If you are contemplating offering your Limits for sale by Auction, bear in mind that the Capital of the Dominion is the greatest lumber centre in America and the place to hold your sale.

Will be pleased to give you all information as to details, etc.

WM. A. COLE,

OFFICES:
63 Sparks Street, Ottawa, Ont.

Established—1895.
References—Any Bank.

21-24

Truck Took Eight Tons up Steep Hill

Some of the controllers and aldermen recently saw a demonstration of the work of the National truck, made by the National Steel Car Company, of Hamilton, Ont. They went to the Beach filtering basins and saw the truck haul three tons of sand from the lake shore. The sand over which it was hauled was very heavy and wet and the truck sank deeply into it, requiring some digging. On the hard road the truck made fine time. The best test was, however, on the mountain side. The truck took an empty wagon up to the quarry chutes, where over three tons of stone were loaded on the wagon and four and a half tons on the truck. This great load was taken up the steep Jolley Cut as easily as a horse would draw an empty wagon. Stops were made at the steepest places and the start made again without the slightest sign of an effort.

The City Engineer of Hamilton is asking the Works Department to buy a truck, believing that it will make a large saving in the cost of hauling sand, stone, drawing a string of garbage wagons and doing other heavy work.

Pulp Company Buys Big Acreage

An announcement is made that the Nashwaak Pulp and Paper Company have bought twenty acres of land at South Devon from Albert J. Myles, paying $250 per acre. The land is located at the mouth of the Nashwaak River, opposite Fredericton, and it is believed it will be utilized for erection of a large pulp and paper plant in accordance with the company's announced intention of removing their main plant nearer to the source of supply of raw materials. The company own the Gibson lumber land on the Nashwaak River.

Gillies New Mill Will Be "Last Word"

The construction of a sawmill of reinforced concrete has been begun by the lumber firm of Gillies Bros., Limited, Braeside, Ont. The mill, which will have a length of 190 feet and a depth of 73 feet, and look out on the Ottawa River, is to replace one of large capacity destroyed by fire on June 23 last. With three double-cut bandsaws and a resaw, the new mill is to be one of even greater capacity than the old one. All of the machinery is to be electrically driven. A. F. Byers & Co., engineers and contractors, of Montreal, have the work in hand and are to finish it on or about May 1 next. The township of McNab has been asked by the company for a fixed assessment of $80,000 for a period of ten years. The new mill will represent the last word in sawmill construction.

Western Lumberman Speaks in Montreal

Mr. L. A. Guertin, of Vancouver, B.C., was the speaker of the afternoon at a recent meeting of the Chambre de Commerce, in Montreal, and as a youthful French-Canadian who has distinctly made good in a western province, he was given a hearty reception by the Montreal body of French-Canadian business men. Mr. Guertin, who was introduced by Mr. A. Lemont, of Le Canada, migrated to the province of British Columbia from Quebec fourteen years ago and is now the head of one of the large lumber manufacturing concerns of the western province. Although for so many years out of touch with his native tongue, he made his address in French, and, despite his own modestly expressed doubts, showed that he had forgotten little of the language of his fathers.

Mr. Guertin's plea was for the development of closer trade relations between the province of his birth and the one which he has chosen for his life's work. He pointed to the fact that Americans control nearly all of the western trade, the possibilities of which, he said, apparently have been overlooked by the eastern part of Canada. He spoke at some length of the natural resources of the west, particularly those of British Columbia, of timber, fruit, mineral and general agricultural and manufacturing possibilities, which are already opened up and which await only capital for development.

Review of Current Trade Conditions

Ontario and the East

Every wholesaler is discussing a shortage of stocks at the present time, and mentally speculating where supplies are going to come from for meeting next year's large requirements. There is not a wholesaler or a manufacturer who has not very much less lumber on hand at the present time than was on stick at this particular period last year, and in not a few instances production was considerably increased during the past operating season. A number are wondering how they are going to bridge the chasm between now and next May, until which time practically no new stock will come on the market. Prices in all lines are holding very firm and it seems to be the prevailing opinion that advances from $5.00 to $10.00 per M will be placed on hemlock and white pine by the producers when seeking to dispose of next year's cut. There is a great shortage in all suplies of hardwood and quotations are advancing all the while. In fact they are soaring amazingly. The automobile industry has been one of the heaviest buyers of Eastern hardwood, and practically all the large makers of cars across the border have bought from Canadian lumber merchants.

The domestic demand for lumber of all kinds has been very active during the past season owing to the extent of house building campaign in various cities and the large amount of repair work carried on. Now many farmers are undertaking to complete alterations to their buildings, which has created good business for the rural retail lumberman in various centres. On top of this there has been a good demand from American consumers for the major portion of the year, which has caused the past season to be one that will be remembered, on the whole, as being one of the most active and satisfactory since the outbreak of the war. November and December are generally comparatively quiet months in wholesale and manufacturing circles.

Practically all sawmills have now closed down for the season, a couple of the largest in Ontario operating until December 1st.

The B. C. market is growing firmer all the time and prices show a tendency to advance. There is also a sharp demand in the West for dressed and rough timbers, and more orders are on the books of most firms for all kinds than there have been for a long while. Timbers cannot be shipped East without considerable delay, owing to the car shortage. Many Coast mills report more inquiries for lumber now than they received last June when the demand was supposed to be at the highest point. 1, 1½ and 2 in. rough clears are very scarce; in fact the upper grades of all lines of fir are limited in quantity at the present time. To use the expression of Eastern representatives British Columbia firms' stocks on the Coast are all "shot to pieces." There are certain odds and ends that may be secured and these are coming through fairly well considering the difficulty in securing cars of which all the Western plants are complaining.

Hardwood flooring firms are very busy and woodworking plants are for the most part rushed with business. Many flooring firms have been offered export trade in large volume, but their sales at home have been so large that they have no offierings for shipment abroad.

There is a scarcity of 2' x 4' and 1½' x 10' white pine. Hemlock is also exceedingly shy and the outlook for any measure of relief is not reassuring. Lath are practically unobtainable and command any figure desired. Then, those who have a stock, do not sell in large quantities and will only give a retail dealer one-third or one-quarter of a car on condition that he purchase enough lumber to make a carload shipment of material; in other words, lath are being used as a bait for the disposal of other products and are not to be secured in the open market.

It is reported that a bank, which had made a seizure of some effects of an Eastern lumber concern, sold nine carloads of No. 1 spruce lath recently at $9.50 per M., f.o.b. mill.

Indications at the present time point to a very heavy cut of lumber in New Brunswick during the winter. The cut will be heavy on both Crown Lands and privately owned lands.

The decision to cut more lumber is said to be the result of prospects in the world-market that there will be a tremendous demand for lumber next year. France and Belgium are expected to have heavy requirements for reconstruction and the United States and British markets also are expected to be under-supplied.

During the past season of navigation there has been a steady movement of manufactured lumber overseas from various New Brunswick ports but scarcity of shipping retarded that movement to quite an extent. The shipping situation will gradually improve, and the expectation is that the huge quantities of manufactured lumber, which has been piled on the millyards all over the province, some of it for more than one season, wil be cleared in 1920, with much of the coming season's cut in addition.

Logging operations and the available supply of men are referred to pretty fully in another column of this issue. The fact that the I.W.W. men and the Bolshevists have made their appearance in Canadian camps calls for the most thorough action, not only in seeing that these clandestine visitors are summarily treated, but also to drive home the fact that eternal vigilance is the price of safety. These gentry are receiving a short shrift in American logging centres, and while they have not grown as bold on this side of the line as in the West, still enough has been seen of their actions and the course they pursue, to earn for them long terms of imprisonment.

United States

General reports from leading centres indicate no particular change in the situation so far as production and demand are concerned. Building activity is naturally falling off and trade slackening down at some centres. However, prices are holding their own and any quietness is seasonal and naturally to be expected as the result of labor troubles, the coal strike, car shortage and other factors which have to be contended with.

In the hardwood market furniture manufacturers continue to take about 60 per cent. of the entire output and quotations are held firmly. Stocks are decreasing all the time and logging operations are interfered with in many centres owing to the excessively wet weather. Box makers are taking about 11 per cent. of the hardwood output, leaving little for the many other concerns. Vehicle firms are also buying quite freely.

Some improvement is seen in regard to the conditions surrounding the Southern Pine. Buyers are more frequently around mills and more sales have taken place during the last few days than for some time past, with advances on certain lines. There are also quite a number of inquiries which is a healthy sign of future activity.

There seems to be no doubt in anybody's mind now that the country will do a great deal of building next year, and the retailers are gradually realizing that it is up to them to get ready for business early, in view of the present stock prospects. There is a very fair demand for finish, but it is practically off the market. With the exception of 2-inch, which seems to have a temporary recession, dimension and timbers are developing great activity in the domestic market, but more particularly in the export field, with large orders for Cuban and South American delivery. In fact, the export business apparently is beginning to materialize more satisfactorily now; prospects at least are much better. Several buyers from Spain, Italy and Great Britain are reported on their way to the United States to negotiate for supplies. Interior shipments are very slow, due to the unsatisfactory car supply.

A very active season is in progress for Douglas Fir and the market has gained considerable strength during the past few days with the result that prices have stiffened. What is taken by lumbermen as an indication that the railroads finally are about to resume their lumber buying is an inquiry for 10,000,000 feet, mostly of car siding, being circulated among the north-western mills by the Northern Pacific Railroad. The railroads, it is believed, will require tremendous amounts of lumber to rehabilitate their lines and equipment after this long period of neglect, and their re-entering the market naturally will be a factor of great force. The Douglas fir mills of Washington and Oregon continue to operate at nearly capacity basis, the production of 125 mills reporting to the West Coast Lumbermen's Association during the week ended Nov. 8 being within 6 per cent. of normal. But the car situation continues such as to interfere seriously with shipments, and there is no definite prospect of relief. That buying has been begun in earnest may be noted from the fact that reports to the association show orders in excess of production.

Some interesting information is forthcoming in regard to the market at Buffalo when it is stated that several sensational advanees have taken place during the past week. The principal increases have been on gum and elm, spruce and hemlock. Lath are practically off the market and Canadian birch prices are regarded as the highest ever known. Buffalo lumbermen complain of an extra shortage of cars. It was reported some time ago that 44,000 Canadian cars were in continued use on the U. S. side of the line. The

matter has been taken up with Washington to see if an adjustment can be made. Lumbermen say it is almost impossible to get cars from New Brunswick and other spruce and cedar districts of Canada.

Great Britain

There has been no particular change in general business conditions during the past fortnight. There is a moderate amount of selling with the demand improving slightly in nearly all parts of the country. A recent report issued by a leading firm shows that stocks of spruce, birch logs and birch planks were higher at Manchester and Liverpool during October than for any similar month during the past three years. The imports of New Brunswick and Nova Scotia spruce and pine at Liverpool was 5,000 stds. during the past month, while consumption was over 3,000 stds., and the stock on hand, 16,000 stds. In Manchester spruce imports were 2,540 stds. with a consumption of 1,410 stds., leaving 11,000 stds. in stock. The combined stock of birch planks at Manchester and Liverpool at the present time is 982 stds.

In regard to the progress of 1920's selling, the "Timber Trade Journal," in a recent issue, says: The 1920 season is opening in a very spasmodic and uncertain manner. Holland made a few early contracts, then the English merchants started, and we now hear that Spain and France, and also Belgium, have taken the plunge. The first sales were concluded at about £2 advance on this year's figures, or on the basis of about £27 for 3 x 9, £25 for 7-in., and so on. and the sellers' ideas have since advanced. It was all along anticipated that 11-in. would be much dearer next year, and every fresh sale confirms this view. Lower Gulf 3 x 11-in. unassorted red have fetched £35 f.o.b.; for 3 x 9 the price to Spain is £30; for 8-in., £28; and for 7-in. battens, £27. In the French market prices appear to be even higher, but the sales are made in kronor. 3 x 9 3rds have made 540 kronor. In spite of all objections which may be raised, we still think that if English firms can obtain good lines of 9-in. and 11-in., they cannot possibly lose by buying in advance. The world supplies must for at least a couple of seasons be short. and firms who do not secure their stocks early will find that there are none left to purchase at any price.

In regard to general business for next open water, it is most difficult to give any opinion as long as uncertainty rules regarding the disposal of Government stocks. Whatever policy is adopted, however, we do not see how the authorities on this side can force down the prices of the Swedish shippers. In the first place, the sellers are not profiteering—the cost of production is enormous; and, in the second place, the demand will so greatly exceed the supply that the British Government's stocks will be absorbed without difficulty, and the market will still be hungry for further goods.

There are also important changes in the method of doing business, and the following outline will be read with considerable interest, particularly by Canadian exporters: It is hard for old-fashioned timber firms, accustomed as they have been for years to regular business, to realize that changes are in the air, and that we may not return again altogether to pre-war methods. The bonds, however, have been loosened, and trading is now carried on in a much more haphazard way. The Federation—rather a conservative body—is doing its utmost to make sharp distinctions, and by strict definitions of importers and retailers to prevent any overlapping between different sections of the trade. At the same time there have lately been bitter complaints that many of the agents are not playing the game. A tendency has arisen among London firms to appoint sub-agents in different ports, and instead of the leading London firms selling merely to one or two large importers at the chief ports, they get their sub-agents to call on the merchants who can purchase 100 standards or so, and to sell to these firms direct. We believe the changes which are now taking place are due in a great measure to the revolutionary rationing scheme instituted by the Controller in July, 1918. On that date, by a stroke of the pen, importers, merchants, and even retailers, were all reduced to the same level, and could purchase from the same source. It would be strange if the trade could survive such an experience, and not feel its effects. The transition stage, however, is very unsettling. If agents are going to sell to the smaller firms, how is the importer to exist? He has to run great risks, he must have command of a large capital, and yet he is in no better position than the merchant who purchases a tenth of the quantity. In what way the situation will develop is very uncertain. There are at the present time, for instance, negotiations proceding abroad for the amalgamation of exporting firms with the idea of opening up offices in this country; and there are also, further combinations among importers for the purpose of making extensive purchases and controlling the market. In spite of all efforts to preserve the old fabric of the trade, changes seem to be inevitable, and new firms with progressive ideas will have opportunities for business on fresh lines.

Market Correspondence

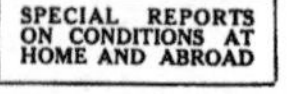

Prices Firm and Outlook Good at Ottawa

Continued firm prices, and a slackened demand as compared with the months of September and October, with a general shortage of high grade stock throughout the Valley, and the prospect of good business being ahead, combined to make the Ottawa lumber market for November, an unusual one in a variety of ways.

The market all around showed strength, both as to firmness of price and as to the outlook for future business. In all branches of the trade hopefulness was expressed. It was generally agreed that the market for the first time since 1914, was rapidly readjusting itself to its pre-war standard. One exception to this, however, was the shortage of high grade stock, which with some of the big companies was practically off the market.

With stocks low, it was expected that with the present and coming demand, prices are going to go up. The "Canada Lumberman" has been reliably advised that stocks in practically all grades will take at least one, if not more, upward jumps in price before the spring months.

A great revival of building activity, equalling if it does not surpass that of the pre-war years, is looked forward to. Already there are signs of it being reflected by the real estate market, and the housing situation at the Capital. It is not expected that any great amount of new building will be commenced during the winter months, but, rather that plans and preparations will be made, for the commencement of a great volume of it in the spring. The expected building boom will include commercial as well as residential buildings.

Shingles and lath, in company with the higher grades of stock, also went off the market with some firms and companies. The stocks of these two building staples were not large at any time during the fall months. The demand of late for them has been such as to about wipe out any stocks there were. Another factor that lent strength to the market were the reports from woodworking plants, which indicated that they already had enough orders on their books to keep them busy until Christmas or the new year. After existing orders have been filled, the indications are that more will be readily forthcoming,, and the factories, according to present signs, are assured of a good business during the winter. The demand for sash and doors increased and plants manufacturing them were kept busy.

Orders especially for export, as was to be expected considering the period of the year, fell off a little. On the other hand inquiries were as numerous if not more so than in October. The principal orders and inquiries came from the United States yards. They were chiefly for the lower grade stocks.

The export situation to England and European ports practically closed down for the year, owing to the port of Montreal closing up. With the exporters, it was taken that the majority of the pine stocks purchased by Sir James Ball, the British Timber Controller, during his visit to Canada, had been shipped. The spruce stocks purchased at the same time, are not yet all across the water. It is expected that some shipments of these will be undertaken during the winter months from the ports of St. John and Halifax.

The outlook toward the purchase and shipment of stocks to the English market for delivery next year, was unsettled. Several important factors exist in this trade. The primary one is the question of ocean freight rates. During the past season Ottawa firms shipping to England had to pay an ocean rate from $36 to $38 per M. feet of lumber, or as judged from the St. Petersburg "standard" —i.e., 1980 feet, about $72 per standard for 2 inch and thicker, and $78 per standard for shipments of inch up to two inch. The question with the exporters now is whether or not the same ocean rates will prevail when shipping opens up next April or May? Shippers believe there is reason for the rates coming down. Another question is what the International rate of exchange will be next spring. The general belief was expressed by exporters that prices would

continue to remain high in the Old Country, largely due to the demand and the shortage of stocks in the Ottawa Valley.

The situation regarding labor for the woods camps remained about the same as it had been. The camps of the Ottawa Valley operators taken all around were not as well filled as some of the operators expected they would have been. Two of the chief difficulties confronting the operators is the still marked deficiency in the quality of woods labor and the ever present problem of transients. Several operators openly state that the relief in the woods labor situation, which was expected to come about through the return of members of the overseas forestry corps, had not shown itself. Some members of this branch of the trade, declare that the members of the forestry corps returning from overseas seemed content to live on their gratuity money rather than go to the bush. Again there was a fairly large percentage of them that took the Governmental vocational training courses, which prevents them from going back to their old occupations as bushmen.

Taken all around, though the operators' plans included the getting out of a fifty or sixty per cent. bigger log output than last year, it was doubtful up to the end of November if this could actually be accomplished. The log output of the Ottawa Valley companies will be higher, but owing to labor and weather conditions, it is not yet known what the percentage of increase will be.

Transportation remained about the same, if it did not show some improvement over October. During the last two weeks of November more foreign cars became available for shipments to the United States. This, the trade believed, was due to the arrangement arrived at whereby the Grand Trunk agreed to let its cars go into American territory.

The soft coal situation in the United States as effecting imports into Canada, causes some concern. Woodworking plants operated by steam will be the most seriously affected. To the trade it also signifies that allied industries using wood or lumber products may have to shut down. The position of the Massey-Harris Company was cited as an instance. Mr. Frank Hawkins, secretary of the Canadian Lumbermen's Association, views the coal import situation as being one of the utmost gravity to the Canadian lumber trade.

Montreal Trade Slackens Toward Close of Year

The Montreal market is without material change. Business locally is only fair, but one looks for a decline at this time, when building is inclined to slacken. Considering all things, trade has been maintained at a satisfactory level, and if reports from architects and contractors are any indication, there should be a pronounced revival next year. There is an optimistic feeling generally, especially as labor troubles are being gradually smoothed out.

The prevalent idea is that lumber will cost more in 1920. While the cut may be heavier, the cost will no doubt increase, based on high wages and expensive provisions for the camps.

Orders for the States are nothing to boast about. Montreal firms have done exceptionally well this season, and as the stocks have been arriving over the border faster than retail sales have been, orders naturally slowed down.

There is a very good demand for hardwoods, with prices on a firm basis.

The B. C. section is strong, with a moderate business passing. The great trouble is that wholesalers are very much at sea as regards prices, and some will not accept orders without telegraphing to the Coast.

Woodworking firms are exceptionally busy, and one of the largest sash and door and interior trim companies has stopped taking orders.

The export season is now over. Practically the whole shipments have been on Government account, the entire stock from this port having been sent to the other side. A comparatively small amount remains in Quebec. There are, however, very large stocks in St. John and Halifax, which are now being shipped.

The pulp market is very firm both for sulphite and mechanical description. There is a world-wide demand for pulp, with indications of this being continued next year. The Riordon Company are exporting to Great Britain, Japan, France and other countries.

J. F. Munro Killed in Plane Crash

James F. Munro, one of the most prominent and valuable citizens of Pembroke, Ont., and Pilot P. E. Dobbin, an aviator of note, who rendered splendid service overseas and whose home is in Medicine Hat, were killed on the outskirts of the village of Eganville recently when the Victory Loan aeroplane in which they were proceeding to Ottawa crashed. Both deaths were instantaneous or almost so, Mr. Munro being dead when first assistance arrived and the pilot drawing his last breath before medical attention could reach the spot.

The late Mr. Munro was the owner of the Pembroke Woollen Mills, which under his stewardship has become one of the town's most valuable industries. Recently he purchased all the stock of that concern, and had built a large addition to the plant. He was a director of the Steel Equipment Company, the Thomas Pink Company, manufacturers of lumbermen's tools, the Superior Electrics and president of the Pembroke Iron Works. For a number of years he was president of the Massey Lumber Company.

Mr. Munro was born in the township of Fitzroy, Carleton County, in the year 1873, and received his early education there, coming to Pembroke in 1880. In 1911 Mr. Munro contested the riding in the Liberal interests and was defeated and he had been asked to run several times since. For three years he sat on the Town Council and was nominated for Mayor at the conclusion of his term, but declined to run.

Annual Meeting of District Six

Secretary J. B. Mackenzie, of Georgetown, Ont., has called the annual gathering of District No. 6 of the Ontario Retail Lumber Dealers' Association to meet in the Council Chamber at Orangeville on Friday, December 5th at 1.30 o'clock in the afternoon. Officers will be elected for the ensuing year, reports presented and a general discussion take place on various matters of importance to retail lumber merchants.

Average Life of Telephone Poles

W. H. Winter, superintendent of plant of the Bell Telephone Co., Montreal, in giving evidence at the inquiry by the Railway Commission into the application by the telegraph companies for increased rates, brought out an interesting fact as to the life of poles. This he put at 14 years on the average and explained that the fast growing British Columbia mountain cedar used on lines west of Moose Jaw is good for only ten years, while the eastern cedar will often give service for eighteen years.

Would Like Our Crown Land Pulpwood

The Resolutions Committee of the American Newspaper Publishers' Association recently made the following recommendation at a special convention of the association which was adopted. "That the White Paper Committee and the Legislative Committee of the A. N. P. A. urge the enactment of such legislation as will permit the development of waterpower that our timber lands may be made fully available for the manufacture of wood pulp, lumber and paper, and we also recommend that Congress be urged to take steps that will induce the Canadian Government to repeal the order-in-cCuncil prohibiting the export of wood cut from Crown lands."

Price Bros. Will Erect New Paper Mill

A big movement for the further development of the pulp and paper industry in Canada will be started in the Province of Quebec shortly by the firm of Price Bros. and Company.

Statistics show that the manufacture of pulp and paper is one of the greatest industries which Canada possesses at the present time, the daily output of paper in this country being 2,200 tons, as compared with 2,900 tons in the United States.

Of Canada's daily output, 260 tons are manufactured at Jonquiere and Kenogami by Price Bros. and Company, and machinery is being installed to bring this output up to over 300 tons a day.

The firm has plans for further expansion and in an interview Sir William Price, the president of the company, outlined his plans as follows:

"My board has definitely decided to start work without delay on a large newsprint mill in the Saguenay district, with a capacity of between four hundred and five hundred tons.

"Work has already been started on the necessary water power and by May of next year, construction of the mill will be under way.

"A further machine is now being erected in our Kenogami mill. This machine would have been working now had it not been for the strike in England. This brings our present output up to 270 tons, or, including Jonquiere, to 325 tons per day of paper and board, in addition to sulphite pulp.

"When our new plant is operating our total output of paper and board will be in the neighborhood of 800 tons per day."

With the erection of the plant a new town will spring into existence. The site is about three or four miles east of Chicoutimi and the town will be called "Saguenay."

It is situated on tide water, and free from the usual tide delays that are experienced at Chicoutimi. An execllent level plain stretches to the south and west, and the whole area is most fittingly adapted for a large manufacturing and industrial centre.

EDGINGS

Ontario

McGibbon, Limited, of Sarnia, are doubling their facilities for handling lumber, and will have one of the largest sheds in the province.

The Peace Tie & Lumber Co., Ltd., Sault Ste. Marie, Ont., have been incorporated to manufacture and deal in timber and lumber and all products thereof. Capital $40,000.

The planing mill of William Gerry & Sons, London, was damaged recently by fire to the extent of $23,000. The blaze is believed to have been caused by a spark from a passing locomotive.

The Bishop Lumber Co. of Nestorville, and the Searchmont Lumber Co. of Searchmont, Ont., are taking out considerable quantities of waney timber at the present time in the Parry Sound district.

Abitibi Power and Paper Company of Iroquois Falls announces that its roduction for three months ending Sept. 30 was 17,002 tons of newsprint, 4,513 tons of pulwood pulp and 1,511 tons of sulphite pulp.

The Elliott Machinery Co., Ltd., Belleville, Ont., has been incorporated to manufacture and deal in woodworking machinery, and to take over the business now known as the Elliott Woodworker Co. of Toronto. The capital is $250,000.

A company, known as Ontario Tie, Timber and Construction Company, Ltd., composing H. H. Davis, E. H. Brower, J. R. Robinson, B. R. Davidson and W. W. Lang, all of Toronto, has been formed with head office at North Bay, and is capitalized at $350,000.

The Matheson Lumber Co. are erecting a new sawmill at Matheson, Ont. The capacity of the plant will be 25,000 ft. a day, and the mill will be of the most modern construction, being built upon a concrete foundation, while power wil be supplied by a 125 H.P. boiler.

The Seaman-Kent Co. of Toronto, who recently purchased the old Tudhope Co. factory, in West Lorne, Ont., for the making of hardwood flooring, intend erecting an addition to the premises. About sixty hands will be employed in the new branch of the company.

Rankin & Company's planing mill and lumber yard, 1536 Dundas St. West, Toronto, was damaged recently to the extent of $2,000, when a fire broke out caused by small boys smoking cigarettes, one of which was dropped in between two logs and set fire to some sawdust.

Hayward Lumber & Tie Co., Ltd., have been incorporated to manufacture, buy and sell and deal in lumber, timber limits, standing timber, etc., and to carry on a lumbering business in all its branches. The capital stock of the company is $100,000, and the head office is at Argolis, Ont.

The Porter Lake Lumber Co., Ltd., Port Arthur, Ont., have been incorporated to carry on business as timber merchants and to manufacture and deal in timber, lumber and wood products of all kinds. Capital $40,000. A. J. McComber and W. F. Langworthy, of Port Arthur, are two of the incorporators.

The Canadian Sault Lumber Co. is conducting extensive operations in the township of Pennyfeather in the Sault Ste Marie district. This is a Chicago firm, of which P. H. Duket is president and W. H. Rath, secretary. The company intend erecting mills for the cutting of hardwood and other timber.

J. F. Paige, general manager of the Port Arthur Shipbuilding Co., Port Arthur, Ont., left recently for Halifax, to take charge of the shipyards in that city. Previous to his departure he was presented with a handsome cabinet of silver by the foremen and shop superintendents of the Port Arthur Shipbuilding Co.

W. L. Card, Nashville, Ont., states that the building trade has been rather slow in his locality for the last few years, but he has hopes that it will improve during the coming season. Last winter he operated his sawmill, but did not have a large quantity of hardwood to cut. The mill will be running again this season if sufficient snow falls.

Kelly Bros., of Bridgenorth, have purchased the old mill site in Lakefield, Ont., where the Lillicrap-Tate Lumber Co. operated from 1902 to 1910. They are moving their Bridgenorth mill to Lakefield and will have everything completed by next summer. The site is an excellent location on the Otonabee River and on the G., T. R siding and dock.

The Bancroft Lumber & Mfg. Co. Ltd. has been incorporated with a capital stock of $40,000, and head office in Bancroft, Hastings County. The company is authorized to carry on a general lumbering and manufacturing business. The incorporators are E. S. Hubbell and U. A. Hubbell of Faraday Township, D. A. Davis of Windsor, D. W. Avey of Detroit and others. The company will erect saw mills at Paudash Lake, Ont., at a cost of $50,000.

James L. Legree, of Calabogie, and John Craig, Darling, have made a purchase of timber rights on the old Rathbun limits up at the Chain rapids and are putting in a camp, with John K. Culhane, of Ashdod, as foreman. Since lumbering operations by the Deseronto Company ceased there, what that firm left standing has grown considerably, and Messrs. Legree and Craig will doubtless take off much good timber for sale in a constantly rising market.

Herman Raney, father of Hon. W. E. Raney, K.C., of Toronto, Attorney-General for Ontario, passed away very suddenly in Rochester, N.Y., where he was spending the winter with his daughters. The remains were brought to his old home in Aultsville for interment. The late Mr. Raney was born in 1835 and for many years was engaged in the lumber business of Cook Bros. at Lawrenceville. He retired from the industry several years ago and went to live in Aultsville.

Carl Sorensen, of the Carl Sorensen Lumber Company, has returned to Fort William from Crozier, near Fort Frances, where he has established a lumber camp, in which twenty-five or thirty men are now at work. Only this camp will be operated this year, but others will be established later on.

The present condition of the bush, he says, is detrimental to the lumber man. There is no frost in the swamps and about a foot of snow covers the ground, making traffic with a horse very hard, and the men are now anxiously waiting for real cold weather. The new company, for the time being, will cut their wood on cedar tracts and will make telegraph poles, fence posts, etc.

Eastern Canada

Frasers Limited which recently purchased the B. A. Mowat mill at Athol, N.B., also all that firm's lumber limits, commenced the construction of their new large mill at Athol, recently.

The sawmill and box factory at Bedford, N.S., owned and operated by Moirs Limited, biscuit makers and confectioners, has been destroyed by fire. The building and machinery were insured for $50,000.

The new saw and planing mill of the Kent Lumber Co., Granby, Que., is about completed. The owners are in the market for the following equipment,——2 horse-power motors, blower and piping, scroll saw, sander and shaper.

La Compagnie de Bois, Fortin Limitee, Chambord, P.Q., have been incorporated to manufacture and deal in lumber, pulp and wood products. Capital $25,000. E. Roy and R. Langlais, both of Quebec, are among the incorporators.

The sawmill and box factory at Bedford, N.S., owned and operated by Moirs, Limited, biscuit makers and confectioners, was destroyed by fire recently. The building, which was fully occupied with modern machinery, was insured for $50,000.

The W. H. Miller Co. of Campbellton, N. B., state they are having no labor shortage in their winter camps and logging operations are proceeding satisfactorily. The hours of work at the sawmills were reduced during the past season from ten to nine a day.

A meeting of the Quebec Forest Protective Association was held in the office of the Minister of Lands and Forests in Quebec on tht 5th of November to discuss needed changes in the fire laws, publicity work and improvements in fire fighting methods.

The "finis" was given recently to the strike of t' Montreal buildng trades which started on Labor Day, and in its early ..ages affected about 12,000 workers. Agreements were gradually reached between the contractors and the men have all returned to work.

An order-in-council was passed at Quebec recently giving to the great dam on the St. Maurice River the official name of the Gouin dam. This barrage of the St. Maurice River is the largest in the world, and is calculated to develop millions of hydro-electric horsepower.

A federal charter has been granted the E. C. Plant Lumber Co., Limited, with a capital stock of $50,000, and headquarters in Montreal. The company is empowered to carry on the business of lumbering in all its branches and to manufacture and deal in logs, lumber, timber, wood, etc.

The Riordon Pulp & Paper Co. intend erecting, in the near future, 100 workmen's houses at Kipawa, Que. The company will secure a loan from the Quebec Housing Commission to put up these workmen's residences on the new town site of this large plant, which will be operating within a few weeks.

A charter has been granted to Royal Roussillon, Limitee, with a capital stock of $49,000, and headquarters in Montreal, to manufacture and sell materials of various kinds, including floorings, wainscottings, mantels, furniture, etc. The incorporators are John P. Hammerdi Joseph R. Papineau and others.

A large sawmill belonging to the Jackman Lumber Company, Quebec, was entirely destroyed by fire recently. For mill hands were badly burned when they were trapped inside an adjoining building that was surrounded by fire, but all are expected to recover. The material damage is estimated at $125,000.

Lumber shipments from Bathurst, N. B., have been brisk the past two months, quite a number of large vessels having loaded and sailed for foreign ports, including the American schooners Margaret Thomas, cleared for Buenos Ayres; Edwin G. Farrar sailed for an Irish port; Charlotte A. Maxwell and Theoline, both in port loading for Havana, Cuba.

The firm of Price Bros. and Company, Quebec, has purchased Kent House, a historic property situated on St. Louis street, oposite the Quebec Court House, for the purpose of erecting a large office building for the firm. The property acquired was at one time the city residence of the Duke of Kent, Queen Victoria's father.

The mill and machinery which was recently purchased by the River Valley Lumber Company from the Flewelling Company at Hampton, N.B., to replace their ill at Oromocto, yhich was burned there some time ago, has been towed up the St. John river to Oromocto on large scows. It will be set up at once on the new site and will be ready for operation early in the spring. It will have a daily capacity of 75,000 superfiicial feet, the building being 40 by 120 feet.

While moose hunting at Upper North River, ten miles from Truro, N.S., Williard C. Lynds made the discovery that between four and five hunded thousand feet of lumber, the property of Hon. W. D. Hill, had been destroyed by fire. The lumber was several miles from the main highway, and owing to being sawed in the late spring, could not be got out till winter. The cook and bunkhouse were not destroyed. The origin of the fire is unknown. This lumber is likely on the MacDonald lot. It carries some insurance.

The Brown Corporation on November 14 and 15 entertained a number of Boston financiers and brokers at Quebec and La Tuque, P.Q. The company have decided to enelarge their pulp and paper production, at La Tuque mills, and the visitors, starting from Quebec city, visited the pulp mills and also La Loutre Dam. On returning to Quebec they were entertained at luncheon at the Chateau Frontenac, Mr. Downing Brown presiding.

Representatives of the Canadian Export Paper Association recently visited the plant of the Belgo-Canadian Pulp & Paper Company at Shawinigan, P.Q. They were welcomed by Messrs. Biermans and Stadler, the general manager and assistant manager of the company. The representatives, after inspecting the plant, were entertained at dinner, at which short speeches were made by Mr. Stadler; Sir William Price, Mr. Apedaile and Mr. John Ball,, of Price Bros., & Company, Limited; Mr. Rossiter of the Brompton Pulp & Paper Company; Mr. Thomas Wark of the St. Maurice Pulp & Paper Company; Mr. Cahoon and Mr. Sabbaton, of Laurentide Ltd.

Peeling Potatoes

requires much labour—all the way from one to five men or more, according to the size of the camp being assigned to this work. Furthermore, there is a great waste in hand peeling—it has been proved from 20% to 30%.

The Cyclone Vegetable Peeler

will peel and wash a bag of potatoes in from three to five minutes, and effect a saving of from 25% to 30% on material alone. Write for circular "L."

JOHN BURNS & CO., MONTREAL

Established 1865

"Beware of Imitations"

There is only one Genuine

CANE MOLA

very heavy 100% pure Sugar Cane Molasses

Sprinkle Cane Mola over your straw, old hay, corn stover, fodder, ensilage, screenings, etc., and reduce cost of feeding.

Cane Mola will keep your horses healthy and improve their appearance. They will winter at hard work and finish in excellent condition in the spring.

Cane Mola is ideal for keeping horses in good shape during the winter in the lumber camps.

Sold in strong iron-hooped barrels at a very reasonable price.

Write for full information and Booklet

ANALYSIS

The value of Cane Mola is principally in its sugar, salts and flavor.

It contains other ingredients of value.

Sugars (average)	56 per cent.
(Guaranteed minimum 52 per cent.)	
Other Carbohydrates (average)	18 per cent.
Natural Salts (average)	3 per cent.
[illegible]	
No fibre.	
Protein	4 per cent.
Moisture	[illegible] per cent.

The Cane Mola Company of Canada, Limited

118 St. Paul Street West, Montreal

Railway and Track Supplies

For Lumber and Contractors' requirements

Rails, Locomotives, Accessories, Cars, Lion Brand Babbitt Metal

Correspondence solicited

Sessenwein Bros., Montreal

ARROW HEAD

Vanadium Steel SAWS

Curve Ground

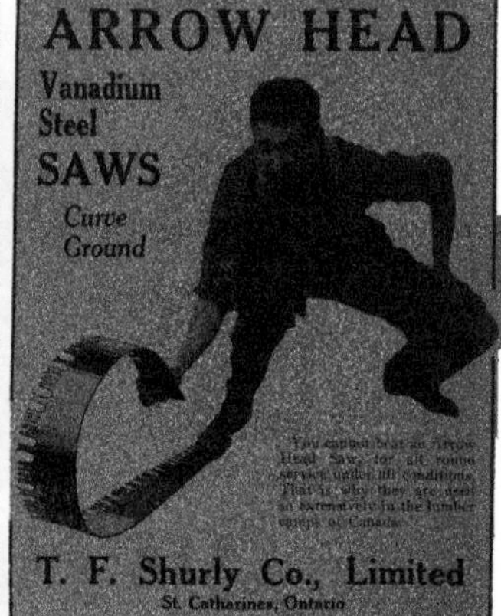

You cannot beat an Arrow Head Saw for all round service under all conditions. That is why they are used so extensively in the lumber camps of Canada.

T. F. Shurly Co., Limited

St. Catharines, Ontario

JOHNSON'S
Veterinary Remedies

are the surest, the most economical and the best medicines with which to equip your stables. They have been on the market for twenty-five years and still retain their superiority over all others.

The quality never varies, it is our first consideration.
Prices in effect at the present time are as follows:

Johnson's Horse Liniment No. 1	Per Gal.	$7.00
Johnson's Horse Liniment No. 1	Quarts, Per Doz.	12.00
Johnson's Horse Liniment No. 1	Pints, Per Doz.	18.00
Johnson's Horse Colic Remedy	Per Gal.	12.50
Johnson's Horse Colic Remedy	Quarts (8 Doses each) Doz.	20.00
Johnson's Horse Colic Remedy	Pints (4 Doses each) Doz.	15.00
Johnson's Veterinary Healing Ointment (Gall Cure)		
2 lb. Tins	each 2.25 Doz.	24.00
½ lb. Tins	Per Doz.	4.00
Johnson's Concentrated Condition Powders, 1 lb. Pkgs.	Doz.	9.00
Johnson's Condition Powder No. 2	Doz.	2.75
Johnson's Horse Worm Powders	Pkgs., Per Doz.	2.00
Johnson's Purging Balls	Per Doz.	5.00
Johnson's Antiseptic Dusting Powder		
(For Drying and Healing Sores, Proud Flesh, etc.)	Per Doz.	8.00
"Kreoline," antiseptic, deodorising	Gal. Tin	1.50

Our Family and Van Remedies are as follows:—

Pine and Tar Cough Syrup	Big 4 Liniment—Mosquito Oil
Purgative Pills	X Ray Liniment
Little Liver Pills	Cholerine Mixture (Diarrhoea)
Porous Plasters	Headache Powders
Stomach Bitters	Sarsaparilla
Laxative Cold Tablets	All Healing White Ointment

All Drugs and Patent Medicines at Market Prices.
Mail orders solicited — Prompt shipments made.

A. H. JOHNSON WHOLESALE DRUGGIST

Collingwood, Ontario

CURRENT LUMBER PRICES—WHOLESALE

TORONTO, ONT.

Prices in Carload Lots, F.O.B. cars Toronto

White Pine:		
1 x 4/7 Good Strips	$70 00	$74 00
1¼ and 1½ x 4/7 Good Strips	73 00	76 00
1 x 8 and up Good Sides	95 00	105 00
2 x 4/7 Goor Strips	75 00	78 00
1¼ and 1½ x 8 and wider Good Sides	100 00	110 00
2 x 8 and wider Good Sides	110 00	113 00
1 in. No. 1, 2 and 3 Cuts	70 00	74 00
5/4 and 6/4 No. 1, 2 and 3 Cuts	73 00	76 00
2 in. No. 1, 2 and 3 Cuts	78 00	80 00
1 x 4 and 5 Mill Run	52 00	53 00
1 x 6 Mill Run	53 00	56 00
1 x 7, 9 and 11 Mill Run	52 00	55 00
1 x 8 Mill Run	54 00	56 00
1 x 10 Mill Run	58 00	60 00
1 x 12 Mill Run	58 00	61 00
5/4 and 6/4 x 4 Mill Run	54 00	55 00
5/4 and 6/4 x 5 Mill Run	54 00	55 00
2 x 4 Mill Run	53 00	54 00
2 x 6 Mill Run	54 00	55 00
2 x 8 Mill Run	54 00	55 00
2 x 10 Mill Run	56 00	58 00
2 x 12 Mill Run	56 00	60 00
1 in. Mill Run Shorts	42 00	45 00
1 x 4 and up 6/16 No. 1 Mill Culls	42 00	45 00
1 x 10 and up 6/16 No. 1 Mill Culls	48 00	40 00
1 x 12 and up 6/16 No. 1 Mill Culls	48 00	40 00
1 x 4 and up 6/16 No. 2 Mill Culls	34 00	36 00
1 x 10 x 12 6/16 No. 2 Mill Culls	37 00	38 00
1 x 4 and up 6/10 No. 3 Mill Culls	25 00	27 00
Red Pine:		
1 x 4 and 5 Mill Run	44 00	46 00
1 x 6 Mill Run	46 00	48 00
1 x 8 Mill Run	47 00	48 00
1 x 10 Mill Run	48 00	50 00
2 x 4 Mill Run	46 00	48 00
2 x 6 Mill Run	47 00	48 00
2 x 8 Mill Run	48 00	49 00
1 in. Clear and Clear Face		Open
2 in. Clear and Clear Face		Open
Spruce:		
1 x 4 Mill Run	43 00	45 00
1 x 6 Mill Run	46 00	48 00
1 x 8 Mill Run	46 00	48 00
1 x 10 Mill Run	49 00	50 00
1 x 12 Mill Run Spruce	51 00	52 00
Mill Culls	37 00	30 00

HEMLOCK, No. 1

(In car load lots f.o.b. Toronto)

1 x 4 and 5 in. x 9 to 16 ft.	30 00	41 00
1 x 6 in. x 9 to 16 ft.	44 00	45 00
1 x 8 in. x 9 to 16 ft.	44 00	45 00
1 x 10 and 12 in. x 9 to 16 ft.	46 00	46 00
1 x 7, 9 and 11 in. x 9 to 16 ft.	42 00	44 00
2 x 4 to 12, 10 and 16 ft.	44 00	45 00
2 x 4 to 12 in., 12 and 14 ft.	44 00	45 00
2 x 4 to 12 in., 18 ft.	46 50	47 00
2 x 4 to 12 in., 20 ft.	47 00	48 00
1 in. No. 2, 6 ft. to 16 ft.	36 00	38 00
2" No. 2, 4" and up, width 6 to 16 ft.	36 00	37 00

DOUGLAS FIR

(Delivered in Toronto)

Dimension Timber up to 32 feet:

6x6 and 8, 10x10 and 12, 12x12		$54 50
6x10, 8x10, 10x14, 12x14, 14x14		55 00
6x12, 8x12		55 00
14x16, 16x16		56 00
6x14, 8x14, 10x16, 12x16		58 00
14x18		58 00
8x16, 10x18, 12x18		59 00
18x18, 20x20		59 50
12x20, 24x24		60 00

Timber in lengths over 32 feet subject to negotiation.

Fir flooring, 1 x 3, edge grain		85 00
Fir flooring, 1 x 4, edge grain		85 00
Fir flooring, 1 x 4, flat grain		69 00
No. 1 & 2, 1-in. clear Fir rough	75 00	82 00
(Depending upon widths).		
No. 1 and 2, 1¼ and 1½ in., clear Fir rough	77 00	81 00
No. 1 and 2 2" clear Fir rough	70 00	77 00
1 x 5 and 1 x 6 Fir casing		80 00
1 x 8 and 1 x 10 Fir base		85 00
1¼ & 1½ x 8, 10 & 12" E. G. stepping		95 00
1¼ & 1½ x 8, 10 & 12" E. G. stepping		85 00
1-in. clear Fir, d 4 sides		75 00
1¼x1¼ in. clear Fir, d 4 sides		78 00
XXX 6 butts to 2 in.		7 10
XXXXX 5 butts to 2 in.		8 00

LATH

No. 1 White Pine, 4 ft.	Open
No. 2 White Pine, 4 ft.	"
No. 3 White Pine, 4 ft.	"
Mill run white pine, 32 in.	"
Merchantable spruce lath, 4 ft.	"

TORONTO HARDWOOD PRICES

The prices given below are for carloads f.o.b. Toronto, from wholesalers to retailers, and are based on a good percentage of long lengths and good widths, without any wide stock having been sorted out. War tax of seven and half per cent. on imported woods, and also the prevailing rate of exchange paid by purchaser.

ASH, WHITE

(Dry weight 3800 lbs. per M. ft.)

	1s & 2s	No. 1 Com.	No. 2 Com.	No. 3 Com.
4/4	$145.00	$90.00	$60.00	$35.00
5/4 & 6/4	160.00	130.00	70.00	40.00
8/4	190.00	160.00	80.00	40.00
10/4 & 12/4	250.00	220.00	120.00	.....
16/4	275.00	240.00	140.00	.....

ASH, BROWN

4/4	$80.00	$60.00	$45.00	$43.00
6/4	85.00	70.00	65.00	55.00
8/4	88.00	75.00	70.00	55.00

BIRCH

(Dry weight 4000 lbs. per M. ft.)

	1s & 2s $		No. 1 Com. $		No. 2 Com. $
4/4	85	90	60	63	55
5/4 & 6/4	90	95	70	75	60
8/4	90	95	70	75	65
10/4 and 12/4	110	115	90	95	75
16/4	125	130	95	100	85

BASSWOOD

(Dry weight 2500 lbs. per M. ft.)

	1s & 2s	No. 1 Com.	No. 2 Com.	No. 3 Com.
4/4	$90.00	$65.00	48.00	$38.00
5/4 & 6/4	95.00	70.00	55.00	40.00
8/4	98.00	72.00	55.00	42.00

CHESTNUT

(Dry weight 2800 lbs. per M. ft.)

	1s & 2s	No. 1 Com.	Sound Wormy
4/4	$105.00	$85.00	$50.00
5/4 & 6/4	115.00	92.00	55.00
8/4	123.00	97.00	55.00

ELM, SOFT

(Dry weight 3100 lbs. per M. ft.)

4/4	$70.00	$55.00	$45.00	$38.00
6/4 & 8/4	85.00	70.00	55.00	45.00
12/4	100.00	85.00	75.00	

GUM, RED

(Dry weight 3300 lbs. per M. ft.)

	Plain 1s & 2s	Plain No. 1 Com.	Quartered 1s & 2s	Quartered No. 1 Com.
4/4	$145.00	$115.00	$160.00	$130.00
5/4	150.00	120.00	170.00	135.00
6/4	155.00	125.00	175.00	140.00
8/4	170.00	145.00	185.00	145.00

Figured Gum, $10 per M. extra, in both plain and quartered.

GUM, SAP

	1s & 2s	No. 1 Com.
4/4	$85.00	$70.00
5/4 & 6/4	90.00	75.00
8/4	100.00	85.00

HICKORY

(Dry weight 4500 lbs. per M. ft.)

	1s & 2s	No. 1 Com.	No. 2 Com.
4/4	$100.00	$70.00	$45.00
5/4	120.00	85.00	55.00
6/4	125.00	85.00	55.00
8/4	135.00	95.00	60.00

MAPLE, HARD

(Dry weight 3900 lbs. per M. ft.)

	1s & 2s	Com. No. 1	Com. No. 2	Com. No. 3
4/4	$75.00	$60.00	$45.000	$35.00
5/4 & 6/4	85.00	70.00	55.00	40.00
8/4	90.00	95.00	60.00	40.00
12/4	110.00	95.00	75.00	
16/4	130.00	115.00	90.00	

SOFT MAPLE

The quantity of soft maple produced in Ontario is small and it is generally sold on a log run basis, the locality governing the prices.

WHITE AND RED OAK

(Plain sawed. Dry weight 4000 lbs. per M. ft.)

	1s & 2s	No. 1 Com.
4/4	$145.00	$105.00
5/4 & 6/4	150.00	110.00
8/4	150.00	110.00
10/4	155.00	115.00
12/4	155.00	115.00
16/4	170.00	120.00

WHITE OAK, Quarter Cut

(Dry weight 4000 lbs. per M. ft.)

	1s & 2s	No. 1 Com.
4/4	$273.00	$194.00
5/4 and 6/4	283.00	204.00
8/4	293.00	214.00

RED OAK, Quarter Cut

	1s & 2s	No. 1 Com.
4/4	$200.00	$150.00
5/4 and 6/4	210.00	165.00
8/4	215.00	170.00

OTTAWA, ONT.

Manufacturers' Prices

Pine good sidings:		
1-in. x 7-in. and up		85 00
1¼-in. and 1½-in., 8-in. & up		110 00
2-in. x 7-in. and up		110 00
No. 2 cuts 2 x 8-in. and up		70 00
Pine good strips:		
1-in.		70 00
1¼-in. and 1½-in.		75 00
2-in.		80 00
Pine good shorts:		
1-in. x 7-in. and up		65 00
1-in. x 4-in. to 6-in.		57 00
1¼-in. and 1½-in.		70 00
2-in.		72 00
7-in. to 9-in. A sidings		56 00
Pine, No. 1 dressing sidings		62 00
Pine, No. 1 dressing strips		58 00
Pine, No. 1 dressing shorts		52 00
Pine, 1-in. x 4-in. s.c. strips		51 00
Pine, 1-in. x 5-in. s.c. strips		52 00
Pine, 1-in. x 6-in. s.c. strips		54 00
Pine, 1-in. x 7-in. s.c. strips		54 00
Pine, 1 x 8-in. s.c., 12 to 16 ft.	48 00	56 00
Pine, 1-in. x 10-in. M.R.		58 00
Pine, s.c. sidings, 1½ and 2-in.		55 00
Pine, s.c. strips, 1-in.	45 00	49 00
1¼, 1½ and 2-in.		56 00
Pine, s.c. shorts, 1 x 4 to 6 in.		45 00
Pine, s.c. and bet., shorts, 1 x 5		45 00
Pine, s.c. and bet., shorts, 1 x 6		47 00
Pine, s.c. shorts, 6'-11', 1"x10"		52 00
Pine box boards:		
1"x4" and up, 6'-11'		40 00
1"x3", 12'-16'		44 00
Pine, mill culls, strips and sidings, 1-in. x 4-in. and up, 12-ft. and up		40 00
Mill cull shorts, 1-in. x 4-in. and up, 6-ft to 11-ft.		38 00
O. culls r & w p		28 00

RED PINE, LOG RUN

mill culls out, 1-in.	36 00	42 00
mill culls out, 1¼-in.	36 00	42 00
mill culls out, 1½-in.	38 00	42 00
mill culls out, 2-in.	40 00	42 00
mill culls, white pine, 1"x7" and up		40 00

MILL RUN SPRUCE

1"x4" and up, 6'-11'		42 00
1"x4" and up, 12'-16'		42 00
1"x9"-10" and up, 12'-16'		48 00
1¼"x7" 8-9" and up, 12'-16'		48 00
1¼ x 10 and up, 12'-16'		50 00
1½" & 2" x 12" and up, 12'-16'		50 00
Spruce, 1-in. clear (fine dressing and B)		55 00
Hemlock, 1-in. cull	23 00	27 00
Hemlock, 1-in. log run	30 00	35 00
Hemlock, 2x4, 6, 8, 10, 12/16'	30 00	35 00
Tamarac	24 00	26 00
Basswood, log run, dead culls out	40 00	48 00
Basswood, log run, mill culls out	45 00	50 00
Birch, log run	48 00	50 00
Soft Elm, common and better, 1, 1½, 2-in.	25 00	30 00
Ash, black, log run	32 00	40 00
1 x 10 No. 1 barn		52 00
1 x 10 No. 2 barn		40 00
1 x 8 and 9 No. 2 barn		42 00
Lath per M:		
No. 1 white pine, 1½-in. x 4 ft.		8 00
No. 2 white pine		7 50
Mill run white pine		7 50
Spruce, mill run 1½-in.		7 00
Red pine, mill run		7 00
Hemlock, mill run		6 00
32-in. lath		3 50
White Cedar Shingles:		
XXXX, 18-in.		7 50
Clear butt, 18-in.		6 50
18-in. xx		5 00
Spruce logs (pulp)	13 00	15 00

QUEBEC, QUE.

WHITE PINE

	Cts. Per Cubic Foot	
First class Ottawa waney, 18-in. average, according to lineal	80	90
19 in. and up average	90	100

SPRUCE DEALS

	Per M. Ft.	
3 in. unsorted Quebec, 4 in. to 6 in. thick	$34 00	$37 00
3 in. unsorted, Quebec, 7 in. to 8 in. thick	38 00	40 00
3 in. unsorted Quebec, 9 in. thick	40 00	45 00

OAK

	Cts. Per Cubic Ft.	
According to average and quality 55 ft. cube	90	1 00

ELM

According to average and quality, 40 to 45 feet, cube	95	1 05
According to average and quality, 30 to 35 feet	75	85

BIRCH PLANKS

1 to 4 in. thick, per M. ft.	40 00	46 00

SARNIA, ONT.

FINE, COMMON AND BETTER

1 x 6 and 8 in.	$85 00
1 in., 8 in. and up wide	90 00
1¼ and 1½ in. and up wide	106 00
2 in. and up wide	106 00

CUTS AND BETTER

4/4 x 8 and up No. 1 and better	82 00
6/4 x 8 and up No. 1 and better	82 00
8/4 x 8 and up No. 1 and better	97 00

No. 1 CUTS

1 in., 8 in. and up wide	72 00
1¼ in., 8 in. and up wide	82 00
1½ in., 8 in. and up wide	82 00
2 in., 8 in. and up wide	87 00
2½ and 3 in., 8 in. and up wide	107 00
4 in., 8 in. and up wide	112 00

No. 1 BARN

1 in., 10 to 16 ft. long	$59 00	$60 00
1¼, 1½ and 2 in., 10/16 ft.	65 00	72 00
2½ to 3 in., 10/16 ft.	77 00	

No. 2 BARN

1 in., 10 to 16 ft. long	56 00	62 00
1¼, 1½ and 2 in., 10/16 ft.	57 00	63 00
2½ in. to 3 in.	70 00	

No. 3 BARN

1 in., 10 to 16 ft. long	52 00	62 00
1¼, 1½ and 2 in., 10/16 ft.	55 00	57 00

BOX

1 in., 1¼ in. & 1½ in., 10/16 ft.	47 00	40 00

MILL CULLS

Mill Run Culls	
1 in., 4 in. and up wide, 6/16 ft.	$30 00
1¼, 1½ and 2 in.	40 00

LATH

No. 1 48 in. White Pine	$8 00
No. 2 48 in. White Pine	7 50
No. 3 48 in. White Pine	7 00
32 in. Pine	3 50
48 in. Hemlock	7 00
32 in. Hemlock	3 00

ST. JOHN, N.B.

ROUGH LUMBER

Wholesale Prices Per M. Sq. Ft.

2x3, 2x4, 3x3, 3x4, Rgh. Merch. Spr.	$47 00
2x3, 2x4, 3x3, 3x4 Dressed 1 edge	49 00
2x3, 2x4, 3x3, 3x4 Dressed 4 sides	53 00
2x6, 2x7, 3x5, 4x4, 4x6, all rough	50 00
2x8, 3x7, 5x5, 6x6	52 00
2x9, 3x8, 6x8, 7x7	55 00
2x10, 3x9	60 00
2x12, 3x10, 3x12, 8x8 and up	62 00
Merch. Spr. Bds. Rough, 1x3-4 & 5	40 00
" " " " 1x6	48 00
" " " " 1x7 & up.	45 00
Refuse Bds., Deals & Setgs.	30 00

Above random lengths up to 18-0 long. Lengths 19-0 & up $5.00 extra per M.

For planing Merch. and Refuse Bds. add $2.00 per M to above prices. Laths $6.50 per M. pieces.

SHINGLES

	Per M.
Cedar, Extras	$6 50
" Clears	6 00
" 2nd Clears	5 50
" Extra No. 1	4 00
Spruce	4 00

WINNIPEG, MANITOBA

No. 1 SPRUCE

Dimension	S.1.S and 1.E 6 ft.	8 ft.	10 ft.
2 x 4	$35 50	$38 50	$42 00
2 x 6	37 50	38 50	42 00
2 x 8	37 50	39 50	42 00
2 x 10	38 50	40 50	43 00

(Continued on page 78)

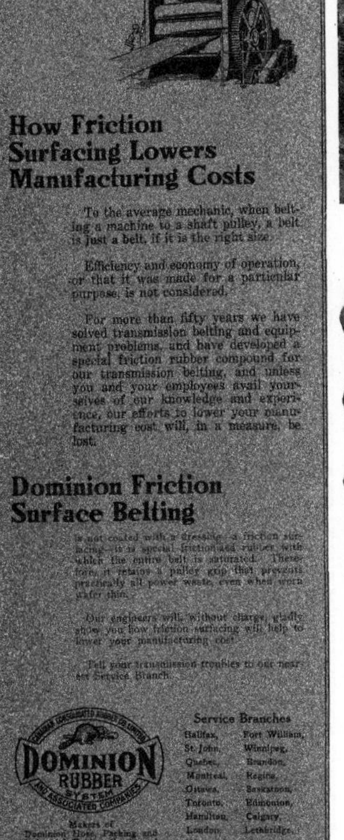

Table of Lumber Trimmer. Note "A" attachments at intervals to push boards past saw.

CURRENT LUMBER PRICES—Continued

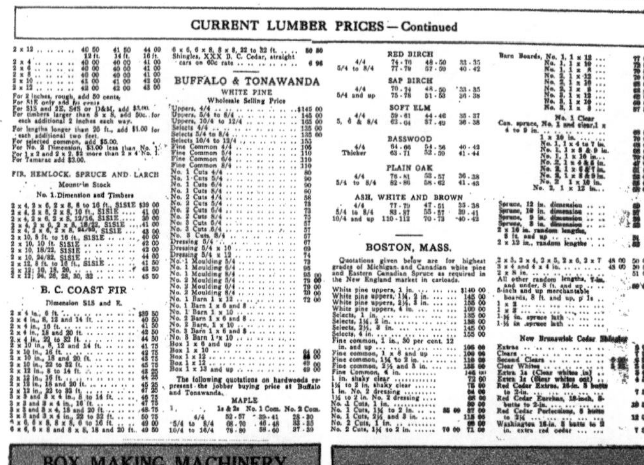

2 x 12	40 50	41 50	44 00
	12 ft.	14 ft.	16 ft.
2 x 4	40 00	40 00	41 00
2 x 6	40 00	40 00	41 00
2 x 8	40 00	40 00	41 00
2 x 10	41 00	41 00	42 00
2 x 12	42 00	42 00	43 00

For 2 inches, rough, add 50 cents.
For S1E only add 50 cents.
For S1S and 2E, S4S or D&M, add $3.00.
For timbers larger than 8 x 8, add 50c. for each additional 2 inches each way.
For lengths longer than 20 ft., add $1.00 for each additional two feet.
For selected common, add $5.00.
For No. 2 Dimension, $3.00 less than No. 1.
For 1 x 2 and 2 x 2, $2 more than 2 x 4 No. 1.
For Tamarac add $3.00.

FIR, HEMLOCK, SPRUCE AND LARCH

Mountain Stock

No. 1 Dimension and Timbers

2 x 4, 2 x 6, 2 x 8, 8 to 16 ft., S1S1E	$39 00
2 x 4, 2 x 6, 2 x 8, 10 ft., S1S1E	41 00
2 x 4, 2 x 6, 2 x 8, 12/16, S1S1E	36 00
2 x 4, 2 x 6, 2 x 8, 18/22, S1S1E	41 00
2 x 4, 2 x 6, 2 x 8, 24/32, S1S1E	43 00
2 x 10, 8 ft. to 16 ft., S1S1E	40 00
2 x 10, 10 ft. S1S1E	42 00
2 x 10, 18/22, S1S1E	42 00
2 x 10, 24/32, S1S1E	44 00
2 x 12, 8 ft. to 16 ft., S1S1E	41 50
2 x 12; 10, 18, 20	43 50
2 x 12; 24, 26, 28, 30, 32	45 50

B. C. COAST FIR

Dimension S1S and E.

2 x 4 in., 6 ft.	$39 50
2 x 4 in., 8, 12 and 14 ft.	40 50
2 x 4 in., 16 ft.	41 50
2 x 4 in., 18 and 20 ft.	42 50
2 x 4 in., 22 to 32 ft.	44 50
2 x 10 in., 8, 12 and 14 ft.	41 75
2 x 10 in., 16 ft.	42 75
2 x 10 in., 18 and 20 ft.	43 75
2 x 10 in., 22 to 32 ft.	45 75
2 x 12 in., 8 to 14 ft.	43 25
2 x 12 in., 16 ft.	44 25
2 x 12 in., 18 and 20 ft.	45 25
2 x 12 in., 22 to 32 ft.	47 25
3 x 3 and 3 x 4 in., 8 to 14 ft.	46 75
3 x 3 and 3 x 4 in., 16 ft.	47 75
3 x 3 and 3 x 4, 18 and 20 ft.	48 75
3 x 3 and 3 x 4 in., 22 to 32 ft.	50 75
4 x 6, 6 x 8, 8 x 8, 6 to 16 ft.	49 00
6 x 6, 6 x 8 and 8 x 8, 18 and 20 ft.	49 50
6 x 6, 6 x 8, 8 x 8, 22 to 32 ft.	50 50
Shingles, XXX B. C. Cedar, straight cars on 60c rate	6 96

BUFFALO & TONAWANDA

WHITE PINE

Wholesale Selling Price

Uppers, 4/4	$145 00
Uppers, 5/4 to 8/4	145 00
Uppers, 10/4 to 12/4	165 00
Selects 4/4	135 00
Selects 5/4 to 8/4	135 00
Selects 10/4 to 12/4	155
Fine Common 4/4	105
Fine Common 5/4	110
Fine Common 6/4	110
Fine Common 8/4	110
No. 1 Cuts 4/4	80
No. 1 Cuts 5/4	90
No. 1 Cuts 6/4	90
No. 1 Cuts 8/4	90
No. 2 Cuts 4/4	58
No. 2 Cuts 5/4	73
No. 2 Cuts 6/4	73
No. 2 Cuts 8/4	73
No. 3 Cuts 5/4	57
No. 3 Cuts 6/4	57
No. 3 Cuts 8/4	57
Dressing 5/4	67
Dressing 5/4 x 10	69
Dressing 5/4 x 12	74
No. 1 Moulding 5/4	73
No. 1 Moulding 6/4	95
No. 1 Moulding 8/4	95 00
No. 2 Moulding 5/4	79 00
No. 2 Moulding 6/4	79 00
No. 2 Moulding 8/4	79 00
No. 1 Barn 1 x 12	72 00
No. 1 Barn 1 x 6 and 8	
No. 1 Barn 1 x 10	
No. 2 Barn 1 x 6 and 8	
No. 2 Barn, 1 x 10	
No. 3 Barn 1 x 6 and 8	
No. 3 Barn 1 x 10	
Box 1 x 6 and up	
Box 1 x 10	64 00
Box 1 x 12	44 00
Box 1 x 12	49 00
Box 1 x 13 and up	49 00

The following quotations on hardwoods represent the jobber buying price at Buffalo and Tonawanda.

	1s & 2s	No. 1 Com.	No. 2 Com.
MAPLE			
4/4	52-57	39-41	28-30
5/4 to 8/4	68-70	46-48	33-35
10/4 to 16/4	78-80	58-60	37-39
RED BIRCH			
4/4	74-76	48-50	33-35
5/4 to 8/4	77-79	57-59	40-42
SAP BIRCH			
4/4	70-74	48-50	33-35
5/4 and up	75-78	51-53	36-38
SOFT ELM			
4/4	59-61	44-46	35-37
5, 6 & 8/4	63-64	37-49	36-38
BASSWOOD			
4/4	64-66	54-56	40-42
Thicker	63-71	52-50	41-44
PLAIN OAK			
4/4	76-81	53-57	36-38
5/4 to 8/4	82-86	58-62	41-43
ASH, WHITE AND BROWN			
4/4	77-79	47-51	35-38
5/4 to 8/4	83-87	55-57	39-41
10/4 and up	110-112	70-73	40-42

BOSTON, MASS.

Quotations given below are for highest grades of Michigan and Canadian white pine and Eastern Canadian Spruce as required in the New England market in carloads.

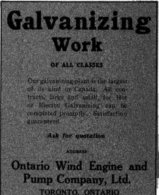

White pine uppers, 1 in.		$140 00
White pine uppers, 1¼, 2 in.		145 00
White pine uppers, 2½, 3 in.		155 00
White pine uppers, 4 in.		100 00
Selects, 1 in.		135 00
Selects, 1¼, 2 in.		138 00
Selects, 2½, 3 in.		145 00
Selects, 4 in.		155 00
Fine common, 1 in., 30 per cent. 12 in. and up		106 00
Fine common, 1 x 8 and up		109 00
Fine common, 1¼ to 2 in.		116 00
Fine common, 2½ and 3 in.		125 00
Fine Common, 4 in.		146 00
1 in. shaky clear		72 00
1¼ to 2 in. shaky clear		75 00
1 in. No. 2 dressing		64 00
1¼ to 2 in. No. 2 dressing		68 00
No. 1 Cuts, 1 in.		80 00
No. 1 Cuts, 1¼ to 2 in.	85 00	87 00
No. 1 Cuts, 2½ and 3 in.		115 00
No. 2 Cuts, 1 in.		69 00
No. 2 Cuts, 1¼ to 2 in.	70 00	71 00

Barn Boards, No. 1, 1 x 12	77 00
No. 1, 1 x 10	72 00
No. 1, 1 x 8	70 00
No. 2, 1 x 12	70 00
No. 2, 1 x 10	[illegible]
No. 2, 1 x 8	[illegible]
No. 3, 1 x 12	[illegible]
No. 3, 1 x 10	60 00
No. 3, 1 x 8	57 00

No. 1 Clear

Can. spruce, No. 1 and clear, 1 x 4 to 9 in.	[illegible]
1 x 10 in.	70 00
No. 1, 1 x 4 to 7 in.	[illegible]
No. 1, 1 x 8 & 9 in.	[illegible]
No. 1, 1 x 10 in.	70 00
No. 2, 1 x 4 & 5 in.	47 00
No. 2, 1 x 6 & 7 in.	[illegible]
No. 2, 1 x 8 & 9 in.	[illegible]
No. 2, 1 x 10 in.	[illegible]
No. 2, 1 x 12 in.	[illegible]

Spruce, 12 in. dimension		60
Spruce, 10 in. dimension		57
Spruce, 9 in. dimension		[illegible]
Spruce, 8 in. dimension		[illegible]
2 x 10 in. random lengths, 8 ft. and up		51
2 x 12 in., random lengths		53
2 x 3, 2 x 4, 2 x 5, 2 x 6, 2 x 7	48 00	50 00
3 x 4 and 4 x 4 in.	48 00	50 00
2 x 8 in.		51 00
All other random lengths, 7-in. and under, 8 ft. and up		60 00
5-inch and up merchantable boards, 8 ft. and up, p 1s		
1 x 2		
1 x 3		
1-⅝ in. spruce lath		
1-½ in. spruce lath		

New Brunswick Cedar Shingles

Extras		[illegible]
Clears		[illegible]
Second Clears	[illegible]	[illegible]
Clear Whites	[illegible]	[illegible]
Extra 1s (Clear whites in)		[illegible]
Extra 1s (Clear whites out)		[illegible]
Red Cedar Extras, 16-in. 5 butts to 2-in.		7 00
Red Cedar Eurekas, 18-inch, 5 butts to 2-in.		10 00
Red Cedar Perfections, 5 butts to 2¼		12 00
Washington 16-in. 5 butts to 2 in. extra red cedar		7 00

ALPHABETICAL INDEX TO ADVERTISERS

FIRE BRICK

We make several brands of fire brick made by every known process of manufacture from a selection of various high grade Pennsylvania clays. This enables us to furnish the best adapted fire brick for your boilers, dutch ovens, refuse burners, kilns, etc.

We specialize in fire brick for power plants and if you will advise us whether your boilers are hand fired or stoker fired and kind of fuel used we can then give you the proper brick for your work.

We carry a large stock of our different brands in various sizes and shapes in our Hamilton warehouse, which enables us to ship at once.

We manufacture the following well-known brands:

"Elkco Special," "Elk Steel," "St. Marys," "Keystone" and "Rotex"

Write for copy of our catalogue, "Refractory Efficiency Engineering."

Elk Fire Brick Co. of Canada, Ltd.

HIGH GRADE FIRE BRICK and CLAY

Sun Life Bldg., Hamilton, Canada

Representatives for Maritime Provinces:
RHODES, CURRY COMPANY, LTD., Head Office, AMHERST, N. S.
Branches at Halifax, Sydney and New Glasgow, N.S.

DIXIE DRAG SAW

A 4 H. P. Portable Single Cylinder 2 Cycle, Gasoline Rig, upon skids. Weight, [illegible] Lbs. Makes [illegible] strokes per minute. Cuts Logs 8" to [illegible] Diameter.

Easily started and moved. Runs as smoothly as the Liberty Motor.

The Solution of the present and future **Fuel, Labor and Car Shortage.**

Economical of fuel and never grows weary.

Saves Labor. May be taken to the Forest for cutting Logs, Fuel and Short Bolts for Stave, Heading, Shingle Bolts, Handle, Charcoal and Alcohol Wood.

When not required for sawing, Dixie Engine may be used for driving Pumps, Dynamos, Churn, Feed Cutters, Mixer, etc.

Price $225.00

Extra 5 ft. or 6 ft. Saws, each $12.00
Extra 6½ ft. or 7 ft. Saws, each $14.00

F. O. B. Cleveland

Manufactured By

The Peter Gerlach Company

Cooperage Machinery and Saw Makers

Established 1854 CLEVELAND, OHIO, U.S.A.

Exhaust Systems

We design and install complete Exhaust Systems for planing and other woodworking plants. Some of the largest mills in the country have been equipped by us.

Send us your enquiries

Geo. W. Reed & Co., Limited

MONTREAL

ASBESTOL REG. IN U.S. PAT. OFF. ASBESTOL REG. IN U.S. PAT. OFF.

His Hands are Clad in "ASBESTOL"

That's why he is smiling and happy. He knows that "ASBESTOL" will protect and guard his hands.

"ASBESTOL" Gloves and Mittens are carefully and scientifically made. They look, fit and wear well.

Once you wear "ASBESTOL" Gloves you will never accept any other kind.

EISENDRATH GLOVE CO.

2001 Elston Ave., CHICAGO, ILL.

Prescott's Valve Controller
Patented June 8, 1918
The Machine You Have Been Waiting for.
To eliminate every trouble with your Steam Feed Valves install one of these machines.
Six Real Reasons for Doing So:
1—Gives the sawyer the easiest kind of control of valve.
2—Hand lever stays put, making them safe against any jerk or kick of valve.
3—Gives the sawyer every confidence in handling valve.
4—Will prevent accidents—is easier on the nerves and carriage runs steadier.
5—Water flowing into valves from foaming boilers does not fret the sawyer.
6—This relief from all troubles of which sawyers have complained enables them to give closer attention to the logs they are cutting and a better inspection of the lumber they produce.
Read what one of the largest lumber companies on the north shore has to say about it.
We are sole Canadian manufacturers of these mahcines.
Pamphlets with full description and prices on application.
Let us quote you also on our new "Hamilton" Vertical Steam Feed Valves.
WHAT IS IT?
PRESCOTT'S VALVE CONTROLLER
Waubaushene, Ont., Sept. 11, 1917.
Messrs. Wm. Hamilton Co.,
Peterborough, Ont.
Gentlemen:—
Replying to your inquiry re Prescott Valve Controller, which you sent us last spring to try out: I beg to say that we installed this machine early in April, just previous to starting the mills, selecting the most difficult valve we have to handle, the steam having to travel through nearly three hundred lineal feet of pipe to reach this valve, and noting the fact that the pipes are well covered, there is necessarily considerable condensation, and every sawyer knows the annoyance caused by water passing through the valves which violently jars or jerks the lever, sometimes wrenching it from the hand and thereby inflicting serious damage to the machinery of the mill. And now after nearly five months of daily use, I am pleased to tell you that this device has put up all that is claimed for it. There is not the slightest jar or vibration to be felt, no matter where the lever is held. It is very easily attached and does not interfere in any way with the free movement of the lever, and the Sawyer, Mr. George Botting, also our Foreman, Mr. W. A. Gill, both speak of your controller in the most glowing terms. I can, therefore, congratulate you on securing an article that will fill many a long felt want.
Yours truly,
(Signed) D. B. Anderson,
Chief Engineer,
The Georgian Bay Lumber Co., Ltd.
William Hamilton Co., Limited
Peterboro, Ontario
Agents: J. L. Neilson & Co., Winnipeg, Man.

CANADA LUMBERMAN BUYERS' DIRECTORY

The following regulations apply to all advertisers:—Eighth page, every issue, three headings; quarter page, six headings; half page, twelve headings; full page, twenty-four headings.

AIR CONDITIONING
Sturtevant Company, B. F.

ASBESTOS GOODS
Atlas Asbestos Company, Ltd.

AXES
Canadian Warren Axe & Tool Co.

BABBITT METAL
Canada Metal Company
General Supply Co. of Canada, Ltd.
United American Metals Corporation

Bale Ties
Laidlaw Bale Tie Company

BAND MILLS
Hamilton Company, William
Waterous Engine Works Company
Yates Machine Company, P. B.

BAND RESAWS
Mershon & Company, W. B.

BELT CEMENT
Graton & Knight Mfg. Company

BELT DRESSING
Atlas Asbestos Company, Ltd.
General Supply Co. of Canada, Ltd.
Graton & Knight Mfg. Company

BELTING
Atlas Asbestos Company, Ltd.
Beardmore Belting Company
Canadian Consolidated Rubber Co.
General Supply Company
Goodhue & Co., J. L.
Goodyear Tire & Rubber Co.
Graton & Knight Mfg. Company
Gutta Percha and Rubber Company
Main Belting Company
Manhattan Rubber Mfg. Co.
D. K. McLaren Limited
McLaren Belting Company, J. C.

BELTING (Transmission, Elevator, Conveyor, Rubber)
Dunlop Tire & Rubber Goods Co.

BLOWERS
Toronto Blower Company
Sturtevant Company, B. F.

BOILERS
Hamilton Company, William
Jenckes Machine Company
Marsh Engineering Works, Limited
Waterous Engine Works Company

BOILER PRESERVATIVE
International Chemical Company

BOX MACHINERY
Garlock-Walker Machinery Co.
Morgan Machine Company
Yates Machine Company, P. B.

BOX SHOOKS
Davison Lumber & Mfg. Company

BUNKS (Steel)
Alaska Bedding Co. of Montreal

CABLE CONVEYORS
Jeffrey Manufacturing Company
Jenckes Machine Company, Ltd.
Waterous Engine Works Company

CAMP SUPPLIES
Burns & Company, John
Canadian Milk Products Limited
Davies Company, William
Dr. Bell Veterinary Wonder Co.
Eckardt & Co.
Gunns Limited
Harris Abattoir Company
Johnson, A. H.
Turner & Sons, J. J.
Woods Manufacturing Company, Ltd.

CANT HOOKS
Canadian Warren Axe & Tool Co.
General Supply Co. of Canada, Ltd.
Pink Company, Thomas

CARS—STEEL BODY
Marsh Engineering Works, Limited

CAR WHEELS AND CASTINGS
Dominion Wheel & Foundries

CEDAR
Fesserton Timber Co.
Foss Lumber Company
Genoa Bay Lumber Company
Muir & Kirkpatrick
Long Lumber Company
Service Lumber Company
Terry & Gordon
Thurston-Flavelle Lumber Company
Vancouver Lumber Company
Victoria Lumber and Mfg. Co.

CHAINS
Canadian Link-Belt Company, Ltd.
General Supply Co. of Canada, Ltd.
Hamilton Company, William
Hobbs Company, Clinton E.
Jeffrey Manufacturing Company
Jenckes Machine Company, Ltd.
Pink & Co., Thomas
Waterous Engine Works Company
Williams Machinery Co., A. R. Vancouver

CHAIN HOISTS
Hobbs Company, Clinton E.

CHINA CLAY
Bowater & Sons, W. V.

CHEMICAL PLANTS
Blair, Campbell & McLean, Ltd.

CLOTHING
Acme Glove Works
Clarke & Company, A. R.
Grant, Holden & Graham
Woods Mfg. Company

COLLAR PADS
American Pad & Textile Co.

CONVEYOR MACHINERY
Canadian Link-Belt Company, Ltd.
Canadian Mathews Gravity Carrier Company
General Supply Co. of Canada, Ltd.
Jeffrey Mfg. Co.
Waterous Engine Works Company

CORDAGE
Consumers Cordage Company

CORN SYRUP
Canada Starch Company

COTTON GLOVES
American Pad & Textile Co.

COUPLING (Shaft)
Jenckes Machine Company, Ltd.

CRANES FOR SHIP YARDS
Canadian Link-Belt Company

CROSS ARMS
Genoa Bay Lumber Company

CUTTER HEADS
Shimer Cutter Head Company

CYPRESS
Chicago Lumber & Coal Company
Long Lumber Company
Wistar, Underhill & Nixon

DERRICKS AND DERRICK FITTINGS
Marsh Engineering Works, Limited

DOORS
Genoa Bay Lumber Company
Long Lumber Co.
Mason, Gordon & Co.
Rutherford & Sons, Wm.
Terry & Gordon

DRAG SAWS
Gerlach Company, Peter
Williams Machinery Co., A. R.

DRIVING BOOTS
Acme Glove Works

DRYERS
Philadelphia Textile Mach. Company

DRY KILNS
Sturtevant Company, B. F.

DUST COLLECTORS
Sturtevant Company, B. F.
Toronto Blower Company

EDGERS
William Hamilton Company, Ltd.
Garlock-Walker Machinery Co.
Green Company, G. Walter
Long Mfg. Company, E.
Waterous Engine Works Company

ELEVATING AND CONVEYING MACHINERY
Canadian Link-Belt Comptny, Ltd.
Jeffery Manufacturing Company
Jenckes Machine Company, Ltd.
Waterous Engine Works Company

ENGINES
Hamilton Company, William
Jenckes Machine Company
Waterous Engine Works, Company

EXCELSIOR MACHINERY
Elmira Machinery and Transmission Company

EXHAUST FANS
Garlock-Walker Machinery Co.
Sturtevant Company, B. F.
Reed & Company, Geo. W.
Toronto Blower Company

EXHAUST SYSTEMS
Reed & Company, Geo. W.
Sturtevant Company, B. F.
Toronto Blower Company

FILES
Disston & Sons, Henry
Simonds Canada Saw Company

FIR
Associated Mills, Limited
Allan-Stoltze Lumber Co.
British American Mills & Timber Co.
Coal Creek Lumber Company
Fesserton Timber Co.
Foss Lumber Company
Grier & Sons, Ltd., G. A.
Heeney, Percy E.
Knox Brothers
Long Lumber Company
Mason, Gordon & Co.
Reynolds Company, Limited
Service Lumber Company
Shearer Company, Jas.
Terry & Gordon
Timberland Lumber Company
Timms, Phillips & Co.
Vancouver Lumber Company
Victoria Lumber and Mfg. Co.
Weller, J. B.

FIRE BRICK
Beveridge Paper Company
Elk Fire Brick Company of Canada

FIRE FIGHTING APPARATUS
Dunlop Tire & Rubber Goods Co.
Pyrene Mfg. Company
Waterous Engine Works Company

FIR FLOORING
Genoa Bay Lumber Company
Rutherford & Sons, Wm.

FLAG STAFFS
Ontario Wind Engine Company

FLOORING (Oak)
Long-Bell Lumber Company

GALVANIZING
Ontario Wind Engine Company

GLOVES
Acme Glove Works
Eisendrath Glove Co.

GASOLINE ENGINES
Ontario Wind Engine Company

GEARS (Cut)
Smart-Turner Machine Co.

GRAIN
Dwyer Company, W. H.

GRAVITY LUMBER CARRIER
Can. Mathews Gravity Carrier Co.

GRINDERS (Bench)
Garlock-Walker Machinery Co.

HARDWOODS
Anderson Lumber Company, C. G.
Atlantic Lumber Co.
Bartram & Ball
Bennett Lumber Company
Blakeslee, Perrin & Darling
Cameron & Co.
Cardinal & Page
Cox, Long & Company
Davison Lumber & Mfg. Company
Dunfield & Company
Edwards & Co., W. C.
Fassett Lumber Company
Fesserton Timber Co.
Fraser Limited
Gall Lumber Company
Gillespie, James
Gloucester Lumber Company
Grier & Son, G. A.
Harris Lumber Co., Frank H
Heeney, Percy E.
Knox Brothers
Long Lumber Company
McLennan Lumber Company
Moores, Jr., E. J.
Pedwell Hardwod Lumber Co.
Powell-Myers Lumber Co.
Russell, Chas. H.
Spencer Limited, C. A.
Stearns & Culver Lumber Co.
Summers, James R.
Taylor Lumber Company, S. K.
Webster & Brother, James

HARDWOOD FLOORING MACHINERY
American Woodworking Machinery Company
Garlock-Walker Machinery Co.

HARDWOOD FLOORING
Grier & Son, G. A.
Long Lumber Company

HAY
Dwyer & Company, W. H.

1851 G&K
TRADE MARK REG. U.S. PAT. OFF.
More than a Catalog
This Catalog of G & K Standardized Series Leather Belting and Leather Products is practically a handbook of leather tannage and manufacture.
It is carefully compiled and indexed for easy reference to the products you want.
It contains mechanical rules, charts and tables that will help you with your transmission problems.
Belt users find this book invaluable. Write for a copy.
Canadian Graton & Knight, Limited, Montreal
Representatives in Canada:
THE CANADIAN FAIRBANKS-MORSE CO., LIMITED
St. John, Quebec, Montreal, Ottawa, Toronto, Hamilton, Vancouver, Victoria.
MADE IN CANADA
G&K

HARNESS
Padgitt Company, Tom

HEMLOCK
Anderson Lumber Company, C. G.
Bartram & Ball
Bourgouin, H.
Canadian General Lumber Company
Cane & Co., Jas. G.
Davison Lumber & Mfg. Company
Dunfield & Company
Edwards & Company, W. C.
Fesserton Timber Co.
Foss Lumber Company
Grier & Sons, Ltd., G. A.
Harris Lumber Co., Frank H
Hart & McDonagh
Hocken Lumber Company
Long Lumber Company
Mason, Gordon & Co.
Roch, Julien
Spencer Limited, C. A.
Terry & Gordon

HOISTING AND HAULING ENGINES
Garlock-Walker Machinery Co.
General Supply Co. of Canada, Ltd.
Marsh Engineering Works, Limited

HORSES
Union Stock Yards

HOSE
Dunlop Tire & Rubber Goods Co.
General Supply Co. of Canada, Ltd.
Goodyear Tire & Rubber Co.
Gutta Percha and Rubber Company

HUMIDIFIERS
Sturtevant Company, B. F.

INDUSTRIAL CARS
Marsh Engineering Works, Limited

INSURANCE
Hardy & Co., E. D.
Walton Company, Walter

INTERIOR FINISH
Eagle Lumber Company
Hay & Co.
Mason, Gordon & Co.
Renfrew Planing Mills
Terry & Gordon

KNIVES
Disston & Sons, Henry
Peter Hay Knife Company
Simonds Canada Saw Company
Waterous Engine Works Company

LARCH
Otis Staples Lumber Co.

LATH
Austin & Nicholson
Canadian General Lumber Company
Cane & Co., Jas. G.
Cardinal & Page
Dupuis Limited, J. P.
Eagle Lumber Company
Fraser Limited
Fraser-Bryson Lumber Company
Genoa Bay Lumber Company
Gloucester Lumber Company
Grier & Sons, Ltd., G. A.
Harris Tie & Timber Company, Ltd.
Long Lumber Company
McLennan Lumber Company
New Ontario Colonization Company
Otis Staples Lumber Co.
River Ouelle Pulp and Lumber Co.
Spencer Limited, C. A.
Terry & Gordon
Union Lumber Company
Victoria Harbor Lumber Company

LATH BOLTERS
Garlock-Walker Machinery Co.
General Supply Co. of Canada, Ltd.
Green Company, C. Walter

LIGHTING APPLIANCES
Hobbs Company, Clinton E.

LOCOMOTIVES
Bell Locomotive Works
General Supply Co. of Canada, Ltd.
Jeffrey Manufacturing Company
Jenckes Machine Company, Ltd.
Climax Manufacturing Company
Montreal Locomotive Works

LATH TWINE
Consumers' Cordage Company

LINK-BELT
Canadian Link-Belt Company
Canadian Mathews Gravity Carrier Company
Jeffrey Mfg. Co.
Williams Machinery Co., A. R., Vancouver

LOGGING COLLARS
Padgitt Company, Tom

LOCOMOTIVE CRANES
Canadian Link-Belt Company, Ltd.

LOGGING ENGINES
Dunbar Engine and Foundry Co.
Jenckes Machine Company
Marsh Engineering Works, Limited

LOG HAULER
Green Company, G. Walter
Jenckes Machine Company, Ltd.

LOGGING MACHINERY AND EQUIPMENT
General Supply Co. of Canada, Ltd.
Hamilton Company, William
Jenckes Machine Company, Ltd.
Marsh Engineering Works, Limited
Waterous Engine Works Company

LOG STAMPS
Superior Mfg. Company

LUMBER TRUCKS
Waterous Engine Works Company

LUMBERMEN'S CLOTHING
Woods Manufacturing Company, Ltd.

METAL REFINERS
Canada Metal Company
Hoyt Metal Company
Sessenwein Brothers

MILLING IN TRANSIT
Renfrew Planing Mills
Rutherford & Sons, Wm.

MOLDINGS
Genoa Bay Lumber Co.
Rutherford & Sons, Wm.

MOTOR TRUCKS
Duplex Truck Company

MOTORS
Sturtevant Company, B. F.

OAK
Chicago Lumber & Coal Company
Long-Bell Lumber Company

OAKUM
Stratford Oakum Co., Geo.

OIL CLOTHING
Leckie Limited, John

OIL ENGINES
Swedish Steel & Importing Co.

OLD IRON AND BRASS
Sessenwein Brothers

OVERALLS
Hamilton Carhartt Cotton Mills

PAPER
Bowater & Sons, W. V.

PACKING
Atlas Asbestos Company, Ltd.
Consumers Cordage Co.
Dunlop Tire & Rubber Goods Co.
Gutta Percha and Rubber Company

PAPER MILL MACHINERY
Bowater & Sons, W. V.

PINE
Anderson Lumber Company, C. G.
Atlantic Lumber Co.
Austin & Nicholson
Bourgouin, H.
Cameron & Co.
Canadian General Lumber Company
Cane & Co., Jas. G.
Cardinal & Page
Chicago Lumber & Coal Company
Cleveland-Sarnia Sawmills Company
Colonial Lumber Company
Cox, Long & Company
Davison Lumber & Mfg. Co.
Dudley, Arthur N.
Dunfield & Company
Eagle Lumber Company
Edwards & Co., W. C.

SPECIAL BELTS

Head Office and Factory
351 St. James St.
Montreal

ST. JOHN, N.B. 90 Germain St.

TORONTO, ONT. 194 King St. W.

VANCOUVER, B. C. 849 Beatty St.

Excelsior Lumber Company
Fesserton Timber Company
Fraser-Bryson Lumber Company
Fraser Limited
Gillies Brothers Limited
Gloucester Lumber Company
Gordon & Co., George
Grier & Sons, Ltd., G. A.
Harris Lumber Co., Frank H
Harris Tie & Timber Company, Ltd.
Hart & McDonagh
Hettler Lumber Company, Herman H.
Hocken Lumber Company
Lloyd, W. Y.
Long-Bell Lumber Company
Long Lumber Company
Mason, Gordon & Co.
McLennan Lumber Company
Montreal Lumber Company
Moores, Jr., E. J.
Muir & Kirkpatrick
Otis Staples Lumber Co.
Parry Sound Lumber Company
Roch, Julien
Russell, Chas. H.
Shearer Company, Pas.
Spencer Limited, C. A.
Summers, James R.
Terry & Gordon
Union Lumber Company
Watson & Todd, Limited
Williams Lumber Company
Wuichet, Louis

PLANING MILL EXHAUSTERS
Garlock-Walker Machinery Co.
Reed & Company, Geo. W.
Toronto Blower Co.

PLANING MILL MACHINERY
American Woodworking Machinery Company
Garlock-Walker Machinery Co.
Mershon & Company, W. B.
Toronto Blower Co.
Yates Machine Company, P. B.

PORK PACKERS
Davies Company, William
Gunns Limited
Harris Abattoir Company

POSTS AND POLES
Auger & Company
Canadian Tie & Lumber Co.
Dupuis Limited, J. P.
Eagle Lumber Company
Harris Tie & Timber Company, Ltd.
Long-Bell Lumber Company
Long Lumber Company
Mason, Gordon & Co.
Terry & Gordon

PULLEYS AND SHAFTING
Canadian Link-Belt Company
Garlock-Walker Machinery Co.
General Supply Co. of Canada, Ltd.
Green Company, G. Walter
Hamilton Company, William
Jeffrey Mfg. Co.
Jenckes Machine Company, Ltd.

PULP MILL MACHINERY
Canadian Link-Belt Company, Ltd.
Hamilton Company, William
Jeffrey Manufacturing Company
Jenckes Machine Company, Ltd.
Waterous Engine Works Company

PUMPS
General Supply Co. of Canada, Ltd.
Hamilton Company, William
Jenckes Machine Company, Ltd.
Smart-Turner Machine Company
Waterous Engine Company

RAILS
Gartshore, John J.
Sessenwein Bros.

ROOFING
Reed & Company, Geo. W.

ROOFINGS
(Rubber, Plastic and Liquid)
International Chemical Company

ROPE
Consumers Cordage Co.
Leckie, Limited, John

RUBBER GOODS
Atlas Asbestos Company
Dunlop Tire & Rubber Goods Co.
Goodyear Tire and Rubber Co.
Gutta Percha & Rubber Company

SASH
Genoa Bay Lumber Company
Renfrew Planing Mills

SAWS
Atkins & Company, E. C.
Disston & Sons, Henry
General Supply Co. of Canada, Ltd.
Gerlach Company, Peter
Green Company, G. Walter
Hoe & Company, R.
Shurly Co., Ltd., T. F.
Shurly-Dietrich Company
Simonds Canada Saw Company

SAW MILL LINK-BELT
Williams Machinery Co., A. R., Vancouver

SAW MILL MACHINERY
Canadian Link-Belt Comptny, Ltd.
Dunbar Engine & Foundry Co.
Firstbrook Bros.
General Supply Co. of Canada, Ltd.
Hamilton Company, William
Huther Bros. Saw Mfg. Company
Jeffrey Manufacturing Company
Long Manufacturing Company, E.
Mershon & Company, W. B.
Parry Sound Lumber Company
Payete Company, P.
Waterous Engine Works Company
Yates Machine Co., P. B.

SHEATHINGS
Goodyear Tire & Rubber Co.

SHINGLE MACHINES
Marsh Engineering Works, Limited

SAW SHARPENERS
Garlock-Walker Machinery Co.
Waterous Engine Works Company

SAW SLASHERS
Waterous Engine Works Company

SAWMILL LINK-BELT
Canadian Link-Belt Company

SHEET METALS
United American Metals Corp'n.

SHINGLES
Allan-Stoltze Lumber Co.
Associated Mills, Limited
Campbell-MacLaurin Lumber Co.
Cardinal & Page
Dominion Lumber & Timber Co.
Eagle Lumber Company
Foss Lumber Company
Fraser Limited
Genoa Bay Lumber Company
Gillespie, James
Gloucester Lumber Company
Grier & Sons, Limited, G. A.
Harris Lumber Co., Frank H
Harris Tie & Timber Company, Ltd.
Heeney, Percy E.
Long Lumber Company
Mason, Gordon & Co.
McLennan Lumber Company
Miller Company, Ltd., W. H.
Reynolds Company, Limited
Service Lumber Company
Shingle Agency of B. C.
Terry & Gordon
Timms, Phillips & Co.
Vancouver Lumber Company
Victoria Lumber and Mfg. Co.

SHINGLE & LATH MACHINERY
Dunbar Engine and Foundry Co.
Garlock-Walker Machinery Co.
Green Company, C. Walter
Hamilton Company, William
Long Manufacturing Company, E.
Payette Company, P.

SHOEPACKS
Acme Glove Works

SILENT CHAIN DRIVES
Canadian Link-Belt Company, Ltd.

SILOS
Ontario Wind Engine Company

SLEEPING ROBES
Woods Mfg. Company, Limited

SLEIGHS
Bateman-Wilkinson Company

SMOKESTACKS
Marsh Enginering Works, Limited
Waterous Engine Works Company

SNOW PLOWS
Bateman-Wilkinson Company
Pink Company, Thomas

SPARK ARRESTORS
Jenckes Machine Company, Ltd.
Reed & Company, Geo. W.
Waterous Engine Works Company

SPRUCE
Bartram & Ball
Bourgouin, H.
Cane & Co., Jas. G.
Cardinal & Page
Cox, Long & Company
Davison Lumber & Mfg. Company
Donogh & Co., John
Dudley, Arthur N.
Dunfield & Company
Exchange Lumber Company
Foss Lumber Company
Fraser Limited
Fraser-Bryson Lumber Company
Gillies Brothers
Gloucester Lumber Company
Grant & Campbell
Grier & Sons, Ltd., G. A.
Harris Lumber Co., Frank H
Hart & McDonagh
Lloyd, W. Y.
Hocken Lumber Company
Long Lumber Company
Mason, Gordon & Co.
McLennan Lumber Company
Muir & Kirpatrick
New Ontario Colonization Company
River Ouelle Pulp and Lumber Co.
Roch, Julien
Russell, Chas. H.
Service Lumber Company
Shearer Company, Jas.
Snowball Co., J. B.
Spencer Limited, C. A.
Terry & Gordon
Rideau Lumber Company

STEEL CHAIN
Canadian Link-Belt Company, Ltd.
Jeffrey Manufacturing Company
Waterous Engine Works Company

STEEL PLATE CONSTRUCTION
Marsh Engineering Works, Limited

STEAM PLANT ACCESSORIES
Waterous Engine Works Company

STEEL BARRELS
Smart-Turner Machine Co.

STEEL DRUMS
Smart-Turner Machine Co.

STOVES
Burns & Company, John

SWEAT PADS
American Pad & Textile Co.

SULPHITE PULP CHIPS
Davison Lumber & Mfg. Company

TANKS
Ontario Wind Engine Company

TARPAULINS
Turner & Sons, J. J.
Woods Manufacturing Company, Ltd.

TAPS AND DIES
Pratt & Whitney Company

TENTS
Turner & Sons, J. J.
Woods Mfg. Company

TENTS, CLOTHING
Grant, Holden & Graham, Limited

TIES
Auger & Company
Austin & Nicholson
Canadian Tie & Lumber Co.
Harris Tie & Timber Company, Ltd.
Long Lumber Company
McLennan Lumber Company
Terry & Gordon

TIMBER BROKERS
Bradley, R. R.
Cant & Kemp
Farnworth & Jardine
Hunter, Herbert F.
Smith & Tyrer, Limited

TIMBER CRUISERS AND ESTIMATORS
Sewall, James W.

TIMBER LANDS
Department of Lands and Forests

TIME RECORDERS
International Business Machines Co.

TRACTORS
British War Mision

TRANSMISSION MACHINERY
Canadian Link-Belt Company, Ltd.
General Supply Co. of Canada, Ltd.
Jenckes Machine Company, Ltd.
Jeffrey Manufacturing Company
Waterous Engine Works Company

TRIMMERS
Garlock-Walker Machinery Co.
Green Company, C. Walter
Waterous Engine Works Company

TUGS
West & Peachey

TURBINES
Hamilton Company, William
Jenckes Machine Company, Ltd.

VALVES
Bay City Foundry & Machine Co.

VENEERS
Webster & Brother, James

VENEER DRYERS
Coe Manufacturing Company
Philadelphia Textile Mach. Co.

VENEER MACHINERY
Coe Machinery Company
Garlock-Walker Machinery Co.
Philadelphia Textile Machinery Co.

VETERINARY REMEDIES
Dr. Bell Veterinary Wonder Co.
Johnson, A. H.

WATER HEATERS
Mason Regulator & Engineering Co.

WATER WHEELS
Hamilton Company, William
Jenckes Machine Company, Ltd.

WIRE
Laidlaw Bale Tie Company

WIRE ROPE
Canada Wire & Cable Co.

WOODWORKING MACHINERY
American Woodworking Machy. Co.
Garlock-Walker Machinery Co.
General Supply Co. of Canada, Ltd.
Jeffrey Manufacturing Company
Long Manufacturing Company, E.
Mershon & Company, W. B.
Waterous Engine Works Company
Yates Machine Company, P. B.

WOOD PRESERVATIVES
International Chemical Company

WOOD PULP
Austin & Nicholson
New Ontario Colonization Co.
River Ouelle Pulp and Lumber Co.

We have an
Edger to suit
Your Mill
32" Edger
36" Edger
Heavy Duty Edger built from 48" to 84" between frames
The E. Long Manufacturing Co., Limited
Orillia Canada
Robert Hamilton & Co., Vancouver,
Gorman, Clancey & Grindley, Ltd., Calgary & Edmonton
A. R. Williams Machy. Co. of Winnipeg Ltd., Winnipeg
Williams and Wilson, Ltd., Montreal.

Pink's Lumbering Tools

The Standard Tools in every province of the Dominion, New Zealand, Australia, etc.
We manufacture all kinds of lumber tools. Light and Durable.

Long Distance Phone, No. 87

Send for Catalogue and Price List.

Sold throughout the Dominion by all Wholesale and Retail Hardware Merchants.

MADE IN CANADA

It's a Pink anyway, you take it, and it's the best Peavey made.

The Thomas Pink Company, Limited

Manufacturers of Lumber Tools

PEMBROKE . . . . ONTARIO

Not altogether what we say, but what users say

"We have used the Alligator or Warping Tug manufactured by you for the last 7 or 8 years, and consider them indispensable to lumbermen on waters of French River or similar streams."

Will move a bag containing 60,000 logs, in calm weather, 30,000 in a head wind.

West & Peachey - Simcoe, Ont.

Montreal Toronto Winnipeg

The J. C. McLaren Belting Co.

Limited

General Mill Supplies MONTREAL

McKinnon Columbus Chain

LIMITED · ST. CATHARINES ONT.

Electric Welded and Fire Welded Chains – All kinds – All sizes

Coil Chain (All Sizes) Loading Chain

Logging Chain Boom Chain

Conveyor or Log Haul up Chain

Vol. 39 Toronto, December 15, 1919 No. 24

Canada Lumberman & Wood Worker

Alphabetical Index to Advertisers, Page 66 Classified Directory to Advertisements, Page 80

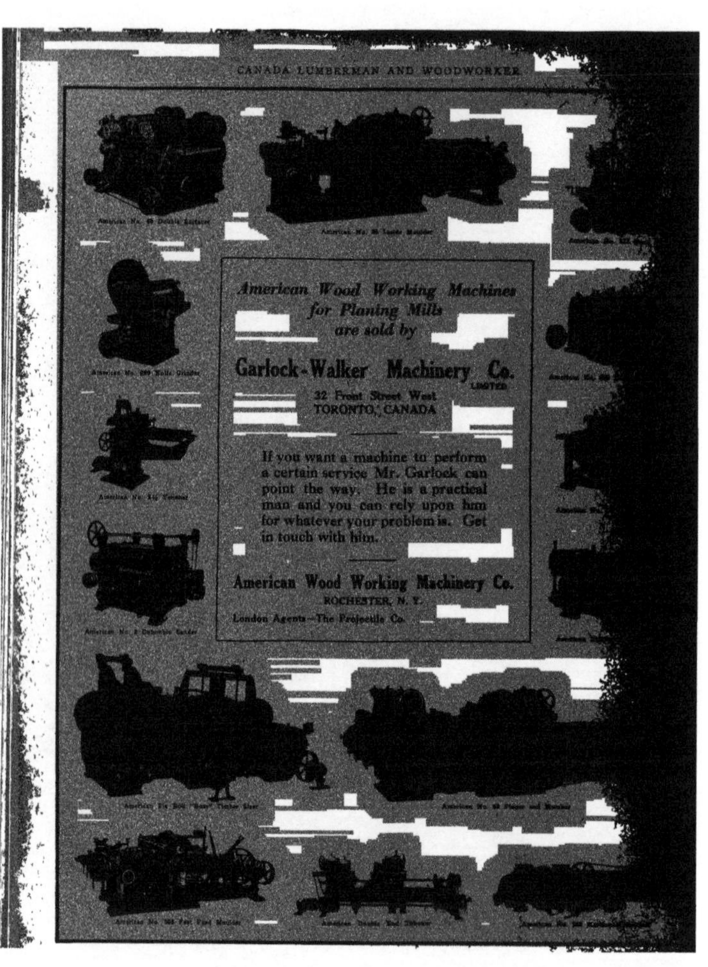
American Wood Working Machines
for Planing Mills
are sold by
Garlock-Walker Machinery Co.
LIMITED
32 Front Street West
TORONTO, CANADA
If you want a machine to perform a certain service Mr. Garlock can point the way. He is a practical man and you can rely upon him for whatever your problem is. Get in touch with him.
American Wood Working Machinery Co.
ROCHESTER, N. Y.
London Agents—The Projectile Co.

View of our Fir Mill from log pond, Vancouver, B.C.

CHRISTMAS
GREETINGS
QUALITY T&G BRAND SERVICE
AS the old year draws to a close, we wish to thank our good friends for their patronage. We hope you may all have a very Merry Christmas, and that your New Year holds untold prosperity, happiness and good fortune.
TERRY & GORDON
Head Office
703 CONFEDERATION LIFE BUILDING,
CABLE ADDRESS "TERIGORD"
TORONTO
ONT.
Vancouver Office—
513 Metropolitan Building.
A. S. Nicholson, Mgr.
Export Agents—
SPENCER, LOCK & CO.,
27 Clements Lane,
London, E.C., 4
Cable Address "Woodfeller"
Representatives in Ontario of
The British Columbia Mills Lumber & Trading Co,
of Vancouver, B.C., Canada

JOHN McKERGOW, President — W. K. GRAFFTEY, Managing-Director

The Montreal Lumber Co. Limited

Wholesale Lumber

Ottawa Office: 46 Elgin St. — Montreal Office: 759 Notre Dame St., W

H. CARDINAL — O. PAGE

Cardinal & Page

180 St. James St.
Montreal, Canada.

Wholesale Dealers and Exporters of All Kinds of

FOREST PRODUCTS

Cable Address "Carpage"

Lake Lumber Co. Ltd.

Manufacturers of

Fir, Cedar, Hemlock, Spruce

QUALICUM QUALITY LUMBER

Rough Fir Timbers

Any size up to 60 feet long

Select Grades a Specialty

FIR PIPE and TANK STOCK

Market wanted for Rough Cedar Timbers
Inquire for prices

Office and Mills:
Qualicum Beach, V. I., B. C.

WE ARE BUYERS OF

Hardwood Lumber
Handles
Staves Hoops
Headings

James WEBSTER & Bro.
Limited

Bootle, Liverpool, England

London Office
Dashwood House 9 New Broad St. E. C.

SPECIALTIES

Sawed Hemlock
Red Cedar Shingles
White Pine Lath
Bass and Poplar Siding

James Gillespie

Pine and Hardwood

Lumber

Lath and Shingles

North Tonawanda, N. Y.

LUMBER

WANTED

ONTARIO HARDWOOD CUTS

ADVANCES MADE DURING OPERATIONS

C. G. Anderson Lumber Company, Limited

Manufacturers and Strictly Wholesale Dealers in Lumber

SALES OFFICE

705 Excelsior Life Building
Toronto

FOR SALE

100M 1" x 3"—6 ft. and up cull boards

130M 1" x 4" and up, 6 ft. and up cull boards

50M 2" x 3" and up culls

1000M 3" Merchantable Hemlock

100M 2" " "

125M 1" " "

With our resawing and planing plant, we are prepared to manufacture any of this stock as may be required by buyers.

We also solicit enquiries for shingles in mixed Carloads. Extras, Clears, Second Clears and Clear Walls.

J. B. Snowball Company
Limited

Chatham, - - New Brunswick

Our NEW TIMBER MILL

(Capacity 100,000 Feet Ten Hours.) NOW IN OPERATION

We solicit your enquiries for

Heavy Construction Material and Yard Stock

ANY SIZE TIMBERS UP TO 100 FT.

Give us an opportunity to prove to you that we have earned a reputation for Quality and Service.

Timberland Lumber Co., Limited

Head Office: Westminster Trust Bldg., NEW WESTMINSTER, B. C.
Mills at South Westminster, on B.C.E.R.
Shipments by C.P.R., C.N.R., G.N.R., N.P.R., and C.M. & St. P. Ry.

British Columbia Red Cedar Shingl

ARROW BRAND

XXX 6/2, Sixteen Inch All
All Vertical Grain XXX

White Pin

Cedar Spruce Heml
Douglas Fir

Manufacturers and Wholesalers

Eastern Representative:
R. G. CHESBRO, 1304 Bank of Hamilton Bldg.
TORONTO, ONT.

Ruskin, Eburne, Nakusp, Summit, Vancouver

ALLEN-STOLTZE LUMBER CO., LTD.

Vancouver, British Columbia

Frank H. Harris Lumber Company, Limited

Manufacturers and Wholesalers of

Yellow Pine and Southern Hardwoods

Yellow Pine in Transit at all Times

Mills: { High Point, Miss. / Lake, Miss.

Office: 814 Excelsior Life Building, TORONTO, Canada.

"Horseshoe" Brand Red Cedar Shingles

Old Growth Fir Logs at Port Moody

Fir Timbers Our Specialty

"IT CAN'T BE DONE"—

You can't build a house on sandstone, neither can you make Quality Lumber out of poor logs. We are able through our own manufacturing facilities to offer the Eastern market the best in B.C. forest products. Send us your enquiries.

REYNOLDS COMPANY LIMITED

General Offices: VANCOUVER, B.C.

SERVICE

Fir, Cedar and Spruce

LUMBER

"Service" Lumber Co.

Pacific Building, VANCOUVER, B.C.

Eastern Representative: A. W. BARNHILL, 20 St. James Street, Montreal.

Ontario Representative: A. E. MASURET, Canada Permanent Bldg., 18 Toronto St., Toronto. Telephone Main 3533

QUICK ACTION

Can be assured if you will let the CANADA LUMBERMAN "Wanted and For Sale" department take care of your miscellaneous business needs.

We receive constant testimony from advertisers as to the value they have received from this far-reaching and inexpensive method of publicity in the lumber trade and allied industries.

Try these columns. The result will surprise you.

CANADA LUMBERMAN

and WOODWORKER

347 Adelaide St. West - - - TORONTO

A Wish—
"May you 'Hew to the Line' during 1920, and your endeavours prove 'all clears.'"

Douglas Fir
Construction Timbers
Dimension Lumber
Flooring
Ceiling

Cedar
Red Cedar Shingle
Bevel Siding
Clear and Common Lumber

Uncertainties
—in most things
Certainty in One

"SERVICE"—Something promised but seldom given—the most common word in the lumber language and the most uncommon in the "getting"—that's uncertainty.

It has been our earnest endeavour during 1919 to render "SERVICE" in all our dealings. We will enter the New Year with the same ambition—that's a certainty.

TIMMS, PHILLIPS & CO.

Head Office: Yorkshire Building, VANCOUVER, B.C.

Canada Lumberman and Woodworker

For Forty Years Canada's National Journal

Issued on the 1st and 15th of every month by
HUGH C. MACLEAN, LIMITED, Publishers
THOS. S. YOUNG, Toronto, General Manager.

OFFICES AND BRANCHES:

TORONTO - - Telephone A. 2700 - - 347 Adelaide Street West
VANCOUVER - - Telephone Seymour 2013 - - Winch Building
MONTREAL - - Telephone Main 2299 - - 119 Board of Trade
WINNIPEG - Telephone Garry 856 - Electric Railway Chambers
NEW YORK - - - - - - - - - - - - 309 Broadway
CHICAGO - Telephone Harrison 5351 - 1413 Great Northern Building
LONDON, ENG. - - - - - - - 16 Regent Street, S. W.

TERMS OF SUBSCRIPTION
Canada, United States and Great Britain, $2.00 per year, in advance; other foreign countries embraced in the General Postal Union, $3.00.
Single copies 15 cents.

"The Canada Lumberman and Woodworker" is published in the interest of, and reaches regularly, persons engaged in the lumber, woodworking and allied industries in every part of Canada. It aims at giving full and timely information on all subjects touching these interests, and invites free discussion by its readers.

Advertisers will receive careful attention and liberal treatment. For manufacturing and supply firms wishing to bring their goods to the attention of owners and operators of saw and planing mills, woodworking factories, pulp mills, etc., "The Canada Lumberman and Woodworker" is undoubtedly the most direct and profitable advertising medium. Special attention is directed to the "Wanted" and "For Sale" advertisements.

Authorized by the Postmaster-General for Canada, for transmission as second-class matter.

Entered as second-class matter July 18th, 1914, at the Postoffice, at Buffalo, N. Y., under the Act of Congress of March 3rd, 1879.

Vol. 39 Toronto, December 15, 1919 No. 24

Lumber Operations of the Closing Year

The past year has been a rather remarkable one in the lumber industry of Canada and affords another illustration of the words of Scotland's famous bard that "the best laid schemes of mice and men gang aft aglee." Many were the predictions made at the commencement of 1919 regarding prospects, prices and production, and out of the myriad of prophecies, possibly not one has come true; in fact the average sawmill man and wholesale lumber dealer, as he sits back during the comparatively quiet days of December in his favorite office chair and, amid the haze of a quiet "pipe" reflects upon how matters have eventuated in comparison with the way he "doped them out" during the initial stages of 1919, shows that our ability to read the future by present conditions and past experiences is anything but reassuring.

It is not the intention to review conditions as they exist in the lumber trade—for these are well-known to every exponent of the industry—but when drifting toward the close of another twelve months, it may be interesting to ask some of the profound prognosticators if, in their expression of views on what would take place during 1919, they thought that shingles would go to their present high price; that lath would be almost as rare as radium and command relatively as high a figure; that mill stocks would be lower than ever known in the history of the trade; that abnormal demand would set in from the other side of the border; that British Columbia forest products would find a brisk requisition over the line; that the market would largely be an auction one; that hardwoods would jump from 50 per cent. to 100 per cent. in quotations; that hemlock and white pine would be used in abundance; that big decline in sterling exchange; that building operations would call for such large quantities of material, and that housing accommodation would be at a premium in every city and town.

Of course it was expected that there would be a pretty fair demand for lumber, but some of the foregoing features were never dreamed of. These are the days when nothing, no matter how colossal, in character, staggers the imagination. We have become used to the surprises, sharp turns, unexpected developments and unparallelled expansion and values. The future appears promising and the question of greatest urgency at the present moment is enlarged production, thrift and efficiency. In these the lumberman will play his part, but just how adequately he will be able to meet the requirements of forest products during next year, it is impossible to foretell.

Many Canadian firms set out this fall with the idea of doubling the quantity of their logging output, but so far, owing to the shortage of help and other drawbacks, have only been able to accomplish a little more than was in evidence at this particular period in 1918. With favorable winter weather and more men in the bush greater stocks of timber will be taken out, and there is no doubt that the demand will be considerably heavier than the production.

There is no sign in the offing that prices will descend. On the contrary it is believed that they will continue to strengthen until the housebuilding and other structural campaigns are further on the way to completion and depleted lumber stocks replenished. Instead of the higher value deterring persons from building, it seems to stimulate activity in many centres, and the rush for materials of all kinds continues. The observation of shrewd followers of the situation bears out the conviction that there is always more building going on in a rising market and when prices are highest than there is when a decline in value takes place. As long as the present healthy and active state of affairs prevails, there can be little doubt that 1920 will be a good one for the manufacturer, the wholesaler and the retailer.

Generally speaking the year just closing has been the most satisfactory one, in spite of the high prices, that the trade has enjoyed since the outbreak of the war, and the coming twelve months bid fair, even in the face of the chaos and clamor, which prevails in certain industrial quarters, to be equally as productive and gratifying in results.

The Expulsion of the Agitator

The labor situation does not seem to improve in many centres. Those who had hoped after the war was over there would be an abunance of men and more evidence of contentment, particularly as the wages paid are the largest ever known in the history of the lumber industry, have been sadly disappointed. While the numbers of laborers available are more numerous, there appears to be more clamor and turmoil in the ranks of the foreigner than ever.

Now the Bolshevist has made his appearance in the camps of the east and his coming may be regarded as a veritable plague. In many centres in the United States and in the West he has been dealt with summarily and sharply. Like a pestilence, this disease on the body politic is hard to suppress and effectively stamp out. The methods of the I. W. W., the Reds, the One Big Union,—call them whatever name you please—are insidious, and clandestine. They play upon the cupidity of the ignorant and the restless, and in the foreigner they have a fruitful ground for cultivation. Many of these, not knowing the language of our country, its institutions, laws and customs, will believe almost any tale that is told them, and then there is the ordinary riff-raff carried about by every breath of opinion or wave of sentiment.

The seeds of dangerous doctrine thus find fruitful soil in many an isolated lumber camp, making it especially difficult to grapple with the problem. In the East practically all the woods superintendents and foremen, clerks and cooks, scalers and teamsters are loyal and hardworking. They have no sympathy with the specious propaganda that is being put forward. The "come on" literature scattered by the Bolsheviki and the I.W.W. is as alluring in tone and deft in touch as any that was ever put out by a wild cat mining concern or a smooth oil well promoter. To read it one would think that the methods propounded were a panacea for all industrial ills, and that when brought into being the millenium was near at hand; that all lumbermen and loggers are tyrants, extortioners and oppressors—not to make use of harsher terms—that, under their direction, no man was given a square deal and the last pound of flesh demanded of all who enter their employ.

The majority of the big operators in lumber and logging in Canada today have come up through the ranks and have won their way to the front by industry, perseverance, energy and courage. The conditions under which they worked have been immeasurably improved, camp facilities, board, sleeping quarters,—everything around a bush operation—has been placed on a higher and better plane and has kept pace with the upward trend of the times and the enlightened advancement of the years.

The Dominion can do without the foreign agitator and the trouble-making alien. If a man is not prepared to become a good Canadian citizen, then his room is preferred to his presence. Law and order must prevail. Conditions similar to those existing in Russia and Mexico will not be tolerated in a progressive young country like Canada. More production is the need of the world today, not only in lumber line but in all other necessities of life, and the homely virtues of labor and thrift must be exercised to an unusual degree if an era of stringent times is to be warded off.

It may be asked what is Bolshevism, what does it stand for and what does it hope to accomplish? Here is what the "Gulf Coast Lumberman" has to say of the sect: The wording is strong and pointed and there is no searching for fine phrases or beautiful similies. Bolshevism is the antithesis of civilization. The Bolshevist is one who stinks for attention. Like the skunk, he has compelled even the noblest of the earth to notice him. From the top to the bottom, Bolshevism is composed chiefly of featherless buzzards, and moral hyenas. Its instincts are a cross between those of Jack-The-Ripper and Lucretia Borgia. Its idealism is that of the foul Harpies who consorted with Medusa. Its sensibilities rival those of the Yahoos whom Gulliver met. Its morality is just two shades darker than that of the South Sea Islander. Its idea of Heaven is a defenseless woman. Its chief God is a rape-fiend. Its coat-of-arms is a vulture, with outstretched wings. It was bred in darkness, conceived in iniquity, and born in the lower left-hand corner of Hell. Its final resting place will be its shameless birthplace. Let's speed the funeral.

Christmas Greeting with Peace & Plenty for the New Year

By the publishers and staff of the Canada Lumberman

A Vigorous Policy of Forestry

A progressive policy has been announced as one of the principal matters to which the new government of Ontario will first give its attention. Such was the statement made by Hon. E. C. Drury, the Premier, in addressing a recent meeting of the Canadian Club in Toronto. His remarks left no doubt in the minds of his hearers that he has thoroughly looked into the situation and will have definite plans to submit at the next session of the provincial legislature. Mr. Drury stated that the treatment of the forests in the past had been sadly neglected and in this oversight both political parties were equally to blame. The sense of the people is being enlightened and timber is now beginning to be appraised at its proper value.

No longer is the wooded wealth of Ontario and the other provinces being looked upon as inexhaustible and the patch of bush on a farm regarded as an "eyesore." The Premier added that logging methods had in the past been most extravagant and wasteful, that the slash had not been burned and only the best trees felled, with little thought given to a second growth and not much consideration to replanting, more particularly those lands which are unsuited for agricultural purposes. He intimated that the lumbermen would probably have to pay higher license fees in order that a more comprehensive and far-reaching policy of conservation and reproduction might be inaugurated. To gain first hand knowledge the Premier, accompanied by the Hon. Beniah Bowman, Minister of Lands and Forests, and others, has been making a tour of the north, visiting the leading towns and making inquiries generally which will doubtless lead to greater development and utilization of the natural resources of that district.

It is gratifying to learn that Ontario, which is known as the white pine province, will continue to husband her resources, and that the forestry policy of the province will be more aggressive and productive than it has been in the past, although splendid work was done during the last few years by Hon. G. Howard Ferguson, the late Minister of Lands, Fore nd Mines. He warmly co-operated with the interests of the lumbermen and instituted many reforms in fire protection and reforestation. Mr. Drury mentioned that a neighbor of his near Crown Hill in Simcoe County has recently sold an acre of hardwood bush for five hundred dollars, which, a few years ago, would not have been thought worth a tithe of this amount.

Ontario has suffered from too many forest fires in the past, and until recent years fire rangers, wardens and other appointments in the forest branch were made on a political basis, rather than on the ground of efficiency and merit. A post of fire ranger was looked upon as a sort of summer vacation, a chance for a life in the open and a general good time on the part of one fortunate enough to exercise the necessary influence to get on the "list." All this has now passed and the forestry administration is more business like, effective and ably managed. The regulations will be enforced impartially and more regard given to better logging methods and in seeing that the province is not denuded of its rich sylvan possessions. Cultivation will be more actively resorted to and greatly extended in the way of replanting the waste lands.

It is pleasing to record that good progress is being made with the timber survey of the province by Roland D. Craig, of the Commission of Conservation, and staff, and that the reconnaissance work is going steadily ahead. The license holders and lumbermen are lending every possible assistance and co-operation and, in this connection, Mr. Craig states that when the job is completed, there will be reasonably accurate information as to the actual timber situation. He adds that very extensive areas have been destroyed by fire. In the last issue of the "Canada Lumberman" views were presented showing the havoc that has been wrought in certain northern districts by the devouring element. It is said that, on the whole, the reproduction of coniferous species is far from satisfactory from the standpoint of sustained yields, but that, in many areas where fire has been kept out, excellent stands of red and white pine are coming up. Mr. Craig concludes a recent progress report on the work in hand by declaring that, in view of the progressive forest policy of the United Farmers of Ontario, he does not anticipate any change in the co-operative arrangement with the Ontario Government.

Canadian Lumbermen to Meet in Quebec City

Twelfth Annual Gathering Takes Place in Ancient Capital on February 4 and 5—Splendid Welcome Will be Accorded—Executive Gets Down to Business

The twelfth annual meeting of the Canadian Lumbermen's Association will take place in the city of Quebec on Wednesday and Thursday, February 4 and 5 next, and preparations for the great gathering of the industry are now under way.

It is probable that the sessions will be held in the Chateau Frontenac, which will be the headquarters of the Association, but if this arrangement is not possible the city hall will be available. Last February the assembly took place in St. John, N.B., where the visitors were royally entertained and extended every courtesy and hospitality. The pleasant associations of that convention will live long in the minds of the members, there being a most representative attendance from all parts of eastern and central Canada.

The Quebec delegates on that occasion extended a hearty invitation for the members to hold their 1920 meeting in Quebec and, it is expected, an equally warm welcome will be accorded the visitors in th Ancient Capital, which for many years has been a great timber and lumber exporting centre, possessing one of the finest shipping ports in the world. The geniality and open heartedness of the people of the quaint, picturesque and historic city is proverbial, and assurances have been received by the directors of the Canadian Lumbermen's Association that everything possible will be done to make the forthcoming conclave one of the greatest and most profitable annual reunions ever held by the lumber exponents of the Dominion.

Of the twenty-two directors of the Association six are from Quebec, including the President, W. Gerard Power. He is a live factor in the industry of that province, being at the head of the River Ouelle Pulp and Lumber Company, of St. Pacome, a busy centre on the Intercolonial Railway, seventy-five miles east of Quebec city. His company also operates mills at Crown Lake, Powerville and River Manie on the National Transcontinental Railway. The other directors from the province of Quebec are H. B. Powlika, Quebec; Geo. W. Grier, Montreal; David Champoux, Restigouche; W. T. Mason, Montreal, and Alex MacLaurin, Montreal.

Many Matters Before the Executive

At a meeting of the Executive of the Association held at the Windsor Hotel, Montreal, on December 2nd, there was a representative attendance. President W. Gerard Power was in the chair and among those present were Dan McLachlin, Arnprior, Ont., and Walter C. Laidlaw, Toronto (Vice-presidents of the Association), W. E. Bigwood, Toronto (former President), A. E. Clark, Toronto; E. R. Bremner, Ottawa; Walter M. Ross, Ottawa; Jas. G. Cane, Toronto; W. T. Mason, Montreal; W. J. Bell, Sudbury, Ont.; Duncan McLaren, Toronto; David Champoux, Restigouche, Que., and Frank Hawkins, Ottawa (Secretary).

The meeting was to determine certain particulars in connection with the coming annual meeting, which will be held in Quebec on Wednesday and Thursday, February 4th and 5th, 1920, and to make arrangements for the presentation of reports, etc.

Amongst other matters presented to the Directors was a communication from the Secretary of the Canadian Forestry Association with regard to placing the entire woods branch under the jurisdiction of the Provincial Forester, and operating members in Ontario have been circularized as follows by Frank Hawkins Secretary of the Canadian Lumbermen's Association:

> We are in receipt of a letter from the Secretary of the Canadian Forestry Association, advising that at the next session of the Ontario Legislature an effort is to be made to bring the entire Woods Branch under the jurisdiction of the Provincial Forestry, whereby the timber scalers would take the chief positions in the fire ranging service during the summer, and act as timber scalers at other times of the year. It is claimed that not only will considerable economy be obtained in this way but that political interference will be eliminated, and as it is proposed to appoint a Forestry Advisory Board consisting of two representatives of limit holders and three representatives of the Government more efficient service can be rendered.
>
> As an Association we have been asked by the Secretary of the Canadian Forestry Association to support them in this matter, but before doing so shall be glad to have your opinion as to the practical value to the trade which such a change would involve.

Some Statistics of Trade Activity

Recent increases in freight rates on lumber in the Ottawa territory were discussed, together with complaints from two of the members with regard to the non-existence of through rates from shipping points on one line of railway to points of destination on another. The matter is to receive the attention of the Transportation Committee.

It was also decided to get out another pamphlet showing the different species of lumber with the name of those who deal in same.

With regard to procuring information as to the aggregate cut of lumber, shipments, and stock on hand during 1919, a new plan was submitted whereby it is hoped that this information will be available shortly after the end of the year.

Clause 88 of the Bank Act is to be reported at the annual meeting by the special committee appointed for this purpose.

A report on the Employment Service of Canada will also be made to the members at the annual meeting.

The Association is in receipt of advice that there will be a British Empire Timber Exhibition held in London, England, from July 5th to 17th, 1920.

The recent deaths of Mr. John Donogh, of Toronto, also of Mrs. MacLaurin, the wife of Mr. Alex. MacLaurin, of Montreal, a former president of this Association, and Mr. G. Harry Askwith, who was connected with the Riordon

Panoramic view of Quebec, the convention city of the Canadian Lumbermen's Association

Pulp & Paper Co., were referred to, and the Secretary instructed to write letters to the immediate relatives, expressing the deep sorrow and sympathy of the Directors.

A communication from Mr. Louis A. Cadieux, 17 Boulevard des Capucines, Paris, France, together with a catalogue and price list of same was presented, but no action was taken as the sizes mentioned therein are all in metrical lengths and do not admit of Canadian lumber being used economically for this trade.

The President and Secretary were deputed to make definite arrangements for the formation of committees, etc., in connection with the annual meeting and banquet, and further announcements will be made in this regard at a later date.

Australian Hardwoods for Canadian Sofiwoods

"The Canadian Trade Commissioner is getting busy with regard to the export of Canadian timbers to Australia," says "Building," which is published in Sydney, Australia.

"It is really no use lamenting the fact that Australia cannot provide timber for her wants, and the trade should therefore be given every encouragement. It has been mentioned that Australia is rich in splendid hardwoods, and it would seem that reciprocation in the matter of timber supply is what is really needed, and no one should complain if Australia could provide hardwood equivalent in price for Canada's softwoods. Visiting the latter country it is really lamentable to see the misuse of soft pines. Jetties, railway bridges and sleepers, and all sorts of construction are put in, only to be replaced in a few years, and expedients have to be adpted to compensate for the softness of the timber used; for instance, in railway practice it is found necessary to use tie plates under the rails to prevent the dogspikes from opening out and causing disaster. There is therefore a wonderful opportunity for the exportation of our hardwoods to be developed as reciprocation of softwood imports. Some idea of the value of the latter can be obtained when it is stated that in the year 1913, roughly 200,000,000 feet were imported into New South Wales from Canada, valued at over £1,000,000, and although the quantity of imports has not been maintained during the war, it is likely to be much exceeded in the coming year; for instance; 500,000 doors are estimated to be required in connection with Government building enterprises, with 70,000,000 feet of flooring per annum.

"It therefore behooves Australian merchants and governments to drop the lamenting about our diminished Australian pine supply, to face the facts, and by every means possible to develop a reciprocal timber trade with our Empire brother—the Dominion."

Good Progress on N. B. Forest Surveys

The Forest Section of the department of Lands and Mines has covered a large area of the Crown lands of the province during the past summer in surveys for the purpose of classification. J. M. Gibson, chief of one of the forest survey parties, returned to Fredericton recently after spending nearly the entire summer on the Little South West Miramichi River, in charge of an eighteen-man cruising party. They cruised upwards of five hundred square miles of timber.

Samvel R. Weston, who was in charge of one of the parties for the department, has returned to the Capital. He ran 230 lineal miles of block lines between the timber lmits, establishing the l purposes of the forest survey. The lines are properly blazed and every quarter of a mile a post or tree is marked with block numbers and the number of chains to the corner, so that a cruiser or lumberman can easily locate himself. A new feature of the survey is the placing of location posts where portages cross the block lines, which makes is easier for a cruiser to locate himself on the map when travelling a portage.

Because of the close of navigation on the St. John river the Fraser Companies, Limited, ended the sawing season of the Victoria Mills in Fredericton last month. While figures were incomplete it was said that the season's cut at the mills amounted to fourteen million feet, and that approximately one million feet of logs are being carried over for next season. It was the intention of the company to cut fifteen million feet. The failure to do so is said to be due to the fact that the working day had been cut from ten to nine hours. Regarding 1920, it is understood that sufficient logs will be cut to keep these mills in full operation during the entire season of 1920.

James Gordon, aged sixty-two years, who belongs to Upper Gagetown, Queens County, N.B., was instantly killed while lumbering in the New Brunswick woods on November 21. He was employed in the woods at Shirley, Sunbury County, and was struck down by a falling tree.

A preliminary report on the lumber industry in Canada has just been completed by the Dominion Bureau of Statistics, Ottawa, covering the returns of 3,086 operating plants for the year 1918.

Capital Investment.—The total capital invested in the industry amounted to $180,017,178, of which logging and timber plants contributed $36,516,701, mill equipment $53,791,373, materials on hand, stocks in process, finished products and miscellaneous supplies $54,147,889, and cash, trading and operating accounts and bills receivable $35,561,215.

Employees' Salaries and Wages.—The number of persons employed on salaries was 3,550, of whom 3,270 were males and 280 females, and the total salaries paid were $4,911,735. The average number of persons working for wages totalled 56,816, of whom 26,736 were employed in operations in the woods and 30,080 in the mills. The total amount paid in wages was $44,490,917, apportioned as follows: woods operations $19,985,553, mills $24,505,364.

Materials, Fuel and Miscellaneous Expenses.—The total cost of these items was $68,498,520, the cost for each being respectively $45,335,526 for materials, $22,570,487 for miscellaneous expenses, and $592,506 for fuel.

Products.—The aggregate value of production for the year was $144,908,864, comprising the following principal items: sawn lumber $102,335,772, shingles $8,124,968, lath $1,560,136, pulpwood $18,416,438, and miscellaneous products, including cooperage stock, poles, cross ties, posts, veneer, etc., to the value of $14,481,550.

Lumber Cut by Kinds of Wood.—The principal kinds of lumber cut during the year were in order of the cut: Spruce 1,140,063 M. ft., white pine 783,482 M. ft., Douglas fir 707,373 M. ft., hemlock 255,356 M. ft., cedar 230,204 M. ft., red pine 99,780 M. ft., balsam fir 94,774, M. ft., and all other varieties, including custom sawn lumber, 618,426 M. ft.

Lumber Cut by Provinces

	Quantity M. Ft. B.M.	Value $
Alberta	22,388	473.694
British Columbia	1,141,197	
Manitoba	54,047	
New Brunswick	439,625	12,189,312
Nova Scotia	166,332	4,089,039
Ontario	1,182.328	
Prince Edward Island	6,393	
Quebec	841,084	
Saskatchewan	75,835	
Yukon	229	

Forest Production—Lumber, Lath, Shingles, Etc., 1918

Provinces	Number of Mills	Capital Invested	Employees on salaries No.	Employees on salaries Salaries	Employees on wages No.	Employees on wages Wages	Cost of miscellaneous supplies	Cost of materials and mill supplies	Value of product
CANADA	3,086	$180,017,178	3,550	$4,911,735	56,820	$44,490,917	$23,162,993	$45,335,527	$144,908,864
Alberta	36	468,534	21	20,760	240	174,177	86,491	101,197	490,572
British Columbia	193	42,186,291	738	1,393,697	13,161	13,536,101	4,891,407	15,443,795	39,041,394
Manitoba	31	2,381,239	41	67,739	917	641,338	353,730	189,768	1,316,792
New Brunswick	224	23,356,855	302	589,606	6,552	4,015,781	2,527,648	5,299,081	14,977,974
Nova Scotia	419	5,057,956	137	91,551	2,478	1,146,240	628,065	1,211,885	4,560,892
Ontario	874	44,846,939	967	1,375,708	16,421	13,090,402	7,093,518	9,941,129	41,852,896
P. E. Island	48	135,290	2	2,200	53	28,511	5,735	67,347	199,684
Quebec	1,247	57,201,820	1,205	1,289,593	15,711		7,111,035	12,771,414	40,199,895
Saskatchewan	13	2,149,109	46	78,461	1,283		463,764	308,079	2,258,450
Yukon	1	33,145	1	2,400	5	3,784	1,600	1,832	10,315

Trend of Lumber Prices and World Events

How Soon Will Canada and United States be Buying From Europe More Than the Countries of Europe Need From Us?

By Geo. H. Holt (Holt Timber Co.) Chicago, Ill.

The question of price absorbed the attention of lumbermen a few months ago. Wholesalers and retailers and line yard men were said to have hatched a conspiracy to keep out of the market and watch the price go down. A month ago they concluded it was time to buy but they very soon found that the hunger for lumber was face to face with famine, and lumber went to a premium, just as silver and pig iron have gone to a premium.

Where there is not enough of a commodity to supply the demand, the people who pay the price get the goods.

Not only has this become a sellers' market but it is a run-away market. The formula is:

"Have you got anything?

"I'll take it.

"What's the price?

"Make your own terms.

"How soon can you deliver it?"

Nobody should have been surprised or deceived. This is no time to make comparisons with former prices or former demands. Never before has the whole world devoted itself to five years of destruction of property and massed its industry to hasten that end.

The Appetite for Accumulated Property

Never before was there so little accumulated property and so vast an appetite for it.

Never before so many millions of people with easy money in their pockets and with an itch to spend it.

How long will it last? That doesn't matter now. At least it will last as long as the conditions last and as long as supply is below the level of demands, and the end of that day is not in sight.

How soon will the demand by foreign governments for loans to pay interest and loans to supply needs come to an end?

How soon will Canada and America be buying from Europe more than Europe needs from us? When will the needs of South America and Asia be supplied? There are others.

The building permits issued in the United States are three times larger than last year. Hardwood for interior finish and furniture and fittings and industry, have jumped so high that the Price List Committee at Chicago recently voted unanimously that the market is from ten to twenty-five dollars per M above last month's published list.

Hemlock lath sold in Chicago, by carload, at $15.00 last week. Pine men have just issued lists at $2.00 to $9.00 per M above previous lists and are not then at the top of the market.

The strike as a weapon to enforce arbitrary and unlimited demand, has slipped from the hands of the Labor Unions. Winnipeg, Man., Gary, Ill., Boston, Mass., and Beaumont, Tex., have shown how to meet that situation. The menace of a general strike no longer exists and the menace of the I.W.W. and the Bolsheviks in this hemisphere is scotched for a long time to come.

There will be a conflict and struggle between opposing interests, but they will be of limited scope, and will not endanger the existence of law and order and private property.

The "Own your own home" movement is not only good for the lumber business, but is good for the community and the state.

The Inter-dependence of Humanity

We are not rid of the self-seeker in society, in politics and in business, but more and more the world is becoming convinced of the inter-dependence of humanity and the workableness of the Law of Love. It is not yet the law of business or the law of the state, but it is tolerated as a working hypothesis, and that is a big advance.

Lincoln's words voice the temper of the new age:

"With malice toward none—With charity for all, with determination to do the right as God gives us to see the right."

Hearts and lips are not yet adjusted to proclaim it but the logic of events leaves no alternative short of chaos, and we cannot choose chaos.

Every considerable community unit ought to have a Housing Association and a Public Welfare Committee to embody and vitalize the principle of the group, as distinguished from the individual.

We know now that the individual is not the unit, that a class is not the unit, that the strong man is not the unit, but

George H. Holt, Chicago, Ill.

that the bundle of strong and weak, wise and simple, employer and employed, men and women and children, is the unit of ultimate consideration and that no individual or class, no matter how aggressive, may seize and permanently hold more than its share of anything.

The Ushering in of a New Era

The finances of the world are badly mussed up but not hopelessly.

Production and barter and intercourse will effect an adjustment that will operate and it will be something broader and better than it used to be.

We mourn and miss the lives that were sacrificed, but more lives have matured during the period of the war than were lost in the war. The world is not better off than it would have been without the war, but as to man-power and woman-power, it is stronger than it was, perhaps vastly stronger.—The training in mass-play will prove a tremendous advantage to the new era. Amplify for yourself the significance of

Demand (world wide)	The new spirit
Supply (limited)	The chastened temper
Buying power	The Will to Righteousness
Man-power	Do not these presage
Mass-play	Progress and
The larger vision	Order, and

A better world to live in? And incidentally, a high level of price for lumber?

With best Wishes for a Happy New Year.

Very cordially yours,

Geo. H. Holt.

Chicago, Ill.,
December 4, 1919.

Will Wooden Shingles be Sold by "Square?"

Proposed Plan Would Provide Simpler Basis of Computation, Eliminate "Short Count" and Comply with All Weights and Measures Laws

At a recent district meeting of lumber retailers held in Ontario the statement was made that farmers and others were buying wooden shingles more and more by the square—100 square feet, five inches to the weather—rather than by the thousand. The term "square" has become familiar to the buyer and the proposal has been put forth by the Shingle Branch of the West Coast Lumbermen's Association that from January 1st next it should be adopted. A letter was sent out lately by J. S. Williams, Secretary of the Shingle Branch of the Association, pointing out the advantage of disposing of shingles by this method and setting forth the simplicity, convenience and other advantages of the plan. It has been stated that the purchaser does not at the present time get a full count of one thousand shingles of certain dimensions but considerably less owing to inability to pack a thousand in the standard packages. It is also contended that if shingles were sold by the square the dealer would pay for the amount of roof covering he bought and not for the number of shingles.

Here is what Secretary Williams has to say on the subject:—

Selling shingles "by the square," in terms of good merchandizing, is selling shingles "on the square."

Ever since Red Cedar Shingles have been shipped out of the Northwest, misunderstandings have arisen as to the "count" or "measure" under which Cedar Shingles are sold. Complaints usually originate with those unacquainted with shingle packing practices ,but this does not lessen the feeling on complainant's part that he has been given "short count."

Legal controversy over the unit of cedar shingle sale in at least three states (California, New York and Kentucky) has been ended only after considerable expenditure of time and money. In fact, a strict interpretation of "weights and measures laws" in a number of states would even now force shingle manufacturers to mark the NET COUNT of shingles on each bundle. It is a further fact that there is a wide disparity in the method of figuring covering capacity of a "so-called" thousand shingles. Dealers, carpenters, contractors and even manufacturers estimate this differently. The result frequently is that a builder hauls to the job either too many or too few shingles.

Where Comparisons are Unfair

It is positively common custom the country over to compare the cost of a "square" of patent roofing with the cost of a "thousand" shingles, despite the fact that the latter has fully 16 per cent. greater covering capacity. Even where this fact is appreciated, bothersome computations are necessary to insure a just price comparison. Patent roofing companies frequently cite the "short count" of shingles as an argument in favor of their own product.

The "apparent" saving in initial cost of some substitute roofing over red cedar shingles, without the slightest doubt, has been directly instrumental in causing thousands to buy the former in preference to cedar shingles. ACTUALLY red cedar shingles are generally cheaper in initial cost, but it doesn't appear that way.

All of the foregoing is leading up to the proposal on the part of your Secretary that:

Beginning January 1st, 1920, Red Cedar Shingles be packed so that four bundles have a covering capacity of one square (100 sq. ft.), based on 4½-inch weather exposure for 16-inch shingles and 5¼-inch exposure for 18-inch shingles.

To summarize points making this change desirable:

1. It provides a directly comparable basis for price comparison with other types of roofing materials.

2. It provides a much simpler basis of computation of "shingles required."

3. It does away with all charges that shingles are "short count."

4. It complies with all weights and measures laws the nation over.

5. It provides a sale unit that takes a lesser selling price —a very desirable aid in merchandizing.

This matter has been taken up with many prominent dealers, shingle salesmen and experts along merchandizing lines the country over. They have recommended the "square" basis unanimously.

The Canadian mills have already taken this matter under advisement and have gone on record favoring the change.

The Proper Time to Make Change

No better time to make this change will ever be presented than "right now" when dealer shingle stocks are lowest in history.

The proposal of this office is to pack the 16-inch shingles 22/22 courses with the openings limited to 1½ inch per course. Laid the standard 4½-inch to the weather four bundles so packed will cover 101.7 sq. ft., providing a margin for overrun of 1.7 per cent.

Eighteen-inch shingles—four bundles to the square, 19/19 courses with openings limited to 1½-inch per course. Laid the standard 5¼-inch to the weather four bundles will cover 102.5 sq. ft., providing a margin for overrun of 2.5 per cent.

This proposal is made to you at this time, so that you may have ample time to ponder this question, both in its broader phases and as to detail, before our Annual Meeting and Shingle Congress. At that time, this matter will be presented for your approval or disapproval.

And remember this—if a change either in a product itself or in its manner of being put up makes that article more "saleable," slight additional costs of manufacture are invariably more than compensated by better prices.

Wealthy Lumberman's Will Probated

A total estate of $2,145,264.35 was left by the late Hiram Robinson, prominent Ottawa Valley lumberman, who died Sept. 9th, 1919, and whose will has been filed for probate at Ottawa. Up to the time of his death Hiram Robinson was the second surviving member of the old school of Ottawa Valley lumberman. John R. Booth aged 92 years, is the oldest and only surviving representative of the lumbering school of nearly a hundred years ago.

The deceased during his lifetime was a genuine product and typical of the lumbering industry in the Ottawa Valley as it existed in its historic days. Big hearted, generous, and considerate always, though possessing a strong aversion to publicity in life, he nevertheless remembered the charitable needs of the community in which he lived, and his will provides that $100,000 be given to the City of Ottawa, for the purpose of building a "Hiram Robinson" wing for children, to its proposed $3,000,000 civic hospital.

Hiram Robinson was chiefly connected in his lumbering activities with the Hawkesbury Lumber Co. in which firm he held at the time of his death 657 shares of stock valued at $558,450. He also held shares in the Lower Ottawa Boom Co. His interests in the Ottawa and Hull Power and Manufacturing Company were valued at $111,100, and his ownership of Victory Loan issues amounted to $571,488.10. He also had $15,149 invested in United Kingdom Gold Notes. Among the other stocks and holdings shown by the will were: Laurentide Power $8,795, Southern Canadian Power Co. $16,032.

The amount of the personal propertywas $1,698,053 and real estate $418,207, book debts amounted to $5,562, moneys secured by mortgage $144,957.62, life insurance $1,000, bank and other stocks $706,213, securities for money $648,389, cash in bank $179,786, personal and other property $10,643. Mr. T. T. McWaters, nephew, is given 200 shares in the Hawkesbury Lumber Co., Dr. James McKay, nephew, 100 shares in Hawkesbury Lumber Co., Hiram McKay one share in Hull and Ottawa Power Co. Other personal bequests are made to relatives and servants. Twenty-nine thousand dollars is left to the Presbyterian Church of Canada and an additional $15,000 to Knox Presbyterian Church, Ottawa, for building a manse. Ten thousand dollars is left the Ottawa branch of the Salvation Army for building a hospital. The Protestants Infants Home is left $2,000, the Day Nursery a like sum. The Perley Home is left $1,000 and the City of Ottawa $100,000 for the building of a children's wing containing seventy beds, in the new civic hospital.

Annual Meeting of Montreal Lumber Trade

Work of Past Year Reviewed—Various Problems with Railways Satisfactorily Adjusted—Geo. W. Grier Elected President—Wharfage Rates Increase

The annual meeting of the Montreal Lumber Association was held at the Board of Trade, Montreal, on December 1, P. D. Gordon presiding.

The annual report referred to the proposed increase in wharfage rates and the action taken by the association in the direction of asking the Federal Government to assume sufficient of the debt of the port to render unnecessary further advances in the port charges.

The question of stop-off and re shipping arrangements on lumber, carloads, for planing, tonguing, grooving, kiln drying, and sorting in transit was again raised by the railways this year, and the views of the trade given to the carriers in a joint letter from the Canadian Lumbermen's Association, Canadian Manufacturers' Association, Toronto Board of Trade, and the Montreal Lumber Association, strong objections being made to any increase in the stop-over charge beyond one cent per 100 pounds, minimum $5 per car. The question was the subject of a further conference with the representatives of the carriers on May 16, since which date nothing further has been heard from them.

Demurrage Rates Pending Stries

The Board of Trade Transportation Bureau made an arrangement with the Canadian Railway War Board on the subject of Canadian car demurrage rules as affected by strikes. The question arose over the strike of Montreal teamsters in April, and the following arrangement was approved by the Board of Railway Commissioners:

"In the case of delay to cars containing cartage freight other than that for delivery of which the railway cartage companies are responsible, resulting in accrual of demurrage and due to inability of consignee to release cars owing to existing strike of teamsters in Montreal, the manager of the Canadian Car Service Bureau is authorized to assess car rental on such cars at a nominal rate not in excess of one dollar per car per day when evidence is satisfactory to Manager of Bureau that consignee is entitled to such concession, is submitted by consignee. This arrangement shall continue until the expiration of five days after date of settlement of strike."

This arrangement terminated on May 5.

On April 20 the railways issued tariffs, naming rates on lumber to Montreal for export, 1c per 100 pounds less than local rates, which had the result of increasing the export lumber rates from many points beyond the advance authorized by Order in Council in the 25 per cent. advance case which became effective on August 12. As a result of the protest made to the Railway Commission the carriers agreed to re-issue their export lumber rates, which came into force on May 16.

A proposal of the carriers that collection of transportation should be made on a cash basis, unless credit was obtained, was the subject of attention by the committee, which met the Canadian Railway War Board to discuss the matter. The result was an arrangement whereby those, whose application for credit accounts are approved, will pay their transportation charges in accordance with the following conditions: (a) All bills or accounts rendered by the carrier to consignor or consignee, as the case may be, from the 1st to the 7th of each month (both dates inclusive), shall be paid on or before the 14th of that month. (b) All bills or acounts rendered by the carrier to consignor or consignee, as the case may be, from the 8th to the 14th of each month (both dates inclusive), shall be paid on or before the 21st of that month. (c) All bills or accounts rendered by the carrier to consignor or consignee, as the case may be, from the 15th to the 21st of each month (both dates inclusive), shall be paid on or before the 21st of that month. (c) All bills or accounts rendered by the carrier to consignor or consignee, as the case may be, from the 15th to the 21st of each month (both dates inclusive) shall be paid on or before the last day of that month. (d) All bills or accounts rendered by the carrier to consignor or consignee, as the case may be, from the 22nd to the last day of each month (both inclusive), shall be paid on or before the 7th of the month following.

The Newly Elected Officers

The following were elected officers for the year 1920:

President—Geo. W. Grier, of G. A. Grier & Sons, Ltd.

Vice-president—D. H. McLennan, McLennan Lumber Co. Ltd.

Treasurer—F. W. Cotter, Dobell, Beckett & Co.

Directors—W. A. Filion; E. H. Lemay; J. P. McLaurin, St. Maurice Paper Co. Ltd.; Geo. E. Goodfellow; S. F. Rutherford, Dominion Box and Package Co., Ltd.

The Storage of Floating Timber

The department of public works has by orders-in-council, granted to the Ontario & Minnesota Power Co. booming rights. The location of the boom extends from the canal to the canal dock at the foot of Portage Ave., Fort Frances. This necessitated the moving of the ferry of Gagne Bros. from Sinclair street to the town dock at Portage avenue. Gagne has been reimbursed by the Power Company for his expense and trouble occasioned by this change of location. The privilege granted the company only gives them the use of this water for storage of floating timber.

P. D. Gordon, Montreal, Retiring President — George W. Grier, Montreal, Newly-elected President — F. W. Cotter, Montreal, Re-elected Treasurer — D. H. McLennan, Montreal, Vice-president of the Association

What Was Doing in the Lumber Industry Thirty Years Ago

The square timber trade is almost a lost art in 1919 and was practically put out of business at the beginning of the war, yet thirty years ago it was one of the big flourishing undertakings of Ontario, and the St. Lawrence, Ottawa and other streams were dotted with huge rafts of square and waney timber on the way to Lachine, Montreal and Quebec. Many old timber men can recall interesting incidents of those halcyon days. In this connection it is interesting to read the attached paragraph from the files of the "Canada Lumberman" of the Fall of 1889:—

The Ottawa lumbermen are making preparations to go heavily into the square timber trade this winter, and the indications are that there will be more square timber taken out during the winter than for many years past. The prospect of high prices and increased demand which a short time ago was looked forward to with certainty, has not been sustained by more recent developments. Should there be an over-production, nothwithstanding there may be an increased demand, it does not necessarily follow that there will be an advance in prices. While some of the lumbermen expect an advance in prices. others again are of the opinion that white pine lumber will be, at least, 10 per cent. below this season's questions.

It is estimated by different lumbermen that the square timber to be taken out in the Ottawa and Matawa districts, will be 8,000,000 feet, which will be chiefly for the Quebec market.

* * *

At Burk's Falls the pulp wood business is in a flourishing condition and shipments have set in in earnest.

Just think of the great strides in pulp and paper making since 1889. It was little thought then that this industry would so develop until to-day the annual production of pulpwood in Ontario is about 800,000 cords, and in Quebec over 1,000,000 cords.

* * *

The forest rangers employed by the government of the province of Quebec, assembled in Hull, Nov. 15, in accordance with a request from the commissioner of crown lands, to receive instructions from Mr. J. B. Charleson, superintendent of rangers, with respect to lumbering operations for the winter. Mr. Charleson pointed out that during the past year the provincial revenue from crown timber dues had increased over $330,000 through careful watching, but remarked that rangers would succeed in stopping fires. Administration of crown lands department, he said, was purely non-political, and every employee of the department was required to do his duty, showing neither fear nor favor, and that no man who failed in the thorough performance of the duty asigned to him need expect political preferences to help him.

Another evidence of progress in 1919, as contrasted with 1889, is the advance which has been made in the protection of the timber wealth of Quebec, including four forest protective associations. Cooperation of the limit holders and lumbermen has been brought to the highest efficiency, including the modern telephone lines, look-out towers, wireless telegraphy and aeroplane patrol.

* * *

Oun more evidence of the advance made in hauling logs is that the tractor is now in general use as well as the motor truck, yet three decades ago it was regarded as somewhat of a novelty.

The "news" in 1889 is revealed in the following paragraphs:

Perley & Pattee of Ottawa, are about to purchase a traction engine for the hauling of logs, similar to those used so extensively in the States. The machine will be the only one of the kind in use in Canada, and is intended to do the work of horses. The engine will be used in one of the limits probably.

Perley & Pattee are about to introduce a Glover steam logger, to be used on their Petawawa limits. This is a giant machine, 28 feet long, weighing 12 tons, that can be driven by steam on a snow road, and is estimated to draw as many as 30,000 to 40,000 logs. The mechanism is simple.

* * *

One more interesting point was that the lumberman had troubles with the railway companies in 1889, the same as to-day, and a shortage of cars was complained of by a number of firms. There was also the ever-present trouble of a scarcity of logs at certain mills, particularly in the West, where a number of plants had to close earlier than usual, not on account of weather conditions but owing to not having any material for the saws.

Thirty years has wrought a great change in industry, and there are very few firms of the present day, the heads of which were in harness in the late 80's. Of course there are many old-timers, but, in looking over the list of names of those present at the various lumber and logging-gatherings there are not many of those hand thirty years ago, who attend these meetings now.

* * *

Another interesting paragraph is that "several Amecicans are preparing for sawmill sites in B. C. with a view to putting up mills, and that British Columbia spruce is being shipped to Guelph for use in the manufacture of organs."

To-day there are millions of dollars invested by enterprising United States capitalists in the Pacific Coast Province, and the forest products from both the Coast and the mountain regions have been spread over all parts of Ontario, many Western firms being represented directly with their own selling organizations, while practically all wholesale lumbermen in the East handle more or less B. C. wood-goods, showing how rapid has been the expansion of the last few years.

Time has wrought many other changes in the base of operations of different mills, the character of their output and cutting capacity and the scenes of logging.

* * *

"The sawdust shoal in the Ottawa river, just below Bronson island, is now fully a foot over water. It is one hundred yards long and fifty wide. Several small pieces of shrubbery have been placed here and there on it to warn approaching tugs of the danger," is another news item of 1889.

One of the live topics of trouble at that time was the deposit of sawdust in the streams of rivers and an agitation was started against the mill-men, which was kept up for a number of years. To-day one hears nothing of this bugbear, as the modern burner consumes all the refuse. Thus a question that was in the air for many years is now numbered among the institutions of the past.

* * *

It is instructive to observe the trend of trade in 1889, showing a few of the ports that were active in the matter of export, and what two or three of the leading places were then doing.

"The lumber shipments of Parrsboro are expected to reach one-third the whole export of the Province of Nova Scotia," says the "Canada Lumberman" of thirty years ago. Places that are not noted to-day for being large export centres were then flourishing shipping points, and many new ports in N. B. have come to the front within the last decade or two.

The export of lumber to Great Britain from the port of Richibucto for the season of 1889, amounts to 10,607,581 s.f. deals, and 7,130 pieces of railway ties containing 192,000 superficial feet. The shipments to Great Britain in 1888 were 9,151,610 s.f. reals and palings. The shipments from Buctouche to Great Britain this year are 3,387,167 s.f. deals, against 667,287 s.f. deals last year. It will therefore, be seen that the shipments of these two Kent ports to Great Britain this season was 4,265,851 s.f. deals, an increase of nearly fifty per cent.

* * *

Other pictures of the great lumber industry, as it was in the late eighties, are presented in the following excerpts of the December (1889) edition of the "Canada Lumberman":—

* * *

Mickle, Dyment & Sons' saw mill, at Bradford, has closed down for the season. The season's cut was as follows: Over 8,000,000 feet of lumber; 4,500 cords of slabs; 3,000,000 pcs. of laths, and 12,000 pickets. They would have continued cutting until the river was frozen, but every available spot was covered, and they could not obtain cars to move the lumber already cut. Seventy men were employed in this mill.

* * *

The annual circular of the Export Lumber Company, Limited, shows the total shipments of lumber for this season from the St. Lawrence, to have been 35,313,573 feet compared with 18,089,716 feet in 1888, and 34,036,076 feet in 1887. This season's shipments were made up of 23,026,135 feet of pine, 11,738,065 feet of spruce, 33,000 feet of hardwood and 516,376 of small stowage.

R. R. Williams, Ottawa — Hugh M. Williams, Ottawa — Lieut. Thos. A. Williams, Ottawa

Greater Expansion in Lumber Line

Well Known Exporting Firm of Ottawa Believe Future is Bright — Record of Williams Lumber Co.

"We are looking forward to greater extension this coming year than any in the past. When reconstruction properly starts there is bound to be a boom in the building line as well as all others," declared R. R. Williams, of the Williams Lumber Co., Ottawa. He stated that the export trade has not been large during the past season outside of the British Government purchases.

When virtually all the available suitable lines were bought up last spring by the timber buyer for the Imperial authorities this took a monopoly on tonnage, which practically closed out private shipments of lumber.

Mr. Williams added that they had to pay during the past summer ocean freight rates over ten times higher than the charges that prevailed before the war started. Whether this move on the part of the British Government will ultimately prove advantageous or not, time alone will tell. However, we look forward for an improvement in the export trade in the near future.

Another matter which militates against export business is the exchange, as any country would, of course, sooner buy in a lower exchange market provided it can get its requirements adequately attended to.

The business of the Williams Lumber Co., wholesalers and exporters, who have offices in the Central Chambers, Ottawa, was started about thirty years ago by Hugh M. Williams, who is to-day the senior member of the firm. Later he admitted A. H. Edwards, of Carleton Place, as a partner. The latter retired in 1909, and Mr. Williams continued the business under the name of the Williams Lumber Company. In 1912 his elder son, R. R. Williams, was taken into partnership. The latter had quite an experience in the manufacturing, wholesaling and retailing lines, having been with W. C. Edwards & Co., Ottawa, the Pembroke Lumber Co., and the Chaudiere Lumber Co., Ottawa. He was treasurer and travelling salesman for the McAuliffe-Davis Lumber Co., Ltd., of Ottawa, when that firm was organized, and continued in this post until becoming associated with his father.

During the past summer Lieut. Thomas A. Williams was admitted into the partnership. He graduated in the spring of 1915 as an electrical engineer from McGill College, Montreal, with the degree of B.Sc. The same year he volunteered for active service with the 26th Battery, C.F.A., later winning a commission on the field, and was thereafter an officer with the 7th Battery, C.F.A. Although wounded three times, Lieut. Williams carried on throughout the war.

The Williams Lumber Co. is to-day composed of Hugh M. Williams, the founder, and his sons R. R. Williams and Thomas A. Williams. They have worked up a large and growing business.

Use of Seaplane in Timber Surveys

Speaking to the Foresters' Club at the Faculty of Forestry, Toronto University, Ellwood Wilson, chief forester of the Laurentide Pulp Company, Grand Mere, Que., declared that as an aid in the development of timberlands the seaplane had a great future. From photographs taken from the air, most accurate maps could be made.

While in new country Mr. Wilson predicted a great future for the seaplane; he was afraid that the airplane would prove of little use. Before an airplane could be operated with safety, landings would have to be arranged every few miles, while nature provided the landings for a seaplane. The forest lands of Quebec and New Brunswick were so thickly covered with lakes that landings abounded everywhere, the speaker said.

Lumber companies are beginning to realize the value of aviation to their business. Mr. Wilson's company was the first in his district to purchase planes. Next year there will be six seaplanes in that district.

Land which his company intended to purchase for reforestation purposes had been thoroughly surveyed from the air. Then when the deal was being put through, Mr. Wilson said, the owner found that the buyers knew more about the land than he did.

New Forestry Policy for Ontario

In the near future a deputation from the Canadian Forestry Association will wait upon Premier Drury of Ontario to urge that all timber and lumber be placed under the control of a Provincial forester, with a staff of technical experts.

It will be pointed out that from eighty to ninety per cent. of forest lands of the Province are Crown lands, are leased yearly to lumber companies, and that the public, therefore, has a direct interest with renewing the leases in 1920 or 1921, and to see that measures are taken to prevent such exploitation of timber areas as would deplete the supplies which will be needed in the future. This policy, now being followed in New Brunswick, Quebec and British Columbia, is said to be getting progressively better results every year.

It is believed that Premier Drury is sympathetic with the plan as well as for permitting the forest once more to regain its hold on lands which have been found unsuitable for agricultural purposes. It is understood that the idea of the Canadian Forestry Association is that anybody given control of the forest wealth of the Province and supervision of cutting by companies, should have three or four Government appointees and two representatives of the lumber industry, so that the object in view might be obtained by co-operative action.

Fassett Co's Mill Now Sawing Hardwoods

The Fassett Lumber Co., Fassett, Que., whose plant has been shut down since the 1st of November, recently resumed operations, and will saw hardwoods this winter. Repairs were made to the mill and two sets of steam set works were installed. The company report that sales are especially good and there is a keen demand for hemlock. The cut of the company this season will be about 20,000,000 ft., 7,000,000 ft. of which will be hardwood. They have also about 5,000 cords of pulpwood and 1,000 cords of hemlock bark. The company contract for their logs direct with one concern, which, in turn, sub-lets to jobbers. The price per thousand this year is just double what it was in pre-war days. As the Fassett Lumber Co. operate their own railroad, they state that their costs are not in proportion to other operators who drive their logs and have to haul their supplies from long distances. Wages are higher than they were last year at this particular period, and men are plentiful in the district, while work is farther advanced than it was in 1919 at this time.

Ontario Retailers Will Convene in Hamilton

The annual meeting of the Ontario Retail Lumber Dealers' Association will be held at the Royal Connaught Hotel, Hamilton, on Tuesday and Wednesday, February 10th and 11th. This is the first time in the history of the Association of a two-days' convention as heretofore the gatherings have been for one day only. It is felt, however, that one day is too short to dispose of the many important matters that will come up for consideration at this particular session, and two days will prove more acceptable all around.

An active membership campaign has been started and each of the 160 members is expected to secure at least one or two new recruits before the February meeting. An interesting program is being prepared and, incidentally, there will be the usual social features. President Thomas Patterson, of Hamilton, gives assurances that all visitors will be given an enthusiastic welcome, and it will well repay any member of the trade to spend two days in conference with his fellow lumbermen.

Last February the convention was held in Toronto and was a splendid success, and it is expected that the gathering on February sentative and enthusiastic in character.

Busy Conditions in Lumber Line

The Labor Gazette of Ottawa in its review of conditions in lumbering for the month of November says:—Charlottetown reported a quiet month. The saw and shingle mills at St. John and Fredericton continued steadily in operation, while towards the end of the month many men were taken on for work in the woods. At the end of the month lumbermen at Quebec were also leaving for the woods. River-driving was concluded for the season, and the saw and shingle mills also approached the end of their season's operations. Sherbrooke reported activity in the camps for timber, ties and poles, also in the saw and shingle mills. Ottawa and Hull reported a scarcity of labor for the lumber camps, several hundreds of shanty men who went to the war having drifted into other occupations on their return. Sawmills had a busy month. Peterborough reported continued activity in the sawmills and many men leaving for the lumber camps. Two shingle mills were idle at Owen Sound, but the sawmills were active and the planing mills and lumber camps were busy. A serious shortage of skilled men was experienced in the lumbering operations at Sault Ste. Marie. At Port Arthur and Fort William the lumbering season opened with strong demand for lumbermen, and it was estimated that 1,500 inexperienced men could be placed in the camps immediately west of Sudbury, pay being $55 to $60 per month. Fernie showed great activity in preparing for extensive work during the coming winter. Important deals took place, insuring, it was said, a revival of the industry for at least ten years. Vancouver reported lumbering and shingle manufacturing good with steady employment expected during winter. At Victoria the lumber industry continued brisk.

Fire Assessors Entitled to Compensation

Mr. Justice Tellier, in the Superior Court, Montreal, maintained the action of the Compagnie d'Arbitrage de Montreal against Wilfrid H. Pauze, lumber merchant, Montreal, for a sum of $802.40, for services rendered as assessors of the defendant's loss by fire in his lumber yard on November 21, 1917. The company plaintiff—composed of Joseph Odilon Dupuis, Alexandre Deschamps, Ludger Clement, and Wilfrid Gadoury—said that it was agreed they should be paid two and a half per cent. of the amount payable to defendant by the fire insurance companies. After a careful assessment it was found that $32,095.44 was recoverable, and this sum was duly paid by the five insurance companies with which defendant held policies.

Plaintiffs claimed $802.40 as two and a half per cent. of this amount, but defendant objected that the claim was too high. He pretended that he was liable for only one per cent., but to avoid litigation he offered plaintiffs $322. This was refused, and in deciding the issue Mr. Justice Tellier said that a proper and careful valuation of the defendant's loss was made by the plaintiffs, and defendant accepted their finding without complaint at the time, and which offer he renewed with his defence—he made no objection to the manner in which the work had been done. His only complaint was that their fees were too high.

In the absence of a special contract fixing the amount of their remuneration, plaintiffs had a right to be paid in accordance with the value of the services rendered and on the basis of the tax generally applied for work of this nature. In the light of the proof, the tax of two and a half per cent. appeared to be proportionate to the value of the services rendered, and did not exceed what assessors in cases of this kind were allowed as a general practice. Moreover this tax of two and a half per cent. appeared to be proportionate to the value of the services rendered, and did not exceed what assessors in cases of this kind were allowed as a general practice. Moreover this tax was exactly what defendant agreed to pay to plaintiffs, and had paid, for services of a like character after a fire that had destroyed his property previously.

Judgment was accordingly given for the plaintiffs for $802.40, with costs. (4839, S.C.M.)

New Regulations in Timber Cutting

The Woodlands section of the Canadian Pulp and Paper Association and the Quebec Timber Limit Holders' Association have jointly appointed the following advisory committee in connection with the proposed changes in the regulation of lands and forests governing the cutting of timber on Crown lands:—Messrs. W. Gerard Power, Ellwood Wilson, R. P. Kernan, and G. C. Piche. Negotiations on the subject are proceeding with the Minister of Lands and Forests.

Lumber Sheds Should be Waterproof

I saw the unloading of a truck load of oak flooring the other day. It came from a shed where the rain had beaten in on the end of the pile. About 500 feet was laid aside so badly stained on the ends that they would have to be cut off, entailing a loss of probably $25.00 or more. You know what quarter-sawed white oak flooring is worth now, don't you? Most of you have open-faced sheds, and some of your stock that has been in them for some time has become more or less damaged by the driving rains, especially at the bottom of the piles. If there have been traces this summer of a leak in the roof it will be worse when the wet snow lies on it. You should go carefully over your whole stock and examine the buildings before winter sets in. Clean up the whole yard, both in back and front of the piles. Clean out the accumulated dust on the upper deck of your sheds and molding racks. When snow drives in and melts, the wet dirt will injure your timber. There is no yard but what needs a housecleaning before winter, for, as it lay's out in the open it catches all the dust and trash blown by the winds, and makes it the dirtiest place in town unless cleaned out frequently.

We have got to take more care of our lumber and buildings than we have been accustomed to; likewise everything else we use. Everybody is going to be forced to have, whether it is his natural inclination or not. Eventually the farmers even will see with an understanding eye that they are losing money by not putting all their working implements under cover. They will see this more and more as they come to understand the computation of the cost of raising their products. The same rules of business apply equally to them as with the town merchant.—Mississippi Valley Lumberman.

Piecework in Logging Operations

The lumber industry has been behind nearly any other manufacturing industry in the proportion of piecework employment to the older system of day wages. The last year or so, however, has seen a very considerable introduction of piecework methods and particularly in logging activities. This branch of lumber manufacture appears to lend itself more particularly to this system, because the individual output is more directly a factor of individual exertion. In the operation of a sawmill the edgerman or trimmer or any of those who work with the product after it leaves the saw carriage can not handle more product than comes to them in the routine process. The volume of output of the mill rests almost entirely with the sawyer and carriageman, says the "American Lumberman."

In the woods, however, the sawyers, swampers, skiddermen and teamsters are "on their own," to use an expressive English idiom. The necessary increase in wages when it came did not bring increased production, and piecework rates have been adopted as the only expedient against seriously rising unit costs of production. Under the piecework rate men have been able to maintain or in some cases very greatly to increase their earnings, doing this, however, through an increased production which has kept the unit cost per thousand feet within reasonable limits. To this plan there have, however, been certain drawbacks. At the Northern Logging Congress one superintendent stated that his men were able to stand their increased rate of work only for three or four weeks, when it became necessary for them to lay off and rest up. Most operators also have preferred to keep teamsters on a monthly wage, not caring to have their own horses overdriven through a piecework incentive.

The piecework method does promote increased individual production where properly applied. In many lines of manufacture it has a detrimental effect upon the quality of product. Unless controlled by proper inspection the piece rate worker is inclined to slight his work. This difficulty is, of course, greater with finished manufactured product than in the cruder operations which go to make up logging.

It is quite probable that a piecework system will be more widely introduced in the next few years in all lines of work where the character of the work gives an opportunity for increased individual production. Its possibilities at least are sufficiently interesting to be worthy of careful consideration.

Hardwood Flooring—"From Forest to Home"

Enterprising Canadian Firm Present Moving Picture Story of Their Industry—Views are Instructive and Tell People how Product is Manufactured

Frank A. Kent, Toronto.

The educative value of moving pictures is being extended in all directions and many industries which heretofore have been known to the general public in name only are now being brought to our very doors and pictorially presented. Films of logging, lumbering and general driving, towing and sorting operations on the way to the sawmill have been displayed on the screen from time to time. The process of showing in every detail a closely allied industry—the making of hardwood flooring—from the bush to the ball room—has just been effected by the Seaman, Kent Co., Limited, of Toronto, who control the output of five plants, the largest of which is located at Meaford, Ont. Pathescope of Canada, Limited, 156 King St. west, Toronto, have been engaged in the work of preparing these films for some months, and the "premiere" was given in the Star Theatre, Meaford, recently, before a large and delighted gathering. The production of "Beaver Brand" hardwood flooring, was depicted in a most comprehensive series of views, and the title of the series of films is "From Forest to Home."

It may be stated that the Seaman, Kent Co. are exceptionally busy at the present time in an effort to keep up with the demand for hardwood flooring of all kinds and lately purchased the West Lorne Wagon Works at West Lorne, Ont., where the buildings are being extended, and the most modern equipment installed for turning out oak flooring exclusively. Owing to the heavy domestic call for maple, oak, beech and birch flooring a large number of orders from the Old Country have had to be declined.

Cutting and Skidding in the Bush

The moving pictures begin with a scene from the forests on the Christian Islands, taken last winter, and show a gang of workmen felling the typical Canadian maples and skidding them in the woods ready for transportation to the saw mills where they are converted into lumber. In many instances the logs were hauled to waterways and put in big booms and towed to the mills. At various dumps some 20,000 hardwood logs were seen awaiting transportation at some point on the Georgian Bay. Upon arrival at the mills, the logs are taken from the water and immediately sawn into lumber of standard lengths and thickness. By labor-saving devices such as chains, carriers, etc., these logs are brought into the mills from the water very quickly and with a minimum of expense. The lumber is placed on trucks and drawn and piled at convenient points for re-handling by water or rail.

The lumber is then ready to be taken to the flooring factory and a boat in the course of loading was shown, which later was unloaded at the Meaford docks by the company's men and men about town. The lumber was later teamed from the docks to the lumber yards and dry kilns.

The manufacture of the real "Beaver Brand" kind of flooring commences when the lumber is put in the kilns, where it remains for at least 15 days under a temperature of from 160 to 200 degrees. Perfect drying is essential to good flooring and great care is taken to see that the flooring gets properly "cured" and away to a good start. When bone dry the lumber is planed and sawed to the desired width and thickness, after which it is tongued and grooved as well as hollowed to prevent warping. The product is so closely matched that it is nearly impossible to see where it is joined. The strips are then conveyed to the end matchers where they are so well end matched that they fit perfectly and avoid waste in laying. The flooring is then sorted into proper lengths and is tied firmly in bundles for quick handling and shipping.

The firm also have a factory at Ste. Agathe, Que., which specializes in hardwood flooring. It is also well equipped and takes care of much Eastern business enjoyed by the company. The premises are not as large as the plant in Meaford, but the product is the same.

How Hardwood Floors are Laid

The next important step in the production of perfect flooring is the laying and in the films workmen demonstrate that the floors are well and truly laid. The matching is the "corner stone" of Beaver Brand flooring and in the production of the material three parts of the trouble of laying is entirely eliminated. Many scenes of dance halls are given as well as parlor floors where entire satisfaction is witnessed with highly polished floors.

The plant of the Seaman, Kent Co. at Meaford, has been operated for nineteen years and the company state they are the largest producers of hardwood flooring in the British Empire. The industry at Meaford now has a capacity of 2,500,000 feet of finished flooring per month, and has now in its employ some 375 hands including both factories and its selling and office force. It is the pioneer flooring establishment in the flooring industry and has already placed orders for additional machinery to extend operations. The wages expended each month in Meaford exceed $10,000 and with orders now on the books for overseas delivery the firm are advertising for sufficient men to run two shifts per day.

One of the two large plants at Meaford, producing hardwood flooring for Seaman, Kent & Co., Limited.

The Seaman, Kent Co., have also placed orders with the Knight Manufacturing Co. to manufacture flooring and some 20 or 30 hands are now operating on flooring in this concern. This addition is likely to continue and may possibly be doubled in the near future.

The company are advertising in the press for hardwood lumber or logs, delivered at Meaford, or at mills within ten or fifteen miles of the town where sawing can be arranged. It is expected that operations will commence in their new plant at West Lorne, Ont., early in 1920. The capacity will be 8,000,000 feet annually. New dry kilns have been built and the very latest equipment installed.

Frank A. Kent of Toronto, managing director of the company, states that with their five plants in operation, the Seaman, Kent Co. will be the largest producers of hardwood flooring in the world. The moving pictures which have been taken and perfected will be shown in all the provinces of Canada through the medium of the film exchanges, and later on it is expected the series will be exhibited in the Old Country and Europe.

Model New Sawmill Erected at Matheson

The new sawmill of the Matheson Lumber Co. at Matheson, Ont., is nearing completion. It is 84 ft. long by 22 ft. wide, with boiler room and trimmer building attached, concrete pillars under mill and heavy concrete floor in boiler room. The company estimate that they will cut somewhere about 25 M. feet per day, with circular saw. They are installing steam feed and steam nigger, and, when completed, the mill will be one of the most modern and up-to-date small plants in the north country. The Matheson Lumber Co., of which R. S. Potter is President, plan on cutting a million and a half feet this coming summer. They commenced their log operations about a month ago and have several men working in the woods. The company have a couple of small limits on the Black River.

Veteran in the Lumber Industry

J. F. Lillicrap, Lakefield, Ont.

"I have managed the lumber business from almost every angle and always find something to learn," stated J. F. Lillicrap, of the Kawatha Lumber Co., Lakefield, Ont. He is one of the most widely known members of the industry in Ontario, having been identified with it for over forty years. Mr. Lillicrap got his first acquaintance with wood products when a clerk in a lumber camp in the township of Harvey, Peterboro County. He kept the books and also the time of the men, measured all the logs and square timber, and for discharging these manifold duties received $12 per month. The wages that prevailed that winter for lumberjacks were $9 to $14 a month, a foreman received $25 and cooks $20. The board consisted of pork, beans, bread and tea without any sugar, and few, if any, potatoes. How different is the menu today!

Until 1882 Mr. Lillicrap measured logs in the winter and then was placed in charge of a large sawmill at Bradford, Ont., where he spent the summer for some years, and during the cold months estimated timber on the limits, located camps, etc. He returned to Lakefield about 1887, where he was employed by the Lakefield Lumber Co., looking after their sawing and shipping. Then for three years he operated a planing mill in that village and, in company with Mr Tate, built and operated a sawmill which they sold in 1909. Mr. Lillicrap next commenced to sell lumber on a commission basis and also to purchase for an American firm. In 1912 he came to Toronto to sell for the Laurentide Lumber Co., of Montreal, but returned to Lakefield in 1917. A year ago, in association with his old partner, E. R. Tate, and G. Elmsley, of Toronto, he formed the Kawatha Lumber Co., Limited, of which he is purchasing agent and salesman. They have had a successful season and expect to largely extend their business next year.

Mr. Lillicrap has made many warm friends during his long connection with the industry and has witnessed many changes in its development during his forty-three years' association with its activities.

Last Block Firm is Very Active

George Willard & Son, of Masonville, Que., who recently purchased the mill and timber limits belonging to the Stewart Estate, will make use of the mill for sawing lumber. They do not expect to employ the output in their business of making last blocks, but intend to work up what soft wood comes from their limits for their own purpose in building camps, keeping up repairs, etc.

The firm have been making shoe last blocks since 1903, doing all work by hand in the woods, and gradually coming to the use of machines run by power. All trade at that time being with the Canadian market, Willard & Son soon discovered the advantage of doing this work with saws driven by steam, and this led the way to rough turned, air dried blocks, which is the principal product of their plants at the present. The firm operate three mills for the manufacture of last blocks, shoe tree blocks, toe pieces and rubber blocks. Their mill at Traver Road, Quebec, has a capacity of 4,000 pieces a day, the one at Bolton Centre 2,500 pieces, and the one at South Bolto the same. The European market which the firm held before the war quickly came to its own as soon as shipping would allow it and is now very keen. About fifty per cent. of the trade of Willard & Son is with the New England States, which abound in shoe factories.

Want Pacific Coast Soft Wood

Australia's need for soft wood for all sorts of commercial purposes, formerly supplied from the Baltic seacoast, must henceforth be met by the Pacific coast, which has ousted the Baltic from the Australian market, said Mark A. Sheldon, commissioner of the Commonwealth of Australia, in an address before the chamber of commerce in San Francisco.

"There is one line that must go on increasing and increasing, and that is the lumber business," he added. "We have no soft woods in Australia. Our woods are heavy and hard, and we want Pacific coast soft woods."

May Build Cargo Vessels for France

Canadian shipyards may have an opportunity to build cargo vessels for the French Government, according to reports in circulation in Ottawa. France, it is said, is anxious to buy or have constructed freight carriers to ply to her colonies, to operate on the Mediterranean, and to build up her commerce generally. If arrangements could be made, it is reported the French Government would be prepared to spend $180,000,000 upon ships of all sizes to the number of more than a hundred, and to pay as much as $170 a ton for them. It would be glad, moreover, to place orders for vessels in this country. Not long ago Hon. C. C. Ballantyne was reported to have told a deputation that Canada, if she wished, could dispose of all the vessels built under the Government construction programme at satisfactory rates. It is now surmised that France would be glad to buy those ships, all of which are of a very high class.

Recently orders for two more ships for the Dominion Government were awarded to the Wallace Shipbuilding Company, of Vancouver, at a price several dollars a ton below $170. J. Coughlan, of J. Coughlan and Sons, of Vancouver, was in the capital seeking orders for two vessels to fill two berths which will soon become vacant at the company's yards.

Progressive Firm Erects New Office Building

Messrs. Millen & Frere, of Montreal, have recently completed a very fine office building in connection with their yards in the north end of the city. This enterprising firm now have attractive executive quarters quite in keeping with their industry and growth, and that are not only a credit to themselves, but to the retail lumber business of Montreal. The building is a two-storey brick one, with concrete basement, and the interior is finished in panels of B. C. fir. The ceiling beams are artistically boxed in and moulded and the entire inside trim is finished natural. The floors are native birch. The office furniture will be made of fir and the whole effect is pleasing but will prove a considerable boost for B. C. fir.

New Sawmill Erected in Peterboro

E. H. Mann & Company have erected a new sawmill on Street, Peterboro. It is equipped with circular saw, edger and trimmer, and will manufacture all kinds of lumber. There has also been installed a shingle machine for turning out heading and while another department will produce lath. The output of the mill will be about 18,000 feet of lumber a day. The building is 24 x 84 ft. and it is expected that operations will start in a few days. Mr. Mann has been in the lumber and planing mill business in Peterboro for many years, and is well known to the trade throughout the Midland district.

Finger Lumber Company Sell Interests

The biggest deal in the history of the lumber business in the province has just been negotiated, the Finger Lumber Company having disposed of its 324 miles of timber limits in The Pas district, Manitoba, for $1,500,000, to C. J. and D. N. Winton, of Minneapolis. This includes a large sawmill, planing plants and logging equipments. The deal becomes effective at once and possession will be taken within a month. H. Finger, head of the retiring company, is a pioneer in the North Country, going to The Pas in 1904, when it was Indian territory. Now the capacity of the company is about 190,000 feet per day.

Canadian Lumber for Japan Market

Writing from Yokohama, Japan, Canadian Trade Commissioner A. E. Bryan says:—Up to the present Canadian lumber has not been imported into Japan in very large quantities, compared to what one would think should be the case. The reason for this is that the Japanese forests have so far been not only supplying the domestic demand, but a certain quantity has been exported as well in the form of logs, railway sleepers, shooks, matchsticks, etc.

It is said, however, that the now available Japanese forests are pretty well exhausted. Most of the forest land of the country is owned by the Imperial Household, and is not allowed to be cut. Only just lately, a forest concession was given over to be cut on account of the available supply of lumber being so low.

Although small parcels of lumber are coming forward from British Columbia quite regularly, it is to be assumed that these will greatly increase in quantity as time goes on. It is of interest to note that one large importer in Kobe told the writer that in his district they always reckoned Canadian lumber as better graded than the American product.

Retail Lumberman Gets Small End of Profit

Carries Larger Stock, Gives Better Service and Works Longer Than Ever Yet is Making Less—District No. 6 O.R.L.D.A. Considers Timely Questions

Matters of vital interest to the retail trade were discussed at the annual meeting of District No. 6 of the Ontario Retail Lumber Dealers' Association, which was held in Orangeville, Ont., on December 5th. Notwithstanding the unfavorable weather there was a representative attendance, and the interchange of thought and opinion on stocks, deliveries, grades, collections, competition, merchandizing methods, cost accounting, profit figuring and other kindred subjects proved to be highly satisfactory and instructive. For nearly three hours the members, who gathered in the Orangeville Council Chamber, had a heart-to-heart discussion. It was a sort of round-table conference, in which everyone took part and expressed his views freely.

One particular feature that the meeting brought out was the scarcity of stocks, particularly in hemlock, the shortage and abnormal demand for shingles, occasioned by the recent severe windstorm in Ontario, when many barns and other buildings were unroofed, and the necessity of securing a fair margin of profit on all materials handled. It was stated that a retail lumberman was doing more work, carrying larger stocks and giving better service to-day than at any period in his history, yet he was earning less money and winding up the year with a smaller sum on the right side of the ledger.

This, one of the members stated, was due to the fact that they were not conversant with their actual costs of doing business, and did not know how to compute profits properly.

Another member declared "we are too fond of exchanging an old dollar for a new one, and there is no satisfaction in that. We buy our lumber for a certain sum and sell it at a certain figure, and think the difference represents profit, when in many cases, considering the prices we have to pay to replenish stocks, it really means a loss. I do not see any particular merit in turning over a stock without being able to make a little money in the transaction, and that is what we have not been doing for a long time. When the market is advancing our prices should be on the basis of current quotations rather than on what the material cost when it was put into our yards.

Retailer Entitled to Better Profits

"Yes," spoke up another member, "we work long hours, have to invest a large amount of money in stock, handle it in small quantities and give the best of service and material, and at the end of the year have little to show for our work and worry. The retail lumberman is entitled to a better profit and should get it, and the sooner he institutes aggressive business methods, the better for him and his future. I believe that the manufacturer and the wholesaler are making all the money that is being cleaned up to-day in the lumber business. It is certainly not the retailer, and I know whereof I speak."

In the discussion it was stated that some dealers were handling cements, and that they had not been protected by the cement manufacturers, who also sold to contractors, but lately, owing to an agitation carried on, the companies had decided to give the retail merchants a slight concession on each sack, so as to make it worth while stocking this material.

The question of closer relations with the farmers, the matter of extending patronage exclusively to those lumber firms who protected the interests of the yardman and did not sell shingles, lath or other supplies to hardware men, blacksmiths, waggon makers, etc., was endorsed. Retail men will naturally support those who stand by the legitimate interests of the trade, and recognize that the yard man is the best, most satisfactory and all-round available means of distributiou.

The question of drawing up some recommendations in regard to better and more uniform grading of lumber was discussed, and some instances were pointed out of the very wide difference in interpretations placed by certain firms upon certain grades of stock and what percentage of good stuff a car should contain. At present there are too many confusing terms without any recognized exact application, and the term "merchantable" had been extended in meaning until it practically took in everything except read culls and scoots. It was, however, deemed advisable not to make any recommendations on this point at the present time in view of the scarcity of stock and the fact that deliveries have been rather slow on a number of lines

The Provincial Gathering in Hamilton

Other live matters discussed were collections, a uniform order form, shipping arrangements, cost of unloading cars, the best method of keeping stock, the Ontario Business Assessment Act, the Mechanics' Lien Act, etc. On some of these questions a definite decision will be reached and brought up at the annual convention of the Ontario Retail Lumber Dealers' Association, which will be held in Hamilton on Tuesday and Wednesday, February 10th and 11th. It is expected that this will be the most representative and interesting meeting ever held in the history of the retail lumber industry of the Province.

One member declared that it might be thought building would stagnate owing to rapidly rising values, but his experience has been that the higher prices went the more activity there generally was in the building line, for the simple reason that there always seemed a large class in any community who did not undertake anything in structural operations until the peak was reached, and then they sud-

J. A. Matthews, Orangeville, Ont., Re-elected Chairman.

Udney Richardson, Elora, Ont., Member of Committee.

J. B. MacKenzie, Georgetown, Ont., Re-elected Secretary.

denly grew very active. It is not thought that the apex of prices has been attained yet by any means, and it is felt that 1920 will be a greater building year than ever. One member from a town of two thousand population stated that indications pointed to the erection of at least fifty dwellings in his burg during next spring and summer.

Among those who delivered addresses was Mr. H. Boultbee, of Toronto, secretary of the Ontario Retail Lumber Dealers' Association, who expressed his gratification at the representative attendance, and dwelt upon some of the good rseults that had been accomplished through organization and co-operation.

Continuing Mr. Boultbee said: We are drawing rapidly towards that delightful season of the year when it is the aim of every person in the Christian world to treat himself to the pleasures growing out of someone else's happiness. The spirit of Christmas is nothing more or less than the spirit upon which our Association is founded. You may say that in co-operating with your fellow retailers you are really actuated by a belief that in so doing you are benefiting yourself and therefore the motive is selfish. But the same thing could just as truthfully be said of the generosity which you display in making your Christmas gifts. It was ever more blessed to give than to receive, and in Association work every effort you make to show the light to your competitor will pay you many times its cost.

Concrete Advantages of Fellowship

After two years of work in connection with the Ontario Retail Lumber Dealers Association, I am still in doubt as to which is the more important result of our efforts—whether it is the concrete advantage to individual members which can be measured in dollars and cents, or the less tangible, but none the less important benefits which accrue to those members who take their Association seriously and reap every advantage they can from the friendships they are thus enabled to secure with those who in former days they looked upon as competitors and therefore enemies.

Possibly this is about enough along this line, but just to drive the point home a little more definitely, let me ask you to look back upon the feelings you had when coming to Orangeville for the meeting a year ago, and to compare them with the feelings you experience to-day. I am satisfied that, no matter how hopefully you may have looked forward to the betterment of trade relationships, you did not indulge in any hopes which to-day can be shown to have been extravagant. You have got rid of the feeling that some of your fellow dealers were not to be trusted, and you have, during the year, co-operated with one another, both informally and at meetings, in a manner which has made your business more pleasant and more successful.

The dealers of this district are to be congratulated upon having formed the first local branch of the Association. Your example has been followed by the dealers of another district who hold their meetings at Stratford. Undoubtedly the formation of these local branches will, in the long run, be the most important factor in the progress of the general Association. It is in the local meetings that the interests of the members are most clearly related, and it is from the local meetings that the suggestions and the inspirations must come that will make for the success of the General Association.

Industrial Relationship of Branch

You should take your relation to the local branch as seriously as possible. It seems to me that there ought to have been more meetings of your branch during the year than there have been. This is by way of suggestion, not criticism. It is more than likely that during the early years of the life of a local branch, the members may, in a sense, feel that they are experimenting and that they will know better how to proceed a year or two later. It is a natural enough feeling, but it does not make for big results. The meetings which I have been able to attend, up to date, have convinced me that the greatest results secured are not the tangible ones, but the personal and intangible ones which elevate your self-respect and improve your appreciation of the good qualities in your fellow dealers. This is why it seems that your branch would have done well to have held more frequent meetings during the past year. Don't let the idea get hold of you that a meeting is not important because very little is done that requires an entry upon the minutes. This thought is likely to creep in as time passes, unless you meet frequently and break through the shell of reserve which forms so quickly around persons who abstain from intercourse with one another. Even a meeting of a half a dozen or so members of a local branch does good. If there are a few definite problems of the trade which require discussion, all the better, but even with an informal programme of friendly discussion, it is possible to make these meetings an inspiration for better business methods after the return home.

This meeting should not confine itself to the presentation of a few reports, the election of officers and an adjournment until the next meeting, possibly several months away. When you have the officers' reports and elections disposed of, I would suggest a discussion of some of your more intimate local problems, such for instance as the education of anyone who may be too fond of cutting prices below cost. If you have a few of these fellows in the district, why not plan out a campaign to show them the light. You will never do much with such men by an occasional call upon them.
ought to make a dead set on them. Every man in the district
to go after them whenever possible, and either get them to do business on a sound basis or make them feel ashamed of themselves.
trouble with these fellows is that they don't feel ashamed of themselves at all. They think they are the only smart ones in the
ness and that all the others are "out of step."

Looking Ahead in Trade Matters

You ought to indulge also in a talk about trade conditions. If you had been able, a year ago, to analyze market conditions properly and had gone ahead and bought good-sized stocks of lumber, you would have made a good thing out of the splendid demand which developed during the present year. You can devote a lot of thought to this subject now, and possibly help one another to see ahead a little more clearly and to decide upon your buying policy for next year. There are indications to-day that the building activity of 1919 is only a forerunner of greater activity in 1920 and that the available stocks of lumber will be in great demand. These are matters which concern you and your bank accounts very closely. Some of you may hold opinions on the subject which are not shared by others. These opinions ought to be brought out and exchanged, so that the best thought on the subject may be available for all.

I don't want to take up much of the time of this meeting, as the dealers present need one another's help more than mine. The work of our Association during the year had been important and productive of results and I could spend an hour or two telling about it. But these are matters which will be best reported at some length at our Annual Meeting. February 10th and 11th are the days which have been selected for the Annual Meeting and it will be held at Hamilton, the home city of our President, Mr. Thomas Patterson.

This meeting of Branch No. 6 comes at a good time to remind you of the Annual Meeting and urge you to do everything you can to make it a success. In a few days you will receive a copy of a circular letter, from the Association, the object of which is to get every member working on a plan for starting next year with a record membership list.

Getting the Other Fellow to Join

Each member is being allotted a few names of prospects for membership and being asked to make a dead set upon them and get them to join the Association. We have nearly 160 members now, but we ought to have twice that number and we can get them if every member puts the right amount of enthusiasm into the work.

One of the chief objects of these branches of the Association is to enable the local members to make more effective use of the general Association. While the members we have, have been pretty keen about the work of the Association, they might have made a great deal more use of it than they have. Some members have been quick to realize the benefits of the service they can get out of the Association, but others have been content to sit back and wait to see results manifest themselves without being gone after. We have been feeling around more or less during the first two years of our existence, and we have learned a great deal about what we can do. From now on we should plan for bigger results. The only way in which this can be done is by getting the local branches to stir things up and force the General Association to take up all those matters which will be to the general interest. I would like to see the members of this district come to the Annual Meeting in a body with a well-mapped out programme of things which they intend to have the Association take up.

Preliminary Action to Get Results

Take, for instance, such matters as plan books, standard sizes, standard moulding designs, standard order forms, standard forms for making claims upon the railway companies, even standard grades for lumber, to say nothing of matters relating to trade ethics. Why not make a list of such matters at this meeting and discuss them one by one, then go to the general meeting prepared to bring them up for discussion and have real action taken. Most of these things have been discussed at one time or another during the past two years and it is time now that on some of them we stirred up enough interest to get action.

It will help to make the Annual Meeting a success if your members will follow this suggestion and have a cut and dried programme ready and make yourselves known at the Annual Meeting by the persistent way in which you stir things up.

Moreover, we must get many other local branches organized

and I think things are about ripe for starting several of them. The example you set at the Annual Meeting by keeping things going, as I have suggested, will be infectious. You will get results out of it. You will be known as the liveliest portion of the Association and the results that grow out of your enthusiasm will ge a long way towards stirring up the rest of the members of other local branches, and in the end make the Association more nearly the important organization that the members should all want it to be.

An address was delivered by J. A. Matthews, of Orangeville, chairman of the district, who warmly welcomed the visitors, and entertained them to dinner.

W. G. Gorvett, Arthur, Ont. Member of Committee.

Eugene Murphy Jr., Mount Forest, Member of Committee.

G. B. Van Blaricom, editor of the "Canada Lumberman," also spoke, touching particularly upon the benefits resulting from association work, and also the annual outings of the Ontario Retail Lumber Dealers' Association. The spirit of good fellowship which characterized these, as well as their educational value and broadening effect, were pointed out.

The Old Officers were Re-elected

All the officers were re-elected for the coming year, Chairman, J. A. Matthews, Orangeville; vice chairman and honorary secretary, J. B. MacKenzie, Georgetown, Ont.; committee, Udney Richardson, ex-M.P.P., Elora, W. G. Gorvett, Arthur, Eugene Murphy, Jr., Mount Forest, and John Howes, Harriston. It was declared that they had done their work worthily and well during the past season, and that the district was one of the livest of any in the Province.

It was decided to hold the next sitting in Toronto during the last week in March, and every member promised to be in attendance. Several matters arising at that particular season of the year will then be taken up.

Among those present at the meeting were J. A. Matthews, Orangeville; J. B. MacKenzie, Georgetown; A. Henderson, Cheltenham; Robert Dixon, Grand Valley; Udney Richardson, ex-M.P.P., Elora; John Howes, Harriston; W. G. Gorvett, Arthur; H. Boultbee, Toronto, (Secretary of the Retail Lumber Dealers' Association), and G. B. VanBlaricom, Toronto, (Editor "Canada Lumberman").

Both Good and Evil Institution

Speaking of the transit car problem, the "American Lumberman" says: Briefs of opposing counsel representing lumbermen who favor and who oppose the per diem charge of $10 a day on cars of lumber held for reconsignment more than forty-eight hours are presented. It is not necessary to review at length the argument pro and con, inasmuch as the briefs are not so abbreviated as the word might imply. An attempt, however, is made in the brief of the National Bureau of Wholesale Lumber Distributors to discuss the subject from a broad economic basis, and a little analysis of that side of the question may be useful.

The brief describes the normal and legitimate function of a wholesaler in gathering up lumber from small mills and finding the buyers for it. It seems to be assumed as axiomatic that the transit car privilege is essential for this purpose. The argument is made that the practice brings the car closer to the consumer at the time he is in the market for it. This is undoubtedly true; but it of course is not true that the average retail lumber dealer can safely let his stocks run down depending upon being able to buy a transit car of lumber of just the kind he wants at the time he wants it. To some extent in the main yard stock items it enables the retailer to do business with a somewhat lower stock on hand.

The claim is made for the transit car that it is a strong factor in keeping the prices of lumber down. The investigations of the United States Forest Service and the Federal Trade Commission into the economics of the lumber business do not suggest that that is any great virtue, averaged over past years, inasmuch as overproduction and overcompetition have often over long periods produced selling prices that were unprofitable and demoralizing. It may well be that the transit car privilege has been a factor in such situations in the past, inasmuch as it has always been with us. No one having the knowledge of the facts would, however, seriously argue that if the case had been otherwise the conditions of market depression would have been transformed into an unreasonable price inflation.

With the brief was put in an exhibit showing average prices for transit car shipments of $40.94 over a period during which the average list of the large mills for mill shipments was $47.48. It is not clearly apparent from these figures that these transit cars were actually bearing the market. There is a material difference in average value between the simpler product of the small mill and the more highly refined and millworked product of the large one.

The transit car is in fact both a good and an evil institution. Confined to its proper legitimate purpose it is a trade convenience, which, however, does not in any such great measure as is sometimes claimed rise to the dignity of a trade necessity. It is, however, subject to abuse and then becomes an economic evil.

In this present case, however, there is no question of doing away with the transit car. The only question is whether those who handle it shall be permitted to hold it indefinitely for reconsignment or whether this pre-reconsignment period shall be limited to forty-eight hours with the $10 a day charge for a longer period.

Increasing Lumber Trade With West Indies

T. B. Macaulay of Montreal is an energetic and persistent advocate of greater trade relations between Canada and the British West Indies. He is of opinion that Canada can supply many of the commodities which the West Indies now purchase in the United States, and that Canada can find in the West Indies sources of supply for which this country is now dependent on the United States. The remedy for this condition is commercial union. Mr. Macaulay asserts that further preference is a necessity. In addressing the members of the Montreal Board of Trade he declared that the United States aims not merely at commercial control of the West Indies, but hopes to annex them politically. He had strong reason to believe American interests were at work in Jamaica to influence public opinion in favor of union with the United States. Closer relations of Canada and the British West Indies is to-day as virtually necessary to the Empire as the union of the provinces of Canada was fifty years ago. Immediate action is imperative. To maintain the commerce of the Empire, and thus maintain its financial independence, the Empire must be commercially consolidated. Lumbermen are, of course, interested in this question as wider markets are of importance to our industry. Canada already does a considerable lumber trade with the West Indies, but there is every reason to believe that the volume could be largely increased if closer commercial union could be arranged.

New Wholesale Lumber Firm in Montreal

A new wholesale lumber firm has been formed in Montreal by Lieut. Col. W. F. Cooke, D.S.O., Canadian Forestry Corps, and his brother, S. P. W. Cooke. They have branched out under the name of Cooke Bros. and are located at 20 St. Alexis St., Montreal. The Cooke brothers hail originally from Ottawa and are sons of Dr. S. P. Cooke of that city.

Lieut.-Col. W. F. Cooke, for many years before and after Prince George, B. C., was blessed with a railway, had a sawmill in that town and was active in the development of the interior of British Columbia. He will be remembered by many old-timers in the district as well as by numerous comrades in the army.

S. P. W. Cooke was with the E. B. Eddy Co. of Hull, Que., on the Ottawa River for a number of years and later with the H. H. Hettler Lumber Co. of Chicago and Midland. Then he took a position with the East Kootenay Lumber Co. of Jaffray, B. C., and for the past eight years has been selling agent on the prairies with headquarters at Moose Jaw, for several leading shippers of B. C. He is favorably known to the trade as "Doc" Cooke of Cooke & Cox, Moose Jaw. Cooke Bros. have a good connection in both the East and West portions of the Dominion and a host of well wishes for their prosperity.

Death of World's Oldest Lumberman

Colon Lafortune at the Advanced Age of 102 Years—Last of a Family of Centenarians

The late Colon Lafortune, Port Dover, Ont.

Colon Lafortune, the oldest lumberman in Canada, and possibly the oldest in the world, died recently at his home at Port Dover, Ont., in his 102nd year. On April 23rd last he passed his 101st milestone and was enjoying excellent health until three days previous to his death when he had the misfortune to trip over a rug in the house of his daughter, Mrs. E. L. Nicolls, and fracture a rib by falling against a table.

In the "Canada Lumberman" from time to time references have been made to the wonderful career of Mr. Lafortune, who, considering his advanced age, was as lively as many men not much more than half his years. He was particularly fond of gardening and poultry raising, and was on his feet a great deal of the time. He had been a total abstainer all his life and did not use tobacco in any form. During the summer he performed many light tasks which were his chief delight.

Mr. Lafortune came of a long-life family, the majority of whom lived to be over 100 years of age and, any who passed away before attaining the century mark, were spoke of as "ending their days very young." Mr. Lafortune was born in 1818, one mile north of Montreal, and was engaged in the lumbering business for many years. When he first came to Port Dover on his way to the district of Port Rowan, where he lived for a long time, there was but one building in Port Dover. Mr. Lafortune followed timber cutting and logdriving for over 65 years and in his day helped to clear many forests, felling very large pine trees. He was an expert with the axe and the saw.

Mr. Lafortune went to Norfolk county in 1836 with four brothers and a sister. Another brother remained at the old home down near Montreal. His sister died at 98, a brother, Fred., at 103, and the other three all went into the middle nineties, except one, of whom Colon was wont to observe: "He died young, had only 92 years."

During his first winter Mr. Lafortune, then eighteen years of age, felled 400 giant pines four feet or over, to fill a Government order for masts. He assisted in getting them to Big Creek by oxen, where they were floated down to the bay, and during the following summer taken to Montreal in a raft. It took months to make the trip. The stalwart lumberman and river driver shot the Lachine Rapids six times on that trip. It is said that once was enough for the most daring of modern years.

When the Lafortunes reached Port Dover over the trail from Hamilton their sleep at the old tavern was broken by the howling of the wolves in the adjacent woods.

He married the daughter of John Lake of Houghton, became a Methodist, and throughout his long life attended the church of his choice regularly.

All of his surviving children reside in Norfolk county, and he has fifteen grandchildren and more than thirty great-grandchildren. The children are Frank Lafortune and Mrs. Ira Whitehead of Simcoe. Mrs. E. L. Nicolls and Mrs. Sarah Osler of Port Dover, and Mrs. Fred Overbaugh of Port Rowan.

Colon Lafortune spent the active part of his life along Big Creek lumbering and rafting. By common consent he was a foremost woodsman. If he had any specialties they were felling spar timber and driving logs down Big Creek. He worked over thousands of acres. He saw docks built in the natural harbors on Norfolk's shore front, and he saw shipbuilding develop till there was quite a fleet of boats plying a coast trade. He witnessed the virgin forect disappear, and with it the shipbuilding, and subsequently the docks. But he followed with pride the development of Canadian manufacturers that drew upon the forest for raw material.

Sudden Demise of Eastern Lumberman

F. W. Sumner of Moncton, N. B., died recently in the Royal Hotel in St. John. The end came very suddenly as a result of an attack of acute indigestion. Early in life he was associated with his father in the hardware and general store business in Moncton and also engaged extensively in the shipping of railroad ties, pulpwood and hemlock bark to the United States. At that time it was not an uncommon sight to see half a dozen or more vessels loading at the port. Mr. Sumner built and owned a number of vessels which were engaged in this trade.

He also for a number of years carried on, in connection with his Moncton business, extensive lumbering and milling operations at Bathurst, but sold his property there some years ago to the Bathurst Lumber Co. Since that time he devoted his attention to his rapidly growing business in Moncton and to the affairs of the various industrial enterprises with which he became connected.

While Agent General for New Brunswick in London he served without salary. In this capacity he made frequent trips to England, at much personal sacrifice and during the war he rendered splendid service in looking after the interests of New Brunswick soldiers overseas.

At one time he was president of the board of directors of the St. John and Quebec Railway company. He was for a time a member of the provincial legislature and in 1908, unsuccessfully contested Westmoreland in the Conservative interests for the federal house, running against the late Hon. H. R. Emmerson. He was mayor of Moncton for six terms, and always took a deep interest in the welfare of that city.

Veteran Lumberman Expires After Long Illness

John O. Donogh, a well-known lumberman, passed away recently at his home, 53 Chestnut Park, Toronto. He has been ailing for many months from a complication of diseases, and for many years had ben a sufferer from asthma.

Mr. Donogh was born in Guelph in March, 1853, and when he was quite young came to Toronto to locate. He took a position as bookkeper in the lumber business of S. R. Briggs & Co., where ex-Mayor Joseph Oliver was then a salesman. They decided to go into business together and the firm of Donogh, McCool and Oliver was formed. In 1880 Mr. McCool withdrew and the style was changed to Donogh & Oliver. This partnership continued until 1896, when the Donogh & Oliver Co. was formed. The headquarters of the organization were removed to Tonawanda, and after a couple of years Mr. Oliver disposed of his interests to Louis H. Swan, and, returning to Toronto, organized the Oliver Lumber Co. The Swan-Donogh Co. operated in Tonawanda until 1901, when Mr. Donogh returned to Toronto and formed the Imperial Lumber Co. This was succeeded by the John Donogh Lumber Co., the Donogh Lumber Co. and the Dargan Lumber Co., at the head of which Mr. Donogh was at the time of his death. He leaves a wife and one sister, while Joseph Oliver of the Oliver Lumber Co, and Rev. Benjamin Greatrix of Peterboro are brothers-in-law.

The late Mr. Donogh was prominently identified with the Masonic Order, the I.O.O.F., the Board of Trade and other organizations, and was a leading member of Sherbourne St. Methodist Church. In his passing there is lost to the industry a firm friend, a thorough gentleman and one who by his cheerful disposition and good-nature endeared himself to all his associates. A brother, William Donogh, who was in the lumber business for a long period, passed away last Spring.

New Secretary Has Extended Experience

F. J. Niven, who was recently appointed Secretary of the Department of Lands, Forests & Mines for Ontario and also Secretary to the Hon. Beniah Bowman, has been in the department for nearly twenty-three years, during which time he was in charge of the issuance of timber licenses throughout the Province and also had the collection of ground rents, bonuses and charges on account of fire protection. The figures relating to the annual report of the department are in course of preparation and will soon be available.

Fernie Sawmill and Limits Sold

John Spence, who conducts a lumber yard in Bradford, Ont., and also does a general contracting business, reports that he has been particularly busy during the past season and has erected a number of cottages at various points along Lake Simcoe. He is a thoroughly practical man and for nearly thirty years was foreman of the Mickle-Dyment planing mill, which operated until a few years ago in Bradford and did an extensive business in that part of the country. The planing mill was taken over later by another concern and run for some time but the venture was not a successful one, and when the stock of lumber, doors, sash, window-frames, etc., was sold Mr. Spence bought the material and has been busy ever since. It is understood that the planing mill, which is a two-storey frame structure, may be put in operation again at an early date, as several parties have been looking over the plant with a view to taking hold of it.

Busy Sawmill Closes its First Year

The Manufacturers Lumber Co., Ltd., of Stratford, are one of the busiest and most progressive wholesale concerns in Western Ontario. The company operate and own a sawmill located in the village of Shakespeare, about seven miles from Stratford and the summer cut of mixed timber was recently finished, being about 600,000 ft., consisting of basswood, maple, cherry, pine and hemlock. The plant has now shut down for the winter but will start sawing again early next spring. The mill is a two-storey one with 100 horse power engine and boiler running a circular saw, edger, butting-saw, slab-saw, etc., and the capacity is about 15,000 ft. a day.

The company find a ready market for a large part of their cut

The sawmill of Manufacturers Lumber Company at Shakespeare, Ont.

in Stratford and haul the product on an eight-ton truck, which they had built for this purpose. The road from the mill to the Classic City is in first-class condition and transportation is not at all difficult.

The company had quite a stand of cedar on their site, from which they cut last winter about 1,000 telephone poles of 25 to 60 ft. in length, 20,000 cedar posts, 20,000 vineyard stakes and 6,000 ties. The accompanying view gives a good illustration of the mill and the facilities for handling lumber.

J. A. McFadgen, head of the company, is well known to the industry in Western Ontario and the sawmill plant at Shakespeare is one of the best-managed of any of the smaller industries in that part of the country. It was started about a year ago by the Manufacturers Lumber Co. Limited, which concern was organized in 1903 and is composed of J. A. McFadgen and his two brothers, G. A. and C. A. McFadgen. The firm carry on a purely wholesale lumber business handling almost entirely native hardwoods. The bulk of their trade is with Western Ontario manufacturers, although a good healthy export business is done with American customers. The Manufacturers Lumber Co. specialize in birch, basswood, maple and elm.

Mr. Johnston Buys Cedar Limit

W. H. Johnston. lumber merchant and manufacturer of Pefferlaw, Ont., accompanied by his son, returned recently from a successful deer-hunting expedition in Nipissing district. They were members of the Round Lake Hunting Club, who succeeded in getting several deer. Mr. Johnston has been remembering a number of his friends with samples of the best brand of venison steak.

During the recent wind storm which swept Ontario, several buildings in North York were unroofed, including a horse-barn belonging to Mr. Johnston. Considerable standing timber was also uprooted. A fine cedar swamp of about 50 acres in the Pefferlaw district was so badly shattered by the gale that the owner decided to place the timber upon the market and it was recently purchased by Mr. Johnston, who expects to cut the material during the winter, and will have several cars of fine stuff for delivery in the spring.

Lumber Shippers Faced with Big Loss

The exchange situation between Canada and Britain is seriously affecting the Canadian lumber trade. A credit of $50,000,000 for purchase of Canadian lumber was arranged, but now the question has arisen regarding payment, whether in British or Canadian currency. In all, $28,000,000 has been expended. Part of this was expended in contracts with fixed exchange, but on the remainder, with the drop in exchange, Canadian shippers are faced from this source with $500,000 loss. The subject is engaging the attention of the Government and it is possible further credits will be refused until there is a guarantee to Canadian shippers against loss from exchange on contracts yet incomplete and those to be arranged.

The only immediate practical remedy to right the British-Canadian exchange situation, according to Lloyd Harris, is for Canada to buy more goods in Great Britain. While an advocate of closer Imperial trade relations, he could not see where an increase in the British preference would produce an immediate result in bettering the exchange situation. An Imperial currency, with fixed exchange rights within the Empire would have a beneficial effect on Canada's export trade.

Enterprising Firm Starting Retail Lumber Yards

Carl Sorensen & Co. of Fort William, Ont., are taking out cedar posts and poles as well as cutting some logs and wood on lands owned by them in the township of Crozier near Fort Frances. They intend to put in a small mill on the land in the spring and ship the products to Port Arthur and Fort William to the retail trade in those cities. Mr. Sorensen states they will have yards in both Fort William and Port Arthur if conditions warrant the undertaking.

Mr. Sorensen has been identified with the lumber business in Minnesota and the Northwestern part of Ontario for the last twenty years and during that time has been connected with no other organization except the Shevlin interests in Minneapolis and Fort William. Carl Sorensen & Co. are an enterprising firm and the way they are going at logging operations and the lumbering business looks as if they are determined to make good in their new ventures.

Optimistic Outlook in Lumber Arena

The annual reports of the superintendents of the Bank of Montreal are optimistic as to lumber conditions. These officers of the bank are generally pretty well informed as to the conditions in the provinces, and their reports may be taken as indicative of the state of the lumber trade in Canada. Thus the superintendent of the Province of Quebec states that practically all stocks have been sold and shipped out. Prices ruled high. Labor conditions show improvement and a larger cut is looked for this winter. The demand for pulpwood from the United States was uneven, but stocks were well disposed of and high prices are expected to be maintained.

From Ontario, the report is to the effect that the production of lumber was seriously reduced owing to shortage of labor; 1919 was an excellent marketing year, with heavy sales to Great Britain and the United States, and a steady domestic demand for all classes of lumber. Prices were unusually high, there is no accumulation of stocks on hand, and notwithstanding the scarcity of labor and increased costs of operating, the year was a successful one. Pulp and paper were in large and increasing demand, with soaring prices for the latter.

In the Maritime Provinces the cut was above that of last year and was largely sold to the British and French Governments at high prices. The demand was good from the United States, but sales were curtailed owing to transportation difficulties. Labor is more plentiful, and notwithstanding high wages and the excessive cost of provisions, indications point to an average cut this coming winter.

Saw mills in the Prairie Provinces were in active operation during the year, their products finding a ready and profitable market. In the opening months of the year the B. C. lumber trade was dull, but in the spring a heavy demand arose in the United States and accumulated stocks were disposed of at rising prices. Great activity prevailed during the summer and autumn. The demand for cedar shingles was good, and prices reached unprecedently high figures. The outlook for the coming year is exceptionally good, both in domestic and foreign markets. The pulp and paper mills were busy, and their product is on the increase. Shipments were largely to the Orient and to the Antipodes.

Would Eliminate Oriental Labor in Mills

An effort is to be made to replace Oriental labor in the saw mills with white men, states Mr. J. C. Child, S. C. R. representative at the government labor bureaus. Mr. Child says this has been done with some success with the mill at Eburne, and in some of the Vancouver mills. Millmen are quite willing to employ white men if a sufficient number is available. The necessary preliminary therefore is to enroll a number of men. Anyone interested is asked to register either with the labor bureau or with one of the S. C. R. representatives. Naturally, the S. C. R. officials are concerned mainly with returned soldiers, but others will be welcomed, as the difficulty is to get a sufficient number of men at one time.

Personal Paragraphs of Interest

R. O. Sweezy, Forestry Engineer, of Montreal, is on a business trip to the Pacific Coast.

Allen S. Nicholson of Vancouver, Western manager of Terry & Gordon, Toronto, is spending a few weeks in the East on business and pleasure and is visiting his old home in Burlington, Ont.

C. Blakeley, the Montreal representative of Cox, Long & Co. Ltd., and Robt. Cox and Co., will, after January 1st next, represent Cox, Long & Co. only. The office will be removed from 113 to 433 Coristine Building, Montreal.

Dr. Judson F. Clark, of Clark & Lyford, Ltd., Forest Engineers, Vancouver, has gone to California for the winter months on account of his health. He still retains his interest in the firm and expects to return to Vancouver during the summer months.

R. R. Bradley, consulting forester and timber cruiser, has formed a partnership with L. R. Avery, and the firm will be known as Bradley & Avery. Their headquarters are 4 Hospital St., Montreal. The new firm will undertake field studies of all kinds, supervision of logging operations, advice on management of woodlands and also make valuation surveys and do timber cruising and forest mapping.

Martin McKee died recently at his home, 450 Jones Ave., Toronto. For a number of years he was engaged in general storekeeping, but later established a planing mill and lumber yard on his premises in Riverdale, Toronto, which he carried on for twenty-five years. Mr. McKee who was born in Belfast, Ireland, came to Canada in 1853 and was highly respected by a wide circle of his friends.

James A. Conners of the James W. Sewall office, Old Town, Maine, timber cruisers and foresters, has returned from northern New Hampshire and Vermont, where he has been cruising large areas of timberlands. Mr. Conners reports considerable optimistic feeling as to the future forest values throughout that part of the country. W. P. Billings of the same office, is engaged in estimating on some 70,000 acres of land in northern Maine.

Major James Brechin, of Victoria, B. C., who for several months past has been British Lumber Commissioner in the East, with offices in the Kent building, Toronto, left recently for the west and it is understood that it is not his intention to return to the East. During his stay in Toronto he made warm friends on all sides in the lumber industry. His duties in Toronto and the East have been assumed by William Robertson of Victoria, who spent several weeks in Toronto during the months of September and October, assisting Major Brechin in the work. Mr. Robertson has been in the forest branch of the Department of Lands as a Commissioner for some time and comes well qualified to fill his new post.

W. Gerard Power of St. Pacome, Que., President of the Canadian Lumbermen's Association, spent a few days recently in Toronto in company with Mrs. Power and called upon many members of the trade. He states that the twelfth annual convention of the Association, which will be held on February 4th and 5th in Quebec City, promises to be the most successful and important of any ever in the history of that body. Logging operations east of Quebec are proceeding satisfactorily and a great deal more timber has been felled than at this time last year. Help is still scarce in some sections and logging jobbers are paying some men as high as a hundred dollars a month and more with board. Mr. Power will operate his mill at Powerville this winter cutting spruce and expects to produce between two and three million feet during the season.

New Brunswick Lumbermen See Premier

The annual meeting of the New Brunswick Lumbermen's Association will be held on Tuesday, March 9th, in Fredericton, when officers and executive for the coming year will be elected. The Association was organized two years ago, and has done excellent work

W. B. Snowball of Chatham, N. B., is the President, Donald Fraser, of Edmundston, N.B., vice-president, and R. W. McLellan, Fredericton, N. B., secretary-treasurer. The executive committee is composed of: W. B. Snowball, F. C. Beatteay, Donald Fraser, J. W. Brankley, Daniel Richards, W. Garfield White, J. B. Gregory, James Robinson and George King.

The association has been engaged for some time perfecting its organization and keeping in touch with the Government. In New Brunswick the Crown owns the greater portion of the holdings of the large lumbermen, which are either licensed or leased to them by the Crown. The executive has been considering questions of great importance along this line, and a few weeks ago held a meeting in St. John and adopted resolutions covering important matters to be submitted to the New Brunswick legislators. Recently these resolutions were submitted to the N. B. authorities, who discussed them in detail. No definite decision was reached, but Premier Foster promised every consideration. The object of the resolutions is clearly set forth in the following, which was submitted:

Resolved:—

That this association, in a fair desire to assist the Government all it possibly can in stablizing the lumber industry of the Province, respectfully urges the rates of stumpage be made operative for a period of ten years, as is the practice of the other neighboring Provinces, thereby enabling manufatcurers to make suitable plans ahead for the good of all concerned, otherwise the very serious labor troubles and the enormous advance in wages will inevitably curtail production, wages and revenue to the Government.

Whereas:—

The Government of this Province has noted on page 2395 of the Consolidated Statutes of New Brunswick, 1903, instructed the Consolidation Commissioners not to reprint or include Chapter 96 of the Revised Statutes (1854) relating to the survey and exportation of lumber in such consolidation, as it was the Government's expressed intention at first opportunity to supersede said Act by legislation; and whereas no such legislation has been enacted:

Therefore resolved that in the absence of any and mutual just and equitable scale of this Province, legal Quebec scale be adopted as being eminently concerned.

Further resolved that the money raised for the prevention of forest fires by a tax levy on license holders be administered, under Government supervision by the license holders, themselves, they being the most deeply and directly interested in fire protection.

Enters Protest About Timber Limit

H. H. Dewart, K.C., M.P.P., the Liberal leader in the Ontario Legislature, has sent a letter to the Hon. Beniah Bowman, Minister of Lands and Forests, regarding timber cutting rights on the area east of Gull River. Mr. Dewart states that too short a time was allowed for tendering, and that the sale of the limits was not advertised. The letter goes on to state that tenders would be received up to December 5th for the right to cut pine and other timber on an area east of Gull River, adjacent to the western boundary of the Nipigon forest reserves. It is declared that the area involves 128 square miles and that the circular letter which was sent out and signed by the Deputy Minister, was dated November 19th, and that all tenders were to be in by December 5th. Mr. Dewart states that the time for receiving bids is "suspiciously short," and in this connection says: The mere sending out of circular letters by a Deputy Minister to Crown Lands Agents is not a method of advertising that can be approved. I am advised that timber contractors did not receive the circular. The Black Sturgeon and Pic River sales are sufficiently fresh in the minds of the people of Port Arthur, and there will be a strong protest against any repetition of that performance.

Fernie Sawmill and Limits Sold

Particulars are to hand regarding the big lumber deal recently made by which O'Neill and Irvine, of Spokane, Wash., have acquired the mill and timber limits of the Fernie Lumber Company.

The Fernie concern, which went into liquidation six years ago, and which has been controlled by the Imperial Bank of Canada, had holdings comprising 9,000 acres of timber containing 230,000,000 ft. merchantable saw timber, cruised as chiefly high grade mountain spruce, but with considerable quantities of Douglas and white fir, cedar, tamarack and lodge pole pine. There are also, estimated, 4,000,000 mine props, 40,000 cedar poles, 700,000 cedar fence posts and all readily accessable for shipping.

The old mill will be rebuilt three miles further up Hartley creek and the standard gauge logging railway will be abandoned and its place taken by a flume nearly five miles in length which will itself cost over $30,000. In their great Washington venture O'Neill & Irvine logged what was considered inaccessable limits by means of a flume 30 miles long and made a gigantic financial success of it. During the winter the flume will be built and by spring their second mill will be ready for logs, with a 10-hour daily capacity of 75,000 feet. Next year's cut is expected to be 15,000,000 feet. The same interests operate mills and camps at Salmo.

W. S. Burley, of the B. C. Fir and Cedar Lumber Company, Ltd., states that the company intend to reconstruct their plant, which was practically wiped out by fire several weeks ago. The new plant will have a nine-hour capacity of 75,000 feet and will be equipped with the most modern type of machinery.

The Logging Camp

How Logging Methods Have Improved

The Laurentide Co., Ltd., Grand Mere, P.Q., have provided facilities for their employees to get an insight into the technical and practical aspects of paper making. The course includes logging, this portion being in the hands of Messrs. Small & Hamilton. Mr. Small dealt with the bush work. He described the actual organization of the gangs—jobbers' gangs and those of the company—incidentally shedding considerable light on the very much improved conditions in logging camps now existing when compared with former times. The enormous supply organization necessary was gone into. Mr. Small described the way in which hundreds of men and horses were broken up into small parties for the actual work of getting out the wood to the logging roads, and so on to the lakes and rivers, to wait for the spring drive. Some details of the drive were also given.

Mr. Small's talk was particularly interesting on account of the comparatively trivial but entertaining details, showing how the element of human nature entered so much into the work and the handling of the gangs. He completed his talk with a few points on the difficulties of the drive, leaving the work at the sorting point to Mr. Hamilton.

Mr. Hamilton sketched the conditions out of which the need for a drive association had arisen, and the moral of his talk seemed to be that since the companies had gone thus far in co-operation they should take another step and abolish sorting altogether.

Mr. George Charters gave an interesting and instructive description of the "wood to mill" departments and the groundwood mill. The wood to mill departments include the slashers, the tumbling barrels, the conveyor and log pile, and the chipper room. A description was given of each essential machine with some of the more important figures connected with it. Mr. Charters had diagrams of the more unfamiliar of the machines described that helped considerably in illustrating his talk.

The Aviation Branch of St. Maurice Forest Protective Association has completed its work for the season, and the two planes loaned by the Government will be thoroughly overhauled and put into condition for further experimental work next season. Four hundred pictures covering 4,000 by 3,200 feet, were taken at an altitude of 5,000 feet. The pictures show all kinds of country, settled districts, villages, swamps, burns, cut-over districts and all sorts of timber types. Those so far developed and printed exceed expectations, and give great promise of an advance in timber mapping.

Important Decision on Logging Rights

An important case interesting to lumbermen, logging companies and sawmill owners in relation to their rights on navigable waters was decided recently in the Court of Review by Justices Demers, Panneton and de Lorimier, Montreal. The Miner Lumber Company, Limited, in initiating the litigation, claimed $8,740 from the Whyte Campbell Lumber Company, being $6,240 for loss of lumber and $2,500 damages resulting, it was alleged, through defendant having opened a boom on Riviere Ouareau to a wider degree than legally allowed.

The court of first instance condemned the defendant company to pay $5,162, but the Court of Review lately held there was error in the original judgment which found defendants at fault. The court, therefore, modified the judgment to the extent of making it virtually a reversal. Defendants were condemned to return to plaintiffs seven and a half cords of wood it was proved had reached defendants' possession, or in default pay the company $90, the value of the wood. In any event they had to pay costs of an action for an amount of $90, and plaintiffs were condemned to pay the costs of review.

Both companies concerned in the action have each a sawmill on river, the one belonging to plaintiffs being about a mile higher up the stream than defendants' mill. In the springtime defendants, in order to sort the mixed logs belonging to both parties, constructed a boom at McGuire's Flat, about two miles higher up the river than plaintiffs' mill, and as the logs arrived they notified plaintiffs in order that they might send men to take part in the sorting. Plaintiffs refused and defendants thereupon put the wood of plaintiffs into the boom and allowed their own to pass down the river. There was some dispute regarding the quantities belonging to the two parties and finally an arrangement was mutually agreed upon. Then plaintiffs, finding that the sorting made at McGuire's Flat was not advantageous, sent their men to open the boom, and the logs became mixed again. The sorting continued by both parties at a boom belonging to plaintiffs just above their mill. Afterwards defendants complained that the sorting of logs and pulp wood was going on too slowly and finally their workmen opened the boom by two feet—from six to eight feet. As a result, plaintiffs alleged, they suffered loss and damage.

Free Passage of Navigable Waters

Mr. Justice Panneton, in pronouncing the judgment of the court, referred to the absolute rights of free passage on navigable waters, with modifications allowed by law for the construction of dams and booms. There was no provision regarding the width of the opening of the booms to allow the passing of the logs, but His Lordship pointed out that because the statute permitted such constructions to facilitate the lumber trade, it did not follow that the party who exercised that right could do so to the detriment of those who had the right to pass their timber down the river. The proprietor of a boom was obliged to give passage to the logs of others, and unless it could be considered that defendants had abused their right by the manner in which that right had been exercised, they could not be held responsible for any damages that plaintiffs had suffered. They had not broken the boom of the plaintiffs, as had been alleged; they had not damaged it, but had simply opened it two feet wider; and it had been done without the least deterioration. They had a right to facilities for the floating of their timber equal to those which the natural flow of the river gave them in order to obtain sufficient timber to keep their mill operating.

As the law did not give plaintiffs right to limit their boom opening to six feet, the court examined their case to see if there had been a tacit understanding between the parties, thus to limit the extent of the opening. The answer was in the negative and the conclusion arrived at was that defendants had done no more than exercise their rights.

Judgment of the court of first instance was accordingly revised in the manner reported above.

Mr. Justice de Lorimier concurred in the finding of Mr. Justice Panneton on the question of law, but was of the opinion that more wood had been lost by plaintiffs than the seven and a half cords which admittedly had been received by defendants. But plaintiffs had failed to establish the responsibility which they charged against defendants, and all that the latter could be held liable for was the quantity now valued at $90.

Recruiting Men for Lumber Camps

The various employment bureaus of Montreal, public and private, are busy these days recruiting men for the lumber camps. While in some quarters it is reported that there is considerable unemployment, the bureaus report that they have openings for more men than are offering themselves, at least for the north woods.

Just now the between season rush is going on. The recent closing of navigation lets loose a large number of men who have spent the summer on the water front, and there is also a large number of farmers' sons who are freed from their summer avocations and anxious to earn money in the winter months by working in the lumber camps.

At the provincial employment bureau Joseph Ainey, the director, stated that there were five or six representatives of lumber companies on the spot recruiting men, and these were finding a shortage. In this rough work there is at present opening for a large number of men.

PUBLISHER'S NOTICE

Advertisements other than "Employment Wanted" or "Employees Wanted" will be inserted in this department at the rate of 20 cents per agate line (14 agate lines make one inch). $2.80 per inch, each insertion, payable in advance. Space measured from rule to rule. When four or more consecutive insertions of the same advertisement are ordered a discount of 25 per cent. will be allowed.

Advertisements of "Wanted Employment" will be inserted at the rate of one cent a word, net. Cash must accompany order. If Canada Lumberman box number is used, enclose ten cents extra for postage in forwarding replies. Minimum charge 25 cents.

Advertisements of "Wanted Employees" will be inserted at the rate of two cents a word, net. Cash must accompany the order. Minimum charge 50 cents.

Advertisements must be received not later than the 10th and 20th of each month to insure insertion in the subsequent issue.

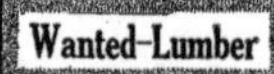

Basswood Wanted

No. 2 Common and Mill Cull. Winter cut preferred. Apply Firstbrook Brothers, Ltd., Toronto, Ont. 8-t.f.

Wanted Lumber

Hardwood Lumber wanted. Birch, Maple, Basswood and other Hardwoods. Dry or sawn to order. We send inspector. Box 14, Canada Lumberman, Toronto. 21-24

Spruce Wanted

One to five cars 2 x 6—16 Merchantable Spruce, S1S to 1¾", for shipment to U. S. any time before February first. Box 81, Canada Lumberman, Toronto. 24

Maple and Spruce

Wanted stock lists and quotations on end dried, white quartered and straight grained action Maple, four and five quarter, also Spruce Lath and Furring, bundled. Box 70, Canada Lumberman, Toronto. 23-2

Basswood and Maple Wanted

Fifteen carload dry 1sts and 2nds or No. 1 Common and Better white winter cut Basswood, plump 1 in. thick.

Twenty carloads dry hard Maple, 1¼" x 3¼" multiples of 9" and 12" in length, one clear face and square edges.

Twenty carloads Hard Maple, 6½" x 6½" and 5¼" x 5¼" x 22" and 26" in length or multiples, practically clear stock and free from checks; can ship green.

For further particulars apply to Box 85, Canada Lumberman, Toronto. 24-t.f.

Wanted To Buy LATH

We are in the market for a large quantity of Lath, including No. 3 grade and 32 in. for immediate shipment or will contract for output. Paying good prices and cash on receipt of B/L.

What have you to offer? Send good description, quote F.O.B. Chicago; state quantity offered.

COVEY DURHAM COMPANY,
431 South Dearborn St.,
24-3 Chicago, Ill.

For Sale–Lumber

SPRUCE KNEES FOR SALE

150 Grown Spruce Knees, 4' x 3' 6", finished 8', 9' and 10" thick; thoroughly sound, ready for immediate delivery. For particulars, apply A. K., Box 78, Canada Lumberman, Toronto. 24

Piling

We can furnish Piling, any length or size, on short notice.

WM. POLLOCK & SON,
23-2 Englehart, Ont.

For Sale

Five to ten cars Selected White Pine Trimmer Ends; 1 x 4 and wider; 1" thick and thicker; 10" long and longer.

JOHN B. SMITH & SONS,
23-24 Toronto, Ont.

PULPWOOD FOR SALE

Ten thousand cords of pulpwood for sale; next summer delivery. Shipping point, Blue River, Canadian National Railway. Apply to

QUEBEC LUMBER CO.,
Phone 329 98 St. Peter Street.
22-25 Quebec, Que.

FOR SALE
Hickory Specials

100 M pcs. ⅞" Dowels, 48" long.
20 M pcs. 1" Squares, 48" long.

Also some shorter stock. All high grade, second growth Hickory. Can ship immediately. Will sell cheap. Address Box 81, Canada Lumberman, Toronto. 23-24

3" Spruce

We hold at Montmagny, Que., 315,000 ft. 5th Quality and Better 3" x 4" and up, 10/14 ft., including 40% 9" and up, piled separately.

Price on application to

Thos. Harling & Son,
406 Board of Trade Bldg.,
24 Montreal, Que.

Dry Lumber For Sale

Shipment latter part of March and later.

430 M 8/4 Hemlock.
175 M 4/4 Hemlock.
160 M 4/4 Birch and Maple.
100 M 4/4 Basswood.
30 M 4/4 Grey Ash.
43 M 4/4 Soft Elm.
12 M 4/4 Pine.
10 M 6/4 Pine.
30 M 8/4 Pine.
6 M 6/4 Rock Elm.
1½ M 8/4 Rock Elm.

Address Box 83, Canada Lumberman, Toronto. 24-1

SIDING FOR SALE

8 M. ft. Elm, Maply and Beech—sidings—mostly 6" wide, ¾ to ¼ thick. Geo. Craik, R. R. No. 2, Mossley, Ont. 24-1

Lumber For Sale

100 M ft. 3 x 4"/up Cull Pine.
100 M ft. 1" Spruce Shorts.
80 M ft. 1" Basswood, No. 3 Com. & Btr.
200 M ft. ¾" Cull Spruce.
500 M ft. 1", 2" and 3" Cull Spruce.
Also 1" Ash, Elm, Birch and Red Oak.

Apply: J. P. ABEL, FORTIN LTD.,
24 Maisonneuve, Montreal.

Wanted–Machinery

Wanted

Barienger brake, either 4 or 6 drum type. Apply Bishop Lumber Co., Ltd., Nesterville, Ont. 23-24

Wanted

To purchase, upright Gang, 44" to 40" wide, 18" stroke. Communicate with The Pembroke Lumber Co., Pembroke, Ont. 23-24

WANTED
Good Alligator Engine

complete including double propellors, with or without usual tackle. Give full particulars.

W. C. EDWARDS & CO., Ltd.
Ottawa, Ont., Canada.
24-1

Band Mill Wanted

1-7 ft. Double Cut Band Mill. Give description and condition, also price. Box 80, Canada Lumberman, Toronto. 24-1

For Sale–Machinery

Good second-hand Hockey Stick Bending Machine for sale. Apply J. H. Still Mfg. Co., St. Thomas, Ont. 23-2

Steam Log Haulers

"Phoenix" make. Have several for sale. Cheap. Also Logging Sleighs.

J. L. NEILSON & CO.,
24 Winnipeg, Man.

FOR SALE

One Waterous double cut Band Mill Complete.
One steam Log Loader.
One steam Kicker.
One Waterous Nigger, 10 and 8" cylinders.
Two Air Cushions.
One 10" Steam Feed, 86 ft. cylinder.
One steam set works, Carriage Wheels and Track. Also a number of steel and wood pulleys, live rolls, etc.

For full information apply Box 74, Canada Lumberman, Toronto. 23-2

Lath Machinery

1 Lath Machine, 1 Bolter, iron frame, strong, good order, with all saws. P. O. Box 5, Papineauville, Que. 24-3

better.

No. 283 "Yates" Band Resaw, 4" or 5" blade. Price $1150.00.

No. 108 "Yates" 12" Four-Sided Inside Moulder or Planer and Matcher. Price $1400.00.

48" "Yates" Three-Drum Sander. Price $1550.00.

The above Machines would be complete with all regular equipment. Apply—

Williams & Wilson, Ltd.,
84 Inspector St.,
24 Montreal Canada.

Wanted–Employment

Advertisements under this heading one cent a word per insertion. Box No. 10 cents extra. Minimum charge 25 cents.

YOUNG MARRIED MAN anxious to secure position giving opportunity of advancement in lumber business. Have already had some experience. Can furnish the best references as to character, etc. First class education. Box 506, Canada Lumberman, Montreal, Que. 23-24

TO LUMBER OPERATORS—I am open to consider position as manager of woods operations, sawmill or selling force; experience in hardwoods in the United States and in New Brunswick Spruce. Can handle men and get results. Box 84, Canada Lumberman, Toronto. 24-1

WANTED—Concern operating in Northern Ontario has opening for active, energetic man to assist in woods operations. Permanent position and advancement for man possessing right qualifications. Address Box 69, Canada Lumberman, Toronto. 23-24

Salesman Wanted

Must be first-class and have good connection with the Lumber Trade in Ontario, Quebec and Maritime Provinces. One well posted in British Columbia woods preferred.

Apply, in confidence, giving full information as to qualifications and salary required, to Box 82, Canada Lumberman, Toronto. 24-1

WANTED: NATIONAL HARDWOOD INSPECTOR for Montreal and vicinity. Permanent position. Knowledge of French preferred. State salary and experience. Apply Box 300, Canada Lumberman, Montreal. 24

Business Chances

For Sale

Fine industrial site, situated near western boundary of Ottawa, Ont. Good property for almost any industry. Mill and storage buildings almost new, with some shafting erected. Five hundred feet siding on C. P. R. If interested apply Box 55, Canada Lumberman, Toronto. 22.1

Saw Mill Plant For Sale

Practically new and modern Saw Mill Plant, capacity about 30 Million feet per annum, located in the Interior of British Columbia on a beautiful inland lake and on the main line of the Grand Trunk Pacific Railway. About 500 Million feet of timber on and adjacent to Lake (about 90% Spruce) and another Billion feet available at reasonable prices. Natural conditions ideal for economical logging, manufacturing, piling and shipping. An advantage of about $4 per thousand feet in freight rates to the Prairie Provinces over Coast shipments.

This property offers unlimited possibilities as a lumber, pulp and paper property. Would consider selling a half interest. Terms reasonable.

A. C. FROST COMPANY,
134 South LaSalle Street,
Chicago, Ill.

5-t.f.

Auction Sale
of Valuable
Quebec Timber Limits

R. H. Klock & Co., through W. A. Cole, Auctioneer, on the Nineteenth day of February, 1920, at the hour of three o'clock p.m., subject to one reserve bid, will offer for sale by Public Auction at the Russell House in the City of Ottawa, in the Province of Ontario, timber berths numbers 176 and 177, Kipawa, are 100 sq. miles more or less. These timber limits contain large quantities of pine, spruce, and other wood goods. For further particulars apply to James B. Klock, 70 St. Matthew St., Montreal; Errol M. McDougall, K.C., Royal Trust Building, Montreal; D. B. Rochester, 145 James Street, Ottawa, and W. A. Cole, Hope Chambers, 63 Sparks Street, Ottawa, Auctioneer. 21-26

To:
Lumbermen—
Trust Companies—
Banks—
Executors of Estates—
Or Private Owners of
Timber and Pulp Lands.

If you are contemplating offering your Limits for sale by Auction, bear in mind that the Capital of the Dominion is the greatest lumber centre in America and the place to hold your sale.

Will be pleased to give you all information as to details, etc.

WM. A. COLE,
Auctioneer.

OFFICES:
63 Sparks Street, Ottawa, Ont.

Established—1806.
References—Any Bank.

21-24

For Sale

Four square miles of Virgin Timber for sale. For desirable information write W. McDonald, LaSalle, N.Y. 23-24

TIMBER LIMITS

I have a number of good Timber Limits for sale. Particulars, Wm. Cooke, Stair Building, Toronto. 20-t.f.

WANTED

To correspond with mills baling softwood chips from logging operations, also baled shavings from planing mills, and clean dry fine hardwood sawdust. Box 68, Canada Lumberman, Toronto. 23-2

For Sale

Sash and Door Factory and Planing Mill, located in one of the busiest and best towns in eastern Ontario. Correspondence solicited. Box 66, Canada Lumberman, Toronto. 23-t.f.

Wanted

Position or interest in wholesale or manufacturing business. Fifteen years' experience stump to market and manager of large mill operations. Excellent references. Box 64, Canada Lumberman, Toronto. 23-24

For Sale

Owner of exceptionally good limit is forced to sell an interest in same or will sell all if desired. Over two hundred million feet of B. C. Cedar, Hemlock and Pine on C. P. Ry. Splendid chance for profitable operation. Write for cruisers' reports, etc. Price very attractive. Box 63, Canada Lumberman, Toronto. 23-24

TIMBER LIMITS

We have some very attractive offerings in Standing Timber, Cedar or Spruce, in Alberta and B. C., with or without sawmills. Lougheed & Taylor, Ltd., Calgary, Alberta. 24-3

Timberland For Sale

Let us prove that we have the best timber proposition on the Pacific Coast: $30,000 cash takes it. Hollis R. Anderson, Fort Jones, Calif. 24-3

For Sale

One million and half feet heavy hardwood timber, Maple, Beech, Basswood, Birch and Rock Elm. Also 25 acres heavy Cedar Swamp. Also Sawmill, 44 x 84—20 ft. high. 7 Bents, all 10 inch square. R. Elm Timber make good barn. All good machinery, nearly new, about 8 miles from loading point. Apply Samuel Leggatt, Gibraltar, Ont., Ravenna R. No. 2. 24-3

Miscellaneous

Wanted

Two patent Snow Plows. State price and time you can make delivery. Apply Bishop Lumber Co., Ltd., Nesterville, Ont. 23-24

For Sale

Sawdust in car lots. Write or phone W. H. Johnston, Pefferlaw, Ont. 24

For Sale

Complete dry-kiln outfit for two kilns, 100 feet long. Guaranteed. Gilpin Bros., Wiarton, Ont. 24-1

Car Wheels For Sale

125 pairs 18" chilled cast iron wheels, fitted to axles with roller bearing. Suitable for piling cars or tram line.

JNO. J. GARTSHORE,
58 Front Street W.,
Toronto, Canada

22-3

Wanted
4-foot LATH
Wire Collect

Charles H. Stewart,
691 Lothrop Avenue,
Detroit, Michigan

24

LOG STAMPS

Write us for particulars and prices

Superior Mfg. Co., Ltd.
93 Church St., Toronto

W. Y. LLOYD

Wholesale Lumber Dealer
51 Yonge St. Toronto, Ont.

PINE, SPRUCE or HARDWOOD LUMBER

To the Mill Man—I'm always in the market for Lumber, Shingles and Lath.
Please mail lists of your stock.

DR. BELL'S
Veterinary Wonder Remedies

10,000 one dollar ($1.00) bottles Free to horsemen who give the Wonder a fair trial. Guaranteed for Colic, Inflammation of the Lungs, Bowels, Kidneys, Fevers, Distemper, etc. Send 25c for Mailing Package, etc. Agents wanted. Write your address plainly. DR. BELL, V.S., Kingston, Ont.

Cut Your Selling Costs

Use MacLean Daily Reports and know where the projects are that offer the most profitable business. Reduce the percentage of wasted time and lost orders by concentrating on the most likely opportunities.

Rates and Samples on Request.

MacLEAN DAILY REPORTS, Ltd.
345 Adelaide Street West, TORONTO

The following limits are offered for sale. Cruiser's Reports and blueprints where available will be sent to Principals or their accredited Agents:—

British Columbia, Prince Rupert District:—

160 acres freehold within ½ mile of Skeena City on the Grand Trunk Pacific Ry. Estimated stand 5,000,000 bd. ft. within a few miles of Prince Rupert.

British Columbia R. R. Belt:—

Estimated stand approximately 300 million bd. ft. Capacity of mill 60,000 bd. ft. per day. The plant is on the main line of the C. P. R. and logs can be driven into the millpond at a minimum cost.

Quebec, Bonaventure County:

A Crownland limit of 4 sq. miles, estimated at 20,000 cords of Spruce and Fir is offered for sale. This limit is on Metapedia waters with a driving distance into the Metapedia, just above the Metapedia boom, of about 25 miles. The limit is about 14 miles from a station on the Intercolonial Ry. and the settlement extends back to within 3 or 4 miles of the northern boundary. Logs can be landed on a drivable stream for $10.00 per M. bd. ft. and can be driven into the Metapedia boom for about $2.00 per M. There should be a minimum profit in operating this tract of $40,000.

Ontario, McMahon Township:

36 sq. miles of Crownland, stand estimated at 50,000,000 bd. ft. with 140,000 cords additional.
Extensive tracts of timberlands for sale in all parts of Canada and Newfoundland.
List your properties with us for quick results.

BRADLEY & AVERY,
Timberland Factors & Cruisers,
4 Hospital Street,
Montreal, P.Q.

HORSES
UNION STOCK YARDS
OF TORONTO, Limited

"Canada's Greatest Live Stock Market" Capital, $1,500,000. Two Hundred Acres. Dundas St. cars to Keele St., West Toronto. Auction Sales every Wednesday. Private Sales Daily.

Correspondence Solicited.

WALTER HARLAND SMITH
Manager Horse Dept.

Geo. A. Velimezis

2 St. Constantin's Street - PIRAEUS. GREECE
Member of Piraeus Chamber of Commerce
ESTABLISHED 1902

Special Soft and Hardwood Agent and Broker

Cable Address: VELIMEZIS, PIRAEUS
Codes Used. A. B. C., 5th Edition, New Zebra

is prepared to consider offers and to accept Agencies for any kind of Canadian and American lumber on commission basis.

ADVANCES ON APPROVED CONSIGNMENTS

Seventeen Years' Experience

Review of Current Trade Conditions

Ontario and the East

December is naturally a quiet month in the lumber arena and consequently there is not a great deal of business going on particularly during the holiday period. Prices in all lines remain firm with a tendency to increase and building activity keeps up in all the leading cities, being practically double in most points to what it was last year.

The chief topic of conversation wherever lumbermen do congregrate is what will be the cut this year in the woods as compared with last winter, how high will prices go next spring, how great will be the demand and will the shortage that is predicted on all sides, be as much accentuated as some are led to believe at the present time. In the meantime, the scarcity of stock is becoming more pronounced all the while. 1 x 4, 5, 6 white pine is almost an unknown quantity and there is an exceptionally brisk demand for 1 in. white pine strips, which have been commanding a high figure at the mill. Hemlock is in brisk requisition and selling at high prices. The scarcity of hardwoods in all lines continues and there is no material change in the situation from that outlined in the last edition of the "Canada Lumberman."

The stocks of many retailers are very low, shingles are advancing and are delayed in delivery owing to the car congestion and the coal shortage, and lath as one wholesaler humorously put it "will soon be as extinct as the dodo." So far as prices on lath are concerned, these are practically open. One leading member of the trade when asked by another what he could get for No. 1 and No. 2 white pine lath, remarked, "Just whatever you have the nerve to ask."

The recent windstorm throughout Ontario created a great deal of havoc and unroofed many buildings of all kinds. The outcome has been an unexpected rush for shingles and other roofing materials, and some lumber merchants have been practically cleaned out of shingles. There has also been a great deal of repair work going on throughout the country and retail lumbermen in most centres were never busier than at the present time.

B. C. stock of all kinds is scarce, particularly rough clears, and only odds and ends are coming through. There have been so many advances in prices that it is hard to keep tab on the situation and it is predicted that values will go much higher by spring owing to the abnormal demand across the border for Coast and mountain stock of all kinds.

There is practically no lumber export business with Great Britain at the present time owing to the close of navigation at Canadian norts and then again matters are in a very uncertain state owing to the sharp decline in exchange and the excellent demand that has been prevailing at home. Some exporters have lost heavily through the low exchange rates existing between England and America.

Many large contracts were accepted last winter when Canada granted a fifty million dollar credit to the British Timber Control. Then the exchange rate was bolstered and stood at $4.86, and it was not expected that it would ever drop as low as it has. The rate dropped and Canadian dealers had to accept payment in pounds, shillings and pence, as the Britons had reserved the right to pay in either coinage.

Canadian exporters had to bring their prices down to compete with Scandinavian exporters, so that the margin of profit allowed them did not also allow for losses on exchange.

One local firm calculates that they are breaking about even by selling to United States and securing the premium on American exchange rates. An official of this company said that Canadian steamship companies cannot provide them with shipping space, so that they have to ship from American ports and on the basis of exchange rates obtaining there. The freight rates on land and sea are so high now that trans-Atlantic commerce is made more difficult than ever.

A leading manufacturer of hardwood flooring states that there is at the present time a great scarcity of rough lumber for flooring work, and that transportation difficulties are not at all favorable. Sales are now limited only by the capacity of machines and ability to secure suitable stock in order to meet the demand.

It is an ill wind that does not blow someone good and the recent hurricane throughout Ontario, which levelled trees, careened buildings and unroofed barns and sheds, has had the result of creating a lively business for retail lumbermen. There has never been such a demand for shingles as during the past fortnight, and the fact that many dealers had just received a car or two proved to be a happy stroke of business. The result of the unusual demand is that some retailers are now practically without stock.

Deliveries of shingles are slow and the price is getting stiffer and many yardmen made the mistake of not buying when they touched low-water mark a few weeks ago. Many expected that the price would fall to $6.00 but in this their hopes were not realized and before the figure got near that mark, it started to climb again. Wholesalers or manufacturers, who have any stocks on hand, will not sell lath without selling lumber and then will give the producers only part of a carload, filling up the rest of the space with other material.

Building activity continues very lively in all the leading centres and the increasing prices do not have any deterrent effect upon demand. More houses than ever will be erected next year, judging by present indications, and how far hemlock and white pine will soar is a matter of conjecture.

The total value of buildings erected in Toronto during the past season will likely reach $17,000,000, which will be just double the amounts spent in structural undertakings in 1918. The aggregate of the permits has of late been running nearly a m llion and a half a month.

United States

Business all over the United States has naturally been more or less affected by the prolonged coal strike, the general tie-up in transportation and also the cessation of activity in many manufacturing industries. The outlook of Mexico is none too reassuring. These and other factors are tending to disturb business, and there is naturally a feeling of uneasiness until a more settled state of affairs prevails. However, building is going on actively in most centres and a record expenditure in structural undertakings is looked for next season. There is very little hardwood stock unsold, and while more or less lumber is moving in the trade, it is mostly on old orders. There is a constant advancing of prices. Much of the advance during the year has been forced by the ever increasing cost of doing business; but a considerable part of it, and more particularly recent advances, have resulted from the bidding of buyers and the law of supply and demand. Fear is expressed in some quarters that the high prices will turn the attention of factory consumers to a search for substitutes which will react injuriously to the trade of the future.

Wholesale buyers are moving with considerable caution. They are afraid to contract for the delivery of lumber far into next year at current prices, for if the market recedes it would mean a considerable loss. The manufacture of northern hardwoods will soon commence, and mill men hope to get in a large supply of logs. The success of their efforts in this direction will depend largely on the labor supply and its efficiency, but the outlook for either is not of the best.

Heavy rains in the southern hardwood districts hold out the prospect of a repetition of this year's experience, when the mills were not able to operate until well along into the busy season of the year in trade.

Speaking of the outlook generally, a leading exchange says: In the three principal producing sections, the south, the north and the west, mills stocks are badly broken. In some places stocks have been practically cleaned out. If there is stock in pile, it is sold and oversold, and still the buyers persist. Failing to get the desirable items they are taking anything they can find, and are trying to contract ahead for stock that will be cut months hence.

Much comment is heard relative to high prices, and there is much expression of opinion that they are higher than is warranted; but the highest prices are being paid by those who are bidding the market up. So keen is the need for some items of lumber and so great the competition that the wholesalers and the factory consumers are, in a large measure, responsible for the flights of the market.

To the statement that high prices will soon have their effect in slowing up business comes the answer that industrial consumers are willing to pay the top of the market for supplies to be delivered in the future, and that they, in turn, are oversold on their products.

In spite of an earnest desire on the part of manufacturers to provide ahead for a large output next year, it looks as though the scarcity of labor and the attitude of available labor would prevent the completion of any such program.

The buying of Southern pine has been very active, and on lines on which have been keen competition, there have been steady ad-

vances. In fact buying is just about upon a level with the heavy buying spurt which normally comes in the early spring or late winter, and is largely due to the desire of foresighted lumbermen to cover their requirements while the "covering is good." Manufacturers restrict sales wherever possible and it is by no means easy to place any great volume of business for future delivery. Labor, weather and shipping conditions remain about the same, though in some localities the car supply is somewhat worse.

England

With the approach of the Christmas holidays there is not a great deal of activity in the lumber market and conditions will slow down until after the Yuletide period. Just what next year will bring forth, no one is prepared to state, but it is believed that conditions generally will become more settled and the industrial outlook more reassuring.

With labor difficulties out of the way and shopping on a normal basis, there is no reason why matters should not progress favorably in every direction. One of the big events of the past few days has been the opening of the timber exchange in London, and speaking of this auspicious event, a trade paper says: Too much stress cannot be laid upon the advantages accruing to the trade by its association with the Exchange, and the general feeling, expressed with enthusiasm, was that an excellent start had been made. Despite the very full publicity given to the trade as to place and time of meeting, it is curious that many of the members were, and are yet, in doubt of the day and hour set apart for the assembly. We desire to impress upon all concerned that the Exchange will be held on Wednesday of each week, between 2 p.m. and 4 p.m., in the Cannon-street Hotel, and, to avoid the possibility of forgetfulness, we shall refer to the fact in each issue of our paper until such time as there can be no misunderstanding. It is our pleasant duty to tender the Chairman and directors an expression of congratulation on the signal success of last Wednesday's meeting. The practical results accruing are not to be measured by the volume of work done at the moment. The seed of success, which was sown months ago, germinated in the formation of the Exchange, and its formal opening the fruition of faith in its future.

There has been little or no improvement in the state of affairs at the Port of London as regards timber. The quays are piled with goods, and fresh boats arrive with larger quantities than are being piled away. Consequently the congestion has become worse instead of better.

Several points of great interest have arisen with regard to the liability of the receivers when quay berths are not available for their steamers, and when the boats are nevertheless admitted into the docks. It appears to be recognized—in fact, we understand there has been a legal decision on the point—that the receivers are bound to provide barges for the discharge, and that if they do not provide them the shipper may do so at the expense of the merchants. It is, in fact, the duty of the receiver to see that the ship is discharged as rapidly as possible, and if circumstances do not permit of her discharge in the most convenient manner, then other arrangements must be made. If neither the shipper nor the receiver can secure barges, then the ship must wait at her own expense.

Firmness prevails in the mahogany market and the substantial upward movement of prices which has been a feature of the past few weeks shows no signs of abatement. All descriptions are in very strong request, and particularly so in the case of African wood, stocks of which are becoming very scarce, while, on the other hand, the inquiry is showing signs of considerable expansion, not only from railway and shipbuilding quarters in the United Kingdom, but also from Continental and U.S.A. sources.

The amount of business done in the timber trade in the Manchester district is well maintained, and the general outlook points to some good trading for a considerable time to come. The great difficulty of transport is causing much annoyance and worry, and orders are not being executed as promptly as desired. The Government scheme of motor haulage has not yet been started in Manchester, although Liverpool has some 80/100 motor lorries now at work at the docks. The shortage of railway wagons is no doubt the cause of the congested state of the quays.

Prices all round are firm, and holders of stocks are not anxious sellers unless at present values. With regard to new f.o.b. or c.i.f. business, there is very little moving, although it is stated that large contracts have been made with Swedish and Finnish shippers at advanced prices by a speculative syndicate.

Market Correspondence

SPECIAL REPORTS ON CONDITIONS AT HOME AND ABROAD

Deals Bring Record Prices on St. John Market

A much better tone prevails in the Eastern Spruce market and, coming, as it does, out of a darkened sky, leads one to believe that the wholesale and retail yards have not been buying through the year as much as they should have, only taking enough to cover the building which they knew was absolutely taking place, or which was in such definite shape in the hands of architects as to be equally safe for bidding.

The market all the season has been spasmodic and led the manufacturers to believe that if any extensive building operations were to take place, a very heavy demand would be made upon the mills to turn out material. The stocks of lumber at St. John, which are unsold to-day are very limited, and buyers, who are in the market are finding difficulty to locate what they need. This condition will become more acute as the mills are about finished sawing for the season, and will not resume operations until opening of navigation next spring. The only mills still running at St. John are Stetson, Cutler & Co., and practically all their stocks are sold to the British Government on old contracts.

In fact, there is not over two million feet of unsold merchantable stock at St. John to-day. This has not been a good fall for logging as it has been extremely wet during the last month and the usual amount of logs has not been put up. No snow has come to allow hauling, therefore the portable mills have not gotten into full swing, and very little new stock has yet been produced. In this immediate section men are asking excessive wages and are not producing up to normal, with supplies high; certainly logs will not be produced within $1.50 to $2.00 per M of last year's prices. Manufacturing will probably be in the same ratio of advance. Prices will assuredly have to be higher than during 1919 to produce any profits for manufacturers. Of course in some localities very little driving has to be done, and the deliveries to the mills are normal. In cases such as these a much cheaper log can be had, which the fortunate manufacturer can sell either lower than his fellows or reap a rich reward on the higher log levels.

Bank log cuts along the St. John will be heavier than for some years past as the farmers have large quantities of fir or balsam, which has been killed by the "bud worm," and unless cut this winter will be a dead loss; therefore, to save the fir, they are cutting extensively. This log, of course, will be very inferior in quality and will turn out a very poor grade of stock and large quantities of refuse. Of this log the manufacturer will be very careful and will not invest his money to any great extent unless he has no other resort. Normal cuts of logs are under contract for all St. John mills, but as a rule a certain amount are hung up each year on the drive and very few mills get a full season's cut.

Locally business is good and the factories are all as busy as possible, some running extra time to try to catch up with the contracts on hand, but as much other work is in need, it does not look as if it is possible to gain much headway. Next year will, no doubt, see the factories more pushed on orders than ever before.

Prices for export remain very firm. English deals have sold this week at the highest price ever realized at St. John. This cleans up about all the deals at this port which were unsold. Steamers are arriving and more deals are moving off the wharves than for some time, and by spring practically all stocks will be removed.

Prices in the American market have improved, ¾, 2/3, 2/4 sized are selling at $41.00 on cars St. John, while 2/6, 4/4, 4/6, 2-7 at $41.00 and 2/8 at $42.00, 2/9, 2/10 at $44.00, all on cars St. John, payment in American funds, which increases the price at least $1.75 per M under present exchange rates.

Laths $7.50 to $8.00 on cars. Not a lath in St. John unsold. Shingles remain very scarce and as high as last quotations. Extras and clears are all sold out.

Ottawa Stocks Decline and Prices Keep Soaring

Unusual stability, as to firmness in price, the keeping up of demand, and the continued decline in practically all stocks, together with another sharp advance in price, for the best grades of pine, and a big jump in the price of lath, provided some of the features of the Ottawa lumber market, for the first two weeks of December.

The outlook on all sides, excepting European export, and the recalling of a greater number of American cars on Canadian rails to the United States, due to the soft coal miners' strike, indicated that the market had a "bed rock" bottom. Business all around was better, prices higher, and the prospect of future trade brighter, than it was a year ago. All indications pointed to the maintenance of present prices till spring, if, in the meantime, they do not go still higher.

It was the best market for its season since the pre-war years, and showed several signs of growing stronger. One of the principal reasons was a report from the real estate market which indicated that a building boom is practically already assured for Ottawa next spring. Hundreds of thousands of dollars worth of works will be undertaken or brought to the stage of completion. Unrestricted export to foreign countries will likely open up in earnest, with a possibility of ocean rates dropping. Stocks are already low and will be lower by spring. There are already some symptoms that the programme of the lumbermen to materially increase their log output this winter, is already keeping up with the expected schedule.

In a nutshell the feeling in the trade was that lumber was going to be lumber, just the same as "pigs are pigs." The question is where are the stocks going to come from, to meet a highly inflated demand next spring? That this demand is coming at Ottawa is pretty well assured by the real estate market, which is stronger than for any year since the war commenced. For the month of November property transfers showed a substantial advance, there being 142 as compared with 98 in November 1918.

The good pine grades with lath, lead in the advance in prices, and established a new high price record. One and a half and one and a quarter to eight inch and up and 2 in. by 7 in. sidings went from $110 to $120 per M. No. 2 cuts, 2 x 8 advanced to $80. One inch by seven in. made the greatest leap of all climbing from $85 to $105 per thousand feet. Little of the latter stock was obtainable.

One and a quarter and 1½ in. good pine strips travelled from $75 to $99. Two inch strips went to $90, and pine good shorts and sidings imitated the product of aviation companies and climbed from $56 to $65. Lath reached the highest quotations it ever had on the Ottawa market. The No. 1 white pine grade went from $8 to $15. There was little or none of it available even at this figure. Lath in all grades was practically out of the market.

Rail transportation tightened up somewhat. Some shippers believed the foreign car situation would grow more acute, due to an apparent desire on the part of the American roads to get their cars back on their rails in the event of the strike of the soft coal miners continuing indefinitely.

Conditions with wood working factories remained good both as to labor and orders. All the factories were busy and reported they had enough business on their books to carry them into 1920. Owing to the increased cost of labor, and material, export prices on sash and door advanced about ten per cent. over previous lists. High class factory labor was somewhat scarce.

The woods operations of the lumbering companies while said on the whole as being generally satisfactory, were according to some reports not going ahead as fast as had been previously expected. A shortage of skilled woods labor was given as the chief cause, and "transients" was another. Weather conditions for camp operations were reported as having been good up to the first week of December. Little or no sickness among the men in the woods camps was reported.

The announcement from London that the pound sterling had dropped to $3.87½ caused considerable speculation in circles of the trade that export to European countries. Exporters agreed that the difference in the exchange rate if it continued would work hardship to them, pointing out if they had to bring out money to pay their ocean freight rates, and prices remained the same, that it would wipe out any margin of profit. Exporters looked for the demand next spring to come for stocks for rebuilding the devastated European countries outside of England.

In connection with the woods operations as regarding the activities of I.W.W. or One Big Union Workers, Ottawa lumbermen are firmly determined that the exponents of such doctrines in their camps will get a short shrift and be told to speedily find other quarters. "We have not been troubled much yet with Bolsheviks. We are, however, on the watch for them, and if we find persons entering our camps who are aiming to spread 'red' propaganda and create unrest, the question of their going or our staying is not going to be very long debated," remarked a well-known woods official of a leading lumbering company.

Market Conditions Generally Good in Montreal

Except for purely local business, Montreal market conditions are very satisfactory. Local trade is interfered with to some extent by the yards taking stock, but taking into consideration this and the season of the year, even this branch may be considered fairly good. The outlook for next year is generally considered to be excellent. There is promise of extensive building and of the Housing Commission getting to work on something like a practical basis. The local Trades and Labor Council have requested that the Housing Act be amended so that the conditions be made more easy for working people to build, and that the financial arrangements in particular be made less burdensome. The building permits for last month totalled $890,864, an increase of $714,819, while for the eleven months the total was $9,375,500, a gain of $4,491,824.

The sash and door manufacturers and allied branches are doing a very large business, much of the work being for out of town buildings. Recently there was an inquiry for several hundred sashes and doors for export.

The hardwood market continues very good, with a strong demand on U. S. account.

The B. C. market has undergone another change. Prices have again taken a further jump, the third since November 1. The greatest advance is in clears, although dimensions and boards are away up. The market is a very uncertain one, and wholesalers will not take orders without first ascertaining the prices asked by the mills. The demand is exceptionally good, especially for clears. Would-be buyers who hesitated found that prices have gone against them, and that delay in closing generally meant stiffer quotations if the goods were to be secured. Owing to a shortage of cars, the amount of stock available is small. A number of circumstances, such as the coal situation, has diverted cars to various purposes other than the transportation of lumber, with the result that only a small quantity can be shipped to the East.

There has been a revival in orders for lumber for the United States. For a time there was a lull in the inquiries, but once more U S. firms have come into the market.

Indications point to a shortage of men for woods operations. The lumber companies have applied to the Provincial Employment Agency for hundreds more men than are at present available, although over 1,100 men have been sent to camps in Quebec and Ontario. Representatives of five or six lumber companies are now in Montreal recruiting men. Wages have gone up from $55 to $60 per month to $60 and $65. Jobbers are willing to pay $90 per month. Reports from the province are to the effect that so far the weather is favorable for logging.

Nothing can be done in the way of exports to the U. K. for some months, but it is anticipated that when the season opens there will be a reduction in freight rates, which were very high, and which exercised a restraining influence on shipments by ordinary export firms during the past season. It was almost impossible to send lumber at the prevailing rates and compete with the lumber placed on the market by the Government.

The exports of pulpwood again declined in September. The total was $884,575, a decrease of $333,060. For the six months of the fiscal year the value was $5,089,693, a falling off of $4,238,208. Paper in September was exported more freely, while chemical pulp increased $647,479, and mechanical pulp $173,837. During the six months chemical pulp exports were smaller by $1,894,801, while mechanical pulp increased by $106,272. Paper was nearly five million and a quarter dollars to the good for the six months.

Larger Exports of Lumber to Britain

During the 1919 season Canada largely increased her exports of lumber to the United Kingdom. The following are the official returns of the quantities and values of the total lumber imports into the United Kingdom for the nine months ending September, 1918 and 1919, together with Canada's share of that trade:

	Quantity Loads	Value £	Quantity Loads	Value £
Wood and timber, hewn—				
Total imports	33,632	795,127	167,133	3,705,266
Canada	4,862	63,180	11,190	202,922
Wood and timber, sawn or split, fir—				
Total imports	996,283	13,334,147	2,749,421	30,257,627
Canada	84,105	886,131	654,087	7,460,133
Wood and timber, sawn or split, planed or dressed, unenumerated—				
Total imports	20,757	374,133	52,299	764,033
Canada	7,771	67,459	20,726	253,673

EDGINGS

Ontario

The Bishopric Wall Board Co., Ltd., Ottawa, Ont., are erecting a factory at a cost of $35,000.

The Bancroft Lumber & Mfg. Company, of which E. S. Hubbell, of Bancroft is manager, will erect sawmills at Paudash Lake, Ont., at a cost of $30,000.

It is reported in Fort William that the Canadian Car & Foundry Company has decided to embark there in the building of ships as one of its chief industries.

Trussler Bros., Limited, of Trout Creek, Ont., have sold out their interest in the lumber business at that point to the Dominion Wood and Lumber Company, Limited.

The O. & W. R. Smith lumber yard, Drayton Avenue, East Toronto, has been taken over by Sheppard & Gill, who propose to enlarge the plant and carry out extensive alterations. The site covers nearly one acre of ground.

The Canadian Cooperage Mfg. Co., Smith's Falls, Ont., are building an up-to-date heading mill to manufacture headings for cheese boxes, stock barrels, etc. The equipment is all in readiness and it will not be long before this plant is in operation.

A charter has been granted to the Canadian-American Resources, Limited, Toronto, with a capital of fifty million dollars. Wide powers are conferred on the new organization, and among them are to carry on the business of lumbermen, timbermen, sawmillers, etc.

Fire recently destroyed the sawmill at Hague's Point, Lakefield, owned and operated by John Charlton. Mr. Charlton had been in Bridgenorth for some time, cutting timber from his timber lot there. The mill was insured for $1,000 and was built about four years ago.

In the recent severe wind-storm, which visited Toronto, considerable damage was done to several lumber companies. The Simpson Planing Mills suffered a loss of some $500, and the Gall Lumber Co., also located at the foot of Spadina Ave., had much damage done to their premises and stock of lumber.

A charter has been granted to Murray Crawford, Limited, with a capital stock of $60,000 and head office in Campbellville, Halton County. The new concern will take over the lumber business conducted by Murray Crawford, and among the incorporators of the organization are Murray Crawford, Lloyd Crawford, Hart Crawford, James K. Mahon and Ed. D. Mahon, all of Campbellville.

Porritts & Spencer (Canada) Limited, with a capital stock of $1,000,000, and headquarters in Hamilton, have been incorporated. The company is empowered to acquire, buy and purchase from John K. Spencer, of Albany, N.Y., a parcel of land situate in Hamilton, and to manufacture and deal in felts and fabrics of all kinds and pulp, paper, and other fibrous substances from the raw material to the finished product.

The Nyando Pulp & Paper Company of Rochester, have commenced pulpwood operations at Windigo, near Port Arthur. Camps have been established and the wood that is taken out during the winter will be shipped across the line in the spring. The Nyando Company a couple of years ago purchased practically all the timber holdings of Hogan Bros., Fort William, on Lac de Mill Lac, said to be one of the finest tracts of spruce in Ontario.

A charter has been granted to the Dominion Rubber System Housing Co. (Waterloo), Limited, with a capital stock of $100,000 and hea doffice in Kitchener, to acquire lands and build dwellings of moderate size and improvements to be sold at a moderate price or rented, under the provisions of the Housing Accommodation Act. Among the incorporators are John A. Martin, Norman M. Davison, Walter Harttung and others, all of Kitchener.

A charter has been granted to the Hanover Lumber Co., Limited, with headquarters at Hanover, and a capital stock of $40,000. The company will take over the business now being conducted in Hanover by Earl F. Abell and Wm. Krauter under the partnership name of the Hanover Lumber Co. Among the incorporators of the company are Earl F. Abell, Wm. Krauter, Alex. Peppler, George Riechen and Norman W. Helwig, all of Hanover.

Complaints have been made to the Board of Control, Toronto, of the inadequacy of the police protection on the property between John Street and Spadina Avenue, where a large number of wholesale lumber yards are located. Thieves have been stealing the stock of late and the owners are demanding better guardianship of their interests. One lumberman stated that he had invested hundreds of thousands of dollars in plant and lumber at the foot of Spadina Avenue and was continually being harassed by burglars.

A series of resolutions affecting the welfare of the settler was presented to Premier Drury and his Ministers at Matheson by President Leith and A. E. Mills, of the District U.F.O. Club. They dealt with colonization and included a suggestion that portable sawmills be sent in by the Government to encourage the settler and to clear up the ground systematically. It was claimed that lumber could be delivered at the railway for twenty dollars per thousand feet. It was also urged that new road work should be planned six months ahead and that the district road inspector should have wider powers.

Eastern Canada

The J. B. A. Martin & Sons Company were recently registered in Montreal as dealers in lumber.

The Fassett Lumber Co., Limited, of Fassett, Que., whose plant has been started up again after alterations will saw hardwood until early in the spring.

George F. Chapman, a well-known lumberman, died recently at Burntland Brook, N.B. He had been ailing for a long time and was in his 57th year. For the past 40 years he had spent most of his time managing lumber camps.

It is stated that the MacLeod Pulp Company at Liverpool, N.S., has been acquired by American interests. The company has two mills on the Mersey River, two miles from Liverpool. The mills have a capacity, together, of fifty tons a day of dry pulp. It is understood that the interests in this deal have taken over large tracts of forest lands in the southern part of Nova Scotia. The purchasers plan to enlarge and extend the operations on a very substantial scale.

Frank W. Pickels, of Annapolis Royal, N.S., has been made a director of the Labrador Pulp & Lumber Co. This company is one whose lands were surveyed by the aerial expedition in Labrador last summer. Major Owen is at the head of the organization.

The St. Lawrence Box Co., Montreal, P.Q., was recently granted a provincial charter to manufacture and deal in boxes and containers of all kinds. Capital $80,000. M. A. Phalen, Westmount, P.Q., and C. G. Ogden, Montreal, P.Q., are two of the incorporators.

Price Bros. & Co., Ltd., Quebec, have filed a bill asking the local legislature to detach a section of Chicoutimi for the purpose of making a separate municipality under the name of Saguenay. The company are carrying out very extensive improvements in this district.

The sale of the controlling interest in the Pejepscott Paper Company and subsidiaries by the W. H. Parsons Company, of New York, to Julius H. Barnes, of Chicago, U. S. Wheat Director, was announced recently at Lewiston, Me. The property includes four mills in Maine and Nova Scotia, timber in Quebec, New Brunswick and Maine, and a fleet of tugs and barges. The sale price was estimated to be in excess of $750,000.

The Glen Falls Pulp Company, of Glen Falls, New York, which recently bought a large area of spruce limits on the Batiscan River, on the line of the Lake St. John Railway, Que., are now taking out logs on these limits and on the River Miguick which flows into the Batiscan. The logs are to be cut into pulpwood, at the mouth of the Batiscan River, and sent by canal boat to Glen Falls, where they will be manufactured into pulp.

The Bathurst Lumber Company, Limited, of Bathurst, N.B., have purchased two large sized barking drums from the Canadian Barking Drum Company, Limited, to take care of extensive alterations they are making in their wood room. The Donnacona Paper Company, Donnacona, Que., and the New Ontario Colonization Company, Jacksonboro, Ont., have also installed extra drums which were secured from the same company.

A federal charter has been granted to the St. Maurice Power Co., Ltd., with a capital stock of $6,500,000, and headquarters in Montreal, to carry on the business of an electric light, heat and power company, to build and construct dams, reservoirs, conduits, flumes, canals, etc. Various other wide powers are conferred upon the company, the incorporators of which are Howard Murray, Wm. S. Hart, Julien C. Smith, James Wilson and Gordon W. McDougall.

The forest belonging to the late E. Stebelin; of Weymouth, N.S., were recently cruised by a party of surveyors who have found in the property 48,000,000 superior feet of merchantable spruce and pine, 70,000 cords of pulp wood, 200,000 feet of hemlock, 3,000,00 superior feet of merchantable hardwood. The surveyors have allowed for farms, burned, etc., 1,000 acres, leaving a solid block of 8,500 acres of green timber. This land, situated on the Tusket River, constitutes the largest block of timber in the west side of lower Nova Scotia.

Western Canada

The Border Lumber Co., of Cascade, B.C., has been granted a charter. The capital stock is $20,000.

The Smith Lumber Co. have purchased the lumber business formerly conducted by Cushing Bros., Limited, at Red Deer, Alta.

The Elliott Shingle and Lumber Co., Limited, of Vancouver, has been granted a charter. The capital stock is $15,000.

The Otis Staples Lumber Company, at Wycliffe, will begin soon the construction of ten new houses for the workers there.

T. H. Tait, manager of the Aetna Saw Works of Vancouver, has taken out a permit for the construction of a saw factory on Industrial Island.

Recent incorporations in Alberta include the McKenna Lath & Lumber Co., Ltd., Chip Lake, Alta., and the Dome Lumber Co., Ltd., Edmonton, Alta.

J. H. Hayes & Son, of Fort Steele, B.C., have gone into the manufacture of lumber and will deal in mining timber, ties, props, etc. The company's mill is located six miles out of Steele.

The Trout Lake Shingle Mills Co., Ltd., of Trout Lake, B.C., is another new organization which has recently taken out letters patent. The capital stock is $50,000.

Miller Saw Trimmer Company, incorporated in the State of Pennsylvania, has registered to do business in British Columbia; capital $500,000, head offices, Pittsburg and Vancouver.

The Clark & Phillips Distributing Company were recently registered in Alberta. This company will deal in lumber and maintain offices in Vancouver, B.C. and Fort Saskatchewan, Alta. The partners are J. L. Phillips and H. W. Clark.

A serious shortage of freight cars is being reported by New Westminster lumber mills who claim they are unable to fill orders for eastern firms on account of the inability to obtain cars. At the Fraser Mills recently over one hundred carloads of lumber were awaiting shipment.

The Small-Bucklin Lumber Co., of New Westminster, B.C., is installing a horizontal band resaw, believed to be the first machine of its kind to be used in a British Columbia sawmill. It is estimated that it will add a matter of 35,000 feet to the daily capacity, bringing it up to 125,000 feet in nine hours.

Reports from various B. C. logging camps are that the supply of logs is away below normal and should an extra demand develop an acute shortage would result. The outlook for the price of lumber in the spring is that all records for British Columbia will be broken.

It is estimated that over 500,000 houses are needed in Great Britain to meet the scarcity there, according to Mr. A. E. Howard, of the War Purchasing Commission, who has just returned from a visit to several of the large British centres, including London, where he discussed with prominent capitalists and members of the government, the part the lumber industry of Canada, more particularly British Columbia, can take in solving the problem existing there. One of the immediate results will be the visit to the West of several British financial men.

Thousands of sawyers will tell you of their experiences with other saws before they permanently selected Disston High-Grade Cross-Cut Saws.

They will tell you of hard work with others saws that "bind" and won't "take hold."

Usually, they also speak of having tried saws that wouldn't hold their set in "hard cutting."

Then, too, they sometimes say they lost much time with saws that had to be sharpened "every time you turn around."

Now these men insist on Disston Cross-Cut Saws—they know that to use an inferior saw is to waste time and energy.

HENRY DISSTON & SONS, INC., TORONTO, CANADA

Branch: Vancouver, B. C.

DISSTON-SAWS

GATES REFRACTORIES,

382 St. James Street - - - MONTREAL

Manufacturing All Kinds of Special Shapes in Refractories

Remember, we are making all our own blocks and making a specialty of special shapes.

We are using a high grade fire clay, which is the factor of supreme importance in all processes of manufacture.

Our burners are experts. When you are in the market be sure and write us as we know you will find our proposition interesting.

Our stoker arches are designed to promote combustion and give longer life.

Our door arches and jambs are made to withstand the strong-armed boy with the slice bar.

Our side wall blocks are made to eliminate the many joints that clinkers stick to, when ordinary fire brick is used. They give longer life and reduce air leaks to a minimum.

We designed these arches and blocks so that any handy man could replace same in half the time that it takes to repair a standard fire brick job.

Remember, Gates' blocks means cutting yo cost of upkeep and fuel bills.

High Temperature Fire Clay for Emergency Repairs.

We specialize in all kinds of POWER PLANT BRICK WORK

The services of our engineers are offered to you without obligation at any time.

Send for our new catalogue describing all kinds of special shapes in fire bricks.

Gates Refractories Limited

382 St. James Street - MONTREAL

Please send your latest catalogue as advertised in the Canada Lumberman.

Name ....

Address ....

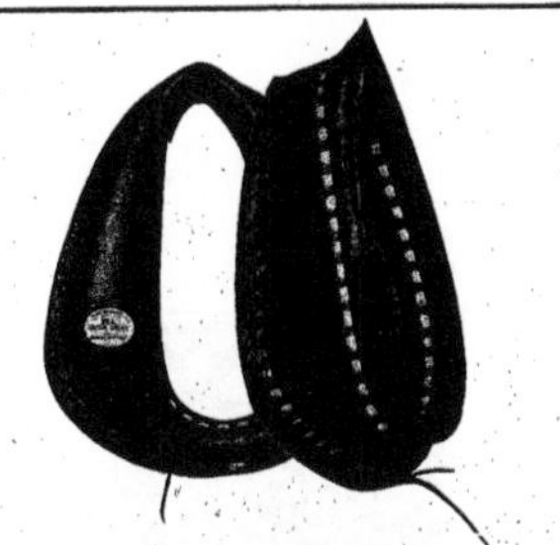

No. 1 IRISH DRAY LOGGING COLLAR

Logging Collars, Harness & Saddles

Send for Special Catalogue of Saw Mill Supplies

TOM PADGITT COMPANY

WACO, TEXAS

"Beware of Imitations"

There is only one Genuine

CANE MOLA

very heavy 100% pure Sugar Cane Molasse

Sold in strong iron-hooped barrels at a very reasonable price

Sprinkle Cane Mola over your straw, old hay, corn stover, fodder, ensilage, screenings, etc., and reduce cost of feeding.

Cane Mola will keep your horses healthy and improve their appearance. They will winter at hard work and finish in excellent condition in the spring.

Cane Mola is ideal for keeping horses in good shape during the winter in the lumber camps.

ANALYSIS

The value of Cane Mola is principally in its sugars, salts and flavor.

It contains other ingredients of value.

Sugars (average) . . . . 55 per cent.
(guaranteed minimum 52 per cent.)
Other Carbohydrates (average) . . . 15 per cent.
Natural Salts (average) . . . . . 5 per cent.
(not over 7 per cent.—just the right amount to act as mild laxative.)
No fibre.
Protein . . . . 4 per cent.
Moisture . . . . 4 per cent.

Write for full Information and Booklet

The Cane Mola Company of Canada, Limited

118 St. Paul Street West, Montreal

Books For Sale

Special Prices

"A Manual for Northern Woodsmen," by Austin Cary. Published in 1918 by The Harvard University Press, Cambridge, Mass. 302 pages and illustrations. Price $2.75.

Baughman's "Buyer & Seller." The handiest labor-saving book for lumbermen ever devised. Desk size, 800 pages, $3.00. Pocket edition, 188 pages, $1.50.

"Baughman's Cost Tables" for figuring cost of any article by the foot, piece, pound or ton. 127 pages, 5¼ in. by 7 in. Price, flexible leather, $1.50; flexible Morocco, $2.50.

Chapin's Lumber Reckoner, valuable in the saving of time, labor and errors. Size 4 in. x 7 in., 171 pages. Price, cloth binding, $2.25, Morocco, $3.25.

"Climax" tally book, bound in sheep, with hand straps. Size 4¼ x 8½, 110 pages. Price $1.75.

"Lumberman's and Logger's Guide," just published by the author, Bernard Brereton, size, 6 in x 9 in., 136 pages, dealing with the merits and uses of Douglas Fir, California Redwood and the leading Commercial Woods of the Pacific Coasts. Contains Log Tables and other useful information. Price $1.00.

"The Kiln Drying of Lumber," a Practical and Theoretical Treatise, by Harry Donald Tiemann, M.E., M.F. Just published by J. B. Lippincott Co. 316 pages, illustrated. Price $4.50.

Seasoning of Wood; A Treatise of the Natural and Artificial Processes Employed in the Preparation of Lumber for Manufacture, with Detailed Explanations of its Uses, Characteristics and Properties, by Joseph Wagner. Published by D. Van Nostrand Co., in 1917. 274 pages, illustrated. Price $3.00.

The Preservation of Structural Timber, by Howard F. Weiss. Published in 1915 by McGraw-Hill Book Company, 312 pages, illustrated. Price $3.

Timber, Its Strength, Seasoning and Grading, by Harold S. Betts. 234 pages, illustrated. Price $3.00.

Utilization of Wood-Waste (Second Revised Edition), by Ernst Hubbard. Published in 1915 by Scott, Greenwood & Sons. 192 pages, illustrated. Price $2.00.

Vest Pocket Ready Reckoner for Lumbermen. 11th edition. Published by the American Lumberman. Price 35 cents.

CANADA LUMBERMAN

347 Adelaide Street West · TORONTO

Special List of

Dr. Bell's Veterinary Wonder Medicines

	Price
Dr. Bell's Veterinary Medical Wonder	$1.00
Dr. Bell's Wonder Fire Blister, per box	1.00
Dr. Bell's Wonder Worm and Indigestion Powder (24 pds.)	.50
Dr. Bell's Wonder Kidney, Water and Blood Powder (24 pds.)	.50
Dr. Bell's Wonder Distemper Cough and Heave Powder (24 pds.)	.50
Dr. Bell's Wonder Condition Powders	.35 and .50
Dr. Bell's Wonder Worm and Physic Ball	.75
Dr. Bell's Wonder Liniment for Horses and Cattle	.75 and 1.00
Dr. Bell's Wonder Lotion for Horses and Cattle	.75 and 1.00
Dr. Bell's Wonder Eye Lotion	.50 and .75
Dr. Bell's Wonder Hoof Ointment and Gall Cure Combined.	.50 and .75
Dr. Bell's Wonder Cow Physic (special)	.50
Dr. Bell's Wonder Pain Stop	(Unquoted)
Dr. Bell's Wonder Gall Cure	.25 and .50
Dr. Bell's Wonder Extract Liniment	per qt., $1.75; per gallon, $6.00
Dr. Bell's Wonder Extract Lotion	per qt., $2.00; per gallon, $6.00
Dr. Bell's Wonder Stock Conditioner and Stock Food.	Send for circular.

Special Household Remedies for Camp use:

Dr. Bell's Wonder Liniment for Man (cures rheumatism and all sprains)	.50 and .75
Dr. Bell's Wonder Ointment	.25
Dr. Bell's Wonder Balsam of Pine Cough Syrup	.35 and .50
Dr. Bell's Wonder Kidney Pills	.25
Dr. Bell's Wonder Stomach and Liver Pills	.25
Dr. Bell's Wonder Rheumatism Tablets (something new).	
Dr. Bell's Wonder Panacea, large bottle	1.00

These medicines are all wonders. Agents wanted in every town and county in Canada. Can make good. Write for terms. Write name and address plainly; also nearest express office.

Dr. Bell's Veterinary Medical Wonder is composed of twenty of the most powerful and costly medicines in the world; and, according to reports from agents and those using it from coast to coast, including all the provinces (old and new) throughout the entire Dominion, also Newfoundland, Medical Wonder has saved in horses, cattle, sheep, and swine over $10,000,000 to the stock-owners of Canada during the past fifteen years, of which $2,500,000 worth were saved by Medical Wonder in 1918.

BANK REFERENCES.—Dr. Bell refers to Northern Crown and Toronto Banks of this city or any bank in Kingston.

A $1.00 bottle free to any Horseman sending 25c for mailing, packing, etc.

Special Wholesale Rates to Lumbermen

Dr. Bell Veterinary Wonder Co.

KINGSTON. ONT.

Reasons Why You Should Use

ATKINS STERLING QUALITY SAWS

Reason No. 1—ATKINS STEEL
Reason No. 2—ATKINS WORKMANSHIP
Reason No. 3—THE TEMPER
Reason No. 4—THE NAME

Reason No. 5 – The Guarantee

IN buying saws a man endeavours to buy service. In choosing Atkins he ensures the very best service. This is not merely a claim; we guarantee it. It is the policy and intention of the E. C. Atkins Company to see to it that any article bearing this name shall be of the highest quality, and we deem it a favor to be advised in regard to any such item which does not give perfect satisfaction.

Atkins represents the surest, safest and most satisfactory saw investment from every standpoint. If we did not implicitly believe this we could not conscientiously carry on business. Our guarantee is absolute satisfaction and you are protected by the Atkins' name.

Watch for Reason No. 6

Send for Free Catalogue

E. C. ATKINS & CO.

Factory: HAMILTON, ONT. Branch: 109 Powell St., VANCOUVER, B.C.

Excelsior Cutting Machinery

Manufactured By

The Elmira Machinery and Transmission Co.

Elmira, Ont.

Write for Circular and Prices

Peeling Potatoes

The Cyclone Vegetable Peeler

JOHN BURNS & CO., MONTREAL

Established 1865

New England Chain Works

Established 1867

Clinton E. Hobbs Co., Proprietors.
Established 1906. Incorporated 1913.

Manufacturers of

All sizes Wrought Iron and Steel Chain for Lumber, Quarry and Railroad requirements, Chain Hoists and Lifting Appliances.

Sales Office:

12 Pearl St. Boston, Mass. U.S.A.

Factories and Warehouses:

Everett - - Mass.

The Largest Veneer Lathe in the World is a Coe

The Coe Manufacturing Co.

Painesville, Ohio, U. S. A.

New RAILS Relaying

12 to 80 pounds per yard.

LOGGING CARS

Jno. J. Gartshore

58 Front St. West, Toronto

International Products

International Chemical Company

44-46 Lombard St. - Toronto, Ontario

ALPHABETICAL INDEX TO ADVERTISERS

CURRENT LUMBER PRICES—WHOLESALE

TORONTO, ONT.

Prices in Carload Lots, F.O.B. cars Toronto

White Pine:

1 x 4/7 Good Strips	$70 00	$74 00
1¼ and 1½ x 4/7 Good Strips	73 00	76 00
1 x 8 and up Good Sides	95 00	103 00
2 x 4/7 Goor Strips	75 00	78 00
1¼ and 1½ x 8 and wider Good Sides	100 00	110 00
2 x 8 and wider Good Sides	110 00	115 00
1 in. No. 1, 2 and 3 Cuts	70 00	74 00
5/4 and 6/4 No. 1, 2 and 3 Cuts	73 00	76 00
2 in. No. 1, 2 and 3 Cuts	80 00	83 00
1 x 4 and 5 Mill Run	52 00	53 00
1 x 6 Mill Run	53 00	56 00
1 x 7, 9 and 11 Mill Run	52 00	55 00
1 x 8 Mill Run	55 00	57 00
1 x 10 Mill Run	58 00	60 00
1 x 12 Mill Run	60 00	64 00
5/4 and 6/4 x 4 Mill Run	54 00	55 00
5/4 and 6/4 x 5 Mill Run	54 00	55 00
2 x 4 Mill Run	53 00	54 00
2 x 6 Mill Run	54 00	55 00
2 x 8 Mill Run	54 00	55 00
2 x 10 Mill Run	56 00	58 00
2 x 12 Mill Run	58 00	62 00
1 in. Mill Run Shorts	42 00	45 00
1 x 4 and up 6/16 No. 1 Mill Culls	42 00	45 00
1 x 10 and up 6/16 No. 1 Mill Culls	48 00	49 00
1 x 12 and up 6/16 No. 1 Mill Culls	48 00	49 00
1 x 4 and up 6/16 No. 2 Mill Culls	34 00	36 00
1 x 10 x 12 6/16 No. 2 Mill Culls	37 00	38 00
1 x 4 and up 6/10 No. 3 Mill Culls	25 00	27 00

Red Pine:

1 x 4 and 5 Mill Run	44 00	46 00
1 x 6 Mill Run	46 00	48 00
1 x 8 Mill Run	47 00	48 00
1 x 10 Mill Run	48 00	50 00
2 x 4 Mill Run	46 00	48 00
2 x 6 Mill Run	47 00	48 00
2 x 8 Mill Run	48 00	49 00
1 in. Clear and Clear Face		Open
2 in. Clear and Clear Face		Open

Spruce:

1 x 4 Mill Run	43 00	45 00
1 x 6 Mill Run	48 00	50 00
1 x 8 Mill Run	48 00	50 00
1 x 10 Mill Run	49 00	51 00
1 x 12 Mill Run Spruce	51 00	52 00
Mill Culls	37 00	39 00

HEMLOCK, No. 1

(In car load lots f.o.b. Toronto)

1 x 4 and 5 in. x 9 to 16 ft.	39 00	41 00
1 x 6 in. x 9 to 16 ft.	44 00	45 00
1 x 8 in. x 9 to 16 ft.	44 00	45 00
1 x 10 and 12 in. x 9 to 16 ft.	45 00	46 00
1 x 7, 9 and 11 in. x 9 to 16 ft.	42 00	44 00
2 x 4 to 12, 10 and 16 ft.	44 00	45 00
2 x 4 to 12 in., 12 and 14 ft.	44 00	45 00
2 x 4 to 12 in., 18 ft.	46 00	47 00
2 x 4 to 12 in., 20 ft.	47 00	48 00
1 in. No. 2, 6 ft. to 16 ft.	36 00	38 00
2" No. 2, 4" and up, width 6 to 16 ft.	36 00	37 00

DOUGLAS FIR

(Delivered in Toronto)

Dimension Timber up to 32 feet:

6x6 and 8, 10x10 and 12, 12x12	$53 00
6x10, 8x10, 10x14, 12x14, 14x14	53 50
6x12, 8x12	54 00
14x16, 16x16	54 50
6x14, 8x14, 10x16, 12x16	55 00
14x18	55 50
8x16, 10x18, 12x18	56 00
18x18, 20x20	56 50
12x20, 24x24	57 00

Timber in lengths over 32 feet subject to negotiation.

Fir flooring, 1 x 3, edge grain		84 50
Fir flooring, 1 x 4, flat grain		69 50
Fir flooring, 1 x 4, edge grain		84 50
No. 1 x 2, 1-in. clear Fir rough	73 75	81 75

(Depending upon widths).

No. 1 and 2, 1¼ and 1½ in., clear Fir rough	85 25	87 25
No. 1 and 2 2" clear Fir rough	76 00	88 00
1 x 5 and 1 x 6 Fir casing		85 50
1 x 8 and 1 x 10 Fir base		87 50
1¼ & 1½ x 8, 10 & 12" E. G. stepping		95 75
1¼ & 1½ x 8, 10 & 12" F.G. stepping		85 75
1-in. clear Fir, d 4 sides	73 25	81 25
1¼x1½ in. clear Fir, d 4 sides	73 25	83 25
XXX 6 butts to 2 in.	7 00	7 40
XXXXX 5 butts to 2 in.	8 00	8 40

LATH

No. 1 White Pine, 4 ft.	Open
No. 2 White Pine, 4 ft.	"
No. 3 White Pine, 4 ft.	"
Mill run white pine, 32 in.	"
Merchantable spruce lath, 4 ft.	"

TORONTO HARDWOOD PRICES

The prices given below are for carloads f.o.b. Toronto, from wholesalers to retailers, and are based on a good percentage of long lengths and good widths, without any wide stock having been sorted out. War tax of seven and half per cent. on imported woods, and also the prevailing rate of exchange paid by purchaser.

ASH, WHITE

(Dry weight 3800 lbs. per M. ft.)

	1s & 2s	No. 1 Com.	No. 2 Com.	No. 3 Com.
4/4	$145.00	$90.00	$60.00	$35.00
5/4 & 6/4	160.00	130.00	70.00	40.00
8/4	190.00	160.00	80.00	40.00
10/4 & 12/4	250.00	220.00	120.00	.....
16/4	275.00	240.00	140.00	.....

ASH, BROWN

4/4	$90.00	$70.00	$55.00	$43.00
6/4	95.00	80.00	75.00	55.00
8/4	98.00	85.00	80.00	55.00

BIRCH

(Dry weight 4000 lbs. per M. ft.)

	1s & 2s $		No. 1 Com. $		No. 2 Com. $
4/4	90	95	65	70	60
5/4 & 6/4	95	100	75	80	65
8/4	95	100	75	80	70
10/4 and 12/4	115	120	95	100	80
16/4	130	135	100	105	90

BASSWOOD

(Dry weight 2500 lbs. per M. ft.)

	1s & 2s	No. 1 Com.	No. 2 Com.	No. 3 Com.
4/4	$90.00	$65.00	48.00	$38.00
5/4 & 6/4	95.00	70.00	53.00	40.00
8/4	98.00	72.00	55.00	42.00

CHESTNUT

(Dry weight 2800 lbs. per M. ft.)

	1s & 2s	No. 1 Com.	Sound Wormy
4/4	$105.00	$85.00	$50.00
5/4 & 6/4	115.00	92.00	53.00
8/4	125.00	97.00	55.00

ELM, SOFT

(Dry weight 3100 lbs. per M. ft.)

4/4	$75.00	$60.00	$50.00	$38.00
6/4 & 8/4	90.00	75.00	60.00	45.00
12/4	105.00	90.00	80.00	

GUM, RED

(Dry weight 3300 lbs. per M. ft.)

	Plain 1s & 2s	Plain No. 1 Com.	Quartered 1s & 2s	Quartered No. 1 Com.
4/4	$145.00	$115.00	$160.00	$130.00
5/4	150.00	120.00	170.00	135.00
6/4	155.00	125.00	175.00	140.00
8/4	170.00	145.00	185.00	145.00

Figured Gum, $10 per M. extra, in both plain and quartered.

GUM, SAP

	1s & 2s	No. 1 Com.
4/4	$85.00	$70.00
5/4 & 6/4	90.00	75.00
8/4	100.00	85.00

HICKORY

(Dry weight 4500 lbs. per M. ft.)

	1s & 2s	No. 1 Com.	No. 2 Com.
4/4	$100.00	$70.00	$45.00
5/4	120.00	85.00	55.00
6/4	125.00	85.00	55.00
8/4	135.00	95.00	60.00

MAPLE, HARD

(Dry weight 3900 lbs. per M. ft.)

	1s & 2s	Com. No. 1	Com. No. 2	Com. No. 3
4/4	$80.00	$65.00	$50.00	$35.00
5/4 & 6/4	90.00	75.00	60.00	40.00
8/4	95.00	100.00	65.00	40.00
12/4	115.00	100.00	80.00	
16/4	135.00	120.00	95.00	

SOFT MAPLE

The quantity of soft maple produced in Ontario is small and it is generally sold on a log run basis, the locality governing the prices.

WHITE AND RED OAK

(Plain sawed. Dry weight 4000 lbs. per M. ft.)

	1s & 2s	No. 1 Com.
4/4	$155.00	$115.00
5/4 & 6/4	160.00	120.00
8/4	160.00	120.00
10/4	165.00	125.00
12/4	165.00	125.00
16/4	180.00	130.00

WHITE OAK, Quarter Cut

(Dry weight 4000 lbs. per M. ft.)

	1s & 2s	No. 1 Com.
4/4	$273.00	$194.00
5/4 and 6/4	283.00	204.00
8/4	293.00	214.00

RED OAK, Quarter Cut

	1s & 2s	No. 1 Com.
4/4	$210.00	$160.00
5/4 and 6/4	220.00	175.00
8/4	225.00	180.00

OTTAWA, ONT.

Manufacturers' Prices

Pine good sidings:

1-in. x 7-in. and up		$105 00
1¼-in. and 1½-in., 8-in. & up		120 00
2-in. x 7-in. and up		120 00
No. 2 cuts 2 x 8-in. and up.		80 00

Pine good strips:

1-in.		80 00
1¼-in. and 1½-in.		90 00
2-in.		90 00

Pine good shorts:

1-in. x 7-in. and up		65 00
1-in. x 4-in. to 6-in.		70 00
1¼-in. and 1½-in.		78 00
2-in.		78 00
7-in. to 9-in. A sidings		63 00
Pine, No. 1 dressing sidings		68 00
Pine, No. 1 dressing strips		65 00
Pine, No. 1 dressing shorts		50 00
Pine, 1-in. x 4-in. s.c. strips		51 00
Pine, 1-in. x 5-in. s.c. strips		52 00
Pine, 1-in. x 6-in. s.c. strips		54 00
Pine, 1-in. x 7-in. s.c. strips		54 00
Pine, 1 x 8-in. s.c., 12 to 16 ft.	48 00	56 00
Pine, 1-in. x 10-in. M.R.		58 00
Pine, s.c. sidings, 1½ and 2-in.		55 00
Pine, s.c. strips, 1-in.	45 00	49 00
1¼, 1½ and 2-in.		56 00
Pine, s.c. shorts, 1 x 4 to 6 in.		45 00
Pine, s.c. and bet., shorts, 1 x 5		45 00
Pine, s.c. and bet., shorts, 1 x 6		47 00
Pine, s.c. shorts, 6'-11', 1"x10"		52 00

Pine box boards:

1"x4" and up, 6'-11'		40 00
1"x3", 12'-16'		44 00
Pine, mill culls, strips and sidings, 1-in. x 4-in. and up, 12-ft. and up		40 00
Mill cull shorts, 1-in. x 4-in. and up, 6-ft to 11-ft.		38 00
O. culls r & w p		28 00

RED PINE, LOG RUN

mill culls out, 1-in.	36 00	42 00
mill culls out, 1¼-in.	36 00	42 00
mill culls out, 1½-in.	38 00	42 00
mill culls out, 2-in.	40 00	42 00
mill culls, white pine, 1"x7" and up		40 00

MILL RUN SPRUCE

1"x4" and up, 6'-11'		42 00
1"x4" and up, 12'-16'		42 00
1"x9"-10" and up, 12'-16'		48 00
1¼"x7" 8-9" and up, 12'-16'		48 00
1¼ x 10 and up, 12'-16'		50 00
1½" & 2" x 12" and up, 12'-16'		50 00
Spruce, 1-in. clear (fine dressing and B)		
Hemlock, 1-in. cull	25	
Hemlock, 1-in. log run	30	
Hemlock, 2x4, 6, 8, 10, 12/16'	30	
Tamarac	24	
Basswood, log run, dead culls out	46	
Basswood, log run, mill culls out	45 00	
Birch, log run	48 [illegible]	[illegible] 00
Soft Elm, common and better, 1, 1½, 2-in.	25 00	30 00
Ash, black, log run	32 00	40 00
1 x 10 No. 1 barn		52 00
1 x 10 No. 2 barn		46 00
1 x 8 and 9 No. 2 barn		42 00

Lath per M:

No. 1 white pine, 1½-in. x 4 ft.	15 00
No. 2 white pine	14 00
Mill run white pine	10 00
Spruce, mill run 1½-in.	12 00
Red pine, mill run	12 00
Hemlock, mill run	10 00
32-in. lath	3 50

White Cedar Shingles:

XXXX, 18-in.		7 50
Clear butt, 18-in.		6 50
18-in. xx		5 00
Spruce logs (pulp)	13 00	15 00

QUEBEC, QUE.

WHITE PINE

	Cts. Per Cubic Foot	
First class Ottawa waney, 18-in. average, according to lineal	80	90
19 in. and up average	90	100

SPRUCE DEALS

	Per M. Ft.	
3 in. unsorted Quebec, 4 in. to 6 in. thick	$34 00	$37 00
3 in. unsorted, Quebec, 7 in. to 8 in. thick	38 00	40 00
3 in. unsorted Quebec, 9 in. thick	40 00	45 00

OAK

	Cts. Per Cubic Ft.	
According to average and quality 55 ft. cube	90	1 00

ELM

According to average and quality, 40 to 45 feet, cube	95	1 05
According to average and quality, 30 to 35 feet	75	85

BIRCH PLANKS

1 to 4 in. thick, per M. ft.	40 00	45 00

SARNIA, ONT.

FINE, COMMON AND BETTER

1 x 6 and 8 in.	00
1 in., 8 in. and up wide	00
1¼ and 1½ in. and up wide	00
2 in. and up wide	00

CUTS AND BETTER

4/4 x 8 and up No. 1 and better	82
6/4 x 8 and up No. 1 and better	82
8/4 x 8 and up No. 1 and better	97

No. 1 CUTS

1 in., 8 in. and up wide	72 00
1¼ in., 8 in. and up wide	82 00
1½ in., 8 in. and up wide	82 00
2 in., 8 in. and up wide	87 00
2½ and 3 in., 8 in. and up wide	107 00
4 in., 8 in. and up wide	112 00

No. 1 BARN

1 in., 10 to 16 ft. long	$59 00	$60 00
1¼, 1½ and 2 in., 10/16 ft.	63 00	72 00
2½ to 3 in., 10/16 ft.	77 00	

No. 2 BARN

1 in., 10 to 16 ft. long	56 00	62
1¼, 1½ and 2 in., 10/16 ft.	57 00	63
2½ in. to 3 in.	70 00	

No. 3 BARN

1 in., 10 to 16 ft. long	52 00	62 00
1¼, 1½ and 2 in., 10/16 ft.	55 00	57 00

BOX

1 in., 1¼ in. & 1½ in., 10/16 ft.	47 00	49 00

MILL CULLS

Mill Run Culls

1 in., 4 in. and up wide, 6/16 ft.	$39 00
1¼, 1½ and 2 in.	40 00

LATH

No. 1 48 in. White Pine	$8 00
No. 2 48 in. White Pine	7 50
No. 3 48 in. White Pine	7 00
32 in. Pine	3 50
48 in. Hemlock	7 00
32 in. Hemlock	3 00

ST. JOHN, N.B.

ROUGH LUMBER

Wholesale Prices Per M. Sq. Ft.

2x3, 2x4, 3x3, 3x4, Rgh. Merch. Spr.	$47 00
2x3, 2x4, 3x3, 3x4 Dressed 1 edge	49 00
2x3, 2x4, 3x3, 3x4 Dressed 4 sides	53 00
2x6, 2x7, 3x5, 4x4, 4x6, all rough	50 00
2x8, 3x7, 5x5, 6x6	52 00
2x9, 3x8, 6x8, 7x7	55 00
2x10, 3x9	60 00
2x12, 3x10, 3x12, 8x8 and up	62 00
Merch. Spr. Bds. Rough, 1x3-4 & 5	40 00
" " " " 1x6	45 00
" " " " 1x7 & up.	45 00
Refuse Bds., Deals & Setgs.	30 00

Above random lengths up to 18-0 long.
Lengths 19-0 & up $5.00 extra per M.

For planing Merch. and Refuse Bds. add $2.00 per M to above prices.
Laths $6,50 per M. pieces.

SHINGLES

	Per M.
Cedar, Extras	$7 00
" Clears	6 50
" 2nd Clears	5 75
" Extra No. 1	4 25
Spruce	4 25

WINNIPEG, MANITOBA

No. 1 SPRUCE

Dimension	S.1.S and 1.E 6 ft.	8 ft.	10 ft.
x [illegible]	$38 50	$41 50	$43 00
x [illegible]	40 50	41 50	45 00
x 8	40 50	42 50	45 00
2 x 10	40 50	43 50	46 00

(Continued on page [illegible])

CURRENT LUMBER PRICES—Continued

2 x 12	43 50	41 50	47 00
	12 ft.	14 ft.	16 ft.
2 x 4	43 00	43 00	44 00
2 x 6	43 00	43 00	44 00
2 x 8	43 00	43 00	44 00
2 x 10	44 00	44 00	45 00
2 x 12	45 00	45 00	46 00

For 2 inches, rough, add 50 cents.
For S1E only add 50 cents.
For S1S and 2E, S4S or D&M, add $3.00.
For timbers larger than 8 x 8, add 50c. for each additional 2 inches each way.
For lengths longer than 20 ft., add $1.00 for each additional two feet.
For selected common, add $5.00.
For No. 2 Dimension, $3.00 less than No. 1.
For 1 x 2 and 2 x 2, $2 more than 2 x 4 No. 1.
For Tamarac add $3.00.

FIR, HEMLOCK SPRUCE AND LARCH

Mountain Stock

No. 1 Dimension and Timbers

2 x 4, 2 x 6, 2 x 8, 8 to 16 ft., S1S1E	$39 00
2 x 4, 2 x 6, 2 x 8, 10 ft, S1S1E	41 00
2 x 4, 2 x 6, 2 x 8, 12/16, S1S1E	39 00
2 x 4, 2 x 6, 2 x 8, 18/22, S1S1E	41 00
2 x 4, 2 x 6, 2 x 8, 24/32, S1S1E	43 00
2 x 10, 8 ft. to 16 ft., S1S1E	40 00
2 x 10, 10 ft. S1S1E	42 00
2 x 10, 18/22, S1S1E	42 00
2 x 10, 24/32, S1S1E	44 00
2 x 12, 8 ft. to 16 ft., S1S1E	41 50
2 x 12; 10, 18, 20,	43 50
2 x 12; 24, 26, 28, 30, 32	45 50

B. C. COAST FIR

Dimension S1S and E.

2 x 4 in., 6 ft.	$44 50
2 x 4 in., 8, 12 and 14 ft.	45 50
2 x 4 in., 16 ft.	46 50
2 x 4 in., 18 and 20 ft.	47 50
2 x 4 in., 22 to 32 ft.	49 50
2 x 10 in., 8, 12 and 14 ft.	46 75
2 x 10 in., 16 ft.	47 75
2 x 10 in., 18 and 20 ft.	48 75
2 x 10 in., 22 to 32 ft.	50 75
2 x 12 in., 8 to 14 ft.	48 25
2 x 12 in., 16 ft.	49 25
2 x 12 in., 18 and 20 ft.	50 25
2 x 12 in., 22 to 32 ft.	52 25
3 x 3 and 3 x 4 in., 8 to 14 ft.	48 75
3 x 3 and 3 x 4 in., 16 ft.	49 75
3 x 3 and 3 x 4, 18 and 20 ft.	50 75
3 x 3 and 3 x 4 in., 22 to 32 ft.	52 75
6 x 6, 6 x 8, 8 x 8, 6 to 16 ft.	51 00
6 x 6, 6 x 8 and 8 x 8, 18 and 20 ft.	51 50
6 x 6, 6 x 8, 8 x 8, 22 to 32 ft.	53 50
Shingles, XXX B. C. Cedar, straight cars on 60c rate	6 90

BUFFALO & TONAWANDA

WHITE PINE

Wholesale Selling Price

Uppers, 4/4	$145 00
Uppers, 5/4 to 8/4	145 00
Uppers, 10/4 to 12/4	165 00
Selects 4/4	135 00
Selects 5/4 to 8/4	135 00
Selects 10/4 to 12/4	155 00
Fine Common 4/4	105 00
Fine Common 5/4	110 00
Fine Common 6/4	110 00
Fine Common 8/4	110 00
No. 1 Cuts 4/4	80 00
No. 1 Cuts 5/4	90 00
No. 1 Cuts 6/4	90 00
No. 1 Cuts 8/4	90 00
No. 2 Cuts 4/4	58 00
No. 2 Cuts 5/4	73 00
No. 2 Cuts 6/4	73 00
No. 2 Cuts 8/4	75 00
No. 3 Cuts 5/4	57 00
No. 3 Cuts 6/4	57 00
No. 3 Cuts 8/4	57 00
Dressing 5/4	67 00
Dressing 5/4 x 10	69 00
Dressing 5/4 x 12	74 00
No. 1 Moulding 5/4	73 00
No. 1 Moulding 6/4	95 00
No. 1 Moulding 8/4	95 00
No. 2 Moulding 5/4	79 00
No. 2 Moulding 6/4	79 00
No. 2 Moulding 8/4	79 00
No. 1 Barn 1 x 12	72 00
No 1 Barn 1 x 6 and 8	64 00
No. 1 Barn 1 x 10	66 00
No. 2 Barn 1 x 6 and 8	60 00
No. 2 Barn, 1 x 10	62 00
No. 3 Barn 1 x 6 and 8	54 00
No. 3 Barn 1 x 10	56 00
Box 1 x 6 and up	48 00
Box 1 x 10	49 00
Box 1 x 12	49 00
Box 1 x 12	49 00
Box 1 x 13 and up	49 00

The following quotations on hardwoods represent the jobber buying price at Buffalo and Tonawanda.

	1s & 2s	No. 1 Com.	No. 2 Com.
MAPLE			
4/4	57-62	44-46	31-33
5/4 to 8/4	73-75	51-53	36-38
10/4 to 10/4	83-85	63-65	40-52
RED BIRCH			
4/4	79-81	53-55	36-38
5/4 to 8/4	82-84	62-64	43-45
SAP BIRCH			
4/4	75-79	53-55	36-38
5/4 and up	80-83	56-58	39-41
SOFT ELM			
4/4	64-65	49-51	38-40
5, 6 & 8/4	67-69	52-54	39-41
BASSWOOD			
4/4	69-71	59-61	43-45
Thicker	68-76	57-64	46-49
PLAIN OAK			
4/4	81-86	58-62	39-41
5/4 to 8/4	87-91	63-67	44-47
ASH, WHITE AND BROWN			
4/4	82-84	52-56	38-41
5/4 to 8/4	88-92	60-62	42-44
10/4 and up	115-117	75-78	43-45

BOSTON, MASS.

Quotations given below are for highest grades of Michigan and Canadian white pine and Eastern Canadian Spruce as required in the New England market in carloads.

White pine uppers, 1 in.		$190 00
White pine uppers, 1¼, 2 in.		185 00
White pine uppers, 2½, 3 in.		165 00
White pine uppers, 4 in		170 00
Selects, 1 in.		145 00
Selects, 1¼, 2 in.		148 00
Selects, 2½, 3 in.		155 00
Selects, 4 in.		165 00
Fine common, 1 in., 30 per cent. 12 in. and up		165 00
Fine common, 1 x 8 and up		100 00
Fine common, 1¼ to 2 in.		119 00
Fine common, 2½ and 3 in		135 00
Fine Common, 4 in.		146 00
1 in. shaky clear		72 00
1¼ to 2 in. shaky clear		76 00
1 in. No 2 dressing		64 00
1¼ to 2 in. No. 2 dressing		68 00
No. 1 Cuts, 1 in.		80 00
No. 1 Cuts, 1¼ to 2 in.	85 00	87 00
No. 1 Cuts, 2½ and 3 in		115 00
No. 2 Cuts, 1 in.		60 00
No. 2 Cuts, 1¼ to 2 in.	70 00	71 00

Barn Boards, No. 1, 1 x 12	79 00
No. 1, 1 x 10	[illegible]
No. 1, 1 x 8	72 00
No. 2, 1 x 12	[illegible]
No. 2, 1 x 10	[illegible]
No. 2, 1 x 8	70 00
No. 3, 1 x 12	[illegible]
No. 3, 1 x 10	[illegible]
No. 3, 1 x 8	[illegible]

No. 1 Clear

Can. spruce, No. 1 and clear, 1 x 4 to 9 in.	[illegible]
1 x 10 in.	[illegible]
No. 1, 1 x 4 to 7 in.	[illegible]
No. 1, 1 x 8 & 9 in.	[illegible]
No. 1, 1 x 10 in.	[illegible]
No. 2, 1 x 4 & 5 in.	[illegible]
No. 2, 1 x 6 & 7 in.	[illegible]
No. 2, 1 x 8 & 9 in.	[illegible]
No. 2 1 x 10 in.	[illegible]
No. 2, 1 x 12 in.	[illegible]
Spruce, 12 in. dimension	
Spruce, 10 in. dimension	
Spruce, 9 in. dimension	
Spruce, 8 in. dimension	
2 x 10 in., random lengths, 8 ft. and up	[illegible]
2 x 12 in., random lengths	[illegible]
2 x 3, 2 x 4, 2 x 5, 2 x 6, 2 x 7	[illegible]
3 x 4 and 4 x 4 in.	[illegible]
2 x 8 in.	
All other random lengths, 7-in. and under, 8 ft. and up	
5-inch and up merchantable boards, 8 ft. and up, p 1s	
1 x 2	
1 x 3	
1-⅝ in. spruce lath	
1-½ in. spruce lath	

New Brunswick Cedar Shingles

Extras	[illegible]
Clears	[illegible]
Second Clears	[illegible]
Clear Whites	[illegible]
Extra 1s (Clear whites in)	[illegible]
Extra 1s (Clear whites out)	[illegible]
Red Cedar Extras, 16-in. 5 butts to 2-in.	[illegible]
Red Cedar Eurekas, 18-inch, 5-butts to 2-in.	[illegible]
Red Cedar Perfections, 5 butts to 2¼	[illegible]
Washington 16-in. 5 butts to 2 in. extra red cedar	

"Brazel Patent" SNOW PLOWS

Known in every Camp from the Atlantic to the Pacific as the most satisfactory Snow Plow made.

Combination Model, Lumberman's Snow Plow, can be used either with or without Rut Cutter.

THE BATEMAN-WILKINSON CO., LIMITED
306 Symington Ave., Toronto

Successors to the WILKINSON PLOW CO. LIMITED

TORONTO, CANADA

Barks from two to three cords per hour

The Moreau Barker

Practice economy and efficiency in barking your pulpwood.

Use the MOREAU BARKER. It barks frozen logs in winter as easily as dry wood in summer. Logs from 3" to 30" in diameter handled with comparative ease with the Moreau Barker.

It has a tension spring which controls the wheels over all irregularities and according to the thickness of the bark.

Only 10 horse power is required to operate the Moreau Barker under all conditions.

Numerous letters in our possession testify to the reliability of the Moreau Barker and the satisfaction given to Canadian lumbermen.

We can prove that the Moreau Barker will do any barking demanded of it.

Write for further particulars.

NOW MADE AND SOLD BY

La Compagnie Manufacturiere F. X. Bertrand

ST. HYACINTHE, QUE.

MANUFACTURERS OF STEAM ENGINES AND WOODWORKING MACHINES

W. G. CRAIG & CO. Ltd.
KINGSTON

WARREN BROS & CO. Ltd.
TORONTO

Wholesale Grocers

SPECIAL ATTENTION GIVEN TO LUMBER TRADE

If you are not receiving our Monthly Catalogue
please notify our *Catalogue Department* and your name will at once be put on our regular mailing list.

Warehouses - TORONTO and KINGSTON, Ont.

Greetings from
Gunns
We wish all our many customers and friends throughout the lumber industry a Christmas replete with happiness and good things, and a New Year of health and prosperity.
In thanking you all for past favors, we solicit your valued patronage during 1920.
Beef, Veal, Mutton
Barrelled Beef
Barrelled Pork
Dry Salt Meats
Butter, Cheese
Oleomargarine
Lard
Eggs, Poultry
Canned Meats
Pork and Beans
Beans, Sausage
Headcheese
Mincemeat
"Easifirst" Shortening
GUNNS LIMITED
WEST TORONTO

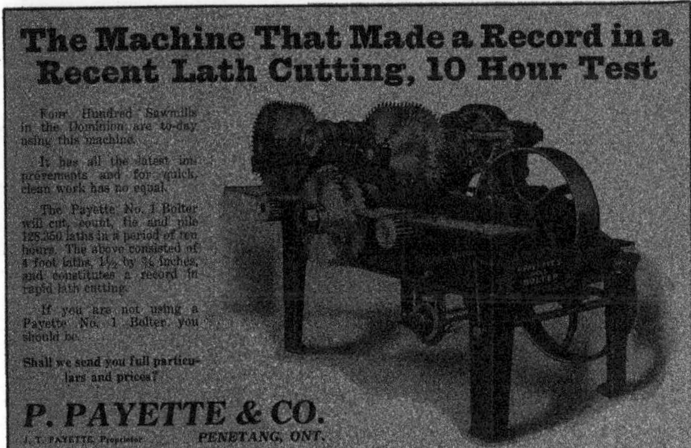
The Machine That Made a Record in a Recent Lath Cutting, 10 Hour Test
Four Hundred Sawmills in the Dominion are to-day using this machine.
It has all the latest improvements and for quick, clean work has no equal.
The Payette No. 1 Bolter will cut, count, tie and pile 125,250 laths in a period of ten hours. The above consisted of 4 foot laths, 1½ by ⅜ inches, and constitutes a record in rapid lath cutting.
If you are not using a Payette No. 1 Bolter, you should be.
Shall we send you full particulars and prices?
P. PAYETTE & CO.
J. T. PAYETTE, Proprietor
PENETANG, ONT.

Gerlach Machinery
PRODUCES THE BEST
as Well as the Cheapest
Tight or Slack Staves,
Headings, Kegs,
Barrels and
Short Box Shooks
100% to 400% profit in Cooperage Stock today. Be wise and purchase the best Machinery.
DIXIE PORTABLE GASOLINE DRAG SAW
Circular, Drag and Cylinder Saws made since 1854
The Peter Gerlach Co.
Cleveland, Ohio

This photograph is exactly as it was taken without any attempt to make it more attractive by retouching.

A "BIG" ONE

This belt is over 8 feet in diameter, 38 inches wide by 4-ply, 1558 feet in length, and 3½ tons in weight; or in other words, one of the longest and largest belts ever made in Canada.

It was purchased by the Montreal Harbor Commissioners for use on one of their huge grain elevators and is only one of dozens we have supplied them from time to time in the past.

Statistics show that the per ton cost of Dunlop Belts for carrying coke, ore, coal, lime, sand, rock, cements, and many other materials is extraordinarily low under all conditions of running.

Expert information is gladly and freely given without obligation to you.

Ask about "Gibraltar" and "Samson" Elevator and Conveyor Belts.

Dunlop Tire & Rubber Goods Company, Limited

Head Office and Factories: TORONTO

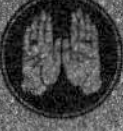

Branches in the Leading Cities.

Survive Every Test

Arrow Head

Vanadium Steel

SAWS

(Curve Ground)

Under all conditions of test, Arrow Head Saws have proved their worth and reliability.

In the lumber camps of the Dominion they have been a big factor in increased output, better quality of work and economical production.

Are you using them?

T. F. Shurly Co., Limited

St. Catharines, Ontario

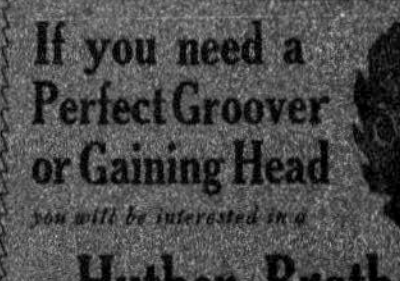

If you need a Perfect Groover or Gaining Head

you will be interested in a

Huther Brothers Dado Head

It will cut perfect grooves of any width either with or across the grain and will not leave the rough edges left by an ordinary groover.

It consists of two outside cutters and enough inside cutters to perform the required cut.

By simplifying intricate grooving Huther Dado Heads are bringing down the overhead costs of many plants.

Send for one on approval. Return it at our expense if unsatisfactory.

HUTHER BROS SAW MFG. CO.
ROCHESTER, N.Y.

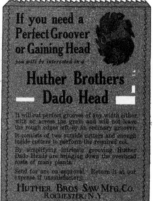

BOLINDER'S HEAV OIL

The Most Efficient and Economical Motive Power FOR TOW BOATS and BARGES

The high efficiency of the Bolinder Engine is evidenced by the fact that during the war the British Admiralty ordered not less than 267 Bolinder Engines, which were installed in

142 Vessels in the British Navy.

All these vessels were in strenuous service during the war and gave a remarkable account of themselves.

The "M 23". One of the Bolinder-engined Motor-Monitors of the British Navy. Equipped with 640 B.H.P. Bolinder Engines

SWEDISH STEEL AND IMPORTING CO., LIMITED

SHAUGHNESSY BUILDING · MONTREAL

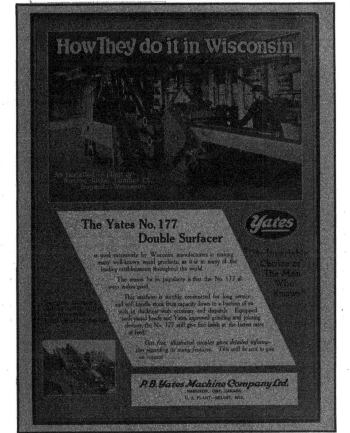

CANADA LUMBERMAN BUYERS' DIRECTORY

The following regulations apply to all advertisers:—Eighth page, every issue, three headings; quarter page, six headings; half page, twelve headings; full page, twenty-four headings.

AIR CONDITIONING
Sturtevant Company, B. F.

ASBESTOS GOODS
Atlas Asbestos Company, Ltd.

AXES
Canadian Warren Axe & Tool Co.

BABBITT METAL
Canada Metal Company
General Supply Co. of Canada, Ltd.
United American Metals Corporation

Bale Ties
Laidlaw Bale Tie Company

BAND MILLS
Hamilton Company, William
Waterous Engine Works Company
Yates Machine Company, P. B.

BAND RESAWS
Mershon & Company, W. B.

BELT CEMENT
Graton & Knight Mfg. Company

BELT DRESSING
Atlas Asbestos Company, Ltd.
General Supply Co. of Canada, Ltd.
Graton & Knight Mfg. Company

BELTING
Atlas Asbestos Company, Ltd.
Beardmore Belting Company
Canadian Consolidated Rubber Co.
General Supply Company
Goodhue & Co., J. L.
Goodyear Tire & Rubber Co.
Graton & Knight Mfg. Company
Gutta Percha and Rubber Company
Main Belting Company
Manhattan Rubber Mfg. Co.
D. K. McLaren Limited
McLaren Belting Company, J. C.

BELTING (Transmission, Elevator, Conveyor, Rubber)
Dunlop Tire & Rubber Goods Co.

BLOWERS
Toronto Blower Company
Sturtevant Company, B. F.

BOILERS
Engineering & Machine Works of Canada
Hamilton Company, William
Marsh Engineering Works, Limited
Waterous Engine Works Company

BOILER PRESERVATIVE
International Chemical Company

BOX MACHINERY
Garlock-Walker Machinery Co.
Morgan Machine Company
Yates Machine Company, P. B.

BOX SHOOKS
Davison Lumber & Mfg. Company

BUNKS (Steel)
Alaska Bedding Co. of Montreal

CABLE CONVEYORS
Engineering & Machine Works of Canada
Jeffrey Manufacturing Company
Waterous Engine Works Company

CAMP SUPPLIES
Burns & Company, John
Canadian Milk Products Limited
Davies Company, William
Dr. Bell Veterinary Wonder Co.
Eckardt & Co.
Gunns Limited
Harris Abattoir Company
Johnson, A. H.
Turner & Sons, J. J.
Woods Manufacturing Company, Ltd.

CANT HOOKS
Canadian Warren Axe & Tool Co.
General Supply Co. of Canada, Ltd.
Pink Company, Thomas

CARS—STEEL BODY
Marsh Engineering Works, Limited

CAR WHEELS AND CASTINGS
Dominion Wheel & Foundries

CEDAR
Fesserton Timber Co.
Foss Lumber Company
Genoa Bay Lumber Company
Muir & Kirkpatrick
Long Lumber Company
Service Lumber Company
Terry & Gordon
Thurston-Flavelle Lumber Company
Vancouver Lumber Company
Victoria Lumber and Mfg. Co.

CHAINS
Canadian Link-Belt Company, Ltd.
General Supply Co. of Canada, Ltd.
Engineering & Machine Works of Canada
Hamilton Company, William
Hobbs Company, Clinton E.
Jeffrey Manufacturing Company
Pink & Co., Thomas
Waterous Engine Works Company
Williams Machinery Co., A. R. Vancouver,

CHAIN HOISTS
Hobbs Company, Clinton E.

CHINA CLAY
Bowater & Sons, W. V.

CHEMICAL PLANTS
Blair, Campbell & McLean, Ltd.

CLOTHING
Acme Glove Works
Clarke & Company, A. R.
Grant, Holden & Graham
Woods Mfg. Company

COLLAR PADS
American Pad & Textile Co.

CONVEYOR MACHINERY
Canadian Link-Belt Company, Ltd.
Canadian Mathews Gravity Carrier Company
General Supply Co. of Canada, Ltd.
Jeffrey Mfg. Co.
Waterous Engine Works Company

CORDAGE
Consumers Cordage Company

CORN SYRUP
Canada Starch Company

COTTON GLOVES
American Pad & Textile Co.

COUPLING (Shaft)
Engineering & Machine Works of Canada

CRANES FOR SHIP YARDS
Canadian Link-Belt Company

CROSS ARMS
Genoa Bay Lumber Company

CUTTER HEADS
Shimer Cutter Head Company

CYPRESS
Chicago Lumber & Coal Company
Long Lumber Company
Wistar, Underhill & Nixon

DERRICKS AND DERRICK FITTINGS
Marsh Engineering Works, Limited

DOORS
Genoa Bay Lumber Company
Long Lumber Co.
Mason, Gordon & Co.
Rutherford & Sons, Wm.
Terry & Gordon

DRAG SAWS
Gerlach Company, Peter
Williams Machinery Co., A.

DRIVING BOOTS
Acme Glove Works

DRYERS
Philadelphia Textile Mach. Company

DRY KILNS
Sturtevant Company, B. F.

DUST COLLECTOR
Sturtevant Company, B. F.
Toronto Blower Company

EDGERS
William Hamilton Company, Ltd.
Garlock-Walker Machinery Co.
Green Company, G. Walter
Long Mfg. Company, E.
Waterous Engine Works Company

ELEVATING AND CONVEYING MACHINERY
Canadian Link-Belt Comptny, Ltd.
Engineering & Machine Works of Canada
Jeffery Manufacturing Gompany
Waterous Engine Works Company

ENGINES
Engineering & Machine Works of Canada
Hamilton Company, William
Waterous Engine Works, Company

EXCELSIOR MACHINERY
Elmira Machinery and Transmission Company

EXHAUST FANS
Garlock-Walker Machinery Co.
Sturtevant Company, B. F.
Reed & Company, Geo. W.
Toronto Blower Company

EXHAUST SYSTEMS
Reed & Company, Geo. W.
Sturtevant Company, B. F.
Toronto Blower Company

FILES
Disston & Sons, Henry
Simonds Canada Saw Company

FIR
Associated Mills, Limited
Allan-Stoltze Lumber Co.
British American Mills & Timber Co.
Coal Creek Lumber Comp
Fesserton Timber Co.
Foss Lumber Company
Grier & Sons, Ltd., G. A.
Heeney, Percy E.
Knox Brothers
Long Lumber Company
Mason, Gordon & Co.
Reynolds Company, Limit
Service Lumber Company
Shearer Company, Jas.
Terry & Gordon
Timberland Lumber Company
Timms, Phillips & Co.
Vancouver Lumber Company
Victoria Lumber and Mfg. Co.
Weller, J. B.

FIRE BRICK
Beveridge Paper Company
Elk Fire Brick Company of Can

Dunlop Tire & Rubber Goods Co.
Pyrene Mfg. Company
Waterous Engine Works Company

FIR FLOORING
Genoa Bay Lumber Company
Rutherford & Sons, Wm.

FLAG STAFFS
Ontario Wind Engine Company

FLOORING (Oak)
Long-Bell Lumber Company

GALVANIZING
Ontario Wind Engine Company

GLOVES
Acme Glove Works
Eisendrath Glove Co.

GASOLINE ENGINES
Ontario Wind Engine Company

GEARS (Cut)
Smart-Turner Machine Co.

GRAIN
Dwyer Company, W. H.

GRAVITY LUMBER CARRIER
Can. Mathews Gravity Carrier Co.

GRINDERS (Bench)
Garlock-Walker Machinery Co.

HARDWOODS
Anderson Lumber Company, C. G.
Atlantic Lumber Co.
Bartram & Ball
Bennett Lumber Company
Blakeslee, Perrin & Darling
Cameron & Co.
Cardinal & Page
Cox, Long & Company
Davison Lumber & Mfg. Company
Dunfield & Company
Edwards & Co., W. C.
Fassett Lumber Company
Fesserton Timber Co.
Fraser Limited
Gall Lumber Company
Gillespie, James
Gloucester Lumber Company
Grier & Son, G. A.
Harris Lumber Co., Frank H
Heeney, Percy E.
Knox Brothers
Long Lumber Company
McLennan Lumber Company

HARDWOOD FLOORING MACHINERY
American Woodworking Machin Company
Garlock-Walker Machinery Co.

HARDWOOD FLOORING
Grier & Son, G. A.
Long Lumber Company

HAY
Dwyer & Company, W. H.

HARNESS
Padgitt Company, Tom

HEMLOCK
Anderson Lumber Company, C. G.
Bartram & Ball
Bourgouin, H.
Canadian General Lumber Company
Cane & Co., Jas. G.
Davison Lumber & Mfg. Company
Dunfield & Company
Edwards & Company, W. C.
Fesserton Timber Co.
Foss Lumber Company
Grier & Sons, Ltd., G. A.
Harris Lumber Co., Frank H
Hart & McDonagh
Hocken Lumber Company
Long Lumber Company
Mason, Gordon & Co.
Roch, Julien
Spencer Limited, C. A.
Terry & Gordon

HOISTING AND HAULING ENGINES
Garlock-Walker Machinery Co.
General Supply Co. of Canada, Ltd.
Marsh Engineering Works, Limited

HORSES
Union Stock Yards

HOSE
Dunlop Tire & Rubber Goods Co.
General Supply Co. of Canada, Ltd.
Goodyear Tire & Rubber Co.
Gutta Percha and Rubber Company

HUMIDIFIERS
Sturtevant Company, B. F.

INDUSTRIAL CARS
Marsh Engineering Works, Limited

INSURANCE
Hardy & Co., E. D.
Walton Company, Walter

INTERIOR FINISH
Eagle Lumber Company
Hay & Co.
Mason, Gordon & Co.
Renfrew Planing Mills
Terry & Gordon

KNIVES
Disston & Sons, Henry
Peter Hay Knife Company
Simonds Canada Saw Company
Waterous Engine Works Company

LARCH
Otis Staples Lumber Co.

LATH
Austin & Nicholson
Canadian General Lumber Company
Cane & Co., Jas. G.
Cardinal & Page
Dupuis Limited, J. P.
Eagle Lumber Company
Fraser Limited
Fraser-Bryson Lumber Company
Genoa Bay Lumber Company
Gloucester Lumber Company
Grier & Sons, Ltd., G. A.
Harris Tie & Timber Company, Ltd.
Long Lumber Company
McLennan Lumber Company
New Ontario Colonization Company
Otis Staples Lumber Co.
River Ouelle Pulp and Lumber Co.
Spencer Limited, C. A.
Terry & Gordon
Union Lumber Company
Victoria Harbor Lumber Company

LATH BOLTERS
Garlock-Walker Machinery Co.
General Supply Co. of Canada, Ltd.
Green Company, C. Walter

LIGHTING APPLIANCES
Hobbs Company, Clinton E.

LOCOMOTIVES
Bell Locomotive Works
Engineering & Machine Works of Canada
General Supply Co. of Canada, Ltd.
Jeffrey Manufacturing Company
Climax Manufacturing Company
Montreal Locomotive Works

LATH TWINE
Consumers' Cordage Company

LINK-BELT
Canadian Link-Belt Company

Canadian Mathews Gravity Carrier Company
Jeffrey Mfg. Co.
Williams Machinery Co., A. R., Vancouver

LOGGING COLLARS
Padgitt Company, Tom

LOCOMOTIVE CRANES
Canadian Link-Belt Company, Ltd.

LOGGING ENGINES
Dunbar Engine and Foundry Co.
Engineering & Machine Works of Canada
Marsh Engineering Works, Limited

LOG HAULER
Green Company, G. Walter
Jenckes Machine Company, Ltd.

LOGGING MACHINERY AND EQUIPMENT
General Supply Co. of Canada, Ltd.
Hamilton Company, William
Jenckes Machine Company, Ltd.
Marsh Engineering Works, Limited
Waterous Engine Works Company

LOG STAMPS
Superior Mfg. Company

LUMBER TRUCKS
Waterous Engine Works Company

LUMBERMEN'S CLOTHING
Woods Manufacturing Company, Ltd.

METAL REFINERS
Canada Metal Company
Hoyt Metal Company
Sessenwein Brothers

MILLING IN TRANSIT
Renfrew Planing Mills
Rutherford & Sons, Wm.

MOLDINGS
Genoa Bay Lumber Co.
Rutherford & Sons, Wm.

MOTOR TRUCKS
Duplex Truck Company

MOTORS
Sturtevant Company, B. F.

OAK
Chicago Lumber & Coal Company
Long-Bell Lumber Company

OAKUM
Stratford Oakum Co., Geo.

OIL CLOTHING
Leckie Limited, John

OIL ENGINES
Swedish Steel & Importing Co.

OLD IRON AND BRASS
Sessenwein Brothers

OVERALLS
Hamilton Carhartt Cotton Mills

PAPER
Bowater & Sons, W. V.

PACKING
Atlas Asbestos Company, Ltd.
Consumers Cordage Co.
Dunlop Tire & Rubber Goods Co.
Gutta Percha and Rubber Company

PAPER MILL MACHINERY
Bowater & Sons, W. V.

PINE
Anderson Lumber Company, C. G.
Atlantic Lumber Co.
Austin & Nicholson
Bourgouin, H.
Cameron & Co.
Canadian General Lumber Company
Cane & Co., Jas. G.
Cardinal & Page
Chicago Lumber & Coal Company
Cleveland-Sarnia Sawmills Company
Colonial Lumber Company
Cox, Long & Company
Davison Lumber & Mfg. Co.
Dudley, Arthur N.
Dunfield & Company
Eagle Lumber Company
Edwards & Co., W. C.

CLIMAX Improved Geared LOCOMOTIVES FOR WOOD AND IRON RAILS

Climax Locomotives are successfully operated on steep grades and sharp curves. Any weight or gauge. Locomotives in stock for immediate shipment. See Catalog "K."

CLIMAX MANUFACTURING CO., 313 W. Main Street, CORRY, PA.
VANCOUVER MACHINERY DEPOT, LTD. VANCOUVER, B. C.

J. J. TURNER & SONS, LIMITED, Peterborough, Ont.

PUT YOUR PROBLEM UP TO US

We are specialists in building locomotives. We build all types and sizes, also all kinds of repair parts for locomotives and tenders.

Our experience puts us in a position to give you expert advice as to what particular type and size of locomotive is best suited to your needs.

Put your locomotive problem up to us.

MONTREAL LOCOMOTIVE WORKS, LIMITED

DOMINION EXPRESS BUILDING, MONTREAL, CANADA.

PRATT & WHITNEY CO.

OF CANADA, LIMITED

SMALL TOOLS

Taps — Dies — Reamers — Cutters — Drills

MADE IN CANADA

As good as money can buy—Guaranteed absolutely!

Head Office and Works, DUNDAS, ONT.

SALES OFFICES:

MONTREAL Drummond Bldg. VANCOUVER WINNIPEG Bank of Hamilton Bldg.

Proctor DRYERS

For Exacting Conditions

Your individual problems of veneer drying may be different or the conditions more exacting. Because it is seldom that two drying problems are the same our engineers make a special study of your particular conditions considering the relation of the drying to preceding and following operations, quantity to be dried, number of men employed, heat available, cost of power, etc.

Proctor Veneer Dryers give a perfectly flat and pliable product without checks or splits

Send for our practical Catalog—It will interest you

PHILADELPHIA TEXTILE MACHINERY CO.

Drying Machine Specialists

SEVENTH STREET AND TABOR ROAD, PHILADELPHIA, PA., U.S.A.

Hamilton, Ont., Canada,—W. J. Westaway, 8 Sun Life Building.

Excelsior Lumber Company
Fesserton Timber Company
Fraser-Bryson Lumber Company
Fraser Limited
Gillies Brothers Limited
Gloucester Lumber Company
Gordon & Co., George
Grier & Sons, Ltd., G. A.
Harris Lumber Co., Frank H
Harris Tie & Timber Company, Ltd.
Hart & McDonagh
Hettler Lumber Company, Herman H.
Hocken Lumber Company
Lloyd, W. Y.
Long-Bell Lumber Company
Long Lumber Company
Mason, Gordon & Co.
McLennan Lumber Company
Montreal Lumber Company
Moores, Jr., E. J.
Muir & Kirkpatrick
Otis Staples Lumber Co.
Parry Sound Lumber Company
Roch, Julien
Russell, Chas. H.
Shearer Company, Pas.
Spencer Limited, C. A.
Summers, James R.
Terry & Gordon
Union Lumber Company
Watson & Todd, Limited
Williams Lumber Company
Wuichet, Louis

PLANING MILL EXHAUSTERS
Garlock-Walker Machinery Co.
Reed & Company, Geo. W.
Toronto Blower Co.

PLANING MILL MACHINERY
American Woodworking Machinery Company
Garlock-Walker Machinery Co.
Mershon & Company, W. B.
Toronto Blower Co.
Yates Machine Company, P. B.

PORK PACKERS
Davies Company, William
Gunns Limited
Harris Abattoir Company

POSTS AND POLES
Auger & Company
Canadian Tie & Lumber Co.
Dupuis Limited, J. P.
Eagle Lumber Company
Harris Tie & Timber Company, Ltd.
Long-Bell Lumber Company
Long Lumber Company
Mason, Gordon & Co.
Terry & Gordon

PULLEYS AND SHAFTING
Canadian Link-Belt Company
Garlock-Walker Machinery Co.
General Supply Co. of Canada, Ltd.
Green Company, G. Walter
Engineering & Machine Works of Canada
Hamilton Company, William
Jeffrey Mfg. Co.

PULP MILL MACHINERY
Canadian Link-Belt Company, Ltd.
Engineering & Machine Works of Canada
Hamilton Company, William
Jeffrey Manufacturing Company
Waterous Engine Works Company

PUMPS
General Supply Co. of Canada, Ltd.
Engineering & Machine Works of Canada
Hamilton Company, William
Smart-Turner Machine Company
Waterous Engine Company

RAILS
Gartshore, John J.
Sessenwein Bros.

ROOFING
Reed & Company, Geo. W.

ROOFINGS
(Rubber, Plastic and Liquid)
International Chemical Company

ROPE
Consumers Cordage Co.
Leckie, Limited, John

RUBBER GOODS
Atlas Asbestos Company
Dunlop Tire & Rubber Goods Co.
Goodyear Tire and Rubber Co.
Gutta Percha & Rubber Company

SASH
Genoa Bay Lumber Company
Renfrew Planing Mills

SAWS
Atkins & Company, E. C.
Disston & Sons, Henry
General Supply Co. of Canada, Ltd.
Gerlach Company, Peter
Green Company, G. Walter
Hoe & Company, R.
Shurly Co., Ltd., T. F.
Shurly-Dietrich Company
Simonds Canada Saw Company

SAW MILL LINK-BELT
Williams Machinery Co., A. R., Vancouver

SAW MILL MACHINERY
Canadian Link-Belt Comptny, Ltd.
Dunbar Engine & Foundry Co.
Firstbrook Bros.
General Supply Co. of Canada, Ltd.
Hamilton Company, William
Huther Bros. Saw Mfg. Company
Jeffrey Manufacturing Company
Long Manufacturing Company, E.
Mershon & Company, W. B.
Parry Sound Lumber Company
Payete Company, P.
Waterous Engine Works Company
Yates Machine Co., P. B.

SHEATHINGS
Goodyear Tire & Rubber Co.

SHINGLE MACHINES
Marsh Engineering Works, Limited

SAW SHARPENERS
Garlock-Walker Machinery Co.
Waterous Engine Works Company

SAW SLASHERS
Waterous Engine Works Company

SAWMILL LINK-BELT
Canadian Link-Belt Company

SHEET METALS
United American Metals Corp'n.

SHINGLES
Allan-Stoltze Lumber Co.
Associated Mills, Limited
Campbell-MacLaurin Lumber Co.
Cardinal & Page
Dominion Lumber & Timber Co.
Eagle Lumber Company
Foss Lumber Company
Fraser Limited
Genoa Bay Lumber Company
Gillespie, James
Gloucester Lumber Company
Grier & Sons, Limited, G. A.
Harris Lumber Co., Frank H
Harris Tie & Timber Company, Ltd.
Heeney, Percy E.
Long Lumber Company
Mason, Gordon & Co.
McLennan Lumber Company
Miller Company, Ltd., W. H.
Reynolds Company, Limited
Service Lumber Company
Shingle Agency of B. C.
Terry & Gordon
Timms, Phillips & Co.
Vancouver Lumber Company
Victoria Lumber and Mfg. Co.

SHINGLE & LATH MACHINERY
Dunbar Engine and Foundry Co.
Garlock-Walker Machinery Co.
Green Company, C. Walter
Hamilton Company, William
Long Manufacturing Company, E.
Payette Company, P.

SHOEPACKS
Acme Glove Works

SILENT CHAIN DRIVES
Canadian Link-Belt Company, Ltd.

SILOS
Ontario Wind Engine Company

SLEEPING ROBES
Woods Mfg. Company, Limited

SLEIGHS
Bateman-Wilkinson Company

SMOKESTACKS
Marsh Enginering Works, Limited
Waterous Engine Works Company

SNOW PLOWS
Bateman-Wilkinson Company
Pink Company, Thomas

SPARK ARRESTORS
Jenckes Machine Company, Ltd.
Reed & Company, Geo. W.
Waterous Engine Works Company

SPRUCE
Bartram & Ball
Bourgouin, H.
Cane & Co., Jas. G.
Cardinal & Page
Cox, Long & Company
Davison Lumber & Mfg. Company
Donogh & Co., John
Dudley, Arthur N.
Dunfield & Company
Exchange Lumber Company
Foss Lumber Company
Fraser Limited
Fraser-Bryson Lumber Company
Gillies Brothers
Gloucester Lumber Company
Grant & Campbell
Grier & Sons, Ltd., G. A.
Harris Lumber Co., Frank H
Hart & McDonagh
Lloyd, W. Y.
Hocken Lumber Company
Long Lumber Company
Mason, Gordon & Co.
McLennan Lumber Company
Muir & Kirpatrick
New Ontario Colonization Company
River Ouelle Pulp and Lumber Co.
Roch, Julien
Russell, Chas. H.
Service Lumber Company
Shearer Company, Jas.
Snowball Co., J. B.
Spencer Limited, C. A.
Terry & Gordon
Rideau Lumber Company

STEEL CHAIN
Canadian Link-Belt Company, Ltd.
Jeffrey Manufacturing Company
Waterous Engine Works Company

STEEL PLATE CONSTRUCTION
Marsh Engineering Works, Limited

STEAM PLANT ACCESSORIES
Waterous Engine Works Company

STEEL BARRELS
Smart-Turner Machine Co.

STEEL DRUMS
Smart-Turner Machine Co.

STOVES
Burns & Company, John

SWEAT PADS
American Pad & Textile Co.

SULPHITE PULP CHIPS
Davison Lumber & Mfg. Company

TANKS
Ontario Wind Engine Company

TARPAULINS
Turner & Sons, J. J.
Woods Manufacturing Company, Ltd.

TAPS AND DIES
Pratt & Whitney Company

TENTS
Turner & Sons, J. J.
Woods Mfg. Company

TENTS, CLOTHING
Grant, Holden & Graham, Limited

TIES
Auger & Company
Austin & Nicholson
Canadian Tie & Lumber Co.
Harris Tie & Timber Company, Ltd.
Long Lumber Company
McLennan Lumber Company
Terry & Gordon

TIMBER BROKERS
Bradley, R. R.
Cant & Kemp
Farnworth & Jardine
Hunter, Herbert F.
Smith & Tyrer, Limited

TIMBER CRUISERS AND ESTIMATORS
Sewall, James W.

TIMBER LANDS
Department of Lands and Forests

TIME RECORDERS
International Business Machines Co

TRACTORS
British War Mision

TRANSMISSION MACHINERY
Canadian Link-Belt Company, Ltd.
Engineering & Machine Works of Canada
General Supply Co. of Canada, Ltd.
Jeffrey Manufacturing Company
Waterous Engine Works Company

TRIMMERS
Garlock-Walker Machinery Co.
Green Company, C. Walter
Waterous Engine Works Company

TUGS
West & Peachey

TURBINES
Engineering & Machine Works of Canada
Hamilton Company, William

VALVES
Bay City Foundry & Machine Co.

VENEERS
Webster & Brother, James

VENEER DRYERS
Coe Manufacturing Company
Philadelphia Textile Mach. Co.

VENEER MACHINERY
Coe Machinery Company
Garlock-Walker Machinery Co.
Philadelphia Textile Machinery Co.

VETERINARY REMEDIES
Dr. Bell Veterinary Wonder Co.
Johnson, A. H.

WATER HEATERS
Mason Regulator & Engineering Co.

WATER WHEELS
Engineering & Machine Works of Canada
Hamilton Company, William

WIRE
Laidlaw Bale Tie Company

WIRE ROPE
Canada Wire & Cable Co.

WOODWORKING MACHINERY
American Woodworking Machy. Co.
Garlock-Walker Machinery Co.
General Supply Co. of Canada, Ltd.
Jeffrey Manufacturing Company
Long Manufacturing Company, E.
Mershon & Company, W. B.
Waterous Engine Works Company
Yates Machine Company, P. B.

WOOD PRESERVATIVES
International Chemical Company

WOOD PULP
Austin & Nicholson
New Ontario Colonization Co.
River Ouelle Pulp and Lumber Co.

The Home of "CONDOR" Belting

Made of 32 oz. duck and the best grade of rubber procurable.

Manufactured on giant presses weighing 550,000 pounds each, giving the greatest friction of any belt on the market.

The General Supply Company of Canada, Limited

OTTAWA MONTREAL TORONTO WINNIPEG VANCOUVER

Large Stocks Carried in Canada

Illustrating portable unit of Mathews Conveyor for unloading cars.

Illustrating permanent installation of Mathews Lumber Conveyor, between mill and shipping and distributing platform.

Write for Catalogue L.

CANADIAN MATHEWS GRAVITY CARRIER COMPANY, LIMITED

PORT HOPE ONTARIO

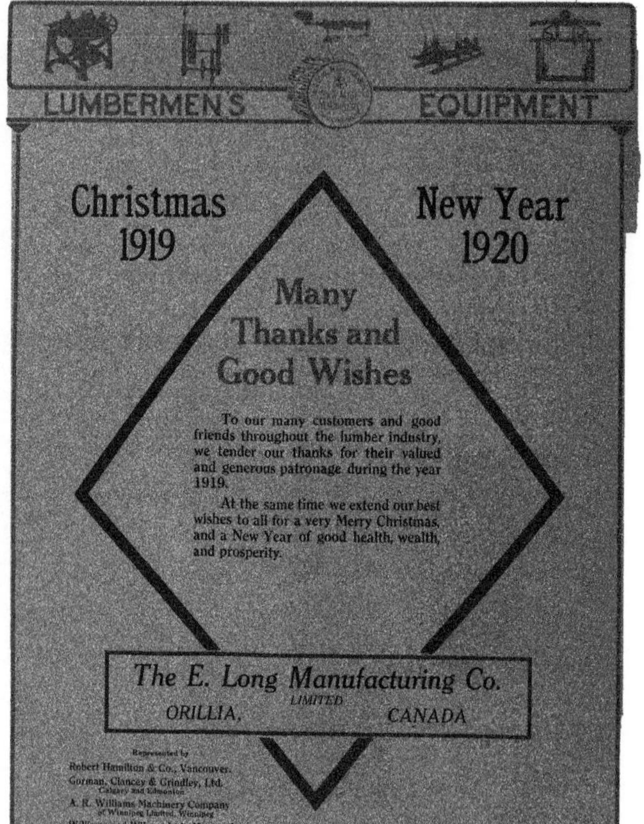
LUMBERMEN'S EQUIPMENT
Christmas 1919
New Year 1920
Many Thanks and Good Wishes
To our many customers and good friends throughout the lumber industry, we tender our thanks for their valued and generous patronage during the year 1919.
At the same time we extend our best wishes to all for a very Merry Christmas, and a New Year of good health, wealth, and prosperity.
The E. Long Manufacturing Co.
LIMITED
ORILLIA, CANADA
Represented by
Robert Hamilton & Co., Vancouver.
Gorman, Clancey & Grindley, Ltd.
Calgary and Edmonton
A. R. Williams Machinery Company
of Winnipeg Limited, Winnipeg
Williams and Wilson, Ltd., Montreal

WATEROUS Steel Carriages are being used in the largest, best equipped Mills in Canada to-day. Built for fast cutting, for accuracy, and to give operating service, they are carefully put together of the best materials obtainable—they stay right.

Increase in cutting efficiency and the increase of cutting speed have been taken care of in the design of these carriages. Improvements in the knee and head blocks and in all moving parts to overcome lost motion; a new setworks—our No. 4—(which may be attached to Steam Setter, or be replaced by trout Power set works) which absolutely prevents and will not develop slack; new style, inserted tooth; quick and easy operating dogs; a friction receder that is operated with the Setworks—these special featues are what keep the Waterous Steel Carriage at its place at the head of the list of "Up-to-date Sawmill Equipment." We build our Steel Carriages in sizes of 36 in. to 72 in. knee opening, in any length and with any number of head blocks—screw or rack motion. They are adaptable for rope or gunshot feed.

Waterous

BRANTFORD, ONTARIO, CANADA

Lightning Source UK Ltd.
Milton Keynes UK
UKHW02n0721150918
328924UK00004B/22/P